T0180306

Lecture Notes in Computer Science   10992

Commenced Publication in 1973
Founding and Former Series Editors:
Gerhard Goos, Juris Hartmanis, and Jan van Leeuwen

More information about this series at http://www.springer.com/series/7410

Hovav Shacham · Alexandra Boldyreva (Eds.)

Advances in Cryptology – CRYPTO 2018

38th Annual International Cryptology Conference
Santa Barbara, CA, USA, August 19–23, 2018
Proceedings, Part II

 Springer

Editors
Hovav Shacham
The University of Texas at Austin
Austin, TX
USA

Alexandra Boldyreva
Georgia Institute of Technology
Atlanta, GA
USA

ISSN 0302-9743   ISSN 1611-3349   (electronic)
Lecture Notes in Computer Science
ISBN 978-3-319-96880-3   ISBN 978-3-319-96881-0   (eBook)
https://doi.org/10.1007/978-3-319-96881-0

Library of Congress Control Number: 2018949031

LNCS Sublibrary: SL4 – Security and Cryptology

This Springer imprint is published by the registered company Springer Nature Switzerland AG
The registered company address is: Gewerbestrasse 11, 6330 Cham, Switzerland

Preface

The 38th International Cryptology Conference (Crypto 2018) was held at the University of California, Santa Barbara, California, USA, during August 19–23, 2018. It was sponsored by the International Association for Cryptologic Research (IACR). For 2018, the conference was preceded by three days of workshops on various topics. And, of course, there was the awesome Beach BBQ at Goleta Beach.

Crypto continues to grow, year after year, and Crypto 2018 was no exception. The conference set new records for both submissions and publications, with a whopping 351 papers submitted for consideration. It took a Program Committee of 46 cryptography experts working with 272 external reviewers almost 2.5 months to select the 79 papers which were accepted for the conference. It also took one program chair about 30 minutes to dig up all those stats.

In order to minimize intentional and/or subconscious bias, papers were reviewed in the usual double-blind fashion. Program Committee members were limited to two submissions, and their submissions were scrutinized more closely and held to higher standards. The two program chairs were not allowed to submit papers. Of course, they were fine with that restriction since they were way too busy to actually write any papers.

The Program Committee recognized two papers and their authors for standing out among the rest. "Yes, There Is an Oblivious RAM Lower Bound!", by Kasper Green Larsen and Jesper Buus Nielsen, was voted best paper of the conference. Additionally, "Multi-Theorem Preprocessing NIZKs from Lattices," by Sam Kim and David J. Wu, was voted Best Paper Authored Exclusively By Young Researchers. There was no award for Best Paper Authored Exclusively by Old Researchers.

Crypto 2018 played host for the IACR Distinguished Lecture, delivered by Shafi Goldwasser. Crypto also welcomed Lea Kissner as an invited speaker from Google.

We would like to express our sincere gratitude to all the reviewers for volunteering their time and knowledge in order to select a great program for 2018. Additionally, we are very appreciative of the following individuals and organizations for helping make Crypto 2018 a success:

Tal Rabin - Crypto 2018 General Chair and Workshops Organizer
Elette Boyle - Workshops Chair
Fabrice Benhamouda - Workshops Organizer
Shafi Goldwasser - IACR Distinguished Lecturer
Lea Kissner - Invited Speaker from Google
Shai Halevi - Author of the IACR Web Submission and Review System
Anna Kramer and her colleagues at Springer
Sally Vito and UCSB Conference Services

We would also like to say thank you to our numerous sponsors, everyone who submitted papers, the session chairs, the rump session chair, and the presenters.

Lastly, a big thanks to everyone who attended the conference at UCSB. Without you, we would have had a lot of leftover potato salad at the Beach BBQ.

August 2018

Alexandra Boldyreva
Hovav Shacham

Crypto 2018

The 38th IACR International Cryptology Conference

University of California, Santa Barbara, CA, USA
August 19–23, 2018

Sponsored by the *International Association for Cryptologic Research*

General Chair

Tal Rabin — IBM T.J. Watson Research Center, USA

Program Chairs

Hovav Shacham — University of Texas at Austin, USA
Alexandra Boldyreva — Georgia Institute of Technology, USA

Program Committee

Shweta Agrawal — Indian Institute of Technology, Madras, India
Benny Applebaum — Tel Aviv University, Israel
Foteini Baldimtsi — George Mason University, USA
Gilles Barthe — IMDEA Software Institute, Spain
Fabrice Benhamouda — IBM Research, USA
Alex Biryukov — University of Luxembourg, Luxembourg
Jeremiah Blocki — Purdue University, USA
Anne Broadbent — University of Ottawa, Canada
Chris Brzuska — Aalto University, Finland
Chitchanok Chuengsatiansup — Inria and ENS de Lyon, France
Dana Dachman-Soled — University of Maryland, USA
Léo Ducas — Centrum Wiskunde & Informatica, The Netherlands
Pooya Farshim — CNRS and ENS, France
Dario Fiore — IMDEA Software Institute, Spain
Marc Fischlin — Darmstadt University of Technology, Germany
Georg Fuchsbauer — Inria and ENS, France
Steven D. Galbraith — University of Auckland, New Zealand
Christina Garman — Purdue University, USA
Daniel Genkin — University of Pennsylvania and University of Maryland, USA
Dov Gordon — George Mason University, USA
Viet Tung Hoang — Florida State University, USA

Tetsu Iwata	Nagoya University, Japan
Stanislaw Jarecki	University of California, Irvine, USA
Seny Kamara	Brown University, USA
Markulf Kohlweiss	University of Edinburgh, UK
Farinaz Koushanfar	University of California, San Diego, USA
Xuejia Lai	Shanghai Jiao Tong University, China
Tancrède Lepoint	SRI International, USA
Anna Lysyanskaya	Brown University, USA
Alex J. Malozemoff	Galois, USA
Sarah Meiklejohn	University College London, UK
Daniele Micciancio	University of California, San Diego, USA
María Naya-Plasencia	Inria, France
Kenneth G. Paterson	Royal Holloway, University of London, UK
Ananth Raghunathan	Google, USA
Mike Rosulek	Oregon State University, USA
Ron Rothblum	MIT and Northeastern University, USA
Alessandra Scafuro	North Carolina State University, USA
abhi shelat	Northeastern University, USA
Nigel P. Smart	Katholieke Universiteit Leuven, Belgium
Martijn Stam	University of Bristol, UK
Noah Stephens-Davidowitz	Princeton University, USA
Aishwarya Thiruvengadam	University of California, Santa Barbara, USA
Hoeteck Wee	CNRS and ENS, France
Daniel Wichs	Northeastern University, USA
Mark Zhandry	Princeton University, USA

Additional Reviewers

Aydin Abadi	Balthazar Bauer	Zvika Brakerski
Archita Agarwal	Carsten Baum	Jacqueline Brendel
Divesh Aggarwal	Amos Beimel	David Butler
Shashank Agrawal	Itay Berman	Matteo Campanelli
Adi Akavia	Marc Beunardeau	Brent Carmer
Navid Alamati	Sai Lakshmi Bhavana	Ignacio Cascudo
Martin Albrecht	Simon Blackburn	Wouter Castryck
Miguel Ambrona	Estuardo Alpirez Bock	Andrea Cerulli
Ghous Amjad	Andrej Bogdanov	André Chailloux
Megumi Ando	André Schrottenloher	Nishanth Chandran
Ralph Ankele	Xavier Bonnetain	Panagiotis Chatzigiannis
Gilad Asharov	Charlotte Bonte	Stephen Checkoway
Achiya Bar-On	Carl Bootland	Binyi Chen
Manuel Barbosa	Jonathan Bootle	Michele Ciampi
Paulo Barreto	Christina Boura	Benoit Cogliati
James Bartusek	Florian Bourse	Gil Cohen
Guy Barwell	Elette Boyle	Ran Cohen

Aisling Connolly
Sandro Coretti
Henry Corrigan-Gibbs
Geoffroy Couteau
Shujie Cui
Ting Cui
Joan Daemen
Wei Dai
Yuanxi Dai
Alex Davidson
Jean Paul Degabriele
Akshay Degwekar
Ioannis Demertzis
Itai Dinur
Jack Doerner
Nico Döttling
Benjamin Dowling
Tuyet Thi Anh Duong
Frédéric Dupuis
Betul Durak
Lior Eldar
Karim Eldefrawy
Lucas Enloe
Andre Esser
Antonio Faonio
Prastudy Fauzi
Daniel Feher
Serge Fehr
Nils Fleischhacker
Benjamin Fuller
Tommaso Gagliardoni
Martin Gagné
Adria Gascon
Pierrick Gaudry
Romain Gay
Nicholas Genise
Marilyn George
Ethan Gertler
Vlad Gheorghiu
Esha Ghosh
Brian Goncalves
Junqing Gong
Adam Groce
Johann Großschädl
Paul Grubbs
Jiaxin Guan

Jian Guo
Siyao Guo
Joanne Hall
Ariel Hamlin
Abida Haque
Patrick Harasser
Gottfried Herold
Naofumi Homma
Akinori Hosoyamada
Jialin Huang
Siam Umar Hussain
Chloé Hébant
Yuval Ishai
Ilia Iliashenko
Yuval Ishai
Håkon Jacobsen
Christian Janson
Ashwin Jha
Thomas Johansson
Chethan Kamath
Bhavana Kanukurthi
Marc Kaplan
Pierre Karpman
Sriram Keelveedhi
Dmitry Khovratovich
Franziskus Kiefer
Eike Kiltz
Sam Kim
Elena Kirshanova
Konrad Kohbrok
Lisa Maria Kohl
Ilan Komargodski
Yashvanth Kondi
Venkata Koppula
Lucas Kowalczyk
Hugo Krawczyk
Thijs Laarhoven
Marie-Sarah Lacharite
Virginie Lallemand
Esteban Landerreche
Phi Hung Le
Eysa Lee
Jooyoung Lee
Gaëtan Leurent
Baiyu Li
Benoit Libert

Fuchun Lin
Huijia Lin
Tingting Lin
Feng-Hao Liu
Qipeng Liu
Tianren Liu
Zhiqiang Liu
Alex Lombardi
Sébastien Lord
Steve Lu
Yiyuan Luo
Atul Luykx
Vadim Lyubashevsky
Fermi Ma
Varun Madathil
Mohammad Mahmoody
Mary Maller
Giorgia Azzurra Marson
Daniel P. Martin
Samiha Marwan
Christian Matt
Alexander May
Sogol Mazaheri
Bart Mennink
Carl Alexander Miller
Brice Minaud
Ilya Mironov
Tarik Moataz
Nicky Mouha
Fabrice Mouhartem
Pratyay Mukherjee
Mridul Nandi
Samuel Neves
Anca Nitulescu
Kaisa Nyberg
Adam O'Neill
Maciej Obremski
Olya Ohrimenko
Igor Carboni Oliveira
Claudio Orlandi
Michele Orrù
Emmanuela Orsini
Dag Arne Osvald
Elisabeth Oswald
Elena Pagnin
Chris Peikert

Léo Perrin
Edoardo Persichetti
Duong-Hieu Phan
Krzysztof Pietrzak
Bertram Poettering
David Pointcheval
Antigoni Polychroniadou
Eamonn Postlethwaite
Willy Quach
Elizabeth Quaglia
Samuel Ranellucci
Mariana Raykova
Christian Rechberger
Oded Regev
Nicolas Resch
Leo Reyzin
M. Sadegh Riazi
Silas Richelson
Peter Rindal
Phillip Rogaway
Miruna Rosca
Dragos Rotaru
Yann Rotella
Arnab Roy
Manuel Sabin
Sruthi Sekar
Amin Sakzad
Katerina Samari
Pedro Moreno Sanchez

Sven Schaege
Adam Sealfon
Yannick Seurin
Aria Shahverdi
Tom Shrimpton
Luisa Siniscalchi
Kit Smeets
Fang Song
Pratik Soni
Jessica Sorrell
Florian Speelman
Douglas Stebila
Marc Stevens
Bing Sun
Shifeng Sun
Siwei Sun
Qiang Tang
Seth Terashima
Tian Tian
Mehdi Tibouchi
Yosuke Todo
Aleksei Udovenko
Dominique Unruh
Bogdan Ursu
María Isabel González
  Vasco
Muthuramakrishnan
  Venkitasubramaniam
Fre Vercauteren

Fernando Virdia
Alexandre Wallet
Michael Walter
Meiqin Wang
Qingju Wang
Boyang Wei
Mor Weiss
Jan Winkelmann
Tim Wood
David Wu
Hong Xu
Shota Yamada
Hailun Yan
LeCorre Yann
Kan Yasuda
Arkady Yerukhimovich
Eylon Yogev
Yang Yu
Yu Yu
Thomas Zacharias
Wentao Zhang
Hong-Sheng Zhou
Linfeng Zhou
Vassilis Zikas
Giorgos Zirdelis
Lukas Zobernig
Adi Ben Zvi

Sponsors

Contents – Part II

Proof Tools

Simplifying Game-Based Definitions

Indistinguishability up to Correctness
and Its Application to Stateful AE

Phillip Rogaway$^{(\boxtimes)}$ and Yusi Zhang

Computer Science Department, University of California Davis,
One Shields Avenue, Davis, USA
rogaway@cs.ucdavis.edu

Abstract. Often the simplest way of specifying game-based crypto-graphic definitions is apparently barred because the adversary would have some trivial win. Disallowing or invalidating these wins can lead to complex or unconvincing definitions. We suggest a generic way around this difficulty. We call it *indistinguishability up to correctness*, or IND|C. Given games G and H and a correctness condition C we define an advantage measure $\mathbf{Adv}^{\mathrm{indc}}_{\mathrm{G,H,C}}$ wherein G/H distinguishing attacks are effaced to the extent that they are inevitable due to C. We formalize this in the language of *oracle silencing*, an alternative to exclusion-style and penalty-style definitions. We apply our ideas to a domain where game-based definitions have been cumbersome: stateful authenticated-encryption (sAE). We rework existing sAE notions and encompass new ones, like replay-free AE permitting a specified degree of out-of-order message delivery.

Keywords: Indistinguishability · Oracle silencing · Provable security
Stateful authenticated encryption

1 Introduction

This paper addresses a common difficulty one encounters in giving game-based cryptographic definitions: the need to ensure that adversaries don't get credit for trivial wins. But what exactly *is* a trivial win? Sometimes answering this is *not* trivial. Our simple but previously unexplored idea is to use a scheme's correctness requirement to automatically determine if a win should or shouldn't count. We believe that this can lead to simpler and more compelling definitions.

Correctness requirements—for example, that a decryption algorithm properly reverses the corresponding encryption algorithm—are normally understood as demands on functionality, not security. Yet we will use correctness to help define security. More specifically, a correctness condition will be used to map a pair of games that an adversary *can* trivially distinguish into a pair of games that it *can't* trivially distinguish. The modified games are identical to the original ones apart from eliminating wins that exploit generic checks on correctness. The adversary's

© International Association for Cryptologic Research 2018
H. Shacham and A. Boldyreva (Eds.): CRYPTO 2018, LNCS 10992, pp. 3–32, 2018.
https://doi.org/10.1007/978-3-319-96881-0_1

advantage in distinguishing the modified games is elevated to a definition for *indistinguishability up to correctness*, or IND|C. In our main elaboration of this, responses to oracle queries are *silenced* when the correctness requirement renders a response *fixed*. A response is fixed when the answer depends only on the query history and the correctness constraint. Once silenced, an oracle will stay so.

Besides developing the idea above, this paper is also about an illustrative application of it. The problem we look at, significant in its own right, is how to find a clean and general treatment for stateful authenticated-encryption (sAE). A sender transmits a sequence of encrypted messages to a receiver. The communication channel might be reliable or not, and the parties might or might not maintain state (stateful AE should encompass conventional AE). If the decrypting party does maintain state, it might have a little or a lot. We seek a metaphorical "knob" with which one can specify precise expectations regarding replays, omissions, and out-of-order delivery. Our definition for sAE security does this. Given a set L specifying exactly which message reorderings are considered permissible, we define a matching correctness condition. From it and a pair of simple games, which do not depend on L, one inherits a security notion, courtesy of IND|C. By appropriately setting L we encompass old sAE notions and significant new ones, like sAE permitting reorderings up to a specified lag in message delivery.

INDISTINGUISHABILITY UP TO CORRECTNESS. In somewhat greater detail, the methodology we suggest works as follows. To define a cryptographic goal one designs a pair of *utopian* games G and H that an adversary must try to distinguish. Game G surfaces the *real* behavior of some underlying protocol Π, while game H surfaces the *ideal* behavior one might wish for. We call the games *utopian* because there is some simple adversarial attack to distinguish them. For example, if we aim to treat public-key encryption (PKE) secure against chosen-ciphertext attack (CCA), then game G might let the adversary encrypt and decrypt with the underlying encryption scheme Π, while H properly answers decryption queries, but answers encryption queries by encrypting zero bits.

The cryptographer next pins down when a scheme is *correct*. Correctness is a validity requirement, not a security requirement. It captures what needs to happen in the *absence* of an adversary. In our PKE example, correctness for a scheme $\Pi = (\mathcal{K}, \mathcal{E}, \mathcal{D})$ says that $(pk, sk) \twoheadleftarrow \mathcal{K}(k)$ and $c \twoheadleftarrow \mathcal{E}(pk, m)$ implies $\mathcal{D}(sk, c) = m$. Formally, saying that a scheme Π is correct just means that it belongs to some class C of correct schemes: for us, a correctness condition *is* a class of scheme.

We generalize conventional indistinguishability (IND) to the notion we call *indistinguishability up to correctness* (IND|C). The idea is this. Suppose that the adversary is interacting with a "real" game G that depends on some underlying cryptographic scheme Π. What it wants is to distinguish G from some "ideal" game H (which might also depend on Π). Suppose, at some point in the adversary's attack, it asks an oracle query x_i. It previously asked $x_1, \ldots, x_{i-1}$ and got answers $y_1, \ldots, y_{i-1}$. If given this query history t there is only one possible reply y across all correct schemes $\Pi \in$ C and all internal coins r that G might use, then we say the oracle's response is *fixed*. The games we denote G$[\psi]$

and H[ψ] behave like G and H except that asking a query that is fixed turns off the oracle: it answers $\lozenge$ from that point on. The symbol ψ in the brackets following G and H denotes the *silencing function*, and we just described defining it by way of fixedness. Correctness-directed *oracle silencing* is the automatic adjustment of games (G, H) to modified games (G[ψ], H[ψ]). Using this method, we generalize the IND advantage $\mathbf{Adv}_{G,H}^{ind}(A) = \Pr[A^G \to 1] - \Pr[A^H \to 1]$ to the INDC-advantage $\mathbf{Adv}_{G,H,C}^{indc}(A) = \mathbf{Adv}_{G[\psi],H[\psi]}^{ind}(A)$.

There is one more needed element: the adversary needs to *know* if an oracle query is going to be silenced—we need ψ to be efficiently computable. One must show that it is. If it's not, the intuition that the adversary shouldn't ask a question because it trivially knows the answer completely falls apart.

APPLICATION: PKE. As a first and simple application of IND|C, we revisit the standard IND-CCA security notion for PKE. We provide a utopian pair of games, G1 and H1, and a correctness class C1, thereby obtaining a security notion PKE.new defined by $\mathbf{Adv}_{G1,H1,C1}^{indc}$. We show, unsurprisingly, that PKE.new is equivalent to PKE.old, the customary definition for IND-CCA secure PKE.

But wait: just what definition is it that we call *customary*? Bellare, Hofheinz, and Kiltz (BHK) describe four variants of IND-CCA secure PKE, which they denote with suffixes SE, SP, BE, and BP [1]. They explain that researchers haven't always been clear as to what version they intend. And they show that it *does* make a difference: while the SE and SP notions are equivalent, all other pairs are inequivalent. BHK suggest that the SE/SP notion is the *right* definitional variant [1, p. 34 & p. 39], implying that the other two notions are *wrong*. We agree. But how can one convincingly justify such a claim? The most convincing response, in our view, is to say that the SE/SP notion coincides with what one gets by invalidating all and only the adversarial wins that one *must* invalidate because of correctness. The BE and BP notions inappropriately invalidate additional wins. This is the response that our work formalizes. Similar reasoning can be used to justify definitional choices that might otherwise seem arbitrary.

APPLICATION: sAE. Our second application of IND|C is more involved: we consider the stateful-AE (sAE) problem, first formalized by Bellare, Kohno, and Namprempre (BKN) [2]. BKN adjust the customary definition of AE to make the decryption process stateful. Trying to model the kind of AE achieved by SSL, they want that ciphertext replays, reorderings, and omissions, as well as forgeries, will all be flagged as invalid. Formalizing this requires care.

Building on the above, Kohno, Palacio, and Black (KPB) describe five *types* of sAE [11], these ranging from a version that forgives all replays, omissions, and reorderings, to one that demands authentication to fail if any of these transgressions occur. Boyd, Hale, Mjølsnes, and Stebila (BHMS) [4] rework the KPB taxonomy, defining four *levels* of sAE. While the games they give are not terribly long, it is not easy to understand their technical constraints [4, Fig. 2]. And perhaps it was not easy for the authors, either, who made a technical adjustment in one of the four definitions about a year after their first publication [5, Recv line 4]. And if one wanted to consider some new sAE variant—and we will explain soon why one might—one would need to start from scratch. The resulting definition might be hard to verify and easy to get wrong.

In our view, sAE is in a muddy state. The BKN, KPB, and BHMS papers use different syntax, making rigorous comparisons problematic. And they live in a sea of disparate and often complex related notions, including UC treatments of secure channels [6,7,12], the ACCE definition of Jager, Kohlar, Schäge, and Schwenk [10], and the notion for stream-based channels from Fischlin, Günther, Marson, and Paterson [8,9].

We go back to the basics for sAE, specifying a scheme's syntax and an extremely simple pair of games for the goal, G2 and H2, which the adversary *will* be able to easily distinguish them. We then "cancel" the trivial wins via IND|C. Given a set L that describes the required level of channel fidelity, we define a corresponding class of correct schemes C2(L). The above induces a security notion sAE[L] via IND|C. The flavors of sAE from BKN, KPB, and BHMS correspond to sAE[L] for specific choices of L. Many further choices are possible. In particular, the set we call L_1^ℓ bans forgeries and replays, but allows omissions and reordering up to some specified lag ℓ. The level we denote L_2^ℓ bans forgeries, replays, and reordering, but allows omissions of up to ℓ messages. The related levels from KPB and BHMS place no limits on ℓ (i.e., $\ell = \infty$). Achieving that aim would normally be impractical, as the decrypting party would need to maintain unlimited state, using it to record every nonce received.

Besides defining sAE[L] security, we show that the natural way to achieve it from nonce-based AE does in fact work. We discuss when this scheme is efficient, and describe efficiency and security improvements that are possible for some L.

ALTERNATIVES. The way we have chosen to define IND|C security is not the only way possible: there are a variety of natural variants. For each, one uses the correctness condition C to automatically edit utopian games G and H to new games G′ and H′. Oracle-editing generalizes oracle-silencing. We look at about half a dozen definitional variants, and evidence the robustness of IND|C by arguing that, under anticipated side conditions, all but one alternative is equivalent to our original formulation. For that final variant, meant to deal with left-or-right style games, we do not know how to prove or disprove equivalence.

2   Indistinguishability up to Correctness

GAMES. We recall the notion of games from Bellare and Rogaway [3], making some minor adjustments. See Fig. 1.

A game G is an always-halting algorithm given by code. It has entry points Initialize, Oracle, and Finalize. The code can obtain successive coin tosses from a uniformly random string $r \twoheadleftarrow \{0,1\}^\infty$. One runs G with an adversary A, which can likewise see coins $\rho \twoheadleftarrow \{0,1\}^\infty$. Both the adversary and game maintain persistent states. A game may depend on an *underlying scheme* $\Pi \colon \{0,1\}^* \to \{0,1\}^*$. We may write G_Π to emphasize G's dependence on Π. Normally this dependence is in the form of black-box access to a Π oracle. A game G may also call out to an arbitrary function ψ whose definition need not be in code.

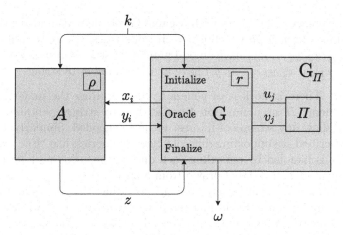

Fig. 1. An adversary interacting with a game. A game G may depend on a cryptographic scheme $\Pi\colon \{0,1\}^* \to \{0,1\}^*$. The game G and adversary A are both provided an initial value k. Adversarial and game randomness are provided by random strings ρ and r. Pairs x_i, y_i and u_j, v_j represent sequences of queries, indexed from 1. The adversary's output is z and the game's outcome is ω.

To execute G with A, the game's Initialize procedure is first run, passing it an initial value k. This is normally assumed to be a number, the security parameter, and presented in unary. Nothing is returned. Next, the adversary A is run, again invoking it on k. The adversary will make a sequence of Oracle calls (oracle queries) $x_1, \ldots, x_q$ obtaining corresponding responses $y_1, \ldots, y_q$. The number of queries q is up to the adversary. When the adversary has asked all the queries it wants to ask, it halts with an output z. The game's Finalize procedure is then called with z. It returns the game outcome ω. Specifying a game entails specifying Initialize, Oracle, and Finalize. If the first is omitted, there is only the default initialization of game variables: 0 for numbers, false for booleans, ε for strings, and the empty vector $\Lambda = (\ )$ for vectors. If Finalize is omitted, it is the algorithm that outputs its input, making the game's outcome the adversary's output. The number $\Pr[A^{\mathrm{G}}(k) \to 1]$ is the probability that A outputs 1 after interacting with game G given the initial input k. The Finalize procedure is irrelevant. The number $\Pr[\mathrm{G}^A(k) \to 1]$ is the probability that G (it's Finalize procedure) outputs 1 after an interaction with A on k.

We can regard G_Π as a function, with $y_i = \mathrm{G}_\Pi(k, x_1, \ldots, x_i, r)$ the value returned by the oracle query when the initial value is k, the queries asked are $x_1, \ldots, x_i$, and the coins are r; while $\omega = \mathrm{G}_\Pi(k, x_1, \ldots, x_q, z, r)$ is similarly construed, employing encoding conventions such that the Finalize call is clear. If we omit r from the arguments then G_Π becomes a randomized function. We omit k whenever the Initialize procedure does not depend on it.

As an adversary A interacts with a game G, oracle calls and responses can be recorded in a *transcript*, which is a vector of strings. Query-terminated transcripts $(x_1, y_1, x_2, y_2 \ldots, x_i)$ have an odd number of strings; response-terminated transcripts $(x_1, y_1, x_2, y_2 \ldots, x_i, y_i)$ have an even number of strings.

DISCUSSION. There is no loss of generality in regarding the underlying cryptographic scheme Π as a function from strings to strings; suitable encoding conventions allow any scheme of interest to be so encoded. Similarly, games are routinely described as supporting different *types* of queries, like "Enc" and "Dec" queries. This is handled by regarding each query x as encoding a vector whose first component, $x[1]$, is a label drawn from a specified set.

An oracle query x might be intended only to adjust the game's internal state, not to elicit any response. Such queries are called *declarative*. All other queries are *investigative*. We do not adopt any special syntax to differentiate declarative and investigative queries, but the designer of a game is always free to adopt some convention to serve this purpose.

CORRECTNESS. What does it mean to say that a scheme Π is correct? The simplest answer is to say Π belongs to some class of schemes C, which are those deemed correct. That is what we will do; for us a *correctness class* is a set C of functions from strings to strings, and defining correctness means specifying C.

Graded notions of correctness, where a scheme is $(1 - \varepsilon)$-correct if some bad event happens with probability at most ε, are outside the scope of our definitions.

SILENCING. Given a correctness class C and a game G we define a predicate on response-terminated transcripts

$$Valid_{C,G}(x_1, y_1, \ldots, x_j, y_j) = (\exists \Pi \in C)(\exists k \in \{0,1\}^*)(\exists r \in \{0,1\}^\infty)(\forall i \in [1..j])$$
$$[\, G_\Pi(k, x_1, x_2, \ldots, x_i, r) = y_i \,] .$$

In English, a response-terminated transcript is valid if there exists a scheme in the specified class that could give rise to it. Since adversaries can ask anything they please, we say that a query-terminated transcript is valid when its longest proper prefix is: $Valid_{C,G}(x_1, y_1, \ldots, x_j, y_j, x) = Valid_{C,G}(x_1, y_1, \ldots, x_j, y_j)$.

Building on the notion of validity, we define a boolean function on query-terminated transcripts

$$Fixed_{C,G}(x_1, y_1, \ldots, x_j, y_j, x) = (\exists! \, y) \; Valid_{C,G}(x_1, y_1, \ldots, x_j, y_j, x, y) .$$

Here $(\exists! \, y)P(y)$ means $(\exists y)P(y) \wedge (\forall y_1)(\forall y_2)((P(y_1) \wedge P(y_2)) \Rightarrow y_1 = y_2)$. In English, a query-terminated transcript is fixed if the last indicated query has exactly one valid response. Note that when the transcript t is invalid then $Fixed_{C,G}(t)$ is false, since $(\exists! \, y)P(y) \Rightarrow (\exists y)P(y)$.

Finally, given a correctness class C and game G, we define our preferred *silencing function* for this pair by

$$Silence_{C,G}(x_1, y_1, \ldots, x_j) = \bigvee_{1 \leq i \leq j} Fixed_{C,G}(x_1, y_1, \ldots, x_i) .$$

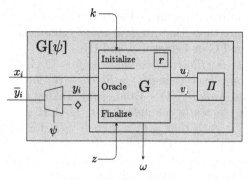

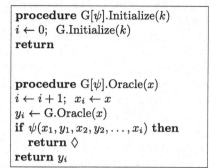

procedure $G[\psi]$.Initialize(k)
$i \leftarrow 0$; $\;$ G.Initialize(k)
return

procedure $G[\psi]$.Oracle(x)
$i \leftarrow i + 1$; $\;$ $x_i \leftarrow x$
$y_i \leftarrow$ G.Oracle(x)
if $\psi(x_1, y_1, x_2, y_2, \ldots, x_i)$ **then**
$\quad$ **return** $\Diamond$
return y_i

Fig. 2. Oracle silencing. Left: Given a game G and a function $\psi\colon \{0,1\}^{**} \to \{0,1\}$ we define the silenced game $G[\psi]$ by silencing the oracle once the boolean value $\psi(x_1, y_1, \ldots, x_i)$ becomes **true**. **Right:** The formal definition for the game $G[\psi]$. The game's Finalize procedure is irrelevant.

That is, we silence an oracle response that terminates a transcript t if that response is now fixed, or was previously. We call this *silence-then-shut-down*.

IND|C SECURITY. Given a game G and a boolean function ψ, which we call a *silencing function*, we define the *silenced game* $G[\psi]$ in Fig. 2. In that game, oracle responses are adjusted according to ψ: when ψ applied to the y_i-terminated transcript is **true**, we return $\Diamond$ instead of y_i.

Now given games G and H and a silencing function ψ, let $\mathbf{Adv}^{\mathrm{indc}}_{\mathrm{G,H},\psi}(A, k) = \Pr[A^{G[\psi]}(k) \to 1] - \Pr[A^{H[\psi]}(k) \to 1]$.

Finally, given games G and H and a correctness class C, let $\mathbf{Adv}^{\mathrm{indc}}_{\mathrm{G,H,C}}(A, k) = \Pr[A^{G[\psi]}(k) \to 1] - \Pr[A^{H[\psi]}(k) \to 1]$ where $\psi = Silence_{\mathrm{C,G}}$. We call this notion INDC security, or, perhaps more pretty, IND|C security. (The vertical bar is meant to suggest conditioning.) Note that the silencing that is applied to the ideal game H is determined by the real game G.

For an asymptotic notion of INDC security, we assert that games G and H are *indistinguishable up to* C if $\mathbf{Adv}^{\mathrm{indc}}_{\mathrm{G,H,C}}(A, k)$ is negligible for any probabilistic polynomial-time (PPT) adversary A. As usual, $\varepsilon(k)$ is negligible if for any polynomial p there exists a number N such that $\varepsilon(k) < 1/p(k)$ for all $k \geq N$.

Remember that games $G = G_\Pi$ and $H = H_\Pi$ may depend on some underlying scheme Π. A cryptographer who specifies G, H and C has specified a security measure on protocols $\Pi \in C$ defined by $\mathbf{Adv}_\Pi(A, k) = \mathbf{Adv}^{\mathrm{indc}}_{G_\Pi, H_\Pi, C}(A, k)$.

COMPUTABILITY OF FIXEDNESS. There is no *a priori* reason to believe that $Fixed_{\mathrm{C,G}}$ or $Silence_{\mathrm{C,G}}$ will be computable, let alone efficiently. Yet for IND|C security to be meaningful, we need $Fixed_{\mathrm{C,G}}$ to be efficiently computable: if the adversary doesn't *know* that the response to its query is determined by the correctness constraint, then the query is *not* trivial, and making it should *not* be disqualifying. The most straightforward way of capturing the stated expectation is to demand that $Fixed_{\mathrm{C,G}}$ be polynomial-time (PT) computable (if one is in the asymptotic setting). This is overkill, however, insofar as the only transcripts t to which $Fixed_{C,G}$ will ever be applied are those that are *legitimate*—those that can arise in an interaction between A and G or between A and H.

Based on this, we say that *fixedness is efficiently computable for* (C, G, H) if there exists a PT-computable function ϕ such that $\phi(t) = Fixed_{C,G}(t)$ for all query-terminated transcripts t satisfying $Valid_{C,G}(t) \vee Valid_{C,H}(t)$. Taking this a step further, we say that *fixedness is efficiently computable for* (C, G, H, q) if there exists a PT-computable function ϕ such that $\phi(t) = Fixed_{C,G}(t)$ for all query-terminated transcripts t satisfying $Valid_{C,G}(t) \vee Valid_{C,H}(t)$ and $|t| < 2q$. The last part says that t involves at most q queries (where $|t|$ is the number of components in t). For positive results, we must verify that fixedness is efficiently computable for (C, G, H), or for (C, G, H, q) with $q(k)$ adequately large.

Further relaxations for efficient computability of fixedness are possible. Since it is safe to silence too little, it is enough to find an efficiently computable function ϕ satisfying $\phi(t) \Rightarrow Silence_{C,G}(t)$ when $Valid_{C,G}(t) \vee Valid_{C,H}(t)$. Our examples won't need this relaxation.

DISCUSSION. We have spoken about the efficient computability of *Fixed*, but we could as well have spoken of the efficient computability of *Silence*. The former is the more basic object, and simpler to think about. In fact, we not only anticipate that the boolean *Fixed* should be efficiently computable, but also the string-valued function $fixed_{G,C}$ that specifies the real-oracle's response when it is in fact fixed (or indicates, alternatively, that it is not). See Sect. 5.

The silencing function ψ used in defining IND|C was not *Fixed* but the logical-or of it applied to all transcript prefixes. Once an oracle is silenced, it stays silenced. An alternative approach, *silence-then-forgive*, is essentially equivalent; see Sect. 5. It is to simplify the description of silence-then-forgive that, in Fig. 2, when a response y_i is silenced, we let the growing "transcript" retain the original (unsilenced) value. This choice is irrelevant for silence-then-shut-down.

As already explained, if fixedness is not efficiently computable the intuition underlying oracle silencing breaks down, and IND|C becomes meaningless. It could even happen that silenced games are harder to distinguish than the utopian ones. For example, given a one-way permutation F with hardcore bit B, game G is constructed to select random values x_0 and x_1 and, on a first oracle query, provide $F(x_0)$ and $F(x_1)$. A second oracle query selects $b \twoheadleftarrow \{0, 1\}$ and returns $B(x_b)$. Now whether or not this query is silenced provides information that the adversary cannot compute. The idea can be elaborated to create indistinguishable games whose silenced versions are distinguishable.

The usual notion of indistinguishability, $\mathbf{Adv}_{G,H}^{\mathrm{ind}}(A, k) = \Pr[A^{\mathrm{G}}(k) \to 1] - \Pr[A^{\mathrm{H}}(k) \to 1]$, coincides with $\mathbf{Adv}_{G,H,\psi}^{\mathrm{indc}}(A, k)$ when $\psi(t) = \mathsf{false}$. Of course IND-security is symmetric: $\mathbf{Adv}_{G,H}^{\mathrm{ind}}(A, k) = \mathbf{Adv}_{H,G}^{\mathrm{ind}}(A, k)$. This is not true of INDC: it may be that $\mathbf{Adv}_{G,H,C}^{\mathrm{indc}}(A, k) \neq \mathbf{Adv}_{H,G,C}^{\mathrm{indc}}(A, k)$. The asymmetry stems from the fact that we silence based on the *real* game, listed first in the subscripts.

Oracle silencing provides an alternative to penalty-style and exclusion-style definitions [1]. We wrap up our discussion by observing that IND|C security could have been defined using those alternatives, too.

```
procedure G⟦ψ⟧.Initialize(k)
q ← 0;  G.Initialize(k)
return

procedure G⟦ψ⟧.Oracle(x)
q ← q + 1;  x_q ← x
return y_q ← G.Oracle(x)

procedure G⟦ψ⟧.Finalize(z)
if ψ(x_1, y_1, x_2, y_2, ..., x_q) then return 0
return z
```

Fig. 3. Penalty-style oracle editing. Oracle queries are answered as usual, but if the final transcript triggers ψ, the game's outcome is set to zero.

PENALTY-STYLE ALTERNATIVE. Instead of turning off an adversary's oracle when it asks an offending question, we could answer the query as usual but, at the end of the game, declare it forfeit. This is what Bellare, Hofheinz, and Kiltz call a *penalty-style* definition [1]. We formalize what is needed in Fig. 3, mapping a game G and a function ψ to a corresponding game $G⟦\psi⟧$. An alternative version of indistinguishability up to correctness, INDC0, is then defined by saying that $\mathbf{Adv}^{indc0}_{G,H,C}(A,k) = \Pr[(G⟦\psi⟧)^A(k) \to 1] - \Pr[(H⟦\psi⟧)^A(k) \to 1]$ where $\psi = Silence_{C,G}$. In effect, the adversary's output z has been replaced by $z \wedge \bigwedge_j \neg Fixed_{C,G}(x_1, y_1, \ldots, x_j)$. For an asymptotic notion of INDC0 security, we say that games G and H are penalty-style indistinguishable up to C if for any PPT adversary A, the function $\mathbf{Adv}^{indc0}_{G,H,C}(A,k)$ is negligible.

What is the relationship between oracle-silencing IND|C and penalty-style INDC0? Assuming fixedness is efficiently computable, the two ways of adjusting games are equivalent. For concision, we give an asymptotic version of the result. The proof, which is easy, is in Appendix A.1.

Theorem 1. *Let G and H be games and let C be a correctness class. Assume fixedness is efficiently computable for (G, H, C). Then G and H are indistinguishable up to C iff they are penalty-style indistinguishable up to C.*

The above might be interpreted as saying that oracle silencing is new language for something that doesn't need it. That misses the point, that oracle-silencing grounds the natural explanation how and why one edits the utopian games.

EXCLUSION-STYLE ALTERNATIVE. And what of exclusion-style definitions [1], where one limits consideration to adversaries that are "well-behaved"? It is possible, although awkward, to describe IND|C in this way. After defining games G_{Π} and H_{Π} and the correctness class C, we restrict attention from all adversaries $\mathcal{U}$ to the subset $\mathcal{A}$ that, when interacting with G_{Π} or H_{Π}, never create a transcript t such that $Fixed_{G,C}(t)$ is true. One attends only to adversaries in $\mathcal{A}$.

The above description might sound problematic because there is no way to inspect an adversary's description and know if it's in $\mathcal{A}$. It doesn't matter. As long as fixedness is efficiently computable for (G, H, C), one can take an adversary

$A \in \mathcal{U}$ and put a "wrapper" around it so that it conforms with $\mathcal{A}$. The wrapped adversary behaves like A unless it is about to ask a query that would make $Fixed_{G,H,C}(t)$ true, in which case it outputs 0 and halts. In this way one names a class of adversaries $\mathcal{A}$ such that the ind-advantage among adversaries in it coincides with the indc-advantage over adversaries in $\mathcal{U}$. So security notions that can be described by oracle silencing can be described exclusion-style. Not that doing so is wise. Exclusion-style definitions compel consideration of adversary classes. They disqualify adversaries that only rarely misbehave. They ignore whether or not an adversary can "know" it has misbehaved. And they promote ambiguity, as the relevant restrictions are not expressed in game code.

FURTHER VARIANTS. Beyond penalty-style and exclusion-style formulations of IND|C, more alternatives are possible. See Sect. 5 for some interesting ones.

3   Public-Key Encryption

Let us consider the well-known IND-CCA security notion for a public-key encryption (PKE) scheme. We first review the syntax. A PKE scheme Π is a tuple of algorithms $\Pi = (\mathcal{K}, \mathcal{E}, \mathcal{D})$ where probabilistic algorithm $\mathcal{K}$ takes in a security parameter k, encoded in unary, and generates a public key pk and a secret key sk; probabilistic algorithm $\mathcal{E}$ takes in a public key pk and a plaintext m, and returns a ciphertext c; and deterministic decryption algorithm $\mathcal{D}$ takes in a secret key sk and a ciphertext c, and returns a message m. For simplicity, we assume a message space of $\{0,1\}^*$. An appropriate encoding of the component algorithms is implicitly assumed whenever we regard Π as a map $\Pi \colon \{0,1\}^* \to \{0,1\}^*$.

To apply our techniques, the first step is to specify the class of correct PKE schemes. This is easily done, letting

$$C1 = \{\Pi = (\mathcal{K}, \mathcal{E}, \mathcal{D}) \mid (\forall k)(\forall m) \; [(pk, sk) \twoheadleftarrow \mathcal{K}(k); c \twoheadleftarrow \mathcal{E}(pk, m) \colon \mathcal{D}(sk, c) = m]\}$$

denote the schemes we consider *correct*. The condition is absolute: decryption of $c \twoheadleftarrow \mathcal{E}(k, m)$ must *always* return m, which is the customary requirement.

The second step is to write down the utopian real and ideal games. For this, we ask the adversary to distinguish between a game that encrypts a message m of the adversary's choice and a game that encrypts an equal length string of zero-bits. For both games, the adversary can request the public key and has access to a proper decryption oracle. See Fig. 4. Those games only allow the adversary a single Enc query. This restriction is unnecessary, but including it reduces the gap between our new notion and the traditional one for IND-CCA that we use.

The games are indeed utopian: if the adversary queries Enc(1), getting back c, then queries Dec(c), getting back m, it will earn advantage 1 by returning m. Naturally this is where oracle silencing comes into play: if Dec is queried with the response c returned by a previous Enc query then $Fixed_{C1,G1}$ will almost always be true, resulting in the query being silenced. Why do we say *almost* always, and not always? The answer is closely related to how one can efficiently compute $Fixed_{C1,G1}$.

procedure Initialize (k) $\quad$ Game G1	procedure Initialize (k) $\quad$ Game H1
111 $(pk, sk) \twoheadleftarrow \mathcal{K}(k)$	121 $(pk, sk) \twoheadleftarrow \mathcal{K}(k)$
procedure Key	procedure Key
112 return pk	122 return pk
procedure Enc (m)	procedure Enc (m)
113 if asked return $\perp$	123 if asked return $\perp$
114 asked $\leftarrow$ true	124 asked $\leftarrow$ true
115 return $\mathcal{E}(pk, m)$	125 return $\mathcal{E}(pk, 0^{|m|})$
procedure Dec (c)	procedure Dec (c)
116 return $\mathcal{D}(sk, c)$	126 return $\mathcal{D}(sk, c)$

Fig. 4. Utopian games used to define PKE.new. The games are easily distinguished in the ind-sense. The problem is fixed by switching to indc-advantage.

COMPUTING FIXEDNESS. As just indicated, even if a transcript t has a Dec(c) follow an Enc(m) that returns c, it is not *always* the case that $Fixed_{C1,G1}(t) =$ true. At issue is the fact that there are some peculiar transcripts that can arise in the ideal setting but would never arise in the real setting. Recall that our formalization demands that we do *not* silence a query ending a transcript t that could never arise in the "real" setting. One such counterexample is a Dec(c) query that returns m, followed by an Enc(m') query that returns c, where $m \neq m'$. This can't happen in the "real" game, since it would violate correctness. Since we only silence valid transcripts, once such an invalid event takes place, in a run with H, we never silence any further queries—even for a Dec(c) following some Enc(m) query that returns c.

The code of Fig. 5 attends to such subtleties. There we write out a formula for a candidate function ϕ that efficiently computes fixedness for (C1, G1, H1). Function ϕ makes sure the mentioned counterexample does not occur (first line), and it also checks for the "usual" concern: a decryption query that asks to decrypt the challenge ciphertext (second line). But there are still some additional, naïve queries to deal with (the last three lines). These are: a Key query subsequent to the first such query; an Enc query subsequent to the first such query; and a repeating Dec(c) query, for some value c. The responses to any of those queries will be silenced. Our result on the computability of fixedness is as follows.

Theorem 2. *There is a PT algorithm that computes fixedness for (C1, G1, H1). In fact, the algorithm of Fig. 5 computes it.*

For a proof, see Appendix A.2.

To define the security of a PKE scheme against IND-CCA attack, we let $\mathbf{Adv}_{\Pi}^{\mathrm{pke.new}}(A, k) = \mathbf{Adv}_{G1[\Pi],H1[\Pi],C1}^{\mathrm{indc}}(A, k)$ for the games and correctness class described. We say that a PKE scheme Π is PKE.new-secure if $\mathbf{Adv}_{\Pi}^{\mathrm{pke.new}}(A, k)$

procedure $\phi(x_1, y_1, \ldots, x_t)$
201 return $\big((\not\exists i, j)\ x_i = (\mathrm{Dec}, y_j) \wedge x_j[1] = \mathrm{Enc} \wedge x_j[2] \neq y_i \big) \wedge$
202 $\big((\exists j)\ (x_j[1] = \mathrm{Enc} \wedge x_t = (\mathrm{Dec}, y_j))\big) \vee$
203    $(\exists j)\ (x_j[1] = \mathrm{Key} \wedge x_t[1] = \mathrm{Key}) \vee$
204    $(\exists j)\ (x_j[1] = \mathrm{Enc} \wedge x_t[1] = \mathrm{Enc}) \vee$
205    $(\exists j, c)\ (x_j = x_t = (\mathrm{Dec}, c))\big)$

Fig. 5. Formula for computing fixedness for PKE.new. Line 201 is the validity check, while line 202–205 are the fixedness checks.

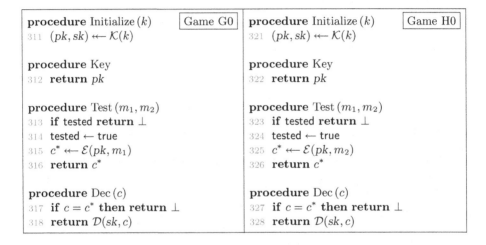

Fig. 6. The PKE.old notion for IND-CCA secure public-key encryption. The formulation is equivalent to the SE and SP notions from BHK [1].

is negligible for all PPT adversaries A. We have already shown that fixedness is efficiently computable for (C1, G1, H1).

How does our PKE.new notion compare with "standard" IND-CCA security for a public-key encryption scheme? By the latter we mean the (equivalent) IND-CCA-SE and IND-CCA-SP notions of BHK [1]. We define it using the G0 and H0 games of Fig. 6. Let $\mathbf{Adv}_\Pi^{\mathrm{pke.old}}(A, k) = \mathbf{Adv}_{\mathrm{G0,H0}}^{\mathrm{ind}}(A, k)$ and define Π as PKE.old-secure if $\mathbf{Adv}_\Pi^{\mathrm{pke.old}}(A, k)$ is negligible for any PPT A.

The new and old PKE security notions are equivalent. Equivalence isn't quite obvious, because the silencing criteria not only includes adversaries querying a Dec on the challenge ciphertext—the sole criterion for PKE.old—but, also, adversaries not having triggered any "invalid" events. Less significantly, we're also looking at a real-vs-ideal game, rather than a left-or-right style one. Still, one can show that the notions are equivalent.

Theorem 3. *A PKE scheme is PKE.new-secure iff it is PKE.old-secure.*

The proof is in Appendix A.3.

Theorem 3 supports the idea that the (equivalent) SE and SP notions of BHK are *right*, while the other two notions are not [1]. One of the uses of IND|C security is to justify or call into question an existing definition by, in effect, looking at what the correctness condition itself has to say.

The structure of the proof of Theorem 3 can be generalized. We observe that *Fixed* can always be decomposed into a *validity check* and a *fixedness check*:

$$Fixed(x_1, y_1, \ldots, x_q) = Valid(x_1, y_1, \ldots, x_{q-1}, y_{q-1}) \qquad \text{(validity)}$$
$$\wedge \big((\forall y_q, y_q') \; Valid(x_1, y_1, \ldots, x_q, y_q) \wedge$$
$$Valid(x_1, y_1, \ldots, x_q, y_q') \Rightarrow y_q = y_q' \big) \qquad \text{(fixedness)}$$

A recapitulation of the proof with the decomposition above allows us to draw the following conclusion: as long as both validity and fixedness checks are efficiently computable, the removal of validity checks will give us an equivalent indistinguishability notion. Related discussions can be found in Sect. 5.

4 Stateful AE

SYNTAX. A scheme for stateful AE (sAE) is a tuple of algorithms $\Pi = (\mathcal{K}, \mathcal{E}, \mathcal{D})$ where key-generation algorithm $\mathcal{K}$ is a probabilistic algorithm that returns a string, while encryption algorithm $\mathcal{E} \colon \mathcal{K} \times \mathcal{A} \times \mathcal{M} \times \mathcal{S} \to (\mathcal{C} \cup \{\bot\}) \times \mathcal{S}$ and decryption algorithm $\mathcal{D} \colon \mathcal{K} \times \mathcal{A} \times \mathcal{C} \times \mathcal{S} \to (\mathcal{M} \cup \{\bot\}) \times \mathcal{S}$ are deterministic. We call $\mathcal{K}, \mathcal{M}, \mathcal{C}, \mathcal{A}$, and $\mathcal{S}$ the key space, message space, ciphertext space, associated-data (AD) space, and state space, respectively. We assume that $\mathcal{K}$ contains the support of $\mathcal{K}$, and that there's a constant τ, the *ciphertext expansion*, such that $(c, s') = \mathcal{E}(k, a, m, s)$ and $c \neq \bot$ implies $|c| = |m| + \tau$. For simplicity, we regard the ciphertext expansion of sAE schemes as a fixed and universal constant (e.g., $\tau = 128$), referring to τ without tying it to any specific scheme.

LEVEL SETS. Suppose a party encrypts messages $1, 2, \ldots, 100$, sending them, encrypted and in order, to some receiver. Due to an active adversary or an unreliable transport, that receiver might recover the sequence of messages $(1, 3, 2)$, or maybe $(1, 10)$, or perhaps $(1, 2, 2, 3)$. In each case, should an authentication error be generated? The answer depends on multiple factors: the anticipated properties of the communication channel; your willingness to have the decrypting party maintain state; how much state you think that party should maintain; and the damage you anticipate from omissions, insertions, and reorderings.

Level	Definition and description
L_0	$\mathbb{N}^*$. This level-set deems all orderings permissible, regardless of omissions, replays, or reorderings. A receiver for this level-set can be stateless. This is the level-set that corresponds to conventional (stateless) AE.
L_1^ℓ	$\{\mathbf{n} \in \mathbb{N}^*: i \neq j \Rightarrow n_i \neq n_j$ and $|n_j - \max_{0 \leq i < j} n_i| \leq \ell + 1$ for all $1 \leq j \leq |\mathbf{n}|\}$. Here we do not permit replays, but do allow omissions and reorderings up to the specified lag. When $\ell = \infty$ there is no limit on the lag and the notion roughly corresponds to level-2 in Kohno et al. [11] and Boyd et al. [4].
L_2^ℓ	$\{\mathbf{n} \in \mathbb{N}^*: 1 \leq n_i - n_{i-1} \leq \ell + 1$ for all $1 \leq i \leq |\mathbf{n}|\}$. This level-set does not permit replays or reorderings, but allows omissions up to ℓ lost packets. When $\ell = \infty$ there is no limit on permissible gaps and the notion roughly corresponds to level-3 in Kohno et al. [11] and Boyd et al. [4]
L_3	$\{\mathbf{n} \in \mathbb{N}^*: n_i = i$ for all $1 \leq i \leq |\mathbf{n}|\}$. This is the strictest level-set: the only permissible receipt order is sending order. This matches the notion for sAE put forward by Bellare et al. [2], level-5 in Kohno et al. [11], and level-4 in Boyd et al. [4]. It is what one expects to achieve over a reliable transport.

Fig. 7. Basic level-sets for sAE. The value $\ell \geq 0$, the maximal *lag*, is a number or the value ∞. The named sets impose increasingly stringent requirements for rejecting replays, omissions, and out-of-order delivery. Throughout, $\mathbf{n} = (n_1, \ldots, n_\beta)$ and $n_0 = 0$.

How might one specify the targeted level of channel fidelity? It can be done by giving a *level-set*, a set $L \subseteq \mathbb{N}^*$ (where $\mathbb{N} = \{1, 2, 3, \ldots\}$ excludes 0). An element $\mathbf{n} \in L$ is called a *permissible ordering*. The intended semantics of $\mathbf{n} = (n_1, \ldots, n_\beta)$ being in L is that *if* the sender transmits a sequence of messages $1, 2, \ldots$, and the receiver recovers, in order, messages $n_1, \ldots, n_\beta$, then this *is* an acceptable degree of fidelity if and only if $\mathbf{n} \in L$. To make sense, we require of any level-set L that $\mathbf{n} \in L$ implies $\mathbf{n}' \in L$ for any prefix $\mathbf{n}'$ of $\mathbf{n}$.

Examples of significant level-sets are given in Fig. 7. We call the level-sets named there the *basic* level-sets. Due to the superscript ℓ, there are infinitely many basic level-sets. The goals associated to levels $L_0, L_1^\infty, L_2^\infty$ and $L_3 = L_1^0 = L_2^0$ are described in prior work [4,11], while the L_1^ℓ and L_2^ℓ goals, for $\ell \in \mathbb{N}$, have not been formalized, although they would seem to be targeted by secure messaging apps like Signal [13].

To apply oracle silencing we need to specify a class of correct sAE schemes. That class will depend on the level-set L. Intuitively, a correct sAE scheme for level-L should satisfy the following condition. Suppose you encrypt a sequence of plaintexts to create ciphertexts we number $1, 2, 3, \ldots$, and then you decrypt, in order, the ciphertexts numbered $n_1, n_2, \ldots, n_\beta$. If $(n_1, \ldots, n_\beta) \in L$ then you must get back the correct sequence of plaintexts. Correctness places no demands on what happens for sequences outside of L. Nor does it levy demands once $\mathcal{E}$ declines to encrypt a string. The correctness class $\mathrm{C2}(L)$ associated to level-set L is formalized at the top of Fig. 8.

UTOPIAN SETTING. We specify the utopian games for sAE in the bottom of Fig. 8, which defines games G2 and H2. The only thing peculiar in the code

$C2(L)$ is the set of all sAE schemes $\Pi = (\mathcal{K}, \mathcal{E}, \mathcal{D})$ that satisfy:

$$\big(\forall k \in \mathcal{K}\big)\big(\forall (a_1, m_1), (a_2, m_2), \ldots \in \mathcal{A} \times \mathcal{M}\big)\big(\forall (n_1, \ldots, n_\beta) \in L\big)$$
$$\big[\; s_0 \leftarrow \varepsilon; \; r_0 \leftarrow \varepsilon; \; \alpha \leftarrow \max(n_1, \ldots n_\beta);$$
$$\textbf{for } i \leftarrow 1 \textbf{ to } \alpha \textbf{ do } (c_i, s_i) \leftarrow \mathcal{E}(k, a_i, m_i, s_{i-1});$$
$$\textbf{for } i \leftarrow 1 \textbf{ to } \beta \textbf{ do } (m'_i, r_i) \leftarrow \mathcal{D}(k, a_{n_i}, c_{n_i}, r_{i-1}):$$
$$((\forall i \in [1..\alpha]) \; (c_i \neq \perp)) \Rightarrow ((\forall i \in [1..\beta]) \; (m'_i = m_{n_i}))\big]$$

procedure Initialize	Game G2	procedure Initialize	Game H2
511 $k \twoheadleftarrow \mathcal{K}$		521 $k \twoheadleftarrow \mathcal{K}$	
procedure Enc(a, m)		**procedure** Enc(a, m)	
512 $(c, s) \twoheadleftarrow \mathcal{E}(k, a, m, s)$		522 $(c, s) \twoheadleftarrow \mathcal{E}(k, a, 0^{|m|}, s)$	
513 **return** c		523 **return** c	
procedure Dec(a, c, σ)		**procedure** Dec(a, c, σ)	
514 $(m, r) \leftarrow \mathcal{D}(k, a, c, r)$		524 **if** σ **then return** $b \twoheadleftarrow \{0,1\}$	
515 **if** σ **then return** $b \twoheadleftarrow \{0,1\}$		525 **return** $\perp$	
516 **return** m			

Fig. 8. Top: Correctness classes for sAE. The function maps a level-set L to a correctness class $C2(L)$. **Bottom: The utopian real and ideal games for sAE.** The games depend on an underlying sAE scheme $\Pi = (\mathcal{K}, \mathcal{E}, \mathcal{D})$.

is the boolean flag σ provided to Dec queries. When set, only a random bit is returned by the game. This is a way for the adversary to mark a *declarative query* (p. 6), meaning an oracle call in which the adversary is not seeking information, but only trying to side-effect the game's internal state. Returning a random bit is just an idiom to exempt a declarative query from getting silenced (as *Fixed* will never be true). Without supporting such an ability, our adversary would effectively be unable to ask a decryption query that it knows the answer to, even if asking such a query would help set the oracle to a state in which the adversary could subsequently cause damage. We call σ the *declarative flag*.

Given an sAE protocol Π and a level-set L, we define $\mathbf{Adv}^{\mathrm{sae}[L]}_{\Pi}(A)$ as $\mathbf{Adv}^{\mathrm{indc}}_{\mathrm{G2}[\Pi], \mathrm{H2}[\Pi], \mathrm{C2}(L)}(A)$. Informally, scheme Π is sAE[L]-secure if $\mathbf{Adv}^{\mathrm{sae}[L]}_{\Pi}(A)$ is small for any reasonable adversary A. Following prevailing traditions in symmetric cryptography, our notion is concrete, not asymptotic, although one could always provide $\mathcal{K}$ with a security parameter and support an asymptotic notion.

COMPUTING FIXEDNESS. It would be nice to give an efficiently computable formula for $Fixed_{C2(L), G2}$, hereinafter abbreviated as $Fixed_L$, for an arbitrary level-set L. But this is not possible—there is no such algorithm—because, in our treatment, level-sets can be arbitrarily bizarre. So we content ourselves with showing efficient computability of fixedness for the basic level-sets. We believe that any "natural" level-set L will have the same property, but stating a sufficient condition on L seems to get rather technical.

Theorem 4. *For any basic level-set L the fixedness function is efficiently computable for* $(C2(L), G2, H2, 2^r - 3)$.

See Appendix A.4 for the proof.

N2S CONSTRUCTION. We now give a simple construction for making an sAE scheme out of a classical nonce-based AE scheme (an nAE scheme) [14]. First we review the syntax and security notions for nonce-based AE.

An nAE scheme $\Pi = (\mathcal{K}, \mathcal{E}, \mathcal{D})$ consists of a probabilistic key-generation algorithm that draws a key from the key space $\mathcal{K}$; a deterministic encryption algorithm $\mathcal{E} \colon \mathcal{K} \times \mathcal{N} \times \mathcal{A} \times \mathcal{M} \to \mathcal{C}$ that takes in a key $k \in \mathcal{K}$, a nonce $n \in \mathcal{N}$, an AD $a \in \mathcal{A}$ and a message $m \in \mathcal{M}$ and outputs a ciphertext $c \in \mathcal{C}$; and a deterministic decryption algorithm $\mathcal{D} \colon \mathcal{K} \times \mathcal{N} \times \mathcal{A} \times \mathcal{C} \to \mathcal{M} \cup \{\bot\}$ that takes in a key $k \in \mathcal{K}$, a nonce $n \in \mathcal{N}$, an AD $a \in \mathcal{A}$ and a ciphertext $c \in \mathcal{C}$ and either outputs a decrypted message $m \in \mathcal{M}$ or a failure symbol $\bot$. Correctness is defined in the natural way: for all $(k, n, a, m) \in \mathcal{K} \times \mathcal{N} \times \mathcal{A} \times \mathcal{M}$ and $c \leftarrow \mathcal{E}(k, n, a, m)$ it holds that $\mathcal{D}(k, n, a, c) = m$. We also assume that for all $(k, n, a, m) \in \mathcal{K} \times \mathcal{N} \times \mathcal{A} \times \mathcal{M}$, the *expansion* $\tau = |\mathcal{E}(k, n, a, m)| - |m|$ is a constant.

For the nAE security definition, let $\$(\cdot, \cdot, \cdot)$ be an oracle that takes in $n \in \mathcal{N}$ and $a \in \mathcal{A}$ and $m \in \mathcal{M}$ and returns a fresh random string of $|m| + \tau$ bits; and let $\bot(\cdot, \cdot, \cdot)$ be an oracle that takes in $n \in \mathcal{N}$ and $a \in \mathcal{A}$ and $c \in \mathcal{C}$ and always returns $\bot$. The advantage of an adversary A against an nAE scheme Π is then defined as

$$\mathbf{Adv}_{\Pi}^{\mathrm{nae}}(A) = \Pr\left[k \in \mathcal{K} \colon A^{\mathcal{E}(k, \cdot, \cdot, \cdot), \mathcal{D}(k, \cdot, \cdot, \cdot)} \to 1\right] - \Pr\left[A^{\$(\cdot, \cdot, \cdot), \bot(\cdot, \cdot, \cdot)} \to 1\right].$$

We require that A never asks (n, a, c) of its right oracle if some previous left oracle query (n, a, m) returned c; and that A does not repeat nonces when asking its left oracle. (The first condition could itself be recovered via IND|C.) Informally, an nAE scheme Π is secure if for all such adversaries with reasonable resources, the advantage $\mathbf{Adv}_{\Pi}^{\mathrm{nae}}(A)$ is small.

Construction N2S turns an nAE scheme Π with key space $\mathcal{K} \subseteq \{0, 1\}^*$, nonce space $\mathcal{N} = \{0, 1\}^\eta$, AD space $\mathcal{A} \subseteq \{0, 1\}^*$ and message space $\mathcal{M} \subseteq \{0, 1\}^*$ and ciphertext expansion τ into an sAE scheme $\overline{\Pi} = (\overline{\mathcal{K}}, \overline{\mathcal{E}}, \overline{\mathcal{D}})$ with the same key space, AD space, and message space. Given an nAE scheme Π and a level-set L, the sAE scheme $\overline{\Pi} = \mathrm{N2S}(\Pi, L)$ is defined and illustrated in Fig. 9.

The construction is quite simple. For encryption, the state is maintained as a counter n that gets incremented with each message sent. When n is used as a string, it is encoded into η bits. The ciphertext is formed by concatenating n and the ciphertext returned by the nAE scheme. For decryption, the state is the vector $\mathbf{n}$ of nonces received so far. The decryption algorithm outputs failure if either the underlying nAE scheme says so *or* the received nonce, when appended to the list of prior ones, does not comprise a permissible ordering in L. We have the following result for the security of N2S:

Theorem 5. *Let* $\Pi = (\mathcal{K}, \mathcal{E}, \mathcal{D})$ *be an nAE scheme with nonce length* η *and ciphertext expansion* τ. *Let* L *be a level-set and let* A *an adversary that asks*

procedure $\overline{\mathcal{K}}$	procedure $\overline{\mathcal{D}}(k, a, nc, \mathbf{n})$
611 **return** $k \twoheadleftarrow \mathcal{K}$	631 **if** $n = \bot$ **then return** $(\bot, \bot)$
	632 $n \| c \leftarrow nc;$ $\mathbf{n} \leftarrow \mathbf{n} \| n$
procedure $\overline{\mathcal{E}}(k, a, m, n)$	633 **if** $\mathbf{n} \notin L$ **then return** $(\bot, \bot)$
621 **if** $n = 2^{\eta} - 1$ **then return** $(\bot, n)$	634 $m \leftarrow \mathcal{D}(k, n, a, c)$
622 $n \leftarrow n + 1$	635 **if** $m = \bot$ **then** $\mathbf{n} \leftarrow \bot$
623 $c \leftarrow \mathcal{E}(k, n, a, m)$	636 **return** $(m, \mathbf{n})$
624 **return** $(n \| c, n)$	

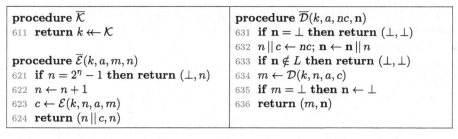

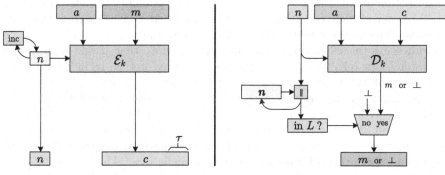

Fig. 9. Top: Definition of the N2S construction. For $\Pi = (\mathcal{K}, \mathcal{E}, \mathcal{D})$ an nAE scheme with η-bit nonces and L a level-set, we construct the sAE scheme $\text{N2S}(\Pi, L) = (\overline{\mathcal{K}}, \overline{\mathcal{E}}, \overline{\mathcal{D}})$. **Bottom: Illustration of the N2S construction.** Messages can be rejected because $\mathcal{D}$ calls for this or because the provided nonce, once concatenated to the prior ones received, is not in L. Various optimizations are possible, depending on L.

$q \leq \min\{2^{\eta}, 2^{\tau} - 3\}$ *queries. Then there exists an adversary* B, *generically described in the proof of this theorem, such that*

$$\mathbf{Adv}_{\Pi}^{nae}(B) \geq \mathbf{Adv}_{N2S[\Pi, L]}^{sae[L]}(A) .$$

Adversary B *is efficient if* A *is efficient and* L *is a basic level-set.*

The efficiency referred to in the theorem statement is made more concrete by the theorem's proof, which is in Appendix A.5.

DISCUSSION. While the decrypting party must, in general, maintain an unbound-edly long state vector $\mathbf{n}$, for many level-sets this is unnecessary: the decryption algorithm will be able to make the decision it needs to make, at line 633, by retaining a finite amount of state. In particular, level-set L_0 needs no retained state; level-set L_1^{ℓ} needs the last $\ell + 1$ nonces; and level-sets L_2^{ℓ} and L_3 need the last nonce received.

Our N2S construction includes in the ciphertext the nonce used for the underlying nAE encryption. This is the usual way to use an nAE scheme, and the choice keeps our construction simple. But it has downsides, both for security and efficiency. The presence of the nonce reveals information that one might wish to hide. It might identify which user a message was sent by (as when one user has sent many messages, and another user has sent few). The presence of the nonces excludes the possibility of achieving IND\$-security, meaning indistinguishability from random bits; it is, in fact, the reason we defined sAE security using the weaker notion of indistinguishability from the encryption of zero-bits (line 522 of Fig. 8). As for efficiency, N2S increases the ciphertext expansion from the nAE scheme's τ bits to $\eta + \tau$ bits, which may be unnecessary.

Addressing the efficiency complaint first, we note that if one is targeting sAE level L_3 (a reliable channel), the nonce n need not be included with the ciphertext, for the receiver will know what it must be if the ciphertext is to be valid. For levels L_1^ℓ and L_2^ℓ, with $\ell \in \mathbb{N}$, we can also reduce the ciphertext length. Instead of including the entire nonce n in the ciphertext, it is sufficient to include $n \bmod (2\ell+2)$ for L_1^ℓ or $n \bmod (\ell+1)$ for L_2^ℓ. From this the receiver can reconstruct the only possible value of n for a valid message. In practical settings, one would expect this information to fit in a single byte. Thus L_1^ℓ and L_2^ℓ are nicer than L_1^∞ and L_2^∞ not only for capping the state of the decrypting party but, also, for reducing ciphertext expansion.

As for security, what change to N2S is needed to achieve the stronger IND\$ definition? (For that, change line 522 to replace c by $|m| + \tau$ many uniformly random bits.) Perhaps the most obvious approach is to include in the ciphertext the enciphered nonce, rather than the nonce itself. One would use a blockcipher and a separate key. If η is small, like 32 or 96, one would need a blockcipher with an unusual block length. And the IND\$ security would now degrade, unpleasantly, with $q^2/2^\eta$. So a better construction, perhaps, is to append the nonce n to the plaintext and encrypt using a zero-nonce MRAE scheme [15], rather than a conventional nAE scheme like we used for N2S. This avoids the quantitative security loss and works for any level-set L. For L_1^ℓ and L_2^ℓ one can use the trick from the last paragraph and include only $n \bmod \ell$ within the scope of what is MRAE-encrypted. It is tempting to try to eliminate this too, using the nonce as the AD value and have the decrypting party employ trial decryptions. But this scheme is problematic because it does not achieve perfect correctness, which is required in our treatment of IND|C.

While it is beyond the scope of this paper to formalize and prove all of the claims made in the last couple of paragraphs, it is our contention that all of them are straightforward to establish within the framework of IND|C.

5   Variants

Formalizations of IND|C are quite robust with respect to definitional adjustments. In this section we describe three IND|C variants and explain in what sense each is equivalent. The three variants are: (1) whether or not to silence oracle responses from the "ideal" game that are invalid in the "real" game; (2) whether to silence-then-shut-down or silence-then-forgive, the latter meaning that oracle responses after silencing will still be returned to the adversary; and (3) whether to silence ideal-side responses, as we have done throughout, or to replace them with the real-side values.

At the end of Sect. 2 we described further alternatives, (0) a penalty-style version of IND|C, and (0′) an exclusion-style variant. One concludes from these examples that many of the definitional choices we have made are not significant.

We go on to look at a more distant alternative to INDC, which we call *symmetric* INDC. Meant to deal with left-or-right games instead of real-or-ideal ones, this variant silences oracle responses whenever the correctness condition dictates fixed but distinct responses from the two sides. We suspect that this approach is, once again, as expressive as our other treatments of IND|C.

Before we describe our IND|C variants, let us clarify what it means to say that one way of defining advantage is equivalent to another. Suppose first that one has defined security measures $\mathbf{Adv}_{\Pi}^{\mathrm{xxx}}(A)$ and $\mathbf{Adv}_{\Pi}^{\mathrm{yyy}}(A)$. Then we may regard them as *equivalent* if any adversary A can be generically converted into an almost-as-efficient adversary B for which $\mathbf{Adv}_{\Pi}^{\mathrm{yyy}}(B)$ is nearly as high as $\mathbf{Adv}_{\Pi}^{\mathrm{xxx}}(A)$; and the other way around.

Now, for our more abstract setting, suppose we have two ways of associating an advantage measure to a primitive Π, a class C containing it, and a pair of Π-dependent games (G, H). Call these $\mathbf{Adv}_{\mathrm{G}_{\Pi},\mathrm{H}_{\Pi},\mathrm{C}}^{\mathrm{xxx}}$ and $\mathbf{Adv}_{\mathrm{G}_{\Pi},\mathrm{H}_{\Pi},\mathrm{C}}^{\mathrm{yyy}}$. Then these approaches for defining security are *equivalently expressive*, or just *equivalent*, if there's a generic method to construct from (G, H) a pair (G′, H′) such that $\mathbf{Adv}_{\mathrm{G}_{\Pi},\mathrm{H}_{\Pi},\mathrm{C}}^{\mathrm{xxx}}$ and $\mathbf{Adv}_{\mathrm{G}'_{\Pi},\mathrm{H}'_{\Pi},\mathrm{C}}^{\mathrm{yyy}}$ are equivalent (in the sense of the last paragraph); and, also, the other way around.

(1) SILENCING INVALID TRANSCRIPTS. Recall that the formula we've been using for $\mathit{Fixed}_{\mathrm{G},\mathrm{C}}(x_1, y_1, \ldots, x_i)$ is $(\exists!\, y_i)\, \mathit{Valid}_{\mathrm{G},\mathrm{C}}(x_1, y_1, \ldots, x_i, y_i)$ where the symbol $\exists!$ means *there exists one and only one*. This choice implies that an adversary, when interacting with the ideal game H, will receive responses y_i (in not yet silenced games) for which the y_i-ending transcript could *not* occur with the real game—that is, when $\mathit{Valid}_{\mathrm{G},\mathrm{C}}(x_1, y_1, \ldots, x_i, y_i) = \mathsf{false}$. The rationale behind this choice is that the adversary should be given a chance to win the distinguishing game by observing that a response is invalid—that it could not occur with the "real" oracle—but that determination should still fall on the adversary.

Yet a natural variant is to silence invalid replies, effectively marking transcripts where the ideal oracle has failed to provide a plausible response. The new silencing condition would define $\mathit{Fixed}_{\mathrm{G},\mathrm{C}}^1(x_1, y_1, \ldots, x_i)$ as

$$(\forall y, y')\, (\mathit{Valid}_{\mathrm{G},\mathrm{C}}(x_1, y_1, \ldots, x_i, y) \wedge \mathit{Valid}_{\mathrm{G},\mathrm{C}}(x_1, y_1, \ldots, x_i, y') \Rightarrow y = y')$$

and would silence by

$$\mathit{Silence}_{\mathrm{G},\mathrm{C}}^1(x_1, y_1, \ldots, x_j) = \bigvee_{1 \leq i \leq j} \mathit{Fixed}_{\mathrm{G},\mathrm{C}}^1(x_1, y_1, \ldots, x_i).$$

In words, we silence whenever there is *at most one* valid response, rather than demanding that there be *exactly one* valid response. We denote the advantage of adversary A under this new silencing condition by $\mathbf{Adv}^{\text{indc1}}_{\text{G,H,C}}(A) = \mathbf{Adv}^{\text{indc}}_{\text{G}[\psi],\text{H}[\psi],\text{C}}$ where $\psi = \text{Silence}^1_{\text{G,C}}$. We call the notion INDC1 security.

We argue that when $\text{Valid}_{\text{G,C}}$ is efficiently computable, this alteration is irrelevant. Given an INDC adversary A, one can construct an INDC1 adversary A' that behaves as A does except when it sees a response y_i for which $\text{Valid}_{\text{G,C}}(x_1, y_1, \ldots, x_i, y_i)$ is false. When this happens, adversary A' halts with a return value of 0. The constructed adversary is about as efficient as the original one (if $\text{Valid}_{\text{G,C}}$ is easily computed) and has advantage no smaller than A's. Conversely, the exact same reduction turns an INDC1 adversary A' to an INDC adversary A of comparable efficiency and undiminished advantage.

(2) SILENCE-THEN-FORGIVE. Our INDC formalization effectively punishes the adversary for triggering silencing: once silencing happens, the oracle shuts down and becomes useless. One might argue that this is overly punitive—that there is no reason to do anything other than silence just the offending query. We call this alternative *silence-then-forgive*. We explain that, when the silencing function is efficiently computable, the difference is inconsequential.

The silence-then-forgive notion is easy to formalize. We use the same *Valid* and *Fixed* predicates as defined in Sect. 2, but for the silencing function, instead of using the logical-or of *Fixed* applied to transcript prefixes, we use *Fixed* directly. That is, we let $\text{Silence}^2 = \text{Fixed}$ and define

$$\mathbf{Adv}^{\text{ind2}}_{\text{G,H,C}}(A) = \Pr[A^{\text{G}[\psi]} \Rightarrow 1] - \Pr[A^{\text{H}[\psi]} \Rightarrow 1]$$

where $\psi = \text{Silence}^2_{\text{C,G}}$. We call this the INDC2 advantage of adversary A.

Given an INDC adversary A differentiating G and H, an INDC2 adversary A' can simply execute A in a black-box manner and whenever A asks a query that will be silenced according to ψ, adversary A' would stop its own interaction and continue simulating the $\Diamond$ response to A. Conversely, given an INDC2 adversary A', an INDC adversary A can simply execute A' and whenever it asks a query that will be silenced according to ψ, adversary A would ask the same query, but setting the declarative flag. It then returns a $\Diamond$ response to A'. Since setting the declarative flag guarantees the response would not be silenced, adversary A would never trigger silencing. The simulation is perfect. The argument implies that the two silencing notions are equally expressive.

(3) IDEAL-SIDE EDITING. So far, all of our INDC variants silence both the real and ideal sides. Consider the following alternative to oracle silencing: the real game G is never changed, while the ideal game H, instead of being silenced when a response is fixed according to G, returns that fixed response.

To formalize this, we change the boolean predicate *Fixed* into a function *fixed* that returns the unique string-valued response that is determined when the original predicate returns true, and returns $*$ (for "not-fixed") otherwise:

$$\text{fixed}_{C,G}(x_1, y_1, \ldots, x_i) = \begin{cases} y & \text{when } (\exists! \, y) \ \text{Valid}_{C,G}(x_1, y_1, \ldots, x_i, y) \\ * & \text{otherwise} \end{cases}$$

We then extend the notion $G[\psi]$ to include the case where ψ is a string-or-$*$-valued function. Specifically, the Oracle procedure of $G[\psi]$ behaves as below.

procedure $G[\psi].\text{Oracle}(x)$
$i \leftarrow i + 1$; $x_i \leftarrow x$; $y_i \leftarrow G.\text{Oracle}(x)$
if $\psi(x_1, y_1, \ldots, x_i) \neq *$ **then** $y_i \leftarrow \psi(x_1, y_1, \ldots, x_i)$
return y_i

Finally, we define INDC3 advantage by $\mathbf{Adv}^{\text{indc3}}_{G,H,C}(A) = \mathbf{Adv}^{\text{ind}}_{G,H[\psi]}(A)$ where $\psi = \text{fixed}_{C,G}$. We call this INDC variant *ideal-side editing*.

We argue that INDC3 is equivalent to INDC assuming $\text{fixed}_{G,C}$ is efficiently computable. Let A be an INDC adversary differentiating a real game G and an ideal game H, where C is the underlying class. One can construct an INDC3 adversary A' executing A in a black-box manner. Whenever A asks a query x_i such that the history so far, when applied to $\text{fixed}_{G,C}$, results in a string response y_i, then A' stops its own interaction and provides the silencing mark $\Diamond$ to A. Conversely, with A' an INDC3 adversary we can construct an INDC adversary A executing A' in a black-box manner. Whenever A' first asks a query x_i such that $\text{fixed}_{G,C}(x_1, y_1, \ldots, x_i) = y_i \neq *$, adversary A would forward x_i to its own game, but would set a declarative flag so that silencing is not triggered. It then returns y_i to A'. Both reductions are perfect in simulating the game interaction.

(4) SYMMETRIC SILENCING. Our last form of game-editing is meant to deal with left-or-right style games instead of real-or-ideal style games. A typical example was given in Sect. 3, the treatment of CCA-secure PKE in which an oracle accepts two equal-length plaintexts and encrypts either the left or the right one of them. Can one directly use our INDC definition in such a setting?

One can, but doing so doesn't make sense. A real game is different from an ideal one, and its privileged position makes it reasonable that $\mathbf{Adv}^{\text{indc}}_{G,H,C}$ is not $\mathbf{Adv}^{\text{indc}}_{H,G,C}$. But a left game and a right game ought not be treated differently: it should be the case that the order of naming them doesn't matter.

Although the rationale just stated is a philosophical one, we have found that trying to apply IND|C to the LR-style games of Sect. 3 just doesn't work.

Here is a way to realize *symmetric* silencing: silence when the responses of the games are distinct fixed strings. Namely, let

$$\text{Fixed}^4_{G,H,C}(t) = \left(\text{fixed}_{C,G}(t) \neq \text{fixed}_{C,H}(t) \ \wedge \ \text{fixed}_{C,G}(t) \neq * \ \wedge \ \text{fixed}_{C,H}(t) \neq * \right).$$

Note that the predicate is symmetric: $Fixed_{G,H,C}^4 = Fixed_{H,G,C}^4$. Define the silencing function $Silence_{G,H,C}^4(t)$ as the logical-or of $Fixed_{G,H,C}^4(t')$ applied to all prefixes t' of t. The INDC-SYM advantage of an adversary A is then defined as $\mathbf{Adv}_{G,H,C}^{\text{indc-sym}}(A) = \mathbf{Adv}_{G[\psi],H[\psi]}^{\text{ind}}(A)$ where $\psi = Silence_{G,H,C}^4$.

We use the games in Sect. 3 to give an example. Let G and H be the left and right games in Fig. 6 with line 317 and line 327 removed, and let C be the class of correct PKE schemes. We remove the two lines so that the decryption does not exclude challenged ciphertext and thus the games become "utopian." The $Fixed_{G,H,C}^4$ predicate, in this case, evaluates to true if (1) no two encryptions of the same-side but distinct plaintexts return identical ciphertexts (validity condition); and (2) a decryption of c is asked while there was a previous $\text{ENC}(m_1, m_2)$ oracle returning c and $m_1 \neq m_2$ (fixedness condition). Therefore, apart from the explicit checking of an additional validity condition, the INDC-SYM notion again coincides with the conventional IND-CCA one.

6   Conclusions

Definitions in cryptography often vary in subtle ways, and deciding among them can seem rather subjective. The IND|C framework may help lessen this subjectivity. It embodies a thesis that a definition is "right" when it attends to the limits imposed by correctness, but goes no further than that in restricting adversarial behavior.

We suspect there are many cryptographers who have written definitions with an implicit view that what they aim to do is to disallow all and only the adversarial behaviors that some correctness condition dictates. The challenge of this work has been in figuring out how to make this vague conception real.

The IND|C approach is rather abstract. Definitions one gets out of it may require significant investigation to concretely characterize or understand. For this reason, one might claim that IND|C doesn't banish complexity so much as hide it. At least with a complicated game, the argument might go, you can see the complexity before your eyes.

We regard the critique as mostly off-base. Most fundamentally, it is unrealistic to think that complex cryptographic goals admit simple formulations when described in low-level terms. A more realistic aim is to find abstraction boundaries that help modularize definitions and enhance intuition.

The situation is reminiscent of UC [6], where an ideal functionality can be simply specified, a definition inherited from it, but it may be quite unclear what that notion means. Yet the hidden complexity behind IND|C isn't remotely at the level of UC. Nor, in our simpler setting, is there much difficulty with rigor. Perhaps IND|C may come to serve as an alternative to UC, for some cryptographic problems, the utopian game H corresponding to the specification of the ideal functionality.

Acknowledgments. Many thanks to anonymous reviewers of this paper, whose questions motivated the addition of Sect. 5. Thanks to the NSF, which provided funding for this work under grants CNS 1314885 and CNS 1717542.

References

1. Bellare, M., Hofheinz, D., Kiltz, E.: Subtleties in the definition of IND-CCA: when and how should challenge decryption be disallowed? J. Cryptol. **28**(1), 29–48 (2015). 5, 10, 11, 14, 15
2. Bellare, M., Kohno, T., Namprempre, C.: Breaking and provably repairing the SSH authenticated encryption scheme: a case study of the encode-then-encrypt-and-MAC paradigm. ACM Trans. Inf. Syst. Secur. **7**(2), 206–241 (2004). https://doi.acm.org/10.1145/996943.996945. 5, 16
3. Bellare, M., Rogaway, P.: The security of triple encryption and a framework for code-based game-playing proofs. In: Vaudenay, S. (ed.) EUROCRYPT 2006. LNCS, vol. 4004, pp. 409–426. Springer, Heidelberg (2006). https://doi.org/10.1007/11761679_25. 6
4. Boyd, C., Hale, B., Mjølsnes, S.F., Stebila, D.: From stateless to stateful: generic authentication and authenticated encryption constructions with application to TLS. In: Sako, K. (ed.) CT-RSA 2016. LNCS, vol. 9610, pp. 55–71. Springer, Cham (2016). https://doi.org/10.1007/978-3-319-29485-8_4. 5, 16
5. Boyd, C., Hale, B., Mjølsnes, S.F., Stebila, D.: From stateless to stateful: generic authentication and authenticated encryption constructions with application to TLS. Cryptology ePrint Archive, Report 2015/1150, revision 20160919:152253 (2016). https://eprint.iacr.org/2015/1150. 5
6. Canetti, R.: Universally composable security: A new paradigm for cryptographic protocols. Cryptology ePrint Archive, Report 2000/067 (2000). http://eprint.iacr.org/2000/067. 6, 24
7. Canetti, R., Krawczyk, H.: Analysis of key-exchange protocols and their use for building secure channels. In: Pfitzmann, B. (ed.) EUROCRYPT 2001. LNCS, vol. 2045, pp. 453–474. Springer, Heidelberg (2001). https://doi.org/10.1007/3-540-44987-6_28. 6
8. Fischlin, M., Günther, F., Marson, G.A., Paterson, K.G.: Data is a stream: security of stream-based channels. In: Gennaro, R., Robshaw, M. (eds.) CRYPTO 2015. LNCS, vol. 9216, pp. 545–564. Springer, Heidelberg (2015). https://doi.org/10.1007/978-3-662-48000-7_27. 6
9. Fischlin, M., Gnther, F., Marson, G.A., Paterson, K.G.: Data is a stream: security of stream-based channels. Cryptology ePrint Archive, Report 2017/1191 (2017). https://eprint.iacr.org/2017/1191. 6
10. Jager, T., Kohlar, F., Schäge, S., Schwenk, J.: On the security of TLS-DHE in the standard model. In: Safavi-Naini, R., Canetti, R. (eds.) CRYPTO 2012. LNCS, vol. 7417, pp. 273–293. Springer, Heidelberg (2012). https://doi.org/10.1007/978-3-642-32009-5_17. 6
11. Kohno, T., Palacio, A., Black, J.: Building secure cryptographic transforms, or how to encrypt and MAC. Cryptology ePrint Archive, Report 2003/177 (2003). http://eprint.iacr.org/2003/177. 5, 16
12. Namprempre, C.: Secure channels based on authenticated encryption schemes: a simple characterization. In: Zheng, Y. (ed.) ASIACRYPT 2002. LNCS, vol. 2501, pp. 515–532. Springer, Heidelberg (2002). https://doi.org/10.1007/3-540-36178-2_32. 6
13. Perrin, T., Marlinspike, M.: The double ratchet algorithm. Open Whisper Systems (2016). https://signal.org/docs/specifications/doubleratchet/. 16
14. Rogaway, P.: Authenticated-encryption with associated-data. In: Atluri, V. (ed.) ACM CCS 2002: 9th Conference on Computer and Communications Security, 18–22 November 2002, pp. 98–107. ACM Press, Washington D.C. (2002). 18

15. Rogaway, P., Shrimpton, T.: A provable-security treatment of the key-wrap problem. In: Vaudenay, S. (ed.) EUROCRYPT 2006. LNCS, vol. 4004, pp. 373–390. Springer, Heidelberg (2006). https://doi.org/10.1007/11761679_23. 20

A   Proofs

A.1   Proof of Theorem 1

It suffices to give mutual reductions between INDC and INDC0 adversaries. Since fixedness is efficiently computable for (G, H, C) we know there exists a PT algorithm ϕ that computes $Fixed_{C,G}$ for all valid transcripts. In the following we give the two reductions.

Let A be an INDC adversary. We construct an INDC0 adversary B that does the following: it runs A as a black-box and forwards every query made by A. Before forwarding a query x_t, however, it appends x_t to the recorded transcript and computes ϕ on it. If ϕ returns true then B stops forwarding and from then on keeps returning $\Diamond$ to A. Clearly B is PPT when A is. In addition, adversary B never triggers the penalty in Finalize, and it perfectly simulates the INDC game for A.

Conversely, let B be an INDC0 adversary. We construct A that does the following: it runs B as a black-box and forwards every query made by B. But A gives up and returns 0 whenever it sees $\Diamond$ returned by the game. When B is PPT then so is A. For the advantage, let bad_G and bad_H denote the events that A sees a $\Diamond$ response when interacting with G and H, then we have $\mathbf{Adv}_{G,H,C}^{indc}(A, k) = \Pr[A^{G[\psi]} \to 1] - \Pr[A^{H[\psi]} \to 1] = \Pr[A^{G[\psi]} \to 1 \cap \neg bad_G] - \Pr[A^{H[\psi]} \to 1 \cap \neg bad_H] = \Pr[G[\![\psi]\!]^B \to 1] - \Pr[H[\![\psi]\!]^B \to 1] = \mathbf{Adv}_{G,H,C}^{indc0}(B, k)$, and the reduction is complete.

A.2   Proof of Theorem 2

First note that the formula ϕ in Fig. 5 is PT-computable. We must show that $Valid_{C1,G1}(x_1, y_1, \ldots, x_t) \vee Valid_{C1,H1}(x_1, y_1, \ldots, x_t)$ implies $\phi(x_1, y_1, \ldots, x_t) = Fixed_{C1,G1}(x_1, y_1, \ldots, x_t)$.

Fix such a transcript. We claim that $Valid_{C1,G1}(x_1, y_1, \ldots, x_{t-1}, y_{t-1})$ if and only if line 201 in Fig. 5 is true. The only-if direction is straightforward: the negation of line 201 violates correctness required by the scheme class C1. For the if direction, consider the artificial scheme $\Pi = (\mathcal{K}, \mathcal{E}, \mathcal{D})$, whose definition depends on the transcript, with the following behavior:

- $\mathcal{K}(k)$: regardless of k, if there is any $(x_i, y_i) = (\text{Key}, pk)$ then output pk. Otherwise output an arbitrary string.
- $\mathcal{E}(pk, m)$: output $c \twoheadleftarrow T[m]$ where $T[m] \subseteq \{0,1\}^*$ are sets of strings, indexed by $m \in \{0,1\}^*$, which satisfy:
  - if there is an $(x_i, y_i) = ((\text{Enc}, m), c)$ then $c \in T[m]$.
  - $(m \neq m') \Rightarrow (T[m] \cap T[m'] = \varnothing)$.

- if there is an $(x_i, y_i) = ((\text{Dec}, c), m)$: when m is not the challenge plaintext then $c \notin T[m']$ for all $m' \in \{0, 1\}^*$; otherwise $c \in T[m]$. (By the *challenge plaintext* we mean the input to the first Enc query in the transcript, if it exists.)
- $\mathcal{D}(sk, c)$: if $(\exists m)\ c \in T[m]$, then output m; else if there exists some $(x_i, y_i) = ((\text{Dec}, c), m)$ then output m; else output an arbitrary string.

It is straightforward to verify that Π as constructed above is correct and can generate the given transcript. It remains to show well-definedness, namely, the existence of indexed sets $T[m]$ for $m \in \{0, 1\}^*$. Note the only possible contradiction in the construction of T is between the first bullet and the third bullet in the description of $\mathcal{E}$. However, such a contradiction can only take place when there is an $(x_i, y_i) = ((\text{Enc}, m), c)$ and an $(x_j, y_j) = ((\text{Dec}, c), m')$ such that $m \neq m'$, exactly the case excluded by line 201 in Fig. 5. The if direction is thus proved.

If $\phi(x_1, y_1, \ldots, x_t)$ is true then one of the lines 202–205 is true. From the code of G1 and the definition of C1, it is straightforward to verify that whichever line in 202–205 is true, the values recorded in the transcript determine the value of $\text{G1}_\Pi(k, x_1, \ldots, x_t, r)$. Additionally, since the above claim says whenever line 201 is true then the transcript is valid, we conclude that the value of $Fixed_{C1,G1}(x_1, y_1, \ldots, x_t)$ is true.

Conversely, if $\phi(x_1, y_1, \ldots, x_t)$ is false then either line 201 or the disjunction of line 202–205 is false. In the former case, our claim implies the falseness of $Valid_{C1,G1}(x_1, y_1, \ldots, x_t)$, so $Fixed_{C1,G1}(x_1, y_1, \ldots, x_t)$ is also false. In the latter case, consider the artificial scheme we just constructed. Since such a scheme can always generate the given history as long as the indexed set T satisfies the required properties, it suffices to give two instantiations of Π which generate distinct responses for x_t. A routine check of the code of G1 concludes that: for all transcripts not falling in the four cases of line 202–205, such instantiations can indeed be given. We conclude that $Fixed_{C1,G1}(x_1, y_1, \ldots, x_t)$ in this case, is also false.

A.3   Proof of Theorem 3

We give reductions for both directions. First, let A be a PPT IND-CCA adversary attacking Π. We construct an INDC-adversary B that does the following. For all Dec queries and Key queries asked by A, forward them to its own game if ψ evaluates to false for the current transcript; otherwise simulate the answers by itself without forwarding (which could be done by an inspection of the code of the four games $(\text{G1}, \text{H1}, \text{G0}, \text{H0})$). For the first Test query (m_1, m_2) queried by A, we let B draw a random coin $b \twoheadleftarrow \{0, 1\}$ and query $\text{Enc}(m_b)$. Now $\mathbf{Adv}_{\text{G1},\text{H1},\text{C1}}^{\text{indc}}(B) = \mathbf{Adv}_\Pi^{\text{ind}}(A)/2$, and B is also PPT.

Next, let B be a PPT IND|C adversary, we construct an IND-CCA adversary A that does the following: forward all Dec queries and Key queries; for the Enc query m, let A query $\text{Test}(m, 0^{|m|})$. In addition A will also silence queries made by B by computing ψ. This reduction simulates perfectly except for one problematic case: when B triggered an invalid event (the negation of line 201 in Fig. 5) and asks for a decryption of the challenged ciphertext, by the formula of ψ he should see an unsilenced response, but the IND-CCA adversary A cannot simulate such a response for him. However, since an invalid event necessarily implies that A is in the ideal world, we could simply let A return 0. Therefore, the advantage of B is preserved.

A.4 Proof of Theorem 4

We introduce some notation first. Given $\mathbf{n} \in \mathbb{N}^*$ and a vector X, we define $X[\mathbf{n}]$ recursively by $X[\emptyset] = \emptyset$ and $X[\mathbf{n} \| i] = X[\mathbf{n}] \| X_i$ if $1 \leq i \leq |X|$, while $X[\mathbf{n}]$ otherwise. For $\mathbf{n} = [i, i+1, \ldots, j]$ we may write $X[i..j]$ instead of $X[\mathbf{n}]$. We use $\boldsymbol{t} = (x_1, y_1, \ldots, x_q)$ to denote a query-terminated transcript that is $\mathsf{Valid}_{\mathrm{C2}(L),\mathrm{G2}}(\boldsymbol{t}) \vee \mathsf{Valid}_{\mathrm{C2}(L),\mathrm{H2}}(\boldsymbol{t})$ and satisfies $q \leq 2^\tau - 3$.

Our proof strategy is as follows. We first give the pseudocode of a function ϕ_L for a general level-set L, and then prove its efficient computability when L is a basic level-set. See Fig. 10 for the code of ϕ_L.

---

procedure $\phi_L(\boldsymbol{t})$

711 $(x_1, y_1, \ldots, x_q) \leftarrow \boldsymbol{t}$

712 **for** $i \leftarrow 1$ **to** $q - 1$ **do**

713   **if** $x_i[1] = \mathsf{Enc}$ **then** $e \leftarrow e + 1$; $(a_e, m_e, c_e) \leftarrow (x_i[2], x_i[3], y_i)$

714 **for** $i \leftarrow 1$ **to** q **then**

715   **if** $x_i[1] = \mathsf{Dec}$ **then** $d \leftarrow d + 1$; $(a'_d, m'_d, c'_d) \leftarrow (x_i[2], y_i, x_i[3])$

716 **if** $(\exists i)(\exists \mathbf{n} \in L)\, (a'[1..i], c'[1..i]) = (a[\mathbf{n}], c[\mathbf{n}]) \wedge m'_i = \bot$ **then return** false

717 **if** $(\exists \mathbf{n}, \mathbf{n}' \in L)\, \big(\mathbf{n} \neq \mathbf{n}' \wedge (m[\mathbf{n}] \neq m[\mathbf{n}']) \wedge (a[\mathbf{n}], c[\mathbf{n}]) = (a[\mathbf{n}'], c[\mathbf{n}'])\big)$

718   **then return** false

719 **return** $x_q[1] = \mathsf{Dec} \wedge x_q[4] = \mathsf{false} \wedge (\exists \mathbf{n} \in L)\, (a', c') = (a[\mathbf{n}], c[\mathbf{n}])$

Fig. 10. Computing fixedness for sAE.

We claim ϕ_L indeed computes fixedness. Let $\boldsymbol{t}$ be such a transcript that satisfies the stated condition in the above, we use $(a_1, c_1), \ldots, (a_e, c_e)$ and $(a'_1, c'_1), \ldots, (a'_d, c'_d)$ to denote its *encryption history* and *decryption history*, defined as in Fig. 10. Given a decryption query (a'_i, c'_i), we say it is $\mathbf{n}$-*honest* if $\mathbf{n} \in L \wedge (a'[1..i], c'[1..i]) = (a[\mathbf{n}], c[\mathbf{n}])$; and it is *honest* if it is $\mathbf{n}$-honest for some $\mathbf{n} \in L$. We use h to denote the largest index of honest decryption queries in the decryption history, namely $h = \max\{i : (a'_i, c'_i) \text{ is honest}\}$.

We try to define an artificial scheme $\Pi \in \mathrm{C2}(L)$, out of two functions $F : \mathbb{N} \times \mathcal{A} \times \mathcal{M} \to \mathcal{C} \cup \{\bot\}$ and $G : \mathbb{N} \times \mathcal{A} \times \mathcal{C} \to \mathcal{M} \cup \{\bot\}$. We require for all $(n, a) \in \mathbb{N} \times \mathcal{A}$, the projected $F_{n,a}(\cdot)$, apart from its possible mapping to $\bot$, is an injection with ciphertext expansion τ: We accordingly write $F_{n,a}^{-1}(c)$ to denote the unique $m \in \mathcal{M}$ such that $F_{n,a}(m) = c$ or $\bot$ if such m does not exist. Basically, the behavior of F has some restrictions that depend on the given transcript $\boldsymbol{t}$,

procedure $\mathcal{K}$	$825 \quad r \leftarrow r + 1;$ **return** $(\mathrm{G}(r,a,c),r)$
811 **return** 0	826 **if** $r = \varepsilon$ **then** $r \leftarrow \{\Lambda\}$
	827 $r' \leftarrow \varnothing$
procedure $\mathcal{E}(k,a,m,s)$	828 **for** $\mathbf{n} \in r$ **do**
821 **if** $s = \varepsilon$ **then** $s \leftarrow 0$	829 **for** $n \in \{n \colon \mathbf{n} \,\|\, n \in L\}$ **do**
822 $s \leftarrow s + 1$	830 **if** $F_{n,a}^{-1}(c) \neq \bot$ **then**
823 **return** $(F_{s,a}(m),s)$	831 $m \leftarrow F_{n,a}^{-1}(c)$
	832 $r' \leftarrow r' \cup \{\mathbf{n} \,\|\, n\}$
procedure $\mathcal{D}(k,a,c,r)$	833 **if** $r' = \varnothing$ **then return** $(\mathrm{G}(0,a,c),0)$
824 **if** isNum(r) **then**	834 **return** (m,r')

Conditions on F for $\Pi \in \mathrm{C2}(L)$ and Π being able to generate the history:

841 $\quad (\forall q)(\forall a_1,\ldots,a_q \in \mathcal{A})(\forall c_1,\ldots,c_q \in \mathcal{C})(\forall \mathbf{n},\mathbf{n}' \in L)$

842 $\quad \Big[\text{For } i \leftarrow 1 \text{ to } q \text{ do } (m_i, m_i') \leftarrow (F_{\mathbf{n}_i,a_i}^{-1}(c_i), F_{\mathbf{n}'_i,a_i}^{-1}(c_i))\colon$

843 $\quad\quad ((\forall i)\, m_i \neq \bot \wedge m_i' \neq \bot) \Rightarrow ((\forall i)\, m_i = m_i') \Big] \bigwedge$

844 $\quad (\forall i \in \{1,\ldots,e\})\, F_{i,a_i}(m_i) = c_i \bigwedge (\forall i \in \mathbb{N})\, c'_{h+1} \notin \mathrm{Range}(F_{i,a'_{h+1}})$

Fig. 11. Code of the artificial sAE scheme.

and such restriction serves its best to make sure Π can generate $\boldsymbol{t}$. Ultimately, we expect Π to have the following properties:

If the validity check is passed (both the if conditions in line 716 and 717 are false) then Π is well-defined, correct, and can generate $\boldsymbol{t}$. On top of that, if the fixedness check does not pass (line 719 returns false), then there are multiple instantiations of Π that generate distinct responses for the last query in $\boldsymbol{t}$.

We call these two properties the *existence property* and the *multiplicity property*. The code of Π is given in Fig. 11. We first make two observations about it:

- When F satisfies line 842–843, the variable m assigned in line 831 is identical across iterations for each decryption in a *correctness experiment* as shown in Fig. 8, and $\Pi \in \mathrm{C2}(L)$. This can be proved by an induction on the number of decryption queries in a correctness experiment. The inductive argument is: after the first i decryptions $(a_1,c_1),(a_2,c_2),\ldots,(a_i,c_i)$ in a correctness experiment, all vectors $\mathbf{n}$ in the receiver state are reorderings in L, and for each $\mathbf{n}$ let $(m_1,\ldots,m_t) \leftarrow (F_{n_1,a_1}^{-1}(c_1),\ldots F_{n_t,a_t}^{-1}(c_t))$ then $(\nexists i)\, m_i = \bot$ and the vector m is identical for all $\mathbf{n}$ in the receiver state.
- When F satisfies all lines 842–844, the scheme Π can generate the encryption history. What's more, as long as the if condition in line 716 in Fig. 10 evaluates to false, then Π, with some instantiation of G, can generate the decryption history as well. The generation of the encryption history is obvious by line 844. For the generation of the decryption history, note that $\mathrm{Valid}_{\mathrm{C2}(L),\mathrm{G2}}(\boldsymbol{t}) \vee \mathrm{Valid}_{\mathrm{C2}(L),\mathrm{H2}}(\boldsymbol{t})$ implies that an $\mathbf{n}$-honest decryption

query (a'_i, c'_i) must have a response either equal to m_{n_i} (in the real world) or $\perp$ (in the ideal world). Since the falseness of the if condition in line 716 of Fig. 10 excludes the latter case, the correctness of Π thus ensures those honest decryption queries' responses can be generated. For those *post-honest* decryption queries, since line 844 implies that the first of those queries c'_{h+1} is not in the range of $F_{i,a'_{h+1}}(\cdot)$ for any i, the updated receiver state r' will be set to $\varnothing$ and from this point the decryption will depend only on G. With the help of the additive state, by simply assigning $G(i - h - 1, a'_i, c'_i) \leftarrow m'_i$ for all $i > h$, we can make Π generate the given decryption history as well.

Based on the above two observations, we first prove the existence property. For a number $i \in \mathbb{N}$, let $\mathsf{num2str}_j(i)$ be the binary representation of i with j bits (leading 0 padded when $i \ll 2^j$). Suppose t is such that both the if conditions in line 716 and 717 evaluate to false then consider the following F:

$$F_{i,a}(m) = \begin{cases} c_i & \text{if } a = a_i \wedge m = m_i; \\ H(i, m) & \text{else if } i \leq e; \\ \perp & \text{otherwise,} \end{cases}$$

where $H: \{1, 2, \ldots, q\} \times \mathcal{M} \to \mathcal{C}$ satisfies

1. $H(i, \cdot)$ is an injection for all i with ciphertext expansion τ;
2. $i \neq j \Rightarrow \mathsf{Range}(H(i, \cdot)) \cap \mathsf{Range}(H(j, \cdot)) = \varnothing$;
3. $t.c_i \notin \mathsf{Range}(H(i, \cdot))$ for all i;
4. $t.c'_{h+1} \notin \mathsf{Range}(H(i, \cdot))$ for all i.

It's easy to see such an H really exists by the condition $q \leq 2^\tau - 3$. We claim that this instantiation satisfies the three conditions in Fig. 11, which would imply the existence property. Indeed, line 844 is obvious. For line 841–843, let $(a_1, a_2, \ldots, a_q)$, $(c_1, c_2, \ldots, c_q)$, $\mathbf{n}$ and $\mathbf{n}'$ be as quantified, then $((\forall i) \, m_i \neq \perp \wedge m'_i \neq \perp)$ implies that for all i, either $c_i \in \mathsf{Range}(H(\mathbf{n}_i, \cdot)) \cap \mathsf{Range}(H(\mathbf{n}'_i, \cdot))$, or c_i is equal to $t.c_j$ for some j (We use the notation $t.c_i$ to differentiate the c_i being quantified in the statement of line 841–843 and the c_i recorded in the transcript t). In the former case, by the second property of H above we have $n_i = n'_i$, hence $m_i = m'_i$. In the latter case, suppose for contradiction that $m_i \neq m'_i$ and let i be the minimal such index. Since by the instantiation of F, for $j \leq i$ either $n_i = n'_i$ (the case we just analyzed) or $(a_i, c_i) = (t.a[n_i], t.c[n_i]) = (t.a[n'_i], t.c[n'_i])$, we conclude $(t.a[\mathbf{n}], t.c[\mathbf{n}]) = (t.a[\mathbf{n}'], t.c[\mathbf{n}'])$. The assumption $m_i \neq m'_i$ therefore contradicts with the condition that line 717 in Fig. 10 returns false.

We next show the multiplicity property. There are three cases of $t.x_q$ to consider. They are: (1) Dec query with the declarative flag set to true; (2) Dec query that is not honest; (3) Enc query. The first case is trivial. For the second case, since our construction depends on an arbitrary function G after a dishonest decryption, there are always multiple ways of specifying different G so as x_q will have distinct outputs. For the third case, it suffices to extend the instantiation of F by H in the above with e replaced by $e+1$. By the condition $q \leq 2^\tau - 3$, the

```
procedure φʲⱼ(t)
911  (x₁, y₁, ..., x_q) ← t
912  if x_q[1] ≠ Dec ∨ x_q[4] ≠ false then return false
913  for i ← 1 to q − 1 do
914      if x_i[1] = Enc then
915          e ← e + 1; (a_e, m_e, c_e) ← (x_i[2], x_i[3], y_i);
916          ac2i[a_e, c_e] ← ac2i[a_e, c_e] ∪ {e}
917  if j = 0 then
918      for i ← 1 to e do
919          if ac2m[a_e, c_e] ≠ ◊ and ac2m[a_e, c_e] ≠ m_e then return false
920          ac2m[a_e, c_e] ← m_e
921  else
922      queue ← ((Λ, Λ))
923      while (n₁, n₂) ← pop(queue) do
924          for (n₁, n₂) ∈ Next(Lʲⱼ, n₁, e) × Next(Lʲⱼ, n₂, e) do
925              if (a[n₁], c[n₁]) = (a[n₂], c[n₂]) then
926                  if m[n₁] ≠ m[n₂] then return false
927                  push(queue, (n₁ ∥ n₁, n₂ ∥ n₂))
928  for i ← 1 to q do
929      if x_i[1] = Dec then
930          d ← d + 1; (a'_d, m'_d, c'_d) ← (x_i[2], y_i, x_i[3])
931  𝒩 ← {Λ}
932  for i ← 1 to d do
933      for n ∈ 𝒩 do
934          for n ∈ ac2i[a'_i, c'_i] do
935              if n ∥ n ∈ Lʲⱼ then
936                  𝒩' ← 𝒩' ∪ {n ∥ n}
937                  if m'_i = ⊥ then return false
938      𝒩 ← 𝒩'; 𝒩' ← ∅
939  return 𝒩 ≠ ∅
```

Fig. 12. Pseudocode of algorithms computing fixedness for sAE. The algorithm ϕ^ℓ_j computes fixedness for $(C2(L^\ell_j), G2, H2, 2^\tau - 3)$ where τ is the ciphertext expansion for sAE schemes. The only dependences on level-sets are in line 924 and line 935, where $\text{Next}(L, \mathbf{n}, e) = \{n \in \{1, \ldots, e\} : \mathbf{n} \| n \in L\}$. The value $\text{Next}(L, \cdot, \cdot)$ is efficiently computable for all $L \in \{L_0, L^\ell_1, L^\ell_2, L_3\}$.

four conditions can still be satisfied by a proper choice of H, and all successive logic thus follows. The different way of instantiating $H(e + 1, \cdot)$ thus guarantees multiplicity property.

To complete the proof, we need to write pseudocode of efficient algorithms for the procedure ϕ_L where L is a basic level set. See Fig. 12 for the concrete code of these algorithms that instantiate ϕ_L.

A.5   Proof of Theorem 5

We describe the code of B in terms of A. See Fig. 13. We claim that this reduction achieves perfect simulation. To see why, note that the only bad event which semantically differs from an otherwise perfect simulation is line 1032, which causes digression from the semantics of H2 but not that of G2, hence it suffices to show in an execution between B and the ideal side, line 1032 is never reached. Suppose for contradiction that it is reached, then by the code semantics, oracle silencing has not taken place, and the nonces in the nc input for Dec queries so far form a reorder $\mathbf{n} \in L$. Consider the first Dec query of which $nc = (n_1, c)$ for some c. Due to the monotonicity of silencing and the event $\mathbf{n} = \bot$, at the point of the query, line 1029 is reached and the if conditions there can be either true or false. If it is true, then in the ideal world H2 we must have m assigned as $\bot$, and accordingly $\mathbf{n}$ gets assigned to $\bot$, contradicting to the assumption that line 1032 is reached later. If it is false, then at this query the vector $\mathbf{n}_1$ already forms a valid reorder of the encryption history at the time, so this query should already have been silenced at line 1024, a contradiction again.

When A queries $\text{Enc}(a, m)$	1025 **if** $\mathbf{n} = \bot$ **then** $m \leftarrow \bot$
1011 **if** silenced **return** $\lozenge$	1026 **else**
1012 $t \leftarrow t \,\|\, (\text{Enc}, a, m)$	1027 $n \,\|\, c \leftarrow nc;\ \mathbf{n} \leftarrow \mathbf{n} \,\|\, n$
1013 **if** $\psi_L(t)$ **then**	1028 **if** $\mathbf{n} \notin L$ **then** $m \leftarrow \bot$
1014 silenced $\leftarrow$ true; **return** $\lozenge$	1029 **else if**
1015 $n \leftarrow n + 1$	1030 $(\nexists m')\ ((\text{Enc}, n, m'), c) = t.x_n$
1016 $c \leftarrow \text{Enc}(n, a, m)$	1031 **then** $m \leftarrow \text{Dec}(n, a, c)$
1017 $t \leftarrow t \,\|\, c$	1032 **else** $m \leftarrow m'$
1018 **return** $n \,\|\, c$	1033 **if** $m = \bot$ **then** $\mathbf{n} \leftarrow \bot$
	1034 $t \leftarrow t \,\|\, m$
When A queries $\text{Dec}(a, nc)$	1035 **return** m
1021 **if** silenced **return** $\lozenge$	
1022 $t \leftarrow t \,\|\, (\text{Dec}, a, c)$	When A outputs b
1023 **if** $\psi_L(t)$ **then**	1036 Output b
1024 silenced $\leftarrow$ true; **return** $\lozenge$	

Fig. 13. Construction of an nAE adversary out of an sAE adversary. The reduction simulates perfectly since the only bad event in line 1032 never takes place in the ideal setting.

We conclude that B simulates for A a perfect execution of the silenced $(\text{G2}_{\text{N2S}[\Pi, L]}, \text{H2}_{\text{N2S}[\Pi, L]})$ games. Adversary B is efficient when A is and the proof is complete.

The Algebraic Group Model
and its Applications

Georg Fuchsbauer[1], Eike Kiltz[2], and Julian Loss[2($\boxtimes$)]

[1] Inria, ENS, CNRS, PSL, Paris, France
`georg.fuchsbauer@ens.fr`
[2] Ruhr University Bochum, Bochum, Germany
{`eike.kiltz,julian.loss`}`@rub.de`

Abstract. One of the most important and successful tools for assessing hardness assumptions in cryptography is the Generic Group Model (GGM). Over the past two decades, numerous assumptions and protocols have been analyzed within this model. While a proof in the GGM can certainly provide some measure of confidence in an assumption, its scope is rather limited since it does not capture group-specific algorithms that make use of the representation of the group.

To overcome this limitation, we propose the Algebraic Group Model (AGM), a model that lies in between the Standard Model and the GGM. It is the first restricted model of computation covering group-specific algorithms yet allowing to derive simple and meaningful security statements. To prove its usefulness, we show that several important assumptions, among them the Computational Diffie-Hellman, the Strong Diffie-Hellman, and the interactive LRSW assumptions, are equivalent to the Discrete Logarithm (DLog) assumption in the AGM. On the more practical side, we prove tight security reductions for two important schemes in the AGM to DLog or a variant thereof: the BLS signature scheme and Groth's zero-knowledge SNARK (EUROCRYPT 2016), which is the most efficient SNARK for which only a proof in the GGM was known. Our proofs are quite simple and therefore less prone to subtle errors than those in the GGM.

Moreover, in combination with known lower bounds on the Discrete Logarithm assumption in the GGM, our results can be used to derive lower bounds for all the above-mentioned results in the GGM.

Keywords: Algebraic algorithms · Generic group model
Security reductions · Cryptographic assumptions

1 Introduction

Starting with Nechaev [Nec94] and Shoup [Sho97], much work has been devoted to studying the computational complexity of problems with respect to generic group algorithms over cyclic groups [BL96, MW98, Mau05]. At the highest level, generic group algorithms are algorithms that do not exploit any special structure

© International Association for Cryptologic Research 2018
H. Shacham and A. Boldyreva (Eds.): CRYPTO 2018, LNCS 10992, pp. 33–62, 2018.
https://doi.org/10.1007/978-3-319-96881-0_2

of the representation of the group elements and can thus be applied in any cyclic group. More concretely, a generic algorithm may use only the abstract group operation and test whether two group elements are equal. This property makes it possible to prove information-theoretic lower bounds on the running time for generic algorithms. Such lower bounds are of great interest since for many important groups, in particular for elliptic curves, no helpful exploitation of the representation is currently known.

The class of generic algorithms encompasses many important algorithms such as the baby-step giant-step algorithm and its generalization for composite-order groups (also known as Pohlig-Hellman algorithm [HP78]) as well as Pollard's rho algorithm [Pol78]. However, part of the common criticism against the generic group model is that many algorithms of practical interest are in fact not generic. Perhaps most notably, index-calculus and some factoring attacks fall outside the family of generic algorithms, as they are applicable only over groups in which the elements are represented as *integers*.

Another example is the "trivial" discrete logarithm algorithm over the additive group $\mathbb{Z}_p$, which is the identity function.

With this motivation in mind, a number of previous works considered extensions of the generic group model [Riv04, LR06, AM09, JR10]. Jager and Rupp [JR10] considered assumptions over groups equipped with a bilinear map $e\colon \mathbb{G}_1 \times \mathbb{G}_2 \longrightarrow \mathbb{G}_3$, where $\mathbb{G}_1$ and $\mathbb{G}_2$ are modeled as generic groups, and $\mathbb{G}_3$ is modeled in the Standard Model. (This is motivated by the fact that in all practical bilinear groups, $\mathbb{G}_1$ and $\mathbb{G}_2$ are elliptic curves whereas $\mathbb{G}_3$ is a sub-group of a finite field). However, none of these models so far capture algorithms that can freely exploit the representation of the group. In this work, we propose a restricted model of computation which does exactly this.

1.1 Algebraic Algorithms

Let $\mathbb{G}$ be a cyclic group of prime order p. Informally, we call an algorithm $\mathsf{A}_{\mathsf{alg}}$ *algebraic* if it fulfills the following requirement: whenever $\mathsf{A}_{\mathsf{alg}}$ outputs a group element $\mathbf{Z} \in \mathbb{G}$, it also outputs a "representation" $\vec{z} = (z_1, \ldots, z_t) \in \mathbb{Z}_p^t$ such that $\mathbf{Z} = \prod_i \mathbf{L}_i^{z_i}$, where $\vec{\mathbf{L}} = (\mathbf{L}_1, \ldots, \mathbf{L}_t)$ is the list of all group elements that were given to $\mathsf{A}_{\mathsf{alg}}$ during its execution so far.

Such algebraic algorithms were first considered by Boneh and Venkatesan [BV98] in the context of straight-line programs computing polynomials over the ring of integers $\mathbb{Z}_n$, where $n = pq$. Later, Paillier and Vergnaud [PV05] gave a more formal and general definition of algebraic algorithms using the notion of an *extractor algorithm* which efficiently computes the representation $\vec{z}$.

In our formalization of algebraic algorithms, we distinguish group elements from all other parameters at a *syntactical level*, that is, other parameters must not depend on any group elements. This is to rule out pathological exploits of the model, see below.

While this class of algebraic algorithms certainly captures a much broader class of algorithms than the class of generic algorithms (e.g., index-calculus algorithms), it was first noted in [PV05] that the class of algebraic algorithms actually *includes* the class of generic algorithms.

Algebraic algorithms have mostly been studied so far in the context of proving *impossibility results* [BV98, Cor02, PV05, BMV08, GBL08, AGO11, KMP16], i.e., to disprove the existence of an algebraic security reduction between two cryptographic primitives (with certain good parameters). Only quite recently, a small number of works have considered the idea of proving statements with respect to *algebraic adversaries* [ABM15, BFW16].

1.2   Algebraic Group Model

We propose the *algebraic group model* (AGM) — a computational model in which all adversaries are modeled as algebraic. In contrast to the GGM, the AGM does not allow for proving information-theoretic lower bounds on the complexity of an algebraic adversary. Similar to the Standard Model, in the AGM one proves security implications via reductions. Specifically, $H \Rightarrow_{\mathsf{alg}} G$ for two primitives H and G means that every algebraic adversary $\mathsf{A}_{\mathsf{alg}}$ against G can be transformed into an algebraic adversary $\mathsf{B}_{\mathsf{alg}}$ against H with (polynomially) related running times and success probabilities. It follows that if H is secure against algebraic adversaries, so is G. While algebraic adversaries have been considered before (see above), to the best of our knowledge, our work is the first to provide a clean and formal framework for security proofs with respect to algebraic adversaries. We elaborate further on our model below.

CONCRETE SECURITY IMPLICATIONS IN THE AGM. Indeed, one can exploit the algebraic nature of an adversary in the AGM to obtain stronger security implications than in the Standard Model. The first trivial observation is that the classical *knowledge of exponent assumption*[1] [Dam92] holds by definition in the AGM.

We are able to show that several important computational assumptions are in fact equivalent to the Discrete Logarithm assumption over prime-order groups in the AGM, including the following:

– Diffie-Hellman assumption [DH76]
– (Interactive) strong Diffie-Hellman assumption [ABR01]
– (Interactive) LRSW assumption [LRSW99, CL04].

The significance of the Strong Diffie-Hellman Assumption comes from its equivalence to the IND-CCA security of Hashed ElGamal encryption (also known as Diffie-Hellman Integrated Encryption Standard) in the random oracle model [ABR01]. The LSRW assumption (named its authors [LRSW99]) is of importance since it is equivalent to the (UF-CMA) security of Camenisch-Lysyanskaya

---

[1] The knowledge of exponent assumption states that for every algorithm A that, given g and $\mathbf{X} = g^x$, outputs $(\mathbf{A}, \mathbf{B})$ with $\mathbf{B} = \mathbf{A}^x$, there exists an extractor algorithms that, given the same input, outputs a satisfying $(\mathbf{A}, \mathbf{B}) = (g^a, \mathbf{X}^a)$.

(CL) signatures [CL04]. CL signatures are a central building block for anonymous credentials [CL04, BCL04, BCS05], group signatures [CL04, ACHdM05], e-cash [CHL05], unclonable functions [CHK+06], batch verification [CHP07], and RFID encryption [ACdM05]. Via our results, the security of all these schemes is implied by the discrete logarithm assumption in the AGM.

Our result can be interpreted as follows. Every algorithm attacking one of the above-mentioned problems and schemes must solve the standard discrete logarithm problem directly, unless the algorithm relies on inherently non-algebraic operations. In particular, powerful techniques such as the index-calculus algorithms do not help in solving these problems any better then they do for solving the discrete logarithm problem directly.

Moreover, we show the *tight* equivalence of the security of the following schemes to the underlying hardness assumptions in the AGM:

- IND-CCA1 (aka lunchtime) security of the standard ElGamal Encryption to a parametrized variant of Decisional Diffie-Hellman assumption where in addition to g^x, g^y the adversary receives $g^{x^2}, \ldots, g^{x^q}$, where q is the maximal number of decryption queries.
- The UF-CMA security of the BLS signature scheme [BLS04] to the discrete logarithm problem in the random oracle model. Previous reductions nontightly reduced from the CDH problem, with a tightness loss linear in the number of signing queries. This loss is known to be inherent [Cor02, KK12], even in the random oracle model.
- The security of the so far most efficient zero-knowledge SNARK scheme by Groth [Gro16] to a parametrized variant of the discrete logarithm problem, where in addition to g^x the adversary receives $g^{x^2}, \ldots, g^{x^{2n-1}}$, where n is the degree of the quadratic arithmetic programs. The only previous proof of the security of this scheme is in the generic group model.

RELATION TO THE GENERIC GROUP MODEL. The AGM is stronger (in the sense that it puts more restrictions on the attackers) than the Standard Model, but weaker than the GGMl. In spite of this, all of our reductions are purely generic algorithms. As mentioned above, any generic algorithm can be modeled within the AGM. In particular, combining arbitrary generic operations with algebraic ones will yield an algebraic algorithm. This suggests the following idea. Let H and G be two computational problems and let $\mathsf{A}_{\mathsf{alg}}$ be an algebraic algorithm that solves problem G. If we can convert $\mathsf{A}_{\mathsf{alg}}$ by means of a generic reduction algorithm $\mathsf{R}_{\mathsf{gen}}$ into an algorithm $\mathsf{B}_{\mathsf{alg}}$ for problem H, then clearly, $\mathsf{B}_{\mathsf{alg}}$ is also an algebraic algorithm. However, we obtain an even stronger statement for free: Namely, if $\mathsf{A}_{\mathsf{gen}}$ is a generic algorithm solving G, then $\mathsf{B}_{\mathsf{gen}}$ is a generic algorithm solving H. This means that results in the AGM directly carry over to the GGM.

For this reason, we believe that our model offers an alternative, perhaps simpler method of proving the hardness of computational problems within the GGM. This applies in particular to interactive assumptions, which can be rather difficult to analyze in the GGM. For example, we prove that the discrete logarithm assumption implies the LRSW assumption in the AGM. As the discrete logarithm assumption holds in the GGM, we instantly obtain that the

LRSW assumption holds in the GGM. The first (rigorous) proof of the LRSW assumption within the GGM was presented in the work of [BFF+14] (the original work [LRSW99] provided only a proof sketch), but was derived from a more general theorem and proven using an automated proof verification tool. We hope that our proof can offer some additional insight over the proof of [BFF+14]. Another example is our tight equivalence of the IND-CCA1 security of ElGamal and our parametrized variant of the Decisional Diffie-Hellman (DDH) assumption in the algebraic group model. Together with the known generic $\sqrt{p/q}$ attack on ElGamal [BG04] for certain primes p (see also [Che06]), our result proves the tight generic bound $\tilde{\Theta}(\sqrt{p/q})$ on the complexity of breaking IND-CCA1 security of ElGamal in the GGM.

We also remark that proofs in the AGM have an inherently different interpretation than proofs in the GGM. To analyze the hardness of an assumption in the GGM, one must explicitly augment the model by any functionality that is offered by the structure of the group. As a simple example, let us consider a group $\mathbb{G}$ which is equipped with a symmetric bilinear map $e \colon \mathbb{G} \times \mathbb{G} \longrightarrow \mathbb{G}_T$. The bilinear map can be modeled in the GGM via an oracle. However, it is not clear whether e can be used to gather even further information about the elements of $\mathbb{G}$. Though it is widely believed that this is not the case, a proof in the GGM provides no answer to this question, because the GGM itself is based on the conjecture that e does not offer any functionality beyond a bilinear map. In contrast, the AGM captures any such exploit without the need of having to model it explicitly and considers the relation between two problems instead of their *individual hardness*. This means that if one can reduce H to G in the AGM and H is conjectured to remain hard with respect to algebraic algorithms, even when given e, then also G remains hard. No similar statement can be inferred in the GGM. Thus, the AGM allows for a more fine grained assessment of the hardness of computational problems than the GGM.

The gap between the two models becomes even more apparent if one considers structural properties of $\mathbb{G}$ which cannot be meaningfully modeled as an oracle in the GGM. As an example, consider the Jacobi symbol, which was shown to be generically hard to compute in [JS09]. Indeed, it was left as an open problem in [AM09] to re-examine the equivalence of factoring and breaking the RSA assumption if an additional oracle for the Jacobi symbol were given. Though their results are stated in the *generic ring model* rather than the GGM, it seems they are similarly confronted with the issue of explicitly modeling such an oracle.

LIMITATIONS OF THE AGM. As already noted, one of the main benefits of our model over the GGM is the ability to reason about algorithms that arbitrarily exploit the structure of the group. So which algorithms are not covered in this manner? Obviously, outputting an obliviously sampled group element (with unknown representation) is forbidden. This coincides with the GGM of Maurer [Mau05] and which also excludes the possibility of obliviously sampling a random group element. For this reason, our model is strictly weaker than the one from [Mau05] in the sense that any security reduction derived in Maurer's GGM also holds in the AGM. In contrast, the GGM defined by Shoup [Sho97] *does* allow for such a sampling process. Similar to Maurer's GGM, we can allow obliviously sampling a random group element **X** through an additional oracle $O()$ that can be called during the execution of A_{alg}. By definition, the outputs of $O()$ are added to the list $\vec{L}$. We have thus argued that both versions of the GGM (i.e., the ones by Maurer and Shoup) are strictly stronger than the AGM. Also note that simulating $O()$ to A_{alg} as part of a reduction is straight-forward and always possible; the reduction simply samples r and returns g^r to the adversary. As the reduction knows r, adding $O()$ to an experiment does not change it and is completely without loss of generality. From a practical point of view, it seems that generating and outputting a random group element without knowing a representation is generally not of much help. We therefore believe that the AGM captures most algorithms of practical interest.

1.3   Related Work and Open Questions

We have already mentioned the semi generic group model (SGGM) [JR10] as related work, but we discuss here some key differences of their model to ours in more detail. First, the SGGM is a very restrictive model in the sense that the class of problems it captures is limited. The main theorem of [JR10] (Theorem 3) holds only for pairing-based computational problems in which the output consists of a single element in either one of the base groups. In contrast, the AGM does not require a pairing group setting and thus applies to a much broader class of computational problems. Second, by extending the AGM to pairing groups, we are able to model all three groups as algebraic and reason again about a broader class of problems, in which the output can also consist of elements in the target group. To extend the AGM to the pairing setting, we allow the algebraic adversary to compute any element in the target group by applying the pairing to elements in the respective base groups.

Dent [Den02] shows that the generic group model as proposed Shoup [Sho97] inherits the known weaknesses in the random oracle model [CGH98]. Thus, there exist schemes which can be proven secure in Shoup's GGM, but are pathologically insecure when viewed in the standard model. An interesting open question is whether the AGM bears similar weaknesses. A promising line of research related to this question has recently been initiated by Bitansky et al. [BCPR16]. Namely, they show that indistinguishability obfuscation (iO) implies the existence of non-extractable one-way functions. If these non-extractable one-way functions were furthermore algebraic (such as the knowledge of exponent assumption [Dam92]), then this would invalidate the AGM (under the assumption that iO exists).

Another promising direction for future research is to prove further reductions between common computational assumptions in the AGM. In particular, it would be interesting to classify different such assumptions within the AGM, for example along the lines of work [SS01, Kil01, Boy08, JR15, CM14, MRV16, GG17].

We leave it as an open problem to come up with a meaningful formalization of the AGM for *decisional assumptions*. At a technical level, the main difficulty in this task arises from the fact that an algorithm, i.e., distinguisher, in a decisional problem is asked to output a *bit* rather than a group element. Therefore, such an algorithm is trivially considered algebraic in our framework. It would therefore be interesting to develop a model which captures the algebraic properties of such algorithms in more detail.

A further potential for follow-up work would be to investigate whether it is possible to automate proofs in the AGM. Indeed, for the case of the GGM this has been considered in [BFF+14, ABS16] and it would be interesting to see if similar automated tools can be derived for the AGM.

Finally, we remark that all of our results require prime-order groups and do not yet extend to the setting of pairing groups. When generalizing our results to composite-order groups, we expect to encounter the following technical difficulty: Given, e.g., an equation of the form $ax \equiv_n b$, where n is composite, there might be (exponentially) many solutions for the unknown x in case $\gcd(a, n) > 1$. This interferes with the proof strategies presented in this work and requires a more involved analysis. In fact, proving a reduction from the discrete logarithm problem to the CDH problem in the AGM for group orders containing multiple prime factors (e.g., $n = p^2$) is excluded by [MW98]. Hardness bounds in the GGM for composite-order groups have been considered in [Sho97, MW98, Mau05]. Generalizing the GGM to pairing groups has been the subject, e.g., of the works of [Boy08, KSW08, RLB+08]. Extending the AGM to either one of these regimes is an interesting line of research for future work.

2 Algebraic Algorithms

ALGORITHMS. We denote by $s \xleftarrow{\$} S$ the uniform sampling of the variable s from the (finite) set S. All our algorithms are probabilistic (unless stated otherwise) and written in uppercase letters A, B. To indicate that algorithm A runs on some inputs $(x_1, \ldots, x_n)$ and returns y, we write $y \xleftarrow{\$} \mathsf{A}(x_1, \ldots, x_n)$. If A has access to an algorithm B (via oracle access) during its execution, we write $y \xleftarrow{\$} \mathsf{A}^\mathsf{B}(x_1, \ldots, x_n)$.

SECURITY GAMES. We use a variant of (code-based) *security games* [BR04, Sho04]. In game $\mathbf{G}_{par}$ (defined relative to a set of parameters par), an adversary A interacts with a challenger that answers oracle queries issued by A. It has a main procedure and (possibly zero) oracle procedures which describe how oracle queries are answered. We denote the output of a game $\mathbf{G}_{par}$ between a challenger and an adversary A via $\mathbf{G}_{par}^\mathsf{A}$. A is said to *win* if $\mathbf{G}_{par}^\mathsf{A} = 1$. We define the *advantage* of A in $\mathbf{G}_{par}$ as $\mathbf{Adv}_{par,\mathsf{A}}^\mathbf{G} := \Pr\left[\mathbf{G}_{par}^\mathsf{A} = 1\right]$ and the running time of $\mathbf{G}_{par}^\mathsf{A}$ as $\mathbf{Time}_{par,\mathsf{A}}^\mathbf{G}$.

$\underline{\mathbf{cdh}_{\mathcal{G}}^{\mathsf{A}}}$	$\underline{\mathbf{cdh}_{\mathcal{G}}^{\mathsf{A}_{\mathsf{alg}}}}$
00 $x, y \xleftarrow{\$} \mathbb{Z}_p$	00 $x, y \xleftarrow{\$} \mathbb{Z}_p$
01 $(\mathbf{X}, \mathbf{Y}) := (g^x, g^y)$	01 $(\mathbf{X}, \mathbf{Y}) := (g^x, g^y)$
02 $\mathbf{Z} \xleftarrow{\$} \mathsf{A}(\mathbf{X}, \mathbf{Y})$	02 $[\mathbf{Z}]_{\vec{z}} \xleftarrow{\$} \mathsf{A}_{\mathsf{alg}}(\mathbf{X}, \mathbf{Y})$
03 Return $(\mathbf{Z} = g^{xy})$	03 Return $(\mathbf{Z} = g^{xy})$

Fig. 1. Left: Algebraic game **cdh** relative to group description $\mathcal{G} = (\mathbb{G}, g, p)$ and adversary A. All group elements are written in bold, uppercase letters. **Right:** Algebraic game **cdh** relative to group description $\mathcal{G} = (\mathbb{G}, g, p)$ and algebraic adversary $\mathsf{A}_{\mathsf{alg}}$. The algebraic adversary $\mathsf{A}_{\mathsf{alg}}$ additionally returns a representation $\vec{z} = (a, b, c)$ of $\mathbf{Z}$ such that $\mathbf{Z} = g^a \mathbf{X}^b \mathbf{Y}^c$.

SECURITY REDUCTIONS. Let $\mathbf{G}, \mathbf{H}$ be security games. We write $\mathbf{H}_{par} \overset{(\Delta_\varepsilon, \Delta_t)}{\Longrightarrow} \mathbf{G}_{par}$ if there exists an algorithm R (called $(\Delta_\varepsilon, \Delta_t)$-*reduction*) such that for all algorithms A, algorithm B defined as $\mathsf{B} := \mathsf{R}^{\mathsf{A}}$ satisfies

$$\mathbf{Adv}_{par,\mathsf{B}}^{\mathbf{H}} \geq \frac{1}{\Delta_\varepsilon} \cdot \mathbf{Adv}_{par,\mathsf{A}}^{\mathbf{G}}, \quad \mathbf{Time}_{par,\mathsf{B}}^{\mathbf{H}} \leq \Delta_t \cdot \mathbf{Time}_{par,\mathsf{A}}^{\mathbf{G}}.$$

2.1 Algebraic Security Games and Algorithms

We consider *algebraic security games* $\mathbf{G}_{\mathcal{G}}$ for which we set *par* to a fixed group description $\mathcal{G} = (\mathbb{G}, g, p)$, where $\mathbb{G}$ is a cyclic group of prime order p generated by g. In algebraic security games, we syntactically distinguish between elements of group $\mathbb{G}$ (written in bold, uppercase letters, e.g., $\mathbf{A}$) and all other elements, which must not depend on any group elements. As an example of an algebraic security game, consider the Computational Diffie-Hellman game $\mathbf{cdh}_{\mathcal{G}}^{\mathsf{A}}$, depicted in Fig. 1 (left).

We now define algebraic algorithms. Intuitively, the only way for an algebraic algorithm to output a new group element $\mathbf{Z}$ is to derive it via group multiplications from known group elements.

Definition 1. *(Algebraic algorithm) An algorithm* $\mathsf{A}_{\mathsf{alg}}$ *executed in an algebraic game* $\mathbf{G}_{\mathcal{G}}$ *is called* algebraic *if for all group elements* $\mathbf{Z}$ *that* $\mathsf{A}_{\mathsf{alg}}$ *outputs (i.e., the elements in bold uppercase letters), it additionally provides the representation of* $\mathbf{Z}$ *relative to all previously received group elements. That is, if* $\vec{\mathbf{L}}$ *is the list of group elements* $\mathbf{L}_0, \ldots, \mathbf{L}_m \in \mathbb{G}$ *that* $\mathsf{A}_{\mathsf{alg}}$ *has received so far (w.l.o.g.* $\mathbf{L}_0 = g$*), then* $\mathsf{A}_{\mathsf{alg}}$ *must also provide a vector* $\vec{z}$ *such that* $\mathbf{Z} = \prod_i \mathbf{L}_i^{z_i}$. *We denote such an output as* $[\mathbf{Z}]_{\vec{z}}$.

REMARKS ON OUR MODEL. Algebraic algorithms were first considered in [BV98, PV05], where they are defined using an additional extractor algorithm which computes for an output group element a representation in basis $\vec{\mathbf{L}}$. We believe that our definition gives a simpler and cleaner definition of algebraic algorithms. If one assumes that the extractor algorithm has constant running time, then our definition is easily seen to be equivalent to theirs. Indeed, this view makes sense for algorithms in the GGM since the representation $\vec{z}$ trivially follows from the description of the algorithm. However, if running the extractor algorithm imposes some additional cost, then this will clearly affect the running times of our reductions. If the cost of the extractor is similar to that of the solver adversary, then reductions in our model that neither call an algebraic solver multiple times nor receive from it a non-constant amount of group elements (along with their representations) will remain largely the same in both models.

For the inputs to algebraic adversaries we syntactically distinguish group elements from other inputs and require that the latter not depend on any group elements. This is necessary to rule out pathological cases in which an algorithm receives "disguised" group elements and is forced to output an algebraic representation of them (which it might not know). To illustrate the issue, consider an efficient algorithm A, which on input $X' := \mathbf{X}\|\bot$ returns $\mathbf{X}$, where $\mathbf{X}$ is a group element, but X' is not. If A is algebraic then it must return a representation of $\mathbf{X}$ in g (the only group element previously seen), which would be the discrete logarithm of $\mathbf{X}$.

Allowing inputs of form X' while requiring algorithms to be algebraic leads to contradictions. (E.g., one could use $\mathsf{A}_{\mathsf{alg}}$ to compute discrete logarithms: given a challenge $\mathbf{X} = g^x$, run $[\mathbf{X}]_x \xleftarrow{\$} \mathsf{A}_{\mathsf{alg}}(\mathbf{X}\|\bot)$ and return x.) We therefore demand that non-group-element inputs must not depend on group elements. (Note that if $\mathsf{A}_{\mathsf{alg}}$'s input contains $\mathbf{X}$ explicitly then it can output $[\mathbf{X}]_{(0,1)}$ with a valid representation of $\mathbf{X}$ relative to $\vec{\mathbf{L}} = (g, \mathbf{X})$.)

Finally, we slightly abuse notation and let an algebraic algorithm also represent output group elements as combinations of previous *outputs*. This makes some of our proofs easier and is justified since all previous outputs must themselves have been given along with an according representation. Therefore, one can always recompute a representation that depends only on the initial inputs to the algebraic algorithm.

INTEGRATING WITH RANDOM ORACLES IN THE AGM. As mentioned above, an algorithm A that samples (and outputs) a group element $\mathbf{X}$ obliviously, i.e., without knowing its representation, is not algebraic. This appears to be problematic if one wishes to combine the AGM with the Random Oracle Model [BR93]. However, group elements output by the random oracle are included by definition in the list $\vec{\mathbf{L}}$. This means that for any such element, a representation is trivially available to $\mathsf{A}_{\mathsf{alg}}$.

2.2 Generic Security Games and Algorithms

Generic algorithms $\mathsf{A}_{\mathsf{gen}}$ are only allowed to use generic properties of group $\mathcal{G}$. Informally, an algorithm is generic if it works regardless of what group it is run in. This is usually modeled by giving an algorithm indirect access to group elements via abstract handles. It is straight-forward to translate all of our algebraic games into games that are syntactically compatible with generic algorithms accessing group elements only via abstract handles.

We say that winning algebraic game $\mathbf{G}_{\mathcal{G}}$ is (ε, t)-*hard in the generic group model* if for every generic algorithm $\mathsf{A}_{\mathsf{gen}}$ it holds that

$$\mathbf{Time}^{\mathbf{G}}_{\mathcal{G}, \mathsf{A}_{\mathsf{gen}}} \leq t \implies \mathbf{Adv}^{\mathbf{G}}_{\mathcal{G}, \mathsf{A}_{\mathsf{gen}}} \leq \varepsilon.$$

We remark that usually in the generic group model one considers group operations (i.e., oracle calls) instead of the running time. In our context it is more convenient to measure the running time instead, assuming every oracle call takes one unit time.

As an important example, consider the algebraic Discrete Logarithm Game $\mathbf{dlog}_{\mathcal{G}}$ in Fig. 2 which is $(t^2/p, t)$-hard in the generic group model [Sho97, Mau05].

We assume that a generic algorithm $\mathsf{A}_{\mathsf{gen}}$ additionally provides the representation of $\mathbf{Z}$ relative to all previously received group elements, for all group elements $\mathbf{Z}$ that it outputs. This assumption is w.l.o.g. since a generic algorithm can only obtain new group elements by multiplying two known group elements; hence it always knows a valid representation. This way, every generic algorithm is also an algebraic algorithm.

Furthermore, if $\mathsf{B}_{\mathsf{gen}}$ is a generic algorithm and $\mathsf{A}_{\mathsf{alg}}$ is an algebraic algorithm, then $\mathsf{B}_{\mathsf{alg}} := \mathsf{B}_{\mathsf{gen}}^{\mathsf{A}_{\mathsf{alg}}}$ is also is an algebraic algorithm. We refer to [Mau05] for more on generic algorithms.

2.3 Generic Reductions Between Algebraic Security Games

Let $\mathbf{G}_{\mathcal{G}}$ and $\mathbf{H}_{\mathcal{G}}$ be two algebraic security games. We write $\mathbf{H}_{\mathcal{G}} \stackrel{(\Delta_\varepsilon, \Delta_t)}{\Longrightarrow}_{\mathsf{alg}} \mathbf{G}_{\mathcal{G}}$ if there exists a generic algorithm $\mathsf{R}_{\mathsf{gen}}$ (called generic $(\Delta_\varepsilon, \Delta_t)$-*reduction*) such that for every algebraic algorithm $\mathsf{A}_{\mathsf{alg}}$, algorithm $\mathsf{B}_{\mathsf{alg}}$ defined as $\mathsf{B}_{\mathsf{alg}} := \mathsf{R}_{\mathsf{gen}}^{\mathsf{A}_{\mathsf{alg}}}$ satisfies

$$\mathbf{Adv}^{\mathbf{H}}_{\mathcal{G}, \mathsf{B}_{\mathsf{alg}}} \geq \frac{1}{\Delta_\varepsilon} \cdot \mathbf{Adv}^{\mathbf{G}}_{\mathcal{G}, \mathsf{A}_{\mathsf{alg}}}, \quad \mathbf{Time}^{\mathbf{H}}_{\mathcal{G}, \mathsf{B}_{\mathsf{alg}}} \leq \Delta_t \cdot \mathbf{Time}^{\mathbf{G}}_{\mathcal{G}, \mathsf{A}_{\mathsf{alg}}}.$$

Note that we deliberately require reduction $\mathsf{R}_{\mathsf{gen}}$ to be generic. Hence, if $\mathsf{A}_{\mathsf{alg}}$ is algebraic, then $\mathsf{B}_{\mathsf{alg}} := \mathsf{R}_{\mathsf{gen}}^{\mathsf{A}_{\mathsf{alg}}}$ is algebraic; if $\mathsf{A}_{\mathsf{alg}}$ is generic, then $\mathsf{B}_{\mathsf{alg}} := \mathsf{R}_{\mathsf{gen}}^{\mathsf{A}_{\mathsf{alg}}}$ is generic. If one is only interested in algebraic adversaries, then it suffices to require reduction $\mathsf{R}_{\mathsf{gen}}$ to be algebraic. But in that case one can no longer infer that $\mathsf{B}_{\mathsf{alg}} := \mathsf{R}_{\mathsf{gen}}^{\mathsf{A}_{\mathsf{alg}}}$ is generic in case $\mathsf{A}_{\mathsf{alg}}$ is generic.

COMPOSING INFORMATION-THEORETIC LOWER BOUNDS WITH REDUCTIONS IN THE AGM. The following lemma explains how statements in the AGM carry over to the GGM.

Lemma 1. *Let* $\mathbf{G}_{\mathcal{G}}$ *and* $\mathbf{H}_{\mathcal{G}}$ *be algebraic security games such that* $\mathbf{H}_{\mathcal{G}} \stackrel{(\Delta_\varepsilon, \Delta_t)}{\Longrightarrow}_{\mathsf{alg}} \mathbf{G}_{\mathcal{G}}$ *and winning* $\mathbf{H}_{\mathcal{G}}$ *is* (ε, t)-*hard in the GGM. Then,* $\mathbf{G}_{\mathcal{G}}$ *is* $(\varepsilon \cdot \Delta_\varepsilon, t/\Delta_t)$-*hard in the GGM.*

Proof. Let $\mathsf{A}_{\mathsf{gen}}$ be a generic algorithm playing in game $\mathbf{G}_{\mathcal{G}}$. Then by our premise there exists a generic algorithm $\mathsf{B}_{\mathsf{alg}} = \mathsf{R}_{\mathsf{gen}}^{\mathsf{A}_{\mathsf{alg}}}$ such that

$$\mathbf{Adv}^{\mathbf{H}}_{\mathcal{G}, \mathsf{B}_{\mathsf{alg}}} \geq \tfrac{1}{\Delta_\varepsilon} \cdot \mathbf{Adv}^{\mathbf{G}}_{\mathcal{G}, \mathsf{A}_{\mathsf{alg}}}, \quad \mathbf{Time}^{\mathbf{H}}_{\mathcal{G}, \mathsf{B}_{\mathsf{alg}}} \leq \Delta_t \cdot \mathbf{Time}^{\mathbf{G}}_{\mathcal{G}, \mathsf{A}_{\mathsf{alg}}}.$$

$\mathbf{dlog}_{\mathcal{G}}^{\mathsf{A}}$	$\mathbf{lc\text{-}dh}_{\mathcal{G}}^{\mathsf{A}}$	$\mathbf{sq\text{-}dh}_{\mathcal{G}}^{\mathsf{A}}$
00 $x \xleftarrow{\$} \mathbb{Z}_p$	00 $x, y \xleftarrow{\$} \mathbb{Z}_p$	00 $x \xleftarrow{\$} \mathbb{Z}_p$
01 $\mathbf{X} := g^x$	01 $(\mathbf{X}, \mathbf{Y}) := (g^x, g^y)$	01 $\mathbf{X} := g^x$
02 $z \xleftarrow{\$} \mathsf{A}(\mathbf{X})$	02 $(\mathbf{Z}, u, v, w) \xleftarrow{\$} \mathsf{A}(\mathbf{X}, \mathbf{Y})$	02 $\mathbf{Z} \xleftarrow{\$} \mathsf{A}(\mathbf{X})$
03 Return $(z = x)$	03 Return $\big(\mathbf{Z} = g^{ux^2 + vxy + wy^2}$	03 Return $\big(\mathbf{Z} = g^{x^2}\big)$
	$\land\, (u \neq 0 \lor v \neq 0 \lor w \neq 0)\big)$	

Fig. 2. Discrete Logarithm Game **dlog**, Square Diffie-Hellman Game **sq-dh**, and Linear Combination Diffie-Hellman Game **lc-dh** relative to group $\mathcal{G}$ and adversary A.

Assume $\mathbf{Time}_{\mathcal{G}, \mathsf{A}_{\mathsf{alg}}}^{\mathbf{G}} \leq t/\Delta_t$; then $\mathbf{Time}_{\mathcal{G}, \mathsf{B}_{\mathsf{alg}}}^{\mathbf{H}} \leq \Delta_t \cdot \mathbf{Time}_{\mathcal{G}, \mathsf{A}_{\mathsf{alg}}}^{\mathbf{G}} \leq t$. Since winning $\mathbf{H}_{\mathcal{G}}$ is (ε, t)-hard in the GGM, it follows that

$$\varepsilon \geq \mathbf{Adv}_{\mathcal{G}, \mathsf{B}_{\mathsf{alg}}}^{\mathbf{H}} \geq \tfrac{1}{\Delta_\varepsilon} \cdot \mathbf{Adv}_{\mathcal{G}, \mathsf{A}_{\mathsf{alg}}}^{\mathbf{G}}$$

and thus $\varepsilon \cdot \Delta_\varepsilon \geq \mathbf{Adv}_{\mathcal{G}, \mathsf{A}_{\mathsf{alg}}}^{\mathbf{G}}$, which proves that $\mathbf{G}_{\mathcal{G}}$ is $(\varepsilon\Delta_\varepsilon, t/\Delta_t)$-hard in the GGM. □

3 The Diffie-Hellman Assumption and Variants

In this section we consider some variants of the standard Diffie-Hellman assumption [DH76] and prove them to be equivalent to the discrete logarithm assumption (defined via algebraic game $\mathbf{dlog}_{\mathcal{G}}$ of Fig. 2) in the Algebraic Group Model.

3.1 Computational Diffie-Hellman

Consider the Square Diffie-Hellman Assumption [MW99] described in algebraic game $\mathbf{sq\text{-}dh}_{\mathcal{G}}$ and the Linear Combination Diffie-Hellman Assumption described in algebraic game $\mathbf{lc\text{-}dh}_{\mathcal{G}}$ (both in Fig. 2), which will be convenient for the proof of Theorem 2.

As a warm-up we now prove that the Discrete Logarithm assumption is tightly equivalent to the Diffie-Hellman, the Square Diffie-Hellman, and the Linear Combination Diffie-Hellman Assumption in the Algebraic Group Model. The equivalence of the Square Diffie-Hellman and Diffie-Hellman problems was previously proven in [MW99, BDZ03].

Theorem 1. $\mathbf{dlog}_{\mathcal{G}} \xRightarrow{(1,1)}_{\mathsf{alg}} \{\mathbf{cdh}_{\mathcal{G}}, \mathbf{sq\text{-}dh}_{\mathcal{G}}\}$ *and* $\mathbf{dlog}_{\mathcal{G}} \xRightarrow{(3,1)}_{\mathsf{alg}} \mathbf{lc\text{-}dh}_{\mathcal{G}}$.

Proof. Let $\mathsf{A}_{\mathsf{alg}}$ be an algebraic adversary executed in game $\mathbf{sq\text{-}dh}_{\mathcal{G}}$; cf. Fig. 3.

As $\mathsf{A}_{\mathsf{alg}}$ is an algebraic adversary, it returns a solution $\mathbf{Z}$ together with a representation $(a, b) \in \mathbb{Z}_p^2$ such that

$$\mathbf{Z} = g^{x^2} = g^a (g^x)^b. \tag{1}$$

$$
\begin{array}{|l|}
\hline
\textbf{sq-dh}_{\mathcal{G}}^{\mathsf{A_{alg}}} \\
\hline
00 \ \ x \xleftarrow{\$} \mathbb{Z}_p \\
01 \ \ \mathbf{X} := g^x \\
02 \ \ [\mathbf{Z}]_{(a,b)} \xleftarrow{\$} \mathsf{A_{alg}}(\mathbf{X}) \\
03 \ \ \text{Return} \ \left(\mathbf{Z} = g^{x^2}\right) \\
\hline
\end{array}
$$

Fig. 3. Algebraic adversary $\mathsf{A_{alg}}$ playing in $\textbf{sq-dh}_{\mathcal{G}}$.

We now show how to construct a generic reduction $\mathsf{R_{gen}}$ that calls $\mathsf{A_{alg}}$ exactly once such that for $\mathsf{B_{alg}} := \mathsf{R_{gen}^{A_{alg}}}$ we have

$$
\mathbf{Adv}_{\mathcal{G},\mathsf{B_{alg}}}^{\mathsf{dlog}} = \mathbf{Adv}_{\mathcal{G},\mathsf{A_{alg}}}^{\mathsf{sq\text{-}dh}}.
$$

$\mathsf{R_{gen}}$ works as follows. On input a discrete logarithm instance $\mathbf{X}$, it runs $\mathsf{A_{alg}}$ on $\mathbf{X}$. Suppose $\mathsf{A_{alg}}$ is successful. Equation (1) is equivalent to the quadratic equation $x^2 - bx - a \equiv_p 0$ with at most two solutions in x. (In general such equations are not guaranteed to have a solution but since the representation is valid and $\mathsf{A_{alg}}$ is assumed to be correct, there exists at least one solution for x.) $\mathsf{R_{gen}}$ can test which one (out of the two) is the correct solution x by testing against $\mathbf{X} = g^x$. Moreover, it is easy to see that $\mathsf{R_{gen}}$ only performs generic group operations and is therefore generic. Hence, $\mathsf{B_{alg}} := \mathsf{R_{gen}^{A_{alg}}}$ is algebraic, which proves

$$
\textbf{dlog}_{\mathcal{G}} \overset{(1,1)}{\underset{\text{alg}}{\Longrightarrow}} \textbf{sq-dh}_{\mathcal{G}}.
$$

The statement $\textbf{dlog}_{\mathcal{G}} \overset{(1,1)}{\underset{\text{alg}}{\Longrightarrow}} \textbf{cdh}_{\mathcal{G}}$ follows, since given an adversary against $\textbf{cdh}_{\mathcal{G}}$ (see Fig. 1), we can easily construct an adversary against $\textbf{sq-dh}_{\mathcal{G}}$ that runs in the same time and has the same probability of success (given $\mathbf{X} = g^x$, sample $r \xleftarrow{\$} \mathbb{Z}_p$, run the $\textbf{cdh}$ adversary on $(\mathbf{X}, \mathbf{X}^r)$, obtain $\mathbf{Z}$ and return $\mathbf{Z}^{\frac{1}{r}}$).

It remains to show that $\textbf{sq-dh}_{\mathcal{G}} \overset{(3,1)}{\underset{\text{alg}}{\Longrightarrow}} \textbf{lc-dh}_{\mathcal{G}}$. Given an algebraic solver $\mathsf{C_{alg}}$ executed in game $\textbf{lc-dh}_{\mathcal{G}}$, we construct an adversary $\mathsf{A_{alg}}$ against $\textbf{sq-dh}_{\mathcal{G}}$ as follows: On input $\mathbf{X} = g^x$, $\mathsf{A_{alg}}$ samples $r \xleftarrow{\$} \mathbb{Z}_p$ and computes either $(\mathbf{X}, g^r)$, $(g^r, \mathbf{X})$, or $(\mathbf{X}, \mathbf{X}^r)$ each with probability $1/3$. Note that this instance is correctly distributed. It then runs $\mathsf{C_{alg}}$ on the resulting tuple $(\mathbf{X}_1, \mathbf{X}_2)$ and receives $(\mathbf{Z}, u, v, w)$ together with (a, b, c) s.t. $\mathbf{Z} = g^a \mathbf{X}_1^b \mathbf{X}_2^c$. If $u \neq 0$, then the choice $\mathbf{X}_1 = \mathbf{X}$, $\mathbf{X}_2 = g^r$ yields $\mathbf{Z} = g^{ux^2 + vxr + wr^2}$, from which g^{x^2} can be computed as $g^{x^2} = (\mathbf{Z}\mathbf{X}^{-vr} g^{-wr^2})^{\frac{1}{u}}$. Clearly, $\mathsf{A_{alg}}$ is able to compute an algebraic representation of g^{x^2} from the values (a, b, c) and thus is algebraic itself. The cases $v \neq 0, w \neq 0$ follow in a similar fashion. $\qed$

Corollary 1. $\textbf{cdh}_{\mathcal{G}}$ and $\textbf{sq-dh}_{\mathcal{G}}$ are $(t^2/p, t)$-hard in the generic group model and $\textbf{lc-dh}_{\mathcal{G}}$ is $(3t^2/p, t)$-hard in the generic group model.

For the subsequent sections and proofs, we will not make explicit the reduction algorithm $\mathsf{R_{gen}}$ every time (as done above).

3.2   Strong Diffie-Hellman

Consider the Strong Diffie-Hellman Assumption [ABR01] described via game $\mathbf{sdh}_{\mathcal{G}}$ in Fig. 4. We now prove that the Discrete Logarithm Assumption (non-tightly) implies the Strong Diffie-Hellman Assumption in the Algebraic Group Model. We briefly present the main ideas of the proof. The full proof of Theorem 2 can be found in the full version of our paper [FKL17]. Let A_{alg} be an algebraic adversary playing in $\mathbf{sdh}_{\mathcal{G}}$ and let $\mathbf{Z} = g^z$ denote the Discrete Logarithm challenge. We show an adversary B_{alg} against $\mathbf{dlog}_{\mathcal{G}}$ that simulates $\mathbf{sdh}_{\mathcal{G}}$ to A_{alg}. B_{alg} appropriately answers A_{alg}'s queries to the oracle $O(\cdot, \cdot)$ by using the algebraic representation of the queried elements provided by A_{alg}. Namely, when $(\mathbf{Y}', \mathbf{Z}')$ is asked to the oracle, B_{alg} obtains vectors $\vec{b}, \vec{c}$ such that $\mathbf{Y}' = g^{b_1} \mathbf{X}^{b_2} \mathbf{Y}^{b_3}$ and $\mathbf{Z}' = g^{c_1} \mathbf{X}^{c_2} \mathbf{Y}^{c_3}$. As long as $b_2 = b_3 = 0$, B_{alg} can answer all of A_{alg}'s queries by checking whether $\mathbf{X}^{b_1} = \mathbf{Z}'$. On the other hand, if $b_2 \neq 0$ or $b_3 \neq 0$, then B_{alg} simply returns 0. Informally, the simulation will be perfect unless A_{alg} manages to compute a valid solution to $\mathbf{lc\text{-}dh}_{\mathcal{G}}$. All of these games can be efficiently simulated by B_{alg}, as we have shown in the previous section.

$\underline{\mathbf{sdh}_{\mathcal{G}}^{\mathsf{A}}}$	$\underline{O(\mathbf{Y}', \mathbf{Z}')}$
00 $x, y \overset{\$}{\leftarrow} \mathbb{Z}_p$	04 Return $\big(\mathbf{Z}' = (\mathbf{Y}')^x\big)$
01 $(\mathbf{X}, \mathbf{Y}) := (g^x, g^y)$	
02 $\mathbf{Z} \overset{\$}{\leftarrow} \mathsf{A}^{O(\cdot, \cdot)}(\mathbf{X}, \mathbf{Y})$	
03 Return $(\mathbf{Z} = g^{xy})$	

Fig. 4. Strong Diffie-Hellman Game $\mathbf{sdh}$ relative to $\mathcal{G}$ and adversary A.

Theorem 2. $\mathbf{dlog}_{\mathcal{G}} \overset{(4q, 1)}{\Longrightarrow}_{\mathsf{alg}} \mathbf{sdh}_{\mathcal{G}}$, where q is the maximum number of queries to oracle $O(\cdot, \cdot)$ in $\mathbf{sdh}_{\mathcal{G}}$.

Corollary 2. $\mathbf{sdh}_{\mathcal{G}}$ is $\big(\frac{t^2}{4pq}, t\big)$-hard in the generic group model.

4   The LRSW Assumption

The interactive LRSW assumption [LRSW99, CL04] is defined via the algebraic security game $\mathbf{lrsw}$ in Fig. 5.

We prove that the LRSW assumption is (non-tightly) implied by the Discrete Logarithm Assumption in the Algebraic Group Model. We give a high-level sketch of the main ideas here; the full proof of Theorem 3 can be found in the full version of our paper [FKL17]. Let A_{alg} be an algebraic adversary playing in $\mathbf{lrsw}_{\mathcal{G}}$ and let $\mathbf{Z} = g^z$ denote the Discrete Logarithm challenge. We construct an adversary B_{alg} against $\mathbf{dlog}_{\mathcal{G}}$, which simulate $\mathbf{lrsw}_{\mathcal{G}}$ to A_{alg} by embedding the value of z in one of three possible ways. Namely, it either sets $\mathbf{X} := \mathbf{Z}$ or $\mathbf{Y} := \mathbf{Z}$, or it chooses a random the query by A_{alg} to the oracle $O(\cdot)$ in $\mathbf{lrsw}_{\mathcal{G}}$ to embed the

$\mathbf{lrsw}_{\mathcal{G}}^{\mathsf{A}}$	$\underline{\mathsf{O}}(m_j)$ //For query j
00 $Q := \emptyset$	05 $r_j \xleftarrow{\$} \mathbb{Z}_p$;
01 $x, y \xleftarrow{\$} \mathbb{Z}_p$	06 $\mathbf{A}_j := g^{r_j}$
02 $\mathbf{X} := g^x, \mathbf{Y} := g^y$	07 $\mathbf{B}_j := g^{r_j y}$
03 $(m^*, \mathbf{A}^*, \mathbf{B}^*, \mathbf{C}^*) \xleftarrow{\$} \mathsf{A}^{\mathsf{O}(\cdot)}(\mathbf{X}, \mathbf{Y})$	08 $\mathbf{C}_j := g^{r_j m_j x y + r_j x}$
04 Return $\big(m^* \notin Q \wedge m^* \neq 0 \wedge \mathbf{A}^* \neq 1$	09 $Q := Q \cup \{m_j\}$
$\wedge\ \mathbf{B}^* = (\mathbf{A}^*)^y \wedge \mathbf{C}^* = (\mathbf{A}^*)^{m^* xy + x}\big)$	10 Return $(\mathbf{A}_j, \mathbf{B}_j, \mathbf{C}_j)$

Fig. 5. Game **lrsw** relative to $\mathcal{G}$ and adversary A.

value of z. These behaviours correspond in our proof to the adversaries $\mathsf{C}_{\mathsf{alg}}, \mathsf{D}_{\mathsf{alg}}$, and $\mathsf{E}_{\mathsf{alg}}$, respectively. After obtaining a solution $(m^*, [\mathbf{A}^*]_{\vec{a}}, [\mathbf{B}^*]_{\vec{b}}, [\mathbf{C}^*]_{\vec{c}})$ on a fresh value $m^* \neq 0$ from $\mathsf{A}_{\mathsf{alg}}$, the adversaries use the algebraic representations $\vec{a}, \vec{b}, \vec{c}$ obtained from $\mathsf{A}_{\mathsf{alg}}$ to suitably rewrite the values of $\mathbf{A}^*, \mathbf{C}^*$. They then make use of the relation $(\mathbf{A}^*)^{(xm^* y + x)} = \mathbf{C}^*$ to obtain an equation mod p, which in turn gives z.

Theorem 3. $\mathbf{dlog}_{\mathcal{G}} \xRightarrow{(6q,1)}_{\mathsf{alg}} \mathbf{lrsw}_{\mathcal{G}}$, where $q \geq 6$ is the maximum number of queries to $\mathsf{O}(\cdot)$ in $\mathbf{lrsw}_{\mathcal{G}}$.

Corollary 3. $\mathbf{lrsw}_{\mathcal{G}}$ is $\big(t, \frac{t^2}{6pq}\big)$-hard in the generic group model.

5 ElGamal Encryption

In this section we prove that the IND-CCA1 (aka. lunchtime security) of the ElGamal encryption scheme (in its abstraction as a KEM) is implied by a parametrized ("q-type") variant of the Decision Diffie-Hellman Assumption in the Algebraic Group Model.

ADVANTAGE FOR DECISIONAL ALGEBRAIC SECURITY GAMES. We parameterize a *decisional* algebraic game **G** (such as the game in Fig. 7) with a parameter bit b. We define the advantage of adversary A in **G** as

$$\mathbf{Adv}_{par,\mathsf{A}}^{\mathbf{G}} := \big| \Pr\big[\mathbf{G}_{par,0}^{\mathsf{A}} = 1\big] - \Pr\big[\mathbf{G}_{par,1}^{\mathsf{A}} = 1\big] \big|.$$

We define $\mathbf{Time}_{par,\mathsf{A}_{\mathsf{alg}}}^{\mathbf{G}}$ independently of the parameter bit b, i.e., we consider only adversaries that have the same running time in both games $\mathbf{G}_{par,0}, \mathbf{G}_{par,1}$. In order to cover games that define the security of schemes (rather than assumptions), instead of $par = \mathcal{G}$, we only require that $\mathcal{G}$ be *included* in par. Let $\mathbf{G}_{par}, \mathbf{H}_{par}$ be decisional algebraic security games. As before, we write $\mathbf{H}_{par} \xRightarrow{(\Delta_\varepsilon, \Delta_t)}_{\mathsf{alg}} \mathbf{G}_{par}$ if there exists a generic algorithm $\mathsf{R}_{\mathsf{gen}}$ (called generic $(\Delta_\varepsilon, \Delta_t)$-*reduction*) such that for algebraic algorithm $\mathsf{B}_{\mathsf{alg}}$ defined as $\mathsf{B}_{\mathsf{alg}} := \mathsf{R}_{\mathsf{gen}}^{\mathsf{A}_{\mathsf{alg}}}$, we have

$$\mathbf{Adv}_{par,\mathsf{B}_{\mathsf{alg}}}^{\mathbf{H}} \geq \frac{1}{\Delta_\varepsilon} \cdot \mathbf{Adv}_{par,\mathsf{A}_{\mathsf{alg}}}^{\mathbf{G}}, \quad \mathbf{Time}_{par,\mathsf{B}_{\mathsf{alg}}}^{\mathbf{H}} \leq \Delta_t \cdot \mathbf{Time}_{par,\mathsf{A}_{\mathsf{alg}}}^{\mathbf{G}}.$$

ind-cca1$^A_{KEM,par,b}$	Dec(C)	Enc() //One time
00 $(pk, sk) \xleftarrow{\$} \text{Gen}(par)$	//Before Enc is called	05 $(K_0^*, C^*) \xleftarrow{\$} \text{Enc}(pk)$
01 $b' \xleftarrow{\$} A^{\text{Dec,Enc}}(pk)$	03 $K \xleftarrow{\$} \text{Dec}(C, sk)$	06 $K_1^* \xleftarrow{\$} \mathcal{K}$
02 Return b'	04 Return K	07 Return (K_b^*, C^*)

Fig. 6. IND-CCA1 Game **ind-cca1** relative to KEM KEM = (Gen, Enc, Dec), parameters par, and adversary A.

KEY ENCAPSULATION MECHANISMS. A *key encapsulation mechanism* (KEM for short) KEM = (Gen, Enc, Dec) is a triple of algorithms together with a symmetric-key space $\mathcal{K}$. The randomized *key generation algorithm* Gen takes as input a set of parameters, par, and outputs a public/secret key pair (pk, sk). The *encapsulation algorithm* Enc takes as input a public key pk and outputs a key/ciphertext pair (K, C) such that $K \xleftarrow{\$} \mathcal{K}$. The deterministic *decapsulation algorithm* Dec takes as input a secret key sk and a ciphertext C and outputs a key $K \in \mathcal{K}$ or a special symbol $\perp$ if C is invalid. We require that KEM be *correct*: For all possible pairs (K, C) output by Enc(pk), we have Dec(sk, C) = K. We formalize IND-CCA1 security of a KEM via the games (for $b = 0, 1$) depicted in Fig. 6.

In the following, we consider the ElGamal KEM EG defined in Fig. 8. We also consider a stronger variant of the well-known Decisional Diffie-Hellman (DDH) assumption that is parametrized by an integer q. In the q-DDH game, defined in Fig. 7, the adversary receives, in addition to (g^x, g^y), the values $g^{x^2}, \ldots, g^{x^q}$.

Lemma 2. *[Che06] For $q < p^{1/3}$,* **q-ddh**$_\mathcal{G}$ *is $\left(\frac{t^2 q}{p \log p}, t\right)$-hard in the generic group model.*

The proof of the following theorem can be found in the full version of our paper [FKL17]. In the proof, we condisder the algebraic games depicted in Fig. 9.

Theorem 4. **ind-cca1**$_{EG,\mathcal{G}} \overset{(1,1)}{\Longleftrightarrow}_{alg}$ **q-ddh**$_\mathcal{G}$, *where $q - 1$ is the maximal number of queries to Dec($\cdot$) in* **ind-cca1**$_{EG,\mathcal{G}}$.

Corollary 4. *For $q < p^{1/3}$,* **ind-cca1**$_{EG,\mathcal{G}}$ *is $\left(\frac{t^2 q}{p \log p}, t\right)$-hard in the generic group model, where $q - 1$ is the maximal number of queries to Dec($\cdot$) in* **ind-cca1**$_{EG,\mathcal{G}}$.

6   Tight Reduction for the BLS Scheme

For this section, we introduce the notion of groups $\mathbb{G}$ equipped with a symmetric, (non-degenerate) bilinear map $e \colon \mathbb{G} \times \mathbb{G} \to \mathbb{G}_T$, where $\mathbb{G}_T$ denotes the so-called *target group*. We now set $\mathcal{G} = (p, \mathbb{G}, \mathbb{G}_T, g, e)$ (Fig. 9).

SIGNATURE SCHEMES. A *signature scheme* SIG = (SIGGen, SIGSig, SIGVer) is a triple of algorithms. The randomized *key generation algorithm* SIGGen takes as input a set of parameters, par, and outputs a public/secret key pair (pk, sk). The randomized *signing algorithm* SIGSig takes as input a secret key sk and a message

$$
\begin{array}{|l|}
\hline
\textbf{q-ddh}^{\mathsf{A}}_{\mathcal{G},b} \\
\hline
00 \quad x, r, z \xleftarrow{\$} \mathbb{Z}_p \\
01 \quad b' \xleftarrow{\$} \mathsf{A}(g^x, g^{x^2}, ..., g^{x^q}, g^r, g^{xr+zb}) \\
02 \quad \text{Return } b' \\
\hline
\end{array}
$$

Fig. 7. q-Decisional Diffie-Hellman Game **q-ddh** relative to $\mathcal{G}$ and adversary A.

$\underline{\mathsf{Gen}(\mathcal{G})}$	$\underline{\mathsf{Enc}(pk)}$:	$\underline{\mathsf{Dec}(\mathbf{C}, sk)}$:
00 $x \xleftarrow{\$} \mathbb{Z}_p$	03 $r \xleftarrow{\$} \mathbb{Z}_p$	07 If $\mathbf{C} \notin \mathbb{G}$
01 $\mathbf{X} := g^x$	04 $\mathbf{C} := g^r$	08 $\quad$ Return $\bot$
02 Return $(pk, sk) := (\mathbf{X}, x)$	05 $\mathbf{K} := \mathbf{X}^r$	09 $\tilde{\mathbf{K}} := \mathbf{C}^x$
	06 Return $(\mathbf{K}, \mathbf{C})$	10 Return $\tilde{\mathbf{K}}$

Fig. 8. ElGamal KEM $\mathsf{EG} = (\mathsf{Gen}, \mathsf{Enc}, \mathsf{Dec})$

$\boxed{\textbf{ind-cca1}^{\mathsf{A}}_{\mathsf{EG},\mathcal{G},0}}$ $\boxed{\textbf{ind-cca1}^{\mathsf{A}}_{\mathsf{EG},\mathcal{G},1}}$	$\underline{\mathsf{Dec}([\mathbf{C}]_{\vec{a}})}$ // Before Enc is called	$\underline{\mathsf{Enc}()}$ // One time
00 $x \xleftarrow{\$} \mathbb{Z}_p$		06 $r \xleftarrow{\$} \mathbb{Z}_p$
01 $\mathbf{X} := g^x$	04 $\mathbf{K} := \mathbf{C}^x$	07 $\mathbf{C}^* := g^r$
02 $b' \xleftarrow{\$} \mathsf{A}^{\mathsf{Dec},\mathsf{Enc}}_{\mathsf{alg}}(\mathbf{X})$	05 Return $\mathbf{K}$	08 $\mathbf{K}^* := \mathbf{X}^r$
03 Return b'		09 $\boxed{\mathbf{K}^* \xleftarrow{\$} \mathcal{K}}$
		10 Return $(\mathbf{K}^*, \mathbf{C}^*)$

Fig. 9. Games **ind-cca1**$^{\mathsf{A}}_{\mathsf{EG},\mathcal{G},0}$ and **ind-cca1**$^{\mathsf{A}}_{\mathsf{EG},\mathcal{G},1}$ with algebraic adversary $\mathsf{A}_{\mathsf{alg}}$. The boxed statement is only executed in **ind-cca1**$^{\mathsf{A}}_{\mathsf{EG},\mathcal{G},1}$.

m in the message space $\mathcal{M}$ and outputs a signature σ in the signature space $\mathcal{S}$. The deterministic *signature verification algorithm* SIGVer takes as input a public key pk, a message m, and a signature σ and outputs $b \in \{0, 1\}$. We require that SIG be *correct*: For all possible pairs (pk, sk) output by SIGGen, and all messages $m \in \mathcal{M}$, we have $\Pr[\mathsf{SIGVer}(pk, m, \mathsf{SIGSig}(m, sk)) = 1] = 1$. We formalize *unforgeability under chosen message attacks* for SIG via game **uf-cma**$_{\mathsf{SIG},par}$ depicted in Fig. 10.

In the following, we show how in the AGM with a random oracle, the security of the BLS signature scheme [BLS04], depicted in Fig. 11, can be tightly reduced to the discrete logarithm problem. Boneh, Lynn and Shacham [BLS04] only prove a loose reduction to the CDH problem. In the AGM we manage to improve the quality of the reduction, leveraging the fact that a forgery comes with a representation in the basis of all previously answered random oracle and signature queries. We embed a discrete logarithm challenge in either the secret key or inside the random oracle queries–a choice that remains hidden from the adversary. Depending on the adversary's behavior we always solve the discrete logarithm challenge in one of the cases.

$\text{uf-cma}^{\mathsf{A}}_{\mathsf{SIG},par}$	$\underline{O}(m)$
00 $(pk, sk) \xleftarrow{\$} \mathsf{SIGGen}$	04 $Q := Q \cup \{m\}$
01 $Q := \emptyset$	05 $\sigma \xleftarrow{\$} \mathsf{SIGSig}(m, sk)$
02 $(m^*, \sigma^*) \xleftarrow{\$} \mathsf{A}^{O(\cdot)}$	06 Return σ
03 Return $\big(m^* \notin Q \wedge \mathsf{SIGVer}(m^*, \sigma^*)\big)$	

Fig. 10. Game **uf-cma** defining (existential) unforgeability under chosen-message attacks for signature scheme SIG, parameters *par* and adversary A.

$\underline{\mathsf{BLSGen}(\mathcal{G})}$	$\underline{\mathsf{BLSSig}(m)}$	$\underline{\mathsf{BLSVer}(m, \Sigma)}$
00 $x \xleftarrow{\$} \mathbb{Z}_p$	05 $\Sigma := H(m)^x$	07 Return $\big(e(H(m), \mathbf{X}) = e(\Sigma, g)\big)$
01 $\mathbf{X} := g^x$	06 Return Σ	
02 $sk := x$		
03 $pk := \mathbf{X}$		
04 Return (pk, sk)		

Fig. 11. Boneh, Lynn and Shacham's signature scheme $\mathsf{BLS}_{\mathcal{G}}$. Here, H is a hash function that is modeled as a random oracle.

Theorem 5. $\mathrm{dlog}_{\mathcal{G}} \overset{(4,1)}{\Longrightarrow}_{\mathsf{alg}} \text{uf-cma}_{\mathsf{BLS},\mathcal{G}}$ *in the random oracle model.*

Proof. Let $\mathsf{A}_{\mathsf{alg}}$ be an algebraic adversary playing in $\mathbf{G} := \text{uf-cma}^{\mathsf{A}_{\mathsf{alg}}}_{\mathsf{BLS},\mathcal{G}}$, depicted in Fig. 12.

As $\mathsf{A}_{\mathsf{alg}}$ is an algebraic adversary, at the end of $\mathbf{G}$, it returns a forgery Σ^* on a message $m^* \notin Q$ together with a representation $\vec{a} = (\hat{a}, a', \bar{a}_1, ..., \bar{a}_q, \tilde{a}_1, ..., \tilde{a}_q)$ s.t.

$$\Sigma^* = H(m^*)^x = g^{\hat{a}} \mathbf{X}^{a'} \prod_{i=1}^{q} \mathbf{H}_i^{\bar{a}_i} \prod_{i=1}^{q} \Sigma_i^{\tilde{a}_i}. \tag{2}$$

Here, the representation is split (from left to right) into powers of the generator g, the public key $\mathbf{X}$, all of the answers to hash queries $\mathbf{H}_i, i \in [q]$, and the signatures $\Sigma_i, i \in [q]$, returned by the signing oracle. In the following, we denote the discrete logarithm of $H(m^*)$ w.r.t. basis g as r^* and for all $i \in [q]$, we denote

$\mathbf{G}^{\mathsf{A}_{\mathsf{alg}}}$	$\underline{O}(m_i)$	$\underline{H}(m_i)$
00 $x \xleftarrow{\$} \mathbb{Z}_p$	05 $Q := Q \cup \{m_i\}$	08 $\mathbf{H}_i \leftarrow H(m_i)$
01 $\mathbf{X} := g^x$	06 $\Sigma_i \leftarrow H(m_i)^x$	09 Return $\mathbf{H}_i$
02 $Q := \emptyset$	07 Return Σ_i	
03 $(m^*, [\Sigma^*]_{\vec{a}}) \xleftarrow{\$} \mathsf{A}^{O(\cdot), H(\cdot)}_{\mathsf{alg}}(\mathbf{X})$		
04 Return $\big(m^* \notin Q \wedge \Sigma^* = H(m^*)^x\big)$		

Fig. 12. Game $\mathbf{G} = \text{uf-cma}^{\mathsf{A}_{\mathsf{alg}}}_{\mathsf{BLS},\mathcal{G}}$ relative to adversary $\mathsf{A}_{\mathsf{alg}}$.

the discrete logarithm of $H(m_i)$ as r_i. Equation (2) is thus equivalent to

$$xr^* \equiv_p x(a' + \Sigma_i r_i \tilde{a}_i) + (\hat{a} + \Sigma_i r_i \bar{a}_i). \tag{3}$$

In the full version of our paper we show how to efficiently compute x from Eq. (3). Again, the main idea is to perform a case distinction over the cases where the coefficient of x is zero, or non-zero, respectively. □

Corollary 5. uf-cma$_{\mathsf{BLS},\mathcal{G}}$ *is* $\left(t, \frac{t^2}{4p}\right)$-*hard in the generic group model with a random oracle.*

7 Groth's Near-Optimal zk-SNARK

In order to cover notions such as knowledge soundness, which are defined via games for two algorithms, we generalize the notion of algebraic games and reductions between them. We write $\mathbf{G}_{par}^{\mathsf{A},\mathsf{X}}$ to denote that A and X play in $\mathbf{G}_{par}$ and define the advantage $\mathbf{Adv}_{par,\mathsf{A},\mathsf{X}}^{\mathbf{G}} := \Pr[\mathbf{G}_{par}^{\mathsf{A},\mathsf{X}} = 1]$ and the running time $\mathbf{Time}_{par,\mathsf{A},\mathsf{X}}^{\mathbf{G}}$ as before. To capture definitions that require that for every A there exists some X (which has black-box access to A) such that $\mathbf{Adv}_{par,\mathsf{A},\mathsf{X}}^{\mathbf{G}}$ is small, we define algebraic reductions for games $\mathbf{G}_{par}$ of this type as follows.

We write $\mathbf{H}_{par} \stackrel{(\Delta_\varepsilon, \Delta_t)}{\Longrightarrow}_{\mathsf{alg}} \mathbf{G}_{par}$ if there exist generic algorithms $\mathsf{R}_{\mathsf{gen}}$ and $\mathsf{S}_{\mathsf{gen}}$ such that for all algebraic algorithms $\mathsf{A}_{\mathsf{alg}}$ we have

$$\mathbf{Adv}_{par,\mathsf{B}_{\mathsf{alg}}}^{\mathbf{H}} \geq \frac{1}{\Delta_\varepsilon} \cdot \mathbf{Adv}_{par,\mathsf{A}_{\mathsf{alg}},\mathsf{X}_{\mathsf{alg}}}^{\mathbf{G}}, \quad \mathbf{Time}_{par,\mathsf{B}_{\mathsf{alg}}}^{\mathbf{H}} \leq \Delta_t \cdot \mathbf{Time}_{par,\mathsf{A}_{\mathsf{alg}},\mathsf{X}_{\mathsf{alg}}}^{\mathbf{G}}.$$

with $\mathsf{B}_{\mathsf{alg}}$ defined as $\mathsf{B}_{\mathsf{alg}} := \mathsf{R}_{\mathsf{gen}}^{\mathsf{A}_{\mathsf{alg}}}$ and $\mathsf{X}_{\mathsf{alg}}$ defined as $\mathsf{X}_{\mathsf{alg}} := \mathsf{S}_{\mathsf{gen}}^{\mathsf{A}_{\mathsf{alg}}}$.

THE q-DISCRETE LOGARITHM ASSUMPTION. We define a parametrized ("q-type") variant of the DLog assumption via the algebraic security game q-**dlog** in Fig. 13. We will show that Groth's [Gro16] scheme, which is the most efficient SNARK system to date, is secure under q-DLog in the algebraic group model.

---

q-**dlog**$_{\mathcal{G}}^{\mathsf{A}}$
00 $x \stackrel{\$}{\leftarrow} \mathbb{Z}_p^*$
01 $z \stackrel{\$}{\leftarrow} \mathsf{A}(g^x, g^{x^2}, ..., g^{x^q})$
02 Return $(z = x)$

Fig. 13. q-Discrete Logarithm Game q-**dlog** relative to $\mathcal{G}$ and adversary A.

NON-INTERACTIVE ZERO-KNOWLEDGE ARGUMENTS OF KNOWLEDGE. Groth [Gro16] considers proof systems for satisfiability of arithmetic circuits, which consist of addition and multiplication gates over a finite field $\mathbb{F}$. As a tool, Gennaro et al. [GGPR13] show how to efficiently convert any arithmetic circuit into a quadratic arithmetic program (QAP) R, which is described by $\mathbb{F}$, integers $\ell \leq m$ and polynomials $u_i, v_i, w_i \in \mathbb{F}[X]$, for $0 \leq i \leq m$, and $t \in \mathbb{F}[X]$, where the degrees of u_i, v_i, w_i are less than the degree n of t. (The relation R can also contain additional information aux.)

A QAP R defines the following binary relation of statements ϕ and witnesses w, where we set $a_0 := 1$:

$$R = \left\{ (\phi, w) \,\middle|\, \begin{array}{l} \phi = (a_1, \ldots, a_\ell) \in \mathbb{F}^\ell, \ w = (a_{\ell+1}, \ldots, a_m) \in \mathbb{F}^{m-\ell} \\ \left(\sum_{i=0}^m a_i u_i(X) \right) \cdot \left(\sum_{i=0}^m a_i v_i(X) \right) \equiv \sum_{i=0}^m a_i w_i(X) \pmod{t(X)} \end{array} \right\}$$

A non-interactive argument system for a class of relations $\mathcal{R}$ is a 3-tuple SNK $=$ (Setup, Prv, Vfy) of algorithms. Setup on input a relation $R \in \mathcal{R}$ outputs a common reference string crs; prover algorithm Prv on input crs and a statement/witness pair $(\phi, w) \in R$ returns an argument π; Verification Vfy on input crs, ϕ and π returns either 0 (reject) or 1 (accept). We require SNK to be *complete*, i.e., for all crs output by Setup, all arguments for true statements produced by Prv are accepted by Vfy.

Knowledge soundness requires that for every adversary A there exists an extractor X_A that extracts a witness from any valid argument output by A. We write $(y; z) \xleftarrow{\$} (A \| X_A)(x)$ when A on input x outputs y and X_A on the same input (including A's coins) returns z. Knowledge soundness is defined via game $\mathbf{knw\text{-}snd}_{\mathsf{SNK}, R}^{\mathsf{A}, \mathsf{X}_A}$ in Fig. 14.

$\underline{\mathbf{knw\text{-}snd}_{\mathsf{SNK}, R}^{\mathsf{A}, \mathsf{X}_A}}$	$\underline{\mathbf{k\text{-}snd\text{-}aff}_{\mathsf{NILP}, R}^{\mathsf{X}, \mathsf{A}}}$
00 $crs \xleftarrow{\$} \mathsf{Setup}(R)$	03 $\vec{\sigma} \xleftarrow{\$} \mathsf{LinSetup}(R)$
01 $((\phi, \pi); w) \xleftarrow{\$} (\mathsf{A} \| \mathsf{X}_\mathsf{A})(R, crs)$	04 $(\phi, P) \xleftarrow{\$} \mathsf{A}(R)$
02 Return $\big((\phi, w) \notin R$	05 $w \xleftarrow{\$} \mathsf{X}(R, \phi, P)$
$\qquad \wedge \mathsf{Vfy}(R, crs, \phi, \pi) = 1 \big)$	06 Return $\big(P \in \mathbb{F}^{\mu \times \kappa} \wedge (\phi, w) \notin R$
	$\qquad \wedge \mathsf{LinVfy}(R, \vec{\sigma}, \phi, P\vec{\sigma}) = 1 \big)$

Fig. 14. Left: Knowledge soundness game **knw-snd** relative to SNK $=$ (Setup, Prv, Vfy), adversary A and extractor X_A. **Right:** Knowledge soundness game **k-snd-aff** relative to NILP $=$ (LinSetup, PrfMtrx, Test), extractor X and *affine* adversary A (right).

Zero-knowledge for SNK requires that arguments do not leak any information besides the truth of the statement. It is formalized by demanding the existence of a simulator which on input a trapdoor (which is an additional output of Setup) and a true statement ϕ returns an argument which is indistinguishable from an argument for ϕ output by Prv (see [Gro16] for a formal definition).

A (preprocessing) *succinct argument of knowledge (SNARK)* is a knowledge-sound non-interactive argument system whose arguments are of size polynomial in the security parameter and can be verified in polynomial time in the security parameter and the length of the statement.

NON-INTERACTIVE LINEAR PROOFS OF DEGREE 2. NILPs (in Groth's [Gro16] terminology) are an abstraction of many SNARK constructions introduced by Bitansky et al. [BCI+13]. We only consider NILPs of degree 2 here. Such a system NILP is defined by three algorithms as follows. On input a quadratic arithmetic program R, LinSetup returns $\vec{\sigma} \in \mathbb{F}^{\mu}$ for some μ. On input R, ϕ and w, algorithm PrfMtrx generates a matrix $P \in \mathbb{F}^{\kappa \times \mu}$ (where κ is the proof length). And on input R and ϕ, Test returns matrices $T_1, \ldots, T_\eta \in \mathbb{F}^{\mu+\kappa}$. The last two algorithms implicitly define a prover and a verification algorithm as follows:

- $\vec{\pi} \xleftarrow{\$} \mathsf{LinPrv}(R, \vec{\sigma}, \phi, w)$: run $P \xleftarrow{\$} \mathsf{PrfMtrx}(R, \phi, w)$; return $\vec{\pi} := P\vec{\sigma}$.
- $b \xleftarrow{\$} \mathsf{LinVfy}(R, \vec{\sigma}, \phi, \vec{\pi})$: $(T_1, \ldots, T_\eta) \xleftarrow{\$} \mathsf{Test}(R, \phi)$; return 1 iff for all $1 \leq k \leq \eta$:

$$(\vec{\sigma}^{\top} \mid \vec{\pi}^{\top}) T_k (\vec{\sigma}^{\top} \mid \vec{\pi}^{\top})^{\top} = 0. \tag{4}$$

Let $T_k =: (t_{k,i,j})_{1 \leq i,j, \leq \mu+\kappa}$; w.l.o.g. we assume that $t_{k,i,j} = 0$ for all k and $i \in \{\mu+1, \ldots, \mu+\kappa\}$ and $j \in \{1, \ldots, \mu\}$.

We require a NILP to satisfy *statistical knowledge soundness against affine prover strategies*, which requires the existence of an (efficient) extractor X that works for all (unbounded) adversaries A. Whenever A returns a proof matrix P which leads to a valid proof $P\vec{\sigma}$ for a *freshly sampled* $\vec{\sigma}$, X can extract a witness from P. The notion is defined via game $\mathbf{k\text{-}snd\text{-}aff}_{\mathsf{NILP},R}^{\mathsf{X},\mathsf{A}}$ in Fig. 14.

NON-INTERACTIVE ARGUMENTS FROM NILPS. From a NILP for a quadratic arithmetic program over a finite field $\mathbb{F} = \mathbb{Z}_p$ for some prime p, one can construct an argument system over a bilinear group $\mathcal{G} = (p, \mathbb{G}, g, e)$. We thus consider QAP relations R of the form

$$R = \left(\mathcal{G}, \mathbb{F} = \mathbb{Z}_p, \ell, \{u_i(X), v_i(X), w_i(X)\}_{i=0}^{m}, t(X)\right), \tag{5}$$

and define the *degree* of R as the degree of n of $t(X)$.

Setup(R)	Prv$(R, \vec{\Sigma}, \phi, w)$	Vfy$(R, \vec{\Sigma}, \phi, \vec{\Pi})$

00 $g \xleftarrow{\$} \mathbb{G}$
 01 $\vec{\sigma} \xleftarrow{\$}$
    LinSetup(R)
 02 Return
    $\vec{\Sigma} := \langle \vec{\sigma} \rangle$
	03 $P \xleftarrow{\$} \mathsf{PrfMtrx}(R, \phi, w)$
	 04 Parse $P = (p_{i,j})_{i,j}$
	 05 For $i = 1 \ldots \kappa$:
	 06 $\quad \Pi_i := \prod_{j=1}^{m} \Sigma_j^{p_{i,j}}$
	 07 $\pi := (\Pi_1, \ldots, \Pi_\kappa)$
	 08 Return π
	 // Note that $\pi := \langle P\vec{\sigma} \rangle$
		09 $T_1, \ldots, T_\eta \xleftarrow{\$} \mathsf{Test}(R, \phi)$
		 10 Return 1 iff for all $1 \leq \ell \leq \eta$:
		 $\quad 0 = \prod_{i=1}^{m} \prod_{j=1}^{m} e(\Sigma_i, \Sigma_j)^{t_{\ell,i,j}}$
		 $\quad \cdot \prod_{i=1}^{m} \prod_{j=1}^{\kappa} e(\Sigma_i, \Pi_j)^{t_{\ell,i,m+j}}$
		 $\quad \cdot \prod_{i=1}^{\kappa} \prod_{j=1}^{\kappa} e(\Pi_i, \Pi_j)^{t_{\ell,m+i,m+j}}$
		 // This evaluates (6) in the exponent

Fig. 15. Argument system (Setup, Prv, Vfy) from a NILP (LinSetup, PrfMtrx, Test).

The construction of $\mathsf{SNK} = (\mathsf{Setup}, \mathsf{Prv}, \mathsf{Vfy})$ from $\mathsf{NILP} = (\mathsf{LinSetup}, \mathsf{PrfMtrx},$ $\mathsf{Test})$ is given in Fig. 15, where we write $\langle \vec{x} \rangle$ for $(g^{x_1}, \ldots, g^{x_{|\vec{x}|}})$. Setup first samples a random group generator g and then embeds the NILP CRS "in the exponent". Using group operations, Prv computes LinPrv in the exponent, and using the pairing, Vfy verifies LinVfy in the exponent.

GROTH'S NEAR-OPTIMAL SNARK FOR QAPS. Groth [Gro16] obtains his SNARK system by constructing a NILP for QAPs and then applying the conversion in Fig. 15. Recall that R, as in (5), defines a language of statements $\phi = (a_1, \ldots, a_\ell) \in \mathbb{F}^\ell$ with witnesses of the form $w = (a_{\ell+1}, \ldots, a_m) \in \mathbb{F}^{m-\ell}$ such that (with $a_0 := 1$):

$$\left(\sum_{i=0}^{m} a_i u_i(X) \right) \cdot \left(\sum_{i=0}^{m} a_i v_i(X) \right) = \sum_{i=0}^{m} a_i w_i(X) + h(X) t(X) \qquad (6)$$

for some $h(X) \in \mathbb{F}[X]$ of degree at most $n - 2$. Groth's NILP is given in Fig. 16.

Theorem 6 ([Gro16, Theorem 1]). *The construction in Fig. 16 in a NILP with perfect completeness, perfect zero-knowledge and statistical knowledge soundness against affine prover strategies.*

Groth embeds his NILP in *asymmetric* bilinear groups, which yields a more efficient SNARK. He then shows that the scheme is knowledge-sound in the generic group model for *symmetric* bilinear groups (which yields a stronger result, as the adversary is more powerful than in asymmetric groups). Since we aim at strengthening the security statement, we also consider the symmetric-group variant (which is obtained by applying the transformation in Fig. 15). We now show how from an algebraic adversary breaking knowledge soundness one can construct an adversary against the q-DLog assumption.

$\mathsf{LinSetup}(R)$

00 $\alpha, \beta, \gamma, \delta, \tau \xleftarrow{\$} \mathbb{F}^*$

01 $\vec{\sigma} := \Big(1, \alpha, \beta, \gamma, \delta, \{\tau^i\}_{i=0}^{n-1}, \big\{ \frac{1}{\gamma} \big(\beta u_i(\tau) + \alpha v_i(\tau) + w_i(\tau) \big) \big\}_{i=0}^{\ell},$

$\qquad \big\{ \frac{1}{\delta} \big(\beta u_i(\tau) + \alpha v_i(\tau) + w_i(\tau) \big) \big\}_{i=\ell+1}^{m}, \big\{ \frac{1}{\delta} (\tau^i t(\tau)) \big\}_{i=0}^{n-2} \Big)$

02 Return $\vec{\sigma}$

$\mathsf{PrfMtrx}(R, \phi, w)$

03 Let $h(X)$ be as in (8)

04 $r, s \xleftarrow{\$} \mathbb{F}$

05 Return $P \in \mathbb{F}^{3 \times (m+2n+4)}$ s.t. $P\vec{\sigma} = (A, B, C)$ with

06 $A := \alpha + \sum_{i=0}^{m} a_i u_i(\tau) + r\delta$

07 $B := \beta + \sum_{i=0}^{m} a_i v_i(\tau) + s\delta$

08 $C := \frac{1}{\delta} \big(\sum_{i=\ell+1}^{m} a_i (\beta u_i(\tau) + \alpha v_i(\tau) + w_i(\tau)) + h(\tau) t(\tau) \big) + As + rB - rs\delta$

$\mathsf{Test}(R, \phi)$

09 Return $T \in \mathbb{F}^{(m+2n+7) \times (m+2n+7)}$ corresponding to the test

$\qquad A \cdot B = \alpha \cdot \beta + \sum_{i=0}^{\ell} a_i \frac{1}{\gamma} \big(\beta u_i(\tau) + \alpha v_i(\tau) + w_i(\tau) \big) \cdot \gamma + C \cdot \delta$

Fig. 16. Groth's NILP $(\mathsf{LinSetup}, \mathsf{PrfMtrx}, \mathsf{Test})$.

Theorem 7. *Let* SNK *denote Groth's [Gro16] SNARK for degree-n QAPs defined over (symmetric) bilinear group* $\mathcal{G}$ *with* $n^2 \leq (p-1)/8$. *Then we have* q-**dlog** $\overset{(3,1)}{\Longrightarrow}_{\mathsf{alg}}$ **knw-snd**$_{\mathsf{SNK}}$ *with* $q := 2n-1$.

Let us start with a proof overview. Consider an algebraic adversary $\mathsf{A}_{\mathsf{alg}}$ against knowledge soundness that returns $(\phi, [\vec{\mathbf{\Pi}}]_P)$ on input $(R, \langle \vec{\sigma} \rangle)$. Since $\mathsf{A}_{\mathsf{alg}}$ is algebraic and its group-element inputs are $\langle \vec{\sigma} \rangle$, we have $\vec{\mathbf{\Pi}} = \langle P\vec{\sigma} \rangle$ with $P \in \mathbb{F}^{3 \times \mu}$. By the definition of Vfy, the proof $\vec{\mathbf{\Pi}}$ is valid iff $P\vec{\sigma}$ satisfies LinVfy. By Groth's theorem (Theorem 6) there exists an extractor X, which on input P such that $P\vec{\sigma}$ satisfies LinVfy extracts a witness (see game **k-snd-aff**$_{\mathsf{NILP},R}$ in Fig. 14).

So it seems this extractor X should also work for $\mathsf{A}_{\mathsf{alg}}$ (which returns P as required). However, X is only guaranteed to succeed if $P\vec{\sigma}$ verifies for a *randomly* sampled $\vec{\sigma}$, whereas for $\mathsf{A}_{\mathsf{alg}}$ in **knw-snd**$_{\mathsf{SNK},R}$ it suffices to return P so that $P\vec{\sigma}$ verifies for the specific $\vec{\sigma}$ for which it received $\langle \vec{\sigma} \rangle$. To prove knowledge soundness, it now suffices to show that an adversary can only output P which works for *all* choices of $\vec{\sigma}$ (from which X will then extract a witness).

In the generic group model this follows rather straight-forwardly, since the adversary has no information about the concrete $\vec{\sigma}$. In the AGM however, A is given $\langle \vec{\sigma} \rangle$. Examining the structure of a NILP CRS $\vec{\sigma}$ (Fig. 16), we see that its components are defined as multivariate (Laurent) polynomials evaluated at a random point $\vec{x} = (\alpha, \beta, \gamma, \delta, \tau)$.

Now what does it mean for $\mathsf{A}_{\mathsf{alg}}$ to output a valid P? By the definition of LinVfy via Test (cf. Eq. (4) with $\vec{\pi} := P\vec{\sigma}$), it means that $\mathsf{A}_{\mathsf{alg}}$ found P such that

$$(\vec{\sigma}^{\top} \mid (P\vec{\sigma})^{\top}) \, T \, (\vec{\sigma}^{\top} \mid (P\vec{\sigma})^{\top})^{\top} = 0. \tag{7}$$

If we interpret the components of $\vec{\sigma}$ as polynomials over $X_1, \ldots, X_5$ (corresponding to $\vec{x} = (\alpha, \beta, \gamma, \delta, \tau)$) then the left-hand side of (7) defines a polynomial $Q_P(\vec{X})$.

On the other hand, what does it mean that $P\vec{\sigma}$ verifies only for the specific $\vec{\sigma}$ from $\mathsf{A}_{\mathsf{alg}}$'s input? It means that $Q_P \not\equiv 0$, that is, Q_P is not the zero polynomial, since otherwise (7) would hold for *any* choice of $\vec{x}$, that is $P\vec{\sigma}'$ would verify for any $\vec{\sigma}'$.

We now bound the probability that $\mathsf{A}_{\mathsf{alg}}$ behaves "badly", that is, it returns a proof that only holds with respect to its specific CRS. To do so, we bound the probability that given $\langle \vec{\sigma} \rangle$, $\mathsf{A}_{\mathsf{alg}}$ returns a nonzero polynomial Q_P which vanishes at $\vec{x}$, that is, the point that defines $\vec{\sigma}$. By factoring Q_P, we can then extract information about $\vec{x}$, which was only given as group elements $\langle \vec{\sigma} \rangle$. In particular, we embed a q-DLog instance into the CRS $\langle \vec{\sigma} \rangle$, for which we need q to be at least the maximum of the total degrees of the polynomials defining σ, which for Groth's NILP is $2n-1$. We then factor the polynomial to obtain its roots, which yields the challenge discrete logarithm.

Proof (of Theorem 7). Let R be a QAP of degree n (cf. (5)). Let NILP $=$ (LinSetup, PrfMtrx, Test) denote Groth's NILP (Fig. 16). By Theorem 6 there exists an extractor X, which on input R, statement $\phi \in L_R$, and $P \in \mathbb{F}^{\mu \times \kappa}$ such that LinVfy$(R, \vec{\sigma}, \phi, P\vec{\sigma}) = 1$ for $\vec{\sigma} \xleftarrow{\$} \text{LinSetup}(R)$ returns a witness w with probability $\mathbf{Adv}_{\text{NILP},R,X,F}^{\text{k-snd-aff}}$ for any affine F.

Let SNK denote Groth's SNARK obtained from NILP via the transformation in Fig. 15 and let A_{alg} be an algebraic adversary in the game $\mathbf{knw\text{-}snd}_{\text{SNK},R}$. From X we construct an extractor X_A for A_{alg} in Fig. 17. Note that since A_{alg} is algebraic, we have $\vec{\mathbf{\Pi}} = \langle P\vec{\sigma} \rangle$. We thus have

$$\text{Vfy}(R, \vec{\mathbf{\Sigma}}, \phi, \vec{\mathbf{\Pi}}) = \text{Vfy}(R, \vec{\mathbf{\Sigma}}, \phi, \langle P\vec{\sigma} \rangle) = \text{LinVfy}(R, \vec{\sigma}, \phi, P\vec{\sigma}), \qquad (8)$$

where the last equality follows from the definition of Vfy (Fig. 15). Game $\mathbf{knw\text{-}snd}_{\text{SNK},R}^{A_{\text{alg}},X_A}$ is written out in Fig. 17 and our goal is to upperbound $\mathbf{Adv}_{\text{SNK},R,A_{\text{alg}},X_A}^{\text{knw-snd}}$.

Consider the affine prover A' in Fig. 18 and $\mathbf{k\text{-}snd\text{-}aff}_{\text{NILP}}^{X,A'}$, with the code of A' written out, also in Fig. 18.

$X_A(R, \langle \vec{\sigma} \rangle)$	$\mathbf{knw\text{-}snd}_{\text{SNK},R}^{A_{\text{alg}},X_A}$
00 $(\phi, [\vec{\mathbf{\Pi}}]_P) \xleftarrow{\$} A_{\text{alg}}(R, \langle \vec{\sigma} \rangle)$	03 $\vec{\sigma} \xleftarrow{\$} \text{LinSetup}(R)$
01 $w \xleftarrow{\$} X(R, \phi, P)$	04 $(\phi, [\vec{\mathbf{\Pi}}]_P) \xleftarrow{\$} A_{\text{alg}}(R, \langle \vec{\sigma} \rangle)$
02 Return w.	05 $w \xleftarrow{\$} X(R, \phi, P)$
	06 Return $\big((\phi, w) \notin R \wedge \text{LinVfy}(R, \vec{\sigma}, \phi, P\vec{\sigma}) = 1 \big)$

Fig. 17. Extractor X_A defined from X and A_{alg} (left) and knowledge soundness game **knw-snd** for a SNARK built from NILP $=$ (LinSetup, PrfMtrx, Test), algebraic adversary A_{alg} and X_A (right).

$A'(R)$	$\mathbf{k\text{-}snd\text{-}aff}_{\text{NILP},R}^{X,A'}$
00 $\vec{\sigma} \xleftarrow{\$} \text{LinSetup}(R)$	03 $\vec{\rho} \xleftarrow{\$} \text{LinSetup}(R);$
01 $(\phi, [\vec{\mathbf{\Pi}}]_P) \xleftarrow{\$} A_{\text{alg}}(R, \langle \vec{\sigma} \rangle)$	04 $\vec{\sigma} \xleftarrow{\$} \text{LinSetup}(R)$
02 Return (ϕ, P).	05 $(\phi, [\vec{\mathbf{\Pi}}]_P) \xleftarrow{\$} A_{\text{alg}}(R, \langle \vec{\sigma} \rangle)$
	06 $w \xleftarrow{\$} X(R, \phi, P)$
	07 If $\big((\phi, w) \notin R \wedge \text{LinVfy}(R, \vec{\sigma}, \phi, P\vec{\sigma}) = 1$
	$\wedge \text{LinVfy}(R, \vec{\rho}, \phi, P\vec{\rho}) = 0 \big)$
	08 Then $\mathbf{bad} := 1$
	09 Return $\big((\phi, w) \notin R \wedge \text{LinVfy}(R, \vec{\rho}, \phi, P\vec{\rho}) = 1 \big)$

Fig. 18. Affine prover A' defined from A_{alg} (left) and game **k-snd-aff** for NILP, extractor X and A' (right).

Comparing the right-hand sides of Figs. 17 and 18, we see that **knw-snd** returns 1 whereas **k-snd-aff** returns 0 if LinVfy returns 0 for $P\vec{\rho}$ w.r.t. $\vec{\rho}$, but it returns 1 for $P\vec{\sigma}$ w.r.t. $\vec{\sigma}$. Let **bad** denote the event when this happens; formally defined as a flag in game **k-snd-aff** in Fig. 18. By definition, we have

$$\mathbf{Adv}^{\mathsf{knw\text{-}snd}}_{\mathsf{SNK},R,A_{\mathsf{alg}},\mathsf{X_A}} \leq \mathbf{Adv}^{\mathsf{k\text{-}snd\text{-}aff}}_{\mathsf{NILP},R,\mathsf{X},A'} + \Pr\left[\mathbf{bad}=1\right]. \tag{9}$$

In order to simplify our analysis, we first make a syntactical change to NILP by multiplying out all denominators, that is, we let LinSetup (cf. Fig. 16) return

$$\vec{\sigma} := \Big(\delta\gamma, \alpha\delta\gamma, \beta\delta\gamma, \delta\gamma^2, \delta^2\gamma, \{\delta\gamma\tau^i\}_{i=0}^{n-1}, \big\{\delta\big(\beta u_i(\tau) + \alpha v_i(\tau) + w_i(\tau)\big)\big\}_{i=0}^{\ell},$$
$$\big\{\gamma\big(\beta u_i(\tau) + \alpha v_i(\tau) + w_i(\tau)\big)\big\}_{i=\ell+1}^{m}, \big\{\gamma\tau^i t(\tau)\big\}_{i=0}^{n-2}\Big). \tag{10}$$

Note that this does not affect the distribution of the SNARK CRS as running the modified LinSetup amounts to the same as choosing $g' \xleftarrow{\$} \mathbb{G}$ and running the original setup with $g := (g')^{\delta\gamma}$, which again is a uniformly random generator.

Observe that the components of LinSetup defined in (10) can be described via multivariate polynomials $S_i(\vec{x})$ of total degree at most $2n-1$ with $\vec{x} := (\alpha, \beta, \gamma, \delta, \tau)$, and LinSetup can be defined as picking a random point $\vec{x} \xleftarrow{\$} (\mathbb{F}^*)^5$ and returning the evaluations $\sigma_i := S_i(\vec{x})$ of these polynomials.

Let T be as defined by Test in Fig. 16. By (4) we have

$$\mathsf{LinVfy}(R, \vec{\sigma}, \phi, P\vec{\sigma}) = 1 \iff \vec{\sigma}^{\top}\big((Id \,|\, P^{\top}) \cdot T \cdot (Id \,|\, P^{\top})^{\top}\big)\vec{\sigma} = 0.$$

Let $\vec{S}$ be the vector of polynomials defined by LinSetup. For a matrix P define the following multivariate polynomial

$$Q_P(\vec{X}) := (\vec{S}(\vec{X}))^{\top}\big((Id \,|\, P^{\top}) \cdot T \cdot (Id \,|\, P^{\top})^{\top}\big)\vec{S}(\vec{X}) \tag{11}$$

of degree at most $(2n-1)^2$. Then for any $\vec{x} \in (\mathbb{F}^*)^5$ and $\vec{\sigma} := \vec{S}(\vec{x})$ we have

$$\mathsf{LinVfy}\big(R, \vec{\sigma}, \phi, P\vec{\sigma})\big) = 1 \iff Q_P(\vec{x}) = 0. \tag{12}$$

Groth [Gro16] proves Theorem 6 by arguing that an affine prover without knowledge of $\vec{\sigma}$ can only succeed in the game **k-snd-aff** $_{\mathsf{NILP},R}$ by making LinVfy return 1 on *every* $\vec{\sigma}$, or stated differently using (12), by returning P with $Q_P \equiv 0$. He then shows that from such P one can efficiently extract a witness.

The adversary's probability of succeeding despite $Q_P \not\equiv 0$ is bounded via the Schwartz-Zippel lemma: the total degree of Q_P is at most $d = (2n-1)^2$ (using the modified $\vec{\sigma}$ from (10)). The probability that $Q_P(\vec{x}) = 0$ for a random $\vec{x} \xleftarrow{\$} (F^*)^5$ is thus bounded by $\frac{d}{p-1}$. This yields

$$\mathbf{Adv}^{\mathsf{k\text{-}snd\text{-}aff}}_{\mathsf{NILP},R,\mathsf{X},A'} \leq \frac{(2n-1)^2}{p-1}. \tag{13}$$

In order to bound $\mathbf{Adv}^{\text{knw-snd}}_{\text{SNK},R,A_{\text{alg}},X_A}$ in (9) we will construct an adversary B_{alg} such that

$$\Pr\left[\mathbf{bad} = 1\right] \leq \left(1 - \tfrac{(2n-1)^2}{p-1}\right) \cdot \mathbf{Adv}^{q\text{-dlog}}_{\mathcal{G},B_{\text{alg}}} \quad \text{with} \quad q = 2n - 1. \qquad (14)$$

For $\mathbf{bad}$ to be set to 1, A_{alg}'s output P must be such that $Q_P \not\equiv 0$: otherwise, LinVfy returns 1 for *any* $\vec{x}$ and in particular $\text{LinVfy}(R, \vec{\rho}, \phi, P\vec{\rho}) = 1$.

$\mathbf{bad} = 1$ implies thus that A_{alg} on input $\langle\vec{\sigma}\rangle = \langle\vec{S}(\vec{x})\rangle$ returns P such that

$$Q_P \not\equiv 0 \quad \text{and} \quad Q_P(\vec{x}) = 0. \qquad (15)$$

We now use such A_{alg} to construct an adversary B_{alg} against q-DLog with $q := 2n - 1$.

Adversary $B_{\text{alg}}(\langle z\rangle, \langle z^2\rangle, ..., \langle z^q\rangle)$: On input a q-DLog instance, B_{alg} simulates $\mathbf{k\text{-snd-aff}}^{X,A'}_{\text{NILP},R}$ for A_{alg}. It first picks a random value $\vec{y} \leftarrow (\mathbb{F}^*)^5$, (implicitly) sets $x_i := y_i z$, that is,

$$\alpha := y_1 z \qquad \beta := y_2 z \qquad \gamma := y_3 z \qquad \delta := y_4 z \qquad \tau := y_5 z$$

and generates a CRS $\langle\vec{\sigma}\rangle := \langle\vec{S}(\vec{x})\rangle = \langle\vec{S}(\alpha, \beta, \gamma, \delta, \tau)\rangle$ as defined in (10). Since the total degree of the polynomials S_i defining $\vec{\sigma}$ is bounded by $2n - 1$ (the degree of the last component of $\vec{\sigma}$), B_{alg} can compute $\vec{\sigma}$ from its q-DLog instance.

Next, B_{alg} runs $(\phi, [\vec{\mathbf{\Pi}}]_P) \xleftarrow{\$} A_{\text{alg}}(R, \langle\vec{\sigma}\rangle)$ and from P computes the multivariate polynomial $Q_P(\vec{X})$ as defined in (11). If $Q_P \equiv 0$ or $Q_P(\vec{x}) \neq 0$ (by (8) and (12) the latter is equivalent to $\text{Vfy}(R, \vec{\Sigma}, \phi, \vec{\mathbf{\Pi}}) = 0$), then B_{alg} aborts. (∗) Otherwise B_{alg} defines the univariate polynomial

$$Q'_P(X) := Q_P(y_1 X, \dots, y_5 X).$$

If $Q'_P \equiv 0$ then B_{alg} aborts. (∗∗)
Otherwise B_{alg} factors Q'_P to obtain its roots (of which by (11) there are at most $(2n-1)^2$), checks them against its DLog instance to determine whether z is among them, and if so, returns z.

First note that B_{alg} perfectly simulates $\mathbf{k\text{-snd-aff}}^{X,A'}_{\text{NILP},R}$ for A_{alg}. Let us analyze the probability that B_{alg} finds the target z provided that $\mathbf{bad} = 1$. In this case B_{alg} will not abort at (∗).

Since $Q'_P(z) = Q_P(y_1 z, \dots, y_5 z) = Q_P(\vec{x})$, by (15) we have $Q'_P(z) = 0$. Thus if $Q'_P \not\equiv 0$ then B_{alg} finds z by factoring Q'_P. It remains to argue that $Q'_P \not\equiv 0$. By (15) we have $Q_P \not\equiv 0$. By the Schwartz-Zippel lemma, the probability that for a random $\vec{y} \xleftarrow{\$} (\mathbb{F}^*)^5$, we have $Q_P(\vec{y}) = 0$ is bounded by $\frac{d}{p-1}$ where d is the total degree of Q_P, which is bounded by $(2n - 1)^2$. Since $Q_P(\vec{y}) = Q'_P(1)$, we have $Q'_P \not\equiv 0$ with probability at least $1 - \frac{(2n-1)^2}{p-1}$. Since the choice of $\vec{y}$ is perfectly hidden from the adversary's view this shows

$$\mathbf{Adv}^{q\text{-dlog}}_{\mathcal{G},B_{\text{alg}}} \geq \left(1 - \tfrac{(2n-1)^2}{p-1}\right) \cdot \Pr\left[\mathbf{bad} = 1\right] \geq \tfrac{1}{2} \cdot \Pr\left[\mathbf{bad} = 1\right],$$

where the last inequality comes from $n^2 \leq (p-1)/8$. Putting this together with (13), we have shown that

$$\mathbf{Adv}^{\mathsf{knw\text{-}snd}}_{\mathsf{SNK},R,\mathsf{A}_{\mathsf{alg}},\mathsf{X}_{\mathsf{A}}} \leq \tfrac{q^2}{p-1} + 2 \cdot \mathbf{Adv}^{q\text{-}\mathbf{dlog}}_{\mathcal{G},\mathsf{B}_{\mathsf{alg}}}.$$

Following the generic bound for Boneh and Boyen's SDH assumption [BB08], we may assume that $\mathbf{Adv}^{q\text{-}\mathbf{dlog}}_{\mathcal{G},\mathsf{B}_{\mathsf{alg}}} \geq \tfrac{q^2}{p-1}$. The above equation thus implies

$$\mathbf{Adv}^{\mathsf{knw\text{-}snd}}_{\mathsf{SNK},R,\mathsf{A}_{\mathsf{alg}},\mathsf{X}_{\mathsf{A}}} \leq 3 \cdot \mathbf{Adv}^{q\text{-}\mathbf{dlog}}_{\mathcal{G},\mathsf{B}_{\mathsf{alg}}},$$

which concludes the proof. $\square$

Corollary 6. *It is $\left(\tfrac{3t^2q+3q^3}{p}, t\right)$-hard to break knowledge soundness of Groth's SNARK [Gro16] in the generic group model.*

The corollary follows from the generic $\left(\tfrac{t^2q+q^3}{p}, t\right)$-hardness of q-**dlog**, which is derived analogously to the bound for Boneh and Boyen's SDH assumption [BB08].

We remark that the above result is not specific to Groth's SNARK; it applies to any SNARK built from a NILP whose setup evaluates multivariate polynomials on a random position. The maximal total degree of these polynomials determines the parameter q in the q-DLog instance.

Acknowledgments. We thank Dan Brown for valuable comments and Pooya Farshim for discussions on polynomials. We also thank Helger Lipmaa for sharing with us his independent security proof for Groth's SNARK. The first author is supported by the French ANR EfTrEC project (ANR-16-CE39-0002). The second author was supported in part by ERC Project ERCC (FP7/615074) and by DFG SPP 1736 Big Data. The third author was supported by ERC Project ERCC (FP7/615074).

References

[ABM15] Abdalla, M., Benhamouda, F., MacKenzie, P.: Security of the J-PAKE password-authenticated key exchange protocol. In: 2015 IEEE Symposium on Security and Privacy, pp. 571–587. IEEE Computer Society Press, May 2015. 35

[ABR01] Abdalla, M., Bellare, M., Rogaway, P.: The oracle Diffie-Hellman assumptions and an analysis of DHIES. In: Naccache, D. (ed.) CT-RSA 2001. LNCS, vol. 2020, pp. 143–158. Springer, Heidelberg (2001). https://doi.org/10.1007/3-540-45353-9_12. 35, 45

[ABS16] Ambrona, M., Barthe, G., Schmidt, B.: Automated unbounded analysis of cryptographic constructions in the generic group model. In: Fischlin, M., Coron, J.-S. (eds.) EUROCRYPT 2016, Part II. LNCS, vol. 9666, pp. 822–851. Springer, Heidelberg (2016). https://doi.org/10.1007/978-3-662-49896-5_29. 39

[ACdM05] Ateniese, G., Camenisch, J., de Medeiros, B.: Untraceable RFID tags via insubvertible encryption. In: Atluri, V., Meadows, C., Juels, A. (eds.) ACM CCS 2005, pp. 92–101. ACM Press, November 2005. 36

[ACHdM05] Ateniese, G., Camenisch, J., Hohenberger, S., de Medeiros, B.: Practical group signatures without random oracles. Cryptology ePrint Archive, Report 2005/385 (2005). http://eprint.iacr.org/2005/385. 36

[AGO11] Abe, M., Groth, J., Ohkubo, M.: Separating short structure-preserving signatures from non-interactive assumptions. In: Lee, D.H., Wang, X. (eds.) ASIACRYPT 2011. LNCS, vol. 7073, pp. 628–646. Springer, Heidelberg (2011). https://doi.org/10.1007/978-3-642-25385-0_34. 35

[AM09] Aggarwal, D., Maurer, U.: Breaking RSA generically is equivalent to factoring. In: Joux, A. (ed.) EUROCRYPT 2009. LNCS, vol. 5479, pp. 36–53. Springer, Heidelberg (2009). https://doi.org/10.1007/978-3-642-01001-9_2. 34, 37

[BB08] Boneh, D., Boyen, X.: Short signatures without random oracles and the SDH assumption in bilinear groups. J. Cryptol. 21(2), 149–177 (2008). 58

[BCI+13] Bitansky, N., Chiesa, A., Ishai, Y., Paneth, O., Ostrovsky, R.: Succinct non-interactive arguments via linear interactive proofs. In: Sahai, A. (ed.) TCC 2013. LNCS, vol. 7785, pp. 315–333. Springer, Heidelberg (2013). https://doi.org/10.1007/978-3-642-36594-2_18. 52

[BCL04] Bangerter, E., Camenisch, J., Lysyanskaya, A.: A cryptographic framework for the controlled release of certified data. In: Security Protocols Workshop, pp. 20–24 (2004). 36

[BCPR16] Bitansky, N., Canetti, R., Paneth, O., Rosen, A.: On the existence of extractable one-way functions. SIAM J. Comput. 45(5), 1910–1952 (2016). 38

[BCS05] Backes, M., Camenisch, J., Sommer, D.: Anonymous yet accountable access control. In: WPES, pp. 40–46 (2005). 36

[BDZ03] Bao, F., Deng, R.H., Zhu, H.F.: Variations of Diffie-Hellman problem. In: Qing, S., Gollmann, D., Zhou, J. (eds.) ICICS 2003. LNCS, vol. 2836, pp. 301–312. Springer, Heidelberg (2003). https://doi.org/10.1007/978-3-540-39927-8_28. 43

[BFF+14] Barthe, G., Fagerholm, E., Fiore, D., Mitchell, J.C., Scedrov, A., Schmidt, B.: Automated analysis of cryptographic assumptions in generic group models. In: Garay, J.A., Gennaro, R. (eds.) CRYPTO 2014, Part I. LNCS, vol. 8616, pp. 95–112. Springer, Heidelberg (2014). https://doi.org/10.1007/978-3-662-44371-2_6. 37, 39

[BFW16] Bernhard, D., Fischlin, M., Warinschi, B.: On the hardness of proving CCA-security of signed ElGamal. In: Cheng, C.-M., Chung, K.-M., Persiano, G., Yang, B.-Y. (eds.) PKC 2016, Part I. LNCS, vol. 9614, pp. 47–69. Springer, Heidelberg (2016). https://doi.org/10.1007/978-3-662-49384-7_3. 35

[BG04] Brown, D.R.L., Gallant, R.P.: The static Diffie-Hellman problem. Cryptology ePrint Archive, Report 2004/306 (2004). http://eprint.iacr.org/2004/306. 37

[BL96] Boneh, D., Lipton, R.J.: Algorithms for black-box fields and their application to cryptography (extended abstract). In: Koblitz, N. (ed.) CRYPTO 1996. LNCS, vol. 1109, pp. 283–297. Springer, Heidelberg (1996). https://doi.org/10.1007/3-540-68697-5_22. 33

[BLS04] Boneh, D., Lynn, B., Shacham, H.: Short signatures from the Weil pairing. J. Cryptol. 17(4), 297–319 (2004). 36, 48

[BMV08] Bresson, E., Monnerat, J., Vergnaud, D.: Separation results on the "one-more" computational problems. In: Malkin, T. (ed.) CT-RSA 2008. LNCS, vol. 4964, pp. 71–87. Springer, Heidelberg (2008). 35

[Boy08] Boyen, X.: The uber-assumption family (invited talk). In: Galbraith, S.D., Paterson, K.G. (eds.) Pairing 2008. LNCS, vol. 5209, pp. 39–56. Springer, Heidelberg (2008). https://doi.org/10.1007/978-3-540-85538-5_3. 38, 39

[BR93] Bellare, M., Rogaway, P.: Random oracles are practical: a paradigm for designing efficient protocols. In: Ashby, V. (ed.) ACM CCS 1993, pp. 62–73. ACM Press, November 1993. 41

[BR04] Bellare, M., Rogaway, P.: Code-based game-playing proofs and the security of triple encryption. Cryptology ePrint Archive, Report 2004/331 (2004). http://eprint.iacr.org/2004/331. 39

[BV98] Boneh, D., Venkatesan, R.: Breaking RSA may not be equivalent to factoring. In: Nyberg, K. (ed.) EUROCRYPT 1998. LNCS, vol. 1403, pp. 59–71. Springer, Heidelberg (1998). https://doi.org/10.1007/BFb0054117. 34, 35, 40

[CGH98] Canetti, R., Goldreich, O., Halevi, S.: The random oracle methodology, revisited (preliminary version). In: 30th ACM STOC, pp. 209–218. ACM Press, May 1998. 38

[Che06] Cheon, J.H.: Security analysis of the strong Diffie-Hellman problem. In: Vaudenay, S. (ed.) EUROCRYPT 2006. LNCS, vol. 4004, pp. 1–11. Springer, Heidelberg (2006). https://doi.org/10.1007/11761679_1. 37, 47

[CHK+06] Camenisch, J., Hohenberger, S., Kohlweiss, M., Lysyanskaya, A., Meyerovich, M.: How to win the clonewars: efficient periodic n-times anonymous authentication. In: Juels, A., Wright, R.N., De Capitani di Vimercati, S. (eds.) ACM CCS 2006, pp. 201–210. ACM Press, October/November 2006. 36

[CHL05] Camenisch, J., Hohenberger, S., Lysyanskaya, A.: Compact e-cash. In: Cramer, R. (ed.) EUROCRYPT 2005. LNCS, vol. 3494, pp. 302–321. Springer, Heidelberg (2005). https://doi.org/10.1007/11426639_18. 36

[CHP07] Camenisch, J., Hohenberger, S., Pedersen, M.Ø.: Batch verification of short signatures. In: Naor, M. (ed.) EUROCRYPT 2007. LNCS, vol. 4515, pp. 246–263. Springer, Heidelberg (2007). https://doi.org/10.1007/978-3-540-72540-4_14. 36

[CL04] Camenisch, J., Lysyanskaya, A.: Signature schemes and anonymous credentials from bilinear maps. In: Franklin, M. (ed.) CRYPTO 2004. LNCS, vol. 3152, pp. 56–72. Springer, Heidelberg (2004). https://doi.org/10.1007/978-3-540-28628-8_4. 35, 45

[CM14] Chase, M., Meiklejohn, S.: Déjà Q: using dual systems to revisit q-type assumptions. In: Nguyen, P.Q., Oswald, E. (eds.) EUROCRYPT 2014. LNCS, vol. 8441, pp. 622–639. Springer, Heidelberg (2014). https://doi.org/10.1007/978-3-642-55220-5_34. 38

[Cor02] Coron, J.-S.: Optimal security proofs for PSS and other signature schemes. In: Knudsen, L.R. (ed.) EUROCRYPT 2002. LNCS, vol. 2332, pp. 272–287. Springer, Heidelberg (2002). https://doi.org/10.1007/3-540-46035-7_18. 35, 36

[Dam92] Damgård, I.: Towards practical public key systems secure against chosen ciphertext attacks. In: Feigenbaum, J. (ed.) CRYPTO 1991. LNCS, vol. 576, pp. 445–456. Springer, Heidelberg (1992). https://doi.org/10.1007/3-540-46766-1_36. 35, 38

[Den02] Dent, A.W.: Adapting the weaknesses of the random oracle model to the generic group model. In: Zheng, Y. (ed.) ASIACRYPT 2002. LNCS, vol. 2501, pp. 100–109. Springer, Heidelberg (2002). https://doi.org/10.1007/3-540-36178-2_6. 38

[DH76] Diffie, W., Hellman, M.E.: New directions in cryptography. IEEE Trans. Inf. Theory **22**(6), 644–654 (1976). 35, 43

[GBL08] Garg, S., Bhaskar, R., Lokam, S.V.: Improved bounds on security reductions for discrete log based signatures. In: Wagner, D. (ed.) CRYPTO 2008. LNCS, vol. 5157, pp. 93–107. Springer, Heidelberg (2008). https://doi.org/10.1007/978-3-540-85174-5_6. 35

[GG17] Ghadafi, E., Groth, J.: Towards a classification of non-interactive computational assumptions in cyclic groups. In: Takagi, T., Peyrin, T. (eds.) ASIACRYPT 2017. LNCS, vol. 10625, pp. 66–96. Springer, Cham (2017). https://doi.org/10.1007/978-3-319-70697-9_3. 38

[GGPR13] Gennaro, R., Gentry, C., Parno, B., Raykova, M.: Quadratic span programs and succinct NIZKs without PCPs. In: Johansson, T., Nguyen, P.Q. (eds.) EUROCRYPT 2013. LNCS, vol. 7881, pp. 626–645. Springer, Heidelberg (2013). https://doi.org/10.1007/978-3-642-38348-9_37. 51

[Gro16] Groth, J.: On the size of pairing-based non-interactive arguments. In: Fischlin, M., Coron, J.-S. (eds.) EUROCRYPT 2016, Part II. LNCS, vol. 9666, pp. 305–326. Springer, Heidelberg (2016). https://doi.org/10.1007/978-3-662-49896-5_11. 36, 50, 52, 53, 54, 56, 58

[HP78] Hellman, M.E., Pohlig, S.C.: An improved algorithm for computing logarithms over $GF(p)$ and its cryptographic significance. IEEE Trans. Inf. Theory **24**(1), 106–110 (1978). 34

[JR10] Jager, T., Rupp, A.: The semi-generic group model and applications to pairing-based cryptography. In: Abe, M. (ed.) ASIACRYPT 2010. LNCS, vol. 6477, pp. 539–556. Springer, Heidelberg (2010). https://doi.org/10.1007/978-3-642-17373-8_31. 34, 38

[JR15] Joux, A., Rojat, A.: Security ranking among assumptions within the *Uber Assumption* framework. In: Desmedt, Y. (ed.) ISC 2013. LNCS, vol. 7807, pp. 391–406. Springer, Cham (2015). https://doi.org/10.1007/978-3-319-27659-5_28. 38

[JS09] Jager, T., Schwenk, J.: On the analysis of cryptographic assumptions in the generic ring model. In: Matsui, M. (ed.) ASIACRYPT 2009. LNCS, vol. 5912, pp. 399–416. Springer, Heidelberg (2009). https://doi.org/10.1007/978-3-642-10366-7_24. 37

[Kil01] Kiltz, E.: A tool box of cryptographic functions related to the Diffie-Hellman function. In: Rangan, C.P., Ding, C. (eds.) INDOCRYPT 2001. LNCS, vol. 2247, pp. 339–349. Springer, Heidelberg (2001). https://doi.org/10.1007/3-540-45311-3_32. 38

[KK12] Kakvi, S.A., Kiltz, E.: Optimal security proofs for full domain hash, revisited. In: Pointcheval, D., Johansson, T. (eds.) EUROCRYPT 2012. LNCS, vol. 7237, pp. 537–553. Springer, Heidelberg (2012). https://doi.org/10.1007/978-3-642-29011-4_32. 36

[KMP16] Kiltz, E., Masny, D., Pan, J.: Optimal security proofs for signatures from identification schemes. In: Robshaw, M., Katz, J. (eds.) CRYPTO 2016, Part II. LNCS, vol. 9815, pp. 33–61. Springer, Heidelberg (2016). https://doi.org/10.1007/978-3-662-53008-5_2. 35

[KSW08] Katz, J., Sahai, A., Waters, B.: Predicate encryption supporting disjunctions, polynomial equations, and inner products. In: Smart, N.P. (ed.) EUROCRYPT 2008. LNCS, vol. 4965, pp. 146–162. Springer, Heidelberg (2008). https://doi.org/10.1007/978-3-540-78967-3_9. 39

[LR06] Leander, G., Rupp, A.: On the equivalence of RSA and factoring regarding generic ring algorithms. In: Lai, X., Chen, K. (eds.) ASIACRYPT 2006. LNCS, vol. 4284, pp. 241–251. Springer, Heidelberg (2006). https://doi. org/10.1007/11935230_16. 34

[LRSW99] Lysyanskaya, A., Rivest, R.L., Sahai, A., Wolf, S.: Pseudonym systems. In: Heys, H.M., Adams, C.M. (eds.) SAC 1999. LNCS, vol. 1758, pp. 184–199. Springer, Heidelberg (2000). https://doi.org/10.1007/3-540-46513-8_14. 35, 37, 45

[Mau05] Maurer, U.M.: Abstract models of computation in cryptography (invited paper). In: Smart, N.P. (ed.) Cryptography and Coding 2005. LNCS, vol. 3796, pp. 1–12. Springer, Heidelberg (2005). https://doi.org/10.1007/11586821_1. 33, 37, 39, 42

[MRV16] Morillo, P., Ràfols, C., Villar, J.L.: The kernel matrix Diffie-Hellman assumption. In: Cheon, J.H., Takagi, T. (eds.) ASIACRYPT 2016, Part I. LNCS, vol. 10031, pp. 729–758. Springer, Heidelberg (2016). https:// doi.org/10.1007/978-3-662-53887-6_27. 38

[MW98] Maurer, U.M., Wolf, S.: Lower bounds on generic algorithms in groups. In: Nyberg, K. (ed.) EUROCRYPT 1998. LNCS, vol. 1403, pp. 72–84. Springer, Heidelberg (1998). https://doi.org/10.1007/BFb0054118. 33, 39

[MW99] Maurer, U., Wolf, S.: The relationship between breaking the Diffie-Hellman protocol and computing discrete logarithms. SIAM J. Comput. **28**(5), 1689–1721 (1999). 43

[Nec94] Nechaev, V.I.: Complexity of a determinate algorithm for the discrete logarithm. Math. Notes **55**(2), 165–172 (1994). 33

[Pol78] Pollard, J.M.: Monte Carlo methods for index computation mod p. Math. Comput. **32**, 918–924 (1978). 34

[PV05] Paillier, P., Vergnaud, D.: Discrete-log-based signatures may not be equivalent to discrete log. In: Roy, B.K. (ed.) ASIACRYPT 2005. LNCS, vol. 3788, pp. 1–20. Springer, Heidelberg (2005). 34, 35, 40

[Riv04] Rivest, R.L.: On the notion of pseudo-free groups. In: Naor, M. (ed.) TCC 2004. LNCS, vol. 2951, pp. 505–521. Springer, Heidelberg (2004). https:// doi.org/10.1007/978-3-540-24638-1_28. 34

[RLB+08] Rupp, A., Leander, G., Bangerter, E., Dent, A.W., Sadeghi, A.-R.: Sufficient conditions for intractability over black-box groups: generic lower bounds for generalized DL and DH problems. In: Pieprzyk, J. (ed.) ASIACRYPT 2008. LNCS, vol. 5350, pp. 489–505. Springer, Heidelberg (2008). https://doi.org/10.1007/978-3-540-89255-7_30. 39

[Sho97] Shoup, V.: Lower bounds for discrete logarithms and related problems. In: Fumy, W. (ed.) EUROCRYPT 1997. LNCS, vol. 1233, pp. 256–266. Springer, Heidelberg (1997). https://doi.org/10.1007/3-540-69053-0_18. 33, 37, 38, 39, 42

[Sho04] Shoup, V.: Sequences of games: a tool for taming complexity in security proofs. Cryptology ePrint Archive, Report 2004/332 (2004). http:// eprint.iacr.org/2004/332

[SS01] Sadeghi, A.-R., Steiner, M.: Assumptions related to discrete logarithms: why subtleties make a real difference. In: Pfitzmann, B. (ed.) EUROCRYPT 2001. LNCS, vol. 2045, pp. 244–261. Springer, Heidelberg (2001). https://doi.org/10.1007/3-540-44987-6_16. 38

[FKL17] Fuchsbauer, G., Kiltz, E., Loss, J.: The algebraic group model and its applications. Cryptology ePrint Archive, Report 2017/620 (2017). http:// eprint.iacr.org/2004/332. 45, 47

Key Exchange

On Tightly Secure Non-Interactive Key Exchange

Julia Hesse[1]([✉]), Dennis Hofheinz[2], and Lisa Kohl[2]

[1] Technische Universität Darmstadt, Darmstadt, Germany
julia.hesse@crisp-da.de
[2] Karlsruhe Institute of Technology, Karlsruhe, Germany
{dennis.hofheinz,lisa.kohl}@kit.edu

Abstract. We consider the reduction loss of security reductions for non-interactive key exchange (NIKE) schemes. Currently, no tightly secure NIKE schemes exist, and in fact Bader et al. (EUROCRYPT 2016) provide a lower bound (of $\Omega(n^2)$, where n is the number of parties an adversary interacts with) on the reduction loss for a large class of NIKE schemes.

We offer two results: the first NIKE scheme with a reduction loss of $n/2$ that circumvents the lower bound of Bader et al., but is of course still far from tightly secure. Second, we provide a generalization of Bader et al.'s lower bound to a larger class of NIKE schemes (that also covers our NIKE scheme), with an adapted lower bound of $n/2$ on the reduction loss. Hence, in that sense, the reduction for our NIKE scheme is optimal.

1 Introduction

TIGHT SECURITY REDUCTIONS. A security reduction relates the security of a cryptographic construction to the difficulty to solve some assumed-to-be-hard problem. In other words, to base the security of a scheme S on the hardness of a problem P, one has to show how to solve P given an adversary that successfully attacks S. As one usually considers asymptotic security, both adversary and problem solver are required to have polynomial running time and non-negligible success probability.

Many security reductions now guess where in S to embed problem P. For example, in case of a signature scheme, the security reduction might guess in which generated signature (an instance of) P is embedded. Asymptotically, this is fine, as an S-attacker can only ask for a polynomial number of signatures.

J. Hesse—Parts of work done while at École Normale Supérieure, Paris, supported by ERC Project CryptoCloud FP7/2007-2013 Grant Agreement no. 339563.
D. Hofheinz—Supported by ERC Project PREP-CRYPTO (724307), and by DFG grants HO 4534/4-1 and HO 4534/2-2.
L. Kohl—Supported by ERC Project PREP-CRYPTO (724307), by DFG grant HO 4534/2-2 and by a DAAD scholarship. Parts of work done while visiting Interdisciplinary Center Herzliya.

H. Shacham and A. Boldyreva (Eds.): CRYPTO 2018, LNCS 10992, pp. 65–94, 2018.
https://doi.org/10.1007/978-3-319-96881-0_3

But when instantiating the scheme with concrete parameters, this guessing step leads to the following paradox: Considering a number of, say, 2^{30} signature queries (which is realistic when thinking of servers) and a security parameter $\lambda = 100$, the concrete loss in success probability introduced by the reduction would actually be larger than a factor of $2^{\lambda/4}$. When aiming at concrete security guarantees (derived from the hardness of P), one thus has to account for the number of expected signatures at the time of set-up, when choosing keylengths.

This makes so called *tight* security reductions a desirable goal. A security reduction is regarded as tight, if (with comparable running times) the success probability of the problem solver is close to the success probability of the under-lying attacker. More precisely, one usually requires the success probabilities to only differ up to a small constant factor (or, for a broader notion of tightness, up to a factor linear in the security parameter). Tight security reductions allow to choose the security parameter for concrete instantiation independently of the number of expected instantiations (or, say, generated signatures in case of a signature scheme).

POSITIVE AND NEGATIVE RESULTS ON TIGHT SECURITY. Schemes with tight security reductions could already be constructed for a variety of cryptographic applications (such as public-key encryption [2,6,19,20,26,28,36,37], identity-based encryption [3,7,11,23,31], digital signature schemes [1,27,34,36,37], or zero-knowledge proofs [20,28]). For public-key encryption schemes, the price to pay for an (almost) tight reduction has been reduced to essentially only one additional group element in ciphertexts [19,20].

On the other hand, starting with the work of Coron [12], a number of works show that certain types of reductions are inherently non-tight (in the sense that a problem solver derived from a given adversary has a significantly reduced success probability). For instance, [4,12,29,32] prove that any "simple" reduction for a sufficiently "structured" signature scheme must lose a factor of $\Omega(q_{\text{sig}})$, where q_{sig} is the number of adversarial signature queries. (Here, the definitions of "simple" and "structured" vary across these papers.) Similar lower bounds exist also for specific schemes and other primitives [4,16,18,35,39]. Particularly interesting to our case is the work of Bader et al. [4], which proves lower bounds on the reduction loss of signature, encryption, and non-interactive key exchange schemes in the standard model.

OUR FOCUS: NON-INTERACTIVE KEY EXCHANGE. In this work, we investigate tight reductions for non-interactive key exchange (NIKE) schemes in the two-party setting[1]. Intuitively, a NIKE scheme enables any two parties P_i and P_j to compute a common shared key K_{ij} using a public-key infrastructure only, but *without any interaction*. (That is, K_{ij} should be an efficiently computable

---

[1] We focus on the two-party setting assuming a public key infrastructure (PKI) since this setting allows for efficient standard-model constructions. Intuitively, stronger settings (multi-party, identity-based with/without setup) appear to require qualita-tively stronger tools to give any construction at all, tightly secure or not. However, since any n-party NIKE can be viewed as a 2-party NIKE by fixing n-2 identities, our lower bound trivially generalizes to multi-user NIKE schemes.

Reference	$|pk|$	model	sec. loss	assumption	uses
Diffie–Hellman [14]	$1 \times \mathbb{G}$	HKR	n^2	DDH	-
Ours, Sec. 3	$3 \times \mathbb{G}$	HKR	$n/2$	DDH	-
CKS08 [10]	$2 \times \mathbb{G}$	DKR	2	CDH	ROM
FHKP13 [17]	$1 \times \mathbb{Z}_N$	DKR	n^2	factoring	ROM
FHKP13 [17]	$2 \times \mathbb{G} + 1 \times \mathbb{Z}_p$	DKR	n^2	DBDH	asymm. pairing
Ours, full version [25]	$12 \times \mathbb{G}$	DKR	$n/2$	DLIN	symm. pairing

Fig. 1. Comparison of existing NIKE schemes. $|pk|$ denotes the size of the public keys, measured in numbers of group elements and exponents. "DKR" or "HKR" denote the CKS-heavy security notion from [17] with dishonest, resp. honest key registrations. Regarding security loss, n denotes the number of honest parties the adversary interacts with and q is the total number of queries made by the adversary. The losses of the two constructions from [17] stems from applying a generic transformation (from the same paper) to level the security guarantees of all compared schemes. Our construction from Sect. 3 is instantiated with the HPS of Cramer–Shoup based on DDH. For more details we refer to the full version [25]. We omit the second scheme from [17] since we focus on non-interactive key registration procedures.

function of P_i's public and P_j's private key, and we require $K_{ij} = K_{ji}$.) Already the original Diffie-Hellman key exchange [14] forms a NIKE scheme (although one that only satisfies a weak form of security). However, the formal investigation of NIKE schemes started with the work of Cash et al. [10], with a more detailed investigation provided in [17].

While there exist highly secure and efficient NIKE schemes (e.g., [10,17]), currently there is no NIKE scheme with a tight security reduction to a standard assumption (and in the standard model). We believe that this is no coincidence: as we will detail below, the rich interdependencies among NIKE keys prevent existing techniques to achieve tight security. Also, it might be interesting to note that the already mentioned work of Bader et al. [4] presents a particularly strong (i.e., *quadratic*) lower bound of $\Omega(n^2)$ on the reduction loss of NIKE schemes, where n is the number of parties that the adversary interacts with. While the scheme of [10] is proven only in the random oracle model, this lower bound applies to the scheme of [17].

OUR RESULTS. In this work, we provide two contributions. First, we construct an efficient and modular NIKE scheme with a reduction significantly tighter than previous reductions. Concretely, our reduction targets the ℓ-Linear assumption in pairing-friendly groups, and has a loss of $n/2$, where n is the number of users an adversary interacts with. Thus, our scheme is the first to break (or, rather, circumvent) the lower bound of Bader et al. [4]. As a technical tool, we also present a generic transformation that turns any mildly secure NIKE scheme (i.e., secure only against passive adversaries) into a strongly secure one (secure against active adversaries).

Second, we show that our security reduction is optimal, in the sense that we can generalize the result of Bader et al. [4] to our scheme, at the price of a smaller lower bound (of precisely $n/2$). Our generalization follows the high-level ideas of Bader et al. (who in turn follow Coron's work [12]). However, unlike their result, we even consider NIKE schemes and reductions that make nontrivial changes to the public-key infrastructure itself. We believe that our second result points out the inherent difference between the public-key or signature settings (in which we already have tightly secure schemes from standard assumptions), and the NIKE setting (in which a broader range of lower bounds holds, and, to our knowledge, no tight schemes exist).

We note that in line with previous works [4,24], our negative result does not consider schemes or reductions in the random oracle model.

1.1   Technical Overview

In order to describe our results, it will be helpful to first recall existing lower bounds results (and in particular the result of Bader et al. [4]). This way, we will be able to detail how we circumvent these lower bounds, and what other obstacles still block the way to a tight reduction.

A CLOSER LOOK ON EXISTING LOWER BOUND RESULTS. It might be interesting to see why these lower bounds do not contradict any of the constructions mentioned above. All mentioned lower bounds use a "meta-reduction" (cf. [9]) that turns any tight reduction into a successful problem solver (even *without* a given successful adversary). To describe how a meta-reduction works, assume a reduction R that interacts with an adversary $\mathcal{A}$. Assume further that R first solves a number of problem instances for $\mathcal{A}$, and then expects $\mathcal{A}$ to solve a new problem instance. (For instance, in the signature setting, R might first generate many signatures for $\mathcal{A}$ on messages of $\mathcal{A}$'s choice, and then expect $\mathcal{A}$ to forge a signature for a fresh message.) R will then try to solve its own input instance using the fresh solution provided by $\mathcal{A}$.

Now a meta-reduction M runs R, and takes the place of $\mathcal{A}$ in an interaction with R. Intuitively, M will try to feed R with R's own problem solutions, and hope that R can use one of those to solve its own input. Of course, security games generally require the adversary to generate a *fresh* problem solution to avoid trivial attacks. (For instance, the standard security game for signatures [22] requires the adversary to forge a signature for a message that has not been signed before.) Hence, M runs R *twice*: in the first run, M asks R for the solutions to, say, q randomly chosen problem instances $z_1, \ldots, z_q$. Then, M rewinds R, asks for solutions to *different* problem instances $\tilde{z}_i$, and submits the previously obtained solution to one z_i as fresh solution.

Of course, R may fail to convert a z_i-solution into a solution to its own input *sometimes* (depending on its reduction loss), and this leaves a "loophole" for R to escape the meta-reduction strategy of M. However, a combinatorial argument of [12] shows that R must have a reduction loss of $\Omega(q_{\mathsf{sig}})$ to use this loophole.

For this strategy of M, it is essential that the reduction R will "accept" a problem solution that it has generated itself. To this end, [12,32] require unique signatures (i.e., problem solutions), and [4,29] require re-randomizable signatures (so that any valid signature produced by R can be converted in a random signature by M). However, this property is violated (in a very strong sense) by many of the tightly secure signature schemes mentioned above (e.g., [1,27,36,37]). Specifically, the corresponding (tight) reductions find a way to produce special valid-looking signatures for an adversary that are however useless to solving a problem instance. (Of course, these signatures are not re-randomizable or unique.)

THE ARGUMENT OF BADER ET AL. FOR NIKE SCHEMES. Bader et al. [4] adapt the above argument to NIKE schemes. To describe their argument, we first recall the NIKE security experiment (according to [10]). A NIKE adversary may request an arbitrary number n of public keys pk_i, and may adaptively corrupt an arbitrary subset of them (in which case the adversary gets the corresponding secret keys sk_i).[2] Finally, the adversary selects two public keys $\mathsf{pk}_{i^*}, \mathsf{pk}_{j^*}$ that have not been corrupted, and then must distinguish between their shared key K_{i^*,j^*}, and an independently random value.[3]

Now assume a reduction R that turns any NIKE adversary into a successful problem solver. This reduction R has to be able to answer adversarial corruption queries, and come up with the corresponding secret keys sk_i. Intuitively, a meta-reduction M can take the role of an adversary, and first obtain some of these keys sk_i from R. Then, M can rewind R, and choose to be challenged on a shared key K_{i^*,j^*} that can be computed from one previously obtained sk_i.

The main difference to the signature case above is that n public keys pk_i give rise to $O(n^2)$ shared keys (or, problem instances/solutions) K_{ij}. In particular, $O(n)$ corruptions enable M to compute $O(n^2)$ shared keys (and thus to potentially solve a quadratic number of shared key challenges). If R turns any of those challenge solutions into a problem solution, then M succeeds. Hence, R must fail with probability $1 - O(1/n^2)$. (Another way to view this is that the reduction's success has to vanish with the failures of the simulation.)

HOW TO CIRCUMVENT THE NIKE LOWER BOUND. However, similar to previous works, Bader et al. assume that any secret key (or, more generally, problem solution) output by R can be used to solve corresponding challenges posed by R. This assumption can in fact be violated easily, e.g., by allowing many different secret keys per public key. (That is, a secret key is not uniquely determined by a given public key and, e.g., R may hand out different secret keys upon a corruption query.) Furthermore, different secret keys (for a given public key) may behave differently in the computation of shared keys, and thus may not necessarily be useful in solving a given challenge. Similar ideas are at the core of known techniques for improving tightness, in particular in the context of corruptions [5].

While this first thought allows to circumvent the lower bound of Bader et al., its concrete implementation is not clear at all in the context of NIKE schemes.

---

[2] We omit additional capabilities of the adversary which are not relevant for this overview.

[3] Like [4], we consider only one challenge pair of public keys (and not an arbitrary number, like the "m-CKS-heavy" notion of [17].

In particular, there should be many secret keys (with different functionality) for a given public key, but the secret keys obtained through corruptions should still satisfy correctness (in the sense that pk_i and sk_j lead to the same shared key as sk_i and pk_j). (We note that this obstacle is specific to NIKE schemes, and in our opinion the main reason why obtaining tightly secure NIKE schemes appears to be particularly difficult.)

OUR SCHEME. To explain our solution, it might be easiest to first outline our scheme (which, in its basic form, is a variation of the password-authenticated key exchange scheme of [21,33]). Let L be a language, and assume a hash proof system (HPS) for L with public keys hpk and secret keys hsk. We write $H_{hsk}(x)$ for hash proof of an L-instance x under key hsk. Then, public and secret keys of our NIKE scheme are of the following form:

$$pk = (hpk, x) \qquad\qquad sk = (hsk, x, w),$$

where $x \in L$ with witness w, and a HPS keypair (hpk, hsk) are randomly chosen. Given $pk_i = (hpk_i, x_i)$ and $sk_j = (hsk_j, x_j, w_j)$, the corresponding NIKE shared key is computed as $K_{ij} = H_{hsk_j}(x_i) \cdot H_{hsk_i}(x_j)$, where the hash value $H_{hsk_i}(x_j)$ is computed from (and uniquely determined by) hpk_i and w_j. We have correctness in the sense $K_{ji} = H_{hsk_i}(x_j) \cdot H_{hsk_j}(x_i) = H_{hsk_j}(x_i) \cdot H_{hsk_i}(x_j) = K_{ij}$.

Recall that there are many HPS secret keys hsk for any given public key hpk. However, all these secret keys act identically on any $x \in L$. Hence, in order to benefit from the non-uniqueness of hsk, a NIKE reduction will have to switch at least one $x \in L$ in a NIKE public key pk_i to a no-instance $x \notin L$. Let us call such a NIKE public key (with $x \notin L$) "invalid". For an invalid pk_i, no (full) secret key exists. This means that our reduction must hope that no invalid pk_i is ever corrupted. Since a NIKE adversary may corrupt all public keys except for the two selected challenge keys pk_{i^*}, pk_{j^*}, this means that our reduction may instead fail with probability $1 - 2/n$.

In other words, already with one invalid public key, our reduction has a loss of at least $n/2$. On the bright side, we will present a strategy that uses precisely one invalid public key to leverage a NIKE security reduction (with loss $n/2$). This reduction is of course far from tight, but it has a loss still considerably better than the $O(n^2)$ lower bound by Bader et al., and thus is significantly tighter than previous constructions. In a nutshell, our security proof proceeds in game hops:

1. We start with the NIKE security game.
2. We guess one index i^*, and hope that pk_{i^*} is one of the challenge public keys finally selected in the adversary's challenge. (If this is not the case, the reduction fails.) Since there are 2 challenge public keys, this step loses a factor of $n/2$.
3. We choose $x_{i^*} \notin L$. Since we may assume that pk_{i^*} is selected as challenge, this change will not be detectable (assuming L has a hard subset membership problem).

4. Finally, we observe that now, *all* keys K_{i*j} (for arbitrary j) are randomized by the smoothness of the underlying HPS. In fact, HPS smoothness implies that K_{i*j} is close to uniform, even given pk_j. In particular, this holds for $j = j^*$ and the final challenge K_{i*j*}.

Note that while [10] also crucially relies on HPSs, there are significant technical differences. Namely, [10] uses hash proof systems mainly as a tool to implement a "replacement decryption method" that allows to forget parts of the secret key. In other words, they use HPSs exclusively in "proof mode". In contrast, for our basic NIKE scheme we use the HPS only in "randomization mode", i.e. to randomize shared keys.

INSTANTIATIONS AND VARIANTS. Our basic scheme only requires a HPS for a language with hard subset membership problem, and thus can be implemented efficiently from various computational assumptions (such as the DDH [13], ℓ-Linear [30], DCR [13], or QR [13] assumptions). However, this basic scheme satisfies only a relatively mild form of security called "honest key registration" or "HKR" security in [17]. Hence, we also present a general transformation that turns *any* mildly secure NIKE scheme into one that satisfies a stronger form of security (dubbed "dishonest key registration" or "DKR" security in [17]). Our scheme requires a suitable non-interactive zero-knowledge proof system, and, very loosely speaking, adapts the Naor-Yung paradigm [38] to NIKE schemes. We finally give a concrete and optimized instance under the ℓ-MDDH assumption [15] (for any $\ell \geq 2$ in pairing-friendly groups). For details we refer to the full version [25].

We note that we view our construction as a "first" that demonstrates how to circumvent existing lower bounds for a particularly challenging application. We do not claim superior efficiency of our (fully secure) scheme over existing state-of-the-art NIKE schemes, not even when taking into account the reduction loss in the choice of group sizes. Still, Fig. 1 provides an overview over existing NIKE schemes, in particular in comparison to our scheme.

OUR NEW LOWER BOUND. Even though it breaks the existing bound of Bader et al. [4], the reduction loss (of $O(n)$) of our scheme might be a bit disappointing. Our second result shows that we can extend the results from [4] to show that the reduction loss (at least for our scheme) is optimal. Specifically, we are able to give new lower bounds on the tightness of NIKE reductions even for schemes with invalid public keys.

In more detail, we show that a weak validity check (on public keys) is sufficient to prove a meaningful lower bound. Namely, we require that validity of a public key (in the sense that two valid public keys admit only one shared key) is verifiable given that public key *and one of its possible secret keys*. Hence, as long as a given public key is not corrupted, its validity may not be efficiently verifiable, and a reduction can hope to substitute it with an invalid key. (Note that this is precisely what happens in the proof of our NIKE scheme.)

On the other hand, this weak validity check allows us to again apply a rewinding argument as in [4]. Namely, as soon as the reduction returns a secret key on an extraction query, we can check whether the given public key was actually valid and in this case use the obtained secret key later to compute the unique shared key. The only case where we fail to do so is if the reduction does not return a valid secret key for a certain public key in all rewinding attempts. But then we can simply abort with high probability, namely in case this public key is part of the extraction queries (which happens with probability $1 - 2/n$). In other words, we prove that the best a reduction can do is to switch one public key to invalid and hope that this public key is not part of the extraction queries. We can thus conclude that a NIKE (such as ours) that admits a non-public validity check still suffers from a security reduction loss of at least $n/2$.

ROADMAP. In Sect. 2 we provide the necessary preliminaries. In Sect. 3 we present our construction of a mildly secure NIKE with a security reduction whose tightness significantly improves upon existing NIKEs. In Sect. 4 we show how to transform a mildly secure NIKE into a strongly secure one. In Sect. 5 we prove a new lower bound for a broad class of NIKE schemes including ours. In the full version [25] we provide a concrete instantiation of our NIKE. Further, we show how to tweak efficiency of the transformation from mild to strong security when using our NIKE construction.

2   Preliminaries

NOTATION. Throughout the paper, λ denotes the security parameter. We say that a function is *negligible in λ* if its inverse vanishes asymptotically faster than any polynomial in λ. If a probabilistic algorithm $\mathcal{A}$ has running time polynomial in λ, we say that $\mathcal{A}$ is *probabilistic polynomial time* (PPT). We use $y \leftarrow \mathcal{A}(x)$ to denote that y is assigned the output of $\mathcal{A}$ running on input x, and we write $y \leftarrow \mathcal{A}(x; r)$ to make the randomness r used by a probabilistic algorithm explicit. We use $y \xleftarrow{\$} X$ to denote sampling from a set X uniformly at random. For $n \in \mathbb{N}$ by $[n]$ we denote the set $\{1, \ldots, n\}$. Let $\varepsilon \in [0, 1]$ and $\mathcal{X}, \mathcal{Y}$ distributions. To denote that $\mathcal{X}$ and $\mathcal{Y}$ have statistical distance at most ε, we write $\mathcal{X} \equiv_\varepsilon \mathcal{Y}$ and say $\mathcal{X}$ and $\mathcal{Y}$ are *ε-close*.

2.1   Hash Proof Systems

Definition 1 (Subset membership problem). *We call* SMP $:=$ Setup *a subset membership problem, if* Setup *is a PPT algorithm with the following properties.*

Setup(1^λ) *outputs a compact (i.e. with length polynomial in λ) description (X, L, R), where $L \subset X$ are sets and R is an efficiently computable relation with*

$$x \in L \iff \exists \ witness \ w \ with \ (x, w) \in R.$$

(We say a relation R is efficiently computable if given a pair (x, w) it can be efficiently checked whether $(x, w) \in R$.)

Further we require for all (X, L, R) in the image of Setup that it is possible to efficiently sample elements x uniformly at random from $X \backslash L$ (written $x \xleftarrow{\$} X \backslash L$) and to sample elements x uniformly random from L together with witness w (written $(x, w) \xleftarrow{\$} R$).

Definition 2 (Subset membership assumption). *Let SMP be a subset membership problem. We say that the* subset membership assumption *holds for SMP, if for all PPT algorithms $\mathcal{A}$ it holds that*

$$\mathrm{Adv}^{\mathrm{smp}}_{\mathcal{A}, \mathit{SMP}}(\lambda) := |\Pr[\mathcal{A}(1^\lambda, (X, L, R), x) = 1 | (x, w) \xleftarrow{\$} R]$$

$$- \Pr[\mathcal{A}(1^\lambda, (X, L, R), x) = 1 | x \xleftarrow{\$} X \backslash L]|$$

is negligible in λ, where $(X, L, R) \xleftarrow{\$} \mathit{SMP}.\mathit{Setup}(1^\lambda)$.

We will employ the notion of a hash proof system based on [13].

Definition 3 (Hash Proof Systems (HPS)). *Let SMP be a subset membership problem. We call HPS := Setup a hash proof system for SMP, if it is a PPT algorithm of the following form.*

Setup(1^λ) *first samples public parameters $\mathcal{PP}_{\mathit{SMP}} := (X, L, R) \leftarrow \mathit{SMP}.\mathit{Setup}(1^\lambda)$ for the underlying subset membership problem. Further Setup chooses sets $\mathcal{HSK}, \Pi, \mathcal{HPK}$ such that elements can be efficiently sampled at random from $\mathcal{HSK}$ (denoted $\mathsf{hsk} \xleftarrow{\$} \mathcal{HSK}$). Further Setup chooses an efficiently computable map*

$$\alpha : \mathcal{HSK} \longrightarrow \mathcal{HPK},$$

a family of efficiently computable functions

$$\mathcal{H} := \{H_{\mathsf{hsk}} : X \longrightarrow \Pi \mid \mathsf{hsk} \in \mathcal{HSK}\}$$

and an efficiently computable map

$$F : R \times \mathcal{HPK} \longrightarrow \Pi$$

such that for all $\mathsf{hsk} \in \mathcal{HSK}, \mathsf{hpk} \in \mathcal{HPK}$ with $\alpha(\mathsf{hsk}) = \mathsf{hpk}$ and for all $(x, w) \in R$ we have

$$H_{\mathsf{hsk}}(x) = F(x, w, \mathsf{hpk}).$$

Finally, Setup outputs $\mathcal{PP} := (\mathcal{PP}_{\mathit{SMP}}, \mathcal{HSK}, \mathcal{H}, \alpha, F)$, which contains $\mathcal{PP}_{\mathit{SMP}}$ together with the compact (i.e. with length polynomial in λ) description of $\mathcal{HSK}, \mathcal{H}, \alpha$ and F.

We need a property of a HPS called smoothness, introduced in [13].

Definition 4 (Smoothness). *Let SMP be a subset membership problem and HPS be a hash proof system for SMP. We call HPS ε-smooth if for all $\mathcal{PP} := ((X, L, R), \mathcal{HSK}, \mathcal{H}, \alpha, F)$ in the image of HPS.Setup, the following distributions are ε-close:*

$$
\left\{ (x, \mathsf{hpk}, H_{\mathsf{hsk}}(x)) \left| \begin{array}{c} \mathsf{hsk} \xleftarrow{\$} \mathcal{K} \\ \mathsf{hpk} := \alpha(\mathsf{hsk}) \\ x \xleftarrow{\$} X \setminus L \end{array} \right. \right\} \equiv_{\varepsilon} \left\{ (x, \mathsf{hpk}, \pi) \left| \begin{array}{c} \mathsf{hsk} \xleftarrow{\$} \mathcal{K} \\ \mathsf{hpk} := \alpha(\mathsf{hsk}) \\ x \leftarrow X \setminus L, \pi \xleftarrow{\$} \Pi \end{array} \right. \right\}.
$$

(Recall that Π is the image set of H_{hsk}.) In other words, on statements x outside the language L, the output of the private evaluation algorithms is ε-close to uniformly random even under knowledge of the public key. Note though that this statement only holds as long as no image of H_{hsk} on input $x \in X \setminus L$ is known.

2.2 Non-Interactive Key Exchange (NIKE)

We formally define the notion of NIKE, following [10,17] and also adopting most of their notation. A NIKE scheme NIKE consists of three algorithms (Setup, KeyGen, SharedKey), an identity space $\mathcal{IDS}$ and a shared key space $\mathcal{K}$ which is the output space of SharedKey.

- Setup: On input 1^{λ}, this probabilistic algorithm outputs the system parameters $\mathcal{PP}$.
- KeyGen: On input $\mathcal{PP}$ and an ID ID, this probabilistic algorithm outputs a tuple $(\mathsf{pk}, \mathsf{sk}) \in \mathcal{PK} \times \mathcal{SK}$.
- SharedKey: On input of the public parameters $\mathcal{PP}$ and two identity, public key pairs $(\mathsf{ID}_1, \mathsf{pk}_1), (\mathsf{ID}_2, \mathsf{sk}_2)$, this deterministic algorithm outputs a shared key $K_{12} \in \mathcal{K}$. We assume that $\mathcal{K}$ contains a failure symbol $\perp$.

Table 1. Types of queries for different security models, taken from [17], where q_x denotes the maximum number of allowed queries of the adversary to oracle $\mathcal{O}_x$. ✓, - and n mean that an adversary is allowed to make arbitrary, zero or n queries of this type, in an arbitrary order.

Model	q_{regH}	q_{regC}	q_{extr}	q_{revH}	q_{revC}	q_{test}
DKR CKS-light	2	✓	-	-	✓	1
DKR CKS	✓	✓	-	-	✓	✓
DKR CKS-heavy	✓	✓	✓	✓	✓	1
DKR m-CKS-heavy	✓	✓	✓	✓	✓	✓
HKR CKS-light	2	-	-	-	-	1
HKR CKS	✓	-	-	-	-	✓
HKR CKS-heavy	✓	-	✓	✓	-	1
HKR m-CKS-heavy	✓	-	✓	✓	-	✓

$\mathrm{Exp}_{\mathcal{A},NIKE}^{[hkr|dkr]-cks-heavy}(\lambda)$:	$\mathcal{O}_{\mathsf{revH}}(ID_1, ID_2)$:
$\mathcal{PP} \xleftarrow{\$} NIKE.Setup(1^\lambda)$ $Q_{\mathsf{regH}} := \emptyset, \boxed{Q_{\mathsf{regC}} := \emptyset}, Q_{\mathsf{extr}} := \emptyset,$ $Q_{\mathsf{rev}} := \emptyset$ $b^* \leftarrow \mathcal{A}^{\mathcal{O}_{\mathsf{H}}, \boxed{\mathcal{O}_{\mathsf{regC}}(\cdot), \mathcal{O}_{\mathsf{revC}}(\cdot, \cdot)}}(\mathcal{PP})$ if $b = b^* \wedge ID_1^*, ID_2^* \notin Q_{\mathsf{extr}}$ $\quad \wedge \{ID_1^*, ID_2^*\} \notin Q_{\mathsf{rev}}$ $\quad$ output 1 else $\quad b' \xleftarrow{\$} \{0,1\}$ $\quad$ output b'	if $\exists sk_1, sk_2 : (ID_1, pk_1, sk_1),$ $\qquad (ID_2, pk_2, sk_2) \in Q_{\mathsf{regH}}$ $\quad Q_{\mathsf{rev}} := Q_{\mathsf{rev}} \cup \{\{ID_1, ID_2\}\}$ $\quad$ return $NIKE.SharedKey(ID_1, pk_1, ID_2, sk_2)$ else return $\perp$
	$\mathcal{O}_{\mathsf{revC}}(ID_1, ID_2)$:
$\mathcal{O}_{\mathsf{regH}}(ID)$: if $(ID, \cdot, \cdot) \notin \mathcal{O}_{\mathsf{regC}} \cup Q_{\mathsf{regH}}$ $\quad (pk, sk) \xleftarrow{\$} NIKE.KeyGen(\mathcal{PP}, ID)$ $\quad Q_{\mathsf{regH}} := Q_{\mathsf{regH}} \cup \{(ID, pk, sk)\}$ $\quad$ return pk else return $\perp$	if $\exists sk_1 : (ID_1, pk_1, sk_1) \in Q_{\mathsf{regH}},$ $\qquad (ID_2, pk_2, \cdot) \in Q_{\mathsf{regC}}$ $\quad Q_{\mathsf{rev}} := Q_{\mathsf{rev}} \cup \{\{ID_1, ID_2\}\}$ $\quad$ return $NIKE.SharedKey(ID_2, pk_2, ID_1, sk_1)$ if $\exists sk_2 : (ID_2, pk_2, sk_2) \in Q_{\mathsf{regH}},$ $\qquad (ID_1, pk_1, \cdot) \in Q_{\mathsf{regC}}$ $\quad Q_{\mathsf{rev}} := Q_{\mathsf{rev}} \cup \{\{ID_1, ID_2\}\}$ $\quad$ return $NIKE.SharedKey(ID_1, pk_1, ID_2, sk_2)$ else return $\perp$
$\mathcal{O}_{\mathsf{regC}}(ID, pk)$: if $(ID, \cdot, \cdot) \notin \mathcal{O}_{\mathsf{regH}} \cup \mathcal{O}_{\mathsf{regC}}$ $\quad Q_{\mathsf{regC}} := Q_{\mathsf{regC}} \cup \{(ID, pk, \perp)\}$ else return $\perp$	$\mathcal{O}_{\mathsf{test}}(ID_1^*, ID_2^*)$:
	$b \xleftarrow{\$} \{0,1\}$ if $\exists sk_1^*, sk_2^* : (ID_1^*, pk_1^*, sk_1^*),$ $\qquad (ID_2^*, pk_2^*, sk_2^*) \in Q_{\mathsf{regH}}$ $\quad K_0 = NIKE.SharedKey(ID_1^*, pk_1^*, ID_2^*, sk_2^*)$ $\quad K_1 \xleftarrow{\$} \mathcal{K}$ $\quad$ return K_b else return $\perp$
$\mathcal{O}_{\mathsf{extr}}(ID)$: if $\exists sk : (ID, pk, sk) \in Q_{\mathsf{regH}}$ $\quad Q_{\mathsf{extr}} := Q_{\mathsf{extr}} \cup \{ID\}$ $\quad$ return sk else return $\perp$	

Fig. 2. Experiment for HKR and DKR CKS-heavy security of a NIKE scheme NIKE with shared key space $\mathcal{K}$. The highlighted parts only occur in the setting of dishonest key registration. The oracle $\mathcal{O}_{\mathsf{test}}$ may only be queried once. $\mathcal{O}_{\mathsf{H}}$ comprises the oracles $\mathcal{O}_{\mathsf{regH}}, \mathcal{O}_{\mathsf{revH}}, \mathcal{O}_{\mathsf{extr}}$ and $\mathcal{O}_{\mathsf{test}}$. We use $\cdot$ to denote an arbitrary entry of a tuple. I.e., $\mathcal{O}_{\mathsf{regH}} \setminus \{(ID, \cdot, \cdot)\}$ denotes the set $\mathcal{O}_{\mathsf{regH}}$ without any tuple that contains ID in the first position.

We always require NIKE to be perfectly correct, meaning that for all corresponding key pairs $(ID_1, pk_1, sk_1), (ID_2, pk_2, sk_2)$ generated by KeyGen it holds

$$SharedKey(ID_1, pk_1, ID_2, sk_2) = SharedKey(ID_2, pk_2, ID_1, sk_1) \neq \perp$$

SECURITY. We quickly recall the game-based security notion from [10], called the *CKS model*, with its refinements from [17]. The model is defined via adversarial queries to oracles implemented by a challenger $\mathcal{C}$. The challenger $\mathcal{C}$ keeps track of all honest and corrupt registered identities and their keys. We informally describe the oracles provided to the adversary attacking a NIKE NIKE below.

- $\mathcal{O}_{\text{regH}}$ for registering an honest user. $\mathcal{C}$ generates a key pair using NIKE.KeyGen and hands the public key to the adversary.
- $\mathcal{O}_{\text{regC}}$ for registering a corrupt user. The adversary may introduce a public key without providing the corresponding secret key.
- $\mathcal{O}_{\text{extr}}$ for extracting a secret key of an honest user.
- $\mathcal{O}_{\text{revH}}$ for revealing a shared key of an honest pair of users.
- $\mathcal{O}_{\text{revC}}$ for revealing a shared key between a corrupted and an honest user.
- $\mathcal{O}_{\text{test}}$ for obtaining a challenge. $\mathcal{A}$ provides a pair of users it wishes to be challenged upon. $\mathcal{C}$ then flips a coin and replies either with their real shared key or a random one.

First, $\mathcal{C}$ runs $\mathcal{PP} \xleftarrow{\$} \text{NIKE.Setup}(1^\lambda)$ and gives $\mathcal{PP}$ to $\mathcal{A}$. Then, the adversary may make an arbitrary number of the above queries, in an arbitrary order. Finally, the adversary outputs a bit $\hat{b}$ and wins if $\hat{b} = b$. Note that the adversary may register each ID only once[4].

To obtain different notions of CKS security, the adversary is restricted in the number of its queries. See Table 1 for a complete list. Notions that admit $\mathcal{O}_{\text{regC}}$ and $\mathcal{O}_{\text{revC}}$ queries are said to *allow dishonest key registrations*, dubbed *DKR*. Notions that do not allow such types of queries are called *with honest key registration*, or *HKR* for short.

In this paper, we are interested in *CKS - heavy* secure NIKE schemes. We provide the corresponding security experiment in Fig. 2.

Definition 5 (HKR- and DKR-CKS-heavy security). *Let NIKE be a NIKE. We say NIKE is* CKS-heavy secure with honest key registration, *or* HKR-CKS-heavy secure, *if for any PPT adversary $\mathcal{A}$ the advantage*

$$\text{Adv}^{\text{hkr}-\text{cks}-\text{heavy}}_{\mathcal{A},NIKE}(\lambda) = |\Pr[\text{Exp}^{\text{hkr}-\text{cks}-\text{heavy}}_{\mathcal{A},NIKE}(\lambda) \Rightarrow 1] - 1/2|$$

is negligible in λ, where $\text{Exp}^{\text{hkr}-\text{cks}-\text{heavy}}_{\mathcal{A},NIKE}$ *is provided in Fig. 2. Similarly, we say that NIKE is* CKS-heavy secure with dishonest key registration, *or* DKR-CKS-heavy secure, *if for any PPT adversary $\mathcal{A}$ the advantage*

$$\text{Adv}^{\text{dkr}-\text{cks}-\text{heavy}}_{\mathcal{A},NIKE}(\lambda) = |\Pr[\text{Exp}^{\text{dkr}-\text{cks}-\text{heavy}}_{\mathcal{A},NIKE}(\lambda) \Rightarrow 1] - 1/2|$$

is negligible in λ.

2.3 Public Key Encryption

Definition 6 (Public key encryption). *We call a tuple of PPT algorithms PKE := (KeyGen, Enc, Dec) a public key encryption scheme if the following holds.*

---

[4] In practice, this can be implemented by appending a counter to an identity string.

$$\boxed{\begin{array}{l} \mathrm{Exp}^{\mathsf{ind-cpa}}_{\mathcal{A}=(\mathcal{A}_1,\mathcal{A}_2),\mathrm{PKE}}(\lambda): \\ \hline (\mathsf{ppk},\mathsf{psk}) \leftarrow \mathrm{PKE.KeyGen}(1^\lambda) \\ (M_0, M_1, st) \leftarrow \mathcal{A}_1(1^\lambda, \mathsf{ppk}) \\ b \xleftarrow{\$} \{0,1\} \\ C := \mathrm{Enc}(\mathsf{ppk}, M_b) \\ b^\star \leftarrow \mathcal{A}_2(st, C) \\ \mathtt{if} \quad b = b^\star \quad \mathtt{output} \quad 1 \\ \mathtt{else\ output\ 0} \end{array}}$$

Fig. 3. IND-CPA experiment.

- *KeyGen*(1^λ) *returns a key pair* $(\mathsf{ppk}, \mathsf{psk})$.
- *Enc*(ppk, M) *returns a ciphertext* C.
- *Dec*(psk, C) *returns a message* M *or a special rejection symbol* $\perp$.

We further require Correctness, *that is for all* $(\mathsf{ppk}, \mathsf{psk})$ *in the range of* *KeyGen*(1^λ), *for all messages* M *and for all* C *in the range of* *Enc*(pk, M) *we require*

$$Dec(\mathsf{sk}, C) = 1.$$

Definition 7 (IND-CPA). *Let* PKE *be a public key encryption scheme. We say* PKE *is* IND-CPA *secure if for all PPT adversaries* $\mathcal{A}$ *we have that*

$$\mathrm{Adv}^{\mathsf{ind-cpa}}_{\mathcal{A},\mathit{PKE}}(\lambda) := |\Pr[\mathrm{Exp}^{\mathsf{ind-cpa}}_{\mathcal{A},\mathit{PKE}}(\lambda) \Rightarrow 1] - 1/2|$$

is negligible in λ, *where* $\mathrm{Exp}^{\mathsf{ind-cpa}}_{\mathcal{A},\mathit{PKE}}(\lambda)$ *is defined as in Fig. 3 and we require* $|M_0| = |M_1|$.

2.4   Non-Interactive Zero Knowledge Proof of Knowledge

The notion of a quasi-adaptive non-interactive zero-knowledge proof was introduced in [8]. The following definition of non-interactive zero-knowledge is an adaptation of [20] with some differences. Note for instance, that we consider computational zero-knowledge instead of perfect zero-knowledge. We will employ such proofs to generically transform a NIKE which is secure in the HKR-CKS-heavy security model to a NIKE which is secure in the DKR-CKS-heavy security model.

Definition 8 (QANIZK). *Let* SMP *be a subset membership problem. Let* $(X, L, R) \leftarrow$ SMP.*Setup*(1^λ). *A quasi adaptive non-interactive zero-knowledge proof* (QANIZK) *for* SMP *is a tuple of PPT algorithms* PS $:= ($*Setup, Gen, Ver, Sim*$)$ *of the following form.*

- *Setup*$(1^\lambda, (X, L, R))$ *generates a common reference string* crs *and a trapdoor* trp. *We assume* (X, L, R) *to be part of the* crs.

$\mathrm{Exp}_{\mathcal{A},\mathrm{PS}}^{\mathrm{extr}}(\lambda):$	$\mathcal{O}_{\mathrm{sim}}(x):$
$\quad (X,L,R) \leftarrow \mathrm{SMP.Setup}(1^\lambda)$	$\quad Q_{\mathrm{sim}} := Q_{\mathrm{sim}} \cup \{x\}$
$\quad (\mathrm{crs},\mathrm{trp},\mathrm{extr}) \xleftarrow{\$} \mathrm{PS.Setup}(1^\lambda, (X,L,R))$	$\quad \Pi \leftarrow \mathrm{PS.Sim}(\mathrm{crs},\mathrm{trp},x)$
$\quad Q_{\mathrm{sim}} := \emptyset$	$\quad \mathrm{return}\ \Pi$
$\quad (x^*, \Pi^*) \leftarrow \mathcal{A}^{\mathcal{O}_{\mathrm{sim}}(\cdot), \mathcal{O}_{\mathrm{extract}}(\cdot,\cdot)}(1^\lambda, \mathrm{crs})$	
$\quad w \leftarrow \mathcal{O}_{\mathrm{extract}}(x^*, \Pi^*)$	$\mathcal{O}_{\mathrm{extract}}(x, \Pi):$
$\quad \mathrm{if}\ \mathrm{PS.Ver}(x^*, \Pi^*) = 1 \wedge (x^*, w) \notin R$	$\quad \mathrm{if}\ x \notin Q_{\mathrm{sim}}$
$\quad \wedge x^* \notin Q_{\mathrm{sim}}$	$\quad\quad w \leftarrow \mathrm{PS.Extract}(\mathrm{crs},\mathrm{extr},x,\Pi)$
$\quad\quad \mathrm{output}\ 1$	$\quad\quad \mathrm{return}\ w$
$\quad \mathrm{else\ output}\ 0$	$\quad \mathrm{else\ return}\ \perp$

Fig. 4. Experiment for a extraction in the presence of simulated proofs. The adversary tries to set up a pair (x, Π) such that a witness w is not extractable from Π.

- **Prove**(crs, x, w) *given a word* $x \in L$ *and a witness* w *with* $R(x, w) = 1$, *outputs a proof* Π.
- **Ver**(crs, x, Π) *on input* crs, $x \in X$ *and* Π *outputs a verdict* $b \in \{0, 1\}$.
- **Sim**$(\mathrm{crs}, \mathrm{trp}, x)$ *given a* crs *with corresponding trapdoor* trp *and a word* $x \in X$, *outputs a proof* Π.

Further we require the following properties to hold.

Perfect completeness: *For all security parameters* λ, *all* (X, L, R) *in the image of* **SMP.Setup**(1^λ), *all* $(\mathrm{crs}, \mathrm{trp})$ *in the range of* **Setup**$(1^\lambda, (X, L, R))$, *all words* $x \in L$, *all witnesses* w *such that* $R(x, w) = 1$ *and all* Π *in the range of* **Prove**(crs, x, w) *we have*

$$\textbf{\textit{Ver}}(\mathrm{crs}, x, \Pi) = 1.$$

Computational zero-knowledge: *For all security parameters* λ, *all* (X, L, R) *in the range of* **SMP.Setup**(1^λ), *all tuples* $(\mathrm{crs}, \mathrm{trp})$ *in the range of* **Setup**$(1^\lambda, (X, L, R))$, *we have for all PPT adversaries* $\mathcal{A}$ *that*

$$\mathrm{Adv}_{\mathcal{A},\mathit{PS}}^{\mathrm{zk}}(\lambda) := |\Pr[\mathcal{A}^{\mathcal{O}_{\mathrm{prv}}(\cdot,\cdot)}(1^\lambda, \mathrm{crs}) = 1] - \Pr[\mathcal{A}^{\mathcal{O}_{\mathrm{sim}}(\cdot,\cdot)}(1^\lambda, \mathrm{crs}) = 1]|$$

is negligible in λ, *where both oracles on input* (x, w) *first check whether* $(x, w) \in R$. *If this is the case,* $\mathcal{O}_{\mathrm{prv}}$ *returns* **Prove**(crs, x, w) *and* $\mathcal{O}_{\mathrm{sim}}$ *returns* **Sim**$(\mathrm{crs}, \mathrm{trp}, x)$ *(and* $\perp$ *otherwise).*

The following definition is tailored to our purposes. We require a strong notion of proof of knowledge in the sense that we need to be able to extract a witness while simulating proofs ourselves.

NIKE.Setup(1^λ)	NIKE.KeyGen$(\mathcal{PP}, \mathsf{ID})$
$(\mathcal{PP}_{\mathrm{SMP}}, \mathcal{HSK}, \mathcal{H}, \alpha, F) \xleftarrow{\$} \mathsf{HPS.Setup}(1^\lambda)$ $\mathcal{PP} := (\mathcal{PP}_{\mathrm{SMP}}, \mathcal{HSK}, \mathcal{H}, \alpha, F)$ return $\mathcal{PP}$	parse $\mathcal{PP} =: (\mathcal{PP}_{\mathrm{SMP}}, \mathcal{HSK}, \mathcal{H}, \alpha, F)$ parse $PP_{\mathrm{SMP}} =: (X, L, R)$ $\mathsf{hsk} \xleftarrow{\$} \mathcal{HSK}$ $\mathsf{hpk} := \alpha(\mathsf{hsk})$ $(x, w) \xleftarrow{\$} R$ $\mathsf{pk} := (\mathsf{hpk}, x)$ $\mathsf{sk} := (\mathsf{hsk}, x, w)$ return $(\mathsf{pk}, \mathsf{sk})$
NIKE.SharedKey$(\mathcal{PP}, \mathsf{ID}_1, \mathsf{pk}_1, \mathsf{ID}_2, \mathsf{sk}_2)$ parse $\mathcal{PP} =: (\mathcal{PP}_{\mathrm{SMP}}, \mathcal{HSK}, \mathcal{H}, \alpha, F)$ parse $\mathsf{pk}_1 =: (\mathsf{hpk}_1, x_1)$ parse $\mathsf{sk}_2 =: (\mathsf{hsk}_2, x_2, w_2)$ $K_{12} := H_{\mathsf{hsk}_2}(x_1) \cdot F(x_2, w_2, \mathsf{hpk}_1)$ return K_{12}	

Fig. 5. Our NIKE scheme. Recall that $\mathcal{H} = \{H_{\mathsf{hsk}} \colon X \to \Pi \mid \mathsf{hsk} \in \mathcal{K}\}$ is a family of functions and $F \colon R \times \mathcal{HPK} \to \Pi$ a function (where $\mathcal{HPK}$ is the image of α).

Definition 9 (QANIZK Proof of knowledge). *Let PS' be a QANIZK for a subset membership problem SMP, where SMP.Setup returns tuples (X, L, R). Let Setup denote an algorithm that, on input $(1^\lambda, (X, L, R))$ runs $(\mathsf{crs}, \mathsf{trp}) \xleftarrow{\$} PS'.Setup(1^\lambda, (X, L, R))$ and outputs $(\mathsf{crs}, \mathsf{trp}, \mathsf{extr})$ with an additional trapdoor extr. Let Gen $:= PS'.Gen, Prove := PS'.Prove, Ver := PS'.Ver, Sim := PS'.Sim. Let further Extract be an algorithm that on input $(\mathsf{crs}, \mathsf{extr}, x, \Pi)$ returns a witness w. We say PS = (Setup, Gen, Prove, Ver, Sim, Extract) is a QANIZK Proof of Knowledge for SMP (QANIZKPoK), if for all PPT adversaries $\mathcal{A}$ the advantage*

$$\mathrm{Adv}^{\mathsf{extr}}_{\mathcal{A}, PS}(\lambda) := \Pr[\mathrm{Exp}^{\mathsf{extr}}_{\mathcal{A}, PS}(\lambda) \Rightarrow 1]$$

is negligible in λ, where $\mathrm{Exp}^{\mathsf{extr}}_{\mathcal{A}, PS}(\lambda)$ is as defined in Fig. 4.

3   Our Construction

We now present a NIKE scheme that is secure in the HKR setting. Our reduction loses a factor of $q_{\mathsf{regH}}/2$, where q_{regH} is the number of honest users. Our scheme uses a hash proof system and its security relies on the hardness of the underlying subset membership problem as well as the smoothness of the HPS. It is presented in Fig. 3.

Let us first elaborate on why our NIKE scheme does not fall under the impossibility result of Bader et al. [4]. To enforce that the output of a successful NIKE attacker can always be used to solve the challenge given to the reduction, Bader et al. require that the NIKE scheme allows only public keys whose corresponding secret keys are uniquely determined. This way, the shared key between two public keys is uniquely determined and will be useful to solve the challenge. Moreover, the uniqueness condition has to be *efficiently checkable given only a public key*. This essentially prevents a reduction from switching public keys to "invalid" public keys that violate the uniqueness condition. Formally, Bader et al. require an efficient algorithm PKCheck for testing uniqueness.

Our scheme does not provide such an algorithm, since essentially deciding uniqueness amounts to deciding a subset membership problem that we assume to be hard. This way, our reduction will have a way to indistinguishably switch one of the public keys to "invalid" by drawing it from outside the subgroup. Note that for such an invalid public key there exist no secret key, since secret keys contain a witness for the public key belonging to the subgroup. While this non-existence of a secret key helps us in arguing security, it also introduces an inherent loss in our reduction; namely, our reduction has to abort whenever the adversary wants to see the secret key corresponding to the invalid key, which occurs with probability $2/q_{\mathsf{regH}}$ and thus results in a loss of $q_{\mathsf{regH}}/2$. We now provide a proof of security that meets exactly this loss.

Theorem 1. *Let SMP be a subset membership problem, and let HPS be a hash proof system for SMP, such that for all $\mathcal{PP} := (\mathcal{PP}_{\mathsf{SMP}}, \mathcal{HSK}, \mathcal{H}, \alpha, F)$ in the range of HPS.Setup the image Π of F and all $H_{\mathsf{hsk}} \in \mathcal{H}$ is a commutative multiplicative group. If the subset membership assumption holds for SMP and if HPS is ε-smooth with ε negligible in λ, then the NIKE scheme NIKE described in Fig. 5 is a perfectly correct, HKR-CKS-heavy secure NIKE. Further, the reduction to SMP loses a factor of $q_{\mathsf{regH}}/2$, where q_{regH} is the number of queries to $\mathcal{O}_{\mathsf{regH}}$ that $\mathcal{A}$ makes. More formally, if $\mathcal{A}$ is an adversary with running time $t_{\mathcal{A}}$ against the scheme in the HKR-CKS-heavy model, there exists an adversary $\mathcal{B}$ with running time $t_{\mathcal{B}} \approx t_{\mathcal{A}}$ breaking the subset membership problem SMP such that*

$$\mathrm{Adv}_{\mathcal{A},NIKE}^{\mathsf{hkr-cks-heavy}}(\lambda) \;\leq\; q_{\mathsf{regH}}/2 \cdot (\mathrm{Adv}_{\mathcal{B},SMP}^{\mathsf{smp}}(\lambda) + \varepsilon)$$

Proof. PERFECT CORRECTNESS. Let the public parameters be $\mathcal{PP} := (\mathcal{PP}_{\mathsf{SMP}}, \mathcal{HSK}, \mathcal{H}, \alpha, F) \overset{\$}{\leftarrow} NIKE.\mathsf{Setup}(1^{\lambda})$ and $(\mathsf{pk}_1, \mathsf{sk}_1) \leftarrow NIKE.\mathsf{KeyGen}(\mathcal{PP}, \mathsf{ID}_1)$, $(\mathsf{pk}_2, \mathsf{sk}_2) \leftarrow NIKE.\mathsf{KeyGen}(\mathcal{PP}, \mathsf{ID}_2)$. Let further $\mathsf{pk}_1 =: (\mathsf{hpk}_1, x_1), \mathsf{pk}_2 =: (\mathsf{hpk}_2, x_2)$ and $\mathsf{sk}_1 =: (\mathsf{hsk}_1, x_1, w_1), \mathsf{sk}_2 =: (\mathsf{hsk}_2, x_2, w_2)$. As HPS is a hash proof system and as $x_1, x_2 \in L$, $\mathsf{hpk}_1 = \alpha(\mathsf{hsk}_1)), \mathsf{hpk}_2 = \alpha(\mathsf{hsk}_2))$ we have

$$H_{\mathsf{hsk}_2}(x_1) = F(x_1, w_1, \mathsf{hpk}_2) \text{ and } H_{\mathsf{hsk}_1}(x_2) = F(x_2, w_2, \mathsf{hpk}_1).$$

This yields

$$K_{12} = H_{\mathsf{hsk}_2}(x_1) \cdot F(x_2, w_2, \mathsf{hpk}_1) = H_{\mathsf{hsk}_1}(x_2) \cdot F(x_1, w_1, \mathsf{hpk}_2) = K_{21}$$

as required.

CKS-HEAVY SECURITY. We prove that the NIKE meets CKS-heavy security with honest key registration in a number of hybrid games. We provide an overview of the games in Fig. 6. By $\Pr[\mathbf{G}_i]$ we denote the probability that $\mathcal{A}$ wins game $\mathbf{G}_i$.

Game $\mathbf{G}_0$: **The real experiment.** Game $\mathbf{G}_0$ is the HKR-CKS-heavy experiment as presented in Fig. 2, where $\mathcal{A}$ plays with a challenger $\mathcal{C}$. We have thus

$$\mathrm{Adv}_{\mathcal{A},NIKE}^{\mathsf{hkr-cks-heavy}}(\lambda) = |\Pr[\mathbf{G}_0] - 1/2|.$$

Game	$\mathcal{O}_{\mathsf{regH}}$ if $i = i^*$	$\mathcal{O}_{\mathsf{extr}}(\mathsf{ID}_{i^*})$	$\mathcal{O}_{\mathsf{revH}}(\{\mathsf{ID}, \mathsf{ID}_{i^*}\})$	$\mathcal{O}_{\mathsf{test}}(\{\mathsf{ID}, \mathsf{ID}_{i^*}\})$	Explanation
$\mathbf{G}_0$	$(x, w) \xleftarrow{\$} R$	sk_{i^*}	$\mathsf{sk}_{i^*}/\mathsf{sk}$	$\mathsf{sk}_{i^*}/\mathsf{sk}$	$= \mathrm{Exp}_{\mathcal{A},\mathtt{NIKE}}^{\mathsf{hkr-cks-heavy}}$
$\mathbf{G}_1$	$(x, w) \xleftarrow{\$} R$	sk_{i^*}	sk	sk	perfect correctness
$\mathbf{G}_2$	$(x, w) \xleftarrow{\$} R$	abort	sk	sk	$q_{\mathsf{regH}}/2$ loss
$\mathbf{G}_3$	$x \xleftarrow{\$} X \setminus L$	abort	sk	sk	SMP assumption
$\mathbf{G}_4$	$x \xleftarrow{\$} X \setminus L$	abort	sk	$K_0 \leftarrow \mathcal{K}$	smoothness HPS

Fig. 6. Games $\mathbf{G}_0$ to $\mathbf{G}_4$ we employ to prove the NIKE presented in Fig. 3 HKR-CKS-heavy secure. From game $\mathbf{G}_1$ on the index $i^* \xleftarrow{\$} q_{\mathsf{regH}}$ is chosen ahead of time. By ID_{i^*} we denote the i^*-th registered honest user. The oracle $\mathcal{O}_{\mathsf{test}}$ may only be queried once. In Column 4 and 5, we give the secret key employed to compute NIKE.SharedKey. By denoting the input as a set $\{\cdot\}$ we want to indicate that we consider both inputs $\mathsf{pk}, \mathsf{pk}_{i^*}$ and $\mathsf{pk}_{i^*}, \mathsf{pk}$. In game $\mathbf{G}_0$ there is thus two possibility secret keys to be employed, depending on the order of the input.

Game $\mathbf{G}_1$: Guess the challenge. Recall that by q_{regH} we denote the number of $\mathcal{O}_{\mathsf{regH}}$ queries of $\mathcal{A}$. From game $\mathbf{G}_1$ on, an index $i^* \leftarrow q_{\mathsf{regH}}$ is chosen ahead of time. The final goal will be to switch the i^*-th registered honest user ID_{i^*} to invalid and hope it is part of the test query. As a first step, from game $\mathbf{G}_1$ on we will make sk_{i^*} redundant for $\mathcal{O}_{\mathsf{revH}}$ and $\mathcal{O}_{\mathsf{test}}$ queries. Namely, if $\mathcal{A}$ asks a query of this form with input $(\mathsf{ID}, \mathsf{ID}_{i^*})$ (for an arbitrary identity ID) we will compute the shared key employing sk, where $(\mathsf{ID}, \mathsf{pk}, \mathsf{sk}) \in Q_{\mathsf{regH}}$, instead of sk_{i^*}. By perfect correctness of NIKE we have

$$\Pr[\mathbf{G}_1] = \Pr[\mathbf{G}_0].$$

Game $\mathbf{G}_2$: Abort upon wrong guess. We change the winning condition of the game as follows. If ID_{i^*} is not included in the test query of $\mathcal{A}$, the experiment returns 1 with probability $1/2$ and aborts. Then it holds

$$\Pr[\mathbf{G}_2] = \Pr[\mathbf{G}_1] \cdot 2/q_{\mathsf{regH}} + 1/2 \cdot (1 - 2/q_{\mathsf{regH}})$$
$$= (\Pr[\mathbf{G}_1] - 1/2) \cdot 2/q_{\mathsf{regH}} + 1/2$$

and thus

$$\Pr[\mathbf{G}_1] - 1/2 = q_{\mathsf{regH}}/2 \cdot (\Pr[\mathbf{G}_2] - 1/2).$$

Game $\mathbf{G}_3$: Remove the secret key. Upon receiving the i^*-th register honest user query, $\mathcal{C}$ deviates from the NIKE.KeyGen procedure as follows: instead of drawing $(x_{i^*}, w_{i^*}) \xleftarrow{\$} R$, $\mathcal{C}$ draws $x_{i^*} \xleftarrow{\$} X \setminus L$. Note that this way there is no w_{i^*} such that $R(x_{i^*}, w_{i^*}) = 1$ and thus $\mathcal{C}$ cannot compute a secret key sk_{i^*}. Instead, $\mathcal{C}$ adds $(\mathsf{ID}_{i^*}, \mathsf{pk}_{i^*}, \mathsf{sk}_{i^*}) := (\mathsf{ID}_{i^*}, (\mathsf{hpk}_{i^*}, x_{i^*}), (\mathsf{hsk}_{i^*}, \bot))$ to Q_{regH}. A distinguisher between both games can be turned directly into a SMP attacker $\mathcal{B}$ putting his challenge in the place of x_{i^*}. If the challenge was in L, Game $\mathbf{G}_2$ was simulated, else it was Game $\mathbf{G}_3$. Observe that it is crucial here that

$\mathcal{C}$ does not make use of w_{i^*} anymore due to the changes made in Game 1. This yields

$$|\Pr[\mathbf{G}_2] - \Pr[\mathbf{G}_3]| \leq \mathsf{Adv}^{\mathsf{smp}}_{\mathcal{B},\mathsf{SMP}}(\lambda).$$

Game $\mathbf{G}_4$: Randomize the test query. $\mathcal{C}$ changes the answer to the query $\mathcal{O}_{\mathsf{test}}(\mathsf{ID}_{i^*}, \mathsf{ID})^5$ by drawing $K_0 \stackrel{\$}{\leftarrow} \mathcal{K}$, where $\mathcal{K} = \Pi$ is the image of the hash functions of the HPS. To analyze the distinguishing advantage, note that in the former game it holds that $K_0 = \mathtt{NIKE.SharedKey}(\mathsf{ID}_{i^*}, \mathsf{pk}_{i^*}, \mathsf{ID}, \mathsf{sk}) = H_{\mathsf{hsk}}(x_{i^*}) \cdot F(x, w, \mathsf{hpk}_{i^*})$ with $(\mathsf{ID}, \mathsf{pk}, \mathsf{sk}) = (\mathsf{ID}, (\mathsf{hpk}, x), (\mathsf{hsk}, w)) \in Q_{\mathsf{regH}}$ and $(\mathsf{ID}_{i^*}, \mathsf{pk}_{i^*}, \mathsf{sk}_{i^*}) = (\mathsf{ID}_{i^*}, (\mathsf{hpk}_{i^*}, x_{i^*}), (\mathsf{hsk}_{i^*}, \perp)) \in Q_{\mathsf{regH}}$. The two distributions $(x_{i^*}, \mathsf{hpk}, H_{\mathsf{hsk}}(x_{i^*})), (x_{i^*}, \mathsf{hpk}, r \stackrel{\$}{\leftarrow} \Pi)$ are ε-close by the ε-smoothness of the HPS, and thus K_0 was already statistically close to the uniform distribution over Π in Game $\mathbf{G}_3$. We thus have

$$|\Pr[\mathbf{G}_3] - \Pr[\mathbf{G}_4]| \leq \varepsilon.$$

We now show that the advantage of $\mathcal{A}$ playing the CKS-heavy game is negligible. We repeatedly use a folklore technique - add zero, then apply the triangle inequality - to go through all the above games until Game $\mathbf{G}_4$, for which the winning probability of $\mathcal{A}$ is $1/2$ since its view does not depend on the challenge bit.

$$
\begin{aligned}
\mathsf{Adv}^{\mathsf{hkr-cks-heavy}}_{\mathcal{A},\mathtt{NIKE}}(\lambda) &= |\Pr[\mathbf{G}_0] - 1/2| = |\Pr[\mathbf{G}_1] - 1/2| \\
&= q_{\mathsf{regH}}/2 \cdot |\Pr[\mathbf{G}_2] - \Pr[\mathbf{G}_3] + \Pr[\mathbf{G}_3] - 1/2| \\
&\leq q_{\mathsf{regH}}/2 \cdot |\Pr[\mathbf{G}_3] - \Pr[\mathbf{G}_4] + \Pr[\mathbf{G}_4] - 1/2| + q_{\mathsf{regH}}/2 \cdot \mathsf{Adv}^{\mathsf{smp}}_{\mathcal{B},\mathsf{SMP}}(\lambda) \\
&\leq q_{\mathsf{regH}}/2 \cdot |\Pr[\mathbf{G}_4] - 1/2| + q_{\mathsf{regH}}/2 \cdot (\mathsf{Adv}^{\mathsf{smp}}_{\mathcal{B},\mathsf{SMP}}(\lambda) + \varepsilon) \\
&= q_{\mathsf{regH}}/2 \cdot (\mathsf{Adv}^{\mathsf{smp}}_{\mathcal{B},\mathsf{SMP}}(\lambda) + \varepsilon)
\end{aligned}
$$

Remark 1. A variant of our NIKE can be obtained if there is a total ordering $<$ on all identities. Then, the shared key of $\mathsf{ID}_1, \mathsf{ID}_2$ can be computed as the hash of the statement provided by the *smaller* identity. More formally, we modify $\mathtt{NIKE.SharedKey}$ as follows:

$$
\begin{aligned}
\mathtt{NIKE.SharedKey}(\mathsf{ID}_1, \mathsf{pk}_1, \mathsf{ID}_2, \mathsf{sk}_2) &:= H_{hsk_2}(x_1) \\
&= F(x_1, w_1, hpk_2) =: \mathtt{NIKE.SharedKey}(\mathsf{ID}_2, \mathsf{pk}_2, \mathsf{ID}_1, \mathsf{sk}_1),
\end{aligned}
$$

where $\mathsf{ID}_1 < \mathsf{ID}_2$. The only change in the proof of security is that in game $\mathbf{G}_2$ the challenger aborts if the guessed i^* is not the *smallest* identity contained in the test query. This yields a reduction loss of q_{regH}.

---

[5] Note that, starting with Game $\mathbf{G}_2$, i^* is always one of the inputs to $\mathcal{O}_{\mathsf{test}}$.

$\text{NIKE}_{\text{dkr}}.\text{Setup}(1^\lambda)$

  $\mathcal{PP} \leftarrow \text{NIKE.Setup}(1^\lambda)$
  $\mathcal{PP}_{\text{PS}} \leftarrow \text{PS.Setup}(1^\lambda, (X_{\text{NIKE}}, L_{\text{NIKE}}, R_{\text{NIKE}}))$
  parse $\mathcal{PP}_{\text{PS}} := (\text{crs}, \text{trp}, \text{extr})$
  $\mathcal{PP}_{\text{dkr}} := (\mathcal{PP}, \text{crs})$
  return $\mathcal{PP}_{\text{dkr}}$

$\text{NIKE}_{\text{dkr}}.\text{SharedKey}(\mathcal{PP}_{\text{dkr}}, \text{ID}_1, \text{pk}_1, \text{ID}_2, \text{sk}_2)$

  parse $\mathcal{PP}_{\text{dkr}} =: (\mathcal{PP}, \text{crs})$
  parse $\text{pk}_1 =: (\text{pk}_1', \Pi_1')$
  if $\text{PS.Ver}(\text{crs}, \text{ID}_1, \text{pk}_1', \Pi_1') = 1$
    return $\text{NIKE.SharedKey}(\text{ID}_1, \text{pk}_1', \text{ID}_2, \text{sk}_2)$
  else return $\perp$

$\text{NIKE}_{\text{dkr}}.\text{KeyGen}(\mathcal{PP}_{\text{dkr}}, \text{ID})$

  parse $\mathcal{PP}_{\text{dkr}} =: (\mathcal{PP}, \text{crs})$
  $r \leftarrow \mathcal{R}_{\text{rand}}$
  $(\text{pk}, \text{sk}) \leftarrow \text{NIKE.KeyGen}(\mathcal{PP}, \text{ID}; r)$
  $\Pi \leftarrow \text{PS.Prove}(\text{crs}, \text{ID}, \text{pk}, \text{sk}, r)$
  return $((\text{pk}, \Pi), \text{sk})$

Fig. 7. A generic transformation from HKR-CKS-heavy security to DKR-CKS-heavy security. $(X_{\text{NIKE}}, L_{\text{NIKE}}, R_{\text{NIKE}})$ is defined as in Remark 2.

4 Security Against Dishonest Key Generation

In this section we want to show how to achieve CKS-heavy security for our scheme allowing dishonest key registrations. That is the adversary is allowed to dishonestly register keys and ask for shared keys where one of the public keys is registered dishonestly.

Due to space limitations we only provide the generic transformation from a HKR-CKS-heavy secure NIKE to a DKR-CKS-heavy secure NIKE. For the proof of security and for a more efficient transformation of an instantiation of our NIKE from Sect. 3 we refer to the full version [25].

Remark 2. Every NIKE induces a SMP as follows. Let NIKE be a NIKE with public key space $\mathcal{PK}$ and secret key space $\mathcal{SK}$ and randomness space $\mathcal{R}_{\text{rand}}$. Then we define an SMP SMP_{NIKE} as follows. On input 1^λ, $\text{SMP}_{\text{NIKE}}.\text{Setup}$ generates $\mathcal{PP} \leftarrow \text{NIKE.Setup}(1^\lambda)$ and sets

$$X_{\text{NIKE}} := \mathcal{IDS} \times \mathcal{PK},$$
$$L_{\text{NIKE}} := \{(\text{ID}, \text{pk}) \in X \mid \exists \text{sk}, r : (\text{pk}, \text{sk}) = \text{NIKE.KeyGen}(\mathcal{PP}, \text{ID}; r)\} \text{ and}$$
$$R_{\text{NIKE}} := \{(\text{ID}, \text{pk}, \text{sk}, r) \mid (\text{pk}, \text{sk}) = \text{NIKE.KeyGen}(\mathcal{PP}, \text{ID}; r)\}.$$

Theorem 2. *If NIKE is a perfectly correct, HKR-CKS-heavy secure NIKE and PS is an QANIZKPoK for the SMP SMP_{NIKE}, then the NIKE_{dkr} presented in Fig. 7 with algorithms $\text{NIKE}_{\text{dkr}}.\text{Setup}, \text{NIKE}_{\text{dkr}}.\text{KeyGen}, \text{NIKE}_{\text{dkr}}.\text{SharedKey}$ is perfectly correct and secure in the DKR-CKS-heavy model. More precisely, if $\mathcal{A}$ is an adversary on NIKE_{dkr} with running time $t_{\mathcal{A}}$, there exists adversaries $\mathcal{B}, \mathcal{B}_1, \mathcal{B}_2$ with running times $t_{\mathcal{B}} \approx t_{\mathcal{B}_1} \approx t_{\mathcal{B}_2} \approx t_{\mathcal{A}}$ such that*

$$\text{Adv}_{\mathcal{A}, \text{NIKE}_{\text{dkr}}}^{\text{dkr}-\text{cks}-\text{heavy}}(\lambda) \leq \text{Adv}_{\mathcal{B}, PS}^{\text{zk}}(\lambda) + \text{Adv}_{\mathcal{B}_1, PS}^{\text{extr}}(\lambda) + \text{Adv}_{\mathcal{B}_2, \text{NIKE}}^{\text{hkr}-\text{cks}-\text{heavy}}(\lambda).$$

$$
\begin{array}{l}
\text{Exp}^{\text{uf}-\text{cks}-\text{heavy}}_{\mathcal{A}=(\mathcal{A}_1,\mathcal{A}_2),n,\text{NIKE}}(\lambda): \\[4pt]
\hline
\mathcal{PP} \xleftarrow{\$} \text{NIKE.Setup}(1^\lambda) \\
\text{ID}_1, ..., \text{ID}_n \xleftarrow{\$} \mathcal{IDS} \text{ (all disjoint)} \\
(\text{pk}_i, \text{sk}_i) \xleftarrow{\$} \text{NIKE.KeyGen}(\mathcal{PP}, \text{ID}_i), i = 1, ..., n \\
(st, \{i^\star, j^\star\}) \leftarrow \mathcal{A}_1(\mathcal{PP}, \text{ID}_1, \text{pk}_1, ..., \text{ID}_n, \text{pk}_n) \\
K^\star \leftarrow \mathcal{A}_2(st, (\text{sk}_i)_{i\in[n]\setminus\{i^\star,j^\star\}}) \\
\text{if } K^\star = \text{NIKE.SharedKey}(\text{ID}_{i^\star}, \text{pk}_{i^\star}, \text{ID}_{j^\star}, \text{sk}_{j^\star}) \\
\quad \text{then output } 1 \\
\text{else output } 0
\end{array}
$$

Fig. 8. Experiment for UF-CKS-$heavy_n$ security of a NIKE scheme NIKE with shared key space $\mathcal{K}$, for any $n \in \mathbb{N}$. The set $C := \{i^\star, j^\star\}$ contains the indices of the two public keys $\mathcal{A}$ wishes to be challenged upon. The set $[n] \setminus C$ contains all indices of the $n - 2$ public keys for which $\mathcal{A}$ learns a secret key from the experiment.

5   Optimality of Our Construction

Our NIKE scheme in Sect. 3 does not meet the lower bound regarding tightness proven in [4]. We can circumvent their result since our scheme does not offer a public and efficient algorithm for checking validity of public keys (called PKCheck in [4]): the reduction introduces invalid public keys where the statement is not from the language. It follows from the hardness of the subset membership problem that this is not detectable given *just the public key*.

This immediately raises the question whether, in this new setting without efficient and public PKCheck, we can still obtain a lower bound for the tightness of HKR-CKS-$heavy$-secure NIKE schemes. We answer this question in the affirmative and prove a new lower bound that meets the loss of our reduction in Sect. 3. To present our result, we first give some definitions.

Since HKR-CKS-$heavy$ security provides several oracles to the adversary which can be queried in an arbitrary order, a reduction to HKR-CKS-$heavy$-security cannot be formalized as an algorithm in a short and easy way. As done in previous impossibility results before, we thus prove our result w.r.t a weaker security notion that is easier to present. Afterwards, we show that our result carries over to HKR-CKS-$heavy$-security. Our weaker notion is called UF-CKS-$heavy_n$[6]. The security experiment is depicted in Fig. 8. Observe that the experiment provides the adversary with all but two secret keys, and thus implicitly with all but one shared key. The adversary chooses which keys he wants to see after obtaining all public keys in the system. The notion is further weakened by letting the number of users in the system be a fixed $n \in \mathbb{N}$ instead of letting the adversary determine it on-the-fly (i.e., via $\mathcal{O}_{\text{regH}}$ queries).

---

[6] We work with an even weaker notion that [4]. The main difference is that our adversary only has a secret key oracle (from which it can compute shared keys itself), while the adversary in [4] is provided with a shared key oracle.

The next lemma allows us to prove a lower bound w.r.t $UF\text{-}CKS\text{-}heavy_n$ instead of $HKR\text{-}CKS\text{-}heavy$. It will become crucial that the reduction is tight.

Lemma 1 ($HKR\text{-}CKS\text{-}heavy \Rightarrow UF\text{-}CKS\text{-}heavy_n$). *For every adversary $\mathcal{A}$ attacking $UF\text{-}CKS\text{-}heavy_n$ in running time $t_{\mathcal{A}}$ with success probability $\varepsilon_{\mathcal{A}}$, there exists an adversary $\mathcal{B}$ attacking $CKS\text{-}heavy$ in running time $t_{\mathcal{B}} \approx t_{\mathcal{A}}$ and success probability $\varepsilon_{\mathcal{B}} = \varepsilon_{\mathcal{A}}$.*

Proof. Let $\mathcal{A} = (\mathcal{A}_1, \mathcal{A}_2)$ be a $UF\text{-}CKS\text{-}heavy_n$ adversary. We show how to construct a $HKR\text{-}CKS\text{-}heavy$ adversary $\mathcal{B}$.

On input $\mathcal{PP}$ by the challenger, the adversary $\mathcal{B}$ first generates random, disjoint identities $\mathsf{ID}_1, ..., \mathsf{ID}_n$ and calls the oracle $\mathcal{O}_{\mathsf{regH}}(\mathsf{ID}_i)$ for all $i \in [n]$. $\mathcal{B}$ thus obtains $\mathsf{pk}_1..., \mathsf{pk}_n$. Now, $\mathcal{B}$ runs $\mathcal{A}_1(\mathcal{PP}, \mathsf{pk}_1, ..., \mathsf{pk}_n)$ and obtains a state $st_{\mathcal{A}}$ and a set $C := \{i^\star, j^\star\}$. Now, for every $i \in [n] \setminus C$, $\mathcal{B}_1$ queries its oracle $\mathcal{O}_{\mathsf{extr}}(\mathsf{ID}_i)$ which returns a secret key sk_i. Next, $\mathcal{B}_1$ runs $\mathcal{A}_2(st_{\mathcal{A}}, (\mathsf{sk}_i)_{i \in [n] \setminus C})$ and obtains a key $K^\star$. The adversary $\mathcal{B}$ finally queries its test oracle on $(\mathsf{ID}_{i^\star}, \mathsf{ID}_{j^\star})$ which returns a key K. It outputs 0 if $K^\star = K$ and 1 otherwise. As we assume the shared key to be uniquely determined and as further $\mathcal{B}$ only queries $\mathcal{O}_{\mathsf{extr}}$ on identities ID_i with $i \notin C$ we obtain $\varepsilon_{\mathcal{B}} = \varepsilon_{\mathcal{A}}$.

We recall the definition of a non-interactive complexity assumption, taken verbatim from [4], Definitions 4 and 5.

Definition 10 (Non-interactive complexity assumption). *A non-interactive complexity assumption (NICA) $N = (T, V, U)$ consists of three turing machines. The instance generation machine $(c, w) \xleftarrow{\$} T(1^\lambda)$ takes the security parameter as input, and outputs a problem instance c and a witness w. U is a PPT machine, which takes as input c and outputs a candidate solution s. The verification TM V takes as input (c, w) and a candidate solution s. If $V(c, w, s) = 1$, then we say that s is a correct solution to the challenge c.*

Definition 11. *We say that $\mathcal{B}$ (t, ε)-breaks a NICA $N = (T, U, V)$ if $\mathcal{B}$ runs in time $t(\lambda)$ and it holds that*

$$|\Pr[\mathrm{Exp}_{\mathcal{B},N}^{\mathsf{nica}}(1^\lambda) \Rightarrow 1] - \Pr[\mathrm{Exp}_{U,N}^{\mathsf{nica}}(1^\lambda) \Rightarrow 1]| \geq \varepsilon(\lambda),$$

where $\mathrm{Exp}_{\mathcal{B},N}^{\mathsf{nica}}$ is the experiment defined in Fig. 9 and the probability is taken over the random coins consumed by T and the uniformly random choices in the experiment.

Now we are ready to formalize what we mean by a reduction Λ from a NICA to the $UF\text{-}CKS\text{-}heavy_n$ security of NIKE. We closely follow the structure of [4] and similar to [4,12,29,32,35] only consider a certain class of reductions.

Definition 12 (Simple reduction). *We call a TM Λ a $(t_\Lambda, n, \varepsilon_\Lambda, \varepsilon_{\mathcal{A}})$-reduction from breaking a NICA $N = (T, U, V)$ to breaking the $UF\text{-}CKS\text{-}heavy_n$ security of NIKE, if Λ turns an adversary $\mathcal{A} = (\mathcal{A}_1, \mathcal{A}_2)$ that runs in time $t_{\mathcal{A}}$ and has advantage $\varepsilon_{\mathcal{A}}$ to break $\mathrm{Exp}_{\mathcal{A},n,NIKE}^{\mathsf{uf-cks-heavy}}$ (as provided in Fig. 8) into a TM $\mathcal{B}$ that runs in time*

$t_\Lambda + t_{\mathcal{A}}$ and has advantage ε_Λ to break N (see Definition 11). We call Λ simple, if Λ has only black-box access to $\mathcal{A}$ and executes $\mathcal{A}$ only once (and in particular without rewinding).

$$
\begin{array}{|l|}
\hline
\mathrm{Exp}^{\mathrm{nica}}_{\mathcal{B},N=(T,U,V)}(\lambda): \\
\hline
(c,w) \xleftarrow{\$} T(1^\lambda) \\
s \leftarrow \mathcal{B}(c) \\
\mathtt{return}\ V(c,w,s) \\
\hline
\end{array}
$$

Fig. 9. Security experiment for a non-interactive complexity assumption (NICA).

In the following we will only consider *simple* reductions. Note that even though this seems to restrict the class of reductions heavily, actually most reductions (including reductions performing hybrid steps) are simple. The security proofs of all existing NIKE schemes [10,14,17] we are aware of[7] are simple reductions.

Since our notion of *UF - CKS - heavy$_n$*-security requires only two rounds of interaction between the adversary and the challenger, we are able to give a very compact formal description of the algorithm $\Lambda := (\Lambda_1, \Lambda_2, \Lambda_3)$ as follows:

- Λ_1 is a probabilistic algorithm that gets as input a (set of) NICA challenge(s) c and outputs public parameters $\mathcal{PP}$, a set of identities and public keys $\mathsf{ID}_1, \mathsf{pk}_1, ..., \mathsf{ID}_n, \mathsf{pk}_n$ and a state st_1.
- Λ_2 is a deterministic algorithmn that receives as input $C \subseteq [n]$ with $|C| = 2$ (else aborts) and st_1 and outputs $(st_2, (sk_i)_{i \in [n] \setminus C})$.
- Λ_3 is a deterministic algorithm that receives as input st_2 and $\tilde{K}$ and outputs an s.

5.1   A Weaker Validity Check

We expand the results from [4] by relaxing the assumptions on the publicly checkable validity of public keys. Recall that [4] requires a method $\mathtt{PKCheck}$ allowing to efficiently verify whether a public key pk was generated by $\mathtt{NIKE.KeyGen}(\mathcal{PP}, \mathsf{ID})$, e.g., whether there exists a secret key sk and random coins r such that $(\mathsf{pk}, \mathsf{sk}) \leftarrow \mathtt{NIKE.KeyGen}(\mathcal{PP}, \mathsf{ID}; r)$. We will only require the following notion of weak checkability of public keys. In particular, we only require it to be checkable whether a public key is valid *given a corresponding secret key*.

Definition 13. *Let NIKE be a NIKE with secret key space $\mathcal{SK}$, identity space $\mathcal{IDS}$ and public key space $\mathcal{PK}$. We say that NIKE satisfies* weak checkability of *public keys, if there exists a efficiently computable function*

$$
\mathtt{wPKCheck} \colon \mathcal{IDS} \times \mathcal{PK} \times \mathcal{SK} \to \{0,1\}
$$

---

[7] Remember that we restrict to 2-party key exchange protocols in the setting where a PKI is available.

with the following properties:

For all $(\mathsf{pk}, \mathsf{sk}) \leftarrow NIKE.KeyGen(\mathcal{PP}, \mathsf{ID})$ *we have* $wPKCheck(\mathsf{ID}, \mathsf{pk}, \mathsf{sk}) = 1$. (1)

For all $(\mathsf{ID}_1, \mathsf{pk}_1, \mathsf{sk}_1), (\mathsf{ID}_1, \mathsf{pk}_1, \mathsf{sk}_1'), (\mathsf{ID}_2, \mathsf{pk}_2, \mathsf{sk}_2)$ *with* $wPKCheck(\mathsf{ID}_1, \mathsf{pk}_1, \mathsf{sk}_1)$
$= wPKCheck(\mathsf{ID}_1, \mathsf{pk}_1, \mathsf{sk}_1') = wPKCheck(\mathsf{ID}_2, \mathsf{pk}_2, \mathsf{sk}_2) = 1$ *it holds*
$$NIKE.SharedKey(\mathsf{ID}_2, \mathsf{pk}_2, \mathsf{ID}_1, \mathsf{sk}_1) = NIKE.SharedKey(\mathsf{ID}_2, \mathsf{pk}_2, \mathsf{ID}_1, \mathsf{sk}_1').$$
(2)

We call a secret key sk *valid for* $(\mathsf{ID}, \mathsf{pk})$ *if* $wPKCheck(\mathsf{ID}, \mathsf{pk}, \mathsf{sk}) = 1$. *We further define the* language of valid public keys

$$L^{\mathrm{valid}} := \{(\mathsf{ID}, \mathsf{pk}) \mid \exists \mathsf{sk} \colon wPKCheck(\mathsf{ID}, \mathsf{pk}, \mathsf{sk}) = 1\}.$$

Property 2 now implies that any two tuples $(\mathsf{ID}_1, \mathsf{pk}_1), (\mathsf{ID}_2, \mathsf{pk}_2) \in L^{\mathrm{valid}}$ *lead to a unique shared key independently of which valid secret key is employed to compute the shared key.*

Remark 3. Note that a NIKE for which it can be efficiently verified whether a pair $(\mathsf{pk}, \mathsf{sk})$ lies in the image of $NIKE.KeyGen(\mathcal{PP}, \mathsf{ID})$ in particular satisfies weak checkability of public keys with

$$\mathsf{wPKCheck}(\mathsf{ID}, \mathsf{pk}, \mathsf{sk}) = \begin{cases} 1 & \text{if } \exists r : (\mathsf{pk}, \mathsf{sk}) = \mathtt{NIKE.KeyGen}(\mathcal{PP}, \mathsf{ID}; r) \\ 0 & \text{else} \end{cases}.$$

5.2 A Lower Bound on Tightness

In this section we show that if a NIKE NIKE satisfies weak checkable uniqueness, then any simple reduction from a NICA to the UF-CKS-$heavy_n$-security of NIKE it has to inherently lose a factor of $n/2$ in reduction, where n is the number of public keys. Further, we show that the NIKE NIKE presented in Fig. 5 satisfies weak checkability of public keys. Note that by definition any NIKE supporting weak checkability of public keys is *perfectly* correct, that is for all $(\mathsf{ID}_i, \mathsf{pk}_i, \mathsf{sk}_i) \xleftarrow{\$}$ $\mathtt{NIKE.KeyGen}(\mathcal{PP}, \mathsf{ID}_i), i \in \{1, 2\}$, we have

$$\mathtt{NIKE.SharedKey}(\mathsf{ID}_1, \mathsf{pk}_1, \mathsf{ID}_2, \mathsf{sk}_2) = \mathtt{NIKE.SharedKey}(\mathsf{ID}_2, \mathsf{pk}_2, \mathsf{ID}_1, \mathsf{sk}_1).$$

Theorem 3. *Let* $N = (T, U, V)$ *be a non-interactive complexity assumption and* $n \in \mathrm{poly}(\lambda)$. *Let* NIKE *be a* UF-CKS-$heavy_n$ *secure NIKE with shared key space* $\mathcal{K}$, *public key space* $\mathcal{PK}$ *and secret key space* $\mathcal{SK}$ *which satisfies weak checkability of public keys via algorithm* wPKCheck. *Let further evaluating* wPKCheck *require time* t_{wPKCheck}. *Then any reduction* $\Lambda = (\Lambda_1, \Lambda_2, \Lambda_3)$ *from* N *to* NIKE *has to lose a factor* $n/2$ *assuming* N *is hard. More formally, for any simple* $(t_\Lambda, n, \varepsilon_\Lambda, 1)$-*reduction from breaking the assumption* N *to breaking the* UF-CKS-$heavy_n$-*security of* NIKE, *there exists an adversary* $\mathcal{B}$ *breaking* N *in running time*

$$t_{\mathcal{B}} \le \frac{n(n-1)}{2}t_\Lambda + \frac{n(n-1)(n-2)}{2}t_{\mathrm{wPKCheck}}$$

with success probability

$$\varepsilon_\mathcal{B} \geq \varepsilon_\Lambda - \frac{2}{n}.$$

Remark 4. We have $\varepsilon_\mathcal{A} = 1$ and $\varepsilon_\mathcal{B} = \eta(\lambda)$ for a negligible function η (as N is assumed to be hard). We can thus transform the last equation into $\varepsilon_\Lambda \leq \frac{2}{n}\varepsilon_\mathcal{A} + \eta(\lambda)$. This implies the claimed reduction loss of $n/2$.

Proof. We follow the proof structure of [4, 29, 35].

THE HYPOTHETICAL ADVERSARY. In the following we describe a hypothetical adversary $\mathcal{A} = (\mathcal{A}_1, \mathcal{A}_2)$. Note that this adversary might not be efficient, but in order to prove the reduction loss of $n/2$ we show how to simulate it efficiently.

$\mathcal{A}_1(\mathcal{PP}, \mathsf{ID}_1, \mathsf{pk}_1, \ldots, \mathsf{ID}_n, \mathsf{pk}_n)$ chooses $C := \{i^\star, j^\star\} \subseteq [n]$ with $|C| = 2$ uniformly at random. It outputs (st, C), where $st = (\mathcal{PP}, \mathsf{ID}_1, \mathsf{pk}_1, \ldots, \mathsf{ID}_n, \mathsf{pk}_n, C)$.

$\mathcal{A}_2(st, (\mathsf{sk}_i)_{i \in [n] \setminus C})$ checks whether $\mathsf{wPKCheck}(\mathsf{ID}_i, \mathsf{pk}_i, \mathsf{sk}_i) = 1$ for all $i \in [n] \setminus C$ and whether $(\mathsf{ID}_i, \mathsf{pk}_i) \in L^{\mathrm{valid}}$ for both $i \in C$. If this is the case $\mathcal{A}_2$ computes a secret key $\mathsf{sk}_{j^\star}$ s.t. $\mathsf{wPKCheck}(\mathsf{ID}_{j^\star}, \mathsf{pk}_{j^\star}, \mathsf{sk}_{j^\star}) = 1$ and outputs $K^\star = \mathsf{NIKE.SharedKey}(\mathsf{ID}_{i^\star}, \mathsf{pk}_{i^\star}, \mathsf{ID}_{j^\star}, \mathsf{sk}_{j^\star})$. Otherwise $\mathcal{A}_2$ outputs $\perp$.

As we have $(\mathsf{ID}, \mathsf{pk}, \mathsf{sk}) \in \mathcal{R}^{\mathrm{unique}}$ for all $(\mathsf{pk}, \mathsf{sk}) \leftarrow \mathsf{NIKE.KeyGen}(\mathcal{PP}, \mathsf{ID})$ and further $\mathsf{NIKE.SharedKey}$ returns a unique key for all tuples passing $\mathsf{wPKCheck}$, due to property 2 of Definition 13 the hypothetical adversary always wins in the $UF\text{-}CKS\text{-}heavy_n$ experiment.

We now describe an adversary $\mathcal{B}$ attempting to break $N = (T, U, V)$. The strategy is to run the reduction $\Lambda = (\Lambda_1, \Lambda_2, \Lambda_3)$ simulating $\mathcal{A}$ efficiently. Let c be the input of $\mathcal{B}$, where $(c, w) \leftarrow T(1^\lambda)$. Let $SK[], SK^\star[]$ be arrays of n entries initialized by $\emptyset$ and maintained throughout the reduction by $\mathcal{B}$.

1. The adversary $\mathcal{B}$ runs $(st_1, \mathcal{PP}, \mathsf{ID}_1, \mathsf{pk}_1, \ldots, \mathsf{ID}_n, \mathsf{pk}_n) \leftarrow \Lambda_1(c)$.
2. The adversary $\mathcal{B}$ samples $\{i^\star, j^\star\} = C^\star \subset [n]$ with $|C^\star| = 2$ uniformly at random.
3. For each $C \subset [n]$ with $|C| = 2$ the adversary $\mathcal{B}$ runs the reduction $\Lambda_2(st_1, C)$. Let $(st_2^C, (\mathsf{sk}_i^C)_{i \in [n] \setminus C})$ denote the output of the respective execution. Whenever $\mathsf{wPKCheck}(\mathsf{ID}_i, \mathsf{pk}_i, \mathsf{sk}_i^C) = 1$ for an $i \in [n] \setminus C$ the adversary sets $SK[i] = \mathsf{sk}_i^C$. If $C = C^\star$, $\mathcal{B}$ additionally sets $SK^\star[i] = \mathsf{sk}_i^{C^\star}$
4. If there exists an $i \in [n] \setminus C^\star$ with $SK^\star[i] = \emptyset$ (i.e. $\mathsf{wPKCheck}(\mathsf{ID}_i, \mathsf{pk}_i, \mathsf{sk}_i^{C^\star}) = 0$) or there exists a $i \in C^\star$ such that $SK[i] = \emptyset$ (i.e. $\mathsf{wPKCheck}(\mathsf{ID}_i, \mathsf{pk}_i, \mathsf{sk}_i^C) = 0$ for all $C \subseteq [n]$ with $|C| = 2$) then $\mathcal{B}$ sets $K^\star = \perp$. Otherwise $\mathcal{B}$ computes $K^\star = \mathsf{NIKE.SharedKey}(\mathsf{ID}_{i^\star}, \mathsf{pk}_{i^\star}, \mathsf{ID}_{j^\star}, SK[j^\star])$.
5. Finally, the adversary $\mathcal{B}$ outputs $s \xleftarrow{\$} \Lambda_3(st_2^{C^\star}, C^\star, K^\star)$.

EFFICIENCY OF $\mathcal{B}$. In the third step Λ_2 has to be executed $\binom{n}{2} = \frac{n(n-1)}{2}$ times. Each time the validity check has to be performed $n - 2$ times. For the running time of $\mathcal{B}$ it thus holds

$$t_\mathcal{B} \leq \frac{n(n-1)}{2} t_\Lambda + \frac{n(n-1)(n-2)}{2} t_{\mathsf{wPKCheck}}.$$

SUCCESS PROBABILITY OF $\mathcal{B}$. Let $C^* = \{i^*, j^*\}$ as before. Consider the following two events:

$$\mathsf{check\text{-}fails} : \quad \exists i \in [n] \setminus C^* \text{ such that } SK^*[i] = \emptyset$$
$$\mathsf{pk\text{-}valid} : \quad \forall i \in C^* \text{ it holds that } SK[i] \neq \emptyset$$

We first want to show that in the case of $\mathsf{check\text{-}fails} \vee \mathsf{pk\text{-}valid}$, $\mathcal{B}$ simulates the hypothetical adversary $\mathcal{A}$ perfectly. If $\mathsf{check\text{-}fails}$ occurs, then $\mathcal{B}$ returns $\perp$. The hypothetical adversary would have returned $\perp$ as well because in this case it holds $\mathsf{wPKCheck}(\mathsf{ID}_i, \mathsf{pk}_i, \mathsf{sk}_i^{C^*}) = 0$ for an $i \in [n] \setminus C^*$. If $\mathsf{pk\text{-}valid}$ occurs, we have $(\mathsf{ID}_i, \mathsf{pk}_i) \in L^{\mathrm{valid}}$ for all $i \in [n]$ (as in this case for each $i \in [n]$ there exists a set $C \subset [n]$ such that the reduction Λ_2 provided an sk_i^C with $\mathsf{wPKCheck}(\mathsf{ID}_i, \mathsf{pk}_i, \mathsf{sk}_i^C) = 1$ at some point). In this case the shared key K^* is unique by property 1 in Definition 13 and can be computed by $\mathcal{B}$ with the secret key $\mathcal{SK}[j^*]$.

We summarize all other possible cases in the event

$$\mathsf{bad} = \neg\mathsf{check\text{-}fails} \wedge \neg\mathsf{pk\text{-}valid},$$

which is well-defined, as Λ_2 is deterministic.

We now bound the probability that bad happens. For this, we observe that $\neg\mathsf{pk\text{-}valid}$ can only occur if the event $E := (\exists i \in [n] \text{ s.t. } \mathcal{SK}[i] = \emptyset)$ occurs. As C^* is chosen uniformly at random and the view of Λ_2 is independent of C^*, we have $i \in [n] \setminus C^*$ with probability $1 - 2/n$. In this case $\mathsf{check\text{-}fails}$ occurs and thus $\Pr[\mathsf{check\text{-}fails}| \; E] \geq 1 - 2/n$. Now since $\neg\mathsf{pk\text{-}valid} \Rightarrow E$ it holds that $\Pr[\neg\mathsf{check\text{-}fails} \wedge \neg\mathsf{pk\text{-}valid}] \leq \Pr[\neg\mathsf{check\text{-}fails} \wedge E] = \Pr[\neg\mathsf{check\text{-}fails}|E] \cdot \Pr[E] \leq \Pr[\neg\mathsf{check\text{-}fails}|E] = 1 - \Pr[\mathsf{check\text{-}fails}|E] \leq 2/n$. We thus obtain

$$\Pr[\mathsf{bad}] \leq 2/n.$$

Let $\varepsilon_\mathcal{B}\big|_{\neg\mathsf{bad}}$ denote the probability of $\mathcal{B}$ to win under the condition that bad does not occur and $\varepsilon_\Lambda\big|_{\neg\mathsf{bad}}$ accordingly. We have

$$|\varepsilon_\mathcal{B} - \varepsilon_\Lambda| \leq \left|\varepsilon_\mathcal{B}\big|_{\neg\mathsf{bad}} - \varepsilon_\Lambda\big|_{\neg\mathsf{bad}}\right| + \Pr[\mathsf{bad}] = \Pr[\mathsf{bad}] \leq \frac{2}{n}.$$

Remark 5. As shown in [4] it is straightforward to generalize Theorem 3 to simple $(t_\Lambda, n, \varepsilon_\Lambda, \varepsilon_\mathcal{A})$-reductions for general $\varepsilon_\mathcal{A}$ by letting the hypothetical adversary (and $\mathcal{B}$ respectively) toss a coin and only return K^* with probability $\varepsilon_\mathcal{A}$.

Remark 6. While Theorem 3 establishes the impossibility of tight security reductions for a large class of NIKE schemes, it thereby also gives a hint about how a tight NIKE scheme has to be constructed. Namely, such a scheme has to violate the assumptions made in the theorem such as the existence of an efficient PKCheck that, given the secret key, decides uniqueness of shared keys. More detailed, a tight NIKE scheme needs to allow a reduction to indistinguishably switch public keys to invalid (in fact, even *tightly* switch many of them in one step), such that invalid public keys admit *many* secret keys that lead do *different* shared keys. It is an interesting open question how to construct such a scheme.

5.3   Weak Checkable Uniqueness of Our NIKE

Lemma 2. *If instantiated with a hash proof system HPS where membership in $\mathcal{HSK}$ is efficient checkable for all sets of secret keys in the image of HPS.Setup, the NIKE NIKE presented in Fig. 5 complies with weak checkability of public keys.*

Proof. Let $\mathcal{PP} := ((X, L, R), \mathcal{HSK}, \mathcal{H}, \alpha, F) \xleftarrow{\$} \text{NIKE.Setup}(1^\lambda)$. We define

$$\texttt{wPKCheck}(\mathsf{ID}, (\mathsf{hpk}, x), (\mathsf{hsk}, x, w)) := \begin{cases} 1 & \text{if } \mathsf{hsk} \in \mathcal{HSK} \wedge \alpha(\mathsf{hsk}) = \mathsf{hpk} \\ & \quad \wedge (x, w) \in R \\ 0 & \text{else} \end{cases}.$$

We have to show that wPKCheck is efficiently computable and further that wPKCheck meets properties 1 and 2 in Definition 13. By prerequisites we have that membership in $\mathcal{HSK}$ is efficiently checkable. Further, by definition of a hash proof system the map α and the relation R are efficiently computable. Property 1 follows straightforward from the definition of wPKCheck. Note that actually we have equality, that is

$$\texttt{wPKCheck}(\mathsf{ID}, \mathsf{pk}, \mathsf{sk}) = 1 \Leftrightarrow \exists r : (\mathsf{pk}, \mathsf{sk}) = \text{NIKE.KeyGen}(\mathcal{PP}, \mathsf{ID}; r).$$

It remains to prove property 2: for all $(\mathsf{ID}_1, \mathsf{pk}_1, \mathsf{sk}_1), (\mathsf{ID}_1, \mathsf{pk}_1, \mathsf{sk}_1'), (\mathsf{ID}_2, \mathsf{pk}_2, \mathsf{sk}_2)$ that all pass wPKCheck we have

$$\text{NIKE.SharedKey}(\mathsf{ID}_2, \mathsf{pk}_2, \mathsf{ID}_1, \mathsf{sk}_1) = \text{NIKE.SharedKey}(\mathsf{ID}_2, \mathsf{pk}_2, \mathsf{ID}_1, \mathsf{sk}_1').$$

Let in the following $\mathsf{pk}_1 =: (\mathsf{hpk}_1, x_1), \mathsf{pk}_2 =: (\mathsf{hpk}_2, x_2), \mathsf{sk}_1 =: (\mathsf{hsk}_1, w_1), \mathsf{sk}_1' =: (\mathsf{hsk}_1', w_1')$ and $\mathsf{sk}_2 =: (\mathsf{hsk}_2, w_2)$. By the properties of the hash proof system we have that for $\mathsf{hsk}_1, \mathsf{hsk}_1' \in \mathcal{HSK}$ with $\alpha(\mathsf{hsk}_1) = \alpha(\mathsf{hsk}_1') = \mathsf{hpk}_1$ and $x_2 \in L$ it holds

$$H_{\mathsf{hsk}_1}(x_2) = F(x_2, w_2, \mathsf{hpk}) = H_{\mathsf{hsk}_1'}(x_2)$$

and for w_1' with $(x_1, w_1') \in \mathcal{R}$ it holds

$$F(x_1, w_1, \mathsf{hpk}_2) = H_{\mathsf{hsk}_2}(x_1) = F(x_1, w_1', \mathsf{hpk}_2).$$

This yields

$$\begin{aligned}
\text{NIKE.SharedKey}(\mathsf{ID}_2, \mathsf{pk}_2, \mathsf{ID}_1, \mathsf{sk}_1) &= H_{\mathsf{hsk}_1}(x_2) \oplus F(x_1, w_1, \mathsf{hpk}_2) \\
&= H_{\mathsf{hsk}_1'}(x_2) \oplus F(x_1', w_1', \mathsf{hpk}_2) \\
&= \text{NIKE.SharedKey}(\mathsf{ID}_2, \mathsf{pk}_2, \mathsf{ID}_1, \mathsf{sk}_1').
\end{aligned}$$

Corollary 1 (Informal). *The security reduction in the proof of Theorem 1 is optimal regarding tightness among all simple reductions.*

Proof. Theorem 3 shows that simple security reductions for a NIKE admitting a weak PKCheck encounter a loss of at least $n/2$. Lemma 2 proves that our NIKE admits such a weak PKCheck and thus from Theorem 3 it follows that

UF - CKS - $heavy_n$-security of our NIKE can only be shown by a simple reduction if the reduction loses at least a factor of $n/2$. Now Lemma 1 shows that a UF - CKS - $heavy_n$ adversary tightly implies a HKR - CKS - $heavy$ adversary. Thus, any reduction with loss M from a NICA to HKR - CKS - $heavy$ security would imply a reduction with loss M to UF - CKS - $heavy_n$ security. It follows that $M \geq n/2$.

Remark 7. Since DKR-CKS-heavy security also tightly implies UF - CKS - $heavy_n$ security, our result carries over to DKR-CKS-heavy secure NIKE schemes that comply with weak checkable uniqueness.

Acknowledgements. We would like to thank Kenny Paterson for collaboration at early stages of this work. Also, we would like to thank the anonymous reviewers of Crypto 2018 for their helpful comments.

References

1. Abe, M., Hofheinz, D., Nishimaki, R., Ohkubo, M., Pan, J.: Compact structure-preserving signatures with almost tight security. In: Katz, J., Shacham, H. (eds.) CRYPTO 2017, Part II. LNCS, vol. 10402, pp. 548–580. Springer, Cham (2017). https://doi.org/10.1007/978-3-319-63715-0_19
2. Abe, M., David, B., Kohlweiss, M., Nishimaki, R., Ohkubo, M.: Tagged one-time signatures: tight security and optimal tag size. In: Kurosawa, K., Hanaoka, G. (eds.) PKC 2013. LNCS, vol. 7778, pp. 312–331. Springer, Heidelberg (2013). https://doi.org/10.1007/978-3-642-36362-7_20
3. Attrapadung, N., Hanaoka, G., Yamada, S.: A framework for identity-based encryption with almost tight security. In: Iwata, T., Cheon, J.H. (eds.) ASIACRYPT 2015, Part I. LNCS, vol. 9452, pp. 521–549. Springer, Heidelberg (2015). https://doi.org/10.1007/978-3-662-48797-6_22
4. Bader, C., Jager, T., Li, Y., Schäge, S.: On the impossibility of tight cryptographic reductions. In: Fischlin, M., Coron, J.-S. (eds.) EUROCRYPT 2016, Part II. LNCS, vol. 9666, pp. 273–304. Springer, Heidelberg (2016). https://doi.org/10.1007/978-3-662-49896-5_10
5. Bader, C., Hofheinz, D., Jager, T., Kiltz, E., Li, Y.: Tightly-secure authenticated key exchange. In: Dodis, Y., Nielsen, J.B. (eds.) TCC 2015, Part I. LNCS, vol. 9014, pp. 629–658. Springer, Heidelberg (2015). https://doi.org/10.1007/978-3-662-46494-6_26
6. Bellare, M., Boldyreva, A., Micali, S.: Public-key encryption in a multi-user setting: security proofs and improvements. In: Preneel, B. (ed.) EUROCRYPT 2000. LNCS, vol. 1807, pp. 259–274. Springer, Heidelberg (2000). https://doi.org/10.1007/3-540-45539-6_18
7. Blazy, O., Kiltz, E., Pan, J.: (Hierarchical) identity-based encryption from affine message authentication. In: Garay, J.A., Gennaro, R. (eds.) CRYPTO 2014, Part I. LNCS, vol. 8616, pp. 408–425. Springer, Heidelberg (2014). https://doi.org/10.1007/978-3-662-44371-2_23
8. Blum, M., Feldman, P., Micali, S.: Non-interactive zero-knowledge and its applications (Extended Abstract). In: Proceedings of 20th ACM STOC, pp. 103–112. ACM Press, May 1988

9. Boneh, D., Venkatesan, R.: Breaking RSA may not be equivalent to factoring. In: Nyberg, K. (ed.) EUROCRYPT 1998. LNCS, vol. 1403, pp. 59–71. Springer, Heidelberg (1998). https://doi.org/10.1007/BFb0054117

10. Cash, D., Kiltz, E., Shoup, V.: The Twin Diffie-Hellman problem and applications. In: Smart, N. (ed.) EUROCRYPT 2008. LNCS, vol. 4965, pp. 127–145. Springer, Heidelberg (2008). https://doi.org/10.1007/978-3-540-78967-3_8

11. Chen, J., Wee, H.: Fully, (almost) tightly secure IBE and dual system groups. In: Canetti, R., Garay, J.A. (eds.) CRYPTO 2013, Part II. LNCS, vol. 8043, pp. 435–460. Springer, Heidelberg (2013). https://doi.org/10.1007/978-3-642-40084-1_25

12. Coron, J.-S.: Optimal security proofs for PSS and other signature schemes. In: Knudsen, L.R. (ed.) EUROCRYPT 2002. LNCS, vol. 2332, pp. 272–287. Springer, Heidelberg (2002). https://doi.org/10.1007/3-540-46035-7_18

13. Cramer, R., Shoup, V.: Universal hash proofs and a paradigm for adaptive chosen ciphertext secure public-key encryption. In: Knudsen, L.R. (ed.) EUROCRYPT 2002. LNCS, vol. 2332, pp. 45–64. Springer, Heidelberg (2002). https://doi.org/10.1007/3-540-46035-7_4

14. Diffie, W., Hellman, M.E.: New directions in cryptography. IEEE Trans. Inf. Theory 22(6), 644–654 (1976)

15. Escala, A., Herold, G., Kiltz, E., Ràfols, C., Villar, J.: An algebraic framework for Diffie-Hellman assumptions. In: Canetti, R., Garay, J.A. (eds.) CRYPTO 2013, Part II. LNCS, vol. 8043, pp. 129–147. Springer, Heidelberg (2013). https://doi.org/10.1007/978-3-642-40084-1_8

16. Fleischhacker, N., Jager, T., Schröder, D.: On tight security proofs for Schnorr signatures. In: Sarkar, P., Iwata, T. (eds.) ASIACRYPT 2014, Part I. LNCS, vol. 8873, pp. 512–531. Springer, Heidelberg (2014). https://doi.org/10.1007/978-3-662-45611-8_27

17. Freire, E.S.V., Hofheinz, D., Kiltz, E., Paterson, K.G.: Non-interactive key exchange. In: Kurosawa, K., Hanaoka, G. (eds.) PKC 2013. LNCS, vol. 7778, pp. 254–271. Springer, Heidelberg (2013). https://doi.org/10.1007/978-3-642-36362-7_17

18. Garg, S., Bhaskar, R., Lokam, S.V.: Improved bounds on security reductions for discrete log based signatures. In: Wagner, D. (ed.) CRYPTO 2008. LNCS, vol. 5157, pp. 93–107. Springer, Heidelberg (2008). https://doi.org/10.1007/978-3-540-85174-5_6

19. Gay, R., Hofheinz, D., Kohl, L.: Kurosawa-Desmedt meets tight security. In: Katz, J., Shacham, H. (eds.) CRYPTO 2017, Part III. LNCS, vol. 10403, pp. 133–160. Springer, Cham (2017). https://doi.org/10.1007/978-3-319-63697-9_5

20. Gay, R., Hofheinz, D., Kiltz, E., Wee, H.: Tightly CCA-secure encryption without pairings. In: Fischlin, M., Coron, J.-S. (eds.) EUROCRYPT 2016, Part I. LNCS, vol. 9665, pp. 1–27. Springer, Heidelberg (2016). https://doi.org/10.1007/978-3-662-49890-3_1

21. Gennaro, R., Lindell, Y.: A framework for password-based authenticated key exchange. In: Biham, E. (ed.) EUROCRYPT 2003. LNCS, vol. 2656, pp. 524–543. Springer, Heidelberg (2003). https://doi.org/10.1007/3-540-39200-9_33

22. Goldwasser, S., Micali, S., Rivest, R.L.: A Digital signature scheme secure against adaptive chosen-message attacks. SIAM J. Comput. 17(2), 281–308 (1988)

23. Gong, J., Chen, J., Dong, X., Cao, Z., Tang, S.: Extended nested dual system groups, revisited. In: Cheng, C.-M., Chung, K.-M., Persiano, G., Yang, B.-Y. (eds.) PKC 2016, Part I. LNCS, vol. 9614, pp. 133–163. Springer, Heidelberg (2016). https://doi.org/10.1007/978-3-662-49384-7_6

24. Guo, F., Chen, R., Susilo, W., Lai, J., Yang, G., Mu, Y.: Optimal security reductions for unique signatures: bypassing impossibilities with a counterexample. In: Katz, J., Shacham, H. (eds.) CRYPTO 2017, Part II. LNCS, vol. 10402, pp. 517–547. Springer, Cham (2017). https://doi.org/10.1007/978-3-319-63715-0_18

25. Hesse, J., Hofheinz, D., Kohl, L.: On tightly secure non-interactive key exchange. In: IACR Cryptology ePrint Archive 2018, p. 237 (2018). http://eprint.iacr.org/2018/237

26. Hofheinz, D.: Adaptive partitioning. In: Coron, J.-S., Nielsen, J.B. (eds.) EUROCRYPT 2017, Part II. LNCS, vol. 10212, pp. 489–518. Springer, Cham (2017). https://doi.org/10.1007/978-3-319-56617-7_17

27. Hofheinz, D.: Algebraic partitioning: fully compact and (almost) tightly secure cryptography. In: Kushilevitz, E., Malkin, T. (eds.) TCC 2016, Part I. LNCS, vol. 9562, pp. 251–281. Springer, Heidelberg (2016). https://doi.org/10.1007/978-3-662-49096-9_11

28. Hofheinz, D., Jager, T.: Tightly secure signatures and public-key encryption. In: Safavi-Naini, R., Canetti, R. (eds.) CRYPTO 2012. LNCS, vol. 7417, pp. 590–607. Springer, Heidelberg (2012). https://doi.org/10.1007/978-3-642-32009-5_35

29. Hofheinz, D., Jager, T., Knapp, E.: Waters signatures with optimal security reduction. In: Fischlin, M., Buchmann, J., Manulis, M. (eds.) PKC 2012. LNCS, vol. 7293, pp. 66–83. Springer, Heidelberg (2012). https://doi.org/10.1007/978-3-642-30057-8_5

30. Hofheinz, D., Kiltz, E.: Secure hybrid encryption from weakened key encapsulation. In: Menezes, A. (ed.) CRYPTO 2007. LNCS, vol. 4622, pp. 553–571. Springer, Heidelberg (2007). https://doi.org/10.1007/978-3-540-74143-5_31

31. Hofheinz, D., Koch, J., Striecks, C.: Identity-based encryption with (almost) tight security in the multi-instance, multi-ciphertext setting. In: Katz, J. (ed.) PKC 2015. LNCS, vol. 9020, pp. 799–822. Springer, Heidelberg (2015). https://doi.org/10.1007/978-3-662-46447-2_36

32. Kakvi, S.A., Kiltz, E.: Optimal security proofs for full domain hash, revisited. In: Pointcheval, D., Johansson, T. (eds.) EUROCRYPT 2012. LNCS, vol. 7237, pp. 537–553. Springer, Heidelberg (2012). https://doi.org/10.1007/978-3-642-29011-4_32

33. Katz, J., Ostrovsky, R., Yung, M.: Efficient password-authenticated key exchange using human-memorable passwords. In: Pfitzmann, B. (ed.) EUROCRYPT 2001. LNCS, vol. 2045, pp. 475–494. Springer, Heidelberg (2001). https://doi.org/10.1007/3-540-44987-6_29

34. Katz, J., Wang, N.: Efficiency improvements for signature schemes with tight security reductions. In: Jajodia, S., Atluri, V., Jaeger, T. (eds.) ACM CCS 03, pp. 155–164. ACM Press, October 2003

35. Lewko, A., Waters, B.: Why proving HIBE systems secure is difficult. In: Nguyen, P.Q., Oswald, E. (eds.) EUROCRYPT 2014. LNCS, vol. 8441, pp. 58–76. Springer, Heidelberg (2014). https://doi.org/10.1007/978-3-642-55220-5_4

36. Libert, B., Peters, T., Joye, M., Yung, M.: Compactly hiding linear spans. In: Iwata, T., Cheon, J.H. (eds.) ASIACRYPT 2015, Part I. LNCS, vol. 9452, pp. 681–707. Springer, Heidelberg (2015). https://doi.org/10.1007/978-3-662-48797-6_28

37. Libert, B., Joye, M., Yung, M., Peters, T.: Concise multi-challenge CCA-secure encryption and signatures with almost tight security. In: Sarkar, P., Iwata, T. (eds.) ASIACRYPT 2014, Part II. LNCS, vol. 8874, pp. 1–21. Springer, Heidelberg (2014). https://doi.org/10.1007/978-3-662-45608-8_1

38. Naor, M., Yung, M.: Public-key cryptosystems provably secure against chosen ciphertext attacks. In: Proceedings of 22nd ACM STOC, pp. 427–437. ACM Press, May 1990
39. Seurin, Y.: On the exact security of Schnorr-type signatures in the random oracle model. In: Pointcheval, D., Johansson, T. (eds.) EUROCRYPT 2012. LNCS, vol. 7237, pp. 554–571. Springer, Heidelberg (2012). https://doi.org/10.1007/978-3-642-29011-4_33

Practical and Tightly-Secure Digital Signatures and Authenticated Key Exchange

Kristian Gjøsteen[1] and Tibor Jager[2(✉)]

[1] NTNU - Norwegian University of Science and Technology, Trondheim, Norway
kristian.gjosteen@ntnu.no
[2] Paderborn University, Paderborn, Germany
tibor.jager@upb.de

Abstract. Tight security is increasingly gaining importance in real-world cryptography, as it allows to choose cryptographic parameters in a way that is supported by a security proof, without the need to sacrifice efficiency by compensating the security loss of a reduction with larger parameters. However, for many important cryptographic primitives, including digital signatures and authenticated key exchange (AKE), we are still lacking constructions that are suitable for real-world deployment.

We construct the first truly practical signature scheme with tight security in a real-world multi-user setting with adaptive corruptions. The scheme is based on a new way of applying the Fiat-Shamir approach to construct tightly-secure signatures from certain identification schemes.

Then we use this scheme as a building block to construct the first practical AKE protocol with tight security. It allows the establishment of a key within 1 RTT in a practical client-server setting, provides forward security, is simple and easy to implement, and thus very suitable for practical deployment. It is essentially the "signed Diffie-Hellman" protocol, but with an additional message, which is crucial to achieve tight security. This additional message is used to overcome a technical difficulty in constructing tightly-secure AKE protocols.

For a theoretically-sound choice of parameters and a moderate number of users and sessions, our protocol has comparable computational efficiency to the simple signed Diffie-Hellman protocol with EC-DSA, while for large-scale settings our protocol has even better computational performance, at moderately increased communication complexity.

1 Introduction

Tight security. In modern cryptography it is standard to propose new cryptographic constructions along with a *proof of security*. The provable security paradigm, which goes back to a seminal work of Goldwasser and Micali [27],

---

K. Gjøsteen—Funded by The Research Council of Norway under Project No. 248166.

H. Shacham and A. Boldyreva (Eds.): CRYPTO 2018, LNCS 10992, pp. 95–125, 2018.
https://doi.org/10.1007/978-3-319-96881-0_4

becomes increasingly relevant for "real-world" cryptosystems today. For instance, the upcoming TLS version 1.3[1] is the first version of this important protocol where formal security proofs were used as a basis for several fundamental design decisions [44].

A security proof usually describes a reduction (in a complexity-theoretic sense), which turns an efficient adversary $\mathcal{A}$ breaking the considered cryptosystem into an efficient adversary $\mathcal{B}$ breaking some underlying complexity assumption, such as the discrete logarithm problem, for example. If $\mathcal{B}$ can be shown to have about the same running time and success probability as $\mathcal{A}$ (up to a constant factor), then the reduction is said to be *tight*. However, many security proofs are not tight. For example, we are often only able to show that if $\mathcal{A}$ runs in time $t_{\mathcal{A}}$ and has success probability $\epsilon_{\mathcal{A}}$, then $\mathcal{B}$ runs in time $t_{\mathcal{B}} \approx t_{\mathcal{A}}$, but we can bound its success probability only as $\epsilon_{\mathcal{B}} \geq \epsilon_{\mathcal{A}}/Q$, where Q is the *security loss*. Q can often be "large", e.g., linear or even quadratic in the number of users.

If Q is polynomially bounded, then this still yields a polynomial-time reduction in the sense of classical asymptotic complexity theory. However, if we want to deploy the cryptosystem in practice, then the size of cryptographic parameters (like for instance the size of an underlying algebraic group, where the discrete logarithm problem is assumed to be hard) must be determined. If we want to choose these parameters in a theoretically-sound way, then a larger loss Q must be compensated by larger parameters, which in turn has a direct impact on efficiency. For example, in the discrete logarithm setting, this would typically require an increase in the group order by a factor Q^2. As a concrete example, 2^{32} users with 2^{32} sessions each and quadratic security loss would force us to use 521 bit elliptic curves instead of 256 bit elliptic curves, which more than quintuples the cost of an exponentiation on one typical platform (as measured by `openssl speed`). Thus, in order to be able to instantiate the cryptosystem with "optimal" parameters, we need a tight security proof.

The possibility and impossibility of tight security proofs has been considered for many primitives, including symmetric encryption [29,31,36], public-key encryption [3,5,24,32], (hierarchical) identity-based encryption [11,16], digital signatures [22,23,32,33,37,43,45,47], authenticated key exchange [2], and more. It also becomes increasingly relevant in "real-world" cryptography. For instance, most recently, Gueron and Lindell [29] improved the tightness of the AES-GCM-SIV nonce misuse-resistant encryption scheme, with a new nonce-based key derivation method. This construction is now part of the current draft of the corresponding RFC proposal,[2] won the best paper award at ACM CCS 2017, and is already used in practice in Amazon's AWS key management scheme.[3]

In many important areas with high real-world relevance, including digital signature schemes and authenticated key exchange protocols, we still do not have any tightly-secure constructions that are suitable for practical deployment. Known schemes either have a security loss which is at least linear in the number

---

[1] See https://tools.ietf.org/html/draft-ietf-tls-tls13-23 for the latest draft.

[2] See https://tools.ietf.org/html/draft-irtf-cfrg-gcmsiv-07.

[3] See https://rwc.iacr.org/2018/Slides/Gueron.pdf.

of users (typical for digital signatures) or even *quadratic* in the number of proto-col sessions (typical for authenticated key exchange), if a real-world multi-user security model is considered. This huge security loss often makes it impossible to choose deployment parameters in a theoretically-sound way, because such parameters would have to be unreasonably large and thus impractical.

1.1 Tightly-Secure Digital Signatures

In the domain of digital signatures, there are two relevant dimensions for tight-ness: (i) the number of signatures issued per public key, and (ii) the number of users (=public keys).

For some important "real-world" schemes, such as Schnorr signatures, impos-sibility results suggest that current proof techniques are not sufficient to achieve tightness [22,23,43,47], not even if only the first dimension is considered in a *single-user* setting. Some other schemes have a tight security proof in the first dimension [10,32,37,45]. However, in a more realistic multi-user setting with adaptive corruptions, which appears to be the "right" real-world security notion for applications of signatures such as key exchange, cryptocurrencies, secure instant messaging, or e-mail signatures, there are only very few constructions with tight security in both dimensions.

One construction is due to Bader [1]. It is in the random oracle model [6], but this seems reasonable, given the objective of constructing simple and effi-cient real-world cryptosystems. However, the construction requires bilinear maps (aka. pairings). Even though bilinear maps have become significantly more effi-cient in the past years, their practical usability is still not comparable to schemes over classical algebraic groups, such as elliptic curves without pairings. Fur-thermore, bilinear maps involve rather complex mathematics, and are therefore rather difficult to implement, and not yet available on many platforms and soft-ware libraries, in particular not for resource-constrained lightweight devices or smartcards. Finally, recent advances in solving the discrete logarithm problem [4] restrain the applicability of bilinear maps in settings with high performance and security requirements.

The other two known constructions are due to Bader *et al.* [2]. Both have a security proof in the standard model (i.e., without random oracles), but are also based on bilinear maps. The first one uses a simulation-sound Groth-Sahai [28] proof system, which internally uses a tree-based signature scheme to achieve tightness. Thus, a signature of the resulting construction consists of hundreds of group elements, and is therefore not suitable for practical deployment. The second scheme is more efficient, but here public keys consist of hundreds of group elements, which is much larger than the public key size of any other schemes currently used in practice, and seems too large for many applications.

In summary, the construction of a practical signature scheme without bilin-ear maps, which provides *tight* security in a realistic multi-user setting with corruptions and in the standard sense of *existential unforgeability under chosen-message attacks*, is an important open problem. A solution would provide a very useful building block for applications where the multi-user setting with adaptive corruptions appears to be the "right" real-world security notion, such as those mentioned above.

The difficulty of constructing tightly-secure signatures. Constructing a tightly-secure signature scheme in a real-world multi-user security model with adaptive corruptions faces the following technical challenge. In the μ-user setting, the adversary $\mathcal{A}$ receives as input a list $pk_1, \ldots, pk_\mu$ of public keys. We denote the corresponding secret keys with $sk_1, \ldots, sk_\mu$. $\mathcal{A}$ is allowed to ask two types of queries. It may either output a tuple (m, i), to request a signature for a chosen message m under secret key sk_i. The security experiment responds with $\sigma \overset{\$}{\leftarrow} \mathsf{Sign}(sk_i, m)$. Or it may "corrupt" keys. To this end, it outputs an index i, and the experiment responds with sk_i. Adversary $\mathcal{A}$ breaks the security, if it outputs (i^*, m^*, σ^*) such that σ^* verifies correctly for a new message m^* and with respect to an uncorrupted key pk_{i^*}. Note that this is the natural extension of *existential unforgeability under chosen-message attacks* (EUF-CMA) to the multi-user setting with corruptions. Following [2], we will call it MU-EUF-CMA^{corr}-*security*. Security in this sense is implied by the standard EUF-CMA security definition, by a straightforward reduction that simply guesses the index i^* of the uncorrupted key, which incurs a security loss of $Q = 1/\mu$ that is linear in the number of users.

Now let us consider the difficulty of constructing a security reduction $\mathcal{B}$ which does not lose a factor $Q = 1/\mu$. On the one hand, in order to avoid the need to guess an uncorrupted key, $\mathcal{B}$ must "know" *all* secret keys $sk_1, \ldots, sk_\mu$, in order to be able to answer key corruption queries.

On the other hand, however, the reduction $\mathcal{B}$ must be able to extract the solution to a computationally hard problem from the forgery (i^*, m^*, σ^*). If $\mathcal{B}$ "knows" sk_{i^*}, then it seems that it could compute (m^*, σ^*) even without the help of the adversary. Now, if $\mathcal{B}$ is then able to extract the solution of a "hard" computational problem from (m^*, σ^*), then this means that the underlying hardness assumption must be false, and thus the reduction $\mathcal{B}$ is not meaningful.

The above argument seems to suggests that achieving tight MU-EUF-CMA^{corr}-security is impossible. One can even turn this intuition into a formal impossibility result, as done in [3]. However, it turns out that the impossibility holds only for schemes where the distribution of signatures that are computable with a secret key sk_{i^*} known to reduction $\mathcal{B}$ is identical to the distribution of signatures (m^*, σ^*) output by adversary $\mathcal{A}$. This provides a leverage to overcome the seeming impossibility. Indeed, the known constructions of tightly MU-EUF-CMA^{corr}-secure schemes [1,2] circumvent the impossibility result. As we describe below in more detail, these constructions essentially ensure that with sufficiently high probability the adversary $\mathcal{A}$ will output a message-signature pair (m^*, σ^*) such that σ^* is *not* efficiently computable, even given sk_{i^*}.

The main technical challenge in constructing signature schemes with tight security in a real-world multi-user security model with corruptions is therefore to build the scheme in a way that makes it possible to argue that the reduction $\mathcal{B}$ is able to extract the solution to a computationally hard problem from the forged signature computed by $\mathcal{A}$, *even though $\mathcal{B}$ knows secret keys for all users.*

On constructing tightly-secure signatures without bilinear maps. All previously known tightly MU-EUF-CMA^{corr}-secure signature schemes [1,2] essentially work as follows. A public key pk consists of two public keys $pk = (pk_0, pk_1)$ of a "base" signature scheme, which is tightly-secure in a multi-user setting *without* corruptions. The secret key sk consists of a random secret key $sk = sk_b$, $b \xleftarrow{\$} \{0,1\}$, for either pk_0 or pk_1. A signature consists of a Groth-Sahai-based [28] witness-indistinguishable OR-proof of knowledge, proving knowledge of a signature that verifies either under pk_0 OR under pk_1. In the security proof, the reduction $\mathcal{B}$ basically knows sk_b (and thus is able to respond to all corruption-queries of $\mathcal{A}$), but it hopes that $\mathcal{A}$ produces a proof of knowledge of a signature under pk_{1-b}, which can then be extracted from the proof of knowledge and be used to break the instance corresponding to pk_{1-b}.

A natural approach to adopt this technique to signatures without pairings would be to use a Fiat-Shamir-like proof of knowledge [21], in combination with the very efficient OR-proofs of Cramer-Damgård-Schoenmakers (CDS) [18]. However, here we face the following difficulties. First, existing signature schemes that use a Fiat-Shamir-like proof *of knowledge*, such as for the Schnorr scheme [46], are already difficult to prove tightly secure in the single-user setting, due to known impossibility results [22,23,43,47]. Second, its tightly-secure variants, such as the DDH-based scheme of Katz-Wang [37] and the CDH-based schemes of Goh-Jarecki [25] or Chevallier-Mames [17], do not use a proof *of knowledge*, but actually a proof of language membership, where we cannot extract a witness along the lines of [1,2]. Thus, adopting the approach of [1,2] to efficient signature schemes without pairings requires additional ideas and new techniques.

Our contributions. We construct the first tightly MU-EUF-CMA^{corr}-secure signature scheme which does not require bilinear maps. We achieve this by describing a new way of combining the efficient EDL signature scheme considered in [25] with Cramer-Damgård-Schoenmakers proofs [18], in order to obtain tightly-secure signatures in the multi-user setting with adaptive corruptions.

The scheme is very efficient, in particular in comparison to previous schemes with tight multi-user security. A public key consists of only two group elements, while the secret key consists of a bit and one integer smaller than the group order. A signature consists of a random nonce, two group elements and four integers smaller than the group order. The computational cost of the algorithms is dominated by exponentiations. Key generation costs a single exponentiation. Signing costs a single exponentiation plus the generation of a proof, for a total of seven exponentiations. Verification costs eight exponentiations.

1.2   Tightly-Secure Authenticated Key Exchange

Modern security models for authenticated key exchange consider very strong adversaries, which control the entire communication network, may adaptively corrupt parties to learn their long-term secret keys, or reveal session keys of certain sessions. This includes all security models that follow the classical

Bellare-Rogaway [7] or Canetti-Krawczyk [14] approach, for instance. The adversary essentially breaks the security, if it is able to distinguish a non-revealed session key from random. Furthermore, in order to achieve desirable properties like *forward security* (aka. *perfect forward secrecy*) [30], the attacker is even allowed to attack session keys belonging to sessions where one or both parties are corrupted, as long as these corruptions do not allow the adversary to trivially win the security experiment (e.g., because it is able to corrupt a communication partner *before* the key is computed, such that the attacker can impersonate this party).

The huge complexity of modern security models for authenticated key exchange makes it difficult to construct tightly-secure protocols. Most examples of modern key exchange protocols even have a *quadratic* security loss in the total number of protocol sessions, which stems from the fact that a reduction has to guess two oracles in the security experiment that belong to the protocol session "tested" by the adversary (cf. the discussion of the "commitment problem" below).

Despite the huge practical importance of authenticated key exchange protocols, we currently know only a single example of a protocol that achieves tight security [2], but it requires complex building blocks, such as one of the tightly-secure signature schemes sketched above, as well as a special key encapsulation mechanisms that is composed of two public-key encryption schemes. Given the huge demand for efficient key exchange protocol in practice, the construction of a simple and efficient, yet tightly-secure, authenticated key exchange protocol *without* these drawbacks is an important open problem.

Our contributions. We describe the first truly practical key exchange protocol with tight security in a standard security model for authenticated key exchange. The construction (but not the security proof) is very simple, which makes the protocol easy to implement and ready to use, even on simple devices.

Our protocol is able to establish a key with very low latency, in three messages and within a single *round-trip time* (1-RTT) in a standard client-server setting. This holds even in a typical real-world situation where both communication partners are initially not in possession of their communication partner's public keys, and therefore have to exchange their certified public keys within the protocol. Furthermore, the protocol provides full *forward security*.

In Sect. 5 we analyse the computational efficiency of our protocol, instantiated with our signature scheme, by comparing it to the simple "signed Diffie-Hellman" protocol, instantiated with EC-DSA. The analysis is based on the benchmark for ECC arithmetic of OpenSSL, and considers a theoretically-sound choice of cryptographic parameters based on the tightness of security proofs. Even though our protocol requires a larger absolute number of exponentiations, already in small-to-medium-scale settings this is quickly compensated by the fact that arithmetic in large groups is significantly more costly than in small groups. In a large-scale setting, our protocol even outperforms signed Diffie-Hellman with EC-DSA with respect to computational performance. This comes at the cost of moderately increased communication complexity, when compared to the (extremely communication-efficient) EC-DSA-signed Diffie-Hellman protocol.

Sketch of our construction and technical difficulties. Our starting point is the standard "signed Diffie-Hellman" protocol, instantiated with our tightly-secure multi-user signature scheme. However, we stress that this is not yet sufficient to achieve tight security, due to the *"commitment problem"* described below. We resolve this problem with an additional message, which is important to achieve tight security, but does not add any additional latency to the protocol.

More precisely, consider the standard "signed Diffie-Hellman" protocol, executed between Alice and Bob, where Bob first sends $v = (g^b, \sigma_B)$, where σ_B is a signature under Bob's secret key over g^b, Alice responds with $w = (g^a, \sigma_A)$, where σ_A is Alice's signature over g^a, and the resulting key is $k = g^{ab}$. Let us sketch why this protocol seems not to allow for a tight security proof.

In a Bellare-Rogaway-style security model, such as the one that we describe in Sect. 4.1, each session of each party is modelled by an oracle π_i^s, where $(i, s) \in [\mu] \times [\ell]$, μ is the number of parties and ℓ is the number of sessions per party. Now, consider a reduction $\mathcal{B}$ which receives as input a DDH challenge (g, g^x, g^y, g^z), and now wants to embed these values into the view of the key exchange adversary $\mathcal{A}$. One way to do this, which is used in most existing security proofs of "signed Diffie-Hellman-like" protocols (such as [34,35,39], for instance) is to guess two oracles π_i^s and π_j^t, embed g^x into the message sent by π_i^s, g^y into the message sent by π_j^t, and then hope that the adversary will forward g^y to π_i^s and "test" the key of oracle π_i^s, where the g^z-value from the DDH challenge is then embedded. Note that the need to guess two out of $\mu\ell$ oracles correctly incurs a quadratic security loss of $O(\mu^2\ell^2)$, which is extremely non-tight.

A natural approach to improve tightness is to use the well-known random self-reducibility of DDH [5], and embed randomised versions of g^x and g^y into the messages of more than one oracle. However, here we face the following difficulty. As soon as an oracle π_i^s has output a Diffie-Hellman share g^a, the reduction $\mathcal{B}$ has essentially committed itself to whether it "knows" the discrete logarithm a.

- If oracle π_i^s outputs a randomised version of g^x, $g^a = g^{x+e_i^s}$ where e_i^s is the randomization, then $\mathcal{B}$ does not "know" the discrete logarithm $a = x + e_i^s$. Now it may happen that the adversary $\mathcal{A}$, which controls the network and possibly also some parties, sends a value h to oracle π_i^s (on behalf of some third party), such that h is *not* controlled by the reduction $\mathcal{B}$. If then $\mathcal{A}$ asks the reduction to reveal the key of oracle π_i^s, then the reduction fails, because it is not able to efficiently compute $k = h^a$.
- This problem does not occur, if $g^a = g^{e_i}$ such that $\mathcal{B}$ "knows" the discrete logarithm a. However, if it now happens that the adversary $\mathcal{A}$ decides to distinguish the key k of oracle π_i^s from random, then again the reduction fails, because it is not able to embed g^z into k.

This *"commitment problem"* is the reason why many classical security proofs, in particular for signed Diffie-Hellman protocols, have a quadratic security loss.

They embed a DDH challenge into the view of adversary $\mathcal{A}$ by guessing two out of $\mu\ell$ oracles, and the reduction will fail if the guess is incorrect.

We resolve the commitment problem in a novel way by adding an additional message. We change the protocol such that Alice initiates the protocol with a message $u = G(g^a)$, where G is a cryptographic hash function (cf. Fig. 3). This message serves as a commitment by Alice to g^a. Then the protocol proceeds as before: Bob sends $v = (g^b, \sigma_B)$, Alice responds with $w = (g^a, \sigma_A)$, and the resulting key is $k = g^{ab}$.[4] However, Bob will additionally check whether the first message u received from Alice matches the third protocol message, that is, $u = G(g^a)$, and abort if not.

As we will prove formally in Sect. 4.2, the additional message u resolves the commitment problem as follows. We will model G as a random oracle. This guarantees that from the point of view of the adversary $\mathcal{A}$, a value $G(h)$ forms a binding and hiding commitment to h. However, for the reduction $\mathcal{B}$, u is not binding, because $\mathcal{B}$ controls the random oracle. We will construct $\mathcal{B}$ such that whenever an oracle π_i^s outputs a first protocol message u, then receives back a message $v = (g^b, \sigma_B)$, and now has to send message $w = (g^a, \sigma_A)$, then $\mathcal{B}$ it is able to *retroactively* decide to embed the element g^x from the DDH challenge into u such that $u = G(g^{x+e_i^s})$, or not and it holds that $u = G(g^{e_i^s})$. This is possible by re-programming the random oracle in a suitable way.[5]

We will explain in Sect. 4.2 that the additional message u does not increase latency to the protocol, when used in a standard client-server setting. This is essentially because Alice can send cryptographically protected payload immediately after receiving message $v = (g^b, \sigma_B)$ from Bob, *along with* message $w = (g^a, \sigma_A)$. Thus, in a typical client-server setting, where the client initiates the protocol and then sends data to the server, the overhead required to establish a key is only 1 RTT, exactly like for ordinary signed Diffie-Hellman.

Outline. Section 2 recalls the necessary background and standard definitions. The signature scheme is described and proven secure in Sect. 3, the AKE protocol is considered in Sect. 4.

2   Background

In this section, we recap some background and standard definitions of Diffie-Hellman problems, the Fiat-Shamir heuristic, and digital signatures.

---

[4] Our actual protocol will compute the key as $k = H(g^{ab})$ for a hash function H, but this is not relevant here.

[5] We note that a programmable random oracle is not inherently necessary here. Instead, we could use an equivocal commitment scheme [19] in place of random oracle G. However, this would make the protocol more complex. Since we want to maximise efficiency and simplicity of the protocol, we consider the random oracle as an adequate choice for our purpose.

Diffie-Hellman Problems. Let $\mathbb{G}$ denote a cyclic group of prime order p and let g be a generator. Let $\mathcal{DDH}$ be the set of *DDH tuples* $\{(g^a, g^b, g^{ab}) \mid a, b \in \{0, 1, \ldots, p-1\}$.

Definition 1. *Let $\mathcal{A}$ be an algorithm that takes two group elements as input and outputs a group element. The* success probability *af $\mathcal{A}$ against the* Computational Diffie-Hellman (CDH) problem *is*

$$\mathrm{Succ}_{\mathbb{G},g}^{\mathsf{CDH}}(\mathcal{A}) = \Pr[\mathcal{A}(x, y) = z \mid (x, y, z) \leftarrow \mathcal{DDH}].$$

We say that $\mathcal{A}$ (t, ϵ)-breaks CDH if $\mathcal{A}$ runs in time t and its success probability $\mathrm{Succ}_{\mathbb{G},g}^{\mathsf{CDH}}(\mathcal{A})$ is at least ϵ.

Definition 2. *Let $\mathcal{A}$ be an algorithm that takes three group elements as input and outputs 0 or 1. The* advantage *of $\mathcal{A}$ against the* Decision Diffie-Hellman (DDH) problem *[12] is*

$$\mathrm{Adv}_{\mathbb{G},g}^{\mathsf{DDH}}(\mathcal{A}) = |\Pr[\mathcal{A}(x, y, z) = 0 \mid (x, y, z) \leftarrow \mathcal{DDH}]-$$
$$\Pr[\mathcal{A}(x, y, z) = 0 \mid (x, y, z) \leftarrow \mathbb{G}^3]|.$$

We say that $\mathcal{A}$ (t, ϵ)-breaks DDH if $\mathcal{A}$ runs in time t and its advantage $\mathrm{Adv}_{\mathbb{G},g}^{\mathsf{DDH}}(\mathcal{A})$ is at least ϵ.

In proofs, it is often convenient to consider an adversary that sees multiple CDH/DDH problems. The n-CDH adversary must solve a CDH problem, but it gets to choose the group elements from two lists of randomly chosen group elements. The n-DDH adversary gets n tuples, all of which are either DDH tuples or random tuples. Again, it is often convenient if some of these DDH tuples share coordinates.

Definition 3. *Let $\mathcal{A}$ be an algorithm that takes as input $2n$ group elements and outputs two integers and a group element. The* success probability *of $\mathcal{A}$ against the n-CDH problem is*

$$\mathrm{Succ}_{\mathbb{G},g}^{n\text{-}\mathsf{CDH}}(\mathcal{A}) = \Pr\left[(x_i, y_j, z) \in \mathcal{DDH} \left| \begin{array}{l} x_1, \ldots, x_n, y_1, \ldots, y_n \leftarrow \mathbb{G}; \\ (i, j, z) \leftarrow \mathcal{A}(x, \ldots, x_n, y_1, \ldots, y_n) \end{array} \right. \right].$$

Definition 4. *Let $\mathcal{A}$ be an algorithm that outputs 0 or 1. $\mathcal{A}$ has access to an oracle that on input of an integer i returns three group elements. If $i > 0$, then the first group element returned will be the same as the first group element in the oracle's ith response. Let $\mathcal{O}_0$ be such an oracle that returns randomly chosen DDH tuples. Let $\mathcal{O}_1$ be such an oracle that returns randomly chosen triples of group elements.*

The advantage *of the algorithm $\mathcal{A}$ against the n-DDH problem is*

$$\mathrm{Adv}_{\mathbb{G},g}^{n\text{-}\mathsf{DDH}}(\mathcal{A}') = |\Pr[\mathcal{A}^{\mathcal{O}_0} = 0] - \Pr[\mathcal{A}^{\mathcal{O}_1} = 0]|.$$

It is clear that 1-CDH and 1-DDH correspond to the ordinary problems. Likewise, it is clear that we can embed a CDH or DDH problem in a n-CDH or n-DDH problem, so a hybrid argument would relate their advantage. However, the DH problems are random self-reducible, which means that we can create better bounds.

Theorem 1. *Let $\mathcal{A}$ be an adversary against n-CDH. Then there exists an adversary $\mathcal{B}$ against CDH such that*

$$\mathrm{Succ}_{\mathbb{G},g}^{n\text{-}\mathsf{CDH}}(\mathcal{A}) = \mathrm{Succ}_{\mathbb{G},g}^{\mathsf{CDH}}(\mathcal{B}).$$

The difference in running time is linear in n.

Theorem 2. *Let $\mathcal{A}$ be an adversary against n-DDH. Then there exists an adversary $\mathcal{B}$ against DDH such that*

$$\mathrm{Adv}_{\mathbb{G},g}^{n\text{-}\mathsf{DDH}}(\mathcal{A}') \leq \mathrm{Adv}_{\mathbb{G},g}^{\mathsf{DDH}}(\mathcal{B}) + \frac{1}{p}.$$

The difference in running time is linear in n.

The proof of the first theorem is straight-forward. A proof of the second theorem can be found in e.g. Bellare, Boldyreva and Micali [5].

Proofs of equality of discrete logarithms. Sigma protocols are special three-move protocols originating in the Schnorr identification protocol [46]. We shall need a proof of equality for discrete logarithms [15] together with the techniques for creating a witness-indistinguishable OR-proof [18].

Let $y, x, z \in \mathbb{G}$ be such that $x = g^a$ and $z = y^a$. The standard sigma protocol [15] for proving that $\log_g x = \log_y z$ works as follows:

Commitment. Sample $\rho \leftarrow \{0, 1, \ldots, p-1\}$. Compute $\alpha_0 = g^\rho$ and $\alpha_1 = y^\rho$. The commitment is (α_0, α_1).
Challenge. Sample $\beta \leftarrow \{0, 1, \ldots, p-1\}$. The challenge is β.
Response. Compute $\gamma \leftarrow \rho - \beta a \bmod p$. The response is γ.
Verification. The verifier accepts the response if

$$\alpha_0 = g^\gamma x^\beta \qquad\qquad \alpha_1 = y^\gamma z^\beta.$$

The usual special honest verifier zero knowledge simulator producing a simulated conversation on public input (x, y, z) and challenge β is denoted by $\mathsf{ZSim}_{\mathrm{eq}}(x, y, z; \beta)$, and it is a perfect simulator. The cost of generating a proof is dominated by the two exponentiations, while the simulation cost is dominated by four exponentiations.

We turn the proofs non-interactive using the standard Fiat-Shamir [21] heuristic, in which case the proof is a pair of integers (β, γ). We denote the algorithm for generating a non-interactive proof π_{eq} that $\log_g x = \log_y z$ by $\mathsf{ZPrv}_{\mathrm{eq}}(a; x, y, z)$. The algorithm for verifying that π_{eq} is a valid proof of this claim is denoted by $\mathsf{ZVfy}_{\mathrm{eq}}(\pi_{\mathrm{eq}}; x, y, z)$, which outputs 1 if and only if the proof is valid.

Based on this proof of equality for a pair of discrete logarithms, an OR-proof for the equality of one out of two pairs of discrete logarithms can be constructed using standard techniques [18].

Briefly, the prover chooses a random challenge β_{1-b} and uses the perfect simulator $\mathsf{ZSim}_{\mathrm{eq}}(\dots)$ to generate a simulated proof for the inequal pair. It then runs the equal d.log. prover which produces a commitment. When the verifier responds with a challenge β, the prover completes the proof for the equal pair using the challenge $\beta_b = \beta - \beta_{1-b}$. It then responds with both challenges and both responses. The verifier checks that the challenges sum to β.

We denote the special honest verifier simulator by

$$\mathsf{ZSim}_{\mathrm{eq,or}}(x_0, x_1, y_0, y_1, z_0, z_1; \beta_0, \beta_1)$$

We note that for any given challenge pair (β_0, β_1), the simulator generates a particular transcript with probability $1/p^2$.

Again, we can turn these proofs non-interactive using Fiat-Shamir and a hash function H_2. In this case, the proof is a tuple $(\beta_0, \beta_1, \gamma_0, \gamma_1)$ of integers, and the verifier additionally checks that the hash value equals the sum of β_0 and β_1. The non-interactive algorithms for generating and verifying proofs are denoted by $\mathsf{ZPrv}_{\mathrm{eq,or}}(b, a_b; x_0, x_1, y_0, y_1, z_0, z_1)$ and $\mathsf{ZVfy}_{\mathrm{eq,or}}(\pi_{\mathrm{eq,or}}; x_0, x_1, y_0, y_1, z_0, z_1)$. The cost of generating a proof is dominated by the two exponentiations for the real equality proof and the four exponentiations for the fake equality proof.

As usual, the simulator is perfect. In addition, these proofs have very strong properties in the random oracle model.

Theorem 3. *Let $\mathcal{A}$ be an algorithm in the random oracle model, making at most l hash queries, that outputs a tuple $(x_0, x_1, y_0, y_1, z_0, z_1)$ of group elements and a proof $\pi_{\mathrm{eq,or}}$. The probability that $\mathsf{ZVfy}_{\mathrm{eq,or}}(\pi_{\mathrm{eq,or}}; x_0, x_1, y_0, y_1, z_0, z_1) = 1$, but $(x_0, y_0, z_0) \notin \mathcal{DDH}$ and $(x_1, y_1, z_1) \notin \mathcal{DDH}$, is at most $\frac{l+1}{p}$.*

The proof of the theorem is straightforward and is implicit in *e.g.* Goh and Jarecki [25].

Digital Signatures. A digital signature scheme consists of a triple $(\mathsf{Gen}, \mathsf{Sign}, \mathsf{Vfy})$ of algorithms. The *key generation* algorithm Gen (possibly taking a set of parameters Π as input) outputs a key pair (vk, sk). The *signing* algorithm Sign takes a signing key sk and a message m as input and outputs a signature σ. The *verification* algorithm Vfy takes a verification key vk, a message m and a signature σ as input and outputs 0 or 1. For correctness, we require that for all $(vk, sk) \leftarrow \mathsf{Gen}$ we have that $\Pr[\mathsf{Vfy}(vk, m, \mathsf{Sign}(sk, m))] = 1$.

3   Signatures with Tight Multi-User Security

Now we are ready to describe our signature scheme with tight multi-user security in a "real-world" security model with adaptive corruptions.

3.1 Security Definition

We define multi-user existential unforgeability under adaptive chosen-message attacks with adaptive corruptions, called MU-EUF-CMA^{corr} security in [2]. Consider the following game between a challenger $\mathcal{C}$ and an adversary $\mathcal{A}$, which is parametrized by the number of public keys μ.

1. For each $i \in [\mu]$, it computes $(pk^{(i)}, sk^{(i)}) \xleftarrow{\$} \text{Gen}(\Pi)$. Furthermore, it initializes a set $\mathcal{S}^{\text{corr}}$ to keep track of corrupted keys, and μ sets $\mathcal{S}_1, \ldots, \mathcal{S}_\mu$, to keep track of chosen-message queries. All sets are initially empty. Then it outputs $(pk^{(1)}, \ldots, pk^{(\mu)})$ to $\mathcal{A}$.
2. $\mathcal{A}$ may now issue two different types of queries. When $\mathcal{A}$ outputs an index $i \in [\mu]$, then $\mathcal{C}$ updates $\mathcal{S}^{\text{corr}} := \mathcal{S}^{\text{corr}} \cup \{i\}$ and returns $sk^{(i)}$. When $\mathcal{A}$ outputs a tuple (m, i), then $\mathcal{C}$ computes $\sigma := \text{Sign}(sk_i, m)$, adds (m, σ) to $\mathcal{S}_i$, and responds with σ.
3. Eventually $\mathcal{A}$ outputs a triple (i^*, m^*, σ^*).

Definition 5. *Let $\mathcal{A}$ be a MU-EUF-CMA^{corr}-adversary against a signature scheme $\Sigma = (\text{Gen}, \text{Sign}, \text{Vfy})$. The advantage of $\mathcal{A}$ is*

$$\text{Adv}_{\Sigma}^{\text{euf-cma}}(\mathcal{A}) = \Pr\left[(m^*, i^*, \sigma^*) \leftarrow \mathcal{A}^{\mathcal{C}} : \begin{array}{c} i^* \notin \mathcal{S}^{\text{corr}} \wedge (m^*, \cdot) \notin \mathcal{S}_{i^*} \\ \wedge \text{Vfy}(vk^{(i^*)}, m^*, \sigma^*) = 1 \end{array}\right].$$

We say that $\mathcal{A}$ (t, ϵ, μ)-breaks the MU-EUF-CMA^{corr}-security of Σ if $\mathcal{A}$ runs in time t and $\text{Adv}_{\Sigma}^{\text{euf-cma}}(\mathcal{A}) \geq \epsilon$. Here, we include the running time of the security experiment into the running time of $\mathcal{A}$.

Remark 1. We include the running time of the security experiment into the running time t of $\mathcal{A}$, because this makes it slightly simpler to analyse the running time of our reduction precisely. Let t_{Exp} denote the time required to run the security experiment alone, and let $t_{\mathcal{A}}$ be the running time of the adversary alone. Given that the experiment can be implemented very efficiently, we may assume $t_{\mathcal{A}} \geq t_{\text{Exp}}$ for any conceivable adversary $\mathcal{A}$, so this increases the running time at most by a small constant factor. It allows us to make the analysis of our reduction more rigorous.

3.2 Construction

Let $H_1 : R \times \{0, 1\}^* \to \mathbb{G}$ be a hash function from a randomness set R and a message space $\{0, 1\}^*$ to the group $\mathbb{G}$. The digital signature scheme Σ_{mu} works as follows:

Key generation. Sample $b \leftarrow \{0, 1\}$, $a_b \leftarrow \{0, 1, \ldots, p - 1\}$ and $x_{1-b} \leftarrow \mathbb{G}$. Compute $x_b \leftarrow g^{a_b}$. The signing key is $sk = (b, a_b)$ and the verification key is $vk = (x_0, x_1)$.

Signing. To sign a message m using signing key $sk = (b, a_b)$, sample $t \leftarrow R$ and $z_{1-b} \leftarrow \mathbb{G}$, let $y = H_1(t, m)$ and compute $z_b \leftarrow y^{a_b}$. Then create a non-interactive zero knowledge proof

$$\pi_{\text{eq,or}} \leftarrow \mathsf{ZPrv}_{\text{eq,or}}(b, a_b; x_0, x_1, y, y, z_0, z_1)$$

proving that $\log_g x_0 = \log_y z_0$ or $\log_g x_1 = \log_y z_1$. The signature is $\sigma = (t, z_0, z_1, \pi_{\text{eq,or}})$.

Verification. To verify a signature $\sigma = (t, z_0, z_1, \pi_{\text{eq,or}})$ on a message m under verification key $vk = (x_0, x_1)$, compute $y = H_1(t, m)$ and verify that $\pi_{\text{eq,or}}$ is a proof of the claim that $\log_g x_0 = \log_y z_0$ or $\log_g x_1 = \log_y z_1$ by checking that $\mathsf{ZVfy}_{\text{eq,or}}(\pi_{\text{eq,or}}; x_0, x_1, y, y, z_0, z_1) = 1$.

The correctness of the scheme follows directly from the correctness of the non-interactive zero knowledge proof.

Theorem 4. *Let $\mathcal{S}$ be a forger for the signature scheme Σ_{mu} in the random oracle model, making at most l hash queries (with no repeating queries), interacting with at most μ users and asking for at most n signatures. Then there exists adversaries $\mathcal{B}$ and $\mathcal{C}$ against DDH and CDH, respectively, such that*

$$\mathrm{Adv}_{\Sigma_{mu}}^{\text{euf-cma}}(\mathcal{A}) \leq \mathrm{Adv}_{\mathbb{G},g}^{\text{DDH}}(\mathcal{B}) + 2\,\mathrm{Succ}_{\mathbb{G},g}^{\text{CDH}}(\mathcal{C}) + \frac{nl}{p^2} + \frac{nl}{|R|} + \frac{1}{p} + \frac{ln}{2p} + \frac{l+1}{p}.$$

The difference in running time is linear in $\mu + l + n$.

3.3 Proof of Theorem 4

The proof proceeds as a sequence of games between a simulator and a forger for the signature scheme. For each game G_i, there is an event E_i corresponding to the adversary "winning" the game. We prove bounds on the differences $\Pr[E_i] - \Pr[E_{i+1}]$ for consecutive games, and finally bound the probability $\Pr[E_5]$ for the last game. Our claim follows directly from these bounds in the usual fashion.

Game 0 The first game is the standard multi-user signature game where μ key pairs are generated. The adversary $\mathcal{S}$ may ask for signatures on any message under any un-revealed key. The adversary may also ask for any signing key.

Let E_0 be the event that the adversary produces a valid forgery (and let E_i be the corresponding event for the remaining games). We have that

$$\mathrm{Adv}_{\Sigma_{mu}}^{\text{euf-cma}}(\mathcal{S}) = \Pr[E_0]. \tag{1}$$

Game 1 In this game, when the adversary asks for a signature on a message, instead of creating the zero knowledge proofs using $\mathsf{ZPrv}_{\text{eq,or}}(\dots)$, we sample challenges β_0, β_1 and create a simulated proof using $\mathsf{ZSim}_{\text{eq,or}}(\dots; \beta_0, \beta_1)$ and then reprogram the random oracle H_2 such that $H_2(\dots) = \beta_0 + \beta_1 \bmod p$.

Since the challenge in the simulated conversation has been chosen uniformly at random, this change is not observable unless the random oracle H_2 had been queried at this exact position before the reprogramming, and the reprogramming attempt fails.

As discussed in Sect. 2, the simulator will choose any particular proof with probability at most $1/p^2$, so the probability that any reprogramming attempt fails is at most l/p^2. The probability of the exceptional event, that at least one of the n attempts fail, is then upperbounded by nl/p^2, giving us

$$|\Pr[E_1] - \Pr[E_0]| \leq nl/p^2. \tag{2}$$

Game 2 Next, when the adversary asks for a signature on a message, instead of just computing the hash of the message directly, we sample $\xi \leftarrow \{0, 1, \ldots, p-1\}$, compute $y \leftarrow g^\xi$ and then reprogram the random oracle H_1 such that $H_1(t, m) = y$.

Since t is sampled from a set R with $|R|$ elements, if there are at most l hash queries in the game, the probability that any one reprogramming attempt fails is at most $l/|R|$. The probability of the exceptional event, that at least one of the n attempts fail, is then upperbounded by $nl/|R|$, giving us

$$|\Pr[E_2] - \Pr[E_1]| \leq \frac{nl}{|R|}. \tag{3}$$

Game 3 We now modify the key generation algorithm used by the simulator, so that instead of sampling x_{1-b} from $\mathbb{G}$, it samples $a_{1-b} \leftarrow \{0, 1, \ldots, p - 1\}$ and computes $x_{1-b} \leftarrow g^{a_{1-b}}$. The experiment stores the a_{1-b} along with a_b as (b, a_0, a_1). However, when the adversary asks for a signing key, the simulator still returns (b, a_b).

In the original key generation algorithm, x_{1-b} is sampled from the uniform distribution on the group. The key value a_{1-b} is sampled from the uniform distribution on $\{0, 1, \ldots, p - 1\}$, so x_{1-b} will also be sampled from the same distribution in this game. Since a_{1-b} is never used and never revealed, this game is indistinguishable from the previous game and

$$\Pr[E_3] = \Pr[E_2]. \tag{4}$$

Game 4 We now modify the signing algorithm used by the simulator, so that instead of sampling z_{1-b} from $\mathbb{G}$, we compute $z_{1-b} \leftarrow y^{a_{1-b}}$.

To bound the difference between this game and the previous one, we need the auxillary $\mu + n$-DDH distinguisher $\mathcal{B}'$ given in Fig. 1.

Regardless of which oracle $\mathcal{B}'$ interacts with, the verification key element x_{1-b} and y are sampled from the uniform distribution on $\mathbb{G}$, just like it is in both this game and the previous game.

When the adversary $\mathcal{B}'$ interacts with the oracle $\mathcal{O}_1$ which returns random tuples, then the oracle samples its third coordinate from the uniform distribution on $\mathbb{G}$, and this value is independent of all other values. Thus z_{1-b} is sampled from the uniform distribution on $\mathbb{G}$, just like in Game 3.

The distinguisher has access to an oracle $\mathcal{O}$.
It proceeds to run Game 4 with $\mathcal{S}$ with the following modifications:

1. The key generation algorithm used by the simulator queries its oracle with 0 and gets the reply (x, y, z). It sets $x_{1-b} \leftarrow x$ and discards y, z.
2. The signing algorithm used by the simulator, when signing with the signing key (b, a_0, a_1) corresponding to the public key (x_0, x_1) with x_{1-b} equal to the first group element of the ith oracle response, the simulator sends i to its oracle and receives the response (x_{1-b}, y, z). It then uses y unchanged as the hash value and sets $z_{1-b} \leftarrow z$.

If $\mathcal{S}$ eventually produces a valid forgery, the distinguisher outputs 0. Otherwise it outputs 1.

Fig. 1. $\mu + n$-DDH distinguisher $\mathcal{B}'$ used in the proof of Theorem 4.

When the adversary $\mathcal{B}'$ interacts with the oracle $\mathcal{O}_0$ which returns DDH tuples, then (x_{1-b}, y, z_{1-b}) is a DDH tuple, just like in Game 4.

We conclude that $\mathcal{B}'$ perfectly simulates the two games, depending on which oracle it has access to, and by Theorem 2 it follows that there exists a DDH adversary $\mathcal{B}$ such that

$$| \Pr[E_4] - \Pr[E_3]| = | \Pr[\mathcal{B}'^{\mathcal{O}_0}] - \Pr[\mathcal{B}'^{\mathcal{O}_1}]| \leq \mathrm{Adv}_{\mathbb{G},g}^{\mathsf{DDH}}(\mathcal{B}) + \frac{1}{p}. \quad (5)$$

At this point, we observe that in this game, the adversary has no information about b for any of the unrevealed keys.

Game 5 We now modify the signing algorithm, so that instead of computing $z_{1-b} \leftarrow y^{a_{1-b}}$, we compute $z_{1-b} \leftarrow x_{1-b}^{\xi}$, where ξ comes from the computation $y \leftarrow g^{\xi}$ introduced in Game 2.

Since $y^{a_{1-b}} = (g^{\xi})^{a_{1-b}} = (g^{a_{1-b}})^{\xi} = x_{1-b}^{\xi}$, the adversary cannot detect this change. Therefore

$$\Pr[E_5] = \Pr[E_4]. \quad (6)$$

Note that in this game, the fake signing key a_{1-b} introduced in Game 3 is no longer actually used for anything except computing x_{1-b}.

Suppose the adversary wins Game 5 by outputting a signature $(t, z_0, z_1, \pi_{\mathsf{eq,or}})$ for a message m and hash $y = H_1(t, m)$ under the verification key (x_0, x_1) with signature key (b, a_0, a_1).

Since we can recover a tuple $(x_0, x_1, y, y, z_0, z_1)$ and a proof $\pi_{\mathsf{eq,or}}$, we would like to apply Theorem 3. But this is tricky because we simulate proofs and reprogram the random oracle involved in the theorem. However, since the adversary's forgery must be on a message that has not been signed by our signature oracle, the forgery cannot involve any value for which we have reprogrammed the random oracle, unless the adversary has found a collision in H_1. This collision must

The solver takes $(x_1, \ldots, x_l, y_1, \ldots, y_l)$ as input.
It proceeds to run Game 5 with $\mathcal{S}$ with the following modifications:

1. When the key generation algorithm used by the simulator generates the ith key pair, it sets $x_{1-b} \leftarrow x_i$.
   The algorithm remembers (x_{1-b}, i).
2. When the forger $\mathcal{S}$ queries the hash oracle with the jth value (t, m) that has not been seen before, the hash oracle sets $y \leftarrow y_j$ and reprograms the hash oracle so that $H_1(t, m) = y$.
   The algorithm remembers (t, m, j).

When the signature forger outputs a valid signature $(t, z_0, z_1, \pi_{\text{eq,or}})$ for a message m under an unrevealed key (b, a_0, a_1) with corresponding public key (x_0, x_1), the solver recalls (x_{1-b}, i) and (t, m, j) and outputs

$$(i, j, z_{1-b}).$$

Fig. 2. l-CDH adversary $\mathcal{C}'$ used in the proof of Theorem 4.

involve a (t, m) pair from a signing query, which means that the probability of a collision is at most $ln/2p$.

When there is no such collision, Theorem 3 applies and we know that either $\log_y z_0 = \log_g x_0$ or $\log_y z_1 = \log_g x_1$ (or both), except with probability $(l+1)/p$.

Since the forger $\mathcal{S}$ has no information about b, it follows that if equality holds for one of the discrete logarithm pairs, then $\log_y z_{1-b} = \log_g x_{1-b}$ at least half the time.

Consider the l-CDH adversary $\mathcal{C}'$ given in Fig. 2. It is clear that it perfectly simulates Game 5 with the adversary $\mathcal{S}$. Furthermore, when the output signature satisfies $\log_y z_{1-b} = \log_g x_{1-b}$, the l-CDH adversary outputs the correct answer. By Theorem 1 there exists a CDH adversary $\mathcal{C}$ such that

$$\Pr[E_5] \leq 2\operatorname{Succ}_{\mathbb{G},g}^{\mathsf{CDH}}(\mathcal{C}) + \frac{ln}{2p} + \frac{l+1}{p}. \tag{7}$$

Theorem 4 now follows from Eqs. (1)–(7).

4   Key Exchange

Now we describe our construction of a tightly-secure key exchange protocol, which uses the signature scheme presented above as a subroutine and additionally resolves the "commitment-problem" sketched in the introduction. This yields the first authenticated key exchange protocol which does not require a trusted setup, has tight security, and truly practical efficiency. The security proof is in the Random Oracle Model [6].

4.1   Security Model

Up to minor notational changes and clarifications, our security model is identical to the model from [2], except that we use the recent approach of Li and Schäge [41] to define "partnering" of oracles. Furthermore, we include a "sender identifier" into the Send query (its relevance is discussed below). As in [2], we let the adversary issue more than one Test-query, in order to achieve tightness in this dimension, too.

Execution Environment. We consider μ parties $P_1, \ldots, P_\mu$. Each party P_i is represented by a set of ℓ oracles, $\{\pi_i^1, \ldots, \pi_i^\ell\}$, where each oracle corresponds to a single protocol execution, and $\ell \in \mathbb{N}$ is the maximum number of protocol sessions per party. Each oracle is equipped with a randomness tape containing random bits, but is otherwise deterministic. Each oracle π_i^s has access to the long-term key pair $(sk^{(i)}, pk^{(i)})$ of party P_i and to the public keys of all other parties, and maintains a list of internal state variables that are described in the following:

- ρ_i^s is the randomness tape of π_i^s.
- Pid_i^s stores the identity of the intended communication partner.
- $\Psi_i^s \in \{\mathtt{accept}, \mathtt{reject}\}$ indicates whether oracle π_i^s has successfully completed the protocol execution and "accepted" the resulting key.
- k_i^s stores the session key computed by π_i^s.

For each oracle π_i^s these variables are initialized as $(\mathsf{Pid}_i^s, \Psi_i^s, k_i^s) = (\emptyset, \emptyset, \emptyset)$, where $\emptyset$ denotes the empty string. The computed session key is assigned to the variable k_i^s if and only if π_i^s reaches the $\mathtt{accept}$ state, that is, we have $k_i^s \neq \emptyset \iff \Psi_i^s = \mathtt{accept}$.

Attacker Model. The attacker $\mathcal{A}$ interacts with these oracles through queries. Following the classical Bellare-Rogaway approach [7], we consider an active attacker that has full control over the communication network, and to model further real world capabilites of an attacker, we provide additionally queries. The Corrupt-query allows the adversary to compromise the long-term key of a party. The Reveal-query may be used to obtain the session key that was computed in a previous protocol instance. The RegisterCorrupt enables the attacker to register maliciously-generated public keys, and we do not require the adversary to know the corresponding secret key. The Test-query does not correspond to any real world capability of an adversary, but it is used to evaluate the advantage of $\mathcal{A}$ in breaking the security of the key exchange protocol. However, we do not allow reveals of ephemeral randomness, as in [8,14]. More precisely:

- Send(i, s, j, m): $\mathcal{A}$ can use this query to send any message m of its choice to oracle π_i^s on behalf of party P_j. The oracle will respond according to the protocol specification and depending on its internal state.

If $(\mathsf{Pid}_i^s, \Psi_i^s) = (\emptyset, \emptyset)$ and $m = \emptyset$, then this means that $\mathcal{A}$ initiates a protocol execution by requesting π_i^s to send the first protocol message to party P_j. In this case, π_i^s will set $\mathsf{Pid}_i^s = j$ and respond with the first message according to the protocol specification.

If $(\mathsf{Pid}_i^s, \Psi_i^s) = (\emptyset, \emptyset)$ and $m \neq \emptyset$, then this means that $\mathcal{A}$ sends a first protocol message from party P_j to π_i^s. In this case, π_i^s will set $\mathsf{Pid}_i^s = j$ and respond with the second message according to the protocol specification. This is the only reason why we include the "partner identifier" j in the Send query.

If $\mathsf{Pid}_i^s = j' \neq \emptyset$ and $j \neq j'$, then this means that the partner id of π_i^s has already been set to j', but the adversary issues a Send-query with $j \neq j'$. In this case, π_i^s will abort by setting $\Psi_i^s = \texttt{reject}$ and responding with $\perp$.

Finally, if π_i^s has already rejected (that is, it holds that $\Psi_i^s = \texttt{reject}$), then π_i^s always responds with $\perp$.

If $\mathsf{Send}(i, s, j, m)$ is the τ-th query asked by $\mathcal{A}$, and oracle π_i^s sets variable $\Psi_i^s = \texttt{accept}$ after this query, then we say that π_i^s has τ-*accepted*.

- Corrupt(i): This query returns the long-term secret key sk_i of party P_i. If the τ-th query of $\mathcal{A}$ is Corrupt(i), then we call P_i τ-corrupted, or simply corrupted. If P_i is corrupted, then all oracles $\pi_i^1, \ldots, \pi_i^\ell$ respond with $\perp$ to all queries.

  We assume without loss of generality that Corrupt(i) is only asked at most once for each i. If Corrupt(i) has not yet been issued by $\mathcal{A}$, then we say that party i is currently ∞-corrupted.

- RegisterCorrupt$(i, pk^{(i)})$: This query allows $\mathcal{A}$ to register a new party $P_i, i > \mu$, with public key $pk^{(i)}$. If the same party P_i is already registered (either via RegisterCorrupt-query or $i \in [\mu]$), a failure symbol $\perp$ is returned to $\mathcal{A}$. Otherwise, P_i is registered, the pair $(P_i, pk^{(i)})$ is distributed to all other parties.

  Parties registered by this query are called *adversarially-controlled*. All parties controlled by the adversary are defined to be 0-corrupted. Furthermore, there are no oracles corresponding to these parties.

- Reveal(i, s): In response to this query π_i^s returns the contents of k_i^s. Recall that we have $k_i^s \neq \emptyset$ if and only if $\Psi_i^s = \texttt{accept}$. If Reveal$(i, s)$ is the τ-th query issued by $\mathcal{A}$, we call π_i^s τ-revealed. If Reveal(i, s) has not (yet) been issued by $\mathcal{A}$, then we say that oracle π_i^s is currently ∞-revealed.

- Test(i, s): If $\Psi_i^s \neq \texttt{accept}$, then a failure symbol $\perp$ is returned. Otherwise π_i^s flips a fair coin b_i^s, samples $k_0 \xleftarrow{\$} \mathcal{K}$ at random, sets $k_1 = k_i^s$, and returns $k_{b_i^s}$. The attacker may ask many Test-queries to different oracles, but not more than one to each oracle. Jumping slightly ahead, we note that there exists a trivial adversary that wins with probability $1/4$, if we allow Test-queries of the above form to "partnered" oracles. In order to address this, we have to define partnering first. Then we will disallow Test-queries to partnered oracles in the AKE security definition (Definition 7).

Partnering and original keys. In order to exclude trivial attacks, we need a notion of "partnering" of two oracles. Bader *et al.* [2] base their security definition on the classical notion of *matching conversations* of Bellare and Rogaway [7]. However, Li and Schäge [41] showed recently that this notion is error-prone and argued convincingly that it captures the cryptographic intuition behind "secure authenticated key exchange" in a very conservative way. This is because the strong requirement of matching conversation even rules out theoretical attacks based on "benign malleability" (e.g., efficient re-randomizability of signatures), which does not match any practical attacks, but breaks matching conversations, and thus seems stronger than necessary. This may hinder the design of simple and efficient protocols.

The new idea of [41] is to based "partnering" on an *original key* of a pair of oracles (π_i^s, π_j^t). Recall that we consider an oracle π_i^s as a deterministic algorithm, but with access to a fixed randomness tape ρ_i^s. The *original key* $K_0(\pi_i^s, \pi_j^t)$ of a pair of oracles (π_i^s, π_j^t) consists of the session key that both oracles would have computed by executing the protocol with each other, and where π_i^s sends the first message. Note that $K_0(\pi_i^s, \pi_j^t)$ depends deterministically on the partner identities i and j and the randomness ρ_i^s and ρ_j^t of both oracles. Note also that for certain protocols it may not necessarily hold that $K_0(\pi_i^s, \pi_j^t) = K_0(\pi_j^t, \pi_i^s)$, thus the order of oracles in the K_0 function matters.

Definition 6 (Partnering). *We say that oracle π_i^s is partnered to oracle π_j^t, if at least one of the following two condition holds.*

1. *π_i^s has sent the first protocol message and it holds that $k_i^s = K_0(\pi_i^s, \pi_j^t)$*
2. *π_i^s has received the first protocol message and it holds that $k_i^s = K_0(\pi_j^t, \pi_i^s)$*

Security experiment. Consider the following game, played between an adversary $\mathcal{A}$ and a challenger $\mathcal{C}$. The game is parameterized by two numbers μ (the number of honest identities) and ℓ (the maximum number of protocol executions per party).

1. $\mathcal{C}$ generates μ long-term key pairs $(sk^{(i)}, pk^{(i)}), i \in [\mu]$. It provides a $\mathcal{A}$ with all public keys $pk^{(1)}, \ldots, pk^{(\mu)}$.
2. The challenger $\mathcal{C}$ provides $\mathcal{A}$ with the security experiment, by implementing a collection of oracles $\{\pi_i^s : i \in [\mu], s \in [\ell]\}$. $\mathcal{A}$ may adaptively issue Send, Corrupt, Reveal, RegisterCorrupt and Test queries to these oracles in arbitrary order.
3. At the end of the game, $\mathcal{A}$ terminates and outputs (i, s, b'), where (i, s) specifies an oracle π_i^s and b' is a guess for b_i^s.

We write $G_\Pi(\mu, \ell)$ to denote this security game, carried out with parameters μ, ℓ and protocol Π.

Definition 7 (AKE Security). *An attacker $\mathcal{A}$ breaks the security of protocol Π, if at least one of the following two events occurs in $G_\Pi(\mu, \ell)$:*

Attack on authentication. Event break_A *denotes that at any point throughout the security experiment there exists an oracle π_i^s such that all the following conditions are satisfied.*

1. *π_i^s has accepted, that is, it holds that $\Psi_i^s = \mathsf{accept}$.*
2. *It holds that $\mathsf{Pid}_i^s = j$ for some $j \in [\mu]$ and party P_j is ∞-corrupted.*
3. *There exists no unique oracle π_j^t that π_i^s is partnered to.*

Attack on key indistinguishability. *We assume without loss of generality that*
$\mathcal{A}$ *issues a* Test(i, s)-*query only to oracles with* $\Psi_i^s =$ accept, *as otherwise the*
query returns always returns $\perp$. *We say that event* break$_{\mathrm{KE}}$ *occurs if* $\mathcal{A}$ *outputs*
(i, s, b') *and all the following conditions are satisfied.*

1. break$_{\mathrm{A}}$ *does not occur throughout the security experiment.*
2. *The intended communication partner of* π_i^s *is not corrupted before the*
   Test(i, s)-*query. Formally, if* Pid$_i^s = j$ *and* π_i^s *is* τ-*tested, then it holds that*
   $j \le \mu$ *and party* P_j *is* τ'-*corrupted with* $\tau' \ge \tau$.
3. *The adversary never asks a* Reveal-*query to* π_i^s. *Formally, we require that* π_i^s
   is ∞-*revealed throughout the security experiment.*
4. *The adversary never asks a* Reveal-*query to the partner oracle of* π_i^s.[6] *For-*
   mally, we demand that π_j^t *is* ∞-*revealed throughout the security experiment.*
5. $\mathcal{A}$ *answers the* Test-*query correctly. That is, it holds that* $b_i^s = b'$, *and if*
   there exists an oracle π_j^t *that* π_i^s *is partnered to, then* $\mathcal{A}$ *must not have asked*
   Test(j, t).

The advantage *of the adversary* $\mathcal{A}$ *against AKE security of* Π *is*

$$\mathrm{Adv}_\Pi^{\mathsf{AKE}}(\mathcal{A}) = \max\left\{\Pr\left[\mathrm{break_A}\right], |\Pr\left[\mathrm{break_{KE}}\right] - 1/2|\right\}.$$

We say that $\mathcal{A}$ $(\epsilon_{\mathcal{A}}, t, \mu, \ell)$-*breaks* Π *if its running time is* t *and* $\mathrm{Adv}_\Pi^{\mathsf{AKE}}(\mathcal{A}) \ge \epsilon_{\mathcal{A}}$.
Again, we include the running time of the security experiment into the running
time of $\mathcal{A}$ *(cf. Remark 1).*

Remark 2. Note that Definition 7 defines event break$_{\mathrm{KE}}$ such that it occurs only
if break$_{\mathrm{A}}$ does *not* occur. We stress that this is without loss of generality. It makes
the two possible ways to break the security of the protocol mutually exclusive,
which in turn makes the reasoning in a security proof slightly simpler.

Remark 3. Note that an oracle π_i^s may be corrupted before the Test(i, s)-query.
This provides security against *key-compromise impersonation* attacks. Furthermore, the communication partner π_j^t may be corrupted as well, but only after
π_i^s has accepted (to prevent the trivial impersonation attack), which provides
forward security (aka. *perfect forward secrecy*).

4.2   Construction

In this section, we construct our protocol, based on a digital signature scheme
$\Sigma = (\mathsf{Gen}, \mathsf{Sign}, \mathsf{Vfy})$, a prime-order group $(\mathbb{G}, g, p)$, and cryptographic hash functions $G : \{0, 1\}^* \to \{0, 1\}^\kappa$ and $H : \mathbb{G} \to \{0, 1\}^d$ for some $d \in \mathbb{N}$.

---

[6] Note that conditions 1 and 2 together imply that there exists a unique oracle π_j^t that
π_i^s is partnered to, as otherwise break$_{\mathrm{A}}$ occurs.

Protocol description. Let us consider a protocol execution between two parties Alice and Bob. The protocol is essentially the classical "signed Diffie-Hellman" with hashed session key, except that there is an additional first message which contains a cryptographic commitment to the Diffie-Hellman share g^a of the initiator of the protocol. This adds another message to the protocol, but is an important ingredient to achieve tightness, along the lines sketched in the introduction. We stress that this additional message does not increase the latency of the protocol. That is, the protocol initiator is able to send cryptographically-protected payload data after one round-trip times (RTTs), exactly as with ordinary signed Diffie-Hellman.

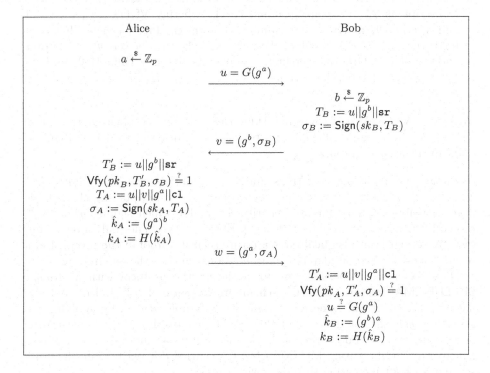

Fig. 3. Basic protocol outline.

Each party is in possession of a long-term key pair $(pk, sk) \overset{\$}{\leftarrow} \mathsf{Gen}(1^\kappa)$ for signature scheme Σ. We write (pk_A, sk_A) and (pk_B, sk_B) to denote the key pair of Alice and Bob, respectively. If Alice initiates a key exchange, then both parties proceed as follows.

1. Alice chooses a random exponent $a \overset{\$}{\leftarrow} \mathbb{Z}_p$, computes $u := G(g^a)$, and sends u to Bob.
2. When Bob receives u, he picks $b \overset{\$}{\leftarrow} \mathbb{Z}_p$ and defines its local transcript of messages as $T_B = u||g^b||\mathsf{sr}$, where sr is a constant that indicates that Bob

acts as a server in this session. Then it computes $\sigma_B := \mathsf{Sign}(sk_B, T_B)$, and responds with $v := (g^b, \sigma_B)$ to Alice.

3. When Alice receives $v := (g^b, \sigma_B)$, she first defines her local view of Bob's transcript as $T'_B = u||g^b||\mathtt{sr}$ and checks $\mathsf{Vfy}(pk_B, T'_B, \sigma_B) \stackrel{?}{=} 1$. If not, then she terminates the protocol execution and sets $\Psi_A := \mathtt{reject}$. Otherwise, she defines her local transcript as $T_A = u||v||g^a||\mathtt{cl}$, where $\mathtt{cl} \neq \mathtt{sr}$ is a constant indicating that Alice acts as a client. Then she computes $\sigma_A := \mathsf{Sign}(sk_A, T_A)$ and sends $w := (g^a, \sigma_A)$ to Bob. Furthermore, she first computes an "internal Diffie-Hellman key" $\hat{k}_A = g^{ab}$, and then the actual session key as $k_A = H(\hat{k}_A)$, and sets $\Psi_A := \mathtt{accept}$.

4. When Bob receives $w := (g^a, \sigma_A)$, he first defines his local view of Alice's transcript as $T'_A = u||v||g^a||\mathtt{cl}$ and checks whether $\mathsf{Vfy}(pk_A, T'_A, \sigma_A) = 1$ and whether g^a matches the commitment from the first message, that is, it holds that $u = G(g^a)$. If one of these checks fails, then he sets $\Psi_B := \mathtt{reject}$ and terminates. Otherwise he first computes its "internal Diffie-Hellman key" $\hat{k}_B = g^{ab}$, and then the actual session key $k_B = H(\hat{k}_B)$, and sets $\Psi_A := \mathtt{accept}$.

Remark 4. We make the "internal Diffie-Hellman key" explicit in the above description, because it will be useful to refer to it in order to define a certain event in the security proof.

Remark 5. We point out that the signatures σ_A and σ_B over $T_A = u||v||g^a||\mathtt{cl}$ and $T_B = u||g^b||\mathtt{sr}$ protect the whole message transcripts, which is more than actually necessary for our security proof (for which signing g^a and g^b, respectively, would actually be sufficient). However, this is not only a more conservative design, but also facilitates a future security proof of the protocol in a security model based on matching conversations, such as the one from [2].

This seems easily possible, by instantiating the protocol with a *strongly* $\mathsf{MU\text{-}EUF\text{-}CMA}^{\mathsf{corr}}$-secure signature scheme in the sense of [13]. Indeed, our signature scheme can easily be made tight strongly-unforgeable, by applying the generic transformation of [49], but this would increase the size of signatures by one group element and one exponent. We leave it as an interesting open problem to prove tight strong $\mathsf{MU\text{-}EUF\text{-}CMA}^{\mathsf{corr}}$-security *directly* for our signature scheme, without increasing the size of signatures.

Correctness. It is straightforward to verify that this protocol is correct.

Efficiency and latency. At a first glance, our protocol seems less efficient than ordinary signed Diffie-Hellman, because the additional message u adds another protocol round and thus latency. We stress that this is actually not the case, for typical applications. Consider a setting where Alice (a client) wants to send cryptographically protected payload data to a server (Bob). To this end, she initiates the protocol by sending message u. Then she waits for message v, which takes about 1 RTT (round trip time). Finally, she computes message w. At this time Alice has already accepted the key exchange, in particular she has computed the key k_A. This means that she can immediately send cryptographically protected payload data along with message w. Thus, the latency overhead of our protocol, defined as the time that Alice has to wait before she can send cryptographically protected payload, is only 1 RTT.

Now let us compare this to standard signed Diffie-Hellman, which essentially corresponds to our protocol restricted to messages v and w, without the additional commitment message u. In the same setting as above, the client Alice would now send the first protocol message v and then wait for w, which again takes 1 RTT. Only then is Alice able to compute the session key, and use it to send cryptographically protected payload. Thus, even though one message less is sent, it still takes 1 RTT before the session key can be used by Alice.

Thus, while our tightly-secure protocol uses an additional message u, this message does not increase the latency of key establishment at all. Furthermore, message u can be as small as 20–32 bytes in practice, such that the total communication overhead incurred by the key exchange protocol is not significantly increased. At the same time, the best known security proof of signed Diffie-Hellman has even *quadratic* security loss. In contrast, our protocol achieves tightness with only constant security loss, without significantly increasing latency or communication complexity.

Efficiency in real-world PKI settings. As usual in cryptographic theory, our security model considers a setting where each party "magically" has access to all public keys of all other parties. In practice, this is not realistic. Instead, in typical real-world protocols like TLS [20] public keys are typically exchanged within the protocol, along with certificates attesting their authenticity. Often this requires additional protocol rounds, and thus adds further messages and latency to the protocol.

We point out that our protocol does not require any such additional protocol rounds when used in a real-world PKI setting. Concretely, we could simply extend message v to $v = (g^b, \sigma_B, pk_B, \text{cert}_B)$, where (pk_B, cert_B) is the certified public key of Bob. Message w would be adopted accordingly to $w = (g^a, \sigma_A, pk_A, \text{cert}_A)$, where $(pk_A, \text{cert}_A B)$ is the certified public key of Alice.

Preventing unknown key-shake (UKS) attacks. Blake-Wilson and Menezes [9] introduced UKS attacks, where a party Alice can be tricked into believing that it shares a key with Eve, even though actually the key is shared with a different party Bob. A simple generic method to prevent such attacks in protocols that use digital signatures for authentication (such as ours) is to include user identities in signatures. In a real-world setting where certified public keys are exchanged during the protocol, one could sign the certificates along with all other messages.

Server-only authentication. Another important real-world application scenario is where only the server is authenticated cryptographically, while the client is not in possession of a long-term cryptographic key pair, and thus the protocol can only achieve unilateral authentication. This setting has been considered e.g.

in [38] for TLS, and in [26, 42, 48] for more general key exchange protocols. While we do not model and prove it formally, we expect that our protocol achieves tight security also for server-only authentication, by an adopting the security model from Sect. 4 and the proof to the unilateral setting. More precisely, in this setting we would consider a security model where we distinguish between client oracles (which are not in possession of a cryptographic long-term key), and server oracles in possession of long-term signature keys. For authentication, the proof is identical, except that event break_A is restricted to accepting client oracles. For key indistinguishability, we would allow Test-queries only for sessions that involve a Diffie-Hellman share that originates from a client oracle controlled by the experiment (as otherwise the adversary is trivially able to win). In this case, we are able to embed a DDH challenge exactly as in the proof for mutual authentication.

Theorem 5. *Consider protocol Π as defined above, where hash functions G and H are modeled as random oracles. Let $\mathcal{A}$ be an adversary that $(t, \mu, \ell, \epsilon_{\mathcal{A}})$-breaks Π. Then we can construct and adversaries $\mathcal{B}_A$ and $\mathcal{B}_{KE}$ such that:*

1. *Either $\mathcal{B}_A$ (t', ϵ', μ)-breaks the $\mathsf{MU\text{-}EUF\text{-}CMA^{corr}}$-security of $(\mathsf{Gen}, \mathsf{Sign}, \mathsf{Vfy})$ with $t' = O(t)$ and $\epsilon' \geq \epsilon_{\mathcal{A}} - \mu^2 \ell^2 / p$.*
2. *Or $\mathcal{B}_{KE}$ (t', ϵ')-breaks the decisional Diffie-Hellman assumption in $(\mathbb{G}, g, p)$ with $t' = O(t)$ and $\epsilon' \geq \epsilon_{\mathcal{A}} - t^2/2^d - \mu^2 \ell^2 / p - \mu^2 \ell^2 / 2^d - \mu \ell t / p$.*

The proof of Theorem 5 consists of two parts. First, we prove that any adversary breaking authentication in the sense of Definition 7 implies an algorithm breaking the $\mathsf{MU\text{-}EUF\text{-}CMA^{corr}}$-security of the signature scheme. This part is standard, with a straightforward reduction. Then we prove key indistinguishability. This result contains the main novelty of our proof. It follows the approach sketched in the introduction very closely. Due to space limitations, the full proofs are given only in the full version, which can be found at the Cryptology ePrint Archive at https://eprint.iacr.org/2018/.

5   Efficiency Analysis

Let us compare an instantiation of our protocol from Sect. 4.2, instantiated with our signature scheme from Sect. 3.2, to plain "signed Diffie-Hellman", instantiated with EC-DSA. The latter is the currently most efficient practical instantiation of an authenticated key exchange protocol over simple groups with *explicit* authentication (in contrast, some protocols, such as NAXOS [40], do not provide explicit authentication via digital signatures, but only implicit authentication via indistinguishability of keys).

We consider a setting where both the signature scheme and the Diffie-Hellman key exchange are instantiated over the same group. This is desirable in practice for many different reasons. Most importantly, it reduces the size of the implementation. This makes the protocol not only faster to implement, but also easier to implement securely (e.g., constant-time and resilient to other side-channels) and easier to maintain, which are very desirable properties, from a real-world security point of view.

Furthermore, an implementation requiring a small codebase or circuit size is particularly desirable for resource-constrained devices, such as IoT devices, where tightness is particularly relevant due to the large number of devices in use.

Computational efficiency. In order to compare the efficiency of protocols, we count the number of exponentiations, as this is the most expensive computation to be performed. Below we will also briefly discuss the potential impact of optimisations.

Our protocol. Each party running our protocol has to perform two exponentiations to perform the Diffie-Hellman key exchange, seven exponentiations to sign a message, and eight exponentiations to verify a signature. In total, this amounts to 17 exponentiations.

Signed Diffie-Hellman. Executing the signed Diffie-Hellman protocol with EC-DSA takes two exponentiations to perform the Diffie-Hellman key exchange, one exponentiation to compute an EC-DSA signature, and two exponentiations to verify a signature. In total, this amounts to 5 exponentiations.

Thus, our protocol requires 3.4 times more exponentiations than signed Diffie-Hellman.

Theoretically-sound instantiations. Let us consider a desired security level equivalent to an 128-bit symmetric key.

Our protocol. The tightness of our security proof allows to instantiate out protocol on a 256-bit elliptic curve group, such as the NIST P-256 curve, independent of the number of users or sessions.

Signed Diffie-Hellman. When instantiating plain "signed Diffie-Hellman", we have to compensate the quadratic security loss of $Q = \mu^2 \ell^2$ of the security proof, depending on the number of users μ and the number of sessions ℓ, by choosing a larger group. For instance:

- In a small-to-medium-scale setting with $\mu = 2^{16}$ and $\ell = 2^{16}$, the security loss amounts already to a factor of $Q = 2^{64}$. In order to compensate this with larger parameters, we have to increase the group size by a factor of $Q^2 = 2^{128}$. We can do this by using the NIST P-384 curve.
- In a large-scale setting with $\mu = 2^{32}$ and $\ell = 2^{32}$, the security loss amounts even to a factor of $Q = 2^{128}$. In order to compensate this with larger parameters, we have to increase the group size by a factor of $Q^2 = 2^{256}$, e.g., by using the NIST P-521 curve.

Remark 6. To justify the numbers chosen above, let us consider Facebook as an example. Facebook lists 2.13 billion active users in December 2017, see https://newsroom.fb.com/company-info/. Even if we assume that each user performs only a single TLS handshake (that is, only a single login) per month, this amounts to about 2^{31} execution of the TLS protocol per month, and about 2^{34} per year (the lifetime of the certified public key). Since known security proofs for TLS have a quadratic security loss, we thus have a security loss of 2^{68} already in the *single-user* setting where only Facebook is considered.

Comparison of computational efficiency. In order to estimate the time required for one exponentiation for different curves, we consider OpenSSL as an example. OpenSSL is a very widely-used and stable cryptographic library with good performance properties. The benchmark tests of elliptic curve Diffie-Hellman, which analyse the performance of different elliptic curves implemented by OpenSSL, can be run on a system where OpenSSL is installed by executing the command `openssl speed ecdh`.

We ran this benchmark on a MacBook Pro computer with 3.3 GHz Intel Core i7 CPU and 16 GB RAM, running Mac OS Version 10.13.2. Figure 1 summarises the results for the considered NIST curves (P256, P384, P521), as well as suitable alternatives. Note that one ECDH operation for the P384 curve takes about 2.7 times longer than for P256, while for P521 it is even about 7.7 times longer. The results for other families of curves (K233/409/571 and B283/409/571) are comparable.

Table 1. OpenSSL Benchmark Results for NIST Curves

Curve	Security level	Time/Operation in s	Operations per s
NIST P256	128	0.0021	476.9
NIST P384	128	0.0056	179.7
NIST P521	128	0.0161	62.0
NIST K233	128	0.0016	640.1
NIST K409	128	0.0068	147.6
NIST K571	128	0.0151	66.4
NIST B283	128	0.0035	284.6
NIST B409	128	0.0074	135.1
NIST B571	128	0.0167	59.8

Comparison of communication complexity. Now let us compare the amount of data to be transmitted for a key exchange. Again, we consider "128-bit security". We assume that each element of an n-bit elliptic group takes $n + 1$ bits, which can be achieved via standard point compression.

Our protocol. This protocol requires the transmission of two group elements for the Diffie-Hellman key exchange, each consisting of 257 bits, plus two signatures (each consisting of a random 256-bit nonce, two group elements, and four 256-bit exponents, which yields 1794 bits), plus the first protocol message, which corresponds to one 256-bit value, if SHA-256 is used. In total, this yields $2 \cdot 257 + 2 \cdot 1794 + 256 = 4358$ bytes, which corresponds to ≈ 545 bytes.

Signed Diffie-Hellman. When instantiating plain "signed Diffie-Hellman" with EC-DSA, each party sends one group element plus one signature consisting of two exponents. This yields:

- When using the NIST P-384 curve, this amounts to $2 \cdot 385 + 4 \cdot 384 = 2306$ bits, which corresponds to ≈ 289 bytes.
- In a large-scale setting with the NIST P-521 curve, this amounts to $2 \cdot 522 + 4 \cdot 521 = 3128$ bits, or ≈ 391 bytes.

Conclusion. Even though the absolute number of exponentiations required to run our protocol is larger than for simple signed Diffie-Hellman, it turns out that for small-to-medium-scale settings the overall computational efficiency is already comparable to signed Diffie-Hellman, if the group order is chosen in a theoretically-sound way. For large-scale settings, it is even significantly better. Concretely, the fact that our protocol requires 3.4 times more exponentiations is already almost compensated by the fact that an exponentiation is about 2.7-times more expensive in the small-to-medium-scale setting. Furthermore, given that in the large-scale setting an exponentiation is about 7.7 times more expensive, it turns out that our protocol is even significantly more efficient by a factor greater than 2.25. We note that this pencil-and-paper analysis considers naïve exponentiation, and does not yet involve optimisations, such as pre-computations, which usually tend to be more effective if more exponentiations are performed.

The improved computational efficiency comes at only very moderate cost of increased communication complexity, amounting to 256 bytes *for the entire protocol* in the small-to-medium-scale setting, and 154 bytes in the large-scale setting. This holds in comparison to the very minimalistic EC-DSA-signed Diffie-Hellman protocol, which is of course extremely communication-efficient in comparison to any other protocol with similar properties.

Given that our protocol is the first proposal for a truly *practical* and tightly-secure key exchange protocol, we expect that future work building upon our techniques will be able to improve this further.

References

1. Bader, C.: Efficient signatures with tight real world security in the random-oracle model. In: Gritzalis, D., Kiayias, A., Askoxylakis, I.G. (eds.) CANS 2014. LNCS, vol. 8813, pp. 370–383. Springer, Cham (2014). https://doi.org/10.1007/978-3-319-12280-9_24
2. Bader, C., Hofheinz, D., Jager, T., Kiltz, E., Li, Y.: Tightly-secure authenticated key exchange. In: Dodis, Y., Nielsen, J.B. (eds.) TCC 2015, Part I. LNCS, vol. 9014, pp. 629–658. Springer, Heidelberg (2015). https://doi.org/10.1007/978-3-662-46494-6_26

3. Bader, C., Jager, T., Li, Y., Schäge, S.: On the impossibility of tight cryptographic reductions. In: Fischlin, M., Coron, J.S. (eds.) EUROCRYPT 2016, Part II. LNCS, vol. 9666, pp. 273–304. Springer, Heidelberg (2016). https://doi.org/10.1007/978-3-662-49896-5_10

4. Barbulescu, R., Duquesne, S.: Updating key size estimations for pairings. J. Cryptol. (2018). https://doi.org/10.1007/s00145-018-9280-5

5. Bellare, M., Boldyreva, A., Micali, S.: Public-key encryption in a multi-user setting: security proofs and improvements. In: Preneel, B. (ed.) EUROCRYPT 2000. LNCS, vol. 1807, pp. 259–274. Springer, Heidelberg (2000). https://doi.org/10.1007/3-540-45539-6_18

6. Bellare, M., Rogaway, P.: Random oracles are practical: a paradigm for designing efficient protocols. In: Ashby, V. (ed.) ACM CCS 1993, pp. 62–73. ACM Press, November 1993

7. Bellare, M., Rogaway, P.: Entity authentication and key distribution. In: Stinson, D.R. (ed.) CRYPTO 1993. LNCS, vol. 773, pp. 232–249. Springer, Heidelberg (1994). https://doi.org/10.1007/3-540-48329-2_21

8. Bergsma, F., Jager, T., Schwenk, J.: One-round key exchange with strong security: an efficient and generic construction in the standard model. In: Katz, J. (ed.) PKC 2015. LNCS, vol. 9020, pp. 477–494. Springer, Heidelberg (2015). https://doi.org/10.1007/978-3-662-46447-2_21

9. Blake-Wilson, S., Menezes, A.: Unknown key-share attacks on the station-to-station (STS) protocol. In: Imai, H., Zheng, Y. (eds.) PKC 1999. LNCS, vol. 1560, pp. 154–170. Springer, Heidelberg (1999). https://doi.org/10.1007/3-540-49162-7_12

10. Blazy, O., Kakvi, S.A., Kiltz, E., Pan, J.: Tightly-secure signatures from chameleon hash functions. In: Katz, J. (ed.) PKC 2015. LNCS, vol. 9020, pp. 256–279. Springer, Heidelberg (2015). https://doi.org/10.1007/978-3-662-46447-2_12

11. Blazy, O., Kiltz, E., Pan, J.: (Hierarchical) identity-based encryption from affine message authentication. In: Garay, J.A., Gennaro, R. (eds.) CRYPTO 2014, Part I. LNCS, vol. 8616, pp. 408–425. Springer, Heidelberg (2014). https://doi.org/10.1007/978-3-662-44371-2_23

12. Boneh, D.: The decision Diffie-Hellman problem. In: Buhler, J.P. (ed.) ANTS 1998. LNCS, vol. 1423, pp. 48–63. Springer, Heidelberg (1998). https://doi.org/10.1007/BFb0054851. Invited paper

13. Boneh, D., Shen, E., Waters, B.: Strongly unforgeable signatures based on computational Diffie-Hellman. In: Yung, M., Dodis, Y., Kiayias, A., Malkin, T. (eds.) PKC 2006. LNCS, vol. 3958, pp. 229–240. Springer, Heidelberg (2006). https://doi.org/10.1007/11745853_15

14. Canetti, R., Krawczyk, H.: Analysis of key-exchange protocols and their use for building secure channels. In: Pfitzmann, B. (ed.) EUROCRYPT 2001. LNCS, vol. 2045, pp. 453–474. Springer, Heidelberg (2001). https://doi.org/10.1007/3-540-44987-6_28

15. Chaum, D., Pedersen, T.P.: Wallet databases with observers. In: Brickell, E.F. (ed.) CRYPTO 1992. LNCS, vol. 740, pp. 89–105. Springer, Heidelberg (1993). https://doi.org/10.1007/3-540-48071-4_7

16. Chen, J., Wee, H.: Fully, (almost) tightly secure IBE and dual system groups. In: Canetti, R., Garay, J.A. (eds.) CRYPTO 2013, Part II. LNCS, vol. 8043, pp. 435–460. Springer, Heidelberg (2013). https://doi.org/10.1007/978-3-642-40084-1_25

17. Chevallier-Mames, B.: An efficient CDH-based signature scheme with a tight security reduction. In: Shoup, V. (ed.) CRYPTO 2005. LNCS, vol. 3621, pp. 511–526. Springer, Heidelberg (2005). https://doi.org/10.1007/11535218_31

18. Cramer, R., Damgård, I., Schoenmakers, B.: Proofs of partial knowledge and simplified design of witness hiding protocols. In: Desmedt, Y. (ed.) CRYPTO 1994. LNCS, vol. 839, pp. 174–187. Springer, Heidelberg (1994). https://doi.org/10.1007/3-540-48658-5_19

19. Di Crescenzo, G., Katz, J., Ostrovsky, R., Smith, A.: Efficient and non-interactive non-malleable commitment. In: Pfitzmann, B. (ed.) EUROCRYPT 2001. LNCS, vol. 2045, pp. 40–59. Springer, Heidelberg (2001). https://doi.org/10.1007/3-540-44987-6_4

20. Dierks, T., Rescorla, E.: The Transport Layer Security (TLS) Protocol Version 1.2. RFC 5246 (Proposed Standard), August 2008. https://www.rfc-editor.org/rfc/rfc5246.txt, updated by RFCs 5746, 5878, 6176, 7465, 7507, 7568, 7627, 7685, 7905, 7919

21. Fiat, A., Shamir, A.: How to prove yourself: practical solutions to identification and signature problems. In: Odlyzko, A.M. (ed.) CRYPTO 1986. LNCS, vol. 263, pp. 186–194. Springer, Heidelberg (1987). https://doi.org/10.1007/3-540-47721-7_12

22. Fleischhacker, N., Jager, T., Schröder, D.: On tight security proofs for Schnorr signatures. In: Sarkar, P., Iwata, T. (eds.) ASIACRYPT 2014, Part I. LNCS, vol. 8873, pp. 512–531. Springer, Heidelberg (2014). https://doi.org/10.1007/978-3-662-45611-8_27

23. Garg, S., Bhaskar, R., Lokam, S.V.: Improved bounds on security reductions for discrete log based signatures. In: Wagner, D. (ed.) CRYPTO 2008. LNCS, vol. 5157, pp. 93–107. Springer, Heidelberg (2008). https://doi.org/10.1007/978-3-540-85174-5_6

24. Gay, R., Hofheinz, D., Kiltz, E., Wee, H.: Tightly CCA-secure encryption without pairings. In: Fischlin, M., Coron, J.S. (eds.) EUROCRYPT 2016, Part I. LNCS, vol. 9665, pp. 1–27. Springer, Heidelberg (2016). https://doi.org/10.1007/978-3-662-49890-3_1

25. Goh, E.J., Jarecki, S.: A signature scheme as secure as the Diffie-Hellman problem. In: Biham, E. (ed.) EUROCRYPT 2003. LNCS, vol. 2656, pp. 401–415. Springer, Heidelberg (2003). https://doi.org/10.1007/3-540-39200-9_25

26. Goldberg, I., Stebila, D., Ustaoglu, B.: Anonymity and one-way authentication in key exchange protocols. Des. Codes Crypt. 67(2), 245–269 (2013). https://doi.org/10.1007/s10623-011-9604-z

27. Goldwasser, S., Micali, S.: Probabilistic encryption. J. Comput. Syst. Sci. 28(2), 270–299 (1984)

28. Groth, J., Sahai, A.: Efficient non-interactive proof systems for bilinear groups. In: Smart, N.P. (ed.) EUROCRYPT 2008. LNCS, vol. 4965, pp. 415–432. Springer, Heidelberg (2008). https://doi.org/10.1007/978-3-540-78967-3_24

29. Gueron, S., Lindell, Y.: Better bounds for block cipher modes of operation via nonce-based key derivation. In: Thuraisingham, B.M., Evans, D., Malkin, T., Xu, D. (eds.) ACM CCS 2017, pp. 1019–1036. ACM Press, October/November 2017

30. Günther, C.G.: An identity-based key-exchange protocol. In: Quisquater, J.J., Vandewalle, J. (eds.) EUROCRYPT 1989. LNCS, vol. 434, pp. 29–37. Springer, Heidelberg (1990). https://doi.org/10.1007/3-540-46885-4_5

31. Hoang, V.T., Tessaro, S.: The multi-user security of double encryption. In: Coron, J., Nielsen, J.B. (eds.) EUROCRYPT 2017, Part II. LNCS, vol. 10211, pp. 381–411. Springer, Cham (2017). https://doi.org/10.1007/978-3-319-56614-6_13

32. Hofheinz, D., Jager, T.: Tightly secure signatures and public-key encryption. In: Safavi-Naini, R., Canetti, R. (eds.) CRYPTO 2012. LNCS, vol. 7417, pp. 590–607. Springer, Heidelberg (2012). https://doi.org/10.1007/978-3-642-32009-5_35

33. Hofheinz, D., Jager, T., Knapp, E.: Waters signatures with optimal security reduction. In: Fischlin, M., Buchmann, J., Manulis, M. (eds.) PKC 2012. LNCS, vol. 7293, pp. 66–83. Springer, Heidelberg (2012). https://doi.org/10.1007/978-3-642-30057-8_5

34. Jager, T., Kohlar, F., Schäge, S., Schwenk, J.: On the security of TLS-DHE in the standard model. In: Safavi-Naini, R., Canetti, R. (eds.) CRYPTO 2012. LNCS, vol. 7417, pp. 273–293. Springer, Heidelberg (2012). https://doi.org/10.1007/978-3-642-32009-5_17

35. Jager, T., Kohlar, F., Schäge, S., Schwenk, J.: Authenticated confidential channel establishment and the security of TLS-DHE. J. Cryptol. 30(4), 1276–1324 (2017)

36. Jager, T., Stam, M., Stanley-Oakes, R., Warinschi, B.: Multi-key authenticated encryption with corruptions: reductions are lossy. In: Kalai, Y., Reyzin, L. (eds.) TCC 2017, Part I. LNCS, vol. 10677, pp. 409–441. Springer, Cham (2017). https://doi.org/10.1007/978-3-319-70500-2_14

37. Katz, J., Wang, N.: Efficiency improvements for signature schemes with tight security reductions. In: Jajodia, S., Atluri, V., Jaeger, T. (eds.) ACM CCS 2003, pp. 155–164. ACM Press, October 2003

38. Krawczyk, H., Paterson, K.G., Wee, H.: On the security of the TLS protocol: a systematic analysis. In: Canetti, R., Garay, J.A. (eds.) CRYPTO 2013, Part I. LNCS, vol. 8042, pp. 429–448. Springer, Heidelberg (2013). https://doi.org/10.1007/978-3-642-40041-4_24

39. Krawczyk, H., Wee, H.: The OPTLS protocol and TLS 1.3. In: IEEE European Symposium on Security and Privacy, EuroS&P 2016, Saarbrücken, Germany, 21–24 March 2016, pp. 81–96. IEEE (2016). https://doi.org/10.1109/EuroSP.2016.18

40. LaMacchia, B.A., Lauter, K., Mityagin, A.: Stronger security of authenticated key exchange. In: Susilo, W., Liu, J.K., Mu, Y. (eds.) ProvSec 2007. LNCS, vol. 4784, pp. 1–16. Springer, Heidelberg (2007). https://doi.org/10.1007/978-3-540-75670-5_1

41. Li, Y., Schäge, S.: No-match attacks and robust partnering definitions: defining trivial attacks for security protocols is not trivial. In: Thuraisingham, B.M., Evans, D., Malkin, T., Xu, D. (eds.) ACM CCS 2017, pp. 1343–1360. ACM Press, October/November 2017

42. Maurer, U., Tackmann, B., Coretti, S.: Key exchange with unilateral authentication: composable security definition and modular protocol design. Cryptology ePrint Archive, Report 2013/555 (2013). http://eprint.iacr.org/2013/555

43. Paillier, P., Vergnaud, D.: Discrete-log-based signatures may not be equivalent to discrete log. In: Roy, B.K. (ed.) ASIACRYPT 2005. LNCS, vol. 3788, pp. 1–20. Springer, Heidelberg (2005). https://doi.org/10.1007/11593447_1

44. Paterson, K.G., van der Merwe, T.: Reactive and proactive standardisation of TLS. In: Chen, L., McGrew, D.A., Mitchell, C.J. (eds.) SSR 2016. LNCS, vol. 10074, pp. 160–186. Springer, Cham (2016). https://doi.org/10.1007/978-3-319-49100-4_7

45. Schäge, S.: Tight proofs for signature schemes without random oracles. In: Paterson, K.G. (ed.) EUROCRYPT 2011. LNCS, vol. 6632, pp. 189–206. Springer, Heidelberg (2011). https://doi.org/10.1007/978-3-642-20465-4_12

46. Schnorr, C.P.: Efficient identification and signatures for smart cards. In: Brassard, G. (ed.) CRYPTO 1989. LNCS, vol. 435, pp. 239–252. Springer, New York (1990). https://doi.org/10.1007/0-387-34805-0_22

47. Seurin, Y.: On the exact security of schnorr-type signatures in the random oracle model. In: Pointcheval, D., Johansson, T. (eds.) EUROCRYPT 2012. LNCS, vol. 7237, pp. 554–571. Springer, Heidelberg (2012). https://doi.org/10.1007/978-3-642-29011-4_33

48. Shoup, V.: On formal models for secure key exchange. Cryptology ePrint Archive, Report 1999/012 (1999). http://eprint.iacr.org/1999/012
49. Steinfeld, R., Pieprzyk, J., Wang, H.: How to strengthen any weakly unforgeable signature into a strongly unforgeable signature. In: Abe, M. (ed.) CT-RSA 2007. LNCS, vol. 4377, pp. 357–371. Springer, Heidelberg (2006). https://doi.org/10.1007/11967668_23

Symmetric Cryptoanalysis

Fast Correlation Attack Revisited
Cryptanalysis on Full Grain-128a, Grain-128, and Grain-v1

Yosuke Todo[1]($\boxtimes$), Takanori Isobe[2], Willi Meier[3], Kazumaro Aoki[1],
and Bin Zhang[4,5]

[1] NTT Secure Platform Laboratories, Tokyo 180-8585, Japan
todo.yosuke@lab.ntt.co.jp
[2] University of Hyogo, Hyogo 650-0047, Japan
[3] FHNW, Windisch, Switzerland
[4] TCA Laboratory, SKLCS, Institute of Software,
Chinese Academy of Sciences, Beijing, China
[5] State Key Laboratory of Cryptology, P.O. Box 5159, Beijing 100878, China

Abstract. A fast correlation attack (FCA) is a well-known cryptanalysis technique for LFSR-based stream ciphers. The correlation between the initial state of an LFSR and corresponding key stream is exploited, and the goal is to recover the initial state of the LFSR. In this paper, we revisit the FCA from a new point of view based on a finite field, and it brings a new property for the FCA when there are multiple linear approximations. Moreover, we propose a novel algorithm based on the new property, which enables us to reduce both time and data complexities. We finally apply this technique to the Grain family, which is a well-analyzed class of stream ciphers. There are three stream ciphers, Grain-128a, Grain-128, and Grain-v1 in the Grain family, and Grain-v1 is in the eSTREAM portfolio and Grain-128a is standardized by ISO/IEC. As a result, we break them all, and especially for Grain-128a, the cryptanalysis on its full version is reported for the first time.

Keywords: Fast correlation attack · Stream cipher · LFSR
Finite field · Multiple linear approximations · Grain-128a
Grain-128 · Grain-v1

1 Introduction

Stream ciphers are a class of symmetric-key cryptosystems. They commonly generate a key stream of arbitrary length from a secret key and initialization vector (iv), and a plaintext is encrypted by XORing with the key stream. Many stream ciphers consist of an initialization and key-stream generator. The secret key and iv are well mixed in the initialization, where a key stream is never output, and the mixed internal state is denoted as the initial state in this paper. After the initialization, the key-stream generator outputs the key stream while updating the internal state. The initialization of stream ciphers generally requires much processing time, but the key-stream generator is very efficient.

© International Association for Cryptologic Research 2018
H. Shacham and A. Boldyreva (Eds.): CRYPTO 2018, LNCS 10992, pp. 129–159, 2018.
https://doi.org/10.1007/978-3-319-96881-0_5

Fig. 1. Model of LFSR-based stream ciphers

LFSRs are often used in the design of stream ciphers, where the update function consists of one or more LFSRs and non-linear functions. Without loss of generality, the key-stream generator of LFSR-based stream ciphers can be represented as Fig. 1, where the binary noise e_t is generated by the non-linear function. LFSR-based stream ciphers share the feasibility to guarantee a long period in the key stream.

A (fast) correlation attack is an important attack against LFSR-based stream ciphers. The initial idea was introduced by Siegenthaler [1], and it exploits the bias of e_t. We guess the initial state $s^{(0)} = (s_0, s_1, \ldots, s_{n-1})$, compute s_t for $t = n, n+1, \ldots, N-1$, and XOR s_t with corresponding z_t. If we guess the correct initial state, highly biased e_t is acquired. Otherwise, we assume that the XOR behaves at random. When we collect an N-bit key stream and the size of the LFSR is n, the simple algorithm requires a time complexity of $N2^n$.

Following up the correlation attack, many algorithms have been proposed to avoid the exhaustive search of the initial state, and they are called as "fast correlation attack." The seminal work was proposed by Meier and Staffelbach [2], where the noise e_t is efficiently removed from z_t by using parity-check equations, and s_t is recovered. Several improvements of the original fast correlation attack have been proposed [3–8], but they have limitations such as the number of taps in the LFSR is significantly small or the bias of the noise is significantly high. Therefore, their applications are limited to experimental ciphers, and they have not been applied to modern concrete stream ciphers.

Another approach of the fast correlation attack is the so-called one-pass algorithm [9,10], and it has been successfully applied to modern concrete stream ciphers [11–13]. Similarly to the original correlation attack, we guess the initial state and recover the correct one by using parity-check equations. To avoid exhaustive search over the initial state, several methods have been proposed to decrease the number of secret bits in the initial state involved by parity-check equations [14,15]. In the most successful method, the number of involved secret bits decreases by XORing two different parity-check equations. Let $e_t = \langle s^{(0)}, a_t \rangle \oplus z_t$ be the parity-check equation, where $\langle s^{(0)}, a_t \rangle$ denotes an inner product between $s^{(0)}$ and a_t, and we assume that e_t is highly biased. Without loss of generality, we first detect a set of pairs (j_1, j_2) such that the first ℓ bits in $a_{j_1} \oplus a_{j_2}$ are 0, where such a set of pairs is efficiently detected from the birthday paradox. Then, $\langle s^{(0)}, a_{j_1} \oplus a_{j_2} \rangle \oplus z_{j_1} \oplus z_{j_2}$ is also highly biased, and the number of involved secret bits decreases from n to $n - \ell$. Later, this method is generalized by the generalized birthday problem [16]. Moreover, an efficient algorithm was proposed to accelerate the one-pass algorithm [14]. They showed that the guess and evaluation procedure can be regarded as a Walsh-Hadamard transform, and the fast Walsh-Hadamard transform (FWHT) can be applied to accelerate the one-pass algorithm. While the naive algorithm for the correlation attack requires $N2^n$, the FWHT enables us to evaluate it with the time complexity of $N + n2^n$. When the number of involved bits decreases from n to $n - \ell$, the time complexity also decreases to $N + (n - \ell)2^{n-\ell}$. The drawback of the one-pass algorithm with the birthday paradox is the increase of the noise. Let p be the probability that $e_t = 1$, and the correlation denoted by c is defined as $c = 1 - 2p$. If we use the XOR of parity-check equations to reduce the number of involved secret bits, the correlation of the modified equations drops to c^2. The increase of the noise causes the increase of the data complexity.

Revisiting Fast Correlation Attack. In this paper, we revisit the fast correlation attack. We first review the structure of parity-check equations from a new point of view based on a finite field, and the new viewpoint brings a new property for the fast correlation attack. A multiplication between $n \times n$ matrices and an n-bit fixed vector is generally used to construct parity-check equations. Our important observation is to show that this multiplication is "commutative" via the finite field, and it brings the new property for the fast correlation attack.

We first review the traditional wrong-key hypothesis, i.e., we observe correlation 0 when incorrect initial state is guessed. The new property implies that we need to reconsider the wrong-key hypothesis more carefully. Specifically, assuming that there are multiple high-biased linear masks, the traditional wrong-key hypothesis does not hold. We then show a modified wrong-key hypothesis.

The new property is directly useful to improve the efficiency of the fast correlation attack when there are multiple high-biased linear masks. In the previous fast correlation attack, the multiple approximations are only useful to reduce the data complexity but are not useful to reduce the time complexity [11]. We propose a new algorithm that reduces both time and data complexities. Our new algorithm is a kind of the one-pass algorithm, but the technique to avoid the exhaustive search of the initial state is completely different from previous ones. The multiple linear masks are directly exploited to avoid the exhaustive search.

Applications. We apply our new algorithm to the Grain family, where there are three well-known stream ciphers: Grain-128a [20], Grain-128 [21], and Grain-v1 [22]. The Grain family is amongst the most attractive stream ciphers, and especially Grain-v1 is in the eSTREAM portfolio and Grain-128a is standardized by ISO/IEC [23]. Moreover the structure is recently used to design a lightweight hash function [24] and stream ciphers [25,26].

Our new algorithm breaks each of full Grain-128a, Grain-128, and Grain-v1. Among them, this is the first cryptanalysis against full Grain-128a[1]. Regarding

---

[1] Grain-128a has two modes of operation: stream cipher mode and authenticated encryption mode. We can break the stream cipher mode under the known-plaintext setting. However we cannot attack the authenticated encryption mode under the reasonable assumption.

Table 1. Summary of results, where the key-stream generator and initialization are denoted as ksg and init, respectively.

Target		Attack	Assumption	Data	Time	Reference
Grain-128a	ksg	fast correlation attack	-	$2^{113.8}$	$2^{115.4}$	Sect. 5
Grain-128	init	dynamic cube attack	chosen IV	2^{63}	2^{90}	[17]
	init	dynamic cube attack	chosen IV	$2^{62.4}$	2^{84}	[18]
	ksg	fast correlation attack	-	$2^{112.8}$	$2^{114.4}$	Sect. 5.4
Grain-v1	ksg	fast near collision attack	-	2^{19}	$2^{86.1}$ †	[19]
	ksg	fast correlation attack	-	$2^{75.1}$	$2^{76.7}$	Sect. 6

† In [19], the time complexity is claimed as $2^{75.7}$ but the unit of the time complexity is 1 update function of reference code on software implementation. Here we adjusted the time complexity for the fair comparison.

full Grain-128, our algorithm is the first attack against the key-stream generator. Regarding full Grain-v1, our algorithm is more efficient than the previous attack [19], and it breaks Grain-v1 obviously faster than the brute-force attack.

To realize the fast correlation attack against all of the full Grain family, we introduce novel linear approximate representations. They well exploit their structure and reveal a new important vulnerability of the Grain family (Table 1).

Comparisons with Previous Attacks Against Grain Family. To understand this paper, it is not necessary to understand previous attacks, but we summarize previous attacks against the Grain family.

Before Grain-v1, there is an original Grain denoted by Grain-v0 [27], and it was broken by the fast correlation attack [11]. Grain-v1 is tweaked to remove the vulnerability of Grain-v0. Nevertheless, our new fast correlation attack can break full Grain-v1 thanks to the new property.

The near collision attack is the important previous attack against Grain-v1 [28], and very recently, an improvement called the fast near collision attack was proposed [19], where the authors claimed that the time complexity is $2^{75.7}$. However, this estimation is controversial because the unit of the time complexity is "1 update function of reference code on software implementation," and they estimated 1 update function to be $2^{10.4}$ cycles. Therefore, the pure time complexity is rather $2^{75.7+10.4} = 2^{86.1}$ cycles, which is greater than 2^{80}. On the other hand, the time complexity of the fast correlation attack is $2^{76.7}$, where the unit of the (dominant) time complexity is at most one multiplication with fixed values over the finite field. It is obviously faster than the brute-force attack, but it requires more data than the fast near collision attack.

Grain-128 is more aggressively designed than Grain-v1, where a quadratic function is adopted for the nonlinear feedback polynomial of the NFSR. Unfortunately, this low degree causes vulnerability against the dynamic cube attack [29]. While the initial work by Dinur and Shamir is a weak-key attack, it was then extended to the single-key attack [17] and recently improved [18]. The dynamic cube attack breaks the initialization, and the fast correlation attack breaks the key-stream generator. Note that different countermeasures are required for attacks against the key-stream generator and initialization. For example, we can avoid the dynamic cube attack by increasing the number of rounds in the initialization, but such countermeasure does not prevent the attack against the key-stream generator.

Grain-128a was designed to avoid the dynamic cube attack. The degree of the nonlinear feedback polynomial is higher than in Grain-128. No security flaws have been reported on full Grain-128a, but there are attacks against Grain-128a whose number of rounds in the initialization is reduced [30–32].

2   Preliminaries

2.1   LFSR-Based Stream Ciphers

The target of the fast correlation attack is LFSR-based stream ciphers, which are modeled as Fig. 1 simply. The LFSR generates an N-bit output sequence as $\{s_0, s_1, \ldots, s_{N-1}\}$, and the corresponding key stream $\{z_0, z_1, \ldots, z_{N-1}\}$ is computed as $z_t = s_t \oplus e_t$, where e_t is a binary noise.

Let

$$f(x) = c_0 + c_1 x^1 + c_2 x^2 + \cdots + c_{n-1} x^{n-1} + x^n$$

be the feedback polynomial of the LFSR and $s^{(t)} = (s_t, s_{t+1}, \ldots, s_{t+n-1})$ be an n-bit internal state of the LFSR at time t. Then, the LFSR outputs s_t, and the state is updated to $s^{(t+1)}$ as

$$s^{(t+1)} = s^{(t)} \times F = s^{(t)} \times \begin{pmatrix} 0 & \cdots & 0 & 0 & c_0 \\ 1 & \cdots & 0 & 0 & c_1 \\ \vdots & \ddots & \vdots & \vdots & \vdots \\ 0 & \cdots & 1 & 0 & c_{n-2} \\ 0 & \cdots & 0 & 1 & c_{n-1} \end{pmatrix},$$

where F is an $n \times n$ binary matrix that represents the feedback polynomial $f(x)$. In concrete LFSR-based stream ciphers, the binary noise e_t is nonlinearly generated from the internal state or another internal state.

2.2   Fast Correlation Attack

The fast correlation attack (FCA) exploits high correlation between the internal state of the LFSR and corresponding key stream [1,2]. We first show the most simple model, where we assume that e_t itself is highly biased. Let p be the probability of $e_t = 1$, and the correlation c is defined as $c = 1 - 2p$. We guess the initial internal state $s^{(0)}$, calculate $\{s_0, s_1, \ldots, s_{N-1}\}$ from the guessed $s^{(0)}$, and evaluate $\sum_{t=0}^{N-1} (-1)^{s_t \oplus z_t}$, where the sum is computed over the set of integers.

If the correct initial state is guessed, the sum is equal to $\sum_{t=0}^{N-1}(-1)^{e_t}$ and follows a normal distribution $\mathcal{N}(Nc, N)^2$. On the other hand, we assume that the sum behaves at random when an incorrect initial state is guessed. Then, it follows a normal distribution $\mathcal{N}(0, N)$. To distinguish the two distributions, we need to collect $N \approx O(1/c^2)$ bits of the key stream.

The FCA can be regarded as a kind of a linear cryptanalysis [33]. The output s_t is linearly computed from $s^{(0)}$ as $s_t = \langle s^{(0)}, A_t \rangle$, where A_t is the 1st row vector in the transpose of F^t denoted by ${}^{\mathrm{T}}F^t$. In other words, A_t is used as linear masks, and the aim of attackers is to find $s^{(0)}$ such that $\sum_{t=0}^{N-1}(-1)^{\langle s^{(0)}, A_t \rangle}$ is far from $N/2$.

Usually, the binary noise e_t is not highly biased in modern stream ciphers, but we may be able to observe high correlation by summing optimally chosen linear masks. In other words, we can execute the FCA if

$$e'_t = \bigoplus_{i \in \mathbb{T}_s} \langle s^{(t+i)}, \Gamma_i \rangle \oplus \bigoplus_{i \in \mathbb{T}_z} z_{t+i}$$

is highly biased by optimally choosing $\mathbb{T}_s$, $\mathbb{T}_z$, and Γ_i, where $s^{(t+i)}$ and Γ_i are n-bit vectors. Recall $s^{(t)} = s^{(0)} \times F^t$, and then, e'_t is rewritten as

$$\begin{aligned} e'_t &= \bigoplus_{i \in \mathbb{T}_s} \left\langle s^{(t+i)}, \Gamma_i \right\rangle \oplus \bigoplus_{i \in \mathbb{T}_z} z_{t+i} \\ &= \bigoplus_{i \in \mathbb{T}_s} \left\langle s^{(0)} \times F^{t+i}, \Gamma_i \right\rangle \oplus \bigoplus_{i \in \mathbb{T}_z} z_{t+i} \\ &= \left\langle s^{(0)}, \left(\bigoplus_{i \in \mathbb{T}_s} (\Gamma_i \times {}^{\mathrm{T}}F^i) \right) \times {}^{\mathrm{T}}F^t \right\rangle \oplus \bigoplus_{i \in \mathbb{T}_z} z_{t+i}. \end{aligned}$$

For simplicity, we introduce Γ denoted by $\Gamma = \bigoplus_{i \in \mathbb{T}_s} (\Gamma_i \times {}^{\mathrm{T}}F^i)$. Then, we can introduce the following parity-check equations as

$$e'_t = \left\langle s^{(0)}, \Gamma \times {}^{\mathrm{T}}F^t \right\rangle \oplus \bigoplus_{i \in \mathbb{T}_z} z_{t+i}. \tag{1}$$

We redefine p as the probability satisfying $e'_t = 1$ for all possible t, and the correlation c is also redefined from the corresponding p. Then, we can execute the FCA by using Eq. (1). Assuming that N parity-check equations are collected, we first guess $s^{(0)}$ and evaluate $\sum_{t=0}^{N-1}(-1)^{e'_t}$. While the sum follows a normal distribution $\mathcal{N}(0, N)$ in the random case, it follows $\mathcal{N}(Nc, N)$ if the correct $s^{(0)}$ is guessed.

The most straightforward algorithm requires the time complexity of $O(N2^n)$. Chose et al. showed that the guess and evaluation procedure can be regarded as a Walsh-Hadamard transform [14]. The fast Walsh-Hadamard transform (FWHT) can be successfully applied to accelerate the algorithm, and it reduces the time complexity to $O(N + n2^n)$.

---

[2] Accurately, when the correct initial state is guessed, it follows $\mathcal{N}(Nc, N + Nc^2)$. However, since N is huge and Nc^2 is small, the normal distribution $\mathcal{N}(Nc, N)$ is enough to approximate the distribution.

Definition 1 (Walsh-Hadamard Transform (WHT)). *Given a function* $w : \{0,1\}^n \to \mathbb{Z}$, *the WHT of* w *is defined as* $\hat{w}(s) = \sum_{x \in \{0,1\}^n} w(x)(-1)^{\langle s,x \rangle}$.

When we guess $s \in \{0,1\}^n$, the empirical correlation $\sum_{t=0}^{N-1}(-1)^{e'_t}$ is rewritten as

$$\sum_{t=0}^{N-1}(-1)^{e'_t} = \sum_{t=0}^{N-1}(-1)^{\langle s, \Gamma \times {}^{\mathsf{T}}F^t \rangle \oplus \bigoplus_{i \in \mathrm{T}_z} z_{t+i}}$$

$$= \sum_{x \in \{0,1\}^n} \left(\sum_{t \in \{0,1,\dots,N-1 | \Gamma \times {}^{\mathsf{T}}F^t = x\}} (-1)^{\langle s,x \rangle \oplus \bigoplus_{i \in \mathrm{T}_z} z_{t+i}} \right)$$

$$= \sum_{x \in \{0,1\}^n} \left(\sum_{t \in \{0,1,\dots,N-1 | \Gamma \times {}^{\mathsf{T}}F^t = x\}} (-1)^{\bigoplus_{i \in \mathrm{T}_z} z_{t+i}} \right) (-1)^{\langle s,x \rangle}.$$

Therefore, from the following public function w as

$$w(x) := \sum_{t \in \{0,1,\dots,N-1 | \Gamma \times {}^{\mathsf{T}}F^t = x\}} (-1)^{\bigoplus_{i \in \mathrm{T}_z} z_{t+i}},$$

we get $\hat{w}$ by using the FWHT, where $\hat{w}(s)$ is the empirical correlation when s is guessed.

3   Revisiting Fast Correlation Attack

We first review the structure of the parity-check equation by using a finite field and show that $\Gamma \times {}^{\mathsf{T}}F^t$ is "commutative." This new observation brings a new property for the FCA, and it is very important when there are multiple linear masks. As a result, we need to reconsider the wrong-key hypothesis carefully, i.e., there is a case that the most simple and commonly used hypothesis does not hold. Moreover, we propose a new algorithm that successfully exploits the new property to reduce the data and time complexities in the next section.

3.1   Reviewing Parity-Check Equations with Finite Field

We review $\Gamma \times {}^{\mathsf{T}}F^t$ by using a finite field $\mathrm{GF}(2^n)$, where the primitive polynomial is the feedback polynomial of the LFSR.

Recall the notation of $A_t \in \{0,1\}^n$, which was defined as the 1st row vector in ${}^{\mathsf{T}}F^t$, and then, the ith row vector of ${}^{\mathsf{T}}F^t$ is represented as A_{t+i-1}. Let α be an element as $f(\alpha) = 0$ and it is a primitive element of $\mathrm{GF}(2^n)$. We notice that α^t becomes natural conversion of $A_t \in \{0,1\}^n$. We naturally convert $\Gamma \in \{0,1\}^n$

to $\gamma \in \mathrm{GF}(2^n)$. The important observation is that $\Gamma \times {}^{\mathrm{T}}F$ also becomes natural conversion of $\gamma\alpha \in \mathrm{GF}(2^n)$ because of

$$\Gamma \times {}^{\mathrm{T}}F = \Gamma \times \begin{pmatrix} 0 & 1 & \cdots & 0 & 0 \\ \vdots & \vdots & \ddots & \vdots & \vdots \\ 0 & 0 & \cdots & 1 & 0 \\ 0 & 0 & \cdots & 0 & 1 \\ c_0 & c_1 & \cdots & c_{n-2} & c_{n-1} \end{pmatrix}.$$

This trivially derives that $\Gamma \times {}^{\mathrm{T}}F^t$ is also natural conversion of $\gamma\alpha^t \in \mathrm{GF}(2^n)$, and of course, the multiplication is commutative, i.e., $\gamma\alpha^t = \alpha^t\gamma$. We finally consider a matrix multiplication corresponding to $\alpha^t\gamma$. Let M_γ be an $n \times n$ binary matrix, where the ith row vector of ${}^{\mathrm{T}}M_\gamma$ is defined as the natural conversion of $\gamma\alpha^{i-1}$. Then, $\alpha^t\gamma$ is the natural conversion of $A_t \times {}^{\mathrm{T}}M_\gamma$, and we acquire $\Gamma \times {}^{\mathrm{T}}F^t = A_t \times {}^{\mathrm{T}}M_\gamma$. The following shows an example to understand this relationship.

Example 1. Let us consider a finite field $\mathrm{GF}(2^8) = \mathrm{GF}(2)[x]/(x^8 + x^4 + x^3 + x^2 + 1)$. When $\Gamma = 01011011$, the transpose matrix of the corresponding binary matrix M_γ is represented as

$$ {}^{\mathrm{T}}M_\gamma = \begin{pmatrix} 0 & 1 & 0 & 1 & 1 & 0 & 1 & 1 \\ 1 & 0 & 0 & 1 & 0 & 1 & 0 & 1 \\ 1 & 1 & 1 & 1 & 0 & 0 & 1 & 0 \\ 0 & 1 & 1 & 1 & 1 & 0 & 0 & 1 \\ 1 & 0 & 0 & 0 & 0 & 1 & 0 & 0 \\ 0 & 1 & 0 & 0 & 0 & 0 & 1 & 0 \\ 0 & 0 & 1 & 0 & 0 & 0 & 0 & 1 \\ 1 & 0 & 1 & 0 & 1 & 0 & 0 & 0 \end{pmatrix}, $$

where the first row coincides with Γ and the second row is natural conversion of $\gamma\alpha$. Then, $\Gamma \times {}^{\mathrm{T}}F^t = A_t \times {}^{\mathrm{T}}M_\gamma$, and for example, when $t = 10$,

$$\Gamma \times {}^{\mathrm{T}}F^{10} = A_{10} \times {}^{\mathrm{T}}M_\gamma,$$

$$\Leftrightarrow (0\,1\,0\,1\,1\,0\,1\,1) \times \begin{pmatrix} 0 & 1 & 0 & 0 & 0 & 0 & 0 & 0 \\ 0 & 0 & 1 & 0 & 0 & 0 & 0 & 0 \\ 0 & 0 & 0 & 1 & 0 & 0 & 0 & 0 \\ 0 & 0 & 0 & 0 & 1 & 0 & 0 & 0 \\ 0 & 0 & 0 & 0 & 0 & 1 & 0 & 0 \\ 0 & 0 & 0 & 0 & 0 & 0 & 1 & 0 \\ 0 & 0 & 0 & 0 & 0 & 0 & 0 & 1 \\ 1 & 0 & 1 & 1 & 1 & 0 & 0 & 0 \end{pmatrix}^{10} = (0\,0\,1\,0\,1\,1\,1\,0) \times \begin{pmatrix} 0 & 1 & 0 & 1 & 1 & 0 & 1 & 1 \\ 1 & 0 & 0 & 1 & 0 & 1 & 0 & 1 \\ 1 & 1 & 1 & 1 & 0 & 0 & 1 & 0 \\ 0 & 1 & 1 & 1 & 1 & 0 & 0 & 1 \\ 1 & 0 & 0 & 0 & 0 & 1 & 0 & 0 \\ 0 & 1 & 0 & 0 & 0 & 0 & 1 & 0 \\ 0 & 0 & 1 & 0 & 0 & 0 & 0 & 1 \\ 1 & 0 & 1 & 0 & 1 & 0 & 0 & 0 \end{pmatrix},$$

and the result is 00010101.

We review Eq. (1) by using the "commutative" feature as

$$\left\langle s^{(0)}, \Gamma \times {}^{\mathrm{T}}F^t \right\rangle = \left\langle s^{(0)}, A_t \times {}^{\mathrm{T}}M_\gamma \right\rangle = \left\langle s^{(0)} \times M_\gamma, A_t \right\rangle,$$

and Eq. (1) is equivalently rewritten as

$$e'_t = \left\langle s^{(0)} \times M_\gamma, A_t \right\rangle \oplus \bigoplus_{i \in \mathbb{T}_z} z_{t+i}.$$

The equation above implies the following new property.

Property 1. We assume that we can observe high correlation when we guess $s^{(0)}$ and parity-check equations are generated from $\Gamma \times {}^{\mathrm{T}}F^t$. Then, we can observe exactly the same high correlation even if we guess $s^{(0)} \times M_\gamma$ and parity-check equations are generated from A_t instead of $\Gamma \times {}^{\mathrm{T}}F^t$.

Hereinafter, $\gamma \in \mathrm{GF}(2^n)$ is not distinguished from $\Gamma \in \{0, 1\}^n$, and we use γ as a linear mask for simplicity.

3.2   New Wrong-Key Hypothesis

We review the traditional and commonly used wrong-key hypothesis, where we assume that the empirical correlation behaves as random when an incorrect initial state is guessed. However, Property 1 implies that we need to consider this hypothesis more carefully.

We assume that the use of a linear mask Γ leads to high correlation, and we simply call such linear masks highly biased linear masks. When we generate parity-check equations from $\Gamma \times {}^{\mathrm{T}}F^t$, let us consider the case that we guess incorrect initial state $s'^{(0)} = s^{(0)} \times M_{\gamma'}$. From Property 1

$$\left\langle s'^{(0)}, \Gamma \times {}^{\mathrm{T}}F^t \right\rangle = \left\langle s^{(0)} \times M_{\gamma'}, A_t \times {}^{\mathrm{T}}M_\gamma \right\rangle = \left\langle s^{(0)}, A_t \times {}^{\mathrm{T}}M_{\gamma\gamma'} \right\rangle$$

In other words, it is equivalent to the case that $\gamma\gamma'$ is used as a linear mask instead of γ. If both γ and $\gamma\gamma'$ are highly biased linear masks, we also observe high correlation when we guess $s^{(0)} \times M_{\gamma'}$. Therefore, assuming that the target stream cipher has multiple linear masks with high correlation, the entire corresponding guessing brings high correlation.

We introduce a new wrong-key hypothesis based on Property 1. Assuming that there are m linear masks whose correlation is high and the others are correlation zero, we newly introduce the following wrong-key hypothesis.

Hypothesis 1 (New Wrong-Key Hypothesis). *Assume that there are m highly biased linear masks as $\gamma_1, \gamma_2, \ldots, \gamma_m$, and parity-check equations are generated from A_t. Then, we observe high correlation when we guess $s^{(0)} \times M_{\gamma_i}$ for any $i \in \{1, 2, \ldots, m\}$. Otherwise, we assume that it behaves at random, i.e., the correlation becomes 0.*

The new wrong-key hypothesis is a kind of extension from the traditional wrong-key hypothesis.

4   New Algorithm Exploiting New Property

Overview. We first show the overview before we detail our new attack algorithm. In this section, let n be the size of the LFSR in the target LFSR-based stream cipher, and we assume that there are m ($\ll 2^n$) highly biased linear masks denoted by $\gamma_1, \gamma_2, \ldots, \gamma_m$. The procedure consists of three parts: constructing parity-check equations, FWHT, and removing γ.

- We first construct parity-check equations. Parity-check equations of the traditional FCA are constructed from $\Gamma \times {}^{\mathrm{T}}F^t$ and $\bigoplus_{i \in \mathbb{T}_z} z_{t+i}$. In our new algorithm, we construct parity-check equations from A_t instead of $\Gamma \times {}^{\mathrm{T}}F^t$.
- We use the fast Walsh-Hadamard transform (FWHT) to get solutions with high correlation. In other words, we evaluate s such that $\langle s, A_t \rangle \oplus \bigoplus_{i \in \mathbb{T}_z} z_{t+i}$ is highly biased. As we explained in Sect. 3.1, we then observe high correlation when $s = s^{(0)} \times M_{\gamma_i}$, and there are m solutions with high correlation. Unfortunately, even if FWHT is applied, we have to guess n bits and it requires $n2^n$ time complexity. It is less efficient than the exhaustive search when the size of the LFSR is greater than or equal to the security level. To overcome this issue, we bypass some bits out of n bits by exploiting m linear masks. Specifically, we bypass β bits, i.e., we guess only $(n - \beta)$ bits and β bits are fixed to constant (e.g., 0). Even if β bits are bypassed, there are $m2^{-\beta}$ solutions with high correlation in average. Therefore, $m > 2^\beta$ is a necessary condition.
- We pick solutions whose empirical correlation is greater than a threshold, where some of solutions are represented as $s = s^{(0)} \times M_{\gamma_i}$. To remove M_{γ_i}, we exhaustively guess the applied γ_i and recover $s^{(0)}$. Assuming that N_p solutions are picked, the time complexity is $N_p \times m$. If the expected number of occurrences that the correct $s^{(0)}$ appears is significantly greater than that for incorrect ones, we can uniquely determine $s^{(0)}$. We simulate them by using the Poisson distribution in detail.

4.1   Detailed Algorithm

Let n be the state size of the LFSR and κ be the security level. We assume that there are m_p ($\ll 2^n$) linear masks $\gamma_1, \gamma_2, \ldots, \gamma_{m_p}$ with positive correlation that is greater than a given c. Moreover we assume that there are m_m ($\ll 2^n$) linear masks $\rho_1, \rho_2, \ldots, \rho_{m_m}$ with negative correlation that is smaller than $-c$. Note that c is close to 0, and $m = m_p + m_m$.

Constructing Parity-Check Equations. We first construct parity-check equations from A_t and $\bigoplus_{i \in \mathbb{T}_z} z_{t+i}$ for $t = 0, 1, \ldots, N-1$, and the time complexity is N. The empirical correlation follows $\mathcal{N}(Nc, N)$ and $\mathcal{N}(-Nc, N)$ when we guess one of $s^{(0)} \times M_{\gamma_i}$ and $s^{(0)} \times M_{\rho_i}$, respectively [3]. Otherwise we assume that the empirical correlation follows $\mathcal{N}(0, N)$.

---

[3]   The correlation c is the lower bound for all γ_i. Therefore, while the empirical correlation may not follow $\mathcal{N}(Nc, N)$, it does not affect the attack feasibility because it is far from $\mathcal{N}(0, N)$.

FWHT with Bypassing Technique. We next pick $s \in \{0,1\}^n$ such that $\left|\frac{\sum_{t=0}^{N-1}(-1)^{e'_t}}{N}\right| \geq th$, where $e'_t = \langle s, A_t \rangle \oplus \bigoplus_{i \in \mathbb{T}_z} z_{t+i}$ and th (> 0) is a threshold. Let ϵ_1 be the probability that values following $\mathcal{N}(0, N)$ is greater than th, and let ϵ_2 be the probability that values following $\mathcal{N}(Nc, N)$ is greater than th. Namely,

$$\epsilon_1 = \frac{1}{\sqrt{2\pi N}} \int_{th}^{\infty} \exp\left(-\frac{x^2}{2N}\right) dx, \quad \epsilon_2 = \frac{1}{\sqrt{2\pi N}} \int_{th}^{\infty} \exp\left(-\frac{(x - Nc)^2}{2N}\right) dx.$$

Note that the probability that values following $\mathcal{N}(0, N)$ is smaller than $-th$ is also ϵ_1 and the probability that values following $\mathcal{N}(-Nc, N)$ is smaller than $-th$ is also ϵ_2. Let $\mathbb{S}_p$ and $\mathbb{S}_m$ be the set of picked solutions with positive and negative correlation, respectively. The expected size of $\mathbb{S}_p$ and $\mathbb{S}_m$ is $(2^n \epsilon_1 + m_p \epsilon_2)$ and $(2^n \epsilon_1 + m_m \epsilon_2)$, respectively, when the whole of n-bit s is guessed.

Unfortunately, if we guess the whole of n-bit s, the time complexity of FWHT is $n2^n$ and it is less efficient than the exhaustive search when $n \geq \kappa$. To reduce the time complexity, we assume multiple solutions. Instead of guessing the whole of s, we guess its partial $(n - \beta)$ bits, where bypassed β bits are fixed to constants, e.g., all 0. Then, the time complexity of the FWHT is reduced from $n2^n$ to $(n - \beta)2^{n-\beta}$. Even if β bits are bypassed, $m_p 2^{-\beta} \epsilon_2$ (resp. $m_m 2^{-\beta} \epsilon_2$) solutions represented as $s^{(0)} \times M_{\gamma_i}$ (resp. $s^{(0)} \times M_{\rho_i}$) remain. Moreover, the size of $\mathbb{S}_p$ and $\mathbb{S}_m$ also decreases to $(2^{n-\beta} \epsilon_1 + m_p 2^{-\beta} \epsilon_2)$ and $(2^{n-\beta} \epsilon_1 + m_m 2^{-\beta} \epsilon_2)$, respectively.

Removing γ. For all $s \in \mathbb{S}_p$ and all $j \in \{1, 2, \ldots, m_p\}$, we compute $s \times M_{\gamma_j}^{-1}$. It computes $s^{(0)} \times M_{\gamma_i} \times M_{\gamma_j}^{-1}$ and becomes $s^{(0)}$ when $i = j$. Since there are $m_p 2^{-\beta} \epsilon_2$ solutions represented as $s^{(0)} \times M_{\gamma_i}$ in $\mathbb{S}_p$, the correct $s^{(0)}$ appears $m_p 2^{-\beta} \epsilon_2$ times. On the other hand, every incorrect initial state appears about $m_p (2^{n-\beta} \epsilon_1 + m_p 2^{-\beta} \epsilon_2) 2^{-n}$ times when we assume uniformly random behavior. In total, every incorrect initial state appears about

$$\lambda_1 = m_p (2^{n-\beta} \epsilon_1 + m_p 2^{-\beta} \epsilon_2) 2^{-n} + m_m (2^{n-\beta} \epsilon_1 + m_m 2^{-\beta} \epsilon_2) 2^{-n}$$
$$= (m 2^{n-\beta} \epsilon_1 + (m_p^2 + m_m^2) 2^{-\beta} \epsilon_2) 2^{-n}$$

times when we assume uniformly random behavior. On the other hand, the correct $s^{(0)}$ appears

$$\lambda_2 = (m_p + m_m) 2^{-\beta} \epsilon_2 = m 2^{-\beta} \epsilon_2$$

times.

The number of occurrences that every incorrect initial state appears follows the Poisson distribution with parameter λ_1, and the number of occurrences that the correct $s^{(0)}$ appears follows the Poisson distribution with parameter λ_2. To recover the unique correct $s^{(0)}$, we introduce a threshold th_p as

$$\sum_{k=th_p}^{\infty} \frac{\lambda_1^k e^{-\lambda_1}}{k!} < 2^{-n}.$$

The probability that the number of occurrences that $s^{(0)}$ appears is greater than th_p is estimated as $\sum_{k=th_p}^{\infty} \frac{\lambda_2^k e^{-\lambda_2}}{k!}$. Therefore, if the probability is close to one, we can uniquely recover $s^{(0)}$ with high probability.

4.2 Estimation of Time and Data Complexities

The procedure consists of three parts: constructing parity-check equations, FWHT, and removing γ. The first step requires the time complexity N, where the unit of the time complexity is a multiplication by α over $GF(2^n)$ and $\bigoplus_{i \in T_z} z_{t+i}$. The second step requires the time complexity $(n - \beta)2^{n-\beta}$, where the unit of the time complexity is an addition or subtraction[4]. The final step requires the time complexity $(m2^{n-\beta}\epsilon_1 + (m_p^2 + m_m^2)2^{-\beta}\epsilon_2)$, where the unit of the time complexity is a multiplication by fixed values over $GF(2^n)$. These units of the time complexity are not equivalent, but at least, they are more efficient than the unit given by the initialization of stream ciphers. Therefore, for simplicity, we regard them as equivalent, and the total time complexity is estimated as

$$N + (n - \beta)2^{n-\beta} + m2^{n-\beta}\epsilon_1 + (m_p^2 + m_m^2)2^{-\beta}\epsilon_2.$$

Proposition 1. *Let n be the size of the LFSR in an LFSR-based stream cipher. We assume that there are m linear masks whose absolute value of correlation is greater than c. When the size of bypassed bits is β, we can recover the initial state of the LFSR with time complexity $3(n - \beta)2^{n-\beta}$ and the required number of parity-check equations is $N = (n - \beta)2^{n-\beta}$, where the success probability is $\sum_{k=th_p}^{\infty} \frac{\lambda_2^k e^{-\lambda_2}}{k!}$, where th_p is the minimum value satisfying*

$$\sum_{k=th_p}^{\infty} \frac{N^k e^{-N}}{k!} < 2^{-n},$$

and

$$\lambda_2 = \frac{m2^{-\beta}}{\sqrt{2\pi N}} \int_{th}^{\infty} \exp\left(-\frac{(x - Nc)^2}{2N}\right) dx,$$

$$th = \sqrt{2N} \times erfc^{-1}\left(\frac{2(n - \beta)}{m}\right).$$

Proof. The total time complexity is estimated as

$$N + (n - \beta)2^{n-\beta} + m2^{n-\beta}\epsilon_1 + (m_p^2 + m_m^2)2^{-\beta}\epsilon_2.$$

In the useful attack parameter, since $(m_p^2 + m_m^2)2^{-\beta}\epsilon_2$ is significantly smaller than the others, we regard it as negligible. We consider the case that other three terms are balanced, i.e.,

$$N = (n - \beta)2^{n-\beta} = m2^{n-\beta}\epsilon_1,$$

---

[4] Since we only use $N < 2^n$ parity-check equations, it is enough to use additions or subtraction on n-bit registers.

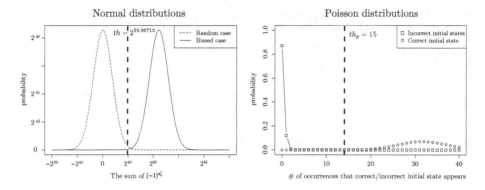

Fig. 2. Theoretical estimation for Example 2.

where ϵ_1 is estimated as

$$\epsilon_1 = \frac{1}{\sqrt{2\pi N}} \int_{th}^{\infty} \exp\left(-\frac{x^2}{2N}\right) dx = \frac{1}{2} \times \mathrm{erfc}\left(\frac{th}{\sqrt{2N}}\right) = \frac{n-\beta}{m}.$$

Thus, when th is

$$th = \sqrt{2N} \times \mathrm{erfc}^{-1}\left(\frac{2(n-\beta)}{m}\right),$$

complexities of the three terms are balanced. We finally evaluate the probability that the initial state of the LFSR is uniquely recovered. The number of occurrences that each incorrect value appears follows the Poisson distribution with parameter $\lambda_1 = N2^{-n}$. To discard all $2^n - 1$ incorrect values, recall th_p satisfying $\sum_{k=th_p}^{\infty} \frac{\lambda_1^k e^{-\lambda_1}}{k!} < 2^{-n}$. Then, the success probability is $\sum_{k=th_p}^{\infty} \frac{\lambda_2^k e^{-\lambda_2}}{k!}$ where λ_2 is

$$\lambda_2 = m2^{-\beta}\epsilon_2 = \frac{m2^{-\beta}}{\sqrt{2\pi N}} \int_{th}^{\infty} \exp\left(-\frac{(x-Nc)^2}{2N}\right) dx$$

□

Example 2. Let us consider an attack against an LFSR-based stream cipher with 80-bit LFSR. We assume that there are 2^{14} linear masks whose correlation is greater than 2^{-36}. For $\beta = 9$, we use $N = (80-9) \times 2^{80-9} \approx 2^{77.1498}$ parity-check equations. The left figure of Fig. 2 shows two normal distributions: random and biased cases. If we use a following threshold

$$th = \sqrt{2N} \times \mathrm{erfc}^{-1}\left(\frac{2(n-\beta)}{m}\right) \approx 2^{39.9672},$$

$\epsilon_1 = (n - \beta)/m \approx 2^{-7.8503}$ and $\epsilon_2 = 0.99957$. The expected number of picked solutions is $2^{80-9}\epsilon_1 + 2^{14-9}\epsilon_2 \approx 2^{63.1498} + 31.98627 \approx 2^{63.1498}$. We apply 2^{14}

inverse linear masks to the picked solutions and recover $s^{(0)}$, and the time complexity is $2^{63.1498+14} = 2^{77.1498}$.

The number of occurrences that each incorrect value appears follows the Poisson distribution with parameter $\lambda_1 = 2^{77.1498-80} = 2^{-2.8502}$. On the other hand, the number of occurrences that $s^{(0)}$ appears follows the Poisson distribution with parameter $\lambda_2 = 2^{14-9} \times 0.99957 \approx 31.98627$. The right figure of Fig. 2 shows two Poisson distributions. For example, when $th_p = 15$ is used, the probability that an incorrect value appears at least 15 is smaller than 2^{-80}. However, the corresponding probability for $s^{(0)}$ is 99.9%. As a result, the total time complexity is $3 \times 2^{77.1498} \approx 2^{78.7348}$.

5 Application to Grain-128a

We apply the new algorithm to the stream cipher Grain-128a [20], which has two modes of operations: stream cipher mode and authenticated encryption mode. We assume that all output sequences of the pre-output function can be observed. Under the known-plaintext scenario, this assumption is naturally realized for the stream cipher mode because the output is directly used as a key stream. On the other hand, this assumption is very strong for the authenticated encryption mode because only even-clock output is used as the key stream. Therefore, we do not claim that the authenticated encryption mode can be broken.

5.1 Specification of Grain-128a

Let $s^{(t)}$ and $b^{(t)}$ be 128-bit internal states of the LFSR and NFSR at time t, respectively, and $s^{(t)}$ and $b^{(t)}$ are represented as $s^{(t)} = (s_t, s_{t+1}, \ldots, s_{t+127})$ and $b^{(t)} = (b_t, b_{t+1}, \ldots, b_{t+127})$. Let y_t be an output of the pre-output function at time t, and it is computed as

$$y_t = h(s^{(t)}, b^{(t)}) \oplus s_{t+93} \oplus \bigoplus_{j \in \mathbb{A}} b_{t+j}, \tag{2}$$

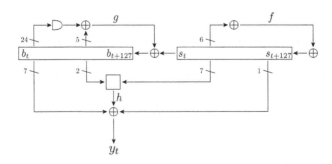

Fig. 3. Specification of Grain-128a

where $\mathbb{A} = \{2, 15, 36, 45, 64, 73, 89\}$, and $h(s^{(t)}, b^{(t)})$ is defined as

$$h(s^{(t)}, b^{(t)}) = h(b_{t+12}, s_{t+8}, s_{t+13}, s_{t+20}, b_{t+95}, s_{t+42}, s_{t+60}, s_{t+79}, s_{t+94})$$
$$= b_{t+12}s_{t+8} \oplus s_{t+13}s_{t+20} \oplus b_{t+95}s_{t+42} \oplus s_{t+60}s_{t+79} \oplus b_{t+12}b_{t+95}s_{t+94}.$$

Moreover, s_{t+128} and b_{t+128} are computed by

$$s_{t+128} = s_t \oplus s_{t+7} \oplus s_{t+38} \oplus s_{t+70} \oplus s_{t+81} \oplus s_{t+96},$$
$$b_{t+128} = s_t \oplus b_t \oplus b_{t+26} \oplus b_{t+56} \oplus b_{t+91} \oplus b_{t+96} \oplus b_{t+3}b_{t+67} \oplus b_{t+11}b_{t+13}$$
$$\oplus b_{t+17}b_{t+18} \oplus b_{t+27}b_{t+59} \oplus b_{t+40}b_{t+48} \oplus b_{t+61}b_{t+65} \oplus b_{t+68}b_{t+84}$$
$$\oplus b_{t+88}b_{t+92}b_{t+93}b_{t+95} \oplus b_{t+22}b_{t+24}b_{t+25} \oplus b_{t+70}b_{t+78}b_{t+82}.$$

Let z_t be the key stream at time t, and $z_t = y_t$ in the stream cipher mode. On the other hand, in the authenticated encryption mode, $z_t = y_{2w+2i}$, where w is the tag size. Figure 3 shows the specification of Grain-128a.

5.2   Linear Approximate Representation for Grain-128a

If there are multiple linear masks with high correlation, the new algorithm can be applied. In this section, we show that Grain-128a has many linear approximate representations, and they produce many linear masks.

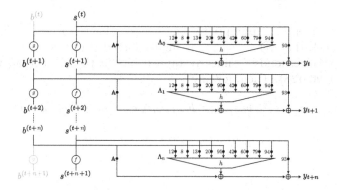

Fig. 4. Linear Approximate Representation for Grain-128a

Figure 4 shows the high-level view of the linear approximate representation. It involves from tth to $(t + n + 1)$th rounds, where $b^{(t)}$ and $b^{(t+n+1)}$ must be linearly inactive to avoid involving the state of NFSR. Moreover, y_{t+i} is linearly active for $i \in \mathbb{T}_z$, and the linear mask of the input of the $(t+i)$-round h function denoted by Λ_i must be nonzero for $i \in \mathbb{T}_z$. Otherwise, it must be zero.

We focus on the structure of the h function, where the input consists of 7 bits from the LFSR and 2 bits from the NFSR. Then, non-zero Λ_i can take several values, and specifically, Λ_i can take 64 possible values (see Table 2) under the condition that a linear mask for 2 bits from NFSR is fixed. Since the sum of y_{t+i} for $i \in \mathbb{T}_z$ is used, it implies that there are $64^{|\mathbb{T}_z|}$ linear approximate representations. These many possible representations are obtained by exploiting the structure of the h function, and this structure is common for all ciphers in the Grain family. In other words, this is a new potential vulnerability of the Grain family.

We first consider $\mathbb{T}_z$ to construct the linear approximate representation, but it is difficult to find an optimal $\mathbb{T}_z$. Our strategy is heuristic and does not guarantee the optimality, but the found $\mathbb{T}_z$ is enough to break full Grain-128a. Once $\mathbb{T}_z$ is determined, we first evaluate the correlation of a linear approximate representation on fixed Λ_i for $i \in \{0, 1, \ldots, n\}$. The high-biased linear mask γ used in our new algorithm is constructed by Λ_i, and the correlation of γ is estimated from the correlation of Λ_i.

Finding Linear Masks with High Correlation. We focus on the sum of key stream bits, i.e., $\bigoplus_{i \in \mathbb{T}_z} y_{t+i}$. From Eq. (2), the sum is represented as

$$\bigoplus_{i \in \mathbb{T}_z} y_{t+i} = \bigoplus_{i \in \mathbb{T}_z} \left(h(s^{(t+i)}, b^{(t+i)}) \oplus s_{t+i+93} \oplus \bigoplus_{j \in A} b_{t+i+j} \right)$$

$$= \bigoplus_{i \in \mathbb{T}_z} \left(h(s^{(t+i)}, b^{(t+i)}) \oplus s_{t+i+93} \right) \oplus \bigoplus_{j \in A} \left(\bigoplus_{i \in \mathbb{T}_z} b_{t+j+i} \right).$$

We first consider an appropriate set $\mathbb{T}_z$. We focus on $\bigoplus_{i \in \mathbb{T}_z} b_{t+j+i}$ and choose $\mathbb{T}_z$ such that $\bigoplus_{i \in \mathbb{T}_z} b_{t+j+i}$ is highly biased. Concretely, we tap 6 bits whose index corresponds to linearly tapped bits in the g function, i.e., $\mathbb{T}_z = \{0, 26, 56, 91, 96, 128\}$. Then, for any j,

$$\bigoplus_{i \in \mathbb{T}_z} b_{t+j+i} = b_{t+j} \oplus b_{t+j+26} \oplus b_{t+j+56} \oplus b_{t+j+91} \oplus b_{t+j+96} \oplus b_{t+j+128}$$

$$= s_{t+j} \oplus g'(b^{(t+j)}),$$

where

$$g'(b^{(t)}) = b_{t+3} b_{t+67} \oplus b_{t+11} b_{t+13} \oplus b_{t+17} b_{t+18} \oplus b_{t+27} b_{t+59} \oplus b_{t+40} b_{t+48}$$
$$\oplus b_{t+61} b_{t+65} \oplus b_{t+68} b_{t+84} \oplus b_{t+88} b_{t+92} b_{t+93} b_{t+95}$$
$$\oplus b_{t+22} b_{t+24} b_{t+25} \oplus b_{t+70} b_{t+78} b_{t+82}.$$

Note that all bits in $g'(b^{(t)})$ are nonlinearly involved, and the correlation may be high. Then

$$\bigoplus_{i \in \mathbb{T}_z} y_{t+i} = \bigoplus_{i \in \mathbb{T}_z} \left(h(s^{(t+i)}, b^{(t+i)}) \oplus s_{t+i+93} \right) \oplus \bigoplus_{j \in A} \left(s_{t+j} \oplus g'(b^{(t+j)}) \right)$$

$$= \bigoplus_{i \in \mathbb{T}_z} s_{t+i+93} \oplus \bigoplus_{j \in A} s_{t+j} \oplus \bigoplus_{i \in \mathbb{T}_z} h(s^{(t+i)}, b^{(t+i)}) \oplus \bigoplus_{j \in A} g'(b^{(t+j)}).$$

Table 2. Correlation of the h function. The horizontal axis shows $\Lambda_{h,i}[1-3]$, the vertical axis shows $\Lambda_{h,i}[5-8]$, and $512 \times cor_{h,i}$ is shown in every cell.

	000	001	010	011	100	101	110	111
0000	-32	-32	-32	32	-32	-32	-32	32
0001	0	0	0	0	0	0	0	0
0010	-32	-32	-32	32	-32	-32	-32	32
0011	0	0	0	0	0	0	0	0
0100	-32	-32	-32	32	-32	-32	-32	32
0101	0	0	0	0	0	0	0	0
0110	32	32	32	-32	32	32	32	-32
0111	0	0	0	0	0	0	0	0
1000	-32	-32	-32	32	0	0	0	0
1001	0	0	0	0	-32	-32	-32	32
1010	-32	-32	-32	32	0	0	0	0
1011	0	0	0	0	-32	-32	-32	32
1100	-32	-32	-32	32	0	0	0	0
1101	0	0	0	0	-32	-32	-32	32
1110	32	32	32	-32	0	0	0	0
1111	0	0	0	0	32	32	32	-32

Case of $\Lambda_{h,i}[0,4] = 00$.

	000	001	010	011	100	101	110	111
0000	-32	-32	-32	32	-32	-32	-32	32
0001	0	0	0	0	0	0	0	0
0010	-32	-32	-32	32	-32	-32	-32	32
0011	0	0	0	0	0	0	0	0
0100	-32	-32	-32	32	-32	-32	-32	32
0101	0	0	0	0	0	0	0	0
0110	32	32	32	-32	32	32	32	-32
0111	0	0	0	0	0	0	0	0
1000	32	32	32	-32	0	0	0	0
1001	0	0	0	0	32	32	32	-32
1010	32	32	32	-32	0	0	0	0
1011	0	0	0	0	32	32	32	-32
1100	32	32	32	-32	0	0	0	0
1101	0	0	0	0	32	32	32	-32
1110	-32	-32	-32	32	0	0	0	0
1111	0	0	0	0	-32	-32	-32	32

Case of $\Lambda_{h,i}[0,4] = 01$.

	000	001	010	011	100	101	110	111
0000	-32	-32	-32	32	32	32	32	-32
0001	0	0	0	0	0	0	0	0
0010	-32	-32	-32	32	32	32	32	-32
0011	0	0	0	0	0	0	0	0
0100	-32	-32	-32	32	32	32	32	-32
0101	0	0	0	0	0	0	0	0
0110	32	32	32	-32	-32	-32	-32	32
0111	0	0	0	0	0	0	0	0
1000	-32	-32	-32	32	0	0	0	0
1001	0	0	0	0	32	32	32	-32
1010	-32	-32	-32	32	0	0	0	0
1011	0	0	0	0	32	32	32	-32
1100	-32	-32	-32	32	0	0	0	0
1101	0	0	0	0	32	32	32	-32
1110	32	32	32	-32	0	0	0	0
1111	0	0	0	0	-32	-32	-32	32

Case of $\Lambda_{h,i}[0,4] = 10$.

	000	001	010	011	100	101	110	111
0000	-32	-32	-32	32	32	32	32	-32
0001	0	0	0	0	0	0	0	0
0010	-32	-32	-32	32	32	32	32	-32
0011	0	0	0	0	0	0	0	0
0100	-32	-32	-32	32	32	32	32	-32
0101	0	0	0	0	0	0	0	0
0110	32	32	32	-32	-32	-32	-32	32
0111	0	0	0	0	0	0	0	0
1000	32	32	32	-32	0	0	0	0
1001	0	0	0	0	-32	-32	-32	32
1010	32	32	32	-32	0	0	0	0
1011	0	0	0	0	-32	-32	-32	32
1100	32	32	32	-32	0	0	0	0
1101	0	0	0	0	-32	-32	-32	32
1110	-32	-32	-32	32	0	0	0	0
1111	0	0	0	0	32	32	32	-32

Case of $\Lambda_{h,i}[0,4] = 11$.

We next consider a linear approximate representation of $h(s^{(t+i)}, b^{(t+i)})$. Let $\Lambda_i \in \{0,1\}^9$ be the input linear mask for the h function at time $t + i$, and $\Lambda_i = (\Lambda_i[0], \Lambda_i[1], \dots, \Lambda_i[8])$. Then,

$$h(s^{(t+i)}, b^{(t+i)})$$
$$\approx \Lambda_i[0]b_{t+i+12} \oplus \Lambda_i[4]b_{t+i+95} \oplus \langle \Lambda_i[1-3], (s_{t+i+8}, s_{t+i+13}, s_{t+i+20}) \rangle$$
$$\oplus \langle \Lambda_i[5-8], (s_{t+i+42}, s_{t+i+60}, s_{t+i+79}, s_{t+i+94}) \rangle,$$

where $\Lambda_i[x-y]$ denotes a sub vector indexed from xth bit to yth bit. Let $cor_{h,i}(\Lambda_i)$ be the correlation of the h function at time $t + i$, and Table 2 summarizes them. From Table 2, $cor_{h,i}(\Lambda_i)$ is 0 or $\pm 2^{-4}$. We have 6 active h functions because

$|\mathbb{T}_z| = 6$, and let $\Lambda_{\mathbb{T}_z} \in \{0,1\}^{9 \times |\mathbb{T}_z|}$ be the concatenated linear mask, i.e., $\Lambda_{\mathbb{T}_z} = (\Lambda_0, \Lambda_{26}, \Lambda_{56}, \Lambda_{91}, \Lambda_{96}, \Lambda_{128})$. The total correlation from all active h functions depends on $\Lambda_{\mathbb{T}_z}$, and it is computed as $cor_h(\Lambda_{\mathbb{T}_z}) = (-1)^{|\mathbb{T}_z|+1} \prod_{i \in \mathbb{T}_z} cor_{h,i}(\Lambda_i)$ because of the piling-up lemma. Therefore, if Λ_i with correlation 0 is used for any $i \in \mathbb{T}_z$, $cor_h(\Lambda_{\mathbb{T}_z}) = 0$. Otherwise, $cor_h(\Lambda_{\mathbb{T}_z}) = \pm 2^{-24}$.

We guess all terms involved in the internal state of the LFSR in the FCA. Under the correlation $\pm 2^{-24}$, we get

$$\bigoplus_{i \in \mathbb{T}_z} y_{t+i} \approx (\text{term by guessings}^{(t)})$$

$$\oplus \bigoplus_{i \in \mathbb{T}_z} (\Lambda_i[0]b_{t+i+12} \oplus \Lambda_i[4]b_{t+i+95}) \oplus \bigoplus_{j \in \mathbb{A}} \left(g'(b^{(t+j)})\right).$$

Therefore, if

$$cor_g(\Lambda_{\mathbb{T}_z}) = \Pr\left[\bigoplus_{i \in \mathbb{T}_z} (\Lambda_i[0]b_{t+i+12} \oplus \Lambda_i[4]b_{t+i+95}) \oplus \bigoplus_{j \in \mathbb{A}} \left(g'(b^{(t+j)})\right) = 0\right]$$

$$- \Pr\left[\bigoplus_{i \in \mathbb{T}_z} (\Lambda_i[0]b_{t+i+12} \oplus \Lambda_i[4]b_{t+i+95}) \oplus \bigoplus_{j \in \mathbb{A}} \left(g'(b^{(t+j)})\right) = 1\right]$$

is high, the FCA can be successfully applied. Note that $cor_g(\Lambda_{\mathbb{T}_z})$ is independent of $\Lambda_i[1-3, 5-8]$ for any $i \in \mathbb{T}_z$. To evaluate its correlation, we divide $\bigoplus_{j \in \mathbb{A}} \left(g'(b^{(t+j)})\right)$ into 20 terms such that b_{t+67} and b_{t+137} are involved by multiple terms. Then, we try out 4 possible values of (b_{t+67}, b_{t+137}) and evaluate correlation independently. As a result, when $(b_{t+67}, b_{t+137}) = (0,0)$ and $(b_{t+67}, b_{t+137}) = (0,1)$, the correlation is $-2^{-33.1875}$ and $-2^{-33.4505}$, respectively. On the other hand, the correlation is 0 when $b_{t+67} = 1$. Therefore

$$cor_g(\Lambda_{\mathbb{T}_z}) = \frac{-2^{-33.1875} - 2^{-33.4505}}{4} = -2^{-34.313}$$

when $\Lambda_i[0,4] = 0$ for all $i \in \mathbb{T}_z$.

We similarly evaluate $cor_g(\Lambda_{\mathbb{T}_z})$ when $\Lambda_i[0,4] \neq 0$ for any $i \in \mathbb{T}_z$. If one of $\Lambda_0[0]$, $\Lambda_{26}[0]$, $\Lambda_{56}[0]$, $\Lambda_{91}[4]$, $\Lambda_{96}[4]$, and $\Lambda_{128}[4]$ is 1, the correlation is always 0 because b_{t+12}, b_{t+38}, b_{t+68}, b_{t+186}, b_{t+191}, and b_{t+223} are not involved to $\bigoplus_{j \in \mathbb{A}} \left(g'(b^{(t+j)})\right)$. Table 3 summarizes $cor_g(\Lambda_{\mathbb{T}_z})$ when $\Lambda_0[0]$, $\Lambda_{26}[0]$, $\Lambda_{56}[0]$, $\Lambda_{91}[4]$, $\Lambda_{96}[4]$, and $\Lambda_{128}[4]$ are 0.

For any fixed Λ_i, we can get the following linear approximate representation

$$\bigoplus_{i \in \mathbb{T}_z} y_{t+i} \approx \bigoplus_{i \in \mathbb{T}_z} s_{t+i+93} \oplus \bigoplus_{j \in \mathbb{A}} s_{t+j} \oplus \bigoplus_{i \in \mathbb{T}_z} \langle \Lambda_i[1-3], (s_{t+i+8}, s_{t+i+13}, s_{t+i+20}) \rangle$$

$$\oplus \bigoplus_{i \in \mathbb{T}_z} \langle \Lambda_i[5-8], (s_{t+i+42}, s_{t+i+60}, s_{t+i+79}, s_{t+i+94}) \rangle. \tag{3}$$

Table 3. Summary of correlations when $\Lambda_i[0,4]$ is fixed. Let $*$ be arbitrary bit.

$\Lambda_0[4]$	$\Lambda_{26}[4]$	$\Lambda_{56}[4]$	$\Lambda_{91}[0]$	$\Lambda_{96}[0]$	$\Lambda_{128}[0]$	$cor_g(\Lambda_{\mathbb{T}_z})$
0	0	0	0	0	0	$-2^{-34.3130}$
0	0	0	0	0	1	$+2^{-36.1875}$
0	0	0	0	1	0	$-2^{-37.5860}$
0	0	0	0	1	1	$+2^{-39.4605}$
0	0	0	1	0	0	$-2^{-34.9230}$
0	0	0	1	0	1	$+2^{-36.7975}$
0	0	0	1	1	0	$+2^{-37.5860}$
0	0	0	1	1	1	$-2^{-39.4605}$
0	0	1	0	0	0	$-2^{-35.8980}$
0	0	1	0	0	1	$+2^{-37.7724}$
0	0	1	0	1	0	$-2^{-39.1710}$
0	0	1	0	1	1	$+2^{-41.0454}$
0	0	1	1	0	0	$-2^{-36.5080}$
0	0	1	1	0	1	$+2^{-38.3825}$
0	0	1	1	1	0	$+2^{-39.1710}$
0	0	1	1	1	1	$-2^{-41.0454}$
0	1	0	0	0	0	$-2^{-35.3636}$
0	1	0	0	0	1	$+2^{-37.2381}$
0	1	0	0	1	0	$-2^{-38.1710}$
0	1	0	0	1	1	$+2^{-40.0454}$
0	1	0	1	0	0	$-2^{-35.8490}$
0	1	0	1	0	1	$+2^{-37.7235}$
0	1	0	1	1	0	$+2^{-38.1710}$
0	1	0	1	1	1	$-2^{-40.0454}$
0	1	1	0	0	0	$-2^{-36.9486}$
0	1	1	0	0	1	$+2^{-38.8230}$
0	1	1	0	1	0	$-2^{-39.7559}$
0	1	1	0	1	1	$+2^{-41.6304}$
0	1	1	1	0	0	$-2^{-37.4340}$
0	1	1	1	0	1	$+2^{-39.3085}$
0	1	1	1	1	0	$+2^{-39.7559}$
0	1	1	1	1	1	$-2^{-41.6304}$
1	$*$	$*$	$*$	$*$	$*$	0

From the piling-up lemma, the correlation is computed as

$$-cor_g(\Lambda_{\mathbb{T}_z}) \times cor_h(\Lambda_{\mathbb{T}_z}),$$

where $cor_g(\mathbb{T}_z)$ is summarized in Table 3 and $cor_h(\Lambda_{\mathbb{T}_z}) = (-1)^{|\mathbb{T}_z|+1} \prod_{i \in \mathbb{T}_z} cor_{h,i}(\Lambda_i)$.

How to Find Multiple γ. The correlation of the linear approximate representation on fixed Λ_i was estimated in the paragraph above. The linear mask γ used in the FCA directly is represented as

$$\gamma = \sum_{i \in \mathbb{T}_z} \left(\Lambda_i[1]\alpha^{i+8} + \Lambda_i[2]\alpha^{i+13} + \Lambda_i[3]\alpha^{i+20} + \Lambda_i[5]\alpha^{i+42} \right.$$
$$\left. + \Lambda_i[6]\alpha^{i+60} + \Lambda_i[7]\alpha^{i+79} + \Lambda_i[8]\alpha^{i+94} + \alpha^{i+93} \right) + \sum_{j \in \mathbb{A}} \alpha^j.$$

If different $\Lambda_{\mathbb{T}_z}$s derive the same γ, we need to sum up corresponding correlations.

Clearly, since this linear approximate representation does not involve $\Lambda_i[0,4]$ for $i \in \mathbb{T}_z$, we need to sum up $2^{2 \times |\mathbb{T}_z|} = 2^{12}$ correlations, where $\Lambda_i[1-3,5-8]$ is identical and only $\Lambda_i[0,4]$ varies for $i \in \mathbb{T}_z$. Let V be a linear span whose basis is 12 corresponding unit vectors.

Moreover, there are special relationships. When we focus on $\Lambda_{56}[6]$ and $\Lambda_{96}[3]$, corresponding elements over $GF(2^{128})$ are identical because $\alpha^{56+60} = \alpha^{96+20} = \alpha^{116}$. In other words, $(\Lambda_{56}[6], \Lambda_{96}[3]) = (0,0)$ and $(\Lambda_{56}[6], \Lambda_{96}[3]) = (1,1)$ derive the same γ, and $(\Lambda_{56}[6], \Lambda_{96}[3]) = (1,0)$ and $(\Lambda_{56}[6], \Lambda_{96}[3]) = (0,1)$ also derive the same γ. We have 3 such relationships as follows.

- $\Lambda_{56}[6]$ and $\Lambda_{96}[3]$. Then, $\alpha^{56+60} = \alpha^{96+20} = \alpha^{116}$.
- $\Lambda_{91}[2]$ and $\Lambda_{96}[1]$. Then, $\alpha^{91+13} = \alpha^{96+8} = \alpha^{104}$.
- $\Lambda_{91}[7]$ and $\Lambda_{128}[5]$. Then, $\alpha^{91+79} = \alpha^{128+42} = \alpha^{170}$.

Therefore, from following three vectors

$$w1(\delta[0]) = (0^9, 0^9, 000000100, 000000000, 000\overline{\delta[0]}00000, 000000000),$$
$$w2(\delta[1]) = (0^9, 0^9, 000000000, 001000000, 0\overline{\delta[1]}0000000, 000000000),$$
$$w3(\delta[2]) = (0^9, 0^9, 000000000, 000000010, \quad 000000000, 00000\overline{\delta[2]}000),$$

a linear span $W(\delta) = \text{span}(w1(\delta[0]), w2(\delta[1]), w3(\delta[2]))$ is defined, where $\overline{\delta[i]} = \delta[i] \oplus 1$. As a result, the correlation for γ denoted by cor_γ is estimated as

$$cor_\gamma = \sum_{w \in W(\delta)} \sum_{v \in V} -cor_g(\Lambda_{\mathbb{T}_z} \oplus v) \times cor_h(\Lambda_{\mathbb{T}_z} \oplus v \oplus w).$$

Note that cor_g is independent of $w \in W(\delta)$.

We heuristically evaluated γ with high correlation. As shown in Table 2, the number of possible Λ_i is at most 64. Otherwise, cor_h is always 0. Therefore, the search space is reduced from 2^{54} to 2^{36}. Moreover, Λ_0 is not involved in $W(\delta)$, and the absolute value of cor_γ is invariable as far as we use Λ_0 satisfying $cor_{h,0} = \pm 2^{-4}$. Therefore, we do not need to evaluate Λ_0 anymore, and the search space is further reduced from 2^{36} to 2^{30}. While Λ_{26} is also not involved to $W(\delta)$, we have non-zero correlation for both cases as $\Lambda_{26}[4] = 0$ and 1 (see Table 3). If the sign of $cor_{h,26}$ for $\Lambda_{26}[4] = 0$ is different from that for $\Lambda_{26}[4] = 1$, they cancel each other out. Therefore, we should use Λ_{26} such that the sign of correlation of Λ_{26} is equal to that of $\Lambda_{26} \oplus (000010000)$, and the number of such candidates is 32. Then, we do not need to evaluate Λ_{26} anymore, and the search space is further reduced from 2^{30} to 2^{24}. We finally evaluated 2^{24} Λ_{T_z} exhaustively. As a result, we found $49152 \times 64 \times 32 \approx 2^{26.58}$ γ whose absolute value of correlation is greater than $2^{-54.2381}$.

5.3   Estimation of Attack Complexity and Success Probability

We apply the attack algorithm described in Sect. 3, and Proposition 1 is used to estimate the attack complexity and success probability. Figure 5 shows the relationship between the time complexity, success probability, and the size of bypassed bits, where $(n, m, c) = (128, 49152 \times 64 \times 32, \pm 2^{-54.2381})$ is used. From Fig. 5, $\beta = 21$ is preferable. The time complexity is $3 \times (128 - 21) \times 2^{128-21} \approx 2^{115.3264}$ and the corresponding success probability is almost 100%. Moreover when $\beta = 22$, the time complexity is $2^{114.3129}$ and the success probability is 60.95%.

The estimation above only evaluates the time complexity to recover the initial state of the LFSR. To recover the secret key, we need to recover the whole of the initial state. Our next goal is to recover the initial state of the NFSR under the condition that the initial state of the LFSR is uniquely determined, but it is not difficult. We have several methods to recover the initial state and explain the most simple method.

The key stream is generated as Eq. (2). We focus on $(y_0, \ldots, y_{34})$, which involves 128 bits as $(b_2, \ldots, b_{129})$. We first guess 93 bits, and the remaining 35 bits are recovered by using corresponding Eq. (2). Specifically, we first guess $(b_{33}, \ldots, b_{75}, b_{80}, \ldots, b_{129})$. Then, $(b_{76}, \ldots, b_{79})$ are uniquely determined by using $(y_{31}, \ldots, y_{34})$. Similarly, we can uniquely determine the remaining 31 bits step by step. While we need to guess 93 bits, the time complexity is negligible compared with that for the FCA.

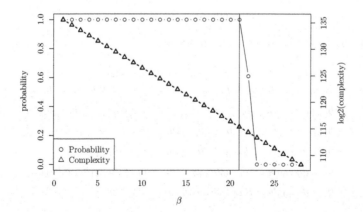

Fig. 5. Time complexity and success probability. FCA against Grain-128a.

5.4   Application to Grain-128

We also applied our technique to Grain-128, but we briefly show the result due to the page limitation. Since Grain-128 is very similar to Grain-128a, we can use the same $\mathbb{T}_z$. Then, $cor_g = -2^{-32}$, where $\Lambda_{26}[4]$ and $\Lambda_{91}[0]$ can be chosen arbitrary but the others must be 0.

We heuristically evaluated γ with high correlation, and we used the same strategy as the case of Grain-128a. As a result, we found $2^{15} \times 64 \times 32 = 2^{26}$ γ with correlation $\pm 2^{-51}$. We apply the attack algorithm described in Sect. 3, and Proposition 1 is used to estimate the attack complexity and success probability. As a result, $\beta = 22$ is preferable, and the time complexity is $3 \times (128 - 22) \times 2^{128-22} \approx 2^{114.3129}$ and the corresponding success probability is 99.0%.

6   Application to Grain-v1

6.1   Specification of Grain-v1

Let $s^{(t)}$ and $b^{(t)}$ be 80-bit internal states of the LFSR and NFSR at time t, respectively, and $s^{(t)}$ and $b^{(t)}$ are represented as $s^{(t)} = (s_t, s_{t+1}, \ldots, s_{t+79})$ and $b^{(t)} = (b_t, b_{t+1}, \ldots, b_{t+79})$, respectively. Then, let z_t be a key stream at time t, and it is computed as

$$z_t = h(s^{(t)}, b^{(t)}) \oplus \bigoplus_{j \in \mathbb{A}} b_{t+j}, \tag{4}$$

where $\mathbb{A} = \{1, 2, 4, 10, 31, 43, 56\}$ and $h(s^{(t)}, b^{(t)})$ is defined as

$$
\begin{aligned}
h(s^{(t)}, b^{(t)}) &= h(s_{t+3}, s_{t+25}, s_{t+46}, s_{t+64}, b_{t+63}) \\
&= s_{t+25} \oplus b_{t+63} \oplus s_{t+3}s_{t+64} \oplus s_{t+46}s_{t+64} \oplus s_{t+64}b_{t+63} \\
&\oplus s_{t+3}s_{t+25}s_{t+46} \oplus s_{t+3}s_{t+46}s_{t+64} \oplus s_{t+3}s_{t+46}b_{t+63} \\
&\oplus s_{t+25}s_{t+46}b_{t+63} \oplus s_{t+46}s_{t+64}b_{t+63}.
\end{aligned}
$$

Moreover, s_{t+80} and b_{t+80} are computed by

$$
\begin{aligned}
s_{t+80} =\ & s_t \oplus s_{t+13} \oplus s_{t+23} \oplus s_{t+38} \oplus s_{t+51} \oplus s_{t+62}, \\
b_{t+80} =\ & s_t \oplus b_{t+62} \oplus b_{t+60} \oplus b_{t+52} \oplus b_{t+45} \oplus b_{t+37} \oplus b_{t+33} \oplus b_{t+28} \oplus b_{t+21} \\
&\oplus b_{t+14} \oplus b_{t+9} \oplus b_t \oplus b_{t+63}b_{t+60} \oplus b_{t+37}b_{t+33} \oplus b_{t+15}b_{t+9} \\
&\oplus b_{t+60}b_{t+52}b_{t+45} \oplus b_{t+33}b_{t+28}b_{t+21} \oplus b_{t+63}b_{t+45}b_{t+28}b_{t+9} \\
&\oplus b_{t+60}b_{t+52}b_{t+37}b_{t+33} \oplus b_{t+63}b_{t+60}b_{t+21}b_{t+15} \\
&\oplus b_{t+63}b_{t+60}b_{t+52}b_{t+45}b_{t+37} \oplus b_{t+33}b_{t+28}b_{t+21}b_{t+15}b_{t+9} \\
&\oplus b_{t+52}b_{t+45}b_{t+37}b_{t+33}b_{t+28}b_{t+21}.
\end{aligned}
$$

6.2 Fast Correlation Attack Against Grain-v1

When we use $\mathbb{T}_z = \{0, 14, 21, 28, 37, 45, 52, 60, 62, 80\}$, we focus on the sum of the key stream bits, i.e., $z_{t+0} \oplus z_{t+14} \oplus z_{t+21} \oplus z_{t+28} \oplus z_{t+37} \oplus z_{t+45} \oplus z_{t+52} \oplus z_{t+60} \oplus z_{t+62} \oplus z_{t+80}$.

$$\bigoplus_{i \in \mathbb{T}_z} z_{t+i} = \bigoplus_{i \in \mathbb{T}_z} h(s^{(t+i)}, b^{(t+i)}) \oplus \bigoplus_{j \in \mathbb{A}} \left(\bigoplus_{i \in \mathbb{T}_z} b_{t+j+i} \right).$$

For any j,

$$\bigoplus_{i \in \mathbb{T}_z} b_{t+j+i} = s_{t+j} \oplus g'(b^{(t+j)}),$$

where $g'(b^{(t)})$ is defined as

$$\begin{aligned}
g'(b^{(t)}) = {} & b_{t+33} \oplus b_{t+9} \oplus b_{t+63}b_{t+60} \oplus b_{t+37}b_{t+33} \oplus b_{t+15}b_{t+9} \oplus b_{t+60}b_{t+52}b_{t+45} \\
& \oplus b_{t+33}b_{t+28}b_{t+21} \oplus b_{t+63}b_{t+45}b_{t+28}b_{t+9} \oplus b_{t+60}b_{t+52}b_{t+37}b_{t+33} \\
& \oplus b_{t+63}b_{t+60}b_{t+21}b_{t+15} \oplus b_{t+63}b_{t+60}b_{t+52}b_{t+45}b_{t+37} \\
& \oplus b_{t+33}b_{t+28}b_{t+21}b_{t+15}b_{t+9} \oplus b_{t+52}b_{t+45}b_{t+37}b_{t+33}b_{t+28}b_{t+21}.
\end{aligned}$$

Then

$$\begin{aligned}
\bigoplus_{i \in \mathbb{T}_z} z_{t+i} &= \bigoplus_{i \in \mathbb{T}_z} h(s^{(t+i)}, b^{(t+i)}) \oplus \bigoplus_{j \in \mathbb{A}} \left(s_{t+j} \oplus g'(b^{(t+j)}) \right) \\
&= \bigoplus_{j \in \mathbb{A}} s_{t+j} \oplus \bigoplus_{i \in \mathbb{T}_z} h(s^{(t+i)}, b^{(t+i)}) \oplus \bigoplus_{j \in \mathbb{A}} g'(b^{(t+j)}).
\end{aligned}$$

We next consider a linear approximate representation of $h(s^{(t+i)}, b^{(t+i)})$. Let Λ_i be the input linear mask for the h function at time $t + i$. Then

$$h(s^{(t+i)}, b^{(t+i)})$$
$$\approx \Lambda_i[4]b_{t+i+63} \oplus \langle \Lambda_i[0-3], (s_{t+i+3}, s_{t+i+25}, s_{t+i+46}, s_{t+i+64}) \rangle.$$

Let $cor_{h,i}(\Lambda_i)$ be the correlation of the h function at time $t + i$, and Table 4 summarizes them. From Table 4, $cor_{h,i}(\Lambda_i)$ is 0 or $\pm 2^{-2}$. Since we have $|\mathbb{T}_z| = 10$ active h functions, the total correlation from all active h functions is computed

Table 4. Correlation of the h function, where $32 \times cor_{h,i}$ is shown in every cell.

	$\Lambda_i[0-3]$															
	0000	0001	0010	0011	0100	0101	0110	0111	1000	1001	1010	1011	1100	1101	1110	1111
$\Lambda_i[4] = 0$	0	0	0	0	0	−8	0	8	0	8	0	−8	−8	8	−8	8
$\Lambda_i[4] = 1$	0	−8	0	8	−8	−8	−8	−8	0	0	0	0	0	−8	0	8

Table 5. Summary of correlations when $\Lambda_i[4]$ is fixed.

$\Lambda_{14}[4]$	$\Lambda_{21}[4]$	$\Lambda_{28}[4]$	$\Lambda_{45}[4]$	$cor_g(\Lambda_{\mathbb{T}_z})$
0	0	0	0	$-2^{-39.7159}$
0	0	0	1	$-2^{-43.4500}$
0	0	1	0	$-2^{-39.6603}$
0	0	1	1	$-2^{-43.7260}$
0	1	0	0	$+2^{-45.1228}$
0	1	0	1	$-2^{-42.9025}$
0	1	1	0	$+2^{-44.3802}$
0	1	1	1	$-2^{-42.6875}$
1	0	0	0	$+2^{-41.9519}$
1	0	0	1	$+2^{-43.5233}$
1	0	1	0	$+2^{-41.8662}$
1	0	1	1	$+2^{-43.6420}$
1	1	0	0	$-2^{-44.9114}$
1	1	0	1	$+2^{-42.8544}$
1	1	1	0	$-2^{-44.5232}$
1	1	1	1	$+2^{-42.7302}$

as $(-1)^{|\mathbb{T}_z|+1}\prod_{i\in\mathbb{T}_z} cor_{h,i}(\Lambda_i) = \pm 2^{-20}$ because of the piling-up lemma. Note that $\Lambda_i[0-3]$ is independent from the state of the NFSR.

All terms involved in the internal state of the LFSR can be guessed in the FCA. Therefore, under the correlation $\pm 2^{-20}$, we get

$$\bigoplus_{i\in\mathbb{T}_z} z_{t+i} = (\text{term by guessing}) \oplus \bigoplus_{i\in\mathbb{T}_z} (\Lambda_i[4]b_{t+i+63}) \oplus \bigoplus_{j\in\mathbb{A}} \left(g'(b^{(t+j)})\right).$$

Therefore, if

$$cor_g(\Lambda_{\mathbb{T}_z}) = \Pr\left[\bigoplus_{i\in\mathbb{T}_z} (\Lambda_i[4]b_{t+i+63}) \oplus \bigoplus_{j\in\mathbb{A}} \left(g'(b^{(t+j)})\right) = 0\right]$$

$$- \Pr\left[\bigoplus_{i\in\mathbb{T}_z} (\Lambda_i[4]b_{t+i+63}) \oplus \bigoplus_{j\in\mathbb{A}} \left(g'(b^{(t+j)})\right) = 1\right]$$

is high, the FCA can be successfully applied.

Similarly to the case of Grain-128a, we evaluate $cor_g(\Lambda_{\mathbb{T}_z})$. If one of $\Lambda_0[4]$, $\Lambda_{37}[4]$, $\Lambda_{52}[4]$, $\Lambda_{60}[4]$, $\Lambda_{62}[4]$, and $\Lambda_{80}[4]$ is 1, the correlation is always 0 because b_{t+63}, b_{t+100}, b_{t+115}, b_{t+123}, b_{t+125}, and b_{t+143} are not involved in $\bigoplus_{j\in\mathbb{A}} \left(g'(b^{(t+j)})\right)$. Table 5 summarizes $cor_g(\Lambda_{\mathbb{T}_z})$ when $\Lambda_i[4] = 0$ for $i \in \{0, 37, 52, 60, 62, 80\}$.

For any fixed Λ_i, we can get the following linear approximate representation

$$\bigoplus_{i \in \mathbb{T}_z} z_{t+i} \approx \bigoplus_{j \in \mathbb{A}} s_{t+j} \oplus \bigoplus_{i \in \mathbb{T}_z} \langle \Lambda_i[0-3], (s_{t+i+3}, s_{t+i+25}, s_{t+i+46}, s_{t+i+64}) \rangle. \quad (5)$$

From the piling-up lemma, the correlation is computed as $-cor_g(\Lambda_{\mathbb{T}_z}) \times cor_h(\Lambda_{\mathbb{T}_z})$.

How to Find Multiple γ. The correlation of the linear approximate representation on fixed Λ_i was estimated in the paragraph above. The linear mask γ used in the FCA directly is represented as

$$\gamma = \sum_{i \in \mathbb{T}_z} \left(\Lambda_i[0]\alpha^{i+3} + \Lambda_i[1]\alpha^{i+25} + \Lambda_i[2]\alpha^{i+46} + \Lambda_i[3]\alpha^{i+64} \right) + \sum_{j \in \mathbb{A}} \alpha^j.$$

If different Λ_h have the same γ, we need to sum up corresponding correlations.

This linear approximate representation does not use $\Lambda_i[4]$ for $i \in \mathbb{T}_z$. Therefore, we need to sum up $2^{|\mathbb{T}_z|} = 2^{10}$ correlations, where $\Lambda_i[0-3]$ is identical and only $\Lambda_i[5]$ varies for $i \in \mathbb{T}_z$. Let V be a linear span whose basis is 12 corresponding unit vectors.

Moreover, there are special relationships similar to the case of Grain-128a, and we have four such relationships as

- $\Lambda_{37}[2]$ and $\Lambda_{80}[0]$. Then, $\alpha^{37+46} = \alpha^{80+3} = \alpha^{83}$.
- $\Lambda_{62}[3]$ and $\Lambda_{80}[2]$. Then, $\alpha^{62+64} = \alpha^{80+46} = \alpha^{126}$.
- $\Lambda_0[2]$ and $\Lambda_{21}[1]$. Then, $\alpha^{0+46} = \alpha^{21+25} = \alpha^{46}$.
- $\Lambda_{21}[3]$ and $\Lambda_{60}[1]$. Then, $\alpha^{21+64} = \alpha^{60+25} = \alpha^{85}$.

Therefore, from following four vectors

$$w1(\delta[0]) = (00000, 0^5, \quad 00000, 0^5, 00100, 0^5, 0^5, 00000, \quad 00000, \overline{\delta[0]}0000),$$
$$w2(\delta[1]) = (00000, 0^5, \quad 00000, 0^5, 00000, 0^5, 0^5, 00000, \quad 00010, 00\overline{\delta[1]}00),$$
$$w3(\delta[2]) = (00100, 0^5, 0\overline{\delta[2]}000, 0^5, 00000, 0^5, 0^5, 00000, \quad 00000, 00000),$$
$$w4(\delta[3]) = (00000, 0^5, \quad 00010, 0^5, 00000, 0^5, 0^5, 0\overline{\delta[3]}000, 00000, 00000),$$

a linear span $W(\delta) = \text{span}(w1(\delta[0]), w2(\delta[1]), w3(\delta[2]), w4(\delta[3]))$ is defined, where $\overline{\delta[i]} = \delta[i] \oplus 1$. Then, let cor_γ be the correlation of γ, and

$$cor_\gamma = \sum_{w \in W(\delta)} \sum_{v \in V} -cor_g(\Lambda_{\mathbb{T}_z} \oplus v) \times cor_h(\Lambda_{\mathbb{T}_z} \oplus v \oplus w).$$

We heuristically evaluated γ with high correlation. For every element in $\mathbb{T}_z$, since the subset $\{14, 28, 45, 52\}$ is independent of the special relationship, we first focus on the subset. Since $b_{t+63+52}$ is not involved in $\bigoplus_{j \in \mathbb{A}} \left(g'(b^{(t+j)}) \right)$, $\Lambda_{52}[4]$ must be 0. Therefore, $\Lambda_{52}[0-3]$ should be chosen as

$$\Lambda_{52}[0-3] \in \{0101, 0111, 1001, 1011, 1100, 1101, 1110, 1111\},$$

and cor_γ is invariable as far as we use Λ_{52} satisfying $cor_{h,52} = \pm 2^{-2}$. We do not need to evaluate Λ_{52} anymore, and the search space is reduced from 2^{40} to 2^{36}. For $i \in \{14, 28, 45\}$, corresponding masks should be chosen as

$$\Lambda_i[0-3] \in \{0101, 0111, 1001, 1011, 1100, 1101, 1110, 1111\}$$

because $cor_g(\Lambda_{T_z})$ is high when $(\Lambda_{14}[4], \Lambda_{21}[4], \Lambda_{28}[4], \Lambda_{45}[4])$ is 0010 or 0000. Let us focus on Table 5. We have three-type linear masks as

- $\Lambda_i[0-3] \in \{1001, 1011, 1100, 1110\}$, where $cor_{h,i} = \pm 2^{-2}$ for $\Lambda_i[4] = 0$ but $cor_{h,i} = 0$ for $\Lambda_i[4] = 1$.
- $\Lambda_i[0-3] \in \{0111, 1101\}$, where the sign of $cor_{h,i}$ is different in each case of $\Lambda_i[4] = 0$ or 1.
- $\Lambda_i[0-3] \in \{0101, 1111\}$, where the sign of $cor_{h,i}$ is the same in both cases of $\Lambda_i[4] = 0$ and 1.

Since cor_γ is invariable in each case, it is enough to evaluate one from each case. Therefore, the search space is reduced from 2^{36} to $3^3 \times 2^{24}$. We finally evaluated 9×2^{24} Λ_{T_z} exhaustively. As a result, we found about 442368 γ whose absolute value of correlation is greater than 2^{-36}.

Estimating Attack Complexity and Success Probability. We apply the attack algorithm described in Sect. 3, and Proposition 1 is used to estimate the attack complexity and success probability. Figure 6 shows the relationship between the time complexity, success probability, and the size of bypassed bits, where $(n, m, c) = (80, 442368, \pm 2^{-36})$ is used. From Fig. 6, $\beta = 11$ is preferable, and the time complexity is $3 \times (80 - 11) \times 2^{80-11} \approx 2^{76.6935}$ and the corresponding success probability is almost 100%.

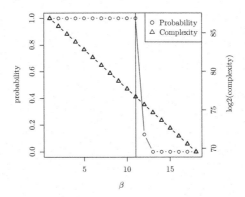

Fig. 6. Time complexity and success probability. FCA against Grain-v1.

7   Verifications, Observations, and Countermeasures

7.1   Experimental Verification

We verify our algorithm by applying it to a toy Grain-like cipher, where the sizes of the LFSR and NFSR are 24 bits, and s_{t+24}, b_{t+24}, and z_t are computed as

$$s_{t+24} = s_t \oplus s_{t+1} \oplus s_{t+2} \oplus s_{t+7},$$

$$b_{t+24} = s_t \oplus b_t \oplus b_{t+5} \oplus b_{t+14} \oplus b_{t+20}b_{t+21} \oplus b_{t+11}b_{t+13}b_{t+15},$$

$$z_t = h(s_{t+3}, s_{t+7}, s_{t+15}, s_{t+19}, b_{t+17}) \oplus \bigoplus_{j \in \{1,3,8\}} b_{t+j},$$

where the h function is as the one used in Grain-v1.

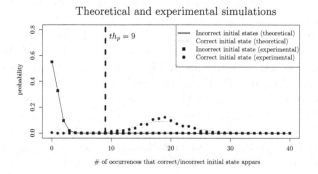

Theoretical and experimental simulations

Fig. 7. Comparison between the theoretical and experimental estimations.

Similarly to the case of Grain-128a, $\mathbb{T}_z$ is used by tapping linear part of the feedback polynomial of NFSR, i.e., $\mathbb{T}_z = \{0, 5, 14, 24\}$. Then, the sum of the key stream is

$$\bigoplus_{i \in \mathbb{T}_z} z_{t+i} = \bigoplus_{i \in \mathbb{T}_z} h(s^{(t+i)}, b^{(t+i)}) \oplus \bigoplus_{j \in \{1,3,8\}} \left(s_{t+j} + g'(b^{(t+j)}) \right),$$

where $g'(b^{(t)}) = b_{t+20}b_{t+21} \oplus b_{t+11}b_{t+13}b_{t+15}$. The ANF of the h function involves b_{t+17}, b_{t+22}, b_{t+31}, and b_{t+41}. If $\Lambda_i[4] = 1$ is used for $i \in \{0, 14, 24\}$, the correlation is always 0 because $\bigoplus_{j \in \{1,3,8\}} g'(b^{(t+j)})$ does not involve b_{t+17}, b_{t+31}, and b_{t+41}. Only b_{t+22} is involved to $\bigoplus_{j \in \{1,3,8\}} g'(b^{(t+j)})$. Therefore, we evaluated correlations of $\bigoplus_{j \in \{1,3,8\}} g'(b^{(t+j)})$ and $\bigoplus_{j \in \{1,3,8\}} g'(b^{(t+j)}) \oplus b_{t+22}$, and they have the correlation $2^{-3.41504}$. For $i \in \{0, 14, 24\}$, we have 8 possible linear masks. Moreover, we should use 0101 and 1111 for the linear mask $\Lambda_{14}[0 - 3]$ because the sign of the correlation is the same in either case of $\Lambda_{14}[4] = 0$ and $\Lambda_{14}[4] = 1$. As a result, we have $8 \times 8 \times 8 \times 2 = 1024$ linear masks whose absolute value of correlations is $2 \times 2^{-8-3.41504} = 2^{-10.41504}$, where the factor 2 is derived from the sum of correlations for $\Lambda_{14}[4] = 0$ and $\Lambda_{14}[4] = 1$.

For example, when $\beta = 5$, the data complexity is $(24 - 5) \times 2^{24-5} \approx 2^{23.25}$. From Proposition 1, when we use $th = 6579$ as the threshold for the normal distribution, the complexities for three steps of the attack algorithm are balanced. Moreover, when we use $th_p = 9$ as the threshold for the Poisson distribution, the probability that incorrect initial state appears at least th_p times is $2^{-26} < 2^{-24}$.

We randomly choose the initial state and repeat the attack algorithm 1000 times. Figure 7 shows the comparison of the Poisson distributions between the theoretical and experimental ones. From this figure, our experimental results almost follow the theoretical one.

7.2   Another View to Find Preferable $\mathbb{T}_z$

In our strategy, we first searched for $\mathbb{T}_z$, which brings the best linear characteristic. A mixed integer linear programming (MILP) is often applied to search for the best linear characteristics of block ciphers [34,35], and this method is naturally applied to search for the best linear characteristic of the fast correlation attack. We first generate an MILP model to represent linear trail with specific number of rounds R. Then, we maximize the probability of the linear characteristic under the condition that $b^{(0)}$ and $b^{(R)}$ are linearly inactive.

We used $\mathbb{T}_z = \{0, 26, 56, 91, 96, 128\}$ and $\mathbb{T}_z = \{0, 14, 21, 28, 37, 45, 52, 60, 62, 80\}$ for Grain-128a and Grain-v1, respectively, and they bring the best linear characteristic. For Grain-128a and Grain-v1, the correlation of the linear characteristic are $\pm 2^{-80.159}$ and $\pm 2^{-38.497}$, respectively. It is not enough to estimate the correlation only from the best characteristic because we need to take into account of the effect by multiple characteristics. For example, assuming that there are two characteristics whose absolute values of correlations are the same but their signs are different, these two characteristics cancel each other. On the other hand, if their signs are the same, we can observe double correlations. Especially, it is very interesting that Grain-128a has significant gain from the best linear characteristic. While the MILP is useful to find the best characteristic, there is no method to find multiple linear characteristics without repeating MILPs. Therefore, we used the MILP only to detect a preferable $\mathbb{T}_z$, and the corresponding correlation is estimated as explained in Sects. 5 and 6.

7.3   Possible Countermeasure Against Our New Attack

The simplest countermeasure is to suppress the output at every second position when the key stream is output. For example, the authenticated encryption mode of Grain-128a has such structure, where the key stream is output only in the even clock. When we attack Grain-128a, we want to use $\mathbb{T}_z = \{0, 26, 56, 91, 96, 128\}$, but we cannot tap 91. As far as we search, we cannot detect a preferable $\mathbb{T}_z$ under the condition that the tapped indices are only even numbers. On the other hand, this countermeasure leads to low throughput.

Another countermeasure would be to limit the length of the key stream for each pair of secret key and iv. It would become difficult to collect enough parity-check equations to execute the FCA. Lightweight stream ciphers often have such restriction, e.g., Plantlet outputs only 2^{30}-bit key stream for each pair of secret key and iv [26]. On the other hand, the advantage of stream ciphers can keep high performance once the initialization finishes, and such restriction does not use the advantage very well.

Acknowledgments. The authors thank the anonymous CRYPTO 2018 reviewers for careful reading and many helpful comments. Takanori Isobe was supported in part by Grant-in-Aid for Young Scientist (B) (KAKENHI 17K12698) for Japan Society for the Promotion of Science. Bin Zhang is supported by the National Key R&D Research programm (Grant No. 2017YFB0802504), the program of the National Natural Science Foundation of China (Grant No. 61572482), National Cryptography Development Fund (Grant No. MMJJ20170107).

References

1. Siegenthaler, T.: Correlation-immunity of nonlinear combining functions for cryptographic applications. IEEE Trans. Inf. Theory **30**(5), 776–780 (1984)
2. Meier, W., Staffelbach, O.: Fast correlation attacks on certain stream ciphers. J. Cryptol. **1**(3), 159–176 (1989)
3. Zeng, K., Yang, C.H., Rao, T.R.N.: An improved linear syndrome algorithm in cryptanalysis with applications. In: Menezes, A.J., Vanstone, S.A. (eds.) CRYPTO 1990. LNCS, vol. 537, pp. 34–47. Springer, Heidelberg (1991). https://doi.org/10.1007/3-540-38424-3_3
4. Mihaljevic, M.J., Golic, J.D.: A fast iterative algorithm for a shift register initial state reconstruction given the noisy output sequence. In: Seberry, J., Pieprzyk, J. (eds.) AUSCRYPT 1990. LNCS, vol. 453, pp. 165–175. Springer, Heidelberg (1990). https://doi.org/10.1007/BFb0030359
5. Chepyzhov, V., Smeets, B.J.M.: On a fast correlation attack on certain stream ciphers. In: Davies, D.W. (ed.) EUROCRYPT 1991. LNCS, vol. 547, pp. 176–185. Springer, Heidelberg (1991). https://doi.org/10.1007/3-540-46416-6_16
6. Johansson, T., Jönsson, F.: Improved fast correlation attacks on stream ciphers via convolutional codes. In: Stern, J. (ed.) EUROCRYPT 1999. LNCS, vol. 1592, pp. 347–362. Springer, Heidelberg (1999). https://doi.org/10.1007/3-540-48910-X_24
7. Johansson, T., Jönsson, F.: Fast correlation attacks based on turbo code techniques. In: Wiener, M. (ed.) CRYPTO 1999. LNCS, vol. 1666, pp. 181–197. Springer, Heidelberg (1999). https://doi.org/10.1007/3-540-48405-1_12
8. Canteaut, A., Trabbia, M.: Improved fast correlation attacks using parity-check equations of weight 4 and 5. In: Preneel, B. (ed.) EUROCRYPT 2000. LNCS, vol. 1807, pp. 573–588. Springer, Heidelberg (2000). https://doi.org/10.1007/3-540-45539-6_40
9. Chepyzhov, V.V., Johansson, T., Smeets, B.J.M.: A simple algorithm for fast correlation attacks on stream ciphers. In: Goos, G., Hartmanis, J., van Leeuwen, J., Schneier, B. (eds.) FSE 2000. LNCS, vol. 1978, pp. 181–195. Springer, Heidelberg (2001). https://doi.org/10.1007/3-540-44706-7_13

10. Mihaljevi, M.J., Fossorier, M.P.C., Imai, H.: Fast correlation attack algorithm with list decoding and an application. In: Matsui, M. (ed.) FSE 2001. LNCS, vol. 2355, pp. 196–210. Springer, Heidelberg (2002). https://doi.org/10.1007/3-540-45473-X_17

11. Berbain, C., Gilbert, H., Maximov, A.: Cryptanalysis of Grain. In: Robshaw, M. (ed.) FSE 2006. LNCS, vol. 4047, pp. 15–29. Springer, Heidelberg (2006). https://doi.org/10.1007/11799313_2

12. Lee, J., Lee, D.H., Park, S.: Cryptanalysis of sosemanuk and SNOW 2.0 using linear masks. In: Pieprzyk, J. (ed.) ASIACRYPT 2008. LNCS, vol. 5350, pp. 524–538. Springer, Heidelberg (2008). https://doi.org/10.1007/978-3-540-89255-7_32

13. Zhang, B., Xu, C., Meier, W.: Fast correlation attacks over extension fields, large-unit linear approximation and cryptanalysis of SNOW 2.0. In: Gennaro, R., Robshaw, M. (eds.) CRYPTO 2015, Part I. LNCS, vol. 9215, pp. 643–662. Springer, Heidelberg (2015). https://doi.org/10.1007/978-3-662-47989-6_31

14. Chose, P., Joux, A., Mitton, M.: Fast correlation attacks: an algorithmic point of view. In: Knudsen, L.R. (ed.) EUROCRYPT 2002. LNCS, vol. 2332, pp. 209–221. Springer, Heidelberg (2002). https://doi.org/10.1007/3-540-46035-7_14

15. Zhang, B., Feng, D.: Multi-pass fast correlation attack on stream ciphers. In: Biham, E., Youssef, A.M. (eds.) SAC 2006. LNCS, vol. 4356, pp. 234–248. Springer, Heidelberg (2007). https://doi.org/10.1007/978-3-540-74462-7_17

16. Wagner, D.A.: A generalized birthday problem. In: Yung, M. (ed.) CRYPTO 2002. LNCS, vol. 2442, pp. 288–304. Springer, Heidelberg (2002). https://doi.org/10.1007/3-540-45708-9_19

17. Dinur, I., Güneysu, T., Paar, C., Shamir, A., Zimmermann, R.: An experimentally verified attack on full grain-128 using dedicated reconfigurable hardware. In: Lee, D.H., Wang, X. (eds.) ASIACRYPT 2011. LNCS, vol. 7073, pp. 327–343. Springer, Heidelberg (2011). https://doi.org/10.1007/978-3-642-25385-0_18

18. Fu, X., Wang, X., Chen, J.: Determining the nonexistent terms of non-linear multivariate polynomials: How to break Grain-128 more efficiently. IACR Cryptol. ePrint Archive 2017, 412 (2017)

19. Zhang, B., Xu, C., Meier, W.: Fast near collision attack on the Grain v1 stream cipher. In: Nielsen, J.B., Rijmen, V. (eds.) EUROCRYPT 2018, Part II. LNCS, vol. 10821, pp. 771–802. Springer, Cham (2018). https://doi.org/10.1007/978-3-319-78375-8_25

20. Ågren, M., Hell, M., Johansson, T., Meier, W.: Grain-128a: a new version of Grain-128 with optional authentication. IJWMC 5(1), 48–59 (2011)

21. Hell, M., Johansson, T., Maximov, A., Meier, W.: A stream cipher proposal: Grain-128. In: IEEE International Symposium on Information Theory (ISIT 2006). IEEE, pp. 1614–1618 (2006)

22. Hell, M., Johansson, T., Meier, W.: Grain: a stream cipher for constrained environments. IJWMC 2(1), 86–93 (2007)

23. ISO/IEC: JTC1: ISO/IEC 29167-13: Information technology - automatic identification and data capture techniques - part 13: Crypto suite Grain-128A security services for air interface communications (2015)

24. Aumasson, J., Henzen, L., Meier, W., Naya-Plasencia, M.: Quark: a lightweight hash. J. Cryptol. 26(2), 313–339 (2013)

25. Armknecht, F., Mikhalev, V.: On lightweight stream ciphers with shorter internal states. In: Leander, G. (ed.) FSE 2015. LNCS, vol. 9054, pp. 451–470. Springer, Heidelberg (2015). https://doi.org/10.1007/978-3-662-48116-5_22

26. Mikhalev, V., Armknecht, F., Müller, C.: On ciphers that continuously access the non-volatile key. IACR Trans. Symmetric Cryptol. 2016(2), 52–79 (2016)

27. Hell, M., Johansson, T., Meier, W.: Grain - a stream cipher for constrained environments (2005). http://www.ecrypt.eu.org/stream
28. Zhang, B., Li, Z., Feng, D., Lin, D.: Near collision attack on the Grain v1 stream cipher. In: Moriai, S. (ed.) FSE 2013. LNCS, vol. 8424, pp. 518–538. Springer, Heidelberg (2014). https://doi.org/10.1007/978-3-662-43933-3_27
29. Dinur, I., Shamir, A.: Breaking Grain-128 with dynamic cube attacks. In: Joux, A. (ed.) FSE 2011. LNCS, vol. 6733, pp. 167–187. Springer, Heidelberg (2011). https://doi.org/10.1007/978-3-642-21702-9_10
30. Lehmann, M., Meier, W.: Conditional differential cryptanalysis of Grain-128a. In: Pieprzyk, J., Sadeghi, A.-R., Manulis, M. (eds.) CANS 2012. LNCS, vol. 7712, pp. 1–11. Springer, Heidelberg (2012). https://doi.org/10.1007/978-3-642-35404-5_1
31. Todo, Y., Isobe, T., Hao, Y., Meier, W.: Cube attacks on non-blackbox polynomials based on division property. In: Katz, J., Shacham, H. (eds.) CRYPTO 2017. LNCS, vol. 10403, pp. 250–279. Springer, Cham (2017). https://doi.org/10.1007/978-3-319-63697-9_9
32. Wang, Q., Hao, Y., Todo, Y., Li, C., Isobe, T., Meier, W.: Improved division property based cube attacks exploiting algebraic properties of superpoly. CRYPTO 2018, Accepted at CRYPTO 2018 (2018). http://eprint.iacr.org/2017/1063
33. Matsui, M.: Linear cryptanalysis method for DES cipher. In: Helleseth, T. (ed.) EUROCRYPT 1993. LNCS, vol. 765, pp. 386–397. Springer, Heidelberg (1994). https://doi.org/10.1007/3-540-48285-7_33
34. Mouha, N., Wang, Q., Gu, D., Preneel, B.: Differential and linear cryptanalysis using mixed-integer linear programming. In: Wu, C.-K., Yung, M., Lin, D. (eds.) Inscrypt 2011. LNCS, vol. 7537, pp. 57–76. Springer, Heidelberg (2012). https://doi.org/10.1007/978-3-642-34704-7_5
35. Sun, S., Hu, L., Wang, P., Qiao, K., Ma, X., Song, L.: Automatic security evaluation and (related-key) differential characteristic search: application to SIMON, PRESENT, LBlock, DES(L) and other bit-oriented block ciphers. In: Sarkar, P., Iwata, T. (eds.) ASIACRYPT 2014, Part I. LNCS, vol. 8873, pp. 158–178. Springer, Heidelberg (2014). https://doi.org/10.1007/978-3-662-45611-8_9

A Key-Recovery Attack
on 855-round Trivium

Ximing Fu[1], Xiaoyun Wang[2,3,4(✉)], Xiaoyang Dong[2], and Willi Meier[5]

[1] Department of Computer Science and Technology,
Tsinghua University, Beijing 100084, China
[2] Institute for Advanced Study, Tsinghua University, Beijing 100084, China
`xiaoyunwang@mail.tsinghua.edu.cn`
[3] School of Mathematics, Shandong University, Jinan 250100, China
[4] Key Laboratory of Cryptologic Technology and Information Security,
Ministry of Education, Shandong University, Jinan 250100, China
[5] FHNW, Windisch, Switzerland

Abstract. In this paper, we propose a key-recovery attack on Trivium reduced to 855 rounds. As the output is a complex Boolean polynomial over secret key and IV bits and it is hard to find the solution of the secret keys, we propose a novel nullification technique of the Boolean polynomial to reduce the output Boolean polynomial of 855-round Trivium. Then we determine the degree upper bound of the reduced nonlinear boolean polynomial and detect the right keys. These techniques can be applicable to most stream ciphers based on nonlinear feedback shift registers (NFSR). Our attack on 855-round Trivium costs time complexity 2^{77}. As far as we know, this is the best key-recovery attack on round-reduced Trivium. To verify our attack, we also give some experimental data on 721-round reduced Trivium.

Keywords: Trivium · Nullification technique · Polynomial reduction
IV representation · Key-recovery attack

1 Introduction

Most symmetric cryptographic primitives can be described by boolean functions over secret variables and public variables. The secret variables are often key bits, the public variables are often plaintext bits for block ciphers and IV bits for stream ciphers. The ANF (algebraic normal form) representation of the output is usually very complex by repeatedly executing a simple iterative function, where the iterative function is a round function for block ciphers or a feedback function for stream ciphers based on nonlinear feedback shift registers. For stream ciphers, obtaining the exact output boolean functions is usually impossible. But if its degree is low, the cipher can not resist on many known attacks, such as higher order differential attacks [13,15], cube attacks [1,4], and integral attacks [14]. Hence, it is important to reduce the degree of polynomials for cryptanalysis of stream ciphers.

© International Association for Cryptologic Research 2018
H. Shacham and A. Boldyreva (Eds.): CRYPTO 2018, LNCS 10992, pp. 160–184, 2018.
https://doi.org/10.1007/978-3-319-96881-0_6

Trivium, based on a nonlinear feedback shift register (NFSR), is one of the finalists by eSTREAM project and has been accepted as ISO standard [2,10]. Trivium has a simple structure, with only bit operations, so that it can be applicable to source restricted applications such as RFID. By iteratively using NFSR, the degree increases rapidly and the output is a complex boolean function over key and IV bits.

There have been lots of cryptanalysis of Trivium since its submission. The early results include the chosen IV statistical attack [6,7], which was applied to key-recovery attack on Trivium reduced to 672 rounds. Inspired by the message modification technique [20,21], Knellwolf et al. invented the conditional differential tool [11], which was applicable to distinguishing stream ciphers based on NFSR. In [12], Knellwolf et al. proposed a distinguishing attack on 961-round Trivium with practical complexity for weak keys.

Cube attacks are the major methods for recent cryptanalysis results of reduced round Trivium. In [4], Dinur and Shamir proposed a practical full key recovery on Trivium reduced to 767 rounds, using cube attacks. Afterwards, Aumasson et al. [1] provided the distinguishers of 790-round Trivium with complexity 2^{30}. Then Fouque and Vannet [8] provided a practical full key recovery for 784/799 rounds Trivium. Todo et al. [19] proposed a key-recovery attack on 832-round Trivium, where one equivalent bit can be recovered with complexity of around 2^{77}, combined with division property [18]. All of these attacks exploited low degree properties of the ANF of the output bit over IV bits. As though the degree is not low, i.e., the degree is equal to the number of variables, there is a possibility to construct distinguishers if there are missing (IV) terms. In [3,5], Dinur and Shamir exploited the density of IV terms, combined with nullification technique, and broke the full-round Grain128. Based on nullification technique [3,5], degree evaluation and IV representation techniques were proposed and the missing IV terms can be obtained with probability 1 [9]. The degree upper bounds of Trivium-like ciphers were obtained [16] using the degree evaluation techniques. Then a key-recovery attack on 835-round Trivium was proposed in [17] using correlation cube attack with a complexity of 2^{75}. Though the cube attack and cube tester tools can be applied to obtain the low-degree information, it is restricted by the computing ability. It is hard to execute cube tester programs of dimension more than 50 on a small cluster of cores.

In this paper, we focus on the cryptanalysis on round-reduced Trivium. We first propose a novel observation of the Boolean polynomial and invent a new nullification technique for reducing the output Boolean polynomial. After nullification, we determine the degree upper bound of the reduced polynomial, which can serve as the distinguishers. In this process, large quantities of state terms arise to be processed. We present a series of techniques to help discard monomials, including degree evaluation and degree reduction techniques. Based on these reduction techniques for boolean polynomials, we propose the first key-recovery attack on 855-round Trivium with time complexity 2^{77}. We summarize the related results in Table 1.

Table 1. Some related key-recovery results for reduced round Trivium.

Rounds	Complexity	Ref.
736	2^{30}	[4]
767	2^{36}	[4]
799	Practical	[8]
832	2^{77}	[19]
835	2^{75}	[17]
855	2^{77}	Sect. 4

The rest of the paper is organised as follows. In Sect. 2, some basic related preliminaries will be shown. The basic techniques used in this paper and the attack framework will be introduced in Sect. 3. Based on the Boolean polynomial reduction techniques and IV representation, a key recovery attack on 855-round Trivium is proposed in Sect. 4, combined with a new nullification technique. Finally, Sect. 5 summarizes the paper.

2 Preliminaries

In this section, some basic notations used in this paper are introduced in the following subsections.

2.1 Notations

ANF   the Algebraic Normal Form
IV bit   public variables of Trivium
IV term   product of certain IV bits
state bit   internal state bit in the initialization of Trivium stream cipher
state term product of certain state bits, IV bits or key bits

2.2 Brief Description of Trivium

Trivium can be described by a 288-bit nonlinear feedback shift register s_i ($1 \leq i \leq 288$). During the initialization stage, s_1 to s_{80} are set to 80 key bits, s_{94} to s_{173} are set with 80 IV bits, $s_{286}, s_{287}, s_{288}$ are set to 1s and the other state bits are set to zeros, i.e.,

$$(s_1, s_2, \ldots, s_{93}) \leftarrow (K_0, \ldots, K_{79}, 0, \ldots, 0)$$
$$(s_{94}, s_{95}, \ldots, s_{177}) \leftarrow (IV_0, \ldots, IV_{79}, 0, \ldots, 0)$$
$$(s_{178}, s_{179}, \ldots, s_{288}) \leftarrow (0, \ldots, 0, 1, 1, 1).$$

Then the NFSR is updated for 1152 rounds with the following updating function, i.e.,

for $i \leftarrow 1 : 4 \cdot 288$ do

$t_1 \leftarrow s_{66} + s_{91} \cdot s_{92} + s_{93} + s_{171}$

$t_2 \leftarrow s_{162} + s_{175} \cdot s_{176} + s_{177} + s_{264}$

$t_3 \leftarrow s_{243} + s_{286} \cdot s_{287} + s_{288} + s_{69}$

$(s_1, s_2, \ldots, s_{93}) \leftarrow (t_3, s_1, \ldots, s_{92})$

$(s_{94}, s_{95}, \ldots, s_{177}) \leftarrow (t_1, s_{94}, \ldots, s_{176})$

$(s_{178}, s_{179}, \ldots, s_{288}) \leftarrow (t_2, s_{178}, \ldots, s_{287})$

end for

After the initialization, the output bits o_i can be generated by the following functions.

for $i \leftarrow 1 : N$ do

$t_1 \leftarrow s_{66} + s_{91} \cdot s_{92} + s_{93} + s_{171}$

$t_2 \leftarrow s_{162} + s_{175} \cdot s_{176} + s_{177} + s_{264}$

$t_3 \leftarrow s_{243} + s_{286} \cdot s_{287} + s_{288} + s_{69}$

$o_i \leftarrow s_{66} + s_{93} + s_{162} + s_{177} + s_{243} + s_{288}$

$(s_1, s_2, \ldots, s_{93}) \leftarrow (t_3, s_1, \ldots, s_{92})$

$(s_{94}, s_{95}, \ldots, s_{177}) \leftarrow (t_1, s_{94}, \ldots, s_{176})$

$(s_{178}, s_{179}, \ldots, s_{288}) \leftarrow (t_2, s_{178}, \ldots, s_{287})$

end for

Then the message can be encrypted by exclusive-or with o_i. To outline our technique more conveniently, we describe Trivium using the following iterative expression. We use s_w^r ($0 \leq w \leq 2$) shown in Eq. 1 to illustrate r-round ($1 \leq r \leq 1152$) s_1, s_{94} and s_{178} separately. Let z_r denote the output bit after r rounds of initialization. Then the initialization process can be illustrated by the following formula

$$
\begin{aligned}
s_0^r &= s_2^{r-66} + s_2^{r-109} s_2^{r-110} + s_2^{r-111} + s_0^{r-69}, \\
s_1^r &= s_0^{r-66} + s_0^{r-91} s_0^{r-92} + s_0^{r-93} + s_1^{r-78}, \\
s_2^r &= s_1^{r-69} + s_1^{r-82} s_1^{r-83} + s_1^{r-84} + s_2^{r-87}.
\end{aligned}
\tag{1}
$$

The s_w^r ($0 \leq w \leq 2$) is denoted as internal **state bit** in this paper. The multiplication of state bits $\prod_{i \in I, j \in J} s_i^j$ is denoted as a **state term**. The output can be described using the state terms as $z_r = s_0^{r-65} + s_0^{r-92} + s_1^{r-68} + s_1^{r-83} + s_2^{r-65} + s_2^{r-110}$.

2.3 Representation of Boolean Functions for Stream Ciphers

Supposing that there are m IV bits, i.e., $v_0, v_1, \ldots, v_{m-1}$ and n key bits, i.e., $k_0, k_1, \ldots, k_{n-1}$, the Algebraic Normal Form (ANF) of the internal state bit or output bit s could be written as the following style:

$$
s = \sum_{I,J} \prod_{i \in I} v_i \prod_{j \in J} k_j,
\tag{2}
$$

where the sum operation is over field $\mathbb{F}_2$. The $\prod_{i \in I} v_i \prod_{j \in J} k_j$ is also denoted as a state term of s and $\prod_{i \in I} v_i$ is denoted as its corresponding IV term. Let IV term $t_I = \prod_{i \in I} v_i$ be the multiplication of v_i whose indices are within I, the ANF of s can be rewritten as

$$s = \sum_I t_I g_I(k), \tag{3}$$

where $g_I(k)$ is the sum of the corresponding coefficient function of terms whose corresponding IV term is t_I. The $|I|$ is denoted as the degree of IV term t_I, $\deg(t_I)$. The degree of s is $\deg(s) = \max_I\{\deg(t_I)\}$.

2.4   Cube Attack and Cube Tester

Cube attack [4] is introduced by Dinur and Shamir at EUROCRYPT 2009. This method is also known as high-order differential attack introduced by Lai [15] in 1994. It assumes the output bit of a cipher is a d-degree polynomial $f(k_0..., k_{n-1}, v_0..., v_{m-1})$ over $GF(2)$. The polynomial can be written as a sum of two polynomials:

$$f(k_0..., k_{n-1}, v_0..., v_{m-1}) = t_I \cdot P + Q_{t_I}(k_0..., k_{n-1}, v_0..., v_{m-1})$$

t_I is called maxterm and is a product of certain public variables, for example $(v_0, ..., v_{s-1}), 1 \le s \le m$, which is called a cube C_{t_I}; P is called superpoly; $Q_{t_I}(k_0..., k_{n-1}, v_0..., v_{m-1})$ is the remainder polynomial and none of its terms is divisible by t_I. The major idea of the cube attack is that the sum of f over all values of the cube C_{t_I} (cube sum) is:

$$\sum_{x'=(v_0,...,v_{s-1}) \in C_{t_I}} f(k_0, ..., k_{n-1}, x', ...v_{m-1}) = P$$

whose degree is at most d-s, where the cube C_{t_I} contains all binary vectors of length s and the other public variables are fixed to constants. In cube attack, P is a linear function over key bits. The key is recovered by solving a system of linear equations derived by different cubes C_{t_I}.

Dynamic cube attack [5] is also introduced by Dinur and Shamir in FSE 2011. The basic idea is to find dynamic variables, which depend on some of the public cube variables and some private variables (the key bits), to nullify the complex function $P = P_1 \cdot P_2 + P_3$, where the degree of P_3 is relatively lower than the degree of P and $P_1 \cdot P_2$ is a complex function. Then guess the involved key bits and compute the dynamic cube variables to make P_1 to be zero and the function is simplified greatly. The right guess of key bits will lead the cube sum to be zero otherwise the cube sums will be random generally.

Cube testers [1] are used to detect non-random properties. Suppose in Eq. 3, an IV term t_I does not exist in the ANF of s, e.g. the coefficient $g_I(k) = 0$. Hence, the cube sum over cube C_{t_I} is definitely zero for different key guessing. However, if the IV term t_I exists, the value of cube sum $g_I(k)$ is dependent on the key guessing. This property was applied to break full-round Grain128 [5,9].

3   Basic Ideas

3.1   New Observation of Boolean Polynomial Reduction

In this paper, we propose a new nullification technique based on a lemma as
follows.

Lemma 1. *Suppose z is the output polynomial of a cipher, and*

$$z = P_1 P_2 + P_3. \tag{4}$$

*Then the polynomial can be reduced to a simpler one $(1 + P_1)z = (1 + P_1)P_3$ by
multiplying $1 + P_1$ in both sides of Eq. (4) if $\deg(P_1 P_2) > \deg((1 + P_1)P_3)$.*

Lemma 1 can be verified by $(P_1 + 1)z = (P_1 + 1)P_1 P_2 + (P_1 + 1)P_3 = (P_1 + 1)P_3$. In our cryptanalysis of Trivium, P_1 is a simple polynomial over several IV
bits and key bits, while P_2 is much more complex than P_3. In our nullification
technique, we multiply $P_1 + 1$ in both sides of Eq. (4) to nullify the most complex
polynomial P_2 without changing P_3. The result $(1 + P_1)z = (1 + P_1)P_3$ could be
analyzed by considering P_3 and $1 + P_1$ independently, and then multiply them
together to get $(1 + P_1)z$.

3.2   Outline of Our Attack

Based on the novel observation in Sect. 3.1, our attack includes two phases, which
are the preprocessing phase and on-line attack phase.
    In the preprocessing phase,

1. We apply the new nullification technique by determining P_1, then multiply
   $1 + P_1$ in both sides of Eq. 4 and obtain the reduced polynomial $(1 + P_1)P_3$.
2. We study the polynomial $(1 + P_1)P_3$ and prove its upper bound degree to be
   d mathematically, then cubes of dimension $d + 1$ lead to distinguishers.

    In the on-line phase, we guess the partial key bits in P_1, and compute the
cube sums of $(P_1 + 1)z$ over $(d + 1)$-degree IV terms:

i For the right key guessing, $(P_1 + 1)z = (P_1 + 1)P_3$. Thus the cube sums must
  be zero.
ii For the wrong key guessing, the equation becomes $(P_1' + 1)z = (P_1' + 1)P_1 P_2 +
  (P_1' + 1)P_3$, which is more complex and dominated by P_2, thus the cube sums
  are not always zero.

    We focus on constructing the distinguishers in the preprocessing phase and
it costs most computing sources.

3.3   Constructing Distinguishers

After obtaining the reduced polynomial $(1 + P_1)P_3$, our major work is to study this polynomial and derive distinguishers. In our analysis, we demonstrate that the degree of the reduced polynomial is strictly lower than 70. As the degree is so high, such a result was hard to achieve in previous works. So we introduce various details of reducing polynomials in an iterative process.

We introduce several techniques to discard monomials in advance during the iterative computation of the ANF representation of the output bit $(1 + P_1)P_3$. Suppose we are proving the upper bound degree of $(1 + P_1)P_3$'s ANF to be d, then the following techniques are used to reduce the Boolean polynomial of $(1 + P_1)P_3$ by discarding monomials in advance. The whole process could be divided into the following three steps shown in Fig. 1.

- **Step 1.** We compute forward to express the ANF of some internal state bits over IV bits and key bits. In Trivium, the internal state bits s_i^j ($0 \le i \le 2$, $0 \le j \le 340$) are computed in a PC.
- **Step 2.** During the iterative computation of the ANF representation of $(1 + P_1)P_3$ in the backward direction (decryption), we introduce the **fast discarding monomial technique** in Sect. 3.4, which includes the following two algorithms:
  - First, we propose the **degree evaluation** algorithm to obtain the degree bounds of internal state bits. As the monomials of $(1 + P_1)P_3$'s ANF is a product of these internal state bits, the degree of a monomial is bounded by the sum of the degrees of the multiplied internal state bits, which is regarded as the degree estimation of the monomial. If the estimated degrees of monomials are lower than d, they are discarded directly.
  - Second, we exploit the iterative structure of Trivium, and find that the $(1 + P_1)P_3$'s ANF contains many products of consecutive internal state bits. Thus, we pre-compute the **degree reduction**s of those products, which is $d_t = \sum_i \deg(x_i) - \deg(\prod_i x_i)$, where x_i is an internal state bit. Thus, the degree of a monomial is upper bounded by the difference value between the sum of the multiplied internal state bits and the corresponding degree reduction d_t. If it is smaller than d, the monomial is discarded.
- **Step 3.** For the left monomials of $(1 + P_1)P_3$'s ANF, we introduce **IV representation technique** in Sect. 3.5 to determine the upper bound degree of $(1 + P_1)P_3$ or find the d-degree missing product of certain IV bits (missing IV term). In IV representation technique, the symbolic key bits in the internal state bits are removed and only IV bits are left. Combining with repeated IV term removing algorithm, we can simplify monomials of $(1 + P_1)P_3$'s ANF without losing the missing IV term information. If we find an IV term is not in the IV representation of $(1 + P_1)P_3$, we can conclude that it is also not in $(1 + P_1)P_3$.

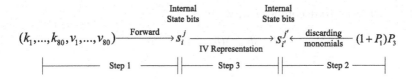

Fig. 1. Framework of constructing distinguishers

3.4 Fast Discarding Monomial Techniques

In Step 2 of Fig. 1, during the iterative computation of the ANF representation of $(1 + P_1)P_3$ in the backward direction (decryption), there arise more and more state terms. We will give several techniques to simplify the polynomial by discarding monomials in advance. In this Step, repeated state terms arise according to the Trivium encryption scheme. The repeated state terms are removed using Algorithm 1. The complexity of Algorithm 1 is $O(n)$, supposing there are n state terms.

Algorithm 1. Repeated-(state)term Removing Algorithm

Input: The vector T with n terms, i.e., $T_1, T_2, \ldots, T_n$.
Output: Updated T with m terms, where $m \leq n$.
1: Initialize an empty Hash Set **H**.
2: **for** $i \leftarrow 1 : n$ **do**
3:     Compute the Hash value of T_i, i.e., $H(T_i)$
4:     **if** $H.contains(T_i)$ is **true then**
5:         $H.delete(T_i)$
6:     **else**
7:         $H.insert(T_i)$
8:     **end if**
9: **end for**

Degree evaluation technique. As we are proving the degree of the Boolean polynomial $(1 + P_1)P_3$ to be d, thus many monomials with lower degree produced during the iterative computation backward (decryption) in Step 3 are deleted without consideration (we do not need to continue the iterative computation over those monomials). We estimate those monomials using degree information of the internal state bits in lower rounds. This section presents a degree evaluation algorithm for the internal state bits. For example, we are going to estimate the degree of $b_i = b_{i-3} + b_{i-1}b_{i-2}$.

$$\begin{aligned}
\deg(b_i) &= \deg(b_{i-3} + b_{i-1}b_{i-2}) \\
&= \max\{\deg(b_{i-3}), \deg(b_{i-1}b_{i-2})\} \\
&\leq \max\{\deg(b_{i-3}), \deg(b_{i-1}) + \deg(b_{i-2})\}
\end{aligned} \tag{5}$$

If we continue to decompose b_i, we find

$$
\begin{aligned}
b_{i-1}b_{i-2} &= (b_{i-4} + b_{i-2}b_{i-3})(b_{i-5} + b_{i-3}b_{i-4}) \\
&= b_{i-4}b_{i-5} + b_{i-3}b_{i-4} + b_{i-2}b_{i-3}b_{i-5} + b_{i-2}b_{i-3}b_{i-4},
\end{aligned}
\tag{6}
$$

If $\deg(b_{i-1}) = \deg(b_{i-2}b_{i-3})$ and $\deg(b_{i-2}) = \deg(b_{i-3}b_{i-4})$, then in Eq. (5), $\deg(b_{i-1}) + \deg(b_{i-2})$ may add $\deg(b_{i-3})$ twice. So in order to obtain a more accurate degree estimation, we are willing to decompose b_i for several rounds backwards.

For Trivium, the ANFs of s_i^j ($0 \le i \le 2, 0 \le j \le 340$) are exactly obtained in a PC and their exact degrees can be obtained. For example, in the cryptanalysis of 855-round Trivium, we compute ANF of s_i^j ($0 \le i \le 2, 0 \le j \le 340$) over 75 free IV variables[1], the degrees are shown in Table 2. To estimate the degree of s_i^r for $r > 340$, we decompose s_i^r until the state terms are the product of internal state bits s_i^j for $j < end = \lfloor \frac{r}{32} \rfloor \times 32 - 128$ considering the efficiency tradeoff of the computation.

Table 2. Degree $\deg(s_i^j)$ of s_i^j for $0 \le i \le 2, 0 \le j \le 340$

j+	0	1	2	3	4	5	6	7	8	9	10	11	12	13	14	15	16	17	18	19	20	21	22	23	24	25	26	27	28	29	30	31	32	33	34
$s_0^{j=0}$	0	0	0	0	0	0	0	0	0	0	0	0	0	0	0	0	0	0	0	0	0	0	0	0	0	0	0	0	0	0	0	0	0	0	0
$s_1^{j=0}$	1	1	1	0	0	1	1	1	1	1	1	1	1	1	1	1	1	1	0	1	1	1	1	1	1	1	1	1	1	0	1	1	1	1	1
$s_2^{j=0}$	0	1	1	1	2	2	2	1	1	0	2	2	2	2	2	2	2	2	2	2	2	2	1	1	2	2	2	2	2	2	2	2	2	2	1
$s_0^{j=35}$	0	0	0	0	0	0	0	0	0	0	0	0	0	0	0	0	0	0	0	0	0	0	0	0	0	0	0	0	0	0	0	0	1	1	1
$s_1^{j=35}$	1	1	1	1	1	1	1	1	1	1	1	1	1	0	1	1	1	1	1	1	1	1	1	1	1	1	1	1	1	1	1	1	1	1	1
$s_2^{j=35}$	1	2	2	2	2	2	2	2	2	2	2	2	2	2	2	2	1	1	2	2	2	2	2	2	2	2	2	2	2	2	2	2	2	2	2
$s_0^{j=70}$	2	2	2	1	1	0	2	2	2	2	2	2	2	2	2	2	2	1	1	2	2	2	2	2	2	2	2	2	1	1	2	2	2	2	2
$s_1^{j=70}$	1	1	1	1	1	1	1	1	1	1	1	0	0	1	1	1	1	1	1	1	1	1	1	1	1	1	0	1	1	1	1	1	1	1	1
$s_2^{j=70}$	2	2	2	2	2	2	2	2	2	2	2	2	2	2	1	1	1	2	2	2	2	2	2	2	2	2	2	2	2	2	2	2	2	2	2
$s_0^{j=105}$	2	2	2	2	2	2	2	3	3	3	3	2	1	1	3	3	3	3	3	3	3	3	3	3	3	3	2	3	3	3	3	3	3	3	3
$s_1^{j=105}$	1	1	1	0	1	1	1	1	1	1	1	1	1	1	1	1	1	1	1	1	0	1	1	1	1	1	1	1	1	1	2	2	2	2	1
$s_2^{j=105}$	2	2	2	2	2	2	2	2	2	2	2	2	2	2	2	2	2	2	2	2	2	2	2	2	2	2	2	2	2	2	2	2	2	2	2
$s_0^{j=140}$	3	3	3	3	2	3	3	3	3	3	3	3	3	3	3	3	3	3	3	3	3	3	2	3	3	3	3	3	3	3	3	3	3	3	3
$s_1^{j=140}$	1	1	2	2	2	2	2	2	2	2	2	2	2	1	1	2	2	2	2	3	3	3	3	2	1	2	3	3	3	3	3	3	3	3	3
$s_2^{j=140}$	2	2	2	2	2	2	2	2	2	2	2	2	2	2	2	2	2	2	2	2	2	2	2	2	2	2	2	2	2	2	2	2	2	2	2
$s_0^{j=175}$	3	3	3	3	3	3	3	3	3	3	3	3	3	3	3	3	3	3	3	3	3	3	3	3	3	4	4	4	4	3	3	4	4	4	4
$s_1^{j=175}$	3	3	3	3	3	3	3	3	3	3	3	3	3	3	3	3	3	3	3	3	3	3	3	3	3	3	3	4	4	5	5	5	5	5	3
$s_2^{j=175}$	2	2	2	2	2	2	2	2	2	2	2	2	2	2	2	2	2	2	2	2	2	2	2	2	2	2	2	2	2	2	2	2	2	2	2
$s_0^{j=210}$	3	4	4	4	4	4	4	4	4	3	4	4	3	4	4	4	4	4	4	4	3	4	4	4	4	4	4	4	3	4	4	4	4	4	4
$s_1^{j=210}$	2	4	5	5	5	5	5	5	5	5	5	5	5	5	5	5	5	5	5	5	5	5	5	5	5	5	5	5	5	5	5	5	5	5	5
$s_2^{j=210}$	2	2	2	2	2	2	2	2	3	3	3	3	2	2	3	3	3	3	3	3	3	3	3	3	3	3	3	3	3	3	4	4	5	5	5
$s_0^{j=245}$	4	4	4	4	3	4	4	4	4	4	4	4	4	4	4	4	4	4	4	4	4	4	4	4	4	4	4	3	3	4	4	4	4	4	4
$s_1^{j=245}$	5	5	5	5	5	5	5	5	5	5	5	5	5	5	5	5	5	5	5	5	5	5	5	5	5	5	5	6	6	6	6	6	6	5	5
$s_2^{j=245}$	5	5	5	3	3	4	5	5	5	5	5	5	5	5	5	6	6	6	6	6	6	5	5	6	6	6	6	6	6	6	6	6	6	6	6
$s_0^{j=280}$	4	4	4	4	4	4	4	4	4	4	4	4	4	4	4	4	4	4	4	4	4	4	4	4	4	4	4	4	5	5	5	5	5	5	4
$s_1^{j=280}$	6	6	6	6	6	6	6	5	5	6	6	7	7	7	7	7	6	7	7	7	7	7	7	7	7	7	7	7	7	7	7	7	7	7	7
$s_2^{j=280}$	6	6	6	6	7	7	8	8	8	8	8	8	5	6	8	8	8	8	8	8	8	8	8	8	8	8	8	8	8	8	8	8	8	8	8
$s_0^{j=315}$	4	4	5	5	5	5	5	5	5	5	5	5	6	6	6	6	6	6	5	6	6	6	6	6	6	6	6								
$s_1^{j=315}$	7	7	7	7	7	7	7	6	6	7	7	7	7	7	7	7	7	7	7	7	7	7	7	7	7	7	7								
$s_2^{j=315}$	8	8	8	8	8	8	8	8	8	8	8	8	8	8	8	8	8	8	8	8	8	8	8	8	8										

---

[1] The other 5 IV bits are fixed as zero and their positions are given in Sect. 4.1.

For example, we estimate the degree upper bound of s_1^{341}, where $end = \lfloor \frac{r}{32} \rfloor \times 32 - 128 = 192$. We first express s_1^{341} using state bits in less rounds, and discard the state terms of degree lower than d.

- **Step 1.** First, we express $s_2^{341} = s_1^{272} + s_1^{259} s_1^{258} + s_1^{257} + s_2^{254}$ according to Eq. (1).
- **Step 2.** According to Table 2 highlighted in red, let $d = \max\{\deg(s_1^{272}),$ $\deg(s_1^{259}) + \deg(s_1^{258}), \deg(s_1^{257}), \deg(s_2^{254}\} = \max\{5, 5 + 5, 5, 5\} = 10$.
- **Step 3.** Discarding the state terms of degree lower than 10, we get $s_2^{341*} = s_1^{259} s_1^{258}$. Iteratively compute s_2^{341*} and discard state terms with degree lower than 10, there is no state term surviving. We reset $d = d - 1$ and repeat the above decomposition and discarding process. We can get the result $s_2^{341**} = s_0^{166} s_0^{167} s_0^{193} + s_0^{167} s_0^{168} s_0^{192} + s_0^{166} s_0^{167} s_0^{168} + s_0^{165} s_0^{167} s_0^{168} + s_0^{167} s_0^{168} s_1^{180} + s_0^{166} s_0^{167} s_1^{181}$.
- **Step 4.** Note that there is still a state bit s_1^{193} in s_2^{341**} that is bigger than $end=192$. So we continue to iteratively compute and discard state terms with degree lower than 9, and we get:

$$
\begin{aligned}
s_2^{341***} = & s_2^{56} s_2^{57} s_2^{83} s_2^{84} s_2^{101} + s_2^{57} s_2^{58} s_2^{83} s_2^{84} s_2^{100} + s_2^{56} s_2^{57} s_2^{58} s_2^{83} s_2^{84} + \\
& s_0^{97} s_2^{57} s_2^{58} s_2^{83} s_2^{84} + s_0^{98} s_2^{56} s_2^{57} s_2^{83} s_2^{84} + s_0^{124} s_2^{56} s_2^{57} s_2^{101} + s_0^{124} s_2^{57} s_2^{58} s_2^{100} + \\
& s_0^{124} s_2^{56} s_2^{57} s_2^{58} + s_0^{124} s_2^{55} s_2^{57} s_2^{58} + s_2^{55} s_2^{57} s_2^{58} s_2^{83} s_2^{84} + s_0^{97} s_0^{124} s_2^{57} s_2^{58} \\
& + s_0^{98} s_0^{124} s_2^{56} s_2^{57} + s_2^{57} s_2^{58} s_2^{82} s_2^{83} s_2^{102} + s_2^{58} s_2^{59} s_2^{82} s_2^{83} s_2^{101} + s_2^{57} s_2^{58} s_2^{59} s_2^{82} s_2^{83} + \\
& s_0^{56} s_2^{58} s_2^{59} s_2^{82} s_2^{83} + s_0^{98} s_2^{58} s_2^{59} s_2^{82} s_2^{83} + s_0^{99} s_2^{57} s_2^{58} s_2^{82} s_2^{83} + s_0^{123} s_2^{57} s_2^{58} s_2^{102} + \\
& s_0^{123} s_2^{58} s_2^{59} s_2^{101} + s_0^{123} s_2^{57} s_2^{58} s_2^{59} + s_0^{123} s_2^{56} s_2^{58} s_2^{59} + s_0^{98} s_0^{123} s_2^{58} s_2^{59} \\
& + s_0^{99} s_0^{123} s_2^{57} s_2^{58} + s_2^{56} s_2^{57} s_2^{58} s_2^{59} s_2^{101} + s_0^{98} s_2^{56} s_2^{57} s_2^{58} s_2^{59} + s_2^{55} s_2^{56} s_2^{57} s_2^{58} s_2^{102} + \\
& s_2^{55} s_2^{56} s_2^{58} s_2^{59} s_2^{101} + s_2^{55} s_2^{56} s_2^{57} s_2^{58} s_2^{59} + s_0^{98} s_2^{55} s_2^{56} s_2^{58} s_2^{59} + s_0^{99} s_2^{55} s_2^{56} s_2^{57} s_2^{58} + \\
& s_2^{114} s_2^{57} s_2^{58} s_2^{102} + s_0^{114} s_2^{58} s_2^{59} s_2^{101} + s_0^{114} s_2^{57} s_2^{58} s_2^{59} + s_2^{114} s_2^{56} s_2^{58} s_2^{59} + s_0^{89} s_0^{90} s_2^{57} s_2^{58} s_2^{100} + \\
& s_0^{98} s_2^{114} s_2^{58} s_2^{59} + s_0^{99} s_2^{114} s_2^{57} s_2^{58} + s_2^{115} s_2^{56} s_2^{57} s_2^{101} + s_2^{115} s_2^{57} s_2^{58} s_2^{100} + s_0^{115} s_2^{56} s_2^{57} s_2^{58} + \\
& s_2^{115} s_2^{55} s_2^{57} s_2^{58} + s_0^{97} s_0^{115} s_2^{57} s_2^{58} + s_0^{98} s_2^{115} s_2^{56} s_2^{57} + s_0^{89} s_0^{90} s_2^{56} s_2^{57} s_2^{101} + \\
& s_0^{89} s_0^{90} s_2^{56} s_2^{57} s_2^{58} + s_0^{89} s_0^{90} s_2^{55} s_2^{57} s_2^{58} + s_0^{89} s_0^{90} s_0^{97} s_2^{57} s_2^{58} + s_0^{89} s_0^{90} s_0^{98} s_2^{56} s_2^{57}.
\end{aligned}
$$

(7)

- **Step 5.** Here, there is no state bit in rounds more than $end = 192$, the expression ends and there are still state terms that survive. Then the current degree $d = 9$ is the estimated degree of s_2^{341}.
- **Step 6.** Note that, if there is no state item in s_2^{341***} surviving, which means the degree added twice or more shown in Eq. (6) happens to the iterative computation of s_2^{341}. So the degree must be less than 9. We reset $d = 8$ and continue the above steps 3–5 to get a more accurate degree bound.

We summarise the above 6 steps as Algorithm 2. We only estimate degree of s_i^r for $r \leq 665$ and list the results in Table 3.

Degree reduction technique. In this part, we formally consider the property in Eq. (6), that $\deg(b_{i-3})$ is added twice. We call it *degree reduction*. Define the degree reduction d_t as

$$
d_t = \sum_{i \in I} \deg(x_i) - \deg(\prod_{i \in I} x_i), \tag{8}
$$

where x_i is a state bit.

Algorithm 2. Degree Evaluation Algorithm ($\mathcal{DEG}$) of State Bit

Input: The value t and r which indicates the state bit s_t^r.
Output: $\mathcal{DEG}(s_t^r)=d$.
1: Initialize the degree bound d similar to the above **Step 2.**, the end point end.
2: $len \leftarrow 0$
3: **while** $len = 0$ **do**
4:     Iteratively express s_t^r using state bits s_i^j, where $0 \leq j \leq 2$ and $0 \leq j < end$. During each expression, discard the state terms of degree lower than d. Let len be the number of remaining state terms.
5:     **if** $len = 0$ **then**
6:         $d \leftarrow d - 1$
7:     **end if**
8: **end while**
9: **Return** d

We pay attention to the degree reduction of the state term $\prod_{j=l}^{l+t-1} s_i^j$ for a specific $i \in [0, 2]$. This state term results from the iteration structure of Trivium scheme, whose high degree state terms come from the multiplication of $s_i^j s_i^{j+1}$ shown in Eq. (1). After several rounds of iteration, the high degree state terms are in the form $\prod_{j=l}^{l+t-1} s_i^j$. Define the degree reduction $d_t = \sum_{j=l}^{l+t-1} \deg(s_i^j) - \deg(\prod_{j=l}^{l+t-1} s_i^j)$.

Table 3. The estimated upper bound degree $\mathcal{DEG}(s_i^j)$ of s_i^r for $r \leq 689$

$\bar{j}+$	0	1	2	3	4	5	6	7	8	9	10	11	12	13	14	15	16	17	18	19	20	21	22	23	24	25	26	27	28	29	30	31	32	33	34
$s_0^{\bar j=340}$	6	6	6	6	6	6	6	6	6	6	7	7	8	9	9	9	9	8	6	7	9	9	9	9	9	9	9	9	9	9	9	9	9	9	9
$s_1^{\bar j=340}$	7	7	7	7	7	7	7	7	7	7	7	7	7	7	7	7	7	7	7	8	8	8	8	7	6	7	8	8	8	8	8	8	8	8	8
$s_2^{\bar j=340}$	8	9	9	9	9	9	9	9	10	10	10	10	10	9	10	10	10	10	10	10	10	10	10	10	11	11	11	11	11	11	10	10	11	12	13
$s_0^{\bar j=375}$	9	9	9	9	9	10	10	11	11	11	11	11	11	9	10	11	11	11	12	13	14	15	15	15	15	13	11	14	15	15	15	15	15	15	15
$s_1^{\bar j=375}$	8	8	8	8	8	8	8	8	8	8	8	8	8	8	8	8	8	8	8	8	8	8	9	9	9	9	9	9	9	9	9	9	9	9	9
$s_2^{\bar j=375}$	13	13	13	12	12	13	13	13	12	12	13	13	13	13	13	13	13	13	12	13	13	12	13	13	13	13	13	13	13	13	12	13	13	13	13
$s_0^{\bar j=410}$	15	15	15	15	15	15	15	15	15	15	15	15	15	15	15	15	15	15	15	15	15	15	15	15	15	15	15	15	15	15	15	15	15	15	15
$s_1^{\bar j=410}$	9	9	9	9	9	9	9	9	10	12	12	12	12	10	10	11	12	12	12	12	12	12	12	12	12	12	12	12	12	12	12	13	14	15	17
$s_2^{\bar j=410}$	13	13	13	12	12	13	13	13	13	13	13	13	13	13	13	13	13	13	13	13	13	13	13	13	13	13	13	13	13	13	13	13	14	14	14
$s_0^{\bar j=445}$	15	15	15	15	15	15	16	16	16	16	16	16	16	16	16	16	16	16	16	17	18	18	18	18	19	18	18	19	19	19	19	19	19	19	18
$s_1^{\bar j=445}$	18	18	18	17	14	12	15	18	18	18	18	18	18	18	18	18	18	18	18	18	18	18	18	18	18	19	20	20	20	20	20	20	20	20	20
$s_2^{\bar j=445}$	14	14	12	12	13	14	15	15	15	15	15	15	15	15	15	15	15	15	15	15	15	15	15	15	15	15	15	15	15	15	15	15	15	15	15
$s_0^{\bar j=480}$	18	19	20	22	22	22	22	21	21	22	22	22	22	22	22	22	22	22	22	22	22	22	22	22	22	22	22	22	22	22	22	22	22	22	21
$s_1^{\bar j=480}$	19	20	20	20	21	22	23	24	24	24	24	24	24	21	22	24	24	24	25	25	25	25	25	25	25	26	26	26	26	26	26	26	26	26	26
$s_2^{\bar j=480}$	15	15	16	16	17	17	17	17	16	15	16	17	17	17	17	17	17	17	17	18	20	21	21	21	20	18	18	20	21	21	21	21	21	21	21
$s_0^{\bar j=515}$	21	22	22	22	22	22	22	22	22	22	22	22	22	22	22	22	22	22	22	22	22	23	23	23	23	23	23	23	24	24	24	24	24	24	24
$s_1^{\bar j=515}$	26	26	26	26	26	26	27	27	27	27	27	27	26	27	28	28	29	29	29	29	29	29	29	29	29	30	31	32	33	33	33	33	33	33	33
$s_2^{\bar j=515}$	21	21	21	21	21	21	21	22	23	24	26	27	28	28	29	28	28	25	27	29	29	29	29	28	29	29	29	30	31	32	33	33	33	33	33
$s_0^{\bar j=550}$	24	25	26	26	26	26	25	23	25	26	27	27	27	27	27	27	26	27	28	29	29	29	29	29	28	29	29	29	29	28	28	29	29	29	29
$s_1^{\bar j=550}$	32	32	32	32	32	33	35	35	35	35	35	35	33	34	35	37	37	37	37	37	37	36	36	38	40	41	41	41	41	40	40	41	41	41	40
$s_2^{\bar j=550}$	31	32	33	34	35	36	37	37	37	36	36	36	35	36	36	36	37	38	39	40	40	40	40	40	40	40	44	45	45	45	45	45	45	45	45
$s_0^{\bar j=585}$	29	29	29	29	29	30	31	31	31	31	31	31	30	30	31	31	31	31	31	31	31	31	31	32	34	36	37	37	37	35	35	34	36	37	37
$s_1^{\bar j=585}$	40	41	41	41	41	41	41	41	41	40	41	41	40	41	41	41	41	41	41	41	41	40	41	41	41	41	42	42	42	41	40	41	42	42	42
$s_2^{\bar j=585}$	45	45	45	45	45	45	42	42	42	42	42	42	42	43	44	44	44	44	45	45	46	46	46	48	47	46	46	48	48	48	48	48	49	49	48
$s_0^{\bar j=620}$	38	38	41	42	42	42	42	41	38	39	42	42	43	45	47	50	53	54	54	54	53	49	45	51	54	54	54	54	54	54	55	56	56	56	56
$s_1^{\bar j=620}$	42	42	42	42	42	43	44	44	44	45	45	45	45	45	45	45	45	44	46	49	50	50	50	50	47	46	48	51	52	52	52	52	52	52	52
$s_2^{\bar j=620}$	49	49	49	49	50	51	51	51	50	51	52	54	54	54	54	54	54	54	56	58	58	58	59	59	59	59	60	62	62	62	62	62	62	60	59
$s_0^{\bar j=655}$	56	56	56	56	56	56	56	57	60	62	64	64	64	64	64	64	63	61	63	64	65	67	70	72	73	73	73	73	74	74	69	72	74	74	75
$s_1^{\bar j=655}$	52	52	52	52	52	52	52	52	52	52	52	52	52	52	52	52	52	52	52	51	52	52	52	52	52	53	54	57	59	61	62	62	62	59	
$s_2^{\bar j=655}$	61	66	68	68	69	69	69	68	68	69	70	70	70	70	70	70	70	70	70	70	70	70	70	70	71	71	71	71	71	71	71	71	71	69	69

The degree reduction can help discard state terms of lower degree dramatically, as it can help predict the change of degree before expression operation[2]. We take the state term $s_1^{340} s_1^{341}$ as an example to illustrate the process to compute the degree reduction d_t. Algorithm 2 is first used to obtain the degree of state bits as shown in Tables 2 and 3.

Let end be $\lfloor \frac{r}{32} \rfloor \times 32 - 128 = 192$, too. The degree bound d is initialized as $d = \mathcal{DEG}(s_1^{340}) + \mathcal{DEG}(s_1^{341})$ and $d_t = 0$. Express the $s_1^{340} s_1^{341}$ by one iteration using Eq. (1). Discard the state terms of degree lower than $d - d_t = d$, there is no state term surviving. Increase the d_t by 1, such that $d_t = 1$. Express $s_1^{340} s_1^{341}$ again and discard the state terms of degree lower than $d - d_t = d - 1$, the result is $s_0^{249} s_0^{250} s_1^{262} + s_0^{248} s_0^{249} s_1^{263}$. Continue to compute iteratively, the remaining state terms are $s_0^{170} s_0^{171} s_0^{180} s_2^{140} s_2^{141} + s_0^{170} s_0^{171} s_0^{181} s_2^{139} s_2^{140} + s_0^{171} s_0^{172} s_0^{179} s_2^{139} s_2^{140} + s_0^{171} s_0^{172} s_0^{180} s_2^{138} s_2^{139}$. There is no state bits s_i^j with j bigger than $end = 192$ in all the state terms, hence the expression ends. Degree reduction $d_t = 1$ is returned. Thus the $\deg(s_1^{340} s_1^{341}) \leq \mathcal{DEG}(s_1^{340}) + \mathcal{DEG}(s_1^{341}) - d_t = 7 + 7 - 1 = 13$. The degree reduction algorithm is shown in Algorithm 3

Algorithm 3. Degree Reduction Algorithm of State Term

Input: The value i, r, t which indicates the state term degree reduction.
Output: The degree reduction $d_t = \sum_{j=l}^{l+t-1} \deg(s_i^j) - \deg(\prod_{j=l}^{l+t-1} s_i^j)$.
1: Initialize the degree bound $d = \sum_{i=l}^{l+t-1} \mathcal{DEG}(s_i^j)$, degree reduction $d_t = 0$, end point end and number of survived state terms len.
2: **while** $len = 0$ **do**
3:   Express the state term $\prod_{j=l}^{l+t-1} s_i^j$ using state bits s_i^j, where $0 \leq i \leq 2$ and $0 \leq j < end$, discard the state terms of degree lower than $d - d_t$. Let len be the number of remaining state terms.
4:   **if** $len = 0$ **then**
5:     $d_t \leftarrow d_t + 1$
6:   **end if**
7: **end while**
8: **Return** d_t

3.5   IV Representation Techniques

In the cryptanalysis of stream ciphers, the output is a boolean function over key and IV bits. But obtaining the exact expression is hard, thus we propose *IV representation* technique to reduce the computation complexity for obtaining the degree information.

Definition 1. *(IV representation) Given a state bit $s = \sum_{I,J} \prod_{i \in I} v_i \prod_{j \in J} k_j$, the IV representation of s is $s_{IV} = \sum_I \prod_{i \in I} v_i$.*

For example, if a boolean polynomial is $s = v_0 k_1 + v_0 k_0 k_2 + v_1 k_1 k_2 + v_0 v_1 k_2$, then its corresponding IV representation is $s_{IV} = v_0 + v_0 + v_1 + v_0 v_1$.

---

[2] The details are given in Sect. 4.2.

IV representation with repeated IV terms Removing Algorithm. Due to neglection of key bits, there are lots of repeated IV terms. Here we give an algorithm to remove the repeated IV terms of s_{IV}. The details of the algorithm are shown in Algorithm 4. This algorithm is based on a Hash function. First, an empty hash set is initialized. For each IV term T_i, compute the hash value as $H(T_i)$ (Line 3), then determine if T_i is already in H. If not, then insert T_i into H (Lines 4–5). Applying Algorithm 4 to the above example, the result is $v_0 + v_1 + v_0 v_1$. Note that this algorithm is slightly different from Algorithm 1. If we apply Algorithm 1 to s_{IV}, the result is $v_1 + v_0 v_1$.

In the iterative computation process of the output bit of Trivium, it should be noted that if an IV term exists in s, it must also exist in s_{IV}, but not the opposite. For example, $x_1 = v_0(k_1 k_2 + k_0 k_2) + v_1 + v_0 v_1 k_2$, $x_2 = v_2 k_0 k_1 + v_1 v_2 k_1$ and $s = x_1 x_2$. We use the IV representations of x_1 and x_2 to approximate the IV representation of s. Thus, $x_{1IV} = v_0 + v_1 + v_0 v_1$, $x_{2IV} = v_2 + v_1 v_2$, and $s_{IV} = x_{1IV} x_{2IV} = v_0 v_2 + v_1 v_2 + v_0 v_1 v_2$. However, $s = x_1 x_2 = v_1 v_2 (k_0 k_1 + k_1)$. *So if we find an IV term is not in s_{IV}, we can conclude that it is not in s either.* We use this to determine the degree upper bound of the output ANF of Trivium.

Algorithm 4. Repeated-IV term Removing Algorithm

Input: The vector T with n IV terms, i.e., T_1, T_2, ..., T_n.
Output: Updated T with m IV terms, where $m \leq n$.
 1: Initialize an empty Hash set **H**.
 2: **for** $i \leftarrow 1 : n$ **do**
 3:    Compute the Hash value of T_i, i.e., $H(T_i)$.
 4:    **if** $H.contains(T_i)$ is **false then**
 5:       $H.insert(T_i)$.
 6:    **end if**
 7: **end for**

After using IV representation combined with Algorithm 4, all the existent IV terms are left by ignoring their repetition. With collision-resistent hash function H, the time complexity of Algorithm 4 is $O(n)$ for processing n IV terms. It needs several minutes to apply Algorithm 4 on 1 billion IV terms on a single core.

4   Key Recovery Attack on 855-round Trivium

In the attack on 855-round Trivium, all the 80-bit IV are initiated with free variables: $IV_i = v_i$, $i \in [0, 79]$.

The output of 855-round Trivium can be described using the internal state bits:

$$z_{855} = s_0^{790} + s_0^{763} + s_1^{787} + s_1^{772} + s_2^{790} + s_2^{745}. \tag{9}$$

As a first step of the attack on 855-round Trivium, we need to determine P_1.

4.1 Determining the Nullification Scheme for the Output Polynomial of 855-round Trivium

For 855-round Trivium, the degree of output bit z is very high, as shown in [19]. So it is not easy to find the missing IV terms in the complex $z = P_1 P_2 + P_3$. However, based on the new observation of Boolean polynomial introduced in Sect. 3.1. we can choose P_1 to reduce the Boolean polynomial $(1 + P_1)z = (1 + P_1)P_3$ such that the degree of $(1 + P_1)P_3$ is lower. The lower, the better. In fact, the lower the degree of a state term, the less high degree IV terms it can deduce.

Degrees of state bits are obtained first in order to determine the high degree state terms. The exact Boolean polynomial of s_i^j for $i \in [0, 2]$ and $j \in [0, 340]$ can be obtained. The other degree upper bounds can be obtained by executing Algorithm 2.

For a search of P_1, we use the decomposition of Trivium and preserve the high degree state terms (bigger than a given bound dependent on our computing ability in a PC), where the degree of state terms means the sum of degrees of each state bit in the earlier rounds involved. We decompose until all the state bits are within the range of $[0, 276]$. The key points to determine P_1 come from 3 criteria: (1) the frequency of P_1 is high; (2) the degree of P_1 is low; (3) the equivalent key guesses in P_1 are minimized. We calculate the frequency of state bits and find that s_1^{210} occurs in about $\frac{3}{4}$ of all the preserved high state terms. The degree of s_1^{210} is 5 and can be reduced to 2 after nullifying the 5 IV bits, and there are only 3 equivalent key bits to be guessed. So we choose $P_1 = s_1^{210}$.

The output polynomial can be rewritten as

$$z = s_1^{210} P_2 + P_3, \tag{10}$$

where P_2 and P_3 do not contain s_1^{210}. Polynomial P_2 is so complex that it is hard to compute its degree and density information while P_3 is relatively simple. Here $P_1 = s_1^{210} = v_{59}v_{60}v_{61} + v_{59}v_{60}v_{76}$
$+v_{17}v_{59}v_{60} + v_{30}v_{31}v_{59}v_{60} + v_{32}v_{59}v_{60} + v_{59}v_{60}v_{62} + v_{59}v_{60}v_{77} + v_{59}v_{60}k_{20}$
$+v_{59}v_{61}v_{73}v_{74} + v_{59}v_{73}v_{74}v_{76} + v_{17}v_{59}v_{73}v_{74} + v_{30}v_{31}v_{59}v_{73}v_{74} + v_{32}v_{59}v_{73}v_{74}+$
$v_{59}v_{62}v_{73}v_{74} + v_{59}v_{73}v_{74}v_{77} + v_{59}v_{73}v_{74}k_{20} + v_{59}v_{60}v_{74}v_{75} + v_{59}v_{60}v_{75}v_{76}+$
$v_{59}v_{73}v_{74}v_{75} + v_{59}v_{73}v_{74}v_{75}v_{76} + v_{59}v_{61}v_{75} + v_{59}v_{74}v_{75} + v_{17}v_{59}v_{75} + v_{30}v_{31}v_{59}v_{75}+$
$v_{32}v_{59}v_{75} + v_{59}v_{62}v_{75} + v_{59}v_{75}v_{77} + v_{59}v_{75}k_{20} + v_{60}v_{61}v_{72}v_{73} + v_{60}v_{72}v_{73}v_{76}+$
$v_{17}v_{60}v_{72}v_{73} + v_{30}v_{31}v_{60}v_{72}v_{73} + v_{32}v_{60}v_{72}v_{73} + v_{60}v_{62}v_{72}v_{73} + v_{60}v_{72}v_{73}v_{77}+$
$v_{60}v_{72}v_{73}k_{20} + v_{61}v_{72}v_{73}v_{74} + v_{72}v_{73}v_{74}v_{76} + v_{17}v_{72}v_{73}v_{74} + v_{30}v_{31}v_{72}v_{73}v_{74}+$
$v_{32}v_{72}v_{73}v_{74} + v_{62}v_{72}v_{73}v_{74} + v_{72}v_{73}v_{74}v_{77} + v_{72}v_{73}v_{74}k_{20} + v_{60}v_{72}v_{73}v_{74}v_{75}+$
$v_{60}v_{72}v_{73}v_{75}v_{76} + v_{72}v_{73}v_{74}v_{75}v_{76} + v_{61}v_{72}v_{73}v_{75} + v_{17}v_{72}v_{73}v_{75} + v_{30}v_{31}v_{72}v_{73}v_{75}+$
$v_{32}v_{72}v_{73}v_{75} + v_{62}v_{72}v_{73}v_{75} + v_{72}v_{73}v_{75}v_{77} + v_{72}v_{73}v_{75}k_{20} + v_{60}v_{61}v_{74} + v_{60}v_{74}v_{76}+$
$v_{17}v_{60}v_{74} + v_{30}v_{31}v_{60}v_{74} + v_{32}v_{60}v_{74} + v_{60}v_{62}v_{74} + v_{60}v_{74}v_{77} + v_{60}v_{74}k_{20}+$
$v_{17}v_{73}v_{74} + v_{30}v_{31}v_{73}v_{74} + v_{32}v_{73}v_{74} + v_{62}v_{73}v_{74} + v_{73}v_{74}v_{77} + v_{73}v_{74}k_{20}+$
$v_{16}v_{60}v_{61} + v_{16}v_{60}v_{74}v_{75} + v_{16}v_{60}v_{76} + v_{16}v_{61}v_{73}v_{74} + v_{16}v_{73}v_{74}v_{75} + v_{16}v_{73}v_{74}v_{76}+$
$v_{16}v_{61}v_{75} + v_{16}v_{74}v_{75} + v_{16}v_{17} + v_{16}v_{30}v_{31} + v_{16}v_{32} + v_{16}v_{62} + v_{16}v_{77} + v_{16}k_{20}+$
$v_{29}v_{30}v_{60}v_{61} + v_{29}v_{30}v_{60}v_{74}v_{75} + v_{29}v_{30}v_{60}v_{76} + v_{29}v_{30}v_{61}v_{73}v_{74} + v_{29}v_{30}v_{73}v_{74}v_{75}+$
$v_{29}v_{30}v_{73}v_{74}v_{76} + v_{29}v_{30}v_{61}v_{75} + v_{29}v_{30}v_{74}v_{75} + v_{17}v_{29}v_{30} + v_{29}v_{30}v_{31} + v_{29}v_{30}v_{32}+$
$v_{29}v_{30}v_{62} + v_{29}v_{30}v_{77} + v_{29}v_{30}k_{20} + v_{31}v_{60}v_{61} + v_{31}v_{60}v_{74}v_{75} + v_{31}v_{60}v_{76}+$

$v_{31}v_{61}v_{73}v_{74} + v_{31}v_{73}v_{74}v_{75} + v_{31}v_{73}v_{74}v_{76} + v_{31}v_{61}v_{75} + v_{31}v_{74}v_{75} + v_{17}v_{31} +$
$v_{30}v_{31} + v_{31}v_{62} + v_{31}v_{77} + v_{31}k_{20} + v_{60}v_{61} + v_{61}v_{75} + v_{61}v_{74}v_{75} + v_{17}v_{61} + v_{30}v_{31}v_{61} +$
$v_{32}v_{61} + v_{61}k_{20} + v_{60}v_{74}v_{75}v_{76} + v_{60}v_{76} + v_{73}v_{74}v_{75}v_{76} + v_{17}v_{76} + v_{30}v_{31}v_{76} +$
$v_{32}v_{76} + v_{76}v_{77} + v_{76}k_{20} + v_{60}v_{61}k_{19} + v_{60}v_{74}v_{75}k_{19} + v_{60}v_{76}k_{19} + v_{61}v_{73}v_{74}k_{19} +$
$v_{73}v_{74}v_{75}k_{19} + v_{73}v_{74}v_{76}k_{19} + v_{61}v_{75}k_{19} + v_{74}v_{75}k_{19} + v_{17}k_{19} + v_{30}v_{31}k_{19} + v_{32}k_{19} +$
$v_{62}k_{19} + v_{77}k_{19} + k_{19}k_{20} + v_{34}v_{35} + v_{34}v_{48}v_{49} + v_{34}v_{50} + v_{35}v_{47}v_{48} + v_{47}v_{48}v_{49} +$
$v_{47}v_{48}v_{50} + v_{35}v_{49} + v_{48}v_{49} + k_{57} + v_{69} + v_4v_5 + v_6 + v_{36} + v_{51} + v_{60} + v_{73}v_{74} +$
$v_{75} + k_{63} + v_{62}v_{74}v_{75} + v_{74}v_{75}v_{77} + v_{75}v_{76} + v_{18} + v_{33} + v_{63} + v_{78} + k_{21} + k_{28}k_{29} +$
$k_3 + k_{30} + k_{12} + k_{37}k_{38} + k_{39} + v_{24}.$

IV Nullification. The degree of s_1^{210} is 5 and the IV bits involved in s_1^{210} are shown in Table 4.

Table 4. Count of IV bits in s_1^{210} before IV nullification.

IV	v_4	v_5	v_6	v_{16}	v_{17}	v_{18}	v_{24}	v_{29}	v_{30}	v_{31}	v_{32}	v_{33}	v_{34}	v_{35}	v_{36}	v_{47}	v_{48}
Count	1	1	1	14	14	1	1	14	27	26	13	1	3	3	1	3	5
IV	v_{49}	v_{50}	v_{51}	v_{59}	v_{60}	v_{61}	v_{62}	v_{63}	v_{69}	v_{72}	v_{73}	v_{74}	v_{75}	v_{76}	v_{77}	v_{78}	
Count	4	2	1	28	44	26	13	1	1	26	56	62	46	26	14	1	

In order to simplify s_1^{210} so that it is easier to obtain the degree bound of $(1 + s_1^{210})P_3$, we nullify v_{74}, v_{60}, v_{75}, v_{30} and v_{48}.

After nullifying the 5 IV bits, we obtain the simplified boolean function:

$$s_1^{210} = v_{16}v_{17} + v_{16}v_{32} + v_{16}v_{62} + v_{16}v_{77} + v_{16}k_{20} + v_{17}v_{31} + v_{31}v_{62} +$$
$$v_{31}v_{77} + v_{31}k_{20} + v_{17}v_{61} + v_{32}v_{61} + v_{61}k_{20} + v_{17}v_{76} + v_{32}v_{76} + v_{76}v_{77} +$$
$$v_{76}k_{20} + v_{17}k_{19} + v_{32}k_{19} + v_{62}k_{19} + v_{77}k_{19} + k_{19}k_{20} + v_{34}v_{35} + v_{34}v_{50} + \quad (11)$$
$$v_{35}v_{49} + k_{57} + v_{69} + v_4v_5 + v_6 + v_{36} + v_{51} + k_{63} + v_{18} + v_{33} + v_{63} +$$
$$v_{78} + k_{21} + k_{28}k_{29} + k_3 + k_{30} + k_{12} + k_{37}k_{38} + k_{39} + v_{24}.$$

Here, the degree of s_1^{210} is 2 and key information equivalent to 3 bits in s_1^{210} are k_{19}, k_{20} and $k_{57} + k_{63} + k_{21} + k_{28}k_{29} + k_3 + k_{30} + k_{12} + k_{37}k_{38} + k_{39}$. The IV bits involved in s_1^{210} are shown in Table 5.

After determining $P_1 = s_1^{210}$, we multiply $1 + s_1^{210}$ in both sides of Eq. (10), then $(1 + s_1^{210})z = (1 + s_1^{210})P_3$. Finding the non-randomness in $(1 + s_1^{210})P_3$ will help us to construct the cube tester of 855-round Trivium. More specifically, we will determine the nonexistent IV terms of degree 70 in $(1 + s_1^{210})P_3$. First, we will reduce the polynomial, then IV presentation technique is applied to determine the nonexistent IV terms. The framework is presented in Fig. 2 and details are shown in the following Sect. 4.2.

Table 5. Frequency of IV bits in s_1^{210} after IV nullification.

IV	v_4	v_5	v_6	v_{16}	v_{17}	v_{18}	v_{24}	v_{31}	v_{32}	v_{33}	v_{34}	v_{35}
Count	1	1	1	5	5	1	1	4	4	1	2	2
IV	v_{36}	v_{49}	v_{50}	v_{51}	v_{61}	v_{62}	v_{63}	v_{69}	v_{76}	v_{77}	v_{78}	
Count	1	1	1	1	3	3	1	1	4	4	1	

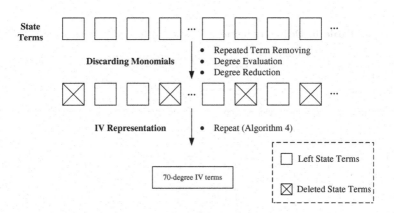

Fig. 2. Framework of determining the missing IV terms

4.2   Determining the Degree Bound of Reduced Polynomial

We are going to iteratively compute $(1 + s_1^{210})P_3$. In each iteration, many state terms of $(1 + s_1^{210})P_3$ are produced. Based on our computing ability, we can compute the IV terms of degree around 70. In computing the 70-degree IV terms, we use a cluster of 600–2400 cores. Since we are finding the 70-degree missing IV terms, state terms with degree less than 70 are removed without consideration, because they do not contain those 70-degree IV terms certainly. The removing process could be divided into 2 steps:

1. Deleting state terms according to degree evaluation;
2. Deleting state terms according to degree reduction.

Degree evaluation phase. After nullifying the 5 IV bits in Sect. 4.1, the exact boolean functions and degrees of state bits s_i^j for $0 \le i \le 2$ and $0 \le j \le 340$ can be updated. Then we execute Algorithm 2 to obtain the degrees of the other state bits, partially in Tables 2 and 3. For example, given a state term $b_1 b_2$, we first find $\mathcal{DEG}(b_1)$ and $\mathcal{DEG}(b_2)$ in Tables 2 and 3, if $\mathcal{DEG}(b_1) + \mathcal{DEG}(b_2) < 70$, then $\deg(b_1 b_2) \le \mathcal{DEG}(b_1) + \mathcal{DEG}(b_2) < 70$, delete $b_1 b_2$.

Degree reduction phase. In the structure of stream ciphers based on NFSR, degree reduction arises often due to the iterative structure. We use Algorithm 3 to obtain the degree reduction, which is shown in Tables 6, 7 and 8 for products of 2 consecutive state bits $s_i^j s_i^{j+1}$ ($t = 2$), 3 consecutive state bits $s_i^j s_i^{j+1} s_i^{j+2}$ ($t = 3$) and 4 consecutive state bits $s_i^j s_i^{j+1} s_i^{j+2} s_i^{j+3}$ ($t = 4$), respectively. Note that we only list the degree reduction when $j \geq 340$. The degree reduction for $j < 340$ is much easier to obtain in a PC.

Table 6. Degree reductions $d_t(s_i^j s_i^{j+1})$ of $s_i^j s_i^{j+1}$ with $t = 2$

j+	0	1	2	3	4	5	6	7	8	9	10	11	12	13	14	15	16	17	18	19	20	21	22	23	24	25	26	27	28	29	30	31	32	33
j = 340, i = 0	0	0	0	0	0	0	0	0	0	0	0	0	0	0	0	0	0	0	0	0	0	0	0	0	0	0	0	0	0	0	0	0	0	0
j = 340, i = 1	1	1	1	1	1	1	1	1	1	1	1	1	1	1	1	1	1	1	0	2	2	2	2	2	2	2	1	1	1	1	1	1		
j = 340, i = 2	1	3	3	3	3	3	2	4	4	4	4	4	4	4	4	4	3	2	2	2	1	3	3	3	3	3	3	3	3	2	2			
j = 374, i = 0	0	0	0	0	0	0	0	0	2	2	2	2	2	2	2	2	2	1	2	3	4	6	6	6	6	6	6	6	6	6	5	5		
j = 374, i = 1	1	1	1	1	1	1	1	1	1	1	1	1	1	1	1	1	1	1	1	1	1	1	1	0	1	1	1	1	1	1	1	1		
j = 374, i = 2	4	4	4	4	4	4	4	4	4	4	4	4	4	4	4	4	4	4	4	4	4	4	4	4	4	4	4	4	4	4	4	4		
j = 408, i = 0	5	5	5	5	5	4	4	4	4	4	4	4	4	4	4	4	4	3	3	3	3	3	3	3	3	3	3	3	3	2	1	1		
j = 408, i = 1	1	1	1	1	1	1	1	1	1	0	0	3	3	3	3	3	3	3	3	3	3	3	3	3	3	3	3	3	3	3	2	3		
j = 408, i = 2	4	4	4	4	4	4	4	4	4	4	4	4	4	4	4	4	4	4	3	3	3	3	3	3	2	2	2	2	2	2	2	2		
j = 442, i = 0	1	1	1	1	1	1	1	0	0	1	1	1	1	0	0	0	0	0	2	1	1	2	2	2	1	3	3	3	3	3	3	3		
j = 442, i = 1	4	4	7	8	8	7	7	7	7	7	7	7	7	6	5	4	3	3	3	3	3	3	3	3	2	3	4	4	4	4				
j = 442, i = 2	3	2	2	2	2	2	2	2	2	3	3	3	3	3	3	3	2	1	1	1	1	1	1	1	1	1	1	1	1	1				
j = 476, i = 0	3	3	1	1	1	0	0	3	3	3	3	3	3	3	3	3	3	6	6	6	6	6	6	6	6	6	6	6	6	6	6	6		
j = 476, i = 1	4	4	4	4	4	4	3	4	5	6	8	8	8	8	8	8	8	8	8	8	7	9	9	9	9	9	8	10	10	10	10	10		
j = 476, i = 2	1	1	1	1	1	0	1	3	3	3	3	3	3	3	3	3	3	3	3	3	3	2	2	5	7	7	7	7	7	7	7	7		
j = 510, i = 0	3	3	3	3	3	3	3	3	2	2	2	2	2	2	2	2	2	2	2	2	2	2	2	1	3	3	3	3	2	1	1			
j = 510, i = 1	10	10	10	10	10	9	8	8	8	8	7	9	8	8	8	8	8	8	8	7	8	10	10	10	9	9	9	9	9	9	10	11	11	
j = 510, i = 2	7	6	4	3	3	3	3	3	3	3	2	3	4	4	7	8	10	9	11	11	11	11	11	11	11	11	10	9	9	9	9			
j = 544, i = 0	3	3	3	3	3	3	2	1	2	2	2	2	2	2	2	1	2	2	2	2	2	2	2	2	4	6	6	6	6	6	6	6		
j = 544, i = 1	11	11	11	10	10	10	10	10	10	10	9	12	12	12	12	12	12	12	12	12	12	12	11	10	12	13	13	13						
j = 544, i = 2	11	11	11	11	11	11	11	11	11	10	9	8	8	10	10	10	8	8	8	8	8	7	7	6	6	7	7	7	7	6	6	6	16	16
j = 578, i = 0	6	6	6	6	6	6	6	6	6	6	6	5	4	3	2	0	0	0	0	0	0	0	0	0	0	0	0	0	0	0	0			
j = 578, i = 1	13	13	13	13	12	12	12	12	12	12	12	12	12	12	12	12	12	12	12	12	11	11	11	11	11	11	11	11	11	11	11	10	12	
j = 578, i = 2	16	15	15	15	15	15	15	15	15	15	15	15	15	9	9	9	9	9	9	9	9	10	12	12	12	13	14	14	14	18	18	17	16	
j = 612, i = 0	0	0	0	0	0	0	0	0	0	0	3	5	5	6	6	6	6	6	6	5	4	5	5	7	11	12	11	10	10	5	5	5	5	5
j = 612, i = 1	12	12	12	12	12	12	11	10	10	10	9	11	12	12	12	11	13	13	13	12	10	9	9	8	7	7	7	6	5	10	12	12		
j = 612, i = 2	16	13	12	12	11	13	13	13	13	13	13	12	13	15	15	15	14	13	12	12	16	16	16	16	15	15	15	18	20	19	18	17	16	16
j = 646, i = 0	5	5	5	5	6	6	4	2	2	4	4	4	4	4	4	4	3	3	7	8	12	12	12	11	11	10	10	10	8	7	7	9	13	16	18
j = 646, i = 1	12	12	12	12	11	9	9	9	9	9	9	9	9	8	8	8	8	8	8	8	8	8	8	8	8	8	8	8	8	8	8	8		
j = 646, i = 2	16	18	18	18	18	18	18	18	17	15	17	19	21	21	21	21	21	21	20	22	21	20	20	20	20	20	19	18	18	18	18	18		

In the cryptanalysis of Trivium, the degree reduction may be more complicated. Further degree reduction for $t > 4$ is hard to be obtained using PC for loop executing Algorithm 3. Some man-made work should be involved to obtain further degree reduction. The degree reduction can help discard state terms of lower degree dramatically. For example, if the state term $b_1 b_2$ goes through degree evaluation phase, that means $\mathcal{DEG}(b_1) + \mathcal{DEG}(b_2) \geq 70$, then we check if $\mathcal{DEG}(b_1) + \mathcal{DEG}(b_2) - d_t(b_1 b_2) < 70$. If yes, $\deg(b_1 b_2) < 70$ and delete it.

For example, the Eq. (9) can be expressed furthermore using state bits: $z_{855} = s_2^{724} + s_2^{680} s_2^{681} + s_2^{679} + s_0^{721} + s_2^{697} + s_2^{653} s_2^{654} + s_2^{652} + s_0^{694} + s_0^{721} + s_0^{695} s_0^{696} + s_0^{694} + s_1^{709} + s_0^{706} + s_0^{680} s_0^{681} + s_0^{679} + s_1^{694} + s_1^{721} + s_1^{707} s_1^{708} + s_1^{706} + s_2^{703} + s_1^{676} + s_1^{662} s_1^{663} + s_1^{661} + s_1^{658}$. Then $s_2^{652}, s_1^{676}, s_1^{661}$, can be discarded because their degree are lower than 68, shown in Table 3 highlighted in red, and the total degree of the multiplication of each one with $(1 + s_{210})$ is lower than 70. In addition, the state terms highlighted in blue can be discarded by removing the repeated state terms. Furthermore, the output can be expressed using state bits in lower rounds and more state terms can be discarded.

Table 7. Degree reductions $d_t(s_i^j s_i^{j+1} s_i^{j+2})$ of $s_i^j s_i^{j+1} s_i^{j+2}$ with $t=3$

$j+$	0	1	2	3	4	5	6	7	8	9	10	11	12	13	14	15	16	17	18	19	20	21	22	23	24	25	26	27	28	29	30	31	32	33
$j=340, i=0$	0	0	0	0	0	0	0	0	0	0	0	0	0	0	0	0	0	0	0	0	0	0	0	0	0	0	0	0	0	0	0	0	0	0
$j=340, i=1$	1	1	1	1	1	1	1	1	1	1	1	1	1	1	1	1	1	1	0	0	2	2	2	2	2	2	2	1	1	1	1	1	1	1
$j=340, i=2$	0	3	3	3	3	3	3	2	2	4	4	4	4	4	4	4	4	4	4	4	3	2	2	1	1	3	3	3	3	3	3	2	0	1
$j=374, i=0$	0	0	0	0	0	0	0	0	1	1	1	1	1	1	1	1	1	0	0	0	1	3	5	5	5	5	5	5	5	5	5	5	5	5
$j=374, i=1$	1	1	1	1	1	1	1	1	1	1	1	1	1	1	1	1	1	1	1	1	0	0	1	0	0	0	0	0	0	0	0	0	0	0
$j=374, i=2$	3	3	3	3	3	3	3	3	3	3	3	3	3	3	3	3	3	3	3	3	3	3	3	3	3	3	3	3	3	3	3	3	3	3
$j=408, i=0$	5	5	5	5	5	3	3	3	3	3	3	3	3	3	3	3	3	3	3	3	2	3	3	3	3	3	3	3	3	2	1	1	1	
$j=408, i=1$	0	0	0	0	0	0	0	0	0	0	0	3	3	3	3	3	3	3	3	3	3	3	3	3	3	3	3	3	3	3	2	1	2	
$j=408, i=2$	3	3	3	3	3	3	3	3	3	3	3	3	3	3	3	3	3	3	3	3	3	3	2	2	2	1	1	1	1	1	1	1	0	
$j=442, i=0$	1	1	1	0	0	0	0	0	0	0	0	0	0	0	0	0	0	0	1	0	0	2	2	1	1	3	3	3	3	3	3	3		
$j=442, i=1$	2	3	7	8	8	7	7	7	7	7	7	7	7	6	5	4	3	3	3	3	3	3	3	2	1	2	4	4	4	4				
$j=442, i=2$	2	2	2	2	2	2	2	1	1	3	3	3	3	3	3	3	2	1	1	1	1	1	1	1	1	1	1	1	1	1	1	0		
$j=476, i=0$	0	0	0	0	0	0	0	0	0	0	2	1	6	6	6	6	6	6	6	6	6	6	6	6	6	6	6	6	6	6	0			
$j=476, i=1$	4	4	4	4	4	4	3	2	3	4	6	8	8	8	8	8	8	8	8	8	7	7	9	9	9	9	9	8	8	10	10	10	10	10
$j=476, i=2$	1	1	1	1	0	0	1	3	3	3	3	3	3	3	3	3	3	3	2	0	1	5	7	7	7	7	7	7	7	0				
$j=510, i=0$	0	0	0	0	0	0	0	0	0	0	0	0	0	2	2	2	2	2	2	2	2	1	1	3	3	3	0	0	0					
$j=510, i=1$	10	10	10	10	10	9	8	8	8	7	7	9	8	7	7	7	7	6	5	7	9	9	9	9	9	9	9	8	8	7	9	11	10	
$j=510, i=2$	7	6	4	3	3	3	3	3	3	3	2	1	2	2	3	7	8	9	9	11	11	11	11	11	11	11	11	11	9	7	7	7	9	
$j=544, i=0$	1	1	1	1	1	0	0	0	0	0	0	0	0	0	0	1	1	1	1	1	1	0	0	2	5	5	5	5	5	5	5	5		
$j=544, i=1$	10	10	10	9	10	10	10	10	10	9	7	8	12	11	10	9	9	9	8	6	8	11	11	11	11	11	11	10	7	7	10	11	11	11
$j=544, i=2$	11	11	11	11	11	11	11	11	10	8	7	6	6	7	7	7	4	4	4	4	4	3	1	1	0	0	1	0	0	0	0	15	15	
$j=578, i=0$	5	5	5	5	5	5	5	5	5	5	5	5	5	0	0	0	0	0	0	0	0	0	0	0	0	0	0	0	0	0	0	0	0	0
$j=578, i=1$	11	11	11	11	11	11	11	11	11	11	11	11	11	11	11	11	11	11	11	11	11	11	11	11	11	11	11	11	11	11	11	10	10	12
$j=578, i=2$	15	15	15	15	15	15	15	15	15	15	15	15	6	6	6	6	6	6	5	8	10	10	10	9	11	10	12	12	12	18	18	17	16	

After the above 2 steps to reduce $(1 + s_1^{210})P_3$, the degrees of the left state terms are possibly higher or equal to 70. As the dimension is high, a cube tester over such a big dimension is far beyond our computing ability. For the left state terms, we use IV representation for each left state terms and remove the repeated IV terms using Algorithm 4 in order to determine the missing 70-degree IV terms. After the above steps, there is no 70-degree IV term in $(1 + s_1^{210})P_3$. So the degree of $(1 + s_1^{210})P_3$ is strictly lower than 70, which is summarized as the following Lemma 2.

Lemma 2. *Set the v_{74}, v_{60}, v_{75}, v_{30} and v_{48} to zeros, then the degree of $(1 + s_1^{210})z_{855}$ is bounded by 70, where z_{855} is the output after 855-round initializations.*

According to Lemma 2, we strictly prove that the degree of the reduced polynomial is lower than 70, so the sum over any selected cube of dimension 70 is zero, such that the distinguishers can be constructed.

Table 8. Degree reductions $d_t(s_i^j s_i^{j+1} s_i^{j+2} s_i^{j+3})$ of $s_i^j s_i^{j+1} s_i^{j+2} s_i^{j+3}$ with $t=4$

$j+$	0	1	2	3	4	5	6	7	8	9	10	11	12	13	14	15	16	17	18	19	20	21	22	23	24	25	26	27	28	29	30	31	32	33
$j=340, i=0$	0	0	0	0	0	0	0	0	0	0	0	0	0	0	0	0	0	0	0	0	0	0	0	0	0	0	0	0	0	0	0	0	0	0
$j=340, i=1$	2	2	2	2	2	2	2	2	2	2	2	2	2	2	1	1	0	4	4	4	4	4	4	3	3	2	2	2	2	2	2	2	2	2
$j=340, i=2$	2	6	6	6	6	5	5	4	8	8	8	8	8	8	8	8	7	6	5	4	3	3	2	6	6	6	6	6	6	5	3	2	4	
$j=374, i=0$	0	0	0	0	0	0	0	0	0	4	4	4	4	4	4	4	3	2	0	2	5	8	12	12	12	12	12	12	12	11	11	10	10	
$j=374, i=1$	2	2	2	2	2	2	2	2	2	2	2	2	2	2	2	2	2	2	2	2	2	1	0	0	2	2	2	2	2	2	2	2	2	
$j=374, i=2$	8	8	8	8	8	8	8	8	8	8	8	8	8	8	8	8	8	8	8	8	8	8	8	8	8	8	8	8	8	8	8	8	8	8
$j=408, i=0$	10	10	10	10	10	9	8	8	8	8	8	8	8	8	8	8	8	8	8	8	7	7	6	6	6	6	6	6	5	4	3	2	2	
$j=408, i=1$	2	2	2	2	2	2	1	0	0	0	6	6	6	6	6	6	6	6	6	6	6	6	6	6	6	6	6	6	5	4	2	3		
$j=408, i=2$	8	8	8	8	8	8	8	8	8	8	8	8	8	8	8	8	8	8	8	7	7	6	6	5	5	4	4	4	4	4	4	3	2	
$j=442, i=0$	2	2	2	2	1	0	0	0	2	2	2	1	0	0	0	0	0	0	1	0	1	4	3	3	2	6	6	6	6	6	6	6		
$j=442, i=1$	5	7	13	15	15	14	14	14	14	14	14	14	14	14	13	12	10	8	7	6	6	6	6	6	6	6	5	4	2	4	8	8	8	8
$j=442, i=2$	5	4	4	4	4	4	4	3	3	6	6	6	6	6	6	5	4	3	2	2	2	2	2	2	2	2	2	2	2	2	2	2	2	2

4.3   Online Phase and Complexity Analysis

We first guess the 3 key bits in s_1^{210}, i.e. k_{19}, k_{20} and $k_{57} + k_{63} + k_{21} + k_{28}k_{29} + k_3 + k_{30} + k_{12} + k_{37}k_{38} + k_{39}$ as shown in Eq. (11), for the right guess the result is 0 while for wrong guesses, the result is 1 with probability $\frac{1}{2}$. If the sum over cubes of dimension 70 is 1, then the key guess is wrong and dropped (Line 7). After the first cube sum, about half key bits remain, and sum over another cube again. The remaining guess is the key. The on-line phase is shown in Algorithm 5.

Algorithm 5. On-line Attack

1: Initialize the possible key space KEY with size of 2^3.
2: **for** $i \leftarrow 1 : 3$ **do**
3:     **for** Each possible key in KEY **do**
4:         Compute the value s_1^{210}, so that obtain the value of $(1 + s_1^{210})z$,
5:         Compute cube sums z_{sum} of $(1 + s_1^{210})z$,
6:         **if** $z_{sum} = 1$ **then**
7:             Delete key from KEY.
8:         **end if**
9:     **end for**
10: **end for**

For each guess, we need to sum over a cube of dimension 70, so that the complexity is $2^3 \cdot 2^{70} + 2^2 \cdot 2^{70} + 2^1 \cdot 2^{70} \approx 2^{74}$.

After the above process, the bits k_{19}, k_{20} and $k_{57} + k_{63} + k_{21} + k_{28}k_{29} + k_3 + k_{30} + k_{12} + k_{37}k_{38} + k_{39}$ can be determined. k_{19} and k_{20} are single master key bits. Let $c = k_{57} + k_{63} + k_{21} + k_{28}k_{29} + k_3 + k_{30} + k_{12} + k_{37}k_{38} + k_{39}$ (c is 0 or 1), then it can be rewritten as $k_{57} = k_{63} + k_{21} + k_{28}k_{29} + k_3 + k_{30} + k_{12} + k_{37}k_{38} + k_{39} + c$. We guess the other 77 key bits excluding k_{19}, k_{20} and k_{57}, the value k_{57} can be obtained directly. So the other 77 key bits excluding k_{19}, k_{20} and k_{57} can be recovered by brute force. Thus the complexity to recover all the key bits is 2^{77}.

4.4   Experimental Verification

We apply a powerful nullification technique to reduce the output polynomial, and prove the degree bound of the reduced polynomial theoretically and recover key bits. To make the attack more clear, we give an attack instance. We give two attacks on 721-round Trivium: a distinguishing attack and a key-recovery attack.

Obtain the Degree Upper Bound of Output of 721-round Trivium. Initial $IV_i = v_i$ with $i \in [0, 79]$. In the example attack on 721-round Trivium, we only use 40 freedom variables, i.e. set $v_{2 \cdot j + 1} = 0$ for $j \in [0, 39]$ and the other 40 IV bits are freedom variables.

The exact boolean functions of the first 340 state bits s_i^j for $i \in [0,2]$ and $j \in [0,340]$ can be obtained directly on PC. Hence, the degrees of them can be obtained directly. Degrees upper bounds of other state bits can be evaluated using Algorithm 2 and are shown in Table 9. Note that in Table 9, the estimated degrees of some state bits are larger than 40, e.g. $\mathcal{DEG}(s_2^{665}) = 41$, which is because the accuracy of Algorithm 2 decreases for state bits with large rounds. Thus we only apply this algorithm to s_i^j for $j \leq 665$.

The output of 721-round Trivium is $z_{721} = s_0^{656} + s_0^{629} + s_1^{653} + s_1^{638} + s_2^{656} + s_2^{611}$. According to Table 9, the 6 state terms (bits) highlighted in red are of degree lower than 40, so the degree of z_{721} is lower than 40, which can serve as distinguishers. This result can be obtained easily by rough computing.

Next, we give a more accurate bound of z_{721}. In the following, we will determine whether z_{721}'s degree is bigger than 37. The 6 state bits are expressed using state bits in lower rounds again and substituted into z_{721}, which is called the substitution or expression process in [9]. Then $z_{721} = s_2^{590} + s_2^{546}s_2^{547} + s_2^{545} + s_0^{587} + s_2^{563} + s_2^{519}s_2^{520} + s_2^{518} + s_0^{560} + s_0^{587} + s_0^{561}s_0^{562} + s_0^{560} + s_1^{575} + s_0^{572} + s_0^{546}s_0^{547} + s_0^{545} + s_1^{560} + s_1^{587} + s_1^{573}s_1^{574} + s_1^{572} + s_2^{569} + s_1^{542} + s_1^{528}s_1^{529} + s_1^{527} + s_2^{524}$. According to degree upper bounds Table 9, $\deg(s_2^{590}) = 27 < 37$ highlighted in blue, so s_2^{590} is removed. Then $\deg(s_2^{546}s_2^{547}) \leq \mathcal{DEG}(s_2^{546}) + \mathcal{DEG}(s_2^{547}) = 20 + 21 = 41$ and $41 \geq 37$, so the degree of $s_2^{546}s_2^{547}$ is possibly bigger than 36 and left. After discarding all the state terms whose degrees are lower than 36, $z_{721}|_{\deg>36} = s_2^{546}s_2^{547} + s_1^{573}s_1^{574}$. Continue substitution and expression process for $z_{721}|_{\deg>36}$ and finally, there remain no state terms with degree bigger than 36, so that the degree bound of z_{721} is 36. The details of the above step are shown in Appendix A.

A Key-Recovery Attack on 721-round Trivium. Similar to the IV setting above for distinguishing 721-round Trivium, we set $v_{2 \cdot j+1} = 0$ for $j \in [0,39]$ and the other 40 IV bits are freedom variables.

According to our attack outline introduced in Sect. 3.2, we need to determine the nullification scheme first. We express the output of 721-round Trivium iteratively and calculate the frequency of state bits in the polynomial. Then we choose s_1^{290} as P_1, the output can be rewritten as $z_{721} = s_1^{290}P_2 + P_3$. Multiply $1 + s_1^{290}$ with z_{721} such that the result is $(1 + s_1^{290})z_{721} = (1 + s_1^{290})P_3$. We study the reduced polynomial $(1 + s_1^{290})P_3$. In order to decrease the number of key bits in s_1^{290}, we choose to nullify v_{58}, v_{64} and v_{72}, so that there are 37 freedom variables. Set the degree bound to 32, we express $(1+s_1^{290})P_3$ using internal state bits furthermore and discard state terms whose degree are lower than $32 + d_t$, where d_t is the corresponding degree reduction. We use IV presentation, combined with Algorithm 4 in order to obtain the IV terms of degree higher than 32. Finally, there is no IV term. Hence, we prove that the degree of $(1 + s_1^{290})z_{721}$ is lower than 32. Then the sum of $(1+s_1^{290})z_{721}$ over any selected cube of dimension 32 is zero. This process can be executed in an hour in a PC.

Table 9. Degree upper bounds $\mathcal{DEG}(s_i^j)$ of the state bits s_i^j for $j \leq 665$

$j+$	1	2	3	4	5	6	7	8	9	10	11	12	13	14	15	16	17	18	19	20	21	22	23	24	25	26	27	28	29	30	31	32	33	34	35
$s_0^{j=0}$	0	0	0	0	0	0	0	0	0	0	0	0	0	0	0	0	0	0	0	0	0	0	0	0	0	0	0	0	0	0	0	0	0	0	0
$s_1^{j=0}$	1	0	1	0	1	0	1	0	1	0	1	0	1	0	1	0	1	0	1	0	1	0	1	0	1	0	1	0	1	0	1	0	1	0	1
$s_2^{j=0}$	0	1	0	1	0	1	1	1	1	1	1	1	1	1	1	1	1	1	1	1	1	1	1	1	1	1	1	1	1	1	1	1	1	1	1
$s_0^{j=35}$	0	0	0	0	0	0	0	0	0	0	0	0	0	0	0	0	0	0	0	0	0	0	0	0	0	0	0	0	0	0	0	0	0	0	0
$s_1^{j=35}$	0	1	0	1	0	1	0	1	0	1	0	1	0	1	0	1	0	1	0	1	0	1	0	1	0	1	0	1	0	1	0	1	0	1	0
$s_2^{j=35}$	1	1	1	1	1	1	1	1	1	1	1	1	1	1	1	1	1	1	1	1	1	1	1	1	1	1	1	1	1	1	1	1	1	1	1
$s_0^{j=70}$	0	1	1	1	1	1	1	1	1	1	1	1	1	1	1	1	1	1	1	1	1	1	1	1	1	1	1	1	1	1	1	1	1	1	1
$s_1^{j=70}$	1	0	1	0	1	0	1	0	1	0	1	0	1	0	1	0	1	0	1	0	1	0	1	0	1	0	1	0	1	0	1	0	1	0	1
$s_2^{j=70}$	1	1	1	1	1	1	1	1	1	1	1	1	1	1	1	1	1	1	1	1	1	1	1	1	1	1	1	1	1	1	1	1	1	1	1
$s_0^{j=105}$	1	1	1	1	1	1	1	1	1	1	2	2	2	2	2	2	2	2	2	2	2	2	2	2	2	2	2	2	2	2	2	2	2	2	2
$s_1^{j=105}$	0	1	0	1	0	1	0	1	0	1	0	1	0	1	0	1	0	1	0	1	0	1	0	1	0	1	0	1	1	1	1	1	1	1	1
$s_2^{j=105}$	1	1	1	1	1	1	1	1	1	1	1	1	1	1	1	1	1	1	1	1	1	1	1	1	1	1	1	1	1	1	1	1	1	1	1
$s_0^{j=140}$	2	2	2	2	2	2	2	2	2	2	2	2	2	2	2	2	2	2	2	2	2	2	2	2	2	2	2	2	2	2	2	2	2	2	2
$s_1^{j=140}$	1	1	1	1	1	1	1	1	1	1	1	1	1	1	1	1	1	1	1	1	1	1	2	2	2	2	2	2	2	2	2	2	2	2	2
$s_2^{j=140}$	1	1	1	1	1	1	1	1	1	1	1	1	1	1	1	1	1	1	1	1	1	1	1	1	1	1	1	1	1	1	1	1	1	1	1
$s_0^{j=175}$	2	2	2	2	2	2	2	2	2	2	2	2	2	2	2	2	2	2	2	2	2	2	2	2	2	2	2	2	2	2	2	2	2	2	2
$s_1^{j=175}$	2	2	2	2	2	2	2	2	2	2	2	2	2	2	2	2	2	2	2	2	2	2	2	2	2	2	2	2	2	2	3	3	3	3	3
$s_2^{j=175}$	1	1	1	1	1	1	1	1	1	1	1	1	1	1	1	1	1	1	1	1	1	1	1	1	1	1	1	1	1	1	1	1	1	1	1
$s_0^{j=210}$	2	2	2	2	2	2	2	2	2	2	2	2	2	2	2	2	2	2	2	2	2	2	2	2	2	2	2	2	2	2	2	2	2	2	2
$s_1^{j=210}$	3	3	3	3	3	3	3	3	3	3	3	3	3	3	3	3	3	3	3	3	3	3	3	3	3	3	3	3	3	3	3	3	3	3	3
$s_2^{j=210}$	1	1	1	1	1	2	2	2	2	2	2	2	2	2	2	2	2	2	2	2	2	2	2	2	2	2	2	2	2	2	2	2	2	2	2
$s_0^{j=245}$	2	2	2	2	2	2	2	2	2	2	2	2	2	2	2	2	2	2	2	2	2	2	2	2	2	2	2	2	2	2	2	2	2	2	2
$s_1^{j=245}$	3	3	3	3	3	3	3	3	3	3	3	3	3	3	3	3	3	3	3	3	3	3	3	3	3	3	3	3	3	4	4	4	4	4	4
$s_2^{j=245}$	3	3	3	3	3	3	3	3	3	3	3	3	3	3	3	3	3	3	3	4	4	4	4	4	4	4	4	4	4	4	4	4	4	4	4
$s_0^{j=280}$	2	2	2	2	2	2	2	2	2	2	2	2	2	2	2	2	2	2	2	2	2	2	2	2	2	2	2	2	2	2	3	3	3	3	3
$s_1^{j=280}$	4	4	4	4	4	4	4	4	4	4	4	4	4	4	4	4	4	4	4	4	4	4	4	4	4	4	4	4	4	4	4	4	4	4	4
$s_2^{j=280}$	4	4	4	4	4	4	4	5	5	5	5	5	5	5	5	5	5	5	5	5	5	5	5	5	5	5	5	5	5	5	5	5	5	5	5
$s_0^{j=315}$	3	3	3	3	3	3	3	3	3	3	3	3	3	4	4	4	4	4	4	4	4	4	4	4	4	4	4	4	4	4	4	4	4	4	4
$s_1^{j=315}$	4	4	4	4	4	4	4	4	4	4	4	4	4	4	4	4	4	4	4	4	4	4	4	4	4	4	4	4	4	4	4	4	4	4	4
$s_2^{j=315}$	5	5	5	5	5	5	5	5	5	5	5	5	5	5	5	5	5	5	5	5	5	5	5	5	5	5	5	5	5	5	5	5	5	5	5
$s_0^{j=350}$	4	4	4	4	5	6	6	6	6	6	6	6	6	6	6	6	6	6	6	6	6	6	6	6	6	6	6	6	6	6	6	6	6	6	7
$s_1^{j=350}$	4	4	4	4	4	4	4	4	4	4	4	4	4	4	4	4	4	4	4	4	4	4	4	4	4	4	4	4	4	4	4	4	4	4	4
$s_2^{j=350}$	5	5	6	6	6	6	6	6	6	6	6	6	6	6	6	6	7	7	7	7	7	7	7	7	7	7	7	7	7	7	7	7	7	7	7
$s_0^{j=385}$	7	7	7	7	7	7	7	7	7	7	7	7	8	9	9	9	9	9	9	9	9	9	9	9	9	9	9	9	9	9	9	9	9	9	9
$s_1^{j=385}$	4	4	4	4	4	4	4	4	4	4	4	4	4	4	4	5	6	6	6	6	6	6	6	6	6	6	6	6	6	6	6	6	6	6	6
$s_2^{j=385}$	7	7	7	7	7	7	7	7	7	7	7	7	7	7	7	7	7	7	7	7	7	7	7	7	7	7	7	7	7	7	7	7	7	7	7
$s_0^{j=420}$	9	9	9	9	9	9	9	9	9	9	9	9	9	9	9	9	9	9	9	9	9	9	9	9	9	9	9	9	9	9	9	9	9	10	10
$s_1^{j=420}$	7	8	8	8	8	8	8	8	8	8	8	8	8	8	8	8	8	8	8	8	8	8	8	8	8	9	11	11	11	11	11	11	11	11	11
$s_2^{j=420}$	7	7	7	7	7	7	7	7	7	7	7	7	7	7	7	7	8	8	8	8	8	8	8	8	8	8	8	8	8	8	8	8	8	8	8
$s_0^{j=455}$	10	10	10	10	10	10	10	10	10	10	10	10	11	12	12	12	12	12	12	12	12	12	12	12	12	12	12	12	12	12	13	13	13	13	13
$s_1^{j=455}$	11	11	11	11	11	11	11	11	11	12	12	12	12	12	12	12	12	12	12	12	13	13	13	13	13	13	13	13	13	13	13	13	13	14	15
$s_2^{j=455}$	8	8	8	8	8	8	8	8	8	8	8	8	8	8	8	8	8	8	8	8	8	8	8	8	8	8	8	8	9	10	10	10	10	10	10
$s_0^{j=490}$	13	13	13	13	13	13	13	13	13	13	13	13	13	13	13	13	13	13	13	13	13	13	13	13	13	13	13	13	13	13	13	13	13	13	13
$s_1^{j=490}$	15	15	15	15	15	15	15	15	15	15	15	15	15	15	15	15	16	16	16	16	16	16	16	16	16	16	16	16	16	16	16	16	16	17	17
$s_2^{j=490}$	10	10	10	10	10	10	10	10	10	10	10	10	10	11	11	14	14	14	14	14	14	14	14	14	14	14	14	14	14	14	14	14	14	14	14
$s_0^{j=525}$	13	13	13	13	13	13	13	13	13	13	13	13	13	13	13	13	13	13	13	13	13	13	13	14	14	14	14	14	14	14	14	14	14	14	14
$s_1^{j=525}$	17	17	17	17	17	17	17	17	17	17	17	17	17	17	17	17	17	17	17	17	17	17	17	17	17	17	17	18	19	19	19	19	20	21	21
$s_2^{j=525}$	14	14	15	17	18	18	18	19	19	19	19	19	19	19	19	19	19	19	19	19	19	**20**	**21**	21	21	21	21	21	21	21	21	21	22	23	23
$s_0^{j=560}$	14	14	15	15	15	15	15	15	15	15	15	15	15	15	15	15	15	15	15	15	15	15	15	15	15	15	15	15	15	15	15	15	15	16	18
$s_1^{j=560}$	21	21	21	21	21	21	22	23	23	23	23	23	23	23	23	23	23	23	23	23	23	23	23	23	23	23	23	23	23	23	23	23	23	23	23
$s_2^{j=560}$	23	23	23	23	23	23	23	23	23	23	24	25	25	25	25	25	27	27	27	27	27	27	27	27	27	27	27	27	27	27	**27**	26	26	26	26
$s_0^{j=595}$	19	19	19	19	20	20	20	20	20	20	20	20	20	20	20	20	20	20	20	20	21	23	24	24	24	24	24	24	24	24	24	25	27	**27**	27
$s_1^{j=595}$	23	23	23	23	23	23	23	23	23	23	23	23	23	23	23	23	23	23	23	23	23	24	24	24	24	24	24	24	24	24	24	24	24	24	24
$s_2^{j=595}$	26	26	26	26	26	26	26	26	26	26	26	27	28	29	29	29	**29**	29	29	29	29	29	30	30	30	30	30	30	30	30	30	30	31	31	31
$s_0^{j=630}$	27	27	27	27	27	27	28	31	33	33	33	34	34	34	34	34	34	34	34	34	34	34	34	34	36	**37**	37	37	37	37	37	37	37	37	37
$s_1^{j=630}$	26	26	26	26	26	26	26	**26**	26	27	28	28	28	28	28	28	28	28	28	28	28	**28**	29	29	29	29	29	29	29	29	29	30	30	30	30
$s_2^{j=630}$	31	31	31	31	32	33	33	33	33	34	36	37	37	37	37	37	37	37	37	38	39	39	39	39	39	**39**	39	40	41	41	41	41	41	41	41

Guess the key bit involved in s_1^{290}. For right guess, sum over a cube of dimension 32 is zero while for wrong guesses, the result is 1 with probability $\frac{1}{2}$. The key bits involved in s_1^{290} are shown in Table 10. After 19 summations over cubes of dimension 32, the 19 key bits can be recovered. The complexity is about $2 \times 2^{19} \times 2^{32} = 2^{52}$. The other key bits can be recovered using brute force with a complexity of 2^{61}. Hence, the total complexity of recovering all key bits of 721-round Trivium is 2^{61}.

Table 10. The key bits involved in s_1^{290}.

Equivalent key bits
$k_{18}, k_{17}, k_{63}, k_{61}, k_{59}, k_{60} + k_{16}k_{17}, k_{35} + k_{60}k_{61} + k_{62}, k_{33} + k_{58}k_{59} + k_{60}, k_{15} + k_{40}k_{41} + k_{42},$
$k_{42}k_{43} + k_{44}, k_{48} + k_{73}k_{74} + k_{75} + k_{61}k_{62}, k_{47} + k_{72}k_{73} + k_{74} + k_{60}k_{61} + k_{62}, k_{46} + k_{71}k_{72}+$
$k_{73} + k_{59}k_{60}, k_{45} + k_{70}k_{71} + k_{72} + k_{58}k_{59} + k_{60}, k_{34}k_{35} + k_{34}k_{60}k_{61} + k_{34}k_{62} + k_{35}k_{59}k_{60}+$
$k_{59}k_{60}k_{61} + k_{59}k_{60}k_{62} + k_{35}k_{61} + k_{60}k_{61} + k_{21} + k_{46}k_{47} + k_{48} + k_{36}, k_{33}k_{34} + k_{33}k_{59}k_{60}+$
$k_{33}k_{61} + k_{34}k_{58}k_{59} + k_{58}k_{59}k_{60} + k_{58}k_{59}k_{61} + k_{34}k_{60} + k_{59}k_{60} + k_{20} + k_{45}k_{46} + k_{47} + k_{35} + k_{62},$
$k_{16}k_{17} + k_{16}k_{42}k_{43} + k_{16}k_{44} + k_{17}k_{41}k_{42} + k_{41}k_{42}k_{43} + k_{41}k_{42}k_{44} + k_{17}k_{43} + k_{42}k_{43} + k_3+$
$k_{28}k_{29} + k_{30} + k_{45} + k_{48} + k_{73}k_{74} + k_{75} + k_{61}k_{62} + k_9, k_{15}k_{16} + k_{15}k_{41}k_{42} + k_{15}k_{43} + k_{16}k_{40}k_{41}+$
$k_{40}k_{41}k_{42} + k_{40}k_{41}k_{43} + k_{16}k_{42} + k_{41}k_{42} + k_2 + k_{27}k_{28} + k_{29} + k_{44} + k_{47} + k_{72}k_{73} + k_{74}+$
$k_{60}k_{61} + k_{62}, k^* (A \ complex \ expression \ of \ key \ bits).$

5   Conclusions

In this paper, we propose the Boolean polynomial reduction techniques and IV representation, which can be applicable to cryptanalysis of stream ciphers based on NFSRs. These techniques can help obtain more accurate degree bounds. We apply these techniques to the cryptanalysis of reduced round Trivium. For recovering the key bits of Trivium, we propose a new nullification technique. Combined with the distinguishers, we propose a key-recovery attack on 855 round Trivium, where 3 equivalent key bits can be recovered with complexity of 2^{74}. The other key bits can be recovered by brute force with a complexity of 2^{77}.

Furthermore, our flexible methods can be applied to attack more round of Trivium by adjustment of P_1, which is our future work. In addition, the degree evaluation and degree reduction techniques can be applicable to other encryption primitives such as Grain family.

Acknowledgement. The authors would like to thank anonymous reviewers for their helpful comments. We also thank National Supercomputing Center in Wuxi for their support of Sunway TaihuLight, which is the most powerful supercomputer. This work was supported by the National Key Research and Development Program of China (Grant No. 2017YFA0303903), and National Cryptography Development Fund (No. MMJJ20170121), and Zhejiang Province Key R&D Project (No. 2017C01062).

References

1. Aumasson, J.-P., Dinur, I., Meier, W., Shamir, A.: Cube testers and key recovery attacks on reduced-round MD6 and Trivium. In: Dunkelman, O. (ed.) FSE 2009. LNCS, vol. 5665, pp. 1–22. Springer, Heidelberg (2009). https://doi.org/10.1007/978-3-642-03317-9_1
2. De Cannière, C., Preneel, B.: Trivium. In: Robshaw, M., Billet, O. (eds.) New Stream Cipher Designs. LNCS, vol. 4986, pp. 244–266. Springer, Heidelberg (2008). https://doi.org/10.1007/978-3-540-68351-3_18
3. Dinur, I., Güneysu, T., Paar, C., Shamir, A., Zimmermann, R.: An experimentally verified attack on full grain-128 using dedicated reconfigurable hardware. In: Lee, D.H., Wang, X. (eds.) ASIACRYPT 2011. LNCS, vol. 7073, pp. 327–343. Springer, Heidelberg (2011). https://doi.org/10.1007/978-3-642-25385-0_18
4. Dinur, I., Shamir, A.: Cube attacks on tweakable black box polynomials. In: Joux, A. (ed.) EUROCRYPT 2009. LNCS, vol. 5479, pp. 278–299. Springer, Heidelberg (2009). https://doi.org/10.1007/978-3-642-01001-9_16
5. Dinur, I., Shamir, A.: Breaking grain-128 with dynamic cube attacks. In: Joux, A. (ed.) FSE 2011. LNCS, vol. 6733, pp. 167–187. Springer, Heidelberg (2011). https://doi.org/10.1007/978-3-642-21702-9_10
6. Englund, H., Johansson, T., Sönmez Turan, M.: A framework for chosen IV statistical analysis of stream ciphers. In: Srinathan, K., Rangan, C.P., Yung, M. (eds.) INDOCRYPT 2007. LNCS, vol. 4859, pp. 268–281. Springer, Heidelberg (2007). https://doi.org/10.1007/978-3-540-77026-8_20
7. Fischer, S., Khazaei, S., Meier, W.: Chosen IV statistical analysis for key recovery attacks on stream ciphers. In: Vaudenay, S. (ed.) AFRICACRYPT 2008. LNCS, vol. 5023, pp. 236–245. Springer, Heidelberg (2008). https://doi.org/10.1007/978-3-540-68164-9_16
8. Fouque, P.-A., Vannet, T.: Improving key recovery to 784 and 799 rounds of Trivium using optimized cube attacks. In: Moriai, S. (ed.) FSE 2013. LNCS, vol. 8424, pp. 502–517. Springer, Heidelberg (2014). https://doi.org/10.1007/978-3-662-43933-3_26
9. Fu, X., Wang, X., Chen, J.: Determining the nonexistent terms of non-linear multivariate polynomials: how to break grain-128 more efficiently. IACR Cryptology ePrint Archive 2017, 412 (2017). http://eprint.iacr.org/2017/412
10. International Organization for Standardization (ISO): ISO/IEC 29192-3:2012, Information technology - Security techniques - Lightweight cryptography - Part 3: Stream ciphers (2012)
11. Knellwolf, S., Meier, W., Naya-Plasencia, M.: Conditional differential cryptanalysis of NLFSR-based cryptosystems. In: Abe, M. (ed.) ASIACRYPT 2010. LNCS, vol. 6477, pp. 130–145. Springer, Heidelberg (2010). https://doi.org/10.1007/978-3-642-17373-8_8
12. Knellwolf, S., Meier, W., Naya-Plasencia, M.: Conditional differential cryptanalysis of Trivium and KATAN. In: Miri, A., Vaudenay, S. (eds.) SAC 2011. LNCS, vol. 7118, pp. 200–212. Springer, Heidelberg (2012). https://doi.org/10.1007/978-3-642-28496-0_12
13. Knudsen, L.R.: Truncated and higher order differentials. In: Preneel, B. (ed.) FSE 1994. LNCS, vol. 1008, pp. 196–211. Springer, Heidelberg (1995). https://doi.org/10.1007/3-540-60590-8_16
14. Knudsen, L., Wagner, D.: Integral cryptanalysis. In: Daemen, J., Rijmen, V. (eds.) FSE 2002. LNCS, vol. 2365, pp. 112–127. Springer, Heidelberg (2002). https://doi.org/10.1007/3-540-45661-9_9

15. Lai, X.: Higher order derivatives and differential cryptanalysis. In: Blahut, R.E., Costello, D.J., Maurer, U., Mittelholzer, T. (eds.) Communications and Cryptography, pp. 227–233. Springer, Boston (1994). https://doi.org/10.1007/978-1-4615-2694-0_23

16. Liu, M.: Degree evaluation of NFSR-based cryptosystems. In: Katz, J., Shacham, H. (eds.) CRYPTO 2017. LNCS, vol. 10403, pp. 227–249. Springer, Cham (2017). https://doi.org/10.1007/978-3-319-63697-9_8

17. Liu, M., Yang, J., Wang, W., Lin, D.: Correlation cube attacks: from weak-key distinguisher to key recovery. Cryptology ePrint Archive, Report 2018/158 (2018). https://eprint.iacr.org/2018/158

18. Todo, Y.: Structural evaluation by generalized integral property. In: Oswald, E., Fischlin, M. (eds.) EUROCRYPT 2015. LNCS, vol. 9056, pp. 287–314. Springer, Heidelberg (2015). https://doi.org/10.1007/978-3-662-46800-5_12

19. Todo, Y., Isobe, T., Hao, Y., Meier, W.: Cube attacks on non-blackbox polynomials based on division property. In: Katz, J., Shacham, H. (eds.) CRYPTO 2017. LNCS, vol. 10403, pp. 250–279. Springer, Cham (2017). https://doi.org/10.1007/978-3-319-63697-9_9

20. Wang, X., Yin, Y.L., Yu, H.: Finding collisions in the full SHA-1. In: Shoup, V. (ed.) CRYPTO 2005. LNCS, vol. 3621, pp. 17–36. Springer, Heidelberg (2005). https://doi.org/10.1007/11535218_2

21. Wang, X., Yu, H.: How to break MD5 and other hash functions. In: Cramer, R. (ed.) EUROCRYPT 2005. LNCS, vol. 3494, pp. 19–35. Springer, Heidelberg (2005). https://doi.org/10.1007/11426639_2

A   The Details of Determining the Degree Upper Bound of Output for 721-round Trivium

For $z_{721}|_{\deg>36} = s_2^{546}s_2^{547} + s_1^{573}s_1^{574}$, the 4 state bits s_2^{546}, s_2^{547}, s_1^{573}, s_1^{574} can be expressed using state bits furthermore. Substitute the 4 state bits using the expression and discard the state terms whose degree is lower than 37, then the resulted $z_{721}|_{\deg>36} = s_1^{463}s_1^{464}s_1^{478} + s_1^{464}s_1^{465}s_1^{477} + s_0^{481}s_0^{482}s_0^{508} + s_0^{482}s_0^{483}s_0^{507} + s_0^{482}s_0^{483}s_1^{495} + s_0^{481}s_0^{482}s_1^{496}$. Then the state bits involved in the polynomial can be expressed using state bits, so that we can obtain
$z_{721}|_{\deg>36} = s_0^{412}s_2^{372}s_2^{373}s_2^{398}s_2^{399} + s_0^{413}s_2^{371}s_2^{372}s_2^{398}s_2^{399} + s_0^{413}s_2^{373}s_2^{374}s_2^{397}s_2^{398} + s_0^{414}s_2^{372}s_2^{373}s_2^{397}s_2^{398} + s_0^{403}s_0^{404}s_2^{372}s_2^{373}s_2^{417} + s_0^{403}s_0^{404}s_2^{373}s_2^{374}s_2^{416} + s_0^{403}s_0^{404}s_2^{372}s_2^{373}s_2^{374} + s_0^{403}s_0^{404}s_2^{371}s_2^{373}s_2^{374} + s_0^{403}s_0^{404}s_0^{413}s_2^{373}s_2^{374} + s_0^{403}s_0^{404}s_0^{414}s_2^{372}s_2^{373} + s_0^{404}s_0^{405}s_2^{371}s_2^{372}s_2^{416} + s_0^{404}s_0^{405}s_2^{372}s_2^{373}s_2^{415} + s_0^{404}s_0^{405}s_2^{371}s_2^{372}s_2^{373} + s_0^{404}s_0^{405}s_2^{370}s_2^{372}s_2^{373} + s_0^{404}s_0^{405}s_0^{412}s_2^{372}s_2^{373} + s_0^{404}s_0^{405}s_0^{413}s_2^{371}s_2^{372}$.

Repeat the process above and we can obtain $z_{721}|_{\deg>36} = s_1^{290}s_1^{291}s_1^{305}s_2^{293} s_2^{294}s_2^{295}s_2^{303}s_2^{304} + s_1^{291}s_1^{292}s_1^{304}s_2^{293}s_2^{294}s_2^{295}s_2^{303}s_2^{304} + s_1^{291}s_1^{292}s_2^{293}s_2^{294}s_2^{295}s_2^{303}s_2^{304} + s_1^{289}s_1^{291}s_1^{292}s_2^{293}s_2^{294}s_2^{295}s_2^{303}s_2^{304} + s_1^{291}s_1^{292}s_2^{286}s_2^{293}s_2^{294}s_2^{295}s_2^{303}s_2^{304} + s_1^{290}s_1^{291}s_1^{287}s_2^{293}s_2^{294}s_2^{295}s_2^{303}s_2^{304} + s_1^{290}s_1^{291}s_1^{305}s_2^{292}s_2^{294}s_2^{295}s_2^{303}s_2^{304} + s_1^{291}s_1^{292}s_2^{304} s_2^{292}s_2^{294}s_2^{295}s_2^{303}s_2^{304} + s_1^{290}s_1^{291}s_1^{292}s_2^{292}s_2^{294}s_2^{295}s_2^{303}s_2^{304} + s_1^{289}s_1^{291}s_1^{292}s_2^{292}s_2^{294}s_2^{295}s_2^{303}s_2^{304} + s_1^{291}s_1^{292}s_2^{286}s_2^{292}s_2^{294}s_2^{295}s_2^{303}s_2^{304} + s_1^{290}s_1^{291}s_1^{287}s_2^{292}s_2^{294}s_2^{295}s_2^{303}s_2^{304} + s_1^{289}s_1^{290}s_2^{304}s_2^{293}s_2^{294}s_2^{295}s_2^{304}s_2^{305} + s_1^{290}s_1^{291}s_2^{303}s_2^{293}s_2^{294}s_2^{295}s_2^{304}s_2^{305} + s_1^{289}s_1^{290}s_1^{291}s_2^{293}s_2^{294}s_2^{295}s_2^{304}s_2^{305} + s_1^{288}s_1^{290}s_1^{291}s_2^{293}s_2^{294}s_2^{295}s_2^{304}s_2^{305} + s_1^{290}s_1^{291}s_2^{285}s_2^{293}s_2^{294}s_2^{295}s_2^{304}s_2^{305} + s_1^{289}s_1^{290}s_2^{286}s_2^{293}s_2^{294}s_2^{295}s_2^{304}s_2^{305} + s_1^{289}s_1^{290}s_2^{304}s_2^{292}s_2^{294}s_2^{295}s_2^{304}s_2^{305} +

$$s_1^{290} s_1^{291} s_1^{303} s_2^{292} s_2^{294} s_2^{295} s_2^{304} s_2^{305} + s_1^{289} s_1^{290} s_1^{291} s_2^{292} s_2^{294} s_2^{295} s_2^{304} s_2^{305} + s_1^{288} s_1^{290} s_1^{291}$$

$$s_2^{292} s_2^{294} s_2^{295} s_2^{304} s_2^{305} + s_1^{290} s_1^{291} s_2^{285} s_2^{292} s_2^{294} s_2^{295} s_2^{304} s_2^{305} + s_1^{289} s_1^{290} s_2^{286} s_2^{292} s_2^{294} s_2^{295}$$

$$s_2^{304} s_2^{305} + s_1^{289} s_1^{290} s_2^{304} s_2^{294} s_2^{295} s_2^{296} s_2^{302} s_2^{303} + s_1^{290} s_1^{291} s_1^{303} s_2^{294} s_2^{295} s_2^{296} s_2^{302} s_2^{303} +$$

$$s_1^{289} s_1^{290} s_1^{291} s_2^{294} s_2^{295} s_2^{296} s_2^{302} s_2^{303} + s_1^{288} s_1^{290} s_1^{291} s_2^{294} s_2^{295} s_2^{296} s_2^{302} s_2^{303} + s_1^{290} s_1^{291} s_2^{285}$$

$$s_2^{294} s_2^{295} s_2^{296} s_2^{302} s_2^{303} + s_1^{289} s_1^{290} s_2^{286} s_2^{294} s_2^{295} s_2^{296} s_2^{302} s_2^{303} + s_1^{289} s_1^{290} s_1^{304} s_2^{293} s_2^{295} s_2^{296}$$

$$s_2^{302} s_2^{303} + s_1^{290} s_1^{291} s_1^{303} s_2^{293} s_2^{295} s_2^{296} s_2^{302} s_2^{303} + s_1^{289} s_1^{290} s_1^{291} s_2^{293} s_2^{295} s_2^{296} s_2^{302} s_2^{303} +$$

$$s_1^{288} s_1^{290} s_1^{291} s_2^{293} s_2^{295} s_2^{296} s_2^{302} s_2^{303} + s_1^{290} s_1^{291} s_2^{285} s_2^{293} s_2^{295} s_2^{296} s_2^{302} s_2^{303} + s_1^{289} s_1^{290} s_2^{286}$$

$$s_2^{293} s_2^{295} s_2^{296} s_2^{302} s_2^{303} + s_1^{288} s_1^{289} s_1^{303} s_2^{294} s_2^{295} s_2^{296} s_2^{303} s_2^{304} + s_1^{289} s_1^{290} s_1^{302} s_2^{294} s_2^{295}$$

$$s_2^{296} s_2^{303} s_2^{304} + s_1^{288} s_1^{289} s_1^{290} s_2^{294} s_2^{295} s_2^{296} s_2^{303} s_2^{304} + s_1^{287} s_1^{289} s_1^{290} s_2^{294} s_2^{295} s_2^{296} s_2^{303}$$

$$s_2^{304} + s_1^{289} s_1^{290} s_2^{284} s_2^{294} s_2^{295} s_2^{296} s_2^{303} s_2^{304} + s_1^{288} s_1^{289} s_2^{285} s_2^{294} s_2^{295} s_2^{296} s_2^{303} s_2^{304} + s_1^{288}$$

$$s_1^{289} s_1^{303} s_2^{293} s_2^{295} s_2^{296} s_2^{303} s_2^{304} + s_1^{289} s_1^{290} s_1^{302} s_2^{293} s_2^{295} s_2^{296} s_2^{303} s_2^{304} + s_1^{288} s_1^{289} s_1^{290} s_2^{293}$$

$$s_2^{295} s_2^{296} s_2^{303} s_2^{304} + s_1^{287} s_1^{289} s_1^{290} s_2^{293} s_2^{295} s_2^{296} s_2^{303} s_2^{304} + s_1^{289} s_1^{290} s_2^{284} s_2^{293} s_2^{295} s_2^{296} s_2^{303}$$

$$s_2^{304} + s_1^{288} s_1^{289} s_2^{285} s_2^{293} s_2^{295} s_2^{296} s_2^{303} s_2^{304}.$$

Substitute once again and there remains no state term, so that the degree of z_{721} is lower than 37, which can be derived as distinguishers with lower complexity.

Improved Key Recovery Attacks on Reduced-Round AES with Practical Data and Memory Complexities

Achiya Bar-On[1], Orr Dunkelman[2(✉)], Nathan Keller[1], Eyal Ronen[3], and Adi Shamir[3]

[1] Department of Mathematics, Bar-Ilan University, Ramat Gan, Israel
[2] Computer Science Department, University of Haifa, Haifa, Israel
orrd@cs.haifa.ac.il
[3] Computer Science Department, The Weizmann Institute, Rehovot, Israel

Abstract. Determining the security of AES is a central problem in cryptanalysis, but progress in this area had been slow and only a handful of cryptanalytic techniques led to significant advancements. At Eurocrypt 2017 Grassi et al. presented a novel type of distinguisher for AES-like structures, but so far all the published attacks which were based on this distinguisher were inferior to previously known attacks in their complexity. In this paper we combine the technique of Grassi et al. with several other techniques to obtain the best known key recovery attack on 5-round AES in the single-key model, reducing its overall complexity from about 2^{32} to about $2^{22.5}$. Extending our techniques to 7-round AES, we obtain the best known attacks on AES-192 which use practical amounts of data and memory, breaking the record for such attacks which was obtained 18 years ago by the classical Square attack.

1 Introduction

The Advanced Encryption Standard (AES) is the best known and most widely used secret key cryptosystem, and determining its security is one of the most important problems in cryptanalysis. Since there is no known attack which can break the full AES significantly faster than via exhaustive search, researchers had concentrated on attacks which can break reduced round versions of AES. Such attacks are important for several reasons. First of all, they enable us to assess the remaining security margin of AES, defined by the ratio between the number of rounds which can be successfully attacked and the number of rounds in the full AES. In addition, they enable us to develop new attack techniques which may become increasingly potent with additional improvements. Finally, there are many proposals for using reduced round AES (and especially its 4 or 5 rounds versions) as components in larger schemes, and thus successful cryptanalysis of these variants can be used to attack those schemes. Examples of such proposals include ZORRO [17], LED [21] and AEZ [22] which use 4-round AES, and WEM [7], Hound [16], and ELmD [3] which use 5-round AES.

© International Association for Cryptologic Research 2018
H. Shacham and A. Boldyreva (Eds.): CRYPTO 2018, LNCS 10992, pp. 185–212, 2018.
https://doi.org/10.1007/978-3-319-96881-0_7

Over the last twenty years, dozens of papers on the cryptanalysis of reduced-round AES were published, but only a few techniques led to significant reductions in the complexity of key recovery attacks. In the standard model (where the attack uses a single key rather than related keys), these techniques include the Square attack [8,15], impossible differential cryptanalysis [1,23], the Demirci-Selçuk attack [10,12], and the Biclique attack [2]. In most of these cases, it took several years — and a series of subsequent improvements — from the invention of the technique until it was developed into its current form. For example, impossible differential cryptanalysis was applied to AES already in 2000 [1] as an attack on 5-round AES, but it was only very recently that Boura et al. [6] improved it into its best currently known variant which breaks 7-round AES with an overall complexity of about 2^{107}. The Demirci-Selçuk attack was presented in 2005 [10] with a huge memory complexity of over 2^{200}, and it took 8 years before Derbez et al. [12] enhanced it in 2013 into an attack on 7-round AES with an overall complexity which is just below 2^{100}. Therefore, the development of any new attack technique is a major breakthrough with potentially far reaching consequences.

The latest such development happened in 2017, when Grassi et al. [20] published a new property of AES, called *multiple-of-8*, which had not been observed before by other researchers. At first, it was not clear whether the new observation can at all lead to attacks on AES which are competitive with respect to previously known results. This question was partially resolved by Grassi [19], who used this observation to develop a new type of attack which can break 5-round AES in data, memory and time complexities of 2^{32}. However, a variant of the Square attack [15] can break the same variant with comparable data and time complexities but with a much lower memory complexity of 2^9. Consequently, the new technique did not improve the best previously known attack on 5 rounds, and its extensions to more than 5 rounds (see [19]) were significantly inferior to other attacks.

In this paper we greatly improve Grassi's attack, and show how to attack 5-round AES in data, memory and time complexities of less than $2^{22.5}$, which is about 500 times faster than any previous attack on the same variant. Due to the exceptionally low complexity of our attack, we could verify it experimentally by running it on real data generated from hundreds of randomly chosen keys. As we expected, the success rate of our full key recovery attack rose sharply from 0.24 to 1 as we increased the amount of available data from 2^{22} to 2^{23} in tiny increments of $2^{0.25}$.

By extending our technique to larger versions of AES, we obtain new attacks on AES-192 and AES-256 which have the best time complexity among all the attacks on 7-round AES which have practical data and memory complexities.

Low data and memory attacks were studied explicitly in a number of papers (e.g., [4,5,12]), but progress in applying such attacks to AES had been even slower than the progress in the "maximum complexity" metric. While some results were obtained on variants with up to 5 rounds, the best such attack on 6 and more rounds is still the improved Square attack presented by

Ferguson et al. [15] in 2000. We use the observation of Grassi et al., along with the *dissection* technique [14] and several other techniques, to beat this 18-year old record and develop the best attacks on 7-round AES in this model. In particular, our attack on 7-round AES with 192-bit keys requires 2^{30} data, 2^{32} memory and 2^{153} time, which outperforms the Square attack in all three complexity measures simultaneously.

A summary of the known and new key recovery attacks in the single key model on 5 and 7 rounds of AES appears in Tables 1 and 2, respectively. The specified complexities describe how difficult it is to find some of the key bytes. Since our new attacks can find with the same complexity any three key bytes which share the same generalized diagonal, we can rerun them several times for different diagonals to find the full key with only slightly elevated complexities.

Table 1. Attacks on 5-Round AES (partial key recovery)

Attack	Data	Memory	Time
	(Chosen plaintexts)	(128-bit blocks)	(encryptions)
MitM [11]	8	2^{56}	2^{64}
Imp. Polytopic [25]	15	2^{41}	2^{70}
Partial Sum [26]	2^8	small	2^{38}
Square [9]	2^{11}	small	2^{44}
Square [9]	2^{33}	2^{32}	2^{34}
Improved Square [15]	2^{33}	small	2^{33}
Yoyo [24]	$2^{11.3}$ ACC	small	2^{31}
Imp. Diff. [1]	$2^{31.5}$	2^{38}	2^{33}
Mixture Diff. [19]	2^{32}	2^{32}	2^{32}
Our Attack (Sect. 4)	$2^{22.25}$	2^{20}	$2^{22.5}$

ACC Adaptive Chosen Plaintexts and Ciphertexts

The paper is organized as follows. In Sect. 2 we briefly describe AES and introduce our notations, and in Sect. 3 we describe the new 4-round distinguisher which was discovered and used by Grassi. In Sect. 4 we show how to exploit this distinguisher in a better way to obtain improved attacks on 5-round AES. We extend the attack to 6-round AES in Sect. 5, and then extend it again to 7 rounds in Sect. 6. In Sect. 7 we explore other points on the time-memory-data tradeoff curve. Section 8 summarizes our paper.

2 Brief Introduction to the AES

2.1 A Short Description of AES

The Advanced Encryption Standard (AES) [9] is a substitution-permutation network which has 128 bit plaintexts and 128, 192, or 256 bit keys. Its 128 bit

Table 2. Attacks on 7-Round AES (full key recovery)

AES Variant	Attack	Data	Memory	Time
		(Chosen Plaintexts)	(128-bit blocks)	(encryptions)
AES-128	Imp. Diff. [6]	2^{105}	2^{74}	$2^{106.88}$
	MitM [13]	2^{97}	2^{98}	2^{99}
AES-192	MitM [13]	2^{97}	2^{98}	2^{99}
	MitM [12]	2^{32}	$2^{129.7}$	$2^{129.7}$
	Collision [18]	2^{32}	2^{80}	2^{140}
	Square [15]	$2^{36.2}$	$2^{36.2}$	2^{155}
	Our Attack (Sect. 6)	2^{30}	2^{32}	2^{153}
	Our Attack (Sect. 7)	2^{32}	2^{40}	2^{145}
AES-256	MitM [13]	2^{97}	2^{98}	2^{99}
	MitM [12]	2^{32}	$2^{133.7}$	$2^{133.7}$
	Collision [18]	2^{32}	2^{80}	2^{140}
	Square [15]	$2^{36.4}$	$2^{36.4}$	2^{172}
	Our Attack (Sect. 6)	2^{30}	2^{48}	$2^{161.6}$

internal state is treated as a byte matrix of size 4×4, where each byte represents a value in $GF(2^8)$. An AES round (described in Fig. 1) applies four operations to this state matrix:

- SubBytes (SB) — applying the same 8-bit to 8-bit invertible S-box 16 times in parallel on each byte of the state,
- ShiftRows (SR) — cyclically shifting the i'th row by i bytes to the left,
- MixColumns (MC) — multiplication of each column by a constant 4×4 matrix over the field $GF(2^8)$, and
- AddRoundKey (ARK) — XORing the state with a 128-bit subkey.

An additional AddRoundKey operation is applied before the first round, and in the last round the MixColumns operation is omitted.

For the sake of simplicity we shall denote AES with n-bit keys by AES-n. The number of rounds depends on the key length: 10 rounds for 128-bit keys, 12 rounds for 192-bit keys, and 14 rounds for 256-bit keys. The rounds are numbered $0, \ldots, Nr - 1$, where Nr is the number of rounds. We use 'AES' to denote all three variants of AES.

The key schedule of AES transforms the key into $Nr + 1$ 128-bit subkeys. We denote the subkey array by $W[0, \ldots, 4 \cdot Nr + 3]$, where each word of $W[\cdot]$ consists of 32 bits. When the length of the key is Nk 32-bit words, the user supplied key is loaded into the first Nk words of $W[\cdot]$, and the remaining words of $W[\cdot]$ are updated according to the following rule:

- For $i = Nk, \ldots, 4 \cdot Nr + 3$, do
  - If $i \equiv 0 \bmod Nk$ then $W[i] = W[i - Nk] \oplus SB(W[i - 1] \lll 8) \oplus RCON[i/Nk]$,

- else if $Nk = 8$ and $i \equiv 4 \bmod 8$ then $W[i] = W[i-8] \oplus SB(W[i-1])$,
- Otherwise $W[i] = W[i-1] \oplus W[i-Nk]$,

where $\lll$ denotes rotation of the word by 8 bits to the left, and $RCON[\cdot]$ is an array of predetermined constants.

2.2   Notations

In the sequel we use the following definitions and notations.

The state matrix at the beginning of round i is denoted by x_i, and its bytes are denoted by $0, 1, 2, \ldots, 15$, as described in Fig. 1. Similarly, the state matrix after the SubBytes and the ShiftRows operations of round i are denoted by x_i' and x_i'', respectively. The difference between two values in state x_i is denoted by $\Delta(x_i)$. We use this notation only when it is clear from the context which are the values whose difference we refer to.

We denote the subkey of round i by k_i, and the first (whitening) key by k_{-1}, i.e., $k_i = W[4 \cdot (i+1)] \| W[4 \cdot (i+1)+1] \| W[4 \cdot (i+1)+2] \| W[4 \cdot (i+1)+3]$. In some cases, we are interested in interchanging the order of the MixColumns operation and the subkey addition. As these operations are linear they can be interchanged, by first XORing the data with an equivalent subkey and only then applying the MixColumns operation. We denote the equivalent subkey for the altered version by u_i, i.e., $u_i = MC^{-1}(k_i)$. The bytes of the subkeys are numbered by $0, 1, \ldots, 15$, in accordance with the corresponding state bytes.

In cases when we interchange the order of the MixColumns operation of round i and the subkey addition, we denote the state right after the subkey addition (and just before the MixColumns operation) by $\bar{x}_i$.

The plaintext is sometimes denoted by x_{-1}, and so $x_0 = x_{-1} \oplus k_{-1}$.

The j'th byte of the state x_i is denoted $x_{i,j}$. When several bytes $j_1, \ldots, j_\ell$ are considered simultaneously, they are denoted $x_{i,\{j_1,\ldots,j_\ell\}}$. When a full column is considered, it is denoted $x_{i,\mathrm{Col}(j)}$, and if several columns are considered simultaneously, we denote them by $x_{i,\mathrm{Col}(j_1,\ldots,j_\ell)}$.

Sometimes we are interested in 'shifted' columns, i.e., the result of the application of ShiftRows to a set of columns. This is denoted by $x_{i,SR(\mathrm{Col}(j_1,\ldots,j_\ell))}$. Similarly, a set of 'inverse shifted' columns (i.e., the result of the application of SR^{-1} to a set of columns) is denoted by $x_{i,SR^{-1}(\mathrm{Col}(j_1,\ldots,j_\ell))}$.

In the attacks on 5-round AES (both Grassi's attack and our attack), we consider encryptions of a quartet of values. To simplify notations, while the plaintext/ciphertext pairs are denoted by (P_j, C_j), $j = 1, \ldots, 4$, we denote the intermediate values by (x_i, y_i, z_i, w_i), where x_i corresponds to the encryption process of P_1 and so $x_{-1} = P_1$, y_i corresponds to the encryption process of P_2 and so $y_{-1} = P_2$, etc.

In the attacks on 6-round and 7-round AES, we consider encryptions of several (e.g., 4 or 8) pairs of values. To simplify notations, in this case we denote the plaintext pairs by $(P_j, \hat{P}_j)$, $j = 1, \ldots, 8$, the corresponding ciphertext pairs by $(C_j, \hat{C}_j)$, $j = 1, \ldots, 8$, and the corresponding pairs of intermediate values by $(x_{i,\ell}^j, \hat{x}_{i,\ell}^j)$, for $j = 1, \ldots, 8$.

In all attacks, we exploit plaintext pairs $(P, \hat{P})$ for which the corresponding intermediate values satisfy $\Delta(x''_{4,SR(\text{Col}(0))}) = 0$ (i.e., have a zero difference in the first shifted column just before the MixColumns operation of round 4). Hence, throughout the paper we call such pairs *good pairs*.

Finally, we measure the time complexity of all the attacks in units which are equivalent to a single encryption operation of the relevant reduced round variant of AES. We measure the space complexity in units which are equivalent to the storage of a single plaintext (namely, 128 bits). To be completely fair, we count all operations carried out during our attacks, and in particular we do not ignore the time and space required to prepare the various tables we use.

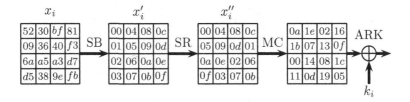

Fig. 1. An AES Round

3   The 4-Round Distinguisher of Grassi

In this section we present the distinguisher for 4-round AES, which serves as the basis to all our attacks. The distinguisher was presented by Grassi [19], as a variant of the 5-round distinguisher introduced at Eurocrypt'17 by Grassi et al. [20]. Note that the distinguisher holds in a more general setting than the one presented here. For sake of simplicity, we concentrate on the special case used in our attacks.

Definition 1. *Let x_i, y_i be two intermediate values at the input to round i of AES, such that $x_{i,\text{Col}(1,2,3)} = y_{i,\text{Col}(1,2,3)}$ (i.e., x_i and y_i may differ only in the first column). We say that (z_i, w_i) is a* mixture *of (x_i, y_i) if for each $j = 0, 1, 2, 3$, the unordered pairs $(x_{i,j}, y_{i,j})$ and $(z_{i,j}, w_{i,j})$ are equal. That is, either the j'th bytes of z_i and w_i are equal to those of x_i and y_i, respectively, or they are swapped. In such a case, (x_i, y_i, z_i, w_i) is called a* mixture quadruple.

Remark 1. Note that for each (x_i, y_i) such that $x_{i,j} \neq y_{i,j}$ for all $j = 0, 1, 2, 3$, there are 7 possible (unordered) mixtures that can be represented by vectors in $\{0, 1\}^4$ which record whether $z_{i,j}$ is equal to $x_{i,j}$ or to $y_{i,j}$, for $j = 0, 1, 2, 3$. For example, (1000) corresponds to the mixture (z_i, w_i) such that $z_{i,\text{Col}(0)} = (x_{i,0}, y_{i,1}, y_{i,2}, y_{i,3})$ and $w_{i,\text{Col}(0)} = (y_{i,0}, x_{i,1}, x_{i,2}, x_{i,3})$.

Observation 1. *Let* (x_i, y_i, z_i, w_i) *be a mixture quadruple of intermediate values at the input to round* i *of AES. Then the corresponding intermediate values* $(x_{i+2}, y_{i+2}, z_{i+2}, w_{i+2})$ *sum up to zero, i.e.,*

$$x_{i+2} \oplus y_{i+2} \oplus z_{i+2} \oplus w_{i+2} = 0. \tag{1}$$

Consequently, if for $j \in \{0, 1, 2, 3\}$ *we have* $x_{i+2,SR^{-1}(\mathrm{Col}(j))} \oplus y_{i+2,SR^{-1}(\mathrm{Col}(j))} = 0$, *then the corresponding intermediate values* $(x''_{i+3}, y''_{i+3}, z''_{i+3}, w''_{i+3})$ *(i.e., just before the MixColumns operation of round* $i + 3$) *satisfy*

$$x''_{i+3,SR(\mathrm{Col}(j))} \oplus y''_{i+3,SR(\mathrm{Col}(j))} = z''_{i+3,SR(\mathrm{Col}(j))} \oplus w''_{i+3,SR(\mathrm{Col}(j))} = 0.$$

Proof. Let (x_i, y_i, z_i, w_i) be as in the assumption. The mixture structure is preserved through the SubBytes operation of round i, and then ShiftRows spreads the active bytes between the columns, such that each column contains exactly one of them. As a result, for each $j \in \{0, 1, 2, 3\}$, the unordered pairs $(x''_{i,\mathrm{Col}(j)}, y''_{i,\mathrm{Col}(j)})$ and $(z''_{i,\mathrm{Col}(j)}, w''_{i,\mathrm{Col}(j)})$ are equal. This property is clearly preserved by MixColumns and by the subsequent AddRoundKey and SubBytes operations. It follows that the intermediate values $(x'_{i+1}, y'_{i+1}, z'_{i+1}, w'_{i+1})$ sum up to zero. As ShiftRows, MixColumns, and AddRoundKey are linear operations, this implies $x_{i+2} \oplus y_{i+2} \oplus z_{i+2} \oplus w_{i+2} = 0$.

Now, if for some j we have $x_{i+2,SR^{-1}(\mathrm{Col}(j))} \oplus y_{i+2,SR^{-1}(\mathrm{Col}(j))} = 0$, then by the round structure of AES we have $x_{i+3,\mathrm{Col}(j)} \oplus y_{i+3,\mathrm{Col}(j)} = 0$, and thus, $x''_{i+3,SR(\mathrm{Col}(j))} \oplus y''_{i+3,SR(\mathrm{Col}(j))} = 0$. Furthermore, by (1) we have $z_{i+2,SR^{-1}(\mathrm{Col}(j))} \oplus w_{i+2,SR^{-1}(\mathrm{Col}(j))} = 0$, and thus by the same reasoning as for (x, y), we get $z''_{i+3,SR(\mathrm{Col}(j))} \oplus w''_{i+3,SR(\mathrm{Col}(j))} = 0$, as asserted.

Grassi [19] used his distinguisher to mount an attack on 5-round AES with data, memory, and time complexities of roughly 2^{32}. The attack algorithm is given in Algorithm 1.

Algorithm 1. Grassi's 5-Round Attack

1: Ask for the encryption of 2^{32} chosen plaintexts in which $SR^{-1}(\mathrm{Col}(0))$ assumes all 2^{32} possible values and the rest of the bytes are constant.
2: Find a pair of ciphertexts $(C_1, C_2) = (x_5, y_5)$ with zero difference in $SR(\mathrm{Col}(0))$.
3: **for** each guess of $k_{-1,SR^{-1}(\mathrm{Col}(0))}$ **do**
4:     Partially encrypt the corresponding plaintexts $(P_1, P_2) = (x_{-1}, y_{-1})$ through AddRoundKey and round 0 to obtain (x_1, y_1).
5:     Let (z_1, w_1) be a mixture of (x_1, y_1), partially decrypt it to find the corresponding plaintext pair $(P_3, P_4) = (z_{-1}, w_{-1})$, and denote the corresponding ciphertexts by $(C_3, C_4) = (z_5, w_5)$.
6:     **if** (z_5, w_5) does not satisfy $z_{5,SR(\mathrm{Col}(0))} \oplus w_{5,SR(\mathrm{Col}(0))} = 0$ **then**
7:         discard the key guess $k_{-1,SR^{-1}(\mathrm{Col}(0))}$.
8:     **end if**
9: **end for**
10: Repeat Steps (1)–(8) for the other three columns, and check the remaining key guesses by trial encryption.

The structure of chosen plaintexts is expected to contain about $2^{63} \cdot 2^{-32} = 2^{31}$ pairs for which the ciphertexts have a zero difference in $SR(\text{Col}(0))$. The adversary can find one of them easily in time 2^{32}, using a hash table. Step 3 of the attack requires only a few operations for each key guess. Since (x_1, y_1, z_1, w_1) form a mixture quadruple, by Observation 1 we know that if (x_5, y_5) have zero difference in $SR(\text{Col}(0))$, then we must have $z_{5, SR(\text{Col}(0))} \oplus w_{5, SR(\text{Col}(0))} = 0$. (Note that the MixColumns operation in the last round is omitted, and thus, the difference in the state z_5 is equal to the difference in the state z_4'' discussed in Observation 1.) Therefore, if the condition fails, we can safely discard the key guess. The probability of a random key to pass this filtering is 2^{-32}, and thus, we expect only a few key guesses to remain. Thus, the data, memory, and time complexities for recovering 32 key bits are 2^{32}, and for recovering the full key are 2^{34}.

4 Improved Attack on 5-Round AES

In this section we present our improved attack on 5-round AES, which requires less than $2^{22.5}$ data, memory, and time to recover 24 key bits and less than $2^{25.5}$ data, memory, and time to recover the full key. This is the first attack on 5-round AES whose all complexities are below 2^{32}. The attack was fully verified experimentally.

Our attack is based on Grassi's attack and enhances it using several observations. First we present and analyze the observations, then we present the attack algorithm and analyze its complexity, and finally we describe the experiments we performed to verify the attack.

4.1 The Observations Behind the Attack

1. Reducing the data complexity to 2^{24}. Our first observation is that we can reduce the amount of data significantly, and still find the mixture quadruple we need for Grassi's attack. Indeed, as mentioned above, when we start with 2^{32} plaintexts, it is expected that the data contains about 2^{31} mixture quadruples, while we need only one mixture quadruple for the attack.

Instead, we may start with 2^{24} plaintexts taken arbitrarily from the structure of size 2^{32} used in Grassi's attack. These plaintexts form 2^{47} pairs, and we expect that in 2^{15} of them, the ciphertexts have zero difference in $SR(\text{Col}(0))$. Fix one such pair, $(C_1, C_2) = (x_5, y_5)$. For each guess of the 32 bits of $k_{-1, SR^{-1}(\text{Col}(0))}$, and for each of the 7 possible types of mixture, the probability that the mixture of (x_1, y_1) is contained in our data set is $(2^{24}/2^{32})^2 = 2^{-16}$. As there are 2^{15} possible pairs (x_5, y_5) and 7 possible types of mixture, we expect that with probability $1 - (1 - 2^{-16})^{7 \cdot 2^{15}} \approx 0.97$, that the data contains a mixture quadruple with respect to the correct value of $k_{-1, SR^{-1}(\text{Col}(0))}$, which is sufficient for mounting the attack. Hence, the data complexity can be reduced to 2^{24} chosen plaintexts. As the memory is used only to store and filter the data, the memory complexity is reduced to 2^{24}, as well.

However, if we simply apply Grassi's attack with the reduced number of plaintexts, its time complexity is increased significantly due to the need to go over the 2^{15} pairs of (x_5, y_5) for each key guess. This will be resolved in the next observations.

2. Reducing the time complexity by changing the order of operations. Our second observation is that if (x_1, y_1, z_1, w_1) is a mixture quadruple then $x_1 \oplus y_1 \oplus z_1 \oplus w_1 = 0$, and consequently, $x_0'' \oplus y_0'' \oplus z_0'' \oplus w_0'' = 0$ as well. This allows to perform a preliminary check of whether (x_1, y_1, z_1, w_1) can be a mixture quadruple, by checking a local condition for each of the bytes in $k_{-1, SR^{-1}(\text{Col}(0))}$ separately (i.e., bytes 0,5,10,15). That is, given a quartet of plaintexts (P_1, P_2, P_3, P_4), we can perform the check whether it is a mixture quadruple using Algorithm 2.

Algorithm 2. Efficient Guessing of $k_{-1, SR^{-1}(\text{Col}(0))}$

1: **for** each guess of $k_{-1,0}$ **do**
2:     Compute the corresponding differences $x_{0,0}'' \oplus y_{0,0}''$ and $z_{0,0}'' \oplus w_{0,0}''$.
3:     **if** $x_{0,0}'' \oplus y_{0,0}'' \neq z_{0,0}'' \oplus w_{0,0}''$ **then**
4:         Discard the guess of $k_{-1,0}$.
5:     **end if**
6: **end for**
7: Repeat the above steps for bytes 5,10,15 of k_{-1} and bytes 1,2,3 of x'', y'', z'', and w'', respectively.
8: **for** each remaining guess of $k_{-1, \{SR^{-1}(\text{Col}(0))\}}$ **do**
9:     Encrypt the quartet through round 0.
10:     Check whether the values (x_1, y_1, z_1, w_1) constitute a mixture quadruple.
11: **end for**

We can use this procedure to replace the guess of $k_{-1, SR^{-1}(\text{Col}(0))}$ performed in Grassi's attack. Specifically, as described above, given 2^{24} plaintexts, we expect 2^{15} pairs in which the ciphertexts have zero difference in $SR(\text{Col}(0))$. We take all 2^{29} pairs of such pairs, and the procedure is applied for each of them.

As Steps 1–7 offer a 32-bit filtering condition, it is expected that only a few suggestions of the key $k_{-1, SR^{-1}(\text{Col}(0)}$ pass to Steps 8–11. Then, each suggestion is checked using a 1-round partial encryption. It is clear that if the data set contains a mixture quadruple (which occurs with a decent probability as described above), then the procedure will succeed for the right guess of $k_{-1, SR^{-1}(\text{Col}(0)}$. For a wrong guess, the probability to pass Steps 1 and 2 is 2^{-64}, and so all wrong guesses are expected to be discarded.

Let us analyze the complexity of the attack. In Steps 1–6 we go over the 2^8 possible values of $k_{-1,0}$, and check the condition for each of them separately. The same goes for each repetition of Step 7. The complexity of Steps 8–11 is even lower. Hence, the overall complexity of the attack is $2^{29} \cdot 2^8 \cdot 4 = 2^{39}$ applications of a single S-box, which are roughly equivalent to 2^{33} encryptions.

3. Reducing the time complexity even further by using a precomputed table. We can further reduce the time complexity of this step using a precomputed table of size $2^{21.4}$ bytes. To construct the table, we consider each quartet of inputs to SubBytes of the form $(0, a, b, c)$, where (a, b, c) are arranged in increasing order (e.g., as numbers in base 2).[1] For each quartet, we go over the 2^8 values of the key byte $\hat{k}$ and store in the entry (a, b, c) of the table the values of $\hat{k}$ for which

$$SB(\hat{k}) \oplus SB(a \oplus \hat{k}) \oplus SB(b \oplus \hat{k}) \oplus SB(c \oplus \hat{k}) = 0. \tag{2}$$

It is expected that a single value of $\hat{k}$ satisfies Condition (2). Now, if we are given a quartet (x, y, z, w) of plaintext bytes and want to find the value of $k_{-1,0}$ such that the four intermediate values after SubBytes sum up to zero, we do the following:

1. Consider the quartet $(0, y \oplus x, z \oplus x, w \oplus x)$.
2. Reorder it using the binary ordering to obtain $(0, a, b, c)$ with $a < b < c$. Then access the table at the entry (a, b, c) and retrieve the value $\hat{k}$.
3. Set $k_{-1,0} = \hat{k} \oplus x$.

The key $k_{-1,0}$ we found is indeed the right one, since the values after the addition of $k_{0,-1}$ are $(\hat{k}, \hat{k} \oplus y, \hat{k} \oplus z, \hat{k} \oplus w)$, and thus Condition (2) means exactly that the four values after SubBytes sum up to zero.

The table requires $2^{24}/3! \approx 2^{21.4}$ bytes of memory. In a naive implementation, its generation requires $2^{21.4} \cdot 2^8 = 2^{29.4}$ applications of a single S-box and a few more XOR operations, which is less than $2^{23.4}$ 5-round encryptions. However, it can be generated much faster, as follows.

Instead of going over all triplets (a, b, c) and for each of them going over all values of $\hat{k}$, we go over triplets $a, b, \hat{k}$. For each of them, we compute $t = SB(\hat{k}) \oplus SB(a \oplus \hat{k}) \oplus SB(b \oplus \hat{k})$. We know that Condition 2 holds for $(a, b, c, \hat{k})$ if and only if $SB(c \oplus \hat{k}) = t$, or equivalently, $c = SB^{-1}(t) \oplus \hat{k}$. (Note that this value may not be unique). Therefore, we write $\hat{k}$ in the table entry/entries of $(a, b, SB^{-1}(t) \oplus \hat{k})$ and move to the next value of $\hat{k}$. In this way, the table generation requires less than 2^{24} S-box applications, which is negligible with respect to other steps of the attack.

Once the table is constructed, Step 1 of the procedure described in Improvement 2 can be performed by 4 table lookups. Hence, the total time complexity of the attack is reduced to 2^{29} times (4 table lookups + one round of encryption), which is less than 2^{29} encryptions.

4. Reducing the overall complexity to $2^{22.25}$ by a wise choice of plaintexts. So far, we reduced the data and memory complexity to 2^{24} and the time complexity to 2^{29}. We show now that all three parameters can be reduced to about $2^{22.25}$ by a specific choice of the plaintexts.

---

[1] As the quartets in which in some byte, not all four values are distinct, are less than 7% of the quartets, we can remove them from the analysis for sake of simplicity, with a negligible effect on the attack's complexity.

Recall that in Improvement 1 we assumed that the 2^{24} plaintexts are arbitrarily taken from the structure of size 2^{32} used in Grassi's attack (in which $SR^{-1}(\text{Col}(0))$ assume all possible values and the rest of the bytes are constant). Instead of doing this, we choose all plaintexts such that byte 0 is constant in all of them. We claim that this significantly increases the probability of a plaintext quartet to form a mixture quadruple.

Indeed, let us fix (P_1, P_2) and a type of mixture, and estimate the probability that for another pair (P_3, P_4), the intermediate values (x_1, y_1, z_1, w_1) form a mixture quadruple of the fixed type. The check can be performed in two steps, like in the procedure described in Improvement 2. First we check whether the corresponding intermediate values (x_1, y_1, z_1, w_1) sum up to zero (a 32-bit condition), and only then we check that the quadruple is indeed a mixture (which is a 31-bit condition, since as we already know that the four values sum up to zero, once the condition for z_1 holds, the condition for w_1 holds for free, and there are two possibilities for the ordering between z_1 and w_1). As described in Improvement 2, the first condition is translated to four independent conditions of the form $x''_{0,j} \oplus y''_{0,j} \oplus z''_{0,j} \oplus w''_{0,j} = 0$, for $j \in \{0, 1, 2, 3\}$. In our case, due to the choice of plaintexts, the condition in byte 0 holds for free! Therefore, the overall probability is boosted from 2^{-63} to 2^{-55}.

On the other hand, we note that only three of the 7 types of mixture are possible in this case. Indeed, in the mixtures of types $(1000), (0100), (0010)$ and (0001), there are two of the values (x_1, y_1, z_1, w_1) which differ in a single byte. As all four values $x''_0, y''_0, z''_0, w''_0$ agree on byte 0, this is impossible since the branching number of the MixColumns operation is 5 (which means that for any pair of inputs/outputs to MC, the number of bytes in which the inputs differ plus the number of bytes in which the outputs differ is at least 5).

Therefore, the probability of (P_3, P_4) taken from our structure to lead into a mixture quadruple with (P_1, P_2) is expected to be $3 \cdot 2^{-55}$. This allows us to reduce the data complexity, and consequently, also the memory and time complexities.

Assume that we start with $2^{22.25}$ plaintexts, taken arbitrarily from the 2^{24} plaintexts that assume all values in bytes $5, 10, 15$ and have all other bytes constant. These plaintexts form $(2^{22.25})^2/2 = 2^{43.5}$ unordered pairs, and thus, 2^{86} unordered pairs of pairs. The probability that a pair-of-pairs gives rise to a mixture quadruple is $3 \cdot 2^{-55}$. Hence, we expect $3 \cdot 2^{-55} \cdot 2^{86} = 3 \cdot 2^{31}$ mix quadruples. With a 'decent' probability, in at least one of them, the ciphertexts (C_1, C_2) have zero difference in $SR(\text{Col}(0))$, and thus, it can be used for the attack.

In the attack, we first insert the ciphertexts into a hash table to find the pairs for which the ciphertexts have zero difference in $SR(\text{Col}(0))$. It is expected that $2^{43.5} \cdot 2^{-32} = 2^{11.5}$ pairs are found. Then, for each of the $(2^{11.5})^2/2 = 2^{22}$ pairs-of-pairs, we check whether the corresponding intermediate values (x_1, y_1, z_1, w_1) constitute a mixture quadruple, as described in Improvement 3. Thus, the time complexity is reduced by a factor of 2^7 (as we have to check 2^{22} quartets instead of 2^{29}), and so the time complexity is less than 2^{22} encryptions, which is less than the time required for encrypting the plaintexts.

5. Reducing the data complexity a bit further by checking several columns instead of one. Finally, the data complexity can be reduced a bit further by considering not only plaintext pairs for which the ciphertexts have zero difference in $SR(\text{Col}(0))$, but also pairs for which the ciphertexts satisfy the same condition for one of the columns 1,2,3. This increases the probability of a quartet to be useful for the attack by a factor of 4, and thus, allows us to reduce the data complexity by another factor of $4^{1/4} = \sqrt{2}$. On the other hand, this requires to use four hash tables to filter the ciphertexts (each corresponding to a different shifted column of the ciphertext), and thus, increases the memory complexity by a factor of 4. As this is not a clear improvement but rather a data/memory tradeoff, we do not include it in the attack algorithm below.

4.2   The Attack Algorithm and Its Analysis

The algorithm of our 5-round attack is given in Algorithm 3.

Algorithm 3. Efficient 5-Round Attack

Preprocessing
1: Initialize an empty table T.
2: **for** all $a < b < c$ **do**
3:     Store in $T[a, b, c]$ all bytes values $\hat{k}$ which satisfy $SB(\hat{k}) \oplus SB(a \oplus \hat{k}) \oplus SB(b \oplus \hat{k}) \oplus SB(c \oplus \hat{k}) = 0$.
4: **end for**
   Online phase
5: Ask for the encryption of $2^{22.25}$ chosen plaintexts in which bytes $5, 10, 15$ assume different values and the rest of the bytes are constant.
6: Store in a list L all ciphertext pairs (C_1, C_2) such that $C_{1,SR(\text{Col}(0))} \oplus C_{2,SR(\text{Col}(0))} = 0$.
7: **for** all pairs of pairs $(C_1, C_2), (C_3, C_4) \in L$ **do**
8:     Let the corresponding plaintexts be $(P_1, P_2, P_3, P_4) = (x_{-1}, y_{-1}, z_{-1}, w_{-1})$, respectively.
9:     Compute the values $(y_{-1,5} \oplus x_{-1,5}, z_{-1,5} \oplus x_{-1,5}, w_{-1,5} \oplus x_{-1,5})$, and sort the three bytes in an increasing order to obtain (a, b, c).
10:     **for** each value $\hat{k}$ in $T[a, b, c]$ **do**
11:         Store in L_5 the value $k_{-1,5} = \hat{k} \oplus x_{-1,5}$.
12:     **end for**
13:     Repeat the above steps for bytes 10 and 15 (with lists L_{10} and L_{15}, respectively).
14:     **for** all subkey candidates $(k_{-1,5} \in L_5, k_{-1,10} \in L_{10}, k_{-1,15} \in L_{15})$ **do**
15:         Partially encrypt (P_1, P_2, P_3, P_4) through round 0 and compute x_1, y_1, z_1, w_1.
16:         **if** (x_1, y_1, z_1, w_1) does not constitute a mixture quadruple **then**
17:             Discard subkey candidate.
18:         **end if**
19:     **end for**
20: **end for**
21: Output all guesses of $k_{-1,5}, k_{-1,10}, k_{-1,15}$ which remained.

As described in Improvement 4, T can be prepared in time of $2^{21.4}$ S-box evaluations, and contains $2^{21.4}$ byte values. Steps 5,6 can be easily performed in time $2^{22.25}$ using a hash table of size $2^{22.25}$ 24-bit values, which are less than 2^{20} 128-bit blocks. The expected size of the list L is $2^{43.5} \cdot 2^{-32} = 2^{11.5}$. Hence, Steps 7–20 are performed for 2^{22} pairs of pairs. As described in Improvement 4, these steps take less than a single encryption for each quartet, and thus, their total complexity is less than 2^{22} encryptions. Therefore, the data complexity of the attack is $2^{22.25}$ chosen plaintexts, the memory complexity is 2^{20} 128-bit blocks, and the time complexity is dominated by encrypting the plaintexts.

It is clear from the algorithm that if the data contains a mixture quadruple for which the ciphertexts (P_1, P_2) have zero difference in $SR(\mathrm{Col}(0))$, then for the right value of $k_{-1,\{5,10,15\}}$, this quadruple will be found and so the right key will remain. The probability of a wrong key suggestion to remain is extremely low, as in the attack we examine $((2^{22.25})^2/2)^2/2 = 2^{86}$ quartets and the filtering condition is on about 117.4 bits (which consist of 64 bits on the ciphertext side – requiring zero difference in $SR(\mathrm{Col}(0))$ for two ciphertext pairs, and 53.4 bits on the plaintext side – requiring that the values (x_1, y_1, z_1, w_1) constitute a mixture quadruple). So, the probability for a wrong key to pass the filtering is $2^{-31.4}$. As there are 2^{24} possible key suggestions, with a high probability no wrong keys remain.

Note that the attack does not recover the value of $k_{-1,0}$ since the question whether a quartet of plaintexts in the structure evolves into a mixture quadruple does not depend on $k_{-1,0}$.

In order to recover the full key, we repeat the attack for each of the four columns on the plaintext side, and apply it once again for the first column, with byte 15 as the 'constant byte' instead of byte 0. This recovers $4 \cdot 24 + 8 = 104$ bits of the key, and the rest of the key can be recovered by exhaustive key search. Therefore, for full key recovery we need data complexity of $5 \cdot 2^{22.25} \approx 2^{24.6}$ chosen plaintexts, memory complexity of 2^{20} 128-bit blocks (as the memory can be reused between the attacks), and time complexity of less than $2^{25.5}$ encryptions.

It is clear from the above analysis that the attack succeeds with a high probability, that can be made very close to 100% by increasing the data complexity by a factor of 2. To achieve the exact value, we fully implemented the attack experimentally.

4.3 Experimental Verification

We have successfully implemented the 5-round attack. To verify our attack success probability and its dependence on the data complexity, we performed the following experiment. We took four possible amounts of data, $2^{22}, 2^{22.25}, 2^{22.5}$, and 2^{23} chosen plaintexts, and for each of them we ran the attack which recovers 3 key bytes for 200 different keys. The results we obtained were the following: For 2^{22} plaintexts, the attack succeeded 100 times. For $2^{22.25}$ plaintexts, the attack succeeded 143 times. For $2^{22.5}$ plaintexts, the attack succeeded 187 times, and for 2^{23} plaintexts, the attack succeeded in all 200 experiments.

Based on these experiments, we calculated the success probability of full key recovery as p^5, where p is the probability of recovering three key bytes (as in order to recover the full key we have to perform 5 essentially independent variants of the attack). Similarly, we calculated the probability when two diagonals in the ciphertext are examined as $1-(1-p)^2$, since the attack fails only if two essentially independent applications of the basic attack fail.

The full details are given in Table 3. As can be seen in the table, with $2^{22.5}$ chosen plaintexts, checking a single diagonal on the ciphertext side is already sufficient for a success rate of over 93% for recovering the first 3 key bytes, and over 70% for recovering the entire key. With $2^{22.25}$ plaintexts, checking a single diagonal in the ciphertext is sufficient for recovering 3 key bytes with success rate of over 70%, but if we want success rate of over 65% for recovering the entire key, we have to check another diagonal on the ciphertext side, which slightly increases the memory complexity to 2^{21} 128-bit blocks.

Table 3. Success probability of the attack for different data complexities

Structure size Key material	One diagonal		Two diagonals	
	3 Bytes	Full key	3 Bytes	Full key
2^{22}	0.5	0.031	0.75	0.24
$2^{22.25}$	0.715	0.187	0.919	0.655
$2^{22.5}$	0.935	0.715	0.996	0.979
2^{23}	1	1	1	1

The experimental results clearly support our analysis presented above. We note that the significant increase of the success rate when the data complexity is increased very moderately follows from the fact that the attack examines quartets, and so multiplying the data by a modest factor of $2^{0.25}$ doubles the number of quartets that can be used in the attack.

5   Attacks on 6-Round AES

In this section we present attacks on 6-round AES. We start with a simple extension of Grassi's attack to 6 rounds, and then we present several improvements that allow reducing the attack complexity significantly. Our best attack has data and memory complexities of $2^{27.5}$ and time complexity of 2^{81}. These results are not very interesting on their own sake, as they are clearly inferior to the improved Square attack on the same variant of AES [15]. However, a further extension of the same attack techniques will allow us obtaining an attack on 7-round AES-192, which clearly outperforms all known attacks on reduced-round AES-192 with practical data and memory complexities (including the improved Square attack).

5.1   An Extension of Grassi's Attack to 6 Rounds

Recall that in Grassi's attack on 5-round AES, we take a structure of 2^{32} plaintexts that differ only in $SR^{-1}(\text{Col}(0))$, and search for ciphertext pairs that have zero difference in $SR(\text{Col}(0))$. Actually, the 4-round distinguisher underlying the attack guarantees a zero difference only in the state $x''_{4,SR(\text{Col}(0))}$, but as the 5th round is the last one, the MixColumns operation is omitted, and so, the zero difference can be seen in the ciphertext.

When we consider 6-round AES, in order to recover the state $x''_{4,SR(\text{Col}(0))}$ by partial decryption we must guess all 128 key bits. However, we can recover one of these 4 bytes by guessing only four equivalent key bytes. Indeed, if we guess $k_{5,SR(\text{Col}(0))}$ and interchange the order between the MixColumns and AddRoundKey operations of round 4, we can partially decrypt the ciphertexts through round 5 and MixColumns to obtain the value of byte 0 before MixColumns. As AddRoundKey does not affect differences, this allows us evaluating differences at the state $x''_{4,0}$.

By the distinguisher, the difference in this byte for both pairs in the mixture quadruple is zero. However, this is only an 16-bit filtering. In order to obtain an additional filtering, we recall that by Remark 1, each pair has 7 mixtures. Checking the condition for all of them, we get a 64-bit filtering, that is sufficient for discarding almost all wrong key guesses. The attack is given in Algorithm 4.

For the right key guess, it is expected that after 2^{32} pairs $(P_1, \hat{P}_1)$, we will encounter a good pair (i.e., a pair for which the difference in the state $x''_{4,SR(\text{Col}(0))}$ is zero), and then by the distinguisher, the difference in the same state for all other 7 mixtures is zero as well. Hence, the right key is expected to be suggested. (Concretely, the probability that the right key is not suggested is $(1-2^{-32})^{2^{32}} \approx e^{-1}$). For wrong key guesses, for each pair $(P_1, \hat{P}_1)$, the probability to pass the filtering of Step 10 is 2^{-64}, and thus, the probability that there exists a guess of $k_{5,SR(\text{Col}(0))}$ that passes it is 2^{-32}. Hence, for all values of $(P_1, \hat{P}_1)$ except a few values, the list L_1 remains empty and the pair is discarded after Step 15. For the few remaining pairs, the probability that there exists a guess of $k_{5,SR(\text{Col}(1))}$ that passes the filtering of Step 17 is again 2^{-32}, and so, for all but very few guesses of $k_{-1,\{SR^{-1}(\text{Col}(0))\}}$, all pairs are discarded. The few remaining guesses are easily checked by trial encryption.

The most time consuming part of the attack is Steps 9,10, which are performed for 2^{64} key guesses and 2^{32} plaintext pairs. (Note that Step 17 is performed for a much smaller number of pairs, and thus is negligible.) Steps 9,10 essentially consist of partial decryption of one column through round 5 for 16 values – which is clearly less than a single 6-round encryption. Therefore, the time complexity of the attack is $2^{64} \cdot 2^{32} = 2^{96}$ encryptions. The memory complexity is 2^{32} (dominated by storing the plaintexts), and the success probability is $1 - e^{-1} = 0.63$. The attack recovers the full subkey k_5, which yields immediately the full secret key via the key scheduling algorithm.[2]

---

[2] We assume, for sake of simplicity, that the attack is mounted on AES-128. When the attack is applied to AES-192 or AES-256, the rest of the key can be recovered easily by auxiliary techniques.

Algorithm 4. Attacking 6-Round AES

1: Ask for the encryption of 2^{32} chosen plaintexts in which $SR^{-1}(\text{Col}(0))$ assumes all 2^{32} possible values and the rest of the bytes are constant.
2: **for** each guess of $k_{-1,SR^{-1}(\text{Col}(0))}$ **do**
3:     Select arbitrarily 2^{32} plaintexts pairs $(P_1^i, \hat{P}_1^i)$ from the structure.
4:     **for** each pair $(x_{-1}^1, y_{-1}^1) = (P_1, \hat{P}_1)$ **do**
5:         Partially encrypt $(x_{-1}^1, \hat{x}_{-1}^1)$ through round 0, obtain $(x_1^1, \hat{x}_1^1)$.
6:         Let the 7 mixtures of $(x_1^1, \hat{x}_1^1)$ be $(x_1^2, \hat{x}_1^2), \ldots, (x_1^8, \hat{x}_1^8)$.
7:         Partially decrypt the 7 mixtures to obtain the plaintext pairs $(P_2, \hat{P}_2) = (x_{-1}^2, \hat{x}_{-1}^2), \ldots, (P_8, \hat{P}_8) = (x_{-1}^8, \hat{x}_{-1}^8)$.
8:         **for** each value of $k_{5,SR(\text{Col}(0))}$ **do**
9:             Take all ciphertext pairs $(C_1, \hat{C}_1), \ldots, (C_8, \hat{C}_8)$.
10:             Partially decrypt them through rounds 5,4.
11:             **if** for all $1 \le j \le 8$: $x_{4,0}^{j''} \oplus \hat{x}_{4,0}^{j''} = 0$ (i.e., all 8 pairs have a zero difference in byte 0 before the MixColumns of round 4) **then**
12:                 Store $k_{5,SR(\text{Col}(0))}$ in a list L_1.
13:             **end if**
14:         **end for**
15:         **if** L_1 is empty **then**
16:             Discard the pair $(P_1, \hat{P}_1)$.
17:         **else**
18:             Repeat the same procedure for $k_{5,SR(\text{Col}(1))}$, with respect to the byte $x_{4,7}''$ and L_2.
19:             **if** L_2 is not empty **then**
20:                 Repeat the same procedure for $k_{5,SR(\text{Col}(2))}$ and $k_{5,SR(\text{Col}(3))}$, with respect to bytes $x_{4,10}''$ and $x_{4,15}''$, respectively.
21:                 Output the remaining key suggestion.
22:             **else**
23:                 Discard the pair $(P_1, \hat{P}_1)$.
24:             **end if**
25:         **end if**
26:     **end for**   ▷ If no pairs remain, move to the next guess of $k_{-1,SR^{-1}(\text{Col}(0))}$.
27: **end for**

5.2   Improvements of the 6-Round Attack

In this section we present two improvements of the 6-round attack described above, which allow us to reduce its complexity significantly. While the resulting attack is still inferior to some previously known attacks on 6-round AES, we describe the improvements here since they will be used in our attack on 7-round AES, and will be easier to understand in the 'simpler' case of the 6-round variant.

1. Using the meet-in-the-middle (MITM) approach. We observe that instead of guessing the subkey $k_{5,\{0,7,10,13\}}$, we can use a MITM procedure. Indeed, the difference in the byte $x_{4,0}''$ (which we want to evaluate in the attack) is a linear combination of the differences in the four bytes $x_{5,0}, x_{5,1}, x_{5,2}, x_{5,3}$.

Specifically, by the definition of MixColumns^{-1}, we have

$$\Delta(x_{4,0}'') = 0E_x \cdot \Delta(x_{5,0}) \oplus 0B_x \cdot \Delta(x_{5,1}) \oplus 0D_x \cdot \Delta(x_{5,2}) \oplus 09_x \cdot \Delta(x_{5,3}),$$

and thus the equation $\Delta(x_{4,0}'') = 0$ can be written in the form

$$0E_x \cdot \Delta(x_{5,0}) \oplus 0B_x \cdot \Delta(x_{5,1}) = 0D_x \cdot \Delta(x_{5,2}) \oplus 09_x \cdot \Delta(x_{5,3}). \quad (3)$$

Hence, instead of guessing the four key bytes $k_{5,\{0,7,10,13\}}$ which allow us to compute the values of $x_{5,0}, x_{5,1}, x_{5,2}, x_{5,3}$ and to check the 64-bit condition on the differences in $x_{4,0}''$, we can do the following:

1. Guess bytes $k_{5,\{0,7\}}$ and compute $x_{5,0}, x_{5,1}$. Store in a table the contribution of these bytes to Eq. (3), i.e., the concatenation of the values $0E_x \cdot \Delta(x_{5,0}^j) \oplus 0B_x \cdot \Delta(x_{5,1}^j)$ for $j = 1, \ldots, 8$.
2. Guess bytes $k_{5,\{10,13\}}$ and compute $x_{5,2}, x_{5,3}$. Compute the contribution of these bytes to Eq. (3), i.e., the concatenation of the values $0D_x \cdot \Delta(x_{5,2}^j) \oplus 09_x \cdot \Delta(x_{5,3}^j)$ for $j = 1, \ldots, 8$, and search it in the table.
3. For each match in the table, store in L_1 the combination $k_{5,\{0,7,10,13\}}$. If there are no matches in the table, discard the pair $(P_1, \hat{P}_1)$.

This meet-in-the-middle procedure is clearly equivalent to guessing $k_{5,\{0,7,10,13\}}$ and checking the condition on $x_{4,0}''$ directly. The time complexity of the procedure, for each pair $(P_1, \hat{P}_1)$, is $2 \cdot 2^{16}$ evaluations of two S-boxes for 16 ciphertexts, and $2 \cdot 2^{16}$ lookups into a table of size 2^{16}, which are less than 2^{16} encryptions.

This procedure can replace Steps 7–10 in the attack presented above, while all other parts of the attack remain unchanged. (Of course, Step 17 can be replaced similarly, but its complexity is anyway negligible.) This reduces the time complexity of the attack to $2^{32} \cdot 2^{32} \cdot 2^{16} = 2^{80}$ encryptions, without affecting the data and memory complexities.

2. Reducing the data complexity by using less mixtures. We would like to reduce the data complexity by considering only part of the structure of size 2^{32}, as we did in Improvement 1 of the 5-round attack. In order to get a significant reduction in the data complexity, we first need to reduce the number of mixtures used in the attack.

We observe that we may use 3 mixtures of each pair instead of all possible 7 mixtures. As a result, the filtering in Step 10 above is reduced to 32 bits, and thus, for each pair $(P_1, \hat{P}_1)$, about one value of $k_{5,\{0,7,10,13\}}$ is inserted into the list L_1. Similarly, in Steps 17, 19 it is expected that a few suggestions of the entire key k_5 remain *for each pair* $(P_1, \hat{P}_1)$. These suggestions are easily checked by trial encryption.

How does this modification affect the time complexity? On the one hand, Steps 9, 10 are now repeated four times for each pair $(P_1, \hat{P}_1)$. On the other hand, each application of this step becomes twice faster since the partial decryptions are performed for 8 ciphertexts instead of 16. Hence, the overall time complexity becomes $4 \cdot \frac{1}{2} \cdot 2^{80} = 2^{81}$ encryptions. The memory complexity remains unchanged, and so is the success probability.

The reduction of the number of mixtures allows us reducing the data complexity effectively, similarly to the reduction we did in Improvement 1 of the 5-round attack. Note that the entire structure of 2^{32} plaintext contains 2^{63} pairs, and about 2^{31} of them are good and so can be used in the attack. Hence, if we take a random subset S of the structure of size $\alpha 2^{32}$, the probability that one of these 2^{31} good pairs, along with at least three of its 7 mixtures, is included in S, is approximately $2^{31} \alpha^8 \cdot \binom{7}{3} \approx 2^{36} \alpha^8$. Hence, if we take $\alpha = 2^{-4.5}$, with a good probability the plaintext set S contains a pair that can be used in the attack.

Formally, the changes required in the attack algorithm are only in Steps 1–6, and are the following:

1. Take a structure of $2^{27.5}$ chosen plaintexts with the same value in all bytes but those of $SR^{-1}(\mathrm{Col}(0))$.
2. For each guess of subkey $k_{-1,SR^{-1}(\mathrm{Col}(0))}$, go over all pairs of plaintexts $(P_1, \hat{P}_1)$ in S, and for each of them do the following:
   (a) Partially encrypt $(P_1, \hat{P}_1) = (x^1_{-1}, \hat{x}^1_{-1})$ through AddRoundKey and round 0 to obtain $(x^1_1, \hat{x}^1_1)$. Consider all 7 mixtures of $(x^1_1, \hat{x}^1_1)$ (denoted by $(x^2_1, \hat{x}^2_1), \ldots, (x^8_1, \hat{x}^8_1)$), and partially decrypt them to find the corresponding plaintext pairs $(P_2, \hat{P}_2) = (x^2_{-1}, \hat{x}^2_{-1}), \ldots, (P_8, \hat{P}_8) = (x^8_{-1}, \hat{x}^8_{-1})$. Check whether for at least three of them, both plaintexts are included in S. If yes, continue as in the original attack. If no, discard the pair $(P_1, \hat{P}_1)$.

The complexity of checking all pairs $(P_1, \hat{P}_1)$ is less than 2^{54} encryptions, which is negligible with respect to other steps of the attack. Since the expected number of pairs that are not discarded instantly is 2^{32}, the attack complexity is the same as the original attack – 2^{81} encryptions. The success probability is $1 - (1 - 2^{-32})^{2^{32}} \approx 1 - e^{-1} = 0.63$, as in the original attack.

To summarize, the data and memory complexity of the improved attack is $2^{27.5}$, and its time complexity is 2^{81} encryptions. Both improvements will be used in the 7-round attacks presented in the next section.

6 Attacks on 7-Round AES-192 and AES-256

In this section we present our new attacks on 7-round AES. First we present the attack on AES-256, which extends the 6-round attack by another round using a MITM technique, and then uses *dissection* [14] to reduce the memory complexity of the attack. Then we show how in the case of AES-192, the key schedule can be used (in conjunction with a more complex dissection attack) to further reduce the data and time complexities of the attack. Our best attack on AES-192 recovers the full key with data complexity of 2^{30}, memory complexity of 2^{32}, and time complexity of 2^{153}, which is better than all previously known attacks on reduced-round AES-192 with practical data and memory complexities.

6.1   Basic Attack on AES-192 and AES-256

The basic attack is a further extension by one round of the 6-round attack. Recall that in the 6-round attack we guess the subkey bytes $k_{5,\{0,7,10,13\}}$ and check whether the state bytes $x_{5,\{0,1,2,3\}}$ satisfy a linear condition (Eq. 3). When we consider 7-round AES, in order to check this condition we have to guess *the entire subkey k_6* and bytes $0, 7, 10, 13$ of the equivalent subkey u_5. Of course, this leads to an extremely high time complexity. In addition, the filtering condition – which is on only 64 bits (i.e., 8 pairs with zero difference in a single byte) – is far from being sufficient for discarding such a huge amount of key material.

In order to improve the filtering condition, we attack *two columns simultaneously*. That is, we guess the entire subkey k_6 and bytes $0, 7, 10, 13$ and $1, 4, 8, 14$ of u_5 and check linear conditions on both state bytes $x_{5,\{0,1,2,3\}}$ (which is Eq. 3) and state bytes $x_{5,\{4,5,6,7\}}$ (which is the following equation:

$$0D_x \cdot \Delta(x_{5,5}) \oplus 09_x \cdot \Delta(x_{5,6}) = 0B_x \cdot \Delta(x_{5,4}) \oplus 0E_x \cdot \Delta(x_{5,7}), \qquad (4)$$

that corresponds to the condition $\Delta(x''_{4,7}) = 0$). Thus, we have 4 more key bytes to guess, but the filtering is increased to 128 bits.

In order to reduce the time complexity, we extend the MITM procedure described in Sect. 5.2 to cover round 6 as well. Specifically, we modify the MITM procedure described in Improvement 1 of Sect. 5.2 as follows:

1. Guess bytes $k_{6,SR(Col(0,3))}$ and $u_{5,\{0,1,13,14\}}$, and compute $x_{5,0}, x_{5,1}$ and $x_{5,5}, x_{5,6}$. Store in a table the contribution of bytes $x_{5,0}, x_{5,1}$ to Eq. (3) (i.e., the concatenation of the values $0E_x \cdot \Delta(x_{5,0}^j) \oplus 0B_x \cdot \Delta(x_{5,1}^j)$ for $j = 1, \ldots, 8$), and the contribution of bytes $x_{5,5}, x_{5,6}$ to Eq. (4) (i.e., the concatenation of the values $0D_x \cdot \Delta(x_{5,5}^j) \oplus 09_x \cdot \Delta(x_{5,6}^j)$ for $j = 1, \ldots, 8$) – 128 bits in total.
2. Guess bytes $k_{6,SR(Col(1,2))}$ and $u_{5,\{4,7,8,10\}}$, and compute $x_{5,2}, x_{5,3}$ and $x_{5,4}, x_{5,7}$. Compute the contribution of bytes $x_{5,2}, x_{5,3}$ to Eq. (3) and the contribution of bytes $x_{5,4}, x_{5,7}$ to Eq. (4), and search it in the table.
3. For each match in the table, store in L_1 the combination k_6, $u_{5,\{0,1,4,7,8,10,13,14\}}$.

After the MITM procedure, for each guess of $k_{-1,SR^{-1}(Col(0))}$ and for each pair $(P_1, \hat{P}_1)$, we remain with $2^{192} \cdot 2^{-128} = 2^{64}$ key suggestions. To discard the wrong ones, we repeat the attack for Col(2) of x_5 (where now the only key bytes we need to guess are $u_{5,\{2,5,8,15\}}$ and we can again use MITM), and for Col(3) of x_5 (where the only key bytes we need to guess are $u_{5,\{3,6,9,12\}}$ and we can again use MITM). In total, we have a 256-bit filtering, and so we obtain on average $2^{256} \cdot 2^{-256} = 1$ suggestions for the entire subkeys u_5, k_6, which of course yield the secret key. The remaining suggestions can be checked easily by trial encryption.

What is the time complexity of the attack? The most time consuming operation is the first MITM procedure which is performed for 2^{32} guesses of $k_{-1,SR^{-1}(Col(0))}$ and for 2^{32} pairs $(P_1, \hat{P}_1)$, and consists of 2^{96} times decrypting a full AES round and one column of another round, for 16 ciphertexts, plus $2 \cdot 2^{96}$ table lookups. Estimating a table lookup as one full AES round (following common practice), the total time complexity is $2^{32} \cdot 2^{32} \cdot 2^{96} \cdot 3 = 2^{161.6}$ encryptions.

The memory complexity is 2^{96}, required for the MITM procedure. The data complexity of the attack is 2^{32} chosen plaintexts. However, it can be reduced using Improvement 2 described in Sect. 5.2. Instead of taking the full structure of 2^{32} plaintexts, we can take an arbitrary subset of 2^{30} plaintexts. As discussed above, there are 2^{31} good pairs that can be used in the attack, and given a pair, the probability that it belongs to S along with all its 7 mixtures is approximately $2^{31} \cdot (2^{-2})^{16} = 1/2$. In addition, if the attack fails for all pairs, we can repeat the attack with other shifted columns of x_4'' instead of $x_{4,SR(0)}''$. As described in Improvement 5 in Sect. 4.1, this increases the number of good pairs by a factor of 4 – which means that on average, 2 pairs will be included in S along with all their 7 mixtures. Therefore, starting with 2^{30} plaintexts, the success probability of the attack is still above $1 - e^{-1} = 0.63$.

We do not present the attack algorithm here, as it will be subsumed by the improved attack algorithm we present in the next subsection.

6.2   Improved Attack on AES-192 and AES-256 Using Dissection

In this section we show that the memory complexity of the attack described above can be reduced from 2^{96} to 2^{48} without affecting the data and time complexities, using the *dissection* technique [14].

For ease of exposition, we first briefly recall the generic dissection attack on 4-encryption (denoted in [14] $Dissect_2(4, 1)$) and then present its application in our case.

The algorithm $Dissect_2(4, 1)$ is given four plaintext/ciphertext pairs (P_1, C_1), $\ldots, (P_4, C_4)$ to a 4-round cipher. It is assumed that the block length is n bits, and that in each round i (for $i = 0, 1, 2, 3$) there is an independent n-bit key k_i. The algorithm finds all values of (k_0, k_1, k_2, k_3) that comply with the 4 plaintext/ciphertext pairs (the expected number of keys is, of course, one), in time $O(2^{2n})$ and memory $O(2^n)$. Instead of using the notations of [14], we will be consistent with our notations, and denote the plaintexts by (x_0, y_0, z_0, w_0) and the intermediate values before round i by (x_i, y_i, z_i, w_i).

The dissection algorithm is the following:

1. Given plaintexts $(x_0, y_0, z_0, w_0) = (P_1, P_2, P_3, P_4)$ and their corresponding ciphertexts $(x_4, y_4, z_4, w_4) = (C_1, C_2, C_3, C_4)$, for each candidate value of x_2:
2. (a) Run a standard MITM attack on 2-round encryption with (x_0, x_2) as a single plaintext/ciphertext pair, to find all keys (k_0, k_1) which 'encrypt' x_0 to x_2. For each of these 2^n values, partially encrypt $y_0 = P_2$ using (k_0, k_1), and store in a table the corresponding values of y_2, along with the values of (k_0, k_1).
   (b) Run a standard MITM attack on 2-round encryption with (x_2, x_4) as a single plaintext/ciphertext pair, to find all keys (k_2, k_3) which 'encrypt' x_2 to x_4. For each of these 2^n values, partially decrypt C_2 using (k_2, k_3) and

check whether the suggested value for y_2 appears in the table. If so, check whether the key (k_0, k_1, k_2, k_3) suggested by the table and the current (k_2, k_3) candidate encrypts P_3 and P_4 into C_3 and C_4, respectively.

We call the two 2-round MITM procedures *internal* ones, and the final MITM step *external*.

The time complexity of each of the two internal 2-round MITM attacks is about 2^n, and so is the time complexity of the external MITM procedure. As these procedures are performed for each value of x_2, the time complexity of the attack is $O(2^{2n})$ operations. The memory complexity is $O(2^n)$, required for each of the MITM procedures. Note that the time complexity of the attack is not better than the complexity of a simple MITM attack on a 4-round cipher with independent round keys. The advantage of dissection is the significant reduction in memory complexity – from 2^{2n} to $O(2^n)$.

While this may not be clear at a first glance, a standard MITM attack can be transformed into a $Dissect_2(4, 1)$ attack whenever each of the two parts of the MITM procedure can be further subdivided into two parts whose contributions are independent, given that a 'partial guess in the middle' (like the guess of x_2 above) can be performed. This is the case in our attack.

Note that the contribution of the first part of the MITM procedure described above to each of Eqs. (3), (4) can be represented as the XOR of two independent contributions: the contribution of state bytes $x_{5,0}$ and $x_{5,5}$, which can be computed by guessing $k_{6,SR(Col(0))}$ and $u_{5,\{0,1\}}$, and the contribution of state bytes $x_{5,1}$ and $x_{5,6}$ which can be computed by guessing $k_{6,SR(Col(3))}$ and $u_{5,\{13,14\}}$. The second half can be divided similarly. The contribution of each side to Eqs. (3), (4) plays the role of the guessed intermediate value. Hence, we introduce the following auxiliary notations. For $1 \leq j \leq 8$, let

$$a_j = 0E_x \cdot \Delta(x_{5,0}^j) \oplus 0B_x \cdot \Delta(x_{5,1}^j) = 0D_x \cdot \Delta(x_{5,2}^j) \oplus 09_x \cdot \Delta(x_{5,3}^j) \quad (5)$$

denote the contributions of the two sides to Eq. (3) for ciphertext pair $(C_j, \hat{C}_j)$, and let

$$b_j = 0D_x \cdot \Delta(x_{5,5}^j) \oplus 09_x \cdot \Delta(x_{5,6}^j) = 0B_x \cdot \Delta(x_{5,4}) \oplus 0E_x \cdot \Delta(x_{5,7}) \quad (6)$$

denote the contributions of the two sides to Eq. (4) for ciphertext pair $(C_j, \hat{C}_j)$.

This allows us to mount the following attack:

1. **Constructing the plaintext pool.** Take a structure S of 2^{30} chosen plaintexts with the same value in all bytes but those of $SR^{-1}(Col(0))$.
2. For each guess of subkey $k_{-1,SR^{-1}(Col(0))}$, go over all chosen pairs of plaintexts $(P_1, \hat{P}_1)$ in S, and for each of them do the following:
   (a) **Checking that the pair can be used in the attack, i.e., the pair and all its 7 mixtures are in the plaintext pool.** Partially encrypt $(P_1, \hat{P}_1) = (x_{-1}^1, \hat{x}_{-1}^1)$ through AddRoundKey and round 0 to obtain $(x_1^1, \hat{x}_1^1)$. Consider all 7 mixtures of $(x_1^1, \hat{x}_1^1)$, which we denote $(x_1^2, \hat{x}_1^2), \ldots, (x_1^8, \hat{x}_1^8)$, and partially decrypt them to find the corresponding

plaintext pairs $(P_2, \hat{P}_2) = (x_{-1}^2, \hat{x}_{-1}^2), \ldots, (P_8, \hat{P}_8) = (x_{-1}^8, \hat{x}_{-1}^8)$. Check whether for all of them, both plaintexts are included in S. If no, discard the pair $(P_1, \hat{P}_1)$.

(b) For each candidate value of $(a_1, a_2, a_3, a_4, a_5, a_6)$ do the following:

(c) **First internal MITM procedure:**

   i. Guess bytes $k_{6,SR(\text{Col}(0))}$ and $u_{5,0}$, and compute $x_{5,0}$. Store in a table the contribution of the byte $x_{5,0}$ to Eq. (3) for the pairs $(C_1, \hat{C}_1), \ldots, (C_6, \hat{C}_6)$, i.e., the concatenation of the values $0E_x \cdot \Delta(x_{5,0}^j) \oplus a_j$ for $j = 1, \ldots, 6 - 48$ bits in total.

   ii. Guess bytes $k_{6,SR(\text{Col}(3))}$ and $u_{5,13}$, and compute $x_{5,1}$. Compute the contribution of the byte $x_{5,1}$ to Eq. (3) for the pairs $(C_1, \hat{C}_1), \ldots, (C_6, \hat{C}_6)$, i.e., the concatenation of the values $0B_x \cdot \Delta(x_{5,1}^j)$ for $j = 1, \ldots, 6$, and check it in the table.

   iii. For each value found in the table, use the suggested value of $k_{6,SR(\text{Col}(0,3))}$ and $u_{5,\{0,13\}}$, guess bytes $u_{5,\{1,14\}}$, and partially decrypt the ciphertexts to obtain the values $(a_7, a_8, b_1, b_2, \ldots, b_8)$. Store them in a table, together with the suggestion for $k_{6,SR(\text{Col}(0,3))}$ and $u_{5,\{0,1,13,14\}}$.

(d) **Second internal MITM procedure:**

   i. Guess bytes $k_{6,SR(\text{Col}(1))}$ and $u_{5,7}$, and compute $x_{5,3}$. Store in a table the contribution of the byte $x_{5,3}$ to Eq. (3) for the pairs $(C_1, \hat{C}_1), \ldots, (C_6, \hat{C}_6)$, i.e., the concatenation of the values $09_x \cdot \Delta(x_{5,3}^j) \oplus a_j$ for $j = 1, \ldots, 6 - 48$ bits in total.

   ii. Guess bytes $k_{6,SR(\text{Col}(2))}$ and $u_{5,10}$, and compute $x_{5,2}$. Compute the contribution of the byte $x_{5,2}$ to Eq. (3) for the pairs $(C_1, \hat{C}_1), \ldots, (C_6, \hat{C}_6)$, i.e., the concatenation of the values $0D_x \cdot \Delta(x_{5,1}^j)$ for $j = 1, \ldots, 6$, and check it in the table.

   iii. For each value found in the table, use the suggested value of $k_{6,SR(\text{Col}(1,2))}$ and $u_{5,\{7,10\}}$, guess bytes $u_{5,\{4,8\}}$, and partially decrypt the ciphertexts to obtain the values $(a_7, a_8, b_1, b_2, \ldots, b_8)$. Check whether the vector exists in the table. If yes, store in a table L the suggested value of k_5 and $u_{5,\{0,1,4,7,8,10,13,14\}}$.

(e) **Completing the attack:** For each remaining key suggestion, repeat the attack for the two last shifted columns of u_5, with respect to the state bytes $x_{4,10}''$ and $x_{4,13}''$, to filter wrong key guesses and obtain suggestions for the entire k_6 and u_5. For each remaining suggestion, use k_6, u_5 to retrieve the full key and check it by trial encryption.

The memory complexity of the attack is 2^{48} 80-bit values (required in Step 2(c)), which are less than 2^{48} 128-bit blocks. As for the time complexity, for each guess of $k_{-1,\{0,5,10,15\}}$, each pair $(P_1, \hat{P}_1)$, and each guessed 48-bit value $(a_1, \ldots, a_6)$, the internal MITM procedures take 2^{40} time and the external MITM procedure consists of 2^{48} times decrypting a full AES round and one column of another round, for 16 ciphertexts, plus $2 \cdot 2^{96}$ table lookups. Estimating a table lookup as one full AES round, the total time complexity of this step is $2^{32} \cdot 2^{32} \cdot 2^{48} \cdot 2^{48} \cdot 3 = 2^{161.6}$ encryptions. The complexity of all other steps is negligible.

Therefore, the data complexity of the attack is 2^{30} chosen plaintexts, the memory complexity is 2^{48} 128-bit blocks, and the time complexity is $2^{161.6}$ encryptions. The success probability is $1 - e^{-1} = 0.63$.

6.3   Improved Attacks on AES-192 Exploiting the Key Schedule

While in the attack on AES-256 the subkeys we guess in the last two rounds are independent, in the case of AES-192 there exists a strong relation between u_5 and k_6. Specifically, by the AES key schedule we have

$$k_{5,\text{Col}(1)} = k_{6,\text{Col}(2)} \oplus k_{6,\text{Col}(3)}, \tag{7}$$

and

$$k_{5,\text{Col}(0)} = k_{6,\text{Col}(2)} \oplus SB(k_{6,\text{Col}(1)} \lll 8) \oplus RCON[5]. \tag{8}$$

Since $u_{5,\text{Col}(j)} = MC^{-1}(k_{5,\text{Col}(j)})$ for each j, two columns of u_5 can be expressed as combinations of bytes of k_6. As these two columns contain half of the bytes of u_5 guessed in the attack, we will be able to use them to enhance the filtering condition. Specifically, this enables us to attack a single column in x_5 (and so guess only bytes $u_{5,SR(\text{Col}(0))}$ and the entire k_6, a total of 160 key bits), and use Eqs. (7) and (8) as additional filtering conditions in the MITM procedure, thus increasing the filtering to 80 bits. This allows us to reduce the time complexity of the attack to 2^{152} and the memory complexity of the attack to 2^{40}, without affecting the data complexity.

By using a much more complex variant of the dissection attack, we can further reduce the memory complexity to 2^{32} without affecting the data and time complexities, thus obtaining an attack which recovers the full secret key in 2^{30} data, 2^{32} memory, and 2^{153} time, which outperforms the classical Square attack in all three complexity parameters. The details will be presented in the full version of the paper.

7   An Alternative Improvement for the 6-Round and 7-Round Attacks

As we mentioned in several places, an obvious point in which Grassi's attack can be enhanced is deploying the fact that while the structure of size 2^{32} contains 2^{31} good pairs, we need only one good pair (along with its mixtures) to apply the attack. So far, we exploited the abundance of good pairs to reduce the data complexity – we took a smaller structure of plaintexts, which was sufficiently large so that at least one good pair, along with the required mixtures, is included in our structure.

In this section we suggest an alternative way to exploit the abundance of good pairs – ask that the good pair we use in the attack will satisfy some additional property, which will allow reducing the *time complexity* of the attack. We first demonstrate the improvement on the 6-round attack, and then we apply it (or more precisely, a variant of it) to the 7-round attack on AES-192.

An alternative improvement to the 6-round attack. Recall that in the 6-round attack, we guess bytes $k_{-1,SR^{-1}(\text{Col}(0))}$, go over 2^{32} plaintext pairs $(P_1, \hat{P}_1)$, and perform a MITM attack on 4 bytes of the subkey k_5. Now, instead of taking any ciphertext pair which corresponds to a plaintext pair $(P_1, \hat{P}_1)$, we add a restriction on the ciphertext pair, that can be checked easily. Specifically, we require that in the ciphertext pair $(C_1, \hat{C}_1)$, there is a zero difference in the entire shifted column $SR(\text{Col}(0))$. Among the 2^{63} ciphertext pairs, about 2^{31} satisfy this extra condition. But importantly, out of the 2^{31} good pairs, about 2^7 satisfy this condition, since in the good pairs, we already know that $\Delta(x''_{4,0}) = 0$, and so 8 bits out of the 32 bits of the extra condition are satisfied for sure. Thus, among the pairs that satisfy the extra condition, the probability of a pair to be good is enhanced from 2^{-32} to 2^{-24}.

This implies that instead of checking 2^{32} pairs $(P_1, \hat{P}_1)$ as we do in the basic attack, it is sufficient to check 2^{24} pairs that satisfy the extra condition. We can thus modify Steps 1–3 of the attack as follows:

1. Consider a structure of 2^{32} chosen plaintexts in which $SR^{-1}(\text{Col}(0))$ assume all 2^{32} possible values and the rest of the bytes are constant. Insert the corresponding ciphertexts into a hash table indexed by bytes $SR(\text{Col}(0))$ of the ciphertext, and extract all plaintext pairs $(P_1, \hat{P}_1)$ for which the corresponding ciphertexts have difference zero in $SR(\text{Col}(0))$.

Then the attack is applied without change, with the advantage that it is sufficient to apply Step 2 for 2^{24} pairs instead of 2^{32}. This reduces the time complexity by a factor of 2^8, without affecting the other parameters of the attack.

While this improvement cannot be completely combined with the data complexity reduction described in Improvement 2 of Sect. 5 (as once we case an additional restriction, the number of good pairs we can use is reduced significantly), the data complexity can still be slightly reduced. Note that after the initial filtering of Step 1, the data still contains 2^7 good pairs, while we need only a single pair. By the same argument as in Improvement 2, if we take a subset S of size $\alpha 2^{32}$, the probability that one of these 2^7 remaining good pairs, along with at least three of its 7 mixtures (that do not need to satisfy the basic filtering condition!), is included in S, is approximately $2^7 \alpha^8 \cdot \binom{7}{3} \approx 2^{12} \alpha^8$. Hence, if we take $\alpha = 2^{-1.5}$, with a good probability the plaintext set S contains a good pair that can be used in the attack.

Therefore, overall we obtain an attack with data and memory complexity of $2^{30.5}$, and time complexity of 2^{73} encryptions.

An alternative improvement to the attack on 7-round AES-192. Recall that in the first step of the attack, we guess bytes $k_{-1,SR^{-1}(\text{Col}(0))}$, go over 2^{32} plaintext pairs $(P_1, \hat{P}_1)$, and perform a MITM attack on 4 bytes of the subkey u_5 and the entire subkey k_6 (a total of 160 subkey bits), with an 80-bit filtering. After that step, we are left with 2^{144} key suggestions and have to find a source for additional filtering. We obtain this filtering by examining $x_{5,\text{Col}(1)}$ and using the condition $\Delta(x''_{4,7}) = 0$. Since we already know the subkey bytes $u_{5,\{1,4\}}$, we can guess bytes $u_{5,\{11,14\}}$, partially decrypt the ciphertexts to find the values $x_{5,\text{Col}(1)}$, and obtain a 64-bit filtering by checking the condition on the state $\Delta(x''_{4,7})$, for all 8 pairs. Naively, this increases the time complexity to 2^{160}. In Sect. 6 we suggested either to perform a MITM procedure on these two key bytes, or to retrieve them instantly using a large precomputed table. The former suggestion increases the time complexity to 2^{153}, while the latter increases the memory complexity to 2^{144}. We show how to obtain the additional filtering without increasing neither the time nor the memory complexity.

As in the 6-round attack, we add a requirement on the good pairs. Specifically, we require that in the ciphertext pair $(C_1, \hat{C}_1)$, there is a zero difference in the entire shifted column $SR(\text{Col}(2))$. As a result, we know that in the intermediate values that correspond to $(C_1, \hat{C}_1)$, we have $\Delta(x_{5,7}) = 0$. In addition, as we know $u_{5,\{1,4\}}$, we can compute $\Delta(x_{5,\{4,5\}})$ for the same pair. Furthermore, assuming that $(C_1, \hat{C}_1)$ is a good pair, we also know that its intermediate values satisfy $\Delta(x''_{4,7}) = 0$. Now, consider the MixColumns operation in round 4, Column 1 in the encryption process of $(C_1, \hat{C}_1)$. We know the difference in three bytes after MixColumns and in one byte before MixColumns. By the structure of MixColumns, this allows to retrieve the input and output differences in all other bytes, by simply solving a system of linear equations. In particular, we retrieve $\Delta(x_{5,6})$. On the other hand, we can obtain the difference $\Delta(x'_{5,6})$ by partial decryption. This gives us the input and output differences to the Sub-Bytes operation in round 5, byte 6, which allows us to retrieve the actual values in the state $x'_{5,6}$ by a single lookup into a precomputed table of size 2^{16}. Finally, from the value $x'_{5,6}$ we can recover $u_{5,14}$ by partial decryption, and then we can repeat the above procedure with one of the other pairs $(C_j, \hat{C}_j)$ to retrieve $u_{5,11}$, using the fact that we can compute the difference $\Delta(x_{5,\{4,5,6\}})$ with the subkey material we already know.

As a result, we obtain the subkey bytes $u_{5,\{11,14\}}$ and can apply the additional filtering, without increasing neither the time nor the memory complexity. To summarize, the data complexity of the attack is 2^{32} (note that we cannot reduce the data complexity in this attack, since only very few good pairs satisfy our additional restriction on $(C_1, \hat{C}_1)$ and so we must keep all of them available), the memory complexity is 2^{40} and the time complexity is $2^{145.6}$ (where both the memory and the time complexities are dominated by the first step of the MITM procedure).

8 Summary

In this paper we developed and experimentally verified the best known key recovery attack on 5-round AES, reducing its total complexity from 2^{32} to $2^{22.5}$. We then extended the attack to 7-round AES, obtaining the best key recovery attacks on the 192 and 256 bit versions of this cryptosystem which have practical data and memory complexities. The main problems left open by our results is whether it is possible to extend our new attacks to larger versions of AES, and whether it is possible to use our results to attack other primitives which use reduced-round AES (e.g., 5-round AES) as a component.

Acknowledgements. The research of Achiya Bar-On and of Nathan Keller was supported by the European Research Council under the ERC starting grant agreement n. 757731 (LightCrypt) and by the BIU Center for Research in Applied Cryptography and Cyber Security in conjunction with the Israel National Cyber Bureau in the Prime Minister's Office. The research of Orr Dunkelman was supported by the Israel Ministry of Science and Technology.

References

1. Biham, E., Keller, N.: Cryptanalysis of Reduced Variants of Rijndael (1999). Unpublished manuscript
2. Bogdanov, A., Khovratovich, D., Rechberger, C.: Biclique cryptanalysis of the full AES. In: Lee, D.H., Wang, X. (eds.) ASIACRYPT 2011. LNCS, vol. 7073, pp. 344–371. Springer, Heidelberg (2011). https://doi.org/10.1007/978-3-642-25385-0_19
3. Bossuet, L., Datta, N., Mancillas-López, C., Nandi, M.: ELmD: a pipelineable authenticated encryption and its hardware implementation. IEEE Trans. Comput. **65**(11), 3318–3331 (2016)
4. Bouillaguet, C., Derbez, P., Dunkelman, O., Fouque, P., Keller, N., Rijmen, V.: Low-data complexity attacks on AES. IEEE Trans. Inf. Theor. **58**(11), 7002–7017 (2012). https://doi.org/10.1109/TIT.2012.2207880
5. Bouillaguet, C., Derbez, P., Fouque, P.-A.: Automatic search of attacks on round-reduced AES and applications. In: Rogaway, P. (ed.) CRYPTO 2011. LNCS, vol. 6841, pp. 169–187. Springer, Heidelberg (2011). https://doi.org/10.1007/978-3-642-22792-9_10
6. Boura, C., Lallemand, V., Naya-Plasencia, M., Suder, V.: Making the impossible possible. J. Cryptol. **31**(1), 101–133 (2018). https://doi.org/10.1007/s00145-016-9251-7
7. Cho, J., et al.: WEM: a new family of white-box block ciphers based on the even-mansour construction. In: Handschuh, H. (ed.) CT-RSA 2017. LNCS, vol. 10159, pp. 293–308. Springer, Cham (2017). https://doi.org/10.1007/978-3-319-52153-4_17
8. Daemen, J., Knudsen, L., Rijmen, V.: The block cipher Square. In: Biham, E. (ed.) FSE 1997. LNCS, vol. 1267, pp. 149–165. Springer, Heidelberg (1997). https://doi.org/10.1007/BFb0052343
9. Daemen, J., Rijmen, V.: The Design of Rijndael: AES - The Advanced Encryption Standard. Information Security and Cryptography. Springer, Heidelberg (2002). https://doi.org/10.1007/978-3-662-04722-4

10. Demirci, H., Selçuk, A.A.: A meet-in-the-middle attack on 8-round AES. In: Nyberg, K. (ed.) FSE 2008. LNCS, vol. 5086, pp. 116–126. Springer, Heidelberg (2008). https://doi.org/10.1007/978-3-540-71039-4_7

11. Derbez, P.: Meet-in-the-middle attacks on AES. Ph.D. thesis, Ecole Normale Supérieure de Paris – ENS Paris (2013)

12. Derbez, P., Fouque, P.-A.: Exhausting Demirci-Selçuk meet-in-the-middle attacks against reduced-round AES. In: Moriai, S. (ed.) FSE 2013. LNCS, vol. 8424, pp. 541–560. Springer, Heidelberg (2014). https://doi.org/10.1007/978-3-662-43933-3_28

13. Derbez, P., Fouque, P.-A., Jean, J.: Improved key recovery attacks on reduced-round, in the single-key setting. In: Johansson, T., Nguyen, P.Q. (eds.) EURO-CRYPT 2013. LNCS, vol. 7881, pp. 371–387. Springer, Heidelberg (2013). https://doi.org/10.1007/978-3-642-38348-9_23

14. Dinur, I., Dunkelman, O., Keller, N., Shamir, A.: Efficient dissection of composite problems, with applications to cryptanalysis, knapsacks, and combinatorial search problems. In: Safavi-Naini, R., Canetti, R. (eds.) CRYPTO 2012. LNCS, vol. 7417, pp. 719–740. Springer, Heidelberg (2012). https://doi.org/10.1007/978-3-642-32009-5_42

15. Ferguson, N.: Improved cryptanalysis of Rijndael. In: Goos, G., Hartmanis, J., van Leeuwen, J., Schneier, B. (eds.) FSE 2000. LNCS, vol. 1978, pp. 213–230. Springer, Heidelberg (2001). https://doi.org/10.1007/3-540-44706-7_15

16. Fouque, P.-A., Karpman, P., Kirchner, P., Minaud, B.: Efficient and provable white-box primitives. In: Cheon, J.H., Takagi, T. (eds.) ASIACRYPT 2016, Part I. LNCS, vol. 10031, pp. 159–188. Springer, Heidelberg (2016). https://doi.org/10.1007/978-3-662-53887-6_6

17. Gérard, B., Grosso, V., Naya-Plasencia, M., Standaert, F.-X.: Block ciphers that are easier to mask: how far can we go? In: Bertoni, G., Coron, J.-S. (eds.) CHES 2013. LNCS, vol. 8086, pp. 383–399. Springer, Heidelberg (2013). https://doi.org/10.1007/978-3-642-40349-1_22

18. Gilbert, H., Minier, M.: A collision attack on 7 rounds of Rijndael. In: Preproceedings of Third AES Candidate Conference, pp. 230–241 (2000)

19. Grassi, L.: Mixture differential cryptanalysis: new approaches for distinguishers and attacks on round-reduced AES. Cryptology ePrint Archive, Report 2017/832 (2017). https://eprint.iacr.org/2017/832

20. Grassi, L., Rechberger, C., Rønjom, S.: A new structural-differential property of 5-round AES. In: Coron, J.-S., Nielsen, J.B. (eds.) EUROCRYPT 2017, Part II. LNCS, vol. 10211, pp. 289–317. Springer, Cham (2017). https://doi.org/10.1007/978-3-319-56614-6_10

21. Guo, J., Peyrin, T., Poschmann, A., Robshaw, M.: The LED block cipher. In: Preneel, B., Takagi, T. (eds.) CHES 2011. LNCS, vol. 6917, pp. 326–341. Springer, Heidelberg (2011). https://doi.org/10.1007/978-3-642-23951-9_22

22. Hoang, V.T., Krovetz, T., Rogaway, P.: Robust authenticated-encryption AEZ and the problem that it solves. In: Oswald, E., Fischlin, M. (eds.) EUROCRYPT 2015, Part I. LNCS, vol. 9056, pp. 15–44. Springer, Heidelberg (2015). https://doi.org/10.1007/978-3-662-46800-5_2

23. Mala, H., Dakhilalian, M., Rijmen, V., Modarres-Hashemi, M.: Improved impossible differential cryptanalysis of 7-round AES-128. In: Gong, G., Gupta, K.C. (eds.) INDOCRYPT 2010. LNCS, vol. 6498, pp. 282–291. Springer, Heidelberg (2010). https://doi.org/10.1007/978-3-642-17401-8_20

24. Rønjom, S., Bardeh, N.G., Helleseth, T.: Yoyo tricks with AES. In: Takagi, T., Peyrin, T. (eds.) ASIACRYPT 2017, Part I. LNCS, vol. 10624, pp. 217–243. Springer, Cham (2017). https://doi.org/10.1007/978-3-319-70694-8_8

25. Tiessen, T.: Polytopic cryptanalysis. In: Fischlin, M., Coron, J.-S. (eds.) EURO-CRYPT 2016, Part I. LNCS, vol. 9665, pp. 214–239. Springer, Heidelberg (2016). https://doi.org/10.1007/978-3-662-49890-3_9

26. Tunstall, M.: Improved "Partial Sums"-based square attack on AES. In: Samarati, P., Lou, W., Zhou, J. (eds.) SECRYPT 2012 - Proceedings of the International Conference on Security and Cryptography, Rome, Italy, 24–27 July 2012, SECRYPT is part of ICETE - The International Joint Conference on e-Business and Telecommunications, pp. 25–34. SciTePress (2012)

Bernstein Bound on WCS is Tight
Repairing Luykx-Preneel Optimal Forgeries

Mridul Nandi$^{(\boxtimes)}$

Indian Statistical Institute, Kolkata, India
mridul.nandi@gmail.com

Abstract. In Eurocrypt 2018, Luykx and Preneel described hash-key-recovery and forgery attacks against polynomial hash based Wegman-Carter-Shoup (WCS) authenticators. Their attacks require $2^{n/2}$ message-tag pairs and recover hash-key with probability about 1.34×2^{-n} where n is the bit-size of the hash-key. Bernstein in Eurocrypt 2005 had provided an upper bound (known as Bernstein bound) of the maximum forgery advantages. The bound says that all adversaries making $O(2^{n/2})$ queries of WCS can have maximum forgery advantage $O(2^{-n})$. So, Luykx and Preneel essentially analyze WCS in a range of query complexities where WCS is known to be perfectly secure. Here we revisit the bound and found that WCS remains secure against all adversaries making $q \ll \sqrt{n} \times 2^{n/2}$ queries. So it would be meaningful to analyze adversaries with beyond birthday bound complexities.

In this paper, we show that *the Bernstein bound is tight* by describing two attacks (one in the *"chosen-plaintext model"* and other in the *"known-plaintext model"*) which **recover the hash-key (hence forges) with probability at least $\frac{1}{2}$ based on $\sqrt{n} \times 2^{n/2}$ message-tag pairs**. We also extend the forgery adversary to the Galois Counter Mode (or GCM). More precisely, we **recover the hash-key of GCM with probability at least $\frac{1}{2}$ based on only $\sqrt{\frac{n}{\ell}} \times 2^{n/2}$ encryption queries**, where ℓ is the number of blocks present in encryption queries.

Keywords: WCS authenticator · GCM · Polynomial hash
Universal hash · AXU · Key-recovery · Forgery

1 Introduction

WEGMAN-CARTER AUTHENTICATION. In 1974 [GMS74], Gilbert, MacWilliams and Sloane considered a coding problem which is essentially an one-time authentication protocol (a fresh key is required for every authentication). Their solutions required a key which is as large as the message to be authenticated. Later in 1981, Wegman and Carter [WC81] proposed a simple authentication protocol based on an almost strongly universal₂ hash function which was described in their early work in [CW79]. The hash-key size is the order of logarithm of message length (which is further reduced by some constant factor due to Stinson [Sti94]).

© International Association for Cryptologic Research 2018
H. Shacham and A. Boldyreva (Eds.): CRYPTO 2018, LNCS 10992, pp. 213–238, 2018.
https://doi.org/10.1007/978-3-319-96881-0_8

The hash-key can be the same for every authentication, but it needs a fresh constant sized random key (used to mask the hash-output). More precisely, let κ be a hash-key of an n-bit hash function ρ_κ and $R_1, R_2, \ldots$ be a stream of secret n-bit keys. Given a message m and its unique message number n (also known as a nonce), the Wegman-Carter (WC) authenticator computes $R_n \oplus \rho_\kappa(m)$ as a tag.

ALMOST XOR-UNIVERSAL OR AXU HASH. In [Kra94] Krawczyk had shown that almost strong universal$_2$ property can be relaxed to a weaker hash (named as AXU or almost-xor universal hash by Rogaway in [Rog95]). The polynomial hashing [dB93, BJKS94, Tay94], division hashing [KR87, Rab81] are such examples of AXU hash functions which were first introduced in a slightly different context. Afterwards, many AXU hash functions have been proposed for instantiating Wegman-Carter authentication [Sho96, HK97, Ber05a, BHK+99, MV04]. A comprehensive survey of universal hash functions can be found in [Ber07, Nan14]. Among all known examples, the polynomial hashing is very popular as it requires hash-key of constant size and, both key generation and hash computation are very fast.

WEGMAN-CARTER-SHOUP OR WCS AUTHENTICATOR. To get rid of onetime masking in Wegman-Carter authenticator, Brassard (in [Bra83]) proposed to use a pseudorandom number generator which generates the keys $R_1, R_2, \ldots$, from a short master key K. However, in some application, message number can come in arbitrary order and so a direct efficient computation of R_n is much desired (it is alternatively known as pseudorandom function or PRF). Brassard pointed out that the Blum-Blum-Shub pseudorandom number generator [BBS86] outputs can be computed directly. As blockciphers are more efficient, Shoup ([Sho96]) considered the following variant of WC authentication:

$$\mathsf{WCS}_{K,\kappa}(n_1, m) := e_K(n) \oplus \rho_\kappa(m)$$

where e_K is a keyed blockcipher modeled as a pseudorandom permutation (PRP). This was named as WCS authenticator by Bernstein in [Ber05b].

The use of PRPs enables practical and fast instantiations of WCS authenticators. The WCS authentication mechanism implicitly or explicitly has been used in different algorithms, such as Poly1305-AES [Ber05a] and Galois Counter Mode or GCM [MV04, AY12]. GCM was adopted in practice, e.g. [MV06, JTC11, SCM08]. GCM and its randomized variants, called RGCM [BT16], are used in TLS 1.2 and TLS 1.3.

1.1   Known Security Analysis of WCS prior to Luykx-Preneel Eurocrypt 2018

HASH-KEY RECOVERY ATTACKS OF WCS. Forgery and key-recovery are the two meaningful security notions for an authenticator. Whenever we recover hash-key, the security is completely lost as any message can be forged. Security of WCS relies on the nonce which should not repeat over different executions [Jou, HP08]. Most of the previously published nonce respecting attacks aim to recover the polynomial key [ABBT15, PC15, Saa12, ZTG13] based on multiple verification attempts. The total number of message blocks in all verification attempts should be about 2^n to achieve some significant advantage.

PROVABLE SECURITY ANALYSIS OF WCS. The WC authenticator based on polynomial hashing has maximum forgery or authenticity advantage $\frac{v\ell}{2^n}$ against all adversaries who make at most q authentication queries and v verification queries consisting of at most ℓ blocks. By applying the standard PRP-PRF switching lemma, WCS (which is based on a random permutation π) has an authenticity advantage at most $\frac{v\ell}{2^n} + \frac{(v+q)^2}{2^n}$. So the bound becomes useless as q approaches $2^{n/2}$ (birthday complexity). Shoup proved that the advantage is at most $\frac{v\ell}{2^n}$ for all $q < 2^{\frac{n-\log \ell}{2}}$ [Sho96]. So, when $\ell = 2^{10}$, $n = 128$, the above bound says that the authenticity advantage is at most $v\ell/2^{128}$, whenever $q \leq 2^{59}$. This is clearly better than the classical bound. However, the application of Shoup's bound would be limited if we allow large ℓ.

Bernstein Bound. Finally, Bernstein [Ber05b] provided an improved bound for WCS which is valid for wider range of q. The maximum authenticity advantage is shown to be bounded above by

$$\mathsf{B}(q, v) := v \cdot \epsilon \cdot (1 - \frac{q}{2^n})^{\frac{-(q+1)}{2}} \tag{1}$$

for all q, where ρ_κ is an ϵ-AXU hash function. Thus, when $q = O(2^{n/2})$, the maximum success probability is $O(v \cdot \epsilon)$ which is clearly negligible for all reasonable choices of v and ϵ. For example, the forgery advantage against 128-bit WCS based on polynomial hashing is at most (1) $1.7v\ell \times 2^{-128}$ when $q \leq 2^{64}$, and (2) $3000v\ell \times 2^{-128}$ when $q = 2^{66}$ (so WCS remains secure even if we go beyond birthday bound query complexity).

1.2   Understanding the Result Due to Luykx and Preneel in [LP18]

FALSE-KEY OR TRUE-KEY SET. All known key-recovery attacks focus on reducing the set of candidate keys, denoted $\mathscr{T}$, which contains the actual key. But the set of candidate keys, also called true-key set, is constructed from verification attempts. Recently, a true-key set (equivalently false-key set which is simply the complement of the true-key set) is constructed from authentication queries only. After observing some authentication outputs of a WCS based on a blockcipher e_K, some choices for the key can be eliminated using the fact that outputs of the blockcipher are distinct. More precisely, we can construct the following false-key set $\mathscr{F}$ based on a transcript $\tau := ((n_1, m_1, t_1), \ldots, (n_q, m_q, t_q))$ where $t_i = e_K(n_i) \oplus \rho_\kappa(m_i)$:

$$\mathscr{F} := \{x \ : \ t_i \oplus \rho_x(m_i) = t_j \oplus \rho_x(m_j), \text{ for some } i \neq j\}. \tag{2}$$

It is easy to see that the hash-key $\kappa \notin \mathscr{F}$, since otherwise, there would exist $i \neq j$, $e_K(n_i) = e_K(n_j)$, which is a contradiction. So, a random guess of a key from outside the false-key set would be a correct guess with probability at least $\frac{1}{2^n - \mathbb{E}(|\mathcal{F}|)}$. This simple but useful observation was made in [LP18]. We also use this idea in our analysis.

– LOWER BOUND ON THE EXPECTED SIZE OF FALSE-KEY SET.
Based on the above discussion, one natural approach would be to maximize the false-key set to obtain higher key-recovery advantage. This has been considered in [LP18]. Proposition 3.1 of [LP18] states that

$$\mathbb{E}(|\mathcal{F}|) \geq \frac{q(q-1)}{4}, \text{ for all } q < \sqrt{2^n - 3}.$$

In other words, expected size of the false-key set grows quadratically. They have stated the following in Sect. 3 of [LP18].

"We describe chosen-plaintext attacks which perfectly match the bounds for both polynomial-based WCS MACs and GCM."

Issue 1: The Luykx-Preneel attack is no better than random guessing. Their attack can eliminate about one fourth keys. In other words, there are still three-fourth candidate keys are left. So, the key-recovery advantage $\mathsf{KR}(q)$ is about $\frac{1.34}{2^n}$ (1.34 times more than a random guess attack without making any query). Naturally, as the key-recovery advantage is extremely negligible, claiming such an algorithm as an attack is definitely under question.

– UPPER BOUND ON THE EXPECTED SIZE OF FALSE-KEY SET.
Now we discuss the other claim of [LP18]. They claimed that (Theorem 5.1 of [LP18]) the size of the false-key set cannot be more than $q(q + 1)/2$ after observing q responses of polynomial-based WCS. In other words, irrespective of the length of queries ℓ, the upper bound of the size of the false-key set is independent of ℓ. At a first glance this seem to be counter-intuitive as the number of roots of a polynomial corresponding to a pair of query-responses can be as large as ℓ. So, at best one may expect the size of the false-key set can be $\binom{q}{2}\ell$. But, on the other extreme there may not be a single root for may pairs of queries. On the average, the number of roots for every pair of messages turns out to be in the order of q^2, independent of ℓ. We investigate the proof of Theorem 5.1 of [LP18] and in the very first line they have mentioned that

"Using Thm. 4.1, Cor. 5.1, and Prop. 5.3, we have..."

However, the Cor 5.1 is stated for all $q \leq M_\gamma$ (a parameter defined in Eq. 41 of [LP18]). They have not studied how big M_γ can be. We provide an estimation which allows us to choose M_γ such that $\ell\binom{M_\gamma}{2} = 2^n - \ell$. With this bound, the Theorem 5.1 can be restated as

$$\mathbb{E}(|\mathcal{F}|) \leq \frac{q(q + 1)}{2} \text{ for all } q < \frac{2^{n/2}}{\sqrt{\ell}}. \tag{3}$$

By combining Proposition 3.1 and a corrected version of Theorem 5.1 as just mentioned, we can conclude that

$$\mathbb{E}(|\mathcal{F}|) = \Theta(q^2), \text{ for all } q < \frac{2^{n/2}}{\sqrt{\ell}}.$$

In other words, authors have found a tight estimate of expected size of the false-key set in a certain range of q.

Issue 2: Usefulness of an upper bound of the false-key set: The lower bound of the expected false-key set immediately leads to a lower bound of key-recovery advantage. However, an upper bound of the expected false-key set does not lead to an upper bound of key-recovery advantage. This is mainly due to the fact, the key-recovery advantage based on q authentication responses can be shown as

$$\mathsf{KR}(q) = \mathbb{E}\left(\frac{1}{2^n - |\mathcal{F}|}\right) \geq \frac{1}{2^n - \mathbb{E}(|\mathcal{F}|)}.$$

The inequality follows from the Jensen inequality. So an upper bound of $\mathbb{E}(|\mathcal{F}|)$ does not give any implication on $\mathsf{KR}(q)$. Moreover, dealing the expression $\mathbb{E}(1/(2^n - |\mathcal{F}|))$ directly is much harder. So the usefulness of an upper bound of the expected size of false-key set is not clear to us (other than understanding tightness of size of the false-key set which could be of an independent interest).

1.3 Our Contributions

In this paper, we resolve the optimality issue of the Bernstein bound. We first provide a tight alternative expression of the Berstein bound. In particular, we observe that $\mathsf{B}(q, v) = \Theta(v \cdot \epsilon \cdot e^{\frac{q^2}{2^{n+1}}})$. So WCS is secure against all adversaries with $q \ll \sqrt{n} \times 2^{n/2}$ queries. An adversary must make about $\sqrt{n} \times 2^{n/2}$ queries to obtain some significant advantage. In this paper we describe three attacks to recover the hash key and analyze their success probabilities.

1. The first two attacks (in the known-plaintext and the chosen-plaintext models) are against WCS based on a polynomial hash; they also work for other hashes satisfying certain regular property. Our attacks are also based a false-key (equivalently a true-key set) as described in the Luykx-Preneel attack. Unlike the Luykx-Preneel attack, we however choose message randomly in case of chosen-plaintext model. The query complexity of our attacks is also beyond the birthday complexity. In particular, these attacks require $\sqrt{n2^n}$ authentication queries. So the bound due to Bernstein is tight (even in the known-plaintext model) when $q \approx \sqrt{n2^n}$.
2. We also extend these attacks to the authentication algorithm of GCM which utilizes the ciphertext of GCM encryption to reduce the complexity of encryption queries. In particular, if each encryption query contains ℓ blocks, then this attack requires $\sqrt{\frac{n}{\ell} \times 2^n}$ encryption queries to recover the hash key used in GCM authentication. We have proved that our forgery is optimum by proving a tight upper bound on the maximum forgery advantage.
3. We also provide a simple proof on the tightness of the false-key set which works for all q. In particular, we show that the expected size of the false-key set is at most $q(q-1)/2^n$.

2   Preliminaries

Notations. We write $X \xleftarrow{\$} \mathcal{X}$ to denote that the random variable X is sampled uniformly (and independently from all other random variables defined so far) from the set $\mathcal{X}$. Let $(a)_b := a(a-1)\cdots(a-b+1)$ for two positive integers $b \leq a$. A tuple $(x_1, \ldots, x_q)$ is simply denoted as x^q. We call x^q *coordinate-wise distinct* if x_i's are distinct. We write the set $\{1, 2, \ldots, m\}$ as $[m]$ for a positive integer m. We use standard asymptotic notations such as $o(\cdot)$, $O(\cdot)$, $\Theta(\cdot)$ and $\Omega(\cdot)$ notations. For real functions $f(x), g(x)$, we write $f = O(g)$ (equivalently $g = \Omega(f)$) if there is some positive constant C such that $f(x) \leq Cg(x)$ for all x. If both $f = O(g)$ and $g = O(f)$ hold then we write $f = \Theta(g)$. We write $f(x) = o(g(x))$ if $\lim\limits_{x \to \infty} \frac{f(x)}{g(x)} = 0$.

Jensen Inequality. We write $\mathbb{E}(X)$ to denote the expectation of a real valued random variable X. A twice differentiable function f is called convex if for all x (from the domain of f), $f''(x) > 0$. For example, (1) $1/x$ is a convex function over the set of all positive real numbers and (2) $\frac{1}{N-x}$ is convex over the set of all positive real number less than N. For every convex function f and a real valued random variable X, $\mathbb{E}(f(X)) \geq f(\mathbb{E}(X))$ (Jensen Inequality). In particular, for all positive random variable X,

$$\mathbb{E}\left(\frac{1}{X}\right) \geq \frac{1}{\mathbb{E}(X)} \tag{4}$$

and for all positive random variable $Y < N$,

$$\mathbb{E}\left(\frac{1}{N-Y}\right) \geq \frac{1}{N-\mathbb{E}(Y)} \tag{5}$$

Lemma 1. *Let $0 < \epsilon \leq \sqrt{2} - 1$. Then, for all positive real $x \leq \epsilon$,*

$$e^{-(1+\epsilon)x} \leq 1 - x.$$

Proof. It is well known (from calculus) that $e^{-x} \leq 1 - x + \frac{x^2}{2}$ for all real x. Let $\eta = 1 + \epsilon < \sqrt{2}$. So

$$\begin{aligned}
e^{-(1+\epsilon)x} &\leq 1 - (1+\epsilon)x + \frac{\eta^2 x^2}{2} \\
&\leq 1 - (1+\epsilon)x + x^2 \\
&= 1 - x - x(\epsilon - x) \leq 1 - x \qquad \qquad \square
\end{aligned}$$

We also know that $1 - x \leq e^{-x}$. So, the above result informally says that $1 - x$ and e^{-x} are "almost" the same whenever x is a small positive real number.

2.1   Security Definitions

PSEUDORANDOM PERMUTATION ADVANTAGE. Let $\mathsf{Perm}_\mathfrak{B}$ be the set of all permutations over $\mathfrak{B}$. A blockcipher over a block set $\mathfrak{B}$ is a function $e : \mathcal{K} \times \mathfrak{B} \to \mathfrak{B}$ such that for all key $k \in \mathcal{K}$, $e(k, \cdot) \in \mathsf{Perm}_\mathfrak{B}$. So, a blockcipher is a keyed family of permutations. A uniform random permutation or URP is denoted as π, where $\pi \leftarrow_\$ \mathsf{Perm}_\mathfrak{B}$. The pseudorandom permutation advantage of a distinguisher $\mathcal{A}$ against a blockcipher e is defined as

$$\mathsf{Adv}_e^{\mathrm{prp}}(\mathcal{A}) := \Big| \Pr_{K \leftarrow_\$ \mathcal{K}} (\mathcal{A}^{e_K} \text{ returns } 1) - \Pr_\pi(\mathcal{A}^\pi \text{ returns } 1) \Big|.$$

Let $\mathbb{A}(q,t)$ denote the set of all adversaries which runs in time at most t and make at most q queries to either a blockcipher or a random permutation. We write $\mathsf{Adv}^{\mathrm{prp}}(q,t) = \max_{\mathcal{A} \in \mathbb{A}(q,t)} \mathsf{Adv}_e^{\mathrm{prp}}(\mathcal{A})$.

Authenticator. A nonce based authenticator with nonce space $\mathcal{N}$, key space $\mathcal{K}$, message space $\mathcal{M}$ and tag space $\mathfrak{B}$ is a function $\gamma : \mathcal{K} \times \mathcal{N} \times \mathcal{M} \to \mathfrak{B}$. We also write $\gamma(k, \cdot, \cdot)$ as $\gamma_k(\cdot, \cdot)$ and hence a nonce based authenticator can be viewed as a keyed family of functions. We say that (n, m, t) is *valid* for γ_k (or for a key k when γ is understood) if $\gamma_k(n, m) = t$. We define a verifier $\mathsf{Ver}_{\gamma_k} : \mathcal{N} \times \mathcal{M} \times \mathfrak{B} \to \{0, 1\}$ as

$$\mathsf{Ver}_{\gamma_k}(n, m, t) = \begin{cases} 1 & \text{if } (n, m, t) \text{ is valid for } \gamma_k, \\ 0 & \text{otherwise.} \end{cases}$$

We also simply write Ver_k instead of Ver_{γ_k}.

An adversary $\mathcal{A}$ against a nonce based authenticator makes authentication queries to γ_K and verification queries to Ver_K for a secretly sampled $K \leftarrow_\$ \mathcal{K}$. An adversary is called

- *nonce-respecting* if nonces in all authentication queries are distinct,
- *single-forgery* (or *multiple-forgery*) if it submits only one (or more than one) verification query,
- *key-recovery* if it finally returns an element from key space.

In this paper we only consider nonce-respecting algorithm. We also assume that $\mathcal{A}$ does not submit a verification query (n, m, t) to Ver_{γ_K} for which (n, m) has already been previously queried to the authentication oracle. Let $\mathbb{A}(q, v, t)$ denote the set of all such nonce-respecting algorithms which runs in time t and make at most q queries to an authenticator and at most v queries to its corresponding verifier. In this paper our main focus on analyzing the information-theoretic adversaries (which can run in unbounded time). So we write $\mathbb{A}(q, v) = \cup_{t < \infty} \mathbb{A}(q, v, t)$.

VIEW OF AN ADVERSARY. An adversary $\mathcal{A} \in \mathbb{A}(q, v)$ makes queries (n_1, m_1), ..., (n_q, m_q) to an authenticator γ_K adaptively and obtain responses $t_1, \ldots, t_q$ respectively. It also makes $(n_1', m_1', t_1'), \ldots, (n_v', m_v', t_v')$ to verifier Ver_K and obtain responses $b_1, \ldots, b_v \in \{0, 1\}$ respectively. The authentication and verification queries can be interleaved and adaptive. Note that all n_i's are distinct as we consider only nonce-respecting adversary, however, n_i''s are not necessarily distinct and can match with n_j values. We also assume that both q and v are fixed and hence non-random. We call the tuple

$$\big((n_1, m_1, t_1), \ldots, (n_q, m_q, t_q), (n_1', m_1', t_1', b_1), \ldots, (n_v', m_v', t_v', b_v)\big)$$

view and denote it as $\mathsf{view}(\mathcal{A}^{\gamma_K, \mathsf{Ver}_K})$ (which is a random variable induced by the randomness of $\mathcal{A}$ and the key of γ). Let

$$\mathcal{V} = (\mathcal{N} \times \mathcal{M} \times \mathcal{B})^q \times (\mathcal{N} \times \mathcal{M} \times \mathcal{B} \times \{0,1\})^v$$

be the set of all possible views. We say that a view $\tau \in \mathcal{V}$ is *realizable* if

$$\Pr_{\mathcal{A}, K}\left(\mathsf{view}(\mathcal{A}^{\gamma_K}) = \tau\right) > 0.$$

AUTHENTICITY ADVANTAGE. Following the notation of the view of an adversary as denoted above, we define the *authenticity advantage* of $\mathcal{A}$ as

$$\mathsf{Auth}_\gamma(\mathcal{A}) := \Pr(\exists i, b_i = 1).$$

In words, it is the probability that $\mathcal{A}$ submits a valid verification query which has not been obtained through a previous authentication query. In this paper, we are interested in the following maximum advantages for some families of adversaries:

$$\mathsf{Auth}_\gamma(q, v, t) = \max_{\mathcal{A} \in \mathbb{A}(q,v,t)} \mathsf{Auth}(\mathcal{A}), \quad \mathsf{Auth}_\gamma(q, v) = \max_{\mathcal{A} \in \mathbb{A}(q,v)} \mathsf{Auth}(\mathcal{A}).$$

So $\mathsf{Auth}_\gamma(q, v)$ is the maximum advantage for all information theoretic adversaries with the limitation that it can make at most q authentication queries and v verification queries. It is shown in [BGM04, Ber05a] that

$$\mathsf{Auth}_\gamma(q, v) \leq v \cdot \mathsf{Auth}_\gamma(q, 1). \tag{6}$$

KEY-RECOVERY ADVANTAGE. A full-key-recovery algorithm $\mathcal{A}$ is an adversary interacting with γ_K and Ver_K and finally it aims to recover the key K. Once the key K is recovered, the full system is broken and so one can forge as many times as it wishes. For some authenticators, we can do the forgeries when a partial key is recovered. Let $\mathcal{K} = \mathcal{K}' \times \mathcal{H}$ for some sets $\mathcal{K}'$ and $\mathcal{H}$. We call $\mathcal{H}$ hash-key space. Let $K = (K', H) \leftarrow_{\$} \mathcal{K}' \times \mathcal{H}$.

Definition 1 (key-recovery advantage). *A hash-key recovery algorithm (or we simply say that a key-recovery algorithm) $\mathcal{A}$ is an adversary interacting with γ_K and Ver_K and finally it returns $\mathbf{h}$, an element from $\mathcal{H}$. We define* key-recovery advantage *of $\mathcal{A}$ against γ as*

$$\mathsf{KR}_\gamma(\mathcal{A}) := \Pr(\mathcal{A}^{\gamma_K, \mathsf{Ver}_K} \Rightarrow \mathbf{h} \wedge \mathbf{h} = H).$$

The above probability is computed under randomness of $\mathcal{A}$ and $K = (K', H)$.

Similar to the maximum authenticity advantages, we define

$$\mathsf{KR}_\gamma(q, v, t) = \max_{\mathcal{A} \in \mathbb{A}(q,v,t)} \mathsf{KR}(\mathcal{A}), \quad \mathsf{KR}_\gamma(q, v) = \max_{\mathcal{A} \in \mathbb{A}(q,v)} \mathsf{KR}(\mathcal{A}).$$

When $v = 0$, we simply write $\mathsf{KR}_\gamma(q, t)$ and $\mathsf{KR}_\gamma(q)$. A relationship between key-recovery advantage and authenticity advantage is the following which can be proved easily $\mathsf{KR}_\gamma(q) \leq \mathsf{Auth}_\gamma(q, 1)$.

AUTHENTICATED ENCRYPTION. In addition to nonce and message, an authenticated encryption γ' takes associated data and returns a ciphertext-tag pair. A verification algorithm $\mathsf{Ver}_{\gamma'}$ takes a tuple of nonce, associated data, ciphertext and tag, and determines whether it is valid (i.e. there is a message corresponding to this ciphertext and tag) or not. A forgery adversary $\mathcal{A}$ submits a fresh tuple (not obtained through encryption queries) of nonce, associated data, ciphertext and tag. Similar to authenticity advantage of an authenticator, authenticity of an adversary $\mathcal{A}$, denoted $\mathsf{Auth}_{\gamma'}(\mathcal{A})$ is the probability that it submits a fresh valid tuple.

ALMOST XOR UNIVERSAL AND Δ-UNIVERSAL HASH FUNCTION. Let $\rho : \mathcal{H} \times \mathcal{M} \to \mathcal{B}$, for some additive commutative group $\mathcal{B}$. We denote the subtraction operation in the group as "$-$". We call ρ ϵ-$\Delta\mathsf{U}$ (ϵ-Δ-universal) if for all $x \neq x' \in \mathcal{M}$ and $\delta \in \mathcal{B}$,

$$\Pr(\rho_\kappa(x) - \rho_\kappa(x') = \delta) \leq \epsilon.$$

Here, the probability is taken under the uniform distribution $\kappa \leftarrow_\$ \mathcal{H}$. Note that $\epsilon \geq 1/N$ (since, for any fixed x, x', $\sum_\delta \Pr(\rho_\kappa(x) - \rho_\kappa(x') = \delta) = 1$). When $\mathcal{B} = \{0,1\}^b$ for some positive integer b and the addition is "$\oplus$" (bit-wise XOR operation), we call ρ ϵ-almost-xor-universal or ϵ-AXU hash function.

3 Known Analysis of WCS

We describe a real and an idealized version of WCS.

Definition 2 (WCS authenticator). *Let e_K be a blockcipher over a commutative group $\mathcal{B}$ of size N with a key space $\mathcal{K}'$ and $\rho_\kappa : \mathcal{M} \to \mathcal{B}$ is a keyed hash function with a key space $\mathcal{K}$. On an input $(n, M) \in \mathcal{B} \times \mathcal{M}$, we define the output of WCS as*

$$\mathsf{WCS}_{K,\kappa}(n, M) = e_K(n) + \rho_\kappa(M). \tag{7}$$

Here, the pair (K, κ), called secret key, is sampled uniformly from $\mathcal{K}' \times \mathcal{K}$.

An idealized version of WCS is based on a uniform random permutation $\pi \leftarrow_\$ \mathsf{Perm}_\mathcal{B}$ (replacing the blockcipher e) and it is defined as

$$\mathsf{iWCS}_{\pi,\kappa}(n, m) = \pi(n) + \rho_\kappa(M) \tag{8}$$

where the hash key $\kappa \leftarrow_\$ \mathcal{K}$ (and independent of the random permutation).

WCS is a nonce based authenticator in which n is the nonce and M is a message. The most popular choice of $\mathfrak{B}$ is $\{0, 1\}^n$ for some positive integer n and the blockcipher is AES [DR05, Pub01] (in which $n = 128$). The WCS and the ideal-WCS authenticators are computationally indistinguishable provided the underlying blockcipher e is a pseudorandom permutation. More formally, one can easily verify the following relations by using standard hybrid reduction;

$$\text{Auth}_{\text{WCS}}(q, v, t) \leq \text{Auth}_{\text{iWCS}}(q, v) + \text{Adv}_e^{\text{prp}}(q + v, t + t'), \tag{9}$$

$$\text{KR}_{\text{WCS}}(q, v, t) \leq \text{KR}_{\text{iWCS}}(q, v) + \text{Adv}_e^{\text{prp}}(q + v, t + t') \tag{10}$$

where t' is the time to compute $q + v$ executions of hash functions ρ_κ.

Polynomial Hash. Polynomial hash is a popular candidate for the keyed hash function in WCS (also used in the tag computation of GCM [MV04]). Here we assume that $\mathfrak{B}$ is a finite field of size N. Given any message $M := (m_1, \ldots, m_d) \in \mathfrak{B}^d$ and a hash key $\kappa \in \mathscr{K} = \mathfrak{B}$, we define the polynomial hash output as

$$\text{Poly}_M(\kappa) := m_d \cdot \kappa + m_{d-1} \cdot \kappa^2 + \cdots + m_1 \cdot \kappa^d. \tag{11}$$

There are many variations of the above definition. Note that it is not an AXU hash function over variable-length messages (as appending zero blocks will not change the hash value). To incorporate variable length message, we sometimes preprocess the message before we run the polynomial hash. One such example is to pad a block which encodes the length of the message. One can simply prepend the constant block 1 to the message. These can be easily shown to be $\frac{\ell}{N}$-AXU over the padded message space $\mathscr{M} = \cup_{i=1}^{\leq \ell} \mathfrak{B}^i$. In this paper we ignore the padding details and for simplicity, we work only on the padded messages. Whenever we use the polynomial hash in the WCS authenticator, we call its hash-key κ the polynomial-key.

Nonce Misuse. The input n is called nonce which should not repeat over different executions. Joux [Jou] and Handschuh and Preneel [HP08] exhibit attacks which recover the polynomial key the moment a nonce is repeated. For any two messages $M \neq M' \in \mathfrak{B}^d$,

$$\text{WCS}_{K,\kappa}(n, M) - \text{WCS}_{K,\kappa}(n, M') = \text{Poly}_M(\kappa) - \text{Poly}_{M'}(\kappa)$$

which is a nonzero polynomial in κ of degree at most d. By solving roots of the polynomial (which can be done efficiently by Berlekamp's algorithm [Ber70] or the Cantor-Zassenhaus algorithm [CZ81]), we can recover the polynomial key. So it is an essential for a WCS authenticator to keep the nonce unique.

3.1   Shoup and Bernstein Bound on WCS

Let iWCS (we simply call it ideal-WCS) be based on a URP and an ϵ-AXU hash function ρ. When we replace the outputs of URP by uniform random values, Wegman and Carter had shown that (in [WC81]) the forgery advantage os less than $v\epsilon$ (independent of the number of authentication queries). So by applying the classical PRP-PRF switching lemma, we obtain

$$\mathsf{Auth_{iWCS}}(q, v) \leq v \cdot \epsilon + \frac{(q+v)^2}{2N}. \tag{12}$$

So the classical bound is useless as q approaches $\sqrt{N}$ or as v approaches to ϵ^{-1}. In [Sho96] Shoup provided an alternative bound (which is improved and valid in a certain range of q). In particular, he proved

$$\mathsf{Auth_{iWCS}}(q, v) \leq v \cdot \epsilon \cdot (1 - \frac{q^2 \epsilon}{2})^{-1}. \tag{13}$$

The above bound is a form of multiplicative (instead of additive form of the classical bounds). Thus, the above bound is simplified as

$$\mathsf{Auth_{iWCS}}(q, v) \leq 2\epsilon_{ver}(v) := 2v \cdot \epsilon, \quad \forall q \leq \sqrt{\epsilon^{-1}}. \tag{14}$$

So the ideal-WCS is secure up to $q \leq \sqrt{\epsilon^{-1}}$ queries. When $\epsilon = 1/N$, it says that authentication advantage is less $2v \cdot \epsilon$ for all $q \leq \sqrt{N}$. In other words, ideal-WCS is secure against birthday complexity adversaries. However, when the hash function is polynomial hash, Shoup's bound says that the ideal-WCS is secure up to $q \leq \sqrt{N/\ell}$. For example, when we authenticate messages of sizes about 2^{24} bytes (i.e. $\ell = 2^{20}$) using AES-based ideal-WCS, we can ensure security up to $q = 2^{54}$ queries. Like the classical bound, it also does not provide guarantees for long-term keys. Bernstein proved the following stronger bound for WCS.

Theorem 1 (Bernstein Bound([Ber05b])). *For all q and v*

$$\mathsf{Auth_{iWCS}}(q, v) \leq B(q, v) := v \cdot \epsilon \cdot (1 - \frac{q}{N})^{-\frac{q+1}{2}}. \tag{15}$$

As a simple corollary (recovering the hash-key implies forgery), for all $v \geq 1$ we have

$$\mathsf{KR_{iWCS}}(q, v) \leq B(q, v), \quad \mathsf{KR_{iWCS}}(q, 0) \leq B(q, 1). \tag{16}$$

The key-recovery bound was not presented in [Ber05b], but it is a simple straightforward corollary from the fact that recovering hash-key implies forgery.

3.2   Interpretation of the Bernstein Bound

We now provide the interpretation of the bound which is crucial for understanding the optimality of ideal-WCS. As $1 - x \leq e^{-x}$, we have

$$B(q, 1) \geq \epsilon \cdot e^{\frac{q(q+1)}{2N}}.$$

Obviously, the Bernstein bound becomes more than one when $q(q+1)/2 \geq N \ln N$ (note that $\epsilon \geq N^{-1}$). So we assume that $q(q+1)/2 \leq N \ln N$. We denote $n = \log_2 N$. By Lemma 1, we have

$$B(q,1) \leq \epsilon \cdot e^{\frac{q(q+1)}{2N}(1+\frac{q}{N})}$$

$$\leq \epsilon \cdot e^{\frac{q(q+1)}{2N}} \times e^{\frac{q \ln N}{N}}$$

$$\leq \epsilon \cdot e^{\frac{q(q+1)}{2N}} \times (1 + \sqrt{\frac{2 \ln^3 N}{N}})$$

$$\leq \epsilon \cdot e^{\frac{q(q+1)}{2N}} \times (1 + \frac{2n^{1.5}}{2^{n/2}}) = \epsilon \cdot e^{\frac{q(q+1)}{2N}} \times (1 + \mathsf{negl}(n))$$

where $\mathsf{negl}(n) = \frac{2n^{1.5}}{2^{n/2}}$. Thus, $B(q,v) = \Theta(v \cdot \epsilon \cdot e^{\frac{q(q+1)}{2N}})$. Let us introduce another parameter δ, called the tolerance level. We would now solve for q and v satisfying $B(q,v) = \delta$ (or the inequality $B(q,v) \geq \delta$) for any fixed constant δ. In other words, we want to get a lower bound of q and v to achieve at least δ authenticity advantage.

1. **Case 1.** When $v \cdot \epsilon = \delta$ and $q \geq 1$ we have $B(q,\ell) \geq \delta$. In other words, one needs to have sufficient verification attempts (and only one authentication query suffices) to have some significant advantage. We would like to note that even when $q = O(\sqrt{N})$, $B(q,v) = \Theta(v \cdot \epsilon)$. So the advantages remain same up to some constant factor for all values of $q = O(\sqrt{N})$. In other words, we can not exploit the number of authentication queries within the birthday-bound complexity.

2. **Case 2.** $v \cdot \epsilon < \delta$. Let us assume that $v\epsilon/\delta = N^\beta$ for some positive real β. In this case one can easily verify that $q = \Omega(\sqrt{\delta N \log N})$ to achieve at least δ advantage. In other words, if $q = o(\sqrt{N \log N})$ and $v = o(\epsilon^{-1})$ then $B(q,v) = o(1)$.

Tightness of the bound for the Case 1. We have seen that when $q = O(\sqrt{N})$, we have $\mathsf{Auth}_\gamma(q,v) = O(v \cdot \epsilon)$. In fact, it can be easily seen to be tight (explained below) when the hash function is the polynomial hash function $\mathsf{Poly}_M(\kappa)$.

KEY GUESS FORGERY/KEY-RECOVERY. Suppose WCS is based on the polynomial hash. Given a tag t of a known nonce-message pair (n, M) with $M \in \mathfrak{B}^\ell$, a simple guess attack works as follows. It selects a subset $\mathfrak{B}_1 \subseteq \mathfrak{B}$ of size ℓ and defines a message $M' \in \mathcal{M}$ and t' such that the following identity as a polynomial in x holds:

$$\mathsf{Poly}_{M'}(x) - t' = \mathsf{Poly}_M(x) - t + \prod_{\alpha \in \mathfrak{B}_1} (x - \alpha).$$

If $\kappa \in \mathfrak{B}_1$ then it is easy to verify that t' is the tag for the nonce-message pair (n, M'). The success probability of the forging attack is exactly ℓ/N. If the forgery is allowed to make v forging attempts, it first chooses v disjoint subsets $\mathfrak{B}_1, \ldots, \mathfrak{B}_v \subseteq \mathfrak{B}$, each of size ℓ. It then performs the above attack for each set $\mathfrak{B}_i$. The success probability of this forgery is exactly $v\ell/N$. The same attack was used to eliminate false keys systematically narrowing the set of potential polynomial keys and searching for "weak" keys.

Remark 1. The tightness of multiple-forgery advantage for WCS based on the polynomial hash can be extended similarly to all those hash functions ρ for which there exist $v + 1$ distinct messages $M_1, \ldots, M_v, M$ and $c_1, \ldots, c_v \in \mathfrak{B}$ such that

$$\Pr(\rho_\kappa(M_i) = \rho_\kappa(M) + c_i, \ \forall i) = v\epsilon_\ell.$$

Why the Bernstein bound is better than the classical birthday bound? One may think the Bernstein bound is very close to the classical birthday bound of the form $q^2/2^n$ and they differ by simply logarithmic factor. However, these two bound are quite different in terms of the data or query limit in the usage of algorithms. We illustrate the difference through an example. Let $n = 128$, and the maximum advantage we can allow is 2^{-32}. Suppose a construction C has maximum forgery advantage $\frac{q^2}{n2^n}$ (a beyond birthday bound with logarithmic factor). Then we must have the constraint $q \leq 2^{51.5}$. Whereas, WCS can be used for at most 2^{64} queries. In other words, Bernstein bound actually provide much better life time of key than the classical birthday bound.

4   False-Key/True-Key Set: A Tool for Key-Recovery and Forgery

Our main goal of the paper is to obtain hash-key-recovery attacks against WCS and GCM. Note that we do not recover the blockcipher key. So key-recovery advantage of whats follows would mean the probability to recover the hash-key only.

Query System and Transcript. A key-recovery (with no verification attempt) or a single forgery adversary has two components. The first component $\mathbf{Q}$, called **query system**, is same for both key-recovery and forgery. It makes queries to $\mathsf{WCS}_{K,\kappa}$ adaptively and obtains responses. Let $(n_1, M_1), \ldots, (n_q, M_q)$ be authentication queries with distinct n_i (i.e., the query system is nonce-respecting) and let t_i denote the response of ith query. Let $\tau := \tau(\mathbf{Q}) = ((n_1, M_1, t_1), \ldots, (n_q, M_q, t_q))$ denote the transcript.

Based on the transcript, a second component of forgery returns a fresh (n, M, t) (not in the transcript). If $n \neq n_i$ for all i then the forgery of WCS is essentially reduced to a forgery of the URP (in particular, forging the value of $\pi(n)$). Hence, the forgery advantage in that case is at most $1/(N-q)$. The most interesting case arises when $n = n_i$ for some i. Similarly, the second component of a key-recovery adversary returns an element $k \in \mathcal{K}$ (key space of the random function) based on the transcript τ obtained by the query system.

Definition 3 (False-key set [LP18]). *With each* $\tau = ((n_1, M_1, t_1), \ldots, (n_q, M_q, t_q))$, *we associate a set*

$$\mathscr{F}_\tau = \{x \in \mathcal{K} \mid \exists i \neq j, \ \rho_x(M_i) - \rho_x(M_j) + t_j - t_i = 0, M_i \neq M_j\}$$

and we call it the **false-key set**.

Note that $\Pr(\kappa \in \mathcal{F}_\tau) = 0$ and so the term false-key set is justified. In other words, the true key κ can be any one of the elements from $\mathcal{T} := \mathcal{K} \setminus \mathcal{F}_\tau$, called the *true-key set*. Given a query system $\mathbf{Q}$, let us consider the key-recovery adversary which simply returns a random key $\mathbf{k}$ from the true-key set. Let us denote the key-recovery adversary as $\mathbf{Q}_{TK}$. The following useful bound is established in [LP18].

Lemma 2 ([LP18]). *Following the notation as described above we have*

$$\mathsf{KR_{WCS}}(\mathbf{Q}_{TK}) \geq \frac{1}{N - \mathbb{E}(|\mathcal{F}_{\tau(\mathbf{Q})}|)}. \tag{17}$$

Proof. Given a transcript τ, the probability that $\mathbf{k} = \kappa$ is exactly $\frac{1}{N-|\mathcal{F}_\tau|}$. Then,

$$\mathsf{KR_{WCS}}(\mathbf{Q}_{TK}) = \sum_\tau \Pr(\mathbf{k} = \kappa \mid \tau) \times \Pr(\tau)$$

$$= \sum_\tau \frac{1}{N - |\mathcal{F}_\tau|} \Pr(\tau)$$

$$= \mathbb{E}\left(\frac{1}{N - |\mathcal{F}_\tau|}\right). \tag{18}$$

Here the expectation is taken under the randomness of the transcript. A transcript depends on the randomness of π, κ and the random coins of the query system. Note that the function $f(x) = \frac{1}{N-x}$ is convex in the interval $(0, N)$ and so by using Jensen inequality, we have $\mathsf{KR_{WCS}}(\mathbf{Q}_{TK}) \geq \frac{1}{N - \mathbb{E}(|\mathcal{F}_{\tau(\mathbf{Q})}|)}$. □

In [LP18], it was also shown that $\mathbb{E}(|\mathcal{F}_{\tau(\mathbf{Q})}| \leq q(q+1)/2$ for all $q < M_\gamma$ where

$$M_\gamma = \max\{q : \min_{m^q, t^q} |\mathcal{T}_\tau| \geq \ell\}$$

where τ denotes the transcript $((m_1, t_1), \ldots, (m_q, t_q))$ (ignoring nonce values as these are redundant). A straight forward estimation of M_γ is $2^{n/2}/\sqrt{\ell}$. Here we give a very simple proof of the above bound for all q.

Lemma 3. *For all q, $\mathbb{E}(|\mathcal{F}_{\tau(\mathbf{Q})}| \leq q(q+1)/2$.*

Proof. We define an indicator random variable I_x which takes value 1 if and only if there exists $i \neq j$ such that $\rho_x(M_i) - \rho_x(M_j) + t_j - t_i = 0$. We observe that $|\mathcal{F}_\tau| = \sum_{x \in \mathcal{K}} \mathsf{I}_x$.

Let us denote $\pi(n_i)$ as V_i. Note that for all i, $t_i = \mathsf{V}_i + \rho_\kappa(M_i)$. Now, $\mathbb{E}(|\mathcal{F}_\tau|) = \sum_{x \in \mathcal{K}} \mathbb{E}(\mathsf{I}_x)$. We write $p_x = \mathbb{E}(\mathsf{I}_x)$ which is nothing but the probability that there exists $i \neq j$ such that $\mathsf{V}_i - \mathsf{V}_j = \rho_x(M_i) - \rho_\kappa(M_i) + \rho_x(M_i) + \rho_\kappa(M_i)$. By using the union bound we have $p_x \leq \binom{q}{2}/(N-1)$. So

$$\mathbb{E}(|\mathcal{F}_\tau|) \leq \frac{Nq(q-1)}{2(N-1)}$$

$$\leq \frac{q(q-1)}{2} + \frac{q(q-1)}{2(N-1)}$$

We can clearly assume that $q < N$ and so by using simple inequality the lemma follows. □

True-key Set. Instead of the false-key set we focus on the true key set. The set $\mathcal{T}_\tau := \mathcal{K} \setminus \mathcal{F}_\tau$ is called the true-key set. In terms of the true-key set, we can write $\mathsf{KR}_{\mathsf{WCS}}(\mathbf{Q}_{TK}) = \mathbb{E}(\frac{1}{|\mathcal{T}_\tau(\mathbf{Q})|})$. Let $\pi(n_i) = \mathsf{V}_i$ and $a_{i,x} := a_{i,x}(\kappa) := \rho_\kappa(M_i) - \rho_x(M_i)$. We can equivalently define the true-key set as

$$\mathcal{T}_\tau = \{x \in \mathcal{K} \mid t_1 - \rho_x(M_1), \ldots, t_q - \rho_x(M_k) \text{ are distinct}\}$$
$$= \{x \in \mathcal{K} \mid \mathsf{V}_1 + a_{1,x}, \ldots, \mathsf{V}_q + a_{q,x} \text{ are distinct}\}. \tag{19}$$

Now we define an indicator random variable I_x as follows:

$$\mathsf{I}_x = \begin{cases} 1, \text{ if } \mathsf{V}_1 + a_{1,x}, \ldots, \mathsf{V}_q + a_{q,x} \text{ are distinct} \\ 0, \text{ otherwise} \end{cases}$$

Let p_x denote the probability that $\mathsf{V}_1 + a_{1,x}, \ldots, \mathsf{V}_q + a_{q,x}$ are distinct. So,

$$\mathbb{E}(|\mathcal{T}_\tau|) = \sum_x \mathbb{E}(\mathsf{I}_x) = \sum_{x \in \mathcal{K}} p_x.$$

When we want to minimize the expected value of the size of the true-key set, we need to upper bound the probability p_x for all x. We use this idea while we analyze our key-recovery attacks.

5   Key-Recovery Security Attacks of WCS

5.1   A Chosen-Plaintext Key-Recovery Attack

In this section we provide a chosen-plaintext attack against any WCS based on any blockcipher and a keyed hash function which satisfies a reasonable assumption, called differential regular. This property is satisfied by the polynomial hash. A function $f : \mathcal{M} \to \mathcal{B}$ is called *regular* if $X \leftarrow_\$ \mathcal{M} \Rightarrow f(X) \leftarrow_\$ \mathcal{B}$. Now we define a special type of keyed hash functions.

Definition 4. *A keyed hash function $\rho_\kappa : \mathcal{K} \to \mathcal{B}$ is called* differential regular *if for all distinct $x, k \in \mathcal{K}$, the function mapping $M \in \mathcal{M}$ to $\rho_k(M) - \rho_x(M)$ is regular.*

The polynomial hash is clearly differential regular. For example, when the message space is $\mathcal{B}$ and $\kappa \neq x$, the function mapping $m \in \mathcal{B}$ to $\rho_\kappa(m) - \rho_x(m) = m(\kappa - x)$ is regular.

Theorem 2. *Suppose WCS is based on a blockcipher and a keyed differential regular hash function ρ. Then,*

$$\mathsf{KR}_{\mathsf{WCS}}(q) \geq \frac{1}{1 + N'e^{-\frac{q(q-1)}{2N}}} \tag{20}$$

where $N' = |\mathcal{K}|$ (size of the hash-key space). In particular, when $q(q-1) = 2N \log N'$ we have $\mathsf{KR}_{\mathsf{WCS}}(q, \ell) \geq 1/2$.

INTERPRETATION OF THE RESULT. When $N' = N$ (key size is same as the block size), we can achieve 0.5 key-recovery advantage after making roughly $\sqrt{2N \log N}$ authentication queries . If $N' = N^c$ for some $c > 1$ (the hash-key size is larger than the block size) we need roughly $\sqrt{2cN \log N}$ (which is a constant multiple of the number queries required for hash-key space of size N) authentication queries.

Proof. Suppose $\mathsf{WCS} := \mathsf{WCS}_{K,\kappa}$ is the WCS authenticator based on a block-cipher e_K and a keyed differential regular hash function ρ_κ. We describe our key-recovery attack[1] $\mathcal{A}$ as follows:

1. Choose q messages $M_1, \ldots, M_q \leftarrow_\$ \mathcal{M}$ and make authentication queries (n_i, M_i), $i \in [q]$ for distinct nonces n_i's.
2. Let $t_1, \ldots, t_q$ be the corresponding responses.
3. Construct the true-key set

$$\mathcal{T}_\tau = \{k \mid (t_i - \rho_k(M_i))'s \text{ are distinct}\}.$$

4. Return a key $\mathbf{k} \leftarrow_\$ \mathcal{T}_\tau$.

Here, $\tau = ((n_1, M_1, t_1), \ldots, (n_q, M_q, t_q))$ is the transcript of the adversary $\mathcal{A}$. We also note that $\Pr(\kappa \in \mathcal{T}_\tau) = 1$ and so we have seen that $\mathsf{KR}_{\mathsf{WCS}}(\mathcal{A}) = \mathbb{E}(\frac{1}{|\mathcal{T}_\tau|})$. Here the expectation is taken under randomness of transcript. The randomness of a transcript depends on the randomness of K, κ and the messages M_i. By using Jensen inequality, we have

$$\mathsf{KR}_{\mathsf{WCS}}(\mathcal{A}) \geq \frac{1}{\mathbb{E}(|\mathcal{T}_\tau|)}.$$

We will now provide an upper bound of $\mathbb{E}(|\mathcal{T}_\tau|)$. In fact, we will provide an upper bound on the conditional expectation after conditioning the blockcipher key K and hash-key κ. Note that $t_i = e_K(n_i) + \rho_\kappa(M_i)$ and hence the true-key set is the set of all x for which $R_{i,x} := e_K(n_i) + \rho_\kappa(M_i) - \rho_x(M_i)$ are distinct for all $i \in [q]$.

Claim. Given K and κ, the conditional distributions of $R_{i,x}$'s are uniform and independent over $\mathfrak{B}$, whenever $x \neq \kappa$.

Proof of the Claim. Once we fix K and κ, for every $x \neq \kappa$, $\rho_\kappa(M_i) - \rho_x(M_i)$ is uniformly distributed (as ρ is differentially regular). So $e_K(n_i) + \rho_\kappa(M_i) - \rho_x(M_i)$'s are also uniformly and independently distributed since $e_K(n_i)$'s are some constants nd M_i's are independently sampled.

---

[1] We note that the similar attack is considered in [LP18] where the messages are fixed and distinct. However in their attacks the analysis is done for $q \leq 2^{n/2}$ whereas, we analyze for all q.

Now we write $|\mathcal{T}_\tau| = \sum_x \mathsf{l}_x$ where l_x is the indicator random variable which takes values 1 if and only if $R_{i,x}$ are distinct for all i. Note that $R_{i,x}$ are distinct for all i has probability exactly $\prod_{i=1}^{q-1}(1 - \frac{i}{N})$ (same as the birthday paradox bound). As $1 - x \le e^{-x}$ for all x, we have $\mathbb{E}(\mathsf{l}_x) = \Pr(\mathsf{l}_x = 1) \le e^{-\frac{q(q-1)}{N}}$. So,

$$\mathbb{E}(|\mathcal{T}| \mid K, \kappa) = 1 + \sum_{x \ne \kappa} \mathbb{E}(\mathsf{l}_x)$$

$$\le 1 + (N' - 1)e^{-\frac{q(q-1)}{2N}}.$$

This bound is true for all K and κ and hence $\mathbb{E}(|\mathcal{T}|) \le 1 + (N' - 1)e^{-\frac{q(q-1)}{2N}}$. This completes the proof. $\qquad\square$

5.2   Known-Plaintext Attack

Now we show a known-plaintext attack for polynomial-based hash in which we do not assume *any randomness of messages*. So our previous analysis does not work in this case. We first describe a combinatorial result which would be used in our known plaintext key-recovery advantage analysis.

Lemma 4. *Let* $V_1, \ldots, V_q$ *be a uniform without replacement sample from* $\mathfrak{B}$ *and* $a_1, \ldots, a_q \in \mathfrak{B}$ *be some distinct elements, for some* $q \le N/6$. *Then,*

$$p_x := \Pr(V_1 + a_1, \ldots, V_q + a_q \ are \ distinct) \le e^{-q^2/4N}.$$

Proof. For $1 \le \alpha \le q$, let h_α denote the number of tuples $v^\alpha = (v_1, \ldots, v_\alpha)$ such that $v_1 + a_1, \ldots, v_\alpha + a_\alpha$ are distinct. Clearly, $h_1 = N$. Now we establish some recurrence relation between $h_{\alpha+1}$ and h_α. We also abuse the term h_α to represent the set of solutions $v^\alpha = (v_1, \ldots, v_\alpha)$ such that $v_1 + a_1, \ldots, v_\alpha + a_\alpha$ are distinct.

Given any solution v^α (among the h_α solutions), we want to estimate the number of ways we can choose $v_{\alpha+1}$. Note that

$$v_{\alpha+1} \notin \{v_1, \ldots, v_\alpha\} \cup \{v_1 + a_1 - a_{\alpha+1}, \ldots, v_\alpha + a_\alpha - a_{\alpha+1}\}.$$

Let $S_\alpha := \{v_1 + a_1 - a_{\alpha+1}, \ldots, v_\alpha + a_\alpha - a_{\alpha+1}\}$. As v^α is one solution from h_α, the size of the set S_α is exactly α. Note that if $v_i = v_j + a_j - a_\alpha$ then j must be different from i as a_i's are distinct. For any $i \ne j \le \alpha$, we denote $h'_\alpha(i, j)$ be the number of v^α such that $v_1 + a_1, \ldots, v_\alpha + a_\alpha$ are distinct and $v_i + a_i = v_j + a_j$ (once again we abuse this term to represent the set of solutions). So by the principle of inclusion and exclusion, we write

$$h_{\alpha+1} = (N - 2\alpha)h_\alpha + \sum_{i \ne j} h'_\alpha(i, j).$$

Claim. For all $i \ne j \le \alpha$, $h'_\alpha(i, j) \le \frac{h_\alpha}{N - 2\alpha}$.

Proof of claim. Let us assume $i = \alpha$ and $j = \alpha - 1$. The proof for the other cases will be similar. Any solution for $h'_\alpha(\alpha, \alpha - 1)$ is a solution for $h_{\alpha-1}$ and $v_\alpha = v_{\alpha-1} + a_{\alpha-1} - a_\alpha$. However, all solutions corresponding to h_α satisfy the solution corresponding to $h_{\alpha-1}$ and v_α is not a member of a set of size at most 2α. So the claim follows.

Now, we have

$$h_{\alpha+1} \leq h_\alpha(N - 2\alpha) + \alpha(\alpha - 1)h_\alpha/(N - 2\alpha).$$

In other words,

$$\frac{h_{\alpha+1}}{h_\alpha} \leq (N - 2\alpha) + \frac{\alpha(\alpha - 1)}{N - 2\alpha} = \frac{N^2 - 4\alpha N + 5\alpha^2 - \alpha}{N - 2\alpha}.$$

Now we simplify the upper bound as follows.

$$\frac{N^2 - 4\alpha N + 5\alpha^2 - \alpha}{N - 2\alpha} = (N - \alpha)\frac{N^2 - 4\alpha N + 5\alpha^2 - \alpha}{N^2 - 3\alpha N + 2\alpha^2}$$

$$= (N - \alpha)(1 - \frac{\alpha N + \alpha - 3\alpha^2}{N^2 - 3\alpha N + 2\alpha^2})$$

$$\leq (N - \alpha)(1 - \frac{\alpha N + \alpha - 3\alpha^2}{N^2})$$

$$\leq (N - \alpha)(1 - \frac{\alpha}{2N})$$

provided $\alpha(N + 1) - 3\alpha^2 \geq \alpha N/2$, equivalently $(N + 2) \geq 6\alpha$. So for all $\alpha \leq q \leq N/6$ we have

$$\frac{h_{\alpha+1}}{h_\alpha} \leq (N - \alpha)(1 - \frac{\alpha}{2N}) \leq (N - \alpha)e^{-\frac{\alpha}{2N}}.$$

By multiplying the ratio for all $1 \leq \alpha \leq q - 1$ and the fact that $h_1 = N$, we have $h_q \leq (N)_q e^{-q^2/4N}$. The lemma follows from the definition that $p_x = \frac{h_q}{(N)_q}$. □

Now we consider the key-recovery adversary considered in [LP18]. However, they considered transcripts with $\sqrt{N}$ queries and were able to show a key-recovery advantage about $1.3/N$. However, we analyze it for all queries q and the key-recovery advantage can reach to $1/2$ for $q = O(\sqrt{N \log N})$.

Theorem 3. *Suppose $m_1, \ldots, m_q \in \mathcal{B}$ be distinct messages and $n_1, \ldots, n_q$ be distinct nonces. Let $t_i = \mathsf{WCS}_{\pi,\kappa}(n_i, m_i)$ where ρ_κ is the polynomial hash. Then, there is an algorithm $\mathcal{A}$ which recovers the hash-key κ with probability at least*

$$\frac{1}{1 + (N - 1)e^{-\frac{q^2}{4N}}}.$$

So when $q = \sqrt{4N \log N}$, the key-recovery advantage is at least $\frac{1}{2}$.

Proof. We denote $\pi(n_i) = \mathsf{V}_i$. So $\mathsf{V}_1, \ldots, \mathsf{V}_q$ forms a without replacement random sample from $\mathcal{B}$. We write $t_i = \mathsf{V}_i + \rho_\kappa(m_i) = \mathsf{V}_i + \kappa \cdot m_i$. As before we define the true-key set as

$$\mathcal{T} := \{x \in \mathcal{B} \mid t_1 - x \cdot m_1, \ldots, t_q - x \cdot m_q \text{ are distinct}\}.$$

Clearly $\kappa \in \mathcal{T}$. Let us fix $x \neq \kappa$ and denote $a_i = (\kappa - x) \cdot m_i$. Note that a_i's are distinct. So given a hash-key κ, we write the size of true-key set $|\mathcal{T}|$ as the sum of the indicator random variables as follows: $|\mathcal{T}| = 1 + \sum_{x \neq \kappa} I_x$ where I_x takes value 1 if and only if $V_1 + a_1, \ldots, V_q + a_q$ are distinct. So,

$$\mathbb{E}(|\mathcal{T}| \mid \kappa) = 1 + \sum_{x \neq \kappa} \mathbb{E}(I_x)$$

$$= 1 + \sum_{x \neq \kappa} p_x$$

where

$$p_x := \Pr(V_1 + a_1, \ldots, V_q + a_q \text{ are distinct}).$$

By Lemma 4, we know that $p_x \leq e^{-\frac{q^2}{4N}}$ and hence $\mathbb{E}(|\mathcal{T}| \mid \kappa) \leq 1 + (N-1)e^{-\frac{q^2}{4N}}$. This is true for all hash-keys κ and hence we have $\mathbb{E}(|\mathcal{T}|) \leq 1 + (N-1)e^{-\frac{q^2}{4N}}$. This completes the proof. □

6   Key-Recovery Security Analysis of GCM

DEFINITION OF GCM. We briefly describe how GCM works. We refer the reader to see [MV04] for details. Here $\mathfrak{B} = \{0,1\}^n$ (with $n = 128$) Let e_K be a blockcipher as before. We derive hash-key as $\kappa = e_K(0^n)$. Given a message $(m_1, \ldots, m_\ell) \in \mathfrak{B}^\ell$ and a nonce $n \in \{0,1\}^{b-s}$ for some s, we define the ciphertext as

$$c_i = V_i' \oplus m_i, \ i \in [\ell], V_i' = e_K(n \| \langle i+1 \rangle)$$

where $\langle i \rangle$ represents s-bit encoding of the integer i. Finally, the tag is computed as xor of $V := e_K(n \| \langle 1 \rangle)$ and the output of the polynomial hash of the associated data and the ciphertext with length encoding. So, $t = V \oplus c_0 \kappa \oplus c_1 \kappa^2 \oplus \cdots$ where c_0 is the block which encodes the length of message (same as the ciphertext) and the associated data.

In other words, the tag is computed as a WCS authentication over the ciphertext with the hash-key derived from the blockcipher. So, one can have a similar key-recovery attack as stated in Theorem 2 which requires roughly $\sqrt{n} \times 2^{n/2}$ authentication queries. More precisely, after making 2^{68} authentication queries with the first message block random we can recover $e_K(0)$ with probability at least $1/2$. Note that the ciphertext blocks are uniformly distributed as it is an XOR of message blocks and some blockcipher outputs independent of the message blocks. Now we show a more efficient algorithm $\mathscr{B}$ which utilize the length of messages as described below.

1. Choose q messages $M_1, \ldots, M_q \xleftarrow{s} \mathfrak{B}^\ell$ and fix some associated data $A_i = A$. Make authentication queries $(n_i, M_i, A), i \in [q]$ for distinct nonces n_i's.
2. Let $(C_1, t_1), \ldots, (C_q, t_q)$ be the corresponding responses.
3. Let $M_i = m_{i,1} \| \cdots m_{i,\ell}$ and $C_i = c_{i,1} \| \cdots c_{i,\ell}$ where $n_{i,j}, c_{i,j} \in \mathfrak{B}$. Construct a set

$$\mathcal{V}' = \{V_{i,j}' := m_{i,j} \oplus c_{i,j} \mid i \in [q], j \in [\ell]\}$$

4. Construct the true-key set

$$\mathcal{T} = \{k \in \mathfrak{B} \mid t_i \oplus \rho_k(A, C_i) \notin \mathcal{V}' \ \forall i \in [q]\}.$$

5. Return a key $\mathbf{k} \leftarrow_\$ \mathcal{T}$.

Remark 2. One may incorporate the relation that $t_i \oplus \rho_k(A, C_i)$'s are distinct while defining the true-key set. We can gain some complexity up to some small constant factor. For the sake of simplicity of the analysis and the attack, we keep the basic simple attack algorithm as described above.

Theorem 4. *Let $N = 2^n$ where n is the block size of the blockcipher used in GCM.*

$$KR_{\mathsf{GCM}}(q, \ell) \geq \frac{1}{1 + Ne^{-\frac{\ell q^2}{N}}} \tag{21}$$

In particular, when $\ell q^2 = N \log N$ we have $KR_{\mathsf{GCM}}(q, \ell) \geq 1/2$.

For example, when $n = 128, \ell = 2^{15}$ we now need $q = 2^{60}$ encryption queries to recover $\kappa = e_K(0)$. Once we recover κ, we can forge as many times as required. Moreover, one can define a universal forgery (for any chosen message and associated data but not the nonce).

Proof. From the permutation nature of the blockcipher, it is easy to see that $e_K(0) \in \mathcal{T}$ as defined in the algorithm. So, as before

$$KR_{\mathsf{GCM}}(\mathcal{A}) \geq \frac{1}{\mathbb{E}(|\mathcal{T}|)}.$$

We will now provide an upper bound of $\mathbb{E}(|\mathcal{T}_\tau|)$. In fact, we will provide an upper bound of the conditional expectation after conditioning the blockcipher key K (so that all blockcipher outputs are fixed). Since message blocks are uniformly distributed, the ciphertext blocks are also uniformly distributed (due to one-time padding). This proves that after conditioning the blockcipher key K,

$$R_{1,x} := t_1 \oplus \rho_x(A, C_1), \ldots, R_{q,x} := t_q \oplus \rho_x(A, C_q) \leftarrow_\$ \mathfrak{B}.$$

Now, we define an indicator random variable I_x to be one if $R_{i,x} \notin \mathcal{V}'$ for all $i \in [q]$ and 0 otherwise. So, from the definition of $\mathcal{T}$, it is easy to see that

$$|\mathcal{T}| = 1 + \sum_{x \neq \kappa} \mathsf{I}_x.$$

Condition a blockcipher key K (and hence the hash-key $\kappa = e_K(0^n)$ is fixed), and fix some $x \neq \kappa$. Now,

$$\mathbb{E}(\mathsf{I}_x \mid K) = \Pr(\mathsf{I}_x = 1 \mid K)$$

$$= \prod_{i=1}^{q} \left(\frac{N - \ell q}{N} \right)$$

$$\leq e^{-\frac{\ell q^2}{N}}.$$

When $x = \kappa$, clearly, $\mathsf{l}_x = 1$. So,

$$\mathbb{E}(|\mathcal{T}| \mid K) = 1 + \sum_{x \neq \kappa} \mathbb{E}(\mathsf{l}_x)$$

$$\leq 1 + Ne^{-\frac{\ell q^2}{N}}.$$

This bound is true for all blockcipher keys K and hence $\mathbb{E}(|\mathcal{T}|) \leq 1 + Ne^{-\frac{\ell q^2}{N}}$. This completes the proof. □

We show that when $\ell q^2 = \sqrt{2N log N}$, we achieve some significant forgery advantage. Bernstein proved an upper bound of the forgery advantage for WCS. A similar proof is also applicable for GCM. In particular, we show that forgery advantage of GCM for single forging attempt is at most $\frac{\ell}{N} \cdot O(e^{\frac{4\ell q^2}{N}})$. So when we consider v forging attempts, the maximum forging advantage is at most $v \cdot \frac{\ell}{N} \cdot O(e^{\frac{4\sigma q}{N}})$. So our forgery algorithm (which is induced from the key-recovery algorithm) is also optimum for GCM. We denote the maximum forging advantage as $\mathsf{Auth}_{\mathsf{GCM}}(q, v, \sigma, \ell)$ where σ denotes the total number of blocks present in message and associated data in all q encryption queries, and ℓ denotes the number of blocks present in associated data and message or ciphertext for the largest query among all encryption and verification attempts. A similar result has been stated in Appendix C of [IOM12a] (full version of [IOM12b]).

Theorem 5. *Let* GCM *be based on the ideal n-bit random permutation* π. *Then, for all* q, v *and* ℓ,

$$\mathsf{Auth}_{\mathsf{GCM}}(q, v, \sigma, \ell) = v \cdot \frac{\ell}{N} \cdot O(e^{\frac{4\sigma q}{N}}) \tag{22}$$

Proof. We use x^q to denote a q tuple $(x_1, \ldots, x_q)$. For positive integers $r \leq m$, we write $(m)_r := m(m - 1) \cdots (m - r + 1)$. Bernstein proved an upper bound of the interpolation probability of a random permutation π as described below. Let $\delta_N(q) = (1 - (q - 1)/N)^{-q/2}$.

Theorem 4.2 in [Ber05b] showed that for all $0 < r \leq N$,

$$\frac{1}{(N)_r} \leq \frac{\delta_N(r)}{N^r} = \frac{(1 - \frac{r-1}{N})^{-\frac{r}{2}}}{N^r}. \tag{23}$$

Note that for any r distinct inputs $x_1, \ldots, x_r$ and outputs $y_1, \ldots, y_r$ the probability that $\pi(x_1) = y_1, \ldots, \pi(x_r) = y_r$ is exactly $\frac{1}{(N)_r}$. We use this result to prove our result.

Without loss of generality we assume that $\mathscr{A}$ is deterministic and the nonce in the forging attempt is one of the nonce in the encryption queries (since otherwise the bound can be shown to be smaller that what we claimed). We also assume that adversary makes single forging attempt (i.e. $v = 1$). Let $\mathscr{A}$ make queries (n_i, m_i, a_i) and obtain response (c_i, t_i) where $m_i = (m_i[1], \ldots, m_i[\ell_i])$, $a_i = (a_i[1], \ldots, a_i[\ell_i'])$ and $c_i = (c_i[1], \ldots, c_i[\ell_i])$ and let $\sigma = \sum_{i=1}^{q}(\ell_i + \ell_i')$

(total number of blocks in all queries). We call $(n^q, m^q, a^q, c^q, t^q)$ transcript (for encryption queries).

Let (n^*, a^*, c^*, t^*) denote the forging attempt where c^* contains ℓ^* blocks. According to our simplification, let $n^* = n_i$ for some i. So c^q, t^q determine the whole transcript including the forging attempt. Let us write $z_i = m_i \oplus c_i$. It is also easy to see that t^q, z^q also determine the transcript.

Let F denote the forgery event, $n^* = n_i$ and $d = t^* \oplus t_i$. Moreover, for every k (a candidate of hash key), we set $y_i(k) = t_i \oplus \rho_k(a_i \| c_i)$. Now, $\Pr(F) = \Pr(\rho_\kappa(a_i \| c_i) \oplus \rho_\kappa(a^* \| m^*) = d)$. This can be written as the following sum

$$\Pr(F) = \sum_{t^q, z^q} \Pr(\rho_\kappa(a_i \| c_i) \oplus \rho_\kappa(a^* \| c^*) = d \ \wedge \ \mathcal{A} \text{ obtains } z^q, t^q)$$

$$= \sum_{t^q, z^q} \Pr(\rho_\kappa(a_i \| c_i) \oplus \rho_\kappa(a^* \| c^*) = d \ \wedge \ E(\kappa))$$

where the sum is taken over all t^q and all those z^q for which all blocks of z_i's are distinct. The event $E(\kappa)$ denotes that $\pi(n_1 \| \langle 1 \rangle) = y_1(\kappa), \ldots, \pi(n_q \| \langle 1 \rangle) = y_q(\kappa)$ and $\pi(n_i \| \langle j \rangle) = z_i[j]$ for all $1 \le i \le q$, $1 \le j \le \ell_i$.

Now conditioning on any $\pi(0) := \kappa = k$ such that $\rho_\kappa(a_i \| c_i) \oplus \rho_\kappa(a^* \| c^*) = d$ (there are at most $\max\{\ell_i + \ell'_i, \ell^* + \ell'^*\} + 1 \le \ell$ choices of k), the conditional probability is reduced to $\Pr(E(k))$ which should be $\frac{1}{(N-1)_{q+\sigma}}$ (note that $\pi(0)$ is conditioned and the event $E(k)$ defines $q + \sigma$ many inputs-outputs of π). So,

$$\Pr(F) = \sum_{t^q, z^q} \Pr(\rho_\kappa(a_i \| c_i) \oplus \rho_\kappa(a^* \| c^*) = d \ \wedge \ E(\kappa))$$

$$= \sum_{t^q, z^q} \Pr(\rho_\kappa(a_i \| c_i) \oplus \rho_\kappa(a^* \| c^*) = d) \times \Pr(E(\kappa) \mid \rho_\kappa(a_i \| c_i) \oplus \rho_\kappa(a^* \| c^*) = d)$$

$$\le \sum_{t^q, z^q} \frac{\ell}{N} \cdot \frac{1}{(N-1)_{q+\sigma}}$$

$$= \frac{\ell \cdot (N)_\sigma \cdot N^q}{(N)_{q+\sigma+1}}$$

Note that in the above sum, we vary all distinct values of z blocks and so there are $(N)_\sigma$ such choices of z. Now it remains to simplify the bound.

$$\Pr(F) \le \frac{\ell \cdot (N)_\sigma \cdot N^q}{(N)_{q+\sigma+1}}$$

$$= \frac{\ell \cdot N^q}{(N-\sigma)_{q+1}}$$

$$\le_{(a)} \frac{\ell \cdot N^q}{(N-\sigma)^{q+1}} \delta_{N-\sigma}(q+1)$$

$$= \frac{\ell}{N} \times (1 - \frac{\sigma}{N})^{-(q+1)} \times (1 - \frac{q}{N-\sigma})^{-(q+1)/2}.$$

The inequality (a) follows from Eq. 23 with N as $N - \sigma$. This provides the forgery bound for GCM (without using the privacy bound for GCM). For the values of q, ℓ and σ of our interest, we can assume that $\sigma \leq N/2$ and $1 - x = \Theta(e^{-x})$ (Lemma 1). So we can rewrite the upper bound of the forgery advantage of GCM as

$$\frac{\ell}{N} \cdot O(e^{\frac{\sigma(q+1)+q(q+1)}{N}}) = \frac{\ell}{N} \cdot O(e^{\frac{(\sigma+q)(q+1)}{N}}) = \frac{\ell}{N} \cdot O(e^{\frac{4\sigma q}{N}}).$$

The proof for v forging attempts simply follows by multiplying above bound by v. $\square$

Remark 3. The above bound says that, as long as $q\sigma = o(N \log N)$, the forgery advantage is negligible and hence we need $q\sigma$ to be in the order of $N \log N$ to get non-negligible advantage. Along with our forgery adversary on GCM, we have shown the above forgery bound of GCM is indeed tight.

7   Conclusion

In this paper we describe key-recover attacks on WCS and GCM. The query complexity of the attack match with the Bernstein bound and hence we prove the tightness of Bernstein bound. Although the query complexity of our attacks are optimal, a straightforward implementation would require $O(N)$ memory and time complexity. Very recently Leurent and Sibleyras [LS18] demonstrated attacks for WCS. They have described a method to recover hash key of WCS (and counter mode encryption) with $O(2^{2n/3})$ query and time complexity. However, the success probability analysis of their attack is heuristic. It would be an interesting problem to see whether our concrete analysis can be adapted to their attacks.

Acknowledgments. The author would like to thank Anirban Ghatak, Eik List, Subhamoy Maitra, Bart Mennink and anonymous reviewers for their useful comments. The author would also like to thank Atul Luykx for the initial discussion of the paper. This work is supported by R. C. Bose Center for Cryptology and Security.

References

[ABBT15] Abdelraheem, M.A., Beelen, P., Bogdanov, A., Tischhauser, E.: Twisted polynomials and forgery attacks on GCM. In: Oswald, E., Fischlin, M. (eds.) EUROCRYPT 2015. LNCS, vol. 9056, pp. 762–786. Springer, Heidelberg (2015). https://doi.org/10.1007/978-3-662-46800-5_29

[AY12] Aoki, K., Yasuda, K.: The security and performance of "GCM" when short multiplications are used instead. In: Kutyłowski, M., Yung, M. (eds.) Inscrypt 2012. LNCS, vol. 7763, pp. 225–245. Springer, Heidelberg (2013). https://doi.org/10.1007/978-3-642-38519-3_15

[BBS86] Blum, L., Blum, M., Shub, M.: A simple unpredictable pseudo-random number generator. SIAM J. Comput. **15**(2), 364–383 (1986)

[Ber70]   Berlekamp, E.R.: Factoring polynomials over large finite fields. Math. Comput. **24**(111), 713–735 (1970)

[Ber05a] Bernstein, D.J.: The Poly1305-AES message-authentication code. In: Gilbert, H., Handschuh, H. (eds.) FSE 2005. LNCS, vol. 3557, pp. 32–49. Springer, Heidelberg (2005). https://doi.org/10.1007/11502760_3

[Ber05b] Bernstein, D.J.: Stronger security bounds for Wegman-Carter-Shoup authenticators. In: Cramer, R. (ed.) EUROCRYPT 2005. LNCS, vol. 3494, pp. 164–180. Springer, Heidelberg (2005). https://doi.org/10.1007/11426639_10

[Ber07]   Bernstein, D.J.: Polynomial evaluation and message authentication. http://cr.yp.to/papers.html#pema. ID b1ef3f2d385a926123e1517392e20f8c. Citations in this document, 2 (2007)

[BGM04]   Bellare, M., Goldreich, O., Mityagin, A.: The power of verification queries in message authentication and authenticated encryption. IACR Cryptology ePrint Archive, 2004:309 (2004)

[BHK+99] Black, J., Halevi, S., Krawczyk, H., Krovetz, T., Rogaway, P.: UMAC: fast and secure message authentication. In: Wiener, M. (ed.) CRYPTO 1999. LNCS, vol. 1666, pp. 216–233. Springer, Heidelberg (1999). https://doi.org/10.1007/3-540-48405-1_14

[BJKS94] Bierbrauer, J., Johansson, T., Kabatianskii, G., Smeets, B.: On families of hash functions via geometric codes and concatenation. In: Stinson, D.R. (ed.) CRYPTO 1993. LNCS, vol. 773, pp. 331–342. Springer, Heidelberg (1994). https://doi.org/10.1007/3-540-48329-2_28. http://cr.yp.to/bib/entries.html#1994/bierbrauer

[Bra83]   Brassard, G.: On computationally secure authentication tags requiring short secret shared keys. In: Chaum, D., Rivest, R.L., Sherman, A.T. (eds.) Advances in Cryptology, pp. 79–86. Springer, Boston, MA (1983). https://doi.org/10.1007/978-1-4757-0602-4_7

[BT16]   Bellare, M., Tackmann, B.: The multi-user security of authenticated encryption: AES-GCM in TLS 1.3. In: Robshaw, M., Katz, J. (eds.) CRYPTO 2016. LNCS, vol. 9814, pp. 247–276. Springer, Heidelberg (2016). https://doi.org/10.1007/978-3-662-53018-4_10

[CW79]   Carter, L., Wegman, M.N.: Universal classes of hash functions. J. Comput. Syst. Sci. **18**(2), 143–154 (1979)

[CZ81]   Cantor, D.G., Zassenhaus, H.: A new algorithm for factoring polynomials over finite fields. Math. Comput. **36**(154), 587–592 (1981)

[dB93]   den Boer, B.: A simple and key-economical unconditional authentication scheme. J. Comput. Secur. **2**, 65–71 (1993). http://cr.yp.to/bib/entries.html#1993/denboer

[DR05]   Daemen, J., Rijmen, V.: Rijndael/AES. In: van Tilborg, H.C.A. (ed.) Encyclopedia of Cryptography and Security, pp. 520–524. Springer, Boston (2005). https://doi.org/10.1007/0-387-23483-7

[GMS74]   Gilbert, E.N., MacWilliams, F.J., Sloane, N.J.A.: Codes which detect deception. Bell Labs Tech. J. **53**(3), 405–424 (1974)

[HK97]   Halevi, S., Krawczyk, H.: MMH: software message authentication in the Gbit/second rates. In: Biham, E. (ed.) FSE 1997. LNCS, vol. 1267, pp. 172–189. Springer, Heidelberg (1997). https://doi.org/10.1007/BFb0052345

[HP08]   Handschuh, H., Preneel, B.: Key-recovery attacks on universal hash function based MAC algorithms. In: Wagner, D. (ed.) CRYPTO 2008. LNCS, vol. 5157, pp. 144–161. Springer, Heidelberg (2008). https://doi.org/10.1007/978-3-540-85174-5_9

[IOM12a] Iwata, T., Ohashi, K., Minematsu, K.: Breaking and repairing GCM security proofs (2012)

[IOM12b] Iwata, T., Ohashi, K., Minematsu, K.: Breaking and repairing GCM security proofs. In: Safavi-Naini, R., Canetti, R. (eds.) CRYPTO 2012. LNCS, vol. 7417, pp. 31–49. Springer, Heidelberg (2012). https://doi.org/10.1007/978-3-642-32009-5_3

[Jou]   Joux, A.: Comments on the draft GCM specification-authentication failures in NIST version of GCM

[JTC11]   JTC1: ISO/IEC 9797–1:2011 information technology - security techniques - message authentication codes (MACs) - part 1: Mechanisms using a block cipher (2011)

[KR87]   Karp, R.M., Rabin, M.O.: Efficient randomized pattern-matching algorithms. IBM J. Res. Dev. **31**, 249–260 (1987). http://cr.yp.to/bib/entries.html#1987/karp

[Kra94]   Krawczyk, H.: LFSR-based hashing and authentication. In: Desmedt, Y.G. (ed.) CRYPTO 1994. LNCS, vol. 839, pp. 129–139. Springer, Heidelberg (1994). https://doi.org/10.1007/3-540-48658-5_15

[LP18]   Luykx, A., Preneel, B.: Optimal forgeries against polynomial-based MACs and GCM. In: Nielsen, J.B., Rijmen, V. (eds.) EUROCRYPT 2018. LNCS, vol. 10820, pp. 445–467. Springer, Cham (2018). https://doi.org/10.1007/978-3-319-78381-9_17

[LS18]   Leurent, G., Sibleyras, F.: The missing difference problem, and its applications to counter mode encryption. In: Nielsen, J.B., Rijmen, V. (eds.) EUROCRYPT 2018. LNCS, vol. 10821, pp. 745–770. Springer, Cham (2018). https://doi.org/10.1007/978-3-319-78375-8_24

[MV04]   McGrew, D.A., Viega, J.: The security and performance of the Galois/Counter Mode (GCM) of operation. In: Canteaut, A., Viswanathan, K. (eds.) INDOCRYPT 2004. LNCS, vol. 3348, pp. 343–355. Springer, Heidelberg (2004). https://doi.org/10.1007/978-3-540-30556-9_27

[MV06]   McGrew, D., Viega, J.: The use of Galois Message Authentication Code (GMAC) in IPsec ESP and AH. Technical report, May 2006

[Nan14]   Nandi, M.: On the minimum number of multiplications necessary for universal hash functions. In: Cid, C., Rechberger, C. (eds.) FSE 2014. LNCS, vol. 8540, pp. 489–508. Springer, Heidelberg (2015). https://doi.org/10.1007/978-3-662-46706-0_25

[PC15]   Procter, G., Cid, C.: On weak keys and forgery attacks against polynomial-based MAC schemes. J. Cryptol. **28**(4), 769–795 (2015)

[Pub01]   NIST FIPS Pub. 197: Advanced encryption standard (AES). Federal information processing standards publication, 197(441):0311 (2001)

[Rab81]   Rabin, M.O.: Fingerprinting by random polynomials (1981). http://cr.yp.to/bib/entries.html#1981/rabin. Note: Harvard Aiken Computational Laboratory TR-15-81

[Rog95]   Rogaway, P.: Bucket hashing and its application to fast message authentication. In: Coppersmith, D. (ed.) CRYPTO 1995. LNCS, vol. 963, pp. 29–42. Springer, Heidelberg (1995). https://doi.org/10.1007/3-540-44750-4_3

238   M. Nandi

[Saa12] Saarinen, M.-J.O.: Cycling attacks on GCM, GHASH and other polynomial MACs and hashes. In: Canteaut, A. (ed.) FSE 2012. LNCS, vol. 7549, pp. 216–225. Springer, Heidelberg (2012). https://doi.org/10.1007/978-3-642-34047-5_13

[SCM08] Salowey, J., Choudhury, A., McGrew, D.: AES Galois Counter Mode (GCM) cipher suites for TLS. Technical report, August 2008

[Sho96] Shoup, V.: On fast and provably secure message authentication based on universal hashing. In: Koblitz, N. (ed.) CRYPTO 1996. LNCS, vol. 1109, pp. 313–328. Springer, Heidelberg (1996). https://doi.org/10.1007/3-540-68697-5_24

[Sti94] Stinson, D.R.: Universal hashing and authentication codes. Des. Codes Cryptogr. **4**(3), 369–380 (1994)

[Tay94] Taylor, R.: An integrity check value algorithm for stream ciphers. In: Stinson, D.R. (ed.) CRYPTO 1993. LNCS, vol. 773, pp. 40–48. Springer, Heidelberg (1994). https://doi.org/10.1007/3-540-48329-2_4

[WC81] Wegman, M.N., Carter, L.: New hash functions and their use in authentication and set equality. J. Comput. Syst. Sci. **22**(3), 265–279 (1981)

[ZTG13] Zhu, B., Tan, Y., Gong, G.: Revisiting MAC forgeries, weak keys and provable security of Galois/Counter Mode of operation. In: Abdalla, M., Nita-Rotaru, C., Dahab, R. (eds.) CANS 2013. LNCS, vol. 8257, pp. 20–38. Springer, Cham (2013). https://doi.org/10.1007/978-3-319-02937-5_2

Hashes and Random Oracles

Correcting Subverted Random Oracles

Alexander Russell[1], Qiang Tang[2(✉)], Moti Yung[3], and Hong-Sheng Zhou[4]

[1] University of Connecticut, Mansfield, USA
acr@cse.uconn.edu
[2] New Jersey Institute of Technology, Newark, USA
qiang@njit.edu
[3] Columbia University, New York City, USA
moti@cs.columbia.edu
[4] Virginia Commonwealth University, Richmond, USA
hszhou@vcu.edu

Abstract. The random oracle methodology has proven to be a powerful tool for designing and reasoning about cryptographic schemes, and can often act as an effective bridge between theory and practice. In this paper, we focus on the basic problem of correcting faulty—or adversarially corrupted—random oracles, so that they can be confidently applied for such cryptographic purposes.

We prove that a simple construction can transform a "subverted" random oracle—which disagrees with the original one at a negligible fraction of inputs—into a construction that is *indifferentiable* from a random function. Our results permit future designers of cryptographic primitives in typical kleptographic settings (i.e., with adversaries who may subvert the implementation of cryptographic algorithms but undetectable via blackbox testing) to use random oracles as a trusted black box, in spite of not trusting the implementation. Our analysis relies on a general rejection re-sampling lemma which is a tool of possible independent interest.

1 Introduction

The random oracle methodology [7] has proven to be a powerful tool for designing and reasoning about cryptographic schemes. It consists of the following two steps: (i) design a scheme Π in which all parties (including the adversary) have oracle access to a common truly random function, and establish the security of Π in this favorable setting; (ii) instantiate the random oracle in Π with a suitable cryptographic hash function (such as SHA256) to obtain an instantiated scheme Π'. The random oracle heuristic states that if the original scheme Π is secure, then the instantiated scheme Π' is also secure. While this heuristic can fail in various settings [19] the basic framework remains a fundamental design and analysis tool. In this work we focus on the problem of correcting faulty—or adversarially corrupted—random oracles so that they can be confidently applied for such cryptographic purposes.

H. Shacham and A. Boldyreva (Eds.): CRYPTO 2018, LNCS 10992, pp. 241–271, 2018.
https://doi.org/10.1007/978-3-319-96881-0_9

Specifically, given a function $\tilde{h}$ drawn from a distribution which agrees in most places with a uniform function, we would like to produce a corrected version that has stronger uniformity properties. Our problem shares some features with the classical "self-checking and self-correcting program" paradigm [9–11]: we wish to transform a program that is faulty at a small fraction of inputs (modeling an evasive adversary) to a program that is correct at all points. In this light, our model can be viewed as an adaptation of the classical theory that considers the problem of "self-correcting a probability distribution." Notably, in our setting the functions to be corrected are structureless—specifically, drawn from the uniform distribution—rather than heavily structured. Despite that, the basic procedure for correction and portions of the technical development are analogous.

One particular motivation for correcting random oracles in a cryptographic context arises from recent work studying security in the *kleptographic* setting. In this setting, the various components of a cryptographic scheme may be subverted by an adversary so long as the tampering cannot be detected via black-box testing. This is a challenging setting for a number of reasons highlighted by [6,49,50]: one particular difficulty is that the random oracle paradigm is directly undermined. In terms of the discussion above, the random oracle—which is eventually to be replaced with a concrete function—is subject to adversarial subversion which complicates even the first step (i) of the random oracle methodology above. Our goal is to provide a generic approach that can rigorously "protect" random oracles from subversion.

1.1 Our Contributions

We first give two concrete attacking scenarios where hash functions are subverted in the kleptographic setting. We then express the security properties by adapting the successful framework of *indifferentiability* [23,41] to our setting with adversarial subversion. This framework provides a satisfactory guarantee of modularity—that is, that the resulting object can be directly employed by other constructions demanding a random oracle. We call this new notion "crooked" indifferentiability to reflect the role of adversary in the modeling; see below. (A formal definition appears in Sect. 2.)

We prove that a simple construction involving only *public* randomness can boost a "subverted" random oracle into a construction that is indifferentiable from a random function (Sects. 3 and 4). We remark that our technical development establishes a novel "rejection re-sampling" lemma, controlling the distribution emerging from adversarial re-sampling of product distributions. This may be a technique of independent interest. We expand on these contributions below.

Consequences of kleptographic hash subversion. We first illustrate the damages that are caused by using hash functions that are subverted at only a negligible fraction of inputs with two concrete examples:

(1) Chain take-over attack on blockchain. For simplicity, consider a proof-of-work blockchain setting where miners compete to find a solution s to the "puzzle"

$h(\mathsf{pre}\|\mathsf{transactions}\|s) \leq d$, where pre denotes the hash of previous block, transactions denotes the set of valid transactions in the current block, and d denotes the difficulty parameter. Here h is intended to be a strong hash function. Note that, the mining machines use a program $\tilde{h}(\cdot)$ (or a dedicated hardware module) which could be designed by a clever adversary. Now if $\tilde{h}$ has been subverted so that $\tilde{h}(*\|z) = 0$ for a randomly chosen z—and $\tilde{h}(x) = h(x)$ in all other cases— this will be difficult to detect by prior black-box testing; on the other hand, the adversary who created $\tilde{h}$ has the luxury of solving the proof of work without any effort for any challenge, and thus can completely control the blockchain. (A fancier subversion can tune the "backdoor" z to other parts of the input so that it cannot be reused by other parties; e.g., $\tilde{h}(w\|z) = 0$ if $z = f(w)$ for a secret pseudorandom function known to the adversary.)

(2) System sneak-in attack on password authentication. In Unix-style system, during system initialization, the root user chooses a master password α and the system stores the digest $\rho = h(\alpha)$, where h is a given hash function normally modeled as a random oracle. During login, the operating system receives input x and accepts this password if $h(x) = \rho$. An attractive feature of this practice is that it is still secure if ρ is accidentally leaked. In the presence of kleptographic attacks, however, the module that implements the hash function h may be strategically subverted, yielding a new function $\tilde{h}$ which destroys the security of the scheme above: for example, the adversary may choose a relatively short random string z and define $\tilde{h}(y) = h(y)$ *unless y begins with z*, in which case $\tilde{h}(zx) = x$. As above, h and $\tilde{h}$ are indistinguishable by black-box testing; on the other hand, the adversary can login as the system administrator using ρ and its knowledge of the backdoor z (without knowing the actual password α, presenting $z\rho$ instead).

The model of "crooked" indifferentiability. The problem of cleaning defective randomness has a long history in computer science. Our setting requires that the transformation must be carried out by a local rule and involve an exponentially small amount of public randomness (in the sense that we wish to clean a defective random function $h : \{0,1\}^n \to \{0,1\}^n$ with only a polynomial length random string). The basic framework of correcting a subverted random oracle is the following:

First, a function $h : \{0,1\}^n \to \{0,1\}^n$ is drawn uniformly at random. Then, an adversary may *subvert* the function h, yielding a new function $\tilde{h}$. The subverted function $\tilde{h}(x)$ is described by an adversarially-chosen (polynomial-time) algorithm $\tilde{H}^h(x)$, with oracle access to h. We insist that $\tilde{h}(x) \neq h(x)$ only at a negligible fraction of inputs.[1] Next, the function $\tilde{h}$ is "publicly corrected" to

---

[1] We remark that tampering with even a negligible fraction of inputs can have devastating consequences in many settings of interest: e.g., the blockchain and password examples above. Additionally, the setting of negligible subversion is precisely the desired parameter range for existing models of kleptographic subversion and security. In these models, when an oracle is non-negligibly defective, this can be easily detected by a watchdog using a simple sampling and testing regimen, see e.g., [49].

a function $\tilde{h}_R$ (defined below) that involves some public randomness R selected after $\tilde{h}$ is supplied.[2]

We wish to show that the resulting function (construction) is "as good as" a random oracle, in the sense of indifferentiability. We say a construction C^H (having oracle access to an ideal primitive H) is indifferentiable from another ideal primitive $\mathcal{F}$, if there exists a simulator $\mathcal{S}$ so that (C^H, H) and $(\mathcal{F}, \mathcal{S})$ are indistinguishable to any distinguisher $\mathcal{D}$.

To reflect our setting, an H-crooked-distinguisher $\widehat{\mathcal{D}}$ is introduced; the H-crooked-distinguisher $\widehat{\mathcal{D}}$ first prepares the subverted implementation $\tilde{H}$ (after querying H first); then a fixed amount of (public) randomness R is drawn and published; the construction C uses only subverted implementation $\tilde{H}$ and R. Now following the indifferentiability framework, we will ask for a simulator $\mathcal{S}$, such that $(C^{\tilde{H}^H}(\cdot, R), H)$ and $(\mathcal{F}, \mathcal{S}^{\tilde{H}}(R))$ are indistinguishable to any H-crooked-distinguisher $\widehat{\mathcal{D}}$ who even knows R. A similar security preserving theorem [23,41] also holds in our model. See Sect. 2 for details.

The construction. The construction depends on a parameter $\ell = \text{poly}(n)$ and public randomness $R = (r_1, \ldots, r_\ell)$, where each r_i is an independent and uniform element of $\{0,1\}^n$. For simplicity, the construction relies on a family of independent random oracles $h_i(x)$, for $i \in \{0, \ldots, \ell\}$. (Of course, these can all be extracted from a single random oracle with slightly longer inputs by defining $\tilde{h}_i(x) = \tilde{h}(i, x)$ and treating the output of $h_i(x)$ as n bits long.) Then we define

$$\tilde{h}_R(x) = \tilde{h}_0 \left(\bigoplus_{i=1}^{\ell} \tilde{h}_i(x \oplus r_i) \right) = \tilde{h}_0 \left(\tilde{g}_R(x) \right).$$

Note that the adversary is permitted to subvert the function(s) h_i by choosing an algorithm $H^{h_*}(x)$ so that $\tilde{h}_i(x) = H^{h_*}(i, x)$. Before diving into the analysis, let us first quick demonstrate how some simpler constructions fail.

Simple constructions and their shortcomings. Although during the stage of manufacturing the hash functions $\tilde{h}_* = \{\tilde{h}_i\}_{i=0}^{\ell}$, the randomness $R := r_1, \ldots, r_\ell$ are not known to the adversary, they become public in the second query phase. If the "mixing" operation is not carefully designed, the adversary could choose inputs accordingly, trying to "peel off" R. We discuss a few examples:

1. $\tilde{h}_R(x)$ is simply defined as $\tilde{h}_1(x \oplus r_1)$. A straightforward attack is as follows: the adversary can subvert h_1 in a way that $\tilde{h}_1(m) = 0$ for a random input m; the adversary then queries $m \oplus r_1$ on $\tilde{h}_R(\cdot)$ and can trivially distinguish $\tilde{h}$ from a random function.

---

[2] We remark that in many settings, e.g., the model of classical self-correcting programs, we are permitted to sample fresh and "private" randomness for each query; in our case, we may only use a single polynomial-length random string for all points. Once R is generated, it is made public and fixed, which implicitly defines our corrected function $\tilde{h}_R(\cdot)$. This latter requirement is necessary in our setting as random oracles are typically used as a public object—in particular, our attacker must have full knowledge of R.

2. $\tilde{h}_R(x)$ is defined as $\tilde{h}_1(x \oplus r_1) \oplus \tilde{h}_2(x \oplus r_2)$. Now a slightly more complex attack can still succeed: the adversary subverts h_1 so that $\tilde{h}_1(x) = 0$ if $x = m||*$, that is, when the first half of x equals to a randomly selected string m with length $n/2$; likewise, h_2 is subverted so that $\tilde{h}_2(x) = 0$ if $x = *||m$, that is, the second half of x equals m. Then, the adversary queries $m_1||m_2$ on $\tilde{h}_R(\cdot)$, where $m_1 = m \oplus r_{1,0}$, and $m_2 = m \oplus r_{2,1}$, and $r_{1,0}$ is the first half of r_1, and $r_{2,1}$ is the second half of r_2. Again, trivially, it can be distinguished from a random function.

This attack can be generalized in a straightforward fashion to any $\ell \le n/\lambda$: the input can be divided in into consecutive substrings each with length λ, and the "trigger" substrings can be planted in each chunk.

Challenges in the analysis. To analyze security in the "crooked" indifferentiability framework, our simulator needs to ensure consistency between two ways of generating output values: one is directly from the construction $C^{\tilde{H}^h}(x, R)$; the other calls for an "explanation" of F—a truly random function—via reconstruction from related queries to H (in a way consistent with the subverted implementation $\tilde{H}$). To ensure a correct simulation, the simulator must suitably answer related queries (defining one value of $C^{\tilde{H}^h}(x, R)$). We develop a theorem establishing an unpredictability property of the internal function $\tilde{g}_R(x)$ to guarantee the success of simulation. In particular, we prove that for any input x (if not yet "fully decided" by previous queries), the output of $\tilde{g}_R(x)$ is unpredicatable to the distinguisher even if she knows the public randomness R (even conditioned on adaptive queries generated by $\hat{\mathcal{D}}$).

Section 4 develops the detailed security analysis for the property of the internal function $\tilde{g}_R(x)$. The proof of correctness for this construction is complicated by the fact that the "defining" algorithm $\tilde{H}$ is permitted to make adaptive queries to h during the definition of $\tilde{h}$; in particular, this means that even when a particular "constellation" of points (the $h_i(x \oplus r_i)$) contains a point that is left alone by $\tilde{H}$ (which is to say that it agrees with $h_i()$) there is no guarantee that $\bigoplus_i h_i(x \oplus r_i)$ is uniformly random. This suggests focusing the analysis on demonstrating that the constellation associated with every $x \in \{0,1\}^n$ will have at least one "good" component, which is (i.) not queried by $\tilde{H}^h(\cdot)$ when evaluated on the other terms, and (ii.) answered honestly. Unfortunately, actually identifying such a good point with certainty appears to require that we examine *all* of the points in the constellation for x, and this interferes with the standard "exposure martingale" proof that is so powerful in the random oracle setting (which capitalizes on the fact that "unexamined" values of h can be treated as independent and uniform values).

To sidestep this difficulty, we prove a "resampling" lemma, which lets us examine all points in a particular constellation, identify one "good" one of interest, and then *resample* this point so as to "forget" about all possible conditioning this value might have. The resampling lemma gives a precise bound on the effects of such conditioning.

Immediate applications: Our correction function can be easily applied to save the faulty hash implementation in several important application scenarios, as explained in the motivational examples.

(1) For proof-of-work based blockchains, as discussed above, miners may rely on a common library $\tilde{h}$ for the hash evaluation, perhaps cleverly implemented by an adversary. Here $\tilde{h}$ is determined before the chain has been deployed. We can then prevent the adversary from capitalizing on this subversion by applying our correction function. In particular, the public randomness R can be embedded in the genesis block; the function $\tilde{h}_R(\cdot)$ is then used for mining (and verification) rather than $\tilde{h}$.

(2) The system sneak-in can also be resolved immediately by applying our correcting random oracle. During system initialization (or even when the operating system is released), the system administrator generates some randomness R and wraps the hash module $\tilde{h}$ (potentially subverted) to define $\tilde{h}_R(\cdot)$. The password α then gives rise to the digest $\rho = \tilde{h}_R(\alpha)$ together with the randomness R. Upon receiving input x, the system first "recovers" $\tilde{h}_R(\cdot)$ based on the previously stored R, and then tests if $\rho = \tilde{h}_R(x)$. The access will be enabled if the test is valid. As the corrected random oracle ensures the output to be uniform for every input point, this remains secure in the face of subversion.[3]

1.2 Related Work

Related work on indifferentiability. The notion of indifferentiability was proposed by Maurer et al. [41], as an extension of the classical concept of indistinguishability when one or more oracles are publicly available (such as a random oracle). It was later adapted by Coron et al. [23] and generalized to several other variants in [29,33,34,47,53]. Notably, a line of elegant work demonstrated the equivalence of the random oracle model and the ideal cipher model; in particular, the Feistel construction (with a small constant number of rounds) is indifferentiable from an ideal cipher, see [24–26]. Our work adapts the indifferentiability framework to the setting where the construction uses only a subverted implementation, which we call "crooked indifferentiability," where the construction aims to be indifferentiable from another repaired random oracle.

Related work on self-correcting programs. The theory of program self-testing, and self-correcting, was pioneered by the work of Blum et al. [9–11]. This theory addresses the basic problem of program correctness by verifying relationships between the outputs of the program on randomly selected inputs; a similar problem is to turn an almost correct program into one that is correct at every point with overwhelming probability. Rubinfeld's thesis [48] is an authoritative survey of the basic framework and results. Our results can be seen as a distributional analogue of this theory but with two main differences: (i). we insist on using

---

[3] Typical authentication of this form also uses password "salt," but this doesn't change the structure of the attack or the solution.

only public randomness drawn once for the entire "correction"; (ii). our target object is a distribution, rather than a particular function.

Related work on random oracles. The random oracle methodology [7] can significantly simplify both cryptographic constructions and proofs, even though there exist schemes which are secure using random oracles, but cannot be instantiated in the standard model, [19]. On the other hand, efforts have been made to identify instantiable assumptions/models in which we may analyze interesting cryptographic tasks [4,12–14,16,18,20,39]. Also, we note that research efforts have also been made to investigate *weakened* idealized models [37,38,40,45]. Finally, there are several recent nice works about random oracle in the auxiliary input model (or with pre-processing) [31,51]. Our model shares some similarities that the adversary may embed some preprocessed information into the subverted implementation, but our subverted implementation can further misbehave. Our results strengthen the random oracle methodology in the sense that using our construction, we can even tolerate a faulty hash implementation.

Related work on kleptographic security. Kleptographic attacks were originally introduced by Young and Yung [54,55]; In such attacks, the adversary provides subverted implementations of the cryptographic primitive, trying to learn secret without being detected. In recent years, several remarkable allegations of cryptographic tampering [42,46], including detailed investigations [21,22], have produced a renewed interest in both kleptographic attacks and in techniques for preventing them [1–3,5,6,8,15,27,28,30,32,43,49,50,52]. None of those work considered how to actually correct a subverted random oracle.

Concurrently, Fischlin et al. [36] also considered backdoored (keyed) hash functions, and how to immunize them particularly for the settings of HMAC and HKDF. They focused on preserving some weaker property of weak pseudorandomness for the building block of the compression function. We aim at correcting all the properties of a subverted random oracle, and moreover, our correction function can be applied to immunize backdoored *public* hash functions, which was left open in [36].

Similar constructions in other context. Our construction follows the simple intuition by mixing and input and output by XORing multiple terms. This share similarities in constructions in several other scenarios, e.g., about hardness amplification, notably the famous Yao XOR lemma, and for weak PRF [44]; and randomizers in the bounded storage model [35]. Our construction has to have an external layer of h_0 to wrap the XOR of terms, and our analysis is very different from them due to that our starting point of a subverted implementation.

2 The Model: Crooked Indifferentiability

2.1 Preliminary: Indifferentiability

The notion of indifferentiability introduced by Maurer et al. [41] has been found very useful for studying the security of hash function and many other primitives, especially model them as idealized objectives. This notion is an extension of the classical notion of indistinguishability, when one or more oracles are publicly available. The indifferentiability notion in [41] is given in the framework of random systems providing interfaces to other systems. Coron et al. [23] demonstrate an equivalent indifferentiability notion for random oracles but in the framework of Interactive Turing Machines (as in [17]). The indifferentiability formulation in this subsection is essentially taken from [23]. In the next subsection, we will introduce our new notion, *crooked indifferentiability*.

Defining indifferentiability. We consider ideal primitives. An ideal primitive is an algorithmic entity which receives inputs from one of the parties and returns its output immediately to the querying party. We now proceed to the definition of indifferentiability [23,41]:

Definition 1 (Indifferentiability [23,41]). *A Turing machine C with oracle access to an ideal primitive $\mathcal{G}$ is said to be $(t_{\mathcal{D}}, t_{\mathcal{S}}, q, \epsilon)$-indifferentiable from an ideal primitive $\mathcal{F}$, if there is a simulator $\mathcal{S}$, such that for any distinguisher $\mathcal{D}$, it holds that :*

$$\left| \Pr[\mathcal{D}^{C,\mathcal{G}} = 1] - \Pr[\mathcal{D}^{\mathcal{F},\mathcal{S}} = 1] \right| \leq \epsilon .$$

The simulator $\mathcal{S}$ has oracle access to $\mathcal{F}$ and runs in time at most $t_{\mathcal{S}}$. The distinguisher $\mathcal{D}$ runs in time at most $t_{\mathcal{D}}$ and makes at most q queries. Similarly, $C^{\mathcal{G}}$ is said to be (computationally) indifferentiable from $\mathcal{F}$ if ϵ is a negligible function of the security parameter λ (for polynomially bounded $t_{\mathcal{D}}$ and $t_{\mathcal{S}}$). See Fig. 1.

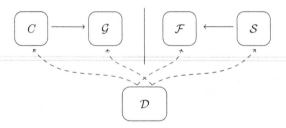

Fig. 1. The indifferentiability notion: the distinguisher $\mathcal{D}$ either interacts with algorithm C and ideal primitive $\mathcal{G}$, or with ideal primitive $\mathcal{F}$ and simulator $\mathcal{S}$. Algorithm C has oracle access to $\mathcal{G}$, while simulator $\mathcal{S}$ has oracle access to $\mathcal{F}$.

As illustrated in Fig. 1, the role of the simulator is to simulate the ideal primitive $\mathcal{G}$ so that no distinguisher can tell whether it is interacting with C and $\mathcal{G}$, or with $\mathcal{F}$ and $\mathcal{S}$; in other words, the output of $\mathcal{S}$ should look "consistent" with what the distinguisher can obtain from $\mathcal{F}$. Note that normally the simulator does not see the distinguisher's queries to $\mathcal{F}$; however, it can call $\mathcal{F}$ directly when needed for the simulation.

Replacement. It is shown in [41] that if $C^{\mathcal{G}}$ is indifferentiable from $\mathcal{F}$, then $C^{\mathcal{G}}$ can replace $\mathcal{F}$ in any cryptosystem, and the resulting cryptosystem is at least *as secure* in the $\mathcal{G}$ model as in the $\mathcal{F}$ model.

We use the definition of [41] to specify what it means for a cryptosystem to be at least as secure in the $\mathcal{G}$ model as in the $\mathcal{F}$ model. A cryptosystem is modeled as an Interactive Turing Machine with an interface to an adversary $\mathcal{A}$ and to a public oracle. The cryptosystem is run by an environment $\mathcal{E}$ which provides a binary output and also runs the adversary. In the $\mathcal{G}$ model, cryptosystem $\mathcal{P}$ has oracle access to C (which has oracle access to $\mathcal{G}$), whereas attacker $\mathcal{A}$ has oracle access to $\mathcal{G}$. In the $\mathcal{F}$ model, both $\mathcal{P}$ and $\mathcal{S}_A$ (the simulator) has direct oracle access to $\mathcal{F}$. The definition is illustrated in Fig. 2.

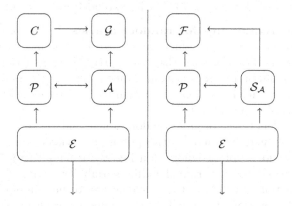

Fig. 2. The environment $\mathcal{E}$ interacts with cryptosystem $\mathcal{P}$ and attacker $\mathcal{A}$. In the $\mathcal{G}$ model (left), $\mathcal{P}$ has oracle access to C whereas $\mathcal{A}$ has oracle access to $\mathcal{G}$. In the $\mathcal{F}$ model, both $\mathcal{P}$ and $\mathcal{S}_A$ have oracle access to $\mathcal{F}$.

Definition 2. *A cryptosystem $\mathcal{P}$ is said to be at least as secure in the $\mathcal{G}$ model with algorithm C, as in the $\mathcal{F}$ model, if for any environment $\mathcal{E}$ and any attacker $\mathcal{A}$ in the $\mathcal{G}$ model, there exists an attacker $\mathcal{S}_A$ in the $\mathcal{F}$ model, such that:*

$$\Pr[\mathcal{E}(\mathcal{P}^C, \mathcal{A}^{\mathcal{G}}) = 1] - \Pr[\mathcal{E}(\mathcal{P}^{\mathcal{F}}, \mathcal{S}_A^{\mathcal{F}}) = 1] \le \epsilon.$$

where ϵ is a negligible function of the security parameter λ, and the notation $\mathcal{E}(\mathcal{P}^C, \mathcal{A}^{\mathcal{G}})$ defines the output of $\mathcal{E}$ after interacting with $\mathcal{P}, \mathcal{A}$ as on the left side of Fig. 2 (similarly we can define the right hand side). Moreover, a cryptosystem is said to be computationally at least as secure, etc., if $\mathcal{E}$, $\mathcal{A}$ and $\mathcal{S}_A$ are polynomial-time in λ.

We have the following security preserving (replacement) theorem, which says that when an ideal primitive is replaced by an indifferentiable one, the security of the "bigger" cryptosystem remains:

Theorem 1 ([23,41]). *Let $\mathcal{P}$ be a cryptosystem with oracle access to an ideal primitive $\mathcal{F}$. Let C be an algorithm such that $C^{\mathcal{G}}$ is indifferentiable from $\mathcal{F}$. Then cryptosystem $\mathcal{P}$ is at least as secure in the $\mathcal{G}$ model with algorithm C as in the $\mathcal{F}$ model.*

2.2   Crooked Indifferentiability

The ideal primitives that we focus on in this paper are random oracles. A random oracle [7] is an ideal primitive which provides a random output for each new query, and for the identical input queries the same answer will be given. Next we will formalize a new notion called crooked indifferentiability to characterize subversion. For simplicity, our formalization here is for random oracles, we remark that the formalization can be easily extended for other ideal primitives.

Crooked indifferentiability for random oracles. Let us briefly recall our goal: as mentioned in the Introduction, we are considering to repair a subverted/faulty random oracle, such that the corrected construction can be used as good as a random oracle. It is thus natural to consider the indifferentiability notion. However, we need to adjust the notion to properly model the subversion and to avoid trivial impossibility.

We use H to denote the original random oracle and $\tilde{H}_z$ to be the subverted implementation (where z could be the potential backdoor hardcoded in the implementation and we often ignore it using $\tilde{H}$ for simplicity). There will be several modifications to the original indifferentiability notion. (1) The deterministic construction C will have the oracle access to the random oracle via the subverted implementation $\tilde{H}$, not via the original ideal primitive H; This creates lots of difficulty (and even impossibility) for us to develop a suitable construction. For that reason, the construction is allowed to access to trusted but public randomness r (see Remark 1 below). (2) The simulator will also have the oracle access to the subverted implementation $\tilde{H}$ and also the public randomness r. Item (2) is necessary as it is clearly impossible to have an indifferentiability definition with a simulator that has no access to $\tilde{H}$, as the distinguisher can simply make query an input such that C will use a value that is modified by $\tilde{H}$ while $\mathcal{S}$ has no way to reproduce it. More importantly, we will show below that, the security will still be preserved to replace an ideal random oracle with a construction satisfying our definition (with an augmented simulator). We will prove the security preserving (i.e., replacement) theorem from [23,41] similarly with our adapted notions. (3) To model the whole process of the subversion and correction, we consider a two-stage adversary: subverting and distinguishing. For simplicity, we simply consider them as parts of one distinguisher, and do not use separate the notations and state passing.

Definition 3 (*H-crooked indifferentiability*). *Consider a distinguisher $\widehat{\mathcal{D}}$ and the following multi-phase real execution. Initially, the distinguisher $\widehat{\mathcal{D}}$ who has oracle access to ideal primitive H, publishes a subverted implementation of H (denoted as $\tilde{H}$). Secondly, a uniformly random string r is sampled and published.*

Thirdly, a deterministic construction C is then developed: the construction C has random string r as input, and has the oracle access to $\tilde{H}$ (the crooked version of H). Finally, the distinguisher $\widehat{\mathcal{D}}$, also having random string r as input, and the oracle access to the pair (C, H), returns a decision bit b. Often, we call $\widehat{\mathcal{D}}$, the H-crooked-distinguisher.

In addition, consider the corresponding multi-phase ideal execution with the same H-crooked-distinguisher $\widehat{\mathcal{D}}$. In the ideal execution, ideal primitive $\mathcal{F}$ is provided. The first two phases are the same (as that in the real execution). In the third phase, a simulator $\mathcal{S}$ will be developed: the simulator has a random string r as input, and has the oracle access to $\tilde{H}$, as well as the ideal primitive $\mathcal{F}$. In the last phase, the H-crooked-distinguisher $\widehat{\mathcal{D}}$, after having random string r as input, and having the oracle access to an alternative pair $(\mathcal{F}, \mathcal{S})$, returns a decision bit b.

We say that construction C, is $(t_{\widehat{\mathcal{D}}}, t_{\mathcal{S}}, q, \epsilon)$-$H$-crooked-indifferentiable from ideal primitive $\mathcal{F}$, if there is a simulator $\mathcal{S}$ so that for any H-crooked-distinguisher $\widehat{\mathcal{D}}$, (let u be the coins of $\widehat{\mathcal{D}}$), it satisfies that the real execution and the ideal execution are indistinguishable. Specifically,

$$\left| \Pr_{u,r,H}\left[\tilde{H} \leftarrow \widehat{\mathcal{D}} : \widehat{\mathcal{D}}^{C^{\tilde{H}}(r),H}(\lambda, r) = 1 \right] - \Pr_{u,r,\mathcal{F}}\left[\tilde{H} \leftarrow \widehat{\mathcal{D}} : \widehat{\mathcal{D}}^{\mathcal{F},\mathcal{S}^{\tilde{H},\mathcal{F}}(r)}(\lambda, r) = 1 \right] \right| \leq \epsilon(\lambda) .$$

Here $H : \{0,1\}^{\lambda} \to \{0,1\}^{\lambda}$ and $\mathcal{F} : \{0,1\}^{k} \to \{0,1\}^{k}$ denote random functions. See Fig. 3 for detailed illustration of the last phase in both real and ideal executions (the distinguishing).

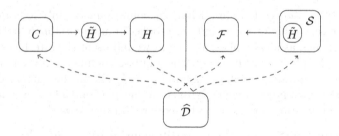

Fig. 3. The H-crooked indifferentiability notion: the distinguisher $\widehat{\mathcal{D}}$, in the first phase, manufactures and publishes a subverted implementation denoted as $\tilde{H}$, for ideal primitive H; then in the second phase, a random string r is published; after that, in the third phase, construction C, or simulator $\mathcal{S}$ is developed; the H-crooked-distinguisher $\widehat{\mathcal{D}}$, in the last phase, either interacting with algorithm C and ideal primitive H, or with ideal primitive $\mathcal{F}$ and simulator $\mathcal{S}$, return a decision bit. Here, algorithm C has oracle access to $\tilde{H}$, while simulator $\mathcal{S}$ has oracle access to $\mathcal{F}$ and $\tilde{H}$.

Remark 1 (The necessity of public randomness). It appears difficult to achieve feasibility without randomness. Intuitively: suppose the corrected hash is represented as $g(\tilde{H}(f(x)))$, i.e., $g(\cdot), f(\cdot)$ are correction functions, f will be applied to each input x before calling $\tilde{H}$, and g will be further applied to the corresponding output; then the attacker can plant a trigger using $f(z)$ for a random backdoor z, such that $\tilde{H}(f(z)) = 0$. It is easy to see that the attacker who has full knowledge of $(z, g(0))$ and can use this pair to distinguish, as $\mathcal{F}(z)$ would be a random value that would not hit $g(0)$ with a noticeable probability. Similarly, we can see that it is also infeasible if the randomness is generated before the faulty implementation is provided. For this reason, we allow the model to have a public randomness that is generated after $\tilde{H}$ is supplied, but such randomness would be available to everyone, including the attacker.

Remark 2 (Comparison with preprocessing). There have been several recent nice works [31,51] about random oracle with preprocessing, in which the adversary can have some auxiliary input compressing the queries. While in the first phase of our model, we also allow the adversary to generate such an auxiliary string as part of the backdoor z (or part of the instruction of $\tilde{H}$). We further allow the crooked implementation to deviate from the original random oracle. In this sense, the preprocessing model for random oracle can be considered to defend against a similar attacker than us, but the attacker would provide an honest implementation (only treating the backdoor as the auxiliary input). We note that their construction using simple salting mechanism [51] cannot correct a subverted random oracle as in our model: the distinguisher plants a trigger z into the inputs that $\tilde{H}(z||*) = 0$ for a randomly chosen z. In this way, the salt would be subsumed into the $*$ part and has no effect on the faulty implementation.

Remark 3 (Extensions). For simplicity, our definition is mainly for random oracle. It is not very difficult to extend our crooked indifferentiability notion to the other setting such as ideal cipher, as long as we represent the interfaces properly, while the multi-phase executions can be similarly defined. Another interesting extension is to consider a global random oracle (while in the current definition, there would be an independent instance in the real and ideal execution). We leave those interesting questions to be explored in future works.

Replacement with crooked indifferentiability. Security preserving (replacement) has been shown in the indifferentiability framework [41]: if $C^{\mathcal{G}}$ is indifferentiable from $\mathcal{F}$, then $C^{\mathcal{G}}$ can replace $\mathcal{F}$ in any cryptosystem, and the resulting cryptosystem in the $\mathcal{G}$ model is at least as secure as that in the $\mathcal{F}$ model. We next show that the replacement property can also hold in our crooked indifferentiability framework. Recall that, in the "standard" indifferentiability framework [23,41], a cryptosystem can be modeled as an Interactive Turing Machine with an interface to an adversary $\mathcal{A}$ and to a public oracle. There the cryptosystem is run by a "standard" environment $\mathcal{E}$ (see Fig. 2). In our crooked indifferentiability framework, a cryptosystem also has the interface to an adversary $\mathcal{A}$ and to a public oracle. However, now the cryptosystem is run by a environment $\widehat{\mathcal{E}}$ that can "crook" the oracle.

Consider an ideal primitive $\mathcal{G}$. Similar to the $\mathcal{G}$-crooked-distinguisher, we can define the $\mathcal{G}$-crooked-environment $\widehat{\mathcal{E}}$ as follows: Initially, the $\mathcal{G}$-crooked-environment $\widehat{\mathcal{E}}$ manufactures and then publishes a subverted implementation of the ideal primitive $\mathcal{G}$, denoted as $\tilde{\mathcal{G}}$. Then $\widehat{\mathcal{E}}$ runs the attacker $\mathcal{A}$, and the cryptosystem $\mathcal{P}$ is developed. In the $\mathcal{G}$ model, cryptosystem $\mathcal{P}$ has oracle access to C whereas attacker $\mathcal{A}$ has oracle access to $\mathcal{G}$; note that, C has oracle access to $\tilde{\mathcal{G}}$, not directly to $\mathcal{G}$. In the $\mathcal{F}$ model, both $\mathcal{P}$ and $\mathcal{S}_\mathcal{A}$ (the simulator) have oracle access to $\mathcal{F}$. Finally, the $\mathcal{G}$-crooked-environment $\widehat{\mathcal{E}}$ returns a binary decision output. The definition is illustrated in Fig. 4.

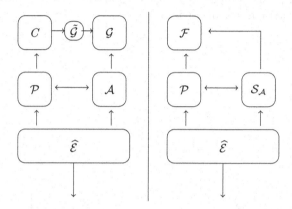

Fig. 4. The environment $\widehat{\mathcal{E}}$ interacts with cryptosystem $\mathcal{P}$ and attacker $\mathcal{A}$. In the $\mathcal{G}$ model (left), $\mathcal{P}$ has oracle access to C (who has oracle access to $\mathcal{G}$) whereas $\mathcal{A}$ has oracle access to $\mathcal{G}$; In the $\mathcal{F}$ model, both $\mathcal{P}$ and $\mathcal{S}_\mathcal{A}$ have oracle access to $\mathcal{F}$.

Definition 4. *Consider ideal primitives $\mathcal{G}$ and $\mathcal{F}$. A cryptosystem $\mathcal{P}$ is said to be at least as secure in the $\mathcal{G}$-crooked model with algorithm C as in the $\mathcal{F}$ model, if for any $\mathcal{G}$-crooked-environment $\widehat{\mathcal{E}}$ and any attacker $\mathcal{A}$ in the $\mathcal{G}$-crooked model, there exists an attacker $\mathcal{S}_\mathcal{A}$ in the $\mathcal{F}$ model, such that:*

$$\Pr[\widehat{\mathcal{E}}(\mathcal{P}^{C^{\tilde{\mathcal{G}}}}, \mathcal{A}^{\mathcal{G}}) = 1] - \Pr[\widehat{\mathcal{E}}(\mathcal{P}^{\mathcal{F}}, \mathcal{S}_\mathcal{A}^{\mathcal{F}}) = 1] \leq \epsilon.$$

where ϵ is a negligible function of the security parameter λ, and $\widehat{\mathcal{E}}(\mathcal{P}^{C^{\tilde{\mathcal{G}}}}, \mathcal{A}^{\mathcal{G}})$ describes the output of $\widehat{\mathcal{E}}$ running the experiment in the $\mathcal{G}$-world (the left side of Fig. 4), and similarly for $\widehat{\mathcal{E}}(\mathcal{P}^{\mathcal{F}}, \mathcal{S}_\mathcal{A}^{\mathcal{F}}).$

We now demonstrate the following theorem which shows that security is preserved when replacing an ideal primitive by a crooked-indifferentiable one:

Theorem 2. *Let $\mathcal{P}$ be a cryptosystem with oracle access to an ideal primitive $\mathcal{F}$. Let C be an algorithm such that $C^{\mathcal{G}}$ is crooked-indifferentiable from $\mathcal{F}$. Then cryptosystem $\mathcal{P}$ is at least as secure in the $\mathcal{G}$-crooked model with algorithm C as in the $\mathcal{F}$ model.*

Proof. The proof is very similar to that in [23, 41]. Let $\mathcal{P}$ be any cryptosystem, modeled as an Interactive Turing Machine. Let $\tilde{\mathcal{E}}$ be any crooked-environment, and $\mathcal{A}$ be any attacker in the $\mathcal{G}$-crooked model. In the $\mathcal{G}$-crooked model, $\mathcal{P}$ has oracle access to C (who has oracle access to $\tilde{\mathcal{G}}$, not directly to $\mathcal{G}$.), whereas $\mathcal{A}$ has oracle access to ideal primitive $\mathcal{G}$; moreover, the crooked-environment $\widehat{\mathcal{E}}$ interacts with both $\mathcal{P}$ and $\mathcal{A}$. This is illustrated in Fig. 5 (left part).

Since C is crooked-indifferentiable from $\mathcal{F}$ (see Fig. 3), one can replace $(C^{\tilde{\mathcal{G}}}, \mathcal{G})$ by $(\mathcal{F}, \mathcal{S})$ with only a negligible modification of the $\mathcal{G}$-crooked-environment $\widehat{\mathcal{E}}$'s output distribution. As illustrated in Fig. 5, by merging attacker $\mathcal{A}$ and simulator $\mathcal{S}$, one obtains an attacker $\mathcal{S}_{\mathcal{A}}$ in the $\mathcal{F}$ model, and the difference in $\widehat{\mathcal{E}}$'s output distribution is negligible. $\square$

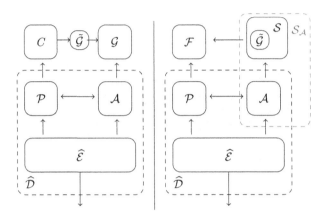

Fig. 5. Construction of attacker $\mathcal{S}_{\mathcal{A}}$ from attacker $\mathcal{A}$ and simulator $\mathcal{S}$.

3   The Construction

Now we proceed to give the construction. Given subverted implementations of the hash functions $\{\tilde{h}_i\}_{i=0,\dots,\ell}$, (the original version of each is $h_i(\cdot)$ could be considered as $h(i, \cdot)$), the corrected function is defined as:

$$\tilde{h}_R(x) = \tilde{h}_0(\tilde{g}_R(x)) = \tilde{h}_0\left(\bigoplus_{i=1}^{\ell} \tilde{h}_i(x \oplus r_i)\right).$$

where $R = (r_1, \dots, r_\ell)$ are sampled uniformly after $\{\tilde{h}_i(\cdot)\}$ is provided, and then revealed to the public, and the internal function $\tilde{g}_R(\cdot)$ is defined below:

$$\tilde{g}_R(x) = \bigoplus_{i=1}^{\ell} \tilde{h}_i(x \oplus r_i).$$

We wish to show that such a construction will be indifferentiable to an actual random oracle (with the proper input/output length). This implies that the distribution of values taken by $\tilde{h}_R(\cdot)$ at inputs that have not been queried have negligible distance from the uniform distribution.

Theorem 3. *Suppose $h : \{0, \ldots, \ell\} \times \{0,1\}^n \to \{0,1\}^n$ defines a family of random oracles $h_i : \{0,1\}^n \to \{0,1\}^n$ as $h(i, \cdot)$, for $i = 0, \ldots, \ell$, and $\ell \geq 3n + 1$. Consider a (subversion) algorithm $\tilde{H}$ and $\tilde{H}^h(x)$ defines a subverted random oracle $\tilde{h}$. Assume that for every h (and every i),*

$$\Pr_{x \in \{0,1\}^n} [\tilde{h}(i, x) \neq h(i, x)] = \mathsf{negl}(n). \tag{1}$$

The construction $\tilde{h}_R(\cdot)$ is $(t_{\widehat{\mathcal{D}}}, t_S, q, \epsilon)$-indifferentiable from a random oracle $F : \{0,1\}^n \to \{0,1\}^n$, for any $t_{\widehat{\mathcal{D}}}$, with $t_S = \mathrm{poly}(q)$, $\epsilon = \mathsf{negl}(n)$ and q is the number of queries made by the distinguisher $\widehat{\mathcal{D}}$ as in Definition 3.

Roadmap for the proof. We first describe the simulator algorithm. The main challenge for the simulator is to ensure the consistency of two ways of generating the output values of $\tilde{h}_R(\cdot)$, (it could also be reconstructed by querying the original random oracle directly together with the subverted implementation $\tilde{h}$ to replace the potentially corrupted terms). The idea for simulation is fairly simple: for an input x, $F(x)$ would be used to program h_0 on input $\tilde{g}_R(x)$.

There are two obstacles that hinder the simulation: (1) for some x, h_0 has been queried on $\tilde{g}_R(x)$ before the actual programing step, thus the simulator has to abort; (2) the distinguisher queries on some input x such that $\tilde{g}_R(x)$ falls into the incorrect portion of inputs to $\tilde{h}_0$.

To bound the probability of these two events, we first establish the property of the internal function $\tilde{g}_R(\cdot)$ that no adversary can find an input value that falls into a small domain (or for any input x, the output is unpredicatable to the adversary if he has not made any related queries.). See Theorem 4 below. Note that the bound is conditioned on adaptive queries of the distinguisher.

Theorem 4 (Informal). *Suppose the subverted implementation disagrees with the original oracle at only a negligible fraction of inputs, then with an overwhelming probability in R, conditioned on the $h(q_1), \ldots, h(q_s)$ (made by any $\widehat{\mathcal{D}}$), for all x outside the "queried" set $\{t \mid h_i(t \oplus r_i)$ was queried$\}$, and every event $E \subset \{0,1\}^n$,*

$$\Pr_h[\tilde{g}_R(x) \in E] \leq \mathrm{poly}(n)\sqrt{\Pr[E]} + \mathsf{negl}(n).$$

In particular, if $|E|$ is exponentially small in $\{0,1\}^n$, the probability $\tilde{g}_R(x)$ falls into E would be negligible for any x.

Next, our major analysis will focus on proving this theorem for $\tilde{g}_R(\cdot)$.

We first set down and prove a "rejection resampling" lemma. This is instrumental in our approach to Theorem 5 (the formal version of Theorem 4), showing that this produces unpredictable values, even to an adaptive adversary with access to the (public) randomness R;

Surveying the proof in more detail, recall that a value $\tilde{g}_R(x)$ is determined as the XOR of a "constellation" of values $\bigoplus \tilde{h}_i(x \oplus r_i)$; intuitively, if we could be sure that **(a)** at least one of these terms, say $x \oplus r_i$, was not queried by $\tilde{H}^h(\cdot)$ when evaluated on the other terms and, **(b)** this isolated term $x \oplus r_i$ was answered "honestly" (that is, $\tilde{h}_i(x \oplus r_i) = h_i(x \oplus r_i)$), then it seems reasonable to conclude that the resulting value, the XOR of the results, is close to uniform.

However, applying this intuition to rigorously prove Theorem 5 faces a few challenges. Perhaps the principal difficulty is that it is not obvious how to "partially expose" the random oracle h to take advantage of this intuition: specifically, a traditional approach to proving such strong results is to expose the values taken by the $h(x)$ "as needed," maintaining the invariant that the unexposed values are uniform and conditionally independent on the exposed values.

In our setting, we would ideally like to expose all but one of the values of a particular constellation $\{h_i(x \oplus r_i)\}$ so as to guarantee that the last (unexposed) value has the properties (a) and (b) above. While randomly guessing an ordering could guarantee this with fairly high probability $\approx 1 - 1/\ell$ we *must have such a favorable event take place for all x*, and so must somehow find a way to guarantee exponentially small failure probabilities. The **rejection resampling lemma**, discussed above, permits us to examine all the points in a particular constellation, identify a good point (satisfying (a) and (b)) and then "pretend" that we never actually evaluated the point in question. In this sense, the resampling lemma quantifies the penalty necessary for "unexposing" a point of interest.

A less challenging difficulty is that, even conditioned on $\tilde{h}_i(x \oplus r_i) = h_i(x \oplus r_i)$, this value may not be uniform, as the adversary may choose to be "honest" based on some criteria depending on x or, even, other adaptively-queried points. Finally, of course, the subversion algorithm $\tilde{H}^h(\cdot)$ is fully-adaptive, and only needs to disrupt $\tilde{g}_R(x)$ at a single value of x.

4   Security Proof

We begin with an abstract formulation of the properties of our construction and the analysis, and then transition to the detailed description of the simulator algorithm and its effectiveness.

4.1   The Simulator Algorithm

The main task of the simulator is to ensure the answers to $\{h_i\}$-queries to be consistent with the value of $F(\cdot)$, since for each input x, $\tilde{h}_R(x)$ is determined by a sequence of related queries to $\{h_i\}$ and $\tilde{H}$, (or simply the backdoor z) and the value of R. The basic idea is to program the external layer h_0 using values of $F(x)$, such that the value $F(x)$ is set for $h_0(\tilde{g}_R(x))$. The value $\tilde{g}_R(x)$ is obtained by $\mathcal{S}$ executing the subverted implementations $\{\tilde{h}_i\}$.

Let us define the simulator $\mathcal{S}$ (answering queries in two stages) as below:

In the first stage, $\mathcal{A}$ makes random oracle queries when manufacturing the subverted implementations $\{\tilde{h}_i\}_{i=0,\dots,\ell}$.

On input queries $x_1, \ldots, x_{q_1}$ (at $\mathcal{A}$'s choice on which random oracle to query) that $\mathcal{A}$ makes before outputting the implementations (and the backdoor), $\mathcal{S}$ answers all those using uniform strings respectively. $\mathcal{S}$ maintains a table. See Table 1. (w.l.o.g, we simply assume the adversary asks all the hash queries for each value x_i, if not, the simulator asks himself to prepare the table.) $\mathcal{S}$ and $\mathcal{D}$ also both receive a random value for R.

Table 1. RO queries in phase-I

RO query x_i	$h_0(x_i)$	$h_1(x_i)$	$\ldots$	$h_\ell(x_i)$
x_1	$v_{1,0}$	$v_{1,1}$	$\ldots$	$v_{1,\ell}$
x_2	$v_{2,0}$	$v_{2,1}$	$\ldots$	$v_{2,\ell}$
$\vdots$	$\vdots$	$\vdots$	$\vdots$	$\ldots$
x_{q_1}	$v_{q_1,0}$	$v_{q_1,1}$	$\ldots$	$v_{q_1,\ell}$

In the second stage, the distinguisher $\mathcal{D}$ now having input R, will ask both queries to the construction and the random oracles. The simulator $\mathcal{S}$ now also has these extra information of R and oracle access to the implementation $\tilde{h}$ and will answer the random oracle queries to ensure consistency. In particular:

On input query m_j to the k_j-th random oracle h_{k_j}, $\mathcal{S}$ defines the adjusted query $m'_j := m_j \oplus r_{k_j}$, and prepares answers for all related queries, i.e., for each i, the input $m'_j \oplus r_i$ to h_i; and the input $\tilde{g}_R(m'_j)$ to h_0.

– If $k_j > 0$:
  $\mathcal{S}$ runs the implementation $\tilde{h}_i$ on $m'_j \oplus r_i = m_j \oplus r_{k_j} \oplus r_i$, for all $i \in \{1, \ldots, \ell\}$, to derive the value $\tilde{g}_R(m'_j) = \bigoplus_{i=1}^{\ell} \tilde{h}_i(m'_j \oplus r_i)$. During the execution of $\tilde{h}_i$ on those inputs, $\mathcal{S}$ also answers the random oracle queries (or read from Table 1) on those values if the implementation makes any. In more detail,
  1. $\mathcal{S}$ first checks in both tables whether $m'_j \oplus r_i$ has been queried for h_i (Table 2 first), if queried in either of them, $\mathcal{S}$ returns the corresponding answer; if not queried, $\mathcal{S}$ simply returns a random value $u_{j,i}$ as answer and records it in Table 2;
  2. $\mathcal{S}$ checks whether $\tilde{g}_R(m'_j)$ has been queried for h_0. If not, $\mathcal{S}$ queries F on m'_j and gets a response $F(m'_j)$. $\mathcal{S}$ then checks whether m'_j has been queried in stage-I, (i.e., check Table 1). If yes and the corresponding value $v_{j,0}$ does not equal to $F(m'_j)$, $\mathcal{S}$ aborts; otherwise, $\mathcal{S}$ sets $F(m'_j) = u_{j,0}$ as the answer for $h_0(\tilde{g}_R(m'_j))$.
– If $k_j = 0$:
  $\mathcal{S}$ checks whether m_j has been queried for h_0 in stage-II, i.e., there exists an m'_t in Table 2 such that $\tilde{g}_R(m'_t) = m_j$. If yes, $\mathcal{S}$ simply uses the corresponding value $u_{t,0}$ as answer; If not, $\mathcal{S}$ checks whether it has been queried in stage-I, $\mathcal{S}$ returns the value of $v_{i,0}$ if m_j has been queried. Otherwise, $\mathcal{S}$ chooses a random value $v_{j,0}$ as the response and records it in Table 2.

Table 2. Phase-II queries: The headers are adjusted random oracle queries $m_i' = m_i \oplus r_{k_i}$ if m_i is queried for h_{k_i}, and $u_{i,0} = F(m_i)$.

Adjusted query m_i'	$h_1(m_i' \oplus r_1)$	$\ldots$	$h_\ell(m_i' \oplus r_\ell)$	$\tilde{g}_R(m_i')$	$h_0\Big(\tilde{g}_R(m_i')\Big)$
$m_1' = m_1 \oplus r_{k_1}$	$u_{1,1}$	$\ldots$	$u_{1,\ell}$	$\tilde{g}_R(m_1')$	$u_{1,0}$
$m_2' = m_2 \oplus r_{k_2}$	$u_{2,1}$	$\ldots$	$u_{2,\ell}$	$\tilde{g}_R(m_2')$	$u_{2,0}$
$\vdots$	$\vdots$	$\ldots$	$\vdots$	$\vdots$	$\vdots$
$m_q' = m_q \oplus r_{k_q}$	$u_{q,1}$	$\ldots$	$u_{q,\ell}$	$\tilde{g}_R(m_q')$	$u_{q,0}$

Probability analysis. Let us define the event that $\mathcal{S}$ aborts as Abort. According to the description, $\mathcal{S}$ aborts only when the distinguisher $\mathcal{D}$ finds an input m such that the $\tilde{g}_R(m) = x$ has either been queried for h_0 in stage-I, or queried in stage-II before any of $\{m \oplus r_i\}_{i=1,\ldots,\ell}$ has been queried for h_i. We can define $T_0 = \{x | x$ is queried for $h_0\}$, and following Theorem 5 (to be proven below), $\Pr[\text{Abort}] \leq \frac{|T_0|}{2^n} \leq \frac{q+q_1}{2^n} \leq \mathsf{negl}(n)$ for any polynomially large q, q_1.

We also define the event Bad as that the distinguisher finds an input m, such that $\tilde{h}_0(\tilde{g}_R(m)) \neq h_0(\tilde{g}_R(m))$, also we define $T_1 = \{m | \tilde{h}_0(\tilde{g}_R(m)) \neq h_0(\tilde{g}_R(m))\}$. Following Theorem 5, $\Pr[\text{Bad}] \leq \frac{|T_1|}{2^n} + \mathsf{negl}(n) \leq \mathsf{negl}(n)$. The latter inequality comes from the condition $\tilde{h}$ disagrees with h only at negligible fraction of inputs.

Furthermore, it is easy to see, conditioned on $\mathcal{S}$ does not abort, and Bad does not happen, the simulation is perfect.

In the rest of the paper, we will focus on proving our main theorem about the property of the internal function $\tilde{g}_R(\cdot)$.

4.2   A Rejection Resampling Lemma

We first prove a general rejection re-sampling lemma, and use it as a machinery to prove our main theorem for $\tilde{g}_R(\cdot)$. Let $\Omega_1, \ldots, \Omega_k$ be a family of sets and let $\Omega = \Omega_1 \times \cdots \times \Omega_k$. We treat Ω as a probability space under the uniform probability law: for an event $E \subset \Omega$, we let $\mu(E) = |E|/|\Omega|$ denote the probability of E. For an element $x = (x_1, \ldots, x_k) \in \Omega$ and an index i, we define the random variable $R_i x = (x_1, \ldots, x_{i-1}, y, x_{i+1}, \ldots, x_k)$ where y is drawn uniformly at random from Ω_i. We say that such a random variable arises by "resampling" x at the index i.

We consider the effect that arbitrary "adversarial" resampling can have on the uniform distribution. Specifically, for a function $A : \Omega \to \{1, \ldots, k\}$, we consider the random variable $R_{A(X)}X$, where X is a uniformly distributed random variable and the index chosen for resampling is determined by A (as a function of X). By this device, the function A implicitly defines a probability law μ_A on Ω, where the probability of an event E is given by

$$\mu_A(E) = \Pr[R_{A(X)}X \in E].$$

Lemma 1 (Rejection re-sampling). *Let X be a random variable uniform on $\Omega = \Omega_1 \times \cdots \times \Omega_k$. Let $A : \Omega \to \{1, \ldots, , k\}$ and define $Z = R_{A(X)}X$ and μ_A as above. Then, for any event E,*

$$\frac{\mu(E)^2}{k} \leq \mu_A(E) \leq k \cdot \mu(E).$$

Remark 4. Jumping ahead, such a resampling lemma will be used to define a good event E such that one term of $\tilde{h}_i(x \oplus r_i)$ will be uniformly chosen (not correlated with any other term), thus yields a uniform distribution for the summation. The actual adversarial distribution $\mu_A(E)$ is thus bounded not too far from $\mu(E)$. Let us first prove this useful lemma.

Proof. Consider an event $E \subset X$. To simplify our discussion of the adversarial resampling process discussed above, we remark that the random variables R_iX and $R_{A(X)}X$ can be directly defined over the probability space $\Omega \times \Omega$: Consider two independent random variables, X and Y, each drawn uniformly on Ω; then, for any i the random variable R_iX can be described $(X_1, \ldots, X_{i-1}, Y_i, X_{i+1}, \ldots, X_k)$ and $R_{A(X)}X = (Z_1, \ldots, Z_k)$ where

$$Z_i = \begin{cases} Y_i & \text{if } i = A(X), \\ X_i & \text{otherwise.} \end{cases}$$

Note that for any fixed i, the probability law of R_iX is the uniform law on Ω.

Upper bound. It follows that for an event E

$$\mu_A(E) = \Pr_{X,Y}[R_{A(X)}X \in E] \leq \Pr_{X,Y}[\exists i, R_iX \in E] \leq k \cdot \mu(E),$$

which establishes the claimed upper bound on $\mu_A(E)$.

Lower bound. As for the lower bound, define

$$B_i = \{x \in \Omega \mid A(x) = i\} \qquad \text{and} \qquad E_i = E \cap B_i.$$

As the B_i, E_i partition Ω, E respectively, and $\sum_i \mu_A(E_i) = \mu_A(E)$. Observe that

$$\Pr_{X,Y}[R_{A(X)}X \in E] = \sum_i \Pr_{X,Y}[R_{A(x)}X \in E_i] \geq \sum_i \Pr_{X,Y}[X \in B_i \text{ and } R_iX \in E_i]$$

$$\geq \sum_i \Pr_{X,Y}[X \in E_i \text{ and } R_iX \in E_i].$$

$$(2)$$

To complete the proof, we will prove that for any i and for any event F

$$\Pr_{X,Y}[X \in F \text{ and } R_iX \in F] \geq \Pr[F]^2.$$

$$(3)$$

Putting aside the proof of (3) for a moment, observe that applying (3) to the events E_i in the expansion (2) above yields the following by Cauchy-Schwarz.

$$\Pr_{X,Y}[R_{A(X)}X \in E] \geq \sum_i \Pr[E_i]^2 \geq \frac{\Pr[E]^2}{k}$$

Finally, we return to establish (3). Observe that for an event F,

$$\Pr_{X,Y}[X \in F \text{ and } R_i X \in F]$$

$$= \frac{1}{|\Omega_i|} \sum_{(x_1,\ldots,x_k)\in\Omega} \Pr[X \in F \text{ and } R_i X \in F \mid \forall j \neq i, X_j = x_j] \Pr[\forall j \neq i, X_j = x_j].$$

(The leading $1/|\Omega_i|$ term cancels the sum over x_i, which not referenced in the argument of the sum.) Under such strong conditioning, however, the two events $X \in F$ and $R_i X \in F$ are independent and, moreover, have the same probability. (Conditioned on the other coordinates, the event depends only on coordinate i of the result that is uniform and independent for the two random variables.) As

$$\Pr[\forall j \neq i, X_j = x_j] = \frac{1}{\prod_{i \neq j} |\Omega_j|}$$

we may rewrite the sum above as

$$\Pr_{X,Y}[X \in F \text{ and } R_i X \in F]$$

$$= \frac{1}{|\Omega_i|} \sum_{(x_1,\ldots,x_k)\in\Omega} \Pr[X \in F \text{ and } R_i X \in F \mid \forall j \neq i, X_j = x_j] \cdot \frac{1}{\prod_{i \neq j} |\Omega_j|}$$

$$= \frac{1}{|\Omega|} \sum_{(x_1,\ldots,x_k)\in\Omega} \Pr[X \in F \text{ and } R_i X \in F \mid \forall j \neq i, X_j = x_j]$$

$$= \frac{1}{|\Omega|} \sum_{(x_1,\ldots,x_k)\in\Omega} \Pr[X \in F \mid \forall j \neq i, X_j = x_j]^2$$

$$\geq \frac{1}{|\Omega|^2} \left(\sum_{(x_1,\ldots,x_k)\in\Omega} \Pr[X \in F \mid \forall j \neq i, X_j = x_j] \right)^2 = \Pr[X \in F]^2,$$

where the inequality is Cauchy-Schwarz. $\square$

We remark that these bounds are fairly tight. For the lower bound—the case of interest in our applications—let $E_i \subset \Omega_i$ be a family of events with small probability ϵ and $E = \{(\omega_1,\ldots,\omega_k,\omega_{k+1}) \mid \exists \text{ unique } i \leq k, \omega_i \in E_i\} \subset \prod_i^{k+1} \Omega_i$. When $\epsilon \ll 1/k$, $\Pr[E] \approx k\epsilon$ while $\Pr[R_{A(X)} X \in E] \approx k\epsilon^2 = (k\epsilon)^2/k$ for the strategy which, in case the event occurred, redraws the offending index and, in case the event did not occur, redraws the $k + 1$st "dummy" index. For the upper bound, consider an event E consisting of a single point x in the hypercube $\{0,1\}^k$; then $\Pr[E] = 2^{-k}$ and $\Pr[R_{A(X)} X \in E] \geq 2^{-k}(k+1)/2$ for the strategy which re-randomizes any coordinate on which the sample and x disagree (the strategy can be defined arbitrarily on the point x itself).

4.3   Establishing Pointwise Unpredictability

In this section, we focus our attention on the "internal" function (for $\ell > 3n$)

$$\tilde{g}_R(x) = \bigoplus_{i=1}^{\ell} \tilde{h}_i(x \oplus r_i) \,.$$

In particular, we will prove that for each x, the probability that the adversary can force the output of $\tilde{g}_R(x)$ to fall into some range E is polynomial in the density of the range (that is, the probability that a uniform element lies in E). Thus, the output will be unpredictable to the adversary if she has not queried the corresponding random oracles.

Intuition about the analysis. As discussed above, we want to show that for every x, there exist at least one term $h_i(x \oplus r_i)$ satisfying: (i) $h_i(x \oplus r_i)$ is answered honestly (that is, $h_i(x \oplus r_i) = \tilde{h}_i(x \oplus r_i)$); (ii) $h_i(x \oplus r_i)$ is not correlated with other terms. In order to ensure condition (ii), we proceed in two steps. We first turn to analyze the probability that $h_i(x \oplus r_i)$ has not been queried by $H^{h_*}(x \oplus r_j)$ for all other index j. This is still not enough to demonstrate perfect independence, as the good term is subject to the condition of (i), but it suffices for our purposes. As discussed above, for analytical purposes we consider an exotic distribution that calls for this "good" term to be independently re-sampled and apply rejection re-sampling lemma to ensure the original (adversarial) distribution is not too far from the exotic one. We first recall the theorem for the internal function:

Theorem 5. *Suppose* $h : \{0, \dots, \ell\} \times \{0,1\}^n \to \{0,1\}^n$ *defines a family of random oracles* $h_i : \{0,1\}^n \to \{0,1\}^n$ *as* $h(i, \cdot)$, *for* $i = 0, \dots, \ell$, *and* $\ell \geq 3n + 1$. *Consider a (subversion) algorithm* H *and* $H^h(x)$ *defines a subverted random oracle* $\tilde{h}$. *Assume that for every* h *(and every* i),

$$\Pr_{x \in \{0,1\}^n} [\tilde{h}(i, x) \neq h(i, x)] = \mathsf{negl}(n) \,.$$

Then, with overwhelming probability in R, h, *and conditioned on the* $h(q_1), \dots,$ $h(q_s)$ *(made by any* $\widehat{D}$) *, for all* x *outside the "queried" set* $\{t \mid h_i(t \oplus r_i)$ *was queried$\}$ *and every event* $E \subset \{0,1\}^n$,

$$\Pr_h[\tilde{g}_R(x) \in E] \leq \mathrm{poly}(n)\sqrt{\Pr[E]} + \mathsf{negl}(n).$$

Proof. Throughout the estimates, we will assume that $\ell > 3n$. Here, we overload the notation h_* to denote the collection of functions $h_1, \dots, h_\ell$.

We begin by considering the simpler case where no queries are made, and just focus on controlling the resulting values vis-a-vis a particular event E. At the end of the proof, we explain how to handle an adaptive family of queries.

Guaranteeing honest answers. First, we ensure that with high probability in R and h_*, for every x, there is a contributing term $\tilde{h}_i(x \oplus r_i)$ that is likely (if the random variable $h_i(x \oplus r_i)$ is *redrawn* according to the uniform distribution) to be "honest" in the sense that $\tilde{h}_i(x \oplus r_i) = h_i(x \oplus r_i)$. The reason that this simple property does not follow straightforwardly is due to the fact that $\tilde{h}_i$ may adaptively define the "dishonest" points which are not fixed during the manufacturing of $\tilde{h}_i$.

To begin, let us consider the following random variables defined by random selection of h_* (denoting the $\{h_i\}$) and R, (later used to bound the number of dishonest terms):

$$d_i(\alpha) = \begin{cases} 1 & \text{if } \tilde{h}_i(\alpha) \neq h_i(\alpha), \\ 0 & \text{otherwise;} \end{cases} \qquad \text{and} \qquad D_i(\alpha) = \mathbb{E}_{h_i(\alpha)}[d_i(\alpha)].$$

(Throughout $\mathbb{E}[\cdot]$ denotes expectation. For a given h_* and an element α, the value $D_i(\alpha)$ is defined by redrawing the value of $h_i(\alpha)$ uniformly at random; equivalently, $D_i(\alpha)$ is the conditional expectation of $d_i(\alpha)$ obtained by setting all other values of $h_*()$ except $h_i(\alpha)$.) Note that by assumption, for each i,

$$\mathbb{E}_{h_*}\mathbb{E}_\alpha[D_i(\alpha)] = \mathbb{E}_{h_*}\mathbb{E}_\alpha\mathbb{E}_{h_i(\alpha)}[d_i(\alpha)] = \mathbb{E}_{h_*}\mathbb{E}_\alpha[d_i(\alpha)] \leq \epsilon,$$

where α is chosen uniformly and ϵ is the (negligible) disagreement probability of (1) above.

We introduce several events that play a basic role in the proof.

– Flat functions. We say that h_* is *flat* if, for each i, $\mathbb{E}_\alpha[D_i(\alpha)] \leq \epsilon^{1/3}$, where α is drawn uniformly.

Note that $\Pr[h_* \text{ not flat}] = \Pr[\exists i \in [\ell], \mathbb{E}_\alpha[D_i(\alpha)] > \epsilon^{1/3}]$, thus

$$\Pr[h_* \text{ not flat}] \leq \ell \cdot \mathbb{E}_{h_*}\mathbb{E}_\alpha[D_i(\alpha)]/\epsilon^{1/3} = \ell\epsilon^{2/3}$$

by Markov's inequality and the union bound. Further, observe that if h_* is flat, then for any $x \in \{0,1\}^n$, any $0 < k \leq \ell$, and random choices of $R = \{r_1, \ldots, r_\ell\}$,

$$\mathbb{E}_R \sum_{\substack{I \subset [\ell], \\ |I|=k}} \prod_i D_i(x \oplus r_i) = \sum_{\substack{I \subset [\ell], \\ |I|=k}} \prod_i \mathbb{E}_{r_i} D_i(x \oplus r_i) \leq \binom{\ell}{k} \epsilon^{k/3} \leq (\ell^3\epsilon)^{k/3}.$$

Next, we will use this property to show that with a sufficiently large ℓ, e.g., $\ell = 3n$, then for each x, we can find an index i such that $D_i(x \oplus r_i)$ is small.

– Honesty under resampling. For a tuple $R = (r_1, \ldots, r_\ell)$, functions h_*, and an element $x \in \{0,1\}^n$, we say that the triple (R, h_*, x) is *honest* if

$$\sum_{\substack{I \subset [\ell], \\ |I|=3n}} \prod_i D_i(x \oplus r_i) \leq 2^{3n}(\ell^3\epsilon)^n.$$

If R and h_* are "universally" honest, which is to say that (R, h_*, x) is honest for all $x \in \{0,1\}^n$, we simply say (R, h_*) is honest. Then $\Pr_R[(R, h_*)$ is not honest$] = \Pr_R[\exists x, (R, h_*, x)$ is not honest$]$. When h_* is flat, we have the following:

$$\Pr_R[(R, h_*) \text{ is not honest}] \leq 2^n \cdot \mathbb{E}_R \left(\sum_{\substack{I \subset [\ell], \\ |I|=3n}} \prod_i D_i(x \oplus r_i) \right)/2^{3n}(\ell^3\epsilon)^n \leq 2^{-2n}$$

by Markov's inequality (on the random variable $\sum_{\substack{I \subset [\ell], \\ |I|=3n}} \prod_i D_i(x \oplus r_i)$) and the union bound. Observe that if (R, h_*) is honest, then for every x,

$$\max_{\substack{I \subset [\ell] \\ |I|=3n}} \prod_i D_i(x \oplus r_i) \le 2^{3n}(\ell^3 \epsilon)^n.$$

It follows that, for every set I of size $3n$, there exists an element $i \in I$ so that

$$D_i(x \oplus r_i) \le \sqrt[3n]{2^{3n}(\ell^3 \epsilon)^n} = 2\ell \sqrt[3]{\epsilon}.$$

That said, *conditioned on h_* being flat*, with an overwhelming probability (that is, $1 - \mathsf{negl}(n)$) in R, the pair (R, h_*) is honest and so gives rise to at least one small $D_i(x \oplus r_i)$ for each x (recall that the smaller $D_i(\alpha)$ is, the fewer points that h_i disagrees $\tilde{h}_i$).

Unfortunately, merely ensuring that some term of each "constellation" $\{\tilde{h}_i(x \oplus r_i)\}$ is honest with high probability is not enough—it is possible that a clever adversary can adapt other terms to an honest term to interfere with the final value of $\tilde{g}_R(x)$. The next part focuses on controlling these dependencies.

Controlling dependence among the terms. We now transition to controlling dependence between various values of $\tilde{h}_i(x)$. In particular, for every x we want to ensure that there exists some i so that $h_i(x \oplus r_i)$ was never queried by $\tilde{H}^{h_*}(\cdot)$ when evaluated on all other $x \oplus r_j$, i.e., for all $j \in [\ell]$ and $j \ne i$.

Note that the set of queries made by $\tilde{H}^{h_*}(u)$ is determined entirely by h_* and u: thus, conditioned on a particular h_*, the event (over R) that $\tilde{H}^{h_*}(u)$ queries $h_s(x \oplus r_s)$ and the event that $\tilde{H}^{h_*}(u')$ queries $h_t(x \oplus r_t)$ are independent (for any u, u' and $s \ne t$). We introduce the following notation for these events: for a pair of indices i, j ($i \ne j$), we define

$$Q_{i \to j}(x) = \begin{cases} 1 & \text{if } \tilde{H}^{h_*}(x \oplus r_i) \text{ queries } h_j(x \oplus r_j), \\ 0 & \text{otherwise.} \end{cases}$$

In light of the discussion above, for an element x and a fixed value of h_*, consider a subset $T \subset [\ell]$ and a function $s : T \to [\ell]$; we treat such a function as a representative for the event that each "target" $t \in T$ was queried by a "source" $s(t)$. (Note that there could be multiple such functions $s(\cdot)$ for T). We define

$$Q_s(x) = \prod_{t \in T} Q_{s(t) \to t}(x).$$

We also introduce a couple of new notions for the ease of presentation:

– Independent fingerprints. We say that a representative $s : T \to [\ell]$ is *independent* if $s(T) \cap T = \emptyset$, which is to say that the range of the function lies in $[\ell] \setminus T$. For any such *independent* fingerprint $s(\cdot)$, note that (for any x, h_*):

$$\mathbb{E}_R[Q_s(x)] = \mathbb{E}_R \left[\prod_{t \in T} Q_{s(t) \to t}(x) \right] = \prod_{t \in T} \mathbb{E}_R \left[Q_{s(t) \to t}(x) \right] \le \left(\frac{\tau(n)}{2^n} \right)^{|T|}, \quad (4)$$

where $\tau(n)$ denotes the running time (and, hence, an upper bound on the number of queries) of $\tilde{H}^h(x)$ on inputs of length n.

We will next use such notion to bound the number of bad terms that were queried by some other term.

– Dangerous set. For a fixed x, h_*, and R, we say that a set $T \subset [\ell]$ is *dangerous* if every element t in T is queried by some $\tilde{H}^{h_*}(x \oplus r_i)$ for $i \neq t$.

We claim that if T is a dangerous set then we can always identify an *independent* fingerprint $s : T' \to [\ell]$ for a subset $T' \subset T$ with $|T'| \geq |T|/2$.

To see this, we build T' as follows: write $T = \{t_1, \ldots, t_m\}$ and consider the elements in order $t_1, \ldots, t_m$; for each element t_i, we add it to T', if t_i is queried by some elements in T[4], pick one of them, denoted as t_j (for $j > i$), define $s(t_i) = t_j$, and remove t_j from T. Observe now that (i) each element in T' maps to a value (or was queried by a term) outside of T'; (ii) each element t_i added to T' removes at most two elements of T (t_i and $s(t_i)$), and hence $|T'| \geq |T|/2$.

If follows that for a set T the number of such possible independent fingerprints (whose image is at least half the size of T) is bounded by:

$$\sum_{m \geq |T|/2} \binom{|T|}{m} (\ell - 1) \cdots (\ell - m) \leq 2^{|T|} \ell^{|T|}$$

We conclude from (4) that for any fixed set T (and any fixed x and h_*)

$$\Pr_R[T \text{ is dangerous}] \leq \Pr[Q_s(x) \text{ occurs for some independent fingerprint}]$$

$$\leq 2^{|T|} \ell^{|T|} \left(\frac{\tau(n)}{2^n} \right)^{|T|/2} = \left(\frac{4\ell^2 \tau(n)}{2^n} \right)^{|T|/2}.$$

By taking the union bound over all sets T of size k, it follows immediately that

$$\Pr_R\left[k \text{ of the } h_i(x \oplus r_i) \text{ are queried by some other } \{\tilde{h}_j(x \oplus r_j)\}_{j \neq i, j \in [\ell]} \right]$$

$$\leq \binom{\ell}{k} \left(\frac{4\ell^2 \tau(n)}{2^n} \right)^{k/2} \leq \ell^k \left(\frac{4\ell^2 \tau(n)}{2^n} \right)^{k/2} \leq \left(\frac{4\ell^4 \tau(n)}{2^n} \right)^{k/2}. \tag{5}$$

The above bound guarantees that, for any fixed x, with overwhelming probability, there are $\ell - k$ terms that were never queried by *any* other terms.

– k-sparsity: Finally, we say that the pair (R, h_*) is *k-sparse* if for all x, the set of queries made by $H^{h_*}(x \oplus r_i)$ includes no more than k of the $h_i(x \oplus r_i)$.

Applying the union bound over all 2^n strings x to (5), we conclude that, for even constant k (say $k = 5$), we have

$$\Pr_{h_*, R}[(R, h_*) \text{ is not } k\text{-sparse}] \leq 2^n \left(\frac{4\ell^4 \tau(n)}{2^n} \right)^{k/2} \leq 2^{-n^{\Theta(k)}}.$$

---

[4] We overload the notation a bit, here the elements in T simply denote the indices of the terms.

With the preparatory work behind us, we turn to guaranteeing that each x possesses a good term (one that is both well behaved under resampling and not queried by other terms).

Establishing existence of a good term. Next, we wish to show that for any event E with $\Pr[E] = \mu(E)$, and for any x,

$$\Pr_{h_*, R}[\tilde{g}_R(x) \in E] \leq \mathsf{poly}(n)\sqrt{\mu(E)} + \mathsf{negl}(n).$$

In particular, if E has negligible density, the probability that $\tilde{g}_R(x) \in E$ is likewise negligible.

We say that R is *flat-honest* if $\Pr_{h_*}[(R, h_*) \text{ not honest} \mid h_* \text{ is flat}] \leq 2^{-n}$. Observe that by Markov's inequality a uniformly selected R is flat-honest with probability $1 - 2^{-n}$.

We also say R is *uniformly-k-sparse* if $\Pr_{h_*}[(R, h_*) \text{ is not} k - \text{sparse}] \leq 2^{-n}$. Assuming k is a sufficiently large constant (e.g., 5), note that by Markov's inequality a random R is uniformly-k-sparse with probability $1 - 2^{-n}$.

Now we know that selection of a uniformly random $R = (r_1, \ldots, r_\ell)$, with probability $1 - 2^{n-1}$, is *both* uniformly-k-sparse (for the constant k discussed above) and flat-honest. We condition, for the moment, on such a choice of R. In this case, a random function h_* is likely to be *both k-sparse and honest*: it follows that for every x there is some term $h_i(x \oplus r_i)$ that is not queried by H to determine the value of the other terms and, moreover, it is equal to $\tilde{h}_i(x \oplus r_i)$ with an overwhelming probability. We say that such a pair (R, h_*) is *unpredictable*; otherwise, we say that (R, h_*) is *predictable*.

$$\begin{aligned}
\Pr_{h_*}[h_* \text{ predictable (for } R)] &= \Pr_{h_*}[(R, h_*) \text{ not } k\text{-sparse or not honest}] \\
&\leq \Pr_{h_*}[(R, h_*) \text{ not } k\text{-sparse}] + \\
&\quad \Pr_{h_*}[(R, h_*) \text{ not honest and } h_* \text{ flat}] + \\
&\quad \Pr_{h_*}[(R, h_*) \text{ not honest and } h_* \text{ not flat}] \\
&\leq \Pr_{h_*}[(R, h_*) \text{ not } k\text{-sparse}] + \\
&\quad \Pr_{h_*}[(R, h_*) \text{ not honest} \mid h_* \text{ flat}] + \\
&\quad \Pr_{h_*}[h_* \text{ not flat}] \\
&\leq 2^{-n} + 2^{-n} + \ell\epsilon^{2/3}.
\end{aligned} \tag{6}$$

For each x, we can be sure there is at least one term $\tilde{h}_i(x \oplus r_i)$ which is typically answered according to $h_i(x \oplus r_i)$ (i.e., answered honestly) and never queried by the other terms. Unfortunately, to identify this term, we needed to evaluate $\tilde{h}$ on the whole constellation of points; the rejection resampling lemma lets us correct for this with a bounded penalty.

To complete the analysis, we consider the following experiment: conditioned on R, consider the probability that $\tilde{g}_R(x) \in E$ when h_* is drawn as follows:

- if (R, h_*) is unpredictable, there is a (lexicographically first) index i for which $h_i(x \oplus r_i)$ is queried by no other $\tilde{h}_j(x \oplus r_j)$ and is honest. Now, *redraw* the value of $h_i(x \oplus r_i)$ uniformly at random.

These rules define a distribution on h_* that is no longer uniform. Note, however, that redrawing $h_i(x \oplus r_i)$ does not affect the values of $\tilde{h}_i(x \oplus r_j)$ (for distinct j); as $\tilde{g}_R(x) = \bigoplus_i \tilde{h}_i(x \oplus r_i)$, under this exotic distribution (for any x),

$$\Pr_{\text{resampled } h_*} \left[\tilde{g}_R(x) \in E \middle| \begin{array}{l} R \text{ unif. } k\text{-sparse} \\ \& \text{ flat honest} \end{array} \right] \leq \mu(E) + (2 \cdot 2^{-n} + \ell \epsilon^{2/3}) + 2\ell \epsilon^{1/3},$$

where the $2\ell \epsilon^{1/3}$ term arises because we have only the guarantee that $D_i(x) \leq 2\ell \epsilon^{1/3}$ from the condition on honesty.

However, based on the **rejection resampling lemma** above, we conclude

$$\Pr_{h_*} \left[\tilde{g}_R(x) \in E \middle| \begin{array}{l} R \text{ unif. } k\text{-sparse} \\ \& \text{ flat honest} \end{array} \right] \leq \sqrt{\ell \left(\mu(E) + 2 \cdot 2^{-n/2} + 3\ell \epsilon^{1/3} \right)}$$
$$\leq O(\sqrt{\ell \mu(E)} + \sqrt{\ell} 2^{-n/4} + \ell \epsilon^{1/6}). \tag{7}$$

and, hence, that

$$\Pr_{h_*, R} [\tilde{g}_R(x) \in E] \leq 2^{-n} + O \left(\sqrt{\ell \mu(E)} + \sqrt{\ell} 2^{-n/4} + \ell \epsilon^{1/6} \right)$$
$$= O \left(\sqrt{\ell \mu(E)} + \sqrt{\ell} 2^{-n/4} + \ell \epsilon^{1/6} \right),$$

where the 2^{-n} term comes from the cases that a randomly chosen R is not flat-honest or universal-k-sparse.

Conditioning on adaptive queries. Finally, we return to the problem of handling adaptive queries. With R and z fixed, the queries generated by $Q^{h_*}(R, z)$ depend only on h_* and we may ramify the probability space of h according to the queries and responses of Q; we say $\alpha = ((q_1, a_1), \ldots, (q_t, a_t))$ is a *transcript* for Q if Q queries h_* at $q_1, \ldots, q_t$ and receives the responses $a_1, \ldots, a_t$. We remark that if E is an event for which $\Pr_h[E \mid R, z] \leq \epsilon$, then by considering the natural martingale given by iterative exposure of values of h_* at the points queried by $Q^h(R, z)$, we have that $\epsilon \geq \Pr[E \mid R, z] = \sum_\alpha \Pr[E \mid \alpha, R, z] \cdot \Pr[\alpha \mid R, z]$. In particular, events with negligible probability likewise occur with negligible probability for all but a negligible fraction of transcripts α. Thus, the global properties of h discussed in the previous proof are retained even conditioned on a typical transcript α.

We require one amplification of the high-probability structural statements developed above. Note that, with overwhelming probability in R and h, every constellation $\{x \oplus r_i\}$ (an argument to h_i) contains only a constant number of points that are queried by more than a 2^{-n} fraction of other points in the domain of h_*. (Indeed, the fraction of points in the domain of h_* that are queried by $H^h(z,x)$ for at least $w(n)$ values of x can be no more than $\text{poly}(n)/w(n)$, where the polynomial is determined by the running time of H.) We say that a pair R, z is *diffuse* if a randomly selected h has this property with probability $1 - 2^{-n/2}$; note that a random pair (R, z) is diffuse with probability $1 - 2^{-n/2}$.

Consider then conditioning on the event that (R, z) is flat-honest, uniformly-4-sparse, and diffuse; note that in this case, with high probability in h every x has an member of its constellation which is not queried by other members of the constellation, only queried by $H()$ at a vanishing fraction of other points in the domain, and has $D_i(x \oplus r_i) \leq 2\ell \sqrt[3]{\epsilon}$. We emphasize that these properties are global properties, holding for all x in the domain of h. In particular, we can apply the argument above to any x for which none of the q_i touch its constellation $\{x \oplus r_i\}$. This concludes the proof. $\square$

5   Conclusions

We initiate the study of correcting subverted random oracles, where each subverted version disagrees with the original random oracle at a negligible fraction of inputs. We demonstrate that such an attack is devastating in several real-world scenarios. We give a simple construction that can be proven indifferentiable from a random oracle. Our analysis involves developing a new machinery of rejection resampling lemma which may be with independent interests. Our work provides a general tool to transform a buggy implementation of random oracle into a well-behaved one which can be directly applied to the kleptographic setting.

There are many interesting problems worth further exploring, such as better constructions, correcting other ideal objectives under subversion and more.

Acknowledgement. The authors thank Jonathan Katz for suggesting the indifferentiability framework as a modeling tool, and we thank anonymous reviewers for valuable comments.

References

1. Abelson, H., et al.: Keys under doormats. Commun. ACM **58**(10), 24–26 (2015)
2. Ateniese, G., Magri, B., Venturi, D.: Subversion-resilient signature schemes. In: Ray, I., Li, N., Kruegel, C. (eds.) ACM CCS 15, pp. 364–375. ACM Press, October 2015
3. Bellare, M., Hoang, V.T.: Resisting randomness subversion: fast deterministic and hedged public-key encryption in the standard model. In: Oswald, E., Fischlin, M. (eds.) EUROCRYPT 2015. LNCS, vol. 9057, pp. 627–656. Springer, Heidelberg (2015). https://doi.org/10.1007/978-3-662-46803-6_21
4. Bellare, M., Hoang, V.T., Keelveedhi, S.: Instantiating random oracles via UCEs. In: Canetti, R., Garay, J.A. (eds.) CRYPTO 2013. LNCS, vol. 8043, pp. 398–415. Springer, Heidelberg (2013). https://doi.org/10.1007/978-3-642-40084-1_23
5. Bellare, M., Jaeger, J., Kane, D.: Mass-surveillance without the state: strongly undetectable algorithm-substitution attacks. In: Ray, I., Li, N., Kruegel, C. (eds.) ACM CCS 15, pp. 1431–1440. ACM Press, October 2015

6. Bellare, M., Paterson, K.G., Rogaway, P.: Security of symmetric encryption against mass surveillance. In: Garay, J.A., Gennaro, R. (eds.) CRYPTO 2014. LNCS, vol. 8616, pp. 1–19. Springer, Heidelberg (2014). https://doi.org/10.1007/978-3-662-44371-2_1

7. Bellare, M., Rogaway, P.: Random oracles are practical: a paradigm for designing efficient protocols. In: Ashby, V. (ed.) ACM CCS 93, pp. 62–73. ACM Press, Nov. (1993)

8. Bellovin, S.M., Blaze, M., Clark, S., Landau, S.: Going bright: wiretapping without weakening communications infrastructure. IEEE Secur. Priv. $11(1)$, 62–72 (2013)

9. Blum, M.: Designing programs that check their work. Technical report TR-88-009, International Computer Science Institure, November 1988. http://www.icsi.berkeley.edu/pubs/techreports/tr-88-009.pdf

10. Blum, M., Kannan, S.: Designing programs that check their work. In: 21st ACM STOC, pp. 86–97. ACM Press, May 1989

11. Blum, M., Luby, M., Rubinfeld, R.: Self-testing/correcting with applications to numerical problems. In: 22nd ACM STOC, pp. 73–83. ACM Press, May 1990

12. Boldyreva, A., Cash, D., Fischlin, M., Warinschi, B.: Foundations of non-malleable hash and one-way functions. In: Matsui, M. (ed.) ASIACRYPT 2009. LNCS, vol. 5912, pp. 524–541. Springer, Heidelberg (2009). https://doi.org/10.1007/978-3-642-10366-7_31

13. Boldyreva, A., Fischlin, M.: Analysis of random oracle instantiation scenarios for OAEP and other practical schemes. In: Shoup, V. (ed.) CRYPTO 2005. LNCS, vol. 3621, pp. 412–429. Springer, Heidelberg (2005). https://doi.org/10.1007/11535218_25

14. Boldyreva, A., Fischlin, M.: On the security of OAEP. In: Lai, X., Chen, K. (eds.) ASIACRYPT 2006. LNCS, vol. 4284, pp. 210–225. Springer, Heidelberg (2006). https://doi.org/10.1007/11935230_14

15. Camenisch, J., Drijvers, M., Lehmann, A.: Anonymous attestation with subverted TPMs. In: Katz, J., Shacham, H. (eds.) CRYPTO 2017, Part III. LNCS, vol. 10403, pp. 427–461. Springer, Cham (2017). https://doi.org/10.1007/978-3-319-63697-9_15

16. Canetti, R.: Towards realizing random oracles: hash functions that hide all partial information. In: Kaliski, B.S. (ed.) CRYPTO 1997. LNCS, vol. 1294, pp. 455–469. Springer, Heidelberg (1997). https://doi.org/10.1007/BFb0052255

17. Canetti, R.: Universally composable security: a new paradigm for cryptographic protocols. In: 42nd FOCS, pp. 136–145. IEEE Computer Society Press, October 2001

18. Canetti, R., Dakdouk, R.R.: Extractable perfectly one-way functions. In: Aceto, L., Damgård, I., Goldberg, L.A., Halldórsson, M.M., Ingólfsdóttir, A., Walukiewicz, I. (eds.) ICALP 2008, Part II. LNCS, vol. 5126, pp. 449–460. Springer, Heidelberg (2008). https://doi.org/10.1007/978-3-540-70583-3_37

19. Canetti, R., Goldreich, O., Halevi, S.: The random oracle methodology, revisited (preliminary version). In: 30th ACM STOC, pp. 209–218. ACM Press, May 1998

20. Canetti, R., Micciancio, D., Reingold, O.: Perfectly one-way probabilistic hash functions (preliminary version). In: 30th ACM STOC, pp. 131–140. ACM Press, May 1998

21. Checkoway, S., et al.: A systematic analysis of the Juniper Dual EC incident. In: Proceedings of ACM CCS 2016 (2016). http://eprint.iacr.org/2016/376

22. Checkoway, S., et al.: On the practical exploitability of dual EC in TLS implementations. In: Proceedings of the 23rd USENIX Security Symposium, San Diego, CA, USA, 20–22 August 2014, pp. 319–335 (2014)

23. Coron, J.-S., Dodis, Y., Malinaud, C., Puniya, P.: Merkle-Damgård revisited: how to construct a hash function. In: Shoup, V. (ed.) CRYPTO 2005. LNCS, vol. 3621, pp. 430–448. Springer, Heidelberg (2005). https://doi.org/10.1007/11535218_26
24. Coron, J.-S., Holenstein, T., Künzler, R., Patarin, J., Seurin, Y., Tessaro, S.: How to build an ideal cipher: the indifferentiability of the Feistel construction. J. Cryptol. **29**(1), 61–114 (2016)
25. Dachman-Soled, D., Katz, J., Thiruvengadam, A.: 10-round Feistel is indifferentiable from an ideal cipher. In: Fischlin, M., Coron, J.-S. (eds.) EUROCRYPT 2016, Part II. LNCS, vol. 9666, pp. 649–678. Springer, Heidelberg (2016). https://doi.org/10.1007/978-3-662-49896-5_23
26. Dai, Y., Steinberger, J.: Indifferentiability of 8-round Feistel networks. In: Robshaw, M., Katz, J. (eds.) CRYPTO 2016, Part I. LNCS, vol. 9814, pp. 95–120. Springer, Heidelberg (2016). https://doi.org/10.1007/978-3-662-53018-4_4
27. Degabriele, J.P., Farshim, P., Poettering, B.: A more cautious approach to security against mass surveillance. In: Leander, G. (ed.) FSE 2015. LNCS, vol. 9054, pp. 579–598. Springer, Heidelberg (2015). https://doi.org/10.1007/978-3-662-48116-5_28
28. Degabriele, J.P., Paterson, K.G., Schuldt, J.C.N., Woodage, J.: Backdoors in pseudorandom number generators: possibility and impossibility results. In: Robshaw, M., Katz, J. (eds.) CRYPTO 2016, Part I. LNCS, vol. 9814, pp. 403–432. Springer, Heidelberg (2016). https://doi.org/10.1007/978-3-662-53018-4_15
29. Demay, G., Gaži, P., Hirt, M., Maurer, U.: Resource-restricted indifferentiability. In: Johansson, T., Nguyen, P.Q. (eds.) EUROCRYPT 2013. LNCS, vol. 7881, pp. 664–683. Springer, Heidelberg (2013). https://doi.org/10.1007/978-3-642-38348-9_39
30. Dodis, Y., Ganesh, C., Golovnev, A., Juels, A., Ristenpart, T.: A formal treatment of backdoored pseudorandom generators. In: Oswald, E., Fischlin, M. (eds.) EUROCRYPT 2015, Part I. LNCS, vol. 9056, pp. 101–126. Springer, Heidelberg (2015). https://doi.org/10.1007/978-3-662-46800-5_5
31. Dodis, Y., Guo, S., Katz, J.: Fixing cracks in the concrete: random oracles with auxiliary input, revisited. In: Coron, J.-S., Nielsen, J.B. (eds.) EUROCRYPT 2017, Part II. LNCS, vol. 10211, pp. 473–495. Springer, Cham (2017). https://doi.org/10.1007/978-3-319-56614-6_16
32. Dodis, Y., Mironov, I., Stephens-Davidowitz, N.: Message transmission with reverse firewalls–secure communication on corrupted machines. In: Robshaw, M., Katz, J. (eds.) CRYPTO 2016. Part I, volume 9814 of LNCS, pp. 341–372. Springer, Heidelberg (2016). https://doi.org/10.1007/978-3-662-53018-4_13
33. Dodis, Y., Puniya, P.: On the relation between the ideal cipher and the random oracle models. In: Halevi, S., Rabin, T. (eds.) TCC 2006. LNCS, vol. 3876, pp. 184–206. Springer, Heidelberg (2006). https://doi.org/10.1007/11681878_10
34. Dodis, Y., Puniya, P.: Feistel networks made public, and applications. In: Naor, M. (ed.) EUROCRYPT 2007. LNCS, vol. 4515, pp. 534–554. Springer, Heidelberg (2007). https://doi.org/10.1007/978-3-540-72540-4_31
35. Dziembowski, S., Maurer, U.M.: Optimal randomizer efficiency in the bounded-storage model. J. Cryptol. **17**(1), 5–26 (2004)
36. Fischlin, M., Janson, C., Mazaheri, S.: Backdoored hash functions: immunizing HMAC and HKDF. Cryptology ePrint Archive, Report 2018/362 (2018). http://eprint.iacr.org/2018/362
37. Katz, J., Lucks, S., Thiruvengadam, A.: Hash functions from defective ideal ciphers. In: Nyberg, K. (ed.) CT-RSA 2015. LNCS, vol. 9048, pp. 273–290. Springer, Cham (2015). https://doi.org/10.1007/978-3-319-16715-2_15

38. Kawachi, A., Numayama, A., Tanaka, K., Xagawa, K.: Security of encryption schemes in weakened random oracle models. In: Nguyen, P.Q., Pointcheval, D. (eds.) PKC 2010. LNCS, vol. 6056, pp. 403–419. Springer, Heidelberg (2010). https://doi.org/10.1007/978-3-642-13013-7_24

39. Kiltz, E., O'Neill, A., Smith, A.: Instantiability of RSA-OAEP under Chosen-plaintext attack. In: Rabin, T. (ed.) CRYPTO 2010. LNCS, vol. 6223, pp. 295–313. Springer, Heidelberg (2010). https://doi.org/10.1007/978-3-642-14623-7_16

40. Liskov, M.: Constructing an ideal hash function from weak ideal compression functions. In: Biham, E., Youssef, A.M. (eds.) SAC 2006. LNCS, vol. 4356, pp. 358–375. Springer, Heidelberg (2007). https://doi.org/10.1007/978-3-540-74462-7_25

41. Maurer, U., Renner, R., Holenstein, C.: Indifferentiability, impossibility results on reductions, and applications to the random oracle methodology. In: Naor, M. (ed.) TCC 2004. LNCS, vol. 2951, pp. 21–39. Springer, Heidelberg (2004). https://doi.org/10.1007/978-3-540-24638-1_2

42. Menn, J.: Exclusive: secret contract tied NSA and security industry pioneer. Reuters, December 2013

43. Mironov, I., Stephens-Davidowitz, N.: Cryptographic reverse firewalls. In: Oswald, E., Fischlin, M. (eds.) EUROCRYPT 2015, Part III. LNCS, vol. 9057, pp. 657–686. Springer, Heidelberg (2015). https://doi.org/10.1007/978-3-662-46803-6_22

44. Myers, S.: Efficient amplification of the security of weak pseudo-random function generators. In: Pfitzmann, B. (ed.) EUROCRYPT 2001. LNCS, vol. 2045, pp. 358–372. Springer, Heidelberg (2001). https://doi.org/10.1007/3-540-44987-6_22

45. Numayama, A., Isshiki, T., Tanaka, K.: Security of digital signature schemes in weakened random oracle models. In: Cramer, R. (ed.) PKC 2008. LNCS, vol. 4939, pp. 268–287. Springer, Heidelberg (2008). https://doi.org/10.1007/978-3-540-78440-1_16

46. Perlroth, N., Larson, J., Shane, S.: N.S.A. able to foil basic safeguards of privacy on web. The New York Times (2013). http://www.nytimes.com/2013/09/06/us/nsa-foils-much-internet-encryption.html

47. Ristenpart, T., Shacham, H., Shrimpton, T.: Careful with composition: limitations of the indifferentiability framework. In: Paterson, K.G. (ed.) EUROCRYPT 2011. LNCS, vol. 6632, pp. 487–506. Springer, Heidelberg (2011). https://doi.org/10.1007/978-3-642-20465-4_27

48. Rubinfeld, R.A.: A mathematical theory of self-checking, self-testing and self-correcting programs. Ph.D. thesis, University of California at Berkeley, Berkeley, CA, USA (1991). UMI Order No. GAX91-26752

49. Russell, A., Tang, Q., Yung, M., Zhou, H.-S.: Cliptography: clipping the power of kleptographic attacks. In: Cheon, J.H., Takagi, T. (eds.) ASIACRYPT 2016, Part II. LNCS, vol. 10032, pp. 34–64. Springer, Heidelberg (2016). https://doi.org/10.1007/978-3-662-53890-6_2

50. Russell, A., Tang, Q., Yung, M., Zhou, H.-S.: Generic semantic security against a kleptographic adversary. In: Thuraisingham, B.M., Evans, D., Malkin, T., Xu, D. (eds.) ACM CCS 17, pp. 907–922. ACM Press, October 2017

51. Coretti, S., Dodis, Y., Guo, S., Steinberger, J.: Random oracles and non-uniformity. In: Nielsen, J.B., Rijmen, V. (eds.) EUROCRYPT 2018. LNCS, vol. 10820, pp. 227–258. Springer, Cham (2018). https://doi.org/10.1007/978-3-319-78381-9_9

52. Schneier, B., Fredrikson, M., Kohno, T., Ristenpart, T.: Surreptitiously weakening cryptographic systems. Cryptology ePrint Archive, Report 2015/097 (2015). http://eprint.iacr.org/2015/097

53. Soni, P., Tessaro, S.: Public-seed pseudorandom permutations. In: Coron, J.-S., Nielsen, J.B. (eds.) EUROCRYPT 2017, Part II. LNCS, vol. 10211, pp. 412–441. Springer, Cham (2017). https://doi.org/10.1007/978-3-319-56614-6_14

54. Young, A., Yung, M.: The dark side of "black-box" cryptography, or: should we trust capstone? In: Koblitz, N. (ed.) CRYPTO 1996. LNCS, vol. 1109, pp. 89–103. Springer, Heidelberg (1996). https://doi.org/10.1007/3-540-68697-5_8

55. Young, A., Yung, M.: Kleptography: using cryptography against cryptography. In: Fumy, W. (ed.) EUROCRYPT 1997. LNCS, vol. 1233, pp. 62–74. Springer, Heidelberg (1997). https://doi.org/10.1007/3-540-69053-0_6

Combiners for Backdoored Random Oracles

Balthazar Bauer[1,2], Pooya Farshim[1,2(✉)], and Sogol Mazaheri[3]

[1] DI/ENS, CNRS, PSL University, Paris, France
`balthazar.bauer@ens.fr, pooya.farshim@gmail.com`
[2] Inria, Paris, France
[3] Cryptoplexity, Technische Universität Darmstadt, Darmstadt, Germany
`sogol.mazaheri@cryptoplexity.de`

Abstract. We formulate and study the security of cryptographic hash functions in the *backdoored random-oracle* (BRO) model, whereby a big brother designs a "good" hash function, but can also see *arbitrary functions* of its table via backdoor capabilities. This model captures intentional (and unintentional) weaknesses due to the existence of collision-finding or inversion algorithms, but goes well beyond them by allowing, for example, to search for structured preimages. The latter can easily break constructions that are secure under random inversions.

BROs make the task of bootstrapping cryptographic hardness somewhat challenging. Indeed, with only a single arbitrarily backdoored function no hardness can be bootstrapped as any construction can be inverted. However, when two (or more) independent hash functions are available, hardness emerges *even with unrestricted and adaptive access to all backdoor oracles*. At the core of our results lie new reductions from cryptographic problems to the *communication complexities* of various two-party tasks. Along the way we establish a communication complexity lower bound for set-intersection for cryptographically relevant ranges of parameters and distributions and where set-disjointness can be easy.

Keywords: Random oracle · Combiner · Communication complexity
Set-disjointness · Set-intersection · Lower bounds

1 Introduction

Hash functions are one of the most fundamental building blocks in the design of cryptographic protocols. From a provable security perspective, a particularly successful methodology to use hash functions in protocols has been the introduction of the random-oracle (RO) model [5,15]. This model formalizes the intuition that the outputs of a well-designed hash function look random by giving all parties, honest or otherwise, oracle access to a uniformly chosen random function. The strong randomness properties inherent in the oracle, in turn, facilitate the security analyses of many protocols.

© International Association for Cryptologic Research 2018
H. Shacham and A. Boldyreva (Eds.): CRYPTO 2018, LNCS 10992, pp. 272–302, 2018.
https://doi.org/10.1007/978-3-319-96881-0_10

The cryptanalytic validation of hash functions can strengthen our confidence in this RO-like behavior. On the other hand, as such analyses improve, (unintentional) weaknesses in hash functions are discovered, which can lead to their partial or total break of security. However, cryptanalytic validation might also fail to detect *intentional* weaknesses that are built into systems. For example such backdoors might be themselves built using cryptographic techniques, which make them hard to detect. Prominent examples show that such backdoors exist and can be exploited in various ways [6,10,11].

In this work we revisit a classical question on protecting against failures of hash functions. Numerous works in this area have studied if, and to what level, by *combining* different hash functions one can offer such protections; see [7,16,17,20] for theoretical treatments and [13,26,30] for cryptanalytic work. However, most work has their focus on unintentional failures (to protect against cryptanalytic advances). In this work, we consider a more adversarial view of hash function failures and ask if well-designed, but possibly *backdoored* hash functions can be used to build backdoor-free hash functions?

Depending on what well-designed means, what adversarial powers the backdoors provide, and what security goals are targeted, different solutions emerge. Hash-function combiners in the works above typically convert two or more hash functions into a new one that is secure as long as *any* of the underlying hash functions is secure. For example, the concatenation combiner builds a collision-resistant hash function given k hash functions as long as one function is collision resistant. Multi-property combiners for other notions, such as PRG, MAC or PRF security, also exist [17].

Typical combiners, however, do not necessarily offer protection when *all* hash functions fail. Intuitively, the goal here is more challenging as all "sources of hardness" have been rendered useless. Despite this, a number of works [20,23,26, 27,33] take a more practical approach and introduce an intermediate *weakened* RO model, where hash functions are vulnerable to strong forms of attack, but are otherwise random.

This is an approach that we also adopt here. Since our goal is to protect against *adversarial* weaknesses (aka. backdoors), we place no assumptions on hash-function weaknesses—they can go well beyond computing random preimages or collisions.

1.1   Contributions

We introduce a substantially weakened RO model where an adversary, on top of hash values, can also obtain *arbitrary functions* of the table of the hash function. We formalize this capability via access to a *backdoor oracle* $\mathrm{BD}(f)$ that on input a function f returns $f(\langle \mathsf{H} \rangle)$, arbitrary auxiliary information about the function table of the hash function H. We call this the *backdoored random-oracle* (BRO) model.

Such backdoors are powerful enough to allow for point inversions—simply hardwire the point y that needs to be inverted into a function $f[y]$ that searches for a preimage of y under H—or finding collisions. But they can go well beyond

274 B. Bauer et al.

them. For example, although Liskov [27] proves one-way security of the combiner $H(0|x_1|x_2)|H(1|x_2|x_1)$ under *random* inversions, it becomes insecure when inverted points are not assumed to be random: given $y_1|y_2$ simply look for an inverse $0|x_1'|x_2'$ for y_1 such that $1|x_2'|x_1'$ also maps to y_2. BRO can also model arbitrary *preprocessing* attacks (aka. non-uniform attacks) as any auxiliary information about $\langle H \rangle$ can be computed via a one-time oracle access at the onset. This means that collisions (without salting) can be easily found. Furthermore, since BD calls can be adaptive, salting does not help in our setting at all. Indeed, with a single hash function and arbitrary backdoor capabilities no combiner can exist as any construction $C^H(x)$ can be easily inverted by a function that sees the entire $\langle H \rangle$ and searches for inversions.

In practice it is natural to assume that independent hash functions are available. We can easily model this by an extension to the k-BRO model, whereby k independent ROs and their respective backdoor oracles are made available.[1] The interpretation in our setting is that different "trusted" authorities have designed and made public hash functions that display good (i.e., RO-like) behaviors, but their respective backdoors enable computing any function of the hash tables. We ask if these hash functions can be combined in way that renders their backdoors useless. We observe that the result of Hoch and Shamir [20] can be seen as one building a collision-resistant hash function in the 2-BRO model assuming backdoor oracles that allow for random inversions only.

From a high-level point of view, our main result shows that in the 2-BRO model cryptographic hardness *can* be bootstrapped, even with access to *both* backdoor oracles and even when *arbitrary* backdoor capabilities are provided. In other words, there are secure constructions in the 2-BRO model that can tolerate arbitrary weaknesses in all underlying hash functions. At the core of our results lies new links with hard problems in the area of *communication complexity*.

COMMUNICATION COMPLEXITY. The communication complexity [24,38] of a two-party task $f(S,T)$ is the minimum communication cost over two-party protocols that compute $f(S,T)$. Two rich and well-studied problems in this area are the *set-disjointness* and *set-intersection* problems (see [9] for a survey). Here two parties hold sets S and T respectively. In set-disjointness, their goal is to decide whether or not $S \cap T = \emptyset$; in set-intersection they need to compute at least one element in this intersection. Typically, work in communication complexity studies communication cost over all inputs, that is, the *worst-case* communication complexity of a problem, as the focus is on lower bounds. Cryptographic applications, on the other hand, usually require *average-case* hardness. Distributional (average-case) communication complexity of a problem averages the communication cost over random choices of (S,T) from some distribution μ. We will rely on average-case lower bounds in this work.

---

[1] Note that k-BRO can be viewed as a *restricted* version of the 1-BRO model where k ROs are built from a single RO acting on k separate domains and backdoor capabilities are restricted to these domains only.

THE BASIC IDEAS. In this work, we focus on the parallel (concatenation) and sequential (cascade) composition of hash functions H_1 and H_2 and consider the combiners:

$$C_|^{H_1,H_2}(x) := H_1(x)|H_2(x) \qquad \text{and} \qquad C_o^{H_1,H_2}(x) := H_2(H_1(x)) \ .$$

Here $H_1 : \{0,1\}^n \to \{0,1\}^{n+s_1}$ and $H_2 : \{0,1\}^n \to \{0,1\}^{n+s_2}$ in the first construction, and $H_1 : \{0,1\}^n \to \{0,1\}^{n+s_1}$ and $H_2 : \{0,1\}^{n+s_1} \to \{0,1\}^{n+s_1+s_2}$ in the second.

Consider the one-way security of the concatenation combiner in the 2-BRO model. An adversary is given a point $y^* := y_1^*|y_2^* := H_1(x^*)|H_2(x^*)$ for a random x^*. It has access to the backdoor oracles BD_1 and BD_2 for functions H_1 and H_2 respectively. Its goal is to compute a preimage x for y^* under $C_|^{H_1,H_2}$. This is the case iff $H_1(x) = y_1^*$ and $H_2(x) = y_2^*$. Now define two sets $S := H_1^-(y_1^*)$, the set of preimages of y_1^* under H_1, and $T := H_2^-(y_2^*)$, the set of preimages of y_2^* under H_2. *Thus the adversary wins iff $x \in S \cap T$.*

The two backdoor oracles respectively know S and T as they are part of the descriptions of the two hash functions. This allows us to convert a successful one-way adversary to a two-party protocol that computes an element x of the intersection $S \cap T$. Put differently, if the communication complexity of set-intersection for sets that are distributed as above has a high lower bound, then the adversary has to place a large number of queries, which, in turn, allows us to conclude that the concatenation combiner is one-way in the 2-BRO model.

The question is: for which sets S and T is set-intersection hard? Suppose the hash functions $H_1, H_2 : \{0,1\}^n \to \{0,1\}^m$ are compressing and $m = n - s$. Then on average the sets S and T would each have 2^s elements. We can of course communicate these sets in $\mathcal{O}(2^s)$ bits and find a preimage. However, the cost of this attack when s is linear in n (or even super-logarithmic in n) becomes prohibitive. This raises the question if set-intersection is hard for, say, $s = n/2$ and where the distribution over (S,T) is induced by the two hash functions, where except a single element in common (guaranteed to exist by the rules of the one-way game) all others are sampled uniformly and independently at random and included in the sets.

We observe that hardness of the set-disjointness problem implies hardness of set-intersection as the parties can verify that a given element is indeed in both their sets.[2] Set-disjointness is a better studied problem. To the best of our knowledge two results on set-disjointness with parameters and distributions close to those in our setting have been proven. First, a classical (and technical) result of Babai, Simon and Frankl [1] which shows an $\Omega(\sqrt{N})$ lower bound for random and independent sets S and T of size *exactly* $\sqrt{N}$ in a universe of size N. Second, a result based on information-theoretic arguments due to Bar-Yossef et al. [2], for dependent sets S and T, which has been adapted to *Bernoulli product distributions* in lectures by Moshkovitz and Barak [32, Lecture 9] and

---

[2] On the other hand, for sufficiently large sets that intersect with high probability, set-disjointness is easy whereas set-intersection can remain hard.

Guruswami and Cheraghchi [19, Lecture 21]. The distribution is as follows: for each of the N elements in the universe, independent $\text{Ber}(1/\sqrt{N})$ bits are sampled. (The probability of 1 is $1/\sqrt{N}$.) The sets then consist of all elements for which the bit is set to 1.[3] The authors again prove an $\Omega(\sqrt{N})$ lower bound (which is tight up to logarithmic factors). We note that both these results only hold for protocols that err with probability at most $\varepsilon \leq 1/100$. However, we only found incomplete proofs of set-disjointness for product Bernoulli distributions, and thus have included a self-contained proof in the full version of this paper [4, Appendix C]. We also prove a distributional communication complexity lower bound for set-*intersection* for parameters where set-disjointness can be *easy*.

The second result is better suited for our purposes as the size restriction in the first one would restrict us to regular random oracles. Indeed, the distribution induced on the preimages of y_1^* (resp. y_2^*) by the hash function outside the common random point *is* Bernoulli: $\Pr[\mathsf{H}_1(x) = y_1^*] = 1/2^m$ (resp. $\Pr[\mathsf{H}_2(x) = y_2^*] = 1/2^m$) for any x and independently for values of x. We use this fact to show that set-intersection and set-disjointness problems are, respectively, sufficient to prove it is hard to invert random co-domain points (a property that we call random preimage resistance, rPre) or even decide if a preimage exists (which we call oblivious PRG, oPRG). The main benefit of these games is that they do away with the common point guaranteed to exist by the rules of one-way game (and also similar technicalities associated with the standard PRG game). These games can then be related to the one-way and PRG games via cryptographic reductions.

Our lower bound for set-intersection allows us to prove strong one-way security for some parameters, while the set-disjointness bound only enables proving weak PRG security. Using amplification techniques we can then convert the weak results to strong one-way functions [18] or strong PRGs [29]. Note that the reductions for all these results are fully black-box and thus would relativize [34]. This implies that the same proofs also hold in the presence of backdoor oracles. Construction of other primitives in minicrypt also relativize. This means we also obtain backdoor-free PRFs, MACs, PRPs, and symmetric encryption schemes in our model. The resulting constructions, however, are often too inefficient to be of any practical use. The bottleneck for PRG efficiency here is the proven lower bounds for set-disjointness. New lower bounds that give trade-offs between protocol error and communication complexity will enable more efficient/secure constructions. We discuss in Sect. 4 why the current proof does not permit this.

Recall that collision resistance can *not* be based on one-way functions [36]. The concatenation combiner, on the other hand, appears to be collision resistant as *simultaneous collisions* seem hard to find, even with respect to arbitrary backdoors for each hash function. Indeed, an analysis of collision resistance for this combiner reveals a natural *multi-instance* analogue of the set-intersection problem, which to the best of our knowledge has not been studied yet. Assuming the hardness of this problem (which we leave open) we get collision resistance.

---

[3] The expected size of such Bernoulli sets is $N/\sqrt{N} = \sqrt{N}$, but this size can deviate from the mean and this distribution is *not* identical to that by Babai et al. [1].

Table 1. Overview of results for concatenation and cascade. Functions H_i have stretch s_i. The parameters for collision resistance are conjectural.

Combiner	Strong OW	Weak PRG	Strong CR
Concatenation	$s_1, s_2 = -(\epsilon + 1) \cdot n/2$ for $0 < \epsilon < 1/3$	$s_1 = -n/2 + 1,$ $s_2 = -n/2$	$s_1, s_2 \leq -n/2 - 1$
Cascade	$s_1 = (1+\epsilon) \cdot n, s_2 = -n$ for $-1/2 < \epsilon < 0$	$s_1 = 2n, s_2 = -2n + 1$	$s_1 = 2n,$ $s_2 = -2n - 1$

We note that fully black-box amplification for collision-resistance also exists [8], and it is sufficient to prove hardness for small values of protocol error ε (should this be the case as in the case single-instance set-disjointness).

We carry out similar analyses for the *cascade* combiner, for which different choices of parameters lead to security. Although the overall approach remains the same, we need to deal with difficulties arising from one of the sets being the *image* of a hash function. The latter distribution is somewhat different to Bernoulli sets (as elements are not chosen independently). We show, however, that by addition of noise one-way and PRG security can be based on *known* lower bounds. For collision-resistance we give a reduction to a multi-instance analogue of set-intersection (whose hardness remains open). We analyze the security of the XOR combiner in the full version of this paper [4].

We summarize our results in Table 1. Roughly speaking, strong security demands that the advantage of adversaries in the corresponding security game is negligible, while for weak security it suffices that the advantage is not overwhelming. In the table, concatenation is with respect to hash function $H_1 : \{0,1\}^n \rightarrow \{0,1\}^{n+s_1}$ and $H_2 : \{0,1\}^n \rightarrow \{0,1\}^{n+s_2}$, while cascade is with respect to hash function $H_1 : \{0,1\}^n \rightarrow \{0,1\}^{n+s_1}$ and $H_2 : \{0,1\}^{n+s_1} \rightarrow \{0,1\}^{n+s_1+s_2}$. The stretch values s_1 and s_2 can assume negative values (compressing), positive values (expanding), or be zero (length-preserving).

1.2 Discussion

BACKDOORS AS WEAKNESSES. One of the main motivations for the works of Liskov [27] and Hoch and Shamir [20] is the study of design principles for symmetric schemes that can offer protections against weaknesses in their underlying primitives. For example, Hoch and Shamir study the failure-friendly double-pipe hash construction of Lucks [28]. Similarly, Liskov shows that his *zipper hash* is indifferentiable from a random oracle even with an inversion oracle for its underlying compression function. Proofs of security in the unrestricted BRO model would strengthen these results as they place weaker assumptions on the types of weaknesses that are discovered.

AUXILIARY INPUTS. As mentioned above, a closely related model to BRO is the Auxiliary-Input RO (AI-RO) model, introduced by Unruh [37] and recently refined by Dodis, Guo, and Katz [14] and Coretti et al. [12]. Here the result of a one-time preprocessing attack with access to the full table of the random oracle is made available to an adversary. The BRO and AI-RO models are similar in that they both allow for arbitrary functions of the random oracle to be computed. However, BRO allows for adaptive, instance-dependent auxiliary information, whereas the AI-RO model only permits a one-time access at the onset.[4] Thus AI-RO is identical to BRO when only a single BD query at the onset is allowed. Extension to multiple ROs can also be considered for AI-ROs, where independent preprocessing attacks are performed on the hash functions. A corollary is that any positive result in the k-BRO model would also hold in the k-AI-RO model. Results in k-AI-RO model can be proven more directly using the decomposition of high-entropy densities as the setting is non-interactive.

FEASIBILITY IN 1-BRO. As already observed, any combiner in 1-BRO is insecure with respect to arbitrary backdoors. We can, however, consider a model where backdoor capabilities are restricted to inversions only. Security in such models will depend on the exact specification of backdoor functionalities $\mathcal{F}$. For example, under random inversions positive results can be established using standard lazy sampling techniques. But another natural choice is to consider functions which output possibly adversarial preimages, i.e., functions $f[y]$ whose outputs are restricted to those x for which $\mathsf{H}(x) = y$. As we have seen, under such generalized inversions provably secure constructions can fail. Moreover, proving security under general inversions seems to require techniques from communication complexity as we do here.

OTHER SETTINGS. Proofs in the random-oracle model often proceed via direct information-theoretic analyses. Here we give cryptographic reductions (somewhat similarly to the standard model) that isolate the underlying communication complexity problems. These problems have diverse applications in other fields (such as circuit complexity, VLSI design, and combinatorial auctions), which motivate their study outside cryptographic contexts. Any improvement in lower bounds for them would also lead to improvements in the security/efficiency of cryptographic constructions. We discussed the benefits of proofs for arbitrary error above. As other examples, results in multi-party communication complexity would translate to the k-BRO model for $k > 2$ or those in quantum communication complexity can be used to built quantum-secure BRO combiners.

1.3   Future Work

Our work leaves a number of problems open, some of which are closer to work in communication complexity. We discuss these below.

Lower bounds for set-disjointness that do not assume a small error would improve the security and/or efficiency of our PRG constructions. Moreover, we do not currently have a lower bound for the multi-instance analogue of set-intersection that we need for proving collision resistance. Finding the "maximal" backdoor

---

[4] Arguably, the AI-RO model is better named the Non-Uniform RO model: auxiliary input is often instance dependent whereas non-uniform input is not.

capabilities in the 1-BRO model under which hardness can be bootstrapped remains an interesting open problem. Katz, Lucks, and Thiruvengadam [22] study the construction of collision-resistant hash functions from ideal ciphers that are vulnerable to differential related-key attacks. We leave the study of combiners for other backdoored primitives, such as ideal ciphers, for future work.

2   Preliminaries

We let $\mathbb{N}$ denote the set of non-negative integers and $\{0,1\}^n$ be the set of all binary strings of length $n \in \mathbb{N}$. For two bit strings x and y, we denote their concatenation by $x|y$. We let $[N]$ denote the set $\{1,\ldots,N\}$. For a finite set S, we denote by $s \twoheadleftarrow S$ the uniform random variable over S. The Bernoulli random variable $x \twoheadleftarrow \mathrm{Ber}(p)$ takes value 1 with probability p and 0 with probability $1-p$. The Binomial random variable $x_1,\ldots,x_n \twoheadleftarrow \mathrm{Bin}(n,p)$ constitutes a sequence of n independent Bernoulli samples. We will sometimes use $e^{-x} := \lim_{n\to\infty}(1-x/n)^n$.

2.1   Random Oracles

A hash function H with n-bit inputs and m-bit outputs is simply a function with signature $\mathsf{H} : \{0,1\}^n \to \{0,1\}^m$. We let $\mathrm{Fun}[n,m]$ denote the set of all such functions. $\mathrm{Fun}[n,m]$ is finite and we endow it with the uniform distribution. For a hash function H, we let $\langle \mathsf{H} \rangle$ denote the function table of H encoded as a string of length $m2^n$. We see the x-th m-bit block of $\langle \mathsf{H} \rangle$ as $\mathsf{H}(x)$, identifying strings $x \in \{0,1\}^n$ with integers in $[1,2^n]$. The random-oracle (RO) model (for a given n and m) is a model of computation where all parties have oracle access to a function $\mathsf{H} \twoheadleftarrow \mathrm{Fun}[n,m]$.

BACKDOOR FUNCTIONS. A backdoor function for $\mathsf{H} \in \mathrm{Fun}[n,m]$ is a function $f : \mathrm{Fun}[n,m] \to \{0,1\}^t$. A backdoor capability class $\mathcal{F}$ is a set of such backdoor functions. The unrestricted class contains all functions. But the class can be also restricted, for example, functions $f[y]$ for $y \in \{0,1\}^m$ whose outputs x are restricted to be in $\mathsf{H}^-(y)$, where $\mathsf{H}^-(y)$ is the set preimages of y under H. Randomness can also be hardwired.

THE BRO MODEL. In the backdoored random-oracle (BRO) model, a random function $\mathsf{H} \twoheadleftarrow \mathrm{Fun}[n,m]$ is sampled. All parties are provided with oracle access to H. Adversarial parties are additionally given access to the procedure

$$\text{Proc. } \mathrm{BD}(f) : \textbf{ return } f(\langle \mathsf{H} \rangle)$$

for $f \in \mathcal{F}$. Formally, we denote this model by $\mathrm{BRO}[n,m,\mathcal{F}]$, but will omit $[n,m,\mathcal{F}]$ when it is clear from the context. When $\mathcal{F} = \emptyset$, we recover the conventional RO model. As discussed in the introduction, when the adversarial parties call the backdoor oracle only once and before any hash queries, we recover random oracles with auxiliary input, the AI-RO model [12, Definition 2]. Thus, BRO also models oracle-dependent auxiliary input or pre-computation

Game $\mathrm{OW}_{\mathsf{C}}^{\mathcal{A}}$	Game $\mathrm{PRG}_{\mathsf{C}}^{\mathcal{A}}$	Game $\mathrm{CR}_{\mathsf{C}}^{\mathcal{A}}$
for $i = 1, 2$ **do**	**for** $i = 1, 2$ **do**	**for** $i = 1, 2$ **do**
$\quad \mathsf{H}_i \twoheadleftarrow \mathrm{Fun}[n_i, m_i]$	$\quad \mathsf{H}_i \twoheadleftarrow \mathrm{Fun}[n_i, m_i]$	$\quad \mathsf{H}_i \twoheadleftarrow \mathrm{Fun}[n_i, m_i]$
$x \twoheadleftarrow \{0,1\}^n; \; y \leftarrow \mathsf{C}^{\mathsf{H}_i}(x)$	$y_0 \twoheadleftarrow \{0,1\}^m; \; b \twoheadleftarrow \{0,1\}$	$(x_1, x_2) \leftarrow \mathcal{A}^{\mathsf{H}_i, \mathrm{BD}_i}$
$x' \twoheadleftarrow \mathcal{A}^{\mathsf{H}_i, \mathrm{BD}_i}(y)$	$x \twoheadleftarrow \{0,1\}^n; \; y_1 \leftarrow \mathsf{C}^{\mathsf{H}_i}(x)$	$y_1 \leftarrow \mathsf{C}^{\mathsf{H}_i}(x_1); \; y_2 \leftarrow \mathsf{C}^{\mathsf{H}_i}(x_2)$
return $(\mathsf{C}^{\mathsf{H}_i}(x') = y)$	$b' \leftarrow \mathcal{A}^{\mathsf{H}_i, \mathrm{BD}_i}(y_b)$	**return** $(x_1 \neq x_2 \wedge y_1 = y_2)$
	return $(b' = b)$	

Fig. 1. The one-way, pseudorandomness, and collision resistance games for $\mathsf{C}^{\mathsf{H}_i} \in \mathrm{Fun}[n, m]$.

attacks as special cases. In the k-BRO model (with the implicit parameters $[n_i, m_i, \mathcal{F}_i]$ for $i = 1, \ldots, k$) access to k independent random oracles $\mathsf{H}_i \in \mathrm{Fun}[n_i, m_i]$ and their respective backdoors BD_i with capabilities $\mathcal{F}_i$ are provided. That is, procedure $\mathrm{BD}_i(f)$ returns $f(\langle \mathsf{H}_i \rangle)$. In this work we are primarily interested in the 1-BRO and 2-BRO models with *unrestricted* $\mathcal{F}$.

We observe that the $2\text{-BRO}[n, m, \mathcal{F}_1, n, m, \mathcal{F}_2]$ model is identical to the $1\text{-BRO}[n+1, m, \mathcal{F}]$ model where for $\mathsf{H} \in \mathrm{Fun}[n+1, m]$ we define $\mathsf{H}_1(x) := \mathsf{H}(0|x)$, $\mathsf{H}_2(x) := \mathsf{H}(1|x)$ and $\mathcal{F}$ to consist of two types of functions: those in $\mathcal{F}_1$ and dependent on values $\mathsf{H}(0|x)$, that is the function table of H_1, only, and those in $\mathcal{F}_2$ and dependent on values of $\mathsf{H}(1|x)$, that is the function table of H_2, only. Thus the adversary in the unrestricted 2-BRO model has less power than in the unrestricted 1-BRO model.

2.2 Cryptographic Notions

We recall the basic notions of one-wayness, pseudorandomness, and collision-resistance for a construction $\mathsf{C}^{\mathsf{H}_1, \mathsf{H}_2}$ in the 2-BRO model in Fig. 1. We omit the implicit parameters from the subscripts and use $\mathsf{C}^{\mathsf{H}_i}$ in place of $\mathsf{C}^{\mathsf{H}_1, \mathsf{H}_2}$ to ease notation. These notions can also be defined in the 1-BRO model analogously by removing access to H_2 and BD_2 throughout. The advantage terms are

$$\mathsf{Adv}_{\mathsf{C}^{\mathsf{H}_i}}^{\mathrm{ow}}(\mathcal{A}) := \Pr[\mathrm{OW}_{\mathsf{C}^{\mathsf{H}_i}}^{\mathcal{A}}], \qquad \mathsf{Adv}_{\mathsf{C}^{\mathsf{H}_i}}^{\mathrm{prg}}(\mathcal{A}) := 2 \cdot \Pr[\mathrm{PRG}_{\mathsf{C}^{\mathsf{H}_i}}^{\mathcal{A}}] - 1,$$

$$\mathsf{Adv}_{\mathsf{C}^{\mathsf{H}_i}}^{\mathrm{cr}}(\mathcal{A}) := \Pr[\mathrm{CR}_{\mathsf{C}^{\mathsf{H}_i}}^{\mathcal{A}}] .$$

All probabilities in this model are also taken over random choices of H_i. Informally $\mathsf{C}^{\mathsf{H}_1, \mathsf{H}_2}$ is OW, PRG, or CR if the advantage of any adversary $\mathcal{A}$ querying its oracles, such that the total length of the received responses remains "reasonable", is "small". Note that if one only considers backdoor functions with 1-bit output lengths, the total length of the oracle responses directly translates to the number of queries made by $\mathcal{A}$. We denote by $\mathsf{Q}(\mathcal{A})$ the number of oracle queries

Game $\text{rPre}_{\mathsf{C}}^{\mathcal{A}}$	Game $\text{oPRG}_{\mathsf{C}}^{\mathcal{A}}$	Game $\text{IU}_{\mathsf{C}}^{\mathcal{A}}$
for $i = 1, 2$ **do**	**for** $i = 1, 2$ **do**	**for** $i = 1, 2$ **do**
$\quad \mathsf{H}_i \twoheadleftarrow \text{Fun}[n_i, m_i]$	$\quad \mathsf{H}_i \twoheadleftarrow \text{Fun}[n_i, m_i]$	$\quad \mathsf{H}_i \twoheadleftarrow \text{Fun}[n_i, m_i]$
$y \twoheadleftarrow \{0,1\}^m$	$y \twoheadleftarrow \{0,1\}^m$	$y_1 \twoheadleftarrow \text{Img}(\mathsf{C}^{\mathsf{H}_i}); \ b \twoheadleftarrow \{0,1\}$
$x' \leftarrow \mathcal{A}^{\mathsf{H}_i, \text{BD}_i}(y)$	$b' \leftarrow \mathcal{A}^{\mathsf{H}_i, \text{BD}_i}(y)$	$x \twoheadleftarrow \{0,1\}^n; \ y_0 \leftarrow \mathsf{C}^{\mathsf{H}_i}(x)$
if $y \in \overline{\text{Img}}(\mathsf{C}^{\mathsf{H}_i})$	**return** $(b' = (y \in \text{Img}(\mathsf{C}^{\mathsf{H}_i})))$	$b' \leftarrow \mathcal{A}^{\mathsf{H}_i, \text{BD}_i}(y_b)$
$\quad$ **return** $(x' = \bot)$		**return** $(b' = b)$
return $(\mathsf{C}^{\mathsf{H}_i}(x') = y)$		

Fig. 2. The random preimage resistance (rPre), oblivious PRG (oPRG), and image uniformity (IU) games for $\mathsf{C}^{\mathsf{H}_i} \in \text{Fun}[n, m]$.

made by an adversary $\mathcal{A}$ to H_i and BD_i. Weak security in each case means that the corresponding advantage is less than 1 and not overwhelming.

We define variants of the above games which will be helpful in our analyses. For a function $\mathsf{H} \in \text{Fun}[n, m]$, define $\text{Img}(\mathsf{H}) := \mathsf{H}(\{0,1\}^n)$ and $\overline{\text{Img}}(\mathsf{H}) := \{0,1\}^m \setminus \text{Img}(\mathsf{H})$. The *random preimage-resistance* (rPre) game is defined similarly to everywhere preimage-resistance (ePre) [35] except that a random co-domain point (as opposed to any such point) must be inverted. This definition differs from one-way security in two aspects: the distribution of $\mathsf{H}(x)$ for a uniform x might not be uniform. Furthermore, some points in the co-domain might not have any preimages. We also define a decisional variant, called *oblivious PRG* (oPRG), where the adversary has to decide if a random co-domain point has a preimage. We formalize these games in Fig. 2. The advantage terms are defined as:

$$\text{Adv}_{\mathsf{C}^{\mathsf{H}_i}}^{\text{rpre}}(\mathcal{A}) := \Pr[\text{rPre}_{\mathsf{C}^{\mathsf{H}_i}}^{\mathcal{A}}] \qquad \text{Adv}_{\mathsf{C}^{\mathsf{H}_i}}^{\text{oprg}}(\mathcal{A}) := \Pr[\text{oPRG}_{\mathsf{C}^{\mathsf{H}_i}}^{\mathcal{A}}]$$

Weak analogues of the above security notions (for example weak rPre or weak oPRG) are defined by requiring the advantage to be bounded away from 1 (i.e., not to be overwhelming). These definitions can be formalized in the asymptotic language, but we use concrete parameters here.

We state two lemmas that relate OW and rPre, resp. PRG and oPRG: for functions that have *uniform images*, as defined below, we show that OW security is implied by rPre security and PRG security is implied by oPRG security.

IMAGE UNIFORMITY. Let $\mathsf{C}^{\mathsf{H}_i} \in \text{Fun}[n, m]$ be a construction in the 2-BRO model. In the image uniformity game IU defined in Fig. 2, an adversary, given access to all backdoor oracles, must decide whether a given value is chosen uniformly at random from the image of $\mathsf{C}^{\mathsf{H}_i}$ or computed as the image of a value x chosen uniformly at random from the domain. The advantage term is

$$\text{Adv}_{\mathsf{C}^{\mathsf{H}_i}}^{\text{iu}}(\mathcal{A}) := 2 \cdot \Pr[\text{IU}_{\mathsf{C}^{\mathsf{H}_i}}^{\mathcal{A}}] - 1 ,$$

where the probability is taken over random choices of H_i.

The following lemma upper bounds the advantage of adversaries playing the image uniformity game for combiners with different stretch values. We denote by $\mathcal{U}_S$ the uniform distribution over a set S. We also let $\mathcal{U}_f^{\mathsf{p}}$ denote the distribution defined by $\mathcal{U}_f^{\mathsf{p}}(x) = |f^{-1}(x)|/2^n$, where $f \in \mathrm{Fun}[n, m]$ is a uniform function. We refer the readers to [4, Appendix A] for proofs.

Lemma 1 (Combiner image uniformity). *Let* $\mathsf{C}_t^{\mathsf{H}_1, \mathsf{H}_2} : \{0, 1\}^n \rightarrow \{0, 1\}^m$ *be a combiner for* $t \in \{|, \circ\}$. *Let* $\mathsf{H} : \{0, 1\}^n \rightarrow \{0, 1\}^m$ *be a hash function. Then*

$$\mathsf{Adv}_{\mathsf{C}_t^{\mathsf{H}_i}}^{\mathrm{iu}}(\mathcal{A}) \leq \mathbb{E}_{\mathsf{H}} \left[\Delta_{\mathsf{TV}} \left(\mathcal{U}_{\mathrm{Img}(\mathsf{H})}, \mathcal{U}_{\mathsf{H}}^{\mathsf{p}} \right) \right] + 2 \cdot p_t \; ,$$

where $p_| = 0$ *and* $p_\circ \leq 2^{2n_1 - m_1}$ *is the probability that* $\mathsf{H}_1 : \{0, 1\}^{n_1} \rightarrow \{0, 1\}^{m_1}$ *is not injective (i.e., it has at least one collision). Let* $2^n = C \cdot 2^{m \cdot \gamma}$ *for constants* C *and* γ. *Then the above statistical distance is negligible for* $\gamma > 1$ *and* $0 < \gamma < 1$ *when* $C = 1$, *while for* $\gamma = 1$ *and* $C \leq 1$ *it less than* $e^{-C} \cdot \left(C/(1 - e^{-C}) - 1 \right)$ *plus negligible terms.*

Now we can relate our notions of rPre and oPRG with their classical variants, i.e., one-way and PRG security. Proofs of both lemmas are included in the full version [4, Appendix B].

Lemma 2 (rPre + IU $\implies$ OW). *Let* $\mathsf{C}^{\mathsf{H}_i} \in \mathrm{Fun}[n, m]$ *be a construction in the 2-BRO model. Then for any adversary* $\mathcal{A}$ *against the one-way security of* $\mathsf{C}^{\mathsf{H}_i}$, *there is an adversary* $\mathcal{B}$ *against the image uniformity and an adversary* $\mathcal{C}$ *against the rPre security of* $\mathsf{C}^{\mathsf{H}_i}$, *all in the 2-BRO model and using identical backdoor functionalities, such that*

$$\mathsf{Adv}_{\mathsf{C}^{\mathsf{H}_i}}^{\mathrm{ow}}(\mathcal{A}) \leq \mathsf{Adv}_{\mathsf{C}^{\mathsf{H}_i}}^{\mathrm{iu}}(\mathcal{B}) + \frac{1}{\alpha} \cdot \mathsf{Adv}_{\mathsf{C}^{\mathsf{H}_i}}^{\mathrm{rpre}}(\mathcal{C}) - \frac{1 - \alpha}{\alpha} \; ,$$

where $\alpha := \Pr[y \in \mathsf{Img}(\mathsf{C}^{\mathsf{H}_i})]$ *over a random choice of* $y \in \{0, 1\}^m$ *and* H_i.

An analogous result also holds for oPRG security.

Lemma 3 (oPRG + IU $\implies$ PRG). *Let* $\mathsf{C}^{\mathsf{H}_i} \in \mathrm{Fun}[n, m]$ *be a construction in the 2-BRO model which is expanding with* $m - n \geq 0.53$. *Then for any adversary* $\mathcal{A}$ *against the PRG security of* $\mathsf{C}^{\mathsf{H}_i}$, *there is an adversary* $\mathcal{B}$ *against the image uniformity and an adversary* $\mathcal{C}$ *against the oPRG security of* $\mathsf{C}^{\mathsf{H}_i}$, *both in the 2-BRO model and using identical backdoor functionalities, such that*

$$\mathsf{Adv}_{\mathsf{C}^{\mathsf{H}_i}}^{\mathrm{prg}}(\mathcal{A}) \leq \mathsf{Adv}_{\mathsf{C}^{\mathsf{H}_i}}^{\mathrm{iu}}(\mathcal{B}) + \frac{1 - \alpha}{\alpha} \cdot \mathsf{Adv}_{\mathsf{C}^{\mathsf{H}_i}}^{\mathrm{oprg}}(\mathcal{C}) - (1 - \alpha) \; ,$$

where $\alpha := \Pr[y \in \mathsf{Img}(\mathsf{C}^{\mathsf{H}_i})]$ *over a random choice of* $y \in \{0, 1\}^m$ *and* H_i.

3   Black-Box Combiners

A standard way to build a good hash function from a number of possibly "faulty" hash functions is to combine them [25]. For instance, given k hash functions

$H_1, \ldots, H_k$, the classical concatenation combiner is guaranteed to be collision resistant as long as one out of the k hash functions is collision resistant. More formally, a black-box collision-resistance combiner C is a pair of oracle circuits (C^{H_i}, R^A) where C^{H_i} is the construction and R^A is a reduction that given as oracle any procedure A that finds a collision for C^{H_i}, returns collisions for *all* of the underlying H_i's. We are interested in a setting where *none* of the available hash functions is good. Under this assumption, however, a secure hash function must be built from scratch, implying that the source of cryptographic hardness must lie elsewhere. As we discussed above, this question has been studied in the RO model.

We briefly explore the difficulty in the standard model here. We consider a variant of this problem where the hash functions are weak due to the existence of *backdoors*. A generation algorithm Gen outputs keys (hk, bk), where hk is used for hashing and bk enables an unspecified backdoor capability (such as finding preimages or collisions). Our hardness assumption is that the hash function with key hk is collision resistant without access to bk. However, when bk is available, no security is assumed. In this setting, the definition of a combiner can be simplified: instead of requiring the existence of a reduction R^A as above, we can proceed in the standard way and require that the advantage of any adversary $A(S)$ that gets any subset $S \subset \{bk_1, \ldots, bk_k\}$ of the backdoors of size $|S| \leq k-1$ to be small.[5] Let us call a combiner secure against any set of at most t backdoors a $\binom{k}{k-t}$-combiner.

It is trivial to see that a $\binom{k}{0}$-combiner is also a $\binom{k}{1}$-combiner. It is also easy to see that a black-box combiner is also a $\binom{k}{1}$-combiner. We are, however, interested in the feasibility of $\binom{k}{0}$-combiners. In this setting there *is* an assumed source of hardness, namely the collision resistance of hash functions without backdoors. But constructions that have to work with a *provided* set of keys seem hard.[6] We next give a simple impossibly result that formalizes this intuition under fully black-box constructions.

Theorem 1. *For any positive $k \in \mathbb{N}$, there are no fully black-box constructions of compressing collision-resistant $\binom{k}{0}$-combiners.*

Proof idea. Let (H, A) be a pair of oracles such that $H(hk, \cdot)$ implements a random function and $A(\langle C \rangle, hk_1, \ldots, hk_k, bk_1, \ldots, bk_k)$ is a break oracle that operates as

---

[5] The classical setting can be viewed as one where bk's are *fixed*, which leads to a difficulty when the new definition is used: a combiner (formally speaking) can "detect" which hash functions are the good ones and use them. Since this detection procedure is not considered practical, one instead asks for the existence of a reduction R as discussed above.

[6] Without this restriction, a trivial construction exists: generate a fresh hash key and "forget" its backdoor. In practice, however, hash keys model sampling of a (unkeyed) hash function from a family. Moreover, it is unclear if the designer of the combiner will securely erase the generated backdoor. Thus, we assume that for any generated key its backdoor is also available.

follows. It interprets $\langle C \rangle$ as the description of a combiner. It then checks that each bk_i indeed enables generating collisions under hk_i. If so, it (inefficiently) finds a random collision for $C^{H(hk_1,\cdot),\ldots,H(hk_k,\cdot)}$ and returns it. An efficient reduction R is given oracle access to $\mathcal{A}$ and H as well as a key hk^* (without its backdoor bk^*). It should find a collision for $H(hk^*, \cdot)$ while making a small (below birthday) number of queries to the two oracles $\mathcal{A}$ and H. We show that any such reduction R must have a negligible success probability.   □

We distinguish between two cases based on whether the reduction R uses the provided break oracle $\mathcal{A}$ or not. Without the use of $\mathcal{A}$, the reduction would break collision resistance for hk^* on its own, contradicting the collision resistance of hk^* beyond the birthday bound. To use $\mathcal{A}$ the reduction has to provide it with k keys hk_i and some other keys bk_i that enable finding collisions (since $\mathcal{A}$ checks this). However, none of the provided keys hk_i can be hk^*, since R must also provide some $\tilde{bk}^*$ that enables finding collisions under hk^*, which means that R can directly use $\tilde{bk}^*$ to compute a collision for $H(hk^*, \cdot)$, once again contradicting the assumed collision resistance of hk^* beyond the birthday bound. Thus, R does not use hk^*. A random oracle $H(hk^*, \cdot)$, however, is collision resistant even in the presence of random collisions for $H(hk, \cdot)$ for $hk \neq hk^*$. This means that R, which places a small number of oracle queries, will have a negligible success probability.

There is room to circumvent this result by considering non-black-box constructions. Here, we will study hash function combiners in the k-BRO model, where the hash oracles model access to different hk and the backdoor oracles model access to the corresponding bk's. As mentioned above, this approach has also been adapted in a number of previous works, both from a provable security as well as a cryptanalytic view [20,21,23,26,31]. In this work we will focus on basic security properties of the concatenation (parallel) and cascade (sequential) combiners in the *unrestricted* 2-BRO model.

4   Communication Complexity

The communication cost [24,38] of a two-party deterministic protocol π on inputs (x, y) is the number of bits that are transmitted in a run of the protocol $\pi(x, y)$. We denote this by $\mathsf{CC}(\pi(x, y))$. The worst-case communication complexity of π is $\max_{(x,y)} \mathsf{CC}(\pi(x, y))$. A protocol π computes a task (function) $f : X \times Y \to Z$ if the last message of $\pi(x, y)$ is $f(x, y)$. The communication complexity of a task f is the minimum communication complexity of any protocol π that computes f. Protocols can also be randomized and thus might err with probability $\Pr[\pi(x, y) \neq f(x, y)]$. Following cryptographic conventions, we denote protocol correctness by $\mathsf{Adv}_\mu^{\mathsf{f}}(\pi)$, where f is a placeholder for the name of the task f.

In the cryptographic setting we are interested in distributional (aka. average-case) communication complexity measured by averaging the communication cost over random choices of inputs and coins. A standard coin-fixing argument shows that in the *distributional* setting any protocol can be derandomized with no change in communication complexity, and thus we can focus on deterministic protocols. For a given distribution μ over the inputs (x, y), the protocol error and correctness are computed by taking the probability over the choice of (x, y). We define the distributional communication cost of a deterministic protocol π as

$$\mathsf{D}_\mu(\pi) := \mathbb{E}_{(x,y)\sim\mu}[\mathsf{CC}(\pi(x, y))].$$

The distributional communication complexity of a task f with error ε is

$$\mathsf{D}_\mu^\varepsilon(f) := \min_\pi \mathsf{D}_\mu(\pi) ,$$

where the minimum is taken over all deterministic protocols π which err with probability at most ε. In this work, we need to slightly generalize functional tasks to relational tasks $R(x, y) \subseteq Z$ and define error as $\Pr[\pi(x, y) \notin R(x, y)]$.

Two central problems in communication complexity that have received substantial attention are the *set-disjointness* and the *set-intersection* problems. In set-disjointness two parties, holding sets S and T respectively, compute the binary function $\mathrm{DISJ}(S, T) := (S \cap T = \emptyset)$. In set-intersection, their goal is to compute the relation $\mathrm{INT}(S, T) := S \cap T$; that is, the last message of the protocol should be equal to some element in the intersection. Note that set-disjointness can be seen as a decisional version of set-intersection and is easier. As mentioned, we are interested in average-case lower bounds for these tasks and moreover we focus on *product* distributions, where the sets are chosen independently.

Two main results to this end have been proven.[7] A classical result of Babai, Frankl, and Simon [1] establishes an $\Omega(\sqrt{N})$ lower bound for set-disjointness where the input sets S and T are independent random subsets of $[N]$ of size exactly $\sqrt{N}$. This result, however, is restrictive for us as it roughly translates to regular functions in the cryptographic setting. Moreover, its proof uses intricate combinatorial arguments, which are somewhat hard to work with.

A second result considers the following distribution. Each element $x \in [N]$ is thrown into S independently with probability p. (And similarly for T with probability q.) We can view S as a N-bit string X where its i-th bit x_i is 1 iff $i \in S$. Thus the distribution can be viewed as N i.i.d. Bernoulli random variables $x_i \sim \mathrm{Ber}(p)$ where $p := \Pr[x_i = 1]$. Thus the elements of the sets form a binomial distribution, and accordingly we write $S \sim \mathrm{Bin}(N, p)$ and $T \sim \mathrm{Bin}(N, q)$. We define $\mu(p, q)$ as the *product* of these distributions. When $p = q = 1/2$ we get the product uniform distribution over the subsets of $[N] \times [N]$, but typically we will be looking at much smaller values of p and q of order $1/\sqrt{N}$.

---

[7] We note that most of the work on distributional communication complexity is driven by Yao's min-max lemma, which lower bounds worst-case communication complexity using distributional communication complexity for *some* (often non-uniform) distribution.

Using information-theoretic techniques [2], the following lower bound can be established.

Theorem 2 (Set-Disjointness Lower Bound). *Let $N \in \mathbb{N}$ and assume $p, q \in (0, 1/2]$ with $p \leq q$ and $pq = 1/(\delta N)$ for some $\delta > 1$. Let $\mu(p, q)$ be the product binomial distribution over subsets $S, T \subseteq [N]$. Assume $\varepsilon < \frac{(\delta-1)p_0}{(4+\delta)}$ and let $p_0 := \Pr[\mathrm{DISJ}(S, T) = 0]$. Then*

$$D_{\mu(p,q)}^{\varepsilon}(\mathrm{DISJ}) \geq \frac{Np}{8} \cdot \left((\delta - 1)p_0 - (4 + \delta)\varepsilon\right)^2 .$$

We have included a detailed proof of the above theorem in the full version [4, Appendix C], which follows those in [19,32]. Our proof generalizes the original result, which was only claimed for $p = q = 1/\sqrt{N}$.[8] Roughly speaking, the proof proceeds along the following lines. We can lower bound the communication complexity of any protocol by the total information leaked by its transcripts about each coordinate (x_i, y_i). The latter can be lower bounded based on the statistical distance in protocol transcripts when $x_i = 1 \wedge y_i = 0$ and $x_i = 0 \wedge y_i = 1$. This step uses a number of information-theoretic inequalities, which we include with proofs in the full version. Finally, we show that a highly correct protocol can be used as a distinguisher with constant advantage: When $x_i = 0 \wedge y_i = 0$, for a constant fraction of the inputs the sets will be disjoint. However, when $x_i = 1 \wedge y_i = 1$ they necessarily intersect, but this condition happens for a constant fraction of the inputs. We get a $\sqrt{N}$ lower bound by averaging over the i's.

In this section we also prove a communication complexity lower bound for the set-intersection problem over Bernoulli sets for which set-disjointness can be *easy*. Although the overall proof structure will be similar to that in [19,32], we will differ in a number of places. First, as above we leave the Bernoulli parameters free so as to be able to compute a feasible region where the lower bound will be non-trivial. We also use the fact that a candidate element can be checked to belong to the intersection (whereas a decision bit for disjointness cannot be checked for correctness). This ensures that the protocol error is one-sided, and allows us to remove the requirement of ε being sufficiently small. Finally, we will bound the probability that the protocol outputs a *random element* in the intersection. This leads to a distinguisher that succeeds with smaller advantage, but overall will lead to a non-trivial bound. We state and prove the formal result next.

---

[8] In the full version of this paper [4, Appendix C.3] we give a new refined proof that extends the theorem to $\delta \geq 0.8$.

Theorem 3 (Set-Intersection Lower Bound). *Let $N \in \mathbb{N}$ and assume $p, q \in (0, 1/2]$ with $p \leq q$. Let $\mu(p, q)$ be the product binomial distribution over subsets $S, T \subseteq [N]$. Let ε be the protocol error and set $p_0 := \Pr[\mathrm{DISJ}(S, T) = 0]$. If $\varepsilon \leq p_0$ then*

$$D_{\mu(p,q)}^{\varepsilon}(\mathrm{INT}) \geq \frac{Np}{8} \cdot \left(\frac{p_0 - \varepsilon}{Npq} \right)^2 .$$

For sufficiently large N we have $p_0 = 1 - (1 - pq)^N \approx 1 - e^{-Npq}$. If $pq \gg 1/N$ we get that $p_0 \approx 1$ (the sets intersect with overwhelming probability) and for the theorem we would need that $\varepsilon \leq 1$.

Let us first give some preliminaries and state two lemmas that are used in the proof of Theorem 3. For random variables X and Y, their statistical distance (aka. total variance) is denoted by $\Delta_{\mathsf{TV}}(X, Y)$, their mutual information is denoted by $I(X; Y)$, and their Hellinger distance is denoted by $\Delta_{\mathsf{Hel}}(X, Y)$:

$$\Delta_{\mathsf{Hel}}(X, Y) := \sqrt{1 - \sum_{z \in D} \sqrt{\Pr[X = z] \Pr[Y = z]}} .$$

Statistical and Hellinger distance are related (cf. proofs in [4, Appendix C.1]) via:

$$\Delta_{\mathsf{Hel}}^2(X, Y) \leq \Delta_{\mathsf{TV}}(X, Y) \leq \sqrt{2} \cdot \Delta_{\mathsf{Hel}}(X, Y) .$$

Below, Lemma 4, proven in the full version [4, Appendix C.1], relates the mutual information of two random variables with their Hellinger distance.

Lemma 4 (Information to Hellinger). *Let X and Y be random variables and $Y_x := Y | X = x$, i.e., Y conditioned on $X = x$. Then*

$$\mathbb{E}_{x \in X}[\Delta_{\mathsf{Hel}}^2(Y, Y_x)] \leq I(X; Y) .$$

Next we state the cut-and-paste lemma from communication complexity. A proof is included in [4, Appendix C.2].

Lemma 5 (Cut-and-Paste). *Let $\Pi(X, Y)$ denote a random variable for the transcripts of a deterministic protocol on input bit strings (X, Y) such that the corresponding sets S and T are drawn from μ, i.e., $S, T \sim \mu$. Let $a, b \in \{0, 1\}$ and define $\Pi_{a,b}^i(X, Y) := \Pi(X, Y) \mid x_i = a \wedge y_i = b$. Then for each i, it holds that*

$$\Delta_{\mathsf{Hel}}^2(\Pi_{0,0}^i, \Pi_{1,1}^i) = \Delta_{\mathsf{Hel}}^2(\Pi_{0,1}^i, \Pi_{1,0}^i) .$$

Now we can prove the claimed lower bound on the communication complexity of set-intersection.

Proof of Theorem 3. Let π be a deterministic protocol with error at most ε, i.e.,

$$\Pr_{(S,T) \sim \mu} [\pi(X, Y) \in \mathrm{INT}(S, T)] \geq 1 - \varepsilon ,$$

where X and Y are bit string representations of S and T as explained above. Let $\Pi(X, Y)$ denote a random variable for the transcripts of protocol π on inputs (X, Y) with corresponding sets $(S, T) \sim \mu$. We write $X = (x_1, \ldots, x_N)$ and $Y = (y_1, \ldots, y_N)$ where $x_i, y_i \in \{0, 1\}$. For random variables A and B, let $\mathrm{supp}(A)$ denote the support of A (i.e., the set of values that have a non-zero probability of happening), and $H(A)$ denote the Shannon entropy. We have

$$D^\varepsilon_{\mu(p,q)}(\mathrm{INT}) \geq \log |\mathrm{supp}(\Pi(X, Y))|$$
$$\geq H(\Pi(X, Y)) = H(\Pi(X, Y)) + H(X, Y) - H(X, Y, \Pi(X, Y))$$
$$= I(X, Y; \Pi) = I(x_1, \ldots, x_N, y_1, \ldots, y_N; \Pi) \geq \sum_{i=1}^{N} I(x_i, y_i; \Pi) \ ,$$

where the last inequality holds due to the independence of $x_1, \ldots, x_N, y_1, \ldots, y_N$ (cf. [4, Appendix C.1]). Let $\Pi^i_{a,b}$ be Π conditioned on the i-th coordinates of X and Y being fixed to a and b respectively:

$$\Pi^i_{a,b}(X, Y) := \Pi(X, Y) \mid x_i = a \wedge y_i = b \ .$$

By Lemma 4 we know

$$I(x_i, y_i; \Pi) \geq \mathbb{E}_{(a,b)}[\Delta^2_{\mathsf{Hel}}(\Pi^i_{a,b}, \Pi)] \ ,$$

where $(a, b) \sim \mathrm{Ber}(p) \times \mathrm{Ber}(q)$ and Δ_{Hel} is the Hellinger distance.

Since $q \geq p$ we have that $q(1 - p) \geq p(1 - q)$ and since $q \leq 1/2$, we also have that $p(1 - q) \geq p/2$. Thus

$$I(x_i, y_i; \Pi) \geq p(1 - q) \cdot \Delta^2_{\mathsf{Hel}}(\Pi^i_{1,0}, \Pi) + q(1 - p) \cdot \Delta^2_{\mathsf{Hel}}(\Pi^i_{0,1}, \Pi)$$
$$\geq p(1 - q) \cdot \left(\Delta^2_{\mathsf{Hel}}(\Pi^i_{1,0}, \Pi) + \Delta^2_{\mathsf{Hel}}(\Pi^i_{0,1}, \Pi) \right)$$
$$\geq p/2 \cdot \left(\Delta^2_{\mathsf{Hel}}(\Pi^i_{1,0}, \Pi) + \Delta^2_{\mathsf{Hel}}(\Pi^i_{0,1}, \Pi) \right)$$
$$\geq p/4 \cdot \left(\Delta_{\mathsf{Hel}}(\Pi^i_{1,0}, \Pi) + \Delta_{\mathsf{Hel}}(\Pi^i_{0,1}, \Pi) \right)^2$$
$$\geq p/4 \cdot \Delta^2_{\mathsf{Hel}}(\Pi^i_{1,0}, \Pi^i_{0,1}) \ .$$

The last inequality is by the triangle inequality for the metric Δ_{Hel}, and the penultimate inequality uses $x^2 + y^2 \geq (x + y)^2/2$. Hence,

$$D^\varepsilon_{\mu(p,q)}(\mathrm{INT}) \geq N \cdot \mathbb{E}_i[I(x_i, y_i; \Pi)]$$
$$\geq Np/4 \cdot \mathbb{E}_i[\Delta^2_{\mathsf{Hel}}(\Pi^i_{1,0}, \Pi^i_{0,1})]$$
$$= Np/4 \cdot \mathbb{E}_i[\Delta^2_{\mathsf{Hel}}(\Pi^i_{0,0}, \Pi^i_{1,1})]$$
$$\geq Np/8 \cdot \mathbb{E}_i[\Delta^2_{\mathsf{TV}}(\Pi^i_{0,0}, \Pi^i_{1,1})]$$
$$\geq Np/8 \cdot \left(\mathbb{E}_i[\Delta_{\mathsf{TV}}(\Pi^i_{0,0}, \Pi^i_{1,1})] \right)^2 \ ,$$

where the third inequality uses the cut-and-paste lemma of communication complexity (Lemma 5) which states that $\Delta^2_{\mathsf{Hel}}(\Pi^i_{1,0}, \Pi^i_{0,1}) = \Delta^2_{\mathsf{Hel}}(\Pi^i_{0,0}, \Pi^i_{1,1})$ for any deterministic protocol π. The penultimate inequality uses $\Delta_{\mathsf{TV}}(A,B) \leq \sqrt{2}\Delta_{\mathsf{Hel}}(A,B)$, which implies $\Delta^2_{\mathsf{Hel}}(\Pi^i_{0,0}, \Pi^i_{1,1}) \geq 1/2\Delta^2_{\mathsf{TV}}(\Pi^i_{0,0}, \Pi^i_{1,1})$, and the last inequality is by Jensen. Thus it remains to lower bound $\Delta_{\mathsf{TV}}(\Pi^i_{0,0}, \Pi^i_{1,1})$.

For every i we have

$$\Pr[\Pi^i_{0,0}(X,Y) = i] = 0 \ .$$

This is because we have conditioned on $x_i = y_i = 0$ and the two parties can check whether or not i belongs to their sets.

Now we look at $x_i = y_i = 1$. We show that the protocol over a *random* choice of i should output i with the expected probability, that is, $1/|S \cap T|$. Note that the expected size of the intersection is

$$\mathbb{E}[|S \cap T|] = \mathbb{E}[\sum_{i=1}^{N} x_i y_i] = \sum_{i=1}^{N} \mathbb{E}[x_i y_i] = Npq \ ,$$

where we have used the linearity of expectation and independence of x_i and y_i.

We proceed as follows.

$$\mathbb{E}_i[\Pr[\Pi^i_{1,1}(X,Y) = i]] =$$

$$= \frac{1}{N} \sum \Pr[\Pi(X,Y) = i | x_i = y_i = 1]$$

$$= \frac{1}{Npq} \sum \Pr[\Pi(X,Y) = i \wedge x_i = y_i = 1]$$

$$= \frac{1}{Npq} \sum_i \sum_{(x,y): \ x_i = y_i = 1 \wedge \pi(x,y) = i} \Pr[(X,Y) = (x,y)]$$

$$= \frac{1}{Npq} \sum_{(x,y): \ \pi(x,y) \ \text{correct and} \ x \cap y \neq \emptyset} \Pr[(X,Y) = (x,y)]$$

$$= \frac{1}{Npq} \left(\sum_{(x,y)} \Pr[(x,y)] - \sum_{x \cap y = \emptyset} \Pr[(x,y)] - \sum_{\pi(x,y) \ \text{fails}} \Pr[(x,y)] \right)$$

$$\geq \frac{1 - \Pr[\mathsf{DISJ}(S,T) = 1] - \varepsilon}{Npq} = \frac{p_0 - \varepsilon}{Npq} \ .$$

Thus we get that

$$\mathbb{E}_i[\Delta_{\mathsf{TV}}(\Pi^i_{0,0}, \Pi^i_{1,1})] \geq (p_0 - \varepsilon)/(Npq) \ ,$$

and overall we obtain

$$\mathsf{D}^\varepsilon_{\mu(p,q)}(\mathsf{INT}) \geq \frac{Np}{8} \cdot \left(\frac{p_0 - \varepsilon}{Npq} \right)^2 ,$$

as required. $\square$

Letting $p = 1/N^{\alpha}$ and $q = 1/N^{\beta}$ with $\alpha \geq \beta$ (since we assumed $p \leq q$), for a non-trivial lower bound—that is an exponentially large right-hand side in the displayed equation above—we would need to have that $\alpha + 2\beta > 1$. We also require that $1 - \alpha - \beta > 0$ so that the expected intersection size Npq is exponentially large, in which case $p_0 \approx 1$ and set-disjointness is *easy*. These inequalities lead to the feasibility region shown in Fig. 3. We have included the symmetric region for $\alpha \leq \beta$.

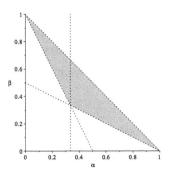

Fig. 3. Region where set intersection is hard with $p = 1/N^{\alpha}$ and $q = 1/N^{\beta}$.

In this work, we will rely on set-disjointness and set-intersection problems, as well as the following *multi-set* extensions of them. These problems are additionally parameterized by the number of sets. Here Alice holds M_1 sets $S_i \sim \text{Bin}(N, p)$ for $i \in [M_1]$ and Bob holds M_2 sets $T_j \sim \text{Bin}(N, q)$ for $j \in [M_2]$. Their goal is to solve the following problems.

1. Find (i, x) such that $x \in S_i \cap T_i$, or return $\perp$ if all the intersections are empty. We call this the (M_1, M_2)-INT problem, a natural multi-instance version of INT. A decisional variant would ask for an index i and a decision bit indicating if $S_i \cap T_i = \emptyset$. When $M_1 = M_2 = 1$, these problems are the usual INT and DISJ problems.

2. Find (i, j, x, x') with $x \neq x'$ such that $x, x' \in S_i \cap T_j$, or return $\perp$ if no such tuple exists. We call this the (M_1, M_2)-2INT problem. When $M_1 = M_2 = 1$ this problem is at least as hard as the INT problem since finding two distinct elements in the intersection is harder than finding one.

REMARK. Intuitively, the INT problem is a harder task than (M_1, M_2)-2INT. One can solve the (M_1, M_2)-2INT problem using a protocol for INT as follows. Alice chooses a random point x in one of its sets S_i and sends it to Bob. Bob will then search through his sets to find a set T_j such that $x \in T_j$. With high probability such a set exists if the number of sets and/or the probability parameters are large enough. Alice and Bob will then run the protocol for INT on sets S_i and T_j to find an $x' \in S_i \cap T_j$. This element will be different from x with good probability (again under appropriate choices of parameters). Indeed, this is simply the communication complexity way of saying "collision-resistance implies one-wayness." However, we are interested in a reduction in the converse direction (as we already have lower bounds for INT). This seems hard as from a cryptographic point of view, as a classical impossibility by Simon [36] shows that collision resistance cannot be based on one-way functions (or even permutations) in a black-box way. Despite this, it is conceivable that direct information-theoretic analyses (similar to those for set-disjointness and set-intersection) can lead to non-trivial lower bounds. We leave proving hardness for this "collision resistance" analogue of set-intersection as an interesting open problem for future work.[9]

5   The Concatenation Combiner

In this section we study the security of the concatenation combiner

$$\mathsf{C}^{\mathsf{H}_1,\mathsf{H}_2}(x) := \mathsf{H}_1(x)|\mathsf{H}_2(x)$$

in the 2-BRO model, where $\mathsf{H}_1 \in \mathrm{Fun}[n, n + s_1]$ and $\mathsf{H}_2 \in \mathrm{Fun}[n, n + s_2]$. We will prove one-way security, pseudorandomness, and collision resistance for this construction. Our results will rely on the hardness of set-intersection and set-disjointness for the first two properties, and the presumed hardness of finding two elements in the intersection given multiple instances.

5.1   One-Way Security

In the full version of this paper [4, Appendix D] we show that when H_1 or H_2 is (approximately) length preserving or somewhat expanding the concatenation combiner is not (strongly) one-way in the 2-BRO model. In both cases preimage sets will be only polynomially large and can be communicated. Accordingly, only when both hash functions are (somewhat) compressing we can achieve one-way security.

To this end, we first give a direct reduction from random preimage resistance (rPre, as defined in Fig. 2) to set-intersection. By Lemma 2 we know that any (weak) rPre-secure function is also a (weak) OW-secure function. In particular, for the highly compressing setting where $s_1, s_2 \leq -n/2 - 4$ we show *strong* one-way security. For settings where the parameters only enable weak security according to the set-intersection theorem, we can apply hardness amplification [18] to get a strongly one-way function.

In our reductions to communication complexity protocols throughout the paper, we make the following simplifying assumptions. (1) The adversary is deterministic; (2) It does not query H_i at all and instead computes hash values via the BD_i oracles; (3) It queries BD_i with functions that have 1-bit outputs; and (4) It starts with a query to BD_1.

We are now ready to prove our first cryptographic hardness result.

Theorem 4. *Let* $\mathsf{H}_1 \in \mathrm{Fun}[n, n + s_1]$ *and* $\mathsf{H}_2 \in \mathrm{Fun}[n, n + s_2]$ *and* $\mathsf{C}^{\mathsf{H}_1,\mathsf{H}_2}(x) :=$ $\mathsf{H}_1(x)|\mathsf{H}_2(x)$. *Then for any adversary* $\mathcal{A}$ *against the* rPre *security of* $\mathsf{C}^{\mathsf{H}_1,\mathsf{H}_2}$ *in the 2-BRO model there is a 2-party protocol* π *against set-intersection with* $\mu :=$ $\mu(p, q)$ *where* $p := 1/2^{n+s_1}$ *and* $q := 1/2^{n+s_2}$ *and such that*

$$\mathsf{Adv}_{\mathsf{C}^{\mathsf{H}_1,\mathsf{H}_2}}^{\mathrm{rpre}}(\mathcal{A}) \leq \mathsf{Adv}_{\mu}^{\mathrm{int}}(\pi) \qquad and \qquad \mathsf{D}_\mu(\pi) \leq \mathsf{Q}(\mathcal{A}) + 3n + s_1 + s_2 .$$

---

[9] We note that our setting is different to direct sum/product theorems where the focus is on hardness amplification. One shows, for example, that computing n independent copies of a function requires n times the communication for one copy for product distributions [3].

Proof. Let $\mathcal{A}$ be an adversary against the rPre security of C^{H_1,H_2} in the 2-BRO model for H_1 and H_2. Adversary $\mathcal{A}$ is given a random point $y := y_1|y_2 \in \{0,1\}^{2n+s_1+s_2}$ and needs to either find an x such that $H_1(x)|H_2(x) = y_1|y_2$ or say that no such x exists. Let

$$S_1 := H_1^-(y_1) \qquad \text{and} \qquad S_2 := H_2^-(y_2) \ .$$

Hence $\mathcal{A}$ outputs an $x \in S_1 \cap S_2$ as long as $S_1 \cap S_2 \neq \emptyset$. We note that these sets are Bernoulli. Indeed, for each x we have that $\Pr[x \in S_1] = 1/2^{n+s_1}$ and $\Pr[x \in S_2] = 1/2^{n+s_2}$, and these events are independent for different values of x.

We use $\mathcal{A}$ to build a 2-party protocol for set-intersection over a product distribution $\mu := \mu(p,q)$ with $p := 1/2^{n+s_1}$ and $q := 1/2^{n+s_2}$ as follows. Alice holds a set $S_1 \subseteq \{0,1\}^n$ and Bob holds a set $S_2 \subseteq \{0,1\}^n$ distributed according to μ. Alice (resp., Bob) samples hash function H_1 (resp., H_2) as follows. Alice picks a random $y_1 \in \{0,1\}^{n+s_1}$ and Bob picks a random $y_2 \in \{0,1\}^{n+s_2}$. Alice defines H_1 to map all points in S_1 to y_1. She maps $x \in \{0,1\}^n \setminus S_1$ to random points in $\{0,1\}^{n+s_1} \setminus \{y_1\}$. Similarly Bob defines H_2 to map all points $x \in S_2$ to y_2 and $x \in \{0,1\}^n \setminus S_1$ to random points in $\{0,1\}^{n+s_2} \setminus \{y_2\}$. As a result, Alice knows the full function table of H_1 and similarly Bob knows the full function table of H_2.

Alice and Bob now run two copies of $\mathcal{A}$ in tandem as follows, where the state values st_A and st_B are initially set to $y_1|y_2$ (with only $2n + s_1 + s_2$ bits of communication).

Alice: It resumes/starts $\mathcal{A}(st_A)$. It terminates if it receives a final guess x from Bob. It answers all pending BD_2 queries—there are none to start with— using the values just received from Bob. It answers all BD_1 queries using the function table of H_1 until $\mathcal{A}$ queries BD_2 or terminates. If $\mathcal{A}$ terminates with a final guess x, it forwards x to Bob and terminates. Else it saves the current state st_A of $\mathcal{A}$ locally and forwards all BD_1 answers that it has provided to $\mathcal{A}$ since the last resumption to Bob. It hands the execution over to Bob.

Bob: It resumes $\mathcal{A}(st_B)$. It terminates if it receives a final guess x from Alice. It answers all pending BD_1 queries using the values received from Alice. It answers all BD_2 queries using the function table of H_2 until $\mathcal{A}$ queries BD_1 or terminates. If $\mathcal{A}$ terminates with a final guess x, it forwards x to Alice and terminates. Else it saves the current state st_B of $\mathcal{A}$ locally and forwards all BD_2 answers that it has provided to $\mathcal{A}$ since the last resumption to Alice. It hands the execution over to Alice.

We claim that Alice and Bob run $\mathcal{A}$ in an environment that is identical to the rPre game in the 2-BRO model. The hash functions H_1 and H_2 sampled by Alice and Bob are uniformly distributed. To see this note that for any (x,y) the probability that $H_1(x) = y$ is $1/|\{0,1\}^{n+s_1}|$ (and similarly for H_2). Furthermore, this event is independent of the hash values that are set for all other values $x' \neq x$. Thus, Alice and Bob faithfully run $\mathcal{A}$ in the environment that it expects by answering its backdoor queries using their knowledge of the full tables of the two functions.

Whenever $\mathcal{A}$ succeeds in breaking the rPre security of C^{H_1,H_2}, the protocol above computes an $x \in S_1 \cap S_2$ or says that no such x exists. In either case, the protocol solves the set-intersection problem. Thus the correctness of this protocol is at least the advantage of the adversary $\mathcal{A}$.

This execution of $\mathcal{A}$ by Alice and Bob ensures that oracle *queries* do not affect the communication cost of Alice and Bob. It is only their answers (plus the final x) that affects the communication cost, since the queried functions f are locally computed and only their answers are communicated. If $\mathcal{A}$ makes $Q(\mathcal{A})$ queries to BD_1 and BD_2 in total and each query has a 1-bit output, the total communication complexity of the protocol is $Q(\mathcal{A})$ plus those bits needed to communicate y_1 and y_2 and the final guess x.   □

We now check that the parameters for hash functions can be set such that their concatenation is a one-way function.

Corollary 1. *For* $H_1, H_2 \in \text{Fun}[n, (1-\epsilon)n/2]$ *with* $0 < \epsilon < 1/3$ *the concatenation combiner is a strongly one-way compressing function in* $\text{Fun}[n, (1-\epsilon)n]$.

Proof. The feasible region in Fig. 3 for $\alpha = \beta$ consists of $1/3 < \alpha < 1/2$. In our setting $\alpha = \beta = (1-\epsilon)/2$, which means concatenation is strongly rPre secure when $0 < \epsilon < 1/3$. Since the combined function is compressing (where $\gamma = 1/(1-\epsilon) > 1$), the image-uniformity bound is negligible and also $\Pr[y \in \text{Img}(C^{H_i})]$ in Lemma 2 is overwhelming. Using these bounds and Lemma 2 we get that strong rPre security implies strong OW security.   □

We conjecture that concatenation is strongly one-way even for $1/3 \leq \epsilon < 1$. The intuition is that in the one-way game a point is "planted" in a large intersection, which seems hard to discover without essentially communicating the entire intersection. Tighter lower bounds for set-intersection can be used to establish this.

5.2 PRG Security

We now consider the PRG security of the concatenation combiner. Our reduction in Theorem 4 from rPre to set-intersection can be easily adapted to the decisional setting. That is, we can show that a decisional variant of rPre can be reduced to the set-disjointness problem. The decisional variant of rPre asks the adversary to decide whether or not a random co-domain point $y_1|y_2$ has a preimage. This is exactly the oblivious PRG (oPRG) notion that we defined in Sect. 2. We get the following result.

Theorem 5. *Let* $H_1 \in \text{Fun}[n, n+s_1]$ *and* $H_2 \in \text{Fun}[n, n+s_2]$ *and* $C^{H_1,H_2}(x) := H_1(x)|H_2(x)$. *Then for any adversary* $\mathcal{A}$ *against the oblivious PRG security of* C^{H_1,H_2} *in the 2-BRO model there is a 2-party protocol* π *against set-disjointness with* $\mu := \mu(p,q)$ *where* $p := 1/2^{n+s_1}$ *and* $q := 1/2^{n+s_2}$ *and such that*

$$\text{Adv}_{C^{H_1,H_2}}^{\text{oprg}}(\mathcal{A}) \leq \text{Adv}_{\mu}^{\text{disj}}(\pi) \quad \text{and} \quad D_{\mu}(\pi) \leq Q(\mathcal{A}) + 2n + s_1 + s_2 + 1 .$$

We next check if concrete parameters can be set to obtain an expanding PRG.

Corollary 2. *For $s_1 = -n/2 + 1$ and $s_2 = -n/2$, the concatenation combiner gives a weak PRG in* $\mathsf{Fun}[n, n+1]$.

Proof. The theorem gives a reduction to set-disjointness with parameters $p = 1/2^{n/2+1}$ and $q = 1/2^{n/2}$. For large n we get, $\delta = 2$, $p_0 = 1 - e^{-1/2}$ and $(\delta-1)p_0/(4+\delta) < 0.0656$, which means we can set $\varepsilon = 0.065$. By set-disjointness lower bound, this means any adversary with advantage at least 0.935 must place at least $\mathcal{O}(2^{n/2})$ queries in total to its oracles.

By Lemma 1 we have that $\mathsf{Adv}^{\mathsf{iu}}_{\mathsf{C}^{\mathsf{H}_i}}(\mathcal{B}) \leq e^{-C} \cdot \left(C/(1 - e^{-C}) - 1\right)$. In our case $C = 1/2 < 1$, and the right hand side above is upper bounded by ≤ 0.165. (We have removed the negligible terms and instead approximated the constants by slightly larger values.)

In Lemma 3 in order to meet the bound $\mathsf{Adv}^{\mathsf{oprg}}_{\mathsf{C}^{\mathsf{H}_i}}(\mathcal{C}) < (2 - \alpha - \mathsf{Adv}^{\mathsf{iu}}_{\mathsf{C}^{\mathsf{H}_i}}(\mathcal{B})) \cdot \alpha/(1-\alpha)$, we would need $0.935 \leq (2 - \alpha - 0.165) \cdot \alpha/(1-\alpha)$. After some algebra this gives $\alpha \geq 0.39343$. With $m = n + s$, we need to have $1 - e^{-2^{-s}} \geq 0.39343$, which means $s \leq 1.00018$. Thus we can set $s = 1$ (which also satisfies $s \geq 0.53$ as required in the lemma). □

We can obtain a strong PRG by amplification. However, we need an amplifier that woks on PRGs with (very) *small* stretch. Such a construction is given by Maurer and Tessaro [29]. In their so-called Concatenate-and-Extract (CaE) construction one sets

$$\mathsf{PRG}(r, x_1, \ldots, x_m) := r|\mathsf{Ext}\big(r, \mathsf{C}^{\mathsf{H}_1, \mathsf{H}_2}(x_1)|\cdots|\mathsf{C}^{\mathsf{H}_1, \mathsf{H}_2}(x_m)\big) \ ,$$

where Ext is a sufficiently good randomness extractor, for instance a two-universal hash function. We refer to the original work for concrete parameters. It is safe to assume the extractor is backdoor-free, since it is an information-theoretic object and relatively easy to implement.

5.3 Collision Resistance

The classical result of Simon [36] shows that collision-resistance relies on qualitatively stronger assumptions than one-way functions. In the theorem below we prove collision resistance based on the hardness of the multi-instance 2INT problem as defined in Sect. 4. As discussed in the final remark of that section, we do not expect that a reduction to the INT problem exists.

Theorem 6. *Let $\mathsf{H}_1 \in \mathsf{Fun}[n, n + s_1]$ and $\mathsf{H}_2 \in \mathsf{Fun}[n, n + s_2]$ and $\mathsf{C}^{\mathsf{H}_1, \mathsf{H}_2}(x) := \mathsf{H}_1(x)|\mathsf{H}_2(x)$. Then for any adversary $\mathcal{A}$ against the collision resistance of $\mathsf{C}^{\mathsf{H}_1, \mathsf{H}_2}$ in the 2-BRO model there is a 2-party protocol π' against multi-instance two-element set-intersection problem over $\mu' := \mu(p', q')$ with $p' := 2n \ln 2/2^{n+s_1}$ and $q' := 2n \ln 2/2^{n+s_2}$ and where Alice holds $M_1 := 2^{n+s_1}$ sets and Bob holds $M_2 := 2^{n+s_2}$ sets such that*

$$\mathsf{Adv}^{\mathsf{cr}}_{\mathsf{C}^{\mathsf{H}_1, \mathsf{H}_2}}(\mathcal{A}) \leq \mathsf{Adv}^{\mathsf{mi\text{-}2int}}_{\mu'}(\pi') + 2 \cdot 2^{-n} \qquad and \qquad \mathsf{D}_{\mu'}(\pi') \leq \mathsf{Q}(\mathcal{A}) + 4n + s_1 + s_2 \ .$$

Proof. We follow an overall strategy that is similar to one for the rPre reduction. For each $i \in \{0,1\}^{n+s_1}$, Alice sets $\mathsf{H}_1^-(i) := S_i$ and for each $j \in \{0,1\}^{n+s_2}$ Bob sets $\mathsf{H}_2^-(j) := T_j$ and they simulate the two hash functions. However, this leads to a problem: S_i are not necessarily disjoint and furthermore their union does not cover the entire domain $\{0,1\}^n$. (The same is true for T_j.) Put differently, the distributions of sets formed by hash preimages of co-domain points do not match independently chosen sets from a Bernoulli distribution.

We treat this problem in two step. The first step is a direct reduction to a "partitioned" modification of the multi-instance set-intersection. In this partitioned problem Alice gets sets $S_i := \mathsf{H}_1^-(i)$ for $i \in \{0,1\}^{n+s_1}$ and a random oracle $\mathsf{H}_1 \in \mathsf{Fun}[n, n+s_1]$. Similarly, Bob gets sets $T_j := \mathsf{H}_2^-(j)$ for $j \in \{0,1\}^{n+s_2}$ and an independent random oracle $\mathsf{H}_2 \in \mathsf{Fun}[n, n+s_2]$. Their goal is to find a tuple (i, j, x, x') with $x \neq x'$ such that $x, x' \in S_i \cap T_j$. Thus, these sets exactly correspond to hash preimages as needed in the reduction above, and a solution would translate to a collision for the combined hash function.

We then show that hardness of the (standard) multi-instance two-element set-intersection problem implies the hardness of the partitioned problem with an increase in the Bernoulli *parameter*.[10] □

Lemma 6 (Partitioned $\Longrightarrow$ Independent). *For any two-party protocol π against the partitioned multi-instance set-intersection problem there is a two-party protocol π' against multi-instance set-intersection problem such that*

$$\mathsf{Adv}_{\mu'}^{\mathrm{mi\text{-}2int}}(\pi') \geq \mathsf{Adv}_{\mu}^{\mathrm{part\text{-}2int}}(\pi) - 2 \cdot 2^{-n} \quad \text{and} \quad \mathsf{D}_{\mu'}(\pi') \leq \mathsf{D}_{\mu}(\pi) .$$

Here $\mu := \mu(p,q)$ is the distribution induced by hash preimages and $\mu' := \mu'(p',q')$ is a product Bernoulli with $p' := 2n \ln 2 \cdot p$ and $q' := 2n \ln 2 \cdot q$.

Proof. To focus on the core ideas, we simplify and let $M_1 = M_2 = M = 2^{n+s}$ and $p = q = 1/2^{n+s}$. Suppose we have sets S_i and T_j for $i = 1, \ldots, M$ and $j = 1, \ldots, M$ as an instance for the multi-instance intersection. Let $p' = q' = 2n \ln 2 \cdot p$. Then

$$\Pr[\exists x \in \{0,1\}^n \; \forall i \in [M] : x \notin S_i] \leq 2^n \Pr[\forall i \in [M] : x \notin S_i]$$
$$\leq 2^n (1 - p')^{1/p} \leq 2^n e^{-2n \ln 2} = 2^{-n} .$$

Thus with these parameters the sets S_i (and similarly T_j) will cover the full domain, that is $\bigcup_{i=1}^M S_i = \{0,1\}^n$.

Note that with these parameters any two sets S_i and T_j will intersect with overwhelming probability. However, finding an element in the intersection may still be hard; see conjecture below.

Our next step it to redistribute the elements among the sets so that they form partitions. We do this via the algorithm ReDist shown in Fig. 4. ReDist iterates through elements x in the domain and leaves x in exactly one of the sets. (By the above covering property such a set always exits.)

---

[10] Another strategy would be to change the *number* of sets involved. But this runs into a problem as this number must match the size of the co-domain of the hash function.

$$
\begin{array}{|l|}
\hline
\text{Algo. ReDist}(S_1, \ldots, S_M) \\
\hline
\textbf{for } x \in \{0,1\}^n \textbf{ do} \\
\quad A_x := \{i \in [M] : x \in S_i\} \\
\quad i_x \twoheadleftarrow A_x \\
\quad \textbf{for } j \in [M] \wedge j \neq i_x \textbf{ do} \\
\quad\quad \widetilde{S}_j \leftarrow \widetilde{S}_j \setminus \{x\} \\
\textbf{return } (\widetilde{S}_1, \ldots, \widetilde{S}_M) \\
\hline
\end{array}
$$

Fig. 4. Redistribution of elements to form a partition.

This procedure will be applied to S_i (resp., T_j) to produce non-overlapping sets $\tilde{S}_i$ (resp. $\tilde{T}_j$). Furthermore, we always have that $\tilde{S}_i \subseteq S_i$ and $\tilde{T}_i \subseteq T_i$, since elements are only deleted from the sets and never added to them. Thus $\tilde{S}_i \cap \tilde{T}_j \subseteq S_i \cap T_j$ as well, and this means that any solution with respect to the tweaked sets will also be a valid solution for the original (Bernoulli) sets.

We still need to show that the distribution of the tweaked sets is identical to that given by hash preimages under a random oracle. Let $E_{x,i}$ be the event that $x \in \tilde{S}_i$. Since the algorithm does not treat any of the i's in a special way, we claim that $\Pr[E_{x,i}]$ is independent of i. Indeed for any i, j we have

$$\Pr[E_{x,i}] = \Pr[x \in S_i]\Pr[i_x = i | x \in S_i] = \Pr[x \in S_j]\Pr[i_x = j | x \in S_j] = \Pr[E_{x,j}].$$

This is because $\Pr[x \in S_i] = \Pr[x \in S_j]$ and $\Pr[i_x = i | x \in S_i] = \Pr[i_x = j | x \in S_j]$. If we call this common probability e_x, since x is guaranteed belongs to one of the M sets, we have that $\sum_{i \in [M]} e_x = 1$. Thus $e_x = 1/M = \Pr[\mathsf{H}_1(x) = i]$. Note that the algorithm assigns different values of x independently of all other values already assigned, we get that the event $\mathsf{H}_1(x) = i$ is independent for different x.

Finally, solutions with respect to the tweaked sets always exist when $s_1 + s_2 < 0$. This is because the problem is equivalent to finding collisions for a function $\mathsf{H}_1(x)|\mathsf{H}_2(x)$ that is compressing, which necessarily exist. $\square$

The birthday attack gives a $2^{\min(n+s_1, n+s_2)/2}$ upper bound on the security of the combined hash function. Balancing the digest lengths with $s_1 = s_2 = n/2$, leads to a maximum collision security of at most $2^{n/4}$. Proving a lower bound, on the other hand, remains an interesting open problem. We formulate a conjecture towards proving this next.

Conjecture 1. The multi-instance 2-element set-intersection problem over Bernoulli sets in a universe of size N with $p = q = 1/\sqrt{N}$ and $\sqrt{N}$ sets for each party has communication complexity

$$\mathsf{D}_{\mu(p,q)}^{\varepsilon}((\sqrt{N}, \sqrt{N})\text{-2INT}) \geq \tilde{\Omega}(N^{1/4})$$

for a sufficiently small protocol error ε and where $\tilde{\Omega}$ hides logarithmic factors.

We note that a lower bound for protocols with a sufficiently small error would be sufficient for feasibility results as collision resistance can also be amplified in a black-box way [8].

6   The Cascade Combiner

We now look at the security of the cascade combiner

$$C^{H_1,H_2}(x) := H_2(H_1(x))$$

in the 2-BRO model, where $H_1 \in \text{Fun}[n, n + s_1]$ and $H_2 \in \text{Fun}[n + s_1, n + s_1 + s_2]$. We will prove one-way security and pseudorandomness based on set-intersection and set-disjointness respectively, and collision resistance based on a variant finding two intersecting points given multiple instances for one party and a single set for the other.

6.1   One-Way Security

Similarly to the concatenation combiner, we can reduce the random preimage resistance (rPre) security of the cascade combiner to set-intersection.

Theorem 7. *Let* $H_1 \in \text{Fun}[n, n + s_1]$ *and* $H_2 \in \text{Fun}[n + s_1, n + s_1 + s_2]$ *and* $C^{H_1,H_2}(x) := H_2(H_1(x))$. *Then for large enough* n *and any adversary* $\mathcal{A}$ *against the* rPre *security of* C^{H_1,H_2} *in the 2-BRO model there is a 2-party protocol* π *against set-intersection with* $\mu := \mu(p, q)$ *where* $p := 1/2^{s_1}$ *and* $q := 1/2^{n+s_1+s_2}$ *and such that*

$$\text{Adv}^{\text{rpre}}_{C^{H_1,H_2}}(\mathcal{A}) \leq \text{Adv}^{\text{int}}_{\mu}(\pi) + \sqrt{n}2^{-n/2}(1 + 2^{s_2-s_1}) \quad \text{and} \quad D_\mu(\pi) \leq Q(\mathcal{A}) + 3n + s_1 + s_2.$$

Proof. We follow a strategy similar to the reductions in Sect. 5. Given a random $y^* \in \{0,1\}^{n+s_1+s_2}$ the task of the adversary $\mathcal{A}$ against rPre security of C^{H_1,H_2} is to a find a z such that $C^{H_1,H_2}(z) = y^*$. With such a z, one can then also compute $x := H_1(z)$ and conclude that $x \in I \cap T$ where

$$I := H_1(\{0,1\}^n) \quad \text{and} \quad T := H_2^-(y^*)$$

with $I, T \subseteq \{0,1\}^{n+s_1}$. The set T is Bernoulli with parameter $\Pr[y \in T] = 1/2^{n+s_1+s_2}$. Although set I appears to be Bernoulli,

$$\Pr[x \in I] = 1 - \Pr[\forall z : H_1(z) \neq x] = 1 - (1 - 1/2^{n+s_1})^{2^n}$$

it is not, since these probabilities are not independent for different values of x.

Our strategy to deal with this and ultimately construct a protocol π for solving set-intersection is to start with a Bernoulli set S (Alice's input), and program H_1 on all $x \in \{0,1\}^n$ to values y that will be taken from S, but are also set to *collide* with the right probability. This will ensure that the image of H_1 contains most of S and is also distributed as the image of a random oracle.

We proceed as follows. Initially the set of assigned domain points X and assigned co-domain points Y are empty. We then iterate through $x \in \{0,1\}^n$ in a random order. A bit b decides at each iteration decides if the hash value y for x should collide with a previously assigned value or not. If so, we sample y from the set of already assigned values Y. Otherwise, y should be a non-colliding value and we sample it from S if S is non-empty (and remove y from S), or otherwise we sample it outside the already assigned points Y. The pseudo-code for this algorithm, which we call HashSam, is shown in Fig. 5.

Algo. HashSam(S)

$X \leftarrow \emptyset; \ Y \leftarrow \emptyset$

for $i = 1, \ldots, 2^n$ **do**

$\quad x \twoheadleftarrow \{0,1\}^n \setminus X; X \leftarrow X \cup \{x\}$

$\quad b \twoheadleftarrow \mathrm{Ber}(|Y|/2^m)$

$\quad$ **if** $b = 1$ **then** $y \twoheadleftarrow Y$

$\quad$ **if** $b = 0 \wedge S = \emptyset$ **then**

$\quad\quad y \twoheadleftarrow \{0,1\}^m \setminus Y; \ Y \twoheadleftarrow Y \cup \{y\}$

$\quad$ **if** $b = 0 \wedge S \neq \emptyset$ **then**

$\quad\quad y \twoheadleftarrow S; \ Y \leftarrow Y \cup \{y\}; \ S \leftarrow S \setminus \{y\}$

$\quad \mathsf{H}_1 \leftarrow \mathsf{H}_1 : [x \mapsto y]$

return H_1

Fig. 5. Hash sampler centered around a Bernoulli set S.

Setting $m := n + s_1$, we now need to check that (1) the returned hash function H_1 is distributed as a random oracle $\{0,1\}^n \to \{0,1\}^m$ when S is Bernoulli with parameter $p = 1/2^{s_1}$, and (2) if $x \in \mathsf{H}_1(\{0,1\}^n) \cap \mathsf{H}_2^-(y^*)$, then we also have that $x \in S \cap T$ with good probability.

We first prove (1). The intuition is that the algorithm treats all inputs and outputs in a uniform way, and hence no particular values are special. Formally, let x^* and y^* be any fixed values. We show that $\Pr[\mathsf{H}_1(x^*) = y^*] = 1/2^m$, even given the previously assigned values. We use a subscript i to denote the values of various variables in the i-th iteration. Looking at different execution branches of the algorithm we can calculate $\Pr[y_i = y^* | x_i = x^*, Y_i, X_i]$ as

$$\Pr[b_i = 1]\Pr[y^* \in Y_i]\frac{1}{|Y_i|} + \Pr[b_i = 0]\Big(\Pr[S_i = \emptyset]\Pr[y^* \notin Y_i]\frac{1}{2^m - |Y_i|} +$$
$$+ \Pr[S_i \neq \emptyset]\Pr[y^* \in S_i]\frac{1}{|S_i|}\Big).$$

Letting $\theta_i := \Pr[S_i = \emptyset]$ we can simplify to

$$\frac{|Y_i|}{2^m}\frac{|Y_i|}{2^m}\frac{1}{|Y_i|} + \Big(1 - \frac{|Y_i|}{2^m}\Big)\Big(\theta_i\Big(1 - \frac{|Y_i|}{2^m}\Big)\frac{1}{2^m - |Y_i|} + \Big(1 - \theta_i\Big)\frac{|S_i|}{2^m}\frac{1}{|S_i|}\Big) = \frac{1}{2^m}.$$

Note we have used the fact that S_i is a Bernoulli set in $\Pr[y^* \in S_i] = \frac{|S_i|}{2^m}$. Hence

$$\Pr[\mathsf{H}_1(x^*) = y^* | Y_i, X_i] = \sum_{i=1}^{2^n} \Pr[y_i = y^* | x_i = x^*, Y_i, X_i] \Pr[x_i = x^*] = \frac{1}{2^m}.$$

Therefore the probability of sampling any given hash function is $(1/2^m)^{2^n}$, as required.

Let us now consider (2). When $I \subseteq S$, any solution with respect to I is also one with respect to S (that is, solutions are not lost). Hence we only look at the case $S \subseteq I$ and bound $|I \setminus S| = |I| - |S|$. Since $|I| \leq 2^n$ and $\mathbb{E}[|S|] = 2^{n+s_1}/2^{s_1} = 2^n$, we get that for any t

$$\Pr[|I| - |S| > t] \leq \Pr[2^n - |S| > t] = \Pr[\mathbb{E}[|S|] - |S| > t].$$

Applying the Chernoff bounds we obtain

$$\Pr\left[\mathbb{E}[|S|] - |S| > t\,\mathbb{E}[|S|]\right] \leq e^{-\frac{t^2}{2+t}\mathbb{E}[|S|]}.$$

Setting $t := \sqrt{n/2^n}$, we get with overwhelming probability that $|I \setminus S| \leq \sqrt{n}2^{n/2}$. Hence $T \cap (I \setminus S)$ will be non-empty with negligible probability $\sqrt{n}2^{-n/2-s_1-s_2}$, in which case if $x \in I \cap T \implies x \in S \cap T$.   □

If $\mathsf{H}_1 \in \mathsf{Fun}[n, (2 + \epsilon)n]$ and $\mathsf{H}_2 \in \mathsf{Fun}[(2 + \epsilon)n, (1 + \epsilon)n])$, we have a reduction to set-intersection with parameters $N = 2^{(2+\epsilon)n}$, $p = 1/2^{(1+\epsilon)n}$, and $q = 1/2^{(1+\epsilon)n}$. Thus with notation as in the description of the feasible in Fig. 3 we have that $\alpha = \beta = (1 + \epsilon)/(2 + \epsilon)$. As in Corollary 1 we would need The point (α, β) lies in the feasible region for $1/3 < (1 + \epsilon)/(2 + \epsilon) < 1/2$, which means $-1/2 < \epsilon < 0$. Since the combined function is compressing (with $\gamma = 1/(1+\epsilon) > 1$) and $p_o \approx 1 - e^{-2^{-\epsilon \cdot n}}$ is negligible, the image uniformity bound is negligible and hence, similarly to Corollary 1 we get strong OW security.

6.2   PRG and CR Security

We briefly outline how to treat the PRG security and collision resistance of cascade. We omit the proofs as the techniques and proof structures are similar to our other results above.

PRG SECURITY. We can prove an analogous result for the oblivious PRG security of the cascade construction. Its reduction is identical to that for rPre security given above, except that the underlying assumption is set-disjointness. Setting $s_1 = 2n$ (H_1 is length doubling) and $s_2 = -2n + 1$ (H_2 compresses by almost a factor of 3) leads to a reduction to an instance of set-intersection with parameters $N = 2^{3n}$, $p = 1/2^{2n}$, and $q = 1/2^{n+1}$. In this case $\delta = 2$ and $p_0 = 1 - e^{-1/2}$. With these parameters we can carry out an analysis similar to Corollary 2: We set the error $\varepsilon = 0.065$ which is smaller than $(\delta - 1)p_0/(4 + \delta) < 0.0656$ as required in Theorem 2 for an exponential number of queries. The combined hash function maps n bits to $n + 1$ bits and hence $C = 1/2$. Furthermore, p_o is negligible as a function from n bits to $3n$ bits is injective with overwhelming probability. Thus we can apply Lemma 3 with $s = 1$ as in Corollary 2 to get a weak PRG.

COLLISION RESISTANCE. We can treat the collision resistance of cascade similarly. The difference is that in the reduction Alice will use the HashSam algorithm in Fig. 5 to adapt a (single) Bernoulli set S that she holds to a hash image set I. On the other hand, Bob uses the ReDist algorithm in Fig. 4 to redistribute elements in multiple Bernoulli sets that he holds so that they form a partition of the entire domain of H_2. The rest of the proof, which is included in the full version [4, Appendix E], proceeds similarly to Lemma 6. For setting parameters, observe that any collision for H_1 is necessarily a collision for $H_2(H_1(\cdot))$. Since collisions for H_1 can be easily found using BD_1, we need H_1 to be injective. For example, $s_1 = 2n$ (co-domain points are $3n$ bits) would lead to an injective H_1 with overwhelming probability.

Acknowledgments. We thank Marc Fischlin for participating in the early stages of this work. We also thank the CRYPTO'18 (sub)reviewers for their valuable comments. Bauer was supported by the French ANR Project ANR-16-CE39-0002 EfTrEC. Farshim was supported by the European Research Council under the European Community's Seventh Framework Programme (FP7/2007-2013 Grant Agreement no. 339563 - CryptoCloud). Mazaheri was supported by the German Federal Ministry of Education and Research (BMBF) and by the Hessian State Ministry for Higher Education, Research and the Arts, within CRISP.

References

1. Babai, L., Frankl, P., Simon, J.: Complexity classes in communication complexity theory (preliminary version). In: 27th FOCS, pp. 337–347 (1986)
2. Bar-Yossef, Z., Jayram, T.S., Kumar, R., Sivakumar, D.: An information statistics approach to data stream and communication complexity. In: 43rd FOCS, pp. 209–218 (2002)
3. Barak, B., Braverman, M., Chen, X., Rao, A.: How to compress interactive communication. In: 42nd ACM STOC, pp. 67–76 (2010)
4. Bauer, B., Farshim, P., Mazaheri, S.: Combiners for backdoored random oracles. Cryptology ePrint Archive (2018)
5. Bellare, M., Rogaway, P.: Random oracles are practical: a paradigm for designing efficient protocols. In: ACM CCS 1993, pp. 62–73 (1993)
6. Bernstein, D.J., Lange, T., Niederhagen, R.: Dual EC: a standardized back door. Cryptology ePrint Archive, Report 2015/767 (2015). http://eprint.iacr.org/2015/767
7. Boneh, D., Boyen, X.: On the impossibility of efficiently combining collision resistant hash functions. In: Dwork, C. (ed.) CRYPTO 2006. LNCS, vol. 4117, pp. 570–583. Springer, Heidelberg (2006). https://doi.org/10.1007/11818175_34
8. Canetti, R., Rivest, R.L., Sudan, M., Trevisan, L., Vadhan, S.P., Wee, H.: Amplifying collision resistance: a complexity-theoretic treatment. In: Menezes, A. (ed.) CRYPTO 2007. LNCS, vol. 4622, pp. 264–283. Springer, Heidelberg (2007). https://doi.org/10.1007/978-3-540-74143-5_15

9. Chattopadhyay, A., Pitassi, T.: The story of set disjointness. SIGACT News **41**(3), 59–85 (2010)
10. Checkoway, S., Maskiewicz, J., Garman, C., Fried, J., Cohney, S., Green, M., Heninger, N., Weinmann, R.-P., Rescorla, E., Shacham, H.: A systematic analysis of the juniper dual EC incident. In: ACM CCS 2016, pp. 468–479 (2016)
11. Checkoway, S., et al.: On the practical exploitability of dual EC in TLS implementations. In: 23rd USENIX Security Symposium (USENIX Security 14), pp. 319–335 (2014)
12. Coretti, S., Dodis, Y., Guo, S., Steinberger, J.: Random oracles and non-uniformity. Cryptology ePrint Archive, Report 2017/937 (2017). http://eprint.iacr.org/2017/937
13. Dinur, I.: New attacks on the concatenation and XOR hash combiners. In: Fischlin, M., Coron, J.-S. (eds.) EUROCRYPT 2016, Part I. LNCS, vol. 9665, pp. 484–508. Springer, Heidelberg (2016). https://doi.org/10.1007/978-3-662-49890-3_19
14. Dodis, Y., Guo, S., Katz, J.: Fixing cracks in the concrete: random oracles with auxiliary input, revisited. In: Coron, J.-S., Nielsen, J.B. (eds.) EUROCRYPT 2017, Part II. LNCS, vol. 10211, pp. 473–495. Springer, Cham (2017). https://doi.org/10.1007/978-3-319-56614-6_16
15. Fiat, A., Shamir, A.: How to prove yourself: practical solutions to identification and signature problems. In: Odlyzko, A.M. (ed.) CRYPTO 1986. LNCS, vol. 263, pp. 186–194. Springer, Heidelberg (1987). https://doi.org/10.1007/3-540-47721-7_12
16. Fischlin, M., Lehmann, A.: Security-amplifying combiners for collision-resistant hash functions. In: Menezes, A. (ed.) CRYPTO 2007. LNCS, vol. 4622, pp. 224–243. Springer, Heidelberg (2007). https://doi.org/10.1007/978-3-540-74143-5_13
17. Fischlin, M., Lehmann, A., Pietrzak, K.: Robust multi-property combiners for hash functions. J. Cryptol. **27**(3), 397–428 (2014)
18. Goldreich, O.: Foundations of Cryptography: Basic Tools, vol. 1. Cambridge University Press, Cambridge (2001)
19. Guruswami, V., Cheraghchi, M.: Set disjointness lower bound via product distribution. Scribes for Information theory and its applications in theory of computation (2013). http://www.cs.cmu.edu/~venkatg/teaching/ITCS-spr2013/
20. Hoch, J.J., Shamir, A.: On the strength of the concatenated hash combiner when all the hash functions are weak. In: Aceto, L., Damgård, I., Goldberg, L.A., Halldórsson, M.M., Ingólfsdóttir, A., Walukiewicz, I. (eds.) ICALP 2008, Part II. LNCS, vol. 5126, pp. 616–630. Springer, Heidelberg (2008). https://doi.org/10.1007/978-3-540-70583-3_50
21. Joux, A.: Multicollisions in iterated hash functions. Application to cascaded constructions. In: Franklin, M. (ed.) CRYPTO 2004. LNCS, vol. 3152, pp. 306–316. Springer, Heidelberg (2004). https://doi.org/10.1007/978-3-540-28628-8_19
22. Katz, J., Lucks, S., Thiruvengadam, A.: Hash functions from defective ideal ciphers. In: Nyberg, K. (ed.) CT-RSA 2015. LNCS, vol. 9048, pp. 273–290. Springer, Cham (2015). https://doi.org/10.1007/978-3-319-16715-2_15
23. Kawachi, A., Numayama, A., Tanaka, K., Xagawa, K.: Security of encryption schemes in weakened random oracle models. In: Nguyen, P.Q., Pointcheval, D. (eds.) PKC 2010. LNCS, vol. 6056, pp. 403–419. Springer, Heidelberg (2010). https://doi.org/10.1007/978-3-642-13013-7_24
24. Kushilevitz, E., Nisan, N.: Communication Complexity. Cambridge University Press, New York (1997)
25. Lehmann, A.: On the security of hash function combiners. Ph.D. thesis, TU Darmstadt (2010)

26. Leurent, G., Wang, L.: The sum can be weaker than each part. In: Oswald, E., Fischlin, M. (eds.) EUROCRYPT 2015, Part I. LNCS, vol. 9056, pp. 345–367. Springer, Heidelberg (2015). https://doi.org/10.1007/978-3-662-46800-5_14

27. Liskov, M.: Constructing an ideal hash function from weak ideal compression functions. In: Biham, E., Youssef, A.M. (eds.) SAC 2006. LNCS, vol. 4356, pp. 358–375. Springer, Heidelberg (2007). https://doi.org/10.1007/978-3-540-74462-7_25

28. Lucks, S.: A failure-friendly design principle for hash functions. In: Roy, B. (ed.) ASIACRYPT 2005. LNCS, vol. 3788, pp. 474–494. Springer, Heidelberg (2005). https://doi.org/10.1007/11593447_26

29. Maurer, U.M., Tessaro, S.: A hardcore lemma for computational indistinguishability: security amplification for arbitrarily weak PRGs with optimal stretch. In: Micciancio, D. (ed.) TCC 2010. LNCS, vol. 5978, pp. 237–254. Springer, Heidelberg (2010). https://doi.org/10.1007/978-3-642-11799-2_15

30. Mendel, F., Rechberger, C., Schläffer, M.: MD5 is weaker than weak: attacks on concatenated combiners. In: Matsui, M. (ed.) ASIACRYPT 2009. LNCS, vol. 5912, pp. 144–161. Springer, Heidelberg (2009). https://doi.org/10.1007/978-3-642-10366-7_9

31. Mittelbach, A.: Cryptophia's short combiner for collision-resistant hash functions. In: Jacobson, M., Locasto, M., Mohassel, P., Safavi-Naini, R. (eds.) ACNS 2013. LNCS, vol. 7954, pp. 136–153. Springer, Heidelberg (2013). https://doi.org/10.1007/978-3-642-38980-1_9

32. Moshkovitz, D., Barak, B.: Communication complexity. Scribes for Advanced Complexity Theory (2012). https://people.csail.mit.edu/dmoshkov/courses/advcomp/

33. Numayama, A., Isshiki, T., Tanaka, K.: Security of digital signature schemes in weakened random Oracle models. In: Cramer, R. (ed.) PKC 2008. LNCS, vol. 4939, pp. 268–287. Springer, Heidelberg (2008). https://doi.org/10.1007/978-3-540-78440-1_16

34. Reingold, O., Trevisan, L., Vadhan, S.P.: Notions of reducibility between cryptographic primitives. In: Naor, M. (ed.) TCC 2004. LNCS, vol. 2951, pp. 1–20. Springer, Heidelberg (2004). https://doi.org/10.1007/978-3-540-24638-1_1

35. Rogaway, P., Shrimpton, T.: Cryptographic hash-function basics: definitions, implications, and separations for preimage resistance, second-preimage resistance, and collision resistance. In: Roy, B., Meier, W. (eds.) FSE 2004. LNCS, vol. 3017, pp. 371–388. Springer, Heidelberg (2004). https://doi.org/10.1007/978-3-540-25937-4_24

36. Simon, D.R.: Finding collisions on a one-way street: can secure hash functions be based on general assumptions? In: Nyberg, K. (ed.) EUROCRYPT 1998. LNCS, vol. 1403, pp. 334–345. Springer, Heidelberg (1998). https://doi.org/10.1007/BFb0054137

37. Unruh, D.: Random oracles and auxiliary input. In: Menezes, A. (ed.) CRYPTO 2007. LNCS, vol. 4622, pp. 205–223. Springer, Heidelberg (2007). https://doi.org/10.1007/978-3-540-74143-5_12

38. Yao, A.C.-C.: Some complexity questions related to distributive computing (preliminary report). In: Proceedings of the Eleventh Annual ACM Symposium on Theory of Computing, pp. 209–213 (1979)

On Distributional Collision Resistant Hashing

Ilan Komargodski[1]([✉]) and Eylon Yogev[2]

[1] Cornell Tech, New York, NY 10044, USA
komargodski@cornell.edu
[2] Weizmann Institute of Science, 76100 Rehovot, Israel
eylon.yogev@weizmann.ac.il

Abstract. Collision resistant hashing is a fundamental concept that is the basis for many of the important cryptographic primitives and protocols. Collision resistant hashing is a family of compressing functions such that no efficient adversary can find *any* collision given a random function in the family.

In this work we study a relaxation of collision resistance called *distributional* collision resistance, introduced by Dubrov and Ishai (STOC '06). This relaxation of collision resistance only guarantees that no efficient adversary, given a random function in the family, can *sample* a pair (x, y) where x is uniformly random and y is uniformly random conditioned on colliding with x.

Our first result shows that distributional collision resistance can be based on the existence of *multi*-collision resistance hash (with no additional assumptions). Multi-collision resistance is another relaxation of collision resistance which guarantees that an efficient adversary cannot find any tuple of $k > 2$ inputs that collide relative to a random function in the family. The construction is non-explicit, non-black-box, and yields an infinitely-often secure family. This partially resolves a question of Berman et al. (EUROCRYPT '18). We further observe that in a black-box model such an implication (from multi-collision resistance to distributional collision resistance) does not exist.

Our second result is a construction of a distributional collision resistant hash from the average-case hardness of SZK. Previously, this assumption was not known to imply any form of collision resistance (other than the ones implied by one-way functions).

1 Introduction

Collision resistant hashing (CRH) is one of the most fundamental building blocks in any cryptographic protocol. Collision resistance is associated with a family of

I. Komargodski—Supported in part by a Packard Foundation Fellowship and by an AFOSR grant FA9550-15-1-0262.
E. Yogev—Supported in part by a grant from the Israel Science Foundation (no. 950/16).

© International Association for Cryptologic Research 2018
H. Shacham and A. Boldyreva (Eds.): CRYPTO 2018, LNCS 10992, pp. 303–327, 2018.
https://doi.org/10.1007/978-3-319-96881-0_11

compressing functions $\mathcal{H} = \{h\colon \{0,1\}^{2n} \to \{0,1\}^n\}$ and it assures us that while it is easy to compute $h(x)$ for any $h \in \mathcal{H}$ and $x \in \{0,1\}^{2n}$, for any polynomial time algorithm it is hard to find $x_1 \neq x_2$ such that $h(x_1) = h(x_2)$ for a random $h \leftarrow \mathcal{H}$. Families of functions with the above presumed hardness exist based on a variety of assumptions such as the hardness of factoring integers, finding discrete logs in finite groups, learning with errors (LWE), and more. On the other hand there is no known construction of CRHs based solely on the existence of one-way functions or even one-way permutations and, furthermore, such a construction does not exist in a black-box model [34].

Recently, [22] introduced a relaxation of collision resistance called *multi-collision resistance* (MCRH). In multi-collision resistance, the family of compressing functions $\mathcal{H}$ is associated with a parameter $k = k(n)$ and the security requirement is that for any polynomial-time algorithm and a random $h \leftarrow \mathcal{H}$ it is hard to find distinct $x_1, \ldots, x_k$ such that $h(x_1) = \ldots = h(x_k)$. In follow-up works [5,7,23], multi-collision resistance was studied as an independent primitive and shown to have many applications.

CRH trivially implies MCRH for any $k \geq 2$ and the latter implies one-way functions. Furthermore, in a black-box model, MCRH for any $k > 2$ cannot be used to get a CRH, yet MCRH cannot be constructed from one-way permutations [5,23]. In terms of constructions, [5] gave a construction of an MCRH from the (average-case) *min-max entropy approximation* assumption first studied in [13]. This is a strengthening of the entropy approximation assumption that is known to be complete for (average-case) non-interactive statistical zero-knowledge (NISZK) [17]. The applications of MCRH in [5,7,23] are broad, showing that not only it is a natural relaxation of CRH, but it is also a useful replacement in several key applications such as constant-round statistically-hiding succinct commitments and various zero-knowledge protocols.

In this work we study yet another relaxation of CRH, called *distributional collision resistance* (dCRH), introduced by Dubrov and Ishai [12] (see more on their work below). The security notion of this primitive says that it may be possible to find some specific collision, but it is computationally hard to sample a *random* collision. More precisely, given a random hash function $h \leftarrow \mathcal{H}$, it is computationally hard to sample a pair (x_1, x_2) such that x_1 is uniform and x_2 is uniform in the set $h^{-1}(x_1) = \{x\colon h(x_1) = h(x)\}$. This definition is reminiscent of the *distributional* version of one-way function, where we require hardness of coming up with a uniform preimage of a random image. In the world of one-way functions, by a result of Impagliazzo and Luby [20], the distributional version is known to be existentially equivalent to plain one-way functions (by an explicit and black-box transformation).

Very little is known about dCRH function families. Intuitively, this is a very weak notion of collision resistance since an adversary may be able to actually find *all* collisions (but with a skewed distribution). Nevertheless, as observed by Dubrov and Ishai [12], in a black-box model, dCRH cannot be constructed from one-way permutations. (The oracle of Simon [34] that finds a random collision is actually an oracle that breaks dCRH.) The main question we are interested in is the power of dCRH and its relation to MCRH and CRH. Can CRH be constructed from dCRH? Can dCRH be constructed from weak assumptions that are not known to imply CRH or MCRH? In what scenarios does the notion of dCRH suffice? What is the relation between MCRH and dCRH? (The latter question was explicitly asked by Berman et al. [5]).

1.1   Our Results

We begin by observing that the separation of [23] of CRH from MCRH uses the same oracle of Simon [34] that finds a random collision. Thus, the separation actually applies to dCRH, thereby implying that there is **no black-box construction** of a dCRH from an MCRH.

MCRH ⇒ DCRH. Our first result is that the existence of MCRH for any constant $k \in \mathbb{N}$ implies the existence of dCRH (and no further assumptions). Our proof is non-constructive and uses an adversary in a **non-black-box** way. Actually, our proof results in an infinitely-often dCRH, and should merely serve as evidence that multi-collision resistance is a stronger assumption than distributional collision resistance. This partially resolves the question of Berman et al. [5] mentioned above.

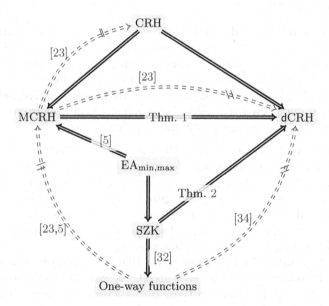

Fig. 1. An illustration of the known results and our new implications. Solid lines mean positive implications, namely, a solid arrow from A to B means that the existence of A implies the existence of B. Crossed out dashed red lines mean black-box separations, namely, such a line from A to B means that there is an impossibility for a black-box construction of B from A. (Color figure online)

SZK ⇒ DCRH. Our second result is an **explicit construction** of a dCRH from the average-case hardness of the class of problems that posses a statistical zero-knowledge (SZK) proof. More concretely, our construction is based on the average-case hardness of the *statistical difference* problem, that is known to be complete for SZK, by a result of Sahai and Vadhan [33]. This assumption is known to imply one-way functions by a result of Ostrovsky [32], but is not known to imply multi-collision resistance (let alone plain collision resistance). It is also weaker than the assumption used by Berman et al. [5] to construct an MCRH.

As an application, we obtain that indistinguishability obfuscation and one-way permutations (and thus their many derivatives) do not imply hardness in SZK via black-box reductions. We use the result of Asharov and Segev [1] that shows that indistinguishability obfuscation and one-way permutations do not imply (in a black-box model) collision resistance. We observe that their separation applies to distributional collision resistance as well (again, because they use the oracle of Simon [34] that finds a random collision) which immediately implies our result. Previously, a direct proof of this result (i.e., not going through [1]) was shown by Bitansky et al. [6].

A summary of the known results together with ours appears in Fig. 1.

1.2   Related Work

The work of Dubrov and Ishai. Dubrov and Ishai [12] studied the question of whether every efficiently samplable distribution can be efficiently sampled, up to a small statistical distance, using roughly as much randomness as the length of its output. They gave a positive answer to this question under various assumptions. They further showed that a negative answer to their question gives rise to a construction of a *distributional* collision resistant hash from any one-way permutation, thus bypassing the separation of Simon [34].

Overcoming black-box barriers. The framework of black-box constructions was introduced by Impagliazzo and Rudich [21] in order to capture "natural" constructions of one primitive from another. This framework has been extensively used to capture the limits of cryptographic primitives under this sort of constructions. Black-box constructions are not only the most natural ones, but often they result with more efficient and scalable construction since each building block is treated independently as a "black-box".

A black-box separation does not mean that one primitive cannot be constructed from another, but rather that *specific* or *natural* types of constructions cannot work. Due to the nature of these constructions, in many cases it is hard to imagine a construction that circumvents the separation. Indeed, we have only a few examples where a black-box barrier was circumvented.

A well known tool that enables to bypass such limitations is using *garbled circuits* on circuits with embedded cryptography (e.g., a one-way function). This technique was used by Beaver [4] to construct round-efficient OT extension protocols (see also the recent work of Garg et al. [15]). They have also been recently used by Döttling and Garg [11] to construct an IBE scheme from the computational Diffie-Hellman assumption.

Another technique, introduced by Barak et al. [3], is via derandomization. Mahmoody and Pass [31] showed a black-box separation for constructions of non-interactive commitments from a stronger notion of one-way functions, which they called *hitting* one-way functions. Then, using the derandomization technique, they showed that there exists a non-black-box construction of non-interactive commitments from hitting one-way functions. Note that the notion of a hitting one-way function was introduced especially for this purpose.

Another technique inspired by complexity theory is due to Harnik and Naor [19] who introduced the task of compressibility of NP instances. Here, the task is to come up with a compression scheme that preserves the solution to an instance of a problem rather than preserving the instance itself. One of their results is a construction of a collision resistant hash function from any one-way function, assuming a compression algorithm for SAT. (Recall that there is no black-box construction of collision resistant hash functions from one-way functions [34].) Fortnow and Santhanam [14] showed that such a compression algorithm cannot exist unless $NP \subseteq coNP/poly$. The result of Dubrov and Ishai [12] discussed above can be viewed as complementary to the one of Harnik and Naor [19], as they show consequences of the non-existence of (strong forms of) such algorithms.

A more recent technique comes from the area of program obfuscation. There, it was first shown by Asharov and Segev [1] that a private-key functional encryption scheme cannot be used to construct a public-key encryption scheme in a black-box way. Here, the definition of black-box is more delicate as we do not want to limit the obfuscation to circuits that have no cryptography in them. So, the actual separation is from an even stronger primitive called private-key functional encryption for *oracle-aided* circuits which are allowed to have one-way function gates. This separation was bypassed by Bitansky et al. [8] using a non-black-box component of Brakerski et al. [10] (see also [24]), where they generate a functional key for a function that calls the encryption/key-generation procedure of the same scheme. In the same line of works and the same high-level non-black-box use, indistinguishability obfuscation was constructed from a primitive called constant-degree multilinear maps in works by Lin, Vaikuntanathan, and Tessaro [25–28], while such constructions were proven impossible in a black-box model by Mahmoody et al. [30].

Lastly, we mention that there is a rich line of work, starting with Barak [2], on non-black-box *simulation*. Here, the construction is black-box but only the simulator (which is constructed to prove the security of the scheme) is allowed to be non-black-box (usually in a potential adversary).

Statistical zero-knowledge. The notion of statistical zero-knowledge (SZK) proofs was introduced in the seminal work of Goldwasser, Micali and Rackoff [18]. It is known that homomorphic encryption schemes and non-interactive computational private-information retrieval schemes imply hard problems in SZK [9,29].

Concrete assumptions such as Discrete Log, QR, lattices, and more, are also known to imply SZK hardness.

The class of (promise problems) with SZK proofs is characterized by the problems *statistical difference* (SD) and *entropy difference* (ED) by results of Sahai and Vadhan [33] and Goldreich and Vadhan [17]. Statistical difference is the problem of deciding whether two distributions (specified by circuits that sample from them) are close or far in statistical distance. Entropy difference is the problem of deciding which of two given distributions (specified by circuits that sample from them) has noticeably higher Shannon entropy than the other.

There are closely related problems that are known to be complete for the class NISZK – the class that contains all (promise) problems for which there is a *non-interactive* statistical zero-knowledge proof. The complete problems, presented by Goldreich et al. [16], are *statistical difference from uniform* (SDU) and *entropy approximation* (EA). The former is the SD problem but where one of the distributions is the uniform one. The latter is the ED problem but where one of the distributions has known entropy k (so the goal is to decide whether the other distribution has entropy bigger than $k + 1$ or smaller than $k - 1$).

The assumption of Berman et al. [5] (leading to a construction of MCRH) is the average-case hardness of the promise problem to distinguish between distributions (specified by circuits) whose min-entropy is at least k from ones with max-entropy at most $k-1$. It is a strengthening of the (average-case) EA assumption which is in turn stronger than (average-case) ED and (average-case) SD.

1.3   Our Techniques

We give an overview of our proof of existence of a dCRH family based on MCRH. It is instructive to give the idea of the construction and proof first in an idealized world where we have an (imaginary) oracle MAGIC. This oracle MAGIC, given any efficiently samplabe distribution D over pairs (x_1, x_2) and any particular value x_1^*, samples x_2 from the marginal of D conditioned on x_1^* being the first output. Using this oracle, we show how to transform an MCRH family to a dCRH family. Then, we show how to replace the oracle with an efficient procedure; this is the non-black-box part in our construction. Notice that in general this oracle cannot be implemented in polynomial time (unless $P = NP$). Our implementation will not exactly be of the oracle MAGIC, but of a much weaker one which is still enough to carry out the proof.

To simplify the argument even further let us start with a 3-MCRH function family $\mathcal{H}$ where each function maps $2n$ bits to n bits. By definition, no polynomial-time algorithm, given $h \leftarrow \mathcal{H}$, can find a triple of values that are mapped to the same image. We assume towards contradiction that dCRH families do not exist. In particular, $\mathcal{H}$ is not a dCRH and thus there *exists* an adversary $\mathcal{A}$ that can break its security. Namely, $\mathcal{A}$ can sample random pairs of collisions relative to $h \leftarrow \mathcal{H}$. We show that given $\mathcal{A}$ and the oracle MAGIC we can find a 3-collision relative to a given h.

Given h, we run $\mathcal{A}$ to get a collision (x_1, x_2), i.e., $h(x_1) = h(x_2)$. We treat $\mathcal{A}$ as describing a distribution over pairs of inputs that collide and run the oracle

MAGIC on $\mathcal{A}$ with $x_1^* = x_1$ to sample another pair of collision (x_1, x_3), i.e., $h(x_1) = h(x_2)$. This results with three values x_1, x_2, x_3 that collide relative to h, that is, $h(x_1) = h(x_2) = h(x_3)$. Are they all distinct? We argue that indeed this is the case.

The first pair (x_1, x_2) was sampled uniformly at random, namely, x_1 is uniformly random and x_2 is uniformly random conditioned on colliding with x_1. Since our hash function is compressing enough, with high probability we have that the set of preimages $h^{(-1)}(x_1)$ is exponentially large and thus the probability that $x_1 = x_2$ is negligible. What about x_3? Recall that x_3 is also sampled uniformly at random conditioned on colliding with x_1, that is, uniformly at random from all the preimages of $h(x)$. Thus, the probability that x_3 is either x_1 or x_2 is negligible, which completes the argument that x_1, x_2 and x_3 are a 3-way collision.

We have shown that if $\mathcal{H}$ is not a dCRH family, then the adversary together with the oracle MAGIC can be used to find a 3-way collision. It remains to explain how we implement this oracle. Our key observation is that in the (false) world where dCRH do not exist and MCRH does exist, we can actually implement an efficient yet limited version of this oracle (where x^* is uniform rather than arbitrary) which suffices for the purposes of our proof. This is the non-constructive (and non-black-box) part of the proof and is our main new insight.

We define a new hash family $\mathcal{H}'$ that depends not only on $\mathcal{H}$ but also on the adversary $\mathcal{A}$. Each $h' \in \mathcal{H}'$ uses the input x as *random coins* to run the adversary $\mathcal{A}$. If the adversary needs ℓ random coins then our hash function h' will map ℓ bits to n bits (w.l.o.g. $\ell > 2n$). First, let $\mathcal{A}^1$ be the adversary $\mathcal{A}$ that outputs only the first element of the collision that $\mathcal{A}$ finds. That is, $\mathcal{A}^1(h; r)$ on input a hash function $h \leftarrow \mathcal{H}$ and random coins r, runs $\mathcal{A}(h; r)$ on h with coins r to get a collision (x, y) and it outputs *only* x. Using $\mathcal{A}^1$ and a key $h \in \mathcal{H}$ we define a key $h' \in \mathcal{H}'$ as follows:

$$h'(x) = h(\mathcal{A}^1(h; x)).$$

This is why our construction is non-explicit: we do not know who the adversary $\mathcal{A}$ is, but we only know it exists.

Since $\mathcal{H}'$ is also not a dCRH function family, there exists an adversary $\mathcal{A}'$ that can sample a random collision relative to $h' \leftarrow \mathcal{H}'$. We use $\mathcal{A}'$ in order to implement (some version of) the oracle MAGIC. First, we run $\mathcal{A}'$ on h' to get a collision (x_1, x_2). Since x_1 is uniform, we have that $\mathcal{A}^1$ gets random bits and will output u_1 which is part of a pair (u_1, u_2) that collides relative to h. Moreover, x_2 is chosen such that it collides with x_1. Thus, if we let $(u_3, u_4) \leftarrow \mathcal{A}(h; x_2)$, then it must be that $h(u_1) = h(u_3)$, and therefore $h(u_1) = h(u_2) = h(u_3)$. Can we show that u_1, u_2, and u_3 are all distinct?

Let U_y be the set of all u's that h maps to $y = h(u_1)$. Since h is compressing enough, the set U_y is exponentially large. Moreover, since x_1 is uniformly random, then (u_1, u_2) is a random collision (under the right distribution) which implies that $u_1 \neq u_2$ with high probability. Arguing distinctness of u_3 is slightly more involved. Our goal is to show that indeed u_3 is sampled uniformly from the set U_y and thus will be distinct from u_1, u_2 with high probability.

Recall that x_2 is sampled uniformly at random conditioned on $h'(x_2) \in U_y$. Thus, the distribution of the element u_3 depends on the adversary $\mathcal{A}$, and how he uses his random coins to output a pair (u_3, u_4) that collide relative to h and where $h(u_3) = y$. Since $\mathcal{A}$ is an adversary for $\mathcal{H}$, we know that $\mathcal{A}^1$ "maps" randomnesses x to elements u. For a string u, denote by X_u the set of all x's such that $\mathcal{A}^1(h; x) = u$. By the guarantee on the output distribution of $\mathcal{A}$, this mapping is regular in the sense that for each $u, u' \in U_y$, it holds that $|X_u| = |X_{u'}|$. Thus, the probability that $u_3 = u_1$ (and similarly $u_3 = u_2$) is bounded by the probability that x_2 comes from X_{u_1}. By the above, x_2 comes (uniformly) from one of the X_u's where $u \in U_y$. But, U_y is exponentially large and all the X_u's are of the same size, implying that the probability that $u_3 = u_1$ is exponentially small. Altogether, indeed u_1, u_2, and u_3 form a 3-way collision.

The above argument is slightly over-simplified since it does not take into account errors that $\mathcal{A}$ or $\mathcal{A}'$ can make. In addition, we assumed that $\mathcal{A}$ and $\mathcal{A}'$ above output uniformly random collisions in the corresponding families, while in reality they can only be used to sample a collision which is statistically close to a random one. In the formal proof we handle these issues.

Finding larger collisions. In the proof above we used an adversary $\mathcal{A}$ that can find random pairs of collisions to construct a new hash function family, for which there is an adversary $\mathcal{A}'$ with which we designed an algorithm that finds 3-way collisions in the alleged 3-MCRH function family $\mathcal{H}$. Let us call this algorithm by BreakMCRH. We first observe that BreakMCRH actually finds an (almost) random 3-way collision, namely, breaking the security of $\mathcal{H}$ as a *distributional* 3-MCRH. The distribution of our 3-way collision (x_1, x_2, x_3) is such that x_1 is uniformly random and x_2 and x_3 are independent uniformly random conditioned on colliding with x_1.

We thus use BreakMCRH in a recursive manner to replace the adversary $\mathcal{A}$ (that finds pairs) and define a new hash function family. Finally, we modify the final algorithm BreakMCRH to find a 4-way collision. To this end, we define a new hash function family $\mathcal{H}'$ such that each $h' \in \mathcal{H}'$ is defined as

$$h'(x) = h(\mathsf{BreakMCRH}^1(h; x)),$$

where $\mathsf{BreakMCRH}^1(h; x)$ is the algorithm BreakMCRH but outputs only the first element from the triple. Since (distributional) 3-MCRH do not exist, there is an adversary that can find a triple of collisions in a random h'. Similarly to the proof above, we use the first two elements to get a 3-way collision. Then, since the extra third element in the collision is sampled uniformly from a large set of pre-images it can be used to find the fourth colliding input.

This process can be generalized and continued for several iterations. The cost of each iteration is a polynomial blow-up in the running time of the hash function and the reduction (and also the success probability). Thus, we can apply this iteratively for k times where $k \in \mathbb{N}$ is any fixed constant, resulting with the statement that k-MCRH implies a dCRH.

A construction from statistical difference. To present the idea behind the construction let us assume first that we have circuits $C_0, C_1 \colon \{0, 1\}^n \to \{0, 1\}^n$

such that it is computationally hard to distinguish whether they describe distributions that are identical or disjoint. This corresponds to the statistical difference problem with parameters 0 and 1. We will overload C_0 and C_1 and let them denote (also) the corresponding distributions.

Our hash function $h\colon \{0,1\}^{n+1} \to \{0,1\}^n$ is indexed by both circuits C_0 and C_1, and it operates as follows

$$h_{C_0,C_1}(x,b) = C_b(x).$$

Let us assume that it is not a dCRH. Namely, there is an efficient adversary $\mathcal{A}$ that gets C_0 and C_1, and finds $(x,b),(x',b')$ that collide relative to h_{C_0,C_1}, as defined above. We claim that if the collision is such that $b \neq b'$ then the circuits C_0 and C_1 must be identically distributed. Indeed, if $b \neq b'$, this means that we have x,x' such that, say, $C_0(x) = C_1(x')$ which means that the induced distributions are not disjoint (and hence must be identical). The other case, if $b = b'$, can occur in both cases that the distributions are identical or disjoint, but each will happen only with probability $1/2$. Thus, to distinguish the two cases we run the adversary $\mathcal{A}$ and check whether $b \neq b'$. If the distributions are identical, it will always be that $b = b'$, while if they are disjoint this will happen only with probability $1/2$. This is enough to distinguish between whether C_0 and C_1 are disjoint or identical with noticeable probability.

The case where the statistical distance is not 0 or 1 but is ϵ vs. $(1 - \epsilon)$ for a small constant $\epsilon > 0$ follows the same high-level idea but requires a slightly more involved analysis. The goal is to relate the probability that $b = b'$ to the statistical distance between C_0 and C_1 and show that these values are correlated. We choose to use a specific f-divergence called the *triangular discrimination*[1] measure which is defined by

$$\Delta_{\mathsf{TD}}(C_0,C_1) = \sum_y \frac{(\Pr[C_0 = y] - \Pr[C_1 = y])^2}{\Pr[C_0 = y] + \Pr[C_1 = y]}.$$

We first related the probability that $b' = b$ to the triangular discrimination between C_0 and C_1 by (simple) algebraic manipulations. Concretely, we show that

$$\Pr[b' = b] = \frac{1}{2} + \frac{\Delta_{\mathsf{TD}}(C_0,C_1)}{4}.$$

Then, we use the fact that the triangular discrimination can be bounded both from above and from below by a function that depends on the statistical distance.[2] More precisely, it holds that

$$2\Delta(C_0,C_1)^2 \leq \Delta_{\mathsf{TD}}(C_0,C_1) \leq 2\Delta(C_0,C_1).$$

---

[1] f-divergence is a family of measures of distance between probability distributions defined by $D_f(P\|Q) = \sum_x Q(x) \cdot f(P(x)/Q(x))$. Statistical distance is a special case with $f(x) = |1 - x|$ and triangular discrimination is a special case with $f(x) = (x - 1)^2/(x + 1)$.

[2] This is why we use the triangular discrimination measure as opposed to more well-known measures such as the Kullback-Leibler divergence. The latter is only lower-bounded by a function that depends on the statistical distance.

We use this to get our separation between the value of $\Pr[b' = b]$ in the case that C_0 and C_1 are close and in the case that they are far.

2 Preliminaries

Unless stated otherwise, the logarithms in this paper are base 2. For an integer $n \in \mathbb{N}$ we denote by $[n]$ the set $\{1, \dots, n\}$. For a distribution X we denote by $x \leftarrow X$ an element chosen from X uniformly at random. We denote by $\circ$ the string concatenation operation. A function $\mathsf{negl} \colon \mathbb{N} \to \mathbb{R}^+$ is *negligible* if for every constant $c > 0$, there exists an integer N_c such that $\mathsf{negl}(n) < n^{-c}$ for all $n > N_c$. Throughout the paper, we denote by n the security parameter.

2.1 Distance Measures

Definition 1 (Statistical distance). *The statistical distance between two random variables X, Y over a finite domain Ω, is defined by*

$$\Delta(X, Y) \triangleq \frac{1}{2} \cdot \sum_{x \in \Omega} |\Pr[X = x] - \Pr[Y = x]|.$$

We say that X and Y are δ-close (resp. -far) if $\Delta(X, Y) \leq \delta$ (resp. $\Delta(X, Y) \geq \delta$).

We will use another (less well-known) distance measure called the *triangular discrimination* (a.k.a Le Cam Divergence).

Definition 2 (Triangular discrimination). *The triangular discrimination between two random variables X, Y over a finite domain Ω, is defined by*

$$\Delta_{\mathsf{TD}}(X, Y) = \sum_{x \in \Omega} \frac{(\Pr[X = x] - \Pr[Y = x])^2}{\Pr[X = x] + \Pr[Y = x]}$$

It is known that the triangular discrimination is bounded from above by the statistical distance and from below by the statistical distance squared (see, for example, [35, Eq. (2.11)]).

Proposition 1. *For any two random variables X, Y over the same finite domain, it holds that*

$$2 \cdot \Delta(X, Y)^2 \leq \Delta_{\mathsf{TD}}(X, Y) \leq 2 \cdot \Delta(X, Y).$$

2.2 Efficient Function Families

A function f, with input length $m_1(n)$ and outputs length $m_2(n)$, specifies for every $n \in \mathbb{N}$ a function $f_n \colon \{0, 1\}^{m_1(n)} \to \{0, 1\}^{m_2(n)}$. We only consider functions with polynomial input lengths (in n) and occasionally abuse notation and write $f(x)$ rather than $f_n(x)$ for simplicity. The function f is computable in polynomial time (efficiently computable) if there exists an algorithm that for any $x \in \{0,1\}^{m_1(n)}$ outputs $f_n(x)$ and runs in time polynomial in n.

A function family ensemble is an infinite set of function families, whose elements (families) are indexed by the set of integers. Let $\mathcal{F} = \{\mathcal{F}_n \colon \mathcal{D}_n \to \mathcal{R}_n\}_{n \in \mathbb{N}}$ stand for an ensemble of function families, where each $f \in \mathcal{F}_n$ has domain $\mathcal{D}_n$ and range $\mathcal{R}_n$. An efficient function family ensemble is one that has an efficient sampling and evaluation algorithms.

Definition 3 (Efficient function family ensemble). *A function family ensemble $\mathcal{F} = \{\mathcal{F}_n \colon \mathcal{D}_n \to \mathcal{R}_n\}_{n \in \mathbb{N}}$ is efficient if:*

- *$\mathcal{F}$ is samplable in polynomial time: there exists a probabilistic polynomial-time machine that given 1^n, outputs (the description of) a uniform element in $\mathcal{F}_n$.*
- *There exists a deterministic algorithm that given $x \in \mathcal{D}_n$ and (a description of) $f \in \mathcal{F}_n$, runs in time $\mathsf{poly}(n, |x|)$ and outputs $f(x)$.*

2.3 Distributional Collision Resistant Hash Functions

A distributional collision resistant hash function is a hash function with the security guarantee that no efficient adversary can sample a uniform collision. This relaxation of classical collision resistance was introduced by Dubrov and Ishai [12].

For $h \colon \{0,1\}^m \to \{0,1\}^n$, we associate a random variable $\mathsf{COL}_h \subseteq \{0,1\}^m \times \{0,1\}^m$ over pairs of inputs (x_1, x_2) to h sampled by the following process: x_1 is chosen uniformly at random from $\{0,1\}^m$ and then x_2 is chosen uniformly at random from the set $\{x \in \{0,1\}^m \colon h(x) = h(x_1)\}$. Note that it is possible that $x_1 = x_2$.

Definition 4 (Distributional collision resistant hashing). *Let $\mathcal{H} = \{\mathcal{H}_n \colon \{0,1\}^{m(n)} \to \{0,1\}^n\}_{n \in \mathbb{N}}$ be an efficient function family ensemble, where $m(n) < n$. We say that $\mathcal{H}$ is a secure distributional collision resistant hash (dCRH) function family if for any probabilistic polynomial-time algorithm $\mathcal{A}$ and any two negligible functions $\delta(\cdot)$ and $\epsilon(\cdot)$, it holds that*

$$\Pr_{h \leftarrow \mathcal{H}} [\Delta(\mathcal{A}(1^n, h), \mathsf{COL}_h) \le \delta(n)] \le 1 - \epsilon(n)$$

for all sufficiently large $n \in \mathbb{N}$. Note that the probability above is only over the choice of $h \leftarrow \mathcal{H}$.

We say that a dCRH as above is infinitely-often secure if the above security only holds for infinitely many n's rather than for all large enough n's.

2.4 Multi-collision Resistant Hash Functions

A multi-collision resistant hash function is a relaxation of standard notion of collision resistant hash function in which it is hard to find *multiple* distinct values that all collide on the same value. This primitive has been recently studied in several works [5,7,22,23].

Definition 5 (Multi-collision resistant hashing). *Let $k = k(n)$ be a polynomial function. An efficient function family ensemble $\mathcal{H} = \{\mathcal{H}_n \colon \{0,1\}^{2n} \to \{0,1\}^n\}_{n \in \mathbb{N}}$ is a secure k-multi-collision resistant hash (MCRH) function family if for any probabilistic polynomial-time algorithm $\mathcal{A}$ there exists a negligible function $\mathsf{negl}(\cdot)$ such that for all $n \in \mathbb{N}$, it holds that*

$$\Pr\left[\begin{array}{c} x_1, \ldots, x_k \text{ are distinct and} \\ h(x_1) = \cdots = h(x_k) \end{array} \middle| \begin{array}{c} h \leftarrow \mathcal{H}_n \\ (x_1, \ldots, x_k) \leftarrow \mathcal{A}(h) \end{array}\right] \leq \mathsf{negl}(n).$$

We call such $x_1, \ldots, x_k$ that map to the same value under h a k-way collision.

3   Constructing dCRH from MCRH

In this section we present our main result. The theorem states that the existence of any MCRH implies the existence of a dCRH. Our construction is *non-black-box*.

Theorem 1. *Assuming the existence of a secure 3-MCRH function family that compresses $2n$ bits to n bits, then there exists an (infinitely often) secure d CRH function family.*

Proof. Let $\mathcal{H} = \{h \colon \{0,1\}^{2n} \to \{0,1\}^n\}$ be a secure 3-MCRH function family. Assume towards contradiction that infinitely-often dCRH function families do not exist, and we will show that 3-MCRH families do not exist as well (which is a contradiction). Since there are no dCRH function families, in particular, $\mathcal{H}$ is not a dCRH and there exists an adversary $\mathcal{A}$ and two negligible functions $\delta(\cdot)$ and ϵ such that for all large enough n's it holds that

$$\Pr_{h \leftarrow \mathcal{H}}\left[\Delta\left(\mathcal{A}(1^n, h), \mathsf{COL}_h\right) \leq \delta(n)\right] > 1 - \epsilon(n)$$

That is, $\mathcal{A}$ gets $h \in \mathcal{H}$ as input, and randomness r and outputs a collision (x_1, x_2) that is distributed as a random collision from COL_h. We denote this process by $(x_1, x_2) \leftarrow \mathcal{A}(h; r)$ (notice that we omit the 1^n argument to simplify notation). Denote by $\mathcal{A}^1$ the same adversary that outputs only x_1. That is, $x_1 \leftarrow A^1(h; r)$.

Our key observation is that we can use A^1 to define a new family $\mathcal{H}'$ of hash functions which will be an infinitely-often secure dCRH function family. The keys in this family are denoted by h' and have the same representation as $h \in \mathcal{H}$ but perform a different operation. Let $\ell = \ell(n)$ be an upper bound on the number of random bits that $\mathcal{A}$ uses, and assume that $\ell > 2n$ without loss of generality. We define a new hash family where the input x is used as random coins to run the adversary $\mathcal{A}^1$. Formally, we define each function in the family $\mathcal{H}' = \{h' \colon \{0,1\}^\ell \to \{0,1\}^n\}$ by

$$h'(x) = h(A^1(h; x)).$$

Again, since there are no infinitely-often dCRH function families, then in particular, $\mathcal{H}'$ is not a dCRH. Thus, again again there is an adversary $\mathcal{A}'$ and two negligible functions $\delta'(\cdot)$ and $\epsilon'(\cdot)$ such that

$$\Pr_{h' \leftarrow \mathcal{H}'} [\Delta (\mathcal{A}'(1^n, h'), \mathsf{COL}_{h'}) \le \delta(n)] > 1 - \epsilon(n) .$$

We show how to construct an adversary $\mathsf{Break}\mathcal{H}$ that uses *both* $\mathcal{A}$ and $\mathcal{A}'$ to break the security of the given MCRH. The full description of $\mathsf{Break}\mathcal{H}(1^n, h)$ is given in Fig. 2.

Algorithm $\mathsf{Break}\mathcal{H}(1^n, h)$:

1. Define h' such that $h'(x) = h(\mathcal{A}^1(h; x))$.
2. $(x_1, x_2) \leftarrow \mathcal{A}'(h')$ with fresh randomness.
3. $(u_1, u_2) \leftarrow \mathcal{A}(h; x_1)$.
4. $(u_3, u_4) \leftarrow \mathcal{A}(h; x_2)$.
5. Output (u_1, u_2, u_3).

Fig. 2. The description of the adversary $\mathsf{Break}\mathcal{H}$ that uses $\mathcal{A}$ and $\mathcal{A}'$ to break the security of the MCRH function family $\mathcal{H}$.

To simplify the analysis we will analyze a different adversary called $\widetilde{\mathsf{Break}\mathcal{H}}$. This adversary is *inefficient* but its output distribution is negligibly close (in statistical distance) to the output distribution of $\mathsf{Break}\mathcal{H}$. So, once we show that $\widetilde{\mathsf{Break}\mathcal{H}}$ breaks $\mathcal{H}$, we will get that $\mathsf{Break}\mathcal{H}$ breaks $\mathcal{H}$ with almost the same probability which is a contradiction.

Let us set-up some notation first. Recall that COL_h is a distribution over pairs of inputs (x_1, x_2) to h such that x_1 is chosen uniformly at random and x_2 is chosen uniformly at random conditioned on $h(x_1) = h(x_2)$. Let COL_h^1 be a distribution that outputs the first element in the collision, namely x_1. Let COL_{h,x_1}^2 be the distribution that outputs the second elements conditioned on colliding with the first, namely, a random x_2 conditioned on $h(x_1) = h(x_2)$. We also denote by $\mathsf{COL}_h(r)$ a sample from COL_h using randomness r.

Algorithm $\widetilde{\mathsf{Break}\mathcal{H}}(1^n, h)$:

1. Define h' such that $h'(x) = h(\mathcal{A}^1(h; x))$.
2. $(u_1, u_2) \leftarrow \mathsf{COL}_h(x_1)$, where $x_1 \leftarrow \mathsf{COL}_{h'}^1$.
3. $(u_3, u_4) \leftarrow \mathcal{A}(h; x_2)$, where $x_2 \leftarrow \mathsf{COL}_{h', x_1}^2$.
4. Output (u_1, u_2, u_3).

Fig. 3. The description of the adversary $\widetilde{\mathsf{Break}\mathcal{H}}$ that uses $\mathcal{A}$ and $\mathcal{A}'$ to break the security of the MCRH function family $\mathcal{H}$.

Claim 1. If $\widetilde{\mathsf{Break}}\mathcal{H}$ breaks the security of $\mathcal{H}$, then so does $\mathsf{Break}\mathcal{H}$.

Proof. We prove the claim by defining a hybrid adversaries $\mathsf{Break}\mathcal{H}^*$ and show the following sequence of implications:

1. If $\widetilde{\mathsf{Break}}\mathcal{H}$ breaks the security of $\mathcal{H}$, then so does $\mathsf{Break}\mathcal{H}^*$.
2. If $\mathsf{Break}\mathcal{H}^*$ breaks the security of $\mathcal{H}$, then so does $\mathsf{Break}\mathcal{H}$.

The adversary $\mathsf{Break}\mathcal{H}^*$ is the same as $\widetilde{\mathsf{Break}}\mathcal{H}$ except that we change Item 3 to the following:

2. $(u_1, u_2) \leftarrow \mathcal{A}(h; x_1)$, where $x_1 \leftarrow \mathsf{COL}_{h'}^1$.

First, we argue that if $\widetilde{\mathsf{Break}}\mathcal{H}$ breaks the security of $\mathcal{H}$, then so does $\mathsf{Break}\mathcal{H}^*$. Denote by $\widetilde{\mu}(n)$ the success probability of $\widetilde{\mathsf{Break}}\mathcal{H}$ in breaking the security of $\mathcal{H}$. With probability $1 - \epsilon(n)$ over the choice of $h \leftarrow \mathcal{H}$ we sample a "good" h, that is, a h for which the adversary $\mathcal{A}$ outputs a collision that is $\delta(n)$-close to one from COL_h. Then, for any such "good" h, the success probability of $\mathsf{Break}\mathcal{H}^*$ is $\widetilde{\mu}(n) - \delta(n)$. So, overall, the success probability of $\mathsf{Break}\mathcal{H}^*$ is $\mu^*(n) = \widetilde{\mu}(n) - \delta(n) - \epsilon(n)$. To simplify the analysis we will analyze a different adversary called $\widetilde{\mathsf{Break}}\mathcal{H}$, described in Fig. 3.

Second, we argue that if $\mathsf{Break}\mathcal{H}^*$ breaks the security of $\mathcal{H}$, then so does $\mathsf{Break}\mathcal{H}$. Denote by $\mu^*(n)$ the success probability of $\mathsf{Break}\mathcal{H}^*$ in breaking the security of $\mathcal{H}$. With probability $1 - \epsilon'(n)$ (over the choice of $h' \leftarrow \mathcal{H}'$) the adversary $\mathcal{A}'$ outputs a collision that is $\delta'(n)$-close to one from $\mathsf{COL}_{h'}$. Then, for any such "good" h, the success probability of $\mathsf{Break}\mathcal{H}$ is $\mu^*(n) - \delta'(n)$. So, overall, the success probability of $\mathsf{Break}\mathcal{H}$ is $\mu(n) = \mu^*(n) - \delta'(n) - \epsilon'(n)$.

Combining both of the above, we have that if $\widetilde{\mathsf{Break}}\mathcal{H}$ breaks the security of $\mathcal{H}$ with probability $\widetilde{\mu}(n)$, then $\mathsf{Break}\mathcal{H}$ breaks it with probability

$$\mu(n) = \widetilde{\mu}(n) - \delta(n) - \epsilon(n) - \delta'(n) - \epsilon'(n). \qquad \blacksquare$$

By the definition of $x_1 \leftarrow \mathsf{COL}_h^1$ and $x_2 \leftarrow \mathsf{COL}_{h,x_1}^2$, we have that x_1 is uniformly random in the domain of h' (namely, $\{0,1\}^\ell$) and x_2 is a uniform element in $\{0,1\}^\ell$ conditioned on satisfying $h(x_1) = h(x_2)$.

Lemma 1. *With all but negligible probability we have that* $h(u_1) = h(u_2) = h(u_3)$.

Proof. By the union bound

$$\Pr[h(u_1) = h(u_2) = h(u_3)] \geq 1 - \Pr[h(u_1) \neq h(u_2) \text{ or } h(u_1) \neq h(u_3)]$$
$$\geq 1 - \Pr[h(u_1) \neq h(u_2)] - \Pr[h(u_1) \neq h(u_3)].$$

If (x_1, x_2) is a collision under h', by definition of h', then it holds that

$$h(u_1) = h(\mathcal{A}^1(h; x_1)) = h(\mathcal{A}^1(h; x_2)) = h(u_3).$$

Thus, since by the definition of $\mathsf{COL}_{h'}$, the inputs x_1 and x_2 are a collision relative to h', then u_1 and u_3 are a collision relative to h. That is,

$$\Pr[h(u_1) \neq h(u_3)] = 0.$$

Additionally, recall that the pair (x_1, x_2) is a random collision sampled via COL_h. Namely, x_1 is uniformly random in $\{0,1\}^\ell$. Since $\mathcal{A}$ outputs a collision relative to h for all but a $\delta(n)$-fraction of possible randomnesses, it must be that $h(u_1) = h(u_2)$, except with probability $\delta(n)$. That is,

$$\Pr[h(u_1) \neq h(u_2)] \leq \delta(n). \qquad \blacksquare$$

What is left to show, and is the most technical part of the proof, is that all three elements u_1, u_2, u_3 are *distinct*. An illustration of the main ideas and the notations used in the proof is given in Fig. 4.

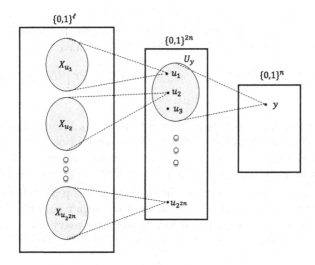

Fig. 4. An illustration of the ideas and notations used in the proof of the proof.

Lemma 2. *With all but negligible probability we have that u_1, u_2, u_3 are distinct.*

Proof. To argue distinctness, we first show that set of inverses of $h(u_1)$ is large with high probability. We use the following claim.

Claim 2. For any $h \in \mathcal{H}$, it holds that

$$\Pr_{x \leftarrow \{0,1\}^{2n}}[|h^{-1}(h(x))| > 2^{n/2}] \geq 1 - 2^{-n/2}.$$

Proof. We count how many x's might there be that satisfy $|\{h^{-1}(h(x))\}| \leq 2^{n/2}$. Let us denote by $U_1, \ldots, U_k$ a partition of $\{0,1\}^{2n}$ into sets according to the output of h. That is, $\forall i \; \forall x, y \in U_i \colon h(x) = h(y)$ and for all $i \neq j$ and $x \in U_i, y \in U_j$ it holds that $h(x) \neq h(y)$. Each set U_i that is larger than $2^{n/2}$ is called "good" and others are called "bad". The total number of sets k is bounded by 2^n and thus, there can be at most 2^n bad sets U_i. Namely, the total number of elements in the bad sets is bounded by $2^n \cdot 2^{n/2} = 2^{3n/2}$. Thus, the number of elements in good sets is $2^{2n} - 2^{3n/2} = (1 - 2^{-n/2}) \cdot 2^{2n}$ and each such good element x satisfies $|\{h^{-1}(h(x))\}| > 2^{n/2}$. ∎

Let $y = h(u_1)$ and let us denote all the values u that are mapped to y by:

$$U_y = \{u \mid h(u) = y\}.$$

Note that, by Claim 2, with very high probability over the choice of x_1, it holds that

$$|U_y| \geq 2^{n/2}. \tag{1}$$

The elements u_1 and u_2 are a sample of COL_h using fresh randomness x_1. Since x_2 is sampled from the set of all preimages of x_1, we have that

$$\Pr[u_1 \neq u_2] \geq \Pr\left[u_1 \neq u_2 \mid |U| > 2^{n/2}\right] \cdot \Pr\left[|U| > 2^{n/2}\right]$$

$$\geq 1 - \mathsf{negl}(n).$$

We continue to show that u_3 is distinct from u_1, u_2. From now on, let us condition on x_1 being such that Eq. (1) holds. We also condition on $h \in \mathcal{H}$ being such that $\Delta(\mathcal{A}(1^n, h), \mathsf{COL}_h) \leq \delta(n)$. The former happens with probability $1 - 2^{-\Omega(n)}$ and the latter happens with probability $1 - \epsilon(n)$. Overall, by the conditioning we will lose an additive $\mathsf{negl}(n)$ term in the overall success probability of $\mathsf{Break}\mathcal{H}$.

The algorithm $\mathcal{A}^1$ (i.e., $\mathcal{A}$ when restricted to output only the first element) gives us a mapping between x's and u's. Namely, for every $x \in \{0,1\}^\ell$, there is a $u \in \{0,1\}^{2n}$ such that $(u, \cdot) = \mathcal{A}(h; x)$. For $u \in \{0,1\}^{2n}$, denote

$$X_u = \{x \mid \mathcal{A}^1(h; x) = u\}.$$

We claim that for any two u, u', the sizes of X_u and $X_{u'}$ are roughly the same.

Claim 3. For any $u, u' \in U_y$,

$$\Pr_{(x_1, x_2) \leftarrow \mathsf{COL}_{h'}}[x_2 \in X_u] \in \Pr_{(x_1, x_2) \leftarrow \mathsf{COL}_{h'}}[x_2 \in X_{u'}] \pm \delta(n).$$

Proof. Since $\mathcal{A}(h; \cdot)$ outputs a pair that is distributed statistically close to a pair coming from COL_h and in the latter the first element is uniformly random in $\{0,1\}^{2n}$, it must be that $\mathcal{A}^1(h; \cdot)$ is distributed almost uniformly at random. Hence, the mapping between x's and u's is regular, except with probability $\delta(n)$. Namely,

$$\frac{|X_u|}{2^\ell} \in \frac{|X_{u'}|}{2^\ell} \pm \delta(n).$$

The claim now follows since x_2 is chosen uniformly at random from the set of all values that go to y. ∎

By the definition of X_u, by Claim 3, and by Eq. (1), we have that

$$\Pr[u_3 = u_1] \le \Pr[x_2 \in X_{u_1}] \le \frac{1}{|U_y|} + \delta(n) \le \mathsf{negl}(n).$$

By a similar reasoning, it holds that

$$\Pr[u_3 = u_2] \le \Pr[x_2 \in X_{u_2}] \le \frac{1}{|U_y|} + \delta(n) \le \mathsf{negl}(n).$$

Therefore, we get that $u_3 \notin \{u_1, u_2\}$ with all but negligible probability. ∎

Combining Lemmas 1 and 2 we get that we will find a 3-way collision with high probability which concludes the proof. ∎

Distributional MCRH. One can also defined a *distribution* notion for a k-MCRH. Here, the task of the adversary is to find, given a hash function $h \leftarrow \mathcal{H}$, not an arbitrary k-way collision, but one that is statistically close to a random one. By a random k-way collision we mean the following distribution. First, sample x_1 uniformly at random and then sample $x_2, \ldots, x_k$ independently uniformly at random conditioned on $h(x_i) = h(x_1)$ for every $2 \le i \le k$. We call this distribution COL_h^k.

We observe that in the proof above we get an algorithm that finds a 3-way collision that is statistically close to a random one from COL_h^3. That is, the proof above shows that existence of dCRH can be based on the existence of the seemingly weaker notion of *distributional* 3-MCRH.

3.1 Going Beyond 3-MCRH

In the previous section we have shown how to construct a dCRH from a 3-MCRH family. Our construction and proof inherently relied on the fact that an adversary cannot find a 3-way collision. In this part, we show how to extend the ideas from the above proof to give a recursive construction that shows the existence of a dCRH from the existence of a k-MCRH for any constant k. We will exemplify the idea for $k = 4$ next and explain the general afterwards.

Suppose that we are given a 4-MCRH family $\mathcal{H}$ and assume towards contradiction that dCRH function families do not exist. As in the proof above, there is an adversary $\mathcal{A}$ that breaks $\mathcal{H}$ as a dCRH and finds a random collision from COL_h, where $h \leftarrow \mathcal{H}$. We define $\mathcal{H}' = \{h' : \{0,1\}^\ell \to \{0,1\}^n\}$ as in the proof above

$$h'(x) = h(\mathcal{A}^1(h; x)).$$

Since $\mathcal{H}'$ do not exist, the adversary $\mathsf{Break}\mathcal{H}_3 \triangleq \mathsf{Break}\mathcal{H}$ from Fig. 2 can be used to find a random 3-way collision (u_1, u_2, u_3) for a random key $h \leftarrow \mathcal{H}$. Denote by $\ell' = \ell'(n)$ an upper bound on the number of bits of randomness used by $\mathsf{Break}\mathcal{H}_3$.

The key observation is that we can use $\mathsf{Break}\mathcal{H}_3$ recursively to get an algorithm $\mathsf{Break}\mathcal{H}_4$ that find a 4-way collision. We define an new hash function family $\mathcal{H}'' = \{h'' \colon \{0,1\}^{\ell'} \to \{0,1\}^n\}$ by

$$h''(x) = h(\mathsf{Break}\mathcal{H}_3^1(h;x)),$$

where $\mathsf{Break}\mathcal{H}_3^1$ is a modified version of the algorithm $\mathsf{Break}\mathcal{H}_3$ that outputs only the first element from its output triple. Since the function family $\mathcal{H}''$ is not a dCRH, there is an algorithm $\mathcal{A}''$ that can find a collision in $h'' \leftarrow \mathcal{H}''$ that is statistically close to one from $\mathsf{COL}_{h''}$. We construct an algorithm $\mathsf{Break}\mathcal{H}_4(1^n, h)$ that is similar to $\mathsf{Break}\mathcal{H}_3(1^n, h)$, except that it uses $\mathsf{Break}\mathcal{H}_3(1^n, h)$ instead of the adversary $\mathcal{A}$ to find a 4-way collision.

That is, $\mathsf{Break}\mathcal{H}_4$ runs $\mathcal{A}''$ to get a random collision (x_1, x_2). Then, x_1 is used as randomness to $\mathsf{Break}\mathcal{H}_3(1^n, h)$ to get a 3-way collision (u_1, u_2, u_3), and x_2 is used to get (u_4, u_5, u_6). Similarly to the arguments in the original proof, here we claim that u_4 will also hash to the same value as u_1, u_2, and u_3, and since it is random in the set of all elements that collide with u_1, the probability that it is distinct from u_1, u_2, and u_3 is very high. Thus, u_1, u_2, u_3, u_4 is a 4-way collision with high probability. (Not only that, it is actually negligibly-close to a random 4-way collision.)

The general case. The above idea extends to starting with a k-MCRH for higher values of k. Namely, our transformation allows one to go from k-MCRH to dCRH. But, there is a cost in parameters since in each step, the algorithm we construct and the construction itself incur a polynomial blowup in the running time (and also a decrease in the success probability). Thus, we can apply this iteratively k times for any constant $k \in \mathbb{N}$. This results with the statement that the existence of k-MCRH for any constant k implies the existence of dCRH. The resulting algorithm is denoted $\mathsf{Break}\mathcal{H}_{k+1}(1^n, h)$ and is given in Fig. 5.

Algorithm $\mathsf{Break}\mathcal{H}_{k+1}(1^n, h)$:

1. Define $h^{(k)}$ such that $h^{(k)}(x) = h(\mathsf{Break}\mathcal{H}_k^1(h;x))$.
2. $(x_1, x_2) \leftarrow \mathcal{A}^{(k)}(h^{(k)})$.
3. Let $(u_1, \ldots, u_k) \leftarrow \mathsf{Break}\mathcal{H}_k(h;x_1)$.
4. Let $(u_{k+1}, \ldots, u_{2k}) \leftarrow \mathsf{Break}\mathcal{H}_k(h;x_2)$.
5. Output $(u_1, u_2, \ldots, u_{k+1})$.

Fig. 5. The description of the adversary $\mathsf{Break}\mathcal{H}_{k+1}$.

Remark 1 (A note on non-uniformity). Notice that the first step in the above argument from 3-MCRH to dCRH results with an infinitely-often dCRH. This can be circumvented by having a non-uniform construction. In particular, instead of having a single adversary $\mathcal{A}$ that works for infinitely many input length, we can hardwire an adversary that works for each input length. The result is a standard dCRH (as opposed to an infinitely-often one) that is computed by circuits instead of Turing machines. This is important for our recursive argument, as otherwise each step of the reduction might work on a different sequence of input lengths.

Remark 2 (Distributional multi-collision resistance). The above idea can be summarized as a transformation from k-dMCRH to a $(k-1)$-dMCRH. A k-dMCRH is the distributional analog of MCRH, where the goal of the adversary is to come up with a *random* k-way collision $(x_1, \ldots, x_k)$. The distribution of such a collision relative to a hash function h is that x_1 is chosen uniformly at random and $x_2, \ldots, x_k$ are all chosen independently and uniformly at random conditioned on colliding with x_1 on h.

4   Constructing dCRH from SZK

In this section we show how to construct a dCRH from the average-case hardness of SZK. The statistical difference problem, which is complete for SZK [33], is a promise problem where one is given two distributions, described by circuits that sample from them, and the goal is to decide whether the distributions are close or far in statistical distance. The hardness of SZK implies the hardness of SD. For our application we will need the *average-case* hardness of this problem, where there is an underlying efficient sampler that samples the two aforementioned circuits.

Definition 6 (Distributions encoded by circuits). *Let $C : \{0,1\}^n \to \{0,1\}^n$ be a Boolean circuit. The distribution encoded by C is the distribution induced on $\{0,1\}^n$ by evaluating the circuit C on a uniformly sampled string of length n. We abuse notation and sometimes write C for the distribution defined by C.*

Definition 7 (The statistical difference problem). *Statistical Difference is the promise problem $\mathsf{SD}^{\epsilon,1-\epsilon} = (\mathsf{SD}_Y, \mathsf{SD}_N)$ over all pairs of circuits $C_0, C_1 : \{0,1\}^n \to \{0,1\}^n$, where the "Yes" instances are those that encode statistically far distributions*

$$\mathsf{SD}_Y = \{(C_0, C_1) : \Delta(C_0, C_1) \geq 1 - \epsilon\}$$

and the "No" instances are those that encode statistically close distributions

$$\mathsf{SD}_N = \{(C_0, C_1) : \Delta(C_0, C_1) \leq \epsilon\}.$$

Definition 8 (Average-case hardness). *We say that the $\mathsf{SD}^{\epsilon,1-\epsilon}$ problem is hard-on-the-average if there exists a probabilistic polynomial-time sampler S that outputs pairs of circuits $C_0, C_1 : \{0,1\}^n \to \{0,1\}^n$ such that for any (non-uniform) probabilistic polynomial-time decider D that outputs "Y" or "N", there exists a negligible function $\mathsf{negl}(\cdot)$ such that for all $n \in \mathbb{N}$ it holds that*

$$\Pr_{(C_0,C_1) \leftarrow S(1^n)} [x \leftarrow D(C_0, C_1) \text{ and } (C_0, C_1) \in \mathsf{SD}_x] \leq \frac{1}{2} + \mathsf{negl}(n).$$

The beautiful result of Sahai and Vadhan [33] shows that (average-case) $\mathsf{SD}^{\frac{1}{3},\frac{2}{3}}$ is complete for (average-case) SZK. Not only that, they showed that the constants $1/3$ and $2/3$ in the Statistical Difference problem are somewhat arbitrary and the gap can be amplified. In more detail, they showed that given two distributions D_0, D_1, and a number k, then in polynomial time (in k) one can sample from distributions D_0' and D_1' such that if $\Delta(D_0, D_1) \leq 1/3$, then $\Delta(D_0', D_1') \leq 2^{-k}$, and if $\Delta(D_0, D_1) \geq 2/3$, then $\Delta(D_0', D_1') \leq 1 - 2^{-k}$.

Our main result in this section is a construction of a dCRH that compresses by 1 bit from the average-case hardness of SZK.

Theorem 2. *There exists an explicit* dCRH *mapping* n *bit to* $(n-1)$ *bits assuming the average-case hardness of SZK.*

Proof. Since SZK is hard-on-the-average, $\mathsf{SD}^{\frac{1}{3},\frac{2}{3}}$ is hard-on-the-average. Also, $\mathsf{SD}^{\epsilon, 1-\epsilon}$ for $\epsilon = 0.01$ is average-case hard [33]. Let S be the sampler for $\mathsf{SD}^{\epsilon, 1-\epsilon}$.

We define our dCRH family $\mathcal{H}$ next. The key sampler for $\mathcal{H}$ runs the simulator S and outputs the two circuits (that describe distributions). Given a key (C_0, C_1) we define the hash function $h_{(C_0, C_1)} \colon \{0,1\}^n \to \{0,1\}^{n-1}$ in by

$$h_{C_0, C_1}(x, b) = C_b(x). \tag{2}$$

In the rest of the proof we shall prove that this function family is a dCRH. We will do so by contradiction, showing that if it were insecure, then we would get a statistical-distance distinguisher for circuits that are output by S. This is a contradiction to the average-case hardness of $\mathsf{SD}^{\epsilon, 1-\epsilon}$.

Suppose (towards contradiction) that $\mathcal{H}$ is not a dCRH. This means that there is a probabilistic polynomial-time adversary $\mathcal{A}$ and two negligible functions $\delta(\cdot)$ and $\epsilon(\cdot)$ such that $\mathcal{A}$ with probability at least $1 - \epsilon(n)$ over the choice of $h \leftarrow \mathcal{H}$ can generate a collision which is δ-close to a uniform one from COL_h. That is,

$$\Pr_{h \leftarrow \mathcal{H}} \left[\Delta \left(\mathcal{A}(1^n, h), \mathsf{COL}_h \right) \leq \delta(n) \right] > 1 - \epsilon(n).$$

We design an algorithm BreakSD that uses $\mathcal{A}$ and solves SD on circuits given by $S(1^n; \cdot)$. The idea is pretty simple: we run $\mathcal{A}$ to get a collision pair $((x, b), (x', b'))$. If $b = b'$, then we output "Y" (i.e., far) and otherwise, we output "N" (i.e., close). This algorithm is described in Fig. 6.

Algorithm BreakSD($1^n, (C_0, C_1)$):

1. Run $(x, b), (x', b') \leftarrow \mathcal{A}(1^n, h_{C_0, C_1})$ with fresh randomness.
2. If $b = b'$ then output "Y", and otherwise output "N".

Fig. 6. The description of the adversary BreakSD.

We next prove that when the statistical distance between C_0 and C_1 is large, then with high probability the collision will be such that $b = b'$. On the other hand, when the distributions are far, the collision will be with $b = b'$ only with bounded probability. If the gap between the events is noticeable, then our algorithm is able to decide whether C_0 and C_1 are close or far with noticeable probability which violates the average-case hardness of SD.

Before we formalize this intuition, let us set up some notation. We say that $h \in \mathcal{H}$ is "good" if the adversary $\mathcal{A}$ acts well on this h, namely,

$$\Delta\left(\mathcal{A}(1^n, h), \mathsf{COL}_h\right) \leq \delta(n).$$

Since $\mathcal{A}$ succeeds to come up with a uniform collision for all but a negligible fraction of the h's, we have that

$$\Pr_{h \leftarrow \mathcal{H}}\left[h \text{ is "good"}\right] \geq 1 - \frac{1}{n}.$$

From now on, we condition on the case that h is "good" and lose a factor of n^{-1} in the success probability. Moreover, we know that for good functions h it holds that $\mathcal{A}$ outputs a collision that is negligibly-close to COL_h. Thus, we can analyze the success probability of BreakSD with COL_h instead of $\mathcal{A}$, and at the end lose another factor of $\delta(n)$. Together, these two lost factors will not be significant since our distinguishing gap will be $\Omega(1)$.

In the following lemma we show that the probability that the adversary outputs a collision in which $b = b'$ is related to the triangular discrimination between C_0 and C_1 (see Definition 2).

Lemma 3. *It holds that*

$$\Pr[b' = b] = \frac{1}{2} + \frac{\Delta_{\mathsf{TD}}(C_0, C_1)}{4}.$$

By this lemma together with Proposition 1 (that says that the triangular discrimination is bounded from above by the statistical distance and from below by the square of the statistical distance), we get that when the statistical distance between C_0 and C_1 is at least $1 - \epsilon = 0.99$, then $\Pr[b' = b] > 0.6$, while when the statistical distance between C_0 and C_1 is at most $\epsilon = 0.01$, then $\Pr[b' = b] < 0.55$. Overall, our adversary has a noticeable distinguishing gap, as required. We prove Lemma 3 next.

Proof of Lemma 3. Let $P_y = \Pr_{x \leftarrow \{0,1\}^n}[C_0(x) = y]$ be the probability that C_0 outputs y and similarly define $Q_y = \Pr_{x \leftarrow \{0,1\}^n}[C_1(x) = y]$.

It happens that $b' = b$ if $b = b' = 0$ or if $b = b' = 1$. So, by the rule of total probability

$$\Pr[b' = b] = \Pr[b = 0] \cdot \Pr[b' = 0 \mid b = 0] + \Pr[b = 1] \cdot \Pr[b' = 1 \mid b = 1].$$

Expanding the LHS (the RHS is expanded analogously):

$$\Pr[b = 0] \cdot \Pr[b' = 0 \mid b = 0]$$

$$= \frac{1}{2} \cdot \sum_{y \in \{0,1\}^n} \Pr[b' = 0 \wedge y' = y \mid b = 0]$$

$$= \frac{1}{2} \cdot \sum_{y \in \{0,1\}^n} \Pr[b' = 0 \mid b = 0 \wedge y' = y] \cdot \Pr[y' = y \mid b = 0]$$

$$= \frac{1}{2} \cdot \sum_{y \in \{0,1\}^n} P_y \cdot \frac{P_y}{P_y + Q_y}.$$

Thus,

$$\Pr[b' = b] = \frac{1}{2} \cdot \sum_{y \in \{0,1\}^n} \frac{P_y^2}{P_y + Q_y} + \frac{1}{2} \cdot \sum_{y \in \{0,1\}^n} \frac{Q_y^2}{P_y + Q_y}. \qquad (3)$$

Let us expand the LHS (again, the RHS is expanded analogously):

$$\sum_{y \in \{0,1\}^n} \frac{P_y^2}{P_y + Q_y} = \sum_{y \in \{0,1\}^n} \frac{P_y^2 - Q_y^2 + Q_y^2}{P_y + Q_y}$$

$$= \sum_{y \in \{0,1\}^n} (P_y - Q_y) + \sum_{y \in \{0,1\}^n} \frac{Q_y^2}{P_y + Q_y}$$

$$= \sum_{y \in \{0,1\}^n} \frac{Q_y^2}{P_y + Q_y}.$$

Hence,

$$\sum_{y \in \{0,1\}^n} \frac{P_y^2}{P_y + Q_y} = \frac{1}{2} \cdot \sum_{y \in \{0,1\}^n} \frac{P_y^2 + Q_y^2}{P_y + Q_y}$$

$$= \frac{1}{4} \cdot \sum_{y \in \{0,1\}^n} \frac{(P_y + Q_y)^2}{P_y + Q_y} + \frac{1}{4} \cdot \sum_{y \in \{0,1\}^n} \frac{(P_y - Q_y)^2}{P_y + Q_y}$$

$$= \frac{1}{2} + \frac{1}{4} \cdot \sum_{y \in \{0,1\}^n} \frac{(P_y - Q_y)^2}{P_y + Q_y}.$$

By plugging this into Eq. (3), we finish the proof.

5   Open Questions and Further Research

In this work, we presented two constructions of DCRH from different assumptions. The first construction is from the existence of an MCRH. This construction is non-black-box which is necessary due to a black-box separation between the two. The other construction is from the average-case hardness of SZK. This construction is fully black-box. There are many questions still left open regarding the power of DCRH and its relation to other notions of collision resistance.

We do not know how to construct an MCRH from a dCRH. We also do not know how to separate MCRH from dCRH or even CRH from dCRH. The latter questions require coming up with a new oracle that can only be used to find collision that are far from random ones.

Another question we did not address in this work is the applicability of dCRH. Does it (existentially) imply any useful cryptographic primitive that is not implied by one-way functions?

Acknowledgments. We thank the anonymous reviewers of CRYPTO 2018 for their elaborate and useful comments. We are grateful to Itay Berman and Ron Rothblum for explaining how to use triangular discrimination in the analysis in Theorem 2. We also thank Moni Naor and Rafael Pass for useful discussions.

References

1. Asharov, G., Segev, G.: Limits on the power of indistinguishability obfuscation and functional encryption. SIAM J. Comput. **45**(6), 2117–2176 (2016)
2. Barak, B.: How to go beyond the black-box simulation barrier. In: 42nd Annual Symposium on Foundations of Computer Science, FOCS, pp. 106–115 (2001)
3. Barak, B., Ong, S.J., Vadhan, S.P.: Derandomization in cryptography. SIAM J. Comput. **37**(2), 380–400 (2007)
4. Beaver, D.: Correlated pseudorandomness and the complexity of private computations. In: Proceedings of the Twenty-Eighth Annual ACM Symposium on the Theory of Computing, pp. 479–488. ACM (1996)
5. Berman, I., Degwekar, A., Rothblum, R.D., Vasudevan, P.N.: Multi-collision resistant hash functions and their applications. In: Nielsen, J.B., Rijmen, V. (eds.) EUROCRYPT 2018. LNCS, vol. 10821, pp. 133–161. Springer, Cham (2018). https://doi.org/10.1007/978-3-319-78375-8_5
6. Bitansky, N., Degwekar, A., Vaikuntanathan, V.: Structure vs. hardness through the obfuscation lens. In: Katz, J., Shacham, H. (eds.) CRYPTO 2017. LNCS, vol. 10401, pp. 696–723. Springer, Cham (2017). https://doi.org/10.1007/978-3-319-63688-7_23
7. Bitansky, N., Kalai, Y.T., Paneth, O.: Multi-collision resistance: a paradigm for keyless hash functions. IACR Cryptology ePrint Archive 2017, 488 (2017). (To appear in STOC 2018)
8. Bitansky, N., Nishimaki, R., Passelègue, A., Wichs, D.: From cryptomania to obfustopia through secret-key functional encryption. In: Hirt, M., Smith, A. (eds.) TCC 2016. LNCS, vol. 9986, pp. 391–418. Springer, Heidelberg (2016). https://doi.org/10.1007/978-3-662-53644-5_15
9. Bogdanov, A., Lee, C.H.: Limits of provable security for homomorphic encryption. In: Canetti, R., Garay, J.A. (eds.) CRYPTO 2013. LNCS, vol. 8042, pp. 111–128. Springer, Heidelberg (2013). https://doi.org/10.1007/978-3-642-40041-4_7
10. Brakerski, Z., Komargodski, I., Segev, G.: Multi-input functional encryption in the private-key setting: stronger security from weaker assumptions. In: Fischlin, M.,

Coron, J.-S. (eds.) EUROCRYPT 2016. LNCS, vol. 9666, pp. 852–880. Springer, Heidelberg (2016). https://doi.org/10.1007/978-3-662-49896-5_30

11. Döttling, N., Garg, S.: Identity-based encryption from the Diffie-Hellman assumption. In: Katz, J., Shacham, H. (eds.) CRYPTO 2017. LNCS, vol. 10401, pp. 537–569. Springer, Cham (2017). https://doi.org/10.1007/978-3-319-63688-7_18

12. Dubrov, B., Ishai, Y.: On the randomness complexity of efficient sampling. In: Proceedings of the 38th Annual ACM Symposium on Theory of Computing, pp. 711–720. ACM (2006)

13. Dvir, Z., Gutfreund, D., Rothblum, G.N., Vadhan, S.P.: On approximating the entropy of polynomial mappings. In: Innovations in Computer Science - ICS, pp. 460–475 (2011)

14. Fortnow, L., Santhanam, R.: Infeasibility of instance compression and succinct pcps for NP. J. Comput. Syst. Sci. **77**(1), 91–106 (2011)

15. Garg, S., Mahmoody, M., Mohammed, A.: Lower bounds on obfuscation from all-or-nothing encryption primitives. In: Katz, J., Shacham, H. (eds.) CRYPTO 2017. LNCS, vol. 10401, pp. 661–695. Springer, Cham (2017). https://doi.org/10.1007/978-3-319-63688-7_22

16. Goldreich, O., Sahai, A., Vadhan, S.: Can statistical zero knowledge be made non-interactive? Or on the relationship of SZK and NISZK. In: Wiener, M. (ed.) CRYPTO 1999. LNCS, vol. 1666, pp. 467–484. Springer, Heidelberg (1999). https://doi.org/10.1007/3-540-48405-1_30

17. Goldreich, O., Vadhan, S.P.: Comparing entropies in statistical zero knowledge with applications to the structure of SZK. In: Proceedings of the 14th Annual IEEE Conference on Computational Complexity, p. 54. IEEE Computer Society (1999)

18. Goldwasser, S., Micali, S., Rackoff, C.: The knowledge complexity of interactive proof systems. SIAM J. Comput. **18**(1), 186–208 (1989)

19. Harnik, D., Naor, M.: On the compressibility of NP instances and cryptographic applications. SIAM J. Comput. **39**(5), 1667–1713 (2010)

20. Impagliazzo, R., Luby, M.: One-way functions are essential for complexity based cryptography (extended abstract). In: 30th Annual Symposium on Foundations of Computer Science, FOCS, pp. 230–235. IEEE Computer Society (1989)

21. Impagliazzo, R., Rudich, S.: Limits on the provable consequences of one-way permutations. In: Proceedings of the 21st Annual ACM Symposium on Theory of Computing, 14–17 May 1989, Seattle, Washington, USA, pp. 44–61. ACM (1989)

22. Komargodski, I., Naor, M., Yogev, E.: White-box vs. black-box complexity of search problems: ramsey and graph property testing. In: 58th IEEE Annual Symposium on Foundations of Computer Science, FOCS, pp. 622–632 (2017)

23. Komargodski, I., Naor, M., Yogev, E.: Collision resistant hashing for paranoids: dealing with multiple collisions. In: Nielsen, J.B., Rijmen, V. (eds.) EUROCRYPT 2018. LNCS, vol. 10821, pp. 162–194. Springer, Cham (2018). https://doi.org/10.1007/978-3-319-78375-8_6

24. Komargodski, I., Segev, G.: From minicrypt to obfustopia via private-key functional encryption. In: Coron, J.-S., Nielsen, J.B. (eds.) EUROCRYPT 2017. LNCS, vol. 10210, pp. 122–151. Springer, Cham (2017). https://doi.org/10.1007/978-3-319-56620-7_5

25. Lin, H.: Indistinguishability obfuscation from constant-degree graded encoding schemes. In: Fischlin, M., Coron, J.-S. (eds.) EUROCRYPT 2016. LNCS, vol. 9665, pp. 28–57. Springer, Heidelberg (2016). https://doi.org/10.1007/978-3-662-49890-3_2

26. Lin, H.: Indistinguishability obfuscation from SXDH on 5-linear maps and locality-5 PRGs. In: Katz, J., Shacham, H. (eds.) CRYPTO 2017. LNCS, vol. 10401, pp. 599–629. Springer, Cham (2017). https://doi.org/10.1007/978-3-319-63688-7_20

27. Lin, H., Tessaro, S.: Indistinguishability obfuscation from trilinear maps and block-wise local PRGs. In: Katz, J., Shacham, H. (eds.) CRYPTO 2017. LNCS, vol. 10401, pp. 630–660. Springer, Cham (2017). https://doi.org/10.1007/978-3-319-63688-7_21

28. Lin, H., Vaikuntanathan, V.: Indistinguishability obfuscation from DDH-like assumptions on constant-degree graded encodings. In: IEEE 57th Annual Symposium on Foundations of Computer Science, FOCS, pp. 11–20. IEEE Computer Society (2016)

29. Liu, T., Vaikuntanathan, V.: On basing private information retrieval on NP-hardness. In: Kushilevitz, E., Malkin, T. (eds.) TCC 2016. LNCS, vol. 9562, pp. 372–386. Springer, Heidelberg (2016). https://doi.org/10.1007/978-3-662-49096-9_16

30. Mahmoody, M., Mohammed, A., Nematihaji, S., Pass, R., Shelat, A.: Lower bounds on assumptions behind indistinguishability obfuscation. In: Kushilevitz, E., Malkin, T. (eds.) TCC 2016. LNCS, vol. 9562, pp. 49–66. Springer, Heidelberg (2016). https://doi.org/10.1007/978-3-662-49096-9_3

31. Mahmoody, M., Pass, R.: The curious case of non-interactive commitments – on the power of black-box vs. non-black-box use of primitives. In: Safavi-Naini, R., Canetti, R. (eds.) CRYPTO 2012. LNCS, vol. 7417, pp. 701–718. Springer, Heidelberg (2012). https://doi.org/10.1007/978-3-642-32009-5_41

32. Ostrovsky, R.: One-way functions, hard on average problems, and statistical zero-knowledge proofs. In: Structure in Complexity Theory Conference, pp. 133–138. IEEE Computer Society (1991)

33. Sahai, A., Vadhan, S.P.: A complete problem for statistical zero knowledge. J. ACM **50**(2), 196–249 (2003)

34. Simon, D.R.: Finding collisions on a one-way street: can secure hash functions be based on general assumptions? In: Nyberg, K. (ed.) EUROCRYPT 1998. LNCS, vol. 1403, pp. 334–345. Springer, Heidelberg (1998). https://doi.org/10.1007/BFb0054137

35. Topsøe, F.: Some inequalities for information divergence and related measures of discrimination. IEEE Trans. Inf. Theory **46**(4), 1602–1609 (2000). https://doi.org/10.1109/18.850703

Trapdoor Functions

Fast Distributed RSA Key Generation for Semi-honest and Malicious Adversaries

Tore Kasper Frederiksen[1], Yehuda Lindell[2,3(✉)], Valery Osheter[3], and Benny Pinkas[2]

[1] Security Lab, Alexandra Institute, Aarhus, Denmark
`tore.frederiksen@alexandra.dk`
[2] Department of Computer Science, Bar-Ilan University, Ramat Gan, Israel
`yehuda.lindell@biu.ac.il, benny@pinkas.net`
[3] Unbound Tech Ltd., Petach Tikva, Israel
`valery.osheter@unboundtech.com`

Abstract. We present two new, highly efficient, protocols for securely generating a distributed RSA key pair in the two-party setting. One protocol is semi-honestly secure and the other maliciously secure. Both are constant round and do not rely on any specific number-theoretic assumptions and improve significantly over the state-of-the-art by allowing a slight leakage (which we show to not affect security).

For our maliciously secure protocol our most significant improvement comes from executing most of the protocol in a "strong" semi-honest manner and then doing a single, light, zero-knowledge argument of correct execution. We introduce other significant improvements as well. One such improvement arrives in showing that certain, limited leakage does not compromise security, which allows us to use lightweight subprotocols. Another improvement, which may be of independent interest, comes in our approach for multiplying two large integers using OT, in the malicious setting, without being susceptible to a selective-failure attack.

Finally, we implement our malicious protocol and show that its performance is an order of magnitude better than the best previous protocol, which provided only *semi-honest* security.

1 Introduction

RSA [RSA78] is the oldest, publicly known, public key encryption scheme. This scheme allows a server to generate a public/private key pair, s.t. any client

T. K. Frederiksen—The majority of the work was done while at Bar-Ilan University, Israel.

Tore, Yehuda and Benny were supported by the BIU Center for Research in Applied Cryptography and Cyber Security in conjunction with the Israel National Cyber Bureau in the Prime Minsters Office. Yehuda and Benny were also been funded by the Israel Science Foundation (grant No. 1018/16). Tore has also received funding from the European Union's Horizon 2020 research and innovation programme under grant agreement No. 731583.

H. Shacham and A. Boldyreva (Eds.): CRYPTO 2018, LNCS 10992, pp. 331–361, 2018.
https://doi.org/10.1007/978-3-319-96881-0_12

knowing the public key can use this to encrypt a message, which can only be decrypted using the private key. Thus the server can disclose the public key and keep the private key secret. This allows anyone to encrypt a message, which only the server itself can decrypt. Even though RSA has quite a few years on its back, it is still in wide use today such as in TLS, where it keeps web-browsing safe through HTTPS. Its technical backbone can also be used to realize digital signatures and as such is used in PGP. However, public key cryptography, RSA in particular, is also a primitive in itself, widely used in more complex cryptographic constructions such as distributed signature schemes [Sho00], (homomorphic) threshold cryptosystems [HMRT12] and even general MPC [CDN01]. Unfortunately, these complex applications are not in the client-server setting, but in the setting of several distrusting parties, and thus require the private key to be secretly shared between the parties. This is known as *distributed key generation* and in order to do this, without a trusted third party, is no easy feat. Even assuming the parties act semi-honestly, and thus follow the prescribed protocol, it is a slow procedure as the fastest known implementation takes 15 min for 2048 bit keys [HMRT12]. For the malicious setting we are unaware of previous implementation. However, in many practical settings such a key sharing only needs to be done once for a static set of parties, where the key pair is then used repeatedly afterwards. Thus, a setup time of 15 min is acceptable, even if it is not desirable. Still, there are concrete settings where this is not acceptable.

Motivation. In the world of MPC there are many cases where a setup time of more than a few seconds is unacceptable. For example consider the case of a static server and a client, with a physical user behind it, wishing to carry out some instant, ad-hoc computation. Or the setting where several users meet and want to carry out an auction of a specific item. In these cases, and any case where a specific set of participating parties will only carry out few computations, it is not acceptable for the users to wait more than 15 min before they start computing. In such cases only a few seconds would be acceptable.

However, if a maliciously secure shared RSA key pairs could be generated in a few seconds, another possible application appears as well: being able to generate public key pairs in an enterprise setting, without the use of a Hardware Security Module (HSM). A HSM is a trusted piece of hardware pervasively used in the enterprise setting to construct and store cryptographic keys, guaranteed to be correct and leakage free. However, these modules are slow and expensive, and in general reflects a single point of failure. For this reason several companies, such as Unbound and Sepior have worked on realizing HSM functionality in a distributed manner, using MPC and secret-sharing. This removes the single point of failure, since computation and storage will be distributed between physically separated machines, running different operating systems and having different system administrators. Thus if one machine gets fully compromised by an adversary, the overall security of the generated keys will not be affected. This has been done successfully for the generation of symmetric keys, which usually does not need a specific mathematical structure. Unfortunately, doing this for RSA keys is not so easy. However, being able to generate a key pair with the private key secretly shared will realize this functionality. But for such a distributed system to be able to work properly in an enterprise setting such generation tasks must be completed in a matter of seconds.

In this paper we take a big step towards being able to generate a shared RSA key between two parties in a matter of seconds, *even* if one of the parties is acting maliciously and not following the prescribed protocol. Thus opening up for realizing the applications mentioned above.

The Setting. We consider two parties P_1 and P_2 whose goal is to generate an RSA modulus of a certain length, such that the knowledge of the private key is additively shared among them. Namely, the parties wish to compute the following:

Common input: A parameter ℓ describing the desired bits of the primes in an RSA modulus, and a public exponent e.

Common output: A modulus N of length 2ℓ bits.

Private outputs: P_1 learns outputs p_1, q_1, d_1, and P_2 learns outputs p_2, q_2, d_2, for which it holds that
- $(p_1 + p_2)$ and $(q_1 + q_2)$ are prime numbers of length ℓ bits.
- $N = (p_1 + p_2) \cdot (q_1 + q_2)$.
- $e \cdot (d_1 + d_2) = 1 \mod \phi(N)$.
  (Namely, $(d_1 + d_2)$ is the RSA private key for (N, e).)

Furthermore, we want the functionality to work (or abort) even if one of the parties is not following the protocol. That is, in the *malicious* setting.

Distributed RSA Key Generation. It turns out that all prior work follows a common structure for distributed RSA key generation. Basically, since there is no efficient algorithm for constructing random primes, what is generally done is simply to pick random, odd numbers, and hope they are prime. However, the Prime Number Theorem tells us that this is not very likely. In fact, for numbers of the size needed for RSA, the probability that a random odd number is prime is around one in 350. Thus to generate an RSA key, many random prime candidates must be generated and tested in some way. Pairs of prime candidates must then be multiplied together to construct a modulus candidate. Depending on whether the tests of the prime candidates involve ensuring that a candidate is prime except with negligible probability, or only that it is somewhat likely to be prime, the modulus candidate must also be tested to ensure that it is the product of two primes. We briefly outline this general structure below:

Candidate Generation: The parties generate random additive shares of potential prime numbers. This may involve ensuring that a candidate is prime except with negligible probability, insuring that the candidate does not contain small prime factors, or simply that it is just an odd number.

Construct Modulus: Two candidates are multiplied together to construct a candidate modulus.

Verify Modulus: This involves ensuring that the public modulus is the product of two primes. However, this is not needed if the prime candidates were guaranteed to be prime (except with negligible probability).

Construct Keys: Using the additive shares of the prime candidates, along with the modulus, the shared RSA key pair is generated.

With this overall structure in mind we consider the chronology of efficient distributed RSA key generation.

Related Work. Work on efficient distributed RSA key generation was started with the seminal result of Boneh and Franklin [BF01]. A key part of their result is an efficient algorithm for verifying biprimality of a modulus without knowledge of its factors. Unfortunately, their protocol is only secure in the semi-honest setting, against an honest majority. Several followup works handle both the malicious and/or dishonest majority setting [PS98, FMY98, Gil99, ACS02, DM10, HMRT12, Gav12]. First Frankel *et al.* [FMY98] showed how to achieve malicious security against a dishonest minority. Their protocol proceeds like Boneh and Franklin's scheme [BF01], but uses different types of secret sharing along with zero-knowledge arguments to construct the modulus and do the biprimality test in a malicious secure manner. Furthermore, for their simulation proof to go through, they also require that all candidate shares are committed to using an equivocable commitment. Poupard and Stern [PS98] strengthened this result to achieve security against a malicious majority (specifically the two-party setting) using 1-out-of-β OT, with some allowed leakage though. Later Gilboa [Gil99] showed how to get semi-honest security in the dishonest majority (specifically two-party) setting. Gilboa's approach follows along the lines of Boneh and Franklin's protocol [BF01], by using their approach for biprimality testing, but also introduces three new efficient approaches for computing the modulus from additive shares: one based on homomorphic encryption, one based on oblivious polynomial evaluation and one based on oblivious transfer. Both Algesheimer *et al.* [ACS02] and Damgård and Mikkelsen [DM10] instead do a full primality test of the prime candidates individually, rather than a biprimality test of the modulus. In particular the protocol of Algesheimer *et al.* [ACS02] is secure in the semi-honest setting (but can be made malicious secure) against a dishonest minority, and executes a distributed Rabin-Miller primality test using polynomial secret sharing with $\Theta(\log(N))$ round complexity, where N is the public modulus. On the other hand Damgård and Mikkelsen's protocol [DM10] is maliciously secure against a dishonest minority and also executes a distributed Rabin-Miller test, using a special type of verifiable secret sharing called replicated secret sharing which allows them to achieve constant round complexity. Later Hazay *et al.* [HMRT12] introduced a practical protocol maliciously secure against a dishonest majority (in the two-party setting), which is leakage-free. More specifically their protocol is based on the homomorphic encryption approach from Gilboa's work [Gil99], but adds zero-knowledge proofs on top of all the steps to ensure security against malicious parties. However, they conjectured that it would be sufficient to only prove correctness of a constructed modulus. This conjecture was confirmed correct by Gavin [Gav12]. In his work Gavin showed how to build a maliciously secure protocol against a dishonest majority (the two-party setting) by having black-box access to methods for generating a modulus candidate which might be incorrect, but is guaranteed to not leak info on the honest party's shares. The protocol then verifies the execution for every failed candidate and for the success modulus a variant of the Boneh and Franklin biprimality test [BF01] is carried out in a maliciously secure manner by using homomorphic encryption and zero-knowledge.

Contributions. We present two new protocols for distributed RSA key generation. One for the semi-honest setting and one for the malicious setting. Neither of our protocols rely on any specific number theoretic assumptions, but instead are based on oblivious transfer (OT), which can be realized efficiently using an OT extension protocol [KOS15, OOS17]. The malicious secure protocol also requires access to an IND-CPA encryption scheme, coin-tossing, zero-knowledge and secure two-party computation protocols. In fact, using OT extension significantly reduces the amount of public key operations required by our protocols. This is also true for the maliciously secure protocol as secure two-party computation (and thus zero-knowledge) can be done black-box based on OT.

We show that our maliciously secure protocols is more than an order of magnitude faster than its competitor. We achieve malicious security so cheaply mainly by executing a slightly stronger version of our semi-honest protocol and adding a new, lightweight zero-knowledge argument at the end, to ensure that the parties have behaved honestly. This overall idea has been hypothesized [HMRT12] and affirmed [Gav12]. However, unlike previous approaches in this paradigm [DM10, Gav12] our approach does not require rerunning and verifying the honesty of candidates that are discarded, thus increasing efficiency. We achieve this by introducing a new ideal functionality which gives the adversary slightly more (yet useless) power than normally allowed. This idea may be of independent interest as it is relevant for other schemes where many candidate values are constructed and potentially discarded throughout the protocol. We furthermore show how to eliminate much computation in the malicious setting by allowing a few bits of leakage on the honest party's prime shares. We carefully argue that this does not help an adversary in a non-negligible manner.

We also introduce a new and efficient approach to avoid selective failure attacks when using Gilboa's protocol [Gil99] for multiplying two large integers together. We believe this approach may be of independent interest as well.

Finally, we present an implementation of our maliciously secure protocol, showing it to be an order of magnitude faster than the most efficient previous *semi-honest* protocol [HMRT12]. In particular, a four thread implementation takes on average less than 40 s to generate a maliciously secure 2048 bit key, whereas the protocol of Hazay *et al.* [HMRT12] on average required 15 min for a *semi-honestly* secure 2048 bit key.

2   Preliminaries

Our protocols use several standard building blocks, namely oblivious transfer, and for the maliciously secure protocol, coin-tossing, an IND-CPA encryption scheme, a zero-knowledge protocol along with secure two-party computation. We here formalize these building blocks.

FIGURE 2.1 $(\mathcal{F}_{\mathsf{OT}}^{\ell,\beta})$

Functionality interacts with a sender **snd** and receiver **rec**. It is initialized with the public values $\ell, \beta \in \mathbb{N}$. It proceeds as follows:

- Upon receiving (**transfer**) from **snd** and (**receive**, i) from **rec** with $i \in \{0, \ldots, \beta - 1\}$ the functionality picks uniformly random values $m_0, \ldots, m_{\beta-1} \in \{0,1\}^{\ell}$ and sends (**transfer**, $m_0, \ldots, m_{\beta-1}$) to **snd** and (**transfer**, m_i) to **rec**.
- If a party is maliciously corrupted then it will receive its output first and if it returns the message (**deliver**) then the functionality will give the honest party its output, otherwise if the corrupted party returns the message (**abort**), then output (**abort**) to the honest party.

Ideal functionality for random oblivious transfer

Random OT. Our protocol relies heavily on random OT both in the candidate generation and construction of modulus phases. The functionality of random OT is described in Fig. 2.1. Specifically we suffice with a functionality that samples the sender's messages at random and lets the receiver choose which one of these random messages it wishes to learn. Random OTs of this form can be realized highly efficiently based on an *OT extension*, which uses a small number of "base" OTs to implement any polynomial number of OTs using symmetric cryptography operations alone. The state-of-the-art 1-out-of-2 OT extension is given by Keller *et al.* [KOS15] and for 1-out-of-β OT, by Orrù *et al.* [OOS17]. In some cases we need the sender to be able to specifically choose its messages. However, this is easily achieved by using the random OT-model as a black box and we will sometimes abuse notation and assume that $\mathcal{F}_{\mathsf{OT}}^{\ell,\beta}$ supports specific messages, by allowing the sender to input the message (**transfer**, $a_0, \ldots, a_{\beta-1}$), and the receiver receiving message (**transfer**, a_i).

AES. Our maliciously secure scheme also requires usage of AES. However, any symmetric encryption scheme will do as long as it is a block-cipher (with blocks of at least κ bits) and can be assumed to be a pseudo-random permutation (PRP) and used in a mode that is IND-CPA secure. We will denote this scheme by $\mathsf{AES} : \{0,1\}^{\kappa} \times \{0,1\}^* \to \{0,1\}^*$ and have that $\mathsf{AES}_K^{-1}(\mathsf{AES}_K(M)) = M$ when $K \in \{0,1\}^{\kappa}, M \in \{0,1\}^*$.

Coin-tossing. We require a coin-tossing functionality several places in our maliciously secure protocols. Such a functionality samples a uniformly random element from a specific set and hands it to both parties. We formally capture the needed functionality in Fig. 2.2.

Zero-Knowledge Argument-of-Knowledge. As part of the setup phase of our malicious protocol we need both parties to prove knowledge of a specific piece of information. For this purpose we require a zero-knowledge argument-of-knowledge. More formally, let $L \subset \{0,1\}^*$ be a publicly known language in NP and M_L be a language verification function of this language i.e. for all $x \in L$ there exist

---

FIGURE 2.2 ($\mathcal{F}_{\mathsf{CT}}$)

Functionality interacts with P_1 and P_2. Upon receiving (**toss**, $\mathbb{R}$) from both parties, where $\mathbb{R}$ is a description of a ring, sample a uniformly random element $x \in \mathbb{R}$ and send (**random**, x) to both parties.

Corruption: If a party is corrupt, then send (**random**, x) to this party first, and if it returns the message (**deliver**) then send (**random**, x) to the other party, otherwise if the corrupted party returns the message (**abort**) then output (**abort**) to the honest party.

Ideal functionality for coin-tossing

FIGURE 2.3 ($\mathcal{F}_{\mathsf{ZK}}^{M_L}$)

Functionality interacts with two parties P and V. It is initialized on a deterministic polytime language verification function $M_L : \{0,1\}^* \times \{0,1\}^* \to \{\top, \bot\}$. It proceeds as follows:

- On input (**prove**, x, w) from P and (**verify**, x') from V. If $x = x'$ and $M_L(x, w) = \top$ output ($\top$) to V, otherwise output ($\bot$).

Ideal functionality for zero-knowledge argument-of-knowledge

a string w of length polynomial in the size of x s.t. $M_L(x, w) = \top$ and for all $x \notin L, w \in \{0,1\}^*$ then $M_L(x, w) = \bot$. Thus this function outputs $\top$ if and only if w is a string that verifies that x belongs to the language L. We use this to specify the notion of a zero-knowledge argument-of-knowledge that a publicly known value $x \in L$. Specifically one party, P the prover, knows a witness w and wish to convince the other party, V the verifier, that $M_L(x, w) = \top$ without revealing any information on w.

We formalize this in Fig. 2.3 and note that such a functionality can be realized very efficiently using garbled circuits [JKO13] or using the "MPC-in-the-head" approach [GMO16].

Two-party Computation. We use a maliciously secure two-party computation functionality in our protocol. For completeness we here formalize the ideal functionality we need for this in Fig. 2.4. Such a functionality can be implemented efficiently in constant rounds using a garbled circuit protocol [Lin16].

Notation. We let κ be the computational security parameter and s the statistical security parameter. We use ℓ to denote the amount of bits in a prime factor of an RSA modulus. Thus $\ell \geq \kappa$. We use $[a]$ to denote the list of integers $1, 2, \ldots, a$. We will sometimes abuse notation and implicitly view bit strings as a non-negative integer.

FIGURE 2.4 ($\mathcal{F}_{\mathsf{2PC}}^{f}$)

Functionality interacts with two parties P_1 and P_2. It is initialized on a deterministic polytime function $f : \{0,1\}^{n_1+n_2} \rightarrow \{0,1\}^{m_1+m_2}$. It proceeds as follows:

Input: On input $(\texttt{input}, x_{\mathcal{I}})$ from $P_{\mathcal{I}}$ where $x_{\mathcal{I}} \in \{0,1\}^{n_{\mathcal{I}}}$, where no message $(\texttt{input}, \cdot)$ was given by $P_{\mathcal{I}}$ before, store $x_{\mathcal{I}}$.

Output: After having received messages $(\texttt{input}, \cdot)$ from both P_1 and P_2, compute $y_1 \| y_2 = y = f(x)$ where $x = x_1 \| x_2$ and $y_1 \in \{0,1\}^{m_1}$, $y_2 \in \{0,1\}^{m_2}$. Then return $(\texttt{output}, y_1)$ to P_1 and $(\texttt{output}, y_2)$ to P_2.

Corruption: If party $P_{\mathcal{I}}$ is corrupt, then it is given $y_{\mathcal{I}}$ from the functionality before $y_{3-\mathcal{I}}$ is given to $P_{3-\mathcal{I}}$. If $P_{\mathcal{I}}$ returns the message $(\texttt{deliver})$ then send $y_{3-\mathcal{I}}$ to party $P_{\mathcal{I}}$, otherwise if $P_{3-\mathcal{I}}$ returns the message $(\texttt{abort})$ then output $(\texttt{abort})$ to $P_{\mathcal{I}}$.

Ideal functionality for two-party computation

3 Construction

This section details constructions of protocols for two-party RSA key generation. We first describe in Sect. 3.1 the general structure of our protocols. We describe in Sect. 3.2 a protocol for the semi-honest setting which is considerably more efficient than previous protocols for this task. Finally, we describe in Sect. 3.3 our efficient protocol which is secure against a malicious adversary.

3.1 Protocol Structure

Following previous protocols for RSA key generation, as described in Sect. 1, the key generation protocol is composed of the following phases:

Candidate Generation: In this step, the two parties choose random shares p_1 and p_2, respectively, with the hope that $p_1 + p_2$ is prime. For our maliciously secure protocol they also commit to their choices. The parties then run a secure protocol, based on 1-out-of-β OT, which rules out the possibility that $p_1 + p_2$ is divisible by any prime number smaller than some pre-agreed threshold B_1. We call this the first *trial division*.

If $p_1 + p_2$ is not divisible by any such prime then it passed on to the next stage, otherwise it is discarded.

Construct Modulus: Given shares of two candidate primes p_1, p_2 and q_1, q_2, the parties run a secure protocol, based on 1-out-of-2 OT, which computes the candidate modulus $N = (p_1 + p_2)(q_1 + q_2)$. The output N is learned by both parties.

Verify Modulus: This step consists of two phases in our semi-honest protocol and three phases in the malicious protocol. Both protocols proceeds s.t. once N is revealed and in the open, the parties run a second *trial division*, by locally checking that no primes smaller than a threshold B_2 ($B_1 < B_2$) are a factor of N. If N is divisible by such a number then N is definitely not a valid RSA modulus and is discarded. For an N not discarded, the parties run a secure *biprimality test* which verifies that N is the product of two primes. If it is not, it is discarded. For the malicious protocol, a *proof of honesty* phase is added to ensure that N is constructed in accordance with the commitments from *Candidate Generation* and that N is indeed a biprime, constructed using the "correct" shares, even if one party has acted maliciously.

Construct Keys: Up to this point, the parties generated the modulus N. Based on the value $\Phi(N) \bmod e$ and their prime shares p_1, q_1, respectively p_2, q_2, the parties can locally compute their shares of the secret key d_1, respectively d_2 s.t. $e \cdot (d_1 + d_2) = 1 \bmod \phi(N)$.

In principle, the protocol could run without the first and second trial division phases. Namely, the parties could choose their shares, compute N and run the biprimality test to check whether N is the product of two primes. The goal of the trial division tests is to reduce the overall run time of the protocol: Checking whether p is divisible by β, filters out $1/\beta$ of the candidate prime factors, and reduces, by a factor of $1 - 1/\beta$, the number of times that the other phases of the protocol need to run. It is easy to see that trial divisions provide diminishing returns as β increases. The thresholds B_1, B_2 must therefore be set to minimize the overall run time of the protocol.

The phases of the protocol are similar to those in previous work that was described in Sect. 1. Our protocol has two major differences: (1) Almost all cryptographic operations are replaced by the usage of OT extension, which is considerably more efficient than public key operations was has been used previously. (2) Security against malicious adversaries is achieved efficiently, by observing that most of checks that are executed in the protocol can be run while being secure only against semi-honest adversaries, assuming privacy is kept against malicious attacks and as long as the final checks that are applied to the chosen modulus N are secure against malicious adversaries.

3.2   The Semi-honest Construction

The protocol consists of the phases described in Sect. 3.1, and is described in Figs. 3.2 and 3.3. These phases are implemented in the following way:

Candidate Generation: The parties P_1 and P_2 choose private random strings p_1 and p_2, respectively, of length $\ell - 1$ bits, subject to the constraint that the two least significant bits of p_1 are 11, and the two least significant bits of p_2 are 0 (this ensures that the sum of the two shares is equal to 3 modulo 4).

The parties now check, for each prime number $3 \leq \beta \leq B_1$, that $(p_1 + p_2) \neq 0 \bmod \beta$. In other words, if we use the notation $a_1 = p_1 \bmod \beta$ and $a_2 = -p_2 \bmod \beta$, then the parties need to run a secure protocol verifying that $a_1 \neq a_2$.

Previous approaches for doing this involved using a modified BGW protocol [BF01], Diffie-Hellman based public key operations (which have to be implemented over relatively long moduli, rather than in elliptic-curve based groups) [HMRT12], and using a 1-out-of-β OT [PS98]. We take our point of

---

FIGURE 3.1 (OT-divisibility Test)

The parties have common input $\beta \in \mathbb{N}$ and P_1 has $p_1 \in \mathbb{N}$ and P_2 has $p_2 \in \mathbb{N}$. The procedure returns $\perp$ iff $\beta | (p_1 + p_2)$, otherwise it returns $\top$.

1. P_2 inputs (**transfer**) to $\mathcal{F}_{\mathsf{OT}}^{\kappa,\beta}$ and learns random messages $\{m_i\}_{i \in [\beta]}$.
2. P_1 computes $a_1 = p_1 \bmod \beta$ and inputs (**receive**, a_1) to $\mathcal{F}_{\mathsf{OT}}^{\kappa,\beta}$ and gets output (**deliver**, m_{a_1}).
3. P_2 lets $a_2 = -p_2 \bmod \beta$ and sends m_{a_2} to P_1.
4. P_1 checks whether $m_{a_1} = m_{a_2}$ and outputs $\perp$ and sends it to P_2 if this is the case, otherwise it outputs $\top$ and sends this to P_2.

The 1-out-of-β OT based trial division procedure

departure in the latter approach, but improve the efficiency by having a lower level of abstraction and using an efficient random OT extension. We describe our approach by procedure Div-OT in Fig. 3.1.

The parties run this test for each prime $3 \leq \beta \leq B_1$ in increasing order (where B_1 is the pre-agreed threshold). Note that the probability that the shares are filtered by the test is $1/\beta$ and therefore the test provides diminishing returns as β increases. The threshold B_1 is chosen to optimize the overall performance of the entire protocol.

Construct Modulus: Once two numbers pass the previous test, the parties have shares of two candidate primes p_1, p_2 and q_1, q_2. They then run a secure protocol which computes the candidate modulus

$$N = (p_1 + p_2)(q_1 + q_2) = p_1 q_1 + p_2 q_2 + p_1 q_2 + p_2 q_1.$$

The multiplication $p_1 q_1$ (resp. $p_2 q_2$) is computed by P_1 (resp. P_2) by itself. The other two multiplications are computed by running a protocol by Gilboa [Gil99], which reduces the multiplication of $\ell - 1$ bit long numbers to $\ell - 1$ invocations of 1-out-of-2 OTs, implemented using an efficient OT extension. The protocol works as follows: Assume that the sender's input is a and that the receiver's input is b, and that they must compute shares of $a \cdot b$. Let the binary representation of b be $b = b_{\ell-1}, \ldots, b_2, b_1$. For each bit the two parties run a 1-out-of-2 OT protocol where the sender's inputs are $(r_i, (r_i + a) \bmod 2^{2\ell})$, and the receiver's input is b_i, where r_i is a random $2^{2\ell}$ bit integer. Denote the receiver's output as $c_i = r_i + a \cdot b_i \bmod 2^{2\ell}$. It is easy to verify that

$$a \cdot b = \left(\sum_{i \in [\ell-1]} 2^{i-1} \cdot c_i \right) + \left(\sum_{i \in [\ell-1]} -2^{i-1} \cdot r_i \right).$$

These will therefore be the two outputs of the multiplication protocol. We implement this protocol based on random OT.

After constructing the modulus, the parties verify that the public exponent e will work with this specific modulus. I.e. that $\gcd(\phi(N), e) = 1$. Namely, that $\gcd(N - p - q + 1, e) = 1$. This is done in the same manner as Boneh and Franklin [BF01], where P_1 computes $w_1 = N + 1 - p_1 - q_1 \bmod e$ and P_2

computes $w_2 = p_2 + q_2 \mod e$. The parties exchange the values w_1 and w_2 and then verify that $w_1 \neq w_2$. If instead $w_1 = w_2$ it means that e is a factor of $\phi(N)$ and the parties discard the candidate shares.

PROTOCOL 3.2 (Semi-honest Key Generation $\Pi_{\text{RSA-semi}}$ - Part 1)

Candidate Generation

1. P_1 picks a uniformly random value $\tilde{p}_1 \in \mathbb{Z}_{2^{\ell-3}}$ and defines $p_1 = 4 \cdot \tilde{p}_1 + 3$.
2. P_2 picks a uniformly random value $\tilde{p}_2 \in \mathbb{Z}_{2^{\ell-3}}$ and defines $p_2 = 4\tilde{p}_2$.
3. Let $\mathcal{B} = \{\beta \leq B_1 | \beta \text{ is prime}\}$. The parties execute procedure Div-OT in Fig. 3.1 for each $\beta \in \mathcal{B}$, where P_1 uses input p_1 and P_2 input p_2. If any of these calls output $\perp$, then discard the candidate pair p_1, p_2.

Construct Modulus

Let p_1, q_1, p_2, q_2 be two candidates that passed the generation phase above, where P_1 knows $p_1 = 4 \cdot \tilde{p}_1 + 3, q_1 = 4 \cdot \tilde{q}_1 + 3$ and P_2 knows $p_2 = 4 \cdot \tilde{p}_2, q_2 = 4 \cdot \tilde{q}_2$.

1. The parties execute the following steps for each $\alpha \in \{p, q\}$ and $i \in [\ell - 1]$:
   (a) P_2 chooses a uniformly random value $r_{\alpha,i} \in \mathbb{Z}_{2^{2\ell}}$ and sets $c_{0,\alpha,i} = r_{\alpha,i}$ and
   $$c_{1,\alpha,i} = \begin{cases} r_{\alpha,i} + q_2 \mod 2^{2\ell} & \text{if } \alpha = p \\ r_{\alpha,i} + p_2 \mod 2^{2\ell} & \text{if } \alpha = q \end{cases}$$
   (b) P_2 invokes $\mathcal{F}_{\text{OT}}^{2\ell,2}$ with input $(\texttt{transfer}, c_{0,\alpha,i}, c_{1,\alpha,i})$.
   (c) P_1 inputs $(\texttt{receive}, \alpha_{1,i})$ to $\mathcal{F}_{\text{OT}}^{2\ell,2}$, $\alpha_{1,i}$ is the i'th bit of α_1. P_1 thus receives the message $(\texttt{deliver}, c_{\alpha_{1,i},i})$ from $\mathcal{F}_{\text{OT}}^{2\ell,2}$ for $i \in [\ell - 1]$.
2. P_1 computes $z_1^\alpha = \sum_{i \in [\ell-1]} c_{\alpha_{1,i},i} \cdot 2^{i-1} \mod 2^{2\ell}$ and P_2 computes $z_2^{\alpha,i} = -\sum_{i \in [\ell-1]} r_{\alpha,i} \cdot 2^{i-1} \mod 2^{2\ell}$.
3. P_2 computes $a_2 = p_2 q_2 + z_2^p + z_2^q \mod 2^{2\ell}$ and sends this to P_1.
4. P_1 computes $a_1 = p_1 q_1 + z_1^p + z_1^q \mod 2^{2\ell}$ and sends this to P_2.
5. P_1 and P_2 then compute $(p_1 + p_2)(q_1 + q_2) = N = (a_1 + a_2 \mod \mathcal{P}) \mod 2^{2\ell}$.
6. P_1 computes $w_1 = N + 1 - p_1 - q_1 \mod e$ and sends this to P_2. Similarly P_2 computes $w_2 = p_2 + q_2 \mod e$ and sends this to P_1.
7. P_1 and P_2 checks if $w_1 = w_2$. If this is the case they discard the candidate N and its associated shares p_1, q_1, p_2, q_2. Otherwise they define the value $w = w_1 - w_2 \mod e$ for later use.

Protocol for semi-honestly secure RSA key generation in the $\mathcal{F}_{\text{OT}}$-hybrid model

Verify Modulus: As previously mentioned, for our semi-honest protocol the verification of the modulus consists of two phases in a pipelined manner; first a *trial division* phase and then a full *biprimality test*. Basically, the full biprimality test is significantly slower than the trial division phase, thus, the trial division phase weeds out unsuitable candidates much cheaper than the biprimality test. Thus, overall we expect to execute the biprimality test much fewer times when doing trial division first.

PROTOCOL 3.3 (Semi-honest Key Generation $\Pi_{\text{RSA-semi}}$ - Part 2)

Trial Division

Let $\mathcal{B} = \{B_1 < p \leq B_2 | p \text{ is prime}\}$ for some previously decided B_2. P_2 then executes trial division of the integers up to B_2. If a factor is found then send $\perp$ to P_1 and discard N and its associated prime shares p_1, q_1, p_2, q_2. Otherwise send $\top$ to P_1.

Biprimality Test

The parties execute the biprimality test described in Fig. 3.4 and discard the candidate N if the test fails.

Generate Shared Key

1. Both parties use the value w computed in 7 in **Construct Modulus** associated with the candidate N to compute $b = w^{-1} \mod e$, and then finally P_1 computes $d_1 = \lfloor \frac{-b \cdot (N+1-p_1-q_1)+1}{e} \rfloor$. If $e | - p_2 - q_2$ then P_2 computes $d_2 = 1 + \lfloor \frac{-b \cdot (-p_2-q_2)}{e} \rfloor$, otherwise P_2 computes $d_2 = \lfloor \frac{-b \cdot (-p_2-q_2)}{e} \rfloor$.

2. P_1 outputs (N, p_1, q_1, d_1) and P_2 outputs (N, p_2, q_2, d_2).

Protocol for semi-honestly secure RSA key generation in the $\mathcal{F}_{\text{OT}}$-hybrid model

---

FIGURE 3.4 (Biprimality test [BF01])

1. The parties execute following test s times.
   (a) P_1 samples a random value $\gamma \in \mathbb{Z}_N^{\times}$ with Jacobi symbol 1 over N.
   (b) P_1 sends γ to P_2.
   (c) P_1 computes $\gamma_1 = \gamma^{\frac{N+1-p_1-q_1}{4}} \mod N$ and sends this value to P_2.
   (d) P_2 checks if $\gamma_1 \cdot \gamma^{\frac{-p_2-q_2}{4}} \mod N \neq \pm 1$. In this case P_2 sends $\perp$ to P_1 and the parties break the loop and discard the candidate N.
2. The parties verify that $\gcd(N, p+q-1) = 1$.
   (a) P_1 chooses a random number $\bar{r}_1 \in \mathbb{Z}_{2^{\ell+s}}$ and P_2 chooses a random $\bar{r}_2 \in \mathbb{Z}_{2^{\ell+s}}$. (The parties will verify that $\gcd((\bar{r}_1 + \bar{r}_2) \cdot (p+q-1), N) = 1$.)
   (b) The parties run a multiplication protocol (similar to that run in the "Construct Modulus" step modulo $2^{2\ell+s+2}$) where they compute shares α_1, α_2 (known to P_1, P_2 respectively) of $\bar{r}_1 \cdot (p_2 + q_2 - 1) \mod 2^{2\ell+s+2}$, and shares β_1, β_2 of $\bar{r}_2 \cdot (p_1 + q_1) \mod 2^{2\ell+s+2}$.
   (c) P_1 sends to P_2 the value $s_1 = \bar{r}_1(p_1 + q_1) + \alpha_1 + \beta_1 \mod 2^{2\ell+s+2}$.
   (d) P_2 computes $s_2 = \bar{r}_2(p_2 + q_2 - 1) + \alpha_2 + \beta_2 \mod 2^{2\ell+s+2}$, and verifies that $\gcd(s_1 + s_2, N) = 1$. If this is not the case then it sends $\perp$ to P_1 and discard the candidate N.

The biprimality test of Boneh and Franklin [BF01]

The trial division phase itself is very simple: since both parties know the candidate modulus N, one party simply try to divide it by all primes numbers in the range $B_1 < \beta \leq B_2$. If successful, then N is discarded.

If N passes the trial division, we must still verify that it is in fact a biprime, except with negligible probability. To do this we use a slightly modified version

---

FIGURE 3.5 ($\mathcal{F}_{\text{RSA-semi}}$)

Functionality interacts with parties P_1 and P_2. Upon query of an integer $\ell \in \mathbb{N}$ and a prime e from both parties the functionality proceeds as follows:

- Sample random values p_1, p_2, q_1, q_2 of $\ell - 1$ bits each s.t. $p_1 \equiv q_1 \equiv 3$ mod 4 and $p_2 \equiv q_2 \equiv 0$ mod 4, $p = p_1 + p_2$ and $q = q_1 + q_2$ are prime, and $\gcd((p-1)(q-1), e) = 1$.
- Compute $d = e^{-1} \mod (p-1)(q-1)$, let $b = ((p-1)(q-1))^{-1} \mod e$ and set $d_2 = \lfloor \frac{-b \cdot (-p_2 - q_2)}{e} \rfloor$ and $d_1 = d - d_2$.
- Output $(N = pq, b, p_1, q_1, d_1)$ to P_1 and $(N = pq, b, p_2, q_2, d_2)$ to P_2.

Ideal functionality for generating a shared RSA key semi-honestly

of the biprimality suggested by Boneh and Franklin [BF01], which relies on number-theoretic properties of $N = pq$ where $p = 3 \mod 4$ and $q = 3 \mod 4$. (Note that in the prime-candidate generation, p and q were guaranteed to have this property.) The test is described in Fig. 3.4. By slightly modified, we mean that step 2), which ensures that $\gcd(N, p+q-1) = 1$, is computed without the need of doing operations in the group $\mathbb{Z}_N[x]/(x^2 + 1))^* / \mathbb{Z}_N^*$.

Construct Keys: This phase is a simplified version of what is done by Boneh and Franklin [BF01]. Using the values w_1 and w_2 defined in *construct modulus* the parties compute $w = w_1 - w_2 \mod e$ and then $b = w^{-1} \mod e$. P_1 defines its share of the private key as $d_1 = \lfloor \frac{-b \cdot (N+1-p_1-q_1)+1}{e} \rfloor$. P_2 defines its share of the private key as $d_2 = 1 + \lfloor \frac{-b \cdot (-p_2 - q_2)}{e} \rfloor$ or $d_2 = \lfloor \frac{-b \cdot (-p_2 - q_2)}{e} \rfloor$ or depending on whether $e | p_2 + q_2$ or not.

We formally describe the full semi-honest protocol in Figs. 3.2 and 3.3.

Ideal functionality. The exact ideal functionality, $\mathcal{F}_{\text{RSA-semi}}$, our semi-honest protocol realizes is expressed in Fig. 3.5. The functionality closely reflects the specific construction of the modulus and the shares of the private key of our protocol. In particular, we notice that both primes of the public modulus are congruent to 3 modulo 4, which is needed for the Boneh and Franklin biprimality test to work. Based on these shared primes, the shares of the private keys are generated and handed to the parties. This part of the functionality closely follows the previous literature [BF01, Gil99, ACS02, DM10, Gav12]. First notice using primes congruent to 3 modulo 4 does not decrease security. This follows since all primes suitable for RSA are odd this means that only about half of potential primes are not used. Thus the amount of possible moduli are reduced by around 75%. However, this is similar to all previous approaches. Furthermore, this does not give an adversary any noticeable advantage in finding primes used in key generation.

Next notice that the value $\phi(N) \mod e$ is leaked. This leakage comes implicitly from how the shares d_1 and d_2 are constructed (although it is made explicit in the ideal functionality). We note that since we use the method of Boneh and Franklin [BF01] for this computation, this leakage is also present in their work and any other protocol that uses this approach to generate the shared keys.

Specifically this means that at most $\log(e)$ bits of information on the honest party's secret shares are leaked. Thus when e is small, this does not pose any issue. However, using the common value of $e = 2^{16} + 1$ this could pose a problem. We show how to avoid leaking $\phi(N) \mod e$ in our maliciously secure protocol.

Using this functionality we get the following theorem:

Theorem 3.6. *The protocol $\Pi_{\text{RSA-semi}}$ in Figs. 3.2 and 3.3 securely realizes the ideal functionality $\mathcal{F}_{\text{RSA-semi}}$ in Fig. 3.5 against a static and semi-honest adversary in the $\mathcal{F}_{\text{OT}}^{\cdot\cdot}$-hybrid model.*

We will not prove this theorem directly. The reason being that the following section will make it apparent that *all* steps of the semi-honest protocol is also part of the malicious protocol. Now remember that a simulator for a semi-honest protocol receives the output of the corrupt party. In our protocol this will in particular mean the prime shares. Thus our semi-honest simulator will proceed like the malicious one for the same steps, using the corrupt party's prime shares.

3.3 Malicious Construction

The malicious protocol follows the semi-honest one with the following exceptions:

- The underlying OT functionality must be maliciously secure.
- An extractable commitment to each party's choice of shares is added to the *construct candidate* phase. This is needed since the simulator must be able to extract the malicious party's choice of shares in order to construct messages indistinguishable from the honest party, consistent with any cheating strategy of the malicious party.
- A new and expanded version of the Gilboa protocol is used to compute a candidate modulus. This is done since a malicious P_2 (the party acting as the sender in the OTs) might launch a *selective failure attack* (details below).
- We use OT to implement an equality check of $w_1 = N + 1 - p_1 - q_1 \mod e$ and $w_2 = p_2 + q_2 \mod e$ to ensure that $\gcd(\phi(N), e) = 1$ without leaking w_1 and w_2, and thus avoid leaking $\phi(N) \mod e$ which is leaked in the semi-honest protocol.
- A *proof of honesty* step is added to the *verify modulus* phase, which is used to have the parties prove to one another that they have executed the protocol correctly.
- The private key shares are randomized and computed using a secure protocol.

For OT we simply assume access to any ideal functionalities as described in Sect. 2. Regarding the AES-based commitments, the expanded Gilboa protocol and the proof of honesty, we give further details below.

AES-based commitments. We implement these "commitments" as follows: Before *Candidate Generation*, in a phase we will call *Setup* each party "commits" to a random AES key K by sending $c = \text{AES}_{\text{AES}_r(K)}(0)$ for a random r (chosen by coin-tossing). This unusual "double encryption" ensure that c is not only *hiding* K, through the encryption, but also *binding* to K. The key K is then used to implement a committing functionality. This is done by using K as the key in an AES encryption, where the value we want to commit to is the message encrypted. However, for our proof to go through we require this "commitment" to be extractable. Fortunately this is easily achievable if the simulator knows K and to ensure this we do a zero-knowledge argument of knowledge of K s.t. $c = \mathsf{AES}_{\mathsf{AES}_r(K)}(0)$. By executing this zero-knowledge argument the simulator can clearly extract K (assuming the zero-knowledge argument is an ideal functionality).

Expanded Gilboa Protocol. The usage of OT in the malicious setting is infamous for selective failure vulnerabilities [KS06, MF06] and our setting is no different. Specifically, what a malicious P_2 can do is to guess that P_1's choice bit is 0 (or 1) in a given step of the Gilboa protocol. In this case, P_2 inputs the correct message for choice 0, i.e. the random string r. But for the message for a choice of 1 it inputs the 0-string. If P_2's guess was correct, then the protocol executes correctly. However, if its guess was wrong, then the result of the Gilboa protocol, i.e. the modulus, will be incorrect. If this happens then the protocol will abort during the proof of honesty. Thus, two distinct and observable things happen dependent on whether P_2's guess was correct or not and so P_2 learns the choice bit of P_1 by observing what happens. In fact, P_2 can repeat this as many times as it wants, each time succeeding with probability $1/2$ (when P_1's input is randomly sampled). This means that with probability 2^{-x} it can learn x of P_1's secret input bits.

To prevent this attack we use the notion of *noisy encodings*. A noisy encoding is basically a linear encoding with some noise added s.t. decoding is *only* possible when using some auxiliary information related to the noise. We have party P_1 noisily encode its true input to the Gilboa protocol. Because of the linearity it is possible to retrieve the true output in the last step of the Gilboa protocol (where the parties send their shares to each other in order to learn the result N) without leaking anything on the secret shares of P_1, even in the presence of a selective failure attack.

In a bit more detail, we define a 2^{-s}-statistically hiding noisy encoding of a value $a \in \mathbb{Z}_{2^{\ell-1}}$ as follows:

- Let $\mathcal{P}$ be the smallest prime larger than $2^{2\ell}$.
- Pick random values $h_1, \ldots, h_{2\ell+3s}, g \in \mathbb{F}_{\mathcal{P}}$ and random bits $d_1, \ldots, d_{2\ell+3s}$ under the constraint that $g + \sum_{i \in [2\ell+3s]} h_i \cdot d_i \bmod \mathcal{P} = a$.
- The noisy encoding is then $(h_1, \ldots, h_{2\ell+3s}, g)$ and the decoding info is $(d_1, \ldots, d_{2\ell+3s})$.

Now for each of its shares, p_1 and q_1, P_1 noisily encodes as described and sends the noisy encodings $(h_{p,1}, \ldots, h_{p,2\ell+3s}, g_p)$ and $(h_{q,1}, \ldots, h_{q,2\ell+3s}, g_q)$ to P_2. Next, when they execute the OT steps, P_1 uses the decoding info $(d_{p,1}, \ldots, d_{p,2\ell+3s})$ and $(d_{q,1}, \ldots, d_{q,2\ell+3s})$ of p_1 and q_1 respectively and uses this as input the OTs instead of the bits of p_1 and q_1. For each such bit of p_1, P_2 inputs to the OT a random value $c_{0,p,i} = r_i$ and the value $c_{1,p,i} = r_i + q_2$ (and also operates in a similar way for q). P_1 then receives the values $c_{d_{p,i},p,i}, c_{d_{q,i},q,i} \in \mathbb{Z}_P$ and P_2 holds the values $c_{0,p,i}, c_{1,p,i}, c_{0,q,i}, c_{1,q,i} \in \mathbb{Z}_P$. It turns out that leaking at most s bits of $(d_{p,1}, \ldots, d_{p,2\ell+3s})$ and $(d_{q,1}, \ldots, d_{q,2\ell+3s})$ to P_2 does not give more than a 2^{-s} advantage in finding the value encoded. Thus, even if P_2 launches s selective failure attacks it gains no significant knowledge on P_1's shares.

After having completed the OTs, the parties compute their shares of the modulus N by using the linearity of the encodings. We believe that this approach to thwart selective failure attacks, when multiplying large integers, could be used other settings as well. In particular, we believe that for certain choices of parameters our approach could make a protocol like MASCOT [KOS16] more efficient since it would be possible to eliminate (in their terminology) the *combining step*.

Proof of Honesty. The proof of honesty has three responsibilities: first, it is a maliciously secure execution of the full biprimality test of Boneh and Franklin [BF01]; second, it verifies that the modulus is constructed from the values committed to in *candidate generation*. Finally it generates a random sharing of the private key. The proof of honesty is carried out twice. Once where party P_1 acts as the prover and P_2 the verifier, and once where P_2 acts the prover and P_1 the verifier. Thus each party gets convinced of the honesty of the other party and learns their respective shares of the private key.

To ensure a correctly executed biprimality test, a typical zero-knowledge technique is used, where coin-tossing is used to sample public randomness and the prover randomizes its witness along with the statement to prove. The verifier then gets the option to decide whether he wants to learn the value used for randomizing or the randomized witness. This ensures that the prover can only succeed with probability $1/2$ in convincing the verifier if it does not know a witness.

To ensure that the modulus was constructed from the values committed to, a small secure two-party computation is executed which basically verifies that this is the case. Since the commitments are AES-based, this can be carried out in a very lightweight manner. Furthermore, to ensure that the values used in the maliciously secure biprimality test are also consistent with the shares committed to, we have the prover commit to the randomization values as well and verify these, along with their relation to the shares. Finally, we let the proving party input some randomness which is used to randomize the verifying party's share of the private key. We formally describe the full protocol in Figs. 3.7, 3.8, 3.9 and 3.10.

Ideal Functionality. We express the ideal functionality that our protocol realizes in Fig. 3.12 When there is no corruption the functionality simply proceeds almost as the semi-honest functionality in Fig. 3.5. That is, making a shared key based on random primes congruent to 3 modulo 4, *but* where the shares of the secret key are sampled at random in the range between $-2^{2\ell+s}$ and $2^{2\ell+s}$. This means that the value $\phi(N) \mod e$ is *not* leaked. When a party is corrupted the adversary is allowed certain freedoms in its interaction with the ideal functionality. Specifically the adversary is given access to several commands, allowing it and the functionality to generate a shared RSA key through an interactive game.

PROTOCOL 3.7 (Malicious Key Generation Π_{RSA} - Part 1)

Setup

1. The parties call $(\mathbf{toss}, \{0,1\}^\kappa)$ on $\mathcal{F}_{\mathsf{CT}}$ twice to sample uniformly random bitvectors $r_1, r_2 \in \{0,1\}^\kappa$. (Note that these outputs are known to both parties.)

2. For $\mathcal{I} \in \{1,2\}$ party $P_\mathcal{I}$ picks a uniformly random value $K_\mathcal{I} \in \{0,1\}^\kappa$, computes and sends $\mathsf{AES}_{\mathsf{AES}_{r_\mathcal{I}}(K_\mathcal{I})}(0) = c_\mathcal{I}$ to $P_{3-\mathcal{I}}$.

3. Let M_L be the function outputting $\top$ on input $((r_\mathcal{I}, c_\mathcal{I}), K_\mathcal{I})$ if and only if $\mathsf{AES}_{\mathsf{AES}_{r_\mathcal{I}}(K_\mathcal{I})}(0) = c_\mathcal{I}$. For $\mathcal{I} \in \{1,2\}$ party $P_\mathcal{I}$ inputs $(\mathbf{prove}, (r_\mathcal{I}, c_\mathcal{I}), K_\mathcal{I})$ on $\mathcal{F}_{\mathsf{ZK}}^{M_L}$ and party $P_{3-\mathcal{I}}$ inputs $(\mathbf{verify}, (r_\mathcal{I}, c_\mathcal{I}))$. (The simplest way of implementing these proofs is probably using garbled circuits [JKO13].)

4. If any of these calls output $(\bot)$ then the parties abort. Otherwise they continue.

Candidate Generation

1. P_1 picks a uniformly random value $\tilde{p}_1 \in \mathbb{Z}_{2^{\ell-3}}$, defines $p_1 = 4 \cdot \tilde{p}_1 + 3$, computes and sends $H_{\tilde{p}_1} = \mathsf{AES}_{K_1}(\tilde{p}_1)$ to P_2.

2. P_2 picks a uniformly random value $\tilde{p}_2 \in \mathbb{Z}_{2^{\ell-3}}$ and defines $p_2 = 4 \cdot \tilde{p}_2$, computes and sends $H_{\tilde{p}_2} = \mathsf{AES}_{K_2}(\tilde{p}_2)$ to P_1.

3. Let $\mathcal{B} = \{\beta \leq B_1 | \beta \text{ is prime}\}$. The parties execute procedure Div-OT in Fig. 3.1 for each $\beta \in \mathcal{B}$, where P_1 uses input p_1 and P_2 input p_2. If any of these calls output $\bot$, then discard the candidate pair p_1, p_2.

Protocol for maliciously secure RSA key generation.

The functionality closely reflects what the adversary can do in our protocol. Specifically we allow a malicious party to repeatedly query the functionality to learn a random modulus, based on its choice of prime shares. This is reflected by commands *sample* and *construct*. *Sample* lets the adversary input its desired share of a prime and the functionality then samples a random share for the honest party s.t. the sum is prime. This command also ensures that the primes work with the choice of public exponent e. I.e., that $\gcd(e, (p-1)(q-1)) = 1$. Specifically it verifies that the gcd of e and the prime candidate minus one is equal to one. This implies that no matter which two primes get paired to construct a modulus, it will always hold that $\gcd(e, \phi(N)) = 1$. *Construct* lets the adversary decide on two primes (of which it only knows its own shares) that should be used to construct a modulus and generate shares of the secret key in the same manner as done by Boneh and Franklin [BF01]. Finally, the adversary can then decide which modulus it wishes to use, which is reflected in the command *select*.

However, the functionality does allow the adversary to learn a few bits of information of the honest party's prime shares. In particular, the trial division part of our *candidate generation* phase, allows the adversary to gain some knowledge on the honest party's shares, as reflected in command *leak*. Specifically the adversary gets to guess the remainder of the honest party's shares modulo β, for each $\beta \in \mathcal{B}$ and is informed whether its guess was correct or not. In case the malicious party is P_2 then if any of its guesses for a particular prime is wrong, the adversary loses the option of selecting the modulus based on this prime.

PROTOCOL 3.8 (Malicious Key Generation Π_{RSA} - Part 2)

Construct Modulus

Let p_1, q_1, p_2, q_2 be two candidates that passed the generation phase above, where P_1 knows $p_1 = 4\tilde{p}_1 + 3, q_1 = 4\tilde{q}_1 + 3$ and $H_{\tilde{p}_2}, H_{\tilde{q}_2}$ and P_2 knows $p_2 = 4\tilde{p}_2, q_2 = 4\tilde{q}_2$ and $H_{\tilde{p}_1}, H_{\tilde{q}_1}$. Furthermore, let $\mathcal{P}$ be the smallest prime number greater than $2^{2\ell}$.

1. For each $\alpha \in \{p, q\}$ party P_1 picks a list of values $h_{\alpha,1}, \ldots, h_{\alpha,2\ell+3s}, g_\alpha \in \mathbb{Z}_{\mathcal{P}}$ and a list of bits $d_{\alpha,1}, \ldots, d_{\alpha,2\ell+3s} \in \{0,1\}$ uniformly at random under the constraint that $g_\alpha + \sum_{i\in[2\ell+3s]} h_{\alpha,i} \cdot d_{\alpha,i} \mod \mathcal{P} = \alpha_1$.

2. The parties execute the following steps for each $\alpha \in \{p, q\}$ and $i \in [2\ell + 3s]$:
   (a) P_2 chooses a uniformly random value $r_{\alpha,i} \in \mathbb{Z}_{\mathcal{P}}$ and sets

   $$c_{0,\alpha,i} = r_{\alpha,i} \quad \text{and} \quad c_{1,\alpha,i} = \begin{cases} r_{\alpha,i} + q_2 & \mod \mathcal{P} \quad \text{if } \alpha = p \\ r_{\alpha,i} + p_2 & \mod \mathcal{P} \quad \text{if } \alpha = q \end{cases}.$$

   (b) P_2 invokes $\mathcal{F}_{\mathsf{OT}}^{2\ell+3s,2}$ with input $(\mathtt{transfer}, c_{0,\alpha,i}, c_{1,\alpha,i})$.
   (c) P_1 inputs $(\mathtt{receive}, d_{\alpha,i})$ to $\mathcal{F}_{\mathsf{OT}}^{2\ell+3s,2}$. P_1 thus receives the message $(\mathtt{deliver}, c_{d_{\alpha,i},i})$ from $\mathcal{F}_{\mathsf{OT}}^{2\ell+3s,2}$.

3. P_1 sends the values $h_{\alpha,1}, \ldots, h_{\alpha,2\ell+3s}, g_\alpha$ to P_2 for $\alpha \in \{p, q\}$.

4. P_1 computes $z_1^\alpha = \sum_{i\in[2\ell+3s]} c_{d_{\alpha,i},i} \cdot h_{\alpha,i} \mod \mathcal{P}$ and P_2 computes $z_2^\alpha = -\sum_{i\in[2\ell+3s]} r_{\alpha,i} \cdot h_{\alpha,i} \mod \mathcal{P}$.

5. P_2 computes $a_2 = p_2 q_2 + z_2^p + g_p \cdot q_2 + z_2^q + g_q \cdot p_2 \mod \mathcal{P}$ and sends this to P_1.

6. P_1 computes $a_1 = p_1 q_1 + z_1^p + z_1^q \mod \mathcal{P}$ and sends this to P_2.

7. P_1 and P_2 then compute $N = (a_1 + a_2 \mod \mathcal{P}) \mod 2^{2\ell}$.

8. P_1 computes $w_1 = N + 1 - p_1 - q_1 \mod e$ and similarly P_2 computes $w_2 = p_2 + q_2 \mod e$.

9. P_2 inputs $(\mathtt{transfer})$ to $\mathcal{F}_{\mathsf{OT}}^{\kappa,\lceil\log(e)\rceil}$ and learns $r_0, \ldots, r_{\beta-1} \in \{0,1\}^\kappa$.

10. P_1 inputs $(\mathtt{receive}, w_1)$ and thus learns r_{w_1}.

11. P_2 sends r_{w_2} to P_1.

12. If $r_{w_1} = r_{w_2}$ then P_1 informs P_2 of this and they both discard the candidate N and its associated shares p_1, q_1, p_2, q_2.

Protocol for maliciously secure RSA key generation.

The functionality keeps track of the adversary's queries and what was leaked to it, through the set J and dictionary C. Basically the set J stores the unique ids of primes the simulator has generated and which the adversary can use to construct an RSA modulus. Thus the ids of primes already used to construct a modulus are removed from this set. The same goes for primes a malicious P_2 have tried to learn extra bits about, but failed (as reflected in *leak*). The dictionary C on the other hand, maps prime ids already used to construct an RSA modulus, into this modulus. This means that once two primes have been used, using *construct*, to construct a modulus, their ids are removed from J and instead inserted into C. After the construction we furthermore allow the

---

PROTOCOL 3.9 (Malicious Key Generation Π_{RSA} - Part 3)

Trial Division

Let $\mathcal{B} = \{B_1 < p \leq B_2 | p \text{ is prime}\}$. P_2 then executes trial division of the integers up to B_2. If a factor is found then send $\perp$ to P_1 and discard N and its associated prime shares p_1, q_1, p_2, q_2. Otherwise send $\top$ to P_1.

Biprimality Test

The parties execute the biprimality test described in Fig. 3.4. However after step 2.a P_1 sends $H_{\bar{r}_1} = \text{AES}_{K_1}(\bar{r}_1)$ and P_2 sends $H_{\bar{r}_2} = \text{AES}_{K_2}(\bar{r}_2)$. Furthermore in step 2.b they use the maliciously secure version of the multiplication protocol from "Construct Modulus" (modulo the smallest prime larger than $2^{2\ell+s+2}$).

Proof of Honesty

The parties call $(\textbf{toss}, \mathbb{Z}_N^\times)$ on $\mathcal{F}_{\text{CT}}$ enough times to get s distinct random elements, denoted by $\gamma_i \in \mathbb{Z}_N^\times$ s.t. $\mathcal{J}_N(\gamma_i) = 1$ for $i \in [s]$.

(Recall that $\tilde{p}$ denotes $p \gg 2$, i.e. p shifted to the right two steps.) Execute the following steps where $P = P_1, V = P_2$ with $\tilde{p}_P = \tilde{p}_1$ and $\tilde{p}_V = \tilde{p}_2$ and where $P = P_2, V = P_1$ with $\tilde{p}_P = \tilde{p}_2$ and $\tilde{p}_V = \tilde{p}_1$. Similarly for $\tilde{q}_1, \tilde{q}_2$:

1. For each $i \in [s]$, P computes $\gamma_{i,P} = \gamma_i^{\frac{N-5}{4} - \tilde{p}_P - \tilde{q}_P} \mod N$
2. P sends $\gamma_{1,P}, \ldots, \gamma_{s,P}$ to V.
3. For each $i \in [s]$, V then verifies that $\gamma_i^{-\tilde{p}_V - \tilde{q}_V} \cdot \gamma_{i,P} \equiv \pm 1 \mod N$.
4. If *any* of the checks do not pass then V sends $\perp$ to P, outputs $\perp$ and aborts.
5. For each $j \in [s]$, P picks a random value $t_j \in \{0,1\}^{\ell-2+s}$. It then computes $\text{AES}_{K_P}(t_j) = H_{t_j}$ and sends this to V.
6. For each $i, j \in [s]$, P then sends the values $\bar{\gamma}_{i,j} = \gamma_i^{t_j} \mod N$ to V.
7. The parties call $(\textbf{toss}, \{0,1\})$ on $\mathcal{F}_{\text{CT}}$ s times to sample uniformly random bits $b_1, \ldots, b_s \in \{0,1\}$.
8. For each $j \in [s]$, P then sends $v_j = b_j \cdot (-\tilde{p}_P - \tilde{q}_P) + t_j$ to V.
9. For each $i, j \in [s]$ V checks that

$$\gamma_i^{v_j} \mod N =^? \bar{\gamma}_{i,j} \cdot \gamma_{i,P}^{b_j} \cdot \gamma_i^{-b_j \cdot \frac{N-5}{4}} \mod N$$

If this is not the case then it sends $\perp$ to P, outputs $\perp$ and aborts.

Protocol for maliciously secure RSA key generation.

adversary $P_\mathcal{I}$ to pick a value $w'_\mathcal{I} \in [0, e[$ and learn if $w'_\mathcal{I} = w_{3-\mathcal{I}}$ when $w_{3-\mathcal{I}}$ is constructed according to the protocol using the honest party's shares. However, if the corrupt party is P_2 and it guesses *correctly* then it won't be allowed to use the candidate.

Finally we have the command *abort* which allows an adversary to abort the functionality at any point it wishes, as is the norm in maliciously secure dishonest majority protocols.

Security. If there is no corruption we have the same security as described for the semi-honest protocol in Sect. 3.2, except that $\phi(N) \mod e$ is *not* implicitly leaked by party's secret key share. Next we see that allowing the adversary to query the functionality for moduli before making up its mind does not influ-

---

PROTOCOL 3.10 (Malicious Key Generation Π_{RSA} - Part 4)

Proof of Honesty *(continued)*

11. P picks uniformly at random a value $\rho_P \in \{0,1\}^{2\ell+s}$.
12. The parties define the following function f, where P gives private input $(\tilde{p}_P, \tilde{q}_P, K_P, \bar{r}_P, \rho_P)$, V gives private input $(\tilde{p}_V, \tilde{q}_V, K_V, \bar{r}_V)$. Let $\sigma = s_P + s_V \mod \mathcal{P}$, based on the values from step 2 of the biprimality test, where $\mathcal{P}$ is the smallest prime larger than $2^{2\ell+s+2}$. They both give public input $(N, e, c_P, r_P, c_V, r_V, \sigma, H_{\tilde{p}_P}, H_{\tilde{q}_P}, H_{\bar{r}_P}, H_{\tilde{p}_V}, H_{\tilde{q}_V}, H_{\bar{r}_V},$ $\{b_j, v_j, H_{t_j}\}_{i \in [s]})$:

$$w := N - 5 - 4(\tilde{p}_P + \tilde{q}_P + \tilde{p}_V + \tilde{q}_V) \mod e \ ,$$

$$\chi := (H_{\tilde{p}_P} =^? \mathsf{AES}_{K_P}(\tilde{p}_P)) \wedge (H_{\tilde{q}_P} =^? \mathsf{AES}_{K_P}(\tilde{q}_P))$$
$$\wedge \, (c_P =^? \mathsf{AES}_{\mathsf{AES}_{r_P}(K_P)}(0)) \wedge (H_{\bar{r}_P} =^? \mathsf{AES}_{K_P}(\bar{r}_P))$$
$$\wedge \, (H_{\tilde{p}_V} =^? \mathsf{AES}_{K_V}(\tilde{p}_V)) \wedge (H_{\tilde{q}_V} =^? \mathsf{AES}_{K_V}(\tilde{q}_V))$$
$$\wedge \, (c_V =^? \mathsf{AES}_{\mathsf{AES}_{r_V}(K_V)}(0)) \wedge (H_{\bar{r}_V} =^? \mathsf{AES}_{K_V}(\bar{r}_V))$$
$$\wedge \, (\forall j \in [s] : \mathsf{AES}_{K_P}(v_j + b_j \cdot (\tilde{p}_P + \tilde{q}_P)) =^? H_{t_j})$$
$$\wedge \, (N =^? (4(\tilde{p}_V + \tilde{p}_P) + 3) \cdot (4(\tilde{q}_V + \tilde{q}_P) + 3))$$
$$\wedge \, \sigma =^? (\bar{r}_P + \bar{r}_V) \cdot (4(\tilde{p}_1 + \tilde{p}_2 + \tilde{q}_1 + \tilde{q}_2) + 5)$$
$$\wedge \, w \neq 0$$

$$\text{if } V = P_1 : d_V := \left\lfloor \frac{-(w^{-1} \mod e) \cdot (N - 5 - 4\tilde{p}_1 - 4\tilde{q}_1) + 1}{e} \right\rfloor$$

$$\text{else} : d_V := \left\lfloor \frac{-(w^{-1} \mod e) \cdot (-4\tilde{p}_2 - 4\tilde{q}_2)}{e} \right\rfloor$$

$$\text{if } \chi = 1 : \bar{d}_V := d_V - \rho_P$$
$$\text{else} : \bar{d}_V = \bot$$

Output $(\chi, \bar{d}_V)$ to V and $(\bot)$ to P

13. The parties then use $\mathcal{F}_{\mathsf{2PC}}$ to compute the output of f and abort if $\chi = 0$.[a]

Generate Shared Key

1. P_1 computes and outputs $d_1 = \bar{d}_1 + \rho_1$.
2. If $e \mid -4\tilde{p}_2 - 4\tilde{q}_2$ then P_2 computes and outputs $d_2 = \bar{d}_2 + \rho_2$, else it computes and outputs $d_2 = \bar{d}_2 + \rho_2 + 1$.

---

[a] This step must be done in parallel for both the cases where P_1 is the prover and P_1 the verifier.

Protocol for maliciously secure RSA key generation.

ence security. Since the adversary is polytime bounded, it can only query for polynomially many moduli. Furthermore, as the honest party's shares are randomly sampled by the functionality, and since they are longer than the security parameter (e.g. 1021 vs. 128) the adversary will intuitively not gain anything from having this ability. Arguments for why this is the case have been detailed by Gavin [Gav12].

Regarding the allowed leakage we show in the full version that (for standard parameters) at most $\log_2(e/(e-1)) + 2\log_2(B_1/2)$ bits are leaked to a malicious party without the protocol aborting, no matter if P_1 or P_2 is malicious. If P_2 is malicious it may choose to *try* to learn $(1+\epsilon)x$ bits of the honest party's prime shares for a small $\epsilon \leq 1$ with probability at most 2^{-x}. However, if it is unlucky and does not learn the extra bits then it will not be allowed to use a modulus based on the prime it tried to get some leakage on.

We now argue that this leakage is not an issue, neither in theory nor in practice. For the theoretical part, assume learning some extra bits on the honest party's prime shares would give the adversary a non-negligible advantage in finding the primes of the modulus. This would then mean that there exists a polytime algorithm breaking the security of RSA with non-negligible probability by simply exhaustively guessing what the leaked bits are and then running the adversary algorithm on each of the guesses. Thus if the amount of leaked bits is $O(\text{polylog}(\kappa))$, for the computational security parameter κ, then such an algorithm would also be polytime, and cannot exist under the assumption that RSA is secure. So from a theoretical point of view, we only need to argue that the leakage is $O(\text{polylog}(\kappa))$. To do so first notice that B_1 is a constant tweaked for efficiency. But for concreteness assume it to be somewhere between two constants, e.g., 31 and 3181.[1] Since B_1 is a constant it also means that the leakage is constant and thus $O(1) \in O(\text{polylog}(\kappa))$.

However, if the concrete constant is greater than κ this is not actually saying much, since we then allow a specific value greater than 2^κ time to be polynomial in κ. However, it turns out that for $B_1 = 31$ the exact leakage is only 3.4 bits and for $B_1 = 3181$ it is 5.7 bits.

Formally we prove the following theorem in the full version.

Theorem 3.11. *The protocol Π_{RSA} in Figs. 3.7, 3.8, 3.9 and 3.10 securely realizes the ideal functionality $\mathcal{F}_{RSA}$ in Fig. 3.12 against a static and malicious adversary in the $\mathcal{F}_{OT}^{\cdot\cdot}$-, $\mathcal{F}_{CT}$-, $\mathcal{F}_{ZK}$-, $\mathcal{F}_{2PC}$-hybrid model assuming AES is IND-CPA and a PRP on the first block per encryption.*

3.4 Outline of Proof

Efficient Malicious Security. One of the reasons we are able to achieve malicious security in such an efficient manner is because of our unorthodox ideal functionality. In particular, by giving the adversary the power to discard some valid moduli, we can prove our protocol secure using a simulation argument *without* having to simulate the honest party's shares of potentially valid moduli discarded throughout the protocol. This means, that we only need to simulate for the candidate N and its shares p_1, q_1, p_2, q_2 that actually get accepted as an output of the protocol.

---

[1] We find it unrealistic that the a greater or smaller choice will be yield a more efficient execution of our protocol.

FIGURE 3.12 ($\mathcal{F}_{\mathsf{RSA}}$)

Upon query of bitlength 2ℓ and public exponent e from parties P_1 and P_2 proceed as functionality $\mathcal{F}_{\mathsf{RSA\text{-}semi}}$ in Fig. 3.5. Otherwise, letting $P_{\mathcal{I}}$ for $\mathcal{I} \in \{1, 2\}$ denote the corrupt party, the functionality initializes an empty set J and a dictionary C mapping IDs to a tuple of elements. Allow the adversary to execute any combination of the following commands:

Sample. On input $(j, p_{\mathcal{I},j})$ where $j \notin J$, $p_{\mathcal{I},j} \leq 2^{\ell-1}$ and $p_{\mathcal{I},j} \equiv 3 \mod 4$ if $\mathcal{I} = 1$ or $p_{\mathcal{I},j} \equiv 0 \mod 4$ if $\mathcal{I} = 2$: select a random value $p_{3-\mathcal{I},j}$ of $\ell - 1$ bits, under the constraint that $p_j = p_{1,j} + p_{2,j} \equiv 3 \mod 4$ is prime and $\gcd(e, p_j - 1) = 1$. Add j to J.

Leak. For each $j \in J$ and for each $\beta \leq B_1$ where β is prime, let $P_{\mathcal{I}}$ input a value $a_{j,\beta}$ and if $\mathcal{I} = 1$ return a bit indicating if $a_{j,\beta} \neq -p_{2,j} \mod \beta$. If $\mathcal{I} = 2$ return a bit indicating if $a_{j,\beta} \neq p_{1,j} \mod \beta$ and set $J = J \backslash \{j\}$ if $a_{j,\beta} = p_{1,j} \mod \beta$.

Construct. On input $(j, j', w'_{\mathcal{I}})$ from $P_{\mathcal{I}}$ where $j, j' \in J$ but $j, j' \notin C$ then compute
$d = e^{-1} \mod (p_j - 1)(p_{j'} - 1)$. Pick a random integer $d_1 \in [2^{2\ell+s}]$ and set $d_2 = d - d_1$. Return $(N = p_j \cdot p_{j'}, p_{\mathcal{I}}, d_{\mathcal{I}})$ to $P_{\mathcal{I}}$ and set $C[j] = C[j'] = (N, d_{3-\mathcal{I}}, j, j')$ and $J = J \backslash \{j, j'\}$. If $P_{\mathcal{I}}$ returns a value $w'_{\mathcal{I},j,j'} \in [0, e-1]$, proceed as follows: If $\mathcal{I} = 1$ notify P_1 whether $w'_{1,j,j'} = p_{2,j} + p_{2,j'} \mod e$ or not. If instead $\mathcal{I} = 2$ then notify P_2 whether $w'_{2,j,j'} = N + 1 - (p_{1,j} + p_{1,j'}) \mod e$ or not. Furthermore, if $\mathcal{I} = 2$ and $\top$ was returned set $C = C \backslash \{j, j'\}$.

Select. On the first input (j, j') with $j, j' \in C$ from $P_{\mathcal{I}}$, where $C[j] = (N, d_{3-\mathcal{I}}, j, j')$ send $(N, p_{3-\mathcal{I},j}, q_{3-\mathcal{I},j}, d_{3-\mathcal{I}})$ to $P_{3-\mathcal{I}}$ and stop accepting commands.

Abort. If $P_{\mathcal{I}}$ inputs $\bot$ at any time then output $\bot$ to both parties and abort.

Ideal functionality for generating shared RSA key

Another key reason for our efficiency improvements is the fact that almost all of the protocol is executed in a "strong" semi-honest manner. By this we mean that only privacy is guaranteed when a party is acting maliciously, but correctness is not. This makes checking a candidate modulus N much more efficient than if full malicious security was required. At the end of the protocol, full malicious security is ensured for a candidate N by the parties proving that they have executed the protocol correctly.

The Simulator. With these observations about the efficiency of the protocol in mind, we see that the overall strategy for our simulator is as follows, assuming w.l.o.g. that $P_{\mathcal{I}}$ is the honest party and $P_{3-\mathcal{I}}$ is corrupted.

For the *Setup* phase the simulator simply emulates the honest party's choice of key $K_{\mathcal{I}}$ by sampling it at random. The reason this is sufficient is that because AES is a permutation and $K_{\mathcal{I}}$ is random, thus $\mathsf{AES}_{r_{\mathcal{I}}}(K_{\mathcal{I}})$ is random in the view of the adversary. The crucial thing to notice is that nothing is leaked about this when using it as key in the second encryption under the PRP property. We do strictly need the second encryption since the encryption key $r_{\mathcal{I}}$ is public, thus if we didn't have the second encryption an adversary could decrypt and learn $K_\mathcal{I}$! Regarding the zero-knowledge proof we notice that the simulator can extract the adversary's input $K'_{3-\mathcal{I}}$. We notice that the simulator can emulate $\mathcal{F}^{ML}_{ZK}$ by verifying $K'_{3-\mathcal{I}}$ in the computation of $c_{3-\mathcal{I}}$. Again we rely on AES being a PRP to ensure that if $K'_{3-\mathcal{I}}$ is not the value used in computing $c_{3-\mathcal{I}}$ then the check will always fail because it would require the adversary to find $K'_{3-\mathcal{I}} \neq K_{3-\mathcal{I}}$ s.t. $\mathsf{AES}_{r_{3-\mathcal{I}}}(K'_{3-\mathcal{I}}) = \mathsf{AES}_{r_{3-\mathcal{I}}}(K_{3-\mathcal{I}})$. Thus the adversary is committed to some specific key $K_{3-\mathcal{I}}$ extracted by the simulator.

For *Candidate Generation* the simulator starts by sampling a random value $\tilde{p}_\mathcal{I}$ and extracts the malicious party's share $\tilde{p}_{3-\mathcal{I}}$ from its "commitment" $H_{\tilde{p}_{3-\mathcal{I}}}$, since the simulator knows the key $K_{3-\mathcal{I}}$. Furthermore, since we use AES in a mode s.t. it is IND-CPA secure the adversary cannot distinguish between the values $H_{\tilde{p}_\mathcal{I}}$ simulated or the values sent in the real protocol.

Next see that if $4(\tilde{p}_1 + \tilde{p}_2) + 3$ is *not* a prime, then the simulator will emulate the rest of the protocol using the random value it sampled. This simulation will be statistically indistinguishable from the real world since the simulator and the honest party both sample at random and follow the protocol. Furthermore, since the shares don't add up to a prime, any modulus based on this will never be output in the real protocol since the *proof of honesty* will discover if N is not a biprime.

On the other hand, if the shares *do* sum to a prime then the simulator uses *sample* on the ideal functionality $\mathcal{F}_{RSA}$ to construct a prime based on the malicious party's share $\tilde{p}_{3-\mathcal{I}}$. It then simulates based on the value extracted from the malicious party. Specifically for the OT-based trial division, the simulator extracts the messages of the malicious party and uses these as input to *leak* on the ideal functionality. This allows the simulator to learn whether the adversary's input to the trial division plus the true and internal random value held by the ideal functionality is divisible by β.

To simulate construction of a modulus, we first consider a hybrid functionality, which is the same as $\mathcal{F}_{RSA}$, except that a command *full-leak* is added. This command allows the simulator to learn the honest party's shares of a prime candidate, under the constraint that it is not used in the RSA that key the functionality outputs. It is easy to see that adding this method to the functionality does not give the adversary more power, since it can only learn the honest party's shares of primes which are independent of the output.

With this expanded, hybrid version of $\mathcal{F}_{RSA}$ in place, the simulator emulates the construction of a modulus by first checking if one of the candidate values were prime and the other was not. In this case it uses *full-leak* to learn the value that is prime and then simulates the rest of the protocol like an honest party. This will be statistically indistinguishable from the real execution since the modulus will never be used as output since it is not a biprime and so will be discarded, at the latest, in the *proof of honesty* phase.

However, if both candidate values are marked as prime the simulator simulates the extended Gilboa protocol for construction of the modulus. It does so by extracting the malicious party's input to the calls to $\mathcal{F}^{\kappa,\beta}_{OT}$. Based on this it can simulate the values of the honest party. This is pretty straightforward, but what is key is that no info on the honest party's prime shares is leaked to the adversary in case of a selective failure attack (when the adversary is the sender in $\mathcal{F}_{\mathsf{OT}}^{\kappa,\beta}$). To see this, first notice that selecting $h_1, \ldots, h_{2\ell+2s}, g$ at random and computing $g + \sum_{i \in [2\ell+2s]} h_i \cdot d_i \bmod \mathcal{P}$ is in fact a 2-universal hash function. This implies, using some observations by Ishai *et al.* [IPS09], that whether these values are picked at random s.t. they hash to the true input or are just random, is 2^{-s} indistinguishable. Thus extending the function with $h_{2\ell+2s+1}, \ldots g_{2\ell+3s}$, allows the adversary to learn s of the bits d_i without affecting the indistinguishable result. Since s is the statistical security parameter and each d_i is picked at random, this implies that the adversary cannot learn anything non-negligible.

The proof of security of the remaining steps is quite straightforward. For *trial division* the simulator basically acts as an honest party since all operations are local. For the *biprimality test* the simulation is also easy. For step 1, it is simply following the proof by Boneh and Franklin [BF01], for step 2, simulation can be done using the same approach as for the Gilboa protocol. Regarding *proof of honesty* the simulation follows the steps for the simulation of the biprimality test and uses the emulation of the coin-tossing functionality to learn what challenge it needs to answer and can thus adjust the value sent to the verifier that will make the proof accept. Finally the *key generation* is also unsurprising as all the computations are local.

4   Instantiation

Optimizations. *Fail-fast.* It is possible to limit the amount of tests carried out on composite candidates, in all of the OT-based trial division, the second trial division and the biprimality test, by simply employing a *fail-fast* approach. That is, to simply break the loop of any of these tests, as soon as a candidate fails. This leads to significantly fewer tests, as in all three tests a false positive is more likely to be discovered in the beginning of the test. (For example, a third of the candidates are likely to fail in the first trial division test, which checks for divisibility by 3.)

Maximum runtime. In the malicious protocol an adversary can cheat in such a way that a legitimate candidate (either prime or modulus) gets rejected. In particular this means that the adversary could make the protocol run forever. For example, if he tries to learn 1024 bits of the honest party's shares by cheating then we expect to discard 2^{1023} good candidate moduli! Thus, tail-bounds for the choice of parameters should be computed s.t. the protocol will abort once it has considered more candidate values than would be needed to find a valid modulus e.w.p. 2^{-s}. In fact, it is strictly needed in order to limit the maximum possible leakage from selective failure attacks.

Synchronous execution. To ensure that neither party P_1 nor party P_2 sits idle at any point in time of the execution of the protocol, we can have them exchange roles for every other candidate. Thus, every party performs both roles, but on two different candidates at the same time, throughout the execution of the protocol. For example, while Alice executes as P_1 in the *candidate generation* on one candidate, she simultaneously executes the candidate generation as P_2 for another candidate. Similarly for Bob. The result of this is that no party will have to wait for the other party to complete a step as they will both do the same amount of computation in each step.

Leaky two-party computation. We already discussed in Sect. 3.3 how leaking a few bits of information on the honest party's prime shares does not compromise the security of the protocol. Along the same line, we can make the observation that learning a predicate on the honest party's share will in expectation not give more than a single bit of information to the adversary. In particular it can learn at most x bits of information with probability at most 2^{-x}. This is the same leakage that is already allowed to P_2, and thus allowing this would not yield any significant change to the leakage of our protocol. This means that it can suffice to construct only two garbled circuits to implement $\mathcal{F}_{2PC}$ by using the *dual-execution* approach [MF06]. This is compared to the s garbled circuits needed in the general case where no leakage is allowed [Lin16].

Constant rounds. We note that the way our protocols $\Pi_{RSA\text{-semi}}$ and Π_{RSA} are presented in Figs. 3.2 and 3.3, respectively Figs. 3.7, 3.8, 3.9 and 3.10 does not give constant time. This is because they are expressed iteratively s.t. candidate primes are sampled until a pair passing all the tests is found. However it is possible to simply execute each step of the protocols once for many candidates in parallel. This is because, based on the Prime Number Theorem, we can find the probability of a pair of candidates being good. This allows us to compute the amount of candidate values needed to ensure that a good modulus is found, except with negligible probability. Unfortunately this will in most situations lead to many candidate values being constructed unnecessarily. For this reason it is in practice more desirable to construct batches of candidates in parallel instead to avoid doing a lot of unnecessary work, yet still limit the amount of round of communication.

Efficiency Comparison. We here try to compare the efficiency of our protocol with previous work. This is done in Table 1.

With regards to more concrete efficiency we recall that both our protocols and previous work have the same type of phases, working on randomly sampled candidates in a pipelined manner. Because of this feature, all protocols limit the amount of unsuitable candidates passing through to the expensive phases, by employing trial division. This leads to fewer executions of expensive phases and thus to greater concrete efficiency. In some protocols this filtering is applied both to individual prime candidates *and* to candidate moduli, leading to minimal executions of the expensive phases. Unfortunately this is not possible in all protocols. For this reason we also show in Table 1 which protocols manage to improve the expected execution time by doing trial division of the prime candidates, respectively the moduli.

Table 1. Comparison of the different protocols for distributed RSA key generation. The best possible values are highlighted in bold. All values assume a constant, and minimal, amount of participating parties; i.e. 2 or 3. The column *Amount of candidates* expresses the expected amount of random candidates that must be generated before finding a suitable modulus. The column *Candidate generation* expresses the computational bit complexity required to construct a *single* candidate prime. The column *Construct modulus* expresses the computational bit complexity required to construct a *single* potential modulus, based on two prime candidates. The column *(Bi)primality test* expresses the computational bit complexity required to verify that a *single* prime candidate is prime except with negligible probability or (depending on the protocol) to verify that a *single* modulus is the product of two primes except with negligible probability. The column *Leakage* expresses how many bits of information of the honest party's shares of the primes that is leaked to the adversary. Here τ means that $\sum_{\beta \in B_1} \log\left(\frac{\beta}{\beta-1}\right)$ bits can be leaked to a malicious adversary. Furthermore, the adversary is allowed to pick a probability x with which it learns $(1+\epsilon)x$ extra bits. However, if the adversary does not learn the extra bits then the honest party learns that the adversary has acted maliciously.

Scheme	Assumptions	Dishonest majority	Malicious secure	Prime trial division	Modulus trial division	Rounds	Amount of candidates	Candidate generation	Construct modulus	(Bi)primality test	Leakage
Our result*	IND-CPA, $\mathcal{F}_{OT}$, $\mathcal{F}_{CT}$	✓	✓	✓	✓	$O(1)$	$O(\ell^2/\log^2(\ell))$	$O(\ell)$	$O(\ell^2)$	$O(s \cdot \ell^3)$	$\tau+2$
[BF01]	None	✗	✗	✓	✓	$O(1)$	$O(\ell^2/\log^2(\ell))$	$O(\ell)$	$O(\ell^2)$	$O(s \cdot \ell^3)$	2
[FMY98]	DL	✗	✓	✗	✓	$O(1)$	$O(\ell^2/\log^2(\ell))$	$O(\ell^3)$	$O(\ell^3)$	$O(s^2 \cdot \ell^3)$	2
[PS98]†	$\mathcal{F}_{OT}$	✓	✓	✓	✓	$O(1)$	$O(\ell^2/\log^2(\ell))$	$O(\ell)$	$O(\ell^2)$	?	$\tau+2$
[Gil99]	PRG, $\mathcal{F}_{OT}$	✓	✗	✓	✓	$O(1)$	$O(\ell^2/\log^2(\ell))$	$O(\ell)$	$O(\ell^2)$	$O(s \cdot \ell^3)$	2
[ACS02]	None	✗	✗	✓	✗	$O(\ell)$	$O(\ell/\log(\ell))$	$O(\ell)$	$O(\ell^2)$	$O(s \cdot \ell^3)$	2
[DM10]	CRS, Strong RSA	✗	✓	✓	✓	$O(1)$	$O(\ell^2/\log^2(\ell))$	$O(\ell^3)$	$O(\ell^3)$	$o(s \cdot \ell^3)$	2
[HMRT12]	DCR, DDH	✓	✓	✓	✓	$O(1)$‡	$O(\ell^2/\log^2 \ell)$	$O(\ell^3)$	$O(\ell^3)$	$O(s \cdot \ell^3)$	2

*: For the malicious protocol $O(s^2 \cdot \ell^3)$ operations are executed *once* per successful key pair generation.

†: The authors do not describe how to ensure biprimality in case of a malicious adversary.

‡: Constant round on average.

To give a proper idea of the efficiency of the different protocols we must also consider the asymptotics. However, because of the diversity in primitives used in the previous protocols, and in the different phases, we try to do this by comparing the computational bit complexity. Furthermore to make the comparison as fair as possible we assume the best possible implementations available *today* are used for underlying primitives. In particular we assume an efficient OT extension is used for OTs [KOS15].

Based on the table we can make the following conclusions regarding the efficiency of our protocols. First, considering the semi-honest protocol; we see that the only real competition is Algesheimer *et al.* as they expect to test asymptotically fewer prime candidates than us. However, this comes at the price of a large amount of rounds requires, making it challenging to use efficiently over the Internet. Furthermore, unlike our protocol, they require an honest majority making it possible for them to leverage efficient information theoretic constructions.

For the malicious security model we see that the only real competition lies in the work of Poupard and Stern [PS98]. However, we note that they don't provide a full maliciously secure protocol. In particular they do not describe how to do a biprimality test secure against a malicious and dishonest majority. Thus the only other protocol considering the same setting as us is the one by Hazay *et al.*. This is also the newest of the schemes and is considered the current state-of-the-art in this setting. However, this protocol requires asymptotically more operations for candidate generation, construction of modulus and the biprimality test.

Implementation. Below we outline the concrete implementation choices we made. We implement AES in counter mode, using AES-NI, with $\kappa = 128$ bit keys. For 1-out-of-2 OT (needed during the *Construct Modulus* phase) we use the maliciously secure OT extension of Keller *et al.* [KOS15]. For the base OTs we use the protocol of Peikert *et al.* [PVW08] and for the internal PRG we use AES-NI with the seed as key, in counter mode. For the random 1-out-of-β OT we use the random 1-out-of-2 OT above using the protocol of Naor and Pinkas [NP99]. For the coin-tossing we use the standard "commit to randomness and then open" approach.

In the *Construct Modulus* phase, instead of having each party sample the values $h_{\alpha,1}, \ldots, h_{\alpha.2\ell+3s}, g_\alpha \in \mathbb{Z}_\mathcal{P}$ and send them to the other party, we instead have it sample a seed and generate these values through a PRG. The party then only needs to send the seed to the other party. This saves a large amount of communication complexity without making security compromises.

Our implementation implemented **OT extension** in batches of 8912 OTs. Whenever a batch of OTs is finished, the program calls a procedure which generates a new block of 8192 OTs. Most of the cryptographic operations were implemented using OpenSSL, but big-integer multiplication was implemented in assembler instead of using the OpenSSL implementation for efficiency reasons.

We did not implement yet the **zero-knowledge argument** or the two-party computation since they can be efficiently realized using existing implementations of garbled circuits (such as JustGarble [BHKR13] or TinyGarble [SHS+15]) by using the protocol of Jawurek *et al.* [JKO13] for zero-knowledge and the dual-execution approach [MF06] for the two-party computation. These protocols are only executed *once* in our scheme using well tested implementations, and thus, as is described later in this section, we can safely estimate that the effect on the total run time is marginal.

Experiments. We implemented our maliciously secure protocol and ran experiments on Azure, using Intel Xeon E5-2673 v.4 - 2.3 Ghz machines with 64 Gb RAM, connected by a 40.0 Gbps network. are pretty strong servers).

We used the code to run 50 computations of a shared 2048 bit modulus, and computed the average run time. The results are as follows:

- With a single threaded execution, the average run time was 134 s.
- With four threads, the average run time was 39.1 s.
- With eight threads, the average run time was 35 s.

The run times showed a high variance (similar to the results of the implementation reported by Hazay *et al.* [HMRT12] for their protocol). For the single thread execution, the average run time was 134 s while the median run time was 84.9 s (the fastest execution took 8.2 s and the slowest execution took 542 s).

Focusing on the single thread execution, we measured the time consumed by different major parts of the protocol. The preparation of the OT extension tables took on average 12% of the run time, the multiplication protocol computing N took 66%, and the biprimality test took 7%. (These percentages were quite stable across all executions and showed little variance.) Overall these parts took 85% of the total run time. The bulk of the time was consumed by the secure multiplication protocol. In that protocol, most time was spent on computing the values z_1^α, z_2^α (line 4 in Fig. 3.8). This is not surprising since each of these computations computes $2\ell + 3s = 2168$ bignum multiplications.

Note that these numbers exclude the time required to do the zero-knowledge argument of knowledge in *Setup* and the two-party computation in *Proof of Honesty*. The zero-knowledge argument of knowledge requires about 12,000 AND gates (for two AES computations), and our analysis in Appendix A shows that the number of AND gates that need to be evaluated in the circuits of the honesty proof is at most 22 million. We also measured a throughput of computing about 3.2 million AND gates in Yao's protocol on the machines that we were using. Therefore we estimate that implementing these computations using garbled circuits will contribute about 7 s to the total time.

Comparing to previous work, the only other competitive protocol (for 2048 bit keys) with implementation work is the one by Hazay *et al.* [HMRT12]. Unfortunately their implementation is not publicly available and thus we are not able to make a comparison on the same hardware. However, we do not that the fastest time they report is 15 min on a 2.3 GHz dual-core Intel desktop, for their *semi-honestly secure* protocol.

References

[ACS02] Algesheimer, J., Camenisch, J., Shoup, V.: Efficient computation modulo a shared secret with application to the generation of shared safe-prime products. In: Yung, M. (ed.) CRYPTO 2002. LNCS, vol. 2442, pp. 417–432. Springer, Heidelberg (2002). https://doi.org/10.1007/3-540-45708-9_27

[BF01] Boneh, D., Franklin, M.K.: Efficient generation of shared RSA keys. J. ACM 48(4), 702–722 (2001)

[BHKR13] Bellare, M., Hoang, V.T., Keelveedhi, S., Rogaway, P.: Efficient garbling from a fixed-key blockcipher. In: IEEE Symposium on Security and Privacy, pp. 478–492. IEEE Computer Society (2013)

[CDN01] Cramer, R., Damgård, I., Nielsen, J.B.: Multiparty computation from threshold homomorphic encryption. In: Pfitzmann, B. (ed.) EUROCRYPT 2001. LNCS, vol. 2045, pp. 280–300. Springer, Heidelberg (2001). https://doi.org/10.1007/3-540-44987-6_18

[DM10] Damgård, I., Mikkelsen, G.L.: Efficient, robust and constant-round distributed RSA key generation. In: Micciancio, D. (ed.) TCC 2010. LNCS, vol. 5978, pp. 183–200. Springer, Heidelberg (2010). https://doi.org/10.1007/978-3-642-11799-2_12

[FMY98] Frankel, Y., MacKenzie, P.D., Yung, M.: Robust efficient distributed RSA-key generation. In: STOC, pp. 663–672 (1998)

[Gav12] Gavin, G.: RSA modulus generation in the two-party case. IACR Cryptology ePrint Archive 2012:336 (2012)

[Gil99] Gilboa, N.: Two party RSA key generation. In: Wiener, M. (ed.) CRYPTO 1999. LNCS, vol. 1666, pp. 116–129. Springer, Heidelberg (1999). https://doi.org/10.1007/3-540-48405-1_8

[GMO16] Giacomelli, I., Madsen, J., Orlandi, C.: ZKBoo: faster zero-knowledge for boolean circuits. In: Holz, T., Savage, S. (eds.) USENIX Security Symposium, pp. 1069–1083. USENIX Association (2016)

[HMRT12] Hazay, C., Mikkelsen, G.L., Rabin, T., Toft, T.: Efficient RSA key generation and threshold paillier in the two-party setting. In: CT-RSA, pp. 313–331 (2012)

[IPS09] Ishai, Y., Prabhakaran, M., Sahai, A.: Secure arithmetic computation with no honest majority. In: Reingold, O. (ed.) TCC 2009. LNCS, vol. 5444, pp. 294–314. Springer, Heidelberg (2009). https://doi.org/10.1007/978-3-642-00457-5_18

[JKO13] Jawurek, M., Kerschbaum, F., Orlandi, C.: Zero-knowledge using garbled circuits: how to prove non-algebraic statements efficiently. In: Sadeghi, A.-R., Gligor, V.D., Yung, M. (eds.) ACM SIGSAC, pp. 955–966. ACM (2013)

[KOS15] Keller, M., Orsini, E., Scholl, P.: Actively secure OT extension with optimal overhead. In: Gennaro, R., Robshaw, M. (eds.) CRYPTO 2015. LNCS, vol. 9215, pp. 724–741. Springer, Heidelberg (2015). https://doi.org/10.1007/978-3-662-47989-6_35

[KOS16] Keller, M., Orsini, E., Scholl, P.: MASCOT: faster malicious arithmetic secure computation with oblivious transfer. In: Weippl, E.R., Katzenbeisser, S., Kruegel, C., Myers, A.C., Halevi, S. (eds.) ACM SIGSAC, pp. 830–842. ACM (2016)

[KS06] Kiraz, M.S., Schoenmakers, B.: A protocol issue for the malicious case of Yao's garbled circuit construction. In: Proceedings of 27th Symposium on Information Theory in the Benelux, pp. 283–290 (2006)

[Lin16] Lindell, Y.: Fast cut-and-choose-based protocols for malicious and covert adversaries. J. Cryptology **29**(2), 456–490 (2016)

[MF06] Mohassel, P., Franklin, M.: Efficiency tradeoffs for malicious two-party computation. In: Yung, M., Dodis, Y., Kiayias, A., Malkin, T. (eds.) PKC 2006. LNCS, vol. 3958, pp. 458–473. Springer, Heidelberg (2006). https://doi.org/10.1007/11745853_30

[NP99] Naor, M., Pinkas, B.: Oblivious transfer and polynomial evaluation. In: Vitter, J.S., Larmore, L.L., Leighton, F.T. (eds.) STOC, pp. 245–254. ACM (1999)

[OOS17] Orrù, M., Orsini, E., Scholl, P.: Actively secure 1-out-of-n OT extension with application to private set intersection. In: CT-RSA, pp. 381–396 (2017)

[PS98] Poupard, G., Stern, J.: Generation of shared RSA keys by two parties. In: Ohta, K., Pei, D. (eds.) ASIACRYPT 1998. LNCS, vol. 1514, pp. 11–24. Springer, Heidelberg (1998). https://doi.org/10.1007/3-540-49649-1_2

[PVW08] Peikert, C., Vaikuntanathan, V., Waters, B.: A framework for efficient and composable oblivious transfer. In: Wagner, D. (ed.) CRYPTO 2008. LNCS, vol. 5157, pp. 554–571. Springer, Heidelberg (2008). https://doi.org/10.1007/978-3-540-85174-5_31

[RSA78] Rivest, R.L., Shamir, A., Adleman, L.M.: A method for obtaining digital signatures and public-key cryptosystems. Commun. ACM **21**(2), 120–126 (1978)

[Sch12] Schneider, T.: Engineering Secure Two-Party Computation Protocols: Design, Optimization, and Applications of Efficient Secure Function Evaluation. Springer, Heidelberg (2012). https://doi.org/10.1007/978-3-642-30042-4

[Sho00] Shoup, V.: Practical threshold signatures. In: Preneel, B. (ed.) EUROCRYPT 2000. LNCS, vol. 1807, pp. 207–220. Springer, Heidelberg (2000). https://doi.org/10.1007/3-540-45539-6_15

[SHS+15] Songhori, E.M., Hussain, S.U., Sadeghi, A.-R., Schneider, T., Koushanfar, F.: TinyGarble: highly compressed and scalable sequential garbled circuits. In: IEEE Symposium on Security and Privacy, pp. 411–428. IEEE Computer Society (2015)

A   The Size of the Circuit for the Proof of Honesty

The circuit that is evaluated in the honesty proof contains the following components:

- AES computation: Four AES encryptions of single blocks (for verifying the commitments to the keys in Step 2), and $s + 6$ encryptions of values of length $|N|/2 + s$ bits. For $|N| = 2048$ bits this translates to $4 + 46 \cdot 9 = 418$ AES blocks. With an AES circuit of size 6000 AND gates, this translates to $2.5M$ gates.
- Multiplications: The circuit computes two multiplications where each of the inputs is $|N|/2$ bits long. For $|N| = 2048$ using Karatsuba multiplication this takes 1.040M gates [Sch12].
- Division: The circuit computes a division of an $|N|$ bit value by $e = 2^{16} + 1$. For $|N| = 2048$ the size of this component is about 900K AND gates.

- Computing the inverse of an $|N|$ bit number modulo e: This operation is done by first reducing the number modulo e and then raising the result to the power of $e - 2$ modulo e. The first step takes about 900K AND gates, and the second step takes 64K AND gates.
- Comparisons, additions, and multiplications by small numbers (smaller than e): These operations are implemented with a number of gates that is linear in the size of their inputs, and is therefore quite small. We estimate an upper bound of 100 K for the number of AND gates in all these operations.

The total size of the circuit is therefore less than 5.5M AND gates. The honesty proof should be carried out by each of the parties, and dual execution requires computing the circuit twice. Therefore the total number of AND gates computed is less than 22M.

Trapdoor Functions from the Computational Diffie-Hellman Assumption

Sanjam Garg[1]([✉]) and Mohammad Hajiabadi[1,2]

[1] University of California, Berkeley, USA
{sanjamg,mdhajiabadi}@berkeley.edu
[2] University of Virginia, Charlottesville, USA

Abstract. Trapdoor functions (TDFs) are a fundamental primitive in cryptography. Yet, the current set of assumptions known to imply TDFs is surprisingly limited, when compared to public-key encryption. We present a new general approach for constructing TDFs. Specifically, we give a generic construction of TDFs from any Chameleon Encryption (Döttling and Garg [CRYPTO'17]) satisfying a novel property which we call recyclability. By showing how to adapt current Computational Diffie-Hellman (CDH) based constructions of chameleon encryption to yield recyclability, we obtain the first construction of TDFs with security proved under the CDH assumption. While TDFs from the Decisional Diffie-Hellman (DDH) assumption were previously known, the possibility of basing them on CDH had remained open for more than 30 years.

Keywords: Trapdoor functions
Computational Diffie-Hellman assumption · Hash encryption

1 Introduction

Trapdoor functions (TDFs) are a fundamental primitive in cryptography, historically pre-dating the complexity-based development of public key encryption (PKE) [11,28]. Informally, TDFs are a family of functions, where each function in the family is easy to compute given the function's index key, and also easy to invert given an associated trapdoor key. The security requirement is that a randomly chosen function from the family should be hard to invert without knowledge of a trapdoor key.

Research supported in part from DARPA/ARL SAFEWARE Award W911NF15C0210, AFOSR Award FA9550-15-1-0274, AFOSR YIP Award, DARPA and SPAWAR under contract N66001-15-C-4065, a Hellman Award and research grants by the Okawa Foundation, Visa Inc., and Center for Long-Term Cybersecurity (CLTC, UC Berkeley). The views expressed are those of the author and do not reflect the official policy or position of the funding agencies.

H. Shacham and A. Boldyreva (Eds.): CRYPTO 2018, LNCS 10992, pp. 362–391, 2018.
https://doi.org/10.1007/978-3-319-96881-0_13

A salient difference between TDFs and PKE lies in their inversion (decryption) algorithms: while the inversion algorithm of a TDF recovers the entire pre-image in full, the decryption algorithm of a PKE only recovers the corresponding plaintext, and not necessarily the randomness. This full-input recovery feature of TDFs is useful in may applications. For example, suppose we have two image points $y_1 := \mathsf{F}(\mathsf{ik}_1, x_1)$ and $y_2 := \mathsf{F}(\mathsf{ik}_2, x_2)$ of a trapdoor function F, and we want to convince Alice — who is given both y_1 and y_2 but only a trapdoor key tk_1 for ik_1 — that $x_1 = x_2$. This will be easy for Alice to do herself: retrieve x_1 from y_1 using the trapdoor key tk_1 and check whether $y_1 = \mathsf{F}(\mathsf{ik}_1, x_1)$ and $y_2 = \mathsf{F}(\mathsf{ik}_2, x_1)$.[1] This is a very useful property, especially in the context of chosen-ciphertext (CCA2) security, and is in fact the main reason behind the success of building CCA2-secure PKE in a black-box way from various forms of TDFs [23,27,29]. In contrast, enabling this technique based on PKE [25] requires the use of expensive non-interactive zero knowledge proofs [4,16], which in turn require strong assumptions and lead to non-black-box constructions.

The deterministic structure of TDFs, however, comes with a price, making the construction of TDFs more challenging than that of PKE. This belief is justified by an impossibility result of Gertner, Malkin and Reingold [18] showing that TDFs cannot be built from PKE in a black-box way. As another evidence, while it was known from the 80's how to build semantically-secure PKE from the Decisional Diffie-Hellman (DDH) assumption [15,20,32], it took two decades to realize TDFs based on DDH [27].

Despite the fundamental nature of TDFs and extensive research on this notion [1–3,17,23,27,29,31] a long-standing question has remained open:

Can trapdoor functions be based on the Computational Diffie-Hellman (CDH) Assumption?

The main difficulty of the above question is that all known DDH-based constructions of TDFs, e.g., [17,27], exploit properties of DDH, such as pseudorandomness of low rank matrices of group elements, which do not hold in the CDH setting (see Sect. 1.1).

Apart from being a natural question, it has the following theoretical motivation: since we know that TDFs are not necessary in a black-box sense for PKE [18], there may be computational assumptions that imply PKE but not TDFs. Thus, it is important to understand whether TDFs can be obtained from all existing computational assumptions that imply PKE. This provides insights into the hardness nature of TDFs as well as our computational assumptions.

1.1 Lack of CDH-Based Techniques for TDF

Diffie-Hellman related assumptions (even DDH) do not naturally lend themselves to a TDF construction. The main reason why it is more difficult to build TDFs

---

[1] Here we also need to assume that certifying whether a given point is in the domain of a trapdoor function can be done efficiently.

from such assumptions, compared to, say, factoring related assumptions, is that we do not know of any generic trapdoors for the *discrete log* problem. Indeed, a long standing open problem in cryptography is whether PKE can be based on the sole hardness of the discrete log problem. To see how this makes things more difficult, consider ElGamal encryption: to encrypt a group element g_m under a public key (g, g_1), we return $(g^r, g_1^r \cdot g_m)$, where r is a random exponent. The decryption algorithm can recover g_m but not r because computing r is as hard as solving the discrete log problem.

Known DDH-based TDF constructions [17,27] get around the above obstacle by designing their TDFs in such a way that during inversion, one will only need to solve the discrete log problem over a small space, e.g., recovering a bit b from g^b. The main idea is as follows: the index key ik of their TDF is g^M, where g is a generator of the group $\mathbb{G}$ of order p and $M \in \mathbb{Z}_p^{n \times n}$ is a random $n \times n$ invertible matrix and g^M denotes entry-wise exponentiation. Let $tk := M^{-1}$ be the trapdoor key. Using ik, the evaluation algorithm on input $x \in \{0,1\}^n$ may use the algebraic property of the group to compute $y := g^{Mx} \in \mathbb{G}^n$. Now using tk and y one can compute $g^x \in \mathbb{G}^n$, hence retrieving x.

To argue about one-wayness, one uses the following property implied by DDH: the matrix g^M is computationally indistinguishable from a matrix g^{M_1}, where M_1 is a random matrix of rank one. If the index key is now set to g^{M_1} and if we have $2^n \gg p$, then even an unbounded adversary cannot retrieve the original x from y. This argument is used to establish one-wayness for the TDF.

Unfortunately, the above rank indistinguishability property used to prove one-wayness is not known (and not believed) to be implied by CDH. Thus, designing TDFs based on CDH requires new techniques.

Finally, we mention that even from the Computational Bilinear Assumption [6] (i.e., pairing-based CDH) no TDF constructions are known. The closest is a result of Wee [30], showing that trapdoor relations, which are much weaker than TDFs, can be built from CDH. Roughly, trapdoor relations are a relaxed version of TDFs, in that the function might not be efficiently computable on individual points but one may sample efficiently a *random* input element together with its corresponding image.

1.2   Our Results and Techniques

We give the first construction of TDFs under the CDH assumption. Our construction is black-box and is obtained through a general construction of TDFs from a primitive we call a *recyclable one-way function with encryption (OWFE)*. Moreover, we show that an *adaptive* strengthening of our notion of recyclable OWEF yields a black-box construction of CCA2-secure PKE.

An OWFE is described by a one-way function $f_{pp} \colon \{0,1\}^n \to \{0,1\}^\nu$, where pp is a public parameter, together with encapsulation/decapsulation algorithms (E, D). Specifically, E takes as input pp, an image $y \in \{0,1\}^\nu$ of f_{pp}, an index $i \in [n]$ and a selector bit $b \in \{0,1\}$, and produces an encapsulated ciphertext ct and a corresponding *key bit* $e \in \{0,1\}$. The algorithm D allows anyone to retrieve e from ct using any pre-image x of y whose ith bit is b. For security, letting $y := f_{pp}(x)$, we require if $(ct, e) \xleftarrow{\$} E(pp, y, (i, b))$ and $x_i \neq b$, then even knowing x one cannot recover e from ct with probability better than $\frac{1}{2} + negl(\lambda)$, where λ is the security parameter. That is, for any $x \in \{0, 1\}^n$, $i \in [n]$, we have $(x, ct, e) \stackrel{c}{\equiv} (x, ct, e')$, where $e' \xleftarrow{\$} \{0, 1\}$, $(ct, e) \xleftarrow{\$} E(pp, f(pp, x), (i, 1 - x_i))$ and $\stackrel{c}{\equiv}$ denotes computational indistinguishability. Our OWFE notion is a weakening of the hash encryption notion [13] in that we do not require f to be collision resistant. The following is a variant of the CDH-based construction of [13].

CDH-based instantiation of OWFE *[13].* Let $\mathbb{G}$ be a group of prime order p. The public parameter is a $2 \times n$ matrix of random group elements $pp := \left(\begin{smallmatrix} g_{1,0}, g_{2,0}, \ldots, g_{n,0} \\ g_{1,1}, g_{2,1}, \ldots, g_{n,1} \end{smallmatrix} \right)$ and $y := f(pp, x \in \{0, 1\}^n) = \prod_{j \in [n]} g_{j, x_j}$.

To perform $E(pp, y, (i, b))$, sample $\rho \xleftarrow{\$} \mathbb{Z}_p$ and return (ct, e), where

$$ct := \left(\begin{matrix} g'_{1,0}, g'_{2,0}, \ldots, g'_{n,0} \\ g'_{1,1}, g'_{2,1}, \ldots, g'_{n,1} \end{matrix} \right), \text{ where } g'_{i,1-b} := \bot, g'_{i,b} := g^{\rho}_{i,b}$$

$$\text{and for all } j \neq i : g'_{j,0} := g^{\rho}_{j,0} \text{ and } g'_{j,1} := g^{\rho}_{j,1}$$

and $e := HC(y^{\rho})$, where HC is a hardcore bit function. The function D is now derived easily. See the main body for the proof of security.

Recyclability. Our recyclability notion asserts that the ciphertext part output, ct, of the key encapsulation algorithm E is independent of the corresponding image input part y. That is, letting E_1 and E_2 refer to the first and second output of E, for any values of y_1 and y_2, we always have $E_1(pp, y_1, (i, b); \rho) = E_1(pp, y_2, (i, b); \rho)$. It is easy to verify that the above CDH-based OWFE satisfies this property. Thus, we may drop y as an input to E_1 and obtain the following:

Property 1. Letting $x \in \{0, 1\}^n$, $x_i = b$, $ct := E_1(pp, (i, b); \rho)$ and $y := f(pp, x)$:

$$D(pp, x, ct) = E_2(pp, y, (i, b); \rho).$$

1.3 Sketch of Our OWFE-Based Construction and Techniques

Let (K, f, E, D) be a recyclable OWFE scheme.[2] Our TDF construction is based on a new technique that we call *bits planting*. Briefly, the input X to our TDF consists of a domain element $x \in \{0, 1\}^n$ of $f(pp, \cdot)$ and a *blinding* string $\mathbf{b} \in \{0, 1\}^{n \times r}$, for some r that we will specify later. The output Y is comprised of $y := f(pp, x)$, as well as a matrix of bits in which we copy all the bits of $\mathbf{b}$ in the clear but in hidden spots determined by x; we fill up the rest of the matrix with key bits that somehow correspond to bit-by-bit encryption of x under y. To an adversary, the matrix is "unrevealing," with no indicative signs of what spots corresponding to the blinding part — which contain $\mathbf{b}$ in the clear. However, using our designed trapdoor, an inverter can pull out both x and $\mathbf{b}$ from Y with all but negligible probability.

---

[2] K is the public-parameter generation algorithm. See Definition 3.

Warm-up Construction. We first give a warm up construction in which our inversion algorithm only recovers half of the input bits (on average). Our TDF input is of the form $(x, \mathbf{b}) \in \{0,1\}^n \times \{0,1\}^n$. This warm-up construction contains most of the ideas behind the full-blown construction.

- **Key generation**: The trapdoor key is $\mathsf{tk} := \left(\begin{smallmatrix} \rho_{1,0}, \dots, \rho_{n,0} \\ \rho_{1,1}, \dots, \rho_{n,1} \end{smallmatrix}\right)$ a matrix of randomness values, and the index key is $\mathsf{ik} := \mathsf{pp}, \left(\begin{smallmatrix} \mathsf{ct}_{1,0}, \dots, \mathsf{ct}_{n,0} \\ \mathsf{ct}_{1,1}, \dots, \mathsf{ct}_{n,1} \end{smallmatrix}\right)$, formed as:

$$\mathsf{ik} := \mathsf{pp}, \begin{pmatrix} \mathsf{ct}_{1,0} := \mathsf{E}_1(\mathsf{pp}, (1,0); \rho_{1,0}), \dots, \mathsf{ct}_{n,0} := \mathsf{E}_1(\mathsf{pp}, (n,0); \rho_{n,0}) \\ \mathsf{ct}_{1,1} := \mathsf{E}_1(\mathsf{pp}, (1,1); \rho_{1,1}), \dots, \mathsf{ct}_{n,1} := \mathsf{E}_1(\mathsf{pp}, (n,1); \rho_{n,1}) \end{pmatrix}.$$

- **Evaluation** $\mathsf{F}(\mathsf{ik}, \mathsf{X})$: Parse $\mathsf{ik} := \mathsf{pp}, \left(\begin{smallmatrix} \mathsf{ct}_{1,0}, \dots, \mathsf{ct}_{n,0} \\ \mathsf{ct}_{1,1}, \dots, \mathsf{ct}_{n,1} \end{smallmatrix}\right)$ and parse the input X as $(x \in \{0,1\}^n, \mathbf{b} := b_1 \cdots b_n \in \{0,1\}^n)$. Set $y := f(\mathsf{pp}, x)$. For $i \in [n]$ set M_i as follows:

$$\mathsf{M}_i := \begin{pmatrix} \mathsf{D}(\mathsf{pp}, x, \mathsf{ct}_{i,0}) \\ b_i \end{pmatrix} \overset{*}{=} \begin{pmatrix} \mathsf{E}_2(\mathsf{pp}, y, (i,0); \rho_{i,0}) \\ b_i \end{pmatrix} \text{ if } x_i = 0$$

$$\mathsf{M}_i := \begin{pmatrix} b_i \\ \mathsf{D}(\mathsf{pp}, x, \mathsf{ct}_{i,1}) \end{pmatrix} \overset{*}{=} \begin{pmatrix} b_i \\ \mathsf{E}_2(\mathsf{pp}, y, (i,1); \rho_{i,1}) \end{pmatrix} \text{ if } x_i = 1 \qquad (1)$$

The matrix M_i is computed using the *deterministic* algorithm D and the equalities specified as $\overset{*}{=}$ follow by Property (1).
Return $\mathsf{Y} := (y, \mathsf{M}_1 || \dots || \mathsf{M}_n)$.

- **Inversion** $\mathsf{F}^{-1}(\mathsf{tk}, \mathsf{Y})$: Parse $\mathsf{Y} := (y, \mathsf{M}_1 || \dots || \mathsf{M}_n)$ and $\mathsf{tk} := \left(\begin{smallmatrix} \rho_{1,0}, \ \dots, \ \rho_{n,0} \\ \rho_{1,1}, \ \dots, \ \rho_{n,1} \end{smallmatrix}\right)$. Set

$$(\mathsf{M}'_1 || \dots || \mathsf{M}'_n) := \begin{pmatrix} \mathsf{E}_2(\mathsf{pp}, y, (1,0); \rho_{1,0}), \dots, \mathsf{E}_2(\mathsf{pp}, y, (n,0); \rho_{n,0}) \\ \mathsf{E}_2(\mathsf{pp}, y, (1,1); \rho_{1,1}), \dots, \mathsf{E}_2(\mathsf{pp}, y, (n,1); \rho_{n,1}) \end{pmatrix}. \qquad (2)$$

Output $(x, \mathbf{b} := b_1 \dots b_n)$, where we retrieve x_i and b_i as follows. If $\mathsf{M}'_{i,1} = \mathsf{M}_{i,1}$ and $\mathsf{M}'_{i,2} \neq \mathsf{M}_{i,2}$ (where $\mathsf{M}_{i,1}$ is the first element of M_i), then set $x_i := 0$ and $b_i := \mathsf{M}_{i,2}$. If $\mathsf{M}'_{i,1} \neq \mathsf{M}_{i,1}$ and $\mathsf{M}'_{i,2} = \mathsf{M}_{i,2}$, then set $x_i := 1$ and $b_i := \mathsf{M}_{i,1}$. Else, set $x_i := \bot$ and $b_i := \bot$.

One-Wayness (Sketch). We show $(\mathsf{ik}, \mathsf{Y}) \overset{c}{\equiv} (\mathsf{ik}, \mathsf{Y}_{\mathrm{sim}})$, where $(\mathsf{ik}, \mathsf{Y})$ is as above and

$$\mathsf{Y}_{\mathrm{sim}} := y, \begin{pmatrix} \mathsf{E}_2(\mathsf{pp}, y, (1,0); \rho_{1,0}), \dots, \mathsf{E}_2(\mathsf{pp}, y, (n,0); \rho_{n,0}) \\ \mathsf{E}_2(\mathsf{pp}, y, (1,1); \rho_{1,1}), \dots, \mathsf{E}_2(\mathsf{pp}, y, (n,1); \rho_{n,1}) \end{pmatrix}.$$

Noting that we may produce $(\mathsf{ik}, \mathsf{Y}_{\mathrm{sim}})$ using only pp and y, the one-wayness of $f(\mathsf{pp}, \cdot)$ implies it is hard to recover x from $(\mathsf{ik}, \mathsf{Y}_{\mathrm{sim}})$, and so also from $(\mathsf{ik}, \mathsf{Y})$.

Why $(\mathsf{ik}, \mathsf{Y}) \overset{c}{\equiv} (\mathsf{ik}, \mathsf{Y}_{\mathrm{sim}})$? Consider $\mathsf{Y}_{\mathrm{sim},1}$, whose first column is the same as $\mathsf{Y}_{\mathrm{sim}}$ and whose subsequent columns are the same as Y. We prove $(x, \mathsf{ik}, \mathsf{Y}) \overset{c}{\equiv} (x, \mathsf{ik}, \mathsf{Y}_{\mathrm{sim},1})$; the rest will follow using a hybrid argument.

Letting M_1 be formed as in Eq. 1, to prove $(x, ik, Y) \overset{c}{\equiv} (x, ik, Y_{\text{sim},1})$ it suffices to show

$$
x, \begin{pmatrix} E_1(pp, y, (1, 0); \rho_{1,0}) \\ E_1(pp, (1, 1); \rho_{1,1}) \end{pmatrix}, M_1 \overset{c}{\equiv} x, \begin{pmatrix} E_1(pp, (1, 0); \rho_{1,0}) \\ E_1(pp, (1, 1); \rho_{1,1}) \end{pmatrix}, \begin{pmatrix} E_2(pp, y, (1, 0); \rho_{1,0}) \\ E_2(pp, y, (1, 1); \rho_{1,1}) \end{pmatrix}.
$$
(3)

We prove Eq. 3 using the security property of OWFE, which says

$$
(x, E_1(pp, (1, 1 - x_1); \rho), b') \overset{c}{\equiv} (x, E_1(pp, (1, 1 - x_1); \rho), E_2(pp, y, (1, 1 - x_1); \rho)),
$$
(4)

where $b' \overset{\$}{\leftarrow} \{0, 1\}$ and ρ is random. We give an algorithm that converts a sample from either side of Eq. 4 into a sample from the same side of Eq. 3. On input (x, ct_1, b_1), sample $(ct_2, b_2) \overset{\$}{\leftarrow} E(pp, y, (1, x_1))$ and

- if $x_1 = 0$, then return $x, \left(\begin{smallmatrix} ct_2 \\ ct_1 \end{smallmatrix} \right), \left(\begin{smallmatrix} b_2 \\ b_1 \end{smallmatrix} \right)$;
- else if $x_1 = 1$, then return $x, \left(\begin{smallmatrix} ct_1 \\ ct_2 \end{smallmatrix} \right), \left(\begin{smallmatrix} b_1 \\ b_2 \end{smallmatrix} \right)$.

The claimed property of the converter follows by inspection. Finally, we mention that the argument used to prove Eq. 3 builds on a technique used by Brakerski et al. [7] to build circularly-secure PKE.

Correctness. F^{-1} recovers on average half of the input bits: F^{-1} fails for an index $i \in [n]$ if $b_i = E_2(pp, y, (i, 1 - x_i); \rho_{i,1-x_i})$. This happens with probability $\frac{1}{2}$ because b_i is a completely random bit.

Boosting correctness. To boost correctness, we provide r blinding bits for each index i of $x \in \{0, 1\}^n$. That is, the input to the TDF is $(x, \mathbf{b}) \in \{0, 1\}^n \times \{0, 1\}^{rn}$. We will also expand ik by providing r encapsulated ciphertexts for each position $(i, b) \in [n] \times \{0, 1\}$. This extra information will bring the inversion error down to 2^{-r}. We will show that one-wayness is still preserved.

On the role of blinding. One may wonder why we need to put a blinding string $\mathbf{b}$ in the TDF input. Why do not we simply let the TDF input be x and derive multiple key bits for every index i of x by applying D to the corresponding ciphertexts provided for that position i in the index key ik; the inverter can still find the matching bit for every index. The reason behind our design choice is that by avoiding blinders, it seems very difficult (if not impossible) to give a reduction to the security of the OWFE scheme.

1.4   CCA2 Security

Rosen and Segev [29] show that an extended form of one-wayness for TDFs, which they term k-*repetition security*, leads to a black-box construction of CCA2-secure PKE. Informally, a TDF is k-repetition secure if it is hard to recover a random input X from $F(ik_1, X), \ldots, F(ik_k, X)$, where $ik_1, \ldots, ik_k$ are sampled independently. They show that k-repetition security, for $k \in \Theta(\lambda)$, suffices for CCA2 security.

We give a CCA2 secure PKE by largely following [29], but we need to overcome two problems. The first problem is that our TDF is not k-repetition secure, due to the blinding part of the input. We overcome this by observing that a weaker notion of k-repetition suffices for us: one in which we should keep x the same across all k evaluations but may sample **b** freshly each time. A similar weakening was also used in [26].

The second problem is that our inversion may fail with negligible probability for every choice of (ik, tk) and a bit care is needed here. In particular, the simulation strategy of [29] will fail if the adversary can create an image Y, which is a true image of a domain point X, but which the inversion algorithm fails to invert. To overcome this problem, we slightly extend the notion of security required by OWFE, calling it *adaptive OWFE*, and show that if our TDF is instantiated using this primitive, it satisfies all the properties needed to build CCA2 secure PKE.

Comparison with related CCA2 constructions. We note that CCA2-secure PKE constructions from CDH are already known, e.g., [9,22,30], which are more efficient than the one obtained by instantiating our construction using CDH. We presented a CCA-2 secure construction just to show the black-box utility of our base general primitive. The recent results of [7,12–14], combined with [8], show that CCA-secure PKE can be built from a related primitive called chameleon/batch encryption, but in a non-black-box way.

1.5   Discussion

Black-box power of chameleon encryption. Our work is a contribution toward understanding the black-box power of the notion of chameleon encryption. Recent works [7,12,13] show that chameleon encryption (and its variants) may be used in a non-black-box way to build strong primitives such as identity-based encryption (IBE). The work of Brakerski et al. [7] shows also black-box applications of (a variant of) this notion, obtaining in turn circularly-secure and leakage-resilient PKE from CDH. Our work furthers the progress in this area, by giving a black-box construction of TDFs.

Related work. Hajiabadi and Kapron [21] show how to build TDFs from any *reproducible* circularly secure single-bit PKE. Informally, a PKE is reproducible if given a public key pk', a public/secret key (pk, sk) and a ciphertext c := PKE.E(pk', b'; r), one can recycle the randomness of c to obtain PKE.E(pk, b; r) for any bit $b \in \{0, 1\}$. Brakerski et al. [7] recently built a circularly secure single-bit PKE using CDH. Their construction is not reproducible, however. (The following assumes familiarity with [7].) In their PKE, a secret key x of their PKE is an input to their hash function and the public key y is its corresponding image. To encrypt a bit b they (a) additively secret-share b into $(b_1, \ldots, b_n)$, where $n = |x|$ and (b) form $2n$ ciphertext $ct_{i,b}$, where $ct_{i,b}$ encrypts b_i using y relative to (i, b). Their scheme is not reproducible because the randomness used for step (a) cannot be recycled and also half of the randomness used to create hash encryption ciphertexts in step (b) cannot be recycled. (This half corresponds to the bits of the target secret key w.r.t. which we want to recycle randomness.) It is not clear whether their scheme can be modified to yield reproducibility.

Open problems. Our work leads to several open problems. Can our TDF be improved to yield perfect correctness? Our current techniques leave us with a negligible inversion error. Can we build lossy trapdoor functions (LTDF) [27] from recyclable-OWFE/CDH? Given the utility of LTDFs, a construction based on CDH will be interesting. Can we build deterministic encryption based on CDH matching the parameters of those based on DDH [5]?

2 Preliminaries

Notation. We use λ for the security parameter. We use $\overset{c}{\equiv}$ to denote computational indistinguishability between two distributions and use $\equiv$ to denote two distributions are identical. For a distribution D we use $x \overset{\$}{\leftarrow} D$ to mean x is sampled according to D and use $y \in D$ to mean y is in the support of D. For a set S we overload the notation to use $x \overset{\$}{\leftarrow} S$ to indicate that x is chosen uniformly at random from S.

Definition 1 (Trapdoor Functions (TDFs)). *Let* $w = w(\lambda)$ *be a polynomial. A family of trapdoor functions* TDF *with domain* $\{0,1\}^w$ *consists of three PPT algorithms* TDF.K, TDF.F *and* TDF.F^{-1} *with the following syntax and security properties.*

- TDF.K(1^λ): *Takes the security parameter* 1^λ *and outputs a pair* (ik, tk) *of index/trapdoor keys.*
- TDF.F(ik, X): *Takes an index key* ik *and a domain element* X $\in \{0,1\}^w$ *and outputs an image element* Y.
- TDF.F^{-1}(tk, Y): *Takes a trapdoor key* tk *and an image element* Y *and outputs a value* X $\in \{0,1\}^w \cup \{\bot\}$.

We require the following properties.

- ***Correctness:*** *For any* (ik, tk) $\in$ TDF.K(1^λ)

$$\Pr[\mathsf{TDF.F}^{-1}(\mathsf{tk}, \mathsf{TDF.F}(\mathsf{ik}, \mathsf{X})) \neq \mathsf{X}] = \mathsf{negl}(\lambda), \tag{5}$$

where the probability is taken over X $\overset{\$}{\leftarrow} \{0,1\}^w$.
- ***One-wayness:*** *For any PPT adversary* $\mathcal{A}$

$$\Pr[\mathcal{A}(\mathsf{ik}, \mathsf{Y}) = \mathsf{X}] = \mathsf{negl}(\lambda), \tag{6}$$

where (ik, tk) $\overset{\$}{\leftarrow}$ TDF.K(1^λ), X $\overset{\$}{\leftarrow} \{0,1\}^w$ *and* Y = TDF.F(ik, X).

A note about the correctness condition. Our correctness notion relaxes that of perfect correctness by allowing the inversion algorithm to fail (with respect to any trapdoor key) for a negligible fraction of evaluated elements. This relaxation nonetheless suffices for all existing applications of perfectly-correct TDFs. Our correctness notion, however, implies a weaker notion under which the correctness probability is also taken over the choice of the index/trapdoor keys. This makes our result for constructing TDFs stronger.

Definition 2 (Computational Diffie-Hellman (CDH) Assumption). *Let* G *be a group-generator scheme, which on input* 1^λ *outputs* $(\mathbb{G}, p, g)$, *where* $\mathbb{G}$ *is the description of a group, p is the order of the group which is always a prime number and g is a generator of the group. We say that G is CDH-hard if for any PPT adversary $\mathcal{A}$:* $\Pr[\mathcal{A}(\mathbb{G}, p, g, g^{a_1}, g^{a_2}) = g^{a_1 a_2}] = \mathsf{negl}(\lambda)$, *where* $(\mathbb{G}, p, g) \xleftarrow{\$} \mathsf{G}(1^\lambda)$ *and* $a_1, a_2 \xleftarrow{\$} \mathbb{Z}_p$.

3   Recyclable One-Way Function with Encryption

We will start by defining the notion of a one-way function with encryption. This notion is similar to the chameleon encryption notion of Döttling and Garg [13]. However, it is weaker in the sense that it does not imply collision-resistant hash functions.

Next, we will define a novel *ciphertext-randomness recyclability* property for one-way function with encryption schemes. We will show that a variant of the chameleon encryption construction of Döttling and Garg [13] satisfies this ciphertext-randomness recyclability property.

3.1   Recyclable One-Way Function with Encryption

We provide the definition of a one-way function with encryption. We define the notion as a key-encapsulation mechanism with single bit keys.

Definition 3 (One-Way Function with Encryption (OWFE)). *An OWFE scheme consists of four PPT algorithms* $\mathsf{K}, \mathsf{f}, \mathsf{E}$ *and* D *with the following syntax.*

- $\mathsf{K}(1^\lambda)$: *Takes the security parameter* 1^λ *and outputs a public parameter* pp *for a function* f *from n bits to ν bits.*
- $\mathsf{f}(\mathsf{pp}, \mathsf{x})$: *Takes a public parameter* pp *and a preimage* $\mathsf{x} \in \{0,1\}^n$, *and outputs* $\mathsf{y} \in \{0,1\}^\nu$.
- $\mathsf{E}(\mathsf{pp}, \mathsf{y}, (i, b); \rho)$: *Takes a public parameter* pp, *a value* y, *an index* $i \in [n]$, *a bit* $b \in \{0,1\}$ *and randomness* ρ, *and outputs a ciphertext* ct *and a bit* e.[3]
- $\mathsf{D}(\mathsf{pp}, \mathsf{x}, \mathsf{ct})$: *Takes a public parameter* pp, *a value* x *and a ciphertext* ct, *and deterministically outputs* $\mathsf{e}' \in \{0,1\} \cup \{\bot\}$.

We require the following properties.

- **Correctness**: *For any* $\mathsf{pp} \in \mathsf{K}(1^\lambda)$, *any* $i \in [n]$, *any* $\mathsf{x} \in \{0,1\}^n$ *and any randomness value* ρ, *the following holds: letting* $\mathsf{y} := \mathsf{f}(\mathsf{pp}, \mathsf{x})$, $b := \mathsf{x}_i$ *and* $(\mathsf{ct}, \mathsf{e}) := \mathsf{E}(\mathsf{pp}, \mathsf{y}, (i, b); \rho)$, *we have* $\mathsf{e} = \mathsf{D}(\mathsf{pp}, \mathsf{x}, \mathsf{ct})$.

---

[3] ct is assumed to contain (i, b).

- **One-wayness:** *For any PPT adversary $\mathcal{A}$:*

$$\Pr[f(pp, \mathcal{A}(pp, y)) = y] = negl(\lambda),$$

where $pp \xleftarrow{\$} K(1^\lambda)$, $x \xleftarrow{\$} \{0,1\}^n$ *and* $y := f(pp, x)$.
- **Security for encryption:** *For any* $i \in [n]$ *and* $x \in \{0,1\}^n$:

$$(x, pp, ct, e) \overset{c}{\equiv} (x, pp, ct, e')$$

where $pp \xleftarrow{\$} K(1^\lambda)$, $(ct, e) \xleftarrow{\$} E(pp, f(pp, x), (i, 1 - x_i))$ *and* $e' \xleftarrow{\$} \{0,1\}$.

Definition 4 (Recyclability). *We say that an OWFE scheme (f, K, E, D) is recyclable if the following holds. Letting E_1 and E_2 refer to the first and second output of E, the value of $E_1(pp, y, (i, b); \rho)$ is always independent of y. That is, for any $pp \in K(1^\lambda)$, $y_1, y_2 \in \{0,1\}^\nu$, $i \in [n]$, $b \in \{0,1\}$ and randomness ρ: $E_1(pp, y_1, i, b); \rho) = E_1(pp, y_2, (i, b); \rho)$.*

We now conclude the above definitions with two remarks.

Note 1 (Simplified Recyclability). *Since under the recyclability notion the ciphertext output ct of E is independent of the input value y, when referring to E_1, we may omit the inclusion of y as an input and write $ct = E_1(pp, (i, b); \rho)$.*

Note 2. *If the function $f(pp, \cdot)$ is length decreasing (e.g., $f(pp, \cdot): \{0,1\}^n \mapsto \{0,1\}^{n-1}$), then the one-wayness condition of Definition 3 is implied by the combination of the security-for-encryption and correctness conditions. In our definition, however, we do not place any restriction on the structure of the function f, and it could be, say, a one-to-one function. As such, under our general definition, the one-wayness condition is not necessarily implied by those two other conditions.*

3.2 Adaptive One-Way Function with Encryption

For our CCA application we need to work with an adaptive version of the notion of OWFE. Recall by Note 1 that a ciphertext ct does not depend on the corresponding y. The security for encryption notion (Definition 3) says if (ct, e) is formed using an image $y := f(pp, x)$ and parameters (i, b), and if $x_i \neq b$, then even knowing x does not help an adversary in distinguishing e from a random bit. The adaptive version of this notion allows the adversary to choose x after seeing ct. This notion makes sense because ct does not depend on the image y, and so ct may be chosen first.

Definition 5 (Adaptive OWFE). *We say that $\mathcal{E} = (K, f, E, D)$ is an adaptive one-way function with encryption scheme if $\mathcal{E}$ is correct in the sense of Definition 3, f is one-way in the sense of Definition 3 and that $\mathcal{E}$ is adaptively secure in the following sense.*

Experiment AdapOWFE$[t]$($\mathcal{E}, \mathcal{A} := (\mathcal{A}_1, \mathcal{A}_2, \mathcal{A}_3)$):

1. $(i^* \in [n], b^* \in \{0,1\}, \mathsf{st}_1) \overset{\$}{\leftarrow} \mathcal{A}_1(1^\lambda)$
2. Sample $\mathsf{pp} \overset{\$}{\leftarrow} \mathsf{K}(1^\lambda)$ and $\rho_1, \ldots, \rho_t \overset{\$}{\leftarrow} \{0,1\}^*$
3. Set $\mathsf{ct}_1 := \mathsf{E}_1(\mathsf{pp}, (i^*, b^*); \rho_1), \ldots, \mathsf{ct}_t := \mathsf{E}_1(\mathsf{pp}, (i^*, b^*); \rho_t)$
4. $(\mathsf{x}, \mathsf{st}_2) \overset{\$}{\leftarrow} \mathcal{A}_2(\mathsf{st}_1, \mathsf{pp}, \mathsf{ct}_1, \ldots, \mathsf{ct}_t)$.
5. If $\mathsf{x}_{i^*} = b^*$, HALT.
6. For $j \in [t]$: $e_j := \mathsf{E}_2(\mathsf{pp}, \mathsf{y}, (i^*, b^*); \rho_j)$, where $\mathsf{y} = \mathsf{f}(\mathsf{pp}, \mathsf{x})$.
7. $\mathsf{ch} \overset{\$}{\leftarrow} \{0,1\}$. If $\mathsf{ch} = 0$, set $\mathbf{e}' := (e_1, \ldots, e_t)$; else, $\mathbf{e}' \overset{\$}{\leftarrow} \{0,1\}^t$.
8. $\mathsf{out} \overset{\$}{\leftarrow} \mathcal{A}_3(\mathsf{st}_2, \mathbf{e}')$.
9. Output 1 if $\mathsf{out} = \mathsf{ch}$ and 0 otherwise.

Fig. 1. The AdapOWFE$[t]$($\mathcal{E}, \mathcal{A}$) Experiment

– **Adaptive Security:** *For any PPT adversary $\mathcal{A}$, we have the following: the probability that* AdapOWFE$[t = 1]$($\mathcal{E}, \mathcal{A}$) *outputs 1 is $\frac{1}{2} + \mathsf{negl}(\lambda)$, where the experiment* AdapOWFE$[t]$ *is defined in Fig. 1.*

We remind the reader that in Step 3 of Fig. 1 the algorithm E_1 does not take any y as input because of Note 1. The following lemma is obtained using a straightforward hybrid argument, so we omit the proof.

Lemma 1. *Let $\mathcal{E} = (\mathsf{K}, \mathsf{f}, \mathsf{E}, \mathsf{D})$ be an adaptive OWFE scheme. For any polynomial $t := t(\lambda)$ and any PPT adversary $\mathcal{A}$, we have $\Pr[\mathsf{AdapOWFE}[t](\mathcal{E}, \mathcal{A}) = 1] \leq \frac{1}{2} + \mathsf{negl}(\lambda)$.*

3.3 Construction from CDH

We give a CDH-based construction of a recyclable adaptive OWFE based on a group scheme G (Definition 2), which is a close variant of constructions given in [10,13].

– $\mathsf{K}(1^\lambda)$: Sample $(\mathbb{G}, p, g) \overset{\$}{\leftarrow} \mathsf{G}(1^\lambda)$. For each $j \in [n]$ and $b \in \{0,1\}$, choose $g_{j,b} \overset{\$}{\leftarrow} \mathbb{G}$. Output

$$\mathsf{pp} := \mathbb{G}, p, g, \begin{pmatrix} g_{1,0}, g_{2,0}, \ldots, g_{n,0} \\ g_{1,1}, g_{2,1}, \ldots, g_{n,1} \end{pmatrix}. \tag{7}$$

– $\mathsf{f}(\mathsf{pp}, \mathsf{x})$: Parse pp as in Eq. 7, and output $\mathsf{y} := \prod_{j \in [n]} g_{j, \mathsf{x}_j}$.

– $\mathsf{E}(\mathsf{pp}, \mathsf{y}, (i,b))$: Parse pp as in Eq. 7. Sample $\rho \overset{\$}{\leftarrow} \mathbb{Z}_p$ and proceed as follows:

1. For every $j \in [n]\setminus\{i\}$, set $c_{j,0} := g_{j,0}^{\rho}$ and $c_{j,1} := g_{j,1}^{\rho}$.
2. Set $c_{i,b} := g_{i,b}^{\rho}$ and $c_{i,1-b} := \bot$.
3. Set $e := HC(y^{\rho})$.[4]
4. Output (ct, e) where $ct := \begin{pmatrix} c_{1,0}, c_{2,0}, \ldots, c_{n,0} \\ c_{1,1}, c_{2,1}, \ldots, c_{n,1} \end{pmatrix}$.

- $D(pp, x, ct)$: Parse $ct := \begin{pmatrix} c_{1,0}, c_{2,0}, \ldots, c_{n,0} \\ c_{1,1}, c_{2,1}, \ldots, c_{n,1} \end{pmatrix}$. Output $HC(\prod_{j \in [n]} c_{j,x_j})$.

Lemma 2. *Assuming that G is CDH-hard and $n \in \omega(\log p)$, the construction described above is an adaptive one-way function with encryption scheme satisfying the recyclability property.*

Proof. We start by proving one-wayness.

One-wayness. The fact that f_{pp} for a random pp is one-way follows by the discrete-log hardness (and hence CDH hardness) of G. Let g^* be a random group element for which we want to find r^* such that $g^{r^*} = g^*$. Sample $i_1 \xleftarrow{\$} [n]$ and $b_1 \xleftarrow{\$} \{0,1\}$ and set $g_{i_1,b_1} := g^*$. For all $i \in [n]$ and $b \in \{0,1\}$ where $(i,b) \neq (i_1,b_1)$, sample $r_{i,b} \xleftarrow{\$} \mathbb{Z}_p$ and set $g_{i,b} := g^{r_{i,b}}$. Set $pp := \begin{pmatrix} g_{1,0}, \ldots, g_{n,0} \\ g_{1,1}, \ldots, g_{n,1} \end{pmatrix}$. Sample x' at random from $\{0,1\}^n$ subject to the condition that $x'_{i_1} = 1 - b_1$. Set $y := \prod_{j \in [n]} g_{j,x'_j}$. Call the inverter adversary on (pp, y) to receive $x \in \{0,1\}^n$. Now if $n \in \omega(\log p)$, then by the leftover hash lemma with probability negligibly close to $\frac{1}{2}$ we have $x_{i_1} = b_1$, allowing us to find r^* from $r_{i,b}$'s.

Recyclability. We need to show that the ciphertext output ct of E is independent of the input value y. This follows immediately by inspection.

Notation. For a matrix $M := \begin{pmatrix} a_{1,0}, a_{2,0}, \ldots, a_{n,0} \\ a_{1,1}, a_{2,1}, \ldots, a_{n,1} \end{pmatrix}$, $i \in [n]$ and $b \in \{0,1\}$, we define the matrix $M' := M|(i,b)$ to be the same as M except that instead of $a_{i,b}$ we put $\bot$ in M'. If M is matrix of group elements, then M^r denotes element-wise exponentiation to the power of r.

Security for encryption. We show if G is CDH-hard, then the scheme is adaptively secure. Suppose that there exists an adversary A for which we have $\Pr[AdapOWFE[t=1](E,A)] = \frac{1}{2} + \frac{1}{q} > \frac{1}{2} + negl(\lambda)$. Using standard techniques we may transform A into a predictor B who wins with probability at least $\frac{1}{2} + \frac{1}{q}$ in the following experiment:

1. $(i^*, b^*) \xleftarrow{\$} B(1^\lambda)$.
2. Sample
$$pp := \begin{pmatrix} g_{1,0}, g_{2,0}, \ldots, g_{n,0} \\ g_{1,1}, g_{2,1}, \ldots, g_{n,1} \end{pmatrix} \xleftarrow{\$} G^{2 \times n}. \tag{8}$$

---

[4] We assume that the $HC(\cdot)$ is a hardcore bit function. If a deterministic hard-core bit for the specific function is not known then we can use the Goldreich-Levin [19] construction. We skip the details of that with the goal of keeping exposition simple.

3. Sample $\rho \xleftarrow{\$} \mathbb{Z}_p$ and set $\mathsf{ct} := \mathsf{pp}^\rho | (i^*, b^*)$.
4. $(\mathsf{x}, b) \xleftarrow{\$} \mathcal{B}(\mathsf{pp}, \mathsf{ct})$.
5. $\mathcal{B}$ wins if $\mathsf{x}_{i^*} = b^*$ and $b = \mathsf{HC}(\mathsf{y}^\rho)$, where $\mathsf{y} := \displaystyle\prod_{j \in [n]} g_{j, \mathsf{x}_j}$.

Using the Goldreich-Levin theorem we know that there should be an adversary $\mathcal{B}_1$ that wins with non-negligible probability in the following:

1. $(i^*, b^*) \xleftarrow{\$} \mathcal{B}_1(1^\lambda)$.
2. Sample

$$\mathsf{pp} := \begin{pmatrix} g_{1,0}, g_{2,0} \cdots, g_{n,0} \\ g_{1,1}, g_{2,1}, \ldots, g_{n,1} \end{pmatrix} \xleftarrow{\$} \mathbb{G}^{2 \times n}. \tag{9}$$

3. Sample $\rho \xleftarrow{\$} \mathbb{Z}_p$ and set $\mathsf{ct} := \mathsf{pp}^\rho | (i^*, b^*)$.
4. $(\mathsf{x}, g^*) \xleftarrow{\$} \mathcal{B}_1(\mathsf{pp}, \mathsf{ct})$.
5. $\mathcal{B}_1$ wins if $\mathsf{x}_{i^*} = b^*$ and $g^* = \mathsf{y}^\rho$, where $\mathsf{y} := \displaystyle\prod_{j \in [n]} g_{j, \mathsf{x}_j}$.

We now show how to use $\mathcal{B}_1$ to solve the CDH problem.

CDH Adversary $\mathcal{A}_1(g, g_1, g_2)$:

- Run $\mathcal{B}_1(1^\lambda)$ to get (i^*, b^*).
- For any $j \in [n] \setminus \{i^*\}$ and $b \in \{0, 1\}$ sample $\alpha_{j,b} \xleftarrow{\$} \mathbb{Z}_p$ and set $g_{j,b} = g^{\alpha_{j,b}}$. Set $g_{i^*, b^*} := g_1$ and $g_{i^*, 1-b^*} = g^\alpha$, where $\alpha \xleftarrow{\$} \mathbb{Z}_p$. Set

$$\mathsf{pp} := \begin{pmatrix} g_{1,0}, g_{2,0} \cdots, g_{n,0} \\ g_{1,1}, g_{2,1}, \ldots, g_{n,1} \end{pmatrix}.$$

- Set $g'_{i^*, 1-b^*} = g_2$ and $g'_{i^*, b^*} = \bot$. For any $j \in [n] \setminus \{i^*\}$ and $b \in \{0, 1\}$ set $g'_{j,b} = g_2^{(\alpha^{-1} \cdot \alpha_{j,b})}$. Set

$$\mathsf{ct} := \begin{pmatrix} g'_{1,0}, g'_{2,0} \cdots, g'_{n,0} \\ g'_{1,1}, g'_{2,1}, \ldots, g'_{n,1} \end{pmatrix}. \tag{10}$$

- Run $\mathcal{B}_1(\mathsf{pp}, \mathsf{ct})$ to get (x, g^*). If $\mathsf{x}_i \neq b_i^*$ then return $\bot$. Otherwise
  - Set

$$g_u := \frac{g^*}{\prod_{j=1}^{i^*-1} g'_{j, \mathsf{x}_j} \cdot \prod_{j=i^*+1}^{n} g'_{j, \mathsf{x}_j}}.$$

  - Return g_u^α.

By inspection one may easily verify that whenever $\mathcal{B}_1$ wins, $\mathcal{A}_1$ also wins. The proof is now complete. $\qquad \square$

4   TDF Construction

In this section we describe our TDF construction. We first give the following notation.

Extending the notation for D. For a given pp, a sequence $\mathsf{ct} := (\mathsf{ct}_1, \ldots, \mathsf{ct}_r)$ of encapsulated ciphertexts and a value x, we define $\mathsf{D}(\mathsf{pp}, \mathsf{x}, \mathsf{ct})$ to be the concatenation of $\mathsf{D}(\mathsf{pp}, \mathsf{x}, \mathsf{ct}_i)$ for $i \in [r]$.

Algorithm Perm. For two lists $\mathbf{u_1}$ and $\mathbf{u_2}$ and a bit b we define $\mathsf{Perm}(\mathbf{u_1}, \mathbf{u_2}, b)$ to output $(\mathbf{u_1}, \mathbf{u_2})$ if $b = 0$, and $(\mathbf{u_2}, \mathbf{u_1})$ otherwise.

Construction 3 (TDF Construction).

Base Primitive. *A recyclable OWFE scheme* $\mathcal{E} = (\mathsf{K}, \mathsf{f}, \mathsf{E}, \mathsf{D})$. *Let* Rand *be the randomness space of the encapsulation algorithm* E.

Construction. *The construction is parameterized over two parameters* $n = n(\lambda)$ *and* $r = r(\lambda)$, *where* n *is the input length to the function* f, *and* r *will be instantiated in the correctness proof. The input space of each TDF is* $\{0, 1\}^{n+nr}$. *We will make use of the fact explained in Note 1.*

- $\mathsf{TDF.K}(1^\lambda)$:
  - *Sample* $\mathsf{pp} \leftarrow \mathsf{K}(1^\lambda)$.
  - *For each* $i \in [n]$ *and selector bit* $b \in \{0, 1\}$:

$$\boldsymbol{\rho}_{i,b} := (\rho_{i,b}^{(1)}, \ldots, \rho_{i,b}^{(r)}) \xleftarrow{\$} \mathsf{Rand}^r$$

$$\mathbf{ct}_{i,b} := (\mathsf{E}_1(\mathsf{pp}, (i, b); \rho_{i,b}^{(1)}), \ldots, \mathsf{E}_1(\mathsf{pp}, (i, b); \rho_{i,b}^{(r)})).$$

  - *Form the index key* ik *and the trapdoor key* tk *as follows:*

$$\mathsf{ik} := (\mathsf{pp}, \mathbf{ct}_{1,0}, \mathbf{ct}_{1,1}, \ldots, \mathbf{ct}_{n,0}, \mathbf{ct}_{n,1}) \tag{11}$$

$$\mathsf{tk} := (\mathsf{pp}, \boldsymbol{\rho}_{1,0}, \boldsymbol{\rho}_{1,1}, \ldots, \boldsymbol{\rho}_{n,0}, \boldsymbol{\rho}_{n,1}). \tag{12}$$

- $\mathsf{TDF.F}(\mathsf{ik}, \mathsf{X})$:
  - *Parse* ik *as in Eq. 11 and parse*

$$\mathsf{X} := (\mathsf{x} \in \{0, 1\}^n, \mathbf{b}_1 \in \{0, 1\}^r, \ldots, \mathbf{b}_n \in \{0, 1\}^r).$$

  - *Set* $\mathsf{y} := \mathsf{f}(\mathsf{pp}, \mathsf{x})$.
  - *For all* $i \in [n]$ *set*

$$\mathbf{e}_i := \mathsf{D}(\mathsf{pp}, \mathsf{x}, \mathbf{ct}_{i, \mathsf{x}_i}).$$

  - *Return*

$$\mathsf{Y} := (\mathsf{y}, \mathsf{Perm}(\mathbf{e}_1, \mathbf{b}_1, \mathsf{x}_1), \ldots, \mathsf{Perm}(\mathbf{e}_n, \mathbf{b}_n, \mathsf{x}_n)).$$

- $\mathsf{TDF.F}^{-1}(\mathsf{tk}, \mathsf{Y})$:
  - *Parse* tk *as in Eq. 12 and* $\mathsf{Y} := (\mathsf{y}, \widetilde{\mathbf{b}_{1,0}}, \widetilde{\mathbf{b}_{1,1}}, \ldots, \widetilde{\mathbf{b}_{n,0}}, \widetilde{\mathbf{b}_{n,1}})$.
  - *Reconstruct* $\mathsf{x} := \mathsf{x}_1 \cdots \mathsf{x}_n$ *bit-by-bit and* $\mathbf{b} := (\mathbf{b}_1, \ldots, \mathbf{b}_n)$ *vector-by-vector as follows. For* $i \in [n]$:

* Parse $\boldsymbol{\rho}_{i,0} := (\rho_{i,0}^{(1)}, \ldots, \rho_{i,0}^{(r)})$ and $\boldsymbol{\rho}_{i,1} := (\rho_{i,1}^{(1)}, \ldots, \rho_{i,1}^{(r)})$.
* If

$$\widetilde{\mathbf{b}_{i,0}} = \left(\mathsf{E}_2(\mathsf{pp}, \mathsf{y}, (i,0); \rho_{i,0}^{(1)}), \ldots, \mathsf{E}_2(\mathsf{pp}, \mathsf{y}, (i,0); \rho_{i,0}^{(r)}) \right) \text{ and}$$

$$\widetilde{\mathbf{b}_{i,1}} \neq \left(\mathsf{E}_2(\mathsf{pp}, \mathsf{y}, (i,1); \rho_{i,1}^{(1)}), \ldots, \mathsf{E}_2(\mathsf{pp}, \mathsf{y}, (i,1); \rho_{i,1}^{(r)}) \right), \quad (13)$$

then set $\mathsf{x}_i = 0$ and $\mathbf{b}_i = \widetilde{\mathbf{b}_{i,1}}$.
* Else, if

$$\widetilde{\mathbf{b}_{i,0}} \neq \left(\mathsf{E}_2(\mathsf{pp}, \mathsf{y}, (i,0); \rho_{i,0}^{(1)}), \ldots, \mathsf{E}_2(\mathsf{pp}, \mathsf{y}, (i,0); \rho_{i,0}^{(r)}) \right) \text{ and}$$

$$\widetilde{\mathbf{b}_{i,1}} = \left(\mathsf{E}_2(\mathsf{pp}, \mathsf{y}, (i,1); \rho_{i,1}^{(1)}), \ldots, \mathsf{E}_2(\mathsf{pp}, \mathsf{y}, (i,1); \rho_{i,1}^{(r)}) \right), \quad (14)$$

then set $\mathsf{x}_i = 1$ and $\mathbf{b}_i = \widetilde{\mathbf{b}_{i,0}}$.
* Else, halt and return $\perp$.
• If $\mathsf{y} \neq \mathsf{f}(\mathsf{pp}, \mathsf{x})$, then return $\perp$. Otherwise, return $(\mathsf{x}, \mathbf{b})$.

We will now give the correctness and one-wayness statements about our TDF, and will prove them in subsequent subsections.

Lemma 3 (TDF Correctness). *The inversion error of our constructed* TDF *is at most* $\frac{n}{2^r}$. *That is, for any* $(\mathsf{ik}, \mathsf{tk}) \in \mathsf{TDF.K}(1^\lambda)$ *we have*

$$\beta := \Pr[\mathsf{TDF.F}^{-1}(\mathsf{tk}, (\mathsf{TDF.F}(\mathsf{ik}, X))) \neq X] \leq \frac{n}{2^r}, \quad (15)$$

where the probability is taken over $X := (\mathsf{x}, \mathbf{b}_1, \ldots, \mathbf{b}_n) \xleftarrow{\$} \{0,1\}^{n+nr}$. *By choosing* $r \in \omega(\log \lambda)$ *we will have a negligible inversion error.*

For one-wayness we will prove something stronger: parsing $X := (\mathsf{x}, \ldots)$, then recovering any x' satisfying $\mathsf{f}(\mathsf{pp}, \mathsf{x}) = \mathsf{f}(\mathsf{pp}, \mathsf{x}')$ from $(\mathsf{ik}, \mathsf{TDF.F}(\mathsf{ik}, X))$ is infeasible.

Lemma 4 (One-Wayness). *The TDF* $(\mathsf{TDF.K}, \mathsf{TDF.F}, \mathsf{TDF.F}^{-1})$ *given in Construction 3 is one-way. That is, for any PPT adversary* $\mathcal{A}$

$$\Pr[\mathcal{A}(\mathsf{ik}, Y) = \mathsf{x}' \text{ and } \mathsf{f}(\mathsf{pp}, \mathsf{x}') = \mathsf{y}] = \mathsf{negl}(\lambda), \quad (16)$$

where $(\mathsf{ik} := (\mathsf{pp}, \ldots), \mathsf{tk}) \xleftarrow{\$} \mathsf{TDF.K}(1^\lambda)$, $X := (\mathsf{x}, \ldots) \xleftarrow{\$} \{0,1\}^{n+nr}$ *and* $Y := (\mathsf{y}, \ldots) := \mathsf{TDF.F}(\mathsf{ik}, X)$.

By combining Lemmas 2, 3 and 4 we will obtain our main result below.

Theorem 4 (CDH Implies TDF). *There is a black-box construction of TDFs from CDH-hard groups.*

4.1 Proof of Correctness: Lemma 3

Proof Let $X := (x, \mathbf{b}_1, \ldots, \mathbf{b}_n) \xleftarrow{\$} \{0,1\}^{n+nr}$ be as in the lemma and

$$Y := \mathsf{TDF.F}(ik, X) := (y, \widetilde{\mathbf{b}_{1,0}}, \widetilde{\mathbf{b}_{1,1}}, \ldots, \widetilde{\mathbf{b}_{n,0}}, \widetilde{\mathbf{b}_{n,1}}). \tag{17}$$

By design, for all $i \in [n]$: $\widetilde{\mathbf{b}_{i,1-x_i}} = \mathbf{b}_i$. Parse

$$\mathsf{tk} := (\boldsymbol{\rho}_{1,0}, \boldsymbol{\rho}_{1,1}, \ldots, \boldsymbol{\rho}_{n,0}, \boldsymbol{\rho}_{n,1}),$$
$$\boldsymbol{\rho}_{i,b} := (\rho_{i,b}^{(1)}, \ldots, \rho_{i,b}^{(r)}), \text{ for } i \in [n] \text{ and } b \in \{0,1\}.$$

Consider the execution of $\mathsf{TDF.F}^{-1}(\mathsf{tk}, Y)$. By the correctness of our recyclable OWFE $\mathcal{E}$ we have the following: the probability that $\mathsf{TDF.F}^{-1}(\mathsf{tk}, Y) \neq X$ is the probability that for some $i \in [n]$:

$$\mathbf{b}_i = \left(E_2(\mathsf{pp}, y, (i, 1 - x_i); \rho_{i,1-x_i}^{(1)}), \ldots, E_2(\mathsf{pp}, y, (i, 1 - x_i); \rho_{i,1-x_i}^{(r)}) \right). \tag{18}$$

Now since $\mathbf{b}_i$, for all i, is chosen uniformly at random and independently of x, the probability of the event in Eq. 18 is $\frac{1}{2^r}$. A union bound over $i \in [n]$ gives us the claimed error bound. ∎

4.2 Proof of One-wayness: Lemma 4

We will prove Lemma 4 through a couple of hybrids, corresponding to the real and a simulated view. We first give the following definition which will help us describe the two hybrids in a compact way.

Definition 6 *Fix* pp, $x \in \{0,1\}^n$ *and* $y := f(\mathsf{pp}, x)$. *We define two PPT algorithms* Real *and* Sim, *where* Real *takes as input* (pp, x) *and* Sim *takes as input* (pp, y). *We stress that* Sim *does not take* x *as input.*

The algorithm Real(pp, x) *outputs* $(\mathbf{CT}, \mathbf{E})$ *and the algorithm* Sim(pp, y) *outputs* $(\mathbf{CT}, \mathbf{E}_{\mathrm{sim}})$, *sampled in the following way.*

- *Sample* $\begin{pmatrix} \rho_{1,0}, \ldots, \rho_{n,0} \\ \rho_{1,1}, \ldots, \rho_{n,1} \end{pmatrix} \xleftarrow{\$} \mathsf{Rand}^{2 \times n}$.
- *Set*

$$\mathbf{CT} := \begin{pmatrix} ct_{1,0}, \ldots, ct_{n,0} \\ ct_{1,1}, \ldots, ct_{n,1} \end{pmatrix} := \begin{pmatrix} E_1(\mathsf{pp}, (1,0); \rho_{1,0}), \ldots, E_1(\mathsf{pp}, (n,0); \rho_{n,0}) \\ E_1(\mathsf{pp}, (1,1); \rho_{1,1}), \ldots, E_1(\mathsf{pp}, (n,1); \rho_{n,1}) \end{pmatrix}.$$

- *Set*

$$\mathbf{E} := \begin{pmatrix} b_{1,0}, \ldots, b_{n,0} \\ b_{1,1}, \ldots, b_{n,1} \end{pmatrix},$$

where, for all $i \in [n]$:
- *if* $x_i = 0$, *then* $b_{i,0} := D(\mathsf{pp}, x, ct_{i,0})$ *and* $b_{i,1} \xleftarrow{\$} \{0,1\}$.
- *if* $x_i = 1$, *then* $b_{i,0} \xleftarrow{\$} \{0,1\}$ *and* $b_{i,1} := D(\mathsf{pp}, x, ct_{i,1})$.

– *Set*

$$\mathbf{E}_{\text{sim}} := \begin{pmatrix} \mathsf{E}_2(\mathsf{pp}, \mathsf{y}, (1,0); \rho_{1,0}), \dots, \mathsf{E}_2(\mathsf{pp}, \mathsf{y}, (n,0); \rho_{n,0}) \\ \mathsf{E}_2(\mathsf{pp}, \mathsf{y}, (1,1); \rho_{1,1}), \dots, \mathsf{E}_2(\mathsf{pp}, \mathsf{y}, (n,1); \rho_{n,1}) \end{pmatrix}$$

We now prove the following lemma which will help us to prove the indistinguishability of the two hybrids in our main proof.

Lemma 5. *Fix polynomial* $r := r(\lambda)$ *and let* $\mathsf{x} \in \{0,1\}^n$. *We have*

$$(\mathsf{pp}, \mathsf{x}, \mathbf{CT}_1, \mathbf{E}_1, \dots, \mathbf{CT}_r, \mathbf{E}_r) \stackrel{c}{\equiv} (\mathsf{pp}, \mathsf{x}, \mathbf{CT}_1, \mathbf{E}_{\text{sim},1}, \dots, \mathbf{CT}_r, \mathbf{E}_{\text{sim},r}), \qquad (19)$$

where $\mathsf{pp} \stackrel{\$}{\leftarrow} \mathsf{K}(1^\lambda)$, *and for all* $i \in [r]$, *we sample* $(\mathbf{CT}_i, \mathbf{E}_i) \stackrel{\$}{\leftarrow} \mathsf{Real}(\mathsf{pp}, \mathsf{x})$ *and* $(\mathbf{CT}_i, \mathbf{E}_{\text{sim},i}) \stackrel{\$}{\leftarrow} \mathsf{Sim}(\mathsf{pp}, \mathsf{f}(\mathsf{pp}, \mathsf{x}))$.

Proof. Fix $\mathsf{x} \in \{0,1\}^n$ and let $\mathsf{y} := \mathsf{f}(\mathsf{pp}, \mathsf{x})$. For the purpose of doing a hybrid argument we define two algorithms SReal and SSim below.

– $\mathsf{SReal}(i, \mathsf{pp}, \mathsf{x})$: sample $\rho_0, \rho_1 \stackrel{\$}{\leftarrow} \mathsf{Rand}$ and return $(\mathbf{ct}, \mathbf{e})$, where

$$\mathbf{ct} := \begin{pmatrix} \mathsf{ct}_0 \\ \mathsf{ct}_1 \end{pmatrix} := \begin{pmatrix} \mathsf{E}_1(\mathsf{pp}, (i,0); \rho_0) \\ \mathsf{E}_1(\mathsf{pp}, (i,1); \rho_1) \end{pmatrix} \qquad (20)$$

and $\mathbf{e}$ is defined as follows:
  • if $\mathsf{x}_i = 0$, then $\mathbf{e} := \begin{pmatrix} \mathsf{D}(\mathsf{pp}, \mathsf{x}, \mathsf{ct}_0) \\ b \end{pmatrix}$, where $b \stackrel{\$}{\leftarrow} \{0,1\}$;
  • if $\mathsf{x}_i = 1$, then $\mathbf{e} := \begin{pmatrix} b \\ \mathsf{D}(\mathsf{pp}, \mathsf{x}, \mathsf{ct}_1) \end{pmatrix}$, where $b \stackrel{\$}{\leftarrow} \{0,1\}$.
– $\mathsf{SSim}(i, \mathsf{pp}, \mathsf{y})$: Return $(\mathbf{ct}, \mathbf{e}_{\text{sim}})$, where $\mathbf{ct}$ is sampled as in Eq. 20 and $\mathbf{e}_{\text{sim}}$ is sampled as

$$\mathbf{e}_{\text{sim}} := \begin{pmatrix} \mathsf{E}_2(\mathsf{pp}, \mathsf{y}, (i,0); \rho_0) \\ \mathsf{E}_2(\mathsf{pp}, \mathsf{y}, (i,1); \rho_1) \end{pmatrix}.$$

We will show that for all $i \in [n]$ and $\mathsf{x} \in \{0,1\}^n$

$$(\mathsf{pp}, \mathsf{x}, \mathbf{ct}, \mathbf{e}) \stackrel{c}{\equiv} (\mathsf{pp}, \mathsf{x}, \mathbf{ct}, \mathbf{e}_{\text{sim}}), \qquad (21)$$

where

$$\mathsf{pp} \stackrel{\$}{\leftarrow} \mathsf{K}(1^\lambda), \ (\mathbf{ct}, \mathbf{e}) \stackrel{\$}{\leftarrow} \mathsf{SReal}(i, \mathsf{pp}, \mathsf{x}) \ \text{and} \ (\mathbf{ct}, \mathbf{e}_{\text{sim}}) \stackrel{\$}{\leftarrow} \mathsf{SSim}(i, \mathsf{pp}, \mathsf{f}(\mathsf{pp}, \mathsf{x})).$$

From Eq. 21 using a simple hybrid argument the indistinguishability claimed in the lemma (Eq. 19) is obtained. Note that for the hybrid argument we need to make use of the fact that that x is provided in both sides of Eq. 21, because we need to know x to be able to build the intermediate hybrids between those of Eq. 19. Thus, in what follows we will focus on proving Eq. 21.

To prove Eq. 21, first note that by the correctness of the OWFE scheme $\mathcal{E}$, we have

$$(\mathsf{pp}, \mathsf{x}, \mathbf{ct}, \mathbf{e}) \equiv (\mathsf{pp}, \mathsf{x}, \mathbf{ct}, \mathbf{e}'),$$

where $\mathbf{ct}$ and $\mathbf{e}$ are sampled according to $\mathsf{SReal}(i, \mathsf{pp}, \mathsf{x})$ as above (using randomness values ρ_0 and ρ_1), and $\mathbf{e}'$ is sampled as:

- if $x_i = 0$, then $\mathbf{e}' := \begin{pmatrix} E_2(\mathsf{pp}, \mathsf{y}, (i, 0); \rho_0) \\ b \end{pmatrix}$, where $b \xleftarrow{\$} \{0, 1\}$;

- if $x_i = 1$, then $\mathbf{e}' := \begin{pmatrix} b \\ E_2(\mathsf{pp}, \mathsf{y}, (i, 1); \rho_1) \end{pmatrix}$, where $b \xleftarrow{\$} \{0, 1\}$.

Thus, we will prove

$$(\mathsf{pp}, \mathsf{x}, \mathbf{ct}, \mathbf{e}') \overset{c}{\equiv} (\mathsf{pp}, \mathsf{x}, \mathbf{ct}, \mathbf{e}_{\mathsf{sim}}). \tag{22}$$

We derive Eq. 22 from the security-for-encryption requirement of the scheme $(\mathsf{K}, \mathsf{f}, \mathsf{E}, \mathsf{D})$.

Recall that the security for encryption requirement asserts that no PPT adversary can distinguish between $(\mathsf{x}, \mathsf{ct}_1, \mathsf{e}_1)$ and $(\mathsf{x}, \mathsf{ct}_1, \mathsf{e}_2)$, where $\mathsf{pp} \xleftarrow{\$} \mathsf{K}(1^\lambda)$, $(\mathsf{ct}_1, \mathsf{e}_1) \xleftarrow{\$} \mathsf{E}(\mathsf{pp}, \mathsf{f}(\mathsf{pp}, \mathsf{x}), (i, 1 - x_i))$ and $\mathsf{e}_2 \xleftarrow{\$} \{0, 1\}$. Let us call $(\mathsf{x}, \mathsf{ct}_1, \mathsf{e}_1)$ the simulated challenge and $(\mathsf{x}, \mathsf{ct}_1, \mathsf{e}_2)$ the random challenge.

To build the reduction we show the existence of a procedure Turn that generically turns a simulated challenge into a sample of $\mathsf{SSim}(i, \mathsf{pp}, \mathsf{x})$ and turns a random challenge into a sample of $\mathsf{SReal}(i, \mathsf{pp}, \mathsf{y})$.

The algorithm $\mathsf{Turn}(\mathsf{x}, \mathsf{ct}, \mathsf{e})$ returns $(\mathbf{ct}_1, \mathbf{e}_1)$, formed as follows:

- Sample $\rho \xleftarrow{\$} \mathsf{Rand}$. Then
  - if $x_i = 0$, then return

$$\mathbf{ct}_1 = \begin{pmatrix} E_1(\mathsf{pp}, (i, 0); \rho) \\ \mathsf{ct} \end{pmatrix} \qquad \mathbf{e}_1 = \begin{pmatrix} E_2(\mathsf{pp}, \mathsf{y}, (i, 0); \rho) \\ \mathsf{e} \end{pmatrix}$$

  - if $x_i = 1$, then return

$$\mathbf{ct}_1 = \begin{pmatrix} \mathsf{ct} \\ E_1(\mathsf{pp}, (i, 0); \rho) \end{pmatrix} \qquad \mathbf{e}_1 = \begin{pmatrix} \mathsf{e} \\ E_2(\mathsf{pp}, \mathsf{y}, (i, 0); \rho) \end{pmatrix}$$

It should be clear by inspection that the output of $\mathsf{Turn}(\mathsf{x}, \mathsf{ct}, \mathsf{e})$ is identically distributed to $\mathsf{SReal}(i, \mathsf{pp}, \mathsf{x})$ if $(\mathsf{x}, \mathsf{ct}, \mathsf{e})$ is a random challenge (defined above), and identically distributed to $\mathsf{SSim}(i, \mathsf{pp}, \mathsf{x})$ if $(\mathsf{x}, \mathsf{ct}, \mathsf{e})$ is a simulated challenge. The proof is now complete. □

Proof (of Lemma 4). To prove Lemma 4 we define two hybrids and will use the notation view_i to refer to the view sampled in **Hybrid** i.

Hybrid 0. The view $(\mathsf{ik}, \mathsf{Y})$ is produced honestly as in the real executions of the scheme TDF. That is,

- Sample $\mathsf{pp} \xleftarrow{\$} \mathsf{K}(1^\lambda)$, $\mathsf{x} \xleftarrow{\$} \{0, 1\}^n$ and let $\mathsf{y} := \mathsf{f}(\mathsf{pp}, \mathsf{x})$.
- For all $j \in [r]$ sample $(\mathbf{CT}^{(j)}, \mathbf{E}^{(j)}) \xleftarrow{\$} \mathsf{Real}(\mathsf{pp}, \mathsf{x})$. Parse

$$\mathbf{CT}^{(j)} := \begin{pmatrix} \mathsf{ct}_{1,0}^{(j)}, \ldots, \mathsf{ct}_{n,0}^{(j)} \\ \mathsf{ct}_{1,1}^{(j)}, \ldots, \mathsf{ct}_{n,1}^{(j)} \end{pmatrix} \qquad \mathbf{E}^{(j)} := \begin{pmatrix} b_{1,0}^{(j)}, \ldots, b_{n,0}^{(j)} \\ b_{1,1}^{(j)}, \ldots, b_{n,1}^{(j)} \end{pmatrix}.$$

– For all $i \in [n]$ and $d \in \{0, 1\}$ set

$$\mathbf{ct}_{i,d} := (\mathsf{ct}_{i,d}^{(1)}, \dots, \mathsf{ct}_{i,d}^{(r)})$$
$$\mathbf{b}_{i,d} := (\mathsf{b}_{i,d}^{(1)}, \dots, \mathsf{b}_{i,d}^{(r)}).$$

– Form the view $(\mathsf{ik}, \mathsf{Y})$ as follows:

$$(\underbrace{(\mathsf{pp}, \mathbf{ct}_{1,0}, \mathbf{ct}_{1,1}, \dots, \mathbf{ct}_{n,0}, \mathbf{ct}_{n,1})}_{\mathsf{ik}}, \underbrace{(\mathsf{y}, \mathbf{b}_{1,0}, \mathbf{b}_{1,1}, \dots, \mathbf{b}_{n,0}, \mathbf{b}_{n,1})}_{\mathsf{Y}}) \qquad (23)$$

Hybrid 1. The view $(\mathsf{ik}, \mathsf{Y})$ is produced the same as **Hybrid** 0 except that for all $j \in [r]$ we sample $(\mathbf{CT}^{(j)}, \mathbf{E}^{(j)})$ now as $(\mathbf{CT}^{(j)}, \mathbf{E}^{(j)}) \xleftarrow{\$} \mathsf{Sim}(\mathsf{pp}, \mathsf{y})$.

We prove that the two views are indistinguishable and then we will show that inverting the image under view$_1$ is computationally infeasible.

Indistinguishability of the views: By Lemma 5 we have $\mathsf{view}_0 \stackrel{c}{\equiv} \mathsf{view}_1$. The reason is that the view in either hybrid is produced entirely based on $(\mathbf{CT}^{(1)}, \mathbf{E}^{(1)}, \dots, \mathbf{CT}^{(r)}, \mathbf{E}^{(r)})$ and that this tuple is sampled from the distribution $\mathsf{Real}(\mathsf{pp}, \mathsf{x})$ in one hybrid and from $\mathsf{Sim}(\mathsf{pp}, \mathsf{y})$ in the other.

One-wayness in Hybrid 1: We claim that for any PPT adversary $\mathcal{A}$

$$\Pr[\mathcal{A}(\mathsf{view}_1) = \mathsf{x}' \text{ and } \mathsf{f}(\mathsf{pp}, \mathsf{x}') = \mathsf{y}] = \mathsf{negl}(\lambda). \qquad (24)$$

Recall that $\mathsf{view}_1 := (\mathsf{ik}, \mathsf{Y})$ is the view in **Hybrid** 1 and that the variables pp and y are part of $\mathsf{ik} := (\mathsf{pp}, \dots)$ and $\mathsf{Y} := (\mathsf{y}, \dots)$. The proof of Eq. 24 follows from the one-wayness of f, taking into account the fact that view_1 in its entirety is produced solely based on pp and $\mathsf{y} := \mathsf{f}(\mathsf{pp}, \mathsf{x})$ (and especially without knowing x). This is because all the underlying variables $(\mathbf{CT}^{(j)}, \mathbf{E}^{(j)})$ — for all j — are produced as $(\mathbf{CT}^{(j)}, \mathbf{E}^{(j)}) \xleftarrow{\$} \mathsf{Sim}(\mathsf{pp}, \mathsf{y})$, which can be formed without knowledge of x.

Completing the Proof of Lemma 4. Let $\mathsf{view}_0 := (\mathsf{ik}, \mathsf{Y})$ and parse $\mathsf{ik} := (\mathsf{pp}, \dots)$ and $\mathsf{Y} := (\mathsf{y}, \dots)$. For any PPT adversary $\mathcal{A}$ we need to show that the probability that $\mathcal{A}$ on input view_0 outputs $\mathsf{x}' \in \{0, 1\}^n$ such that $\mathsf{f}(\mathsf{pp}, \mathsf{x}') = \mathsf{y}$ is negligible. We know that $\mathcal{B}$ fails to compute such a string x' with non-negligible probability if the view $((\mathsf{pp}, \dots), (\mathsf{y}, \dots))$ is sampled according to view_1. Since $\mathsf{view}_0 \stackrel{c}{\equiv} \mathsf{view}_1$, the claim follows. $\qquad \square$

4.3   Extended One-Wayness

For our CCA2 application we need to prove a stronger property than the standard one-wayness for our constructed TDF. This extension requires that if we evaluate m correlated inputs under m independent functions from the TDF family, the result still cannot be inverted.

Lemma 6 (Extended One-Wayness). *Let* TDF $= ($TDF.K, TDF.F, TDF.F$^{-1})$
be the TDF built in Construction 3 based on an arbitrary parameter $r = r(\lambda)$.
Let $m := m(\lambda)$. *For any PPT adversary* $\mathcal{A}$

$$\Pr[\mathcal{A}(\text{view} := (\text{ik}_1, \ldots, \text{ik}_m, Y_1, \ldots, Y_m)) = x] = \text{negl}(\lambda),$$

where $x \xleftarrow{\$} \{0,1\}^n$ *and for* $i \in [m]$, $(\text{ik}_i, \text{tk}_i) \xleftarrow{\$} \text{TDF.K}(1^\lambda)$, $\mathbf{b}_i \xleftarrow{\$} \{0,1\}^{nr}$
and $Y_i := \text{TDF.F}(\text{ik}_i, x || \mathbf{b}_i)$. *Thus, there exists a hardcore function* HC *such that*
$\text{HC}(x)$ *remains pseudorandom in the presence of* view.

Proof. For any PPT adversary $\mathcal{A}$ we need to show that the probability that
$\mathcal{A}(\text{view})$ outputs x is negligible. It is easy to verify by inspection that the distribution of view can be perfectly formed based on the view (ik^*, Y^*) of an inverter
against the one-wayness of the trapdoor function (TDF.K, TDF.F, TDF.F^{-1}) of
Construction 3 but under the new parameter $r' = m \times r$. Invoking Lemma 4 our
claimed one-wayness extension follows.   □

5   CCA2-Secure Public-Key Encryption

In this section we show how to use our constructed TDF to build a CCA2 secure
PKE. For the proof of CCA2 security we need to assume that the OWFE scheme
underlying the TDF is adaptively secure (Definition 5).

Notation. Let TDF $:= ($TDF.K, TDF.F, TDF.F$^{-1})$ be as in Sect. 4. We will interpret the input X to the TDF as (x, s), where $x \in \{0,1\}^n$ corresponds to f's preimage part and $s \in \{0,1\}^{n_1}$ corresponds to the *blinding* part. In particular, if r
is the underlying parameter of the constructed TDF as in Construction 3, then
$n_1 = n \times r$.

Ingredients of our CCA2-secure PKE. Apart from a TDF with the above
syntax, our CCA2 secure construction also makes use of a one-time signature
scheme SIG $= ($SIG.K, SIG.Sign, SIG.Ver$)$ with prefect correctness, which in turn
can be obtained from any one-way function. A one-time signature scheme SIG
with message space $\{0,1\}^\eta$ is given by three PPT algorithms SIG.K, SIG.Sign and
SIG.Ver satisfying the following syntax. The algorithm SIG.K on input a security
parameter 1^λ outputs a pair (vk, sgk) consisting of a verification key vk and a
signing key sgk. The signing algorithm SIG.Sign on input a signing key sgk and
a message $m \in \{0,1\}^\eta$ outputs a signature σ. For correctness, we require that
for any (vk, sgk) $\in$ SIG.K(1^λ), any message $m \in \{0,1\}^\eta$ and any signature $\sigma \in$
SIG.Sign(sgk, m): SIG.Ver(vk, m, σ) $= \top$. The one-time unforgeability property
requires that the success probability of any PPT adversary $\mathcal{A}$ in the following
game be at most negligible. Sample (vk, sgk) $\xleftarrow{\$}$ SIG.K(1^λ) and give vk to $\mathcal{A}$.
Now, $\mathcal{A}(\text{vk})$ may call a signing oracle SgnOracle[sgk]$(\cdot)$ only once, where the
oracle SgnOracle[sgk]$(\cdot)$ on input m returns $\sigma \xleftarrow{\$}$ SIG.Sign(sgk, m). Finally, $\mathcal{A}(\text{vk})$
should return a pair (m', σ') of message/signature and will win if $(m, \sigma) \neq (m', \sigma')$
and that SIG.Ver(vk, m', σ') $= \top$.

Our CCA2 primitive. We will build a CCA2 secure single-bit PKE, which by the result of [24] can be boosted into many-bit CCA2 secure PKE. Since we deal with single-bit CCA2 PKE, we may assume without loss of generality that the CCA adversary issues all her CCA oracles after seeing the challenge ciphertext. We will now describe our CCA2-secure PKE scheme.

Construction 5 (CCA2 Secure PKE). *The construction is parameterized over a parameter $m := m(\lambda)$, which denotes the size of the verification key of the underlying signature scheme* SIG. *Let* HC *be a bit-valued hardcore function whose existence was proved in Lemma 6.*

- PKE.K(1^λ): *For $i \in [m]$ and $b \in \{0,1\}$, sample $(\mathsf{ik}_i^b, \mathsf{tk}_i^b) \overset{\$}{\leftarrow}$* TDF.K($1^\lambda$). *Form* (pk, sk) *the public/secret key as follows:*

$$\mathsf{pk} := (\mathsf{ik}_1^0, \mathsf{ik}_1^1, \ldots, \mathsf{ik}_m^0, \mathsf{ik}_m^1), \;\; \mathsf{sk} := (\mathsf{tk}_1^0, \mathsf{tk}_1^1, \ldots, \mathsf{tk}_m^0, \mathsf{tk}_m^1). \tag{25}$$

- PKE.E(pk, b): *Parse* pk *as in Eq. 25. Sample* $(\mathsf{vk}, \mathsf{sgk}) \overset{\$}{\leftarrow}$ SIG.K(1^λ), $\mathsf{x} \overset{\$}{\leftarrow} \{0,1\}^n$ *and set*

$$X_1 := (\mathsf{x}, \mathsf{s}_1 \overset{\$}{\leftarrow} \{0,1\}^{n_1}), \;\; \ldots, \;\; X_m := (\mathsf{x}, \mathsf{s}_m \overset{\$}{\leftarrow} \{0,1\}^{n_1}). \tag{26}$$

Let $\mathsf{b}' = \mathsf{b} \oplus \mathsf{HC}(\mathsf{x})$ *and for $i \in [m]$ let $Y_i = $* TDF.F($\mathsf{ik}_i^{\mathsf{vk}_i}, X_i$). *Return*

$$\mathsf{c} := (\mathsf{vk}, Y_1, \ldots, Y_m, \mathsf{b}', \mathsf{Sign}(\mathsf{sgk}, Y_1 || \ldots || Y_m || \mathsf{b}')). \tag{27}$$

- PKE.D(sk, c): *Parse* sk *as in Eq. 25 and parse*

$$\mathsf{c} := (\mathsf{vk}, Y_1, \ldots, Y_m, \mathsf{b}', \sigma). \tag{28}$$

   • *Set* msg $:= Y_1 || \cdots Y_m || \mathsf{b}'$. *If* SIG.Ver($\mathsf{vk}, \mathsf{msg}, \sigma$) $= \bot$, *then return $\bot$.*
   • *Otherwise, for $i \in [m]$ set $X_i := $* TDF.F^{-1}($\mathsf{tk}_i^{\mathsf{vk}_i}, Y_i$). *Check that for all $i \in [n]$: $Y_i = $* TDF.F($\mathsf{ik}_i^{\mathsf{vk}_i}, X_i$). *If not, return $\bot$.*
   • *If there exists $\mathsf{x} \in \{0,1\}^n$ and $\mathsf{s}_1, \ldots, \mathsf{s}_m \in \{0,1\}^{n_1}$ such that for all $i \in [m]$, $X_i = (\mathsf{x}, \mathsf{s}_i)$, then return $\mathsf{b}' \oplus \mathsf{HC}(\mathsf{x})$. Otherwise, return $\bot$.*

Correctness. If the underlying signature scheme SIG = (SIG.K, SIG.Sign, SIG.Ver) is correct and also that the underlying TDF (TDF.K, TDF.F, TDF.F^{-1}) is correct in the sense of Definition 1, the above constructed PKE is correct in a similar sense: for any $(\mathsf{pk}, \mathsf{sk}) \in$ PKE.K(1^λ) and plaintext bit $\mathsf{b} \in \{0,1\}$ we have $\Pr[\mathsf{PKE.D}(\mathsf{sk}, \mathsf{PKE.E}(\mathsf{pk}, \mathsf{b}))] = \mathsf{negl}(\lambda)$. The proof of this is straightforward.

6   Proof of CCA2 Security

We will prove the following theorem.

Theorem 6 (CCA2 security). *Let* (TDF.K, TDF.F, TDF.F^{-1}) *be the TDF that results from Construction 3 based on a recyclable OWFE* (K, f, E, D). *Assuming* (K, f, E, D) *is adaptively secure, the PKE given in Construction 5 is CCA2 secure.*

We need to show that the probability of success of any CCA2 adversary is the CCA2 game is at most $\frac{1}{2} + \mathsf{negl}(\lambda)$. Fix the adversary $\mathcal{A}$ in the remainder of this section. We give the following event that describes exactly the success of $\mathcal{A}$.

Event Success. Let $(\mathsf{pk}, \mathsf{sk}) \xleftarrow{\$} \mathsf{PKE.K}(1^\lambda)$, $\mathsf{b_{plain}} \xleftarrow{\$} \{0, 1\}$, $\mathsf{c} \xleftarrow{\$} \mathsf{PKE.E}(\mathsf{pk},$ $\mathsf{b_{plain}})$. Run the adversary $\mathcal{A}$ on $(\mathsf{pk}, \mathsf{c})$ and reply to any query $\mathsf{c'} \neq \mathsf{c}$ of $\mathcal{A}$ with $\mathsf{PKE.D}(\mathsf{sk}, \mathsf{c'})$. We say that the event Success holds if $\mathcal{A}$ outputs $\mathsf{b_{plain}}$.

Road Map. To prove Theorem 6, in Sect. 6.1 we define a simulated experiment Sim and we show that the probability of success of any CCA2 adversary in this experiment is $\frac{1}{2} + \mathsf{negl}(\lambda)$. Next, in Sect. 6.2 we will show that the probabilities of success of any CCA2 adversary in the real and simulated experiments are negligibly close, establishing Theorem 6.

6.1   Simulated CCA2 Experiment

We now define a simulated way of doing the CCA2 experiment. Roughly, our simulator does not have the full secret key (needed to reply to CCA2 queries of the adversary), but some part of it. Our simulation is enabled a syntactic property of our constructed TDF. We first state the property and then prove that it is satisfied by our TDF. We require the existence of an efficient algorithm Recover for our constructed TDF $(\mathsf{TDF.K}, \mathsf{TDF.F}, \mathsf{TDF.F^{-1}})$ that satisfies the following property.

Algorithm Recover: The input to the algorithm is an index key ik, a pre-fix input $\mathsf{x} \in \{0,1\}^n$ and a possible image Y. The output of the algorithm is $X \in \{0,1\}^{n+n_1} \cup \{\bot\}$. As for correctness we requite the following. For any $(\mathsf{ik}, *) \in \mathsf{TDF.K}(1^\lambda)$, $\mathsf{x} \in \{0,1\}^n$ and Y both the following two properties hold:

- if for no $\mathsf{s} \in \{0,1\}^{n_1}$ $\mathsf{TDF.F}(\mathsf{ik}, \mathsf{x}||\mathsf{s}) = Y$, then $\mathsf{Recover}(\mathsf{ik}, \mathsf{x}, Y) = \bot$
- if for some s, $\mathsf{TDF.F}(\mathsf{ik}, \mathsf{x}||\mathsf{s}) = Y$, then $\mathsf{Recover}(\mathsf{ik}, \mathsf{x}, Y)$ returns (x, s).

Lemma 7 (Existence of Recover). *There exists an efficient algorithm* Recover *with the above properties for our constructed TDF .*

Proof. To build Recover, first parse the given inputs as follows: $\mathsf{ik} = (\mathsf{pp}, \dots)$, $\mathsf{x} \in \{0,1\}^n$ and $Y := (y, \widetilde{\mathbf{b}_{1,0}}, \widetilde{\mathbf{b}_{1,1}}, \dots, \widetilde{\mathbf{b}_{n,0}}, \widetilde{\mathbf{b}_{n,1}})$. Do the following steps:

1. For all $i \in [n]$ set $\mathbf{b}_i := \widetilde{\mathbf{b}_{i,1-\mathsf{x}_i}}$.
2. Let $\mathsf{s} = \mathbf{b}_1 || \cdots || \mathbf{b}_n$.
3. Check if $Y = \mathsf{TDF.F}(\mathsf{ik}, \mathsf{x}||\mathsf{s})$. If the check holds, return (x, s). Otherwise, return $\bot$.

The correctness of the algorithm Recover follows by inspection.   □

$\mathsf{Sim}(\mathsf{ik}_1, \dots, \mathsf{ik}_m, Y_1, \dots, Y_m, \mathsf{b})$: The simulated experiment differs from the real experiment in that the challenger does not know the trapdoor keys of half of the index keys that are given to the CCA adversary as part of the public key. The challenger, however, tries to produce accurate answers based on her partial knowledge.

Formally, do the following steps.

1. **Initializing the CCA Adversary:**
   (a) Sample $(\mathsf{vk}, \mathsf{sgk}) \overset{\$}{\leftarrow} \mathsf{SIG.K}(1^\lambda)$.
   (b) For all $i \in [m]$ set $\mathsf{ik}_i^{\mathsf{vk}_i} := \mathsf{ik}_i$ and sample $(\mathsf{ik}_i^{1-\mathsf{vk}_i}, \mathsf{tk}_i^{1-\mathsf{vk}_i}) \overset{\$}{\leftarrow} \mathsf{TDF.K}(1^\lambda)$.
   (c) Sample a challenge bit $\mathsf{b}_{\mathsf{plain}} \overset{\$}{\leftarrow} \{0,1\}$ and let $\mathsf{b}_1 := \mathsf{b}_{\mathsf{plain}} \oplus \mathsf{b}$. Set

$$\mathsf{msg} := \mathsf{Y}_1 || \cdots || \mathsf{Y}_m || \mathsf{b}_1.$$

Sample $\sigma \overset{\$}{\leftarrow} \mathsf{SIG.Sign}(\mathsf{sgk}, \mathsf{msg})$ and set

$$\mathsf{pk} := (\mathsf{ik}_1^0, \mathsf{ik}_1^1, \ldots, \mathsf{ik}_m^0, \mathsf{ik}_m^1), \quad \mathsf{c} := (\mathsf{vk}, \mathsf{Y}_1, \ldots, \mathsf{Y}_m, \mathsf{b}_1, \sigma).$$

Run the CCA2 adversary $\mathcal{A}$ on $(\mathsf{pk}, \mathsf{c})$.
2. **Simulating the CCA responses:**
   Respond to a CCA2-oracle query $\mathsf{c}' := (\mathsf{vk}', \mathsf{Y}_1', \ldots, \mathsf{Y}_m', \mathsf{b}', \sigma')$ as follows:
   (a) Letting $\mathsf{msg}' := \mathsf{Y}_1' || \cdots || \mathsf{Y}_m' || \mathsf{b}'$ if $\mathsf{Ver}(\mathsf{vk}', \mathsf{msg}', \sigma') = \bot$, then return $\bot$. Otherwise, if $\mathsf{vk}' = \mathsf{vk}$, then halt and return $\bot$.
   (b) Otherwise, let Q consist all of all indices $i \in [m]$ for which we have $\mathsf{vk}_i' \neq \mathsf{vk}_i$. For $i \in Q$ set $\mathsf{X}_i' := \mathsf{TDF.F}^{-1}(\mathsf{tk}_i^{\mathsf{vk}_i'}, \mathsf{Y}_i')$ and check if $\mathsf{Y}_i' = \mathsf{TDF.F}(\mathsf{ik}_i^{\mathsf{vk}_i'}, \mathsf{X}_i')$; if this fails for any $i \in Q$, then return $\bot$. Now if there exists $x' \in \{0,1\}^n$ such that for all $i \in Q$ we have $\mathsf{X}_i' = (x', *)$ then continue with the following steps and otherwise return $\bot$.
      (I) for all $j \in [m] \setminus Q$, let $\mathsf{X}_j' := \mathsf{Recover}(\mathsf{ik}_j^{\mathsf{vk}_j'}, x', \mathsf{Y}_j')$. Reply to the query c' with $\mathsf{HC}(x')$ if for all j we have $\mathsf{X}_j' \neq \bot$; otherwise, reply to the query with $\bot$.
3. **Forming the output of the experiment:** The experiment outputs 1 if $\mathcal{A}$ outputs $\mathsf{b}_{\mathsf{plain}}$; otherwise, the experiments outputs 0.

Event $\mathsf{Success}_{\mathsf{sim}}$. The event that $\mathsf{Sim}(\mathsf{ik}_1, \ldots, \mathsf{ik}_m, \mathsf{Y}_1, \ldots, \mathsf{Y}_m, \mathsf{b})$ outputs 1 where $x \overset{\$}{\leftarrow} \{0,1\}^n$, $\mathsf{b} := \mathsf{HC}(x)$ and for $i \in [m]$, $(\mathsf{ik}_i, \mathsf{tk}_i) \overset{\$}{\leftarrow} \mathsf{TDF.K}(1^\lambda)$, $\mathsf{s}_i \overset{\$}{\leftarrow} \{0,1\}^{nr}$ and $\mathsf{Y}_i := \mathsf{TDF.K}(\mathsf{ik}_i, x || \mathsf{s}_i)$.

We now show that the probability of the event $\mathsf{Success}_{\mathsf{sim}}$ is $\frac{1}{2} + \mathsf{negl}(\lambda)$. We will then show in the next section that the probability of the event $\mathsf{Success}$ is close to that of $\mathsf{Success}_{\mathsf{sim}}$, hence obtaining our main result.

Lemma 8.
$$\alpha := \Pr[\mathsf{Success}_{\mathsf{sim}}] \leq \frac{1}{2} + \mathsf{negl}(\lambda). \tag{29}$$

Proof. This lemma follows by Lemma 6. Suppose the input to Sim is sampled exactly as done in the event $\mathsf{Success}_{\mathsf{sim}}$, except that we sample $\mathsf{b} \overset{\$}{\leftarrow} \{0,1\}$ (instead of setting $\mathsf{b} := \mathsf{HC}(x)$). In this case the output of the simulation is 1 with probability $1/2$. Now Lemma 6 implies that $\alpha = \frac{1}{2} + \mathsf{negl}(\lambda)$ (Eq. 29), and the proof is complete. $\square$

6.2   Relating the Simulated and Real Experiments

We will now show that the probabilities of the events Success and Success$_{sim}$ are negligibly close, hence obtaining Theorem 6 from Lemma 8. To this end, we define below two events Forge and Spoof, and show that the difference of the probabilities of Success and Success$_{sim}$ is at most the sum of the probabilities of Forge and Spoof. We will then show that both these events happen with negligible probability.

Event Forge: In the experiment $Sim(ik_1, \ldots, ik_m, Y_1, \ldots, Y_m, b)$ we let Forge be the event that $\mathcal{A}$ issues a CCA2 query

$$c' := (vk', Y'_1, \ldots, Y'_m, b', \sigma')$$

such that $vk = vk'$ and $Ver(vk, Y'_1 || \cdots || Y'_m || b', \sigma') = \top$. Recall that vk is part of the challenge ciphertext $c := (vk, \ldots)$ given to the adversary.

Informally, the event Spoof below describes a situation in which a decryption query during the execution of Sim is answered with a non $\perp$ string, but the same query may be replied to with $\perp$ under the real decryption oracle.

Event Spoof: Let $c := (vk, \ldots)$ be the challenge ciphertext formed during $Sim(ik_1, \ldots, ik_m, Y_1, \ldots, Y_m, b)$. We let Spoof be the event that $\mathcal{A}$ issues a CCA2 query

$$c' := (vk', Y'_1, \ldots, Y'_m, b', \sigma')$$

for which the following holds. Let Q be the set of indices $i \in [m]$ for which we have $vk_i \neq vk'_i$. For some $h \in Q$ and for some $w \in [m] \setminus Q$ we have

- $TDF.F^{-1}(tk_h^{vk'_h}, Y'_h) = (x', *) \neq \perp$; and
- $s'_j := Recover(ik_w^{vk'_w}, x', Y'_w) \neq \perp$ but $TDF.F^{-1}(tk_w^{vk'_w}, Y'_w) = \perp$.

We will now prove the following three lemmas.

Lemma 9. *We have*

$$|\Pr[Success] - \Pr[Success_{sim}]| \leq \Pr[Forge] + \Pr[Spoof].$$

Lemma 10.
$$\Pr[Forge] \leq negl(\lambda).$$

Lemma 11.
$$\Pr[Spoof] \leq negl(\lambda).$$

Let us first derive the proof of Theorem 6 and then prove each of the lemmas.

Proof of Theorem 6. Follows from Lemmas 8 and 9, taking into account the fact that the experiment $Real(1^\lambda)$ is the real CCA2 experiment.   □

We prove Lemmas 9 and 10 and will prove Lemma 11 in Sect. 6.3.

Proof (of Lemma 9). First of all, note that the input $(\mathsf{pk}, \mathsf{c})$ given to the CCA2 adversary under the simulated experiment is identically distributed to that under the real CCA2 experiment. Thus, any possible difference between the simulated and real experiments must be due to the ways in which decryption queries are answered. We will now show that if at any point a decryption query is answered to differently under Sim and Real, then either Forge or Spoof must happen. First, in order for a query c' to be answered differently, either (1) the query c' is replied to with $\perp$ under Sim and with some $\mathsf{b}' \in \{0, 1\}$ under Real; or (2) c' is replied to with some $\mathsf{b}' \in \{0, 1\}$ under Sim and with $\perp$ under Real. In particular, we cannot have a situation in which c' is replied to with some $\mathsf{b}' \in \{0, 1\}$ under Sim and with $1 - \mathsf{b}'$ under Real. The reason for this is that if both experiments reply to a query with something other than $\perp$, then the underlying recovered pre-image x' must be the same, hence both will end up replying with the same bit.

Let $\mathsf{c} := (\mathsf{vk}, \dots)$ be the challenge ciphertext of the underlying CCA2 adversary and $\mathsf{c}' := (\mathsf{vk}', \mathsf{msg}', \sigma')$ be an issued query. We now consider all possible cases:

- If Sim replies to $\mathsf{c}' := (\mathsf{vk}', \mathsf{msg}', \sigma')$ with $\perp$, then one of the following must hold.
    - $\mathsf{SIG.Ver}(\mathsf{vk}', \mathsf{msg}', \sigma') = \perp$: in this case Real also replies to with $\perp$;
    - $\mathsf{SIG.Ver}(\mathsf{vk}', \mathsf{msg}', \sigma') = \top$ and $\mathsf{vk} = \mathsf{vk}'$: in this case the event Forge happens;
    - Sim returns $\perp$ as a result of Step 2b of the execution of Sim: that is, $\mathsf{TDF.F}^{-1}(\mathsf{tk}_i^{vk_i'}, Y_i') = \perp$: in this case Real also replies with $\perp$
    - Sim replies with $\perp$ as a result of Step (I): in this case by correctness of Recover we will know Real will also reply with $\perp$.
- If Real replies to c' with $\perp$ and Sim replies to c' with some $\mathsf{b}' \in \{0, 1\}$, then we may easily verify that the event Spoof must necessarily hold. We omit the details.   □

Proof (of Lemma 10). Suppose $\Pr[\mathsf{Forge}] > \mathsf{negl}(\lambda)$. We show how to build an adversary $\mathcal{B}$ against the one-time unforgeability of $\mathsf{SIG} = (\mathsf{SIG.K}, \mathsf{SIG.Sign}, \mathsf{SIG.Ver})$. Build $\mathcal{B}^{\mathsf{SgnOracle[sgk]}(\cdot)}(\mathsf{vk})$ as follows. Sample the input $(\mathsf{ik}_1, \dots, \mathsf{ik}_m, Y_1, \dots, Y_m, \mathsf{b})$ to Sim and form the tuple msg as in the execution of Sim on this input. Then request a signature σ for the message msg by calling $\mathsf{SgnOracle[sgk]}(\cdot)$ on msg. Form $(\mathsf{pk}, \mathsf{c})$ as in Sim and run the CCA2 adversary $\mathcal{A}$ on $(\mathsf{pk}, \mathsf{c})$. Let q be the number queries that $\mathcal{A}$ asks. Choose $i \xleftarrow{\$} [q]$ to be a guess for the index of the first query for which the event Forge occurs and output the pair of message/signature contained in that query. Note that $\mathcal{B}$ can perfectly reply to all the previous $i - 1$ queries of $\mathcal{A}$, because all of those can be replied to without knowing sgk. If $\alpha := \Pr[\mathsf{Forge}]$, then $\mathcal{B}$ will win with probability at least $\frac{\alpha}{q}$.   □

6.3   Proof of Lemma 11

The proof of Lemma 11 is based on a property of our TDF that we now state and prove. Informally, if the OWFE scheme used in our TDF construction is adaptively secure, then the constructed TDF has the property that given a random index key ik, it is infeasible to produce an image element which is in the range of the trapdoor function TDF.F(ik, ·), but which "inverts" to $\perp$.

Lemma 12. *Let* $\mathsf{TDF} = (\mathsf{TDF.K}, \mathsf{TDF.F}, \mathsf{TDF.F}^{-1})$ *be the TDF built in Sect. 4, with the underlying parameter* $r := r(\lambda) \in \omega(\log \lambda)$, *based on a recyclable OWFE scheme* $\mathsf{OWFE} = (\mathsf{K}, \mathsf{f}, \mathsf{E}, \mathsf{D})$. *Assuming* OWFE *is adaptive (Definition 5), for any PPT adversary* $\mathcal{A}$:

$$\Pr[(X, Y) \xleftarrow{\$} \mathcal{A}(\mathsf{ik}) \text{ s.t. } Y = \mathsf{TDF.F}(\mathsf{ik}, X), \mathsf{TDF.F}^{-1}(\mathsf{tk}, Y) = \perp] = \mathsf{negl}(\lambda), \quad (30)$$

where $(\mathsf{ik}, \mathsf{tk}) \xleftarrow{\$} \mathsf{TDF.K}(1^\lambda)$.

Proof. Let Surprise be the event of the lemma. Parse

$$\mathsf{ik} := (\mathsf{pp}, \mathbf{ct}_{1,0}, \mathbf{ct}_{1,1}, \dots, \mathbf{ct}_{n,0}, \mathbf{ct}_{n,1}), \mathsf{tk} := (\boldsymbol{\rho}_{1,0}, \boldsymbol{\rho}_{1,1}, \dots, \boldsymbol{\rho}_{n,0}, \boldsymbol{\rho}_{n,1}), \quad (31)$$

and for all $i' \in [n]$ and $b' \in \{0, 1\}$ parse

$$\mathbf{ct}_{i',b'} := (\mathsf{ct}_{i',b'}^{(1)}, \dots, \mathsf{ct}_{i',b'}^{(r)}) \quad (32)$$

$$\boldsymbol{\rho}_{i',b'} := (\rho_{i',b'}^{(1)}, \dots, \rho_{i',b'}^{(r)}).$$

Recall that for all $i' \in [n]$, $b' \in \{0, 1\}$ and $j \in [r]$ we have

$$\mathsf{ct}_{i',b'}^{(j)} = \mathsf{E}_1(\mathsf{pp}, (i', b'); \rho_{i',b'}^{(j)}). \quad (33)$$

Also, parse (X, Y), the output of $\mathcal{A}(\mathsf{ik})$, as

$$X := (x \in \{0, 1\}^n, \mathbf{b}_1 \in \{0, 1\}^r, \dots, \mathbf{b}_n \in \{0, 1\}^r) \quad (34)$$

$$Y := (y, \mathbf{b}_{1,0} \in \{0, 1\}^r, \mathbf{b}_{1,1} \in \{0, 1\}^r, \dots, \mathbf{b}_{n,0} \in \{0, 1\}^r, \mathbf{b}_{n,1} \in \{0, 1\}^r).$$

If the event Surprise happens, then by definition we have $Y = \mathsf{TDF.F}(\mathsf{ik}, X)$ and $\mathsf{TDF.F}^{-1}(\mathsf{tk}, Y) = \perp$. Thus, by definition of $\mathsf{TDF.F}^{-1}$, for some $i \in [n]$ we must have

$$\mathbf{b}_i = \left(\mathsf{E}_2(\mathsf{pp}, y, (i, 1 - \mathsf{x}_i); \rho_{i,1-\mathsf{x}_i}^{(1)}), \dots, \mathsf{E}_2(\mathsf{pp}, y, (i, 1 - \mathsf{x}_i); \rho_{i,1-\mathsf{x}_i}^{(r)}) \right). \quad (35)$$

We show how to use Eq. 35 to break the adaptive security of OWFE.

We show how to build an adversary against the adaptive security of OWFE in the sense of Lemma 1. Sample $i \xleftarrow{\$} [n]$ and $b \xleftarrow{\$} \{0, 1\}$ — The value of b will serve as a guess bit for $1 - \mathsf{x}_i$ (see Eq. 35). Give the pair (i, b) to the challenger to receive $(\mathsf{pp}, \mathsf{ct}_1, \dots, \mathsf{ct}_r)$. Set $\mathbf{ct}_{i,b} := (\mathsf{ct}_1, \dots, \mathsf{ct}_r)$ and sample all other $\mathbf{ct}_{i',b'}$, for $(i', b') \neq (i, b)$, as in Eq. 32 and form the index ik as in Eq. 31. Call $\mathcal{A}(\mathsf{ik})$ to receive (X, Y) and parse them as in Eq. 34. If $\mathsf{x}_i = b$ then return $\perp$. Otherwise, give x to the challenger to receive some $\mathbf{e}' \in \{0, 1\}^r$. If $\mathbf{e}' = \mathbf{b}_i$ then return 0, and otherwise return 1.

If the probability of the event Surprise is non-negligible, then $\mathcal{A}$ wins with a probability non-negligibly greater than $\frac{1}{2}$. The reason is if $\mathbf{e}'$ was generated uniformly at random from $\{0, 1\}^r$, then the probability that $\mathbf{e}' = \mathbf{b}_i$ is $\frac{1}{2^r} = \mathsf{negl}(\lambda)$. On the other hand, if $\mathbf{e}'$ was generated as a result of true encapsulation encryptions (see the description of the game in Lemma 1), then the probability that $\mathbf{e}' = \mathbf{b}_i$ is the probability of the event in Eq. 35, which is non-negligible. Thus, we break the adaptive security of OWFE, a contradiction to Lemma 1. $\square$

Proof (of Lemma 11). The proof of this lemma follows easily from Lemma 12, so we will give a sketch of the proof. Let $\beta := \Pr[\mathsf{Spoof}]$. We show how to build an adversary $\mathcal{B}$ in the sense of Lemma 12 that wins with probability $\frac{\beta}{poly(\lambda)}$.

Recall h and w from the event Spoof. The adversary $\mathcal{B}(\mathsf{ik})$ acts as follows.

- Sample $(\mathsf{vk}, \mathsf{sgk}) \xleftarrow{\$} \mathsf{SIG.K}(1^\lambda)$.
- Guess $w \xleftarrow{\$} [m]$
- Set $\mathsf{ik}_w^{\mathsf{vk}_w} := \mathsf{ik}$. Also, sample $(\mathsf{ik}_w^{1-\mathsf{vk}_w}, \mathsf{tk}_w^{1-\mathsf{vk}_w}) \xleftarrow{\$} \mathsf{TDF.K}(1^\lambda)$
- For all $i \in [m] \setminus \{w\}$ and $b \in \{0, 1\}$, sample $(\mathsf{ik}_i^b, \mathsf{tk}_i^b) \xleftarrow{\$} \mathsf{TDF.K}(1^\lambda)$.
- Sample $\mathsf{x} \xleftarrow{\$} \{0, 1\}^n$, $\mathbf{b} := \mathsf{HC}(\mathsf{x})$ and for $i \in [m]$, $\mathsf{Y}_i := \mathsf{TDF.K}(\mathsf{ik}_i^{\mathsf{vk}_i}, \mathsf{x}||\mathsf{s}_i)$.
- Sample $\mathsf{b}_{\mathrm{plain}} \xleftarrow{\$} \{0, 1\}$ and set $\mathsf{b}_1 := \mathsf{b}_{\mathrm{plain}} \oplus \mathbf{b}$.
- Set the challenge public key and ciphertext $(\mathsf{pk}, \mathsf{c})$ as in Sim and run the CCA2 adversary $\mathcal{A}$ on $(\mathsf{pk}, \mathsf{c})$.

Now guess η to be the index of the first query of $\mathcal{A}$ that causes Spoof to happen and guess $\mathsf{h} \xleftarrow{\$} [m]$ be the underlying index defined in the event Forge. Note that $\mathcal{B}$ can perfectly simulate the response all the first $\eta - 1$ queries of $\mathcal{A}$ as in Sim. The reason is that $\mathcal{B}$ has the trapdoor key for all $\mathsf{ik}_i^{1-\mathsf{vk}_i}$, and so it can perform as in Sim.

The ηth query. Letting the ηth query be

$$c' := (\mathsf{vk}', \mathsf{Y}_1', \ldots, \mathsf{Y}_m', \mathsf{b}_{ciph}', \sigma')$$

$\mathcal{B}$ acts as follows: set $(\mathsf{x}', \mathsf{s}_h) := \mathsf{TDF.F}^{-1}(\mathsf{tk}_h^{\mathsf{vk}_h'}, \mathsf{Y}_h')$ and $\mathsf{X}_w' := \mathsf{Recover}(\mathsf{ik}, \mathsf{x}', \mathsf{Y}_w')$. Finally, $\mathcal{B}$ returns $(\mathsf{X}_w', \mathsf{Y}_w')$.

It is now easy to verify if Spoof occurs and that all the guesses of the adversary $\mathcal{B}$ were correct (i.e., the guessed values for h, w and vk_w') — which happens with probability $\frac{1}{poly(\lambda)}$ — the adversary $\mathcal{B}$ wins in the sense of Lemma 12. $\square$

Acknowledgments. We would like to thank the anonymous reviewers for their useful comments, and thank Mohammad Mahmoody and Adam O'Neill for useful discussions.

References

1. Bellare, M., Boldyreva, A., O'Neill, A.: Deterministic and efficiently searchable encryption. In: Menezes, A. (ed.) CRYPTO 2007. LNCS, vol. 4622, pp. 535–552. Springer, Heidelberg (2007). https://doi.org/10.1007/978-3-540-74143-5_30
2. Bellare, M., Fischlin, M., O'Neill, A., Ristenpart, T.: Deterministic encryption: definitional equivalences and constructions without random oracles. In: Wagner, D. (ed.) CRYPTO 2008. LNCS, vol. 5157, pp. 360–378. Springer, Heidelberg (2008). https://doi.org/10.1007/978-3-540-85174-5_20
3. Bellare, M., Halevi, S., Sahai, A., Vadhan, S.P.: Many-to-one trapdoor functions and their relation to public-key cryptosystems. In: Krawczyk, H. (ed.) CRYPTO 1998. LNCS, vol. 1462, pp. 283–298. Springer, Heidelberg (1998). https://doi.org/10.1007/BFb0055735
4. Blum, M., Feldman, P., Micali, S.: Proving security against chosen ciphertext attacks. In: Goldwasser, S. (ed.) CRYPTO 1988. LNCS, vol. 403, pp. 256–268. Springer, New York (1990). https://doi.org/10.1007/0-387-34799-2_20
5. Boldyreva, A., Fehr, S., O'Neill, A.: On notions of security for deterministic encryption, and efficient constructions without random oracles. In: Wagner, D. (ed.) CRYPTO 2008. LNCS, vol. 5157, pp. 335–359. Springer, Heidelberg (2008). https://doi.org/10.1007/978-3-540-85174-5_19
6. Boneh, D., Boyen, X.: Secure identity based encryption without random oracles. In: Franklin, M. (ed.) CRYPTO 2004. LNCS, vol. 3152, pp. 443–459. Springer, Heidelberg (2004). https://doi.org/10.1007/978-3-540-28628-8_27
7. Brakerski, Z., Lombardi, A., Segev, G., Vaikuntanathan, V.: Anonymous IBE, leakage resilience and circular security from new assumptions. In: Nielsen, J.B., Rijmen, V. (eds.) EUROCRYPT 2018, Part I. LNCS, vol. 10820, pp. 535–564. Springer, Cham (2018). https://doi.org/10.1007/978-3-319-78381-9_20
8. Canetti, R., Halevi, S., Katz, J.: Chosen-ciphertext security from identity-based encryption. In: Cachin, C., Camenisch, J.L. (eds.) EUROCRYPT 2004. LNCS, vol. 3027, pp. 207–222. Springer, Heidelberg (2004). https://doi.org/10.1007/978-3-540-24676-3_13
9. Cash, D., Kiltz, E., Shoup, V.: The twin Diffie-Hellman problem and applications. In: Smart, N.P. (ed.) EUROCRYPT 2008. LNCS, vol. 4965, pp. 127–145. Springer, Heidelberg (2008). https://doi.org/10.1007/978-3-540-78967-3_8
10. Cho, C., Döttling, N., Garg, S., Gupta, D., Miao, P., Polychroniadou, A.: Laconic oblivious transfer and its applications. In: Katz, J., Shacham, H. (eds.) CRYPTO 2017, Part II. LNCS, vol. 10402, pp. 33–65. Springer, Cham (2017). https://doi.org/10.1007/978-3-319-63715-0_2
11. Diffie, W., Hellman, M.E.: New directions in cryptography. IEEE Trans. Inf. Theory **22**(6), 644–654 (1976)
12. Döttling, N., Garg, S.: From selective IBE to full IBE and selective HIBE. In: Kalai, Y., Reyzin, L. (eds.) TCC 2017, Part I. LNCS, vol. 10677, pp. 372–408. Springer, Cham (2017). https://doi.org/10.1007/978-3-319-70500-2_13
13. Döttling, N., Garg, S.: Identity-based encryption from the Diffie-Hellman assumption. In: Katz, J., Shacham, H. (eds.) CRYPTO 2017, Part I. LNCS, vol. 10401, pp. 537–569. Springer, Cham (2017). https://doi.org/10.1007/978-3-319-63688-7_18
14. Döttling, N., Garg, S., Hajiabadi, M., Masny, D.: New constructions of identity-based and key-dependent message secure encryption schemes. In: Abdalla, M., Dahab, R. (eds.) PKC 2018, Part I. LNCS, vol. 10769, pp. 3–31. Springer, Cham (2018). https://doi.org/10.1007/978-3-319-76578-5_1

15. ElGamal, T.: A public key cryptosystem and a signature scheme based on discrete logarithms. In: Blakley, G.R., Chaum, D. (eds.) CRYPTO 1984. LNCS, vol. 196, pp. 10–18. Springer, Heidelberg (1985). https://doi.org/10.1007/3-540-39568-7_2

16. Feige, U., Lapidot, D., Shamir, A.: Multiple non-interactive zero knowledge proofs based on a single random string (extended abstract). In: 31st FOCS, St. Louis, Missouri, 22–24 October 1990, pp. 308–317. IEEE Computer Society Press (1990)

17. Freeman, D.M., Goldreich, O., Kiltz, E., Rosen, A., Segev, G.: More constructions of lossy and correlation-secure trapdoor functions. In: Nguyen, P.Q., Pointcheval, D. (eds.) PKC 2010. LNCS, vol. 6056, pp. 279–295. Springer, Heidelberg (2010). https://doi.org/10.1007/978-3-642-13013-7_17

18. Gertner, Y., Malkin, T., Reingold, O.: On the impossibility of basing trapdoor functions on trapdoor predicates. In: 42nd FOCS, Las Vegas, NV, USA, 14–17 October 2001, pp. 126–135. IEEE Computer Society Press (2001)

19. Goldreich, O., Levin, L.A.: A hard-core predicate for all one-way functions. In: 21st ACM STOC, Seattle, WA, USA, 15–17 May 1989, pp. 25–32. ACM Press (1989)

20. Goldwasser, S., Micali, S.: Probabilistic encryption and how to play mental poker keeping secret all partial information. In: 14th ACM STOC, San Francisco, CA, USA, 5–7 May 1982, pp. 365–377. ACM Press (1982)

21. Hajiabadi, M., Kapron, B.M.: Reproducible circularly-secure bit encryption: applications and realizations. In: Gennaro, R., Robshaw, M.J.B. (eds.) CRYPTO 2015, Part I. LNCS, vol. 9215, pp. 224–243. Springer, Heidelberg (2015). https://doi.org/10.1007/978-3-662-47989-6_11

22. Haralambiev, K., Jager, T., Kiltz, E., Shoup, V.: Simple and efficient public-key encryption from computational Diffie-Hellman in the standard model. In: Nguyen, P.Q., Pointcheval, D. (eds.) PKC 2010. LNCS, vol. 6056, pp. 1–18. Springer, Heidelberg (2010). https://doi.org/10.1007/978-3-642-13013-7_1

23. Kiltz, E., Mohassel, P., O'Neill, A.: Adaptive trapdoor functions and chosen-ciphertext security. In: Gilbert, H. (ed.) EUROCRYPT 2010. LNCS, vol. 6110, pp. 673–692. Springer, Heidelberg (2010). https://doi.org/10.1007/978-3-642-13190-5_34

24. Myers, S., Shelat, A.: Bit encryption is complete. In: 50th FOCS, Atlanta, GA, USA, 25–27 October 2009, pp. 607–616. IEEE Computer Society Press (2009)

25. Naor, M., Yung, M: Public-key cryptosystems provably secure against chosen ciphertext attacks. In: 22nd ACM STOC, Baltimore, MD, USA, 14–16 May 1990, pp. 427–437. ACM Press (1990)

26. Peikert, C.: Public-key cryptosystems from the worst-case shortest vector problem: extended abstract. In: Mitzenmacher, M. (ed.) 41st ACM STOC, Bethesda, MD, USA, 31 May–2 June 2009, pp. 333–342. ACM Press (2009)

27. Peikert, C., Waters, B.: Lossy trapdoor functions and their applications. In: Ladner, R.E., Dwork, C. (eds.) 40th ACM STOC, Victoria, British Columbia, Canada, 17–20 May 2008, pp. 187–196. ACM Press (2008)

28. Rivest, R.L., Shamir, A., Adleman, L.M.: A method for obtaining digital signature and public-key cryptosystems. Commun. Assoc. Comput. Mach. **21**(2), 120–126 (1978)

29. Rosen, A., Segev, G.: Chosen-ciphertext security via correlated products. In: Reingold, O. (ed.) TCC 2009. LNCS, vol. 5444, pp. 419–436. Springer, Heidelberg (2009). https://doi.org/10.1007/978-3-642-00457-5_25

30. Wee, H.: Efficient chosen-ciphertext security via extractable hash proofs. In: Rabin, T. (ed.) CRYPTO 2010. LNCS, vol. 6223, pp. 314–332. Springer, Heidelberg (2010). https://doi.org/10.1007/978-3-642-14623-7_17

31. Wee, H.: Dual projective hashing and its applications — lossy trapdoor functions and more. In: Pointcheval, D., Johansson, T. (eds.) EUROCRYPT 2012. LNCS, vol. 7237, pp. 246–262. Springer, Heidelberg (2012). https://doi.org/10.1007/978-3-642-29011-4_16

32. Yao, A.C.-C: Theory and applications of trapdoor functions (extended abstract). In: 23rd FOCS, pp. 80–91. IEEE Computer Society Press, Chicago, 3–5 November 1982

Round Optimal MPC

Round-Optimal Secure Multiparty Computation with Honest Majority

Prabhanjan Ananth[1]([✉]), Arka Rai Choudhuri[2], Aarushi Goel[2], and Abhishek Jain[2]

[1] Massachusetts Institute of Technology, Cambridge, USA
prabhanjan@csail.mit.edu
[2] Johns Hopkins University, Baltimore, USA
{achoud,aarushig,abhishek}@cs.jhu.edu

Abstract. We study the exact round complexity of secure multiparty computation (MPC) in the honest majority setting. We construct several *round-optimal* n-party protocols, tolerating any $t < \frac{n}{2}$ corruptions.

1. **Security with abort:** We give the first construction of two round MPC for general functions that achieves security with abort against *malicious* adversaries in the plain model. The security of our protocol only relies on one-way functions.

2. **Guaranteed output delivery:** We also construct protocols that achieve security with guaranteed output delivery: **(i)** Against *fail-stop* adversaries, we construct two round MPC either in the (bare) public-key infrastructure model with no additional assumptions, or in the plain model assuming two-round semi-honest oblivious transfer. In three rounds, however, we can achieve security assuming only one-way functions. **(ii)** Against *malicious* adversaries, we construct three round MPC in the plain model, assuming public-key encryption and Zaps.

Previously, such protocols were only known based on specific learning assumptions and required the use of common reference strings.

All of our results are obtained via general compilers that may be of independent interest.

1 Introduction

The notion of secure multiparty computation (MPC) [20,31] is fundamental in cryptography. Informally speaking, an MPC protocol allows mutually distrusting parties to jointly evaluate a function over their private inputs in such a manner that the protocol execution does not leak anything beyond the function output.

A fundamental measure of efficiency in MPC is *round complexity*, i.e., the number of rounds of communication between the parties. Protocols with smaller round complexity are more desirable so as to minimize the effect of network latency, which in turn decreases the time complexity of the protocol. Over the last three decades, the round complexity of MPC has been extensively studied in various security models.

© International Association for Cryptologic Research 2018
H. Shacham and A. Boldyreva (Eds.): CRYPTO 2018, LNCS 10992, pp. 395–424, 2018.
https://doi.org/10.1007/978-3-319-96881-0_14

MPC with Honest Majority. In this work, we study the exact round complexity of MPC in the *honest majority* setting, where an adversary may corrupt up to t parties out of $n = 2t+1$ total parties. We seek to construct round-optimal protocols in the plain model without any trusted setup assumptions.

The study of MPC in the honest majority model was initiated in the works of [5,9]. We recall the main security notions that have been studied over the years in this model:

- **Security with Abort:** In this notion, an adversary may learn the function output but prevent the honest parties from doing so by prematurely aborting the protocol. This is the most well-studied notion in the dishonest majority setting, where four rounds are known to be necessary for security against malicious adversaries [15,27]. Interestingly, this lower bound does not hold in the honest majority setting, which opens doors to achieving this notion in fewer rounds.
- **Guaranteed Output Delivery:** This notion guarantees that the honest parties always learn the function output (computed over the inputs of "active" parties) even if some parties prematurely abort the protocol. A relaxation of this notion, referred to as fairness, guarantees that either all the parties learn the output or no one does.

  It is well known that fairness and guaranteed output delivery are impossible to realize for general functions in the dishonest majority setting [10]. In the honest majority setting, however, these notions are indeed possible (see, e.g., [5,11]).

Our Questions. We now summarize the state of the art results for the aforementioned security notions and state our motivating questions. We refer the reader to Sect. 1.2 for a more comprehensive survey of prior work.

We first focus on security with abort. Ishai et al. [26] constructed two round protocols in a "super" honest majority model where a malicious adversary can corrupt up to $t \leqslant \frac{n}{3}$ parties (see also [24,29] for efficiency improvements when $n = 3$, $t = 1$). Their protocol achieves a weaker notion of *selective security with abort*, where the adversary can choose which honest parties learn the output. This is necessary since their protocol only uses private channels.

We ask whether it is possible to handle the optimal corruption threshold of $t < \frac{n}{2}$ in two rounds (which are known to be optimal [23]), while also achieving standard notion of security with abort (with the additional use of broadcast):

> **Q1:** *Does there exist a two round MPC protocol in the plain model that achieves security with abort against any $t < \frac{n}{2}$ malicious corruptions?*

For the case of *semi-honest* adversaries, Ishai and Kushilevitz [25] constructed two-round MPC in the super honest majority model assuming only one-way functions for general computations, and with unconditional security for NC^1 computations. More recently, several new two-round MPC protocols have been constructed (see [6,16] and references therein); however, these protocols necessarily require at least semi-honest oblivious transfer since they can also handle a dishonest majority of corruptions. We ask whether it is possible to construct two-round (semi-honest) MPC with honest majority, from weaker assumptions:

Q2: *Does there exist a two round MPC protocol for general computations in the plain model against any $t < \frac{n}{2}$ corruptions, based only on one-way functions?*

We next consider the stronger notion of guaranteed output delivery. In this setting, Gennaro et al. [18] established the impossibility of two round protocols against $t \geqslant 2$ malicious adversaries in the plain model. More recently, Dov Gordon et al. [21] established the impossibility of two round protocols over broadcast channel (but no private channels) against fail-stop[1] adversaries in the common reference string (CRS) model. Put together, these works leave open the possibility of achieving guaranteed output delivery against fail-stop adversaries in two rounds using private channels in the plain model or just using broadcast channels in the bare public-key (BPK) model.[2]

Q3: *Does there exist a two round MPC protocol that achieves guaranteed output delivery against any $t < \frac{n}{2}$ fail-stop corruptions?*

In the broadcast-only model, Dov Gordon et al. [21] also constructed a three round protocol with guaranteed output delivery tolerating $t < \frac{n}{2}$ fail-stop corruptions.[3] Their protocol, however, requires the use of a CRS and its security is based on the learning with errors assumption. To achieve security against malicious adversaries, they compile their protocol with non-interactive zero-knowledge (NIZK) proofs [7,14]. Their work leaves open the possibility of constructing three round protocols in the plain model, based on general assumptions:

Q3: *Does there exist a three round MPC protocol over broadcast channel that achieves guaranteed output delivery against any $t < \frac{n}{2}$ malicious corruptions based on general assumptions, in the plain model?*

1.1   Our Results

In this work, we resolve all of the aforementioned questions in the affirmative. Below, we elaborate upon our results in more detail. Unless mentioned otherwise, all of our results are in the *plain model*, and do not require any trusted setup.

Security with Abort. We construct two-round MPC for general computations that achieves security with abort against any minority of malicious corruptions, based on one-way functions.

---

[1] A fail-stop adversary behaves like a semi-honest adversary, except that it may choose to abort at any point (on all the communication channels) based on its view.

[2] The BPK model was proposed in [8] where, prior to the start of the protocol, every player is required to declare a public key and store it in a public file. Since no assumptions are made on whether or not the public keys deposited are unique or "bad", this is considered a weaker model than the standard PKI model.

[3] Assuming a special-purpose public-key infrastructure, their protocol can be collapsed to two rounds.

Theorem 1 (Informal). *Assuming one-way functions, there exists a two round MPC protocol for general circuits that achieves security with abort against any* $t < \frac{n}{2}$ *malicious corruptions.*

We emphasize that our protocol in the above theorem only makes *black-box* use of one-way functions. In order to prove the above theorem, we devise a general compiler that "compresses" an arbitrary polynomial round MPC protocol (that may use both broadcast and private point-to-point channels) that achieves security with abort against any minority of malicious corruptions [5,9] into a two round MPC protocol. Our compiler builds upon the recent beautiful work of Garg and Srinivasan [16] who construct two-round UC secure MPC with dishonest majority from two-round UC secure oblivious transfer, in the CRS model. Indeed, our compiler can be viewed as an honest-majority analogue of their work (in the plain model).

Guaranteed Output Delivery. We next turn our attention to constructing protocols with guaranteed output delivery. We first consider security against *fail-stop* adversaries. In this case, we devise a round-preserving compiler that accepts any two-round semi-honest MPC protocol with a "delayed-function" property[4] and outputs a new protocol that achieves guaranteed output delivery against non-rushing fail-stop adversaries. If the underlying protocol tolerates semi-malicious[5] corruptions, then the resulting protocol achieves security against rushing, semi-malicious fail-stop adversaries. Our compiler only requires the use of one-way functions.

Theorem 2 (Informal). *Assuming one-way functions, there exists a general compiler that transforms any two round semi-honest (resp., semi-malicious) MPC protocol with delayed-function property into a two-round protocol that achieves guaranteed output delivery against non-rushing fail-stop (resp., rushing, semi-malicious fail-stop) adversaries.*

Our compiler yields the following two kinds of protocols: (i) Protocols in the plain model that use only *private* channels, if the underlying protocol only uses broadcast channels. (ii) Protocols in the (bare) public-key model that only use *broadcast* channels, if the underlying protocol uses private channels. We note that in the latter case, the use of BPK model is necessary due to the impossibility result of [21].

By applying our compiler from Theorem 2 on a variant of the protocol from Theorem 1 that achieves delayed-function[6] property, we obtain the following result in the BPK model:

---

[4] Roughly, a two-round MPC protocol satisfies the delayed-function property if the first round messages of the honest parties are computed independent of the function and the number of parties.

[5] A semi-malicious adversary is similar to a semi-honest adversary, except that it may choose its input and randomness arbitrarily [1].

[6] In the technical sections, we describe a simply modification to achieve this property. The same idea also works for the protocols of [16].

Corollary 1 (Informal). *There exists a two round MPC protocol over broadcast channels in the BPK model that achieves guaranteed output delivery against any $t < \frac{n}{2}$ (semi-malicious) fail-stop corruptions.*

Furthermore, the above protocol can also be easily modified to obtain a three round protocol in the plain model based only on one-way functions.

Next, by applying the compiler from Theorem 2 on a delayed-function variant of the semi-honest protocol from [16] (that only uses broadcast channels, unlike the protocol in Theorem 1), we get the following result:

Corollary 2 (Informal). *Assuming the existence of semi-honest (resp., semi-malicious), two-round oblivious transfer, there exists a two round MPC protocol over private channels that achieves guaranteed output delivery against any $t < \frac{n}{2}$ fail-stop (resp., semi-malicious fail-stop) corruptions in the plain model.*

We next consider security against *malicious* adversaries. We devise another compiler that accepts any two-round MPC protocol with guaranteed output delivery against semi-malicious fail-stop adversaries and outputs a three-round protocol that achieves guaranteed output delivery against malicious adversaries. The main tool used in our compiler is a new notion of *multi-verifier zero-knowledge* (MVZK) proofs, which may be of independent interest. Briefly, an MVZK protocol is a multiparty interactive protocol between a single prover and multiple verifiers where the soundness and zero knowledge properties only hold when a majority of the parties are honest. An MVZK must also achieve a *strong completeness* property such that the honest verifiers always accept the proof given by an honest prover even if some of the verifiers (who constitute a minority) are dishonest.

Theorem 3 (Informal). *Assuming public-key encryption and two round delayed-input[7] multi-verifier zero-knowledge arguments, there exists a general compiler that transforms any two round MPC protocol with guaranteed output delivery against semi-malicious fail-stop adversaries into a three round protocol with guaranteed output delivery against malicious adversaries.*

Our compiler only requires broadcast channels, and is therefore optimal in the number of rounds, in keeping with the impossibility result of [21]. We next give a simple construction of delayed-input MVZK arguments based on Zaps [13] (i.e., two round witness indistinguishable proofs), following the construction of NIZKs in the multi-CRS model [22]. Then, applying our compiler on the protocol from Corollary 1, we obtain the following result:

Corollary 3 (Informal). *Assuming Zaps and public-key encryption, there exists a three round MPC protocol over broadcast channels that achieves guaranteed output delivery against any $t < \frac{n}{2}$ malicious corruptions.*

---

[7] Delayed-input property for MVZK is defined in the same manner as two-party interactive proofs [28], namely, by allowing the prover to choose the instance after the first round of the protocol.

1.2   Related Work

Over the years, the round complexity of MPC has been extensively studied both in the honest majority and dishonest majority settings. Here, we focus on the honest majority setting and refer the reader to [2] for a comprehensive survey of the literature in the dishonest majority setting.

The study of constant-round MPC was initiated by Beaver et al. [3]. They constructed such protocols against malicious adversaries in the honest majority setting using pseudorandom generators (PRGs). Damgård and Ishai [12] later achieved a similar result by making only black-box use of PRGs.

In a seminal work, Ishai and Kushilevitz [25] constructed two round and three round semi-honest MPC protocols that tolerate $t \leqslant \frac{n}{3}$ and $t < \frac{n}{2}$ corruptions, respectively. Subsequently, Ishai et al. [26] constructed two round protocols against $t \leqslant \frac{n}{3}$ malicious corruptions, achieving selective security with abort. More recently, Ishai et al. [24,29] constructed simpler two round protocols for $n = 3$ parties that tolerate any single, malicious corruption.

While the work of [5] already achieved fairness, several subsequent works also achieve guaranteed output delivery (see, e.g., [11] for references). We highlight a few results in this regime. Damgård and Ishai [12] constructed a three round MPC protocol with guaranteed output delivery for $t < \frac{n}{5}$. Ishai et al. [26] constructed a two round protocol with guaranteed output delivery using only private channels for the special case of $t = 1$, $n \geqslant 5$. Further, they also constructed a two-round protocol in the client server model, with n clients and $m > 2$ servers, that tolerates a single corrupted client and $t \leqslant \frac{n}{5}$ colluding servers. Subsequently, Asharov et al. [1] constructed five round protocols with guaranteed delivery for $t < N/2$, assuming learning with errors (LWE) and NIZKs. More recently, Ishai et al. [24] constructed several protocols with guaranteed output delivery for the case of $t = 1$ and $n = 4$: a two round statistically secure protocol for linear functionalities, a two round computationally secure protocol for general functionalities with guaranteed output delivery from injective one-way functions, and a two round unconditionally secure protocol for general functionalities with guaranteed output delivery in the preprocessing model. Dov Gordon et al. [21] constructed a three round protocol with guaranteed output delivery in the CRS model with broadcast-only messages assuming LWE and NIZKs.

Gennaro et al. [18] established a lower bound for achieving guaranteed output delivery against malicious adversaries. They ruled out the existence of two round protocols in the plain model that achieve guaranteed output delivery against $t \geqslant 2$ malicious parties. More recently, Dov Gordon et al. [21] established a stronger lower bound for protocols that only use broadcast channels. Specifically, they ruled out the existence of two round protocols over broadcast channels that achieve guaranteed output delivery against (non-rushing) fail-stop adversaries in the CRS model.

2   Preliminaries

In our constructions, we make use of some well studied primitives like *garbled circuits* [31] and *threshold secret sharing* [30]. While garbled circuits with selective security suffice for our application in Sect. 4, we require *adaptive garbled circuits* in Sect. 5. An adaptively secure garbled circuit is one where the adversary first gets to see a garbling for any circuit of his choice. After seeing this garbled circuit, he can adaptively choose an input and obtain labels corresponding to that input. For our application, the online complexity (i.e., size of input wire labels) is not important; as such it suffices to use one-time pads with Yao's garbled circuits as suggested in the work of Bellare et al. [4] to obtain adaptively secure garbled circuits from one-way functions. We refer the reader to [4] or the full version of our paper for a formal definition of this primitive.

We use various notions of security for secure multiparty computation (MPC) in our constructions. Apart from the standard notion of *security with abort* that guarantees correctness of output of the honest parties (when the adversary does not prematurely abort), we also consider a relaxed notion of security called *privacy with knowledge of output* [26]. The only difference from the definition for security with abort is that in the ideal world, on receiving outputs from the trusted party, the adversary can choose the output it wants to send to the honest parties. It is easy to see that this is a weaker notion since the correctness of output for the honest parties is no longer guaranteed. A formal definition of this can be found in the full version of our paper, or in [26]. We also consider security with *guaranteed output delivery* against both fail-stop and malicious adversaries.

For our application in Sect. 5, we also consider MPC protocols with a *delayed function property*, i.e., protocols where the first round messages of all parties are independent of the function and the number of parties in the protocol.

3   Definitions

In this section, we define some new notions that we consider in this work.

3.1   Multiparty Oblivious Transfer Protocol

A multiparty oblivious transfer (OT) protocol consists of n-parties, where one of the parties P_n is the receiver and every other party $P_1, \ldots, P_{n-1}$ is a sender. Sender P_i has inputs $m_{i,0}, m_{i,1}$ and the receiver R has a private input σ_1. At the end of this protocol every party learns only $\{m_{i,\sigma_1}\}_{i\in[n-1]}$.

Before proceeding we note that every player gets the output. Therefore, on completion of the protocol there is no receiver security. For our applications this is completely fine. On the other hand, we will insist that if the second round of the protocol is not executed the receiver privacy is maintained. We should also point out that we have given a general definition, but this can be appropriately modified to let only the receiver obtain the output by setting every other party's output to be $\perp$.

We consider protocols that have both broadcast and private messages m_B and m_{priv}. But for convenience of notation we denote this as $m := (m_B, m_{\text{priv}})$. When we say such a message is sent, we indicate that m_B is sent by broadcast and m_{priv} is sent privately.

We consider a variant of the multiparty OT protocol, which we shall denote as *multiparty homomorphic oblivious transfer protocol*. In this variant there is a special designated sender $\widehat{S}$ $(=P_{n-1})$ with an additional input σ_2. At the end of the protocol, every party learns only $\{m_{i,\sigma_1 \oplus \sigma_2}\}_{i \in [n-1]}$. The regular multi-party OT can be thought of as a special mode of the homomorphic oblivious transfer where the additional input from this special designated sender is ignored (or set to 0). Hence, it is convenient to formally define the homomorphic notion of the multiparty OT, but we shall use both these notions:

Definition 1 (Multiparty Homomorphic OT Protocol). *A two round 1-out-of-2 multiparty homomorphic oblivious transfer protocol* $\mathsf{OT} = (\mathsf{OT}_1^R, \mathsf{OT}_1^{\widehat{S}}, \mathsf{OT}_1^S, \mathsf{OT}_2, \mathsf{OT}_3)$ *is an interactive protocol between n parties, where one of the parties is the receiver, one of the parties is a special designated sender and the others are senders. The sender parties P_i for $i \in [n-1]$ have inputs $m_{i,0}, m_{i,1} \in \{0,1\}^\lambda$, the receiver party P_n has an input bit $\sigma_1 \in \{0,1\}$, and the special designated sender P_{n-1} has an additional input $\sigma_2 \in \{0,1\}$.*

First round. The parties compute their first round messages as follows:

- ***Receiver:*** $\left\{ \mathsf{ot}_n[j]_{\to n,n-1}^1 \right\}_{j \in [n]} \leftarrow \mathsf{OT}_1^R(\sigma_1)$ *where* $\mathsf{ot}_n[j]_{\to n,n-1}^1$ *refers to the message that the party j receives from the receiver (party P_n). The subscript $\to n, n-1$ denotes that the designated special sender is P_{n-1} while the receiver is P_n.*

- ***Special sender:*** $\left\{ \mathsf{ot}_{n-1}[j]_{\to n,n-1}^1 \right\}_{j \in [n]} \leftarrow \mathsf{OT}_1^{\widehat{S}}((m_{n-1,0}, m_{n-1,1}), \sigma_2)$. *The notation is almost identical to the previous case, but the notation here identifies this as a message from the special sender (party P_{n-1}).*

- ***Senders:*** *Each party $i \in [n-2]$ computes* $\left\{ \mathsf{ot}_i[j]_{\to n,n-1}^1 \right\}_{j \in [n]} \leftarrow \mathsf{OT}_1^S (m_{i,0}, m_{i,1})$. *The notation is almost identical to the previous case, but the notation here identifies this as the message from the corresponding sender (party P_i).*

Each party sends P_j its corresponding message. Thus, at the end of the first round each party P_j has $\left\{ \mathsf{ot}_i[j]_{\to n,n-1}^1 \right\}_{i \in [n]}$.

Second Round. Each party P_i computes their second round message

$\mathsf{ot}_i[\perp]_{\to n,n-1}^2 \leftarrow \mathsf{OT}_2 \left(\left\{ \mathsf{ot}_j[i]_{\to n,n-1}^1 \right\}_{j \in [n]} \right)$. *Here by $\perp$ we denote that the message is broadcast to every party.*

Output Computation. Every party computes the output as follows

$$\left(\{\widetilde{m}_i\}_{i \in [n-1]} \right) := \mathsf{OT}_3 \left(\left\{ \mathsf{ot}_i[\perp]_{\to n,n-1}^2 \right\}_{i \in [n]} \right)$$

We require the following properties from the protocol:

1. **Correctness:** *For every $\sigma_1, \sigma_2 \in \{0,1\}$, and sender input messages $\forall i \in [n], b \in \{0,1\}$ $m_{i,b} \in \{0,1\}^\lambda$, $\Pr\left[\forall i \in [n-1] \quad \tilde{m}_i = m_{i,\sigma_1 \oplus \sigma_2}\right] = 1$ where the randomness is over the coins used to compute the first and second round messages of the protocol.*

2. **Security:** *We consider two notions of security depending on whether or not the second round of the protocol is executed:*

    -   **Privacy.** *If the protocol terminates at the end of the first round, then the notion of privacy is satisfied;*

    -   **Privacy with Knowledge of Outputs against Malicious Minority:** *If the second round is executed (by the honest parties at least), then for any PPT adversary $\mathcal{A}$ controlling a minority set of the parties, there exists a PPT simulator $\mathsf{Sim} = (\mathsf{Sim}_{OT}, \mathsf{Ext}_{OT})$ satisfying the security notion of privacy with knowledge of outputs (defined in Sect. 2).*
        The role of the extractor Ext_{OT} is to extract the adversary's input from its first round messages. On the other hand, the role of the Sim_{OT} is to generate the transcript for the protocol.

Instantiation. The multiparty homomorphic oblivious transfer protocol with inputs $(\{m_{i,b}[\ell]\}_{i \in [n-1], b \in \{0,1\}, \ell \in [\lambda]}, \sigma_1, \sigma_2)$, where $\sigma_1, \sigma_2, m_{i,b[\ell]} \in \{0,1\}$, can be thought of as a vector of degree 2 polynomials in $\mathbb{F}_2$: $\forall i \in [n-1], \ell \in [\lambda]$ $m_{i,0[\ell]} \cdot (1 + \sigma_1 + \sigma_2) + m_{i,1}[\ell] \cdot (\sigma_1 + \sigma_2)$. The work of Ishai et al. [26] gives us an explicit construction for such a degree 2 polynomial computation protocol:

Theorem 4 ([26]). *For $n = 2t + 1$, where t is the number of corrupted parties, there exists a 2 round protocol that computes a vector of polynomials of degree 2 and satisfies statistical t-privacy with knowledge of outputs.*

We note that the original stated lemma in [26] requires $|\mathbb{F}| > n$, but this condition can be relaxed to computing polynomials in $\mathbb{F}_2$ if we can construct a 2-multiplicative $(2t+1, t)$ linear secret sharing scheme that is pairwise verifiable (see [26] for details). In fact, [26] discusses how to construct such a scheme, which in turn suffices for our notion of the multiparty homomorphic OT.

3.2   Multi-Verifier Zero Knowledge Proof System

A multi-verifier zero-knowledge proof system consists of a prover P and n verifiers $V_1, \ldots, V_n$. The prover and the verifiers share a statement x that belongs to an NP-language. The prover additionally holds a private input w. If w is a valid witness for the statement x, all honest verifiers must be able to output 1. If x does not belong to the NP-language, honest verifiers should not output 1 with a very high probability. The verifiers should not learn anything about w in either case.

Consider n verifiers, where t can be corrupted. For completeness, $t \leqslant n$, for soundness, $t \leqslant n - 1$, and for ZK, $t \leqslant n$. Note that in the extreme case, the definition subsumes the standard ZK definition since all the verifiers can be combined into one. In our constructions, we will focus on the honest-majority case, where for soundness, $t \leqslant \frac{n-1}{2}$ and for ZK, $t \leqslant \frac{n}{2}$. For our constructions, we require a two round multi-verifier zero knowledge protocol that satisfies delayed input property, i.e., first round messages of both the prover and verifier and second round messages of verifier are independent of the statement.

A formal definition of this primitive is as follows:

Definition 2 (Two Round Multi-Verifier Zero Knowledge). *A two round multi-verifier zero-knowledge proof system associated with an NP relation $\mathcal{R}$ is an interactive zero-knowledge protocol with a prover P and n verifiers $V_1, \ldots, V_n$. The prover and the verifiers hold an instance x of the language $\mathcal{L}(\mathcal{R})$ defined by the relation $\mathcal{R}$. The prover also holds a string $w \in \{0,1\}^{\lambda}$. It can be defined as a tuple of PPT algorithms* $\mathsf{mvzk} := (\mathsf{P}^1_{\mathsf{mvzk}}, \mathsf{V}^1_{\mathsf{mvzk}}, \mathsf{P}^2_{\mathsf{mvzk}}, \mathsf{V}^2_{\mathsf{mvzk}}, \mathsf{Verify}_{\mathsf{mvzk}})$.

- $\mathsf{pMsg}^1 \leftarrow \mathsf{P}^1_{\mathsf{mvzk}}(1^{\lambda})$: $\mathsf{P}^1_{\mathsf{mvzk}}$ *takes the security parameter λ as input and outputs first round messages of the prover.*
- $\mathsf{vMsg}^1_i \leftarrow \mathsf{V}^1_{\mathsf{mvzk}}(1^{\lambda}, i)$: $\mathsf{V}^1_{\mathsf{mvzk}}$ *takes the security parameter λ and index i of the verifier as input and outputs first round messages of the verifier.*
- $\mathsf{pMsg}^2 \leftarrow \mathsf{P}^2_{\mathsf{mvzk}}(\mathsf{trans}^1_{\mathsf{mvzk}}, x, w)$: $\mathsf{P}^2_{\mathsf{mvzk}}$ *takes the first round transcript of mvzk,* $\mathsf{trans}^1_{\mathsf{mvzk}} := (\mathsf{pMsg}^1, \{\mathsf{vMsg}^1_i\}_{i \in [n]})$, *the statement x and the witness w as input and outputs second round messages of the prover.*
- $\mathsf{vMsg}^2_i \leftarrow \mathsf{V}^2_{\mathsf{mvzk}}(i, \mathsf{trans}^1_{\mathsf{mvzk}})$: $\mathsf{V}^2_{\mathsf{mvzk}}$ *takes index i of the verifier and the first round transcript of mvzk,* $\mathsf{trans}^1_{\mathsf{mvzk}} := (\mathsf{pMsg}^1, \{\mathsf{vMsg}^1_i\}_{i \in [n]})$ *as input and outputs second round messages of the verifier.*
- $b := \mathsf{Verify}_{\mathsf{mvzk}}(i, \{\mathsf{trans}^r_{\mathsf{mvzk}}\}_{r \in [2]}, x)$: $\mathsf{Verify}_{\mathsf{mvzk}}$ *takes index i of the verifier, the entire transcript of the protocol and the statement x as input and outputs a bit b.*

We want the multi-verifier zero-knowledge proof system to satisfy the following properties:

1. **Completeness:** *For every n.u. PPT adversary $\mathcal{A}$ that corrupts up to t verifiers, let $H \subset [n]$ be the set of honest verifiers, then for every $x \in \mathcal{L}(\mathcal{R})$ and for all honest verifiers V_i, where $i \in H$,*

$$\Pr[\mathsf{Verify}_{\mathsf{mvzk}}(i, \{\mathsf{trans}^r_{\mathsf{mvzk}}\}_{r \in [2]}, x) = 1] = 1$$

2. **Soundness:** *For every adversary $\mathcal{A}$ controlling the prover (P^*) and upto t verifiers, let $H \subseteq [n]$ be the set of honest verifiers, then for every $x \notin \mathcal{L}(\mathcal{R})$ and for all honest verifiers V_i where $i \in H$,*

$$\Pr[\mathsf{Verify}_{\mathsf{mvzk}}(i, \{\mathsf{trans}^r_{\mathsf{mvzk}}\}_{r \in [2]}, x) = 1] \leqslant \mu(\lambda)$$

for some negligible function μ.

We require a slightly stronger notion of soundness, where soundness holds, even if an adversarial prover is allowed to choose the statement after looking at the first round messages of honest verifiers.

3. **Zero-Knowledge:** *For every n.u. PPT adversary $\mathcal{A}$, that corrupts upto t verifiers, let $H \subseteq [n]$ be the set of honest verifiers, then there exists a PPT Simulator* $\mathsf{Sim}_{\mathsf{mvzk}} := (\mathsf{Sim}^1_{\mathsf{mvzk}}, \mathsf{Sim}^2_{\mathsf{mvzk}})$, *s.t., for every $x \in \mathcal{L}(\mathcal{R}), w \in \mathcal{R}(x), \mathbf{z} \in \{0,1\}^*$ and a negligible function $\mu(.)$,*

$$| \Pr[\mathsf{Exp}^{\mathsf{ZK}}_{\mathcal{A},\mathsf{Sim}_{\mathsf{mvzk}}}(1^\lambda, 0) = 1] - \Pr[\mathsf{Exp}^{\mathsf{ZK}}_{\mathcal{A},\mathsf{Sim}_{\mathsf{mvzk}}}(1^\lambda, 1) = 1]| \leqslant \mu(\lambda)$$

where the experiment $\mathsf{Exp}^{\mathsf{ZK}}_{\mathcal{A},\mathsf{Sim}_{\mathsf{mvzk}}}(1^\lambda, \mathsf{b})$ *is defined as follows:*

(a) *The adversary $\mathcal{A}$ gets* $(\mathsf{pMsg}^1, \{\mathsf{vMsg}^1_i\}_{i \in H})$, *which are computed as follows:*
   - *If $b = 0$:* $\mathsf{pMsg}^1 \leftarrow \mathsf{P}^1_{\mathsf{mvzk}}(1^\lambda)$, $\{\mathsf{vMsg}^1_i\}_{i \in H} \leftarrow \{\mathsf{V}^1_{\mathsf{mvzk}}(1^\lambda, i)\}_{i \in H}$
   - *If $b = 1$:* $(\mathsf{pMsg}^1, \{\mathsf{vMsg}^1_i\}_{i \in H}) \leftarrow \mathsf{Sim}^1_{\mathsf{mvzk}}(1^\lambda, H)$.

(b) *The adversary $\mathcal{A}$ sends* $\{\mathsf{vMsg}^1_i\}_{i \notin H}$ *and specifies x, w and gets* $(\mathsf{pMsg}^2, \{\mathsf{vMsg}^2_i\}_{i \in H})$, *which are computed as follows:*
   - *If $b = 0$:* $\mathsf{pMsg}^2 \leftarrow \mathsf{P}^2_{\mathsf{mvzk}}(\mathsf{trans}^1_{\mathsf{mvzk}}, x, w)$, $\{\mathsf{vMsg}^2_i\}_{i \in H} \leftarrow \{\mathsf{V}^2_{\mathsf{mvzk}}(i, \mathsf{trans}^1_{\mathsf{mvzk}})\}_{i \in H}$.
   - *If $b = 1$:* $(\mathsf{pMsg}^2, \{\mathsf{vMsg}^2_i\}_{i \in H}) \leftarrow \mathsf{Sim}^2_{\mathsf{mvzk}}(H, \mathsf{trans}^1_{\mathsf{mvzk}}, x)$.

(c) *The adversary outputs a bit b', which is the output of the experiment.*

If the soundness property only holds against polynomial-time adversaries, then we refer to the above system as an *argument* system.

In the full version, we provide a construction of multi-verifier ZK arguments based on Zaps. Our protocol is based on the multi-CRS NIZK construction of [22], with some changes to achieve the strong completeness property.

4 Security with Abort Against Malicious Adversaries

Overview. We start by providing an overview of our construction. Our starting point is the recent beautiful work of Garg and Srinivasan [16].

Recap of [16]. Garg and Srinivasan [16] constructed two-round maliciously secure MPC against dishonest majority based on any two-round OT in the CRS model with some specific security properties (that we discuss below). At a high level, their protocol works by compiling a multi-round maliciously secure protocol of a very specific syntactic structure (where each round only consists of a single bit broadcast by one party to all the other parties), which they refer to as a *conforming protocol*, into a two round protocol using OT.

The compiler of Garg and Srinivasan uses a two-round OT protocol in the CRS model with the following properties: (1) simulation-based security against malicious receivers (which implies that the simulator can extract the input bit from a malicious receiver); and (2) equivocation of the honest receiver bit. Unfortunately, in two rounds, these properties can only be achieved in the common random string (CRS) model in the dishonest majority setting.

At a high level, OT is used to transmit garbled circuit labels for a single input (that corresponds to a message in the underlying conforming protocol) to an evaluator. Loosely speaking, a "speaker" party in any round of the underlying conforming protocol sends a receiver's OT message in the first round of the two-round protocol. The receiver's message is computed using as input the bit b which is supposed to be broadcast in the underlying protocol. Note that these messages are not actually known in the first round, so the "speaker" party actually prepares multiple OT messages. Every other party (unaware of this bit ahead of time) computes the OT protocol message with the two labels for its own garbled circuit as its sender input. At a later point, when the message bit is broadcast, the OT receiver also reveals the randomness used to compute the appropriate first OT message. This enables an evaluator, different from the receiver, to obtain the appropriate labels for each garbled circuit and then evaluate them correctly.

However, this release of the randomness used to compute the OT receiver messages creates a problem during simulation against a rushing adversary since a simulator, who computes an OT receiver message on behalf of an honest party, does not know what inputs to use. For this reason, the compiler in [16] requires the ability to equivocate receiver's randomness.

Challenges. We face some challenges in adopting the template of [16] to achieve our goal of constructing a maliciously secure two-round MPC protocol in the honest majority setting from one-way functions. We highlight a couple of them below.

- *Issue #1. Replacing Oblivious Transfer:* If we have any hope of basing our construction on one-way functions, we first need to figure out how to replace the oblivious transfer protocols in [16] for the honest majority setting. Note that the oblivious transfer protocols are used in two places in [16]: (i) in the interactive secure MPC protocol and, (ii) in the transformation of conforming protocols into two-round secure MPC protocols. We handle both (i) and (ii) separately.
- *Issue #2. Private Channels:* We first handle (i) by starting with a interactive secure MPC protocol in the honest majority setting. The existence of such a protocol achieving perfect security is known in literature [5,9]. However such protocols, in addition to broadcast channels, inherently use private channels – every pair of parties has a channel designated to them such that any communication on this channel cannot be observed by an external entity. However, the approach of [16] starts with an interactive secure MPC protocol that uses only broadcast channels. Hence, we need to modify their approach that will enable us to handle private channels in the underlying interactive secure MPC protocol.

Multiparty Homomorphic Oblivious Transfer. Towards solving both the above issues, we introduce the notion of multiparty homomorphic oblivious transfer. For simplicity, we first focus on achieving the weaker goal of semi-honest secure two-round MPC in the honest majority setting.

As the name suggests, this notion is a multiparty protocol where only three of the parties have inputs and the rest of the parties have no inputs. These three parties are termed as sender, receiver and designated sender. The sender[8], has inputs (m_0, m_1), receiver has input a bit σ_1 and the designated sender has input a mask σ_2. At the end of the protocol, every party receives the output $m_{\sigma_1 \oplus \sigma_2}$. We can also consider a weaker notion where the designated sender does not supply any input and we term such a notion as multiparty OT (in particular, not homomorphic). In this case, every party receives m_{σ_1}.

We can use this protocol to replace the oblivious transfer protocols in the transformation from conforming protocols to two-round secure MPC protocols. Moreover this protocol can be instantiated from two-round perfectly secure MPC protocols for quadratic polynomials [5,9][9]. To see how this can be used to solve the issue of private channels, we make the following modifications to the framework of [16].

- We start with an interactive perfectly secure MPC protocol that uses only broadcast channels in the pre-processing setting. By pre-processing, we mean that the parties can exchange information with each other over private channels before seeing any input. Once pre-processing phase is over, the parties receive the inputs in the online phase and during this phase, they perform secure computation only using broadcast channels. Such a protocol can be achieved by starting with an perfectly secure protocol without pre-processing but using private channels: the parties can exchange one-time pads (of suitable length) in the pre-processing phase to emulate the private channels in the online phase. In particular, whenever a party P_i has to send a message to another party P_j, it encrypts its message using the one-time pad P_j sent to P_i during the online phase. We transform such a interactive MPC protocol into a conforming protocol in the pre-processing setting.
- To transform a conforming protocol in the pre-processing setting into a two-round protocol, the main challenge we encounter is to get rid of the pre-processing phase. Specifically, every party in the two-round protocol is required to commit to all its actions (corresponding to the conforming protocol) in the first round. This is not possible if we start with a conforming protocol in the pre-processing setting since the actions of the parties depend on the output of the pre-processing phase which cannot be computed before the first round in the two-round protocol. This is where we crucially use the homomorphism property of the multiparty homomorphic OT protocol.

Malicious Security. While the use of multiparty homomorphic OT protocol can be used to achieve a semi-honest secure two-round MPC protocol in the honest majority setting, we need additional mechanisms to prove security against malicious adversaries. We start by incorporating the equivocation mechanism inside our multiparty homomorphic protocol.

---

[8] For simplicity, we explain the main ideas using just a single sender. We use a generalized version with multiple senders.

[9] Note that [5,9] dealt with computations over large fields while we need to securely compute quadratic polynomials over boolean fields. By suitably using extension fields in [5] we can solve this issue.

Equivocation. Instead of using an OT protocol that explicitly allows for randomness equivocation, we achieve a similar effect from the fact that an honest receiver's input in the multiparty OT protocol is not fixed in the adversary's view when it can corrupt only a minority of parties.

Given a maliciously secure multiparty homomorphic OT protocol satisfying these properties, one could obtain the required compiler following the above strategy. However, we do not know of such a protocol in only two rounds.

Towards this, we note that the work of Ishai, Kushilevitz and Paskin [26] construct a two round protocol for degree 2 polynomial computation, in the honest majority setting. While their protocol does not achieve full malicious security, it achieves a weaker notion they refer to as *privacy with knowledge of outputs*. Roughly, this notion is similar to standard malicious security, except that it does not guarantee correctness of outputs received by the honest parties. In particular, the adversary can explicitly set the output of the honest parties to any value of its choice (in this sense, it "knows" the honest party outputs). Since a multi-party OT can be represented as a degree 2 polynomial computation, a two-round multi-party OT protocol achieving this weaker security notion can be obtained from [26].

Our main insight is that this weaker notion of multiparty homomorphic OT can still be used to obtain our desired compiler. In the protocol by Garg and Srinivasan [16], it is essential that OT security holds against malicious receivers that attempt to equivocate their receiver bit. It would seem that in our weaker model, since the adversary can set the output to be a value of its choice, it could potentially change the output from say m_b to m_{1-b}, where b was its input to the OT protocol. This would completely break simulation since the adversary could essentially equivocate its input, and thus the guarantees of the protocol in [16] would no longer apply. This is where we use the knowledge of output property of the protocol, i.e. the output that the honest parties receive is known to the adversary. In the case of the OT protocol, when the sender is honest, an ideal world adversary receives only m_b and m_{1-b} remains hidden. Thus the output of honest parties forced by the adversary are independent of m_{1-b}. This does not stop the adversary to from setting it to a random value. However, since messages m_b and m_{1-b} correspond to wire keys of a garbled circuit, we can rely on the security of the garbling scheme which ensures that a garbled circuit cannot be evaluated unless the evaluator has one of the keys.

4.1   Conforming Protocols

Let Φ be an n-party deterministic MPC protocol with honest majority. Let $\mathcal{P} = \{P_1, \ldots, P_n\}$ be the set of parties in the protocol with inputs $x_1, \ldots, x_n$ respectively. A conforming protocol can be defined by a tuple of 3 functions (pre, comp, post).

Pre-processing Phase: For each $(i \in [n])$, party P_i computes the following: $(z_i, \widehat{v}_i) \leftarrow \mathsf{pre}(1^\lambda, i, x_i)$. The randomized algorithm pre takes as input, the index

i of the party, its input x_i and outputs $z_i \in \{0,1\}^{\ell/n}$ and $\widehat{v}_i \in \{0,1\}^{\ell}$. $\widehat{v}_i$ is private information, that it retains with itself. We require that $\widehat{v}_i[k] = 0$ for all $k \in [\ell] \setminus \{(i-1)\ell/n, \cdots, i\ell/n\}$. z_i is a public value that is broadcast to every other party in the protocol.

Each party P_i additionally samples masks $r_{k \to i}$ for all $k \in [n] \setminus \{i\}$ of appropriate length (to be discussed shortly). The mask $r_{k \to i}$ is sent privately to P_k.

Computation Phase: The computation phase can be viewed as a series of T actions $\Phi_1, \ldots, \Phi_T$. Each action Φ_r, for $t \in [T]$, can be parsed as tuple of 5 indices, $\Phi_t = (i^*, j^*, f, g, h)$, where $i^* \in [n], j^* \in [n] \cup \{\bot\}$, and $f, g, h \in [\ell]$. Since Φ is a deterministic protocol, $\Phi_1, \ldots, \Phi_T$, are known to each party in advance.

- For all $j \in [n] \setminus \{i\}$, $\mathbb{I}_{j \to i} = \{h \mid \Phi.(j, i, \cdot, \cdot, h)\}$, and $\mathbb{I}_i := \cup_{j \in [n] \setminus \{i\}} \mathbb{I}_{j \to i}$[10].
  Hence, for each $k \in [n] \setminus \{i\}$, $r_{k \to i} \in \{0,1\}^{|\mathbb{I}_{k \to i}|}$. From each $r_{k \to i}$, we want to refer to the bit in $r_{k \to i}$ that is associated with the index h. This is achieved by defining the following function $r_{k \to i}(h) := r_{k \to i}[\rho(h)]$, where $\rho(h)$ is the index of h in $\mathbb{I}_{k \to i}$. We are able to do so because we are treating as an ordered set.
- We now create the vector $v \in \{0,1\}^{\ell}$ from $\widehat{v}$ and masks $r_{k \to i}$.

$$
v_i[k] := \begin{cases}
\widehat{v}[k] & \text{if } k \in \{(i-1)\ell/n, \cdots, i\ell/n\} \\
r_{\pi(k) \to i}[k] & \text{if } k \in \mathbb{I}_i \\
0 & \text{otherwise}
\end{cases}
$$

where $\pi(k)$ is j such that $k \in \mathbb{I}_{j \to i}$. We simply update $\widehat{v}$ to include the mask bits at the appropriate position. It is important to note that these updates make sense only if for every i the sets $\mathbb{I}_{j \to i}$ are disjoint. This will indeed be enforced in the conforming protocol (see below).

Let For each $i \in [n]$, party P_i does the following:
Sets, $\mathsf{st}_i = (z_1 \| \ldots \| z_n) \oplus v_i$
For each $t \in \{1, \ldots, T\}$,

1. Parse Φ_t as (i^*, j, f, g, h)
2. **If** $i = i^*$, compute $\mathsf{st}_i[h] = \mathsf{NAND}(\mathsf{st}_i[f], \mathsf{st}_i[g]) \oplus r_{i \to j}(h)$ (where $r_{i \to j}(h) = 0$ if $j = \bot$) and broadcast $\mathsf{st}_i[h] \oplus v_i[h]$ to all other parties.
3. **Else,** updates $\mathsf{st}_i[h]$ to the bit value received from P_{i^*}.

We require each action Φ_t, for $t \in [T]$, to update a unique position h in the state. More specifically, $\forall t, t' \in [T]$ such that $t \neq t'$, if $\Phi_t = (., ., ., ., h)$ and $\Phi_{t'} = (., ., ., ., h')$, then $h \neq h'$. Additionally, for every party P_i we require that a bit at index h sent privately to a party P_j is not used as a input to a NAND computation by P_i. Formally, $\forall t \in [T]$ if $\Phi_t = (i, j, \cdot, \cdot, h)$ where $j \neq \bot$ then $\nexists t' \in [t, T]$ such that $\Phi_{t'} = (i, \cdot, h, \cdot, \cdot)$ or $\Phi_{t'} = (i, \cdot, \cdot, h, \cdot)$. We denote $A_i \subset [T]$ be set of rounds in which party P_i sends a bit.

---

[10] We abuse notation slightly and consider each $\mathbb{I}_{j \to i}$ to be an ordered set, ordered increasingly by h.

We note that the non-repetition of h ensures that for every i, k the sets $\mathbb{I}_{i \to k}$ are disjoint.

Output Phase: For each $i \in [n]$, party P_i outputs $\mathsf{post}(\mathsf{st}_i)$.

Transformation to a Conforming Protocol. Let Π be an n-party deterministic MPC protocol with honest majority. Let $\mathcal{P} = \{P_1, \ldots, P_n\}$ be the parties in the protocol Π. Let each party P_i have input $x_i \in \{0,1\}^m$. We want to transform this protocol Π to a conforming protocol Φ, while preserving its security and correctness. We allow the protocol Π to use both broadcast and private channels.

We can assume w.l.o.g. that only a single bit is communicated by one party in each round of Π. This can trivially be achieved by increasing the round complexity of the protocol. As discussed, this bit can be broadcast or sent to a specific party. Since only a single bit is communicated in each round by one party, the message complexity in this case is equivalent to the round complexity. Let the message/round complexity of Π after increasing the round complexity be p. Let C_r be the circuit computed in round $r \in [p]$. Again we can assume without loss of generality that this circuit is only composed of NAND gates with fan-in two and each C_r is composed of q NAND gates.

We now describe how to transform Π into a conforming protocol Φ. There are $T = pq$ rounds in Φ. Let $\ell = mn + pq$ and $\ell' = pq/n$

- $\mathsf{pre}(1, x_i)$:
    1. Samples $r_i \leftarrow \{0,1\}^m$ and $s_i \leftarrow (\{0,1\}^{g-1}||0)^{p/n}$.
    2. Output $z_i := x_i \oplus r_i||0^{\ell'}$ and $v_i := 0^{\ell/n}|| \ldots ||r_i||s_i|| \ldots ||0^{\ell/n}$
- $\mathsf{comp} := \{\Phi_1, \ldots, \Phi_T\}$: As specified in the transformation above, each round $r \in [p]$ in Π is expanded into q actions in Φ. Each of these actions $\{\Phi_t\}_t$, where $t \in \{(r-1)q + 1, \ldots, rq\}$ is a single NAND computation. For each t, Φ_t is set as (i^*, j^*, f, g, h). f, g are the locations in st_{i^*} that the tth NAND gate in C_r is computed on. h is the first location in st_{i^*} amongst the locations $(i^* - 1)\ell/n + m + 1$ to $i\ell/n$ that has not been updated before. For $t \in \{(r-1)q + 1, \ldots, rq - 1\}$, $j^* := \bot$, and for $t = rq$, j^* is set to be the recipient of the bit in the round r of Π. If the bit is to be broadcast in round r of Π, j^* is set to $\bot$.
- $\mathsf{post}(i, \mathsf{st}_i)$ Party P_i gathers messages sent by other parties in Π from the final st_i and runs the output phase of Π to output the output.

To ensure the global invariant property (defined shortly) when there are private channels involved, we require the second property described in the conforming protocol. Namely, if a player P_i sends a bit in index h over a private channel, P_i cannot subsequently use the index h as an input to a NAND gate. This is easily fixed by "copying" the bit at index h by recomputing the bit to a new position h' in the subsequent round of P_i. This increases the number of NAND gate in each round by 1, and does not affect the transformation above.

The changes in the conforming protocol, and the transformation is to accommodate underlying protocols that use both broadcast and private channels. The conforming protocol in [16] relies on the underlying protocol to use only broadcast channels.

4.2   Our Compiler

Building Blocks. The main primitives required in this construction are:

1. A maliciously secure conforming protocol Φ with honest majority.
2. A garbling scheme (Garble, Eval) for circuits.
3. A 2 round Multiparty Homomorphic Oblivious Transfer Protocol that works in the honest majority setting.

Theorem 5. *Assuming maliciously secure conforming protocol Φ, secure garbling scheme* (Garble, Eval) *and a 2 round multiparty homomorphic OT protocol the two round protocol Π described below achieves security with abort against any $t < \frac{n}{2}$ malicious corruptions.*

We instantiate the underlying MPC protocol with an information-theoretic honest majority MPC protocol such as [5,9]. Further, our compiler makes only black-box use of one-way functions.

While we describe our complier for malicious adversaries using both broadcast and private channels, it is easy to see that our protocol is secure against semi-honest adversaries that use only private channels.

Protocol. Let $\mathcal{P} = \{P_1, \ldots, P_n\}$ be the set of parties in the protocol and let $\{x_1, \ldots, x_n\}$ and $\{\widetilde{r}_1, \ldots, \widetilde{r}_n\}$ be their respective inputs and randomness. Next, we describe the protocol Π in detail:

Round 1. Each party P_i does the following:

1. Run the pre-computation phase to compute (z_i, v_i): $(z_i, \widehat{v}_i,) \leftarrow \mathsf{pre}(1^\lambda, i, (x_i, \widetilde{r}_i))$. Sample masks $\{r_{j \to i}\}_{j \in [n] \setminus \{i\}}$ of appropriate length and construct v_i as in the conforming protocol (see Subsect. 4.1). Broadcast z_i and send each $r_{j \to i}$ to P_j.
2. **For** each round $t \in [T]$:
   - Parse Φ_t as (i^*, j^*, f, g, h)
   - **If** P_i is the speaker, i.e., $i = i^*$, we compute the first round OT receiver messages. Specifically, for each $\alpha, \beta \in \{0, 1\}$:

   $$\left\{ \mathsf{ot}_i[j]_{\to i^*, j^*}^{1, t, \alpha, \beta} \right\}_{j \in [n]} \leftarrow \mathsf{OT}_1^R \left(v_{i,h} \oplus \mathsf{NAND}\left(v_{i,f} \oplus \alpha, v_{i,g} \oplus \beta \right) \right).$$

   In the case that $j^* = \bot$, this is the regular OT (without the special designated sender). Send P_j its corresponding message.
   - **Else** (if $i \neq i^*$),
     - it computes the sender OT messages. First, it generates labels for the t-th round: $\left\{ \mathsf{lab}_{k,0}^{i,t}, \mathsf{lab}_{k,1}^{i,t} \right\}_{k \in [\ell]} \leftarrow \mathsf{Gen}(1^\lambda)$. Next, it computes the OT messages: $\forall \alpha, \beta \in \{0, 1\}$
       - if $i = j^*$,[11]

       $$\left\{ \mathsf{ot}_i[j]_{\to i^*, j^*}^{1, t, \alpha, \beta} \right\}_{j \in [n]} \leftarrow \mathsf{OT}_1^{\widehat{S}} \left(\mathsf{lab}_{h, r_{i^* \to i}(h)}^{i,t}, \mathsf{lab}_{h, 1 \oplus r_{i^* \to i}(h)}^{i,t}, r_{i^* \to i}(h) \right)$$

---

[11] The labels are ordered such that when $\sigma_1 \oplus \sigma_2 = r_{i^* \to i}(h) \oplus \gamma$, the selected label would be $\mathsf{lab}_{h,\gamma}^{i,t}$.

– else, $\left\{ \mathsf{ot}_i[j]_{\to i^*,j^*}^{1,t,\alpha,\beta} \right\}_{j\in[n]} \leftarrow \mathsf{OT}_1^S \left(\mathsf{lab}_{h,0}^{i,t}, \mathsf{lab}_{h,1}^{i,t} \right)$

where h is the index specified by Φ_t.

Send $\left\{ \mathsf{ot}_i[j]_{\to i^*,j^*}^{1,t,\alpha,\beta} \right\}_{\alpha,\beta\in\{0,1\}}$ to party P_j.

Round 2. Each party P_i does the following:

1. **Set state.** The local state is defined as $\mathsf{st}_i := (z_1||\dots||z_i||\dots||z_n) \oplus v_i$
2. **For** each t from T to 1,
   (a) Parse Φ_t as (i^*, j^*, f, g, h)
   (b) Compute the second round OT messages as follows:

$$\forall \alpha, \beta \in \{0,1\}, \quad \mathsf{ot}_i[\bot]_{\to i^*,j^*}^{2,t,\alpha,\beta} \leftarrow \mathsf{OT}_2 \left(\left\{ \mathsf{ot}_j[i]_{\to i^*,j^*}^{1,t,\alpha,\beta} \right\}_{j\in[n]} \right)$$

   (c) Compute the garbled circuit as

$$\tilde{\mathsf{P}}^{i,t} \leftarrow \mathsf{Garble} \left(\mathsf{P}\left[i, \Phi_t, v_i, \left\{ \mathsf{ot}_i[\bot]_{\to i^*,j^*}^{2,t,\alpha,\beta} \right\}_{\alpha,\beta\in\{0,1\}}, \overline{\mathsf{lab}}^{i,t+1}, \{r_{i\to j}\}_{j\in[n]\setminus\{i\}} \right], \right.$$
$$\left. \left\{ \mathsf{lab}_{k,b}^{i,t} \right\}_{k\in[\ell],b\in\{0,1\}} \right).$$

   where the program P is defined in Fig. 1.
3. Broadcast the garbled program, and the keys to the first circuit:

$$\left(\{\tilde{\mathsf{P}}^{i,t}\}_{t\in[T]}, \left\{ \mathsf{lab}_{k,\mathsf{st}_{i,k}}^{i,1} \right\}_{k\in[\ell]} \right) \text{ to every other party.}$$

Evaluation. To compute the output of the protocol, each party P_i does the following:

1. For each $j \in [n]$, let $\widetilde{\mathsf{lab}}^{j,1} := \left\{ \mathsf{lab}_k^{j,1} \right\}_{k\in[\ell]}$ be the labels received from party P_j at the end of Round 2.
2. **For** each t from 1 to T do:
   (a) Parse Φ_t as (i^*, j^*, f, g, h)
   (b) Evaluate the t-th garbled circuit received from party i^*

$$\left((\alpha, \beta, \gamma), \widetilde{\mathsf{lab}}^{i^*,t+1}, \mathsf{ot}_{i^*}[\bot]_{\to i^*,j^*}^{2,t} \right) := \mathsf{Eval} \left(\tilde{\mathsf{P}}^{i^*,t}, \widetilde{\mathsf{lab}}^{i^*,t} \right)$$

   (c) Update the h-th bit in the local state: $\mathsf{st}_{i,h} := \gamma \oplus v_{i,h}$.
   (d) Evaluate the t-th garbled circuits for each other party.
      For each $j \neq i^*$ compute:

$$\left(\left\{ \mathsf{lab}_k^{j,t+1} \right\}_{k\in[\ell]\setminus\{h\}}, \mathsf{ot}_j[\bot]_{\to i^*,j^*}^{2,t} \right) := \mathsf{Eval} \left(\tilde{\mathsf{P}}^{j,t}, \widetilde{\mathsf{lab}}^{j,t} \right)$$

(e) To compute the label of the h-th input wire, of the $(t+1)$-th garbled circuit, for each party other than i^*, we apply the OT output function OT_3. Recover

$$\left(\left\{\mathsf{lab}_h^{j,t+1}\right\}_{j\in[n]\setminus\{i^*\}}\right) := \mathsf{OT}_3\left(\left\{\mathsf{ot}_j[\bot]_{\to i^*,j^*}^{2,t}\right\}_{j\in[n]}\right)$$

For each $j \neq i^*$ set $\widetilde{\mathsf{lab}}^{j,t+1} := \left\{\mathsf{lab}_k^{j,t+1}\right\}_{k\in[\ell]}$.

3. Compute the output as $\mathsf{post}(i,\mathsf{st}_i)$.

Program P .

Input. st_i

Hardcoded. The index i of the party, the action $\Phi_t = (i^*, j^*, f, g, h)$, the secret value v_i, the OT messages $\left\{\mathsf{ot}_i[\bot]_{\to i^*,j^*}^{2,t,\alpha,\beta}\right\}_{\alpha,\beta\in\{0,1\}}$, a set of labels $\overline{\mathsf{lab}}^{i,t+1} = \{\mathsf{lab}_{k,0}^{i,t+1}, \mathsf{lab}_{k,1}^{i,t+1}\}_{k\in[\ell]}$ and masks $\{r_{i\to j}\}_{j\in[n]\setminus\{i\}}$.

1. **If** $i = i^*$ **then:**
   (a) Compute $\mathsf{st}_i[h] := r_{i^*\to j^*}(h) \oplus \mathsf{NAND}\,(\mathsf{st}_i[f], \mathsf{st}_i[g])$, $\alpha := \mathsf{st}_i[f] \oplus v_i[f]$, $\beta := \mathsf{st}_i[g] \oplus v_i[g]$ and $\gamma := \mathsf{st}_i[h] \oplus v_i[h]$.
   (b) **Output** $\left((\alpha,\beta,\gamma), \left\{\mathsf{lab}_{k,\mathsf{st}_i[k]}^{i,t+1}\right\}_{k\in[\ell]}, \left\{\mathsf{ot}_i[\bot]_{\to i^*,j^*}^{2,t,\alpha,\beta}\right\}_{j\in[n]\setminus\{i\}}\right)$

2. **Else:**
   (a) **Output** $\left(\left\{\mathsf{lab}_{k,\mathsf{st}_i[k]}^{i,t+1}\right\}_{k\in[\ell]\setminus\{h\}}, \mathsf{ot}_i[\bot]_{\to i^*,j^*}^{2,t,\mathsf{st}_i[f],\mathsf{st}_i[g]}\right)$

Fig. 1. Program P

Correctness. An important property of the protocol is that $\forall i,j \in [n]$ and $k \in \ell$, we have $\mathsf{st}_i[k] \oplus v_i[k] = \mathsf{st}_j[k] \oplus v_j[k]$. This is denoted by a value st^*, which we shall refer to as the *global invariant*. In addition, the transcript of the execution in the computation phase is denoted by $Z \in \{0,1\}^T$. Correctness of the protocol in [16] follows from this global invariant property and the structure of v_i.

From the correctness of the multiparty homomorphic OT, the difference from the protocol in [16] arises when there exists $t \in [T]$ such that $\Phi_t = (\cdot, j, \cdot, \cdot, h)$ such that $j \neq \bot$. Or in other words, when there is a private message to be sent. In this case, every P_i for $i \in [n] \setminus \{j\}$ sets their respective state $\mathsf{st}_i[h]$ to be $r_{i\to j} \oplus \delta$ where δ is the computation of the NAND functionality, and $r_{i\to j}$ is the mask selected by P_j. From the structure of v_i, for every $i \in [n] \setminus \{j\}, v_i[h] = 0$. On the other hand, P_j updates its state to be $\mathsf{st}_j[h] = \delta$, but from the structure of v_j, we have $v_j[h] = r_{i\to j}$. Thus this maintains the global invariant, $\forall i,j \in [n]$ and $k \in \ell$, we have $\mathsf{st}_i[k] \oplus v_i[k] = \mathsf{st}_j[k] \oplus v_j[k]$.

In addition, since P_j knows $v_j[h]$ in the first round, it can compute the OT receiver message in the first round to subsequently use position h in the protocol.

But this is not true for P_i, which is why we incorporate the process of "copying" the bit sent to get around this issue (see Subsect. 4.1).

The proof of our construction can be found in the full version of our paper.

4.3 Achieving Function-Delayed Property

A conforming protocol Φ is defined by computation steps or *actions* $\Phi_i, \ldots, \Phi_T$ where T is the total number of rounds of this conforming protocol. The pre-processing phase in [16] depends only on T, and is otherwise independent of Φ. We shall leverage this fact to construct protocols for functions that require at most T rounds in the conforming protocol. The function itself can be decided after the pre-processing phase, but must be fixed prior to the computation phase.

An action for a given round t is denoted by a five-tuple (i, f, g, h), where $i \in [n], j \in [n] \cup \{\perp\} f, g, h \in [\ell]$. Given that the state is of length ℓ^{12}, there can be at most $n \cdot (n + 1) \cdot \ell^3$ actions. While there are further restrictions on the choices of (f, g, h), we are satisfied with a loose upper bound. When we compress the protocol, as in [16], we seem to run into a problem since we send messages for the computation phase in the first round of the compressed protocol, prior to the function being decided.

To account for this, we compute first round OT messages for all possible actions in each round.

For instance, party P_i computes receiver OT messages as follows: $\forall j \in [n] \cup \{\perp\}, f, g, h \in [\ell], \forall \alpha, \beta \in \{0, 1\}$ $\mathsf{ot}_{1,t,\alpha,\beta}^{i,j,f,g,h} \leftarrow \mathsf{OT}_1^R (v_{i,h} \oplus \mathsf{NAND} (v_{i,f} \oplus \alpha, v_{i,g} \oplus \beta))$ Similarly P_i computes the first round OT messages when it takes the roles of the special designate sender, and the sender. These OT messages are indexed by the tuple (i, j, f, g, h). Thus for each round t, there are $4 \cdot n \cdot (n+1) \cdot \ell^3$ (polynomially many) first round OT messages that are computed. These are sent to the respective parties in the first round.

By the second round, when the parties are creating the garbled circuit they are aware of the function Φ being computed. Let the action in the t-th round be $(\hat{i}, \hat{j}, \hat{f}, \hat{g}, \hat{h})$. Thus, when party P_i is preparing its garbled circuit, it will compute its second round OT message accordingly.

While we have described how to achieve the function delayed property in our protocol, the same ideas hold for the protocol in [16]. In fact, we will use the function delayed property of both our protocol, and that of [16] to achieve subsequent results. Further discussion, and the security sketch can be found in the full version.

5   Guaranteed Output Delivery: Fail-Stop Adversaries

In this section we describe a general compiler to get a two-round MPC protocol with guaranteed output delivery against semi-malicious fail stop adversaries, from any 2 round semi-malicious MPC protocol that satisfies the delayed function property and only uses broadcast channels.

---

[12] It is typically polynomial in the security parameter.

Overview. A semi-malicious fail stop adversary may choose to abort at any point in the protocol. To achieve security with guaranteed output delivery, we want to implement a mechanism that enables the honest parties to continue the execution, even if some parties abort prematurely. In a two-round protocol, a corrupted party might choose to abort either in the first round or in the second round. If a party aborts in the first round, the honest parties should be able to alter the functionality and continue execution while ignoring its input. However, if a party only aborts in the second round, we cannot ignore its input because such a protocol would clearly not be secure.[13] Let us say that a party is "active", if it does not abort in the first round. In order to achieve guaranteed output delivery, we need to make sure that the honest parties have sufficient information about the input of all the active parties (in some encoded manner) by the end of the first round, so that even if an active party aborts in the second round, the honest parties can still include its input in the computation of the output.

Let us first focus on adversaries who only abort in the first round. In order to give the honest parties enough liberty to modify the functionality in case some parties abort, a secure protocol with guarantee of output must have a *delayed function* property, namely, where the first round message of an honest party is independent of the function and the number of parties. Indeed, for this reason, our starting point is a two-round semi-malicious protocol with delayed function property.

In order to handle adversaries who abort in the second round, our main idea is to require each party to send, in the first round itself, a garbled circuit of an *augmented* second-round next-message function. This augmented next-message function takes a list of active and inactive parties as input and computes second round messages for the appropriate functionality (namely, where the inputs of the inactive parties are set to some default values). To enable the honest parties to continue execution in the second round, we also require each party to send $(t+1, n)$ secret shares of all the labels for its garbled circuit over private channels (in particular, each party only receives one of the shares for each label). At the end of the first round, each party prepares of list of active and inactive parties based on who aborted the protocol. In the second round, each party simply broadcasts the appropriate shares for each garbled circuit, based on its list of active and inactive parties. Since we use a $(t+1, n)$ secret sharing scheme, even if some parties abort in the second round, the honest parties have sufficient information to compute the output.

Finally, we remark that our techniques can be seen as a generalization of the techniques used by Dov Gordon et al. in [21], who constructed a three round protocol with guaranteed output delivery using threshold fully homomorphic encryption with special properties. In contrast, we develop a general compiler using only one-way functions.

---

[13] Indeed, such a protocol would allow an adversary to "ignore" the input of one or more honest parties and learn multiple outputs, which would clearly break security.

5.1   Our Construction

Building Blocks. The main primitives required in this construction are:

1. A two-round semi-malicious MPC protocol Φ, with delayed function property that only uses broadcast channels.
2. An adaptive garbling scheme (AdapGarble, AdapEval) for circuits.
3. A threshold secret sharing scheme. We denote this by SS(Share, Reconstruct).

Next, we establish some notations that are used in our construction.

Active Parties. For any two-round semi-malicious protocol Φ, we say that a party is 'active' in an execution of Φ, if it does not abort in the first round. Let active $\in \{0, 1\}^n$ be an n-bit binary string that denotes which parties are active in the last round of the protocol. For each $i \in [n]$, we set $\text{active}_i := 1$, if party P_i is active and $\text{active}_i := 0$ otherwise.

Augmented Next Message Function. Let Φ be a 2 round MPC protocol that supports delayed function property (i.e, where the first round messages of each honest party is independent of the function). Let $\text{Msg}_\Phi^j(i, x_i, \text{trans}_\Phi^{j-1}; r_i)$ be the next message function for round j. It takes as input, party index i, it's input x_i, previous round transcripts trans_Φ^{j-1} and randomness r_i. Delayed function property ensures that $\text{Msg}_\Phi^1(\cdot, \cdot, \cdot; \cdot)$ is independent of the function $\mathcal{F}$ that the MPC computes and only $\text{Msg}_\Phi^2(\cdot, \cdot, \cdot; \cdot)$ depends on it.

We define an 'augmented' second round next message function, that additionally takes a list of active parties (active) in the protocol as input, and computes the second round messages. More specifically, this augmented next message function has the function $\mathcal{F}$ and default inputs for all parties hard coded inside it. Given a list active, it substitutes the actual input of an inactive party with this default input in $\mathcal{F}$ and computes the second round messages. We denote this augmented second round next message function by $\text{AugMsg}_\Phi^2(i, x_i, \text{trans}_\Phi^1, \text{active}; r_i)$.

Theorem 6. *Let Φ be any two-round semi-honest (resp., semi-malicious) broadcast channel MPC protocol with delayed function property, (AdapGarble, AdapEval) be an adaptively secure garbling scheme for circuits and SS(Share, Reconstruct) be a threshold secret sharing scheme. There exists a general compiler that transforms Φ into a two-round protocol that achieves guaranteed output delivery against non-rushing fail-stop (resp., rushing, semi-malicious fail-stop) adversaries.*

A few corollaries of the above theorem are in order:

- The protocol from Theorem 5 (with the function-delayed property) can be easily transformed into a protocol that only uses broadcast channels in the BPK model [8]. Applying the compiler from Theorem 6 to this protocol, we obtain a two-round broadcast-channel MPC protocol in the BPK model that achieves guaranteed output delivery against any $t < \frac{n}{2}$ (semi-malicious) fail-stop corruptions.

- The semi-honest construction from [16] can be modified to support the function-delayed property as discussed in Sect. 4.3. Applying the compiler from Theorem 6 to this modified construction, we obtain a two round MPC protocol over private point to point channels, that achieves guaranteed output delivery against any $t < \frac{n}{2}$ non-rushing fail-stop (resp., rushing, semi-malicious fail-stop) corruptions in the plain model, based on two round semi-honest oblivious transfer.

We now describe our protocol in detail. For simplicity, we describe a compiler that uses both broadcast and private channels. But since this protocol is only secure against fail-stop adversaries, it can be easily modified to work only using private channels in the plain model. If the underlying protocol works in the (bare) public key model, then the compiler can be modified to work only using broadcast channels. We specify these modifications in the protocol description.

Protocol. Let $\mathcal{P} = \{P_1, \ldots, P_n\}$ be the set of parties in the protocol. Let $\{x_1, \ldots, x_n\}$ be their respective inputs and $\{r_1, \ldots, r_n\}$ be their respective randomness used in the underlying protocol Φ. If the underlying program assumes existence of the BPK model, then let $\{\mathsf{pk}_1, \ldots, \mathsf{pk}_n\}$ and $\{\mathsf{sk}_1, \ldots, \mathsf{sk}_n\}$ be the respective public and secret keys of the parties. Let λ be the security parameter.

Round 1. Each party P_i does the following in the first round:

1. Computes the first round message Φ_i^1 using its input x_i and randomness r_i, i.e., $\Phi_i^1 := \mathsf{Msg}_\Phi^1(i, x_i, \bot; r_i)$
2. Computes an adaptive garbling of the augmented second round next message function $\mathsf{AugMsg}_\Phi^2[i, x_i; r_i](\cdot, \cdot)$ with it's index i, input x_i and randomness r_i hardcoded inside it. This function only takes the first round transcript (trans_Φ^1) and the list active as input, i.e., $(\widetilde{\mathsf{NMF}}_i, \{\mathsf{lab}_i^{w,b}\}_{w \in [\mathsf{inp}], b \in \{0,1\}}) \leftarrow \mathsf{AdapGarble}(1^\lambda, \mathsf{AugMsg}_\Phi^2[i, x_i; r_i])$, where inp is the length of input to $\mathsf{AugMsg}_\Phi^2[i, x_i; r_i]$.
3. Uses a threshold secret sharing scheme to compute $(t+1, n)$ shares of the input labels, i.e., $\{\mathsf{lab}_{i,1}^{w,b}, \ldots, \mathsf{lab}_{i,n}^{w,b}\}_{w \in \mathsf{inp}, b \in \{0,1\}} \leftarrow \mathsf{Share}(1^\lambda, \{\mathsf{lab}_i^{w,b}\}_{w \in \mathsf{inp}, b \in \{0,1\}})$
4. Broadcasts $M_i^1 := (\Phi_i^1, \widetilde{\mathsf{NMF}}_i)$ to all other parties.
5. Sends $\{\mathsf{lab}_{i,j}^{w,b}\}_{w \in \mathsf{inp}, b \in \{0,1\}}$ to party P_j (for $j \in [n] \backslash \{i\}$) over private channels. (In the BPK model, the message for party P_j is encrypted under pk_j and then sent over the broadcast channel.)

At the end of Round 1. Each party P_i does the following:

1. **For** j from 1 to n:
   (a) **If** party P_j sent its first round messages, parse M_j^1 as $(\Phi_j^1, \widetilde{\mathsf{NMF}}^j)$ and set $\mathsf{active}_j := 1$
   (b) **If** party P_j aborts in the first round, set $\Phi_j^1 := 0^\ell$, where ℓ is the length of each party's first round message in Φ and set $\mathsf{active}_j := 0$
2. Sets $\mathsf{trans}_\Phi^1 := \{\Phi_j^1\}_{j \in [n]}$.

3. In the BPK model, it decrypts the encrypted labels sent by other parties using its secret key sk_i.

Round 2. Each party P_i does the following in the second round:

1. It sets $z = \mathsf{trans}_{\Phi}^1 || \mathsf{active}$.
2. For each garbled circuit $\{\widetilde{\mathsf{NMF}}_j\}_{j \in [n]}$, it sends shares for the key and the labels corresponding to active and trans_{Φ}^1 i.e., $M_i^2 := \{\mathsf{lab}_{j,i}^{w,z[w]}\}_{w \in [\mathsf{inp}], j \in [n]}$. We assume that $\mathsf{lab}_{j,i}^{\mathsf{trans}_{\Phi}^1 || \mathsf{active}} = \perp$ for a party P_j that aborts in the second round.

Output Phase. Let $\mathbf{Y}$ be the set of any $t+1$ parties that send first and second round. messages. Each party P_i does the following:

1. **For** $j \in \mathbf{Y}$:
   (a) Parse M_j^2 as $\{\mathsf{lab}_{k,j}^{w,z[w]}\}_{w \in [\mathsf{inp}], k \in [n]}$
   (b) **If** $\mathsf{active}_j = 1$, reconstruct the input labels and evaluate the garbled circuit, i.e., $\{\mathsf{lab}_j^{w,z[w]}\}_{w \in [\mathsf{inp}]} := \{\mathsf{Reconstruct}(\{\mathsf{lab}_{j,k}^{w,z[w]}\}_{k \in \mathbf{Y}})\}_{w \in [\mathsf{inp}]}$ and $\Phi_j^2 := \mathsf{AdapEval}(\widetilde{\mathsf{NMF}}_j, \{\mathsf{lab}_j^{w,z[w]}\}_{w \in [\mathsf{inp}]})$
2. Let $\mathbf{A}$ be the set of 'active' parties in the protocol.
3. Runs the output phase of Φ, $\mathsf{Out}_{\Phi}(\{\Phi_j^2\}_{j \in \mathbf{A}})$ to learn the output.

Remark. The above compiler can also be modified to get a three-round protocol in the plain model only assuming one-way functions. This main idea is to divide the first round messages of the above compiler into two. More specifically, the parties exchange their first round messages of Φ (which may include private channel messages) in the first round. In the second round, each party P_i computes an adaptive garbled circuit on the augmented second round next message function $\mathsf{AugMsg}_{\Phi}^2[i, x_i, \mathsf{trans}_{\Phi,i}^1; r_i](.)$ of Φ, that has it's index i, input x_i, it's first round transcript $\mathsf{trans}_{\Phi,i}^1$ and randomness r_i hard wired inside it. Since the first round messages are already hard-wired, this garbled circuit only takes the list of 'active' parties as input. Each party also secret shares all the input labels to this garbled circuit. The third round proceeds similar to the second round in the above compiler, with the only difference that all the parties who participate in the first two rounds constitute the list of 'active' parties. Instantiating this modified compiler with the protocol from Theorem 5 (with the function-delayed property), we get the following corollary:

Corollary 4. *Assuming one-way functions, there exists a three round MPC protocol that achieves guaranteed output delivery against any $t < \frac{n}{2}$ (semi-malicious) fail-stop corruptions.*

6   Guaranteed Output Delivery: Malicious Adversaries

In this section we describe a general compiler to get a three-round malicious MPC protocol with guaranteed output delivery in the plain model from our two round semi-malicious MPC protocol with guaranteed output delivery.

Overview. In order to compile our semi-malicious protocol from the previous section into a maliciously secure one, we use the standard "commit-and-prove" methodology of [20], where the adversary initially commits to his input and randomness and then gives a zero-knowledge proof of "honest behavior" together with each round of the underlying semi-malicious protocol. We note, however, that implementing this methodology in the setting of guaranteed output delivery requires extra care. In particular, we need to ensure that all the honest parties have a *consistent view of which parties aborted in a given round* since the behavior of an honest party in the next round depends upon this view.

Note that if the underlying semi-malicious protocol uses private channels, then a party may need to prove different statements to different parties in order to establish honest behavior, and in particular, the statement being proven by party i to party j may not be known to another party k. This presents a problem in ensuring that the honest parties have consistent views (of the form as discussed above). Therefore, as a first step, we transform the two-round semi-malicious protocol into a three-round protocol that only uses broadcast channels, using public-key encryption. However, if the underlying semi-malicious protocol works in the (bare) public key model and only uses broadcast channels, we can transform this two-round semi-malicious protocol into a three-round semi-malicious protocol in the plain model by exchanging public keys in the first round.

Next we note that zero-knowledge proofs with black-box simulation are known to require at least four rounds [19]. To overcome this lower bound, and in order to obtain a three round maliciously secure protocol, we leverage the fact that we are in the honest majority setting. Towards this, we define a new notion of *multi-verifier zero-knowledge* (MVZK) proofs. Briefly, an MVZK proof system is an interactive multiparty protocol between a prover and multiple verifiers. Similar to standard ZK, we require MVZK to achieve soundness and zero knowledge properties. In particular, we require the soundness property to hold as long as the honest verifiers constitute a majority. Similarly, we require ZK property to hold as long as the honest prover and the honest verifiers, together constitute a majority. In order to use MVZK in our setting, we also require a "strong completeness" property which guarantees that any set of dishonest verifiers (who constitute a minority) cannot prevent the honest verifiers from accepting a proof from an honest prover.

We implement our compiler using two-round MVZK arguments with a delayed input property, namely, where the first round messages of the honest parties are independent of the statement. We note that while our two-round MPC protocol from Sect. 4 can be used to construct a two-round MVZK without the aforementioned strong completeness property; therefore it does not suffice here. Instead, in the full version, we give a construction of two round delayed-input

MVZK (that achieves strong completeness) from Zaps, following the construction of multi-CRS NIZKs by Groth and Ostrovsky [22]. We then use this MVZK to implement our compiler.

6.1 Our Construction

Building Blocks. The main primitives required in this construction are:

1. A two-round MPC protocol Π that achieves guaranteed output delivery against semi-malicious fail-stop adversaries. Let $\mathsf{Msg}_\Pi^j(i, x_i, \{\mathsf{trans}_\Pi^k\}_{k \in [j-1]}; r_i)$ be the next message function for round j. It takes as input, index i of the party, it's input x_i, previous round transcripts $\{\mathsf{trans}_\Pi^k\}_{k \in [j-1]}$ and randomness r_i.
2. A threshold secret sharing scheme. We denote this by $\mathsf{SS} := (\mathsf{Share}, \mathsf{Reconstruct})$.
3. Two-round delayed-input multi-verifier zero-knowledge arguments $\mathsf{mvzk} := (\mathsf{P}_{\mathsf{mvzk}}^1, \mathsf{V}_{\mathsf{mvzk}}^1, \mathsf{P}_{\mathsf{mvzk}}^2, \mathsf{V}_{\mathsf{mvzk}}^2, \mathsf{Verify}_{\mathsf{mvzk}})$.
4. A public-key encryption scheme $\mathcal{E} := (\mathsf{Gen}, \mathsf{Enc}, \mathsf{Dec})$

Theorem 7. *Let Π be a two-round MPC protocol with guaranteed output delivery against semi-malicious fail-stop adversaries, $(\mathsf{AdapGarble}, \mathsf{AdapEval})$ be an adaptively secure garbling scheme, $\mathsf{mvzk} := (\mathsf{P}_{\mathsf{mvzk}}^1, \mathsf{V}_{\mathsf{mvzk}}^1, \mathsf{P}_{\mathsf{mvzk}}^2, \mathsf{V}_{\mathsf{mvzk}}^2, \mathsf{Verify}_{\mathsf{mvzk}})$ be a delayed-input MVZK argument system and $\mathcal{E} := (\mathsf{Gen}, \mathsf{Enc}, \mathsf{Dec})$ be a PKE scheme. Then there exists a general compiler that transforms Π into a three round protocol with guaranteed output delivery against malicious adversaries.*

Applying the compiler from Theorem 7 to the two-round BPK model protocol from Sect. 5, we get a three round protocol based on Zaps and public-key encryption. Next, we describe the protocol in detail:

Protocol. Let $\mathcal{P} = \{P_1, \ldots, P_n\}$ be the set of parties in the protocol and let $\{x_1, \ldots, x_n\}$ be their respective inputs. Let λ be the security parameter.

Round 1. Each party P_i does the following in the first round:

1. Generates a key pair for the public key encryption scheme, i.e., $(\mathsf{pk}_i, \mathsf{sk}_i) := \mathsf{Gen}(1^\lambda; q_i)$
2. Computes the first round prover message of MVZK and verifier messages for all other parties, i.e., $\mathsf{pMsg}^{1,i} \leftarrow \mathsf{P}_{\mathsf{mvzk}}(1^\lambda)$ and $\{\mathsf{vMsg}_i^{1,j}\}_{j \in [n] \setminus i} \leftarrow \{\mathsf{V}_{\mathsf{mvzk}}(1^\lambda, i)\}_{j \in [n] \setminus i}$
3. Broadcasts $M_i^1 := (\mathsf{pk}_i, \mathsf{pMsg}^{1,i}, \{\mathsf{vMsg}_i^{1,j}\}_{j \in [n] \setminus i})$ to all other parties.

At the end of Round 1. Each Party P_i for $i \in [n]$ does the following:

1. **For** j from 1 to n:
   (a) **If** Party P_j sends its first round messages, parse M_j^1 as $(\mathsf{pk}_j, \mathsf{pMsg}^{1,j}, \{\mathsf{vMsg}_j^{1,k}\}_{k \in [n] \setminus j})$
   (b) **Else**, set $\mathsf{pMsg}^{1,j} := \perp$ and $\{\mathsf{vMsg}_j^{1,k}\}_{k \in [n] \setminus j} := \perp$

2. **For** j from 1 to n, set $\text{trans}_{\text{mvzk}}^{1,j} := (\text{pMsg}^{1,j}, \{\text{vMsg}_k^{1,j}\}_{k\in[n]\setminus j})$.

Round 2. Each party P_i does the following in the first round:

1. Computes the first round message Π_i^1 using its input x_i and randomness r_i, i.e., $\Pi_i^1 := \text{Msg}_{\Pi}^1(i, x_i, \perp; r_i)$
2. Uses a threshold secret sharing scheme to compute $(t+1, n)$ shares of $X_i = (x_i, r_i)$, i.e., $\{X_{i,1}, \ldots, X_{i,n}\} := \text{Share}(1^\lambda, X_i; s_i)$
3. For each $j \in [n]$, it encrypts the share $X_{i,j}$ under public key pk_j, i.e., $c_{i,j} := \text{Enc}(\text{pk}_j, X_{i,j}; t_{i,j})$
4. Proves the following:
   (a) The public key pk_i was honestly generated **AND**
   (b) Each ciphertext $c_{i,j}$ is an honestly computed encryption **AND**
   (c) The first round messages of Π are computed honestly using the input x_i and randomness r_i that were honestly secret shared and each of these shares were honestly encrypted.

   Using the language:

   $$L = \{(\Pi_i^1, \{\text{pk}_j\}_{j\in[n]}, \{c_{i,j}\}_{j\in[n]}) \mid \exists (x_i, r_i, s_i, q_i, \{t_{i,j}\}_{j\in[n]})$$
   $$\text{s.t. } ((\text{pk}_i, \cdot) = \text{Gen}(1^\lambda; q_i)) \text{ AND } (\Pi_i^1 = \text{Msg}_{\Pi}^1(i, x_i, \perp; r_i))$$
   $$\text{AND } (\{X_{i,j}, \ldots, X_{i,n}\} := \text{Share}(1^\lambda, X_i; s_i))$$
   $$\text{AND } (\{c_{i,j}\}_{j\in[n]} := \{\text{Enc}(\text{pk}_j, X_{i,j}; t_{i,j})\}_{j\in[n]}))\}$$

   It computes second round prover messages of mvzk as follows:
   Let $Y_i = (\Pi_i^1, \{\text{pk}_j\}_{j\in[n]}, \{c_{i,j}\}_{j\in[n]})$ and $W_i = (x_i, r_i, s_i, q_i, \{t_{i,j}\}_{j\in[n]})$, i.e., $\text{pMsg}^{2,i} \leftarrow \text{P}_{\text{mvzk}}(\text{trans}_{\text{mvzk}}^{1,i}, Y_i, W_i)$
5. Computes second round verifier messages of mvzk for all other parties for the same language, i.e., $\{\text{vMsg}_i^{2,j}\}_{j\in[n]\setminus i} \leftarrow \{\text{V}_{\text{mvzk}}(i, \text{trans}_{\text{mvzk}}^{1,j})\}_{j\in[n]\setminus i}$
6. Computes another set of first round prover message of MVZK and verifier messages for all other parties, i.e., $\widetilde{\text{pMsg}}^{1,i} \leftarrow \text{P}_{\text{mvzk}}(1^\lambda)$ and $\{\widetilde{\text{vMsg}_i}^{1,j}\}_{j\in[n]\setminus i} \leftarrow \{\text{V}_{\text{mvzk}}(1^\lambda, i)\}_{j\in[n]\setminus i}$
7. Broadcasts $M_i^2 := (\Pi_i^1, \{c_{i,j}\}_{j\in[n]}, \text{pMsg}^{2,i}, \{\text{vMsg}_i^{2,j}\}_{j\in[n]\setminus i}, \widetilde{\text{pMsg}}^{1,i}, \{\widetilde{\text{vMsg}_i}^{1,j}\}_{j\in[n]\setminus i})$ to all other parties.

At the end of Round 2. Each party does the following:

1. **For** j from 1 to n:
   (a) **If** Party P_j sent its first and second round messages, parse M_j^2 as $(\Pi_i^2, \{c_{j,k}\}_{j\in[n]}, \text{pMsg}^{2,j}, \{\text{vMsg}_i^{2,k}\}_{k\in[n]\setminus j}, \widetilde{\text{pMsg}}^{1,j}, \{\widetilde{\text{vMsg}_i}^{1,k}\}_{k\in[n]\setminus j})$
   (b) **Else** set $\text{pMsg}^{2,j}, \widetilde{\text{pMsg}}^{1,j} := \perp$ and $\{\text{vMsg}_j^{2,k}, \widetilde{\text{vMsg}_j}^{1,k}\}_{k\in[n]\setminus j} := \perp$
2. **For** j from 1 to n:
   (a) Set $Y_j := (\Pi_j^1, \{\text{pk}_k\}_{k\in[n]}, \{c_{j,k}\}_{k\in[n]})$
   (b) **If** $\text{Verify}_{\text{mvzk}}(i, \{\text{trans}_{\text{mvzk}}^{r,j}\}_{r\in[2]}, Y_j) = 1$, decrypt $c_{j,i}$, i.e., $m_{j,i} := \text{Dec}(\text{sk}_i, c_{j,i})$ and parse $m_{j,i}$ as $X_{j,i}$

(c) **Else:**
  i. Set $\Pi_j^1 := 0^\ell$, where ℓ is the length first round messages in Π.
  ii. Set $\widetilde{\mathsf{pMsg}}^{1,j} := \bot$ and $\{\widetilde{\mathsf{vMsg}}_j^{1,k}\}_{k\in[n]\backslash j} := \bot$
3. **For** j from 1 to n, set $\mathsf{trans}_{\underset{\mathsf{mvzk}}{\longleftarrow}}^{1,j} := (\widetilde{\mathsf{pMsg}}^{1,j}, \{\widetilde{\mathsf{vMsg}}_k^{1,j}\}_{k\in[n]\backslash j})$.
4. Set $\mathsf{trans}_\Pi^1 := \{\Pi_j^1\}_{j\in[n]}$.

Round 3. Each party P_i does the following in the third round:

1. Computes second round messages of Π, i.e., $\Pi_i^2 := \mathsf{Msg}_\Pi^2(i, x_i, \mathsf{trans}_\Pi^1; r_i)$
2. Proves that the second round message Π_i^2 was computed honestly using the language $L = \{(\Pi_i^2, \mathsf{trans}_\Pi^1) \mid \exists(x_i, r_i) \text{ s.t. } \Pi_i^2 := \mathsf{Msg}_\Pi^2(i, x_i, r_i, \mathsf{trans}_\Pi^1)\}$.
   It computes second round prover messages of mvzk as follows; Let $Z_i = (\Pi_i^2, \mathsf{trans}_\Pi^1)$ and $W_i = (x_i, r_i)$, i.e., $\widetilde{\mathsf{pMsg}}^{2,i} \leftarrow \mathsf{P}_{\mathsf{mvzk}}(\mathsf{trans}_{\underset{\mathsf{mvzk}}{\longleftarrow}}^{1,i}, Z_i, W_i)$
3. Computes second round verifier messages of mvzk for all other parties for the same language, i.e., $\{\widetilde{\mathsf{vMsg}}_i^{2,j}\}_{j\in[n]\backslash i} \leftarrow \{\mathsf{V}_{\mathsf{mvzk}}(i, \mathsf{trans}_{\underset{\mathsf{mvzk}}{\longleftarrow}}^{1,j})\}_{j\in[n]\backslash i}$
4. Broadcasts $M_i^3 := (\Pi_i^2, \widetilde{\mathsf{pMsg}}^{2,i}, \{\widetilde{\mathsf{vMsg}}_i^{2,j}\}_{j\in[n]\backslash i})$ to all other parties.

Output Phase. Each party P_i does the following:

1. **For** j from 1 to $[n]$
   (a) **If** party P_j sent a message in the third round, parse M_i^3 as $(\Pi_j^2, \widetilde{\mathsf{pMsg}}^{2,j}, \{\widetilde{\mathsf{vMsg}}_j^{2,k}\}_{k\in[n]\backslash j})$
   (b) **Else** set $\Pi_j^2 := \bot$, $\widetilde{\mathsf{pMsg}}^{2,j} := \bot$ and $\{\widetilde{\mathsf{vMsg}}_j^{2,k}\}_{k\in[n]\backslash j} := \bot$
2. **For** j from 1 to n:
   (a) Set $Z_j := (\Pi_j^2, \mathsf{trans}_\Pi^1)$
   (b) **If** $\mathsf{Verify}_{\mathsf{mvzk}}(i, \{\mathsf{trans}_{\underset{\mathsf{mvzk}}{\longleftarrow}}^{r,j}\}_{r\in[2]}, Z_j) = 0$, set $\Pi_j^2 := \bot$
3. Set $\mathsf{trans}_\Pi^2 = \{\Pi_j^2\}_{j\in[n]}$ and run the output phase of Π, $\mathsf{Out}_\Pi(\mathsf{trans}_\Pi^1, \mathsf{trans}_\Pi^2)$ to learn the output.

Acknowledgments. This research was supported in part by a DARPA/ARL Safeware Grant W911NF-15-C-0213, and a subaward from NSF CNS-1414023. We would like to thank Sanjam Garg, Yuval Ishai and Akshayaram Srinvisan for pointing out the limitation of using conforming protocols of [17] towards achieving information-theoretic security for our first construction. The second author would like to thank Ignacio Cascudo for helpful discussions.

References

1. Asharov, G., Jain, A., López-Alt, A., Tromer, E., Vaikuntanathan, V., Wichs, D.: Multiparty computation with low communication, computation and interaction via threshold FHE. In: Pointcheval, D., Johansson, T. (eds.) EUROCRYPT 2012. LNCS, vol. 7237, pp. 483–501. Springer, Heidelberg (2012). https://doi.org/10. 1007/978-3-642-29011-4_29
2. Badrinarayanan, S., Goyal, V., Jain, A., Kalai, Y.T., Khurana, D., Sahai, A.: Promise zero knowledge and its applications to round optimal MPC. In: CRYPTO (2018). https://eprint.iacr.org/2017/1088
3. Beaver, D., Micali, S., Rogaway, P.: The round complexity of secure protocols (extended abstract). In: 22nd ACM STOC, pp. 503–513. ACM Press, May 1990
4. Bellare, M., Hoang, V.T., Rogaway, P.: Adaptively secure garbling with applications to one-time programs and secure outsourcing. In: Wang, X., Sako, K. (eds.) ASIACRYPT 2012. LNCS, vol. 7658, pp. 134–153. Springer, Heidelberg (2012). https://doi.org/10.1007/978-3-642-34961-4_10
5. Ben-Or, M., Goldwasser, S., Wigderson, A.: Completeness theorems for non-cryptographic fault-tolerant distributed computation (extended abstract). In: 20th ACM STOC, pp. 1–10. ACM Press, May 1988
6. Benhamouda, F., Lin, H.: k-round multiparty computation from k-round oblivious transfer via garbled interactive circuits. In: Nielsen, J.B., Rijmen, V. (eds.) EURO-CRYPT 2018, Part II. LNCS, vol. 10821, pp. 500–532. Springer, Cham (2018). https://doi.org/10.1007/978-3-319-78375-8_17
7. Blum, M., Feldman, P., Micali, S.: Non-interactive zero-knowledge and its applications (extended abstract). In: 20th ACM STOC, pp. 103–112. ACM Press, May 1988
8. Canetti, R., Goldreich, O., Goldwasser, S., Micali, S.: Resettable zero-knowledge (extended abstract). In: 32nd ACM STOC, pp. 235–244. ACM Press, May 2000
9. Chaum, D., Crépeau, C., Damgård, I.: Multiparty unconditionally secure protocols (extended abstract). In: 20th ACM STOC, pp. 11–19. ACM Press, May 1988
10. Cleve, R.: Limits on the security of coin flips when half the processors are faulty (extended abstract). In: 18th ACM STOC, pp. 364–369. ACM Press, May 1986
11. Cohen, R., Lindell, Y.: Fairness versus guaranteed output delivery in secure multiparty computation. In: Sarkar, P., Iwata, T. (eds.) ASIACRYPT 2014, Part II. LNCS, vol. 8874, pp. 466–485. Springer, Heidelberg (2014). https://doi.org/10. 1007/978-3-662-45608-8_25
12. Damgård, I., Ishai, Y.: Constant-round multiparty computation using a black-box pseudorandom generator. In: Shoup, V. (ed.) CRYPTO 2005. LNCS, vol. 3621, pp. 378–394. Springer, Heidelberg (2005). https://doi.org/10.1007/11535218_23
13. Dwork, C., Naor, M.: Zaps and their applications. In: 41st FOCS, pp. 283–293. IEEE Computer Society Press, November 2000
14. Feige, U., Lapidot, D., Shamir, A.: Multiple non-interactive zero knowledge proofs based on a single random string (extended abstract). In: 31st FOCS, pp. 308–317. IEEE Computer Society Press, October 1990
15. Garg, S., Mukherjee, P., Pandey, O., Polychroniadou, A.: The exact round complexity of secure computation. In: Fischlin, M., Coron, J.-S. (eds.) EUROCRYPT 2016, Part II. LNCS, vol. 9666, pp. 448–476. Springer, Heidelberg (2016). https:// doi.org/10.1007/978-3-662-49896-5_16

16. Garg, S., Srinivasan, A.: Two-round multiparty secure computation from minimal assumptions. In: Nielsen, J.B., Rijmen, V. (eds.) EUROCRYPT 2018, Part II. LNCS, vol. 10821, pp. 468–499. Springer, Cham (2018). https://doi.org/10.1007/978-3-319-78375-8_16

17. Garg, S., Srinivasan, A.: Two-round multiparty secure computation from minimal assumptions. In: Nielsen, J.B., Rijmen, V. (eds.) EUROCRYPT 2018. LNCS, vol. 10821, pp. 468–499. Springer, Cham (2018). https://doi.org/10.1007/978-3-319-78375-8_16

18. Gennaro, R., Ishai, Y., Kushilevitz, E., Rabin, T.: On 2-round secure multiparty computation. In: Yung, M. (ed.) CRYPTO 2002. LNCS, vol. 2442, pp. 178–193. Springer, Heidelberg (2002). https://doi.org/10.1007/3-540-45708-9_12

19. Goldreich, O., Krawczyk, H.: On the composition of zero-knowledge proof systems. SIAM J. Comput. **25**(1), 169–192 (1996). https://doi.org/10.1137/S0097539791220688

20. Goldreich, O., Micali, S., Wigderson, A.: How to play any mental game or a completeness theorem for protocols with honest majority. In: Aho, A. (ed.) 19th ACM STOC, pp. 218–229. ACM Press, May 1987

21. Dov Gordon, S., Liu, F.-H., Shi, E.: Constant-round MPC with fairness and guarantee of output delivery. In: Gennaro, R., Robshaw, M. (eds.) CRYPTO 2015, Part II. LNCS, vol. 9216, pp. 63–82. Springer, Heidelberg (2015). https://doi.org/10.1007/978-3-662-48000-7_4

22. Groth, J., Ostrovsky, R.: Cryptography in the multi-string model. In: Menezes, A. (ed.) CRYPTO 2007. LNCS, vol. 4622, pp. 323–341. Springer, Heidelberg (2007). https://doi.org/10.1007/978-3-540-74143-5_18

23. Halevi, S., Lindell, Y., Pinkas, B.: Secure computation on the web: computing without simultaneous interaction. In: Rogaway, P. (ed.) CRYPTO 2011. LNCS, vol. 6841, pp. 132–150. Springer, Heidelberg (2011). https://doi.org/10.1007/978-3-642-22792-9_8

24. Ishai, Y., Kumaresan, R., Kushilevitz, E., Paskin-Cherniavsky, A.: Secure computation with minimal interaction, revisited. In: Gennaro, R., Robshaw, M. (eds.) CRYPTO 2015, Part II. LNCS, vol. 9216, pp. 359–378. Springer, Heidelberg (2015). https://doi.org/10.1007/978-3-662-48000-7_18

25. Ishai, Y., Kushilevitz, E.: Randomizing polynomials: a new representation with applications to round-efficient secure computation. In: 41st FOCS, pp. 294–304. IEEE Computer Society Press, November 2000

26. Ishai, Y., Kushilevitz, E., Paskin, A.: Secure multiparty computation with minimal interaction. In: Rabin, T. (ed.) CRYPTO 2010. LNCS, vol. 6223, pp. 577–594. Springer, Heidelberg (2010). https://doi.org/10.1007/978-3-642-14623-7_31

27. Katz, J., Ostrovsky, R.: Round-optimal secure two-party computation. In: Franklin, M. (ed.) CRYPTO 2004. LNCS, vol. 3152, pp. 335–354. Springer, Heidelberg (2004). https://doi.org/10.1007/978-3-540-28628-8_21

28. Lapidot, D., Shamir, A.: Publicly verifiable non-interactive zero-knowledge proofs. In: Menezes, A.J., Vanstone, S.A. (eds.) CRYPTO 1990. LNCS, vol. 537, pp. 353–365. Springer, Heidelberg (1991). https://doi.org/10.1007/3-540-38424-3_26

29. Mohassel, P., Rosulek, M., Zhang, Y.: Fast and secure three-party computation: the garbled circuit approach. In: Ray, I., Li, N., Kruegel, C. (eds.) ACM CCS 2015, pp. 591–602. ACM Press, October 2015

30. Shamir, A.: How to share a secret. Commun. Assoc. Comput. Mach. **22**(11), 612–613 (1979)

31. Yao, A.C.C.: How to generate and exchange secrets (extended abstract). In: 27th FOCS, pp. 162–167. IEEE Computer Society Press, October 1986

On the Exact Round Complexity
of Secure Three-Party Computation

Arpita Patra[✉] and Divya Ravi

Indian Institute of Science, Bangalore, India
{arpita,divyar}@iisc.ac.in

Abstract. We settle the exact round complexity of three-party computation (3PC) in honest-majority setting, for a range of security notions such as selective abort, unanimous abort, fairness and guaranteed output delivery. Selective abort security, the weakest in the lot, allows the corrupt parties to selectively deprive some of the honest parties of the output. In the mildly stronger version of unanimous abort, either all or none of the honest parties receive the output. Fairness implies that the corrupted parties receive their output only if all honest parties receive output and lastly, the strongest notion of guaranteed output delivery implies that the corrupted parties cannot prevent honest parties from receiving their output. It is a folklore that the implication holds from the guaranteed output delivery to fairness to unanimous abort to selective abort. We focus on two network settings– pairwise-private channels without and with a broadcast channel.

In the minimal setting of pairwise-private channels, 3PC with selective abort is known to be feasible in just two rounds, while guaranteed output delivery is infeasible to achieve irrespective of the number of rounds. Settling the quest for exact round complexity of 3PC in this setting, we show that three rounds are necessary and sufficient for unanimous abort and fairness. Extending our study to the setting with an additional broadcast channel, we show that while unanimous abort is achievable in just two rounds, three rounds are necessary and sufficient for fairness and guaranteed output delivery. Our lower bound results extend for any number of parties in honest majority setting and imply tightness of several known constructions.

The fundamental concept of garbled circuits underlies all our upper bounds. Concretely, our constructions involve transmitting and evaluating only constant number of garbled circuits. Assumption-wise, our constructions rely on injective (one-to-one) one-way functions.

1 Introduction

In secure multi-party computation (MPC) [19,37,67], n parties wish to jointly perform a computation on their private inputs in a secure way, so that no adversary $\mathcal{A}$ actively corrupting a coalition of t parties can learn more information than their outputs (*privacy*), nor can they affect the outputs of the computation other than by choosing their own inputs (*correctness*). MPC has been a subject

© International Association for Cryptologic Research 2018
H. Shacham and A. Boldyreva (Eds.): CRYPTO 2018, LNCS 10992, pp. 425–458, 2018.
https://doi.org/10.1007/978-3-319-96881-0_15

of extensive research and has traditionally been divided into two classes: MPC with dishonest majority [2,12,16,27,28,31,37] and MPC with honest majority [6–8,10,11,18,25,26,64]. While the special case of MPC with dishonest majority, namely the two-party computation (2PC) has been at the focus of numerous works [1,42,46,54,59,65–67], the same is not quite true for the special case of MPC protocols with honest majority.

The three-party computation (3PC) and MPC with small number of parties maintaining an honest majority make a fascinating area of research due to myriad reasons as highlighted below. First, they present useful use-cases in practice, as it seems that the most likely scenarios for secure MPC in practice would involve a small number of parties. In fact, the first large scale implementation of secure MPC, namely the Danish sugar beet auction [15] was designed for the three-party setting. Several other applications solved via 3PC include statistical data analysis [14], email-filtering [52], financial data analysis [14] and distributed credential encryption service [60]. The practical efficiency of 3PC has thus got considerable emphasis in the past and some of them have evolved to technologies [3,13,20,30,33,52,53]. Second, in practical deployments of secure computation between multiple servers that may involve long-term sensitive information, three or more servers are preferred as opposed to two. This enables recovery from faults in case one of the servers malfunctions. Third and importantly, practical applications usually demand strong security goals such as fairness (corrupted parties receive their output only if all honest parties receive output) and guaranteed output delivery (corrupted parties cannot prevent honest parties from receiving their output) which are feasible *only* in honest majority setting [22]. Fourth and interestingly, there are evidences galore that having to handle a single corrupt party can be leveraged conveniently and taken advantage of to circumvent known lower bounds and impossibility results. A lower bound of three rounds has been proven in [35] for *fair* MPC with $t \geq 2$ and arbitrary number of parties, even in the presence of broadcast channels. [43] circumvents the lower bound by presenting a *two-round* 4PC protocol tolerating a *single* corrupt party that provides guaranteed output delivery without even requiring a broadcast channel. Verifiable secret sharing (VSS) which serves as an important tool in constructing MPC protocols are known to be impossible with $t \geq 2$ with one round in the sharing phase irrespective of the computational power of the adversary [5,34,62]. Interestingly enough, a perfect VSS with $(n = 5, t = 1)$ [34], statistical VSS with $(n = 4, t = 1)$ [43,62] and cryptographic VSS with $(n = 4, t = 1)$ [5] are shown to be achievable with one round in the sharing phase.

The world of MPC for small population in honest majority setting witnesses a few more interesting phenomena. Assumption-wise, MPC with 3, 4 and 5 parties can be built from just One-way functions (OWF) or injective one-way functions/permutations [17,43,60], shunning public-key primitives such as Oblivious Transfer (OT) entirely, which is the primary building block in the 2-party setting. Last but not the least, the known constructions for small population in the honest majority setting perform arguably better than the constructions with two parties while offering the same level of security. For instance, 3PC with honest majority [43,60] allows to circumvent certain inherent challenges in malicious 2PC such as enforcing correctness of garbling which incurs additional communication.

The exact round complexity is yet another measure that sets apart the protocols with three parties over the ones with two parties. For instance, 3PC protocol is achievable just in two rounds with the minimal network setting of pairwise-private channels [43]. The 2PC (and MPC with dishonest majority) protocols achieving the same level of security (with abort) necessarily require 4 rounds [50] and have to resort to a common reference string (CRS) to shoot for the best possible round complexity of 2 [41].

With the impressive list of motivations that are interesting from both the theoretical and practical viewpoint, we explore 3PC in the honest majority setting tolerating a malicious adversary. In this work, we set our focus on the exact round complexity of 3PC. To set the stage for our contributions, we start with a set of relevant works below.

Related Works. Since round complexity is considered an important measure of efficiency of MPC protocols, there is a rich body of work studying the round complexity of secure 2PC and MPC protocols under various adversarial settings and computational models. We highlight some of them below. Firstly, it is known that two rounds of interaction are essential for realizing an MPC protocol irrespective of the setting. This is because in a 1-round protocol, a corrupted party could repeatedly evaluate the "residual function" with the inputs of the honest parties fixed on many different inputs of its own (referred as "residual function" attack) [41]. In the plain model, any actively secure 2PC is known to require 5 rounds in non-simultaneous message model [50] (under black-box simulation). The bound can be improved to 4 even in the dishonest majority setting [32] in simultaneous message model and tight upper bounds are presented in [2,16,40]. With a common reference string (CRS), the lower bound can be further improved to 2 rounds [41]. Tight upper bounds are shown in [31] under indistinguishability obfuscation (assumption weakened to witness encryption by [39]), and in [61] under a variant of Fully Homomorphic Encryption (FHE) and Non-interactive Zero-knowledge.

In the honest majority setting which is shown to be necessary [22] and sufficient [10,18,24] for the feasibility of protocols with fairness and guaranteed output delivery, the study on round complexity has seen the following interesting results. Three is shown to be the lower bound for fair protocols in the stand-alone model (surprisingly even with access to a CRS), assuming *non-private* channels [39]. The same work presents a matching upper bound that provides guaranteed output delivery, uses a CRS and a broadcast channel and relies on a 'special' FHE. Their protocol can be collapsed to two rounds given access to PKI where the infrastructure carries the public keys corresponding to the 'special' FHE. In the plain model, three rounds are shown to be necessary for MPC with fairness and $t \geq 2$, even in the presence of a broadcast channel and arbitrary number of parties [35]. In an interesting work, [43] circumvents the above result by considering 4PC with *one* corruption. The protocol provides guaranteed output delivery, yet does not use a broadcast channel. In the same setting (plain model and no broadcast), [43] presents a 2-round 3PC protocol tolerating single corruption; whose communication and computation efficiency was improved by the 3-round protocol of [60]. Both these protocols achieve a weaker notion of security known as security with selective abort. Selective abort security [44] (referred as 'security with abort and no fairness' in [38]) allows the corrupt parties to selectively deprive some of the honest parties of the output. In the mildly stronger version of unanimous abort (referred as 'security with unanimous abort and no fairness' in [38]), either all or none of the honest parties receive the output. An easy observation concludes that the 3PC of [60] achieves unanimous abort, when its third round message is broadcasted, albeit for functions giving the same output to all. The works relevant to honest majority setting are listed below.

3PC has been studied in different settings as well. High-throughput MPC with non-constant round complexity are studied in [3,30]. [21] studies 3PC with dishonest majority. Recently, [17] presents a practically efficient 5-party MPC protocol in honest majority setting, going beyond 3-party case, relying on distributed garbling technique based on [7].

Ref.	Setting	Round	Network Setting/Assumption	Security	Comments
[4]	$t < n/2$	≥ 5	private channel, Broadcast/CRS, FHE, NIZK	fairness	upper bound
[39]	$t < n/2$	3	non-private channel, Broadcast/CRS, FHE	guaranteed output delivery	upper bound
[39]	$t < n/2$	2	non-private channel, Broadcast/CRS, PKI, FHE	guaranteed output delivery	upper bound
[44]	$n = 5, t = 1$	2	private channel/OWF	guaranteed output delivery	upper bound
[43]	$n = 3, t = 1$	2	private channel/OWF	selective abort	upper bound
[43]	$n = 4, t = 1$	2	private channel/(injective) OWF	guaranteed output delivery	upper bound
[60]	$n = 3, t = 1$	3	private channel, Broadcast/PRG	unanimous abort	upper bound
[39]	$t < n/2$	3	non-private channel, Broadcast/CRS	fairness	lower bound
[35]	$n; t > 1$	3	private channel, Broadcast	fairness	lower bound

1.1 Our Results

In this paper, we set our focus on the exact round complexity of 3PC protocols with one active corruption achieving a range of security notions, namely selective abort, unanimous abort, fairness and guaranteed output delivery in a setting with pair-wise private channels and without or with a broadcast channel (and no additional setup). In the minimal setting of pair-wise private channels, it is known that 3PC with selective abort is feasible in just two rounds [43], while guaranteed output delivery is infeasible to achieve irrespective of the number of rounds [23]. No bound on round complexity is known for unanimous abort or fairness. In the setting with a broadcast channel, the result of [60] implies 3-round 3PC with unanimous abort. Neither the round optimality of the [60] construction, nor any bound on round complexity is known for protocols with fairness and guaranteed output delivery.

This work settles all the above questions via two lower bound results and three upper bounds. Both our lower-bounds extend for general n and t with strict honest majority i.e. $n/3 \leq t < n/2$. They imply tightness of several known constructions of [43] and complement the lower bound of [35] which holds for only $t > 1$. Our upper bounds are from injective (one-to-one) one-way functions. The fundamental concept of garbled circuits (GC) contributes as their key basis, following several prior works in this domain [21,43,60]. The techniques in our upper bounds do not seem to extend for $t > 1$, leaving open designing round-optimal protocols for the general case with various security notions. We now elaborate on the results below:

Without Broadcast Channel. In this paper, we show that three rounds are necessary to achieve 3PC with unanimous abort and fairness, in the absence of a broadcast channel. The sufficiency is proved via a 3-round fair protocol (which also achieves unanimous abort security). Our lower bound result immediately implies tightness of the 3PC protocol of [43] achieving selective abort in two rounds, in terms of security achieved. This completely settles the questions on exact round complexity of 3PC in the minimal setting of pair-wise private channels. Our 3-round fair protocol uses a sub-protocol that is reminiscent of Conditional Disclosure of Secrets (CDS) [36], with an additional property of authenticity that allows a recipient to detect the correct secret. Our implementation suggests a realisation of authenticated CDS from privacy-free GCs.

With Broadcast Channel. With access to a broadcast channel, we show that it takes just two rounds to get 3PC with unanimous abort, implying non-optimality of the 3-round construction of [60]. On the other hand, we show that three rounds are necessary to construct a 3PC protocol with fairness and guaranteed output delivery. The sufficiency for fairness already follows from our 3-round fair protocol without broadcast. The sufficiency for guaranteed output delivery is shown via yet another construction in the presence of broadcast. The lower bound result restricted for $t = 1$ complements the lower bound of [35] making three rounds necessary for MPC with fairness in the honest majority setting for all the values of t. The lower bound further implies that for two-round fair (or guaranteed output delivery) protocols with one corruption, the number of parties needs to be at least four, making the 4PC protocol of [43] an optimal one. Notably, our result does not contradict with the two-round protocol of [39] that assumes PKI (where the infrastructure contains the public keys of a 'special' FHE), CRS and also broadcast channel.

The table below captures the complete picture of the round complexity of 3PC. The necessity of two rounds for any type of security follows from [41] via the 'residual attack'. Notably, broadcast facility only impacts the round complexity of unanimous abort and guaranteed output delivery, leaving the round complexity of selective abort and fairness unperturbed.

Security	Without Broadcast	References Necessity/ Sufficiency	With Broadcast	References Necessity/ Sufficiency
Selective Abort	2	[41]/[43]	2	[41]/[43]
Unanimous Abort	3	**This paper/This paper**	2	[41]/**This paper**
Fairness	3	**This paper/This paper**	3	**This paper/This paper**
Guaranteed output delivery	Impossible	[23]	3	**This paper/This paper**

1.2 Techniques

Lower Bounds. We present two lower bounds– **(a)** three rounds are necessary for achieving fairness in the presence of pair-wise channels and a broadcast channel; **(b)** three rounds are necessary for achieving unanimous abort in the presence of just pair-wise channels. The lower bounds are shown by taking a special 3-party function and by devising a sequence hybrid executions under different adversarial strategies, allowing to conclude any 3PC protocol computing the considered function cannot be simultaneously private and fair or secure with unanimous abort.

Upper Bounds. We present three upper bounds– **(a)** 3-round fair protocol; **(b)** 2-round protocol with unanimous abort and **(c)** 3-round protocol with guaranteed output delivery. The former in the presence of just pairwise channels, the latter two with an additional broadcast channel. The known generic transformations such as, unanimous abort to (identifiable) fairness [45] or identifiable fairness to guaranteed output delivery [24], does not help in any of our constructions. For instance, any 3-round fair protocol without broadcast cannot take the former route as it is not round-preserving and unanimous abort in two rounds necessarily requires broadcast as shown in this work. A 3-round protocol with guaranteed output delivery cannot be constructed combining both the transformations due to inflation in round complexity.

Building on the protocol of [60], the basic building block of our protocols needs two of the parties to enact the role of the garbler and the remaining party to carry out the responsibility of circuit evaluation. Constrained with just two or three rounds, our protocols are built from the parallel composition of three sub-protocols, each one with different party enacting the role of the evaluator (much like [43]). Each sub-protocol consumes two rounds. Based on the security needed, the sub-protocols deliver distinct flavours of security with 'identifiable abort'. For the fair and unanimous abort, the identifiability is in the form of conflict that is local (privately known) and public/global (known to all) respectively, while for the protocol with guaranteed output delivery, it is local identification of the corrupt. Achieving such identifiability in just two rounds (sometime without broadcast) is challenging in themselves. Pulling up the security guarantee of these subprotocols via entwining three executions to obtain the final goals of fairness, unanimous abort and guaranteed output delivery constitute yet another novelty of this work. Maintaining the input consistency across the three executions pose another challenge that are tackled via mix of novel techniques (that consume no additional cost in terms of communication) and existing tricks such as 'proof-of-cheating' or 'cheat-recovery' mechanism [21,54]. The issue of input consistency does not appear in the construction of [60] at all, as it does not deal with parallel composition. On the other hand, the generic input consistency technique adopted in [43] can only (at the best) detect a conflict locally and cannot be extended to support the stronger form of identifiability that we need.

Below, we present the common issues faced and approach taken in all our protocols before turning towards the challenges and way-outs specific to our constructions. Two of the major efficiency bottlenecks of 2PC from garbled circuits, namely the need of multiple garbled circuits due to cut-and-choose approach and Oblivious Transfer (OT) for enabling the evaluator to receive its input in encoded form are bypassed in the 3PC scenario through two simple tricks [43,60]. First, the garblers use common randomness to construct the same garbled circuit individually. A simple comparison of the GCs received from the two garblers allows to conclude the correctness of the GC. Since at most one party can be corrupt, if the received GCs match, then its correctness can be concluded. Second, the evaluator shares its input additively among the garblers at the onset of the protocol, reducing the problem to a secure computation of a function on the garblers' inputs alone. Specifically, assuming P_3 as the evaluator, the computation now takes inputs from P_1 and P_2 as (x_1, x_{31}) and (x_2, x_{32}) respectively to compute $C(x_1, x_2, x_{31}, x_{32}) = f(x_1, x_2, x_{31} \oplus x_{32})$. Since the garblers possess all the inputs needed for the computation, OT is no longer needed to transfer the evaluator's input in encoded form to P_3.

Next, to force the garblers to input encoding and decoding information (the keys) that are consistent with the GCs, the following technique is adopted. Notice that the issue of input consistency where a corrupt party may use different inputs as an evaluator and as a garbler in different instances of the sub-protocols is distinct and remains to be tackled separately. Together with the GC, each garbler also generates the commitment to the encoding and decoding information using the common shared randomness and communicates to the evaluator. Again a simple check on whether the set of commitments are same for both the garblers allows to conclude their correctness. Now it is infeasible for the garblers to decommit the encoded input corresponding to their own input and the evaluator's share to something that are inconsistent to the GC without being caught. Following a common trick to hide the inputs of the garblers, the commitments on the encoding information corresponding to every bit of the garblers' input are sent in permuted order that is privy to the garblers. The commitment on the decoding information is relevant only for the fair protocol where the decoding information is withheld to force a corrupt evaluator to be fair. Namely, in the third round of the final protocol, the evaluator is given access to the decoding information only when it helps the honest parties to compute the output. This step needs us to rely on the obliviousness of our garbling scheme, apart from privacy. The commitment on the decoding information and its verification by crosschecking across the garblers are needed to prevent a corrupt party to lie later. Now we turn to the challenges specific to the constructions.

Achieving fairness in 3 rounds. The sub-protocol for our fair construction only achieves a weak form of identifiability, a local conflict to be specific, in the absence of broadcast. Namely, the evaluator either computes the encoded output ('happy' state) or it just gets to know that the garblers are in conflict ('confused' state) in the worst case. The latter happens when it receives conflicting copies of GCs or commitments to the encoding/decoding information. In the composed protocol, a corrupt party can easily breach fairness by keeping one honest evaluator happy and the other confused in the end of round 2 and *selectively* enable the happy party to compute the output by releasing the decoding information in the third round (which was withheld until Round 2). Noting that the absence of a broadcast channel ensues conflict and confusion, we handle this using a neat trick of 'certification mechanism' that tries to enforce honest behaviour from a sender who is supposed to send a common information to its fellow participants.

A party is rewarded with a 'certificate' for enacting an honest sender and emulating a broadcast by sending the same information to the other two parties, for the common information such as GCs and commitments. This protocol internally mimics a CDS protocol [36] for equality predicate, with an additional property of 'authenticity', a departure from the traditional CDS. An authenticated CDS allows the receiver to detect correct receipt of the secret/certificate (similar to authenticated encryption where the receiver knows if the received message is the desired one). As demonstrated below, the certificate allows to identify the culprit behind the confusion on one hand, and to securely transmit the decoding information from a confused honest party to the happy honest party in the third round, on the other. The certificate, being a proof of correct behaviour, when comes from an honest party, say P_i, the other honest party who sees conflict in the information distributed by P_i communicated over point-to-point channel, can readily identify the corrupt party responsible for creating the conflict in Round 3. This aids the latter party to compute the output using the encoded output of the former honest party. The certificate further enables the latter party to release the decoding information in Round 3 in encrypted form so that the other honest party holding a certificate can decrypt it. The release of encryption is done only for the parties whose distributed information are seen in conflict, so that a corrupt party either receives its certificate or the encryption but *not* both. Consequently, it is forced to assist at least one honest party in getting the certificate and be happy to compute the output, as only a happy party releases the decoding information on clear. In a nutshell, the certification mechanism ensures that when one honest party is happy, then no matter how the corrupt party behaves in the third round, both the honest parties will compute the output in the third round. When no honest party is happy, then none can get the output. Lastly, the corrupt party must keep one honest party happy, for it to get the output.

Yet again, we use garbled circuits to implement the above where a party willing to receive a certificate acts as an evaluator for a garbled circuit implementing 'equality' check of the inputs. The other two parties act as the garblers with their inputs as the common information dealt by the evaluator. With no concern of input privacy, the circuit can be garbled in a privacy-free way [29,49]. The certificate that is the key for output 1 is accessible to the evaluator only when it emulates a broadcast by dealing identical copies of the common information to both the other parties. Notably, [47] suggests application of garbling to realise CDS.

Achieving unanimous abort in 2 rounds. Moving on to our construction with unanimous abort, the foremost challenge comes from the fact that it must be resilient to any corrupt Round 2 private communication. Because there is no time to report this misbehaviour to the other honest party who may have got the output and have been treated with honest behaviour all along. Notably, in our sub-protocols, the private communication from both garblers in second round inevitably carries the encoded share of the evaluator's input (as the share themselves arrives at the garblers' end in Round 1). This is a soft spot for a corrupt garbler to selectively misbehave and cause selective abort. While the problem of transferring encoded input shares of the evaluator without relying on second round private communication seems unresolvable on the surface, our take on the problem uses a clever 'two-part release mechanism'. The first set of encoding information for random inputs picked by the garblers themselves is released in the first round privately and any misbehaviour is brought to notice in the second round. The second set of encoding information for the offsets of the random values and the actual shares of the evaluator's input is released in the second round via broadcast without hampering security, while allowing public detection. Thus the sub-protocol achieves global/public conflict and helps the final construction to exit with ⊥ unanimously when any of the sub-protocol detects a conflict.

Achieving guaranteed output delivery in 3 rounds. For achieving this stronger notion, the sub-protocol here needs a stronger kind of identifiability, identifying the corrupt locally to be specific, to facilitate all parties to get output within an additional round no matter what. To this effect, our sub-protocol is enhanced so that the evaluator either successfully computes the output or identifies the corrupt party. We emphasise that the goals of the sub-protocols for unanimous abort and guaranteed output delivery, namely global conflict vs. local identification, are orthogonal and do not imply each other. The additional challenge faced in composing the executions to achieve guaranteed output delivery lies in determining the appropriate 'committed' input of the corrupt party based on which round and execution of sub-protocol it chooses to strike. *Tackling input consistency.* We take a uniform approach for all our protocols. We note that a party takes three different roles across the three composed execution: an evaluator, a garbler who initiate the GC generation by picking the randomness, a co-garbler who verifies the sanity of the GC. In each instance, it gets a chance to give inputs. We take care of input consistency in two parts. First, we tie the inputs that a party can feed as an evaluator and as a garbler who initiates a GC construction via a mechanism that needs no additional communication at all. This is done by setting the permutation strings (used to permute the commitments of encoding information of the garblers) to the shares of these parties' input in a certain way.

The same trick fails to work in two rounds for the case when a party acts as a garbler and a co-garbler in two different executions. We tackle this by superimposing two mirrored copies of the sub-protocol where the garblers exchange their roles. Namely, in the final sub-protocol, each garbler initiates an independent copy of garbled circuit and passes on the randomness used to the fellow garbler for verification. The previous trick is used to tie the inputs that a party feeds as an evaluator and as a garbler for the GC initiated by it (inter-execution consistency). The input consistency of a garbler for the two garbled circuits (one initiated by him and the other by the co-garbler) is taken care using 'proof-of-cheating' mechanism [54] where the evaluator can unlock the clear input of both the other parties using conflicting output wire keys (intra-execution consistency). While this works for our protocols with unanimous abort and guaranteed output delivery, the fair protocol faces additional challenges. First, based on whether a party releases a clear or encoded input, a corrupt garbler feeding two different inputs can conclude whether f leads to the same output for both his inputs, breaching privacy. This is tackled by creating the ciphertexts using conflicting input keys. Second, inspite of the above change, a corrupt garbler can launch 'selective failure attack' [51,58] and breach privacy of his honest co-garbler. We tackle this using 'XOR-tree approach' [55] where every input bit is broken into s shares and security is guaranteed except with probability $2^{-(s-1)}$ per input bit. We do not go for the refined version of this technique, known as probe-resistant matrix, [55,66] for simplicity.

On the assumption needed. While the garbled circuits can be built just from OWF, the necessity of injective OWF comes from the use of commitments that need binding property for any (including adversarially-picked) public parameter. Our protocols, having 2–3 rounds, seem unable to spare rounds for generating and communicating the public parameters by a party who is different from the one opening the commitments.

On concrete efficiency. Though the focus is on the round complexity, the concrete efficiency of our protocols is comparable to Yao [67] and require transmission and evaluation of few GCs (upto 9) (in some cases we only need privacy-free GCs which permit more efficient constructions than their private counterparts [29,49]). The broadcast communication of the optimized variants of our protocols is independent of the GC size via applying hash function. We would like to draw attention towards the new tricks such as the ones used for input consistency, getting certificate of good behaviour via garbled circuits, which may be of both theoretical and practical interest. We believe the detailed take on our protocols will help to lift them or their derivatives to practice in future.

1.3   Roadmap

We present a high-level overview of the primitives used in Sect. 2. We present our 3-round fair protocol, 2-round protocol with unanimous abort and 3-round protocol with guaranteed output delivery in Sects. 3, 4 and 5 respectively. Our lower bound results appear in Sect. 6. The security definitions, complete security proofs and optimizations appear in the full version [63]. We define authenticated CDS and show its realisation from one of the sub-protocols used in our fair protocol in the full version.

2 Preliminaries

2.1 Model

We consider a set of $n = 3$ parties $\mathcal{P} = \{P_1, P_2, P_3\}$, connected by pair-wise secure and authentic channels. Each party is modelled as a probabilistic polynomial time Turing (PPT) machine. We assume that there exists a PPT adversary $\mathcal{A}$, who can actively corrupt at most $t = 1$ out of the $n = 3$ parties and make them behave in any arbitrary manner during the execution of a protocol. We assume the adversary to be static, who decides the set of t parties to be corrupted at the onset of a protocol execution. For our 2-round protocol achieving unanimous abort and 3-round protocol achieving guaranteed output delivery, a broadcast channel is assumed to exist.

We denote the cryptographic security parameter by κ. A negligible function in κ is denoted by $\mathsf{negl}(\kappa)$. A function $\mathsf{negl}(\cdot)$ is *negligible* if for every polynomial $p(\cdot)$ there exists a value N such that for all $m > N$ it holds that $\mathsf{negl}(m) < \frac{1}{p(m)}$. We denote by $[x]$, the set of elements $\{1, \ldots, x\}$ and by $[x, y]$ for $y > x$, the set of elements $\{x, x + 1, \ldots, y\}$. For any $x \in_R \{0,1\}^m$, x^i denotes the bit of x at index i for $i \in [m]$. Let S be an infinite set and $X = \{X_s\}_{s \in S}, Y = \{Y_s\}_{s \in S}$ be distribution ensembles. We say X and Y are computationally indistinguishable, if for any PPT distinguisher $\mathcal{D}$ and all sufficiently large $s \in S$, we have $|\Pr[\mathcal{D}(X_s) = 1] - \Pr[\mathcal{D}(Y_s) = 1]| < 1/p(|s|)$ for every polynomial $p(\cdot)$.

2.2 Primitives

Garbling Schemes. The term 'garbled circuit' (GC) was coined by Beaver [7], but it had largely only been a technique used in secure protocols until they were formalized as a primitive by Bellare et al. [9]. 'Garbling Schemes' as they were termed, were assigned well-defined notions of security, namely *correctness*, *privacy*, *obliviousness*, and *authenticity*. A garbling scheme $\mathcal{G}$ is characterised by a tuple of PPT algorithms $\mathcal{G} = (\mathsf{Gb}, \mathsf{En}, \mathsf{Ev}, \mathsf{De})$ described below.

- $\mathsf{Gb}(1^\kappa, C)$ is invoked on a circuit C in order to produce a 'garbled circuit' $\mathbf{C}$, 'input encoding information' e, and 'output decoding information' d.
- $\mathsf{En}(x, e)$ encodes a clear input x with encoding information e in order to produce a garbled/encoded input $\mathbf{X}$.
- $\mathsf{Ev}(\mathbf{C}, \mathbf{X})$ evaluates $\mathbf{C}$ on $\mathbf{X}$ to produce a garbled/encoded output $\mathbf{Y}$.
- $\mathsf{De}(\mathbf{Y}, d)$ translates $\mathbf{Y}$ into a clear output y as per decoding information d.

We give an informal intuition of the notion captured by each of the security properties, namely *correctness*, *privacy*, *obliviousness*, and *authenticity*. Correctness enforces that a correctly garbled circuit, when evaluated, outputs the correct output of the underlying circuit. Privacy aims to protect the privacy of encoded inputs. Authenticity enforces that the evaluator can only learn the output label that corresponds to the value of the function. Obliviousness captures the notion that when the decoding information is withheld, the garbled circuit evaluation leaks no information about *any* underlying clear values; be they of the input, intermediate, or output wires of the circuit. The formal definitions are presented in the full version [63].

We are interested in a class of garbling schemes referred to as *projective* in [9]. When garbling a circuit $C : \{0,1\}^n \mapsto \{0,1\}^m$, a projective garbling scheme produces encoding information of the form $e = \left(e_i^0, e_i^1\right)_{i \in [n]}$, and the encoded input $\mathbf{X}$ for $x = (x_i)_{i \in [n]}$ can be interpreted as $\mathbf{X} = \mathsf{En}(x, e) = (e_i^{x_i})_{i \in [n]}$.

Our 3-round fair protocol relies on garbling schemes that are simultaneously correct, private and oblivious. One of its subroutine uses a garbling scheme that is only authentic. Such schemes are referred as *privacy-free* [29,49]. Our protocols with unanimous abort and guaranteed output delivery need a correct, private and authentic garbling scheme that need not provide obliviousness. Both these protocols as well as the privacy-free garbling used in the fair protocol further need an additional decoding mechanism denoted as *soft decoding* algorithm sDe [60] that can decode garbled outputs without the decoding information d. The soft-decoding algorithm must comply with correctness: $\mathsf{sDe}(\mathsf{Ev}(\mathbf{C}, \mathsf{En}(e, x))) = C(x)$ for all $(\mathbf{C}, e, d)$. While both sDe and De can decode garbled outputs, the authenticity needs to hold only with respect to De. In practice, soft decoding in typical garbling schemes can be achieved by simply appending the truth value to each output wire label.

Non-interactive Commitment Schemes. A non-interactive commitment scheme (NICOM) consists of two algorithms (Com, Open) defined as follows. Given a security parameter κ, a common parameter pp, message x and random coins r, PPT algorithm Com outputs commitment c and corresponding opening information o. Given κ, pp, a commitment and corresponding opening information (c, o), PPT algorithm Open outputs the message x. The algorithms should satisfy correctness, binding (i.e. it must be hard for an adversary to come up with two different openings of any c and *any* pp) and hiding (a commitment must not leak information about the underlying message) properties. We need this kind of strong binding as the same party who generates the pp and commitment is required to open later. Two such instantiations of NICOM based on symmetric key primitives (specifically, injective one-way functions) and the formal definitions of the properties are given in the full version. We also need a NICOM scheme that admits equivocation property. An equivocal non-interactive commitment (eNICOM) is a NICOM that allows equivocation of a certain commitment to any given message with the help of a trapdoor. The formal definitions and instantiations appear in the full version [63].

Symmetric-Key Encryption (SKE) with Special Correctness. Our fair protocol uses a SKE $\pi = (\mathsf{Gen}, \mathsf{Enc}, \mathsf{Dec})$ which satisfies CPA security and a special correctness property [48,56]– if the encryption and decryption keys are different, then decryption fails with high probability. The definition and an instantiation appear in the full version.

3   3-round 3PC with Fairness

This section presents a tight upper bound for 3PC achieving fairness in the setting with just pair-wise private channels. Our lower bound result showing necessity of three rounds for unanimous abort assuming just pairwise private channels (appears in the full version [63]) rules out the possibility of achieving fairness in 2 rounds in the same setting. Our result from Sect. 6.1 further shows tightness of 3 rounds even in the presence of a broadcast channel.

Building on the intuition given in the introduction, we proceed towards more detailed discussion of our protocol. Our fair protocol is built from parallel composition of three copies of each of the following two sub-protocols: (a) fair_i where P_i acts as the evaluator and the other two as garblers for computing the desired function f. This sub-protocol ensures that honest P_i either computes its encoded output or identifies just a conflict in the worst case. The decoding information is committed to P_i, yet not opened. It is released in Round 3 of the final composed protocol under subtle conditions as elaborated below. (b) cert_i where P_i acts as the evaluator and the other two as garblers for computing an equality checking circuit on the common information distributed by P_i in the first round of the final protocol. Notably, though the inputs come solely from the garblers, they are originated from the evaluator and so the circuit can be garbled in a privacy-free fashion. This sub-protocol ensures either honest P_i gets its certificate, the key for output 1 (meaning the equality check passes through), or identifies a conflict in the worst case. The second round of cert_i is essentially an 'authenticated' CDS for equality predicate tolerating one active corruption. Three *global* variables are maintained by each party P_i to keep tab on the conflicts and the corrupt. Namely, $\mathcal{C}_i$ to keep the identity of the corrupt, flag_j and flag_k (for distinct $i, j, k \in [3]$) as indicators of detection of conflict with respect to information distributed by P_j and P_k respectively. The sub-protocols fair_i and cert_i assure that if neither the two flags nor $\mathcal{C}_i$ is set, then P_i must be able to evaluate the GC successfully and get its certificate respectively.

Once $\{\text{fair}_i, \text{cert}_i\}_{i \in [3]}$ complete by the end of round 2 of the final protocol fair, any honest party will be in one of the three states: (a) no corruption and no conflict detected $((\mathcal{C}_i = \emptyset) \wedge (\text{flag}_j = 0) \wedge (\text{flag}_k = 0))$; (b) corruption detected $(\mathcal{C}_i \neq \emptyset)$; (c) conflict detected $(\text{flag}_j = 1) \vee (\text{flag}_k = 1)$. An honest party, guaranteed to have computed its encoded output and certificate *only* in the first state, releases these as well as the decoding information for both the other parties unconditionally in the third round. In the other two states, an honest party conditionally releases only the decoding information. This step is extremely crucial for maintaining fairness. Specifically, a party that belongs to the second state, releases the decoding information only to the party identified to be honest. A party that belongs to the third state, releases the decoding information in encrypted form *only* to the party whose distributed information are not agreed upon, so that the encryption can be unlocked only via a valid certificate. A corrupt party will either have its certificate or the encrypted decoding information, but *not* both. The former when it distributes its common information correctly and the latter when it does not. The only way a corrupt party can get its decoding information is by keeping one honest party in the first state, in which case both the honest parties will be able to compute the output as follows. The honest party in state one, say P_i, either gets it decoding information on clear or in encrypted form. The former when the other honest party, P_j is in the first or second state and the latter when P_j is in the third state. P_i retrieves the decoding information no matter what, as it also holds the certificate to open the encryption. An honest party P_j in the second state, on identifying P_i as honest, takes the encoded output of P_i and uses its own decoding information to compute the output. The case for an honest party P_j in the third state is the most interesting. Since honest P_i belongs to the first state, a corrupt party must have distributed its common information correctly as otherwise P_i will find a conflict and would be in third state. Therefore, P_j in the third state must have found P_i's information on disagreement due the corrupt party's misbehaviour. Now, P_i's certificate that proves his correct behaviour, allows P_j to identify the corrupt, enter into the second state and compute the output by taking the encoded output of honest P_i. In the following, we describe execution fair_i assuming input consistency, followed by cert_i. Entwining the six executions, tackling the input consistency and the final presentation of protocol fair appear in the end.

3.1   Protocol fair_i

At a high level, fair_i works as follows. In the first round, the evaluator shares its input additively between the two garblers making the garblers the sole input contributors to the computation. In parallel, each garbler initiates construction of a GC and commitments on the encoding and decoding information. While the GC and the commitments are given to the evaluator P_i, the co-garbler, acting as a verifier, additionally receives the source of the used randomness for GC and openings of commitments. Upon verification, the co-garbler either approves or rejects the GC and commitments. In the former case, it also releases its own encoded input and encoded input for the share of P_i via opening the commitments to encoding information in second round. In the latter case, P_i sets the flag corresponding to the generator of the GC to true. Failure to open a verified commitment readily exposes the corrupt to the evaluator. If all goes well, P_i evaluates both circuits and obtains encoded outputs. The correctness of the evaluated GC follows from the fact that it is either constructed or scrutinised by a honest garbler. The decoding information remains hidden (yet committed) with P_i and the obliviousness of GC ensures that P_i cannot compute the output until it receives the correct opening.

To avoid issues of adaptivity, the GCs are not sent on clear in the first round to P_i who may choose its input based on the GCs. Rather, a garbler sends a commitment to its GC to P_i and it is opened only by the co-garbler after successful scrutiny. The correctness of evaluated GC still carries over as a corrupt garbler cannot open to a different circuit than the one committed by an honest garbler by virtue of the binding property of the commitment scheme. We use an eNICOM for committing the GCs and decoding information as equivocation is needed to tackle a technicality in the security proof. The simulator of our final protocol needs to send the commitments on GC, encoding and decoding information without having access to the input of an evaluator P_i (and thus also the output), while acting on behalf of the honest garblers in fair_i. The eNICOM cannot be used for the encoding information, as they are opened by the ones who generate the commitments and eNICOM does not provide binding in such a case. Instead, the GCs and the decoding information are equivocated based on the input of the evaluator and the output.

Protocol fair_i appears in Fig. 1 where P_i returns encoded outputs $\mathbf{Y}_i = (\mathbf{Y}_i^j, \mathbf{Y}_i^k)$ (initially set to $\perp$) for the circuits created by P_j, P_k, the commitments to the respective decoding information $C_j^{\mathsf{dec}}, C_k^{\mathsf{dec}}$ and the flags $\mathsf{flag}_j, \mathsf{flag}_k$ (initially set to false) to be used in the final protocol. The garblers output their respective corrupt set, flag for the fellow garbler and opening for the decoding information corresponding to its co-garbler's GC and *not* its own. This is to ensure that it cannot break the binding of eNICOM which may not necessarily hold for adversarially-picked public parameter.

Lemma 1. *During* fair_i, $P_\beta \notin \mathcal{C}_\alpha$ *holds for honest* P_α, P_β.

Proof. An honest P_α would include P_β in $\mathcal{C}_\alpha$ only if one of the following hold: (a) Both are garblers and P_β sends commitments to garbled circuit, encoding and decoding information inconsistent with the randomness and openings shared privately with P_α (b) P_α is an evaluator and P_β is a garbler and either (i) P_β's opening of a committed garbled circuit fails or (ii) P_β's opening of a committed encoded input fails. It is straightforward to verify that the cases will never occur for honest (P_α, P_β). □

Lemma 2. *If honest* P_i *has* $\mathcal{C}_i = \emptyset$ *and* $\mathsf{flag}_j = \mathsf{flag}_k = 0$, *then* $\mathbf{Y}_i = (\mathbf{Y}_i^j, \mathbf{Y}_i^k) \neq \perp$.

Proof. According to fair_i, P_i fails to compute $\mathbf{Y}_i$ when it identifies the corrupt or finds a mismatch in the common information $\mathcal{D}_j$ or $\mathcal{D}_k$ or receives a nOK signal from one of its garblers. The first condition implies $\mathcal{C}_i \neq \emptyset$. The second condition implies, P_i would have set either flag_j or flag_k to true. For the third condition, if P_j sends nOK then P_i would set $\mathsf{flag}_k = 1$. Lastly, if P_k sends nOK, then P_i sets $\mathsf{flag}_j = 1$. Clearly when $\mathcal{C}_i = \emptyset \wedge \mathsf{flag}_j = 0 \wedge \mathsf{flag}_k = 0$, P_i evaluates both $\mathbf{C}_j, \mathbf{C}_k$ and obtains $\mathbf{Y}_i = (\mathbf{Y}_i^j, \mathbf{Y}_i^k) \neq \perp$. □

3.2   Protocol cert_i

When a party P_i in fair_i is left in a confused state and has no clue about the corrupt, it is in dilemma on whether or whose encoded output should be used to compute output and who should it release the decoding information (that

---

Protocol fair$_i$()

Inputs: Party P_α has x_α for $\alpha \in [3]$.

Common Inputs: The circuit $C(x_1, x_2, x_3, x_4)$ that computes $f(x_1, x_2, x_3 \oplus x_4)$.

Output: A garbler P_l ($l \in \{j, k\}$) outputs corrupt set $\mathcal{C}_l$, flag$_{\{j,k\}\setminus l}$ and O_i^{dec}. P_i outputs ($\mathcal{C}_i$, $\mathbf{Y}_i = (\mathbf{Y}_i^j, \mathbf{Y}_i^k), C_j^{\text{dec}}, C_k^{\text{dec}}$, flag$_j$, flag$_k$) where $\mathbf{Y}_i$ denote a pair of encoded outputs or $\perp$.

Primitives: A garbling scheme $\mathcal{G} = (\mathsf{Gb}, \mathsf{En}, \mathsf{Ev}, \mathsf{De})$ that is correct, private and oblivious, a NICOM (Com, Open), an eNICOM (eGen, eCom, eOpen, Equiv) and a PRG G.

Round 1:

– P_i randomly secret shares his input x_i as $x_i = x_{ij} \oplus x_{ik}$ and sends x_{ij} to P_j and x_{ik} to P_k.

– P_l for $l \in \{j, k\}$ samples $s_l \in_R \{0,1\}^\kappa$, epp$_l$ and pp$_l$ for G, eNICOM and NICOM resp. and:

  ○ compute garbled circuit $(\mathbf{C}_l, e_l, d_l) \leftarrow \mathsf{Gb}(1^\kappa, C)$ using randomness from $\mathsf{G}(s_l)$. Assume $\{e_{l\alpha}^0, e_{l\alpha}^1\}_{\alpha \in [\ell]}$, $\{e_{l(\ell+\alpha)}^0, e_{l(\ell+\alpha)}^1\}_{\alpha \in [\ell]}$, $\{e_{l(2\ell+\alpha)}^0, e_{l(2\ell+\alpha)}^1\}_{\alpha \in [2\ell]}$ denote the encoding information for the input of P_j, P_k and the secret shares of P_i respectively.

  ○ compute commitments for GC and decoding information. $(c_l, o_l) \leftarrow \mathsf{eCom}(\mathsf{epp}_l, \mathbf{C}_l)$ and $(c_l^{\text{dec}}, o_l^{\text{dec}}) \leftarrow \mathsf{eCom}(\mathsf{epp}_l, d_l)$.

  ○ sample permutation strings $p_{lj}, p_{lk} \in_R \{0,1\}^\ell$ for the inputs of P_j and P_k. Compute commitments to encoding information as: for $b \in \{0,1\}$, $(c_{l\alpha}^b, o_{l\alpha}^b) \leftarrow \mathsf{Com}(\mathsf{pp}_l, e_{l\alpha}^{p_{lj}^\alpha \oplus b})$, $(c_{l(\ell+\alpha)}^b, o_{l(\ell+\alpha)}^b) \leftarrow \mathsf{Com}(\mathsf{pp}_l, e_{l(\ell+\alpha)}^{p_{lk}^\alpha \oplus b})$ when $\alpha \in [\ell]$, $(c_{l(2\ell+\alpha)}^b, o_{l(2\ell+\alpha)}^b) \leftarrow \mathsf{Com}(\mathsf{pp}_l, e_{l(2\ell+\alpha)}^b)$ when $\alpha \in [2\ell]$.

  ○ send $\mathcal{D}_l = (\mathsf{epp}_l, \mathsf{pp}_l, c_l, \{c_{l\alpha}^b\}_{\alpha \in [4\ell], b \in \{0,1\}}, c_l^{\text{dec}})$ to both the other parties and send $\{s_l, p_{lj}, p_{lk}, o_l, \{o_{l\alpha}^b\}_{\alpha \in [4\ell], b \in \{0,1\}}, o_l^{\text{dec}}\}$ only to co-garbler $P_{\{j,k\}\setminus l}$.

– P_j sets $\mathcal{C}_j = P_k$ if $\mathcal{D}_k$ and $\{s_k, p_{kj}, p_{kk}, o_k, \{o_{k\alpha}^b\}_{\alpha \in [4\ell], b \in \{0,1\}}, o_k^{\text{dec}}\}$ are inconsistent. Else, set $O_i^{\text{dec}} = o_k^{\text{dec}}$. P_k performs similar steps for the values received from P_j.

Round 2:

– P_i sends $\mathcal{D}_j$ to P_k and $\mathcal{D}_k$ to P_j. P_j sets flag$_k = 1$ if $\mathcal{D}_k$ received from P_i and P_k does not match. Similar step is executed by P_k.

– P_j computes the indicator strings $m_{jj} = p_{jj} \oplus x_j, m_{kj} = p_{kj} \oplus x_j$ for its inputs. If $P_k \notin \mathcal{C}_j$, then send $\left(\mathsf{OK}, \mathcal{D}_k, (o_k, \{o_{k\alpha}^{m_{kj}^\alpha}, o_{k(2\ell+\alpha)}^{x_{ij}^\alpha}\}_{\alpha \in [\ell]}, m_{kj}), (\{o_{j\alpha}^{m_{jj}^\alpha}, o_{j(2\ell+\alpha)}^{x_{ij}^\alpha}\}_{\alpha \in [\ell]}, m_{jj})\right)$ to P_i. Else, send nOK to P_i. P_k performs similar steps.

– (Local Computation) P_i sets $\mathbf{Y}_i^j = \perp$ and flag$_j = 1$ when **(a)** P_k sent nOK or **(b)** $\mathcal{D}_j$ sent by P_j and P_k do not match. Otherwise, P_i sets $C_j^{\text{dec}} = c_j^{\text{dec}} \in \mathcal{D}_j$ and does:

  ○ open $\mathbf{C}_j \leftarrow \mathsf{eOpen}(\mathsf{epp}_j, c_j, o_j)$ with o_j received from P_k. Set $\mathcal{C}_i = P_k$ if $\mathbf{C}_j = \perp$.

  ○ open $\mathbf{X}_j^\alpha = \mathsf{Open}(\mathsf{pp}_j, c_{j\alpha}^{m_{jj}^\alpha}, o_{j\alpha}^{m_{jj}^\alpha})$, $\mathbf{X}_{ij}^\alpha = \mathsf{Open}(\mathsf{pp}_j, c_{j(2\ell+\alpha)}^{x_{ij}^\alpha}, o_{j(2\ell+\alpha)}^{x_{ij}^\alpha})$, for $\alpha \in [\ell]$, for the opening received from P_j and the commitments taken from $\mathcal{D}_j$. Include P_j in $\mathcal{C}_i$ if any of the opened input labels above is opened to $\perp$.

  ○ open $\mathbf{X}_k^\alpha = \mathsf{Open}(\mathsf{pp}_j, c_{j(\ell+\alpha)}^{m_{jk}^\alpha}, o_{j(\ell+\alpha)}^{m_{jk}^\alpha})$ and $\mathbf{X}_{ik}^\alpha = \mathsf{Open}(\mathsf{pp}_j, c_{j(3\ell+\alpha)}^{x_{ik}^\alpha}, o_{j(3\ell+\alpha)}^{x_{ik}^\alpha})$ for $\alpha \in [\ell]$, for the opening received from P_k and the commitments taken from $\mathcal{D}_j$. Include P_k in $\mathcal{C}_i$ if any of the opened input labels above is opened to $\perp$.

  ○ If $\mathcal{C}_i = \emptyset$, set $\mathbf{X} = \mathbf{X}_j | \mathbf{X}_k | \mathbf{X}_{ij} | \mathbf{X}_{ik}$, run $\mathbf{Y}_i^j \leftarrow \mathsf{Ev}(\mathbf{C}_j, \mathbf{X})$. Else set $\mathbf{Y}_i^j = \perp$.

Similar steps for $\mathbf{C}_k$ will be executed to compute $\mathbf{Y}_i^k$, populate $\mathcal{C}_i$ and update flag$_k$.

Fig. 1. Protocol fair$_i$

it holds as a garbler) to in the final protocol. Protocol cert_i, in a nutshell, is introduced to help a confused party to identify the corrupt and take the honest party's encoded output for output computation, on one hand, and to selectively deliver the decoding information only to the other honest party, on the other. Protocol cert_i implements evaluation of an equality checking function that takes inputs from the two garblers and outputs 1 when the test passes and outputs the inputs themselves otherwise. In the final protocol, the inputs are the common information (GCs and commitments) distributed by P_i across all executions of fair_j. The certificate is the output key corresponding to output 1. Since input privacy is not a concern here, the circuit is enough to be garbled in privacy-free way and authenticity of garbling will ensure a corrupt P_i does not get the certificate. cert_i follows the footstep of fair_i with the following simplifications: (a) Input consistency need not be taken care across the executions implying that it is enough one garbler alone initiates a GC and the other garbler simply extends its support for verification. To divide the load fairly, we assign garbler P_j where $i = (j+1) \mod 3$ to act as the generator of GC in cert_i. (b) The decoding information need not be committed or withheld. We use soft decoding that allows immediate decoding.

Similar to fair_i, at the end of the protocol, either P_i gets its certificate (either the key for 1 or the inputs themselves), or sets its flags (when GC and commitment do not match) or sets its corrupt set (when opening of encoded inputs fail). P_i outputs its certificate, the flag for the GC generator and corrupt set, to be used in the final protocol. The garblers output the key for 1, flag for its fellow garbler and the corrupt set. Notice that, when cert_i is composed in the bigger protocol, P_i will be in a position to identify the corrupt when the equality fails and the certificate is the inputs fed by the garblers. The protocol appears in Fig. 2.

Lemma 3. *During* cert_i, $P_\beta \notin \mathcal{C}_\alpha$ *holds for honest* P_α, P_β.

Proof. An honest P_α would include P_β in $\mathcal{C}_\alpha$ only if one of the following holds: (a) P_β sends inconsistent $(s_\beta, \mathcal{W}_\beta)$ to P_α. (b) P_β's opening of committed encoded input or garbled circuit fails. It is straightforward to verify that the cases will never occur for honest (P_β, P_α). □

Lemma 4. *If an honest* P_i *has* $\mathcal{C}_i = \emptyset$ *and* $\mathsf{flag}_j = \mathsf{flag}_k = 0$, *then,* $\mathsf{cert}_i \neq \bot$.

Proof. The proof follows easily from the steps of the protocol. □

3.3 Protocol fair

Building on the intuition laid out before, we only discuss input consistency that is taken care in two steps: Inter-input consistency (across executions) and intra-input consistency (within an execution). In the former, P_i's input as an evaluator in fair_i is tied with its input committed as garblers for its own garbled circuits in fair_j and fair_k. In the latter, the consistency of P_i's input for both garbled circuits in fair_j (and similarly in fair_k) is tackled. We discuss them one by one.

$\mathsf{cert}_i()$

Common Inputs: The circuit $C(\gamma_j, \gamma_k)$ that outputs 1 if $(\gamma_j = \gamma_k)$ and $(0, \gamma_j, \gamma_k)$ otherwise. For distinct $i, j, k \in [3]$, P_i is assumed to be the evaluator and (P_j, P_k) as the garblers. We assume $i = (j + 1) \mod 3, k = (j + 2) \mod 3$.

Primitives: A correct, authentic, privacy-free garbling scheme $\mathcal{G} = (\mathsf{Gb, En, Ev, De})$ that has the property of *soft decoding*, a PRG G, a NICOM $(\mathsf{Com, Open})$

Output: A garbler P_l for $l \in \{j, k\}$ outputs corrupt set $\mathcal{C}_l$ and $\mathbf{key}_i$. P_i outputs $(\mathsf{cert}_i, \mathcal{C}_i, \mathsf{flag}_j, \mathsf{flag}_k)$. Garbler P_k additionally outputs flag_j.

Round 1: P_j does the following:

- Choose a seed $s_i \in_R \{0, 1\}^\kappa$ for G and construct a garbled circuit $(\mathbf{C}_i, e_i, d_i) \leftarrow \mathsf{Gb}(1^\kappa, C)$. Generate commitment on garbled circuit $\mathbf{C}_i$ as $(c_i, o_i) \leftarrow \mathsf{Com}(\mathbf{C}_i)$ and on the encoding information e_i as $(c_i, o_i) \leftarrow \mathsf{Com}(e_i)$ using randomness from $\mathsf{G}(s_i)$. Let $\mathcal{W}_i = \{c_i, c_i\}$. Send $(s_i, \mathcal{W}_i)$ to P_k and $\mathcal{W}_i$ to P_i.
- (Local Computation by P_k) P_k adds P_j to $\mathcal{C}_k$ if $(s_i, \mathcal{W}_i)$ are inconsistent and is not as per what an honest P_j should do. P_j and P_k output $\mathbf{key}_i$ equals to the key for output 1 of $\mathbf{C}_i$.

Round 2:

- P_i sends $\mathcal{W}_i$ to P_k. P_k sets $\mathsf{flag}_j = 1$ if $\mathcal{W}_i$ received from P_i and P_j is not identical.
- P_j opens its encoded input $\mathbf{X}_j$ (corresponding to γ_j) to P_i by sending the opening of the corresponding commitment in c_i.
- If $P_j \in \mathcal{C}_k$, P_k sends nOK to P_i. Else P_k sends $\mathcal{W}_i$, opening for garbled circuit o_i and its encoded input $\mathbf{X}_k$ (for γ_k) to P_i.
- (Local Computation by P_i) If P_i does not receive identical $\mathcal{W}_i$ from P_j and P_k or receives nOK from P_k, P_i sets $\mathsf{cert}_i = \bot$ and $\mathsf{flag}_j = 1$. Else, P_i uses the opening information sent by P_j, P_k to retrieve $\mathbf{X}_j, \mathbf{X}_k$. P_i adds P_l ($l \in \{j, k\}$) to $\mathcal{C}_i$ and sets $\mathsf{cert}_i = \bot$ if any of the openings sent by P_l result in $\bot$. Else, P_i runs $\mathbf{Y} \leftarrow \mathsf{Ev}(\mathbf{C}_i, \mathbf{X}_j, \mathbf{X}_k)$. If $\mathsf{sDe}(\mathbf{Y}) = 1$, then set $\mathsf{cert}_i = \mathbf{Y}$, else set $\mathsf{cert}_i = (\gamma'_j, \gamma'_k)$ where these two are decoded from $\mathbf{Y}$.

Fig. 2. Protocol cert_i

We tackle the former in a simple yet clever way without incurring any additional overhead. We explain the technique for enforcing P_1's input consistency on input x_1 as an evaluator during fair_1 and as a garbler during $\mathsf{fair}_2, \mathsf{fair}_3$ with respect to his GC $\mathbf{C}_1$. Since the protocol is symmetric in terms of the roles of the parties, similar tricks are adopted for P_2 and P_3. Let in the first round of fair_1, P_1 shares its input x_1 by handing x_{12} and x_{13} to P_2 and P_3 respectively. Now corresponding to $\mathbf{C}_1$ during fair_2, P_1 and P_3 who act as the garblers use x_{13} as the permutation vector p_{11} that defines the order of the commitments of the bits of x_1. Now input consistency of P_1's input is guaranteed if m_{11} transferred by P_1 in fair_2 is same as x_{12}, P_1's share for P_2 in fair_1. For an honest P_1, the above will be true since $m_{11} = p_{11} \oplus x_1 = x_{13} \oplus x_1 = x_{12}$. If the check fails, then P_2 identifies P_1 as corrupt. This simple check forces P_1 to use the same input in both fair_1 and fair_2 (corresponding to $\mathbf{C}_1$). A similar trick is used to ensure input consistency of the input of P_1 across fair_1 and fair_3 (corresponding to $\mathbf{C}_1$) where

P_1 and P_2 who act as the garblers use x_{12} as the permutation vector p_{11} for the commitments of the bits of x_1. The evaluator P_3 in fair$_3$ checks if m_{11} transferred by P_1 in fair$_3$ is same as x_{13} that P_3 receives from P_1 in fair$_1$. While the above technique enforces the consistency with respect to P_1's GC, unfortunately, the same technique cannot be used to enforce P_1's input consistency with respect to $\mathbf{C}_2$ in fair$_3$ (or fair$_2$) since p_{21} cannot be set to x_{12} which is available to P_2 only at the end of first round. While, P_2 needs to prepare and broadcast the commitments to the encoding information in jumbled order as per permutation string p_{21} in the first round itself. We handle it differently as below.

The consistency of P_i's input for both garbled circuits in fair$_j$ (and similarly in fair$_k$) is tackled via 'cheat-recovery mechanism' [54]. We explain with respect to P_1's input in fair$_3$. P_2 prepares a ciphertext (cheat recovery box) with the input keys of P_1 corresponding to the mismatched input bit in the two garbled circuits, $\mathbf{C}_1$ and $\mathbf{C}_2$ in fair$_3$. This ciphertext encrypts the input shares of garblers that P_3 misses, namely, x_{12} and x_{21}. This would allow P_3 to compute the function on clear inputs directly. To ensure that the recovered missing shares are as distributed in fair$_1$ and fair$_2$, the shares are not simply distributed but are committed via NICOM by the input owners and the openings are encrypted by the holders. Since there is no way for an evaluator to detect any mismatch in the inputs to and outputs from the two GCs as they are in encoded form, we use encryption scheme with special correctness to enable the evaluator to identify the relevant decryptions. Crucially, we depart from the usual way of creating the cheat recovery boxes using conflicting encoded outputs. Based on whether the clear or encoded output comes out of honest P_3 in round 3, corrupt garbler P_1 feeding two different inputs to $\mathbf{C}_1$ and $\mathbf{C}_2$ can conclude whether its two different inputs lead to the same output or not, breaching privacy. Note that the decoding information cannot be given via this cheat recovery box that uses conflicting encoded outputs as key, as that would result in circularity.

Despite using the above fix, the mechanism as discussed above is susceptible to 'selective failure attack', an attack well-known in the 2-party domain. While in the latter domain, the attack is launched to breach the privacy of the evaluator's input based on whether it aborts or not. Here, a corrupt garbler can prepare the ciphertexts in an incorrect way and can breach privacy of its honest co-garbler based on whether clear or encoded output comes out of the evaluator. We elaborate the attack in fair$_3$ considering a corrupt P_1 and single bit inputs. P_1 is supposed to prepare two ciphertexts corresponding to P_2's input bit using the following key combinations– (a) key for 0 in $\mathbf{C}_1$ and 1 in $\mathbf{C}_2$ and (b) vice-versa. Corrupt P_1 may replace one of the ciphertexts using key based on encoded input 0 of P_2 in both the GCs. In case P_2 indeed has input 0 (that he would use consistently across the 2 GCs during fair$_3$), then P_3 would be able to decrypt the ciphertext and would send clear output in Round 3. P_1 can readily conclude that P_2's input is 0. This attack is taken care via the usual technique of breaking each input bit to s number of xor-shares, referred as 'XOR-tree approach' [55] (probe-resistance matrix [55,66] can also be used; we avoid it for simplicity). The security is achieved except with probability $2^{-(s-1)}$. Given that input consistency is enforced, at the end of round 2, apart from the three states– (a) no corruption and no conflict detected (b) corrupt identified (c) conflict detected, a party can be in yet another state. Namely, no corruption and no conflict detected and the party is able to open a ciphertext and compute f on clear. A corrupt party cannot be in this state since the honest parties would use consistent inputs and therefore the corrupt would not get access to conflicting encoded inputs that constitute the key of the ciphertexts. If any honest party is in this state, our protocol results in all parties outputting this output. In Round 3, this party can send the computed output along with the opening of the shares he recovered via the ciphertexts as 'proof' to convince the honest party of the validity of the output. The protocol fair appears in Figs. 3 and 4.

We now prove the correctness of fair. The intuitive proof of fairness and formal proof of security are presented in the full version [63].

Lemma 5. *During* fair, $P_j \notin \mathcal{C}_i$ *holds for honest* P_i, P_j.

Proof. An honest P_i will not include P_j in its corrupt set in the sub-protocols $\{\text{fair}_\alpha, \text{cert}_\alpha\}_{\alpha \in [3]}$ following Lemmas 1 and 3. Now we prove the statement individually investigating the three rounds of fair.

In Round 1 of fair, P_i includes P_j as corrupt only if (a) P_i, P_j are garblers and P_j sets $p_{jj} \neq x_{ji}$ or (b) P_j sends $\text{pp}_j, c_{ji}, o_{ji}, x_{ji}$ to P_i such that $\text{Open}(\text{pp}_j, c_{ji}, o_{ji}) \neq x_{ji}$. None of them will be true for an honest P_j. In Round 2 of fair, P_i includes P_j as corrupt only if (a) P_j is a garbler and P_i is an evaluator and $m_{jj} \neq x_{ji}$ or (b) P_i obtains $\text{cert}_i = (\gamma'_j, \gamma'_k)$ and detects P_j's input γ'_j in cert_i to be different from the information sent by him. The former will not be true for an honest P_j. The latter also cannot hold for honest P_j by correctness of the privacy-free garbling used. In the last round of fair, P_i will identify P_j as corrupt, if it has $\text{flag}_k = 1$ and yet receives cert_k which is same as key_k from P_k. A corrupt P_k receives key_k only by handing out correct and consistent common information to P_i and P_j until the end of Round 1. Namely, the following must be true for P_k to obtain key_k (except for the case when it breaks the authenticity of the GC): (i) γ_i and γ_j for cert_k must be same and (ii) P_k must not be in the corrupt set of any honest party at the end of Round 1. In this case, flag_k cannot be 1. $\qquad\square$

Lemma 6. *No corrupt party can be in* st_1 *by the end of Round 1, except with negligible probability.*

Proof. For a corrupt P_k, its honest garblers P_i and P_j creates the ciphertexts cts using keys with opposite meaning for their respective inputs from their garbled circuits. Since honest P_i and P_j use the same input for both the circuits, P_k will not have a key to open any of the ciphertexts. The openings (o_{ij}, o_{ji}) are therefore protected due to the security of the encryption scheme. Subsequently, P_k cannot compute y. $\qquad\square$

Definition 1. A party P_i is said to be 'committed' to a unique input x_i, if P_j holds $(c_{ij}, c_{ik}, o_{ij}, x_{ij})$ and P_k holds $(c_{ij}, c_{ik}, o_{ik}, x_{ik})$ such that: (a) $x_i = x_{ij} \oplus x_{ik}$ and (b) c_{ij} opens to x_{ij} via o_{ij} and likewise, c_{ik} opens to x_{ik} via o_{ik}.

Protocol fair()

Inputs: Party P_i has x_i for $i \in [3]$.
Output: $y = f(x_1, x_2, x_3)$ or $\bot$ where the inputs and the function output belong to $\{0,1\}^\ell$.
Subprotocols: fair_i for $i \in [3]$ (Figure 1), cert_i for $i \in [3]$ (Figure 2), SKE (Enc, Dec) with 'special correctness'.

Round 1: For $i \in [3]$ and for distinct indices $j, k \in [3] \setminus \{i\}$

- Each P_i computes an encoding of length ℓs corresponding to its input x_i. For each bit b of x_i, the encoding $b_1, \ldots b_s$ is such that $b = \oplus_{\alpha=1}^s b_\alpha$. Reusing the notation, we refer to this encoding as P_i's input x_i and its length by ℓ.
- **Round 1** of cert_i is run.
- **Round 1** of fair_i are run with the following amendments: **(1)** The circuit in fair_i is changed as follows: each input wire is replaced by a gate whose input consists of s new input wires and whose output is the exclusive-or of these wires. **(2)** P_j and P_k work with the permutation strings p_{jj} and p_{kk} respectively as x_{jk} and x_{kj}.
- P_i samples pp_i, generates $(c_{ij}, o_{ij}) \leftarrow \text{Com}(\text{pp}_i, x_{ij})$, $(c_{ik}, o_{ik}) \leftarrow \text{Com}(\text{pp}_i, x_{ik})$ and sends $\{\text{pp}_i, c_{ij}, c_{ik}\}$ to P_j, P_k. Additionally, P_i sends o_{ij}, o_{ik} to P_j, P_k respectively.
- (Local Computation by P_i) P_i adds P_ℓ in C_i if $\text{Open}(c_{li}, o_{li}) \neq x_{li}$. P_j adds P_k in C_j if: **(a)** p_{kk} not taken as x_{kj} or **(b)** the check in fair_i or cert_i fails. P_k adds P_j in C_k if: **(a)** p_{jj} not taken as x_{jk} or **(b)** the check in fair_i or cert_i fails.

Round 2: For $i \in [3]$ and for distinct indices $j, k \in [3] \setminus \{i\}$:

- If $P_i \notin C_j$, P_j sends $(\text{pp}_i, c_{ij}, c_{ik})$ to P_k. If $P_i \notin C_k$, P_k sends $(\text{pp}_i, c_{ij}, c_{ik})$ to P_j. They set $\text{flag}_i = 1$ in case of mismatch or no communication.
- If $P_i \notin C_j$, P_j participates in cert_i as a garbler with input γ_j as $\{\mathcal{D}_i^j, \mathcal{D}_i^k, \mathcal{W}_k, \text{pp}_i, c_{ij}, c_{ik}\}$ where $\mathcal{D}_i^j, \mathcal{D}_i^k, \mathcal{W}_k$ and $(\text{pp}_i, c_{ij}, c_{ik})$ was received from P_i during Round 1 of $\text{fair}_j, \text{fair}_k$, cert_k (assuming $k = (i+1) \mod 3$) and fair respectively. Similar step is taken by P_k.
- If $\text{cert}_i = (\gamma_j', \gamma_k')$, P_i sets $C_i = P_l$ if $\gamma_l' \neq \{\mathcal{D}_i^j, \mathcal{D}_i^k, \mathcal{W}_k, \text{pp}_i, c_{ij}, c_{ik}\}$ for $l \in \{j, k\}$.
- If $P_i \notin C_j$, P_j participates in **Round 2** of fair_i. When $P_k \notin C_j$, P_j additionally sends the ciphertexts $\text{ct}_{j\alpha}^\beta$ for $\beta \in \{0,1\}$ and $\alpha \in [\ell]$ created as follows. Let $\{\mathbf{X}_{l(\ell+\alpha)}^0, \mathbf{X}_{l(\ell+\alpha)}^1\}$, denote the encoding information of co-garbler P_k's input wire α corresponding to C_l ($l \in \{j, k\}$). Then $\text{ct}_{j\alpha}^\beta = \text{Enc}_{\text{sk}_\alpha^\beta}(o_{jk}, o_{kj})$ for $\text{sk}_\alpha^0 = \mathbf{X}_{j(\ell+\alpha)}^0 \oplus \mathbf{X}_{k(\ell+\alpha)}^1$ and $\text{sk}_\alpha^1 = \mathbf{X}_{j(\ell+\alpha)}^1 \oplus \mathbf{X}_{k(\ell+\alpha)}^0$. P_k takes similar steps.
- (Local Computation by P_i) Include P_l in C_i if $m_{ll} \neq x_{li}$ for $l \in \{j, k\}$. If $C_i = \emptyset$, $\text{flag}_j = 0, \text{flag}_k = 0$, then use key $\mathbf{X}_{j(\ell+\alpha)}^{m_{jk}^\alpha} \oplus \mathbf{X}_{k(\ell+\alpha)}^{m_{kk}^\alpha}$ ($\alpha \in [\ell]$) to decrypt the ciphertexts $\text{ct}_{j\alpha}^0$ or $\text{ct}_{j\alpha}^1$ obtained from P_j. If the decryption succeeds, retrieve o_{kj}, o_{jk}. Execute $x_{kj} \leftarrow \text{Open}(c_{kj}, o_{kj})$ and $x_{jk} \leftarrow \text{Open}(c_{jk}, o_{jk})$. If the opening succeeds, then evaluate f on $(x_i, x_{ji} \oplus x_{jk}, x_{ki} \oplus x_{kj})$ to obtain y. Similarly, steps are taken with respect to P_j's input, using the key $\mathbf{X}_{j\alpha}^{m_{jj}^\alpha} \oplus \mathbf{X}_{k\alpha}^{m_{kj}^\alpha}$ to decrypt the ciphertexts $\text{ct}_{k\alpha}^0$ or $\text{ct}_{k\alpha}^1$ obtained from P_k.

Fig. 3. A Three-Round Fair 3PC protocol

We next prove that a corrupt party must have committed its input if some honest party is in st_1 or st_2. To prove correctness, the next few lemmas then show that an honest party computes its output based on its own output or encoded output if it is in st_1 or st_2 or relies on the output or encoded output of the other

A party P_i is said to be in st_α for $\alpha \in [4]$ if the following conditions are satisfied. Let $(\mathbf{Y}_i, C_j^{\mathsf{dec}}, C_k^{\mathsf{dec}})$, O_j^{dec} and O_k^{dec} denote the output of P_i in fair_i, fair_j and fair_k, respectively. Let $\mathbf{cert}_i$, $\mathbf{key}_j$, and $\mathbf{key}_k$ denotes the output of P_i in cert_i, cert_j and cert_k respectively.

(i) st_1(output is already computed): If y and proofs (o_{jk}, o_{kj}) are computed in Round 2.
(ii) st_2 (no corruption and no conflict detected): If $((C_i = \emptyset) \wedge (\mathsf{flag}_j = 0) \wedge (\mathsf{flag}_k = 0))$
(which implies $\mathbf{Y}_i \neq \perp$ and $\mathbf{cert}_i \neq \perp$)
(iii) st_3 (corruption detected): If $(C_i \neq \emptyset)$
(iv) st_4 (conflict detected, but no corruption detected): If $(\mathsf{flag}_j = 1) \vee (\mathsf{flag}_k = 1)$

Round 3: Each P_i for $i \in [3]$ does the following based one of the four states that it belongs to.

- If in st_1, then send y to P_j, P_k. Send o_{jk} to P_j and o_{kj} to P_k as proofs.
- If in st_2, then send $(\mathbf{Y}_i, \mathbf{cert}_i, O_l^{\mathsf{dec}})$ to P_l for $l \in \{j, k\}$.
- If in st_3, then send O_l^{dec} to P_l for $l \in \{j, k\}$ only if $P_l \notin C_i$.
- If in st_4, then send $z_l = \mathsf{Enc}_{\mathbf{key}_l}(O_l^{\mathsf{dec}})$ to P_l only if $\mathsf{flag}_l = 1$. If $\mathsf{flag}_j = 1$ and $\mathbf{cert}_j$ received from P_j is same as $\mathbf{key}_j$, then set $C_i = P_k$. Similar steps are taken to check and identify if P_j is corrupt. Update state from st_4 to st_3 if corrupt is identified.
- If in st_1, then output y.
- If in $\{\mathsf{st}_2, \mathsf{st}_3, \mathsf{st}_4\}$ and if any other party is identified to be in st_1, namely if y is received from P_j or P_k with o_{ki} or o_{ji} respectively such that $\mathsf{Open}(\mathsf{pp}_i, c_{li}, o_{li}) \neq \perp$ for $l \in \{j, k\}$, then output the received y.
- If in st_2, then compute y as follows: Retrieve O_i^{dec} from either z_i (with $\mathbf{cert}_i$ as the key) received from P_j or from direct communication of P_j. If $d \leftarrow \mathsf{eOpen}(\mathsf{epp}_k, C_k^{\mathsf{dec}}, O_i^{\mathsf{dec}})$ is not $\perp$, then use d to compute $y \leftarrow \mathsf{De}(\mathbf{Y}_i^k, d)$. Similar steps are executed with respect to P_k's communication if y is not computed yet.
- If in st_3, then output $y \leftarrow \mathsf{De}(\mathbf{Y}_l^i, d)$ where $\mathbf{Y}_l$ is received from (honest) $P_l \notin C_i$ and decoding information d is known as garbler during fair_l. Otherwise output $y = \perp$.
- If in st_4, output $y = \perp$.

Fig. 4. A Three-Round Fair 3PC protocol

honest party. In all cases, the output will correspond to the committed input of the corrupt party.

Lemma 7. *If an honest party is in $\{\mathsf{st}_1, \mathsf{st}_2\}$, then corrupt party must have committed a unique input.*

Proof. An honest P_i is in $\{\mathsf{st}_1, \mathsf{st}_2\}$ only when $C_i = \emptyset$, $\mathsf{flag}_j = 0$, $\mathsf{flag}_k = 0$ hold at the end of Round 2. Assume P_k is corrupt. P_k has not committed to a unique x_k implies either it has distributed different copies of commitments (c_{ki}, c_{kj}) to the honest parties or distributed incorrect opening information to some honest party. In the former case, flag_k will be set by P_i. In the latter case, at least one honest party will identify P_k to be corrupt by the end of Round 1. If it is P_i, then $C_i \neq \emptyset$. Otherwise, P_j populates its corrupt set with P_k, leading to P_i setting $\mathsf{flag}_k = 1$ in Round 2. □

Lemma 8. *If an honest party is in st_1, then its output y corresponds to the unique input committed by the corrupt party.*

Proof. An honest P_i is in st_1 only when $C_i = \emptyset$, $\mathsf{flag}_j = 0, \mathsf{flag}_k = 0$ hold at the end of Round 2 and it computes y via decryption of the ciphertexts ct sent by either P_j or P_k. Assume P_k is corrupt. By Lemma 7, P_k has committed to its input. The condition $\mathsf{flag}_j = 0$ implies that P_k exchanges the commitments on the shares of P_j's input, namely $\{c_{ji}, c_{jk}\}$, honestly. Now if P_i opens honest P_j's ciphertext, then it unlocks the opening information for the missing shares, namely (o_{kj}, o_{jk}) corresponding to common and agreed commitments (c_{kj}, c_{jk}). Using these it opens the missing shares $x_{kj} \leftarrow \mathsf{Open}(c_{kj}, o_{kj})$ and $x_{jk} \leftarrow \mathsf{Open}(c_{jk}, o_{jk})$ and finally computes output on $(x_i, x_{ji} \oplus x_{jk}, x_{ki} \oplus x_{kj})$. Next, we consider the case when P_i computes y by decrypting a ct sent by corrupt P_k. In this case, no matter how the ciphertext is created, the binding property of NICOM implies that P_k will not be able to open c_{jk}, c_{kj} to anything other than x_{jk}, x_{kj} except with negligible probability. Thus, the output computed is still as above and the claim holds. $\qquad\square$

Lemma 9. *If an honest party is in* st_2*, then its encoded output* $\mathbf{Y}$ *corresponds to the unique input committed by the corrupt party.*

Proof. An honest P_i is in st_2 only when $C_i = \emptyset$, $\mathsf{flag}_j = 0, \mathsf{flag}_k = 0$ hold at the end of Round 2. The conditions also imply that P_i has computed $\mathbf{Y}_i$ successfully (due to Lemma 2) and P_k has committed to its input (due to Lemma 7). Now we show that $\mathbf{Y}_i$ correspond to the unique input committed by the corrupt P_k. We first note that P_k must have used the same input for both the circuits $\mathbf{C}_j$ and $\mathbf{C}_k$ in fair_i. Otherwise one of the ciphertexts prepared by honest P_j must have been opened and y would be computed, implying P_i belongs to st_1 and not in st_2 as assumed. We are now left to show that the input of P_k for its circuit $\mathbf{C}_k$ in fair_i is the same as the one committed.

In fair, honest P_j would use permutation string $p_{kk} = x_{kj}$ for permuting the commitments in $\mathcal{D}_k$ corresponding to x_k. Therefore, one can conclude that the commitments in $\mathcal{D}_k$ are constructed correctly and ordered as per x_{kj}. Now the only way P_k can decommit x'_k is by giving $m_{kk} = p_{kk} \oplus x'_k$. But in this case honest P_i would add P_k to C_i as the check $m_{kk} = x_{ki}$ would fail ($m_{kk} = p_{kk} \oplus x'_k \neq p_{kk} \oplus x_k$) and will be in st_3 and not in st_2 as assumed. $\qquad\square$

Lemma 10. *If an honest party is in* st_2*, then its output* y *corresponds to the unique input committed by the corrupt party.*

Proof. Note that an honest party P_i in st_2 either uses y of another party in st_1 or computes output from its encoded output $\mathbf{Y}_i$. The proof for the former case goes as follows. By Lemma 6, a corrupt P_k can never be in st_1. The correctness of y computed by an honest P_j follows directly from Lemma 8. For the latter case, Lemma 9 implies that $\mathbf{Y}_i$ corresponds to the unique input committed by the corrupt party. All that needs to be ensured is that P_i gets the correct decoding information. The condition $\mathsf{flag}_j = \mathsf{flag}_k = 0$ implies that the commitment to the decoding information is computed and distributed correctly for both $\mathbf{C}_j$ and $\mathbf{C}_k$. Now the binding property of eNICOM ensures that the decoding information received from either P_j (for $\mathbf{C}_k$) or P_k (for $\mathbf{C}_j$) must be correct implying correctness of y (by correctness of the garbling scheme). $\qquad\square$

Lemma 11. *If an honest party is in* st_3 *or* st_4, *then its output* y *corresponds to the unique input committed by the corrupt party.*

Proof. An honest party P_i in st_3 either uses y of another party in st_1 or computes output from encoded output $\mathbf{Y}_j$ of P_j who it identifies as honest. For the latter case note that an honest P_j will never be identified as corrupt by P_i, due to Lemma 5. The claim now follows from Lemma 6, Lemma 8 and the fact that corrupt P_k cannot forge the 'proof' o_{ij} (binding of NICOM) for the former case and from Lemma 9 and the fact that it possesses correct decoding information as a garbler for $\mathbf{Y}_j$ for the latter case. An honest party P_i in st_4 only uses y of another party in st_1. The lemma follows in this case via the same argument as before.   □

Theorem 1. *Protocol* fair *is correct.*

Proof. In order to prove the theorem, we show that if an honest party, say P_i outputs y that is not $\perp$, then it corresponds to x_1, x_2, x_3 where x_j is the input committed by P_j (Definition 1). We note that an honest P_i belong to one among $\{\mathsf{st}_1, \mathsf{st}_2, \mathsf{st}_3, \mathsf{st}_4\}$ at the time of output computation. The proof now follows from Lemmas 7, 8, 10, 11.   □

4   2-round 3PC with Unanimous Abort

This section presents a tight upper bound for 3PC achieving unanimous abort in the setting with pair-wise private channels and a broadcast channel. The impossibility of one-round protocol in the same setting follows from "residual function" attack [41]. Our lower bound result presented in the full version [63] rules out the possibility of achieving unanimous abort in the absence of a broadcast channel in two rounds. This protocol can be used to yield a round-optimal fair protocol with broadcast (lower bound in Sect. 6.1) by application of the transformation of [45] that compiles a protocol with unanimous abort to a fair protocol via evaluating the circuits that compute shares (using error-correcting secret sharing) of the function output using the protocol with unanimous abort and then uses an additional round for reconstruction of the output.

In an attempt to build a protocol with unanimous abort, we note that any protocol with unanimous abort must be robust to any potential misbehaviour launched via the private communication in the second round. Simply because, there is no way to report the abort to the other honest party who may have seen honest behaviour from the corrupt party all along and has got the output, leading to selective abort. Our construction achieves unanimity by leveraging the availability of the broadcast channel to abort when a corrupt behaviour is identified either in the first round or in the broadcast communication in the second round, and behaving robustly otherwise. In summary, if the corrupt party does not strike in the first round and in the broadcast communication of the second round, then our construction achieves robustness.

Turning to the garbled circuit based constructions such as the two-round protocol of [43] achieving selective abort or the composition of three copies of the sub-protocol fair_i of fair, we note that the second round private communication that involves encoding information for inputs is crucial for computing the output and cannot transit via broadcast because of input privacy breach. A bit elaborately, the transfer of the encoding information for the inputs of the garblers can be completed in the first round itself and any inconsistency can be handled via unanimous abort in the second round. However, a similar treatment for the encoding information of the shares of the evaluator seems impossible as they are transferred to garblers only in the first round. We get past this seemingly impossible task via a clever 'two-part release mechanism' for the encoding information of the shares of the evaluator. Details follow.

Similar to protocol fair, we build our protocol ua upon three parallel executions of a sub-protocol ua_i $(i \in [3])$, each comprising of two rounds and with each party P_i enacting the role of the evaluator once. With fair_i as the starting point, each sub-protocol ua_i allows the parties to reach agreement on whether the run was successful and the evaluator got the output or not. A flag flag_i is used as an indicator. The protocol ua then decides on unanimous abort if at least one of the flags from the three executions ua_i for $i \in [3]$ is set to true. Otherwise, the parties must have got the output. Input consistency checks ensure that the outputs are identical. Intra-execution input consistency is taken care by cheat-recovery mechanism (similar and simplified version of what protocol fair uses), while inter-execution input consistency is taken care by the same trick that we use in our fair protocol. Now looking inside ua_i, the challenge goes back to finding a mechanism for the honest evaluator to get the output when a corrupt party behaves honestly in the first round and in the broadcast communication of the second round. In other words, its private communication in the second round should not impact robustness. This is where the 'two-part release mechanism' for the encoding information of the shares of the evaluator kicks in. It is realized by tweaking the function to be evaluated as $f(x_j, x_k, (z_j \oplus r_j) \oplus (z_k \oplus r_k))$ in the instance ua_i where P_i enacts the role of the evaluator. Here r_j, r_k denote random pads chosen by the garblers P_j, P_k respectively in the first round. The encoding information for these are released to P_i *privately* in the first round itself. Any inconsistent behaviour in the first round is detected, the flag is set and the the protocol exits with $\bot$ unanimously. Next, z_j and z_k are the offsets of these random pads with the actual shares of P_i's input and are available only at the end of first round. The encoding information for these offsets and these offsets themselves are transferred via broadcast in the second round for public verification. As long as the pads are privately communicated, the offsets do not affect privacy of the shares of P_i's input. Lastly, note that the encoding information for a garbler's input for its own generated circuit can be transferred in the first round itself. This ensures that a corrupt garbler misbehaves either in the first round or in the broadcast communication in the second round or lets the evaluator get the output via its own GC. The formal description and proof of security of ua appear in the full version [63].

450   A. Patra and D. Ravi

5   3-round 3PC with Guaranteed Output Delivery

In this section, we present a three-round 3PC protocol, given access to pairwise-private channels and a broadcast channel. The protocol is round-optimal following 3-round lower bound for fair 3PC proven in Sect. 6.1. The necessity of the broadcast channel for achieving guaranteed output delivery with strict honest majority follows from [23].

Our tryst starts with the known generic transformations that are relevant such as the transformations from the unanimous abort to (identifiable) fair protocol [45] or identifiable fair to guaranteed output delivery [24]. However, these transformations being non-round-preserving do not turn out to be useful. Turning a 2-round protocol offering unanimous (or even selective) abort with identifiability (when the honest parties learn about the identity of the corrupt when deprived of the output) to a 3-round protocol with guaranteed output delivery in a black-box way show some promise. The third round can be leveraged by the honest parties to exchange their inputs and compute output on the clear. We face two obstacles with this approach. First, there is neither any known 2-round construction for selective/unanimous abort with identifiability nor do we see how to transform our unanimous abort protocol to one with identifiability in two rounds. Second, when none of the parties (including the corrupt) receive output from the selective/unanimous abort protocol and the honest parties compute it on the clear in the third round by exchanging their inputs and taking a default value for the input of the corrupt party, it is not clear how the corrupt party can obtain the same output (note that the ideal functionality demands delivering the output to the adversary).

We get around the above issues by taking a non-blackbox approach and tweaking ua_i and $fair_i$ to get yet another sub-protocol god_i that achieves a form of local identifiability. Namely, the evaluator P_i in god_i either successfully computes the output or identifies the corrupt party. As usual, our final protocol god is built upon three parallel executions of god_i ($i \in [3]$), each comprising of two rounds and with each party P_i enacting the role of the evaluator once. Looking ahead, the local identifiability helps in achieving guaranteed output delivery as follows. In a case when both honest parties identify the corrupt party and the corrupt party received the output by the end of Round 2, the honest parties can exchange their inputs and reconstruct the corrupt party's input using the shares received during one of the executions of god_i and compute the function on clear inputs in the third round. Otherwise, the honest party who identifies the corrupt can simply accept the output computed and forwarded by the other honest party. The issue of the corrupt party getting the same output as that of the honest parties when it fails to obtain any in its instance of god_i is taken care as follows. First, the only reason a corrupt party in our protocol does not receive its output in its instance of god_i is due to denial of committing its input. In this case it is detected early and the honest parties exchange inputs in the second round itself so that at least one honest party computes the output using a default input of the corrupt party by the end of Round 2 and hands it over to others in Round 3. The protocol and the proof appear in the full version [63].

6   Lower Bounds

In this paper, we present two lower bounds– **(a)** three rounds are necessary for achieving fairness in the presence of pair-wise private channels and a broadcast channel; **(b)** three rounds are necessary for achieving unanimous abort in the presence of just pair-wise private channels (and no broadcast). The second result holds even if broadcast was allowed in the first round. Our results extend for any n and t with $3t \geq n > 2t$ via standard player-partitioning technique [57]. Our results imply the following. First, selective abort is the best amongst the four notions (considered in this work) that we can achieve in two rounds without broadcast (from **(b)**). Second, unanimous abort as well as fairness require 3 rounds in the absence of broadcast (from **(b)**). Third, broadcast does not help to improve the round complexity of fairness (from **(a)**). Lastly, guaranteed output delivery requires 3 rounds with broadcast (from **(a)**). The first lower bound appears below. We prove the second lower bound in the full version [63].

6.1   The Impossibility of 2-round Fair 3PC

In this section, we show that it is impossible to construct a fair 2-round 3PC for general functions. [39] presents a lower bound of three rounds assuming *non-private* point-to-point channels and a broadcast channel (their proof crucially relies on the assumption of non-private channels). [35] presents a three-round lower bound for fair MPC with $t \geq 2$ (arbitrary number of parties) in the same network setting as ours. Similar to the lower bounds of [35,39] (for the function of conjunction of two input bits), our lower bound result does not exploit the rushing nature of the adversary and hence holds for non-rushing adversary as well. Finally, we observe that the impossibility of 2-round 3PC for the information-theoretic setting follows from the impossibility of 2-round 3-party statistical VSS of [62] (since VSS is a special case of MPC). We now prove the impossibility formally.

Theorem 2. *There exist functions f such that no two-round fair 3PC protocol can compute f, even in the honest majority setting and assuming access to pairwise-private and broadcast channel.*

Proof. Let $\mathcal{P} = \{P_1, P_2, P_3\}$ denote the set of 3 parties and the adversary $\mathcal{A}$ may corrupt any one of them. We prove the theorem by contradiction. We assume that there exists a two-round fair 3PC protocol π that can compute $f(x_1, x_2, x_3)$ defined below for P_i's input x_i:

$$f(x_1, x_2, x_3) = \begin{cases} 1 & \text{if } x_2 = x_3 = 1 \\ 0 & \text{otherwise} \end{cases}$$

At a high level, we discuss two adversarial strategies $\mathcal{A}_1$ and $\mathcal{A}_2$ of $\mathcal{A}$. We consider party P_i launching $\mathcal{A}_i$ in execution Σ_i ($i \in [2]$) of π. Both the executions are assumed to be run for the same input tuple (x_1, x_2, x_3) and the same random inputs (r_1, r_2, r_3) of the three parties. (Same random inputs are considered for simplicity and without loss of generality. The same arguments hold for distribution ensembles as well.) When strategy $\mathcal{A}_1$ is launched in execution Σ_1, we would claim that by correctness of π, $\mathcal{A}$ corrupting P_1 should learn the output $y = f(x_1, x_2, x_3)$. Here, we note that the value of $f(x_1, x_2, x_3)$ depends only on the inputs of honest P_2, P_3 (i.e. input values x_2, x_3) and is thus well-defined. We refer to $f(x_1, x_2, x_3)$ as the value determined by this particular combination of inputs (x_2, x_3) henceforth. Now, since $\mathcal{A}$ corrupting P_1 learnt the output, due to fairness, P_2 should learn the output too in Σ_1. Next strategy $\mathcal{A}_2$ is designed so that P_2 in Σ_2 can obtain the same view as in Σ_1 and therefore it gets the output too. Due to fairness, we can claim that P_3 receives the output in Σ_2. A careful observation then lets us claim that P_3 can, in fact, learn the output at the end of Round 1 itself in π. Lastly, using the above observation, we show a strategy for P_3 that explicitly allows P_3 to breach privacy.

We use the following notation: Let $\mathsf{p}^r_{i \to j}$ denote the pairwise communication from P_i to P_j in round r and b^r_i denote the broadcast by P_i in round r, where $r \in [2], \{i, j\} \in [3]$. V_i denotes the view of party P_i at the end of execution of π. Below we describe the strategies $\mathcal{A}_1$ and $\mathcal{A}_2$.

$\mathcal{A}_1$: P_1 behaves honestly during Round 1 of the protocol. In Round 2, P_1 waits to receive the messages from other parties, but does not communicate at all.

$\mathcal{A}_2$: P_2 behaves honestly towards P_3 in Round 1, i.e. sends the messages $\mathsf{p}^1_{2 \to 3}, \mathsf{b}^1_2$ according to the protocol specification. However P_2 does not communicate to P_1 in Round 1. In Round 2, P_2 waits to receive messages from P_3, but does not communicate to the other parties.

Next we present the views of the parties in the two executions Σ_1 and Σ_2 in Table 1. The communications that could potentially be different from the communications in an honest execution (where all parties behave honestly) with the considered inputs and random inputs of the parties are appended with $\star$ (e.g. $\mathsf{p}^2_{1 \to 3}(\star)$). We now prove a sequence of lemmas to complete our proof.

Lemma 12. *A corrupt P_1 launching $\mathcal{A}_1$ in Σ_1 should learn the output $y = f(x_1, x_2, x_3)$.*

Proof. The proof follows easily. Since P_1 behaved honestly during Round 1, it received all the desired communication from honest P_2 and P_3 in Round 2 (refer to Table 1 for the view of P_1 in Σ_1 in the end of Round 2). So it follows from the correctness property that his view at the end of the protocol i.e. V_1 should enable P_1 to learn the correct function output $f(x_1, x_2, x_3)$.   □

Lemma 13. *A corrupt P_2 launching $\mathcal{A}_2$ in Σ_2 should learn the output y.*

Proof. We prove the lemma with the following two claims. First, the view of P_2 in Σ_2 subsumes the view of honest P_2 in Σ_1. Second, P_2 learns the output in Σ_1 due to the fact that the corrupt P_1 learns it and π is fair. We

Table 1. Views of P_1, P_2, P_3 in Σ_1 and Σ_2

	Σ_1			Σ_2		
	V_1	V_2	V_3	V_1	V_2	V_3
Initial Input	(x_1, r_1)	(x_2, r_2)	(x_3, r_3)	(x_1, r_1)	(x_2, r_2)	(x_3, r_3)
Round 1	$p^1_{2\to 1}, p^1_{3\to 1}, b^1_2, b^1_3$	$p^1_{1\to 2}, p^1_{3\to 2}, b^1_1, b^1_3$	$p^1_{1\to 3}, p^1_{2\to 3}, b^1_1, b^1_2$	$-, p^1_{3\to 1}, b^1_2, b^1_3$	$p^1_{1\to 2}, p^1_{3\to 2}, b^1_1, b^1_3$	$p^1_{1\to 3}, p^1_{2\to 3}, b^1_1, b^1_2$
Round 2	$p^2_{2\to 1}, p^2_{3\to 1}, b^2_2, b^2_3$	$-, p^2_{3\to 2}, b^2_3$	$-, p^2_{2\to 3}, b^2_2$	$-, p^2_{3\to 1}, b^2_3$	$p^2_{1\to 2}(\star), p^2_{3\to 2}, b^2_1(\star), b^2_3$	$-, p^2_{1\to 3}(\star), b^2_1(\star)$

now prove our first claim. In Σ_1, we observe that P_2 has received communication from both P_1 and P_3 in the first round, and only from P_3 in the second round. So $V_2 = \{x_2, r_2, p^1_{1\to 2}, b^1_1, p^1_{3\to 2}, b^1_3, p^2_{3\to 2}, b^2_3\}$ (refer to Table 1). We now analyze P_2's view in Σ_2. Both P_1 and P_3 are honest and must have sent $\{p^1_{1\to 2}, b^1_1, p^1_{3\to 2}, b^1_3\}$ according to the protocol specifications in Round 1. Since P_3 received the expected messages from P_2 in Round 1, P_3 must have sent $\{p^2_{3\to 2}, b^2_3\}$ in Round 2. Note that we can rule out the possibility of P_3's messages in this round having been influenced by P_1 possibly reporting P_2's misbehavior towards P_1. This holds since P_3 would send the messages in the beginning of Round 2. We do not make any assumption regarding P_1's communication to P_2 in Round 2 since P_1 has not received the expected message from P_2 in Round 1. Thus, overall, P_2's view V_2 comprises of $\{x_2, r_2, p^1_{1\to 2}, b^1_1, p^1_{3\to 2}, b^1_3, p^2_{3\to 2}, b^2_3\}$ (refer to Table 1). Note that there may also be some additional messages from P_1 to P_2 in Round 2 which can be ignored by P_2. These are marked with '$(\star)$' in Table 1. A careful look shows that the view of P_2 in Σ_2 subsumes the view of honest P_2 in Σ_1. This concludes our proof. $\qquad\square$

Lemma 14. P_3 in Σ_2 should learn the output y by the end of Round 1.

Proof. According to the previous lemma, P_2 should learn the function output in Σ_2. Due to fairness property, it must hold that an honest P_3 learns the output as well (same as obtained by P_2 i.e. y with respect to x_2). First, we note that as per strategy $\mathcal{A}_2$, P_2 only communicates to P_3 in Round 1. Second, we argue that the second round communication from P_1 does not impact P_3's output computation as follows.

We observe that the function output depends only on (x_2, x_3). Clearly, Round 1 messages $\{p^1_{1\to 3}, b^1_1\}$ of P_1 does not depend on x_2. Next, since there is no private communication to P_1 from P_2 as per strategy $\mathcal{A}_2$, the only information that can possibly hold information on x_2 and can impact the round 2 messages of P_1 is b^1_2. However, since this is a broadcast message, P_3 holds this by the end of Round 1 itself. $\qquad\square$

Lemma 15. A corrupt P_3 violates the privacy property of π.

Proof. The adversary corrupting P_3 participates in the protocol honestly by fixing input $x_3 = 0$. Since P_3 can get the output from P_2's and P_1's round 1 communication (Lemma 14), it must be true that P_3 can evaluate the function

f locally by plugging in any value of x_3. (Note that P_2 and P_1's communication in round 1 are independent of the communication of P_3 in the same round.) Now a corrupt P_3 can plug in $x_3 = 1$ locally and learn x_2 (via the output $x_2 \wedge x_3$). In the ideal world, corrupt P_3 must learn nothing beyond the output 0 as it has participated in the protocol with input 0. But in the execution of π (in which P_3 participated honestly with input $x_3 = 0$), P_3 has learnt x_2. This is a clear breach of privacy as P_3 learns x_2 regardless of his input. $\square$

Hence, we have arrived at a contradiction, completing the proof of Theorem 2.
                                                                                    $\square$

Acknowledgement. The first author would like to acknowledge partial support from Google Inc. and SERB Women Excellence Award from Science and Engineering Research Board of India. The second author would like to acknowledge partial support from Indian Association for Research in Computing Science (IARCS) and Microsoft Research India.

References

1. Afshar, A., Mohassel, P., Pinkas, B., Riva, B.: Non-interactive secure computation based on cut-and-choose. In: Nguyen, P.Q., Oswald, E. (eds.) EUROCRYPT 2014. LNCS, vol. 8441, pp. 387–404. Springer, Heidelberg (2014). https://doi.org/10.1007/978-3-642-55220-5_22

2. Ananth, P., Choudhuri, A.R., Jain, A.: A new approach to round-optimal secure multiparty computation. In: Katz, J., Shacham, H. (eds.) CRYPTO 2017. LNCS, vol. 10401, pp. 468–499. Springer, Cham (2017). https://doi.org/10.1007/978-3-319-63688-7_16

3. Araki, T., Furukawa, J., Lindell, Y., Nof, A., Ohara, K.: High-throughput semi-honest secure three-party computation with an honest majority. In: ACM CCS (2016)

4. Asharov, G., Jain, A., López-Alt, A., Tromer, E., Vaikuntanathan, V., Wichs, D.: Multiparty computation with low communication, computation and interaction via threshold FHE. In: Pointcheval, D., Johansson, T. (eds.) EUROCRYPT 2012. LNCS, vol. 7237, pp. 483–501. Springer, Heidelberg (2012). https://doi.org/10.1007/978-3-642-29011-4_29

5. Backes, M., Kate, A., Patra, A.: Computational verifiable secret sharing revisited. In: Lee, D.H., Wang, X. (eds.) ASIACRYPT 2011. LNCS, vol. 7073, pp. 590–609. Springer, Heidelberg (2011). https://doi.org/10.1007/978-3-642-25385-0_32

6. Beaver, D.: Efficient multiparty protocols using circuit randomization. In: Feigenbaum, J. (ed.) CRYPTO 1991. LNCS, vol. 576, pp. 420–432. Springer, Heidelberg (1992). https://doi.org/10.1007/3-540-46766-1_34

7. Beaver, D., Micali, S., Rogaway, P.: The round complexity of secure protocols (extended abstract). In: ACM STOC (1990)

8. Beerliová-Trubíniová, Z., Hirt, M.: Efficient multi-party computation with dispute control. In: Halevi, S., Rabin, T. (eds.) TCC 2006. LNCS, vol. 3876, pp. 305–328. Springer, Heidelberg (2006). https://doi.org/10.1007/11681878_16

9. Bellare, M., Hoang, V.T., Rogaway, P.: Foundations of garbled circuits. In: CCS (2012)

10. Ben-Or, M., Goldwasser, S., Wigderson, A.: Completeness theorems for non-cryptographic fault-tolerant distributed computation (extended abstract). In: STOC (1988)
11. Ben-Sasson, E., Fehr, S., Ostrovsky, R.: Near-linear unconditionally-secure multiparty computation with a dishonest minority. In: Safavi-Naini, R., Canetti, R. (eds.) CRYPTO 2012. LNCS, vol. 7417, pp. 663–680. Springer, Heidelberg (2012). https://doi.org/10.1007/978-3-642-32009-5_39
12. Bendlin, R., Damgård, I., Orlandi, C., Zakarias, S.: Semi-homomorphic encryption and multiparty computation. In: Paterson, K.G. (ed.) EUROCRYPT 2011. LNCS, vol. 6632, pp. 169–188. Springer, Heidelberg (2011). https://doi.org/10.1007/978-3-642-20465-4_11
13. Bogdanov, D., Laur, S., Willemson, J.: Sharemind: a framework for fast privacy-preserving computations. In: Jajodia, S., Lopez, J. (eds.) ESORICS 2008. LNCS, vol. 5283, pp. 192–206. Springer, Heidelberg (2008). https://doi.org/10.1007/978-3-540-88313-5_13
14. Bogdanov, D., Talviste, R., Willemson, J.: Deploying secure multi-party computation for financial data analysis. In: Keromytis, A.D. (ed.) FC 2012. LNCS, vol. 7397, pp. 57–64. Springer, Heidelberg (2012). https://doi.org/10.1007/978-3-642-32946-3_5
15. Bogetoft, P., et al.: Secure multiparty computation goes live. In: Dingledine, R., Golle, P. (eds.) FC 2009. LNCS, vol. 5628, pp. 325–343. Springer, Heidelberg (2009). https://doi.org/10.1007/978-3-642-03549-4_20
16. Brakerski, Z., Halevi, S., Polychroniadou, A.: Four round secure computation without setup. In: Kalai, Y., Reyzin, L. (eds.) TCC 2017. LNCS, vol. 10677, pp. 645–677. Springer, Cham (2017). https://doi.org/10.1007/978-3-319-70500-2_22
17. Chandran, N., Garay, J.A., Mohassel, P., Vusirikala, S.: Efficient, constant-round and actively secure MPC: beyond the three-party case. In: ACM CCS (2017)
18. Chaum, D., Crépeau, C., Damgård, I.: Multiparty unconditionally secure protocols (extended abstract). In: ACM STOC (1988)
19. Chaum, D., Damgård, I.B., van de Graaf, J.: Multiparty computations ensuring privacy of each party's input and correctness of the result. In: Pomerance, C. (ed.) CRYPTO 1987. LNCS, vol. 293, pp. 87–119. Springer, Heidelberg (1988). https://doi.org/10.1007/3-540-48184-2_7
20. Chida, K., et al.: Implementation and evaluation of an efficient secure computation system using 'R' for healthcare statistics. J. Am. Med. Inform. Assoc. (2014)
21. Choi, S.G., Katz, J., Malozemoff, A.J., Zikas, V.: Efficient three-party computation from cut-and-choose. In: Garay, J.A., Gennaro, R. (eds.) CRYPTO 2014. LNCS, vol. 8617, pp. 513–530. Springer, Heidelberg (2014). https://doi.org/10.1007/978-3-662-44381-1_29
22. Cleve, R.: Limits on the security of coin flips when half the processors are faulty (extended abstract). In: ACM STOC (1986)
23. Cohen, R., Haitner, I., Omri, E., Rotem, L.: Characterization of secure multiparty computation without broadcast. In: Kushilevitz, E., Malkin, T. (eds.) TCC 2016. LNCS, vol. 9562, pp. 596–616. Springer, Heidelberg (2016). https://doi.org/10.1007/978-3-662-49096-9_25
24. Cohen, R., Lindell, Y.: Fairness versus guaranteed output delivery in secure multiparty computation. In: Sarkar, P., Iwata, T. (eds.) ASIACRYPT 2014. LNCS, vol. 8874, pp. 466–485. Springer, Heidelberg (2014). https://doi.org/10.1007/978-3-662-45608-8_25

25. Cramer, R., Damgård, I., Dziembowski, S., Hirt, M., Rabin, T.: Efficient multiparty computations secure against an adaptive adversary. In: Stern, J. (ed.) EUROCRYPT 1999. LNCS, vol. 1592, pp. 311–326. Springer, Heidelberg (1999). https://doi.org/10.1007/3-540-48910-X_22

26. Damgård, I., Nielsen, J.B.: Scalable and unconditionally secure multiparty computation. In: Menezes, A. (ed.) CRYPTO 2007. LNCS, vol. 4622, pp. 572–590. Springer, Heidelberg (2007). https://doi.org/10.1007/978-3-540-74143-5_32

27. Damgård, I., Orlandi, C.: Multiparty computation for dishonest majority: from passive to active security at low cost. In: Rabin, T. (ed.) CRYPTO 2010. LNCS, vol. 6223, pp. 558–576. Springer, Heidelberg (2010). https://doi.org/10.1007/978-3-642-14623-7_30

28. Damgård, I., Pastro, V., Smart, N., Zakarias, S.: Multiparty computation from somewhat homomorphic encryption. In: Safavi-Naini, R., Canetti, R. (eds.) CRYPTO 2012. LNCS, vol. 7417, pp. 643–662. Springer, Heidelberg (2012). https://doi.org/10.1007/978-3-642-32009-5_38

29. Frederiksen, T.K., Nielsen, J.B., Orlandi, C.: Privacy-free garbled circuits with applications to efficient zero-knowledge. In: Oswald, E., Fischlin, M. (eds.) EUROCRYPT 2015. LNCS, vol. 9057, pp. 191–219. Springer, Heidelberg (2015). https://doi.org/10.1007/978-3-662-46803-6_7

30. Furukawa, J., Lindell, Y., Nof, A., Weinstein, O.: High-throughput secure three-party computation for malicious adversaries and an honest majority. In: Coron, J.-S., Nielsen, J.B. (eds.) EUROCRYPT 2017. LNCS, vol. 10211, pp. 225–255. Springer, Cham (2017). https://doi.org/10.1007/978-3-319-56614-6_8

31. Garg, S., Polychroniadou, A.: Two-round adaptively secure MPC from indistinguishability obfuscation. In: Dodis, Y., Nielsen, J.B. (eds.) TCC 2015. LNCS, vol. 9015, pp. 614–637. Springer, Heidelberg (2015). https://doi.org/10.1007/978-3-662-46497-7_24

32. Garg, S., Mukherjee, P., Pandey, O., Polychroniadou, A.: The exact round complexity of secure computation. In: Fischlin, M., Coron, J.-S. (eds.) EUROCRYPT 2016. LNCS, vol. 9666, pp. 448–476. Springer, Heidelberg (2016). https://doi.org/10.1007/978-3-662-49896-5_16

33. Geisler, M.: Viff: Virtual ideal functionality framework (2007)

34. Gennaro, R., Ishai, Y., Kushilevitz, E., Rabin, T.: The round complexity of verifiable secret sharing and secure multicast. In: ACM STOC (2001)

35. Gennaro, R., Ishai, Y., Kushilevitz, E., Rabin, T.: On 2-round secure multiparty computation. In: Yung, M. (ed.) CRYPTO 2002. LNCS, vol. 2442, pp. 178–193. Springer, Heidelberg (2002). https://doi.org/10.1007/3-540-45708-9_12

36. Gertner, Y., Ishai, Y., Kushilevitz, E., Malkin, T.: Protecting data privacy in private information retrieval schemes. J. Comput. Syst. Sci. (2000)

37. Goldreich, O., Micali, S., Wigderson, A.: How to play any mental game or a completeness theorem for protocols with honest majority. In: ACM STOC (1987)

38. Goldwasser, S., Lindell, Y.: Secure computation without agreement. In: Malkhi, D. (ed.) DISC 2002. LNCS, vol. 2508, pp. 17–32. Springer, Heidelberg (2002). https://doi.org/10.1007/3-540-36108-1_2

39. Dov Gordon, S., Liu, F.-H., Shi, E.: Constant-round MPC with fairness and guarantee of output delivery. In: Gennaro, R., Robshaw, M. (eds.) CRYPTO 2015. LNCS, vol. 9216, pp. 63–82. Springer, Heidelberg (2015). https://doi.org/10.1007/978-3-662-48000-7_4

40. Halevi, S., Hazay, C., Polychroniadou, A., Venkitasubramaniam, M.: Round-optimal secure multi-party computation. Cryptology ePrint Archive, Report 2017/1056 (2017). https://eprint.iacr.org/2017/1056

41. Halevi, S., Lindell, Y., Pinkas, B.: Secure computation on the web: computing without simultaneous interaction. In: Rogaway, P. (ed.) CRYPTO 2011. LNCS, vol. 6841, pp. 132–150. Springer, Heidelberg (2011). https://doi.org/10.1007/978-3-642-22792-9_8

42. Huang, Y., Katz, J., Kolesnikov, V., Kumaresan, R., Malozemoff, A.J.: Amortizing garbled circuits. In: Garay, J.A., Gennaro, R. (eds.) CRYPTO 2014. LNCS, vol. 8617, pp. 458–475. Springer, Heidelberg (2014). https://doi.org/10.1007/978-3-662-44381-1_26

43. Ishai, Y., Kumaresan, R., Kushilevitz, E., Paskin-Cherniavsky, A.: Secure computation with minimal interaction, revisited. In: Gennaro, R., Robshaw, M. (eds.) CRYPTO 2015. LNCS, vol. 9216, pp. 359–378. Springer, Heidelberg (2015). https://doi.org/10.1007/978-3-662-48000-7_18

44. Ishai, Y., Kushilevitz, E., Paskin, A.: Secure multiparty computation with minimal interaction. In: Rabin, T. (ed.) CRYPTO 2010. LNCS, vol. 6223, pp. 577–594. Springer, Heidelberg (2010). https://doi.org/10.1007/978-3-642-14623-7_31

45. Ishai, Y., Kushilevitz, E., Prabhakaran, M., Sahai, A., Yu, C.-H.: Secure protocol transformations. In: Robshaw, M., Katz, J. (eds.) CRYPTO 2016. LNCS, vol. 9815, pp. 430–458. Springer, Heidelberg (2016). https://doi.org/10.1007/978-3-662-53008-5_15

46. Ishai, Y., Prabhakaran, M., Sahai, A.: Founding cryptography on oblivious transfer – efficiently. In: Wagner, D. (ed.) CRYPTO 2008. LNCS, vol. 5157, pp. 572–591. Springer, Heidelberg (2008). https://doi.org/10.1007/978-3-540-85174-5_32

47. Ishai, Y., Wee, H.: Partial garbling schemes and their applications. In: Esparza, J., Fraigniaud, P., Husfeldt, T., Koutsoupias, E. (eds.) ICALP 2014. LNCS, vol. 8572, pp. 650–662. Springer, Heidelberg (2014). https://doi.org/10.1007/978-3-662-43948-7_54

48. Jafargholi, Z., Wichs, D.: Adaptive security of Yao's garbled circuits. In: Hirt, M., Smith, A. (eds.) TCC 2016. LNCS, vol. 9985, pp. 433–458. Springer, Heidelberg (2016). https://doi.org/10.1007/978-3-662-53641-4_17

49. Jawurek, M., Kerschbaum, F., Orlandi, C.: Zero-knowledge using garbled circuits: how to prove non-algebraic statements efficiently. In: CCS (2013)

50. Katz, J., Ostrovsky, R.: Round-optimal secure two-party computation. In: Franklin, M. (ed.) CRYPTO 2004. LNCS, vol. 3152, pp. 335–354. Springer, Heidelberg (2004). https://doi.org/10.1007/978-3-540-28628-8_21

51. Kiraz, M.S., Schoenmakers, B.: A protocol issue for the malicious case of Yao's garbled circuit construction. In: 27th Symposium on Information Theory in the Benelux (2006)

52. Launchbury, J., Archer, D., DuBuisson, T., Mertens, E.: Application-scale secure multiparty computation. In: Shao, Z. (ed.) ESOP 2014. LNCS, vol. 8410, pp. 8–26. Springer, Heidelberg (2014). https://doi.org/10.1007/978-3-642-54833-8_2

53. Launchbury, J., Diatchki, I.S., DuBuisson, T., Adams-Moran, A.: Efficient lookup-table protocol in secure multiparty computation. In: ACM SIGPLAN ICFP 2012 (2012)

54. Lindell, Y.: Fast cut-and-choose based protocols for malicious and covert adversaries. In: Canetti, R., Garay, J.A. (eds.) CRYPTO 2013. LNCS, vol. 8043, pp. 1–17. Springer, Heidelberg (2013). https://doi.org/10.1007/978-3-642-40084-1_1

55. Lindell, Y., Pinkas, B.: An efficient protocol for secure two-party computation in the presence of malicious adversaries. In: Naor, M. (ed.) EUROCRYPT 2007. LNCS, vol. 4515, pp. 52–78. Springer, Heidelberg (2007). https://doi.org/10.1007/978-3-540-72540-4_4

56. Lindell, Y., Pinkas, B.: A proof of security of Yao's protocol for two-party computation. J. Cryptol. (2009)
57. Lynch, N.A.: Distributed Algorithms. Morgan Kaufmann (1996)
58. Mohassel, P., Franklin, M.: Efficiency tradeoffs for malicious two-party computation. In: Yung, M., Dodis, Y., Kiayias, A., Malkin, T. (eds.) PKC 2006. LNCS, vol. 3958, pp. 458–473. Springer, Heidelberg (2006). https://doi.org/10.1007/11745853_30
59. Mohassel, P., Rosulek, M.: Non-interactive secure 2PC in the offline/online and batch settings. In: Coron, J.-S., Nielsen, J.B. (eds.) EUROCRYPT 2017. LNCS, vol. 10212, pp. 425–455. Springer, Cham (2017). https://doi.org/10.1007/978-3-319-56617-7_15
60. Mohassel, P., Rosulek, M., Zhang, Y.: Fast and secure three-party computation: the garbled circuit approach. In: ACM CCS (2015)
61. Mukherjee, P., Wichs, D.: Two round multiparty computation via multi-key FHE. In: Fischlin, M., Coron, J.-S. (eds.) EUROCRYPT 2016. LNCS, vol. 9666, pp. 735–763. Springer, Heidelberg (2016). https://doi.org/10.1007/978-3-662-49896-5_26
62. Patra, A., Choudhary, A., Rabin, T., Rangan, C.P.: The round complexity of verifiable secret sharing revisited. In: Halevi, S. (ed.) CRYPTO 2009. LNCS, vol. 5677, pp. 487–504. Springer, Heidelberg (2009). https://doi.org/10.1007/978-3-642-03356-8_29
63. Patra, A., Ravi, D.: On the exact round complexity of secure three-party computation. Cryptology ePrint Archive, Report 2018/481 (2018). https://eprint.iacr.org/2018/481
64. Rabin, T., Ben-Or, M.: Verifiable secret sharing and multiparty protocols with honest majority (extended abstract). In: ACM STOC (1989)
65. Rindal, P., Rosulek, M.: Faster malicious 2-party secure computation with online/offline dual execution. In: USENIX Security Symposium (2016)
66. Shelat, A., Shen, C.-H.: Fast two-party secure computation with minimal assumptions. In: ACM CCS (2013)
67. Yao, A.C.-C.: Protocols for secure computations (extended abstract). In: FOCS (1982)

Promise Zero Knowledge and Its Applications to Round Optimal MPC

Saikrishna Badrinarayanan[1]([✉]), Vipul Goyal[2], Abhishek Jain[3],
Yael Tauman Kalai[4], Dakshita Khurana[1], and Amit Sahai[1]

[1] UCLA, Los Angeles, USA
{saikrishna,dakshita,sahai}@cs.ucla.edu
[2] CMU, Pittsburgh, USA
goyal@cs.cmu.edu
[3] JHU, Baltimore, USA
abhishek@cs.jhu.edu
[4] Microsoft Research, MIT, Cambridge, USA
yael@microsoft.com

Abstract. We devise a new *partitioned simulation* technique for MPC where the simulator uses different strategies for simulating the view of aborting adversaries and non-aborting adversaries. The protagonist of this technique is a new notion of *promise zero knowledge* (ZK) where the ZK property only holds against non-aborting verifiers. We show how to realize promise ZK in three rounds in the simultaneous-message model assuming polynomially hard DDH (or QR or N^{th}-Residuosity).

We demonstrate the following applications of our new technique:

- We construct the first round-optimal (i.e., four round) MPC protocol for general functions based on polynomially hard DDH (or QR or N^{th}-Residuosity).
- We further show how to overcome the four-round barrier for MPC by constructing a three-round protocol for "list coin-tossing" – a slight relaxation of coin-tossing that suffices for most conceivable applications – based on polynomially hard DDH (or QR or N^{th}-Residuosity). This result generalizes to randomized input-less functionalities.

S. Badrinarayanan, D. Khurana and A. Sahai—Research supported in part from a DARPA/ARL SAFEWARE award, NSF Frontier Award 1413955, NSF grants 1619348, 1228984, 1136174, and 1065276, BSF grant 2012378, a Xerox Faculty Research Award, a Google Faculty Research Award, an equipment grant from Intel, and an Okawa Foundation Research Grant. This material is based upon work supported by the Defense Advanced Research Projects Agency through the ARL under Contract W911NF-15-C-0205. The views expressed are those of the authors and do not reflect the official policy or position of the Department of Defense, the National Science Foundation, or the U.S. Government. Fifth author's research also supported by the UCLA Dissertation Year Fellowship.

V. Goyal—Work supported in part by a grant from Northrop Grumman.

A. Jain—Supported in part by a DARPA/ARL Safeware Grant W911NF-15-C-0213, and a subaward from NSF CNS-1414023.

© International Association for Cryptologic Research 2018
H. Shacham and A. Boldyreva (Eds.): CRYPTO 2018, LNCS 10992, pp. 459–487, 2018.
https://doi.org/10.1007/978-3-319-96881-0_16

Previously, four round MPC protocols required sub-exponential-time hardness assumptions and no multi-party three-round protocols were known for any relaxed security notions with polynomial-time simulation against malicious adversaries.

In order to base security on polynomial-time standard assumptions, we also rely upon a *leveled rewinding security* technique that can be viewed as a polynomial-time alternative to leveled complexity leveraging for achieving "non-malleability" across different primitives.

1   Introduction

Provably secure protocols lie at the heart of the theory of cryptography. How can we design protocols, not only so that we cannot devise attacks against them, but so that we can *prove* that no such attacks exist (under well-studied complexity assumptions)? The goal of achieving a proof of security has presented many challenges and apparent trade-offs in secure protocol design. This is especially true with regards to the goal of minimizing rounds of interaction, which has been a long-standing driver of innovation in theoretical cryptography. We begin by focusing on one such challenge and apparent trade-off in the context of *zero-knowledge* (ZK) protocols [19], one of the most fascinating and broadly applicable notions in cryptography.

Recall that in a ZK protocol, a prover should convince a verifier that some statement is true, without revealing to the verifier anything beyond the validity of the statement being proven. It is known that achieving zero knowledge with black-box simulation[1] is impossible with three or fewer rounds of simultaneous message exchange [14,17]. A curious fact emerges, however, when we take a closer look at the proof of this impossibility result. It turns out that three-round ZK is impossible when considering verifiers that essentially behave completely honestly, but that sometimes probabilistically refuse to finish the protocol. This is bizarre: ZK protocols are supposed to prevent the verifier from learning information from the prover; how can behaving honestly but aborting the protocol early possibly help the verifier learn additional information? Indeed, one might think that we can prove that such behavior cannot possibly help the verifier learn additional information. Counter-intuitively, however, it turns out that such early aborts are critical to the impossibility proofs of [14,17]. This observation is the starting point for our work; now that we have identified a key (but counter-intuitive) reason behind the impossibility results, we want to leverage this understanding to bypass the impossibility result in a new and useful way.

---

[1] In this work, we focus on black-box simulation. However, no solutions for three-round ZK from standard assumptions with non-black-box simulation [2] are presently known either. [6] showed how to construct 3 round ZK using non-black-box simulation from the non-standard assumption that keyless multi-collision resistant hash functions exist.

Promise Zero Knowledge. Our main idea is to consider adversarial verifiers that promise not to abort the protocol early with noticeable probability. However, we do not limit ourselves only to adversarial verifiers that behave honestly; we consider adversarial verifiers that may deviate from the prescribed protocol arbitrarily, as long as this deviation does not cause the protocol to abort. A *promise zero-knowledge* protocol is one that satisfies the correctness and soundness guarantees of ordinary zero-knowledge protocols, but only satisfies the zero knowledge guarantee against adversarial verifiers that "promise" not to abort with noticeable probability. The centerpiece of our work is a construction of three-round promise zero-knowledge protocol, in the simultaneous message model, for proving statements where the statement need not be decided until the last (third) round, but where such statements should come from a distribution such that both a statement and a witness for that statement can be sampled in the last round. We call this primitive a *distributional delayed-input promise zero-knowledge argument.* Our construction requires only on DDH/QR/N^{th}-Residuosity assumption. Interestingly, in our construction, we rely upon information learned from the verifier in the third round, to simulate its view in the third round!

Partitioned Simulation, and Applications to MPC. But why should we care about promise ZK? Actual adversaries will not make any promise regarding what specific types of adversarial behavior they will or will not engage in. However, recall our initial insight – early aborting by an adversary should, generally speaking, only hurt the adversary, not help it. We know due to the impossibility results of [14,17], that we cannot leverage this insight to achieve three-round standard ZK (with black-box simulation). Our goal instead, then, is to use our insight to replace ZK with promise ZK for the construction of other secure protocols. Specifically, we consider the most general goal of secure protocol design: secure multi-party computation (MPC), as we discuss further below.

To do so, we devise a novel *partitioned simulation* strategy for leveraging promise ZK. At a high-level, we split the simulation into two disjoint cases, *depending upon whether or not the adversary is an aborting adversary* (i.e., one who aborts with high probability). In one case, we will exploit promise ZK. In the other, we exploit the intuition that early aborting should only harm the adversary, to devise alternate simulation strategies that bypass the need for ZK altogether, and instead essentially rely on a weaker notion called strong witness indistinguishability, that was recently constructed in three rounds (in the "delayed-input" setting) in [24].

Secure Multi-Party Computation. The notion of secure multiparty computation (MPC) [18,34] is a unifying framework for general secure protocols. MPC allows mutually distrusting parties to jointly evaluate any efficiently computable function on their private inputs in such a manner that each party does not learn anything beyond the output of the function.

The round complexity of MPC has been extensively studied over the last three decades in a long sequence of works [1,4,7,8,14,18,20,25,26,29]. In this work, we study the problem of *round-optimal* MPC against malicious adversaries who may corrupt an arbitrary subset of parties, in the plain model without any trust assumptions. The state-of-the-art results on round-optimal MPC for general functions are due to Ananth et al. [1] and Brakerski et al. [7], both of which rely on sub-exponential-time hardness assumptions. (See Sect. 1.2 for a more elaborate discussion on related works.) Our goal, instead is to base security on standard, *polynomial-time* assumptions.

We now highlight the main challenge in basing security on polynomial-time assumptions. In the setting of four round protocols in the simultaneous-message model, a rushing adversary may always choose to abort after receiving the honest party messages in the last round. At this point, the adversary has already received enough information to obtain the purported output of the function being computed. This suggests that we must enforce "honest behavior" on the parties within the first three rounds in order to achieve security against malicious adversaries. As discussed above, three-round zero knowledge is impossible, and this is precisely why we look to our new notion of promise ZK and partitioned simulation to resolve this challenge.

However, this challenge is exacerbated in the setting of MPC as we must not only enforce honest behavior but also ensure non-malleability *across different cryptographic primitives* that are being executed in parallel within the first three rounds. We show how to combine our notions of promise ZK with new simulation ideas to overcome these challenges, relying only on polynomial-time assumptions.

Coin Tossing. Coin-tossing allows two or more participants to agree on an unbiased coin (or a sequence of unbiased coins). Fair multiparty coin-tossing is known to be impossible in the dishonest majority setting [10]. Therefore, while current notions of *secure coin-tossing* require that the protocol have a (pseudo)-random outcome, the adversary is additionally allowed to abort depending on the outcome of the toss.

Presently, secure multiparty coin-tossing is known to require at least four rounds w.r.t. black-box simulation [14, 25]. In this work, we seek to overcome this barrier.

Towards this, our key observation is that coin-tossing is perfectly suited for application of partitioned simulation. The definition of secure coin-tossing roughly requires the existence of a simulator that successfully forces externally sampled random coin, and produces a distribution over adversary's views that is indistinguishable from a real execution. To account for the adversary aborting or misbehaving based on the outcome, the simulator is allowed to either force an external coin, or force an abort as long as the simulated distribution remains indistinguishable from the real one. Crucially, in the case of an adversary that always aborts before the end of the protocol, the prescribed output of any secure coin-tossing protocol is also abort: therefore, the simulator never needs to force *any external coin* against such an adversary! Simulating the view of such adversaries that always abort is thus completely trivial. This leaves the case of non-aborting adversaries, which is exactly the setting that promise ZK was designed for.

Using promise ZK, we design a three-round protocol for "list coin-tossing" – a notion that is slightly weaker that regular coin-tossing, but nevertheless, suffices for nearly all important applications of coin-tossing (see below for a discussion). Therefore, promise ZK gives us a way to overcome the four-round barrier for secure coin-tossing [14,25].

1.1   Our Results

We introduce the notion of promise ZK proof systems and devise a new partitioned simulation strategy for round-efficient MPC protocols. Our first result is a three-round distributional delayed-input promise ZK argument system based on DDH/QR/N^{th}-Residuosity.

Theorem 1 (Informal). *Assuming DDH/QR/N^{th}-Residuosity, there exists a three round distributional delayed-input promise ZK argument system in the simultaneous-message model.*

Round-Optimal MPC. We present two applications of partitioned simulation to round-optimal MPC. We first devise a general compiler that converts any three-round semi-malicious MPC protocol, where the first round is public-coin (i.e., the honest parties simply send random strings in the first round), into a four-round malicious secure MPC protocol. Our compiler can be instantiated with standard assumptions such as DDH or Quadratic Residuosity or N^{th}-Residuosity. The resulting protocol is optimal in the number of rounds w.r.t. black-box simulation [14]. A three round semi-malicious protocol with the aforementioned property can be obtained based on DDH/QR/N^{th} Residuosity [5,15].

Theorem 2 (Informal). *Assuming DDH/QR/N^{th}-Residuosity, there exists a four round MPC protocol for general functions with black-box simulation.*

List Coin-Tossing. We also study the feasibility of multiparty coin-tossing in only three rounds. While three round coin-tossing is known to be impossible [14], somewhat surprisingly, we show that a slightly relaxed variant that we refer to as *list coin-tossing* is, in fact, possible in only three rounds.

Very briefly, in list coin-tossing, the simulator is allowed to receive polynomially many random string samples from the ideal functionality (where the exact polynomial may depend upon the adversary), and it may choose any one of them as its output. It is not difficult to see that this notion already suffices for most conceivable applications of coin-tossing, such as implementing a common random string setup. For example, consider the setting where we want to generate a CRS in the setup algorithm of a non-interactive zero knowledge (NIZK) argument system. Now, in the ideal world, instead of running a simulator which "forces" one particular random string given by the ideal functionality, we can substitute it with the simulator of a list coin tossing protocol that receives polynomially many random strings from the ideal functionality and "forces" one of them as the CRS. This would still suffice for the NIZK argument system.

We achieve the following result:

Theorem 3 (Informal). *Assuming $DDH/QR/N^{th}$-Residuosity, there exists a three round multiparty list coin-tossing protocol with black-box simulation. This can be generalized to randomized inputless functionalities where security is defined analogously to list coin-tossing.*

Finally, we note that by applying the transformation[2] of [14] on the protocol from Theorem 3 for the two-party case, we can obtain a four round two-party list coin-tossing protocol in the *unidirectional-message* model. This result overcomes the barrier of five rounds for standard two-party coin-tossing established by [25].

Corollary 1 (Informal). *Assuming $DDH/QR/N^{th}$-Residuosity, there exists a four round two-party list coin-tossing protocol in the unidirectional-message model with black-box simulation.*

Leveled Rewinding Security. While promise ZK addresses the issue of proving honest behavior within three rounds, it does not address non-malleability issues that typically plague security proofs of constant-round protocols in the simultaneous-message model. In particular, when multiple primitives are being executed in parallel, we need to ensure that they are non-malleable w.r.t. each other. For example, we may require that a primitive A remains "secure" while the simulator (or a reduction) is (say) trying to extract adversary's input from primitive B via rewinding.

In the works of [1,7], such issues are addressed by using complexity leveraging. In particular, they rely upon multiple levels of complexity leveraging to establish non-malleability relationships across primitives, e.g., by setting the security parameters such that primitive X is more secure than primitive Y that is more secure than primitive Z, and so on. Such a use a complexity leveraging is, in fact, quite common in the setting of limited rounds (see, e.g., [9]).

We instead rely upon a *leveled rewinding security* technique to avoid the use of complexity leveraging and base security on polynomial-time assumptions. Roughly, in our constructions, primitives have various levels of "bounded rewinding" security that are carefully crafted so that they enable non-malleability relationships across primitives, while still enabling rewinding-based simulation and reductions. E.g., a primitive X may be insecure w.h.p. against 1 rewind, however, another primitive Y may be secure against 1 rewind but insecure against 2 rewinds. Yet another primitive Z may be secure against 2 rewinds but insecure against 3 rewinds, and so on. We remark that leveled rewinding security with a "single level" was previously used in [22]; here we extend this idea to "multiple levels".

---

[2] The work of Garg et al. [14] establishes an impossibility result for three round multiparty coin-tossing by transforming any three round two-party coin-tossing protocol in the simultaneous-message model into a four round two-party coin-tossing protocol in the unidirectional-message model, and then invoking [25] who proved the impossibility of four round two-party coin-tossing.

1.2 Related Work

Concurrent Work. In a concurrent and independent work, Halevi et al. [23] construct a four round MPC protocol against malicious adversaries in the plain model based on different assumptions than ours. In particular, they rely upon enhanced trapdoor permutations and public-key encryption schemes that admit affine homomorphisms with equivocation (which in turn can be based on LWE/DDH/QR; see [23]). They do not consider the problems of promise ZK and list coin-tossing. We discuss more related work in the full version of the paper.

2 Technical Overview

In this section, we provide an overview of the main ideas underlying our results.

2.1 Promise Zero Knowledge

Recall that the notion of promise ZK is defined in the simultaneous-message model, where in every round, both the prover and the verifier send a message simultaneously.[3] Crucially, the ZK property is only defined w.r.t. a set of admissible verifiers that promise to send a "valid" non-aborting message in the last round with some noticeable probability.

We construct a three round distributional promise ZK protocol with black-box simulation based on DDH/QR/N^{th}-Residuosity. We work in the delayed-input setting where the statement being proven is revealed to the (adversarial) verifier only in the last round.[4] Further, we work in the distributional setting, where statements being proven are sampled from an efficiently sampleable public distribution, i.e., it is possible to efficiently sample a statement together with a witness.

For simplicity of presentation, here we describe our construction using an additional assumption of two-round WI proofs, a.k.a. Zaps [12]. In our actual construction of promise ZK, we replace the Zaps with three round delayed-input WI proofs with some additional security guarantees that we construct based on Assuming DDH/QR/N^{th}-Residuosity.[5]

---

[3] An adversarial prover or verifier can be rushing, i.e., it may wait to receive a message from the honest party in any round before sending its own message in that round.

[4] In our actual construction, we consider a slightly more general setting where a statement x has two parts (x_1, x_2): the first part x_1 is revealed in the second round while the second part x_2 is revealed in the third round. This generalization is used in our applications of promise ZK, but we ignore it here for simplicity of presentation.

[5] In particular, replacing Zaps with delayed-input WI proofs relies on *leveled rewinding security* technique with multiple levels that we describe in Sect. 2.2. We do not discuss it here to avoid repetition.

Our construction of promise ZK roughly follows the FLS paradigm [13] for ZK:

- First, the prover and the verifier engage in a three round "trapdoor generation phase" that determines a secret "trapdoor" that is known to the verifier but not the prover.
- Next, in a proof phase, the prover commits to 0 in a (three round) delayed-input extractable commitment and proves via a Zap that either the purported statement is true or that it committed to the trapdoor (instead of 0).

By appropriately parallelizing both of these phases, we obtain a three round protocol in the simultaneous-message model. Below, we discuss the challenges in proving soundness and promise ZK properties.

Proving Soundness. In order to argue soundness, a natural strategy is to rewind the cheating prover in the second and third round to extract the value it has committed in the extractable commitment. If this value is the trapdoor, then we can (hopefully) break the hiding property of the trapdoor generation phase to obtain a contradiction. Unfortunately, this strategy doesn't work as is since the trapdoor generation phase is parallelized with the extractable commitment. Thus, while extracting from the extractable commitment, we may inadvertently also break the security of the trapdoor generation phase! Indeed, this is the key problem that arises in the construction of non-malleable protocols.

To address this, we observe that in order to prove soundness, it suffices to extract the trapdoor from the cheating prover with some noticeable probability (as opposed to overwhelming probability). Now, suppose that the extractable commitment scheme is such that it is possible to extract the committed value via k rewinds (for some small integer k) if the "main thread" of execution is non-aborting with noticeable probability. Then, we can still argue soundness if the trapdoor generation has a stronger hiding property, namely, security under k rewinds (but is insecure under more than k rewinds to enable simulation; see below). This is an example of leveled rewinding security technique with a single level; later we discuss its application with multiple levels.

We note that standard extractable commitment schemes such as [31,32] (as well as their delayed-input variants) achieve the above extraction property for $k = 1$. This means that we only require the trapdoor generation phase to maintain hiding property under 1 rewinding. Such a scheme can be easily constructed from one-way functions.

Proving Promise ZK. In order to prove the promise ZK property, we construct a simulator that learns information from the verifier in the third round, in order to simulate its view in the third round! Roughly, our simulator first creates multiple "look-ahead" execution threads[6] with the adversarial verifier in order to extract the trapdoor from the trapdoor generation phase. Note that unlike

---

[6] Throughout, whenever the simulator rewinds, we call each rewound execution a look-ahead thread. The messages that are eventually output by the simulator constitute the main thread.

typical ZK protocols where such a look-ahead thread only consists of partial protocol transcript, in our case, each look-ahead thread must contain a full protocol execution since the trapdoor generation phase completes in the third round.

Now, since the adversarial verifier may be rushing, the simulator must first provide its third round message (namely, the second message of Zap) on each look-ahead thread in order to learn the verifier's third round message. Since the simulator does not have a trapdoor yet, the only possibility for the simulator to prepare a valid third round message is by behaving honestly. However, the simulator does not have a witness for the statement proven by the honest prover. Thus, it may seem that we have run into a circularity.

This is where the distributional aspect of our notion comes to the rescue. Specifically, on the look-ahead execution threads, the simulator simply samples a fresh statement together with a witness from the distribution and proves the validity of the statement like an honest prover. Once it has extracted the trapdoor, it uses its knowledge to cheat (only) on the main thread (but continues to behave honestly on each look-ahead thread).[7]

2.2   Four Round Secure Multiparty Computation

We now describe the main ideas underlying our compiler from any three round semi-malicious MPC protocol Π (where the first round is public coin) to a four round malicious-secure MPC protocol Σ. For simplicity of presentation, in the discussion below, we ignore the first round of Π, and simply treat it as a *two round* protocol.

Starting Ideas. Similar to several previous works, our starting idea is to follow the GMW paradigm [18] for malicious security. This entails two main steps: (1) Enabling extraction of adversary's inputs, and (2) Forcing honest behavior on the adversary in each round of Π. A natural idea to implement the first step is to require each party to commit to its input and randomness via a three round extractable commitment protocol. To force honest behavior, we require each party to give a delayed-input ZK proof together with every message of Π to establish that it is "consistent" with the input and randomness committed in the extractable commitment.

In order to obtain a four-round protocol Σ, we need to parallelize all of these sub-protocols appropriately. This means that while the proof for the second message of Π can be given via a four round (delayed-input) regular ZK proof, we need a *three round* proof system to prove the well-formedness of the first message of Π. However, as discussed earlier, three-round ZK proofs are known to be impossible w.r.t. black-box simulation [14,17] and even with non-black box simulation, are not known from standard assumptions.

Promise ZK and Partitioned Simulation. While [1,7] tackled this issue by using sub-exponential hardness, we address it via partitioned simulation to base

---

[7] The idea of using a witness to continue simulation is an old one [3]. Most recently, [24] used this idea in the distributional setting.

security on polynomial-time assumptions. Specifically, we use different mechanisms for proving honest behavior depending upon whether or not the adversary is aborting in the third round. For now, let us focus on the case where the adversary does not abort in the third round of Σ; later we discuss the aborting adversary case.

For the non-aborting case, we rely upon a three-round (delayed-input) distributional promise ZK to prove well-formedness of the first message of Π. As we discuss below, however, integrating promise ZK in our construction involves overcoming several technical challenges due to specific properties of the promise ZK simulator (in particular, its requirement to behave honestly in look-ahead threads).[8] We also remark that in our actual construction, to address non-malleability concerns [11], the promise ZK and the standard ZK protocols that we use are suitably "hardened" using three-round non-malleable commitments [21,27] to achieve *simulation soundness* [33] in order to ensure that the proofs given by the adversarial parties remain sound even when the proofs given by honest parties are simulated. For simplicity of discussion, however, here we largely ignore this point, and instead focus on the technical ideas that are more unique to our construction.

We now proceed to discuss the main technical challenges underlying our construction and its proof of security.

How to do "Non-Malleable" Input Extraction? Let us start with the issue of extraction of adversary's input and trapdoors (for simulation of ZK proofs). In the aforementioned protocol design, in order to extract adversary's input and trapdoors, the simulator rewinds the second and third rounds. Note, however, that this process also rewinds the input commitments of the honest parties since they are executed in parallel. This poses the following fundamental challenge: we must somehow maintain privacy of honest party's inputs *even under rewinds*, while still extracting the inputs of the adversarial parties.

A plausible strategy to address this issue is to cheat in the rewound executions by sending random third round messages in the input commitment protocol on behalf of each honest party. This effectively nullifies the effect of rewinding on the honest party input commitments. However, in order to implement such a strategy, we need the ability to cheat in the ZK proofs since they are proving "well-formedness" of the input commitments.[9]

Unfortunately, such a strategy is not viable in our setting. As discussed in the previous subsection, in order to simulate the promise ZK on the main thread, the simulator must behave "honestly" on the rewound execution threads. This suggests that we cannot simply "sidestep" the issue of rewinding and instead must somehow make the honest party input commitments immune to rewinding.

---

[8] Our construction of four round MPC, in fact, uses promise ZK in a non-black-box manner for technical reasons. We ignore this point here as it is not important to the discussion.

[9] Indeed, [1] implement such a strategy in their security proof by relying on sub-exponential hardness assumptions.

Yet, we must do this while still keeping the adversary input commitments extractable. Thus, it may seem that we have reached an impasse.

Leveled Rewinding Security to the Rescue. In order to break the symmetry between input commitments of honest and adversarial parties, we use the following sequence of observations:

- The security of the honest party input commitments is only invoked when we switch from a hybrid experiment (say) H_i to another experiment H_{i+1} inside our security proof. In order to argue indistinguishability of H_i and H_{i+1} by contradiction, it suffices to build an adversary that breaks the security of honest party input commitments with some noticeable probability (as opposed to overwhelming probability).
- This means that the reduction only needs to generate the view of the adversary in hybrids H_i and H_{i+1} with some noticeable probability. This, in turn, means that the reduction only needs to successfully extract the adversary's inputs and trapdoor (for generating its view) with noticeable probability.
- Now, recall that the trapdoor generation phase used in our promise ZK construction is secure against one rewind. However, if we rewind two times, then we can extract the trapdoor with noticeable probability.
- Now, suppose that we can construct an input commitment protocol that maintains hiding property even if it is rewound two times, but guarantees extraction with noticeable probability if it is rewound three times. Given such a commitment scheme, we resolve the above problem as follows: the reduction rewinds the adversary three times, which ensures that with noticeable probability, it can extract *both* the trapdoor and the inputs from the adversary. In the first two rewound executions, the reduction generates the third round messages of the honest party input commitments honestly. At this point, the reduction already has the trapdoor. Now, in the third rewound execution, it generates random third messages in the honest party input commitments and uses the knowledge of the trapdoor to cheat in the proof.

The above strategy allows us to extract the adversary's inputs with noticeable probability while still maintaining privacy of honest party inputs. To complete this idea, we construct a new extractable commitment scheme from injective one-way functions that achieves the desired "bounded-rewinding security" property.

Taking a step back, note that in order to implement the above strategy, we created two levels of rewinding security: while the trapdoor generation phase is secure against one rewind (but insecure against two rewinds), the input commitment protocol is secure against two rewinds (but insecure against three rewinds). We refer to this technique as *leveled rewinding security* with multiple levels, and this is precisely what allows us to avoid the use of leveled complexity leveraging.

Using Promise ZK. In the works of [1,7], the simulator behaves honestly in the first three rounds using random inputs for the honest parties. *We depart from this proof strategy, and instead, require our simulator to cheat even in the first three* *rounds on the main thread.*[10] Indeed, such a simulation strategy seems necessary for our case since the recent two-round semi-malicious MPC protocols of [5, 15] – which we use to instantiate our compiler – require a cheating simulation strategy even in the first round.

To implement this proof strategy, we turn to promise ZK. However, recall that promise ZK simulator works by behaving honestly in the look-ahead threads. When applied to our MPC construction, this means that we must find a way to behave honestly on the look-ahead threads that are used for extracting inputs and trapdoors from the adversary. However, at first it is not immediately clear how to implement such a strategy. Clearly, our final simulator cannot use honest party inputs on the look-ahead threads to behave honestly.

Instead, our simulator uses random inputs to behave honestly on the look-ahead threads. The main challenge then is to argue that when we switch from using real honest inputs (in an intermediate hybrid) to random inputs on the look-ahead threads, the probability of extraction of adversary's inputs and trapdoors remains unchanged. Crucially, here, we do not need to consider a joint view across all the look-ahead threads, and instead, it suffices to argue the indistinguishability of adversary's view on each look-ahead thread (when we switch from real input to random input) one at a time. We rely upon techniques from the work of Jain et al. [24] for this indistinguishability argument. The same proof technique is also used to argue security in the case when the adversary aborts in the third round with overwhelming probability. We discuss this next.

Aborting Adversary Case. In the case where the adversary aborts in the third round with overwhelming probability, we cannot rely upon promise ZK since there is no hope for extraction from such an aborting adversary (which is necessary for simulating promise ZK). Therefore, in this case, the simulator simply behave honestly on the main thread using random inputs (as in [1,7]). The main challenge then is to switch in an indistinguishable manner from honest behavior in the first three rounds using real inputs to honest behavior using random inputs, while relying only on polynomial-time assumptions.

We address this case by relying upon techniques from [24]. We remark that we cannot directly use the three-round strong WI argument system of [24] since it requires the instance being proven to be disclosed to the verifier only in the third round of the protocol. This is not true in our case, since the instance also consists of the transcript of the three-round extractable commitment (and other sub-protocols like the trapdoor generation). Nevertheless, we are able to use ideas from [24] in a non-black-box manner to enable our security proof; we refer the reader to the technical sections for more details.

Other Issues. We note that since our partitioned simulation technique crucially relies upon identifying whether an adversary is aborting or not, we have to take precaution during simulation to avoid the possibility of the simulator running in

---

[10] We emphasize that this strategy is only used in the case where the adversary does not abort in the third round. As we discuss below, we use a different strategy in the aborting adversary case.

exponential time. For this reason, we use ideas first developed in [17] and later used in many subsequent works, to ensure that the running time of our simulator is expected polynomial-time.

Finally, we note that the above discussion is oversimplified, and omits several technical points. We refer the reader to the technical sections for full details.

2.3 List Coin-Tossing

We now describe the main ideas underlying our construction of three round multiparty list coin-tossing. We start by describing the basic structure of our protocol:

- We start with a two-round semi-honest multiparty coin-tossing protocol based on injective one-way functions. Such a protocol can be constructed as follows: In the first round, each party i commits to a string r_i chosen uniformly at random, using a non-interactive commitment scheme. In the second round, each party reveals r_i without the decommitment information. The output is simply the XOR of all the r_i values.
- To achieve malicious security, we "compile" the above semi-honest protocol with a (delayed-input) distributional promise ZK protocol. Roughly speaking, in the third round, each party i now proves that the value r_i is the one it had committed earlier. By parallelizing the two sub-protocols appropriately, we obtain a three round protocol.

We first note that as in the case of our four round MPC protocol, here also we need to "harden" the promise ZK protocol with non-malleability properties. We do so by constructing a three-round simulation-extractable promise ZK based on DDH/QR/N^{th}-Residuosity and then using it in the above compiler. Nevertheless, for simplicity of discussion, we do not dwell on this issue here, and refer the reader to the technical sections for further details.

We now describe the main ideas underlying our simulation technique. As in the case of four round MPC, we use partitioned simulation strategy to split the simulation into two cases, depending upon whether the adversary aborts or not in the third round.

Aborting Case. If the adversary aborts in the third round, then the simulator simply behaves honestly using a uniformly random string r_i on behalf of each honest party i. Unlike the four round MPC case, indistinguishability can be argued here in a straightforward manner since the simulated transcript is identically distributed as a real transcript. The main reason why such a strategy works is that since the parties do not have any input, there is no notion of "correct output" that the simulator needs to enforce on the (aborting) adversary. This is also true for any randomized inputless functionality, and indeed for this reason, our result extends to such functionalities. Note, however, that this is not true for general functionalities where each party has an input.

Non-Aborting Case. We next consider the case where the adversary does not abort in the third round with noticeable probability. Note that in this case, when one execution thread completes, the simulator learns the random strings r_j committed to by the adversarial parties by simply observing the adversary's message in the third round.

At this point, the simulator queries the ideal functionality to obtain the random output (say) R and then attempts to "force" it on the adversary. This involves simulating the simulation-extractable promise ZK and sending a "programmed" value r_i' on behalf of one of the honest parties so that it leads to the desired output R. Now, since the adversary does not abort in the last round with noticeable probability, it would seem that after a polynomial number of trials, the simulator should succeed in forcing the output. At this point, it may seem that we have successfully constructed a three round multiparty coin-tossing protocol, which would contradict the lower bound of [14]!

We now explain the flaw in the above argument. As is typical to security with abort, an adversary's aborting behavior may depend upon the output it receives in the last round. For example, it may always choose to abort if it receives an output that starts with 00. Thus, if the simulator attempts to repeatedly force the same random output on the adversary, it may never succeed.

This is where list coin-tossing comes into the picture. In list coin-tossing, the simulator obtains a polynomial number of random strings from the ideal functionality, as opposed to a single string in regular coin-tossing. Our simulator attempts to force each of (polynomially many) random strings one-by-one on the adversary, in the manner as explained above. Now, each of the trials are independent, and therefore the simulator is guaranteed to succeed in forcing one of the random strings after a polynomial number of attempts.

Organization. We define some preliminaries in Sect. 3 and some building blocks for our protocols in Sect. 4. In Sect. 5, we define and construct Simulation-Extractable Promise ZK. Due to lack of space, our three round List Coin Tossing protocol and our four round maliciously secure MPC protocol are described in the full version of the paper.

3   Preliminaries

Here, we recall some preliminaries that will be useful in the rest of the paper. Throughout this paper, we will use λ to denote the security parameter, and $\mathsf{negl}(\lambda)$ to denote any function that is asymptotically smaller than $\frac{1}{\mathsf{poly}(\lambda)}$ for any polynomial $\mathsf{poly}(\cdot)$. We will use PPT to describe a probabilistic polynomial time machine. We will also use the words "rounds" and "messages" interchangeably, whenever clear from context.

3.1   Secure Multiparty Computation

In this work we follow the standard real/ideal world paradigm for defining secure multi-party computation. We refer the reader to [16] for the precise definition.

Semi-malicious adversary. An adversary is said to be semi-malicious if it follows the protocol correctly, but with potentially maliciously chosen randomness.

3.2 Delayed-Input Interactive Arguments

In this section, we describe delayed-input interactive arguments.

Definition 1 (Delayed-Input Interactive Arguments). *An n-round delayed-input interactive protocol* (P, V) *for deciding a language* L *is an argument system for* L *that satisfies the following properties:*

- **Delayed-Input Completeness.** *For every security parameter* $\lambda \in \mathbb{N}$, *and any* $(x, w) \in R_L$ *such that* $|x| \leq 2^\lambda$,

$$\Pr[(P, V)(1^\lambda, x, w) = 1] = 1 - \mathsf{negl}(\lambda).$$

  where the probability is over the randomness of P *and* V. *Moreover, the prover's algorithm initially takes as input only* 1^λ, *and the pair* (x, w) *is given to* P *only in the beginning of the* n'th *round.*
- **Delayed-Input Soundness.** *For any PPT cheating prover* P^* *that chooses* x^* *(adaptively) after the first* $n - 1$ *messages, it holds that if* $x^* \notin L$ *then*

$$\Pr[(P^*, V)(1^\lambda, x^*) = 1] = \mathsf{negl}(\lambda).$$

  where the probability is over the random coins of V.

Remark 1. We note that in a delayed-input interactive argument satisfying Definition 1, completeness and soundness also hold when (part of) the instance is available in the first $(n - 1)$ rounds.

We will also consider delayed-input interactive arguments in the simultaneous-message setting, that satisfy soundness against rushing adversaries.

3.3 Extractable Commitments

Here onwards until Sect. 5, we will discuss protocols where only one party sends a message in any round.

Definition 2 (Extractable Commitments). *Consider any statistically binding, computationally hiding commitment scheme* $\langle C, R \rangle$. *Let* $\mathsf{Trans}\langle C(m, r_C),$ $R(r_R)\rangle$ *denote a commitment transcript with committer input* m, *committer randomness* r_C *and receiver randomness* r_R, *and let* $\mathsf{Decom}(\tau, m, r_C)$ *denote the algorithm that on input a commitment transcript* τ, *committer message* m *and randomness* r_C *outputs 1 or 0 to denote whether or not the decommitment was accepted (we explicitly require the decommitment phase to not require receiver randomness* r_R). *Then* $\langle C, R \rangle$ *is said to be extractable if there exists an expected PPT oracle algorithm* $\mathcal{E}$, *such that for any PPT cheating committer* C^* *the following holds.*

Let $\mathsf{Trans}\langle C^*, R(r_R)\rangle$ denote a transcript of the interaction between C^* and R. Then $\mathcal{E}^{C^*}(\mathsf{Trans}\langle C^*, R(r_R)\rangle)$ outputs m, r_C such that over the randomness of $\mathcal{E}$ and of sampling $\mathsf{Trans}\langle C^*, R(r_R)\rangle$:

$$\Pr[(\exists \widetilde{m} \neq m, \widetilde{r}_C) \text{ such that } \mathsf{Decom}(\tau, \widetilde{m}, \widetilde{r}_C) = 1] = \mathsf{negl}(\lambda)$$

Remark 2. The notion of extraction described in Definition 2 is often referred to as over-extraction. This is because the extractor $\mathcal{E}$ is allowed to output any arbitrary value if $\mathsf{Trans}\langle C^*, R(r_R)\rangle$ does not contain a commitment to any valid message. On the other hand, if $\mathsf{Trans}\langle C^*, R(r_R)\rangle$ is a valid commitment to some message m, $\mathcal{E}$ must output the correct committed message m.

Definition 3 (k-Extractable Commitments). *An extractable commitment satisfying Definition 2 is said to be k-extractable if there exists a polynomial $p(\cdot)$ such that the extractor $\mathcal{E}^{C^*}(\mathsf{Trans}\langle C^*, R(r_R)\rangle)$ with $k-1$ queries to C^*, outputs m, r_C such that over the randomness of $\mathcal{E}$ and of sampling $\mathsf{Trans}\langle C^*, R(r_R)\rangle$:*

$$\Pr[\mathsf{Decom}(\tau, m, r_C) = 1] \geq p(\lambda)$$

Delayed-Input Extractable Commitments. We say that an extractable commitment is *delayed-input* if the committer uses the input message m only in the last round of the protocol.

Theorem 4. *[31,32] For any constant $K > 0$, assuming injective one-way functions, there exists a three round delayed-input K-extractable commitment scheme satisfying Definition 3.*

3.4 Non-Malleable Commitments

We start with the definition of non-malleable commitments by Pass and Rosen [30] and further refined by Lin et al. [28] and Goyal [20]. (All of these definitions build upon the original definition of Dwork et al. [11]).

In the real experiment, a man-in-the-middle adversary MIM interacts with a committer C in the left session, and with a receiver R in the right session. Without loss of generality, we assume that each session has identities or tags, and require non-malleability only when the tag for the left session is different from the tag for the right session.

At the start of the experiment, the committer C receives an input val and MIM receives an auxiliary input z, which might contain a priori information about val. Let $\mathsf{MIM}_{\langle C,R\rangle}(\mathsf{val}, z)$ be a random variable that describes the value $\widetilde{\mathsf{val}}$ committed by MIM in the right session, jointly with the view of MIM in the real experiment.

In the ideal experiment, a PPT simulator $\mathcal{S}$ directly interacts with MIM. Let $\mathsf{Sim}_{\langle C,R\rangle}(1^\lambda, z)$ denote the random variable describing the value $\widetilde{\mathsf{val}}$ committed to by $\mathcal{S}$ and the output view of $\mathcal{S}$.

In either of the two experiments, if the tags in the left and right interaction are equal, then the value $\widetilde{\mathsf{val}}$ committed in the right interaction, is defined to be $\perp$.

We define a strengthened version of non-malleable commitments for use in this paper.

Definition 4 (Special Non-malleable Commitments). *A three round commitment scheme* $\langle C, R \rangle$ *is said to be special non-malleable if:*

- *For every* synchronizing[11] *PPT MIM, there exists a PPT simulator* S *such that the following ensembles are computationally indistinguishable:*

$$\{\mathsf{MIM}_{\langle C,R \rangle}(\mathsf{val}, z)\}_{\lambda \in \mathbb{N}, \mathsf{val} \in \{0,1\}^\lambda, z \in \{0,1\}^*} \text{ and } \{\mathsf{Sim}_{\langle C,R \rangle}(1^\lambda, z)\}_{\lambda \in \mathbb{N}, \mathsf{val} \in \{0,1\}^\lambda, z \in \{0,1\}^*}$$

- $\langle C, R \rangle$ *is delayed-input, that is, correctness holds even when the committer obtains his input only in the last round.*
- $\langle C, R \rangle$ *satisfies* last-message pseudorandomness, *that is, for every non-uniform PPT receiver* R^*, *it holds that* $\{\mathsf{REAL}_0^{R^*}(1^\lambda)\}_\lambda$ *and* $\{\mathsf{REAL}_1^{R^*}(1^\lambda)\}_\lambda$ *are computationally indistinguishable, where for* $b \in \{0,1\}$, *the random variable* $\mathsf{REAL}_b^{R^*}(1^\lambda)$ *is defined via the following experiment.*
  1. *Run* $C(1^\lambda)$ *and denote its output by* (com_1, σ), *where* σ *is its secret state, and* com_1 *is the message to be sent to the receiver.*
  2. *Run the receiver* $R^*(1^\lambda, \mathsf{com}_1)$, *who outputs a message* com_2.
  3. *If* $b = 0$, *run* $C(\sigma, \mathsf{com}_2)$ *and send its message* com_3 *to* R^*. *Otherwise, if* $b = 1$, *compute* $\mathsf{com}_3 \xleftarrow{\$} \{0,1\}^m$ *and send it to* R^*. *Here* $m = m(\lambda)$ *denotes* $|\mathsf{com}_3|$.
  4. *The output of the experiment is the output of* R^*.
- $\langle C, R \rangle$ *satisfies* 2-extractability *according to Definition 3.*

Goyal et al. [21] construct three-round special non-malleable commitments satisfying Definition 4 based on injective OWFs.

Imported Theorem 1 ([21]). *Assuming injective one-way functions, there exists a three round non-malleable commitment satisfying Definition 4.*

4   Building Blocks

We now describe some of the building blocks we use in our constructions.

4.1   Trapdoor Generation Protocol

In this section, we define and construct a primitive called Trapdoor Generation Protocol. In such a protocol, a sender S (a.k.a. trapdoor generator) communicates with a receiver R. The protocol satisfies two properties: (i) Sender security, i.e., no cheating PPT receiver can learn a valid trapdoor, and (ii) Extraction, i.e., there exists an expected PPT algorithm (a.k.a. extractor) that can extract a trapdoor from an adversarial sender via rewinding.

---

[11] A synchronizing adversary is one that sends its message for every round before obtaining the honest party's message for the next round.

We construct a three-round trapdoor generation protocol where the first message sent by the sender determines the set of valid trapdoors, and in the next two rounds the sender proves that indeed it knows a valid trapdoor. Such schemes are known in the literature based on various assumptions [8,31,32]. Here, we consider trapdoor generation protocols with a stronger sender security requirement that we refer to as *1-rewinding security*. Below, we formally define this notion and then proceed to give a three-round construction based on one-way functions. Our construction is a minor variant of the trapdoor generation protocol from [8].

Syntax. A trapdoor generation protocol

$$\mathsf{TDGen} = (\mathsf{TDGen}_1, \mathsf{TDGen}_2, \mathsf{TDGen}_3, \mathsf{TDOut}, \mathsf{TDValid}, \mathsf{TDExt})$$

is a three round protocol between two parties - a sender (trapdoor generator) S and receiver R that proceeds as below.

1. **Round 1 - $\mathsf{TDGen}_1(\cdot)$:**
   S computes and sends $\mathsf{td}_1^{S \to R} \leftarrow \mathsf{TDGen}_1(r_S)$ using a random string r_S.
2. **Round 2 - $\mathsf{TDGen}_2(\cdot)$:**
   R computes and sends $\mathsf{td}_2^{R \to S} \leftarrow \mathsf{TDGen}_2(\mathsf{td}_1^{S \to R}; r_R)$ using randomness r_R.
3. **Round 3 - $\mathsf{TDGen}_3(\cdot)$:**
   S computes and sends $\mathsf{td}_3^{S \to R} \leftarrow \mathsf{TDGen}_3(\mathsf{td}_2^{R \to S}; r_S)$
4. **Output - $\mathsf{TDOut}(\cdot)$**
   The receiver R outputs $\mathsf{TDOut}(\mathsf{td}_1^{S \to R}, \mathsf{td}_2^{R \to S}, \mathsf{td}_3^{S \to R})$.
5. **Trapdoor Validation Algorithm - $\mathsf{TDValid}(\cdot)$:**
   Given input $(\mathsf{t}, \mathsf{td}_1^{S \to R})$, output a single bit 0 or 1 that determines whether the value t is a valid trapdoor corresponding to the message td_1 sent in the first round of the trapdoor generation protocol.

In what follows, for brevity, we set td_1 to be $\mathsf{td}_1^{S \to R}$. Similarly we use td_2 and td_3 instead of $\mathsf{td}_2^{R \to S}$ and $\mathsf{td}_3^{S \to R}$, respectively. Note that the algorithm $\mathsf{TDValid}$ does not form a part of the interaction between the trapdoor generator and the receiver. It is, in fact, a public algorithm that enables public verification of whether a value t is a valid trapdoor for a first round message td_1.

Extraction. There exists a PPT extractor algorithm TDExt that, given a set of values[12] $(\mathsf{td}_1, \{\mathsf{td}_2^i, \mathsf{td}_3^i\}_{i=1}^3)$ such that $\mathsf{td}_2^1, \mathsf{td}_2^2, \mathsf{td}_2^3$ are distinct and $\mathsf{TDOut}(\mathsf{td}_1, \mathsf{td}_2^i, \mathsf{td}_3^i) = 1$ for all $i \in [3]$, outputs a trapdoor t such that $\mathsf{TDValid}(\mathsf{t}, \mathsf{td}_1) = 1$.

1-Rewinding Security. We define the notion of *1-rewinding security* for a trapdoor generation protocol TDGen. Consider the following experiment between a sender S and any (possibly cheating) receiver R^*.

---

[12] These values can be obtained from the malicious sender via an expected PPT rewinding procedure. The expected PPT simulator in our applications performs the necessary rewindings and then feeds these values to the extractor TDExt.

Experiment E:

- R^* interacts with S and completes one execution of the protocol TDGen. R^* receives values $(\mathsf{td}_1, \mathsf{td}_3)$ in rounds 1 and 3 respectively.
- Then, R^* rewinds S to the beginning of round 2.
- R^* sends S a new second round message td_2^* and receives a message td_3^* in the third round.
- At the end of the experiment, R^* outputs a value t^*.

Definition 5 (1-Rewinding Security). *A trapdoor generation protocol* TDGen $=$ (TDGen$_1$, TDGen$_2$, TDGen$_3$, TDOut, TDValid) *achieves 1-rewinding security if, for every non-uniform PPT receiver R^* in the above experiment E,*

$$\Pr\big[\mathsf{TDValid}(\mathsf{t}^*, \mathsf{td}_1) = 1\big] = \mathsf{negl}(\lambda),$$

where the probability is over the random coins of S, and where t^* is the output of R^* in the experiment E, and td_1 is the message from S in round 1.

Construction. We describe our construction of a three round trapdoor generation protocol based on one way functions in the full version of the paper.

4.2 WI with Non-adaptive Bounded Rewinding Security

We define the notion of three-round delayed-input witness indistinguishable (WI) argument with "bounded-rewinding security," and construct such a primitive assuming the existence of polynomially hard DDH (or QR or N^{th}-Residuosity). In the non-delayed-input setting, such a primitive was implicitly constructed and used previously by Goyal et al. [22].[13]

We formally define three-round delayed-input WI with *non-adaptive* bounded-rewinding security here. In the full version, we describe a construction for the same. For our applications, we instantiate the rewinding parameter B with the value 6.

Definition 6 (3-Round Delayed-Input WI with Non-adaptive Bounded Rewinding Security). *Fix a positive integer B. A delayed-input 3-round inter-active argument (as defined in Definition 1) for an NP language L, with an NP relation R_L is said to be WI with Non-adaptive B-Rewinding Security if for every non-uniform PPT interactive Turing Machine V^*, it holds that $\{\mathsf{REAL}_0^{V^*}(1^\lambda)\}_\lambda$ and $\{\mathsf{REAL}_1^{V^*}(1^\lambda)\}_\lambda$ are computationally indistinguishable, where for $b \in \{0, 1\}$ the random variable $\mathsf{REAL}_b^{V^*}(1^\lambda)$ is defined via the following experiment. In what follows we denote by P_1 the prover's algorithm in the first round, and similarly we denote by P_3 his algorithm in the third round.*

Experiment $\mathsf{REAL}_b^{V^*}(1^\lambda)$:

---

[13] Specifically, they consider non-delayed-input WI with 1-rewinding security.

1. *Run $P_1(1^\lambda)$ and denote its output by (rwi_1, σ), where σ is its secret state, and rwi_1 is the message to be sent to the verifier.*
2. *Run the verifier $V^*(1^\lambda, \mathsf{rwi}_1)$, who outputs $\{(x^i, w^i)\}_{i \in [B-1]}$, x^B, w_0^B, w_1^B and a set of messages $\{\mathsf{rwi}_2^i\}_{i \in [B]}$.*
3. *For each $i \in [B-1]$, run $P_3(\sigma, \mathsf{rwi}_2^i, x^i, w^i)$, and for $i = B$, run $P_3(\sigma, \mathsf{rwi}_2^i, x^i, w_b^i)$ where P_3 is the (honest) prover's algorithm for generating the third message of the WI protocol, and send its message $\{\mathsf{rwi}_3^i\}_{i \in [B]}$ to V^*.*

In the full version, we prove the following theorem:

Theorem 5. *Assuming $DDH/QR/N^{th}$-Residuosity, there exists a three round delayed-input witness-indistinguishable argument system with non-adaptive ($B = 6$)-rewinding security.*

5   Promise Zero Knowledge

In this section, we introduce our new notion of promise zero knowledge interactive arguments. Unlike the standard notion of zero knowledge interactive arguments that is defined in the unidirectional-message model of communication, promise ZK is defined in the simultaneous-message model, where in every round, both the prover and the verifier simultaneously send a message to each other. Crucially, in promise ZK, the zero knowledge property is only required to hold against a specific class of "valid" verifiers (that do not send invalid messages).

Validity Check. First, we enhance the syntax for simultaneous-message interactive arguments to include an additional algorithm Valid. That is, a simultaneous-message interactive argument is denoted by (P, V, Valid). The notions of completeness and soundness remain intact as before. Looking ahead, the intuition behind introducing the new algorithm is that we want to capture those verifiers who send a "valid" message in every round (including the last round). We do this by using the Valid algorithm.

This algorithm Valid is protocol specific. For example, if the honest verifier is instructed to prove knowledge of a trapdoor that he generated, and the proof fails, then his messages are not valid. Importantly, even if only the verifier's last message is invalid, and even though the prover does not need to explicitly respond to this message[14] we refer to this transcript as invalid. We denote by Valid the (public verification) algorithm which checks whether the transcript, including the verifier's last message, is valid or not, that is,

$$\mathsf{Valid}(\mathsf{Trans}(P(x, w), V^*)) = 1$$

---

[14] We use this promise ZK protocol as a building block in our MPC protocols, and in these protocols, the party acting as prover does indeed read this last ZK message sent by the verifier, and based on its validity decides whether to abort the MPC protocol.

if and only if all the messages sent by V^* appear to be valid, given the transcript. The correctness requirement of this algorithm is that if the verifier's messages are generated honestly according to the protocol, then

$$\Pr[\mathsf{Valid}(\mathsf{Trans}(P(x, w), V)) = 1] = 1.$$

Looking ahead, in our protocols, at the end of each execution of the ZK protocol, the prover will check whether the verifier sent "valid" messages, and if not, the prover will abort.

5.1 Definitions

We now proceed to describe our notion of promise zero knowledge. Roughly speaking, we define promise ZK similarly to standard ZK, with two notable differences: First, promise ZK is defined in the simultaneous-message model. Second, the zero knowledge property is only defined w.r.t. a special class of verifiers who generate a valid transcript, with some noticeable probability. In order to define this notion, we need to have an estimation of the probability that the cheating verifier sends an invalid message throughout the protocol.

Validity Approximation. Consider a delayed-input simultaneous message interactive argument system (P, V, Valid). Consider any verifier V^*, and any efficiently sampleable distribution $\mathcal{D} = \{\mathcal{D}_\lambda\}$, where $\mathcal{D}_\lambda$ samples pairs (x, w) such that $x \in \{0, 1\}^\lambda$ and $(x, w) \in R_L$

In what follows we denote by $P = (P_1, P_2)$, a prover that is split into two parts. First, $(\mathsf{view}_{V^*,1}, \mathsf{st}) \leftarrow P_1(1^\lambda)$ is obtained, and then $P_2(x, w, \mathsf{st})$ continues the rest of the P algorithm with V^*. This is done primarily because we would like to approximate the the validity probability of V^* conditioned on $\mathsf{view}_{V^*,1}$.

Let $\mathsf{Trans}(P_2(x, w, \mathsf{st}), V^*)$ denote the protocol transcript between P_2 and V^*: that is, $\mathsf{Trans}(P, V^*) = (\mathsf{view}_{V^*,1}, \mathsf{Trans}(P_2(x, w, \mathsf{st}), V^*))$. Let

$$q_{\mathsf{view}_{V^*,1}} = \Pr[\mathsf{Valid}(\mathsf{view}_{V^*,1}, \mathsf{Trans}(P_2(x, w, \mathsf{st}), V^*)) = 1 | (\mathsf{view}_{V^*,1}, \mathsf{st}) \leftarrow P_1(1^\lambda)]$$

where the probability is over the generation of $(x, w) \leftarrow \mathcal{D}_\lambda$ and the coins of P_2. We emphasize that $q_{\mathsf{view}_{V^*,1}}$ depends on $\mathcal{D}$ and on V^*, we omit this dependence from the notation to avoid cluttering.

Definition 7. *For any constant $c \in \mathbb{N}$, a PPT oracle algorithm $\mathsf{pExtract}_c$ is said to be a validity approximation algorithm, if the following holds for all malicious verifiers V^* and for all efficiently sampleable distributions $\mathcal{D} = \{\mathcal{D}_\lambda\}$:*

- *If $\mathsf{pExtract}_c^{V^*, \mathcal{D}}(\mathsf{view}_{V^*,1}, \mathsf{st}) = 0$, then $q_{\mathsf{view}_{V^*,1}} < 2 \cdot \lambda^{-c}$.*
- *Otherwise, if $\mathsf{pExtract}_c^{V^*, \mathcal{D}}(\mathsf{view}_{V^*,1}, \mathsf{st}) = p$, then $p \geq \lambda^{-c}$ and $\frac{p}{2} < q_{\mathsf{view}_{V^*,1}} < 2 \cdot p$.*

We now formalize our notion of promise ZK. We note that this only considers the delayed-input distributional setting. For simplicity of exposition, we restrict ourselves to 3-round protocols since this work is only concerned with constructions and applications of 3-round promise zero-knowledge. We note that this definition can be extended naturally to any number of rounds.

Definition 8 (Promise Zero Knowledge). *A 3-round distributional delayed-input simultaneous-message interactive argument* (P, V, Valid) *for a language* L *is said to be* promise zero knowledge against delayed-input verifiers *if there exists an oracle machine* $\mathsf{Sim} = (\mathsf{Sim}_1, \mathsf{Sim}_2, \mathsf{Sim}_3)$ *such that for every constant* $c \in \mathbb{N}$, *and any validity approximation algorithm* $\mathsf{pExtract}_c$, *for every polynomials* $\nu = \nu(\lambda)$ *and* $\widetilde{\nu} = \widetilde{\nu}(\lambda)$, *for every efficiently sampleable distribution* $\mathcal{D} = \{\mathcal{D}_\lambda\}$ *such that* $\mathsf{Supp}(\mathcal{D}_\lambda) = \{(x, w) : x \in L \cap \{0, 1\}^\lambda, w \in R_L(x) \text{ where } x = (x_2, x_3), w = (w_2, w_3)\}$, *for any delayed-input PPT verifier* V^* *that obtains* x_i *in round* i *and any* $z \in \{0, 1\}^{\mathsf{poly}(\lambda)}$, *conditions 1 and 2 (defined below) hold for* REAL_{V^*} *and* IDEAL_{V^*} *(defined below).*

- REAL_{V^*} *is computed as follows:*
  - *Sample* $(\mathsf{view}_{V^*, 1}, \mathsf{st}) \leftarrow P_1(1^\lambda)$.
  - *Sample* $(x, w) \leftarrow \mathcal{D}_\lambda$ *where* $x = (x_2, x_3)$.
  - *Execute the interaction* $(\mathsf{view}_{V^*, 1}, \langle P_2(x, w, \mathsf{st}), V^*(\mathsf{view}_{V^*, 1}) \rangle)$, *where* V^* *obtains* x_i *in round* i.
  - *The output of the experiment is the view of* V^* *in the execution* $(x, \langle P(x, w), V^*(\mathsf{view}_{V^*, 1}) \rangle)$.
- IDEAL_{V^*} *is computed as follows:*
  - *Sample* $(\mathsf{view}_{V^*, 1}, \mathsf{st}) \leftarrow P_1(1^\lambda)$.
  - *Compute* $p = \mathsf{pExtract}_c^{V^*}(\mathsf{view}_{V^*, 1}, \mathsf{st})$.
  - *Sample* $(x, w) \leftarrow \mathcal{D}_\lambda$ *where* $x = (x_2, x_3)$.
  - *If* $p = 0$,
    - *Execute the interaction* $(\mathsf{view}_{V^*, 1}, \langle P_2(x, w, \mathsf{st}), V^*(\mathsf{view}_{V^*, 1}) \rangle)$, *where* V^* *obtains* x_i *in round* i.
    - *The output of the experiment is* $(x, \langle P(x, w), V^*(\mathsf{view}_{V^*, 1}) \rangle)$.
  - *Else, execute* $\mathsf{Sim}^{V^*}(x, \mathsf{view}_{V^*, 1}, \mathsf{st}, p) \to (\mathsf{view}_{V^*, 2}, \mathsf{view}_{V^*, 3})$, *which operates as follows:*
    - *Compute* $\mathsf{Sim}_1^{V^*}(\mathsf{view}_{V^*, 1}, \mathsf{st}, p) \to \mathsf{st}_1$.
    - *Then compute* $\mathsf{Sim}_2^{V^*}(x_2, \mathsf{view}_{V^*, 1}, \mathsf{st}_1) \to (\mathsf{view}_{V^*, 2}, \mathsf{st}_2)$.
    - *Finally, compute* $\mathsf{Sim}_3^{V^*}(x_3, \mathsf{view}_{V^*, 1}, \mathsf{view}_{V^*, 2}, \mathsf{st}_2)$ *to output* $(\mathsf{view}_{V^*, 3})$.

Conditions 1 and 2 are defined as follows:

1. *No PPT distinguisher can distinguish* REAL_{V^*} *from* IDEAL_{V^*} *with advantage greater than* λ^{-c}.
2. *For any input* $x = (x_2, x_3)$, *the running time of* $\mathsf{Sim}_1^{V^*}(\mathsf{view}_{\mathsf{MIM}, 1}, \mathsf{st}, p)$ *is polynomial in* λ *and linear in* $\frac{1}{p}$, *and the running times of* $\mathsf{Sim}_2^{V^*}(x_2, \mathsf{view}_{V^*, 1}, \mathsf{st})$ *and* $\mathsf{Sim}_3^{V^*}(x_3, \mathsf{view}_{V^*, 1}, \mathsf{view}_{V^*, 2}, \mathsf{st}_2)$ *are polynomial in* λ *and independent of* p.

Going forward, we use *promise ZK argument* to refer to a distributional promise zero-knowledge simultaneous-message argument system, satisfying delayed-input completeness and soundness, as well as zero-knowledge against delayed-input verifiers according to Definition 8.

Defining Simulation-Sound Promise ZK in the multi-party setting. We now consider a man-in-the-middle adversary that interacts in promise zero-knowledge protocols as follows: It opens polynomially many sessions where it plays the role of the verifier interacting with an honest prover; these are called "left" sessions, and we denote by ν the number of such left sessions. We note that in all left sessions, the honest prover proves the same statement with the same witness. It can simultaneously initiate polynomially many sessions where it plays the role of the prover interacting with an honest verifier: these are called "right" sessions, and we denote by $\tilde{\nu}$ the number of such right sessions. We restrict ourselves to *synchronous* (rushing) adversaries, that for each round j, send all their j'th round messages (in all sessions), before observing any of the honest parties messages for the next round of the protocol.

We formalize the notion of simulation-soundness against a rushing man-in-the-middle adversary below, where we use $\tilde{a}$ to denote any random variable a that corresponds to a right session.

Redefining Validity Approximation. Similarly to before, we need to approximate the probability that the messages sent by a man-in-the-middle adversary in the left execution are valid, conditioned on all messages in the first round of the protocol. We consider ν "left" sessions and $\tilde{\nu}$ "right" sessions. Similar to the setting of promise ZK, we denote by $P = (P_1, P_2)$, an honest prover for the "left" sessions that is split into two parts, P_1 generates the first round message, and P_2 generates the messages of the second and third rounds. Below, we abuse notation and use P, P_1, P_2 not only to denote the interaction of the honest prover in a single session, but also to denote the interaction of the honest prover in all ν left sessions, using independent randomness for each such execution. Let $\mathsf{Trans}_{\mathsf{left}}(P_2(x, w, \mathsf{view}_{\mathsf{MIM},1}, \mathsf{st}), \mathsf{MIM})$ denote all the transcripts in the "left" sessions between $P_2(x, w, \mathsf{view}_{\mathsf{MIM},1}, \mathsf{st})$ and MIM, which can be decomposed as follows: $\mathsf{Trans}_{\mathsf{left}}(P, \mathsf{MIM}) = (\mathsf{view}_{\mathsf{MIM},1}, \mathsf{Trans}_{\mathsf{left}}(P_2(x, w, \mathsf{view}_{\mathsf{MIM},1}, \mathsf{st}), \mathsf{MIM}))$. For any $\mathsf{view}_{\mathsf{MIM},1}$ sampled according to honest prover and verifier strategy as described above, let $q_{\mathsf{view}_{\mathsf{MIM},1}} =$

$$\Pr[\mathsf{Valid}(\mathsf{view}_{\mathsf{MIM},1}, \mathsf{Trans}_{\mathsf{left}}(P_2(x, w, \mathsf{view}_{\mathsf{MIM},1}, \mathsf{st}), \mathsf{MIM})) = 1 | (\mathsf{view}_{\mathsf{MIM},1}, \mathsf{st}) \leftarrow P_1(1^\lambda)]$$

where Valid above refers to the AND of all the validity tests for each of the ν left sessions, and the probability is over the generation of $(x, w) \leftarrow \mathcal{D}_\lambda$ and the coins of each of the ν instantiations of P_2. We emphasize that $q_{\mathsf{view}_{\mathsf{MIM},1}}$ depends on $\mathcal{D}$ and on MIM, we omit this dependence from the notation to avoid cluttering. We re-define the algorithm $\mathsf{pExtract}_c$ from Definition 8 to depend additionally on the honest verifier first messages in the right sessions.

Definition 9. *For any constant $c \in \mathbb{N}$, a PPT oracle algorithm $\mathsf{pExtract}_c$ is said to be a* validity approximation *algorithm, if the following holds for all MIM and for all efficiently sampleable distributions $\mathcal{D} = \{\mathcal{D}_\lambda\}$, with probability at least $1 - 2^{-\lambda}$ over the coins of the algorithm, we have that:*

- *If* $\mathsf{pExtract}_c^{\mathsf{MIM},\mathcal{D}}(\mathsf{view}_{\mathsf{MIM},1}, \mathsf{st}) = 0$, *then* $q_{\mathsf{view}_{\mathsf{MIM},1}} < 2 \cdot \lambda^{-c}$.
- *Else, if* $\mathsf{pExtract}_c^{\mathsf{MIM},\mathcal{D}}(\mathsf{view}_{\mathsf{MIM},1}, \mathsf{st}) = p$, *then* $p \geq \lambda^{-c}$ *and* $\frac{p}{2} < q_{\mathsf{view}_{\mathsf{MIM},1}} < 2 \cdot p$.

Remark 3. We briefly describe a canonical polynomial-time validity approximation algorithm for any constant $c \in \mathbb{N}$:

1. $\mathsf{pExtract}_c^{\mathsf{MIM},\mathcal{D}}(\mathsf{view}_{\mathsf{MIM},1}, \mathsf{st})$ executes $\lambda^2 \cdot \lambda^c$ independent executions of all sessions with MIM, using freshly sampled instance-witness pairs from the distribution $\mathcal{D}_\lambda$ to complete the left executions in the role of the honest provers, and acting as honest verifiers in the right sessions.
2. Let ρ be the number of these executions that resulted in *all* left executions begin valid. We call such executions successful trials.
3. If $\rho < \lambda^2$, output 0.
4. Otherwise, output $\rho/(\lambda^2 \cdot \lambda^c)$.

We now informally analyze this algorithm:

- Observe that if $\mathsf{pExtract}_c^{\mathsf{MIM},\mathcal{D}}(\mathsf{view}_{\mathsf{MIM},1}, \mathsf{st})$ outputs zero, this means that fewer than λ^2 trials succeeded. On the other hand, if $q_{\mathsf{view}_{\mathsf{MIM},1}} \geq 2 \cdot \lambda^{-c}$, then the expected number of successful trials is at least $2\lambda^2$. By a Chernoff bound, except with probability at most $2^{-\lambda}$, at least λ^2 trials must succeed if $q_{\mathsf{view}_{\mathsf{MIM},1}} \geq 2 \cdot \lambda^{-c}$. Thus, the first condition is satisfied.
- Observe that if $\mathsf{pExtract}_c^{\mathsf{MIM},\mathcal{D}}(\mathsf{view}_{\mathsf{MIM},1}, \mathsf{st})$ outputs a nonzero value, then this value must be at least λ^{-c} by construction. And again, the required condition on $q_{\mathsf{view}_{\mathsf{MIM},1}}$ follows immediately from a Chernoff bound.

For simplicity, we restrict ourselves to 3 rounds in the definition below. This suffices for our construction and applications.

Definition 10 (Simulation-Sound Promise Zero Knowledge). *A 3-round publicly-verifiable promise zero-knowledge argument against delayed-input verifiers* (P, V, Valid) *is said to be simulation-sound if there exists an oracle machine* $\mathsf{Sim} = (\mathsf{Sim}_1, \mathsf{Sim}_2, \mathsf{Sim}_3)$ *such that, for every constant* $c \in \mathbb{N}$, *and any validity approximation algorithm* $\mathsf{pExtract}_c$, *for every polynomials* $\nu = \nu(\lambda)$ *and* $\widetilde{\nu} = \widetilde{\nu}(\lambda)$, *for every efficiently sampleable distribution* $\mathcal{D} = \{(\mathcal{X}_\lambda, \mathcal{W}_\lambda)\}$ *such that* $\mathsf{Supp}((\mathcal{X}, \mathcal{W})_\lambda) = \{(x, w) : x \in L \cap \{0,1\}^\lambda, w \in R_L(x) \text{ where } x = (x_2, x_3)\}$, *and every distribution* $\mathcal{X}'_\lambda$ *such that* $\mathcal{X}_\lambda$ *and* $\mathcal{X}'_\lambda$ *are computationally indistinguishable, for any PPT synchronous* MIM *that initiates* ν *"left" sessions and* $\widetilde{\nu}$ *"right" sessions, we require the following to hold. Let*

$$\mathsf{Sim}^{\mathsf{MIM}}(x', \mathsf{view}_{\mathsf{MIM},1}, \mathsf{st}, p) \rightarrow (\mathsf{view}_{\mathsf{MIM},2}, \mathsf{view}_{\mathsf{MIM},3}, \{\widetilde{x}_i\}_{i \in [\widetilde{\nu}]})$$

where $\mathsf{view}_{\mathsf{MIM},1}$ *are all the messages sent in the first round (both left and right executions) with* MIM, *and* st *denotes all the corresponding secret states of the honest parties, and* $p = \mathsf{pExtract}_c^{\mathsf{MIM},\mathcal{D}}(\mathsf{view}_{\mathsf{MIM},1}, \mathsf{st})$.

– *For any input* $x' = (x'_2, x'_3)$, *we have that* $\mathsf{Sim}^{\mathsf{MIM}}(x', \mathsf{view}_{\mathsf{MIM},1}, \mathsf{st}, p)$ *operates by first computing*

$$\mathsf{Sim}_1^{\mathsf{MIM}}(\mathsf{view}_{\mathsf{MIM},1}, \mathsf{st}, p) \to \mathsf{st}_1$$

then computing

$$\mathsf{Sim}_2^{\mathsf{MIM}}(x'_2, \mathsf{view}_{\mathsf{MIM},1}, \mathsf{st}_1) \to (\mathsf{view}_{\mathsf{MIM},2}, \mathsf{st}_2)$$

and then computing

$$\mathsf{Sim}_3^{\mathsf{MIM}}(x'_2, x'_3, \mathsf{view}_{\mathsf{MIM},1}, \mathsf{view}_{\mathsf{MIM},2}, \mathsf{st}_2) = (\mathsf{view}_{\mathsf{MIM},3}, \{\widetilde{x}_i\}_{i \in [\widetilde{\nu}]}).$$

Here, $\mathsf{view}_{\mathsf{MIM},2}$ *and* $\mathsf{view}_{\mathsf{MIM},3}$ *denotes the set of all messages sent in the second and third round (respectively) of the multi-party execution with* MIM. *We require that* $\{\widetilde{x}_i\}$ *(which is part of the output of* $\mathsf{Sim}^{\mathsf{MIM}}$*) is consistent[15] with* $(\mathsf{view}_{\mathsf{MIM},2}, \mathsf{view}_{\mathsf{MIM},3})$.

– *For any input* $x' = (x'_2, x'_3)$, *we require that the running time of* $\mathsf{Sim}_1^{\mathsf{MIM}}(\mathsf{view}_{\mathsf{MIM},1}, \mathsf{st}, p)$ *is polynomial in* λ *and linear in* $\frac{1}{p}$, *while the running times of* $\mathsf{Sim}_2^{\mathsf{MIM}}(x'_2, \mathsf{view}_{\mathsf{MIM},1}, \mathsf{st}_1)$ *and* $\mathsf{Sim}_3^{\mathsf{MIM}}(x'_2, x'_3, \mathsf{view}_{\mathsf{MIM},1}, \mathsf{view}_{\mathsf{MIM},2}, \mathsf{st}_2)$ *are polynomial in* λ, *independent of* p.

– *If* $\Pr\left[\mathsf{pExtract}_c^{\mathsf{MIM}}(\mathsf{view}_{\mathsf{MIM},1}, \mathsf{st}) \geq \lambda^{-c}\right] \geq \lambda^{-c}$, *then we have:*

$$\left(x', \mathsf{view}_{\mathsf{MIM},1}, \mathsf{IDEAL}_{\mathsf{MIM}}(x', \mathsf{view}_{\mathsf{MIM},1}, \mathsf{st}) \,\Big|\, \mathsf{pExtract}_c^{\mathsf{MIM}}(\mathsf{view}_{\mathsf{MIM},1}, \mathsf{st}) \geq \lambda^{-c}\right) \approx$$
$$\left(x, \mathsf{view}_{\mathsf{MIM},1}, \mathsf{REAL}_{\mathsf{MIM}}(x, w, \mathsf{view}_{\mathsf{MIM},1}, \mathsf{st}) \,\Big|\, \mathsf{pExtract}_c^{\mathsf{MIM}}(\mathsf{view}_{\mathsf{MIM},1}, \mathsf{st}) \geq \lambda^{-c}\right)$$

where $(x, w) \leftarrow (\mathcal{X}, \mathcal{W})_\lambda$, $x' \leftarrow \mathcal{X}'_\lambda$, *and* $(\mathsf{view}_{\mathsf{MIM},1}, \mathsf{st})$ *is generated by simulating all the messages sent in the first round of the execution with* MIM,[16] *where* $\mathsf{view}_{\mathsf{MIM},1}$ *denotes all the simulated messages and* st *denotes the secret states of all the honest parties, and*

$$\mathsf{IDEAL}_{\mathsf{MIM}}(x', \mathsf{view}_{\mathsf{MIM},1}, \mathsf{st}) = (\mathsf{view}_{\mathsf{MIM},1}, \mathsf{view}_{\mathsf{MIM},2}, \mathsf{view}_{\mathsf{MIM},3}),$$

where the variables $(\mathsf{view}_{\mathsf{MIM},2}, \mathsf{view}_{\mathsf{MIM},3})$ *are computed by running* $\mathsf{Sim}^{\mathsf{MIM}}(x', \mathsf{view}_{\mathsf{MIM},1}, \mathsf{st}, p)$ *for* $p = \mathsf{pExtract}_c^{\mathsf{MIM}, \mathcal{D}}(\mathsf{view}_{\mathsf{MIM},1}, \mathsf{st})$. *The experiment* $\mathsf{REAL}_{\mathsf{MIM}}(x, w, \mathsf{view}_{\mathsf{MIM},1})$ *is computed by running a real world execution with* MIM, *where the provers in the "left" sessions uses the input* (x, w) *and where the first round messages are* $\mathsf{view}_{\mathsf{MIM},1}$, *and by* $\mathsf{Valid}(\mathsf{Trans}_{\mathsf{left}}(P_2(x, w, \mathsf{st})))$ *we mean that all left sessions in the execution of* $\mathsf{REAL}_{\mathsf{MIM}}$ *are valid.*

– *Over the randomness of* Sim, *of generating* $(\mathsf{view}_{\mathsf{MIM},1}, \mathsf{st})$ *and over* $x' \leftarrow \mathcal{X}'_\lambda$,

$$\Pr\left[\bigvee_{i \in [\widetilde{\nu}]}\left(\mathsf{Acc}(\widetilde{\mathsf{Trans}}_i) = 0\right) \bigvee \left(\bigwedge_{i \in [\widetilde{\nu}]} \widetilde{x}_i \in L\right)\right] \geq 1 - \lambda^{-c},$$

---

[15] Note that $(\mathsf{view}_{\mathsf{MIM},2}, \mathsf{view}_{\mathsf{MIM},3})$ includes the instances $\{\widetilde{x}_i\}$, and we add the instances explicitly to the output of $\mathsf{Sim}^{\mathsf{MIM}}$ only so that we will be able to refer to it later.

[16] Note that this can be simulated easily since the protocol is delayed-input which means that the parties do not use their private inputs to compute their first round message.

where $\{\widetilde{\mathsf{Trans}}_i\}$ *is the transcript of the i'th right execution when* $(\mathsf{view}_{\mathsf{MIM},1},$ $\mathsf{view}_{\mathsf{MIM},2}, \mathsf{view}_{\mathsf{MIM},3})$ *are computed in* $\mathsf{IDEAL}_{\mathsf{MIM}}(x', \mathsf{view}_{\mathsf{MIM},1}, \mathsf{st})$ *as above, and* $\mathsf{Acc}(\widetilde{\mathsf{Trans}}_i) = 0$ *denotes the event that the (publicly verifiable) transcript* $\widetilde{\mathsf{Trans}}_i$ *causes an honest verifier to reject.*

5.2 Constructing Simulation Sound Promise ZK

In this section, we describe our construction of Simulation Sound Promise ZK. Formally, we prove the following theorem:

Theorem 6. *Assuming the existence of polynomially hard DDH/QR/N^{th}-Residuosity, there exists a three round simulation-sound promise ZK argument according to Definition 10.*

The Protocol. Let P and V denote the prover and verifier, respectively. Let L be any NP language with an associated relation R_L. Let $\mathcal{D}_\lambda = (\mathcal{X}_\lambda, \mathcal{W}_\lambda)$ be any efficiently sampleable distribution on R_L.

Building Blocks. Our construction relies on the following cryptographic primitives.

- TDGen = $(\mathsf{TDGen}_1, \mathsf{TDGen}_2, \mathsf{TDGen}_3, \mathsf{TDOut})$ is the three-message trapdoor generation protocol from Sect. 4, that is 3-extractable according to Definition 3, with corresponding extractor TDExt.
- RWI = $(\mathsf{RWI}_1, \mathsf{RWI}_2, \mathsf{RWI}_3, \mathsf{RWI}_4)$ is the three round delayed-input witness indistinguishable argument with non-adaptive bounded rewinding security for $B = 6$ from Definition 6. The fourth algorithm RWI_4 is the final verification algorithm.
- NMCom = $(\mathsf{NMCom}_1, \mathsf{NMCom}_2, \mathsf{NMCom}_3)$ denotes a special non-malleable commitment according to Definition 4.

NP Languages. We define the following relation R' that will be useful in our construction. Parse instance $\mathsf{st} = (x, \mathsf{c}, \mathsf{td}_1)$, where $\mathsf{c} = (\mathsf{c}_1, \mathsf{c}_2, \mathsf{c}_3)$. Parse witness $\mathsf{w} = (w, \mathsf{t}, \mathsf{r})$. Then, $R'(\mathsf{st}, \mathsf{w}) = 1$ if and only if :

$$\left(R(x, w) = 1 \right) \vee \left(\mathsf{TDValid}(\mathsf{td}_1, \mathsf{t}) = 1 \wedge \mathsf{c}_1 = \mathsf{NMCom}_1(\mathsf{r}) \wedge \mathsf{c}_3 = \right.$$

$$\left. \mathsf{NMCom}_3(\mathsf{t}, \mathsf{c}_1, \mathsf{c}_2; \mathsf{r}) \right).$$ We denote the corresponding language by L'.

That is, either :

1. x is in the language L with witness w, OR,
2. the third non-malleable commitment $(\mathsf{c}_1, \mathsf{c}_2, \mathsf{c}_3)$ is to a value t that is a valid trapdoor for the message td_1 generated using the trapdoor generation algorithms.

We construct a three round protocol $\pi^{\mathsf{SE-PZK}} = (P, V, \mathsf{Valid})$ for L in Fig. 1. The completeness of this protocol follows from the correctness of the underlying primitives.

Inputs: Prover P with tag **tag** obtains input $(x = (x_2, x_3), w) \leftarrow (\mathcal{X}, \mathcal{W})$ in the second round.

1. **Round 1:**
   - **Prover message:**
     - Compute $\mathsf{rwi}_1 = \mathsf{RWI}_1(1^\lambda, \widehat{r})$.
     - Sample $r \leftarrow \{0, 1\}^*$.
     - Compute $c_1 \leftarrow \mathsf{NMCom}_1(r)$ using NMCom with tag **tag** and uniform randomness[a].
     - Send (rwi_1, c_1).
   - **Verifier message:**
     Sample $r_{td} \overset{\$}{\leftarrow} \{0, 1\}^*$, then compute and send $\mathsf{td}_1 \leftarrow \mathsf{TDGen}_1(r_{td})$.
2. **Round 2:**
   - **Prover message:**
     - Obtain input $(x = (x_2, x_3), w)$ which is a randomly chosen sample from $(\mathcal{X}_\lambda, \mathcal{W}_\lambda)$. Send x_2 to V.
     - Compute and send $\mathsf{td}_2 \leftarrow \mathsf{TDGen}_2(\mathsf{td}_1)$.
   - **Verifier message:**
     Compute and send $\mathsf{rwi}_2 \leftarrow \mathsf{RWI}_2(\mathsf{rwi}_1)$ and $c_2 \leftarrow \mathsf{NMCom}_2(c_1)$.
3. **Round 3:**
   - **Prover message:**
     - Compute $c_3 \leftarrow \{0, 1\}^m$ and let $c = (c_1, c_2, c_3)$.
     - Set $x' = (x, c, \mathsf{td}_1)$ and $w' = (w, \bot, \bot)$. Compute $\mathsf{rwi}_3 \leftarrow \mathsf{RWI}_3(\mathsf{rwi}_1, \mathsf{rwi}_2, x', w')$ for $R'(x', w') = 1$ for R' defined above.
     - Send $(x_3, c_3, \mathsf{rwi}_3)$.
   - **Verifier message:**
     Sample and send $\mathsf{td}_3 \leftarrow \mathsf{TDGen}_3(\mathsf{td}_1, \mathsf{td}_2, r_{td})$ using uniform randomness.
4. **Verifier Output:**
   Output $\mathsf{RWI}_4(\mathsf{rwi}_1, \mathsf{rwi}_2, \mathsf{rwi}_3, \mathsf{st})$.

Valid(Trans):
Given the transcript of the protocol execution, output 1 if $\mathsf{TDOut}(\mathsf{td}_1, \mathsf{td}_2, \mathsf{td}_3) = 1$.

---

[a] We omit explicit dependence of the algorithm on tag to avoid cluttering.

Fig. 1. Three round Simulation-Sound Promise ZK argument.

5.3 Security Proof

Due to lack of space, we defer the proof of our protocol to the full version.

Acknowledgements. We thank Silas Richelson, Shai Halevi, Carmit Hazay, Antigoni Polychroniadou, Muthuramakrishnan Venkitasubramaniam and the anonymous reviewers of STOC 2018 for useful comments in an earlier draft of this paper.

References

1. Ananth, P., Choudhuri, A.R., Jain, A.: A new approach to round-optimal secure multiparty computation. In: Katz, J., Shacham, H. (eds.) CRYPTO 2017. LNCS, vol. 10401, pp. 468–499. Springer, Cham (2017). https://doi.org/10.1007/978-3-319-63688-7_16

2. Barak, B.: How to go beyond the black-box simulation barrier. In: 2001 Proceedings of the 42nd IEEE Symposium on Foundations of Computer Science, pp. 106–115. IEEE (2001)

3. Barak, B., Sahai, A.: How to play almost any mental game over the net - concurrent composition via super-polynomial simulation. In: Proceedings of the 46th Annual IEEE Symposium on Foundations of Computer Science (FOCS 2005), 23–25 October 2005, Pittsburgh, PA, USA, pp. 543–552 (2005). https://doi.org/10.1109/SFCS.2005.43

4. Beaver, D., Micali, S., Rogaway, P.: The round complexity of secure protocols (extended abstract). In: STOC, pp. 503–513 (1990)

5. Benhamouda, F., Lin, H.: k-round multiparty computation from k-round oblivious transfer via garbled interactive circuits. In: Nielsen, J.B., Rijmen, V. (eds.) EUROCRYPT 2018. LNCS, vol. 10821, pp. 500–532. Springer, Cham (2018). https://doi.org/10.1007/978-3-319-78375-8_17

6. Bitansky, N., Kalai, Y.T., Paneth, O.: Multi-collision resistance: a paradigm for keyless hash functions. IACR Cryptology ePrint Archive 2017, 488 (2017). http://eprint.iacr.org/2017/488

7. Brakerski, Z., Halevi, S., Polychroniadou, A.: Four round secure computation without setup. In: Kalai, Y., Reyzin, L. (eds.) TCC 2017. LNCS, vol. 10677, pp. 645–677. Springer, Cham (2017). https://doi.org/10.1007/978-3-319-70500-2_22

8. Ciampi, M., Ostrovsky, R., Siniscalchi, L., Visconti, I.: Delayed-input non-malleable zero knowledge and multi-party coin tossing in four rounds. In: Kalai, Y., Reyzin, L. (eds.) TCC 2017. LNCS, vol. 10677, pp. 711–742. Springer, Cham (2017). https://doi.org/10.1007/978-3-319-70500-2_24

9. Ciampi, M., Ostrovsky, R., Siniscalchi, L., Visconti, I.: Concurrent non-malleable commitments (and more) in 3 rounds. In: Robshaw, M., Katz, J. (eds.) CRYPTO 2016. LNCS, vol. 9816, pp. 270–299. Springer, Heidelberg (2016). https://doi.org/10.1007/978-3-662-53015-3_10

10. Cleve, R.: Limits on the security of coin flips when half the processors are faulty (extended abstract). In: Hartmanis, J. (ed.) STOC, pp. 364–369. ACM (1986)

11. Dolev, D., Dwork, C., Naor, M.: Non-malleable cryptography (extended abstract). In: STOC, pp. 542–552 (1991)

12. Dwork, C., Naor, M.: Zaps and their applications. In: FOCS, pp. 283–293 (2000)

13. Feige, U., Lapidot, D., Shamir, A.: Multiple non-interactive zero knowledge proofs based on a single random string (extended abstract). In: FOCS, pp. 308–317 (1990)

14. Garg, S., Mukherjee, P., Pandey, O., Polychroniadou, A.: The exact round complexity of secure computation. In: Fischlin, M., Coron, J.-S. (eds.) EUROCRYPT 2016. LNCS, vol. 9666, pp. 448–476. Springer, Heidelberg (2016). https://doi.org/10.1007/978-3-662-49896-5_16

15. Garg, S., Srinivasan, A.: Two-round multiparty secure computation from minimal assumptions. In: Nielsen, J.B., Rijmen, V. (eds.) EUROCRYPT 2018. LNCS, vol. 10821, pp. 468–499. Springer, Cham (2018). https://doi.org/10.1007/978-3-319-78375-8_16

16. Goldreich, O.: The Foundations of Cryptography - Volume 2, Basic Applications. Cambridge University Press, New York (2004)
17. Goldreich, O., Kahan, A.: How to construct constant-round zero-knowledge proof systems for NP. J. Cryptol. **9**(3), 167–190 (1996)
18. Goldreich, O., Micali, S., Wigderson, A.: How to play any mental game or A completeness theorem for protocols with honest majority. In: STOC, pp. 218–229 (1987)
19. Goldwasser, S., Micali, S., Rackoff, C.: The knowledge complexity of interactive proof systems. SIAM J. Comput. **18**, 186–208 (1989)
20. Goyal, V.: Constant round non-malleable protocols using one way functions. In: STOC, pp. 695–704 (2011)
21. Goyal, V., Pandey, O., Richelson, S.: Textbook non-malleable commitments. In: STOC, pp. 1128–1141 (2016)
22. Goyal, V., Richelson, S., Rosen, A., Vald, M.: An algebraic approach to non-malleability. In: FOCS, pp. 41–50 (2014)
23. Halevi, S., Hazay, C., Polychroniadou, A., Venkitasubramaniam, M.: Round-optimal secure multi-party computation. IACR Cryptology ePrint Archive. 2017, 1056 (2017). http://eprint.iacr.org/2017/1056. Accepted to CRYPTO 2018
24. Jain, A., Kalai, Y.T., Khurana, D., Rothblum, R.: Distinguisher-dependent simulation in two rounds and its applications. In: Katz, J., Shacham, H. (eds.) CRYPTO 2017. LNCS, vol. 10402, pp. 158–189. Springer, Cham (2017). https://doi.org/10.1007/978-3-319-63715-0_6
25. Katz, J., Ostrovsky, R.: Round-optimal secure two-party computation. In: Franklin, M. (ed.) CRYPTO 2004. LNCS, vol. 3152, pp. 335–354. Springer, Heidelberg (2004). https://doi.org/10.1007/978-3-540-28628-8_21
26. Katz, J., Ostrovsky, R., Smith, A.: Round efficiency of multi-party computation with a dishonest majority. In: Biham, E. (ed.) EUROCRYPT 2003. LNCS, vol. 2656, pp. 578–595. Springer, Heidelberg (2003). https://doi.org/10.1007/3-540-39200-9_36
27. Khurana, D.: Round optimal concurrent non-malleability from polynomial hardness. In: Kalai, Y., Reyzin, L. (eds.) TCC 2017, Part II. LNCS, vol. 10678, pp. 139–171. Springer, Cham (2017). https://doi.org/10.1007/978-3-319-70503-3_5
28. Lin, H., Pass, R., Venkitasubramaniam, M.: Concurrent non-malleable commitments from any one-way function. In: Canetti, R. (ed.) TCC 2008. LNCS, vol. 4948, pp. 571–588. Springer, Heidelberg (2008). https://doi.org/10.1007/978-3-540-78524-8_31
29. Pass, R.: Bounded-concurrent secure multi-party computation with a dishonest majority. In: Proceedings of the 36th Annual ACM Symposium on Theory of Computing, Chicago, IL, USA, 13–16 June 2004, pp. 232–241 (2004)
30. Pass, R., Rosen, A.: Concurrent non-malleable commitments. In: FOCS, pp. 563–572 (2005)
31. Prabhakaran, M., Rosen, A., Sahai, A.: Concurrent zero knowledge with logarithmic round-complexity. In: FOCS, pp. 366–375 (2002)
32. Rosen, A.: A note on constant-round zero-knowledge proofs for NP. In: Naor, M. (ed.) TCC 2004. LNCS, vol. 2951, pp. 191–202. Springer, Heidelberg (2004). https://doi.org/10.1007/978-3-540-24638-1_11
33. Sahai, A.: Non-malleable non-interactive zero knowledge and adaptive chosen-ciphertext security. In: FOCS, pp. 543–553 (1999)
34. Yao, A.C.: Protocols for secure computations (extended abstract). In: FOCS (1982)

Round-Optimal Secure Multi-Party Computation

Shai Halevi[1]([⊠]), Carmit Hazay[2], Antigoni Polychroniadou[3],
and Muthuramakrishnan Venkitasubramaniam[4]

[1] IBM Research, New York, USA
shaih@alum.mit.edu
[2] Bar-Ilan University, Ramat Gan, Israel
carmit.hazay@biu.ac.il
[3] Cornell Tech and University of Rochester, New York, USA
antigoni@cornell.edu
[4] University of Rochester, New York, USA
muthuv@cs.rochester.edu

Abstract. Secure multi-party computation (MPC) is a central cryptographic task that allows a set of mutually distrustful parties to jointly
compute some function of their private inputs where security should hold
in the presence of a malicious adversary that can corrupt any number of
parties. Despite extensive research, the precise round complexity of this
"standard-bearer" cryptographic primitive is unknown. Recently, Garg,
Mukherjee, Pandey and Polychroniadou, in EUROCRYPT 2016 demonstrated that the round complexity of any MPC protocol relying on black-
box proofs of security in the plain model must be at least four. Following
this work, independently Ananth, Choudhuri and Jain, CRYPTO 2017
and Brakerski, Halevi, and Polychroniadou, TCC 2017 made progress
towards solving this question and constructed four-round protocols based
on non-polynomial time assumptions. More recently, Ciampi, Ostrovsky,
Siniscalchi and Visconti in TCC 2017 closed the gap for two-party protocols by constructing a four-round protocol from polynomial-time assumptions. In another work, Ciampi, Ostrovsky, Siniscalchi and Visconti TCC
2017 showed how to design a four-round multi-party protocol for the specific case of multi-party coin-tossing.

In this work, we resolve this question by designing a four-round
actively secure multi-party (two or more parties) protocol for general
functionalities under standard polynomial-time hardness assumptions
with a black-box proof of security.

Keywords: Secure multi-party computation · Garbled circuits
Round complexity · Additive errors

1 Introduction

Secure multi-party computation. A central cryptographic task, *secure multiparty computation* (MPC), considers a set of parties with private inputs that wish

© International Association for Cryptologic Research 2018
H. Shacham and A. Boldyreva (Eds.): CRYPTO 2018, LNCS 10992, pp. 488–520, 2018.
https://doi.org/10.1007/978-3-319-96881-0_17

to jointly compute some function of their inputs while preserving privacy and correctness to a maximal extent [Yao86, CCD87, GMW87, BGW88].

In this work, we consider MPC protocols that may involve two or more parties for which security should hold in the presence of *active* adversaries that may corrupt any number of parties (i.e. dishonest majority). More concretely, *we are interested in identifying the precise round complexity of MPC protocols for securely computing arbitrary functions in the plain model.*

In [GMPP16], Garg, et al., proved a lower bound of four rounds for MPC protocols that relies on black-box simulation. Following this work, in independent works, Ananth et al. [ACJ17] and Brakerski et al. [BHP17] showed a matching upper bound by constructing four-round protocols based on the Decisional Diffie-Hellman (DDH) and Learning With Error (LWE) assumptions, respectively, albeit with super-polynomial hardness. More recently, Ciampi et al. in [COSV17b] closed the gap for two-party protocols by constructing a four-round protocol from standard polynomial-time assumptions. The same authors in another work [COSV17a] showed how to design a four-round multi-party protocol for the specific case of multi-party coin-tossing.

The state-of-affairs leaves the following fundamental question regarding round complexity of cryptographic primitives open:

Does there exist four-round secure multi-party computation protocols for general functionalities based on standard polynomial-time hardness assumptions and black-box simulation in the plain model?

We remark that tight answers have been obtained in prior works where one or more of the requirements in the motivating question are relaxed. In the two-party setting, the recent work of Ciampi et al. [COSV17b] showed how to obtain a four-round protocol based on trapdoor permutations. Assuming trusted setup, namely, a common reference string, two-round constructions can be obtained [GGHR14, MW16] or three-round assuming tamper-proof hardware tokens [HPV16].[1] In the case of passive adversaries, (or even the slightly stronger setting of semi-malicious[2] adversaries) three round protocols based on the Learning With Errors assumption have been constructed by Brakerski et al. [BHP17]. Ananth et al. gave a five-round protocol based on DDH [ACJ17]. Under subexponential hardness assumptions, four-round constructions were demonstrated in [BHP17, ACJ17]. Under some relaxations of superpolynomial simulation, the work of Badrinarayanan et al. [BGJ+17] shows how to obtain three-round MPC assuming subexponentially secure LWE and DDH. For specific multi-party functionalities four-round constructions have been obtained, e.g., coin-tossing by Ciampi et al. [COSV17b]. Finally, if we assume an honest majority, the work of Damgard and Ishai [DI05] provided a three-round MPC protocol. If we allow trusted setup (i.e. not the plain model) then a series of works

---

[1] Where in this model the lower bound is two rounds.

[2] A semi-malicious adversary is allowed to invoke a corrupted party with arbitrary chosen input and random tape, but otherwise follows the protocol specification honestly as a passive adversary.

[CLOS02, GGHR14, MW16, BL18, GS17] have shown how to achieve two-round multiparty computation protocols in the common reference string model under minimal assumptions. In the tamper proof setup model, the work of [HPV16] show how to achieve three round secure multiparty computation assuming only one-way functions.

1.1   Our Results

The main result we establish is a four-round multi-party computation protocol for general functionalities in the plain model based on standard polynomial-time hardness assumptions. Slightly more formally, we establish the following theorem.

Theorem 1.1 (Informal). *Assuming the existence of injective one-way functions, ZAPs and a certain affine homomorphic encryption scheme, there exists a four-round multi-party protocol that securely realizes arbitrary functionalities in the presence of active adversaries corrupting any number of parties.*

This theorem addresses our motivating question and resolves the round complexity of multiparty computation protocols. The encryption scheme that we need admits a homomorphic affine transformation

$$c = \mathsf{Enc}(m) \mapsto c' = \mathsf{Enc}(a \cdot m + b) \text{ for plaintext } a, b,$$

as well as some equivocation property. Roughly, given the secret key and encryption randomness, it should be possible to "explain" the result c' as coming from $c' = \mathsf{Enc}(a' \cdot m + b')$, for any a', b' satisfying $am + b = a'm + b'$. We show how to instantiate such an encryption scheme by relying on standard additively homomorphic encryption schemes (or slight variants thereof). More precisely, we instantiate such an encryption scheme using LWE, DDH, Quadratic Residuosity (QR) and Decisional Composite Residuosity (DCR) hardness assumptions. ZAPs on the other hand can be instantiated using the QR assumption or any (doubly) enhanced trapdoor permutation such as RSA or bilinear maps. Injective one-way functions are required to instantiate the non-malleable commitment scheme from [GRRV14] and can be instantiated using the QR. In summary, all our primitives can be instantiated by the single QR assumptions and therefore we have the following corollary

Corollary 1.2. *Assuming QR, there exists a four-round multi-party protocol that securely realizes arbitrary functionalities in the presence of active adversaries corrupting any number of parties.*

1.2   Our Techniques

Starting point: the [ACJ17] protocol. We begin from the beautiful work of Ananth et al. [ACJ17], where they used randomized encoding [AIK06] to reduce the task of securely computing an arbitrary functionality to securely computing the sum of many three-bit multiplications. To implement the required three-bit multiplications, Ananth et al. used an elegant three-round protocol, consisting of three instances of a two-round oblivious-transfer subprotocol, as illustrated in Fig. 1.

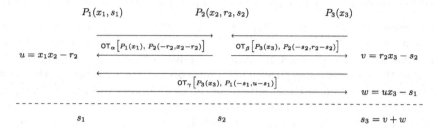

Fig. 1. The three-bit multiplication protocol from [ACJ17], using two-round oblivious transfer. The OT sub-protocols are denoted by $\mathsf{OT}[\text{Receiver}(b), \text{Sender}(m_0, m_1)]$, and u, v, w are the receivers' outputs in the three OT protocols. The outputs of P_1, P_2, P_3 are s_1, s_2, s_3, respectively. The first message in OT_γ can be sent in the second round, together with the sender messages in OT_α and OT_β. The sum of s_1, s_2, s_3 results into the output $x_1 x_2 x_3$.

Using this three-round multiplication subprotocol, Ananth et al. constructed a four-round protocol for the semi-honest model, then enforced correctness in the third and fourth rounds using zero-knowledge proofs to get security against a malicious adversary. In particular, the proof of correct behavior in the third round required a special three-round non-malleable zero-knowledge proof, for which they had to rely on super-polynomial hardness assumptions. (A four-round proof to enforce correctness in the last round can be done based on standard assumptions.) To eliminate the need for super-polynomial assumptions, our very high level approach is to weaken the correctness guarantees needed in the third round, so that we can use simpler proofs. Specifically we would like to be able to use two-round (resettable) witness indistinguishable proofs (aka ZAPs [DN07]).

WI using the Naor-Yung approach. To replace zero-knowledge proofs by ZAPs, we must be able to use the honest prover strategy (since ZAPs have no simulator), even as we slowly remove the honest parties' input from the game. We achieve this using the Naor-Yung approach: We modify the three-bit multiplication protocol by repeating each OT instance twice, with the receiver using the same choice bit in both copies and the sender secret-sharing its input bits between the two. (Thus we have a total of six OT instances in the modified protocol.) Crucially, while we require that the sender proves correct behavior relative to its inputs in both instances, we only ask the receiver to prove that it behaves correctly in *at least one of the two*.

In the security proof, this change allows us to switch in two steps from the real world where honest parties use their real inputs as the choice bit, to a simulated

S. Halevi et al.

world where they are simulated using random inputs. In each step we change the choice bit in just one of the two OT instances, and use the other bit that we did not switch to generate the ZAP proofs on behalf of the honest parties.[3]

We note that intuitively, this change does not add much power to a real-world adversary: Although an adversarial receiver can use different bits in the two OT instances, this will only result in the receiver getting random bits from the protocol, since the sender secret-shares its input bits between the two instances.

Extraction via rewinding. While the adversary cannot gain much by using different bits in different OT instances, we crucially rely on the challenger in our hybrid games to use that option. Hence we must compensate somehow for the fact that the received bits in those OT protocols are meaningless. To that end, the challenger (as well as the simulator in the ideal model) will use rewinding to extract the necessary information from the adversary.

But rewinding takes rounds, so the challenger/simulator can only extract this information at the end of the third round.[4] Thus we must rearrange the simulater so that it does not need the extracted information — in particular the bits received in the OT protocols — until after the third round. Looking at the protocol in Fig. 1, there is only one place where a value received in one of the OTs is used before the end of the third round. To wit, the value u received in the second round by P_1 in OT_α is used in the third round when P_1 plays the sender in OT_γ.

This causes a real problem in the security proof: Consider the case where P_2 is an adversarial sender and P_1 an honest receiver. In some hybrid we would want to switch the choice bit of P_1 from its real input to a random bit, and argue that these hybrids are close by reduction to the OT receiver privacy. Inside the reduction, we will have no access to the values received in the OT, so we cannot ensure that it is consistent with the value that P_1 uses as the sender in OT_γ (with P_3 as the receiver). We would like to extract the value of u from the adversary, but we are at a bind: we must send to the adversary the last message of OT_γ before we can extract u, but we cannot compute that message without knowing u.

Relaxing the correctness guarantees. To overcome the difficulty from above, we relax the correctness guarantees of the three-bit multiplication protocol, allowing the value that P_1 sends in OT_γ (which we denote by u') to differ from the value that it received in OT_α (denoted u). The honest parties will still use $u' = u$, but the protocol no longer includes a proof for that fact (so the adversary can use $u' \neq u$, and so can the challenger). This modification lets us introduce into the proof an earlier hybrid in which the challenger uses $u' \neq u$, even on behalf of an honest P_1. (That hybrid is justified by the sender privacy of OT_γ.)

---

[3] We do not need to apply a similar trick to the sender role in the OT subprotocols, since the sender bits are always random.

[4] To get it by then, the ZAPs are performed in parallel to the second and third rounds of the three-bit multiplication protocol.

Then, we can switch the choice bit of P_1 in OT_α from real to random, and the reduction to the OT receiver privacy in OT_α will not need to use the value u.[5]

Dealing with additive errors. Since the modified protocol no longer requires proofs that $u' = u$, an adversarial P_1 is free to use $u' \neq u$, thereby introducing an error into the three-bit multiplication protocol. Namely, instead of computing the product $x_1 x_2 x_3$, an adversarial P_1 can cause the result of the protocol to be $(x_1 x_2 + (u' - u))x_3$. Importantly, the error term $e = u' - u$ cannot depend on the input of the honest parties. (The reason is that the value u received by P_1 in OT_α is masked by r_2 and hence independent of P_2's input x_2, so any change made by P_1 must also be independent of x_2.).

To deal with this adversarial error, we want to use a randomized encoding scheme which is resilient to such additive attacks. Indeed, Genkin et al. presented transformations that do exactly this in [GIP+14, GIP15, GIW16]. Namely, they described a compiler that transforms an arbitrary circuit C to another circuit C' that is resilient to additive attacks. Unfortunately, using these transformations does not work out of the box, since they do not preserve the degree of the circuit. So even if after using randomized encoding we get a degree-three function, making it resilient to additive attacks will blow up the degree, and we will not be able to use the three-bit multiplication protocol as before.

What we would like, instead, is to first transform the original function f that we want to compute into a resilient form $\hat{f}$, then apply randomized encoding to $\hat{f}$ to get a degree-three encoding g that we can use in our protocol. But this too does not work out of the box: The adversary can introduce additive errors in the circuit of g, but we only know that $\hat{f}$ is resilient to additive attacks, not its randomized encoding g. In a nutshell, we need distributed randomized encoding that has offline (input independent) and online (input dependent) procedures that satisfies the following three conditions:

- The offline encoding has degree-3 (in the randomness);
- The online procedure is decomposable (encodes each bit separately);
- The offline procedure is resilient to additive attacks on the internal wires of the computation.

As such the encoding procedure in [AIK06] does not meet these conditions.

BMR to the rescue. To tackle this last problem, we forgo "generic" randomized encoding, relying instead on the specific multiparty garbling due to Beaver et al. [BMR90] (referred to as "BMR encoding") and show how it can be massaged to satisfy the required properties.[6] For this specific encoding, we carefully align the roles in the BMR protocol to those in the three-bit multiplication protocol, and show that the errors in the three-bit multiplication instances with

---

[5] The reduction will still need to use u in the fourth round of the simulation, but by then we have already extracted the information that we need from the adversary.

[6] We remark that our BMR encoding differs from general randomized encoding as we allow some "local computation" on the inputs before it is fed into the offline encoding procedure.

a corrupted P_1 can be effectively translated to an additive attack against the underlying computation of $\hat{f}$, see Lemma 3.2. Our final protocol, therefore, pre-compiles the original function f to $\hat{f}$ using the transformations of Genkin et al., then applies the BMR encoding to get $\hat{f}'$ which is of degree-three and still resilient to the additive errors by a corrupted P_1. We remark here that another advantage of relying on BMR encoding as opposed to the randomized encoding from [AIK06] is that it can be instantiated based on any one-way function. In contrast the randomized encoding of [AIK06] requires the assumption of PRGs in NC^1.

A Sketch of the Final Protocol. Combining all these ideas, our (almost) final protocol proceeds as follows: Let C be a circuit that we want to evaluate securely, we first apply to it the transformation of Genkin et al. to get resilience against additive attacks, then apply BMR encoding to the result. This gives us a randomized encoding for our original circuit C. We use the fact that the BMR encoding has the form $C_{\mathsf{BMR}}(x; (\lambda, \rho)) = (x \oplus \lambda, g(\lambda, \rho))$ where each output bit of g has degree three (or less) in the (λ, ρ). Given the inputs $x = (x_1, \ldots, x_n)$, the parties choose their respective pieces of the BMR randomness λ^i, ρ^i, and engage in our modified three-bit multiplication protocol Π' (with a pair of OT's for each one in Fig. 1), to compute the outputs of $g(\lambda, \rho)$. In addition to the third round message of Π', each party P_i also broadcasts its masked input $x_i \oplus \lambda^i$.

Let wit_i be a witness of "correct behavior" of party P_i in Π' (where the witness of an OT-receiver includes the randomness for only one of the two instances in an OT pair). In parallel with the execution of Π', each party P_i also engages in three-round non-malleable commitment protocols for wit_i, and two-round ZAP proofs that wit_i is indeed a valid witness for "correct behavior" (in parallel to rounds 2,3). Once all the proofs are verified, the parties broadcast their final messages s_i in the protocol Π', allowing them to complete the computation of the encoding output $g(\lambda, \rho)$. They now all have the BMR encoding $C_{\mathsf{BMR}}(x; (\lambda, \rho))$, so they can locally apply the corresponding BMR decoding procedure to compute $C(x)$.

Other Technical Issues Non-malleable Commitments. Recall that we need a mechanism to extract information from the adversary before the fourth round, while simultaneously providing proofs of correct behavior for honest parties via ZAPs. In fact, we need the stronger property of *non-malleability*, namely the extracted information must not change when the witness in the ZAP proofs changes.

Ideally, we would want to use standard non-malleable commitments and recent work of Khurana [Khu17] shows how to construct such commitments in three rounds. However, our proof approach demands additional properties of the underlying non-malleable commitment, but we do not know how to construct such commitments in three rounds. Hence we relax the conditions of standard non-malleable commitments. Specifically, we allow for the non-malleable commitment scheme to admit invalid commitments. (Such weaker commitments are often used as the main tool in constructing full-fledged non-malleable commitments, see [GRRV14,Khu17] for few examples.)

A consequence of this relaxation is the problem of "over-extraction" where an extractor extracts the wrong message from an invalid commitment. We resolve this in our setting by making each party provide two independent commitments to its witness, and modify the ZAP proofs to show that at least one of these two commitments is a valid commitment to a valid witness.

This still falls short of yeilding full-fledged non-malleable commitments, but it ensures that the witness extracted in at least one of the two commitments is valid. Since the witness in our case includes the input and randomness of the OT subprotocols, the challenger in our hybrids can compare the extracted witness against the transcript of the relevant OT instances and discard invalid witnesses.

Another obstacle is that in some intermediate hybrids, some of the information that the challenger should commit to is only known in later rounds of the protocol, hence we need the commitments to be *input-delayed*. For this we rely on a technique of Ciampi et al. [COSV16] for making non-malleable commitments into input-delayed ones. Finally, we observe that we can instantiate the "weak simulation extractable non-malleable commitments" that we need from the three-round non-malleable commitment scheme implicit in the work of Goyal et al. [GRRV14].

Equivocable oblivious transfer. In some hybrids in the security proof, we need to switch the sender bits in the OT subprotocols. For example in one step we switch the P_2 sender inputs in OT_α from $(-r_2, x_2 - r_2)$ to $(-r_2, \tilde{x}_2 - r_2)$ where x_2 is the real input of P_2 and $\tilde{x}_2$ is a random bit. (We also have a similarly step for P_1's input in OT_γ.)

For every instance of OT, the challenger needs to commit to the OT randomness on behalf of the honest party and prove via ZAP that it behaved correctly in the protocol. Since ZAPs are not simulatable, the challenger can only provide these proofs by following the honest prover strategy, so it needs to actually have the sender randomness for these OT protocols. Recalling that we commit twice to the randomness, our security proof goes through some hybrids where in one commitment we have the OT sender randomness for one set of values and in the other we have the randomness for another set. (This is used to switch the ZAP proof from one witness to another).

But how can there be two sets of randomness values that explain *the same OT transcript*? To this end, we use an *equivocable* oblivious transfer protocol. Namely, given the receiver's randomness, it is possible to explain the OT transcript after the fact, in such a way that the "other sender bit" (the one that the receiver does not get) can be opened both ways. In all these hybrids, the OT receiver gets a random output bit. So the challenger first runs the protocol according to the values in one hybrid, then rewinds the adversary to extract the randomness of the receiver, where it can then explain (and hence prove) the sender's actions in any way that it needs, while keeping the OT transcript fixed.

We show how to instantiate the equivocable OT that we need from (a slightly weak variant of) additive homomorphic encryption, with an additional equivocation property. Such encryption schemes can in turn be constructed under standard (polynomial) hardness assumptions such as LWE, DDH, Quadratic Residuosity (QR) and Decisional Composite Residuosity (DCR).

Premature rewinding. One subtle issue with relying on equivocable OT is that equivocation requires knowing the randomness of the OT receiver. To get this randomness, the challenger in our hybrids must rewind the receiver, so we introduce in some of the hybrids another phase of rewinding, which we call "premature rewinding." This phase has nothing to do with the adversary's input, and it has no effect on the transcript used in the main thread. All it does is extract some keys and randomness, which are needed to equivocate.

No four-round proofs. A side benefit of using BMR garbling is that the authentication properties of BMR let us do away completely with the four-round proofs from [ACJ17]. In our protocol, at the end of the third round the parties hold a secret sharing of the garbled circuit, its input labels, and the translation table to interpret the results of the garbled evaluation. Then in the last round they just broadcast their shares and input labels, then reconstruct the circuit, evaluate the circuit, and recover the result.

Absent a proof in the fourth round, the adversary can report arbitrary values as its shares, even after seeing the shares of the honest parties, but we argue that it still can not violate privacy or correctness. It was observed in prior work [LPSY15] that faulty shares for the garbled circuit itself or the input labels can at worst cause an honest party to abort, and such an event will be independent of the inputs of the honest parties. Roughly speaking, this is because the so called "active path" in the evaluation is randomized by masks from each party. Furthermore, if an honest party does not abort and completes evaluation, then the result is correct. This was further strengthened in [HSS17], and was shown to hold even when the adversary is rushing. One course of action still available to the adversary is to modify the translation tables, arbitrarily making the honest party output the wrong answer. This can be fixed by a standard technique of precompiling f to additionally receive a MAC key from each party and output the MACs of the output under all keys along with the output. Each honest party can then verify the garbled-circuit result using its private MAC key.

A modular presentation with a "defensible" adversary. In order to make our presentation more modular, we separate the issues of extraction and non-malleability from the overall structure of the protocol by introducing the notion of a "defensible" adversary. Specifically, we first prove security in a simpler model in which the adversary voluntarily provides the simulator with some extra information. In a few more details, we consider an "explaining adversary" that at the end of the third round outputs a "defense" (or explanation) for its actions so far.[7]

This model is somewhat similar to the semi-malicious adversary model of Asharov et al. [AJL+12] where the adversary outputs its internal randomness

---

[7] The name "defensible adversaries" is adapted from the work of Haitner et al. [HIK+11].

with every message. The main difference is that here we (the protocol designers) get to decide what information the adversary needs to provide and when. We suspect that our model is also somewhat related to the notion of robust semi-honest security defined in [ACJ17], where, if a protocol is secure against defensible adversaries and a defense is required after the kth round of the protocol, then it is plausible that the first k rounds admits robust semi-honest security.

Once we have a secure protocol in this weaker model, we add to it commitment and proofs that would let us extract from the adversary the same information that was provided in the "defense". As we hinted above, this is done by having the adversary commit to that information using (a weaker variant of) simulation extractable commitments, and also prove that the committed values are indeed a valid "defense" for its actions. While in this work we introduce "defensible" adversaries merely as a convenience to make the presentation more modular, we believe that it is a useful tool for obtaining round-efficient protocols.

1.3 Related and Concurrent Work

The earliest MPC protocol is due to Goldreich et al. [GMW87]. The round complexity of this approach is proportional to the circuit's multiplication depth (namely, the largest number of multiplication gates in the circuit on any path from input to output) and can be non-constant for most functions. In Table 1, we list relevant prior works that design secure multiparty computation for arbitrary number parties in the stand-alone plain model emphasizing on the works that have improved the round complexity or cryptographic assumptions.

Table 1. Prior works that design secure computation protocols for arbitrary number of parties in the plain model where we focus on constant round constructions.

Protocol	Functionality	Round	Assumptions	Sub-exponential
[BMR90, KOS03]	General	$O(1)$	CRHF, ETDP	Yes
[Pas04]	General	$O(1)$	CRHF, ETDP	No
[PW10]	General	$O(1)$	ETDP	Yes
[LP11, Goy11]	General	$O(1)$	ETDP	No
[LPV12]	General	$O(1)$	OT	No
[GMPP16]	General	6	LWE	Yes
		5	iO	Yes
[ACJ17]	General	5	DDH	No
		4	DDH	Yes
[BHP17]	General	4	LWE	Yes
[COSV17b]	Coin Tossing	4	ETDP	No

In concurrent work, simultaneously Benhamouda and Lin [BL18] and Garg and Srinivasan [GS17] construct a five-round MPC protocol based on minimal assumptions. While these protocols rely on the minimal assumption of 4-round OT protocol, they require an additional round to construct their MPC.

In another concurrent work, Badrinarayanan et al. [BGJ+18] establish the main feasibility result presented in this work, albeit with different techniques and slightly different assumptions. Their work compiles the semi-malicious protocol of [BL18, GS17] while we build on modified variants of BMR and the 3-bit multiplication due to [ACJ17]. Both works rely on injective OWFs, and whereas we also need ZAPs and affine homomorphic encryption scheme, they also need dense cryptosystems and two-round OT.

2   Preliminaries

2.1   Affine Homomorphic PKE

We rely on public-key encryption schemes that admit an affine homomorphism and an equivocation property. As we demonstrate via our instantiations, most standard additively homomorphic encryption schemes satisfy these properties. Specifically, we provide instantiations based on Learning With Errors (LWE), Decisional Diffie-Hellman (DDH), Quadratic Residuosity (QR) and Decisional Composite Residuosity (DCR) hardness assumptions.

Definition 2.1 (Affine homomorphic PKE). *We say that a public key encryption scheme* $(\mathcal{M} = \{\mathcal{M}_\kappa\}_\kappa, \mathsf{Gen}, \mathsf{Enc}, \mathsf{Dec})$ *is affine homomorphic if*

- Affine transformation: *There exists an algorithm* AT *such that for every* $(\mathrm{PK}, \mathrm{SK}) \leftarrow \mathsf{Gen}(1^\kappa)$, $m \in \mathcal{M}_\kappa$, $r_c \leftarrow \mathcal{D}_{rand}(1^\kappa)$ *and every* $a, b \in \mathcal{M}_\kappa$, $\mathsf{Dec}_{\mathrm{SK}}(\mathsf{AT}(\mathrm{PK}, c, a, b)) = am + b$ *holds with probability 1, and* $c = \mathsf{Enc}_{\mathrm{PK}}(m; r_c)$, *where* $\mathcal{D}_{rand}(1^\kappa)$ *is the distribution of randomness used by* Enc.
- Equivocation: *There exists an algorithm* Explain *such that for every* $(\mathrm{PK}, \mathrm{SK}) \leftarrow \mathsf{Gen}(1^\kappa)$, *every* $m, a_0, b_0, a_1, b_1 \in \mathcal{M}_\kappa$ *such that* $a_0 m + b_0 = a_1 m + b_1$ *and every* $r_c \leftarrow \mathcal{D}_{rand}(1^\kappa)$, *it holds that the following distributions are statistically close over* $\kappa \in \mathbb{N}$:
  - $\{\sigma \leftarrow \{0,1\}; r \leftarrow \mathcal{D}_{rand}(1^\kappa); c^* \leftarrow \mathsf{AT}(\mathrm{PK}, c, a_\sigma, b_\sigma; r) : (m, r_c, c^*, r, a_\sigma, b_\sigma)\}$, *and*
  - $\{\sigma \leftarrow \{0,1\}; r \leftarrow \mathcal{D}_{rand}(1^\kappa); c^* \leftarrow \mathsf{AT}(\mathrm{PK}, c, a_\sigma, b_\sigma; r);$
    $t \leftarrow \mathsf{Explain}(\mathrm{SK}, a_\sigma, b_\sigma, a_{1-\sigma}, b_{1-\sigma}, m, r_c, r) : (m, r_c, c^*, t, a_{1-\sigma}, b_{1-\sigma})\}$,

  where $c = \mathsf{Enc}_{\mathrm{PK}}(m; r_c)$.

In the full version [HHPV17], we demonstrate how to meet Definition 2.1 under a variety of hardness assumptions.

Definition 2.2 (Resettable reusable WI argument). *We say that a two-message delayed-input interactive argument* (P, V) *for a language* L *is resettable reusable witness indistinguishable, if for every PPT verifier* V^*, *every* $z \in \{0,1\}^*$, $\Pr[b = b'] \leq 1/2 + \mu(\kappa)$ *in the following experiment, where we denote the first round message function by* $m_1 = \mathsf{wi}_1(r_1)$ *and the second round message* *function by* $\mathsf{wi}_2(x, w, m_1, r_2)$. *The challenger samples* $b \leftarrow \{0, 1\}$. V^* *(with auxiliary input* z*) specifies* $(m_1^1, x^1, w_1^1, w_2^1)$ *where* w_1^1, w_2^1 *are (not necessarily distinct) witnesses for* x^1. V^* *then obtains second round message* $\mathsf{wi}_2(x^1, w_b^1, m_1^1, r)$ *generated with uniform randomness* r. *Next, the adversary specifies arbitrary* $(m_1^2, x^2, w_1^2, w_2^2)$, *and obtains second round message* $\mathsf{wi}_2(x^2, w_b^2, m_1^2, r)$. *This continues* $m(\kappa) = \text{poly}(\kappa)$ *times for a-priori unbounded* m, *and finally* V^* *outputs* b.

ZAPs (and more generally, any two-message WI) can be modified to obtain resettable reusable WI, by having the prover apply a PRF on the verifier's message and the public statement in order to generate the randomness for the proof. This allows to argue, via a hybrid argument, that fresh randomness can be used for each proof, and therefore perform a hybrid argument so that each proof remains WI. In our construction, we will use resettable reusable ZAPs. In general, any multitheorem NIZK protocol implies a resettable reusable ZAP which inturn can be based on any (doubly) enhanced trapdoor permutation.

2.2 Additive Attacks and AMD Circuits

In what follows we borrow the terminology and definitions verbatim from [GIP+14, GIW16]. We note that in this work we work with binary fields $\mathbb{F}_2$.

Definition 2.3 (AMD code[CDF+08]). *An* (n, k, ε)*-AMD code is a pair of circuits* (Encode, Decode) *where* Encode $: \mathbb{F}^n \rightarrow \mathbb{F}^k$ *is randomized and* Decode $: \mathbb{F}^k \rightarrow \mathbb{F}^{n+1}$ *is deterministic such that the following properties hold:*

– *Perfect completeness. For all* $\mathbf{x} \in \mathbb{F}^n$,

$$\Pr[\mathsf{Decode}(\mathsf{Encode}(\mathbf{x})) = (0, \mathbf{x})] = 1.$$

– *Additive robustness. For any* $\mathbf{a} \in \mathbb{F}^k, \mathbf{a} \neq 0$, *and for any* $\mathbf{x} \in \mathbb{F}^n$ *it holds that*

$$\Pr[\mathsf{Decode}(\mathsf{Encode}(\mathbf{x}) + \mathbf{a}) \notin \mathsf{ERROR}] \leq \varepsilon.$$

Definition 2.4 (Additive attack). *An additive attack* $\mathbf{A}$ *on a circuit* C *is a fixed vector of field elements which is independent from the inputs and internal values of* C. $\mathbf{A}$ *contains an entry for every wire of* C, *and has the following effect on the evaluation of the circuit. For every wire* ω *connecting gates* a *and* b *in* C, *the entry of* $\mathbf{A}$ *that corresponds to* ω *is added to the output of* a, *and the computation of the gate* b *uses the derived value. Similarly, for every output gate* o, *the entry of* $\mathbf{A}$ *that corresponds to the wire in the output of* o *is added to the value of this output.*

Definition 2.5 (Additively corruptible version of a circuit). *Let* C $: \mathbb{F}^{I_1} \times \ldots \times \mathbb{F}^{I_n} \rightarrow \mathbb{F}^{O_1} \times \ldots \times \mathbb{F}^{O_n}$ *be an* n*-party circuit containing* W *wires. We define the additively corruptible version of* C *to be the* n*-party functionality* $f^{\mathbf{A}} : \mathbb{F}^{I_1} \times \ldots \times \mathbb{F}^{I_n} \times \mathbb{F}^W \rightarrow \mathbb{F}^{O_1} \times \ldots \times \mathbb{F}^{O_n}$ *that takes an additional input from the adversary which indicates an additive error for every wire of* C. *For all* $(\mathbf{x}, \mathbf{A})$, $f^{\mathbf{A}}(\mathbf{x}, \mathbf{A})$ *outputs the result of the additively corrupted* C, *denoted by* $C^{\mathbf{A}}$, *as specified by the additive attack* $\mathbf{A}$ ($\mathbf{A}$ *is the simulator's attack on* C*) when invoked on the inputs* $\mathbf{x}$.

Definition 2.6 (Additively secure implementation). *Let $\varepsilon > 0$. We say that a randomized circuit $\widehat{C} : \mathbb{F}^n \to \mathbb{F}^t \times \mathbb{F}^k$ is an ε-additively-secure implementation of a function $f : \mathbb{F}^n \to \mathbb{F}^k$ if the following holds.*

- Completeness. *For every $\mathbf{x} \in \mathbb{F}^n$, $\Pr[\widehat{C}(\mathbf{x}) = f(\mathbf{x})] = 1$.*
- Additive attack security. *For any additive attack $\mathbf{A}$ there exist $a^{\mathrm{In}} \in \mathbb{F}^n$, and a distribution $\mathbf{A}^{\mathrm{Out}}$ over $\mathbb{F}^k$, such that for every $\mathbf{x} \in \mathbb{F}^n$,*

$$SD(C^{\mathbf{A}}(\mathbf{x}), f(\mathbf{x} + a^{\mathrm{In}}) + \mathbf{A}^{\mathrm{Out}}) \leq \varepsilon$$

where SD denotes statistical distance between two distributions.

Theorem 2.7 ([GIW16], Theorem 2). *For any boolean circuit $C : \{0,1\}^n \to \{0,1\}^m$, and any security parameter κ, there exists a $2^{-\kappa}$-additively-secure implementation $\widehat{C}$ of C, where $|\widehat{C}| = \mathsf{poly}(|C|, n, \kappa)$. Moreover, given any additive attack $\mathbf{A}$ and input $\mathbf{x}$, it is possible to identify a^{In} such that $\widehat{C}^{\mathbf{A}}(\mathbf{x}) = f(\mathbf{x} + a^{\mathrm{In}})$.*

Remark 2.1. Genkin et al. [GIW16] present a transformation that achieves tighter parameters, namely, better overhead than what is reported in the preceding theorem. We state this theorem in weaker form as it is sufficient for our work.

Remark 2.2. Genkin et al. [GIW16] do not claim the stronger version where the equivalent a^{In} is identifiable. However their transformation directly yields a procedure to identify a^{In}. Namely each bit of the input to the function f needs to be preprocessed via an AMD code before feeding it to $\widehat{C}$. a^{In} can be computed as $\mathsf{Decode}(\mathsf{x}_{\mathsf{Encode}} + \mathbf{A}_{\mathrm{In}}) - \mathbf{x}$ where $\mathsf{x}_{\mathsf{Encode}}$ is the encoded input $\mathbf{x}$ via the AMD code and $\mathbf{A}_{\mathrm{In}}$ is the additive attack $\mathbf{A}$ restricted to the input wires. In other words, either the equivalent input is $\mathbf{x}$ or the output of $\widehat{C}$ will be ERROR.

Functionality $\mathcal{F}^{\mathbf{A}}_{\mathrm{MULT}}$

$\mathcal{F}^{\mathbf{A}}_{\mathrm{MULT}}$ runs with parties $\mathcal{P} = \{P_1, P_2, P_3\}$ and an adversary $\mathcal{S}$ who corrupts a subset $I \subset [3]$ of parties.

1. For each $i \in \{1, 2, 3\}$, the functionality receives x_i from party P_i, and P_1 also sends another bit e_{In}.
2. Upon receiving the inputs from all parties, evaluate $y = (x_1 x_2 + e_{\mathrm{In}})x_3$ and sends it to $\mathcal{S}$.
3. Upon receiving $(\mathsf{deliver}, e_{\mathrm{Out}})$ from $\mathcal{S}$, the functionality sends $y + e_{\mathrm{Out}}$ to all parties.

Fig. 2. Additively corruptible 3-bit multiplication functionality.

3   Warmup MPC: The Case of Defensible Adversaries

For the sake of gradual introduction of our technical ideas, we begin with a warm-up, we present a protocol and prove security in an easier model, in which the adversary volunteers a "defense" of its actions, consisting of some of its inputs and randomness. Specifically, instead of asking the adversary to prove an action, in this model we just assume that the adversary reveals all its inputs and randomness for that action.

The goal of presenting a protocol in this easier model is to show that it is sufficient to prove correct behavior in some *but not all* of the "OT subprotocols". Later in Sect. 4 we will rely on our non-malleability and zero-knowledge machinery to achieve similar results. Namely the adversary will be required to prove correct behavior, and we will use rewinding to extract from it the "defense" that our final simulator will need.

3.1   Step 1: 3-Bit Multiplication with Additive Errors

The functionality that we realize in this section, $\mathcal{F}^{\mathsf{A}}_{\mathrm{MULT}}$ is an additively corruptible version of the 3-bit multiplication functionality. In addition to the three bits x_1, x_2, x_3, $\mathcal{F}^{\mathsf{A}}_{\mathrm{MULT}}$ also takes as input an additive "error bit" e_{In} from P_1, and e_{Out} from the adversary, and computes the function $(x_1 x_2 + e_{\mathrm{In}})x_3 + e_{\mathrm{Out}}$. The description of $\mathcal{F}^{\mathsf{A}}_{\mathrm{MULT}}$ can be found in Fig. 2.

Our protocol relies on an equivocable affine-homomorphic-encryption scheme (Gen, Enc, Dec, AT, Explain) (over $\mathbb{F}_2$) as per Definition 2.1, and an additive secret sharing scheme (Share, Recover) for sharing 0. The details of our protocol are as follows. We usually assume that randomness is implicit in the encryption scheme, unless specified explicitly. See Fig. 3 for a high level description of protocol Π_{DMULT}.

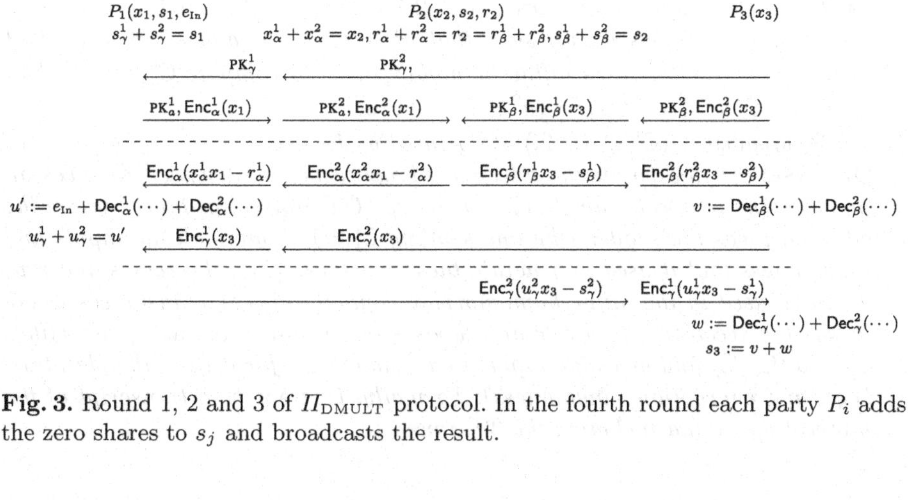

Fig. 3. Round 1, 2 and 3 of Π_{DMULT} protocol. In the fourth round each party P_i adds the zero shares to s_j and broadcasts the result.

Protocol 1 (3-bit Multiplication protocol Π_{DMULT})

Input & Randomness: *Parties* P_1, P_2, P_3 *are given inputs* $(x_1, e_{\text{In}}), x_2, x_3$, *respectively.* P_1 *chooses a random bit* s_1 *and* P_2 *chooses two random bits* s_2, r_2 *(in addition to the randomness needed for the sub-protocols below).*

ROUND 1:

- *Party* P_1 *runs key generation twice,* $(\text{PK}_a^1, \text{SK}_a^1), (\text{PK}_a^2, \text{SK}_a^2) \leftarrow$ Gen, *encrypts* $\mathsf{C}_\alpha^1[1] := \mathsf{Enc}_{\text{PK}_a^1}(x_1)$ *and* $\mathsf{C}_\alpha^2[1] := \mathsf{Enc}_{\text{PK}_a^2}(x_1)$, *and broadcasts* $((\text{PK}_a^1, \mathsf{C}_\alpha^1[1]), (\text{PK}_a^2, \mathsf{C}_\alpha^2[1]))$ *(to be used by* P_2*).*
- P_3 *runs key generation four times,* $(\text{PK}_\beta^1, \text{SK}_\beta^1), (\text{PK}_\beta^2, \text{SK}_\beta^2),$ $(\text{PK}_\gamma^1, \text{SK}_\gamma^1), (\text{PK}_\gamma^2, \text{SK}_\gamma^2) \leftarrow$ Gen(1^κ).

  Next it encrypts using the first two keys, $\mathsf{C}_\beta^1[1] := \mathsf{Enc}_{\text{PK}_\beta^1}(x_3)$ *and* $\mathsf{C}_\beta^2[1] :=$ $\mathsf{Enc}_{\text{PK}_\beta^2}(x_3)$, *and broadcasts* $\left((\text{PK}_\beta^1, \mathsf{C}_\beta^1[1]), (\text{PK}_\beta^2, \mathsf{C}_\beta^2[1])\right)$ *(to be used by* P_2*), and* $(\text{PK}_\gamma^1, \text{PK}_\gamma^2)$ *(to be used in round 3 by* P_1*).*
- *Each party* P_j *samples random secret shares of 0,* $(z_j^1, z_j^2, z_j^3) \leftarrow$ Share$(0, 3)$ *and sends* z_j^i *to party* P_i *over a private channel.*

ROUND 2:

- *Party* P_2 *samples* x_α^1, x_α^2 *such that* $x_\alpha^1 + x_\alpha^2 = x_2$ *and* r_α^1, r_α^2 *such that* $r_\alpha^1 + r_\alpha^2 = r_2$. *It use affine homomorphism to compute* $\mathsf{C}_\alpha^1[2] := (x_\alpha^1 \boxdot \mathsf{C}_\alpha^1[1]) \boxminus r_\alpha^1$ *and* $\mathsf{C}_\alpha^2[2] := (x_\alpha^2 \boxdot \mathsf{C}_\alpha^1[1]) \boxminus r_\alpha^2$.

  Party P_2 *also samples* r_β^1, r_β^2 *such that* $r_\beta^1 + r_\beta^2 = r_2$ *and* s_β^1, s_β^2 *such that* $s_\beta^1 + s_\beta^2 = s_2$, *and uses affine homomorphism to compute* $\mathsf{C}_\beta^1[2] :=$ $(r_\beta^1 \boxdot \mathsf{C}_\beta^1[1]) \boxminus s_\beta^1$ *and* $\mathsf{C}_\beta^2[2] := (r_\beta^2 \boxdot \mathsf{C}_\beta^2[1]) \boxminus s_\beta^2$.

  P_2 *broadcasts* $(\mathsf{C}_\alpha^1[2], \mathsf{C}_\alpha^2[2])$ *(to be used by* P_1*) and* $(\mathsf{C}_\beta^1[2], \mathsf{C}_\beta^2[2])$ *(to be used by* P_3*).*
- *Party* P_3 *encrypt* $\mathsf{C}_\gamma^1[1] := \mathsf{Enc}_{\text{PK}_\gamma^1}(x_3)$ *and* $\mathsf{C}_\gamma^2[1] := \mathsf{Enc}_{\text{PK}_\gamma^2}(x_3)$ *and broadcast* $(\mathsf{C}_\gamma^1[1], \mathsf{C}_\gamma^2[1])$ *(to be used by* P_1*).*

ROUND 3:

- *Party* P_1 *computes* $u := \mathsf{Dec}_{\text{SK}_a^1}(\mathsf{C}_\alpha^1[2]) + \mathsf{Dec}_{\text{SK}_a^2}(\mathsf{C}_\alpha^2[2])$ *and* $u' = u + e_{\text{In}}$. *Then* P_1 *samples* u_γ^1, u_γ^2 *such that* $u_\gamma^1 + u_\gamma^2 = u'$ *and* s_γ^1, s_γ^2 *such that* $s_\gamma^1 + s_\gamma^2 = s_1$. *It uses affine homomorphism to compute* $\mathsf{C}_\gamma^1[2] := (u_\gamma^1 \boxdot \mathsf{C}_\gamma^1[1]) \boxminus s_\gamma^1$ *and* $\mathsf{C}_\gamma^2[2] := (u_\gamma^2 \boxdot \mathsf{C}_\gamma^2[1]) \boxminus s_\gamma^2$.

  P_1 *broadcasts* $(\mathsf{C}_\gamma^1[2], \mathsf{C}_\gamma^2[2])$ *(to be used by* P_3*).*

DEFENSE: *At this point, the adversary broadcasts its "defense:" It gives an input for the protocol, namely* $x_\star$. *For every "OT protocol instance" where the adversary was the sender (the one sending* $\mathsf{C}_\star^*[2]$*), it gives all the inputs and randomness that it used to generate these messages (i.e., the values and randomness used in the affine-homomorphic computation). For instances where it was the receiver, the adversary chooses one message of each pair (either* $\mathsf{C}_\star^1[1]$ *or* $\mathsf{C}_\star^2[1]$*) and gives the inputs and randomness for it (i.e., the plaintext, keys, and encryption randomness). Formally, let* trans *be a transcript of the protocol up to and including the* 3rd *round*

$$\text{trans} \overset{\text{def}}{=} \left(\begin{array}{l} \text{PK}_a^1, \mathsf{C}_\alpha^1[1], \mathsf{C}_\alpha^1[2], \text{PK}_a^2, \mathsf{C}_\alpha^2[1], \mathsf{C}_\alpha^2[2],\ \ \text{PK}_\beta^1, \mathsf{C}_\beta^1[1], \mathsf{C}_\beta^1[2], \text{PK}_\beta^2, \mathsf{C}_\beta^2[1], \mathsf{C}_\beta^2[2], \\ \text{PK}_\gamma^1, \mathsf{C}_\gamma^1[1], \mathsf{C}_\gamma^1[2], \text{PK}_\gamma^2, \mathsf{C}_\gamma^2[1], \mathsf{C}_\gamma^2[2] \end{array} \right)$$

$$\text{trans}_{P_1}^b \overset{\text{def}}{=} \left(\text{PK}_a^b, \mathsf{C}_a^b[1],\ \ \mathsf{C}_\gamma^1[2], \mathsf{C}_\gamma^2[2]\ \right)$$

$$\text{trans}_{P_2}^0 = \text{trans}_{P_2}^1 \overset{\text{def}}{=} \left(\mathsf{C}_\alpha^1[2], \mathsf{C}_\alpha^2[2],\ \ \mathsf{C}_\beta^1[2], \mathsf{C}_\beta^2[2]\ \right)$$

$$\text{trans}_{P_3}^b \overset{\text{def}}{=} \left(\text{PK}_\beta^b, \mathsf{C}_\beta^b[1],\ \ \text{PK}_\gamma^b, \mathsf{C}_\gamma^b[1] \right)$$

we have three NP languages, one per party, with the defense for that party being the witness:

$$\mathcal{L}_{P_1} = \left\{ \text{trans} \ \middle|\ \begin{array}{l} \exists\, (x_1, e_{\text{In}}, \rho_\alpha, \text{SK}_a, \sigma_\alpha, u_\gamma^1, u_\gamma^2, s_\gamma^1, s_\gamma^2) \\ \left((\text{PK}_a^1, \text{SK}_a = \mathsf{Gen}(\rho_\alpha) \wedge \mathsf{C}_\alpha^1[1] = \mathsf{Enc}_{\text{PK}_a^1}(x_1; \sigma_\alpha)) \right. \\ \left. \vee\ (\text{PK}_a^2, \text{SK}_a = \mathsf{Gen}(\rho_\alpha) \wedge \mathsf{C}_\alpha^2[1] = \mathsf{Enc}_{\text{PK}_a^2}(x_1; \sigma_\alpha)) \right) \\ \wedge\ \mathsf{C}_\gamma^1[2] = u_\gamma^1 \boxdot \mathsf{C}_\gamma^1[1] \boxminus s_\gamma^1\ \wedge\ \mathsf{C}_\gamma^2[2] = u_\gamma^2 \boxdot \mathsf{C}_\gamma^2[1] \boxminus s_\gamma^2 \end{array} \right\} \tag{1}$$

$$\mathcal{L}_{P_2} = \left\{ \text{trans} \ \middle|\ \begin{array}{l} \exists\, (x_\alpha^1, x_\alpha^2, s_\beta^1, s_\beta^2, r_\alpha^1, r_\alpha^2, r_\gamma^1, r_\gamma^2)\ \ s.t.\ \ r_\alpha^1 + r_\alpha^2 = r_\gamma^1 + r_\gamma^2 \\ \wedge\ \mathsf{C}_\alpha^1[2] = x_\alpha^1 \boxdot \mathsf{C}_\alpha^1[1] \boxminus r_\alpha^1\ \wedge\ \mathsf{C}_\alpha^2[2] = x_\alpha^2 \boxdot \mathsf{C}_\alpha^2[1] \boxminus r_\alpha^2 \\ \wedge\ \ \mathsf{C}_\beta^1[2] = r_\beta^1 \boxdot \mathsf{C}_\beta^1[1] \boxminus s_\beta^1\ \wedge\ \mathsf{C}_\beta^2[2] = r_\beta^2 \boxdot \mathsf{C}_\beta^2[1] \boxminus r_\beta^2 \end{array} \right\} \tag{2}$$

$$\mathcal{L}_{P_3} = \left\{ \text{trans} \ \middle|\ \begin{array}{l} \exists\, (x_3, \rho_\beta, \text{SK}_\beta, \sigma_\beta, \rho_\gamma, \text{SK}_\gamma, \sigma_\gamma) \\ \left((\text{PK}_\beta^1, \text{SK}_\beta = \mathsf{Gen}(\rho_\beta) \wedge \mathsf{C}_\beta^1[1] = \mathsf{Enc}_{\text{PK}_\beta^1}(x_3; \sigma_\beta)) \right. \\ \left. \vee\ (\text{PK}_\beta^2, \text{SK}_\beta = \mathsf{Gen}(\rho_\beta) \wedge \mathsf{C}_\beta^2[1] = \mathsf{Enc}_{\text{PK}_\beta^2}(x_3; \sigma_\beta)) \right) \\ \wedge\ \left((\text{PK}_\gamma^1, \text{SK}_\gamma = \mathsf{Gen}(\rho_\gamma) \wedge \mathsf{C}_\gamma^1[1] = \mathsf{Enc}_{\text{PK}_\gamma^1}(x_3; \sigma_\gamma)) \right. \\ \left. \vee\ (\text{PK}_\gamma^2, \text{SK}_\gamma = \mathsf{Gen}(\rho_\gamma) \wedge \mathsf{C}_\gamma^2[1] = \mathsf{Enc}_{\text{PK}_\gamma^2}(x_3; \sigma_\gamma)) \right) \end{array} \right\} \tag{3}$$

ROUND 4:

- P_3 computes $v := \mathsf{Dec}_{\text{SK}_\beta^1}(\mathsf{C}_\beta^1[2]) + \mathsf{Dec}_{\text{SK}_\beta^2}(\mathsf{C}_\beta^2[2])$, $w := \mathsf{Dec}_{\text{SK}_\gamma^1}(\mathsf{C}_\gamma^1[2]) + \mathsf{Dec}_{\text{SK}_\gamma^2}(\mathsf{C}_\gamma^2[2])$, and $s_3 := v + w$.
- Every party P_j adds the zero shares to s_j, broadcasting $S_j := s_j + \sum_{i=1}^3 z_i^j$.

– OUTPUT: *All parties set the final output to* $Z = S_1 + S_2 + S_3$.

Lemma 3.1. *Protocol* Π_{DMULT} *securely realizes the functionality* $\mathcal{F}_{\text{MULT}}^{\text{A}}$ *(cf. Fig. 2) in the presence of a "defensible adversary" that always broadcast valid defense at the end of the third round.*

Proof. We first show that the protocol is correct with a benign adversary. Observe that $u' = e_{\text{In}} + x_1(x_\alpha^1 + x_\alpha^2) - (r_\alpha^1 + r_\alpha^2) = e_{\text{In}} + x_1 x_2 - r_2$, and similarly $v = x_3 r_2 - s_2$ and $w = x_3 u' - s_1$. Therefore,

$$\begin{aligned} S_1 + S_2 + S_3 = s_1 + s_2 + s_3 &= s_1 + s_2 + (v + w) \\ &= s_1 + s_2 + (x_3 r_2 - s_2) + (x_3 u' - s_1) \\ &= x_3 r_2 + x_3(x_1 x_2 - r_2 + e_{\text{In}}) \\ &= (x_1 x_2 + e_{\text{In}}) x_3 \end{aligned}$$

as required. We continue with the security proof.

To argue security we need to describe a simulator and prove that the simulated view is indistinguishable from the real one. Below fix inputs $x_1, e_{\text{In}}, x_2, x_3$, and a defensible PPT adversary $\mathcal{A}$ controlling a fixed subset of parties $I \subseteq [3]$ (and also an auxiliary input z).

The simulator $\mathcal{S}$ chooses random inputs for each honest party (denote these values by $\hat{x}_i$), and then follows the honest protocol execution using these random inputs until the end of the 3rd round. Upon receiving a valid "defense" that includes the inputs and randomness that the adversary used to generate (some of) the messages $C^i_*[j]$, the simulator extracts from that defense the effective inputs of the adversary to send to the functionality, and other values to help with the rest of the simulation. Specifically:

- If P_3 is corrupted then its defense (for one of the $C^i_\beta[1]$'s and one of the $C^i_\gamma[1]$'s) includes a value for x_3, that we denote x_3^*. (A defensible adversary is guaranteed to use the same value in the defense for $C^*_\beta[1]$ and in the defense for $C^*_\gamma[1]$'s.)
- If P_2 is corrupted then the defense that it provides includes all of its inputs and randomness (since it always plays the "OT sender"), hence the simulator learns a value for x_2 that we denote x_2^*, and also some values r_2, s_2. (If P_2 is honest then by r_2, s_2 we denote below the values that the simulator chose for it.)
- If P_1 is corrupted then its defense (for either of the $C^i_\alpha[1]$'s) includes a value for x_1 that we denote x_1^*.
    From the defense for both $C^1_\gamma[2], C^2_\gamma[2]$ the simulator learns the u_i^γ's and s_i^γ's, and it sets $u' := u_\gamma^1 + u_\gamma^2$ and $s_1 := s_\gamma^1 + s_\gamma^2$.
    The simulator sets $u := x_1^* x_2^* - r_2$ if P_2 is corrupted and $u := x_1^* \hat{x}_2 - r_2$ if P_2 is honest, and then computes the effective value $e_{\text{In}}^* := u' - u$. (If P_1 is honest then by s_1, u, u' we denote below the values that the simulator used for it.)

Let x_i^* and e_{In}^* be the values received by the functionality. (These are computed as above if the corresponding party is corrupted, and are equal to x_i, e_{In} if it is honest.) The simulator gets back from the functionality the answer $y = (x_1^* x_2^* + e_{\text{In}}^*) x_3^*$.

Having values for s_1, s_2 as described above, the simulator computes $s_3 := y - s_1 - s_2$ if P_3 is honest, and if P_3 is corrupted then the simulator sets $v := r_2 x_3^* - s_2$, $w := u x_3^* - s_1$ and $s_3 := v + w$. It then proceeds to compute the values S_j that the honest parties broadcast in the last round.

Let s be the sum of the s_i values for all the corrupted parties, and let z be the sum of the zero-shares that the simulator sent to the adversary (on behalf of all the honest parties), and z' be the sum of zero-shared that the simulator received from the adversary. The values that the simulator broadcasts for the honest parties in the fourth round are chosen at random, subject to them summing up to $y - (s + z - z')$.

If the adversary sends its fourth round messages, an additive output error is computed as $e_{\text{Out}} := y - \sum_j \tilde{S}_j$ where $\tilde{S}_j$ are the values that were broadcast in the fourth round. The simulator finally sends (deliver, e_{Out}) to the ideal functionality.

This concludes the description of the simulator, it remains to prove indistinguishability. Namely, we need to show that for the simulator $\mathcal{S}$ above, the two distributions $\mathbf{REAL}_{\Pi_{\mathrm{DMULT}},\mathcal{A}(z),I}(\kappa, (x_1, e_{\mathrm{In}}), x_2, x_3)$ and $\mathbf{IDEAL}_{\mathcal{F}_{\mathrm{MULT}}^{\mathbf{A}},\mathcal{S}(z),I}(\kappa, (x_1, e_{\mathrm{In}}), x_2, x_3)$ are indistinguishable. We argue this via a standard hybrid argument. We provide a brief sketch below.

High-level sketch of the proof. On a high-level, in the first two intermediate hybrids, we modify the fourth message of the honest parties to be generated using the defense and the inputs chosen for the honest parties, rather than the internal randomness and values obtained in the first three rounds of the protocol. Then in the next hybrid below we modify the messages S_i that are broadcast in the last round. In the hybrid following this, we modify P_3 to use fake inputs instead of its real inputs where indistinguishability relies on the semantic security of the underlying encryption scheme. In the next hybrid, the value u is set to random u' rather than the result of the computation using $C_\alpha^2[1]$ and $C_\alpha^2[2]$. This is important because only then we carry out the reduction for modifying P_1's input. Indistinguishability follows from the equivocation property of the encryption scheme. Then we modify the input x_1 and indistinguishability relies on the semantic security. Then, we modify the input of P_2 from real to fake which again relies on the equivocation property. Finally we modify the S_i's again to use the output from the functionality $\mathcal{F}_{\mathrm{MULT}}^{\mathbf{A}}$ which is a statistical argument and this is the ideal world. A formal proof appears in the full version [HHPV17].

Between Defensible and Real Security. In Sect. 4 below we show how to augment the protocol above to provide security against general adversaries, not just defensible ones, by adding proofs of correct behavior and using rewinding for extraction.

There is, however, one difference between having a defensible adversary and having a general adversary that proves correct behavior: Having a proof in the protocol cannot ensure correct behavior, it only ensures that deviation from the protocol will be detected (since the adversary cannot complete the proof). So we still must worry about the deviation causing information to be leaked to the adversary before it is caught.

Specifically for the protocol above, we relied in the proof on at least one in each pair of ciphertexts being valid. Indeed for an invalid ciphertext C, it could be the case that $C' := (u \boxdot C) \boxplus s$ reveals both u and s. If that was the case, then (for example) a corrupt P_1 could send invalid ciphertexts $C_\alpha^{1,2}[1]$ to P_2, then learn both $x_\alpha^{1,2}$ (and hence x_2) from P_2's reply.

One way of addressing this concern would be to rely on maliciously secure encryption (as defined in [OPP14]), but this is a strong requirement, much harder to realize than our Definition 2.1. Instead, in our BMR-based protocol we ensure that all the inputs to the multiplication gates are just random bits, and have parties broadcast their real inputs masked by these random bits later in the protocol. We then use ZAP proofs of correct ciphertexts *before the parties broadcast their masked real inputs*. Hence, an adversary that sends two invalid ciphertexts can indeed learn the input of (say) P_2 in the multiplication protocol, but this is just a random bit, and P_2 will abort before outputting anything related to its real input in the big protocol. For that, we consider the following two NP languages:

$$\mathcal{L}'_{P_1} = \left\{ \mathsf{trans}_2 \; \middle| \; \begin{array}{l} \exists\,(x_1, \rho_\alpha, \mathrm{SK}_a, \sigma_\alpha) \\ s.t. \left(\begin{array}{l} (\mathrm{PK}_a^1, \mathrm{SK}_a = \mathsf{Gen}(\rho_\alpha) \wedge \mathsf{C}_\alpha^1[1] = \mathsf{Enc}_{\mathrm{PK}_a^1}(x_1; \sigma_\alpha)) \\ \vee\; (\mathrm{PK}_a^2, \mathrm{SK}_a = \mathsf{Gen}(\rho_\alpha) \wedge \mathsf{C}_\alpha^2[1] = \mathsf{Enc}_{\mathrm{PK}_a^2}(x_1; \sigma_\alpha)) \end{array} \right) \end{array} \right\}$$

$$\mathcal{L}'_{P_3} = \left\{ \mathsf{trans}_2 \; \middle| \; \begin{array}{l} \exists\,(x_3, \rho_\beta, \mathrm{SK}_\beta, \sigma_\beta, \rho_\gamma, \mathrm{SK}_\gamma) \\ s.t. \left(\begin{array}{l} (\mathrm{PK}_\beta^1, \mathrm{SK}_\beta = \mathsf{Gen}(\rho_\beta) \wedge \mathsf{C}_\beta^1[1] = \mathsf{Enc}_{\mathrm{PK}_\beta^1}(x_3; \sigma_\beta)) \\ \vee\; (\mathrm{PK}_\beta^2, \mathrm{SK}_\beta = \mathsf{Gen}(\rho_\beta) \wedge \mathsf{C}_\beta^2[1] = \mathsf{Enc}_{\mathrm{PK}_\beta^2}(x_3; \sigma_\beta)) \end{array} \right) \\ \wedge \left((\mathrm{PK}_\gamma^1, \mathrm{SK}_\gamma = \mathsf{Gen}(\rho_\gamma)) \right) \end{array} \right\}$$

where trans_2 is a transcript of the protocol up to and including the 2rd round. Note that P_2 does not generate any public keys and thus need not prove anything.

3.2 Step 2: Arbitrary Degree-3 Polynomials

The protocol Π_{DMULT} from above can be directly used to securely compute any degree-3 polynomial for any number of parties in this "defensible" model, roughly by just expressing the polynomial as a sum of degree-3 monomials and running Π_{DMULT} to compute each one, with some added shares of zero so that only the sum is revealed.

Namely, party P_i chooses an n-of-n additive sharing of zero $\mathbf{z}_i = (z_i^1, \ldots, z_i^n) \leftarrow \mathsf{Share}(0, n)$, and sends z_i^j to party j. Then the parties run one instance of the protocol Π_{DMULT} for each monomial, up to the end of the third round. Let $s_{i,m}$ be the value that P_i would have computed in the mth instance of Π_{DMULT} (where $s_{i,m} := 0$ if P_i's is not a party that participates in the protocol for computing the mth monomial). Then P_i only broadcasts the single value

$$S_i = \sum_{m \in [M]} s_{i,m} + \sum_{j \in [n]} z_j^i.$$

where M denotes the number of degree-3 monomials. To compute multiple degree-3 polynomials on the same input bits, the parties just repeat the same protocol for each output bit (of course using an independent sharing of zero for each output bit).

In terms of security, we add the requirement that a valid "defense" for the adversary is not only valid for each instance of Π_{DMULT} separately, but all these "defenses" are consistent: If some input bit is a part of multiple monomials (possibly in different polynomials), then we require that the same value for that bit is used in all the corresponding instances of Π_{DMULT}. We denote this modified protocol by Π_{DPOLY} and note that the proof of security is exactly the same as the proof in the previous section.

3.3   Step 3: Arbitrary Functionalities

We recall from the works of [BMR90, DI06, LPSY15] that securely realizing arbitrary functionalities f can be reduced to securely realizing the "BMR-encoding" of the Boolean circuit C that computes f. Our starting point is the observation that the BMR encoding of a Boolean circuit C can be reduced to computing many degree-3 polynomials. However, our protocol for realizing degree-3 polynomials from above lets the adversary introduce additive errors (cf. Functionality $\mathcal{F}_{\mathrm{MULT}}^{\mathbf{A}}$), so we rely on a pre-processing step to make the BMR functionality resilient to such additive attacks. We will immunize the circuit to these attacks by relying on the following primitives and tools:

Information theoretic MAC $\{\mathsf{MAC}_\alpha\}$: This will be required to protect the output translation tables from being manipulated by a rushing adversary. Namely, each party contributes a MAC key and along with the output of the function its authentication under each of the parties keys. The idea here is that an adversary cannot simply change the output without forging the authenticated values.

AMD codes (Definition 2.3): This will be required to protect the inputs and outputs of the computation from an additive attack by the adversary. Namely, each party encodes its input using an AMD code. The original computed circuit is then modified so that it first decodes these encoded inputs, then runs the original computation and finally, encodes the outcome.

Additive attack resilient circuits (i.e. AMD circuits, Sect. 2.2): This will be required to protect the computation of the internal wire values from an additive attack by the adversary. Recall from Sect. 3.1 that the adversary may introduce additive errors to the computed polynomials whenever corrupting party P_1. To combat with such errors we only evaluate circuits that are resilient to additive attacks.

Family of pairwise independent hash functions: We will need this to mask the key values of the BMR encoding. The parties broadcast all keys in a masked format, namely, $h, h(T) \oplus k$ for a random string T, key k and hash function h. Then, when decrypting a garbled row, only T is revealed. T and h can be combined with the broadcast message to reveal k.

Next we explain how to embed these tools in the BMR garbling computation. Let $f(\hat{x}_1, \ldots, \hat{x}_n)$ be an n-party function that the parties want to compute securely. At the onset of the protocol, the parties locally apply the following transformation to the function f and their inputs:

1. Define
$$f_1\big((\hat{x}_1, \alpha_1), \ldots, (\hat{x}_n, \alpha_n)\big) = \big(f(\mathbf{x}), \mathsf{MAC}_{\alpha_1}(f(\mathbf{x})), \ldots, \mathsf{MAC}_{\alpha_n}(f(\mathbf{x}))\big)$$
where $\mathbf{x} = (\hat{x}_1, \ldots, \hat{x}_n)$ are the parties' inputs.

The MAC verification is meant to detect adversarial modifications to output wires (since our basic model allows arbitrary manipulation to the output wires).

2. Let (Encode, Decode) be the encoding and decoding functions for an AMD code, and define

$$\mathsf{Encode}'(\hat{x}_1, \ldots, \hat{x}_n) = (\mathsf{Encode}(\hat{x}_1), \ldots, \mathsf{Encode}(\hat{x}_n))$$

and

$$\mathsf{Decode}'(y_1, \ldots, y_n) = (\mathsf{Decode}(y_1), \ldots, \mathsf{Decode}(y_n)).$$

Then define a modified function

$$f_2(\mathbf{x}) = \mathsf{Encode}'(f_1(\mathsf{Decode}'(\mathbf{x}))).$$

Let C be a Boolean circuit that computes f_2.

3. Next we apply the transformations of Genkin et al. [GIP+14, GIW16] to circuit C to obtain $\widehat{C}$ that is resilient to additive attacks on its internal wire values.

4. We denote by $\mathsf{BMR.Encode}^{\widehat{C}}((x_1, R_1), ..., (x_n, R_n))$ our modified BMR randomized encoding of circuit $\widehat{C}$ with inputs x_i and randomness R_i, as described below. We denote by $\mathsf{BMR.Decode}$ the corresponding decoding function for the randomized encoding, where, for all i, we have

$$\mathsf{BMR.Decode}(\mathsf{BMR.Encode}^{\widehat{C}}((x_1, R_1), ..., (x_n, R_n)), R_i) = \widehat{C}(x_1, \ldots, x_n).$$

In the protocol for computing f, each honest party P_i with input $\hat{x}_i$ begins by locally encoding its input via an AMD code, $x_i := \mathsf{Encode}(\hat{x}_i; \$)$ (where $\$$ is some fresh randomness). P_i then engages in a protocol for evaluating the circuit $\widehat{C}$ (as defined below), with local input x_i and a randomly chosen MAC key α_i. Upon receiving an output y_i from the protocol (which is supposed to be AMD encoded, as per the definition of f_2 above), P_i decodes and parses it to get $y_i' := \mathsf{Decode}(y_i) = (z, t_1, \ldots, t_n)$. Finally P_i checks whether $t_i = \mathsf{MAC}_{\alpha_i}(z)$, outputting z if the verification succeeds, and $\bot$ otherwise.

A modified BMR encoding. We describe the modified BMR encoding for a general circuit D with n inputs $x_1, \ldots, x_n$. Without loss of generality, we assume D is a Boolean circuit comprising only of fan-in two NAND gates. Let W be the total number of wires and G the total number of gates in the circuit D. Let $F = \{\mathsf{F}_k : \{0,1\}^\kappa \to \{0,1\}^{4\kappa}\}_{k \in \{0,1\}^*, \kappa \in \mathbb{N}}$ be a family of PRFs.

The encoding procedure takes the inputs $x_1, \ldots, x_n$ and additional random inputs $R_1, \ldots, R_n$. Each R_j comprises of PRF keys, key masks and hash functions from pairwise independent family for every wire. More precisely, R_j ($j \in [n]$) can be expressed as $\{\lambda_w^j, k_{w,0}^j, k_{w,1}^j, T_{w,0}^j, T_{w,1}^j, h_{w,0}^j, h_{w,1}^j\}_{w \in [W]}$ where λ_w^j are bits, $k_{w,b}^j$ are κ bit PRF keys, $T_{w,b}^j$ are 4κ bits key masks, and $h_{w,b}^j$ are hash functions from a pairwise independent family from 4κ to κ bits.

The encoding procedure $\mathsf{BMR.Encode}^{\widehat{C}}$ on input $((x_1, R_1), ..., (x_n, R_n))$ outputs

$$\begin{cases} (R_{00}^{g,j}, R_{01}^{g,j}, R_{10}^{g,j}, R_{11}^{g,j})_{g \in [G], j \in [n], r_1, r_2 \in \{0,1\}} & \texttt{// Garbled Tables} \\ (h_{w,b}^j, \Gamma_{w,b}^j)_{w \in [W], j \in [n], b \in \{0,1\}}, & \texttt{// masked key values} \\ (\Lambda_w, k_{w, \Lambda_w}^1, \ldots, k_{w, \Lambda_w}^n)_{w \in \mathsf{Inp}}, & \texttt{// keys and masks for input wires} \\ (\lambda_w)_{w \in \mathsf{Out}} & \texttt{// Output translation table} \end{cases}$$

where

$$R^{g,j}_{r_1,r_2} = \Big(\bigoplus_{i=1}^{n} \mathsf{F}_{k^i_{a,r_1}}(g,j,r_1,r_2) \Big) \oplus \Big(\bigoplus_{i=1}^{n} \mathsf{F}_{k^i_{b,r_2}}(g,j,r_1,r_2) \Big) \oplus S^{g,j}_{r_1,r_2}$$

$$S^{g,j}_{r_1,r_2} = T^j_{c,0} \oplus \chi_{r_1,r_2} \cdot (T^j_{c,1} \oplus T^j_{c,0})$$

$$\chi_{r_1,r_2} = \mathsf{NAND}(\lambda_a \oplus r_1, \lambda_b \oplus r_2) \oplus \lambda_c = [(\lambda_a \oplus r_1) \cdot (\lambda_b \oplus r_2) \oplus 1] \oplus \lambda_c$$

$$\Gamma^j_{w,b} = h^j_{w,b}(T^j_{w,b}) \oplus k^j_{w,b}$$

$$\lambda_w = \begin{cases} \lambda^{j_w}_w & \text{if } w \in \mathsf{Inp} \quad \text{// input wire} \\ \lambda^1_w \oplus \cdots \oplus \lambda^n_w & \text{if } w \in [W]/\mathsf{Inp} \text{// internal wire} \end{cases}$$

$$\Lambda_w = \lambda_w \oplus x_w \text{ for all } w \in \mathsf{Inp} \qquad \text{// masked input bit}$$

and wires a, b and $c \in [W]$ denote the input and output wires respectively for gate $g \in [G]$. $\mathsf{Inp} \subseteq [W]$ denotes the set of input wires to the circuit, $j_w \in [n]$ denotes the party whose input flows the wire w and x_w the corresponding input. $\mathsf{Out} \subseteq [W]$ denotes the set of output wires.

We remark that the main difference with standard BMR encoding is that when decrypting a garbled row, a value $T^\star_{\star,\star}$ is revealed and the key is obtained by unmasking the corresponding $h^\star_{\star,\star}, h^\star_{\star,\star}(T^\star_{\star,\star}) \oplus k^\star_{\star,\star}$ value that is part of the encoding. This additional level of indirection of receiving the mask T and then unmasking the key is required to tackle errors to individual bits of the plaintext encrypted in each garbled row.

The decoding procedure basically corresponds to the evaluation of the garbled circuit. More formally, the decoding procedure BMR.Decode is defined iteratively gate by gate according to some standard (arbitrary) topological ordering of the gates. In particular, given an encoding information k^j_{w,Λ_w} for every input wire w and $j \in [n]$, of some input x, then for each gate g with input wires a and b and output wire c compute

$$T^j_c = R^{g,j}_{r_1,r_2} \oplus \bigoplus_{i=1}^{n} \Big(\mathsf{F}_{k^i_{a,\Lambda_a}}(g,j,\Lambda_a,\Lambda_b) \oplus \mathsf{F}_{k^i_{b,\Lambda_b}}(g,j,\Lambda_a,\Lambda_b) \Big)$$

Let Λ_c denote the bit for which $T^j_c = T^j_{c,\Lambda_c}$ and define $k^j_c = \Gamma^j_{c,\Lambda_c} \oplus h^j_{c,\Lambda_c}(T^j_c)$. Finally given Λ_w for every output wire w, compute the output carried in wire w as $\Lambda_w \oplus \Big(\bigoplus_{j=1}^{n} \lambda^j_w \Big)$.

Securely computing BMR.Encode using Π_{DPOLY}. We decompose the computation of BMR.Encode into an offline and online phase. The offline part of the computation will only involve computing the "plaintexts" in each garbled row, i.e. $S^\star_{\star,\star}$ values and visible mask Λ_w values for input wires. More precisely, the parties compute

$$\{(S^{g,j}_{00}, S^{g,j}_{01}, S^{g,j}_{10}, S^{g,j}_{11})_{g\in[G],j\in[n],r_1,r_2\in\{0,1\}}, (\Lambda_w)_{w\in\mathsf{Inp}}\}.$$

Observe that the $S^\star_{\star,\star}$ values are all degree-3 computations over the randomness $R_1, \ldots, R_n$ and therefore can be computed using Π_{DPOLY}. Since the Λ_w values for the input wires depend only on the inputs and internal randomness of party P_{j_w}, the Λ_w value can be broadcast by that party P_{j_w}. The offline phase comprises of executing all instances of Π_{DPOLY} in parallel in the first three rounds. Additionally, the Λ_w values are broadcast in the third round. At the end of the offline phase, in addition to the Λ_w values for the input wires, the parties obtain XOR shares of the $S_{\star,\star}^{\star,\star}$ values.

In the online phase which is carried out in rounds 3 and 4, each party P_j broadcasts the following values:

- $\widetilde{R}_{\star,\star}^{\star,j}$ values that correspond to the shares of the $S_{\star,\star}^{\star,j}$ values masked with P_j's local PRF computations.
- $h_{\star,\star}^{j}, \Gamma_{\star,\star}^{j} = h_{\star,\star}^{j}(T_{\star,\star}^{j}) \oplus k_{\star,\star}^{j}$ that are the masked key values.
- λ_w^j for each output wire w that are shares of the output translation table.

Handling errors. Recall that our Π_{DPOLY} protocol will allow an adversary to introduce errors into the computation, namely, for any degree-3 monomial $x_1 x_2 x_3$, if the party playing the role of P_1 in the multiplication sub-protocol is corrupted, it can introduce an error e_{In} and the product is modified to $(x_1 x_2 + e_{\mathrm{In}})x_3$. The adversary can also introduce an error e_{Out} that is simply added to the result of the computation, namely the $S_{\star,\star}^{\star,\star}$ values. Finally, the adversary can reveal arbitrary values for λ_w^j, which in turn means the output translation table can arbitrarily assign the keys to output values.

Our approach to tackle the "e_{In}" errors is to show that these errors can be translated to additive errors on the wires of $\widehat{\mathsf{C}}$ and then rely on the additive resilience property of $\widehat{\mathsf{C}}$. Importantly, to apply this property, we need to demonstrate the errors are independent of the actual wire value. We show this in two logical steps. First, by carefully assigning the roles of the parties in the multiplication subprotocols, we can show that the shares obtained by the parties combine to yield $S_{r_1,r_2}^{g,j} + e_{r_1,r_2}^{g,j} \cdot (T_{c,0}^{j} \oplus T_{c,1}^{j})$ where $e_{r_1,r_2}^{g,j}$ is a 4κ bit string (and '$\cdot$' is applied bitwise). In other words, by introducing an error, the adversary causes the decoding procedure of the randomized encoding to result in a string where each bit comes from either $T_{c,b}^{j}$ or $T_{c,1-b}^{j}$. Since an adversary can incorporate different errors in each bit of $S_{\star,\star}^{\star,\star}$, it could get partial information from both the T values. We use a pairwise independent hash function family to mask the actual key, and by the left-over hash lemma, we can restrict the adversary from learning at most one key. As a result, if the majority of the bits in $e_{r_1,r_2}^{g,j}$ are 1 then the "value" on the wire flips, and otherwise it is "correct".[8] The second logical step is to rely on the fact that there is at least one mask bit λ_w^j chosen by an honest party to demonstrate that the flip event on any wire will be independent of the actual wire value.

To address the "e_{Out}" errors, following [LPSY15, HSS17], we show that the BMR encoding is already resilient to such adaptive attacks (where the adversary

---

[8] Even if a particular gate computation is correctly evaluated, it does not necessarily mean this is the correct wire value as the input wire values to the gate could themselves be incorrect due to additive errors that occur earlier in the circuit.

may add errors to the garbled circuit even after seeing the complete garbling and then deciding on the error).

Finally, to tackle a rushing adversary that can modify the output of the translation table arbitrarily, we rely on the MACs to ensure that the output value revealed can be matched with the MACs revealed along with the output under each party's private MAC key.

Role assignment in the multiplication subprotocols. As described above, we carefully assign roles to parties to restrict the errors introduced in the multiplication protocol. Observe that χ_{r_1,r_2} is a degree-2 computation, which in turn means the expressions $T_{c,0}^j \oplus \chi_{r_1,r_2}(T_{c,1}^j \oplus T_{c,0}^j)$ over all garbled rows is a collection of polynomials of degree at most 3. In particular, for every $j \in [n]$, every gate $g \in G$ with input wires a, b and an output wire c, $S_{r_1,r_2}^{g,j}$ involves the computation of one or more of the following monomials:

- $\lambda_a^{j_1} \lambda_b^{j_2} (T_{c,1}^j \oplus T_{c,0}^j)$ for $j, j_1, j_2 \in [n]$.
- $\lambda_c^{j_1} (T_{c,1}^j \oplus T_{c,0}^j)$ for $j, j_1 \in [n]$.
- $T_{c,0}^j$.

We first describe some convention regarding how each multiplication triple is computed, namely assign parties with roles P_1, P_2 and P_3 in Π_{DMULT} (Sect. 3.1), and what products are computed. Letting $\Delta_c^j = (T_{c,1}^j \oplus T_{c,0}^j)$, we observe that every product always involves Δ_c^j as one of its operands. Moreover, every term can be expressed as a product of three operands, where the product $\lambda_c^{j_1} \Delta_c^j$ will be (canonically) expressed as $(\lambda_c^{j_1})^2 \Delta_c^j$ and singleton monomials (e.g., the bits of the keys and PRF values) will be raised to degree 3. Then, for every polynomial involving the variables $\lambda_a^{j_1}, \lambda_b^{j_2}$ and Δ_c^j, party P_j will be assigned with the role of P_3 in Π_{DMULT} whereas the other parties P_{j_1} and P_{j_2} can be assigned arbitrarily as P_1 and P_2. In particular, the roles are chosen so as to restrict the errors introduced by a corrupted P_1 in the computation to only additive errors of the form $e_{\mathrm{In}}\delta$ where δ is some bit in Δ_c^j, where it follows from our simulation that e_{In} will be independent of δ for honest P_j.

We now proceed to a formal description of our protocol.

Protocol 2 (Protocol Π_{DMPC} secure against defensible adversaries)

INPUT: *Parties $P_1, \ldots, P_n$ are given input $\hat{x}_1, \ldots, \hat{x}_n$ of length κ', respectively, and a circuit $\widehat{C}$ as specified above.*

LOCAL PRE-PROCESSING: *Each party P_i chooses a random MAC key α_i and sets $x_i = \mathsf{Encode}(\hat{x}_i, \alpha_i)$. Let κ be the length of the resulting x_i's, and we fix the notation $[x_i]_j$ as the jth bit of x_i. Next P_i chooses all the randomness that is needed for the BMR encoding of the circuit $\widehat{C}$. Namely, for each wire w, P_i chooses the masking bit $\lambda_w^i \in \{0,1\}$, random wire PRF keys $k_{w,0}^i, k_{w,1}^i \in \{0,1\}^\kappa$, random functions from a universal hash family $h_{w,0}^i, h_{w,1}^i : \{0,1\}^{4\kappa} \to \{0,1\}^\kappa$ and random hash inputs $T_{w,0}^i, T_{w,1}^i \in \{0,1\}^{4\kappa}$.*

Then, for every non-output wire w and every gate g for which w is one of the inputs, P_i compute all the PRF values $\Theta_{j,r_1,r_2}^{i,w,g} = \mathsf{F}_{k_{w,r_1}^i}(g, j, r_1, r_2)$ for

$j = 1, \ldots, n$ and $r_1, r_2 \in \{0, 1\}$. (The values λ_w^i, $T_{w,r}^i$, and $\Theta_{j,r_1,r_2}^{i,w,g}$, will play the role of P_i's inputs to the protocol that realizes the BMR encoding BMR.Encode$^{\widehat{C}}$.)

The parties identity the set of 3-monomials that should be computed by the BMR encoding BMR.Encode$^{\widehat{C}}$ and index them by $1, 2, \ldots, M$. Each party P_i identifies the set of monomials, denoted by Set_i, that depends on any of its inputs (λ_w^i, $T_{w,r}^i$, or $\Theta_{j,r_1,r_2}^{i,w,g}$). As described above, each P_i also determines the role, denoted by $\mathsf{Role}(t, i) \in \{P_1, P_2, P_3\}$, that it plays in the computation of the t-th monomial (which is set to $\perp$ if P_i does not participate in the computation of the t-th monomial).

- ROUNDS 1,2,3: For each $i \in [M]$, parties $P_1, \ldots, P_n$ execute Π_{DPOLY} for the monomial p_i up until the 3rd round of the protocol with random inputs for the BMR encoding BMR.Encode$^{\widehat{C}}$. Along with the message transmitted in the 3rd round of Π_{DPOLY}, party P_j broadcasts the following:
  - For every input wire $w \in W$ that carries some input bit $[x_j]_k$ from P_j's input, P_j broadcasts $\Lambda_w = \lambda_w \oplus [x_j]_k$.

For every $j \in [n]$, let $\{S_{\ell,j}\}_{\ell \in M}$ be the output of party P_j for the M degree-3 monomials. It reassembles the output shares to obtain $S_{r_1,r_2}^{g,j}$ for every garbled row r_1, r_2 and gate g.

- DEFENSE: At this point, the adversary broadcasts its "defense:" The defense for this protocol is a collection of defenses for every monomial that assembles the BMR encoding. The defense for every monomial is as defined in protocol Π_{DMULT} from Sect. 3. Namely, for each party P_i there is an NP language

$$\mathcal{L}_{P_i}^* = \left\{ (\mathsf{trans}^1, \ldots, \mathsf{trans}^M) \;\middle|\; \begin{array}{l} \mathsf{trans}^j \in \mathcal{L}_{P_1}, \mathcal{L}_{P_2}, \mathcal{L}_{P_3} \text{ if } P_i \text{ is assigned the role} \\ P_1, P_2, P_3, \text{ respectively, in the } j^{th} \text{ instance of } \Pi_{\mathrm{DMULT}} \\ \wedge \text{ all the } \mathsf{trans}^{j'}\text{s are consistent with the same value of } x_i \end{array} \right\}$$

- ROUND 4: Finally for every gate $g \in G$ and $r_1, r_2 \in \{0, 1\}$, P_j ($j \in [n]$) broadcasts the following:
  - $\widetilde{R}_{r_1,r_2}^{g,i} = \mathsf{F}_{k_{a,r_1}^j}(g, j, r_1, r_2) \oplus \mathsf{F}_{k_{b,r_2}^j}(g, i, r_1, r_2) \oplus S_{r_1,r_2}^{g,i}$ for every $i \in [n]$.
  - k_{w,Λ_w}^j for every input wire w.
  - λ_w^j for every output wire w.
  - $(\Gamma_{w,0}^j, \Gamma_{w,1}^j) = (h(T_{w,0}^j) \oplus k_{w,0}^j, h(T_{w,1}^j) \oplus k_{w,1}^j)$ for every wire w.

- OUTPUT: Upon collecting $\{\widetilde{R}_{r_1,r_2}^{g,j}\}_{j \in [n], g \in [G], r_1, r_2 \in \{0,1\}}$, the parties compute each garbled row by $R_{r_1,r_2}^{g,j} = \bigoplus_{j=1}^n \widetilde{R}_{r_1,r_2}^{g,j}$ and run the decoding procedure BMR.Decode on some standard (arbitrary) topological ordering of the gates. Concretely, let g be a gate in this order with input wires a, b and output wire c. If a party does not have masks Λ_a, Λ_b or keys (k_a, k_b) corresponding to the input wires when processing gate g it aborts. Otherwise, it will compute

$$T_c^j = R_{r_1,r_2}^{g,j} \oplus \bigoplus_{i=1}^n \left(\mathsf{F}_{k_{a,\Lambda_a}^i}(g, j, \Lambda_a, \Lambda_b) \oplus \mathsf{F}_{k_{b,\Lambda_b}^i}(g, j, \Lambda_a, \Lambda_b) \right).$$

Party P_j identifies Λ_c such that $T_c^j = T_{c,\Lambda_c}^j$. If no such Λ_c exists the party aborts. Otherwise, each party defines $k_c^i = \Gamma_{c,\Lambda_c}^i \oplus h(T_c^j)$. The evaluation is completed when all the gates in the topological order are processed. Finally given Λ_w for every output wire w, the parties compute for every output wire w, $\Lambda_w \oplus \left(\bigoplus_{j=1}^n \lambda_w^j \right)$ and decode the outcome using Dec.

This concludes the description of our protocol. We next prove the following Lemma.

Lemma 3.2 (MPC secure against defensible adversaries). *Protocol Π_{DMPC} securely realizes any n-input function f in the presence of a "defensible adversary" that always broadcasts valid defense at the end of the third round.*

Proof. Let $\mathcal{A}$ be a PPT defensible adversary corrupting a subset of parties $I \subset [n]$, then we prove that there exists a PPT simulator $\mathcal{S}$ with access to an ideal functionality $\mathcal{F}$ that implements f, and simulates the adversary's view whenever it outputs a valid defense at the end of the third round. We use the terminology of active keys to denote the keys of the BMR garbling that are revealed during the evaluation. Inactive keys are the hidden keys. Denoting the set of honest parties by $\bar{I}$, our simulator $\mathcal{S}$ is defined below.

Description of the simulator.

– *Simulating rounds 1–3.* Recall that the parties engage in an instance of Π_{DPOLY} to realize the BMR encoding BMR.Encode$^{\widehat{C}}$ in the first three rounds. The simulator samples random inputs for the honest parties and generates their messages using these random inputs. For every input wire that is associated with an honest party's input, the simulator chooses a random Λ_w and sends these bits to the adversary as part of the 3rd message. At this point, a defensible adversary outputs a valid defense. Next the simulator executes the following procedure to compute the fourth round messages of the honest parties.

SimGarble(defense):
  1. The simulator extracts from the defense λ_w^j and $T_{w,0}^j, T_{w,0}^j \oplus T_{w,1}^j$ for every corrupted party P_j and internal wire w. Finally, it obtains the vector of errors $e_{r_1,r_2}^{g,j}$ for every gate g, $r_1, r_2 \in \{0,1\}$ and $j \in I$, introduced by the adversary for row (r_1, r_2) in the garbling of gate g.[9]
  2. The simulator defines the inputs of the corrupted parties by using the Λ_w values revealed in round 3 corresponding to the wires w carrying inputs of the corrupted parties. Namely, for each such input wire $w \in W$, the simulator computes $\rho_w = \Lambda_w \oplus \lambda_w$ and the errors in the input wires and fixes the adversary's input $\{x_I\}$ to be the concatenation of these bits incorporating the errors. $\mathcal{S}$ sends Decode(x_I) to the trusted party computing f, receiving the output $\tilde{y}$. $\mathcal{S}$ fixes $y = $ Encode$(\tilde{y})$ (recall that Encode in the encoding of an AMD code). Let $y = (y_1, \ldots, y_m)$.

---

[9] The errors are bits and are extracted for each monomial where the corrupted party plays the role of P_1. For simplicity of notation we lump them all in a single vector.

3. Next, the simulator defines the $S^{\star,\star}_{\star,\star}$ values, i.e the plaintexts in the garbled rows. Recall that the shares of the $S^{\star,\star}_{\star,\star}$ values are computed using the Π_{DPOLY} subprotocol. Then the simulator for the main protocol, uses the $S^{\star,\star}_{\star,\star}$ values that are defined by the simulation of Π_{DPOLY}. Next, S chooses a random $\Lambda_w \leftarrow \{0,1\}$ for every internal wire $w \in W$. Finally, it samples a single key k^j_w for every honest party $j \in \bar{I}$ and wire $w \in W$. We recall that in the standard BMR garbling, the simulator sets the garbled row so that for every gate g with input wires a, b and output wire c, only the row Λ_a, Λ_b is decryptable and decrypting this row gives the single key chosen for wire c (denoted by an active key). In our modified BMR garbling, we will essentially ensure the same, except that we also need to simulate the errors introduced in the computation.

   More formally, the simulator considers an arbitrary topological ordering on the gates. Fix some gate g in this sequence with a, b as input wires and c as the output wire. Then, for every honest party P_j and random values $T^j_{c,0}$ and $T^j_{c,1}$ that were involved in the computation of the $S^{\star,\star}_{\star,\star}$ values for this gate within the above simulation of Π_{DPOLY}, the simulator defines the bits of $S^{g,j}_{\Lambda_a,\Lambda_b}$ to be $(e^{g,j}_{\Lambda_a,\Lambda_b} \cdot T^j_{c,\Lambda_c}) \oplus (\bar{e}^{g,j}_{\Lambda_a,\Lambda_b} \cdot T^j_{c,\bar{\Lambda}_c})$ if the majority of the bits in $e^{g,j}_{\Lambda_a,\Lambda_b}$ is 1 and $(\bar{e}^{g,j}_{\Lambda_a,\Lambda_b} \cdot T^j_{c,\Lambda_c}) \oplus (e^{g,j}_{\Lambda_a,\Lambda_b} \cdot T^j_{c,\bar{\Lambda}_c})$ otherwise. Here $\bar{e}^{g,j}_{\Lambda_a,\Lambda_b}$ refers to the complement of the vector $e^{g,j}_{\Lambda_a,\Lambda_b}$ and "$\cdot$" is bitwise multiplication.

4. Next, it generates the fourth message on behalf of the honest parties. Namely, for every gate g and an active row Λ_a, Λ_b, the shares of the honest parties are computed assuming the output of the polynomials defined in the BMR encoding are $S^{g,j}_{\Lambda_a,\Lambda_b}$ for every j masked with the PRF under the keys k^j_a, k^j_b as defined by $\tilde{R}^{g,j}_{\Lambda_a,\Lambda_b}$. For the remaining three rows the simulator sends random strings. On behalf of every honest party P_j, in addition to the shares, the fourth round message is appended with a broadcast of the message $(r, h(T^j_{w,\Lambda_w}) \oplus k^j_w)$ if $\Lambda_w = 1$ and $(h(T^j_{w,\Lambda_w}) \oplus k^j_w, r)$ if $\Lambda_w = 0$ where r is sampled randomly. Intuitively, upon decrypting $S^{g,j}_{\Lambda_a,\Lambda_b}$ for any gate g, the adversary learns the majority of the bits of T^j_{c,Λ_c} with which it can learn only k^j_c.

- The simulator sends the messages as indicated by the procedure above on behalf of the honest parties. If the adversary provides its fourth message, namely, $\tilde{R}^{g,j}_{r_1,r_2}$ for $j \in [n], g \in [G], r_1, r_2 \in \{0,1\}$, the simulator executes the following procedure that takes as input all the messages exchanged in the fourth round, the Λ_w values broadcast in the third round and the target output y. It determines whether the final output needs to be delivered to the honest parties in the ideal world.

ReconGarble(4th round messages, Λ_w for every input wire w,y):

- The procedure reconstructs the garbling GC_A using the shares and the keys provided. First, the simulator checks that the output key of every key obtained during the evaluation is the active key k^j_{c,Λ_c} encrypted by the simulator. In addition, the simulator checks that the outcome of GC_A is y.

If both events hold, the the procedure outputs the OK message, otherwise it outputs ⊥.

- Finally, if the procedure outputs OK the simulator instructs the trusted party to deliver $\tilde{y}$ to the honest parties.

In the full version [HHPV17], we provide a formal proof of the following claim:

Claim 3.3 $\mathbf{REAL}_{\Pi_{\mathrm{DMPC}},\mathcal{A}(z),I}(\kappa, \hat{x}_1, \ldots, \hat{x}_n) \overset{c}{\approx} \mathbf{IDEAL}_{\mathcal{F},\mathcal{S}(z),I}(\kappa, \hat{x}_1, \ldots, \hat{x}_n).$

4 Four-Round Actively Secure MPC Protocol

In this section we formally describe our protocol.

Protocol 3 (Actively secure protocol Π_{MPC})

INPUT: *Parties $P_1, \ldots, P_n$ are given input $\hat{x}_1, \ldots, \hat{x}_n$ of length κ', respectively, and a circuit $\widehat{\mathsf{C}}$.*

- LOCAL PRE-PROCESSING: *Each party P_i chooses a random MAC key α_i and sets $x_i = \mathsf{Encode}(\hat{x}_i, \alpha_i)$. Let κ be the length of the resulting x_i's, and we fix the notation $[x_i]_j$ as the jth bit of x_i. Next P_i chooses all the randomness that is needed for the BMR encoding of the circuit $\widehat{\mathsf{C}}$. Namely, for each wire w, P_i chooses the masking bit $\lambda_w^i \in \{0,1\}$, random wire PRF keys $k_{w,0}^i, k_{w,1}^i \in \{0,1\}^\kappa$, random functions from a pairwise independent hash family $h_{w,0}^i, h_{w,1}^i : \{0,1\}^{4\kappa} \rightarrow \{0,1\}^\kappa$ and random hash inputs $T_{w,0}^i, T_{w,1}^i \in \{0,1\}^{4\kappa}$.*
  Then, for every non-output wire w and every gate g for which w is one of the inputs, P_i computes all the PRF values $\Theta_{j,r_1,r_2}^{i,w,g} = \mathsf{F}_{k_{w,r_1}^i}(g,j,r_1,r_2)$ for $j = 1, \ldots, n$ and $r_1, r_2 \in \{0,1\}$. (The values λ_w^i, $T_{w,r}^i$, and $\Theta_{j,r_1,r_2}^{i,w,g}$, will play the role of P_i's inputs to the protocol that realizes the BMR encoding $\mathsf{BMR.Encode}^{\widehat{\mathsf{C}}}$.)
  The parties identify the set of 3-monomials that should be computed by the BMR encoding $\mathsf{BMR.Encode}^{\widehat{\mathsf{C}}}$ and enumerate them by integers from $[M]$. Moreover, each party P_i identifies the set of monomials, denoted by Set_i, that depends on any of its inputs (λ_w^i, $T_{w,r}^i$, or $\Theta_{j,r_1,r_2}^{i,w,g}$). As described in Sect. 3.3, each P_i also determines the role, denoted by $\mathsf{Role}(t,i) \in \{P_1, P_2, P_3\}$, that it plays in the computation of the t-th monomial(which is set to $\perp$ if P_i does not participate in the computation of the t-th monomial).
- ROUND 1: *For $i \in [n]$ each party P_i proceeds as follows:*
  - *Engages in an instance of the three-round non-malleable commitment protocol nmcom with every other party P_j, committing to arbitrarily chosen values $w_{0,i}, w_{1,i}$. Denote the messages sent within the first round of this protocol by $\mathsf{nmcom}_{i,j}^0[1], \mathsf{nmcom}_{i,j}^1[1]$, respectively.*
  - *Broadcasts the message $\Pi_{\mathrm{DMPC}}^{i,j}[1]$ to every other party P_j.*

- Engages in a ZAP protocol with every party other P_j for the NP language $\mathcal{L}'_{\text{Role}(t,i)}$ defined in Sect. 3.1, for every monomial in case $\text{Role}(t,i) \in \{P_1, P_3\}$. Note that the first message, denoted by $\text{ZAP}^{\text{ENC}}_{i,j}[1]$ is sent by P_j (so P_i sends the first message to all the P_j's for their respective ZAPs).

- ROUND 2: For $i \in [n]$ each party P_i proceeds as follows:
  - Sends the messages $\text{nmcom}^0_{i,j}[2]$ and $\text{nmcom}^1_{i,j}[2]$ for the second round of the respective non-malleable commitment.
  - Engages in a ZAP protocol with every other party P_j for the NP language $\mathcal{L}_{\text{Role}(t,i)}$ defined in Sect. 3.1 for every monomial M_t. As above, the first message, denoted by $\text{ZAP}^{\text{COM}}_{i,j}[1]$ is sent by P_j (so P_i sends the first message to all the P_j's for their respective ZAPs).
  - Sends the message $\Pi^{i,j}_{\text{DMPC}}[2]$ to every other party P_j.
  - Sends the second message $\text{ZAP}^{\text{ENC}}_{i,j}[2]$ of the ZAP proof for the language $\mathcal{L}'_{\text{Role}(t,i)}$.

- ROUND 3: For $i \in [n]$ each party P_i proceeds as follows:
  - Sends the messages $\text{nmcom}^0_{i,j}[3]$, $\text{nmcom}^1_{i,j}[3]$ for the third round of the respective non-malleable commitment. For $b \in \{0,1\}$ define the NP language:

$$\mathcal{L}_{\text{nmcom}} = \Big\{ \text{nmcom}^*_{i,j}[1], \text{nmcom}^*_{i,j}[2], \text{nmcom}^*_{i,j}[3] |$$
$$\exists\, b \in \{0,1\} \text{ and } (w_i, \rho_i) \text{ s.t. } \text{nmcom}^b_{i,j} = \text{nmcom}(w_i; \rho_i) \Big\}.$$

  - Chooses $\tilde{w}_{0,i}$ and $\tilde{w}_{1,i}$ such that $\forall t \in [Set_i]$, $w_{0,i} + \tilde{w}_{0,i} = w_{1,i} + \tilde{w}_{1,i} = \text{wit}_i$ where wit_i is the witness of transcript $(\text{trans}^0_{\text{Role}(1,i)} || \cdots || \text{trans}^0_{\text{Role}(|Set_i|,i)} || \text{trans}^0_{\text{nmcom}})$ and $\text{Role}(t,i) \in \{P_1, P_2, P_3\}$, where trans^b_* is as defined in Sect. 3.1.
  - Generates the message $\text{ZAP}^{\text{COM}}_{i,j}[2]$ for the second round of the ZAP protocol relative to the NP language

$$\mathcal{L}_{\text{Role}(1,i)} \wedge \ldots \wedge \mathcal{L}_{\text{Role}(|Set_i|,i)} \wedge \mathcal{L}_{\text{nmcom}} \wedge \big(w_{b,i} + \tilde{w}_{b,i} = \text{wit}_i\big)$$

    where $\mathcal{L}_{\text{Role}(\cdot,i)}$ is defined in protocol 1.
  - Broadcasts the message $\Pi^{i,j}_{\text{DMPC}}[3]$ to every other party P_j.
  For every $j \in [n]$, let $\{S_{\ell,j}\}_{\ell \in M}$ be the output of party P_j for the M degree-3 polynomials. It reassembles the output shares to obtain $S^{g,j}_{r_1,r_2}$ for every garbled row r_1, r_2 and gate g.

- ROUND 4: Finally, broadcasts the message $\Pi^{i,j}_{\text{DMPC}}[4]$ to every other party P_j.
- OUTPUT: As defined in Π_{DMPC}.

This concludes the description of our protocol. The proof for the following theorem can be found in [HHPV17].

Theorem 4.1 (Main). *Assuming the existence of affine homomorphic encryption (cf. Definition 2.1) and enhanced trapdoor permutations, Protocol Π_{MPC} securely realizes any n-input function f in the presence of static, active adversaries corrupting any number of parties.*

Acknowledgements. We thank the anonymous reviewers for their valuable feedback. Following Ananth et. al. [ACJ17], we would like to acknowledge Yuval Ishai's contribution in the three-bit three-round multiplication protocol employed in this work. We would also like to thank Daniel Genkin, Yuval Ishai and Mor Weiss for several discussions on binary AMD resilient circuits.

The first author was supported by the Defense Advanced Research Projects Agency (DARPA) and Army Research Office(ARO) under Contract No. W911NF-15-C-0236. The second author was supported by the BIU Center for Research in Applied Cryptography and Cyber Security in conjunction with the Israel National Cyber Bureau in the Prime Minister's Office. The third author was supported by the National Science Foundation under Grant No. 1617676, 1526377 and 1618884, IBM under Agreement 4915013672 and the Packard Foundation under Grant 2015-63124. The last author was supported by the National Science Foundation under Grant No. 1526377 and 1618884, a Google Faculty Research grant and DIMACS Special Focus on Cryptography program. The work was partially done while the fourth author was at Cornell Tech.

The views expressed are those of the authors and do not reflect the official policy or position of the Department of Defense, the National Science Foundation, or the U.S. Government.

References

[ACJ17] Ananth, P., Choudhuri, A.R., Jain, A.: A new approach to round-optimal secure multiparty computation. In: Katz, J., Shacham, H. (eds.) CRYPTO 2017. LNCS, vol. 10401, pp. 468–499. Springer, Cham (2017). https://doi.org/10.1007/978-3-319-63688-7_16

[AIK06] Applebaum, B., Ishai, Y., Kushilevitz, E.: Cryptography in NC^0. SIAM J. Comput. **36**(4), 845–888 (2006)

[AJL+12] Asharov, G., Jain, A., López-Alt, A., Tromer, E., Vaikuntanathan, V., Wichs, D.: Multiparty computation with low communication, computation and interaction via threshold FHE. In: Pointcheval, D., Johansson, T. (eds.) EUROCRYPT 2012. LNCS, vol. 7237, pp. 483–501. Springer, Heidelberg (2012). https://doi.org/10.1007/978-3-642-29011-4_29

[BGJ+17] Badrinarayanan, S., Goyal, V., Jain, A., Khurana, D., Sahai, A.: Round optimal concurrent MPC via strong simulation. In: Kalai, Y., Reyzin, L. (eds.) TCC 2017. LNCS, vol. 10677, pp. 743–775. Springer, Cham (2017). https://doi.org/10.1007/978-3-319-70500-2_25

[BGJ+18] Badrinarayanan, S., Goyal, V., Jain, A., Kalai, Y.T., Khurana, D., Sahai, A.: Promise zero knowledge and its applications to round optimal MPC (2018)

[BGW88] Ben-Or, M., Goldwasser, S., Wigderson, A.: Completeness theorems for non-cryptographic fault-tolerant distributed computation (extended abstract). In: STOC, pp. 1–10 (1988)

[BHP17] Brakerski, Z., Halevi, S., Polychroniadou, A.: Four round secure computation without setup. In: Kalai, Y., Reyzin, L. (eds.) TCC 2017. LNCS, vol. 10677, pp. 645–677. Springer, Cham (2017). https://doi.org/10.1007/978-3-319-70500-2_22

[BL18] Benhamouda, F., Lin, H.: k-round multiparty computation from k-round oblivious transfer via garbled interactive circuits. In: Nielsen, J.B., Rijmen, V. (eds.) EUROCRYPT 2018. LNCS, vol. 10821, pp. 500–532. Springer, Cham (2018). https://doi.org/10.1007/978-3-319-78375-8_17

[BMR90]   Beaver, D., Micali, S., Rogaway, P.: The round complexity of secure protocols (extended abstract). In: STOC, pp. 503–513 (1990)

[CCD87]   Chaum, D., Crépeau, C., Damgård, I.: Multiparty unconditionally secure protocols (abstract). In: Pomerance, C. (ed.) CRYPTO 1987. LNCS, vol. 293, pp. 462–462. Springer, Heidelberg (1988). https://doi.org/10.1007/3-540-48184-2_43

[CDF+08] Cramer, R., Dodis, Y., Fehr, S., Padró, C., Wichs, D.: Detection of algebraic manipulation with applications to robust secret sharing and fuzzy extractors. In: Smart, N. (ed.) EUROCRYPT 2008. LNCS, vol. 4965, pp. 471–488. Springer, Heidelberg (2008). https://doi.org/10.1007/978-3-540-78967-3_27

[CLOS02] Canetti, R., Lindell, Y., Ostrovsky, R., Sahai, A.: Universally composable two-party and multi-party secure computation. In: STOC, pp. 494–503 (2002)

[COSV16] Ciampi, M., Ostrovsky, R., Siniscalchi, L., Visconti, I.: Concurrent non-malleable commitments (and more) in 3 rounds. In: Robshaw, M., Katz, J. (eds.) CRYPTO 2016. LNCS, vol. 9816, pp. 270–299. Springer, Heidelberg (2016). https://doi.org/10.1007/978-3-662-53015-3_10

[COSV17a] Ciampi, M., Ostrovsky, R., Siniscalchi, L., Visconti, I.: Delayed-input non-malleable zero knowledge and multi-party coin tossing in four rounds. In: Kalai, Y., Reyzin, L. (eds.) TCC 2017. LNCS, vol. 10677, pp. 711–742. Springer, Cham (2017). https://doi.org/10.1007/978-3-319-70500-2_24

[COSV17b] Ciampi, M., Ostrovsky, R., Siniscalchi, L., Visconti, I.: Round-optimal secure two-party computation from trapdoor permutations. In: Kalai, Y., Reyzin, L. (eds.) TCC 2017. LNCS, vol. 10677, pp. 678–710. Springer, Cham (2017). https://doi.org/10.1007/978-3-319-70500-2_23

[DI05]   Damgård, I., Ishai, Y.: Constant-round multiparty computation using a black-box pseudorandom generator. In: Shoup, V. (ed.) CRYPTO 2005. LNCS, vol. 3621, pp. 378–394. Springer, Heidelberg (2005). https://doi.org/10.1007/11535218_23

[DI06]   Damgård, I., Ishai, Y.: Scalable secure multiparty computation. In: Dwork, C. (ed.) CRYPTO 2006. LNCS, vol. 4117, pp. 501–520. Springer, Heidelberg (2006). https://doi.org/10.1007/11818175_30

[DN07]   Dwork, C., Naor, M.: Zaps and their applications. SIAM J. Comput. **36**(6), 1513–1543 (2007)

[GGHR14] Garg, S., Gentry, C., Halevi, S., Raykova, M.: Two-round secure MPC from indistinguishability obfuscation. In: Lindell, Y. (ed.) TCC 2014. LNCS, vol. 8349, pp. 74–94. Springer, Heidelberg (2014). https://doi.org/10.1007/978-3-642-54242-8_4

[GIP+14] Genkin, D., Ishai, Y., Prabhakaran, M., Sahai, A., Tromer, E.: Circuits resilient to additive attacks with applications to secure computation. In: STOC, pp. 495–504 (2014)

[GIP15]   Genkin, D., Ishai, Y., Polychroniadou, A.: Efficient multi-party computation: from passive to active security via secure SIMD circuits. In: Gennaro, R., Robshaw, M. (eds.) CRYPTO 2015. LNCS, vol. 9216, pp. 721–741. Springer, Heidelberg (2015). https://doi.org/10.1007/978-3-662-48000-7_35

[GIW16]   Genkin, D., Ishai, Y., Weiss, M.: Binary AMD circuits from secure multiparty computation. In: Hirt, M., Smith, A. (eds.) TCC 2016. LNCS, vol. 9985, pp. 336–366. Springer, Heidelberg (2016). https://doi.org/10.1007/978-3-662-53641-4_14

[GMPP16] Garg, S., Mukherjee, P., Pandey, O., Polychroniadou, A.: The exact round complexity of secure computation. In: Fischlin, M., Coron, J.-S. (eds.) EUROCRYPT 2016. LNCS, vol. 9666, pp. 448–476. Springer, Heidelberg (2016). https://doi.org/10.1007/978-3-662-49896-5_16

[GMW87] Goldreich, O., Micali, S., Wigderson, A.: How to play any mental game or A completeness theorem for protocols with honest majority. In: STOC, pp. 218–229 (1987)

[Goy11] Goyal, V.: Constant round non-malleable protocols using one way functions. In: Proceedings of the 43rd ACM Symposium on Theory of Computing STOC 2011, San Jose, CA, USA, pp. 695–704, 6–8 June 2011 (2011)

[GRRV14] Goyal, V., Richelson, S., Rosen, A., Vald, M.: An algebraic approach to non-malleability. In: FOCS, pp. 41–50 (2014)

[GS17] Garg, S., Srinivasan, A.: Two-round multiparty secure computation from minimal assumptions. IACR Cryptol. ePrint Archive **2017**, 1156 (2017)

[HHPV17] Halevi, S., Hazay, C., Polychroniadou, A., Venkitasubramaniam, M.: Round-optimal secure multi-party computation. IACR Cryptol. ePrint Archive **2017**, 1056 (2017)

[HIK+11] Haitner, I., Ishai, Y., Kushilevitz, E., Lindell, Y., Petrank, E.: Black-box constructions of protocols for secure computation. SIAM J. Comput. **40**(2), 225–266 (2011)

[HPV16] Hazay, C., Polychroniadou, A., Venkitasubramaniam, M.: Composable security in the tamper-proof hardware model under minimal complexity. In: Hirt, M., Smith, A. (eds.) TCC 2016. LNCS, vol. 9985, pp. 367–399. Springer, Heidelberg (2016). https://doi.org/10.1007/978-3-662-53641-4_15

[HSS17] Hazay, C., Scholl, P., Soria-Vazquez, E.: Low cost constant round MPC combining BMR and oblivious transfer. In: Takagi, T., Peyrin, T. (eds.) ASIACRYPT 2017. LNCS, vol. 10624, pp. 598–628. Springer, Cham (2017). https://doi.org/10.1007/978-3-319-70694-8_21

[Khu17] Khurana, D.: Round optimal concurrent non-malleability from polynomial hardness. In: Kalai, Y., Reyzin, L. (eds.) TCC 2017. LNCS, vol. 10678, pp. 139–171. Springer, Cham (2017). https://doi.org/10.1007/978-3-319-70503-3_5

[KOS03] Katz, J., Ostrovsky, R., Smith, A.: Round efficiency of multi-party computation with a dishonest majority. In: Biham, E. (ed.) EUROCRYPT 2003. LNCS, vol. 2656, pp. 578–595. Springer, Heidelberg (2003). https://doi.org/10.1007/3-540-39200-9_36

[LP11] Lin, H., Pass, R.: Constant-round non-malleable commitments from any one-way function. In: STOC, pp. 705–714 (2011)

[LPSY15] Lindell, Y., Pinkas, B., Smart, N.P., Yanai, A.: Efficient constant round multi-party computation combining BMR and SPDZ. In: Gennaro, R., Robshaw, M. (eds.) CRYPTO 2015. LNCS, vol. 9216, pp. 319–338. Springer, Heidelberg (2015). https://doi.org/10.1007/978-3-662-48000-7_16

[LPV12] Pass, R., Lin, H., Venkitasubramaniam, M.: A unified framework for UC from only OT. In: Wang, X., Sako, K. (eds.) ASIACRYPT 2012. LNCS, vol. 7658, pp. 699–717. Springer, Heidelberg (2012). https://doi.org/10.1007/978-3-642-34961-4_42

[MW16] Mukherjee, P., Wichs, D.: Two round multiparty computation via multi-key FHE. In: Fischlin, M., Coron, J.-S. (eds.) EUROCRYPT 2016. LNCS, vol. 9666, pp. 735–763. Springer, Heidelberg (2016). https://doi.org/10.1007/978-3-662-49896-5_26

[OPP14] Ostrovsky, R., Paskin-Cherniavsky, A., Paskin-Cherniavsky, B.: Maliciously circuit-private FHE. In: Garay, J.A., Gennaro, R. (eds.) CRYPTO 2014. LNCS, vol. 8616, pp. 536–553. Springer, Heidelberg (2014). https://doi.org/10.1007/978-3-662-44371-2_30

[Pas04] Pass, R., Wee, H.: Constant-round non-malleable commitments from sub-exponential one-way functions. In: Gilbert, H. (ed.) EUROCRYPT 2010. LNCS, vol. 6110, pp. 638–655. Springer, Heidelberg (2010). https://doi.org/10.1007/978-3-642-13190-5_32

[PW10] Pass, R., Wee, H.: Constant-Round Non-malleable Commitments from Sub-exponential One-Way Functions. In: Gilbert, H. (ed.) EUROCRYPT 2010. LNCS, vol. 6110, pp. 638–655. Springer, Heidelberg (2010)

[Yao86] Yao, A.C.-C: How to generate and exchange secrets (extended abstract). In: FOCS, pp. 162–167 (1986)

Foundations

Yes, There is an Oblivious RAM Lower Bound!

Kasper Green Larsen[1,2]([✉]) and Jesper Buus Nielsen[1,2]

[1] Computer Science, Aarhus University, Aarhus, Denmark
larsen@cs.au.dk
[2] Computer Science and DIGIT, Aarhus University, Aarhus, Denmark

Abstract. An Oblivious RAM (ORAM) introduced by Goldreich and Ostrovsky [JACM'96] is a (possibly randomized) RAM, for which the memory access pattern reveals no information about the operations performed. The main performance metric of an ORAM is the bandwidth overhead, i.e., the multiplicative factor extra memory blocks that must be accessed to hide the operation sequence. In their seminal paper introducing the ORAM, Goldreich and Ostrovsky proved an amortized $\Omega(\lg n)$ bandwidth overhead lower bound for ORAMs with memory size n. Their lower bound is very strong in the sense that it applies to the "offline" setting in which the ORAM knows the entire sequence of operations ahead of time.

However, as pointed out by Boyle and Naor [ITCS'16] in the paper "Is there an oblivious RAM lower bound?", there are two caveats with the lower bound of Goldreich and Ostrovsky: (1) it only applies to "balls in bins" algorithms, i.e., algorithms where the ORAM may only shuffle blocks around and not apply any sophisticated encoding of the data, and (2), it only applies to statistically secure constructions. Boyle and Naor showed that removing the "balls in bins" assumption would result in super linear lower bounds for sorting circuits, a long standing open problem in circuit complexity. As a way to circumventing this barrier, they also proposed a notion of an "online" ORAM, which is an ORAM that remains secure even if the operations arrive in an online manner. They argued that most known ORAM constructions work in the online setting as well.

Our contribution is an $\Omega(\lg n)$ lower bound on the bandwidth overhead of any online ORAM, even if we require only computational security and allow arbitrary representations of data, thus greatly strengthening the lower bound of Goldreich and Ostrovsky in the online setting. Our lower bound applies to ORAMs with memory size n and any word size $r \geq 1$. The bound therefore asymptotically matches the known upper bounds when $r = \Omega(\lg^2 n)$.

K. G. Larsen—Supported by a Villum Young Investigator grant 13163 and an AUFF starting grant.
J. B. Nielsen—Supported by the European Union's Horizon 2020 research and innovation programme under grant agreement #731583 (SODA).

H. Shacham and A. Boldyreva (Eds.): CRYPTO 2018, LNCS 10992, pp. 523–542, 2018.
https://doi.org/10.1007/978-3-319-96881-0_18

1   Introduction

It is often attractive to store data at an untrusted party, and only retrieve the needed parts of it. Encryption can help ensure that the party storing the data has no idea of what it is storing, but still it is possible to get information about the stored data by analyzing the access pattern.

Goldreich and Ostrovsky [GO96] solved this problem in a model with a client that is equipped with a random oracle and small (constant size) memory. The client runs a program while using a (larger) RAM stored on a server, where the access pattern is observed by the adversary. The results from [GO96] shows that any program in the standard RAM model can be transformed using an "oblivious RAM simulator" into a program for the oblivious RAM model, where the access pattern is information theoretically hidden. Whereas it is not reasonable to assume a random oracle in a real implementation, Goldreich and Ostrovsky point out that one can replace it by a pseudorandom function (PRF) that only depends on a short key stored by the client. This way, one obtains a solution that is only computationally secure. The construction in [GO96] had an overhead of $\mathrm{polylog}(n)$, where the overhead is defined to be the number of memory blocks communicated per operation and n is defined as the number of memory blocks of the ORAM. The paper at the same time showed a lower bound on the overhead of $\Omega(\lg n)$.

There has been a surge in research on ORAMs in recent years, both on practical efficiency, asymptotic efficiency, practical applications and theoretical applications. There are literally hundreds of papers on the subject and any list will leave out important results. However, a good starting point for getting an overview of the breadth of the research is [PR10, DMN11, GM11, GMOT12, KLO12, WST12, SS13, CLP14, GHL+14, GLO15, BCP16, LO17, Goo17, Goo18], their references and the papers citing them.

A seminal result was the Path ORAM [SvDS+13], which has an amortized $O(\lg n)$ bandwidth cost (measured in blocks communicated) for blocks of size $\Omega(\lg^2 n)$ bits. It was the first to achieve this overhead. Since the lower bound in [GO96] applies to any block size, this seems to have finished the story by giving matching lower and upper bounds. However, as pointed out by Boyle and Naor [BN16], there are two caveats with the lower bound of Goldreich and Ostrovsky: (1) it only applies to "balls in bins" algorithms, i.e., algorithms where the ORAM may only shuffle blocks around and not apply any sophisticated encoding of the data, and (2), it only applies to statistically secure constructions. This leaves open the question whether a non-"balls in bins" ORAM construction or an inherently computationally secure only ORAM construction could beat the $\lg n$ lower bound. In this work we show that this is not the case.

1.1   Our Contributions

Before we state our result we present the class of ORAM schemes our new lower bound applies to.

Online ORAMs. Boyle and Naor showed that proving lower bounds without the "balls in bins" assumption would result in super-linear lower bounds for sorting circuits, a long standing open problem in circuit complexity. As a way to circumventing this barrier, they proposed a notion of an "online" ORAM, which is an ORAM that remains secure even if the operations arrive in an online manner. They argued that most known ORAM constructions work in the online setting as well. Also, most applications of ORAM schemes require that the scheme is online.

Passive ORAMs. It is implicit in the original definition of ORAMs that the server is passive storage. There are also ORAM constructions (for instance, Onion ORAM [DvDF+16] and the recent proposal in [AFN+16]), which allow the server to perform untrusted computation on behalf of the client. Our lower bound does not apply to such ORAMs. And indeed most of these schemes achieves sub-logarithmic overhead.

Problem Statement. To be a bit more precise, the purpose of the online ORAM is to allow a client to store data on an untrusted server. The online ORAM provides security in the sense that it hides the data access pattern from the server (which blocks are read/written). More formally, an online ORAM supports the following two operations:

- write(a, data): Store data in the block of address a, where a $\in [n]$ and data $\in \{0,1\}^r$.
- read(a): Return the contents of the block of address a.

During operation, the ORAM maybe perform the same type of operations on a memory stored on a server. The server memory space may be larger than that of the ORAM and the block size need not be the same. To distinguish the two, we refer to blocks at the server as *memory cells*, we use w to denote the number of bits in a memory cell and we use r to denote the number of bits in a block, i.e., r is the number of bits in the data arguments of the write(a, data) operations.

An online ORAM is secure in the following sense: Let y be a sequence of operations for the ORAM:

$$y := (op_1, \ldots, op_M)$$

where each op_i is either a write(a, data) or read(a) operation. Let

$$A(y) := (A(op_1), \ldots, A(op_M))$$

denote the memory access pattern to the server from the online ORAM, i.e., each $A(op_j)$ is the list of addresses of the cells accessed at the server while processing op_j. For a randomized construction $A(y)$ is a random variable. Security is defined as follows: for two distinct sequences of operations y and z with the same number of operations, $A(y)$ and $A(z)$ are computationally indistinguishable. In the main text we will give a more formal definition. The present informal definition is only to be able to present our result.

We prove the following theorem.

Theorem 1 (informal). *Any online ORAM with n blocks of memory, consisting of $r \geq 1$ bits each, must have an expected amortized bandwidth overhead of $\Omega(\lg(nr/m))$ on sequences of $\Theta(n)$ operations. Here m denotes the client memory in bits. This holds in the random oracle model, requiring only computational indistinguishability, holds for any server cell size w and allows for arbitrary representations of the data in memory. For the natural setting of parameters $r \leq m \leq n^{1-\varepsilon}$ for an arbitrarily small constant $\varepsilon > 0$, the lower bound simplifies to $\Omega(\lg n)$.*

Discussion 1. Comparing our definition of an online ORAM to that of Boyle and Naor [BN16], our security definition is slightly stricter in the sense that for us, $A(y)$ also lets the adversary see which block accesses belong to which operations. Boyle and Naor simply define $A(y)$ as $A(\mathrm{op}_1) \cdots A(\mathrm{op}_M)$ (without the comma separation). We believe our stricter definition is justifiable as it seems questionable to base security on not knowing when one operation has finished processing, at least in an online setting where operations arrive one at a time and we don't know before hand how many operations we have to process. To the best of our knowledge, all online ORAM implementations also satisfy our stricter security definition.

Discussion 2. Most ORAM constructions have $w = \Theta(r)$, i.e., the server memory cells have the same asymptotic number of bits as the block size of the ORAM. However, this is not a strict requirement, and the Path ORAM [SvDS+13] in fact has $r = \Theta(\lg^2 n)$ and $w = \Theta(\lg n)$ in order to achieve their $O(\lg n)$ amortized bandwidth overhead, i.e., the ORAM block size and the server memory cells have very different sizes. When dealing with w and r that are not asymptotically the same, one defines the bandwidth overhead as the multiplicative factor extra bits that must be accessed from the server compared to just reading the r bits comprising a block. Thus if an ORAM accesses t memory cells per operation, its bandwidth overhead is tw/r. The Path ORAM accesses an amortized $\Theta(\lg^2 n)$ memory cells per operation. This is $\Theta(w \lg^2 n) = \Theta(\lg^3 n)$ bits, which is a multiplicative factor $\Theta((\lg^3 n)/r) = \Theta(\lg n)$ overhead, i.e., its bandwidth overhead is $\Theta(\lg n)$. Our lower bound holds regardless of the memory cell size w.

1.2   Proof Strategy

In the following, we give a brief overview of the ideas in our lower bound proof. Our first observation is that the definition of the online ORAM coincides with the definition of an oblivious data structure, as defined in [WNL+14], solving the following array maintenance problem:

Definition 1. *In the array maintenance problem, we must maintain an array B of n r-bit entries under the following two operations:*

- *write(a, data): Set the contents of $B[a]$ to data, where $a \in [n]$ and data $\in \{0,1\}^r$.*
- *read(a): Return the contents of $B[a]$.*

This data structure view allows us to re-use techniques for proving data structure lower bounds. More concretely, we prove a lower bound for oblivious data structures solving the array maintenance problem and then use the argument above to conclude the same lower bound for online ORAMs.

Data structure lower bounds are typically proved in the cell probe model of Yao [Yao81]. Intuitively, this model is the same as the standard RAM, except that computation is free of charge and we only pay for memory accesses. This matches the ORAM performance metrics perfectly as we care about the bandwidth overhead and the memory accesses revealing no information. We thus tweak the definition of the cell probe model such that it captures client memory and other technical details of the online ORAM not normally found in data structures. We will define our model, which we term the *oblivious cell probe model*, formally in Sect. 2. Another advantage of this data structure view is that it accurately captures the *online* setting of online ORAMs and thus allow us to circumvent the circuit complexity barrier demonstrated by Boyle and Naor [BN16].

The strongest current techniques for proving lower bounds in the cell probe model, can prove lower bounds of the form $\tilde{\Omega}(\lg^2 n)$ [Lar12] for problems with a $\lg n$-bit output, and $\tilde{\Omega}(\lg^{1.5} n)$ for decision problems [LWY18], i.e., one-bit answers to queries. Here $\tilde{\Omega}$ hides polyloglog factors. We did not manage to use these techniques to prove lower bounds for ORAMs, but instead took inspiration from the so-called *information transfer* method of Pătraşcu and Demaine [PD06], which can prove lower bounds of $\Omega(\lg n)$. It would be quite exciting if the techniques in [Lar12,LWY18] could be tweaked to prove $\omega(\lg n)$ lower bounds for e.g. the *worst case* bandwidth overhead of ORAMs. We leave this as intriguing future work.

The basic idea in the *information transfer* method, is to consider a distribution over sequences of M operations on a data structure. One then considers a binary tree $\mathcal{T}$ on top of such a random sequence, having an operation in each leaf. The next step is to consider the memory accesses arising from processing the M operations. Each such memory access is assigned to a node $v \in \mathcal{T}$ as follows: For a memory access p to a memory cell c, let ℓ_i be the leaf of $\mathcal{T}$ containing the operation that caused the memory access p. Let ℓ_j, with $j < i$, be the leaf corresponding to the last time c was accessed prior to p. We associate p with the lowest common ancestor of ℓ_i and ℓ_j. The next step is to prove that for every node $v \in \mathcal{T}$, there has to be many memory accesses assigned to v. Since each memory access is assigned to only one node in $\mathcal{T}$, we can sum up the number of memory accesses assigned to all the nodes of $\mathcal{T}$ and get a lower bound on the total number of accesses.

Now to lower bound the number of memory accesses assigned to a node v, observe that such memory accesses correspond precisely to operations in the right subtree of v accessing memory cells last accessed during the operations in the left subtree. To prove that there must be many such memory accesses, one proves that the answers to the queries (read operations) in the right subtree depends heavily on the updates (write operations) in the left subtree. In this way, one basically shows that every leaf must make a memory access for every ancestor in $\mathcal{T}$, resulting in an $\Omega(\lg M)$ lower bound.

The problem for us, is that the array maintenance problem is trivial for standard data structures. Thus the above approach fails utterly without more ideas. The issue is that for any distribution over read and write operations, we cannot prove that a read operation in some leaf of T has to make memory accesses for every ancestor in T. Basically, for most nodes, the read operations in the right subtree will request array entries not written to in the left subtree and thus will not need to access anything written there. Our key idea for exploiting the security requirement is that, if we *change* the distribution over operations, then the number of memory accesses assigned to the nodes of T cannot change drastically as this would be observable by an adversary who can simply construct T and assign the memory accesses. We can therefore examine the nodes v of T, and for each one, change the distribution over operations such that the read operations in the right subtree requests precisely the array entries written to in the left subtree. By an entropy argument, there has to be many memory accesses under such a distribution. And by our security requirement, this translates back to many memory accesses under the original distribution. We refer the reader to Sect. 3 for the full details.

2   Oblivious Cell Probe Model

In this section, we formally define a lower bound model for proving lower bounds for oblivious data structures. As mentioned earlier, an ORAM immediately gives an oblivious data structure for array maintenance. Hence we set out to prove lower bounds for such data structures.

Our new model is an extension of the cell probe model of Yao [Yao81]. The cell probe model is traditionally used to prove lower bounds for word-RAM data structures and is extremely powerful in the sense that it allows arbitrary computations and only charge for memory accesses. We augment the cell probe model to capture the client side memory of an ORAM. To make clear the distinction between our lower bound model and traditional upper bound models, we call ours the *oblivious cell probe model*. The reason why we introduce this model, is that it allows for a clean proof and definition, plus it brings in all the techniques developed for proving data structure lower bounds. Moreover, we hope that our work inspires other lower bound proofs for oblivious data structures, and thus our thorough definition may serve as a reference.

Problems. A data structure problem in the oblivious cell probe model is defined by a universe $\mathcal{U}$ of update operations, a universe $\mathcal{Q}$ of queries and an output domain $\mathcal{O}$. Furthermore, there is a query function $f : \mathcal{U}^* \times \mathcal{Q} \to \mathcal{O}$. For a sequence of updates $u_1 \ldots u_M \in \mathcal{U}$ and a query $q \in \mathcal{Q}$ we say that the answer to the query q after updates $u_1 \ldots u_M$ is $f(u_1 \ldots u_M, q)$.

As an example, consider the array maintenance problem (Definition 1). Here $\mathcal{U}$ is the set of all write(a, data) operations, $\mathcal{Q}$ is the set of all read(a) operations and $\mathcal{O}$ is $\{0, 1\}^r$.

Oblivious Cell Probe Data Structure. An oblivious cell probe data structure with client memory m bits for a problem $\mathcal{P} = (\mathcal{U}, \mathcal{Q}, \mathcal{O}, f)$ consists of a random access memory of w-bit cells, a client memory of m bits and a random bit string R of some finite length ℓ. We make no restrictions on ℓ, only that it is finite. Note in particular that R can be exponentially long and hence contain all the randomness needed by the oblivious RAM and/or a random oracle. We will call R the *random-oracle bit-string*. Each cell of the memory has an integer address amongst $[K]$ and we typically assume $w \geq \max\{\lg K, \lg M\}$ such that any cell can store the address of any other cell and the index of any operation performed on it.

When processing an operation, an oblivious cell probe data structure may read or write memory cells. The cell to read or write in each step may depend arbitrarily on the client memory contents and all contents of cells read so far while processing the operation. Moreover, after each read or write, the oblivious cell probe data structure may change the contents of the client memory. The performance measure is defined solely as the number of memory cells read/written to while processing an operation, i.e., computation is free of charge. To capture this formally, an oblivious cell probe data structure is defined by a decision tree T_{op} for every operation op $\in \mathcal{U} \cup \mathcal{Q}$, i.e., it has one decision tree for every possible operation in the data structure problem. The tree is meant to capture in a crisp way the operation of the oblivious data structure. Each node represents a "step" of computation which might depend on the local client memory of the oblivious data structure, the randomness R and all server memory positions read so far while processing the operation. It may also read a memory position on the server or write a memory position on the server. The "implementation" of the operation can therefore depend on previous operations to the extent that information about them is stored in the local memory.

More formally, each decision tree T_{op} is a rooted finite tree. Each node v of T_{op} is labelled with an address $i \in [K]$ and it has one child for every triple of the form (m_0, c_0, r) where $m_0 \in \{0,1\}^m$, $c_0 \in \{0,1\}^w$ and $r \in \{0,1\}^\ell$. Each edge to a child is furthermore labelled with a triple (j, m_1, c_1) with $j \in [K]$, $m_1 \in \{0,1\}^m$ and $c_1 \in \{0,1\}^w$. To process an operation op, the oblivious cell probe data structure starts its execution at the root of the corresponding tree T_{op} and traverses a root to leaf path in T_{op}. When visiting a node v in this traversal, labelled with some address $i_v \in [K]$ it *probes* the memory cell of address i_v. If C denotes its contents, M denotes the current contents of the client memory and R denotes the random-oracle bit-string, the process continues by descending to the child of v corresponding to the tuple (M, C, R). If the edge to the child is labelled (j, m_1, c_1), then the memory cell of address j has its contents updated to c_1 and the client memory is updated to m_1. We say that memory cell j is *probed*. We make no requirements that $m_1 \neq M$, $c_1 \neq C$ or $j \neq i$. The execution stops when reaching a leaf of T_{op}.

Finally, each leaf v of a tree T_{op}, where op is in $\mathcal{Q}$, is labelled with a w-bit string L_v (the answer to the query). We say that the oblivious cell probe data structure returns L_v as its answer to the query op.

Definition 2 (Expected Amortized Running Time). *We say that an oblivious cell probe data structure has expected amortized running time $t(M)$ on a sequence y of M operations from $\mathcal{U} \cup \mathcal{Q}$ if the total number of memory probes is no more than $t(M) \cdot M$ in expectation. The expectation is taken over a uniformly random random-oracle string $r \in \{0,1\}^{\ell}$. We say that an oblivious cell probe data structure has expected amortized running time $t(M)$ if it has expected amortized running time $t(M)$ on all sequences y of operations from $\mathcal{U} \cup \mathcal{Q}$.*

We proceed to define security. Let

$$y := (\mathrm{op}_1, \ldots, \mathrm{op}_M)$$

denote a sequence of M operations to the data structure problem, where each $\mathrm{op}_i \in \mathcal{U} \cup \mathcal{Q}$. For an oblivious cell probe data structure, define the (possibly randomized) *probe sequence* on y as the tuple:

$$A(y) := (A(\mathrm{op}_1), \ldots, A(\mathrm{op}_M))$$

where $A(\mathrm{op}_i)$ is the sequence of memory addresses probed while processing op_i. More precisely, let $A(y; R) := (A(\mathrm{op}_1; R), \ldots, A(\mathrm{op}_M; R))$ be the deterministic sequence of operations when the random-oracle bit-string is R and let $A(y)$ be the random variable describing $A(y; R)$ for a uniformly random $R \in \{0,1\}^{\ell}$.

Definition 3 (Correctness). *We say that an oblivious cell probe data structure has failure probability δ if, for every sequence and any operation op in the sequence, the data structure answers op correctly with probability at least $1 - \delta$.*

Definition 4 (Security). *An oblivious cell probe data structure is said to be secure if the following two properties hold:*

Indistinguishability: *For any two data request sequences y and z of the same length M, their probe sequences $A(y)$ and $A(z)$ cannot be distinguished with probability better than $\frac{1}{4}$ by an algorithm which is polynomial time in $M + \lg |\mathcal{U}| + \lg |\mathcal{Q}| + w$.*

Correctness: *The oblivious cell probe data structure has failure probability at most $1/3$.*

Discussion 1. It is clear that for most uses of an ORAM, having indistinguishability of $1/4$ and failure probability $1/3$ is not satisfactory. However, for the sake of a lower bound, allowing these large constant slack parameters just gives a stronger bound. In particular, when $M, \lg |\mathcal{U}|, \lg |\mathcal{Q}|, w \in \mathrm{poly}(k)$ for a security parameter k, then our bound applies to computational indistinguishability by an adversary running in time $\mathrm{poly}(k)$.

Discussion 2. Since the random-oracle bit-string and the decision trees are finite, the model does not capture algorithms which might potentially run for arbitrary many steps with vanishing probability. However, any such algorithm might at the price of an error probability on the output be pruned to a finite decision tree consuming only a finite amount of randomness. By pruning at a sufficiently high depth, an arbitrarily small error probability in $O(2^{-n})$ may be introduced. Since we allow a large constant error probability of $1/3$ our lower bound also applies to algorithms which might potentially run for arbitrary many step with vanishing probability on sequences of length poly(n).

Discussion 3. For online ORAMs, we are typically interested in the *bandwidth overhead*, which is the multiplicative factor extra bits that must be accessed compared to the underlying RAM being simulated. If the underlying RAM/array has r-bit entries, we have that a sequence of M operations can be processed by accessing Mr bits. Thus for ORAMs with (server) cell size w bits, this translates into the minimum number of probes being Mr/w. Thus if an oblivious data structure for the array maintenance problem has expected amortized running time $t(M)$, then the corresponding ORAM has an expected amortized bandwidth overhead of $t(M)w/r$.

3   Lower Bound

In this section, we prove our lower bound for oblivious cell probe data structures solving the array maintenance problem and thus indirectly also prove a lower bound for online ORAMs. The model is recapped in Fig. 1. The formal statement of our result is as follows:

Theorem 2. *Let $\mathcal{D}$ be an oblivious cell probe data structure for the array maintenance problem on arrays of n r-bit entries where $r \geq 1$. Let w denote the cell size of $\mathcal{D}$, let m denote the number of bits of client memory. If $\mathcal{D}$ is secure according to Definition 4, then there exists a sequence y of $\Theta(n)$ operations such that the expected amortized running time of $\mathcal{D}$ on y is $\Omega(\lg(nr/m)r/w)$. In terms of bandwidth overhead, this means that the expected amortized bandwidth overhead is $\Omega(\lg(nr/m))$. For the most natural setting of $r \leq m \leq n^{1-\varepsilon}$, this simplifies to $\Omega(\lg n)$.*

Let $\mathcal{D}$ be as in Theorem 2 and let $[K] \subseteq [2^w]$ be the set of possible addresses of its memory cells. Throughout our lower bound proof, we assume that $\mathcal{D}$ has failure probability at most $1/32$ instead of $1/3$. Note that the lower bound extends to failure probability $1/3$ (or any failure probability bounded away from $1/2$) simply because one can always run a constant number of independent copies in parallel and use a majority vote when answering a read operation.

We prove our lower bound for processing the following fixed sequence of $M = 2n$ operations:

- We perform a sequence y of intermixed read and write operations. The sequence has n of each type and looks as follows:

$$y := \text{write}(0,\bar{0}), \text{read}(0), \text{write}(0,\bar{0}), \text{read}(0), \ldots, \text{write}(0,\bar{0}), \text{read}(0)$$

where $\bar{0}$ denotes the all-zeroes bit string of length r.

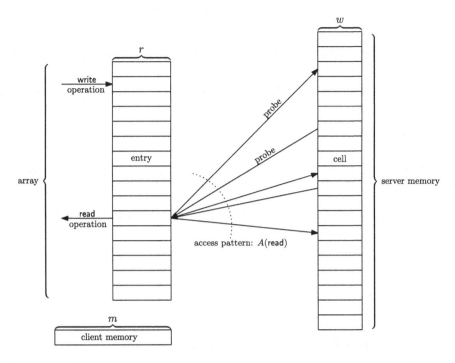

Fig. 1. An ORAM implements an array of r-bit entries. Each operation can be a read or a write. Each operation op makes read and write probes to the server memory. The sequence of probes made during an operation op is called the access pattern of op and is written as $A(\text{op})$. Words in the server memory are called cells. Each cell is w bits. The ORAM is restricted to m bits of storage between two operations. During an operation it can use unlimited storage.

The sequence y is just the sequence of alternating write and read operations that all access the first array entry, and the write operations just store $\bar{0}$ in it. What makes this sequence costly is of course that the probe sequence of $\mathcal{D}$ on y must be computationally indistinguishable from all other sequences of $M = 2n$ operations.

To exploit this, define $A(y)$ as the random variable giving the probe sequence (as defined in Sect. 2) of $\mathcal{D}$ when processing y. Since our sequence has $M = 2n$ operations on an array with r-bit entries, we have a minimum bandwidth usage of $2nr$ bits. The data structure $\mathcal{D}$ has a cell size of w bits, and thus the minimum number of probes is $2nr/w$. Thus by definition, we have that the expected amortized bandwidth overhead is $\mathbb{E}[|A(y)|]w/(2nr)$. Our goal is thus to lower bound $\mathbb{E}[|A(y)|]$. Our proof is an adaptation of the *information transfer* technique by Pǎtraşcu and Demaine [PD06] for proving data structure lower bounds in the cell probe model. The basic proof strategy is as follows:

For any sequence of $M = 2n$ operations z of the form:

$$\text{write}(i_1, d_1), \text{read}(i_2), \text{write}(i_3, d_3), \text{read}(i_4), \ldots, \text{write}(i_{2n-1}, d_{2n-1}), \text{read}(i_{2n}),$$

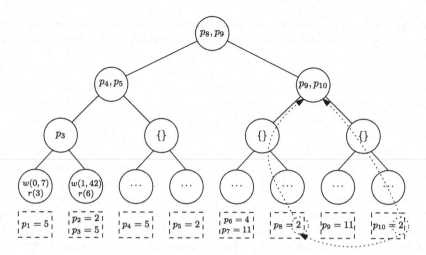

Fig. 2. Illustration of how probes are associated to nodes. The second to bottom layer is a sequence of 16 intermixed read and write operations $\mathrm{write}(0,7), \mathrm{read}(3), \mathrm{write}(1,42),$ $\mathrm{read}(6), \dots$. We only show the two first pairs. Under each pair of commands we show for illustration the probes that they made. In the nodes we illustrate where the probes would be associated. As an example, take leaf number 8 (the right most leaf). It did the 10'th probe. That probe probed cell 2. That happened last time in leaf number 6 by probe p_8. The lowest common ancestor of leafs 6 and 8 therefore contains p_{10}.

we consider a binary tree $\mathcal{T}(z)$ with n leaves, on top of the $2n$ operation. There is one leaf in $\mathcal{T}(z)$ for each consecutive pair $\mathrm{write}(i_j, d_j), \mathrm{read}(i_{j+1})$. Let op_i denote the i'th operation in the sequence z, i.e., op_1 is the first $\mathrm{write}(i_1, d_1)$ operation, op_2 is the first $\mathrm{read}(i_2)$ operation and so on. Consider the probe sequence $A(z) = (A(\mathrm{op}_1), A(\mathrm{op}_2), \dots, A(\mathrm{op}_{2n}))$ where each $A(\mathrm{op}_i)$ is the sequence of memory addresses probed when $\mathcal{D}$ processes $A(\mathrm{op}_i)$ during the sequence of operations z. Let $p_1, \dots, p_T$ denote the concatenation of all the sequences of probed memory addresses, i.e., $p_1, \dots, p_T = A(\mathrm{op}_1) \circ A(\mathrm{op}_2) \circ \dots \circ A(\mathrm{op}_{2n})$ where $\circ$ is concatenation.

We assign each probed address p_i to a node of $\mathcal{T}(z)$. If $p_i = s$ for some address $s \in [K] \subseteq [2^w]$, then let p_j with $j < i$ denote the last time cell s was probed prior to p_i. Let ℓ_i and ℓ_j denote the leaves of $\mathcal{T}(z)$ containing the two operations whose processing caused the probes p_i and p_j, i.e., if p_i is a probe resulting from op_a, then ℓ_i is the leaf containing op_a. We assign p_i to the lowest common ancestor of ℓ_i and ℓ_j. If p_j does not exist, i.e., the memory cell with address s was not probed before, then we do not assign p_i to any node of $\mathcal{T}(z)$. See Fig. 2 for an illustration.

Our goal is to show that for the sequence y, it must be the case that most nodes of $\mathcal{T}(y)$ have a large number of probes assigned to them (in expectation). Since a probe is assigned to only one node of the tree, we can sum up the number of probes assigned to all nodes of $\mathcal{T}(y)$ to get a lower bound on the total number of probes in $A(y)$. In more detail, consider a node $v \in \mathcal{T}(y)$. Our proof will show that the read instructions in the right subtree of v have to probe many cells that were last probed during the operations in the left subtree. This corresponds precisely to the set of probes assigned to v being large.

To gain intuition for why the read operations in the right subtree must make many probes to cells written in the left subtree, observe that from the indistinguishability requirement, the probe sequence must look identical regardless of whether $\mathcal{D}$ is processing y, or if we instead process a random sequence in which the write operations in the left subtree are $\mathrm{write}(1, d_1), \mathrm{write}(2, d_2), \ldots$ and the reads in the right subtree are $\mathrm{read}(1), \mathrm{read}(2), \ldots$, where each d_i is a uniformly random r-bit string. In the latter case, the read operations have to recover all the (random) bits written in the left subtree and thus must probe many cells written in the left subtree by an entropy argument. Since counting the probes assigned to a node v can be done in poly-time in $M + r$ without knowing the arguments to the instructions, it follows from the indistinguishability property that for $A(y)$, there also has to be a large number of probes assigned to the node v. The argument is fleshed out in a bit more detail in Fig. 3.

We proceed to give a formal proof.

Nodes with Large Information Transfer. In the following, we argue that for many nodes in $\mathcal{T}(y)$, there must be a large number of probes assigned to v in expectation. We can then sum this up over all nodes in $\mathcal{T}(y)$. We do this as follows: For a sequence of operations z of the form

$$\mathrm{write}(i_1, d_1), \mathrm{read}(i_2), \mathrm{write}(i_3, d_3), \mathrm{read}(i_4), \ldots, \mathrm{write}(i_{2n-1}, d_{2n-1}), \mathrm{read}(i_{2n}),$$

and for every internal node v in $\mathcal{T}(z)$, let $P_v(z)$ denote the set of probes assigned to v. Using the terminology by Pătraşcu and Demaine [PD06], we refer to the set $P_v(z)$ as the *information transfer* in node v. We thus want to lower bound the size of the information transfer in the nodes of $\mathcal{T}(y)$. To do so, define depth(v) to be the distance from the root of $\mathcal{T}(y)$ to v. We prove the following:

Lemma 1. *If $\mathcal{D}$ has failure probability at most $1/32$, then for every internal node $v \in \mathcal{T}(y)$ with depth $d \in \{5, \ldots, (1/2)\lg(nr/m)\}$, it holds that*

$$\mathbb{E}\left[|P_v(y)|\right] = \Omega(nr/(w2^d)).$$

Let us first briefly give an explanation why the lemma only is proven for $d \in \{5, \ldots, (1/2)\lg(nr/m)\}$. Consider a node at depth d. It has about $nr/2^d$ nodes below it. So a node at depth $d = \lg(nr/m)$ has about m nodes below it. Recall that m is the size of the client memory between two operations. By going only to depth $(1/2)\lg(nr/m)$ we ensure that the node has to transfer much more than m bits such that the client memory plays essentially no role in the information transfer. Starting only from $d = 5$ makes some steps in the proof simpler.

Before proving Lemma 1, we show that it implies our main result. Since every probe in $A(y)$ is assigned to at most one node in $\mathcal{T}(y)$, and using linearity of expectation together with the fact that there are 2^d nodes of depth d in $\mathcal{T}(y)$, we have:

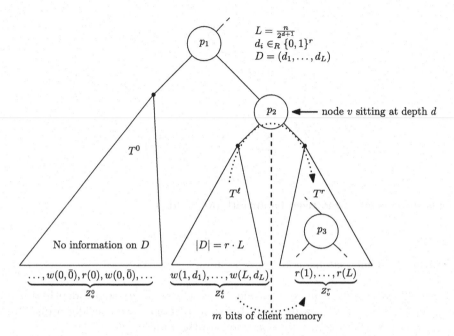

Fig. 3. We sketch the intuition of the proof. Assume for simplicity that the ORAM has perfect correctness, is deterministic and has no client memory. Consider a node v sitting at depth d. It has two sub-tree T^ℓ and T^r. Each of them has $L = \frac{n}{2^{d+1}}$ write and read operations in their leafs. Consider the sequence of operations which in each write in T^ℓ writes a fresh uniform value $d_i \in \{0,1\}^r$ and which in T^r reads these values back. In the sub-tree T^0 preceding T^ℓ the sequence will just write and read zero-values. There is an information transfer of $r \cdot L$ bits from the write operations in T^ℓ to the read operations in T^r, as the string $D = (d_1, \ldots, d_L)$ is being retrieved by the ORAM while in T^r. We argue that this information goes through v in the sense that there must be Lr/w probes assigned to v (illustrated using the dotted arrow in the figure). Namely, there must in T^r clearly be Lr/w probes that give information on D as each probe gives at most w bits of information. A probe in T^r gets assigned either to a node in T^r, to the node v or to an ancestor of v. Consider first a probe p_1 which gets assigned to an ancestor of v. It reads a cell which was last written before D was stored. Hence it cannot give information on D. Consider a probe p_3 assigned to a node in T^r. This node was last written by an operation in T^r. Hence it cannot give new information which was not previously learned by a probe in T^r. Therefore all probes giving information on D are assigned to v, so there are Lr/w probes assigned to v. If the scheme is only correct on a fraction $1 - \delta$ of the reads, proportionally less information is transferred, so only $(1 - \delta)Lr/w$ probes are needed. Also, m bits of information could be transferred via the client memory when moving from T^ℓ to T^r, reducing the needed number of probes to $\delta Lr/w - m/w$. If d is small enough, this will still be $\Omega(Lr/w)$.

$$
\begin{aligned}
\mathbb{E}[|A(y)|] &\geq \sum_{v \in \mathcal{T}(y)} \mathbb{E}[|P_v(y)|] \\
&\geq \sum_{d=5}^{(1/2)\lg(nr/m)} \sum_{v \in \mathcal{T}(y):\mathrm{depth}(v)=d} \mathbb{E}[|P_v|] \\
&= \Omega \left(\sum_{d=5}^{(1/2)\lg(nr/m)} \sum_{v \in \mathcal{T}(y):\mathrm{depth}(v)=d} nr/(w2^d) \right) \\
&= \Omega \left(\sum_{d=5}^{(1/2)\lg(nr/m)} 2^d \cdot nr/(w2^d) \right) \\
&= \Omega \left(nr \lg(nr/m)/w \right).
\end{aligned}
$$

Thus the expected amortized bandwidth overhead is

$$
\mathbb{E}[|A(y)|]w/(2nr) = \Omega(\lg(nr/m))
$$

as claimed. What remains is to prove Lemma 1.

Lower Bounding the Probes. Consider a node v in $\mathcal{T}(y)$ whose depth is $d = \mathrm{depth}(v) \in \{5, \ldots, (1/2)\lg(nr/m)\}$. To prove Lemma 1, we consider a distribution over sequences of $M = 2n$ operations of the form

$$
\mathrm{write}(i_1, d_1), \mathrm{read}(i_2), \mathrm{write}(i_3, d_3), \mathrm{read}(i_4), \ldots, \mathrm{write}(i_{2n-1}, d_{2n-1}), \mathrm{read}(i_{2n}).
$$

Our distribution will be chosen such that if we draw a sequence Z_v from the distribution and run $\mathcal{D}$ on Z_v, then the read operations in v's right subtree must probe many cells last written during the operations in v's left subtree. This means that $P_v(Z_v)$ must be large. We will then use the computational indistinguishability to argue that $P_v(y)$ must be just as large.

In greater detail, let Z_v be the random variable giving a sequence of $2n$ operations chosen as follows: For every $\mathrm{read}(i_j)$ not in the subtree rooted at v's right child, we simply have $i_j = 0$. For every $\mathrm{write}(i_j, d_j)$ not in the subtree rooted at v's left child, we have $i_j = 0$ and $d_j = \bar{0}$. For the $n/2^{d+1}$ read operations in v's right subtree $\mathrm{read}(i_j), \ldots, \mathrm{read}(i_{j+n/2^{d+1}-1})$, we have $i_j = 1, i_{j+1} = 2, \ldots, i_{j+n/2^{d+1}-1} = n/2^{d+1}$, i.e., the read operations in v's right subtree simply read the array entries $1, 2, 3, \ldots, n/2^{d+1}$ in that order. Finally for the $n/2^{d+1}$ write operations in v's left subtree $\mathrm{write}(i_j, d_j), \ldots, \mathrm{write}(i_{j+n/2^{d+1}}, d_{j+n/2^{d+1}-1})$ we have $i_j = 1, j_{j+1} = 2, \ldots, i_{j+n/2^{d+1}-1} = n/2^{d+1}$ and all d_j are independent and uniformly random w-bit strings. Thus for the random sequence Z_v, the read operations in v's right subtree precisely read the $n/2^{d+1}$ array entries that were filled with random bits during the $n/2^{d+1}$ write operations in v's left subtree.

All other operations just read and write array entry 0 as in the fixed sequence y. We prove the following via an entropy argument:

Lemma 2. *If $\mathcal{D}$ has failure probability at most $1/32$, then there exists a universal constant $C > 0$ such that*

$$\Pr[|P_v(Z_v)| \geq Cnr/(w2^d)] \geq 1/2.$$

Before proving Lemma 2, we show that it implies Lemma 1. For this, observe that by averaging, Lemma 2 implies that there must exist a sequence z in the support of Z_v such that

$$\Pr[|P_v(z)| \geq Cnr/(w2^d)] \geq 1/2.$$

From our security definition, $A(y)$ and $A(z)$ must be computationally indistinguishable. We argue that this implies that $\mathbb{E}[|P_v(y)|] \geq (C/4)nr/(w2^d) = \Omega(nr/(w2^d))$. To see this, assume for the sake of contradiction that $\mathbb{E}[|P_v(y)|] < (C/4)nr/(w2^d)$. By Markov's inequality, we get $\Pr[|P_v(y)| \geq Cnr/(w2^d)] \leq 1/4$. An adversary can now distinguish z and y as follows: Given a sequence $a \in \{y, z\}$, run $\mathcal{D}$ on the sequence a to obtain $A(a)$. Construct from $A(a)$ the tree $T(a)$ and the set $P_v(a)$ (an adversary knows precisely which probes belong to which operations and can thus construct all the sets $P_v(a)$ for all nodes v in $T(a)$ in polynomial time in M and w). Output 1 if $|P_v(a)| \geq Cnr/(w2^d)$ and 0 otherwise. This distinguishes y and z with probability at least $1/4$. Thus all that remains is to prove Lemma 2.

Encoding Argument. To prove Lemma 2, we assume for the sake of contradiction that the lemma is false, i.e., $\mathcal{D}$ has failure probability at most $1/32$ but:

$$\Pr[|P_v(Z_v)| \geq (1/100)nr/(w2^d)] < 1/2.$$

We will use this $\mathcal{D}$ to give an impossible encoding of the (random) data

$$d_j, d_{j+1}, \ldots, d_{j+n/2^{d+1}-1}$$

written in the left subtree of v in the sequence Z_v. Let $H(\cdot)$ denote binary Shannon entropy and observe that:

$$H(d_j, d_{j+1}, \ldots, d_{j+n/2^{d+1}-1} \mid R) = nr/2^{d+1} \, ,$$

where R denotes the random bits of the random oracle (these are independent of the input distribution). This is because the variables

$$d_j, d_{j+1}, \ldots, d_{j+n/2^{d+1}-1}$$

are uniformly random and independent r-bit strings. From Shannon's source coding theorem, any (possibly randomized) encoding of

$$d_j, d_{j+1}, \ldots, d_{j+n/2^{d+1}-1},$$

conditioned on R, must use $nr/2^{d+1}$ bits in expectation. This also holds for encoding and decoding algorithms which are not computationally efficient. Our encoding and decoding procedures are as follows:

Encoding. The encoder Alice is given

$$d_j, d_{j+1}, \ldots, d_{j+n/2^{d+1}-1}, R \ .$$

Alice does as follows:

1. From $d_j, d_{j+1}, \ldots, d_{j+n/2^{d+1}-1}$ she constructs the sequence Z_v. She then runs $\mathcal{D}$ on Z_v using the randomness R. While running the sequence Z_v on $\mathcal{D}$, she collects the set F of read operations read(i_j) in v's right subtree which fail to report the correct value d_j written by the write operation write(i_j, d_j) in v's left subtree. If either $|P_v(Z_v)| \geq (1/100)nr/(w2^d)$ or $|F| \geq (1/8)n/2^{d+1}$, then she writes down a 0-bit, followed by $nr/2^{d+1}$ bits giving a straight-forward encoding of $d_j, d_{j+1}, \ldots, d_{j+n/2^{d+1}-1}$. Otherwise, she writes down a 1-bit and proceeds to the next step.

2. She now writes down the contents and addresses of all memory cells whose address is in $P_v(Z_v)$. Let Z_v^ℓ denote operations in v's left subtree and let Z_v^0 denote the prefix of Z_v containing all operations up to just before Z_v^ℓ. The contents she writes down is the contents as they were just after processing the prefix $Z_v^0 \circ Z_v^\ell$. She also writes down the m client memory bits as they were immediately after processing $Z_v^0 \circ Z_v^\ell$. Finally, she also writes down $|F|$ using $\lg n$ bits as well as $\lg \binom{n/2^{d+1}}{|F|}$ bits specifying which read operations in v's right subtree that fail together with $|F|r$ bits specifying the correct answers to the failing read operations. The first part costs $|P_v(Z_v)|(\lg K + w) \leq |P_v(Z_v)|2w \leq (1/25)nr/2^{d+1}$ where $[K]$ is the address space of memory cells. Writing down the client memory costs m bits and writing down the failing read's and their correct answers costs at most

$$
\begin{aligned}
\lg n + |F|r + \lg \binom{n/2^{d+1}}{|F|} &\leq \lg n + (1/8)nr/2^{d+1} + \lg \binom{n/2^{d+1}}{(1/8)n/2^{d+1}} \\
&\leq \lg n + (1/8)nr/2^{d+1} \cdot (1 + \lg(8e)/r) \\
&\leq \lg n + (3/4)nr/2^{d+1} \\
&\leq (4/5)nr/2^{d+1}.
\end{aligned}
$$

Thus Alice's message has length at most $m + (21/25)nr/2^{d+1}$ if we she reaches step 2.

Decoding. The decoder Bob is given the message from Alice as well as R. His task is to recover

$$d_j, d_{j+1}, \ldots, d_{j+n/2^{d+1}-1} \ .$$

He proceeds as follows:

1. He starts by checking the first bit of the encoding. If this is a 0-bit, the remaining part is an encoding of $d_j, d_{j+1}, \ldots, d_{j+n/2^{d+1}-1}$ and he is done. Otherwise, he proceeds to the next step.

2. Bob runs the operations in Z_v^0 on $\mathcal{D}$, using the randomness R. Note that these operations are fixed (they all access array entry 0) and are thus known to Bob. He now skips all the instructions Z_v^ℓ in v's left subtree (which are unknown to him). He sets the client memory to what Alice told him it was after processing $Z_v^0 \circ Z_v^\ell$. He then overwrites all memory cells that appear in $P_v(Z_v)$ (Alice sent the addresses and contents of these as they were right after processing $Z_v^0 \circ Z_v^\ell$). Let Z_v^r denote the operations in v's right subtree. He then starts processing the operations Z_v^r using the randomness R, starting with the client memory contents that Alice sent him. We claim that this will give exactly the same execution as when Alice executed Z_v^r. To see this, consider any memory cell with address s and look at the first time it is probed during Bob's simulation of Z_v^r. There are two cases: either the contents were overwritten due to Alice's message. In this case, the contents are consistent with Alice's execution. Otherwise, the probe must be assigned to some node $w \in \mathcal{T}(Z_v)$ other than v. If w is an ancestor of v, then the cell cannot have been updated during Z_v^ℓ (by definition of how we assign probes to nodes in $\mathcal{T}$) and Bob has the correct contents from his own simulation of Z_v^0. If w is a descendant of v, it means that the cell was already probed during Z_v^r, contradicting that this was the first probe to the cell. Since Bob can finish the simulation (using the randomness R), he gets the same set of answers to all read operations in v's right subtree as Alice did. Finally, he uses the last part of Alice's message to correct the answers to all read operations in Z_v^r which fail. He is now done since the answers to the read operations in Z_v^r reveal $d_j, d_{j+1}, \ldots, d_{j+n/2^{d+1}-1}$.

Analysis. What remains is to show that the above encoding length is less than $nr/2^{d+1}$ in expectation, yielding the sought contradiction. If G denotes the event that Alice writes a 0-bit, we have that the expected length of the encoding is no more than:

$$1 + \Pr[G] \cdot nr/2^{d+1} + (1 - \Pr[G])(m + (21/25)nr/2^{d+1}).$$

Since $5 \leq d \leq (1/2)\lg(nr/m)$, we have

$$m \leq nr/2^{2d} = (nr/2^{d+1})/2^{d-1} \leq (1/16)(nr/2^{d+1}) .$$

Therefore the above is no more than:

$$1 + \Pr[G] \cdot nr/2^{d+1} + (1 - \Pr[G])(1/16 + 21/25)nr/2^{d+1} \leq$$
$$1 + \Pr[G] \cdot nr/2^{d+1} + (1 - \Pr[G])(91/100)nr/2^{d+1}.$$

Since the failure probability of $\mathcal{D}$ is no more than $1/32$, it follows from Markov's inequality and linearity of expectation that $\Pr[|F| \geq (1/8)n/2^{d+1}] \leq 1/4$. By a union bound, we have

$$\Pr[G] \leq \Pr[|P_v(Z_v)| \geq (1/100)nr/(w2^d)] + \Pr[|F| \geq (1/8)n/2^{d+1}]$$
$$\leq 1/2 + 1/4 \leq 3/4.$$

This means that the expected length of our encoding is no more than

$$1 + (3/4) \cdot nr/2^{d+1} + (1/4)(91/100)nr/2^{d+1} < nr/2^{d+1}.$$

This gives our sought contradiction and completes the proof of Theorem 2.

4   Conclusion and Future Work

It is 22 years since Goldreich and Ostrovsky proved the ORAM lower bound [GO96] assuming statistical security and "balls in bins". No progress was done on strengthening the bound for two decades. Two years ago, Boyle and Naor asked the question, *Is There an Oblivious RAM Lower Bound?* [BN16]. We have answered this question in the affirmative by eliminating both restrictions of the Goldreich-Ostrovsky lower bound.

The oblivious cell probe model and our lower bound for the array maintenance problem and online ORAMs open up a number of exciting questions. A number of papers (cf. [WNL+14]) have designed oblivious data structures. There is no reason why our proof technique cannot also be applied to prove lower bounds for such oblivious data structures.

Acknowledgment. Kasper Green Larsen wishes to thank Vinod Vaikuntanathan for introducing him to oblivious RAMs and oblivious data structures during a visit at MIT, eventually leading to the results in this paper.

References

[AFN+16] Abraham, I., Fletcher, C.W., Nayak, K., Pinkas, B., Ren, L.: Asymptotically tight bounds for composing ORAM with PIR. Cryptology ePrint Archive, Report 2016/849 (2016). https://eprint.iacr.org/2016/849

[BCP16] Boyle, E., Chung, K.-M., Pass, R.: Oblivious parallel RAM and applications. In: Kushilevitz, E., Malkin, T. (eds.) [KM16], pp. 175–204 (2016)

[BN16] Boyle, E., Naor, M.: Is there an oblivious RAM lower bound? In: Proceedings of the 2016 ACM Conference on Innovations in Theoretical Computer Science, pp. 357–368 (2016)

[CLP14] Chung, K.-M., Liu, Z., Pass, R.: Statistically-secure ORAM with $\tilde{O}(\lg^2 n)$ Overhead. In: Sarkar, P., Iwata, T. (eds.) ASIACRYPT 2014, Part II. LNCS, vol. 8874, pp. 62–81. Springer, Heidelberg (2014). https://doi.org/10.1007/978-3-662-45608-8_4

[DMN11] Damgård, I., Meldgaard, S., Nielsen, J.B.: Perfectly secure oblivious RAM without random oracles. In: Ishai, Y. (ed.) TCC 2011. LNCS, vol. 6597, pp. 144–163. Springer, Heidelberg (2011). https://doi.org/10.1007/978-3-642-19571-6_10

[DvDF+16] Devadas, S., van Dijk, M., Fletcher, C.W., Ren, L., Shi, E., Wichs, D.: Onion ORAM: a constant bandwidth blowup oblivious RAM. In: Kushilevitz, E., Malkin, T. (eds.) TCC 2016. LNCS, vol. 9563, pp. 145–174. Springer, Heidelberg (2016). https://doi.org/10.1007/978-3-662-49099-0_6

[GHL+14] Gentry, C., Halevi, S., Lu, S., Ostrovsky, R., Raykova, M., Wichs, D.: Garbled RAM revisited. In: Nguyen, P.Q., Oswald, E. (eds.) EUROCRYPT 2014. LNCS, vol. 8441, pp. 405–422. Springer, Heidelberg (2014). https://doi.org/10.1007/978-3-642-55220-5_23

[GLO15] Garg, S., Lu, S., Ostrovsky, R.: Black-box garbled RAM. In: Guruswami, V. (ed.) IEEE 56th Annual Symposium on Foundations of Computer Science, FOCS 2015, Berkeley, CA, USA, 17–20 October 2015, pp. 210–229. IEEE Computer Society (2015)

[GM11] Goodrich, M.T., Mitzenmacher, M.: Privacy-preserving access of outsourced data via oblivious RAM simulation. In: Aceto, L., Henzinger, M., Sgall, J. (eds.) ICALP 2011, Part II. LNCS, vol. 6756, pp. 576–587. Springer, Heidelberg (2011). https://doi.org/10.1007/978-3-642-22012-8_46

[GMOT12] Goodrich, M.T., Mitzenmacher, M., Ohrimenko, O., Tamassia, R.: Privacy-preserving group data access via stateless oblivious RAM simulation. In: Rabani, Y. (ed.) [Rab12], pp. 157–167 (2012)

[GO96] Goldreich, O., Ostrovsky, R.: Software protection and simulation on oblivious RAMs. J. ACM 43(3), 431–473 (1996)

[Goo17] Goodrich, M.T.: BIOS ORAM: improved privacy-preserving data access for parameterized outsourced storage. In: Thuraisingham, B.M., Lee, A.J. (eds.) Proceedings of the 2017 on Workshop on Privacy in the Electronic Society, Dallas, TX, USA, 30 October–3 November 2017, pp. 41–50. ACM (2017)

[Goo18] Goodrich, M.T.: Isogrammatic-fusion ORAM: improved statistically secure privacy-preserving cloud data access for thin clients. In: Proceedings of the 13th ACM ASIA Conference on Information, Computer and Communication Security (2018, to appear)

[KLO12] Kushilevitz, E., Lu, S., Ostrovsky, R.: On the (in)security of hash-based oblivious RAM and a new balancing scheme. In: Rabani, E. (ed.) [Rab12], pp. 143–156 (2012)

[KM16] Kushilevitz, E., Malkin, T. (eds.): TCC 2016, Part II. LNCS, vol. 9563. Springer, Heidelberg (2016). https://doi.org/10.1007/978-3-662-49099-0

[Lar12] Larsen, K.G.: The cell probe complexity of dynamic range counting. In: Proceedings of the 44th ACM Symposium on Theory of Computation, pp. 85–94 (2012)

[LO17] Lu, S., Ostrovsky, R.: Black-box parallel garbled RAM. In: Katz, J., Shacham, H. (eds.) CRYPTO 2017, Part II. LNCS, vol. 10402, pp. 66–92. Springer, Cham (2017). https://doi.org/10.1007/978-3-319-63715-0_3

[LWY18] Larsen, K.G., Weinstein, O., Yu, H.: Crossing the logarithmic barrier for dynamic boolean data structure lower bounds. In: Symposium on Theory of Computing, STOC 2018 (2018, to appear)

[PD06] Pătrașcu, M., Demaine, E.D.: Logarithmic lower bounds in the cell-probe model. SIAM J. Comput. 35(4), 932–963 (2006)

[PR10] Pinkas, B., Reinman, T.: Oblivious RAM revisited. In: Rabin, T. (ed.) CRYPTO 2010. LNCS, vol. 6223, pp. 502–519. Springer, Heidelberg (2010). https://doi.org/10.1007/978-3-642-14623-7_27

[Rab12] Rabani, Y. (ed.) Proceedings of the Twenty-Third Annual ACM-SIAM Symposium on Discrete Algorithms, SODA 2012, Kyoto, Japan, 17–19 January 2012. SIAM (2012)

[SS13]   Stefanov, E., Shi, E.: Oblivistore: high performance oblivious distributed cloud data store. In 20th Annual Network and Distributed System Security Symposium, NDSS 2013, San Diego, California, USA, 24–27 February 2013. The Internet Society (2013)

[SvDS+13]   Stefanov, E., van Dijk, M., Shi, E., Fletcher, C.W., Ren, L., Yu, X., Devadas, S.: Path ORAM: an extremely simple oblivious RAM protocol. In: Sadeghi, A.-R., Gligor, V.D., Yung, M. (eds.) 2013 ACM SIGSAC Conference on Computer and Communications Security, CCS 2013, Berlin, Germany, 4–8 November 2013, pp. 299–310. ACM (2013)

[WNL+14]   Wang, X.S., Nayak, K., Liu, C., Hubert Chan, T.-H., Shi, E., Stefanov, E., Huang, Y.: Oblivious data structures. In: Ahn, G.-J., Yung, M., Li, N. (eds.) Proceedings of the 2014 ACM SIGSAC Conference on Computer and Communications Security, Scottsdale, AZ, USA, 3–7 November 2014, pp. 215–226. ACM (2014)

[WST12]   Williams, P., Sion, R., Tomescu, A.: Privatefs: a parallel oblivious file system. In: Yu, T., Danezis, G., Gligor, V.D. (eds.) The ACM Conference on Computer and Communications Security, CCS 2012, Raleigh, NC, USA, 16–18 October 2012, pp. 977–988. ACM (2012)

[Yao81]   Yao, A.C.-C.: Should tables be sorted? J. ACM 28(3), 615–628 (1981)

Constrained PRFs for $\mathbf{NC}^1$ in Traditional Groups

Nuttapong Attrapadung[1], Takahiro Matsuda[1], Ryo Nishimaki[2(✉)],
Shota Yamada[1], and Takashi Yamakawa[2]

[1] National Institute of Advanced Industrial Science and Technology (AIST),
Tokyo, Japan
{n.attrapadung,t-matsuda,yamada-shota}@aist.go.jp
[2] Secure Platform Laboratories, NTT Corporation, Tokyo, Japan
{nishimaki.ryo,yamakawa.takashi}@lab.ntt.co.jp

Abstract. We propose new constrained pseudorandom functions
(CPRFs) in *traditional groups*. Traditional groups mean cyclic and multiplicative groups of prime order that were widely used in the 1980s and
1990s (sometimes called "pairing free" groups). Our main constructions
are as follows.

- We propose a selectively single-key secure CPRF for *circuits with
  depth $O(\log n)$ (that is, $\mathbf{NC}^1$ circuits) in traditional groups* where n
  is the input size. It is secure under the L-decisional Diffie-Hellman
  inversion (L-DDHI) assumption in the group of quadratic residues
  $\mathbb{QR}_q$ and the decisional Diffie-Hellman (DDH) assumption in a traditional group of order q *in the standard model*.
- We propose a selectively single-key *private bit-fixing* CPRF in *traditional groups*. It is secure under the DDH assumption in any prime-
  order cyclic group *in the standard model*.
- We propose *adaptively* single-key secure CPRF for $\mathbf{NC}^1$ and private
  bit-fixing CPRF in the random oracle model.

To achieve the security in the standard model, we develop a new technique using correlated-input secure hash functions.

1 Introduction

1.1 Background

Pseudorandom functions (PRFs) are one of the most fundamental notions in
cryptography [27]. A PRF is a deterministic function $\mathsf{PRF}(\cdot,\cdot) : \mathcal{K} \times \mathcal{D} \to \mathcal{R}$
where $\mathcal{K}$, $\mathcal{D}$, and $\mathcal{R}$ are its key space, domain, and range, respectively. Roughly
speaking, we say that PRF is a secure PRF if outputs of $\mathsf{PRF}(\mathsf{msk}, \cdot)$ look random
for any input $x \in \mathcal{D}$ and a randomly chosen key $\mathsf{msk} \in \mathcal{K}$. Not only are PRFs
used to construct secure encryption schemes but also they frequently appear in
the constructions of various cryptographic primitives.

© International Association for Cryptologic Research 2018
H. Shacham and A. Boldyreva (Eds.): CRYPTO 2018, LNCS 10992, pp. 543–574, 2018.
https://doi.org/10.1007/978-3-319-96881-0_19

Constrained PRF. Boneh and Waters introduced the notion of *constrained PRFs (CRPFs)* [16] (Kiayias, Papadopoulos, Triandopoulos, and Zacharias [35] and Boyle, Goldwasser, and Ivan [10] also proposed the same notion in their concurrent and independent works). CPRFs are an advanced type of PRFs. Specifically, if we have a master secret key msk of a CPRF PRF, then we can generate a "constrained" key sk_f for a function $f : \mathcal{D} \to \{0, 1\}$. We can compute the value $\mathsf{PRF}(\mathsf{msk}, x)$ from sk_f and x if $f(x) = 0$ holds; otherwise cannot. For an input x such that $f(x) = 1$, the value $\mathsf{PRF}(\mathsf{msk}, x)$ looks pseudorandom.[1]

CPRFs with various types of function classes have been considered. Here, we explain the classes of *bit-fixing functions* and *circuits* since we present new CPRFs for these functions.

Bit-fixing functions: Let $\{0, 1\}^n$ be the domain of a CPRF. Each function in this class is specified by a "constraint vector" $c = (c_1, \ldots, c_n) \in \{0, 1, *\}^n$, from which a *bit-fixing* function $f_c : \{0, 1\}^n \to \{0, 1\}$ is defined as follows. If $c_i = *$ or $x_i = c_i$ holds for all $i \in [n]$, then $f_c(x) = 0$; otherwise $f_c(x) = 1$.

Circuits: This class consists of functions $\{f_C\}$ computable by polynomial-sized boolean circuits C, defined by $f_C(\cdot) := C(\cdot)$. We call a CPRF for this function class simply a CPRF for circuits. If a CPRF supports functions computable by polynomial-sized boolean circuits with depth $O(\log n)$, where n is the input-length of the circuits, then we call it a CPRF for $\mathbf{NC}^1$.

The number of constrained keys that can be released (to a potentially malicious party) is one of the important security measures of CPRFs. If a-priori unbounded polynomially many constrained keys could be released (i.e., the number of queries is not a-priori bounded), then a CPRF is called *collusion-resistant*. If only one constrained key can be released, it is called a *single-key secure* CPRF. Boneh and Waters [16] showed that (collusion-resistant) CPRFs have many applications such as broadcast encryption with optimal ciphertext length. (See their paper and references therein for more details.)

Private CPRF. Boneh, Lewi, and Wu [13] proposed the notion of *privacy* for CPRFs (Kiayias et al. also proposed policy privacy as essentially the same notion [35]). Roughly speaking, private CPRFs do not reveal information about constraints embedded in constrained keys beyond what is leaked from the evaluation results using the constrained keys.

Known instantiations. The first papers on CPRFs [10,16,35] observed that the Goldreich-Goldwasser-Micali [27] PRF yields a puncturable PRF[2] (and a CPRF

---

[1] We note that the role of the constraining function f is "reversed" from the definition by Boneh and Waters [16], in the sense that the evaluation by a constrained key sk_f is possible for inputs x with $f(x) = 1$ in their definition, while it is possible for inputs x for $f(x) = 0$ in our paper. Our treatment is the same as Brakerski and Vaikuntanathan [15].

[2] A constrained key in which a set of points is hard-wired enables us to compute an output if an input is not in the specified set.

for related simple functions). However, it turned out that achieving CPRFs for other types of function classes is quite challenging. Here, we review some prior works on CPRFs whose function classes are related to those we focus on in this study (i.e., bit-fixing functions and $\mathbf{NC}^1$ circuits).

Boneh and Waters [16] constructed a left-right CPRF[3] in the random oracle model (ROM) from bilinear maps, and a collusion-resistant bit-fixing CPRF and collusion-resistant CPRF for circuits from multilinear maps [25] in the standard model. After that, Brakerski and Vaikuntanathan [15] constructed a single-key secure CPRF for circuits from standard lattice-based assumptions, without relying on multilinear maps.

Boneh et al. [13] constructed a collusion-resistant private CPRF for circuits from indistinguishability obfuscation (IO) [9,26], and a single-key private bit-fixing CPRF and puncturable CPRF from multilinear maps [13]. After that, a single-key private puncturable PRF [12], a single-key private CPRF for $\mathbf{NC}^1$ [18], and a single-key private CPRF for circuits [14,37] were constructed from standard lattice assumptions.

Our motivation. (Private) CPRFs have been attracting growing attention as above since they are useful tools to construct various cryptographic primitives [13,16]. A number of other types of CPRFs have been constructed [2,8, 23,32,32,33,33]. However, all of known sufficiently expressive (private) CPRFs (such as bit-fixing, circuits) rely on IO, multilinear maps, or lattices, and there is currently no candidate of secure multilinear maps.

Very recently, Bitansky [11] and Goyal, Hohenberger, Koppula, and Waters [28] proposed sub-string match[4] CPRFs in *traditional groups* to construct verifiable random functions. In this paper, by traditional groups we mean the multiplicative groups of prime order[5] that have been widely used to construct various cryptographic primitives such as the ElGamal public-key encryption scheme, around two decades before bilinear maps dominate the area of cryptography [7]. (Of course, they are still being used for many cryptographic primitives.) However, their CPRFs are not expressive enough and do not satisfy the standard security requirements of CPRFs[6]. See Tables 1 and 2 for comparisons. There is no construction of *expressive enough* (private) CPRF in *traditional groups*. This status might be reasonable since lattices and multilinear maps are stronger tools.

---

[3] There are left and right constrained keys in which v_ℓ and v_r are hard-wired, respectively. We can compute outputs by using the left (resp. right) constrained key if the first (resp. last) half of an input is equal to v_ℓ (resp. v_r).

[4] This is the negation of bit-fixing functions, that is, $f_c(x) = 0$ if there exists an index i such that $x_i \neq c_i$ (i-th bit of a constraint) and $c_i \neq *$. It can be seen as a generalization of punctured predicates.

[5] For example, cyclic group $\mathbb{H} \subset \mathbb{Z}_q^*$ of a prime order p such that $q = 2p + 1$ where q is also a prime.

[6] In their sub-string match CPRFs, adversaries are not given access to the evaluation oracle, which gives outputs of a CPRF for queried inputs. We call such security no-evaluation security in this paper.

Based on the motivation mentioned above, we tackle the following question:

Is it possible to construct sufficiently expressive (private) CPRFs in traditional groups?

In this study, we give affirmative answers to this question and show that traditional groups are quite powerful tools. From the theoretical point of view, the more instantiations of cryptographic primitives are available, the more desirable. One reason is that constructions from different tools can be alternatives when one tool is broken (like multilinear maps). Another reason is that, generally, new instantiations shed light on how to construct the studied primitive, and widen and deepen our insights on it. One remarkable example of this line of research would be the recent work by Döttling and Garg [22], who constructed an identity-based encryption (IBE) scheme and a hierarchical IBE scheme in traditional groups. Another example would be the work by Boyle, Ishai, and Gilboa [17], who constructed communication-efficient secure two-party protocols in traditional groups. It is also expected that new instantiations provide us with insights on how to use the studied primitive in applications (in the real world or in the construction of another primitive as a building block).

1.2 Our Contributions

In this paper, we present new constructions of a CPRF and a private CPRF in *traditional groups* as main contributions.

The properties of our CPRFs are summarized as follows.

- Our first CPRF is a *selectively single-key secure*[7] *CPRF for* NC^1 in traditional groups. It is secure under the L-decisional Diffie-Hellman inversion (L-DDHI) assumption[8] in the group of quadratic residues $\mathbb{QR}_q$ and the decisional Diffie-Hellman (DDH) assumption[9] in a traditional group $\mathbb{G}$ of order q *in the standard model*. Here, $\mathbb{QR}_q$ denotes the group of quadratic residue modulo q, where q is a prime such that $q = 2p + 1$ and p is also a prime. We need to use this specific type of group for technical reasons. See Sects. 1.3 and 4 for the details.
- Our second CPRF is a *selectively single-key private bit-fixing CPRF* in traditional groups. Specifically, it is secure under the standard DDH assumption in any prime-order cyclic group *in the standard model*.

---

[7] Adversaries commit a function to be embedded in a constrained key at the beginning of the security experiment and have access to the evaluation oracle, which gives outputs of CPRFs for queried inputs.

[8] The L-DDHI assumption in a group $\mathbb{H}$ of order p [4,21] says that it is hard to distinguish $(g, g^\alpha, g^{\alpha^2}, \ldots, g^{\alpha^L}, g^{1/\alpha})$ from $(g, g^\alpha, g^{\alpha^2}, \ldots, g^{\alpha^L}, g^z)$ where $g \xleftarrow{\text{R}} \mathbb{H}, \alpha, z \xleftarrow{\text{R}} \mathbb{Z}_p$. See the full version [3] for the rigorous definition.

[9] The DDH assumption in a group $\mathbb{G}$ of order q says that it is hard to distinguish (g, g^x, g^y, g^{xy}) from (g, g^x, g^y, g^z) where $g \xleftarrow{\text{R}} \mathbb{G}, x, y, z \xleftarrow{\text{R}} \mathbb{Z}_q$.

– Our third and fourth CPRFs are an *adaptively*[10] *single-key secure CPRF for* **NC**^{1} *circuits* and an *adaptively single-key private bit-fixing CPRF*, both in the ROM. Our standard model and ROM constructions of CPRFs for **NC**^{1}, share high-level ideas behind the constructions in common, and the same is true for our bit-fixing CPRFs. These connections are explained in Sect. 1.3. Due to the space limit, we omit the constructions in the ROM in this paper.

The main technique that enables us to achieve the above results, is a novel use of *correlated-input secure hash functions*. We will explain the technical overview in Sect. 1.3.

As an application of our results, we can obtain a single-key secret-key attributed-based encryption (ABE) scheme with *optimal ciphertext overhead* in traditional groups. A (multi-key) public-key ABE scheme with optimal ciphertext overhead was presented by Zhandry [39], but it is based on multilinear maps. See the full version [3] for more details.

Table 1. Comparison of CPRFs (we omit constructions based on multilinear maps or IO). In "Function" column, sub-match is sub-string match. Prefix-fixing means that a constrained key with prefix p enables us to compute outputs for inputs $p\|*$. "# keys" column means the number of issuable constrained keys. "Eval.$\mathcal{O}$" column means the evaluation oracle is available for adversaries or not. "Tool" column means what kinds of cryptographic tools are used. GGM, pairing, and group mean the PRF by Goldreich, Goldwasser, and Micali [27], bilinear maps, and traditional groups, respectively. In "Assumptions" column, OWF, BDDH, LWE, and 1D-SIS mean one-way function, bilinear Diffie-Hellman, learning with errors, and one-dimensional short integer solution assumptions, respectively. In "Model" column, Std means the standard model. In "Misc" column, key-hom means key-homomorphic property.

Reference	Function	# keys	Eval.$\mathcal{O}$	Tool	Assumptions	Model	Misc
[16]	puncture[a]	N/A	N/A	GGM	OWF	Std	
[16]	left/right	multi	✓	pairing	BDDH	ROM	
[35]	puncture[a]	N/A	N/A	GGM	OWF	Std	
[10]	puncture[a]	N/A	N/A	GGM	OWF	Std	
[8]	prefix-fixing	multi	✓	lattice	LWE	Std	key-hom
[15]	circuit	single	✓	lattice	LWE, 1D-SIS	Std	
[11]	sub-match	single	no	group	DDH	Std	
[28]	sub-match	single	no	group	L-power DDH	Std	
[28]	sub-match	single	no	group	Φ-hiding	Std	
Ours	**NC**^{1}	single	✓	group	DDH, L-DDHI	Std	

[a] More precisely, they consider slightly different functions, but we write just "puncture" for simplicity since their constructions are based on the GGM PRF. See their papers for details.

---

[10] Adversaries can decide a function for which it makes the key query at any time.

Table 2. Comparison of private CPRFs (we omit constructions based on multilinear maps and IO). See Table 1 for terms.

Reference	Predicate	# keys	Eval.$\mathcal{O}$	Tool	Assumptions	Model
[35]	puncture[a]	N/A	N/A	GGM	OWF	Std
[12]	puncture	N/A	N/A	lattice	LWE, 1D-SIS	Std
[18]	bit-fixing	single	✓	lattice	LWE	Std
[18]	$\mathbf{NC^1}$	single	✓	lattice	LWE	Std
[14]	circuit	single	✓	lattice	LWE	Std
[37]	circuit	single	✓	lattice	LWE, 1D-SIS	Std
Ours	bit-fixing	single	✓	group	DDH	Std

[a] Same as in Table 1.

1.3   Technical Overview

In this section, we provide an overview of our construction ideas. We ignore many subtle issues in this section and focus on the essential ideas for simplicity.

Basic construction satisfying no-evaluation security. To illustrate our ideas in a modular manner, we start with a no-evaluation secure CPRF for $\mathbf{NC^1}$, that is, adversaries do not have access to the evaluation oracle. We denote the PRF by $\mathsf{PRF_{NE}}$. It turns out that even in this simple setting, it is non-trivial to construct a CPRF for $\mathbf{NC^1}$ in traditional groups (or bilinear groups) since known constructions use some sort of "fully homomorphic" properties of lattices or multilinear maps, both of which are not available in traditional groups. In the following, let λ be the security parameter.

The first challenge is how to implement an $\mathbf{NC^1}$ circuit constraint in a key. Our idea is to encode an $\mathbf{NC^1}$ circuit f[11] into a bit string $f = (f_1, \ldots, f_z) \in \{0,1\}^z$ and then embed this into a secret key. When evaluating a PRF value on input $x = (x_1, \ldots, x_n) \in \{0,1\}^n$, we will "homomorphically" evaluate $U(\cdot, x)$ on the secret key, where $U(\cdot, \cdot)$ is a universal circuit that outputs $U(f, x) = f(x)$ on input (f, x). To make the representation of the universal circuit $U(\cdot, \cdot)$ compatible with our algebraic setting, we regard $U(\cdot, \cdot)$ as a degree-D polynomial of the variables $\{f_i\}$ and $\{x_j\}$, such that D is some fixed polynomial of λ.[12] Furthermore, we extend the input space of $U(\cdot, \cdot)$ to be non-binary, where the computation is done over $\mathbb{Z}_p$ using the polynomial representation of $U(\cdot, \cdot)$. Specifically, we allow the input of the form $((b_1, \ldots, b_z), x) \in \mathbb{Z}_p^z \times \{0,1\}^n$.

Now, we give a more detailed description of $\mathsf{PRF_{NE}}$. A master secret key msk of $\mathsf{PRF_{NE}}$ is of the form $(b_1, \ldots, b_z, \alpha, g)$, where $b_i \xleftarrow{\mathsf{R}} \mathbb{Z}_p$ for each $i \in [z]$ and

---

[11] Here, we identify a circuit that computes a function f with f itself.

[12] We can construct a universal circuit U whose depth is only constant times deeper than that of f by the result of Cook and Hoover [20]. It is well known that an $\mathbf{NC^1}$ circuit can be represented by a polynomial with polynomial degree (for example, this fact is used for functional encryption for $\mathbf{NC^1}$ [31]).

$\alpha \xleftarrow{\text{R}} \mathbb{Z}_p^*$, and g is a generator of a traditional group $\mathbb{H}$ of order p. (We will turn to the explanation on this group $\mathbb{H}$ later in this subsection.) The evaluation algorithm of $\mathsf{PRF}_{\mathsf{NE}}$ outputs $g^{x'/\alpha}$, where $x' = U((b_1, \ldots, b_z), x) \in \mathbb{Z}_p$. To compute a constrained key sk_f of an $\mathbf{NC}^1$ circuit f, we set $b_i' := (b_i - f_i)\alpha^{-1}$. The constrained key is $\mathsf{sk}_f = (f, b_1', \ldots, b_z', g, g^\alpha, g^{\alpha^2}, \ldots, g^{\alpha^{D-1}})$.

We then look closer at why this construction achieves the constraint defined by the $\mathbf{NC}^1$ circuit f. When we compute $x' := U((b_1, \ldots, b_z), x)$ by using $b_i = \alpha \cdot b_i' + f_i$, we can write the computation of U in the following way:

$$x' = U((\alpha \cdot b_1' + f_1, \ldots, \alpha \cdot b_z' + f_z), x) = f(x) + \sum_{j=1}^{D} c_j \alpha^j,$$

where the coefficients $\{c_j\}_j$ are efficiently computable from the descriptions of U and f, $\{b_i'\}_i$, and x since the degree D is polynomial in the security parameter. This can be seen by observing that $U((\alpha \cdot b_1' + f_1, \ldots, \alpha \cdot b_z' + f_z), x)$ should be equal to $f(x)$ when $\alpha = 0$ since we have $U((f_1, \ldots, f_z), x) = f(x)$ by the definition of a universal circuit.

- If $f(x) = 0$, then we can compute $g^{x'/\alpha} = g^{f(x)/\alpha + \sum_{j=0}^{D-1} c_j \alpha^j}$ since the $g^{f(x)/\alpha}$ part disappears and the remaining part is computable from $\mathsf{sk}_f = (f, b_1', \ldots, b_z', g, g^\alpha, \ldots, g^{\alpha^{D-1}})$ and x.
- If $f(x) = 1$, then $g^{x'/\alpha} = g^{f(x)/\alpha + \sum_{j=0}^{D-1} c_j \alpha^j}$ looks random since $g^{1/\alpha}$ looks random even if $(g, g^\alpha, \ldots, g^{\alpha^{D-1}})$ is given, due to the $(D-1)$-DDHI assumption in $\mathbb{H}$.

This is a high-level intuition for why $\mathsf{PRF}_{\mathsf{NE}}$ for $\mathbf{NC}^1$ is no-evaluation secure. This CPRF $\mathsf{PRF}_{\mathsf{NE}}$ is our base construction, and the idea behind our construction here is inspired by the affine partitioning function used in the recent construction of a verifiable random function by Yamada [38].

On the other hand, this construction can be broken by making only one evaluation query: Suppose that $x \neq \hat{x}$ satisfy $f(x) = f(\hat{x}) = 1$. Then we can write $\mathsf{PRF}_{\mathsf{NE}}(\mathsf{msk}, x) = g^{1/\alpha + \sum_{j=0}^{D-1} c_j \alpha^j}$ and $\mathsf{PRF}_{\mathsf{NE}}(\mathsf{msk}, \hat{x}) = g^{1/\alpha + \sum_{j=0}^{D-1} \hat{c}_j \alpha^j}$ by using $\{c_j\}_j$ and $\{\hat{c}_j\}_j$ that are efficiently computable by an adversary. Then we have $\mathsf{PRF}_{\mathsf{NE}}(\mathsf{msk}, \hat{x}) = \mathsf{PRF}_{\mathsf{NE}}(\mathsf{msk}, x) \cdot g^{\sum_{j=0}^{D-1} (\hat{c}_j - c_j)\alpha^j}$. Therefore if an adversary obtains $\mathsf{PRF}_{\mathsf{NE}}(\mathsf{msk}, x)$, then it can efficiently compute $\mathsf{PRF}_{\mathsf{NE}}(\mathsf{msk}, \hat{x})$ and break the security of the PRF.

Single-key secure construction in the ROM. To achieve security against adversaries making a-priori unbounded polynomially many evaluation queries (i.e., the number of queries is polynomial, but not fixed in advance), we consider using a random oracle as an intermediate step. (This construction is denoted by $\mathsf{PRF}^{\mathsf{rom}}$.) $\mathsf{PRF}^{\mathsf{rom}}$ is the same as $\mathsf{PRF}_{\mathsf{NE}}$ except that an output is now computed by $H(g^{x'/\alpha})$, instead of $g^{x'/\alpha}$, where $H : \mathbb{H} \to \{0, 1\}^{n'}$ is a cryptographic hash function. In the ROM where H is modeled as a random oracle, adversaries make hash queries and obtain outputs of the hash function H. If $f(x) = 1$, then an adversary cannot compute $g^{x'/\alpha}$ due to the no-evaluation security, and thus $H(g^{x'/\alpha})$ seems uniformly random from the view of the adversary. Therefore evaluation queries from an adversary can be answered with uniformly random strings, and the adversary cannot notice whether this is a correct behavior of the evaluation oracle as long as it does not find a collision (x_1, x_2) such that $g^{x'_1/\alpha} = g^{x'_2/\alpha}$ where $x'_i = U((b_1, \ldots, b_z), x_i)$. Our real construction is slightly modified from the above construction so that such a collision exists only with negligible probability (see Sect. 4.1 for the detail).

The second challenge is how to remove the random oracle and achieve security against a-priori unbounded polynomially evaluation queries in the standard model.

Replacing a random oracle with a correlated-input secure hash function. We observe that we do not need the full power of random oracles to prove the security of CPRFs. Specifically, we can use a *correlated-input secure hash function* (CIH) [5,29,30,34][13], instead of random oracles.

Here, we briefly recall the definition of a CIH whose definition is associated with a class of functions Ψ. At the beginning, the challenger chooses the challenge bit $\text{coin} \overset{\text{R}}{\leftarrow} \{0, 1\}$, a function description CIH,[14] and a random element r from the domain of CIH. The adversary is given CIH and access to an oracle that, upon a query $\psi_i \in \Psi$ from the adversary, answers $\text{CIH}(\psi_i(r))$ if $\text{coin} = 1$; otherwise the oracle answers the query with $\text{RF}(\psi_i(r))$, where RF is a truly random function. If it is hard for adversaries to distinguish the case $\text{coin} = 1$ from the case $\text{coin} = 0$, we say that CIH is correlated-input pseudorandom for Ψ (or simply, a CIH for Ψ).[15]

If there exists a CIH for *group-induced* functions $\psi_\Delta : \mathbb{H} \to \mathbb{H}$ such that $\Delta \in \mathbb{H}$ and $\psi_\Delta(y) := y \cdot \Delta$ (denoted by CIH_0) where $\cdot$ is the group operation of $\mathbb{H}$, then $\text{CIH}_0(\text{PRF}_{\text{NE}}(\text{msk}, x))$ is a secure CPRF. This can be seen as follows: For x satisfying $f(x) = 1$, $\text{PRF}_{\text{NE}}(\text{msk}, x)$ can be written as $g^{1/\alpha} \cdot g^{\sum_{j=0}^{D-1} c_j \alpha^j}$ where $g^{1/\alpha}$ is pseudorandom and $g^{\sum_{j=0}^{D-1} c_j \alpha^j}$ is efficiently computable from the view of an adversary as discussed above. By applying the security of a CIH by setting $y := g^{1/\alpha}$ and $\Delta = g^{\sum_{j=0}^{D-1} c_j \alpha^j}$, we can see that $\text{CIH}_0(\text{PRF}_{\text{NE}}(\text{msk}, x))$ is computationally indistinguishable from $\text{RF}(\text{PRF}_{\text{NE}}(\text{msk}, x))$. This is computationally indistinguishable from a random function as long as $\text{PRF}_{\text{NE}}(\text{msk}, x)$ has no collision, and the actual construction of $\text{PRF}_{\text{NE}}(\text{msk}, x)$ is made collision-free as mentioned in the previous paragraph.

---

[13] Several works defined similar notions in different names such as related-key security. We use the name "correlated-input security" since we think it is the most suitable name for our usage.

[14] In the formal security definition, the function is parameterized by a public parameter generated by some setup procedure. We ignore the public parameter in the explanation below for simplicity. See Sect. 2.2 for the rigorous security definition for CIHs.

[15] The definition of CIHs in this paper can be seen as a hybrid of correlated-input pseudorandom by Goyal et al. [30] and RKA-PRG by Bellare and Cash [5]. See Sect. 2.2 for the formal definition.

However, there is one subtle issue: The only known instantiation of CIH for group induced functions which satisfies our security requirements is the CIH based on the DDH assumption by Bellare and Cash [5] (denoted by $\mathsf{CIH_{BC}}$). In $\mathsf{CIH_{BC}}$, we consider the *m-dimensional, component-wise group-induced functions* $\Psi_m^{\mathsf{g\text{-}indc}} := \{\psi_{\vec{a}} \mid \vec{a} \in (\mathbb{Z}_q^*)^m\}$, where $\psi_{\vec{a}} : (\mathbb{Z}_q^*)^m \to (\mathbb{Z}_q^*)^m$ is defined by $\psi_{\vec{a}}(\vec{r}) := \vec{a} \star \vec{r}$ and $\star$ denotes the component-wise group operation on $\mathbb{Z}_q^*$. Here, the domain of $\mathsf{CIH_{BC}}$ is not compatible with the range of $\mathsf{PRF_{NE}}$ (the output is $g^{x'/\alpha_i} \in \mathbb{H}$). One might think that m-folded parallel running of $\mathsf{PRF_{NE}}$ on $\mathbb{H} := \mathbb{Z}_q^*$ works, but this is not the case. This is because if $\mathbb{H} := \mathbb{Z}_q^*$, then the L-DDHI assumption can be easily broken by computing the Jacobi symbol.

We observe that the attack based on the Jacobi symbol does not work if we consider the group of quadratic residues modulo q, denoted by $\mathbb{QR}_q$ instead of $\mathbb{Z}_q^*$, and it is reasonable to assume the L-DDHI assumption holds on $\mathbb{QR}_q$. However, if we set $\mathbb{H} := \mathbb{QR}_q$, then we cannot simply use the security of $\mathsf{CIH_{BC}}$ since it is not obvious if the security of $\mathsf{CIH_{BC}}$ still holds when we restrict the domain of $\mathsf{CIH_{BC}}$ to $\mathbb{QR}_q^m$. We resolve the issue by proving that the CIH obtained by restricting the domain of $\mathsf{CIH_{BC}}$ to $\mathbb{QR}_q^m$ (denoted by $\mathsf{CIH_{\widehat{BC}}}$) is also secure as a CIH for component-wise group operations on $\mathbb{QR}_q^m$ under the DDH assumption on a group of an order $p = \frac{q-1}{2}$ if p is a prime. See Sect. 3 for more details of $\mathsf{CIH_{\widehat{BC}}}$.

We are now ready to explain our CRPF PRF for **NC**^{1}. It uses multiple instances of $\mathsf{PRF_{NE}}$ and apply a CIH for m-dimensional component-wise group-induced functions to the outputs from those instances. That is, we define

$$\mathsf{PRF_{NC^1}}(\mathsf{msk}, x) := \mathsf{CIH_{\widehat{BC}}}\Big(\mathsf{PRF_{NE}}(\mathsf{msk}_1, x), \ldots, \mathsf{PRF_{NE}}(\mathsf{msk}_m, x) \Big).$$

Now, we look closer at why correlated-input pseudorandomness helps us achieve security in the presence of a-priori unbounded polynomially many evaluation queries. In $\mathsf{PRF_{NE}}$, when the inputs x with $f(x) = 1$ are used, we can view its output as consisting of two separate parts. Specifically, we can write $g^{x'/\alpha} = g^{f(x)/\alpha + \sum_{j=0}^{D-1} c_j \alpha^j} = \mathsf{Aux}(\mathsf{msk}) \cdot \mathsf{SEval}(\mathsf{sk}_f, x)$ if we define $\mathsf{Aux}(\mathsf{msk}) := g^{1/\alpha}$ and $\mathsf{SEval}(\mathsf{sk}_f, x) := g^{\sum_{j=0}^{D-1} c_j \alpha^j}$ (where SEval stands for "semi"-evaluation). The first part is computable only from msk, and the second part is computable from sk_f and x. Thanks to the $(D-1)$-DDHI assumption, it is now easy to see that $\mathsf{Aux}(\mathsf{msk})$ is indistinguishable from a random element even if sk_f is given. Therefore, it holds that

$$\mathsf{PRF_{NC^1}}(\mathsf{msk}, x) \approx_c \mathsf{CIH_{\widehat{BC}}}\Big(r_1 \cdot \mathsf{SEval}(\mathsf{sk}_{f,1}, x), \ldots, r_m \cdot \mathsf{SEval}(\mathsf{sk}_{f,m}, x) \Big),$$

where $r_i \xleftarrow{\mathsf{R}} \mathbb{H}$ for all $i \in [m]$ and $\approx_c$ denotes computational indistinguishability. Furthermore, $\mathsf{sk}_{f,i}$ denotes the secret key associated to f generated from msk_i. (Namely, it corresponds to the i-th instance.) Here, $\phi_i := \mathsf{SEval}(\mathsf{sk}_{f,i}, x) \in \mathbb{H}$ are adversarially chosen correlated values and fall in the component-wise group-induced functions $\Psi_m^{\mathsf{g\text{-}indc}}$ due to $(\phi_1, \ldots, \phi_m) \in \mathbb{H}^m$. Therefore, by applying the correlated-input pseudorandomness of $\mathsf{CIH_{\widehat{BC}}}$, we obtain

$$\mathsf{CIH_{\widehat{BC}}}(r_1 \cdot \phi_1, \ldots, r_m \cdot \phi_m) \approx_c \mathsf{RF}(r_1 \cdot \phi_1, \ldots, r_m \cdot \phi_m).$$

As long as adversaries do not find a collision (x_1, x_2) such that $(\mathsf{SEval}(\mathsf{sk}_{f,1}, x_1),$ $\ldots, \mathsf{SEval}(\mathsf{sk}_{f,m}, x_1)) = (\mathsf{SEval}(\mathsf{sk}_{f,1}, x_2), \ldots, \mathsf{SEval}(\mathsf{sk}_{f,m}, x_2))$, $\mathsf{PRF}_{\mathbf{NC}^1}(\mathsf{msk}, \cdot)$ is pseudorandom since RF is a truly random function. It is not difficult to see that a collision is hard to find by the universality of the modified $\mathsf{PRF}_{\mathsf{NE}}$ (see Lemma 8 for the detail). Therefore, we can prove the pseudorandomness of PRF against a-priori unbounded polynomially many evaluation queries in the standard model by using the security of CIH for (m-dimensional, component-wise) group-induced functions.

How to achieve private constraint. Here, we give a brief explanation on how our single-key private CPRF for bit-fixing functions is constructed. The basic strategy is the same as that of our CPRFs for $\mathbf{NC}^1$. That is, we firstly construct a private bit-fixing CPRF in the ROM, and then convert it into a private bit-fixing CPRF in the standard model via a CIH for an appropriate function class.

Our single-key private bit-fixing CPRF in the ROM is very simple. This is slightly different from what we present in the full version of this paper [3], but we stick to the following construction in this section since it is consistent with the standard model construction in Sect. 5.1. A master secret key is $\mathsf{msk} := \{s_{i,b}\}_{i \in [n], b \in \{0,1\}}$ and a PRF output for input x is $H(\sum_{i=1}^{n} s_{i,x_i})$ where H is a (standard) hash function. For convenience, we define $\mathsf{PRF}_{\mathsf{bf}\text{-}\mathsf{NE}}(\mathsf{msk}, x) := \sum_{i=1}^{n} s_{i,x_i}$. A constrained key for $c \in \{0, 1, *\}^n$ is $\{t_{i,b}\}_{i \in [n], b \in \{0,1\}}$ where $t_{i,b} := s_{i,b}$ if $c_i = *$ or $c_i = b$; otherwise $t_{i,b} \xleftarrow{\mathsf{R}} \mathbb{Z}_p$. If an input does not match the constraint c, then the sum includes completely unrelated values and we cannot compute the correct output. Adversaries are given just random values by the random oracle. Moreover, adversaries cannot distinguish two different constraints as long as a challenge input does not satisfy the constraints since both $s_{i,b}$ and $t_{i,b}$ are uniformly random values in $\mathbb{Z}_p$. This construction satisfies adaptive single-key privacy in the random oracle model, without relying on any complexity assumption.

Now we replace the cryptographic hash function (random oracle) H with a CIH $\mathsf{CIH}_{\mathsf{aff}}$ for *affine functions* $\Phi^{\mathsf{aff}} = \{\phi_{\vec{u}, \vec{v}} : \mathbb{Z}_p^m \to \mathbb{Z}_p^m\}$ where $\vec{u} \in (\mathbb{Z}_p^*)^m$, $\vec{v} \in \mathbb{Z}_p^m$, and $\phi_{\vec{u}, \vec{v}}(\vec{x}) := \vec{u} \odot \vec{x} + \vec{v}$ where $\odot$ is component-wise multiplication in $\mathbb{Z}_p$. Our private bit-fixing CPRF is defined by

$$\mathsf{PRF}_{\mathsf{BF}}(\mathsf{msk}, x) := \mathsf{CIH}_{\mathsf{aff}}\Big(\mathsf{PRF}_{\mathsf{bf}\text{-}\mathsf{NE}}(\mathsf{msk}_1, x), \ldots, \mathsf{PRF}_{\mathsf{bf}\text{-}\mathsf{NE}}(\mathsf{msk}_m, x) \Big).$$

A constrained key sk_c consists of constrained keys for c with respect to msk_j, for all $j \in [m]$. It is easy to see that the correctness holds. For the security, we set $t_{i,b,j} := s_{i,b,j} - \alpha_j$ for $c_i \neq *$ and $b = 1 - c_i$ where $\alpha_j \xleftarrow{\mathsf{R}} \mathbb{Z}_p$. Then, we can write $\sum_{i=1}^{n} s_{i,x_i,j} = u\alpha_j + v_j$ for some $u \in [n]$ (especially $u \neq 0$) where $v_j = \sum_{i=1}^{n} t_{i,x_i,j}$ for an evaluation query x from an adversary, since x is not allowed to satisfy the constraint. For two different constraints, the adversary cannot distinguish which constraint is used in a constrained key (that is, $s_{i,b,j} \approx_{\mathsf{c}} t_{i,b,j} + \alpha_j$) since $t_{i,b,j}$ is uniformly random. Here, α_j's are uniformly random and u and v_j are adversarially chosen values. It is easy to see that this falls into the class of affine functions. Thus, we can use the security of the CIH $\mathsf{CIH}_{\mathsf{aff}}$ for affine functions, and obtain

$$\mathsf{CIH}_{\mathsf{aff}}(u\alpha_1 + v_1, \ldots, u\alpha_m + v_m) \approx_c \mathsf{RF}(u\alpha_1 + v_1, \ldots, u\alpha_m + v_m).$$

As long as a collision of $(\mathsf{PRF}_{\mathsf{bf\text{-}NE}}(\mathsf{msk}_1, \cdot), \ldots, \mathsf{PRF}_{\mathsf{bf\text{-}NE}}(\mathsf{msk}_m, \cdot)$ is not found, $\mathsf{RF}(u\alpha_1 + v_1, \ldots, u\alpha_m + v_m)$ is indistinguishable from a random value. Furthermore, it is not difficult to show that the condition holds by the universality of $F_t(x) := (u\alpha_1 + v_1, \ldots, u\alpha_m + v_m)$. Therefore, we can prove the security of our private bit-fixing CPRF. See the full version of this paper [3] for the details.

1.4 Other Related Works

While we focus on (private) CPRFs without IO and multilinear maps, many expressive (private) CPRFs have been proposed based on IO or multilinear maps: collusion-resistant CPRFs for circuit based on multilinear maps [8,16], adaptively secure CPRFs based on IO [32,33], collusion-resistant CPRFs for Turing machines based on (differing-input) IO [2,23], collusion-resistant private CPRFs for circuits based on IO [13].

Cohen, Goldwasser, and Vaikuntanathan showed a connection between CPRFs for some class of functions and computational learning theory [19]. See the papers and references therein for more details.

Organization. The rest of the paper is organized as follows. After introducing minimum notations, security definitions, and building blocks in Sect. 2, we present our correlated-input secure hash function in Sect. 3, our CPRFs for $\mathbf{NC}^1$ and its security proofs in Sect. 4, and our private bit-fixing CPRF in Sect. 5. Many materials are omitted in this extended abstract due to the space limit. See the full version for all details [3].

2 Preliminaries

In this section, we review some notations and definitions, tools, and cryptographic primitives.

Notations. We denote by "poly$(\cdot)$" an unspecified integer-valued positive polynomial of λ and by "negl(λ)" an unspecified negligible function of λ. For sets $\mathcal{D}$ and $\mathcal{R}$, "Func$(\mathcal{D}, \mathcal{R})$" denotes the set of all functions with domain $\mathcal{D}$ and range $\mathcal{R}$.

Group generator. For convenience, we introduce the notion of a "group generator". We say that a PPT algorithm GGen is a *group generator*, if it takes a security parameter 1^λ as input and outputs a "group description" $\mathcal{G} := (\mathbb{G}, p)$ where $\mathbb{G}$ is a group with prime order $p = \Omega(2^\lambda)$, from which one can efficiently sample a generator uniformly at random.

2.1   Constrained Pseudorandom Function

Here, we give the syntax and security definitions for a constrained pseudorandom function (CPRF). For clarity, we will define a CPRF as a primitive that has a public parameter. However, this treatment is compatible with the standard syntax in which there is no public parameter, because it can always be contained as part of a master secret key and constrained secret keys.

Syntax. Let $\mathcal{F} = \{\mathcal{F}_{\lambda,k}\}_{\lambda,k \in \mathbb{N}}$ be a class of functions[16] where each $\mathcal{F}_{\lambda,k}$ is a set of functions with domain $\{0,1\}^k$ and range $\{0,1\}$, and the description size (when represented by a circuit) of every function in $\mathcal{F}_{\lambda,k}$ is bounded by $\mathrm{poly}(\lambda,k)$.

A CPRF for $\mathcal{F}$ consists of the five PPT algorithms (Setup, KeyGen, Eval, Constrain, CEval) where (Setup, KeyGen, Eval) constitutes a PRF (where a key msk output by KeyGen is called a *master secret key*), and the last two algorithms Constrain and CEval have the following interfaces:

Constrain(pp, msk, f) $\xrightarrow{\text{R}}$ sk$_f$: This is the constraining algorithm that takes as input a public parameter pp, a master secret key msk, and a function $f \in \mathcal{F}_{\lambda,n}$, where $n = n(\lambda) = \mathrm{poly}(\lambda)$ is the input-length specified by pp. Then, it outputs a constrained key sk$_f$.

CEval(pp, sk$_f$, x) $=: y$: This is the deterministic constrained evaluation algorithm that takes a public parameter pp, a constrained key sk$_f$, and an element $x \in \{0,1\}^n$ as input, and outputs an element $y \in \mathcal{R}$.

As in an ordinary PRF, whenever clear from the context, we will drop pp from the inputs of Eval, Constrain, and CEval, and the executions of them are denoted as "Eval(msk, x)", "Constrain(msk, f)", and "CEval(sk$_f$, x)", respectively.

Correctness. For correctness of a CPRF for a function class $\mathcal{F} = \{\mathcal{F}_{\lambda,k}\}_{\lambda,k \in \mathbb{N}}$, we require that for all $\lambda \in \mathbb{N}$, pp $\xleftarrow{\text{R}}$ Setup(1^λ) (which specifies the input length $n = n(\lambda) = \mathrm{poly}(\lambda)$), msk $\xleftarrow{\text{R}}$ KeyGen(pp), functions $f \in \mathcal{F}_{\lambda,n}$, and inputs $x \in \{0,1\}^n$ satisfying $f(x) = 0$, we have CEval(Constrain(msk, f), x) = Eval(msk, x).

Remark 1. We note that in our definition, the role of the constraining functions f is "reversed" from that in the original definition [16], in the sense that correctness (i.e. the equivalence Eval(msk, $\cdot$) = CEval(sk$_f$, $\cdot$)) is required for inputs x with $f(x) = 0$, while it is required for inputs x with $f(x) = 1$ in the original definition [16].

Security. Here, we give the security definitions for a CPRF. We only consider CPRFs that are secure in the presence of a single constrained key, for which we consider two flavors of security: *selective single-key security* and *adaptive single-key security*. The former notion only captures security against adversaries $\mathcal{A}$ that

---

[16] In this paper, a "class of functions" is a set of "sets of functions". Each $\mathcal{F}_{\lambda,k}$ in $\mathcal{F}$ considered for a CPRF is a set of functions parameterized by a security parameter λ and an input-length k.

decide the constraining function f (and the constrained key sk_f is given to $\mathcal{A}$) before seeing any evaluation result of the CPRF, while the latter notion has no such restriction and captures security against adversaries that may decide the constraining function f at any time. Also, in Sect. 4, as a security notion for a CPRF used as a building block, we will use the notion of *no-evaluation security*, which captures security against adversaries that have no access to the evaluation oracle. The definition below reflects these differences.

$$
\begin{array}{l}
\mathsf{Expt}^{\mathsf{cprf}}_{\mathsf{CPRF},\mathcal{F},\mathcal{A}}(\lambda): \\[4pt]
\quad \mathsf{coin} \xleftarrow{\mathsf{R}} \{0,1\} \\
\quad \mathsf{pp} \xleftarrow{\mathsf{R}} \mathsf{Setup}(1^\lambda) \\
\quad \mathsf{msk} \xleftarrow{\mathsf{R}} \mathsf{KeyGen}(\mathsf{pp}) \\
\quad \mathsf{RF}(\cdot) \xleftarrow{\mathsf{R}} \mathsf{Func}(\{0,1\}^n, \mathcal{R}) \\
\quad \mathcal{O}_{\mathsf{Chal}}(\cdot) := \begin{cases} \mathsf{Eval}(\mathsf{msk}, \cdot) & \text{if } \mathsf{coin} = 1 \\ \mathsf{RF}(\cdot) & \text{if } \mathsf{coin} = 0 \end{cases} \\
\quad (f, \mathsf{st}_\mathcal{A}) \xleftarrow{\mathsf{R}} \mathcal{A}_1^{\mathcal{O}_{\mathsf{Chal}}(\cdot), \mathsf{Eval}(\mathsf{msk}, \cdot)}(\mathsf{pp}) \\
\quad \mathsf{sk}_f \xleftarrow{\mathsf{R}} \mathsf{Constrain}(\mathsf{msk}, f) \\
\quad \widehat{\mathsf{coin}} \xleftarrow{\mathsf{R}} \mathcal{A}_2^{\mathcal{O}_{\mathsf{Chal}}(\cdot), \mathsf{Eval}(\mathsf{msk}, \cdot)}(\mathsf{sk}_f, \mathsf{st}_\mathcal{A}) \\
\quad \text{Return } (\widehat{\mathsf{coin}} \overset{?}{=} \mathsf{coin}).
\end{array}
$$

Fig. 1. The experiment for defining single-key security for a CPRF.

Formally, for a CPRF $\mathsf{CPRF} = (\mathsf{Setup}, \mathsf{KeyGen}, \mathsf{Eval}, \mathsf{Constrain}, \mathsf{CEval})$ (with input-length $n = n(\lambda)$) for a function class $\mathcal{F} = \{\mathcal{F}_{\lambda,k}\}_{\lambda,k\in\mathbb{N}}$ and an adversary $\mathcal{A} = (\mathcal{A}_1, \mathcal{A}_2)$, we define the single-key security experiment $\mathsf{Expt}^{\mathsf{cprf}}_{\mathsf{CPRF},\mathcal{F},\mathcal{A}}(\lambda)$ as described in Fig. 1 (left).

In the security experiment, the adversary $\mathcal{A}$'s single constraining query is captured by the function f included in the first-stage algorithm $\mathcal{A}_1$'s output. Furthermore, $\mathcal{A}_1$ and $\mathcal{A}_2$ have access to the *challenge* oracle $\mathcal{O}_{\mathsf{Chal}}(\cdot)$ and the *evaluation* oracle $\mathsf{Eval}(\mathsf{msk}, \cdot)$, where the former oracle takes $x^* \in \{0,1\}^n$ as input, and returns either the actual evaluation result $\mathsf{Eval}(\mathsf{msk}, x^*)$ or the output $\mathsf{RF}(x^*)$ of a random function, depending on the challenge bit $\mathsf{coin} \in \{0,1\}$.

We say that an adversary $\mathcal{A} = (\mathcal{A}_1, \mathcal{A}_2)$ in the security experiment $\mathsf{Expt}^{\mathsf{cprf}}_{\mathsf{CPRF},\mathcal{F},n,\mathcal{A}}(\lambda)$ is *admissible* if $\mathcal{A}_1$ and $\mathcal{A}_2$ are PPT and respect the following restrictions:

- $f \in \mathcal{F}_{\lambda,n}$.
- $\mathcal{A}_1$ and $\mathcal{A}_2$ never make the same query twice.
- All challenge queries x^* made by $\mathcal{A}_1$ and $\mathcal{A}_2$ satisfy $f(x^*) = 1$, and are distinct from any of the evaluation queries x that they submit to the evaluation oracle $\mathsf{Eval}(\mathsf{msk}, \cdot)$.

Furthermore, we say that $\mathcal{A}$ is *selectively admissible* if, in addition to the above restrictions, $\mathcal{A}_1$ makes no challenge or evaluation queries. Finally, we say that $\mathcal{A}$

is a *no-evaluation adversary* if $\mathcal{A}_1$ and $\mathcal{A}_2$ are PPT, and they do not make any queries, except that $\mathcal{A}_2$ is allowed to make only a single challenge query x^* such that $f(x^*) = 1$.

Definition 1 (Security of CPRF). *We say that a CPRF* CPRF *for a function class $\mathcal{F}$ is* adaptively single-key secure, *if for all admissible adversaries $\mathcal{A}$, the advantage* $\mathsf{Adv}_{\mathsf{CPRF},\mathcal{F},\mathcal{A}}^{\mathsf{cprf}}(\lambda) := 2 \cdot |\Pr[\mathsf{Expt}_{\mathsf{CPRF},\mathcal{F},\mathcal{A}}^{\mathsf{cprf}}(\lambda) = 1] - 1/2|$ *is negligible.*

We define selective single-key security *(resp.* no-evaluation security*) of* CPRF *analogously, by replacing the phrase "all admissible adversaries $\mathcal{A}$" in the above definition with "all selectively admissible adversaries $\mathcal{A}$" (resp. "all no-evaluation adversaries $\mathcal{A}$").*

Remark 2. As noted by Boneh and Waters [16], without loss of generality we can assume that $\mathcal{A}$ makes a challenge query only once, because security for a single challenge query can be shown to imply security for multiple challenge queries via a standard hybrid argument. Hence, in the rest of the paper we only use the security experiment with a single challenge query for simplicity.

Remark 3. In some existing works [16,23,24], the term "selective" is used to mean that $\mathcal{A}$ has to make a challenge query at the beginning of the security experiment. On the other hand, in this paper, "selective" means that $\mathcal{A}$ has to make a constraining query at the beginning of the security experiment, which is the same definitional approach by Brakerski and Vaikuntanathan [15].

2.2   Correlated-Input Secure Hash Function

Here, we review the definition of a correlated-input secure hash function (CIH) that was originally introduced in Goyal et al. [30].

Syntactically, a CIH is an efficiently computable deterministic (hash) function that has a public parameter pp that is generated by using some setup procedure, and we refer to such a pair of function and setup procedure as a *publicly parameterized function*. In this paper, we will consider a CIH that is associated with a group generator GGen. Thus, we model its setup algorithm by a "parameter generation" algorithm PrmGen that takes a group description $\mathcal{G}$ generated by GGen as input, and outputs a public parameter pp.

Formally, a publicly parameterized function CIH with respect to a group generator GGen, consists of the two PPT algorithms (PrmGen, Eval) with the following interfaces:

PrmGen$(\mathcal{G}) \xrightarrow{\mathsf{R}}$ pp: This is the parameter generation algorithm that takes as input a group description $\mathcal{G}$ output by GGen(1^λ). Then, it outputs a public parameter pp, where we assume that pp contains $\mathcal{G}$ and the descriptions of the domain $\mathcal{D}$ and the range $\mathcal{R}$.

Eval$(\mathsf{pp}, x) =: y$: This is the deterministic evaluation algorithm that takes a public parameter pp and an element $x \in \mathcal{D}$ as input, and outputs an element $y \in \mathcal{R}$.

When there is no confusion, we will abuse the notation and denote by "CIH(pp, x)" to mean the execution of Eval(pp, x). Furthermore, when pp is clear from the context, we may sometimes drop pp from the input of CIH, and treat as if it is a single function (e.g. "CIH : $\mathcal{D} \to \mathcal{R}$") for more intuitive descriptions.

Security of CIHs. The security definition of a CIH that we use in this paper is a slightly generalized version of *correlated-input pseudorandomness* [30] (see Remark 4 for the differences from related works).

Let GGen be a group generator, and CIH $=$ (PrmGen, Eval) be a publicly parameterized function with respect to GGen. Let $\mathcal{F} = \{\mathcal{F}_{\lambda,z}\}_{\lambda \in \mathbb{N}, z \in \{0,1\}^*}$ be a class of functions, where each $\mathcal{F}_{\lambda,z}$ is a set of functions parameterized by $\lambda \in \mathbb{N}$ and $z \in \{0,1\}^*$,[17] and it is required that for all $\lambda \in \mathbb{N}$, if $\mathcal{G} \xleftarrow{R} \text{GGen}(1^\lambda)$ and pp $\xleftarrow{R}$ PrmGen($\mathcal{G}$), then the domain and the range of functions in $\mathcal{F}_{\lambda,\text{pp}}$ are identical to the domain of Eval(pp, $\cdot$).

For the publicly parameterized function CIH, the group generator GGen, the function class $\mathcal{F}$, and an adversary $\mathcal{A}$, we define the security experiment $\text{Expt}^{\text{cih}}_{\text{CIH},\mathcal{F},\mathcal{A}}(\lambda)$ as described in Fig. 2.

$\text{Expt}^{\text{cih}}_{\text{CIH},\text{GGen},\mathcal{F},\mathcal{A}}(\lambda)$:	$\mathcal{O}(f \in \mathcal{F}_{\lambda,\text{pp}})$:
coin $\xleftarrow{R} \{0,1\}$	$y := \begin{cases} \text{Eval}(\text{pp}, f(x)) & \text{if coin} = 1 \\ \text{RF}(f(x)) & \text{if coin} = 0 \end{cases}$
$\mathcal{G} \xleftarrow{R} \text{GGen}(1^\lambda)$	Return y.
pp $\xleftarrow{R}$ PrmGen($\mathcal{G}$)	
RF($\cdot$) $\xleftarrow{R}$ Func($\mathcal{D}, \mathcal{R}$)	
$x \xleftarrow{R} \mathcal{D}$	
$\widehat{\text{coin}} \xleftarrow{R} \mathcal{A}^{\mathcal{O}(\cdot)}(\text{pp})$	
Return ($\widehat{\text{coin}} \stackrel{?}{=} \text{coin}$).	

Fig. 2. Left: The security experiment for a CIH. **Right:** The definition of the oracle $\mathcal{O}$ in the experiment.

Note that in the experiment, the oracle $\mathcal{O}(\cdot)$ that $\mathcal{A}$ has access to, takes $f \in \mathcal{F}_{\lambda,\text{pp}}$ as input, and returns either the evaluation result CIH(pp, $f(x)$) or the output RF($f(x)$) of the random function RF, depending on the challenge bit coin $\in \{0,1\}$.

Definition 2 (Security of CIH). *Let* CIH *be a publicly parameterized function with respect to a group generator* GGen, *and let* $\mathcal{F}$ *be a function class. We say that* CIH *is a CIH for* $\mathcal{F}$ *(or,* $\mathcal{F}$-*CIH) with respect to* GGen, *if for all PPT adversaries* $\mathcal{A}$, *the advantage* $\text{Adv}^{\text{cih}}_{\text{CIH},\text{GGen},\mathcal{F},\mathcal{A}}(\lambda) := 2 \cdot |\Pr[\text{Expt}^{\text{cih}}_{\text{CIH},\text{GGen},\mathcal{F},\mathcal{A}}(\lambda) = 1] - 1/2|$ *is negligible.*

---

[17] For a class of functions $\mathcal{F}$ considered for CIHs, we allow each member of $\mathcal{F}$ to be parameterized by not only $\lambda \in \mathbb{N}$ but also $z \in \{0,1\}^*$. The role of z is to associate the functions with a public parameter pp generated by Setup(1^λ). See the security experiment in Fig. 2.

Remark 4 (On the difference between CIHs and related-key secure PRFs (or PRGs)). This remark provides additional information for readers who are familiar with related primitives. We note that Definition 2 is essentially the same as the definition of a related-key secure pseudorandom generator (RKA-PRG) by Bellare and Cash [5, Sect. 6, Eq. (27)]. A very minor difference is that we explicitly consider public parameters in the syntax. An RKA-PRG can be seen as a generalized version of correlated-input pseudorandomness by Goyal, O'Neill, and Rao [30, Definition 7]. If $\mathcal{A}$ in the security of a CIH must declare functions that will be queried to the oracle at the beginning of the experiment (i.e., selective security) and $\mathsf{RF}(f(x))$ is replaced by a uniformly random element in $\mathcal{R}$, then it is the same as correlated-input pseudorandomness. The reason why we select the name "CIH" is that it is well-suited for our usage.

Moreover, an RKA-PRF implies an RKA-PRG[18]. Therefore, the RKA-PRF (or RKA-PRG) by Bellare and Cash [5, Theorem 4.2] and the RKA-PRF by Abdalla, Benhamouda, Passelègue, and Paterson [1, Theorem 7] are secure CIHs under our definition. (Of course, supported function classes are the same as theirs.)

In Sects. 3 and 5, we introduce two concrete function classes for CIHs used as building blocks in our proposed CPRFs.

3   Building Block: Correlated-Input Secure Hash

In this section, we construct a CIH for group-induced functions on $\mathbb{QR}_q^n$, Its security under the DDH assumption is proven in the full version [3]. The definition of group-induced functions is given below.

Quadratic Residuosity groups. A safe prime q is a prime such that $q = 2p + 1$ for some p which is also a prime. We denote by $\mathbb{QR}_q$ the subgroup of all quadratic residues in $\mathbb{Z}_q^*$. From an elementary result, we have that $\mathbb{QR}_q$ is a group of prime order p. We denote by $\mathsf{SPGGen}(1^\lambda)$ a group generator that outputs a group description $(\mathbb{G}, q)$ where q is a safe prime and $q = \Omega(2^\lambda)$.

CIH for group-induced functions. The notion of *(component-wise) group-induced functions with respect to a group generator* GGen is a function class $\Psi^{\mathsf{g\text{-}indc}} = \{\Psi_{\lambda,z}^{\mathsf{g\text{-}indc}}\}_{\lambda \in \mathbb{N}, z \in \{0,1\}^*}$ satisfying the following property for all $(\lambda, z) \in \mathbb{N} \times \{0,1\}^*$: If z can be parsed as a tuple $(\mathcal{G}, n, z')$ so that $\mathcal{G} = (\mathbb{G}, q)$ is a group description output by $\mathsf{GGen}(1^\lambda)$, $n \in \mathbb{N}$, and $z' \in \{0,1\}^*$, then we have $\Psi_{\lambda,z}^{\mathsf{g\text{-}indc}} = \{\psi_{\vec{a}} : (\mathbb{Z}_q^*)^n \to (\mathbb{Z}_q^*)^n \mid \vec{a} \in (\mathbb{Z}_q^*)^n\}$, where for each $\vec{a} \in (\mathbb{Z}_q^*)^n$, $\psi_{\vec{a}}(\vec{x}) := \vec{a} \star \vec{x} \in (\mathbb{Z}_q^*)^n$ and $\star$ denotes the component-wise multiplication in $\mathbb{Z}_q^*$.

---

[18] If we fix an input of a PRF and view its key as a seed of a PRG, then the former can be seen as a latter.

Naor-Reingold PRF. We recall the Naor-Reingold PRF [36] denoted by NR. The setup takes 1^λ as input and outputs $\mathsf{pp} = (\mathbb{G}, g, n)$ where $\mathbb{G}$ is a group of prime order q output from $\mathsf{GGen}(1^\lambda)$. The key $\mathsf{msk} = \{x_i\}_{i=0}^n$ is chosen as $x_i \xleftarrow{\mathsf{R}} \mathbb{Z}_q^*$, and the evaluation of the function on input $(u_1, \ldots, u_n) \in \{0,1\}^n$ is defined as $\mathsf{NR}((x_0, \ldots, x_n), (u_1, \ldots, u_n)) := g^{x_0 \prod_{i=1}^n x_i^{u_i}}$. Our PRF used in our CIH, denoted by NR', is a variant of NR. NR' is defined as NR, except that $\mathsf{msk} = \{x_i\}_{i=0}^n$ is chosen as $x_i \xleftarrow{\mathsf{R}} \mathbb{QR}_q$, instead of $x_i \xleftarrow{\mathsf{R}} \mathbb{Z}_q^*$. In particular, the function evaluation of NR' matches NR, but its domain is restricted to $\mathbb{QR}_q^{n+1} \times \{0,1\}^n$.

CIH Construction. We are now ready to describe our CIH for the (component-wise) group-induced functions with respect to SPGGen. It can be considered as a variant of the hash function by Bellare and Cash [5], denoted as $\mathsf{CIH}_{\mathsf{BC}}$, which we recall as follows. The public parameter consists of the description of $\mathbb{G}$, which is a cyclic group of order q, output from the group generator $\mathsf{GGen}(1^\lambda)$, a generator g of $\mathbb{G}$, and a collision-resistant hash function $\mathsf{H}_{\mathsf{cr}} : \mathbb{G}^{n+1} \to \{0,1\}^{n-2}$. The evaluation is defined as follows.

The function is $\mathsf{CIH}_{\mathsf{BC}} : (\mathbb{Z}_q^*)^{n+1} \longrightarrow \mathbb{G}$ and

$$\mathsf{CIH}_{\mathsf{BC}}(\vec{x}) := \mathsf{NR}\Big(\vec{x},\ 11\|\mathsf{H}_{\mathsf{cr}}\Big(\mathsf{NR}(\vec{x}, e_0), ..., \mathsf{NR}(\vec{x}, e_n) \Big) \Big)$$

where $e_0 = 0^n$ and $e_k = 0^{k-1}\|1\|0^{n-k}$ for $k \in [n]$.

Our variant of CIH is exactly the same as $\mathsf{CIH}_{\mathsf{BC}}$ but the domain is restricted. In more detail, our CIH is operated on $\mathbb{QR}_q^{n+1} \to \mathbb{G}$ with exactly the same evaluation as $\mathsf{CIH}_{\mathsf{BC}}$. Note that due to our restriction on the domain, the NR evaluation inside the function is thus restricted to NR'. We denote this CIH as $\mathsf{CIH}_{\widetilde{\mathsf{BC}}}$.

Theorem 1. *If the DDH assumption holds with respect to SPGGen and H_{cr} is a CRHF, then $\mathsf{CIH}_{\widetilde{\mathsf{BC}}}$ is a secure CIH for the (component-wise) group-induced functions with respect to SPGGen.*

The proof of Theorem 1 is given in the full version [3].

4 CPRF for $\mathbf{NC}^1$ Circuits

In this section, we first show a construction of a CPRF for $\mathbf{NC}^1$ circuits with no-evaluation security, where an adversary is not allowed to make evaluation queries (Sect. 4.1). We then show that by combining the scheme with our CIH in Sect. 3, we can upgrade the security to the selective single-key security, where the adversary is allowed to make evaluation queries unbounded times after it is given the secret key (Sect. 4.2). We also show that the adaptive security can be achieved in the random oracle model in the full version [3].

4.1   Our Basic Constrained PRF

Here, we give a construction of a CPRF for $\mathbf{NC}^1$ with no-evaluation security. We then prove that the scheme has additional properties that we call semi-evaluability and universality. These properties will be used in security proofs of our selectively/adaptively secure CPRF for $\mathbf{NC}^1$ in the standard/random-oracle model.

Notations. In the following, we will sometimes abuse notation and evaluate a boolean circuit $C(\cdot) : \{0,1\}^\ell \to \{0,1\}$ on input $y \in \mathbb{R}^\ell$ for some ring $\mathbb{R}$. The evaluation is done by regarding $C(\cdot)$ as the arithmetic circuit whose AND gates $(y_1, y_2) \mapsto y_1 \wedge y_2$ being changed to the multiplication gates $(y_1, y_2) \mapsto y_1 y_2$, NOT gates $y \mapsto \neg y$ changed to the gates $y \mapsto 1 - y$, and the OR gates $(y_1, y_2) \mapsto y_1 \vee y_2$ changed to the gates $(y_1, y_2) \mapsto y_1 + y_2 - y_1 y_2$. It is easy to observe that if the input is confined within $\{0,1\}^\ell \subseteq \mathbb{R}$, the evaluation of the arithmetized version of $C(\cdot)$ equals to that of the binary version. (Here, we identify ring elements $0, 1 \in \mathbb{R}$ with the binary bit.) In that way, we can regard $C(\cdot)$ as an ℓ-variate polynomial over $\mathbb{R}$. The degree of $C(\cdot)$ is defined as the maximum of the total degree of all the polynomials that appear during the computation.

Class of Functions. Let $n = \mathrm{poly}(\lambda)$, $z(n) = \mathrm{poly}(n)$, and $d(n) = O(\log n)$ be parameters. The function class that will be dealt with by the scheme is denoted by $\mathcal{F}^{\mathbf{NC}^1} = \{\mathcal{F}^{\mathbf{NC}^1}_{\lambda, n(\lambda)}\}_{\lambda \in \mathbb{N}}$, where $\mathcal{F}^{\mathbf{NC}^1}_{\lambda, n}$ consists of (Boolean) circuits f whose input size is $n(\lambda)$, the description size is $z(n)$, and the depth is $d(n)$. We can set the parameters arbitrarily large as long as they do not violate the asymptotic bounds above, and thus the function class corresponds to $\mathbf{NC}^1$ circuits with bounded size. The following lemma will be helpful when describing our scheme.

Lemma 1. *Let $n = \mathrm{poly}(\lambda)$. There exists a family of universal circuit $\{U_n\}_{n \in \mathbb{N}}$ of degree $D(\lambda) = \mathrm{poly}(\lambda)$ such that $U_n(f, x) = f(x)$ for any $f \in \mathcal{F}^{\mathbf{NC}^1}_{\lambda, n(\lambda)}$ and $x \in \{0,1\}^n$.*

Proof. Due to the result by Cook and Hoover [20], there exists a universal circuit $U_n(\cdot)$ of depth $O(d) = O(\log n)$ and size $\mathrm{poly}(n, z, d) = \mathrm{poly}(\lambda)$. Furthermore, the degree of $U_n(\cdot)$ is bounded by $2^{O(d)} = \mathrm{poly}(n) = \mathrm{poly}(\lambda)$. ∎

Construction. Let $\mathcal{F}^{\mathbf{NC}^1} = \{\mathcal{F}^{\mathbf{NC}^1}_{\lambda, k}\}_{\lambda, k \in \mathbb{N}}$ be the family of the circuit defined as above and $\{U_n\}_{n \in \mathbb{N}}$ be the family of the universal circuit defined in Lemma 1. Let the parameter $D(\lambda)$ be the degree of the universal circuit (chosen as specified in Lemma 1). Since we will fix n in the construction, we drop the subscripts and just denote $\mathcal{F}^{\mathbf{NC}^1}$ and U in the following. We also let HGen be any group generator. The description of our CPRF $\mathsf{CPRF}_{\mathsf{NE}} = (\mathsf{Setup}, \mathsf{KeyGen}, \mathsf{Eval}, \mathsf{Constrain}, \mathsf{CEval})$ is given below.

Setup(1^λ): It obtains the group description $\mathcal{H} = (\mathbb{H}, p)$ by running $\mathcal{H} \xleftarrow{\text{R}}$ HGen(1^λ). It then outputs the public parameter pp := $\mathcal{H}$.[19]

KeyGen(pp): It chooses $(b_1, ..., b_z) \xleftarrow{\text{R}} \mathbb{Z}_p^z$, $\alpha \xleftarrow{\text{R}} \mathbb{Z}_p^*$, and $g, h_1, \ldots, h_n \xleftarrow{\text{R}} \mathbb{H}$. Then it outputs msk := $(b_1, \ldots, b_z, \alpha, g, h_1, \ldots, h_n)$.

Eval(msk, x): Given input $x \in \{0,1\}^n$, it computes and outputs

$$X := g^{U((b_1,\ldots,b_z),(x_1,\ldots,x_n))/\alpha} \cdot \prod_{i \in [n]} h_i^{x_i}.$$

Constrain(msk, f): It first parses $(b_1, ..., b_z, \alpha, g, h_1, \ldots, h_n) \leftarrow$ msk. Then it sets

$$b_i' := (b_i - f_i)\alpha^{-1} \mod p \quad \text{for } i \in [z]$$

where f_i is the i-th bit of the binary representation of f. It then outputs

$$\mathsf{sk}_f := (f, b_1', \ldots, b_z', g, g^\alpha, \ldots, g^{\alpha^{D-1}}, h_1, \ldots, h_n).$$

CEval(sk_f, x): It parses $(f, b_1', \ldots, b_z', g, g^\alpha, \ldots, g^{\alpha^{D-1}}, h_1, \ldots, h_n) \leftarrow \mathsf{sk}_f$. As proved in Lemma 2 below, it is possible to efficiently compute $\{c_i\}_{i \in [D]}$ that satisfies

$$U((b_1, \ldots, b_z), (x_1, \ldots, x_n)) = f(x) + \sum_{i=1}^{D} c_i \alpha^i \qquad (1)$$

from sk_f and x. If $f(x) = 0$, it computes $X := \prod_{i=1}^{D}(g^{\alpha^{i-1}})^{c_i} \cdot \prod_{j=1}^n h_j^{x_j}$ and outputs X. Otherwise it outputs $\perp$.

Correctness and semi-evaluability. In order to prove the correctness, it suffices to show the following lemma.

Lemma 2. *Given* sk_f, x, *one can efficiently compute* $\{c_i\}_{i \in [D]}$ *satisfying Eq.* (1).

Proof. The algorithm evaluates the circuit $U(\cdot)$ on input $(b_1'\mathsf{Z} + f_1, \ldots, b_z'\mathsf{Z} + f_z, x_1, \ldots, x_n)$ to obtain $\{c_i\}_{i \in \{0,1,\ldots,D\}}$ such that

$$U(b_1'\mathsf{Z} + f_1, \ldots, b_z'\mathsf{Z} + f_z, x_1, \ldots, x_n) = c_0 + \sum_{i \in [D]} c_i \mathsf{Z}^i \qquad (2)$$

where Z denotes the indeterminant of the polynomial ring $\mathbb{Z}_p[\mathsf{Z}]$. Note that the computation is done over the ring $\mathbb{Z}_p[\mathsf{Z}]$ and can be efficiently performed, since we have $D = \mathrm{poly}(\lambda)$. We prove that $\{c_i\}_{i \in [D]}$ actually satisfies Eq. (1). To see this, we first observe that by setting $\mathsf{Z} = 0$ in Eq. (2), we obtain $c_0 = U(f_1, \ldots, f_z, x_1 \ldots, x_n) = f(x)$. To conclude, we further observe that by setting $\mathsf{Z} = \alpha$ in Eq. (2), we recover Eq. (1), since we have $b_j = b_j'\alpha + f_j$ by the definition of b_j'. This completes the proof of the lemma. ∎

---

[19] Here, we intentionally use the symbol $\mathbb{H}$ and HGen instead of $\mathbb{G}$ and GGen. Looking ahead, in Sect. 4.2, the latter symbols will be used to represent yet another group of order q and corresponding group generator. There, we should require $\mathbb{H}$ to be $\mathbb{QR}_q$.

The lemma implies an additional property of the CPRF that we call *semi-evaluability*, which will be useful in our security proof. We formally state it in the following lemma:

Lemma 3. *There exist deterministic and efficient algorithms* SEval *and* Aux *satisfying the following property. For all* $\mathcal{F}^{NC^1}$ *and* x *such that* $f(x) = 1$ *and for all possible* msk $\xleftarrow{\text{R}}$ KeyGen(pp), sk$_f$ $\xleftarrow{\text{R}}$ Constrain(msk, f), *we have*

$$\text{SEval}(\text{sk}_f, x) \cdot \text{Aux}(\text{msk}) = \text{Eval}(\text{msk}, x),$$

where "·" indicates the group operation on $\mathbb{H}$. *(We refer to this property of our CPRF as* semi-evaluability.*)*

Proof. We define SEval and Aux as follows.

SEval(sk$_f$, x): It first parses $(f, b'_1, \ldots, b'_z, g, g^\alpha, \ldots, g^{\alpha^{D-1}}, h_1, \ldots, h_n) \leftarrow$ sk$_f$.
   It then compute $\{c_j\}_{j \in [D]}$ that satisfies Eq. (1). It finally computes $X' := \prod_{i=1}^{D} (g^{\alpha^{i-1}})^{c_i} \cdot \prod_{j \in [n]} h_j^{x_j}$ and outputs X'.
Aux(msk): It parses $(b_1, \ldots, b_z, \alpha, g, h_1, \ldots, h_n) \leftarrow$ msk and outputs $g^{1/\alpha}$.

   The lemma readily follows from Eq. (1) and $f(x) = 1$. ∎

Universality. The following lemma indicates that the above scheme can be seen as a universal hashing. The only reason why we need $h_1, \ldots, h_n$ in pp is to ensure this property. Formally, we have the following lemma. The lemma will be used later in this section.

Lemma 4. *For all* $x, x' \in \{0,1\}^n$ *with* $x \neq x'$ *and* pp *output by* Setup(1^λ), *we have*

$$\Pr[\ \text{msk} \xleftarrow{\text{R}} \text{KeyGen(pp)} \ : \ \text{Eval}(\text{msk}, x) = \text{Eval}(\text{msk}, x') \ ] = \tfrac{1}{p}.$$

Proof. Since $x \neq x'$, there exists an index i such that $x_i \neq x'_i$. Let us fix msk except for h_i. Then, we can see that there exists a unique h_i such that Eval(msk, x) = Eval(msk, x') holds. Since h_i is chosen uniformly at random from $\mathbb{H}$, the lemma follows. ∎

No-evaluation security.

Theorem 2. *If the* $(D-1)$-*DDHI assumption holds with respect to* HGen, *then* CPRF$_{\text{NE}}$ *defined above satisfies no-evaluation security as a CPRF for the circuit class* $\mathcal{F}^{NC^1}$.

Proof. Let $\mathcal{A} = (\mathcal{A}_1, \mathcal{A}_2)$ be any no-evaluation adversary that attacks the no-evaluation security of CPRF. We prove the above theorem by considering the following sequence of games.

Game 0: This is the real single-key security experiment $\text{Expt}^{\text{cprf}}_{\text{CPRF}_{\text{NE}}, \mathcal{F}^{NC^1}, \mathcal{A}}(\lambda)$ against the no-evaluation adversary $\mathcal{A} = (\mathcal{A}_1, \mathcal{A}_2)$. Namely,

$\mathsf{coin} \xleftarrow{\mathsf{R}} \{0,1\}$
$\mathsf{pp} \xleftarrow{\mathsf{R}} \mathsf{Setup}(1^\lambda)$
$\mathsf{msk} \xleftarrow{\mathsf{R}} \mathsf{KeyGen}(\mathsf{pp})$
$X^* \xleftarrow{\mathsf{R}} \mathbb{H}$
$(f, \mathsf{st}_\mathcal{A}) \xleftarrow{\mathsf{R}} \mathcal{A}_1(\mathsf{pp})$
$\mathsf{sk}_f \xleftarrow{\mathsf{R}} \mathsf{Constrain}(\mathsf{msk}, f)$
$\widehat{\mathsf{coin}} \xleftarrow{\mathsf{R}} \mathcal{A}_2^{\mathcal{O}_{\mathsf{Chal}}(\cdot)}(\mathsf{sk}_f, \mathsf{st}_\mathcal{A})$
Return $(\widehat{\mathsf{coin}} \stackrel{?}{=} \mathsf{coin})$

where the challenge oracle $\mathcal{O}_{\mathsf{Chal}}(\cdot)$ is described below.

$\mathcal{O}_{\mathsf{Chal}}(x^*)$: Given $x^* \in \{0,1\}^n$ as input, it returns $\mathsf{Eval}(\mathsf{msk}, x^*)$ if $\mathsf{coin} = 1$ and X^* if $\mathsf{coin} = 0$.

We recall that $\mathcal{O}_{\mathsf{Chal}}(\cdot)$ is queried at most once during the game.

Game 1: In this game, we change the way sk_f is sampled. In particular, we change the way of choosing $\{b_i\}_{i\in[z]}$ and $\{b'_i\}_{i\in[z]}$. Namely, given the constraining query f from $\mathcal{A}_1$, the game picks $(b'_1, \ldots, b'_z) \xleftarrow{\mathsf{R}} \mathbb{Z}_p^z$, $\alpha \xleftarrow{\mathsf{R}} \mathbb{Z}_p^*$, and sets $b_i := b'_i \alpha + f_i \mod p$ for $i \in [z]$.

Game 2 In this game, we change the challenge oracle $\mathcal{O}_{\mathsf{Chal}}(\cdot)$ as follows:
$\mathcal{O}_{\mathsf{Chal}}(x^*)$: Given $x^* \in \{0,1\}^n$ as input, it returns $\mathsf{SEval}(\mathsf{sk}_f, x^*) \cdot \mathsf{Aux}(\mathsf{msk})$ if $\mathsf{coin} = 1$ and X^* if $\mathsf{coin} = 0$.

Game 3: In this game, we further change the challenge oracle as follows:
$\mathcal{O}_{\mathsf{Chal}}(x^*)$: Given $x^* \in \{0,1\}^n$ as input, it first picks $\psi \xleftarrow{\mathsf{R}} \mathbb{H}$ and returns $\mathsf{SEval}(\mathsf{sk}_f, x) \cdot \psi$ if $\mathsf{coin} = 1$ and X^* if $\mathsf{coin} = 0$.

Game 4 In this game, the oracle is changed as follows.
$\mathcal{O}_{\mathsf{Chal}}(x^*)$: Given $x^* \in \{0,1\}^n$ as input, it returns X^* regardless of the value of coin.

Let T_i be the event that Game i returns 1.

Lemma 5. *It holds that* $\Pr[\mathsf{T}_1] = \Pr[\mathsf{T}_0]$, $\Pr[\mathsf{T}_2] = \Pr[\mathsf{T}_1]$, $\Pr[\mathsf{T}_3] = \Pr[\mathsf{T}_4]$, *and* $|\Pr[\mathsf{T}_4] - 1/2| = 0$.

Lemma 6. *If the* $(D-1)$*-DDHI assumption holds, then* $|\Pr[\mathsf{T}_3] - \Pr[\mathsf{T}_2]| = \mathsf{negl}(\lambda)$.

Therefore, the advantage of $\mathcal{A}$ is $\mathsf{Adv}^{\mathsf{cprf}}_{\mathsf{CPRF}_{\mathsf{NE}}, \mathcal{F}^{\mathbf{NC}^1}, \mathcal{A}}(\lambda) = 2 \cdot |\Pr[\mathsf{T}_0] - 1/2| = \mathsf{negl}(\lambda)$. See the full version for proofs of these lemmas. ∎

4.2 Selectively-Secure CPRF in the Standard Model

Here, we give our CPRF for $\mathbf{NC}^1$ with selectively single-key security in the standard model. The scheme is obtained by combining our CPRF $\mathsf{CPRF}_{\mathsf{NE}} = (\mathsf{Setup}_{\mathsf{NE}}, \mathsf{KeyGen}_{\mathsf{NE}}, \mathsf{Eval}_{\mathsf{NE}}, \mathsf{Constrain}_{\mathsf{NE}}, \mathsf{CEval}_{\mathsf{NE}})$ for the function class $\mathcal{F}^{\mathbf{NC}^1}$ in Sect. 4.1 with our CIH $\mathsf{CIH}_{\widetilde{\mathsf{BC}}} = (\mathsf{PrmGen}_{\widetilde{\mathsf{BC}}}, \mathsf{Eval}_{\widetilde{\mathsf{BC}}})$ constructed in Sect. 3. For the simplicity of the notation, we will denote $\mathsf{Eval}_{\widetilde{\mathsf{BC}}}(\mathsf{pp}_{\mathsf{CIH}}, \cdot)$ by $\mathsf{CIH}_{\widetilde{\mathsf{BC}}}(\cdot)$ when $\mathsf{pp}_{\mathsf{CIH}}$ is clear. Let SPGGen denote the group generator defined in Sect. 3. The construction of our scheme $\mathsf{CPRF}_{\mathbf{NC}^1\text{-Sel}} = (\mathsf{Setup}, \mathsf{KeyGen}, \mathsf{Eval}, \mathsf{Constrain}, \mathsf{CEval})$ is as follows:

Setup(1^λ): It first runs $\mathcal{G}_0 \xleftarrow{\text{R}} \text{SPGGen}(1^\lambda)$ to obtain the group description $\mathcal{G}_0 :=$ $(\mathbb{G}, q)$. Recall that $\mathcal{G}_0$ also defines the description of the group $\mathbb{QR}_q \subset \mathbb{Z}_q^*$ of prime order $p = (q-1)/2$. We denote the description of the group by $\mathcal{G}_1 := (\mathbb{QR}_q, p)$. It then samples $\text{pp}_{\text{CIH}} \xleftarrow{\text{R}} \text{PrmGen}_{\widetilde{\text{BC}}}(\mathcal{G}_0)$. Let $\text{pp}_{\text{NE}} := \mathcal{G}_1$. It outputs $\text{pp} := (\text{pp}_{\text{CIH}}, \text{pp}_{\text{NE}})$.

KeyGen(pp): It first parses $(\text{pp}_{\text{CIH}}, \text{pp}_{\text{NE}}) \leftarrow \text{pp}$ and runs $\text{msk}_i \xleftarrow{\text{R}} \text{KeyGen}_{\text{NE}}(\text{pp}_{\text{NE}})$ for $i \in [m]$. It then outputs $\text{msk} := (\text{msk}_1, ..., \text{msk}_m)$.

Eval(msk, x): It first parses $(\text{msk}_1, ..., \text{msk}_m) \leftarrow \text{msk}$ and outputs

$$y := \text{CIH}_{\widetilde{\text{BC}}}\Big(\text{Eval}_{\text{NE}}(\text{msk}_1, x), ..., \text{Eval}_{\text{NE}}(\text{msk}_m, x) \Big).$$

where we recall that we have $\text{CIH}_{\widetilde{\text{BC}}} : (\mathbb{QR}_q)^m \to \mathbb{G}$ and $\text{Eval}_{\text{NE}}(\text{msk}_i, \cdot) :$ $\{0,1\}^n \to \mathbb{QR}_q$ for $i \in [m]$ (for simplicity, we omit writing pp_{CIH} and pp_{NE} here).

Constrain(msk, f): It first parses $(\text{msk}_1, ..., \text{msk}_m) \leftarrow \text{msk}$. It then computes $\text{sk}_{f,i} \xleftarrow{\text{R}} \text{Constrain}_{\text{NE}}(\text{msk}_i, f)$ for $i \in [m]$ and outputs $\text{sk}_f := (\text{sk}_{f,1}, ..., \text{sk}_{f,m})$.

CEval(sk_f, x): It first parses $(\text{sk}_{f,1}, ..., \text{sk}_{f,m}) \leftarrow \text{sk}_f$. It then computes $X_i :=$ $\text{Eval}_{\text{NE}}(\text{sk}_{f,i}, x)$ for $i \in [m]$ and outputs $\text{CIH}_{\widetilde{\text{BC}}}(X_1, ..., X_m)$.

Remark 5. In the above, we need m instances of CPRF_{NE}, which may seem redundant. This is necessary because the domain of the CIH constructed in Sect. 3 is $\mathbb{QR}^m$ for $m = poly(\lambda)$, and thus input of the CIH must be an m-dimensional vector. If we had a CIH for group-induced function on $\mathbb{QR}$, then the m times blowup could be avoided.

Remark 6. The algorithm Setup implicitly uses the group generator SPGGen' that first runs SPGGen to obtain $\mathcal{G} = (\mathbb{G}, q)$ and then outputs the group description $(\mathbb{QR}_q, p)$. Here, from the technical reason, we assume that the description of $\mathbb{QR}_q$ implicitly contains that of $\mathbb{G}$ as well. While our construction in Sect. 4.1 can be instantiated with any prime-order group generator HGen, our scheme above requires to instantiate the scheme with the specific group generator SPGGen'.

It is easy to observe that the correctness of the above scheme follows from that of the underlying schemes. The following theorem addresses the security of the scheme.

Theorem 3. *The above construction $\text{CPRF}_{\text{NC}^1\text{-Sel}}$ is a selective single-key secure CPRF for the function class $\mathcal{F}^{NC^1}$ if the $(D-1)$-DDHI assumption holds with respect to SPGGen' (see Remark 6) and the DDH assumption holds with respect to SPGGen.*

Proof. The security of the scheme will be proven by the no-evaluation security, semi-evaluability, and universality of CPRF_{NE} as well as correlated-input security of $\text{CIH}_{\widetilde{\text{BC}}}$ for (component-wise) group-induced functions. Let $\mathcal{A} = (\mathcal{A}_1, \mathcal{A}_2)$ be any selectively admissible adversary that attacks the selective single-key security of CPRF. For simplicity, we assume that $\mathcal{A}_2$ never makes the same query twice, makes a challenge query only once (see Remark 2), and all evaluation queries x

made by $\mathcal{A}_2$ satisfy $f(x) = 1$. In the following, Q denotes the upper bound on the number of the access to the evaluation oracle $\mathsf{Eval}(\mathsf{msk}, \cdot)$ made by $\mathcal{A}_2$. We prove the theorem by considering the following sequence of games.

Game 0: This is the actual single-key security experiment $\mathsf{Expt}^{\mathsf{cprf}}_{\mathsf{CPRF}_{\mathbf{NC}^1\text{-Sel}}, \mathcal{F}^{\mathbf{NC}^1}, \mathcal{A}}$ (λ) against the selective adversary $\mathcal{A} = (\mathcal{A}_1, \mathcal{A}_2)$ where the coin of the game is fixed to $\mathsf{coin} = 1$. Namely,

$\mathsf{pp} \xleftarrow{\mathsf{R}} \mathsf{Setup}(1^\lambda)$	where we describe $\mathsf{Eval}(\mathsf{msk}, \cdot)$ and $\mathcal{O}_{\mathsf{Chal}}(\cdot)$ below.
$\mathsf{msk} \xleftarrow{\mathsf{R}} \mathsf{KeyGen}(\mathsf{pp})$	
$(f, \mathsf{st}_\mathcal{A}) \xleftarrow{\mathsf{R}} \mathcal{A}_1(\mathsf{pp})$	$\mathsf{Eval}(\mathsf{msk}, \cdot)$: Given $x \in \{0,1\}^n$ as
$\mathsf{sk}_f \xleftarrow{\mathsf{R}} \mathsf{Constrain}(\mathsf{msk}, f)$	input, it returns $\mathsf{Eval}(\mathsf{msk}, x)$.
$\widehat{\mathsf{coin}} \xleftarrow{\mathsf{R}} \mathcal{A}_2^{\mathcal{O}_{\mathsf{Chal}}(\cdot), \mathsf{Eval}(\mathsf{msk}, \cdot)}(\mathsf{sk}_f, \mathsf{st}_\mathcal{A})$	$\mathcal{O}_{\mathsf{Chal}}(\cdot)$: Given $x^* \in \{0,1\}^n$ as input,
Return $\widehat{\mathsf{coin}}$	it returns $y^* = \mathsf{Eval}(\mathsf{msk}, x^*)$.
	(Recall that we set $\mathsf{coin} = 1$ in this game.)

Game 1: In this game, we do not differentiate the challenge oracle $\mathcal{O}_{\mathsf{Chal}}(\cdot)$ from $\mathsf{Eval}(\mathsf{msk}, \cdot)$ and identify them. Namely, $\mathcal{A}_2$ is equipped with the following oracle $\mathcal{O}_{\mathsf{Merge}}(\cdot)$ defined below, instead of $\mathcal{O}_{\mathsf{Chal}}(\cdot)$ and $\mathsf{Eval}(\mathsf{msk}, \cdot)$:

$\mathcal{O}_{\mathsf{Merge}}(\cdot)$: Given the j-th query $x^{(j)} \in \{0,1\}^n$ from $\mathcal{A}_2$, the oracle first computes $X_i^{(j)} := \mathsf{Eval}_{\mathsf{NE}}(\mathsf{msk}_i, x^{(j)})$ for $i \in [m]$, and then returns $y^{(j)} := \mathsf{CIH}_{\widetilde{\mathsf{BC}}}(X_1^{(j)}, \ldots, X_m^{(j)})$.

(We note that $\mathcal{O}_{\mathsf{Merge}}(\cdot)$ simply returns $\mathsf{Eval}(\mathsf{msk}, x)$ given x.) Since we do not differentiate the challenge query x^* from the evaluation queries in this game, we have $x^* = x^{(j)}$ for some $j \in [Q + 1]$.

Game 2: Let Col be the event that there exist $j_1 \neq j_2 \in [Q + 1]$ such that $(X_1^{(j_1)}, \ldots, X_m^{(j_1)}) = (X_1^{(j_2)}, \ldots, X_m^{(j_2)})$. If Col occurs, the game immediately aborts and outputs a uniformly random bit. The rest is the same as the previous game.

Game 3 In this game, we change the way $\{X_i^{(j)}\}_{i \in [m], j \in [Q+1]}$ is created. In particular, $\mathcal{O}_{\mathsf{Merge}}(\cdot)$ works as follows:

$\mathcal{O}_{\mathsf{Merge}}(\cdot)$: Given the j-th query $x^{(j)} \in \{0,1\}^n$ from $\mathcal{A}_2$, it proceeds as follows. There are two cases to consider:

1. For the first query $x^{(1)}$, it first computes

$$X_i^{(1)} := \mathsf{Eval}_{\mathsf{NE}}(\mathsf{msk}_i, x^{(1)}) \quad \text{for } i \in [m].$$

Then, it computes and returns $y^{(1)} := \mathsf{CIH}_{\widetilde{\mathsf{BC}}}(X_1^{(1)}, \ldots, X_m^{(1)})$.

2. To answer queries $x^{(j)}$ with $j > 1$, it first computes

$$X_i^{(j)} := X_i^{(1)} \cdot \mathsf{SEval}_{\mathsf{NE}}(\mathsf{sk}_{f,i}, x^{(1)})^{-1} \cdot \mathsf{SEval}_{\mathsf{NE}}(\mathsf{sk}_{f,i}, x^{(j)}) \tag{3}$$

for $i \in [m]$. Then it computes and returns $y^{(j)} := \mathsf{CIH}_{\widetilde{\mathsf{BC}}}(X_1^{(j)}, \ldots, X_m^{(j)})$.

Note that during the above phase, as soon as the game finds $j_1 \neq j_2 \in [Q+1]$ such that $(X_1^{(j_1)}, \ldots, X_m^{(j_1)}) = (X_1^{(j_2)}, \ldots, X_m^{(j_2)})$, the game aborts and outputs a random bit (as specified in Game 2).

Game 4 We define Col' as the event that there exist $j_1 \neq j_2 \in [Q+1]$ such that

$$\mathsf{SEval}_{\mathsf{NE}}(\mathsf{sk}_{f,i}, x^{(j_1)}) = \mathsf{SEval}_{\mathsf{NE}}(\mathsf{sk}_{f,i}, x^{(j_2)}) \quad \forall i \in [m].$$

In this game, the game aborts when Col' occurs instead of Col.

Game 5: In this game, we change the way $X_i^{(1)}$ is chosen. In particular, the first item of the description of the oracle $\mathcal{O}_{\mathsf{Merge}}(\cdot)$ in Game 3 is changed as follows:

1. For the first query $x^{(1)}$, the oracle sets

$$X_i^{(1)} \xleftarrow{\mathsf{R}} \mathbb{QR}_q \quad \text{for } i \in [m].$$

Then, it computes and returns $y^{(1)} := \mathsf{CIH}_{\widetilde{\mathsf{BC}}}(X_1^{(1)}, \ldots, X_m^{(1)})$.

Game 6 In this game, we further change the oracle $\mathcal{O}_{\mathsf{Merge}}(\cdot)$ as follows:
$\mathcal{O}_{\mathsf{Merge}}(\cdot)$: Given the j-th query $x^{(j)} \in \{0,1\}^n$ from $\mathcal{A}_2$, it picks $y^{(j)} \xleftarrow{\mathsf{R}} \mathbb{G}$ and returns it.

Game 7 This is the real game with the coin being fixed to $\mathsf{coin} = 0$. Namely, $\mathcal{A}_2$ is equipped with the oracles $\mathcal{O}_{\mathsf{Chal}}(\cdot)$ and $\mathsf{Eval}(\mathsf{msk}, \cdot)$ that work as follows. (We do not consider $\mathcal{O}_{\mathsf{Merge}}(\cdot)$ any more.)
$\mathsf{Eval}(\mathsf{msk}, \cdot)$: Given $x \in \{0,1\}^n$ as input, it returns $\mathsf{Eval}(\mathsf{msk}, x)$.
$\mathcal{O}_{\mathsf{Chal}}(\cdot)$: Given $x^* \in \{0,1\}^n$ as input, it picks $y^* \xleftarrow{\mathsf{R}} \mathbb{G}$ and returns it. (Recall that we set $\mathsf{coin} = 0$ in this game.)

Let T_i be the event that Game i returns 1.

Lemma 7. $\Pr[\mathsf{T}_1] = \Pr[\mathsf{T}_0]$.

Proof. Since $\mathsf{coin} = 1$ in Game 0, we have $\mathcal{O}_{\mathsf{Chal}}(\cdot) = \mathsf{Eval}(\mathsf{msk}, \cdot)$. Therefore, this is only the conceptual change. ∎

Lemma 8. *If* $m \geq n$, $|\Pr[\mathsf{T}_2] - \Pr[\mathsf{T}_1]| = \mathsf{negl}(\lambda)$.

See the full version [3] for the proof of this lemma. This is proved by the union bound and the universality of $\mathsf{CPRF}_{\mathsf{NE}}$ (Lemma 4).

Lemma 9. $\Pr[\mathsf{T}_3] = \Pr[\mathsf{T}_2]$.

Proof. We prove that the change is only conceptual. The difference between the games is that $X_i^{(j)}$ is computed as $\mathsf{Eval}_{\mathsf{NE}}(\mathsf{msk}_i, x^{(j)})$ in Game 2, whereas it is computed as the right-hand side of Eq. (3) in Game 3. We show here that they are actually equivalent. The right-hand side of Eq. (3) equals to

$$X_i^{(1)} \cdot \mathsf{SEval}_{\mathsf{NE}}(\mathsf{sk}_{f,i}, x^{(1)})^{-1} \cdot \mathsf{SEval}_{\mathsf{NE}}(\mathsf{sk}_{f,i}, x^{(j)})$$
$$= \mathsf{Aux}_{\mathsf{NE}}(\mathsf{msk}_i) \cdot \mathsf{SEval}_{\mathsf{NE}}(\mathsf{sk}_{f,i}, x^{(1)}) \cdot \mathsf{SEval}_{\mathsf{NE}}(\mathsf{sk}_{f,i}, x^{(1)})^{-1} \cdot \mathsf{SEval}_{\mathsf{NE}}(\mathsf{sk}_{f,i}, x^{(j)})$$
$$= \mathsf{Aux}_{\mathsf{NE}}(\mathsf{msk}_i) \cdot \mathsf{SEval}_{\mathsf{NE}}(\mathsf{sk}_{f,i}, x^{(j)})$$
$$= \mathsf{Eval}_{\mathsf{NE}}(\mathsf{msk}_i, x^{(j)})$$

where we used our simplification assumption that $f(x^{(1)}) = f(x^{(j)}) = 1$ and semi-evaluability (Lemma 3) in the first and the last equations above.   ∎

Lemma 10. $\Pr[\mathsf{T}_4] = \Pr[\mathsf{T}_3]$.

Proof. It suffices to show that the abort conditions Col and Col' are equivalent. We have

$$\mathsf{SEval}_{\mathsf{NE}}(\mathsf{sk}_{f,i}, x^{(j_1)}) = \mathsf{SEval}_{\mathsf{NE}}(\mathsf{sk}_{f,i}, x^{(j_2)}) \quad \forall i \in [m]$$

$$\Leftrightarrow \mathsf{Aux}_{\mathsf{NE}}(\mathsf{msk}_i) \cdot \mathsf{SEval}_{\mathsf{NE}}(\mathsf{sk}_{f,i}, x^{(j_1)})$$

$$= \mathsf{Aux}_{\mathsf{NE}}(\mathsf{msk}_i) \cdot \mathsf{SEval}_{\mathsf{NE}}(\mathsf{sk}_{f,i}, x^{(j_2)}) \quad \forall i \in [m]$$

$$\Leftrightarrow X_i^{(j_1)} = X_i^{(j_2)} \quad \forall i \in [m].$$

Hence, the change is only conceptual. The lemma readily follows.   ∎

Lemma 11. *If* $\mathsf{CPRF}_{\mathsf{NE}}$ *satisfies no-evaluation security when instantiated by the group generator* $\mathsf{HGen} := \mathsf{SPGGen}'$, *we have* $|\Pr[\mathsf{T}_5] - \Pr[\mathsf{T}_4]| = \mathsf{negl}(\lambda)$.

Proof. For the sake of the contradiction, let us assume $|\Pr[\mathsf{T}_5] - \Pr[\mathsf{T}_4]|$ is non-negligible for the adversary $\mathcal{A} = (\mathcal{A}_1, \mathcal{A}_2)$. We consider the following hybrid games for $k \in \{0, 1, \ldots, m\}$:

Game 4.k: This is the same as Game 4 with the following difference. In this game, $X_i^{(1)}$ is set as $X_i^{(1)} = \mathsf{Eval}_{\mathsf{NE}}(\mathsf{msk}_i, x^{(1)})$ when $i > k$ and $\tilde{X}_i \xleftarrow{\mathsf{R}} \mathbb{QR}_q$ when $i \leq k$.

By the definition, we have Game 4.0 (resp. Game 4.m) is equivalent to Game 4 (resp. Game 5). Therefore, we have

$$|\Pr[\mathsf{T}_5] - \Pr[\mathsf{T}_4]| = \Pr[\mathsf{T}_{4.m}] - \Pr[\mathsf{T}_{4.0}]| \geq \sum_{k \in [m]} |\Pr[\mathsf{T}_{4.k}] - \Pr[\mathsf{T}_{4.k-1}]|$$

where $\Pr[\mathsf{T}_i]$ denotes the probability that Game 4.k outputs 1. By the above inequality, we have that there exists an index k^* such that $|\Pr[\mathsf{T}_{4.k^*}] - \Pr[\mathsf{T}_{4.k^*-1}]|$ is non-negligible. We then construct an adversary $\mathcal{B} = (\mathcal{B}_1, \mathcal{B}_2)$ that breaks the no-evaluation security of the underlying scheme $\mathsf{CPRF}_{\mathsf{NE}}$. The description of $\mathcal{B}$ is as follows.

$\mathcal{B}_1(\mathsf{pp}_{\mathsf{NE}})$: Given the group description $\mathsf{pp}_{\mathsf{NE}} = (\mathbb{QR}_q, p)$, $\mathcal{B}_1$ first recovers the group description $\mathcal{G}_0 = (\mathbb{G}, q)$ from $(\mathbb{QR}_q, p)$ (See remark Remark 6). $\mathcal{B}_1$ then samples $\mathsf{pp}_{\mathsf{CIH}} \xleftarrow{\mathsf{R}} \mathsf{PrmGen}_{\widetilde{\mathsf{BC}}}(\mathcal{G}_0)$ and sets $\mathsf{pp} := (\mathsf{pp}_{\mathsf{CIH}}, \mathsf{pp}_{\mathsf{NE}})$. It then runs $(f, \mathsf{st}_{\mathcal{A}}) \xleftarrow{\mathsf{R}} \mathcal{A}_1(\mathsf{pp})$ and outputs $(f, \mathsf{st}_{\mathcal{B}} := \mathsf{st}_{\mathcal{A}})$.

$\mathcal{B}_2^{\mathcal{O}_{\mathsf{Chal}}(\cdot)}(\mathsf{sk}_f, \mathsf{st}_{\mathcal{B}})$: Here, we denote the master secret key of the no-evaluation security game (played for $\mathcal{B}$) by msk'. The task of $\mathcal{B}_2$ is to distinguish whether $\mathcal{O}_{\mathsf{Chal}}(\cdot)$ corresponds to $\mathsf{Eval}_{\mathsf{NE}}(\mathsf{msk}', \cdot)$ or $\mathsf{RF}(\cdot)$. First, $\mathcal{B}_2$ picks $\mathsf{msk}_i \xleftarrow{\mathsf{R}} \mathsf{KeyGen}_{\mathsf{NE}}(\mathsf{pp}_{\mathsf{NE}})$ for $i \in \{k^* + 1, \ldots, m\}$. $\mathcal{B}_2$ then runs $\mathcal{A}_2(\mathsf{sk}_f, \mathsf{st}_{\mathcal{A}})$ and simulates $\mathcal{O}_{\mathsf{Merge}}(\cdot)$ for $\mathcal{A}_2$ as follows:

- To answer the first query $x^{(1)}$ from $\mathcal{A}_2$, $\mathcal{B}_2$ submits the same $x^{(1)}$ to its challenge oracle $\mathcal{O}_{\mathsf{Chal}}(\cdot)$. Then, $\mathcal{B}_2$ is given R. Then, $\mathcal{B}_2$ sets $X_i^{(1)} = \mathsf{SEval}_{\mathsf{NE}}(\mathsf{msk}_i, x^{(1)})$ for $i \geq k^* + 1$, $X_{k^*}^{(1)} = R$, and samples $X_i^{(1)} \xleftarrow{\mathsf{R}} \mathbb{QR}_q$ for $i \leq k^* - 1$. Finally, $\mathcal{B}_2$ returns $y^{(1)} = \mathsf{CIH}_{\widetilde{\mathsf{BC}}}(X_1^{(1)}, \dots, X_m^{(1)})$ to $\mathcal{A}_2$.
- To answer the query $x^{(j)}$ with $j > 1$ from $\mathcal{A}_2$, $\mathcal{B}_2$ first parses $\mathsf{sk}_f \rightarrow (\mathsf{sk}_{f,1}, \dots, \mathsf{sk}_{f,m})$ and computes $X_i^{(j)} := X_i^{(1)} \cdot \mathsf{SEval}_{\mathsf{NE}}(\mathsf{sk}_{f,i}, x^{(1)})^{-1} \cdot \mathsf{SEval}_{\mathsf{NE}}(\mathsf{sk}_{f,i}, x^{(j)})$ for $i \in [m]$. It then returns $y^{(j)} = \mathsf{CIH}_{\widetilde{\mathsf{BC}}}(X_1^{(j)}, \dots, X_m^{(j)})$ to $\mathcal{A}_2$.

Note that during the above phase, as soon as $\mathcal{B}_2$ finds $j_1 \neq j_2 \in [Q]$ such that $(X_1^{(j_1)}, \dots, X_m^{(j_1)}) = (X_1^{(j_2)}, \dots, X_m^{(j_2)})$, $\mathcal{B}_2$ aborts and outputs a random bit. When $\mathcal{A}_2$ terminates with output $\widehat{\mathsf{coin}}$, $\mathcal{B}_2$ outputs $\widehat{\mathsf{coin}}$ as its guess and terminates.

The above completes the description of $\mathcal{B}$. It is straightforward to see that $\mathcal{B}$ makes only single challenge query. It is also easy to see that $\mathcal{B}$ simulates Game $4.(k^* - 1)$ for $\mathcal{A}$ when $\mathcal{B}$'s challenge oracle is $\mathsf{Eval}_{\mathsf{NE}}(\mathsf{msk}', \cdot)$ and Game $4.k^*$ when $\mathcal{B}$'s challenge oracle is $\mathsf{RF}(\cdot)$. Note that in the former case, $\mathcal{B}$ implicitly sets $\mathsf{msk}_{k^*} := \mathsf{msk}'$. Since $\mathcal{B}$ outputs 1 if and only if $\mathcal{A}$ outputs 1, we have that $\mathcal{B}$'s advantage is $|\Pr[\mathsf{T}_{4.k^*-1}] - \Pr[\mathsf{T}_{4.k^*}]|$, which is non-negligible. This completes the proof of the lemma. $\blacksquare$

Lemma 12. *If* $\mathsf{CIH}_{\widetilde{\mathsf{BC}}}$ *is a* $\Psi^{\mathsf{g\text{-}indc}}$*-CIH with respect to* SPGGen*, then we have* $|\Pr[\mathsf{T}_6] - \Pr[\mathsf{T}_5]| = \mathsf{negl}(\lambda)$.

Proof. For the sake of the contradiction, let us assume that $|\Pr[\mathsf{T}_6] - \Pr[\mathsf{T}_5]|$ is non-negligible for the adversary $\mathcal{A} = (\mathcal{A}_1, \mathcal{A}_2)$. We then construct an adversary $\mathcal{B}$ that breaks the security of $\mathsf{CIH}_{\widetilde{\mathsf{BC}}}$ as follows.

$\mathcal{B}^{\mathcal{O}(\cdot)}(\mathsf{pp}_{\mathsf{CIH}})$: At the beginning of the game, $\mathcal{B}$ is given the public parameter $\mathsf{pp}_{\mathsf{CIH}}$ of the CIH. Then it parses the group description $(\mathbb{G}, q)$ from $\mathsf{pp}_{\mathsf{CIH}}$ and obtains the description of another group $\mathsf{pp}_{\mathsf{NE}} := (\mathbb{QR}_q, p)$. It then sets $\mathsf{pp} := (\mathsf{pp}_{\mathsf{CIH}}, \mathsf{pp}_{\mathsf{NE}})$ and runs $(f, \mathsf{st}_{\mathcal{A}}) \xleftarrow{\mathsf{R}} \mathcal{A}_1(\mathsf{pp})$. It further samples $\mathsf{msk}_i \xleftarrow{\mathsf{R}} \mathsf{KeyGen}_{\mathsf{NE}}(\mathsf{pp}_{\mathsf{NE}})$ and $\mathsf{sk}_{f,i} \xleftarrow{\mathsf{R}} \mathsf{Constrain}_{\mathsf{NE}}(\mathsf{msk}_i, f)$ for $i \in [m]$. It then gives the input $\mathsf{sk}_f := (\mathsf{sk}_{f,1}, \dots, \mathsf{sk}_{f,m})$ and $\mathsf{st}_{\mathcal{A}}$ to $\mathcal{A}_2$ and simulates $\mathcal{O}_{\mathsf{Merge}}(\cdot)$ for $\mathcal{A}_2$ as follows:

- To answer the first query $x^{(1)}$ from $\mathcal{A}_2$, $\mathcal{B}$ queries its oracle on input $\vec{\phi}^{(1)} := (1, \dots, 1) \in \mathbb{QR}_q^m$ to obtain $y^{(1)}$. It then passes $y^{(1)}$ to $\mathcal{A}_2$.
- To answer the query $x^{(j)}$ with $j > 1$ from $\mathcal{A}_2$, $\mathcal{B}$ first parses $\mathsf{sk}_f \rightarrow (\mathsf{sk}_{f,1}, \dots, \mathsf{sk}_{f,m})$ and computes $\phi_i^{(j)} := \mathsf{SEval}_{\mathsf{NE}}(\mathsf{sk}_{f,i}, x^{(1)})^{-1} \cdot \mathsf{SEval}_{\mathsf{NE}}(\mathsf{sk}_{f,i}, x^{(j)})$ for $i \in [m]$. $\mathcal{B}$ then sets $\vec{\phi}^{(j)} = (\phi_1^{(j)}, \dots, \phi_m^{(j)})$ and queries $\vec{\phi}^{(j)}$ to its oracle. Given the response $y^{(j)}$ from the oracle, $\mathcal{B}_2$ relays the same value to $\mathcal{A}_2$.

Note that during the above phase, as soon as $\mathcal{B}$ finds $j_1 \neq j_2 \in [Q]$ such that $\mathsf{SEval}_{\mathsf{NE}}(\mathsf{sk}_{f,i}, x^{(j_1)}) = \mathsf{SEval}_{\mathsf{NE}}(\mathsf{sk}_{f,i}, x^{(j_2)})$ for all $i \in [m]$, it aborts and outputs a random bit. When $\mathcal{A}_2$ terminates with output $\widehat{\mathsf{coin}}$, $\mathcal{B}$ outputs the same $\widehat{\mathsf{coin}}$ and terminates.

The above completes the description of $\mathcal{B}$. Here, we prove that $\mathcal{B}$ simulates Game 5 when $\mathcal{B}$'s challenge coin coin$'$ is 1 and Game 6 when coin$' = 0$.

We start by proving the former statement. When coin$' = 1$, the CIH security experiment chooses randomness $\vec{R} := (R_1, \ldots, R_m) \xleftarrow{\text{R}} \mathrm{QR}_q^m$ during the game and the oracle $\mathcal{O}(\cdot)$ returns $\mathsf{CIH}_{\widetilde{\mathsf{BC}}}(\vec{R} \star \vec{\phi})$ on input $\mathcal{B}$'s query $\vec{\phi} = (\phi_1, \ldots, \phi_m) \in \mathrm{QR}_q^m$. The view of $\mathcal{A}_2$ corresponds to Game 5, with $X_i^{(1)}$ being implicitly set as $X_i^{(1)} := R_i$ for $i \in [m]$.

We next show the latter statement. When coin$' = 0$, the CIH security experiment chooses randomness $\vec{R} := (R_1, \ldots, R_m) \xleftarrow{\text{R}} \mathrm{QR}_q^m$ during the game and the oracle $\mathcal{O}(\cdot)$ returns $\mathsf{RF}(\vec{R} \star \vec{\phi})$ on input $\mathcal{B}$'s query $\vec{\phi} = (\phi_1, \ldots, \phi_m)$ where $\mathsf{RF}(\cdot)$ is a random function. In order to prove that $\mathcal{B}$ simulates Game 6, it suffices to show that all the queries made by $\mathcal{B}$ are distinct. We have

$$\phi_i^{(j_1)} = \phi_i^{(j_2)} \iff \mathsf{SEval}_{\mathsf{NE}}(\mathsf{sk}_{f_i}, x^{(j_1)}) = \mathsf{SEval}_{\mathsf{NE}}(\mathsf{sk}_{f,i}, x^{(j_2)})$$

by the definition. Since $\mathcal{B}$ aborts whenever Col$'$ occurs, this implies that $\mathcal{B}$ does not make the same oracle query twice. ∎

Lemma 13. *We have* $|\Pr[T_7] - \Pr[T_6]| = \mathrm{negl}(\lambda)$.

Proof. This can be proven by applying the same game changes as that from Game 0 to Game 6 in a reverse order, with the only difference that the challenge query x^* is always returned by a uniformly random group element $y^* \xleftarrow{\text{R}} \mathbb{G}$. ∎

We have

$$\mathsf{Adv}^{\mathrm{cprf}}_{\mathrm{CPRF}_{\mathbf{NC}^1\text{-Sel}}, \mathcal{F}^{\mathbf{NC}^1}, \mathcal{A}}(\lambda) = |\Pr[T_7] - \Pr[T_0]| \leq \sum_{i=1}^{7} |\Pr[T_i] - \Pr[T_{i-1}]| = \mathrm{negl}(\lambda).$$

This completes the proof of the theorem. ∎

5   Private Constrained PRF for Bit-Fixing

In this section, we construct a single-key private CPRF for bit-fixing. Our scheme is selectively secure under the DDH assumption. We also construct an adaptively secure single-key private CPRF for bit-fixing in the ROM in the full version [3].

Bit-fixing functions. First, we define a function class of bit-fixing functions formally. The class $\mathcal{BF} = \{\mathcal{BF}_n\}_{n \in \mathbb{N}}$ of bit-fixing functions is defined as follows[20]. $\mathcal{BF}_n$ is defined to be the set $\{\mathsf{BF}_c\}_{c \in \{0,1,*\}^n}$ where

$$\mathsf{BF}_c(x) := \begin{cases} 0 & \text{if for all } i, \, c_i = * \text{ or } x_i = c_i \\ 1 & \text{otherwise} \end{cases}.$$

By an abuse of notation, we often write c to mean BF_c when the latter is given as an input to an algorithm.

---

[20] According to the definition given in [3], we should give $\mathcal{BF}_{\lambda,n}$ for all $\lambda \in \mathbb{N}$ and $n \in \mathbb{N}$. However, since $\mathcal{BF}_{\lambda,n}$ is the same for all λ if n is fixed in the case of the bit-fixing, we use this simpler notation.

CIH for affine functions. We introduce the notion of affine functions for CIH since it is used in our private CPRF for bit-fixing. *The class of affine functions with respect to a group generator* GGen, *denoted by* $\Phi^{\mathsf{aff}} = \{\Phi^{\mathsf{aff}}_{\lambda,z}\}_{\lambda\in\mathbb{N},z\in\{0,1\}^*}$, *is a function class satisfying the following property for every* $(\lambda, z) \in \mathbb{N} \times \{0,1\}^*$: If z can be parsed as a tuple $(\mathcal{G}, m, z')$ so that $\mathcal{G} = (\mathbb{G}, p)$ is a group description output by $\mathsf{GGen}(1^\lambda)$, $m \in \mathbb{N}$, and $z' \in \{0,1\}^*$, then we have $\Phi^{\mathsf{aff}}_{\lambda,z} = \{\phi_{\vec{u},\vec{v}} : \mathbb{Z}_p^m \to \mathbb{Z}_p^m \mid \vec{u} \in (\mathbb{Z}_p^*)^m, \vec{v} \in \mathbb{Z}_p^m\}$, where for each $\vec{u}, \vec{v}$, $\phi_{\vec{u},\vec{v}}(\vec{x}) := \vec{u} \odot \vec{x} + \vec{v} \in \mathbb{Z}_p^m$ and $\odot$ denotes the component-wise multiplication in $\mathbb{Z}_p$.

We will use the following theorem that is implicitly proven by Abdalla et al. [1] (see also Remark 4).

Theorem 4. *(implicit in [1, Theorem 7]) Let* GGen *be a group generator. If the DDH assumption holds with respect to* GGen, *then for any polynomial* $m = m(\lambda) \in \Omega(\lambda)$, *there exists a* Φ^{aff}-*CIH* $\mathsf{CIH}_{\mathsf{aff}} = (\mathsf{PrmGen}_{\mathsf{aff}}, \mathsf{Eval}_{\mathsf{aff}})$ *with respect to* GGen, *with the following property: For all* $\lambda \in \mathbb{N}$, *if* $\mathcal{G} = (\mathbb{G}, p) \xleftarrow{\mathsf{R}} \mathsf{GGen}(1^\lambda)$ *and* $\mathsf{pp} \xleftarrow{\mathsf{R}} \mathsf{PrmGen}_{\mathsf{aff}}(\mathcal{G})$, *then* pp *can be parsed as* $(\mathcal{G}, m, z')$ *for some* $z' \in \{0,1\}^*$, *and furthermore* $\mathsf{Eval}_{\mathsf{aff}}(\mathsf{pp}, \cdot)$ *is a function with domain* $\mathbb{Z}_p^m$ *and range* $\mathbb{G}$.

This theorem is derived from the following facts. (1) Abdalla et al. [1] constructed RKA-PRF for affine functions based on the DDH assumption. (2) Bellare and Cash [6] showed that RKA-PRF for a function class implies RKA-PRG for the same function class. (3) Our definition of CIH is the same as that of RKA-PRG (See Remark 4).

5.1 Construction in the Standard Model

Construction. Here, we give a construction of a selectively secure private CPRF for bit-fixing. Our CPRF is built on a Φ^{aff}-CIH, which is known to exist under the DDH assumption [1]. Let GGen be a group generator that given 1^λ, generates a description of group of an ℓ_p-bit prime order, and $\mathsf{CIH}_{\mathsf{aff}} = (\mathsf{PrmGen}_{\mathsf{aff}}, \mathsf{Eval}_{\mathsf{aff}})$ be a Φ^{aff}-CIH. For simplicity, we denote $\mathsf{Eval}_{\mathsf{CIH}}(\mathsf{pp}_{\mathsf{CIH}}, \cdot)$ by $\mathsf{CIH}_{\mathsf{aff}}(\cdot)$ when $\mathsf{pp}_{\mathsf{CIH}}$ is clear. Our scheme $\mathsf{CPRF}_{\mathsf{priv,std}} = (\mathsf{Setup}, \mathsf{KeyGen}, \mathsf{Eval}, \mathsf{Constrain}, \mathsf{CEval})$ is described as follows. Let $n(\lambda)$ (often denoted as n for short) be an integer, which is used as the input length of $\mathsf{CPRF}_{\mathsf{priv,std}}$.

$\mathsf{Setup}(1^\lambda)$: It generates $\mathcal{G} \xleftarrow{\mathsf{R}} \mathsf{GGen}(1^\lambda)$ to obtain the group description $\mathcal{G} := (\mathbb{G}, p)$, and runs $\mathsf{pp}_{\mathsf{CIH}} \xleftarrow{\mathsf{R}} \mathsf{PrmGen}_{\mathsf{aff}}(\mathcal{G})$ to obtain $\mathsf{pp}_{\mathsf{CIH}} := (\mathcal{G}, m, z')$. Recall that $\mathsf{pp}_{\mathsf{CIH}}$ specifies the domain $\mathbb{Z}_p^m$ and the range $\mathcal{R}$ of $\mathsf{CIH}_{\mathsf{aff}}$. It outputs $\mathsf{pp} := (\mathsf{pp}_{\mathsf{CIH}}, 1^n)$.

$\mathsf{KeyGen}(\mathsf{pp})$: It chooses $s_{i,b,j} \xleftarrow{\mathsf{R}} \mathbb{Z}_p$ for $i \in [n]$, $b \in \{0,1\}$ and $j \in [m]$, and outputs $\mathsf{msk} := \{s_{i,b,j}\}_{i\in[n],b\in\{0,1\},j\in[m]}$.

$\mathsf{Eval}(\mathsf{msk}, x)$: It parses $\{s_{i,b,j}\}_{i\in[n],b\in\{0,1\},j\in[m]} \leftarrow \mathsf{msk}$. It computes $X_j := \sum_{i=1}^n s_{i,x_i,j}$ for $j \in [m]$. Then it computes $y := \mathsf{CIH}_{\mathsf{aff}}(X_1, ..., X_m)$ and outputs it.

Constrain$(\mathsf{msk}, c \in \{0, 1, *\}^n)$: It parses $\{s_{i,b}\}_{i \in [n], b \in \{0,1\}} \leftarrow \mathsf{msk}$, picks $\alpha_j \xleftarrow{\mathsf{R}} \mathbb{Z}_p$ for $j \in [m]$. Then it defines $\{t_{i,b,j}\}_{i \in [n], b \in \{0,1\}, j \in [m]}$ as follows. For all $i \in [n]$, $b \in \{0, 1\}$ and $j \in [m]$, it sets

$$t_{i,b,j} := \begin{cases} s_{i,b,j} & \text{If } c_i = * \text{ or } b = c_i \\ s_{i,b,j} - \alpha_j & \text{If } c_i \neq * \text{ and } b = 1 - c_i \end{cases}.$$

Then it outputs $\mathsf{sk}_c := \{t_{i,b,j}\}_{i \in [n], b \in \{0,1\}, j \in [m]}$.

CEval(sk_c, x): It parses $\{t_{i,b,j}\}_{i \in [n], b \in \{0,1\}, j \in [m]} \leftarrow \mathsf{sk}_c$, computes $X_j := \sum_{i=1}^{n} t_{i,x_i,j}$ for $j \in [m]$ and $y := \mathsf{CIH}_{\mathsf{aff}}(X_1, ..., X_m)$, and outputs y.

Theorem 5. *If* CIH *is a* $\Phi^{\mathsf{aff}}\text{-}CIH$ *and* $2^{2n-m\ell_p}$ *is negligible, then the above scheme is a selectively single-key secure CPRF for* $\mathcal{BF}$ *with selective single-key privacy.*

We prove the correctness and Theorem 5 in the full version [3].

Acknowledgement. We thank Keita Xagawa for letting us know the relation between CIH and RKA-PRG. The first, second, and fourth authors were supported by JST CREST Grant No. JPMJCR1688. The fourth author was supported by JSPS KAK-ENHI Grant Number 16K16068.

References

1. Abdalla, M., Benhamouda, F., Passelègue, A., Paterson, K.G.: Related-key security for pseudorandom functions beyond the linear barrier. In: Garay, J.A., Gennaro, R. (eds.) CRYPTO 2014, Part I. LNCS, vol. 8616, pp. 77–94. Springer, Heidelberg (2014). https://doi.org/10.1007/978-3-662-44371-2_5

2. Abusalah, H., Fuchsbauer, G., Pietrzak, K.: Constrained PRFs for unbounded inputs. In: Sako, K. (ed.) CT-RSA 2016. LNCS, vol. 9610, pp. 413–428. Springer, Cham (2016). https://doi.org/10.1007/978-3-319-29485-8_24

3. Attrapadung, N., Matsuda, T., Nishimaki, R., Yamada, S., Yamakawa, T.: Constrained PRFs for NC^1 in traditional groups. IACR Cryptol. ePrint Arch. **2018**, 154 (2018)

4. Boneh, D., Boyen, X.: Short signatures without random oracles. In: Cachin, C., Camenisch, J.L. (eds.) EUROCRYPT 2004. LNCS, vol. 3027, pp. 56–73. Springer, Heidelberg (2004). https://doi.org/10.1007/978-3-540-24676-3_4

5. Bellare, M., Cash, D.: Pseudorandom functions and permutations provably secure against related-key attacks. IACR Cryptol. ePrint Arch., 397 (2010). Version 20150729:233210. Preliminary Version Appeared in CRYPTO 2010

6. Bellare, M., Cash, D.: Pseudorandom functions and permutations provably secure against related-key attacks. In: Rabin, T. (ed.) CRYPTO 2010. LNCS, vol. 6223, pp. 666–684. Springer, Heidelberg (2010). https://doi.org/10.1007/978-3-642-14623-7_36

7. Boneh, D., Franklin, M.K.: Identity-based encryption from the weil pairing. SIAM J. Comput. **32**(3), 586–615 (2003)

8. Banerjee, A., Fuchsbauer, G., Peikert, C., Pietrzak, K., Stevens, S.: Key-homomorphic constrained pseudorandom functions. In: Dodis, Y., Nielsen, J.B. (eds.) TCC 2015, Part II. LNCS, vol. 9015, pp. 31–60. Springer, Heidelberg (2015). https://doi.org/10.1007/978-3-662-46497-7_2

9. Barak, B., Goldreich, O., Impagliazzo, R., Rudich, S., Sahai, A., Vadhan, S.P., Yang, K.: On the (im)possibility of obfuscating programs. J. ACM **59**(2), 601–648 (2012)

10. Boyle, E., Goldwasser, S., Ivan, I.: Functional signatures and pseudorandom functions. In: Krawczyk, H. (ed.) PKC 2014. LNCS, vol. 8383, pp. 501–519. Springer, Heidelberg (2014). https://doi.org/10.1007/978-3-642-54631-0_29

11. Bitansky, N.: Verifiable random functions from non-interactive witness-indistinguishable proofs. In: Kalai, Y., Reyzin, L. (eds.) TCC 2017. LNCS, vol. 10678, pp. 567–594. Springer, Cham (2017). https://doi.org/10.1007/978-3-319-70503-3_19

12. Boneh, D., Kim, S., Montgomery, H.: Private puncturable PRFs from standard lattice assumptions. In: Coron, J.-S., Nielsen, J.B. (eds.) EUROCRYPT 2017, Part I. LNCS, vol. 10210, pp. 415–445. Springer, Cham (2017). https://doi.org/10.1007/978-3-319-56620-7_15

13. Boneh, D., Lewi, K., Wu, D.J.: Constraining pseudorandom functions privately. In: Fehr, S. (ed.) PKC 2017, Part II. LNCS, vol. 10175, pp. 494–524. Springer, Heidelberg (2017). https://doi.org/10.1007/978-3-662-54388-7_17

14. Brakerski, Z., Tsabary, R., Vaikuntanathan, V., Wee, H.: Private constrained PRFs (and mode) from LWE. In: TCC 2017 (2017)

15. Brakerski, Z., Vaikuntanathan, V.: Constrained key-homomorphic PRFs from standard lattice assumptions. In: Dodis, Y., Nielsen, J.B. (eds.) TCC 2015, Part II. LNCS, vol. 9015, pp. 1–30. Springer, Heidelberg (2015). https://doi.org/10.1007/978-3-662-46497-7_1

16. Boneh, D., Waters, B.: Constrained pseudorandom functions and their applications. In: Sako, K., Sarkar, P. (eds.) ASIACRYPT 2013, Part II. LNCS, vol. 8270, pp. 280–300. Springer, Heidelberg (2013). https://doi.org/10.1007/978-3-642-42045-0_15

17. Boyle, E., Gilboa, N., Ishai, Y.: Breaking the circuit size barrier for secure computation under DDH. In: Robshaw, M., Katz, J. (eds.) CRYPTO 2016, Part I. LNCS, vol. 9814, pp. 509–539. Springer, Heidelberg (2016). https://doi.org/10.1007/978-3-662-53018-4_19

18. Canetti, R., Chen, Y.: Constraint-hiding constrained PRFs for NC^1 from LWE. In: EUROCRYPT 2017, Part I, pp. 446–476 (2017)

19. Cohen, A., Goldwasser, S., Vaikuntanathan, V.: Aggregate pseudorandom functions and connections to learning. In: Dodis, Y., Nielsen, J.B. (eds.) TCC 2015, Part II. LNCS, vol. 9015, pp. 61–89. Springer, Heidelberg (2015). https://doi.org/10.1007/978-3-662-46497-7_3

20. Cook, S.A., Hoover, H.J.: A depth-universal circuit. SIAM J. Comput. **14**(4), 833–839 (1985)

21. Camenisch, J., Hohenberger, S., Lysyanskaya, A.: Compact E-Cash. In: Cramer, R. (ed.) EUROCRYPT 2005. LNCS, vol. 3494, pp. 302–321. Springer, Heidelberg (2005). https://doi.org/10.1007/11426639_18

22. Döttling, N., Garg, S.: Identity-based encryption from the diffie-hellman assumption. In: Katz, J., Shacham, H. (eds.) CRYPTO 2017, Part I. LNCS, vol. 10401, pp. 537–569. Springer, Cham (2017). https://doi.org/10.1007/978-3-319-63688-7_18

23. Deshpande, A., Koppula, V., Waters, B.: Constrained pseudorandom functions for unconstrained inputs. In: Fischlin, M., Coron, J.-S. (eds.) EUROCRYPT 2016, Part II. LNCS, vol. 9666, pp. 124–153. Springer, Heidelberg (2016). https://doi.org/10.1007/978-3-662-49896-5_5

24. Fuchsbauer, G., Konstantinov, M., Pietrzak, K., Rao, V.: Adaptive security of constrained PRFs. In: Sarkar, P., Iwata, T. (eds.) ASIACRYPT 2014, Part II. LNCS, vol. 8874, pp. 82–101. Springer, Heidelberg (2014). https://doi.org/10.1007/978-3-662-45608-8_5

25. Garg, S., Gentry, C., Halevi, S.: Candidate multilinear maps from ideal lattices. In: Johansson, T., Nguyen, P.Q. (eds.) EUROCRYPT 2013. LNCS, vol. 7881, pp. 1–17. Springer, Heidelberg (2013). https://doi.org/10.1007/978-3-642-38348-9_1

26. Garg, S., Gentry, C., Halevi, S., Raykova, M., Sahai, A., Waters, B.: Candidate indistinguishability obfuscation and functional encryption for all circuits. SIAM J. Comput. **45**(3), 882–929 (2016)

27. Goldreich, O., Goldwasser, S., Micali, S.: How to construct random functions. J. ACM **33**(4), 792–807 (1986)

28. Goyal, R., Hohenberger, S., Koppula, V., Waters, B.: A generic approach to constructing and proving verifiable random functions. In: Kalai, Y., Reyzin, L. (eds.) TCC 2017. LNCS, vol. 10678, pp. 537–566. Springer, Cham (2017). https://doi.org/10.1007/978-3-319-70503-3_18

29. Goldenberg, D., Liskov, M.: On related-secret pseudorandomness. In: Micciancio, D. (ed.) TCC 2010. LNCS, vol. 5978, pp. 255–272. Springer, Heidelberg (2010). https://doi.org/10.1007/978-3-642-11799-2_16

30. Goyal, V., O'Neill, A., Rao, V.: Correlated-input secure hash functions. In: Ishai, Y. (ed.) TCC 2011. LNCS, vol. 6597, pp. 182–200. Springer, Heidelberg (2011). https://doi.org/10.1007/978-3-642-19571-6_12

31. Gorbunov, S., Vaikuntanathan, V., Wee, H.: Functional encryption with bounded collusions via multi-party computation. In: Safavi-Naini, R., Canetti, R. (eds.) CRYPTO 2012. LNCS, vol. 7417, pp. 162–179. Springer, Heidelberg (2012). https://doi.org/10.1007/978-3-642-32009-5_11

32. Hofheinz, D., Kamath, A., Koppula, V., Waters, B.: Adaptively secure constrained pseudorandom functions. IACR Cryptol. ePrint Arch. **2014**, 720 (2014)

33. Hohenberger, S., Koppula, V., Waters, B.: Adaptively secure puncturable pseudorandom functions in the standard model. In: Iwata, T., Cheon, J.H. (eds.) ASIACRYPT 2015, Part I. LNCS, vol. 9452, pp. 79–102. Springer, Heidelberg (2015). https://doi.org/10.1007/978-3-662-48797-6_4

34. Ishai, Y., Kilian, J., Nissim, K., Petrank, E.: Extending oblivious transfers efficiently. In: Boneh, D. (ed.) CRYPTO 2003. LNCS, vol. 2729, pp. 145–161. Springer, Heidelberg (2003). https://doi.org/10.1007/978-3-540-45146-4_9

35. Kiayias, A., Papadopoulos, S., Triandopoulos, N., Zacharias, T.: Delegatable pseudorandom functions and applications. ACMCCS **2013**, 669–684 (2013)

36. Naor, M., Reingold, O.: Number-theoretic constructions of efficient pseudo-random functions. J. ACM **51**(2), 231–262 (2004)

37. Peikert, C., Shiehian, S.: Privately constraining and programming PRFs, the LWE way. In: Abdalla, M., Dahab, R. (eds.) PKC 2018. LNCS, vol. 10770, pp. 675–701. Springer, Cham (2018). https://doi.org/10.1007/978-3-319-76581-5_23

38. Yamada, S.: Asymptotically compact adaptively secure lattice IBEs and verifiable random functions via generalized partitioning techniques. In: Katz, J., Shacham, H. (eds.) CRYPTO 2017, Part III. LNCS, vol. 10403, pp. 161–193. Springer, Cham (2017). https://doi.org/10.1007/978-3-319-63697-9_6
39. Zhandry, M.: How to avoid obfuscation using witness PRFs. In: Kushilevitz, E., Malkin, T. (eds.) TCC 2016, Part II. LNCS, vol. 9563, pp. 421–448. Springer, Heidelberg (2016). https://doi.org/10.1007/978-3-662-49099-0_16

Lattices

GGH15 Beyond Permutation Branching Programs: Proofs, Attacks, and Candidates

Yilei Chen[1](✉), Vinod Vaikuntanathan[2], and Hoeteck Wee[3]

[1] Boston University, Boston, USA
chenyl@bu.edu
[2] MIT, Cambridge, USA
vinodv@csail.mit.edu
[3] CNRS and ENS, PSL, Paris, France
wee@di.ens.fr

Abstract. We carry out a systematic study of the GGH15 graded encoding scheme used with *general* branching programs. This is motivated by the fact that general branching programs are more efficient than permutation branching programs and also substantially more expressive in the read-once setting. Our main results are as follows:

- **Proofs.** We present new constructions of private constrained PRFs and lockable obfuscation, for constraints (resp. functions to be obfuscated) that are computable by general branching programs. Our constructions are secure under LWE with subexponential approximation factors. Previous constructions of this kind crucially rely on the permutation structure of the underlying branching programs. Using general branching programs allows us to obtain more efficient constructions for certain classes of constraints (resp. functions), while posing new challenges in the proof, which we overcome using new proof techniques.

- **Attacks.** We extend the previous attacks on indistinguishability obfuscation (iO) candidates that use GGH15 encodings. The new attack simply uses the rank of a matrix as the distinguisher, so we call it a "rank attack". The rank attack breaks, among others, the iO candidate for general read-once branching programs by Halevi, Halevi, Shoup and Stephens-Davidowitz (CCS 2017).

- **Candidate Witness Encryption and iO.** Drawing upon insights from our proofs and attacks, we present simple candidates for witness encryption and iO that resist the existing attacks, using GGH15 encodings. Our candidate for witness encryption crucially exploits the fact that formulas in conjunctive normal form (CNFs) can be represented by general, *read-once* branching programs.

1 Introduction

Graph-induced graded encodings – henceforth called GGH15 encodings – were put forth by Gentry, Gorbunov and Halevi [23] as a candidate instantiation of (approximate) cryptographic multilinear maps [8,20], with the hope that these

© International Association for Cryptologic Research 2018
H. Shacham and A. Boldyreva (Eds.): CRYPTO 2018, LNCS 10992, pp. 577–607, 2018.
https://doi.org/10.1007/978-3-319-96881-0_20

encodings could in turn be used to build advanced cryptographic primitives whose security is related to the hardness of the learning with errors (LWE) problem [36]. In addition, following [20,21], the same work presented candidate constructions of multi-party key exchange and indistinguishability obfuscation (iO) starting from these graded encoding schemes.

In the last few years, a very fruitful line of works has shed a great deal of insight into the use of GGH15 encodings in two complementary settings: constructing security reductions from LWE (partially validating the intuition in GGH15), and demonstrating efficient attacks. The former include constructions of private constrained pseudorandom functions (PRFs) [13], lockable obfuscation (aka obfuscating the "compute-then-compare" functionality) [26,38] and encryption schemes that constitute counter-examples for circular security [27,30]. The latter include efficient attacks [15,17] on the key exchange and iO candidates described in [23]. One of the key distinctions between the two settings is whether an adversary can obtain encodings of zero from honest evaluations. For all the applications that can be based on LWE, the adversary cannot trivially obtain encodings of zero; whereas the attacks apply only to settings where the adversary can trivially obtain encodings of zero. There is much grey area in between, where we neither know how to obtain encodings of zero nor are we able to prove security based on LWE (e.g., in the setting of witness encryption).

This work. In this work, we explore the use of GGH15 encodings together with general (non-permutation) matrix branching programs. In particular, we present (i) new constructions of private constrained PRFs and lockable obfuscation from LWE, (ii) new attacks on iO candidates, and (iii) new candidates for iO and witness encryption that resist our new attacks as well as prior attacks. At the core of these results are new techniques and insights into the use of GGH15 encodings for a larger class of branching programs.

Most of the prior constructions and candidates for the primitives we consider follow the template laid out in [21]: start with the class of NC^1 circuits, represented using permutation branching programs, which are specified by a collection of permutation matrices $\{\mathbf{M}_{i,b}\}_{i\in[h],b\in\{0,1\}}$. Computation in such a program proceeds by taking a subset product of these matrices, where the choice of the subset is dictated by the input but the order in which the matrices are multiplied is oblivious to the input. To cryptographically "protect" this computation, we will first pre-process and randomize $\{\mathbf{M}_{i,b}\}$ to obtain a new collection of matrices $\{\hat{\mathbf{S}}_{i,b}\}$, and then encode the latter using graded encodings. Functionality (e.g. evaluation in lockable obfuscation and iO) relies on the fact that we can check whether some subset product of the $\hat{\mathbf{S}}_{i,b}$'s is zero (or the identity matrix) using the underlying graded encodings. Any security proof or attack would of course depend on the class of matrices $\mathbf{M}_{i,b}$'s we start out with, and how the $\hat{\mathbf{S}}_{i,b}$'s are derived.

Beyond permutation matrices. From a feasibility point of view, working with permutation matrices is without loss of generality. We know that any NC^1 circuit (or even a logspace computation) can be represented as a permutation matrix branching program [5]. Moreover, any general branching program, where the underlying matrices are possibly low-rank, can be converted to a permutation branching program with a polynomial blow-up in the number and dimensions of these matrices. Nonetheless, there are advantages to working with more general, not necessarily permutation or full-rank, branching programs:

- The first is concrete efficiency. For instance, representing equality or point functions on ℓ-bit string would use $O(\ell^2)$ constant-width matrices with permutation branching programs, but just 2ℓ width-one matrices (i.e. entries) with general branching programs.
- The second is that in the read-once setting, general branching programs are more expressive than permutation branching programs. The restriction to read-once branching programs is useful in applications such as iO and witness encryption, as they allow us to disregard "multiplicative bundling" factors that protect against mixed-input attacks, which in turn yields much more efficient constructions. This was shown in a recent work of Halevi, Halevi, Shoup and Stephens-Davidowitz (HHSS) [29], which presented an iO candidate for read-once branching programs based on GGH15 encodings. Their candidate is designed for general read-once branching programs, as read-once permutation branching programs only capture an extremely limited class of functions.

This raises the natural question of the security of GGH15-based constructions when applied to general (non-permutation, possibly low-rank) matrix branching programs, as is exactly the focus of this work. Indeed, the afore-mentioned proof techniques *and* attacks break down in this setting. In particular, the HHSS iO candidate appears to resist the existing attacks in [15,17], thanks in part to the use of low-rank matrices (cf. [29, Sect. 1.2]).

We proceed to describe our results and techniques in more detail.

1.1 Our Results I: New Cryptographic Constructions from LWE

We present new constructions of private constrained PRFs and lockable obfuscation that work directly with general matrix branching programs. As with prior works, our constructions are secure under the LWE assumption with subexponential approximation factors. Our result generalizes the previous constructions in [13,26,38] which only work for permutation branching programs, and yields improved concrete efficiency for several interesting classes of functions that can be represented more efficiently using general branching programs, as described next.

- Lockable obfuscation [26,38] refers to the average-case secure virtual blackbox (VBB) obfuscation for a class of functionalities $\mathbf{C}[f, y]$ which, on input x, output 1 if $f(x) = y$ and 0 otherwise. The average-case refers (only) to a uniformly random choice of y (more generally, y with sufficient min-entropy). For lockable obfuscation, we obtain improved constructions for a class of "compute" functions where each output bit is computed using a general branching program applied to the input x (whereas [26,38] require permutation branching programs). To illustrate the efficiency gain, consider the case where each output bit of the underlying function f computes a disjunction or conjunction of the ℓ input bits. In this case, we achieve up to a quadratic gain in efficiency due to our support for general branching programs. This class generalizes the distributional conjunction obfuscator studied in [10,12,38].

– Private puncturable PRFs are an important special case of constrained PRFs, with many applications such as 2-server private information retrieval (PIR) [6]. We obtain a very simple private puncturable PRF with a quadratic efficiency improvement over the recent GGH15-based construction of Canetti and Chen [13]. Nonetheless, our construction is admittedly less efficient –for most settings of parameters– than the more complex constructions in [6,11] that combines techniques from both fully-homomorphic and attribute-based encryption.

Next, we provide a very brief overview of our techniques, and defer a more detailed technical overview to Sect. 2.

New constructions and proof techniques. A GGH15 encoding of a low-norm matrix $\hat{\mathbf{S}}$ w.r.t. two matrices $\mathbf{A}_0$ and $\mathbf{A}_1$ is defined to be along the edge $\mathbf{A}_0 \mapsto \mathbf{A}_1$ and is computed as

$$\mathbf{D} \leftarrow \mathbf{A}_0^{-1}(\hat{\mathbf{S}}\mathbf{A}_1 + \mathbf{E})$$

where for all $\mathbf{A}, \mathbf{Y}$ with proper dimensions, the notation $\mathbf{D} \leftarrow \mathbf{A}^{-1}(\mathbf{Y})$ means that $\mathbf{D}$ is a random low-norm matrix such that $\mathbf{A}\mathbf{D} = \mathbf{Y} \bmod q$.

The constructions in [13,26,27,38] encode any permutation matrix $\mathbf{M} \in \{0,1\}^{w \times w}$ as a GGH15 encoding of $\hat{\mathbf{S}} = \mathbf{M} \otimes \mathbf{S}$, i.e.

$$\mathbf{A}_0^{-1}((\mathbf{M} \otimes \mathbf{S})\mathbf{A}_1 + \mathbf{E})$$

for a random low-norm $\mathbf{S}$. The crux of the analysis is to show that $\mathbf{M}$ is hidden under the LWE assumption, namely: for any *permutation* matrix $\mathbf{M} \in \{0,1\}^{w \times w}$,

$$(\mathbf{A}_0, \mathbf{A}_0^{-1}((\mathbf{M} \otimes \mathbf{S})\mathbf{A}_1 + \mathbf{E})) \approx_c (\mathbf{A}_0, \mathbf{V}) \tag{1}$$

where $\mathbf{A}_0, \mathbf{A}_1$ are uniformly random over $\mathbb{Z}_q$, $\mathbf{S}, \mathbf{V}, \mathbf{E}$ are random low-norm matrices, $\approx_c$ stands for computational indistinguishable. The proof of (1) follows quite readily from the fact that given any permutation matrix $\mathbf{M} \in \{0,1\}^{w \times w}$, we have:

$$(\mathbf{A}, (\mathbf{M} \otimes \mathbf{S})\mathbf{A} + \mathbf{E}) \approx_c (\mathbf{A}, \mathbf{U})$$

under the LWE assumption, where $\mathbf{U}$ is uniformly random.

However, this statement is false for arbitrary matrices $\mathbf{M}$, take for instance $\mathbf{M} = \mathbf{0}^{w \times w}$, the all-0 matrix. Indeed, the reader can easily come up with rank-$(w-1)$ matrices $\mathbf{M}$ for which Eq. (1) fails to hold.

In our construction, we encode an arbitrary matrix $\mathbf{M}$ as a GGH15 encoding of

$$\hat{\mathbf{S}} = \begin{pmatrix} \mathbf{M} \otimes \mathbf{S} & \\ & \mathbf{S} \end{pmatrix}$$

That is, we append $\mathbf{S}$ along the diagonal. We then establish the following analogue of (1) under the LWE assumption: for any *arbitrary* $\mathbf{M} \in \{0,1\}^{w \times w}$,

$$\left(\mathbf{J} \mathbf{A}_0, \mathbf{A}_0^{-1} \left(\begin{pmatrix} \mathbf{M} \otimes \mathbf{S} & \\ & \mathbf{S} \end{pmatrix} \mathbf{A}_1 + \mathbf{E} \right) \right) \approx_c \left(\mathbf{J} \mathbf{A}_0, \mathbf{V} \right) \qquad (2)$$

where $\mathbf{J}$ is any matrix of the form $[\star \mid \mathbf{I}]$, and $\mathbf{A}_0, \mathbf{A}_1, \mathbf{S}, \mathbf{V}, \mathbf{E}$ are distributed as in (1). This statement is qualitatively incomparable with (1): it is stronger in that it works for *arbitrary* $\mathbf{M}$, but weaker in that the distinguisher only sees partial information about $\mathbf{A}_0$.

Proving the statement in (2) requires a new proof strategy where we will treat $\mathbf{S}$ (instead of $\mathbf{A}_0, \mathbf{A}_1$) as a public matrix known to the distinguisher. In particular, we start with taking the bottom part of $\mathbf{A}_1$ as the LWE secret, in conjunction with the public $\mathbf{S}$ in the bottom-right diagonal; then use an extension of the trapdoor sampling lemma by Gentry et al. [25] to produce an "oblique" (while *statistically* indistinguishable) preimage sample using only the trapdoor of the top part of $\mathbf{A}_0$; finally argue that the "oblique" sample is *computationally* indistinguishable from random Gaussian using the top part of $\mathbf{A}_0$ as the LWE secret. Walking through these steps requires new techniques on analyzing the trapdoor sampling detailed in Sect. 4. We refer the readers to Sects. 2.2 and 5.3 for further explanation of the proof techniques.

Next, we show that the weaker guarantee in (2) (in that the distinguisher gets $\mathbf{J} \mathbf{A}_0$ instead of $\mathbf{A}_0$) is sufficient for constructions of constrained PRFs and lockable obfuscation based on GGH15 encodings; this yields new constructions that are directly applicable to general, non-permutation matrix branching programs.

1.2 Our Results II: New Attacks on iO Candidates

Next, we turn our attention to iO, where adversaries can obtain encodings of zero through honest evaluations. Concretely, we focus on iO candidates that follow the [21] template described earlier in the introduction: start with a branching program $\{\mathbf{M}_{i,b}\}$, pre-process and randomize $\{\mathbf{M}_{i,b}\}$ to obtain a matrices $\{\hat{\mathbf{S}}_{i,b}\}$, and encode the latter using GGH15 encodings.

We present an attack that run in time $\mathsf{size}^{O(c)}$ for general read-c branching programs of size size. In particular, we have a polynomial-time attack when c is constant, as is the case for the iO candidate in [29] which corresponds to $c = 1$. Our attack covers various "safeguards" in the literature, such as Kilian-style randomization, multiplicative bundling, and diagonal padding.

Attack overview. Our attack is remarkably simple, and proceeds in two steps:

1. Compute a matrix $\mathbf{V}$ whose (i,j)'th entry correspond to an iO evaluation on input $x^{(i)} \mid y^{(j)}$ that yields an encoding of zero. The dimensions of $\mathbf{V}$ and the number of evaluations is polynomial in size^c.
2. Output the rank of $\mathbf{V}$ (over $\mathbb{Z}$). More precisely, check if $\mathsf{rank}(\mathbf{V})$ is above some threshold.

Step 1 was used in the attack of Coron et al. [17] and Chen et al. [15], both originated from the zeroizing attack of Cheon et al. [16] on CLT13 [19]. The novelty of our analysis lies in showing that $\mathsf{rank}(\mathbf{V})$ leaks information about the $\hat{\mathbf{S}}_{i,b}$'s and thus the plaintext branching program matrices $\mathbf{M}_{i,b}$'s. So we call the attack a "rank attack".

Our attack improves upon the previous attack of Chen et al. [15] on GGH15-based iO candidates in several ways: (i) we have a classical as opposed to a quantum attack, and (ii) it is applicable to a larger class of branching programs, i.e. branching programs that are not necessarily input-partitioned or using permutation matrices.

Why the rank-attack works? To get a taste of the rank-attack, let's consider an oversimplified description of the iO candidates based on GGH15 encodings. Let $\{\hat{\mathbf{S}}_{i,b}\}$ be the randomization of plaintext matrices $\{\mathbf{M}_{i,b}\}$. Then the obfuscated code is the GGH15 encodings of the $\hat{\mathbf{S}}_{i,b}$ matrices

$$\mathbf{A}_0, \{\mathbf{D}_{i,b}\}_{i \in [h], b \in \{0,1\}} \text{ where } \mathbf{D}_{i,b} \leftarrow \mathbf{A}_{i-1}^{-1} \left(\hat{\mathbf{S}}_{i,b} \mathbf{A}_i + \mathbf{E}_{i,b} \right)$$

Evaluation proceeds by first computing the product of $\mathbf{A}_0$ with the subset product of the $\mathbf{D}_{i,b}$ matrices. As an example, for the obfuscation of a 3-step branching program that computes all-0 functionality, the evaluation on input $x = 000$ gives

$$\mathsf{Eval}(x) = \mathbf{A}_0 \cdot \mathbf{D}_{1,0} \cdot \mathbf{D}_{2,0} \cdot \mathbf{D}_{3,0} = \hat{\mathbf{S}}_{1,0}\hat{\mathbf{S}}_{2,0}\mathbf{E}_{3,0} + \hat{\mathbf{S}}_{1,0}\mathbf{E}_{2,0}\mathbf{D}_{3,0} + \mathbf{E}_{1,0}\mathbf{D}_{2,0}\mathbf{D}_{3,0} \quad (3)$$

To give a sense of why computing the rank is useful in an attack, we make a further simplification, that suppose we manage to learn the monomial

$$\hat{\mathbf{S}}_{1,0}\mathbf{E}_{2,0}\mathbf{D}_{3,0} \in \mathbb{Z}^{t \times m}.$$

W.h.p., the Gaussians $\mathbf{E}_{2,0}, \mathbf{D}_{3,0}$ and therefore its product $\mathbf{E}_{2,0}\mathbf{D}_{3,0}$ are full rank (over $\mathbb{Z}$), so the rank of this term is that of $\hat{\mathbf{S}}_{1,0}$, which leaks some information about the rank of $\mathbf{M}_{1,0}$. Note that learning the rank of $\mathbf{M}_{1,0}$ leaks no useful information for permutation branching programs, but is sufficient to break iO for general branching programs.

In actuality, a single evaluation corresponding to an encoding of zero only provides a single value in $\mathbb{Z}$, which is a *sum* of products of the form above, multiplied by some left and right bookend vectors. To extract the important information out of the summation of random-looking terms, we will first form a matrix $\mathbf{V}$ of evaluations on appropriately chosen inputs. The matrix $\mathbf{V}$ has the property that it factors into the product of two matrices $\mathbf{V} = \mathbf{X} \cdot \mathbf{Y}$. We proceed analogously to the toy example in two steps with $\mathbf{X}, \mathbf{Y}$ playing the roles of $\hat{\mathbf{S}}_{1,0}$ and $\mathbf{E}_{2,0} \cdot \mathbf{D}_{3,0}$:

1. argue that $\mathbf{Y}$ is non-singular over $\mathbb{Q}$ so that $\mathsf{rank}(\mathbf{V}) = \mathsf{rank}(\mathbf{X})$, and
2. argue that $\mathsf{rank}(\mathbf{X})$ leaks information about the underlying branching program.

So far we have described what the analysis looks like for the read-once branching programs (i.e. $c = 1$). For the case of $c > 1$, the analysis has the flavor of converting the obfuscated code of a read-c branching program into the read-once setting, using the "tensor switching lemmas" from previous attacks [4,18] on iO candidates that use GGH13 and CLT13.

The code that demonstrates the attack as a proof-of-concept is available at https://github.com/wildstrawberry/cryptanalysesBPobfuscators.

1.3 Our Results III: New Candidates

Given the insights from our proofs and attacks, we present simple candidates for witness encryption and iO based on GGH15 encodings. Our witness encryption candidate relies on the observation from [24] that to build witness encryption for general NP relations, it suffices to build witness encryption for CNF formulas, and that we can represent CNF formulas using general, read-once branching programs. The ciphertext corresponding to a formula Ψ and a message $\mu \in \{0,1\}$ is of the form described in (2), namely

$$\mathbf{J}\mathbf{A}_0, \left\{ \mathbf{A}_{i-1}^{-1} \left(\begin{pmatrix} \mathbf{M}_{i,b} \otimes \mathbf{S}_{i,b} & \\ & \mu \mathbf{S}_{i,b} \end{pmatrix} \mathbf{A}_i + \mathbf{E}_{i,b} \right) \right\}$$

where $\mathbf{J}$ is a specific matrix of the form $[\star \mid \mathbf{I}]$ and the $\mathbf{M}_{i,b}$'s are the read-once branching program representing Ψ.

Starting from the witness encryption candidate, we also present an iO candidate for NC^1 circuits that appear to resist our rank attack as well as all prior attacks. In order to thwart the rank attack, our iO candidate necessarily reads each input bit $\omega(1)$ times. To then prevent mixed-input attacks, we rely on an extension of multiplicative bundling factors used in prior works that uses matrices instead of scalars.

We stress that an important design goal in these candidates is simplicity so as to facilitate the security analysis. We believe and anticipate that any attacks or partial security analysis for these candidates (perhaps in some weak idealized model cf. [22]) would enhance our understanding of witness encryption and obfuscation.

1.4 Discussion and Open Problems

Perspective. The proposal of candidate multilinear maps [20] from lattice-type assumptions in 2013 has triggered a major paradigm shift in cryptography and enabled numerous cryptographic applications, most notably indistinguishability obfuscation [21]. Among the three multilinear maps candidates [19,20,23], GGH15 is the only one that has served as a basis for new cryptographic applications based on established lattice problems, as demonstrated in e.g. [13,26,27,38]. We believe that extending the safe settings of GGH15 (where security can be based on the LWE assumption), as explored in this work through the generalized GGH15 framework as well as both proofs and attacks, will pave the way towards new cryptographic constructions.

Open problems. We conclude with a number of open problems:

- Study the security of our candidate for witness encryption, either prove security under instance-independent assumptions, or find a direct attack on the scheme. For the former (i.e., prove security), the only proof strategy in the existing literature is to build and prove a so-called positional witness encryption scheme [24], for which the security definition allows the adversary to obtain encodings of zeroes. Unfortunately, the natural extensions of our candidate witness encryption scheme to a positional variant are susceptible to the rank attack in the presence of encodings of zeroes. For the latter (i.e., directly attack the scheme), all existing attack strategies on GGH15 encodings as used in our candidate require encodings of zeroes, which are not readily available in the witness encryption setting.
- Find a polynomial-time attack for iO candidates for branching programs where every input repeats $c = O(\lambda)$ time where λ is the security parameter. The analysis of known attacks, including our rank attack, yields running times that grow exponentially with c. There are possibilities that the analysis is not tight and the rank attack or prior attacks could in fact succeed with a smaller running time. However we have not detected such a phenomenon with experiments for small c.
- Note that all our candidate constructions are of the form: $\mathbf{A}_J$, $\{\mathbf{D}_{i,b}\}_{i\in[h],b\in\{0,1\}}$ and evaluation/decryption proceeds by first computing $\mathbf{A}_J\mathbf{D}_{\mathbf{x}'} := \mathbf{A}_J \prod_{i=1}^{h} \mathbf{D}_{i,x_i'}$ for some $\mathbf{x}' \in \{0,1\}^h$. Consider the following restricted class of adversaries that only gets oracle access to $\mathbf{x}' \mapsto \mathbf{A}_J\mathbf{D}_{\mathbf{x}'}$ instead of $\mathbf{A}_j, \{\mathbf{D}_{i,b}\}_{i\in[h],b\in\{0,1\}}$. Note that our rank attack as well as various mixed-input and zeroizing attacks can all be implemented using this restricted adversaries. Can we prove (or break) security of our witness encryption or iO candidates against this restricted class of adversaries under some reasonable instance-independent assumptions?

Independent work. Variants of our new lemmas related to lattice preimage sampling in Sect. 4 were presented in an independent work of Goyal, Koppula and Waters [28], for different purposes from ours. In [28], the lemmas were used as intermediate building blocks en route a collusion resistant traitor tracing scheme based on the LWE assumption.

1.5   Reader's Guide

The rest of the article is organized as follows. Section 2 provides a more detailed overview of our techniques. Section 4 provides new lemmas related to lattice preimage sampling. Section 5 gives a formal construction of the generalized-GGH15 encoding, the security notions, and the main technical proof that suffices for the applications. Due to the page limitation we leave the applications, the attacks, and the witness encryption and iO candidates in the full version available at https://eprint.iacr.org/2018/360.

2   Technical Overview

In this section, we present a more detailed overview of our techniques. We briefly describe the notation used in this overview and the paper, and refer the reader to Sect. 3 for more details. We use boldface upper-case and lower-case letters for matrices and vectors respectively. Given a bit-string $\mathbf{x} \in \{0,1\}^h$, we use $\mathbf{M_x}$ to denote matrix subset product $\prod_{i=1}^{h} \mathbf{M}_{i,x_i}$. Given matrices $\mathbf{A}, \mathbf{B}$, we use $\mathbf{A}^{-1}(\mathbf{B})$ to denote a random low-norm Gaussian $\mathbf{D}$ satisfying $\mathbf{A D} = \mathbf{B} \bmod q$. Two probability distributions are connected by $\approx_s$ or $\approx_c$ if they are statistically close or computationally indistinguishable.

2.1   Generalized GGH15 Encodings

In this work, we think of GGH15 as encoding two collections of matrices, one collection is arbitrary and the other one is random, and computing some function γ of a subset product of these matrices; we refer to this as (generalized) γ-GGH15 encodings.[1] That is, the γ-GGH15 encoding takes as input two collections of matrices $\{\mathbf{M}_{i,b}\}_{i\in[\ell],b\in\{0,1\}}, \{\mathbf{S}_{i,b}\}_{i\in[\ell],b\in\{0,1\}}$, an additional matrix $\mathbf{A}_\ell$, and the output is a collection of matrices

$$\mathbf{A}_0, \{\mathbf{D}_{i,b}\}_{i\in[\ell],b\in\{0,1\}}$$

such that for all $\mathbf{x} \in \{0,1\}^\ell$, we have

$$\mathbf{A}_0 \cdot \mathbf{D_x} \approx \gamma(\mathbf{M_x}, \mathbf{S_x}) \cdot \mathbf{A}_\ell$$

where $\mathbf{M_x}, \mathbf{D_x}, \mathbf{S_x}$ denotes subset-product of matrices as defined earlier. Here,

$$\mathbf{M}_{i,b} \in \{0,1\}^{w\times w}, \mathbf{S}_{i,b} \in \mathbb{Z}^{n\times n}, \mathbf{A}_0, \mathbf{A}_\ell \in \mathbb{Z}_q^{\gamma(w,n)\times m}, \mathbf{D}_{i,b} \in \mathbb{Z}^{m\times m}.$$

Intuitively, we also want to hide the $\mathbf{M}_{i,b}$'s, which we will come back to after describing the choices for γ and the construction.

---

[1] See Remark 5.2 for a comparison with the original GGH15 encodings.

Choices for γ. There are several instantiations for γ in the literature [12, 13, 21, 23, 26, 29, 38]:

$$\gamma_{\times}(\mathbf{M}, \mathbf{S}) = \mathbf{M}\mathbf{S}, \ \gamma_{\otimes}(\mathbf{M}, \mathbf{S}) := \mathbf{M} \otimes \mathbf{S}, \ \gamma_{\mathrm{diag}}(\mathbf{M}, \mathbf{S}) := \begin{pmatrix} \mathbf{M} & \\ & \mathbf{S} \end{pmatrix}$$

where the first $\gamma_{\times}$ requires working with rings so that multiplication commutes. More generally, for the construction, we require that γ be multiplicatively homomorphic, so that

$$\gamma(\mathbf{M}, \mathbf{S})\gamma(\mathbf{M}', \mathbf{S}') = \gamma(\mathbf{M}\mathbf{M}', \mathbf{S}\mathbf{S}')$$

as is clearly satisfied by the three instantiations above.

The γ-GGH15 construction. We briefly describe the construction of γ-GGH15 encodings implicit in [23], from the view-point of "cascaded cancellations" [2, 27, 30]. The starting point of the construction is to expand $\gamma(\mathbf{M_x}, \mathbf{S_x}) \cdot \mathbf{A}_\ell$ using multiplicative homomorphism as a matrix product

$$\gamma(\mathbf{M_x}, \mathbf{S_x}) \cdot \mathbf{A}_\ell = \prod_{i=1}^{\ell} \gamma(\mathbf{M}_{i,x_i}, \mathbf{S}_{i,x_i}) \cdot \mathbf{A}_\ell$$

Next, it randomizes the product by sampling random (wide, rectangular) matrices $\mathbf{A}_0, \ldots, \mathbf{A}_{\ell-1}$ over $\mathbb{Z}_q$ along with their trapdoors, and rewrites the product as a series of "cascaded cancellations":

$$\gamma(\mathbf{M_x}, \mathbf{S_x}) \cdot \mathbf{A}_\ell = \mathbf{A}_0 \cdot \prod_{i=1}^{\ell} \mathbf{A}_{i-1}^{-1}(\gamma(\mathbf{M}_{i,x_i}, \mathbf{S}_{i,x_i})\mathbf{A}_i)$$

where $\mathbf{A}_{i-1}^{-1}(\cdot)$ denotes random low-norm Gaussian pre-images as defined earlier.[2]

For functionality, it suffices to define $\mathbf{D}_{i,b}$ to be $\mathbf{A}_{i-1}^{-1}(\gamma(\mathbf{M}_{i,b}, \mathbf{S}_{i,b})\mathbf{A}_i)$, but that would not be sufficient to hide the underlying $\mathbf{M}_{i,b}$'s. Instead, the construction introduces additional error terms $\{\mathbf{E}_{i,b}\}_{i \in [\ell], b \in \{0,1\}}$, and defines[3]

$$\mathbf{D}_{i,b} \leftarrow \mathbf{A}_{i-1}^{-1}(\gamma(\mathbf{M}_{i,b}, \mathbf{S}_{i,b})\mathbf{A}_i + \mathbf{E}_{i,b})$$

Observe that for all $\mathbf{x} \in \{0, 1\}^\ell$, we have

$$\mathbf{A}_0 \cdot \mathbf{D_x} \approx \gamma(\mathbf{M_x}, \mathbf{S_x}) \cdot \mathbf{A}_\ell$$

---

[2] A reader who is familiar with Kilian's randomization for branching programs should notice the similarity. In Kilian's randomization, we randomize the product

$$\mathbf{M_x} = \prod_{i=1}^{\ell} \mathbf{R}_{i-1}^{-1} \mathbf{M}_{i,x_i} \mathbf{R}_i$$

by picking random invertible matrices $\mathbf{R}_1, \ldots, \mathbf{R}_{\ell-1}$ along with $\mathbf{R}_0 = \mathbf{R}_\ell = \mathbf{I}$. Here, we replace the square matrices $\mathbf{R}_i$'s with wide rectangular matrices $\mathbf{A}_i$'s, and change from left-multiplying $\mathbf{R}_{i-1}^{-1}$ to sampling a random Gaussian preimage of $\mathbf{A}_{i-1}$.

[3] In the GGH15 terminology, $\mathbf{D}_{i,b}$ would be an encoding of $\gamma(\mathbf{M}_{i,b}, \mathbf{S}_{i,b})$ relative to the path $i - 1 \mapsto i$.

where $\approx$ refers to an additive error term that depends on $| \mathbf{D}_{i,b} |, | \mathbf{E}_{i,b} |, | \gamma(\mathbf{M}_{i,b}, \mathbf{S}_{i,b}) |$, which we require to be small.

Semantic security. Following [13,26,27,38], we consider the following notion of semantic security for γ-GGH15 encodings, namely that

(semantic security.) The output $(\mathbf{A}_0, \{\mathbf{D}_{i,b}\}_{i\in[\ell],b\in\{0,1\}})$ computationally hides $\{\mathbf{M}_{i,b}\}_{i\in[\ell],b\in\{0,1\}}$. We only require that security holds "on average" over random $\{\mathbf{S}_{i,b}\}_{i\in[\ell],b\in\{0,1\}}$, $\mathbf{A}_\ell$.

Prior works [13,26,38] showed that the $\gamma_\otimes$-GGH15 encodings achieve semantic security if we restrict the $\mathbf{M}_{i,b}$'s to be permutation matrices. That is,

Informal Lemma. Under the LWE assumption, we have that for all *permutation* matrices $\{\mathbf{M}_{i,b}\}_{i\in[\ell],b\in\{0,1\}}$,

$$(\mathbf{A}_0, \{\mathbf{D}_{i,0}, \mathbf{D}_{i,1}\}_{i\in[\ell]}) \approx_c (\mathbf{A}_0, \{\mathbf{V}_{i,0}, \mathbf{V}_{i,1}\}_{i\in[\ell]}) \qquad (4)$$

where $\mathbf{D}_{i,b} \leftarrow \mathbf{A}_{i-1}^{-1}((\mathbf{M}_{i,b} \otimes \mathbf{S}_{i,b})\mathbf{A}_i + \mathbf{E}_{i,b})$, and $\mathbf{V}_{i,0}, \mathbf{V}_{i,1}$ are random low-norm Gaussians.

As mentioned earlier in the introduction, the proof of security crucially relies on the fact that any permutation matrix $\mathbf{M}$, LWE tells us that $(\mathbf{A}, (\mathbf{M}\otimes\mathbf{S})\mathbf{A}+\mathbf{E}) \approx_c (\mathbf{A}, \mathbf{U})$, where $\mathbf{U}$ is uniformly random. We sketch the proof of the semantic security of $\gamma_\otimes$-GGH15 for $\ell = 1$, which extends readily to larger ℓ (here the major changes in the hybrid arguments are highlighted with boxes):

$$\left(\mathbf{A}_0, \{\mathbf{A}_0^{-1}((\mathbf{M}_{1,b} \otimes \mathbf{S}_{1,b})\mathbf{A}_1 + \mathbf{E}_{1,b})\}_{b\in\{0,1\}}\right)$$
$$\approx_c \left(\mathbf{A}_0, \{\mathbf{A}_0^{-1}(\boxed{\mathbf{U}_{1,b}})\}_{b\in\{0,1\}}\right) \quad // \text{ LWE}$$
$$\approx_s \left(\mathbf{A}_0, \{\boxed{\mathbf{V}_{1,b}}\}_{b\in\{0,1\}}\right) \quad // \text{ GPV}$$

2.2 This Work: Semantic Security for Arbitrary Matrices

Without further modifications, γ-GGH15 encoding does not achieve semantic security for arbitrary matrices. Concretely, given $\mathbf{A}_0, \mathbf{D}_{1,0}$, we can compute

$$\mathbf{A}_0 \cdot \mathbf{D}_{1,0} = \gamma(\mathbf{M}_{1,0}, \mathbf{S}_{1,0})\mathbf{A}_1 + \mathbf{E}_{1,0}$$

which might leak information about the structure of $\mathbf{M}_{1,0}$. In particular, we can distinguish between $\mathbf{M}_{1,0}$ being $\mathbf{I}^{w\times w}$ versus $\mathbf{0}^{w\times w}$ for all of $\gamma_\times, \gamma_\otimes, \gamma_{\text{diag}}$.

The key to our new cryptographic constructions for general branching programs is a new technical lemma asserting semantic security for γ_{diag}-GGH15 encodings with arbitrary matrices where we replace $\mathbf{A}_0$ with $\mathbf{J}\mathbf{A}_0$ for some wide bookend matrix $\mathbf{J}$ that statistically "loses" information about $\mathbf{A}_0$:

New Lemma, Informal. Under the LWE assumption, we have that for all matrices $\{\mathbf{M}_{i,b}\}_{i\in[\ell],b\in\{0,1\}}$ over $\mathbb{Z}$,

$$(\mathbf{J}\mathbf{A}_0, (\mathbf{D}_{i,0}, \mathbf{D}_{i,1})_{i\in\ell}) \approx_c (\mathbf{J}\mathbf{A}_0, (\mathbf{V}_{i,0}, \mathbf{V}_{i,1})_{i\in\ell}) \tag{5}$$

where $\mathbf{J}$ is any matrix of the form $[\star \mid \mathbf{I}]$, $\mathbf{D}_{i,b} \leftarrow \mathbf{A}_{i-1}^{-1}(\begin{pmatrix} \mathbf{M}_{i,b} & \\ & \mathbf{S}_{i,b} \end{pmatrix} \mathbf{A}_i + \mathbf{E}_{i,b})$, and $\mathbf{V}_{i,0}, \mathbf{V}_{i,1}$ are random low-norm Gaussians.

New proof technique. We prove a stronger statement for the semantic security of γ_{diag}-GGH15, namely the semantic security holds even given $\mathbf{S}_{1,0}, \mathbf{S}_{1,1}, \ldots, \mathbf{S}_{\ell,0}, \mathbf{S}_{\ell,1}$ (but not $\mathbf{A}_1, \ldots, \mathbf{A}_\ell$). Our proof departs significantly from the prior analysis – in particular, we will treat $\mathbf{A}_1, \ldots, \mathbf{A}_\ell$ as LWE secrets. Let $\overline{\mathbf{A}}_i, \underline{\mathbf{A}}_i$ denote the top and bottom parts of $\mathbf{A}$, and define $\overline{\mathbf{E}}_{i,b}, \underline{\mathbf{E}}_{i,b}$ analogously. This means that

$$\mathbf{A}_{i-1}^{-1}(\gamma_{\text{diag}}(\mathbf{M}_{i,b}, \mathbf{S}_{i,b})\mathbf{A}_i + \mathbf{E}_{i,b}) = \mathbf{A}_{i-1}^{-1}\begin{pmatrix} \mathbf{M}_{i,b}\overline{\mathbf{A}}_i + \overline{\mathbf{E}}_{i,b} \\ \mathbf{S}_{i,b}\underline{\mathbf{A}}_i + \underline{\mathbf{E}}_{i,b} \end{pmatrix}$$

We will use $\mathbf{A}_1, \ldots, \mathbf{A}_\ell$ as LWE secrets in the following order: $\underline{\mathbf{A}}_\ell, \ldots, \underline{\mathbf{A}}_1, \overline{\mathbf{A}}_0, \ldots, \overline{\mathbf{A}}_{\ell-1}$. We sketch the proof for $\ell = 1$ (and it extends readily to larger ℓ):

$$\left(\mathbf{J}\mathbf{A}_0, \{\mathbf{A}_0^{-1}\begin{pmatrix} \mathbf{M}_{1,b}\overline{\mathbf{A}}_1 + \overline{\mathbf{E}}_{1,b} \\ \mathbf{S}_{1,b}\underline{\mathbf{A}}_1 + \underline{\mathbf{E}}_{1,b} \end{pmatrix}\}_{b\in\{0,1\}}\right)$$

$$\approx_c \left(\mathbf{J}\mathbf{A}_0, \{\boxed{\overline{\mathbf{A}}_0^{-1}(\mathbf{M}_{1,b}\overline{\mathbf{A}}_1 + \overline{\mathbf{E}}_{1,b})}\}_{b\in\{0,1\}}\right)$$

$$\approx_s \left(\boxed{\mathbf{U}_0}, \{\overline{\mathbf{A}}_0^{-1}(\mathbf{M}_{1,b}\overline{\mathbf{A}}_1 + \overline{\mathbf{E}}_{1,b})\}_{b\in\{0,1\}}\right)$$

$$\approx_c \left(\mathbf{U}_0, \{\boxed{\mathbf{V}_{1,b}}\}_{b\in\{0,1\}}\right)$$

where the notations and analysis of hybrid arguments are as follows

- The first $\approx_c$ follow from a more general statement, namely for all i and for any $\mathbf{Z}_{i,b}$, we have

$$\left\{\mathbf{A}_{i-1}^{-1}\begin{pmatrix} \mathbf{Z}_{i,b} \\ \mathbf{S}_{i,b}\underline{\mathbf{A}}_i + \underline{\mathbf{E}}_{i,b} \end{pmatrix}\right\}_{b\in\{0,1\}} \approx_c \left\{\overline{\mathbf{A}}_{i-1}^{-1}(\mathbf{Z}_{i,b})\right\}_{b\in\{0,1\}}$$

even if the distinguisher gets $\mathbf{A}_{i-1}, \mathbf{S}_{i,b}, \mathbf{Z}_{i,b}$. The proof of this statement follows by first applying LWE with $\underline{\mathbf{A}}_i$ as the secret[4] to deduce that

$$\{\mathbf{S}_{i,b}, \mathbf{S}_{i,b}\underline{\mathbf{A}}_i + \underline{\mathbf{E}}_{i,b}\}_{b\in\{0,1\}} \approx_c \{\mathbf{S}_{i,b}, \mathbf{U}_{i,b}\}_{b\in\{0,1\}}$$

---

[4] Here, we could have used $\mathbf{S}_{i,0}, \mathbf{S}_{i,1}$ as the LWE secrets and $\underline{\mathbf{A}}_i$ as the public matrix; however, this strategy would break down when $\mathbf{M}_{i,b}$ depends on $\mathbf{S}_{i,b}$, which is needed in the applications.

where the $\mathbf{U}_{i,b}$ matrices are uniformly random over $\mathbb{Z}_q$, followed by a new statistical lemma about trapdoor sampling which tells us that for all but negligibly many $\mathbf{A}_{i-1}$, we have that for all $\mathbf{Z}_{i,b}$,

$$\mathbf{A}_{i-1}^{-1}\begin{pmatrix}\mathbf{Z}_{i,b}\\\mathbf{U}_{i,b}\end{pmatrix} \approx_s \overline{\mathbf{A}}_{i-1}^{-1}\left(\mathbf{Z}_{i,b}\right)$$

– The $\approx_s$ follows from the structure of $\mathbf{J}$, which implies $(\overline{\mathbf{A}}_0, \mathbf{J}\mathbf{A}_0) \approx_s (\overline{\mathbf{A}}_0, \mathbf{U}_0)$, where $\mathbf{U}_0$ is a uniformly random matrix.
– The final $\approx_c$ follows from a more general statement, which says that under the LWE assumption, we have that for any $\mathbf{Z}$,

$$\mathbf{A}^{-1}(\mathbf{Z}+\mathbf{E}) \approx_c \mathbf{A}^{-1}(\mathbf{U})$$

where the distributions are over random choices of $\mathbf{A}, \mathbf{E}, \mathbf{U}$, provided $\mathbf{A}$ is hidden from the distinguisher. The proof uses the Bonsai technique [14]. Suppose $\mathbf{A}$ is of the form $[\mathbf{A}_1 \mid \mathbf{A}_2]$ where $\mathbf{A}_1$ is uniformly random, $\mathbf{A}_2$ sampled with a trapdoor. Then, we have via the Bonsai technique [14]:

$$\mathbf{A}^{-1}(\mathbf{Z}+\mathbf{E}) \approx_s \begin{pmatrix}-\mathbf{V}\\\mathbf{A}_2^{-1}(\mathbf{A}_1\mathbf{V}+\mathbf{E}+\mathbf{Z})\end{pmatrix}$$

where $\mathbf{V}$ is a random low-norm Gaussian. We then apply the LWE assumption to $(\mathbf{V}, \mathbf{A}_1\mathbf{V}+\mathbf{E})$ with $\mathbf{A}_1$ as the LWE secret. Once we replace $\mathbf{A}_1\mathbf{V}+\mathbf{E}$ with a uniformly random matrix, the rest of the proof follows readily from the standard GPV lemma.

Extension: combining $\gamma_\otimes, \gamma_{diag}$. For the applications to private constrained PRFs and lockable obfuscation, we will rely on $\gamma_{\otimes\mathrm{diag}}$-GGH15 encodings, where

$$\gamma_{\otimes\mathrm{diag}}(\mathbf{M}, \mathbf{S}) := \begin{pmatrix}\mathbf{M}\otimes\mathbf{S} & \\ & \mathbf{S}\end{pmatrix}$$

We observe that our proof of semantic security for γ_{diag} also implies semantic security for $\gamma_{\otimes\mathrm{diag}}$, where we give out $\mathbf{J}\mathbf{A}_0$ instead of $\mathbf{A}_0$. This follows from the fact that our proof for γ_{diag} goes through even if the $\mathbf{M}_{i,b}$'s depend on the $\mathbf{S}_{i,b}$'s, since we treat the latter as public matrices when we invoke the LWE assumption.

2.3 New Cryptographic Constructions from LWE

Using $\gamma_{\otimes\mathrm{diag}}$-GGH15 encodings and the proof that semantic security of $\gamma_{\otimes\mathrm{diag}}$ holds for arbitrary $\mathbf{M}$ matrices, we are ready to construct private constrained PRFs and lockable obfuscation where the constraint/function can be recognized by arbitrary matrix branching programs. Here we briefly explain the private constrained PRF construction as an example.

Before that we recall some terminologies for matrix branching programs. In the overview, we focus on read-once matrix branching programs for notational simplicity, although our scheme works for general matrix branching programs with any input pattern and matrix pattern (possibly low-rank matrices). A (read-once) matrix branching program for a function $f_\Gamma : \{0,1\}^\ell \to \{0,1\}$ is specified by $\Gamma := \left\{ \{\mathbf{M}_{i,b}\}_{i\in[\ell],b\in\{0,1\}}, \mathbf{P}_0, \mathbf{P}_1 \right\}$ such that for all $\mathbf{x} \in \{0,1\}^\ell$,

$$\mathbf{M}_\mathbf{x} = \prod_{i=1}^{\ell} \mathbf{M}_{i,x_i} = \mathbf{P}_{f_\Gamma(x)}$$

We will work with families of branching programs $\{\Gamma\}$, which share the same $\mathbf{P}_0, \mathbf{P}_1$.

Private constrained PRFs. We proceed to provide an overview of our construction of private constrained PRFs using $\gamma_{\otimes\text{diag}}$-GGH15 encodings. As a quick overview of a private constrained PRF, a private constrained PRF allows the PRF master secret key holder to derive a constrained key given a constraint predicate C. The constrained key is required to randomize the output on every input x s.t. $C(x) = 0$, preserve the output on every input x s.t. $C(x) = 1$. In addition, the constraint C is required to be hidden given the description of the constrained key.

Let $\mathbf{e}_i \in \{0,1\}^{1\times w}$ denotes the unit vector with the ith coordinate being 1, the rest being 0. Consider a class of constraints recognizable by branching programs

$$\Gamma_C := \left\{ \{\mathbf{M}_{i,b} \in \{0,1\}^{w\times w}\}_{i\in[\ell],b\in\{0,1\}}, \mathbf{P}_0, \mathbf{P}_1 \right\},$$

where the target matrices $\mathbf{P}_0, \mathbf{P}_1$ satisfy $\mathbf{e}_1\mathbf{P}_0 = \mathbf{e}_1$, $\mathbf{e}_1\mathbf{P}_1 = \mathbf{0}^{1\times w}$.

We use $\gamma_{\otimes\text{diag}}$ to encode $\{\mathbf{M}_{i,b}\}_{i\in[\ell],b\in\{0,1\}}$, which means for $i = 0, ..., \ell$, $\mathbf{A}_i \in \mathbb{Z}_q^{(nw+n)\times m}$. Denote $\underline{\mathbf{A}}_0$ as the bottom n rows of $\mathbf{A}_i$, $\overline{\mathbf{A}}_i$ as the top nw rows of $\mathbf{A}_i$. Inside $\overline{\mathbf{A}}_i$ let $\overline{\mathbf{A}}_i^{(j)}$ denote the $(j-1)n^{th}$ to jn^{th} rows of $\overline{\mathbf{A}}_i$, for $j \in [w]$.

Define the output of the normal PRF evaluation as

$$\mathbf{x} \mapsto \lfloor \mathbf{S}_\mathbf{x}\underline{\mathbf{A}}_\ell \rceil_p$$

where $\lfloor \cdot \rceil_p$ denotes the rounding-to-$\mathbb{Z}_p$ operation used in previous LWE-based PRFs, which we suppress in the rest of this overview for notational simplicity.

We set $\mathbf{J} := (\mathbf{e}_1 \otimes \mathbf{I} \mid \mathbf{I})$ so that $\mathbf{J} \cdot \mathbf{A}_0 = \overline{\mathbf{A}}_0^{(1)} + \underline{\mathbf{A}}_0$, then

$$\mathbf{J} \cdot \gamma_{\otimes\text{diag}}(\mathbf{M}_\mathbf{x}, \mathbf{S}_\mathbf{x}) \cdot \mathbf{A}_\ell = ((\mathbf{e}_1 \cdot \mathbf{M}_\mathbf{x}) \otimes \mathbf{S}_\mathbf{x}) \cdot \overline{\mathbf{A}}_\ell + \mathbf{S}_\mathbf{x}\underline{\mathbf{A}}_\ell = \begin{cases} \mathbf{S}_\mathbf{x}\underline{\mathbf{A}}_\ell & \text{if } f_\Gamma(\mathbf{x}) = 1 \\ \mathbf{S}_\mathbf{x}\overline{\mathbf{A}}_\ell^{(1)} + \mathbf{S}_\mathbf{x}\underline{\mathbf{A}}_\ell & \text{if } f_\Gamma(\mathbf{x}) = 0 \end{cases}$$

Given Γ, the constrained key is constructed as

$$\overline{\mathbf{A}}_0^{(1)} + \underline{\mathbf{A}}_0, (\mathbf{D}_{i,0}, \mathbf{D}_{i,0})_{i\in[\ell]}$$

where $(\mathbf{A}_0, \{\mathbf{D}_{i,b}\}_{i\in[\ell],b\in\{0,1\}}) \leftarrow \text{GGHEnc}_{\otimes\text{diag}}(\{\mathbf{M}_{i,b}\}_{i\in[\ell],b\in\{0,1\}}, \{\mathbf{S}_{i,b}\}_{i\in[\ell],b\in\{0,1\}}, \mathbf{A}_\ell)$.

The constrained evaluation on an input $\mathbf{x}$ gives

$$(\overline{\mathbf{A}}_0^{(1)} + \underline{\mathbf{A}}_0) \cdot \mathbf{D_x} \approx \mathbf{J} \cdot \gamma_{\otimes \mathrm{diag}}(\mathbf{M_x}, \mathbf{S_x}) \cdot \mathbf{A}_\ell$$

which equals to $\mathbf{S_x}\underline{\mathbf{A}}_\ell$ if $f_\Gamma(\mathbf{x}) = 1$, $\mathbf{S_x}\overline{\mathbf{A}}_\ell^{(1)} + \mathbf{S_x}\underline{\mathbf{A}}_\ell$ if $f_\Gamma(\mathbf{x}) = 0$.

A special case: private puncturable PRFs. A private puncturable PRF can be obtained by simply using branching program with 1×1 matrices (i.e. let $w = 1$). The punctured key at $\mathbf{x}^*$ is given by

$$\overline{\mathbf{A}}_0 + \underline{\mathbf{A}}_0, \{\mathbf{D}_{i,b}\}_{i \in [\ell], b \in \{0,1\}}$$

where

$$\mathbf{D}_{i,x_i^*} \leftarrow \mathbf{A}_{i-1}^{-1}\left(\begin{pmatrix}\mathbf{S}_{i,x_i^*} & \\ & \mathbf{S}_{i,x_i^*}\end{pmatrix}\mathbf{A}_i + \mathbf{E}_{i,x_i^*}\right), \mathbf{D}_{i,1-x_i^*} \leftarrow \mathbf{A}_{i-1}^{-1}\left(\begin{pmatrix}\mathbf{0} & \\ & \mathbf{S}_{i,1-x^*}\end{pmatrix}\mathbf{A}_i + \mathbf{E}_{i,1-x_i^*}\right).$$

The construction extends naturally to allow us to puncture at sets of points specified by a wildcard pattern $\{0, 1, \star\}^\ell$.

Security. In the security proof, we will use the fact that whenever $f_\Gamma(\mathbf{x}) = 0$, constrained evaluation outputs $\boxed{\mathbf{S_x}\overline{\mathbf{A}}_\ell^{(1)}} + \mathbf{S_x}\underline{\mathbf{A}}_\ell$, so that the normal PRF output is masked by the boxed term. More formally, in the security game, the adversary gets a constrained key for Γ_C, and oracle access to a PRF evaluation oracle Eval. We consider the following sequence of games:

- Replace the output of the Eval oracle by

$$(\overline{\mathbf{A}}_0^{(1)} + \underline{\mathbf{A}}_0) \cdot \mathbf{D_x} - \mathbf{S_x} \cdot \overline{\mathbf{A}}_\ell^{(1)}$$

  This is statistically indistinguishable from the real game, since $(\overline{\mathbf{A}}_0^{(1)} + \underline{\mathbf{A}}_0) \cdot \mathbf{D_x} \approx \mathbf{S_x} \cdot \overline{\mathbf{A}}_\ell^{(1)} + \mathbf{S_x} \cdot \underline{\mathbf{A}}_\ell$, and the approximation disappears w.h.p. after rounding.
- Apply semantic security to replace $(\mathbf{D}_{i,0}, \mathbf{D}_{i,0})_{i \in [\ell]}$ with random. Here, we require that semantic security holds even if the distinguisher gets $\{\mathbf{S}_{i,b}\}_{i \in [\ell], b \in \{0,1\}}, \overline{\mathbf{A}}_\ell$, where the latter are needed in order to compute $\mathbf{S_x} \cdot \overline{\mathbf{A}}_\ell^{(1)}$. This implies constraint-hiding.
- Now, we can apply the BLMR analysis to deduce pseudorandomness of $\mathbf{S_x} \cdot \overline{\mathbf{A}}_\ell^{(1)}$, where we treat $\overline{\mathbf{A}}_\ell^{(1)}$ as the seed of the BLMR PRF [7]. This implies pseudorandomness of the output of the Eval oracle.

3   Preliminaries

Notations and terminology. In cryptography, the security parameter (denoted as λ) is a variable that is used to parameterize the computational complexity of the cryptographic algorithm or protocol, and the adversary's probability of breaking security. An algorithm is "efficient" if it runs in (probabilistic) polynomial time over λ.

When a variable v is drawn randomly from the set S we denote as $v \xleftarrow{\$} S$ or $v \leftarrow U(S)$, sometimes abbreviated as v when the context is clear. We use $\approx_s$ and $\approx_c$ as the abbreviation for statistically close and computationally indistinguishable.

Let $\mathbb{R}, \mathbb{Z}, \mathbb{N}$ be the set of real numbers, integers and positive integers. Denote $\mathbb{Z}/(q\mathbb{Z})$ by $\mathbb{Z}_q$. The rounding operation $\lfloor a \rceil_p : \mathbb{Z}_q \to \mathbb{Z}_p$ is defined as multiplying a by p/q and rounding the result to the nearest integer.

For $n \in \mathbb{N}$, $[n] := \{1, ..., n\}$. A vector in $\mathbb{R}^n$ (represented in column form by default) is written as a bold lower-case letter, e.g. $\mathbf{v}$. For a vector $\mathbf{v}$, the ith component of $\mathbf{v}$ will be denoted by v_i. A matrix is written as a bold capital letter, e.g. $\mathbf{A}$. The ith column vector of $\mathbf{A}$ is denoted $\mathbf{a}_i$. In this article we frequently meet the situation where a matrix $\mathbf{A}$ is partitioned into two pieces, one stacking over the other. We denote it as $\mathbf{A} = \left(\begin{smallmatrix}\overline{\mathbf{A}} \\ \underline{\mathbf{A}}\end{smallmatrix}\right)$. The partition is not necessarily even. We will explicitly mention the dimension when needed.

The length of a vector is the ℓ_p-norm $\|\mathbf{v}\|_p = (\sum v_i^p)^{1/p}$. The length of a matrix is the norm of its longest column: $\|\mathbf{A}\|_p = \max_i \|\mathbf{a}_i\|_p$. By default we use ℓ_2-norm unless explicitly mentioned. When a vector or matrix is called "small", we refer to its norm.

Subset products (of matrices) appear frequently in this article. For a given $h \in \mathbb{N}$, a bit-string $\mathbf{v} \in \{0,1\}^h$, we use $\mathbf{X}_\mathbf{v}$ to denote $\prod_{i \in [h]} \mathbf{X}_{i,v_i}$ (it is implicit that $\{\mathbf{X}_{i,b}\}_{i \in [h], b \in \{0,1\}}$ are well-defined).

The tensor product (Kronecker product) for matrices $\mathbf{A} \in \mathbb{R}^{\ell \times m}$, $\mathbf{B} \in \mathbb{R}^{n \times p}$ is defined as

$$\mathbf{A} \otimes \mathbf{B} = \begin{bmatrix} a_{1,1}\mathbf{B}, \ldots, a_{1,m}\mathbf{B} \\ \ldots, \ldots, \ldots \\ a_{\ell,1}\mathbf{B}, \ldots, a_{\ell,m}\mathbf{B} \end{bmatrix} \in \mathbb{R}^{\ell n \times mp}. \tag{6}$$

The rank of the resultant matrix satisfies $\mathrm{rank}(\mathbf{A} \otimes \mathbf{B}) = \mathrm{rank}(\mathbf{A}) \cdot \mathrm{rank}(\mathbf{B})$. For matrices $\mathbf{A} \in \mathbb{R}^{\ell \times m}$, $\mathbf{B} \in \mathbb{R}^{n \times p}$, $\mathbf{C} \in \mathbb{R}^{m \times u}$, $\mathbf{D} \in \mathbb{R}^{p \times v}$,

$$(\mathbf{AC}) \otimes (\mathbf{BD}) = (\mathbf{A} \otimes \mathbf{B}) \cdot (\mathbf{C} \otimes \mathbf{D}). \tag{7}$$

Lemma 3.1 (Leftover hash lemma). *Let $\mathcal{H} = \{h : \mathcal{X} \to \mathcal{Y}\}$ be a 2-universal hash function family. Then for any random variable $X \in \mathcal{X}$, for $\epsilon > 0$ s.t. $\log(|\mathcal{Y}|) \le H_\infty(X) - 2\log(1/\epsilon)$, the distributions*

$$(h, h(X)) \text{ and } (h, U(\mathcal{Y}))$$

are ϵ-statistically close.

3.1 Lattices Background

Smoothing parameter. We recall the definition of smoothing parameter and some useful facts.

Definition 3.2 (Smoothing parameter [32]). *For any n-dimensional lattice Λ and positive real $\epsilon > 0$, the smoothing parameter $\eta_\epsilon(\Lambda)$ is the smallest real $\sigma > 0$ such that $\rho_{1/\sigma}(\Lambda^* \setminus \{0\}) \leq \epsilon$.*

Lemma 3.3 (Smoothing parameter bound from [25]). *For any n-dimensional lattice $\Lambda(\mathbf{B})$ and for any $\omega(\sqrt{\log n})$ function, there is a negligible $\epsilon(n)$ for which*

$$\eta_\epsilon(\Lambda) \leq \|\tilde{\mathbf{B}}\| \cdot \omega(\sqrt{\log n})$$

Lemma 3.4 (Smooth over the cosets [25]). *Let Λ, Λ' be n-dimensional lattices s.t. $\Lambda' \subseteq \Lambda$. Then for any $\epsilon > 0$, $\sigma > \eta_\epsilon(\Lambda')$, and $\mathbf{c} \in \mathbb{R}^n$, we have*

$$\Delta(D_{\Lambda,\sigma,\mathbf{c}} \bmod \Lambda',\ U(\Lambda \bmod \Lambda')) < 2\epsilon$$

Lemma 3.5 ([32,35]). *Let $\mathbf{B}$ be a basis of an n-dimensional lattice Λ, and let $\sigma \geq \|\tilde{\mathbf{B}}\| \cdot \omega(\log n)$, then $\Pr_{\mathbf{x} \leftarrow D_{\Lambda,\sigma}}[\|\mathbf{x}\| \geq \sigma \cdot \sqrt{n} \vee \mathbf{x} = \mathbf{0}] \leq \mathrm{negl}(n)$.*

Lemma 3.6 ([9,25]). *There is a p.p.t. algorithm that, given a basis $\mathbf{B}$ of an n-dimensional lattice $\Lambda(\mathbf{B})$, $\mathbf{c} \in \mathbb{R}^n$, $\sigma \geq \|\tilde{\mathbf{B}}\| \cdot \sqrt{\ln(2n+4)/\pi}$, outputs a sample from $D_{\Lambda,\sigma,\mathbf{c}}$.*

Learning with errors. We recall the learning with errors problem.

Definition 3.7 (Decisional learning with errors (LWE) [37]). *For $n, m \in \mathbb{N}$ and modulus $q \geq 2$, distributions for secret vectors, public matrices, and error vectors $\theta, \pi, \chi \subseteq \mathbb{Z}_q$. An LWE sample is obtained from sampling $\mathbf{s} \leftarrow \theta^n$, $\mathbf{A} \leftarrow \pi^{n \times m}$, $\mathbf{e} \leftarrow \chi^m$, and outputting $(\mathbf{A}, \mathbf{s}^T \mathbf{A} + \mathbf{e}^T \bmod q)$.*

We say that an algorithm solves $\mathsf{LWE}_{n,m,q,\theta,\pi,\chi}$ if it distinguishes the LWE sample from a random sample distributed as $\pi^{n \times m} \times U(\mathbb{Z}_q^{1 \times m})$ with probability bigger than $1/2$ plus non-negligible.

Lemma 3.8 (Regularity of Ajtai function [37]). *Fix a constant $c > 1$, let $m \geq cn \log q$. Then for all but $q^{\frac{-(c-1)n}{4}}$ fraction of $\mathbf{A} \in \mathbb{Z}_q^{n \times m}$, the statistical distance between a random subset-sum of the columns of $\mathbf{A}$ and uniform over $\mathbb{Z}_q^n$ is less than $q^{\frac{-(c-1)n}{4}}$.*

Lemma 3.9 (Standard form [9,33,34,37]). *Given $n \in \mathbb{N}$, for any $m = \mathrm{poly}(n)$, $q \leq 2^{\mathrm{poly}(n)}$. Let $\theta = \pi = U(\mathbb{Z}_q)$, $\chi = D_{\mathbb{Z},\sigma}$ where $\sigma \geq 2\sqrt{n}$. If there exists an efficient (possibly quantum) algorithm that breaks $\mathsf{LWE}_{n,m,q,\theta,\pi,\chi}$, then there exists an efficient (possibly quantum) algorithm for approximating SIVP and GapSVP in the ℓ_2 norm, in the worst case, to within $\tilde{O}(nq/\sigma)$ factors.*

We drop the subscripts of LWE when referring to standard form of LWE with the parameters specified in Lemma 3.9. In this article we frequently use the following variant of LWE that is implied by the standard form.

Lemma 3.10 (LWE with small public matrices [7]). *For n, m, q, σ chosen as was in Lemma 3.9, $\mathsf{LWE}_{n',m,q,U(\mathbb{Z}_q),D_{\mathbb{Z},\sigma},D_{\mathbb{Z},\sigma}}$ is as hard as $\mathsf{LWE}_{n,m,q,U(\mathbb{Z}_q),U(\mathbb{Z}_q),D_{\mathbb{Z},\sigma}}$ for $n' \geq 2 \cdot n \log q$.*

Trapdoor and preimage sampling. Given $\mathbf{A} \in \mathbb{Z}_q^{n \times m}$, denote the kernel lattice of $\mathbf{A}$ as

$$\Lambda^\perp(\mathbf{A}) := \{\mathbf{c} \in \mathbb{Z}^m : \mathbf{A} \cdot \mathbf{c} = 0^n \pmod q\}.$$

Given any $\mathbf{y} \in \mathbb{Z}_q^n$, $\sigma > 0$, we use $\mathbf{A}^{-1}(\mathbf{y}, \sigma)$ to denote the distribution of a vector $\mathbf{d}$ sampled from $D_{\mathbb{Z}^m, \sigma}$ conditioned on $\mathbf{Ad} = \mathbf{y} \pmod q$. We sometimes suppress σ when the context is clear.

Lemma 3.11 ([1,3,31]). *There is a p.p.t. algorithm* $\mathsf{TrapSam}(1^n, 1^m, q)$ *that, given the modulus* $q \geq 2$, *dimensions* n, m *such that* $m \geq 2n \log q$, *outputs* $\mathbf{A} \approx_s U(\mathbb{Z}_q^{n \times m})$ *with a trapdoor* τ.

Following Lemmas 3.6 and 3.11,

Lemma 3.12. *There is a p.p.t. algorithm that for* $\sigma \geq 2\sqrt{n \log q}$, *given* $(\mathbf{A}, \tau) \leftarrow \mathsf{TrapSam}(1^n, 1^m, q)$, $\mathbf{y} \in \mathbb{Z}_q^n$, *outputs a sample from* $\mathbf{A}^{-1}(\mathbf{y}, \sigma)$.

Lemma 3.13 ([25]). *For all but negligible probability over* $(\mathbf{A}, \tau) \leftarrow \mathsf{TrapSam}(1^n, 1^m, q)$, *for sufficiently large* $\sigma \geq 2\sqrt{n \log q}$, *the following distributions are efficiently samplable and statistically close:*

$$\{\mathbf{A}, \mathbf{x}, \mathbf{y} : \mathbf{y} \leftarrow U(\mathbb{Z}_q^n), \mathbf{x} \leftarrow \mathbf{A}^{-1}(\mathbf{y}, \sigma)\} \approx_s \{\mathbf{A}, \mathbf{x}, \mathbf{y} : \mathbf{x} \leftarrow D_{\mathbb{Z}^m, \sigma}, \mathbf{y} = \mathbf{Ax}\}.$$

Lemma 3.14 (Bonsai technique [14]**).** *Let* $n, m, m_1, m_2, q \in \mathbb{N}, \sigma \in \mathbb{R}$ *satisfy* $m = m_1 + m_2$, $m_2 \geq 2n \log q$, $\sigma > 2\sqrt{n \log q}$. *For any* $\mathbf{y} \in \mathbb{Z}_q^n$, *the following two distributions are efficiently samplable and statistically close.*

1. *Let* $(\mathbf{A}, \tau) \leftarrow \mathsf{TrapSam}(1^n, 1^m, q)$, $\mathbf{d} \leftarrow \mathbf{A}^{-1}(\mathbf{y}, \sigma)$. *Output* $(\mathbf{A}, \mathbf{d})$.
2. *Let* $\mathbf{A}_1 \leftarrow U(\mathbb{Z}_q^{n \times m_1})$, $(\mathbf{A}_2, \tau_2) \leftarrow \mathsf{TrapSam}(1^n, 1^{m_2}, q)$; $\mathbf{d}_1 \leftarrow D_{\mathbb{Z}^{m_1}, \sigma}$, $\mathbf{d}_2 \leftarrow \mathbf{A}_2^{-1}(\mathbf{y} - \mathbf{A}_1 \cdot \mathbf{d}_1, \sigma)$. *Let* $\mathbf{A} = [\mathbf{A}_1, \mathbf{A}_2]$, $\mathbf{d} = [\mathbf{d}_1^T, \mathbf{d}_2^T]^T$. *Output* $(\mathbf{A}, \mathbf{d})$.

4   New Lemmas on Preimage Sampling

In this section, we present new lemmas related to lattice preimage sampling. These lemmas are essential to the proof of semantic security for non-permutation branching programs, as outlined in Sect. 2.2.

The first is a statistical lemma which states that for all but negligibly many matrix $\mathbf{A}$ (with proper dimensions), for any matrix $\mathbf{Z}$, the following two distributions are statistically indistinguishable:

$$\left(\mathbf{A}, \mathbf{A}^{-1}\begin{pmatrix} \mathbf{Z} \\ \mathbf{U} \end{pmatrix}\right) \approx_s \left(\mathbf{A}, \overline{\mathbf{A}}^{-1}(\mathbf{Z})\right)$$

where the distributions are over random choices of a matrix $\mathbf{U}$ and probability distributions $\mathbf{A}^{-1}(\cdot)$ and $\overline{\mathbf{A}}^{-1}(\cdot)$. This is in essence an extension of the trapdoor sampling lemma from Gentry, Peikert and Vaikuntanathan [25].

The second is a computational lemma which states that for any matrix $\mathbf{Z}$, the following two distributions are computationally indistinguishable:

$$\mathbf{A}^{-1}(\mathbf{Z} + \mathbf{E}) \approx_c \mathbf{A}^{-1}(\mathbf{U})$$

where the distributions are over random private choices of $\mathbf{A}, \mathbf{E}$ and $\mathbf{U}$ and the coins of $\mathbf{A}^{-1}(\cdot)$. The computational indistinguishability relies on the hardness of the decisional learning with errors (LWE) problem.

4.1   The Statistical Lemma

We prove the above statistical lemma for vectors; the setting for matrices follow readily via a hybrid argument.

Lemma 4.1. *Let $\epsilon > 0$. Given $\sigma \in R^+$, $n', n, m, q \in \mathbb{N}$. For all but a $q^{-2n'}$ fraction of $\overline{\mathbf{A}} \in \mathbb{Z}_q^{n' \times m}$, all but a q^{-2n} fraction of $\underline{\mathbf{A}} \in \mathbb{Z}_q^{n \times m}$, let $\mathbf{A} := \left(\begin{smallmatrix} \overline{\mathbf{A}} \\ \underline{\mathbf{A}} \end{smallmatrix}\right)$. For $\sigma > \eta_\epsilon(\Lambda^\perp(\mathbf{A}))$, $m \geq 9(n' + n) \log q$. For a fixed $\mathbf{z} \in \mathbb{Z}_q^{n'}$, for $\mathbf{u} \leftarrow U(\mathbb{Z}_q^n)$, we have*

$$\mathbf{A}^{-1}\left(\begin{pmatrix} \mathbf{z} \\ \mathbf{u} \end{pmatrix}, \sigma\right) \text{ and } \overline{\mathbf{A}}^{-1}(\mathbf{z}, \sigma)$$

are 2ϵ-statistically close.

Proof. We need two lemmas to assist the proof of Lemma 4.1.

Lemma 4.2. *Let $c > 9$. For $n', n, m, q \in \mathbb{N}$ such that $m \geq c(n' + n) \log q$. For all but $q^{-2n'}$ fraction of $\overline{\mathbf{A}} \in \mathbb{Z}_q^{n' \times m}$, all but q^{-2n} fraction of $\underline{\mathbf{A}} \in \mathbb{Z}_q^{n \times m}$, we have $\{\underline{\mathbf{A}} \cdot \mathbf{x} \mid \mathbf{x} \in \{0, 1\}^m \cap \Lambda^\perp(\overline{\mathbf{A}})\} = \mathbb{Z}_q^n$.*

Proof. From Lemma 3.8, we have for all but $q^{-2n'}$ fraction of $\overline{\mathbf{A}} \in \mathbb{Z}_q^{n' \times m}$

$$\left| \Pr_{\mathbf{x} \in \{0,1\}^m}[\overline{\mathbf{A}} \cdot \mathbf{x} = 0^{n'}] - q^{-n'} \right| < 2q^{-2n'} \Rightarrow \Pr_{\mathbf{x} \in \{0,1\}^m}[\overline{\mathbf{A}} \cdot \mathbf{x} = 0^{n'}] > 0.99 \cdot q^{-n'} \quad (8)$$

Let $\mathbf{x} \leftarrow U(\{0, 1\}^m \cap \Lambda^\perp(\overline{\mathbf{A}}))$, we have $H_\infty(\mathbf{x}) > m - 2n' \log q$. For $\delta > 0$, by setting $m \geq n \log q + 2n' \log q + 2 \log(1/\delta)$, we have that for $\underline{\mathbf{A}} \leftarrow U(\mathbb{Z}_q^{n \times m})$,

$$(\underline{\mathbf{A}}, \underline{\mathbf{A}} \cdot \mathbf{x}) \text{ and } (\underline{\mathbf{A}}, U(\mathbb{Z}_q^n))$$

are δ-statistically close following leftover hash lemma (cf. Lemma 3.1).

Then Lemma 4.2 follows by setting $\delta = q^{-4n}$ and take a union bound for $\underline{\mathbf{A}}$.

Lemma 4.3. *For $n', n, m, q \in \mathbb{N}$, $\sigma > 0$. $\overline{\mathbf{A}} \in \mathbb{Z}_q^{n' \times m}$, $\underline{\mathbf{A}} \in \mathbb{Z}_q^{n \times m}$. Assuming the columns of $\mathbf{A} := \left(\begin{smallmatrix} \overline{\mathbf{A}} \\ \underline{\mathbf{A}} \end{smallmatrix}\right)$ generate $\mathbb{Z}_q^{n'+n}$. For any vectors $\mathbf{u} \in \mathbb{Z}_q^n$, $\mathbf{z} \in \mathbb{Z}_q^{n'}$, and $\mathbf{c} \in \mathbb{Z}^m$ where $\mathbf{A} \cdot \mathbf{c} = \left(\begin{smallmatrix} \mathbf{z} \\ \mathbf{u} \end{smallmatrix}\right) \bmod q$. The conditional distribution D of $\mathbf{x} \leftarrow \mathbf{c} + D_{\Lambda^\perp(\overline{\mathbf{A}}), \sigma, -\mathbf{c}}$ given $\underline{\mathbf{A}}\mathbf{x} = \mathbf{u} \bmod q$ is exactly $\mathbf{c} + D_{\Lambda^\perp(\mathbf{A}), \sigma, -\mathbf{c}}$.*

Proof. Observe that the support of D is $\mathbf{c}+\Lambda^{\perp}(\mathbf{A})$. We compute the distribution D: for all $\mathbf{x} \in \mathbf{c} + \Lambda^{\perp}(\mathbf{A})$,

$$D(\mathbf{x}) = \frac{\rho_{\sigma}(\mathbf{x})}{\rho_{\sigma}(\mathbf{c} + \Lambda^{\perp}(\mathbf{A}))} = \frac{\rho_{\sigma,-\mathbf{c}}(\mathbf{x} - \mathbf{c})}{\rho_{\sigma,-\mathbf{c}}(\Lambda^{\perp}(\mathbf{A}))} = D_{\Lambda^{\perp}(\mathbf{A}),\sigma,-\mathbf{c}}(\mathbf{x} - \mathbf{c}). \qquad (9)$$

Finally from Lemma 3.4, let $\Lambda = \Lambda^{\perp}(\overline{\mathbf{A}})$, $\Lambda' = \Lambda^{\perp}(\mathbf{A})$, we have $\Lambda' \subseteq \Lambda$. Since $\sigma > \eta_{\epsilon}(\Lambda')$, $D_{\Lambda^{\perp}(\overline{\mathbf{A}}),\sigma,-\mathbf{c}}$ is 2ϵ-statistically close to uniform over the cosets of the quotient group $(\Lambda^{\perp}(\overline{\mathbf{A}})/\Lambda^{\perp}(\mathbf{A}))$. The rest of the proof of Lemma 4.1 follows Lemma 4.3 and Lemma 4.2.

4.2   The Computational Lemma

Lemma 4.4. *Given $n, m, k, q \in \mathbb{N}$, $\sigma \in \mathbb{R}$ such that $n, m, k \in \mathrm{poly}(\lambda)$, $m \geq 4n \log q$, $\sigma \geq 2\sqrt{n \log q}$. For arbitrary matrix $\mathbf{Z} \in \mathbb{Z}_q^{n \times k}$, the following two distributions are computationally indistinguishable assuming* $\mathsf{LWE}_{m,k,q,U(\mathbb{Z}_q),D_{\mathbb{Z},\sigma},D_{\mathbb{Z},\sigma}}$.

Distribution 1. *Let* $\mathbf{A}, \tau \leftarrow \mathsf{TrapSam}(1^n, 1^m, q)$, $\mathbf{E} \leftarrow D_{\mathbb{Z},\sigma}^{n \times k}$. *Sample* $\mathbf{D} \leftarrow \mathbf{A}^{-1}(\mathbf{Z} + \mathbf{E}, \sigma)$ *using* τ. *Output* $\mathbf{D}$.
Distribution 2. *Sample* $\mathbf{D} = D_{\mathbb{Z},\sigma}^{m \times k}$. *Output* $\mathbf{D}$.

Proof. We prove a stronger statement where the computational indistinguishability holds even when $\mathbf{Z}$ is given to the adversary. The proof uses the Bonsai technique [14]. Let $m = m_1 + m_2$ such that $m_1, m_2 \geq 2n \log q$. We introduce 2 intermediate distributions,

Distribution 1.1. *Let* $\mathbf{A}_1 \leftarrow U(\mathbb{Z}_q^{n \times m_1})$, $(\mathbf{A}_2, \tau_2) \leftarrow \mathsf{TrapSam}(1^n, 1^{m_2}, q)$. *Sample* $\mathbf{D}_1 \leftarrow D_{\mathbb{Z},\sigma}^{m_1 \times k}$. *Let* $\mathbf{E} \leftarrow D_{\mathbb{Z},\sigma}^{n \times k}$, *sample* $\mathbf{D}_2 \leftarrow \mathbf{A}_2^{-1}((-\mathbf{A}_1 \cdot \mathbf{D}_1 + \mathbf{E} + \mathbf{Z}), \sigma)$ *using* τ_2. *Let* $\mathbf{D} := \binom{\mathbf{D}_1}{\mathbf{D}_2}$. *Output* $\mathbf{D}$.
Distribution 1.2. *Let* $\mathbf{A}_1 \leftarrow U(\mathbb{Z}_q^{n \times m_1})$, $(\mathbf{A}_2, \tau_2) \leftarrow \mathsf{TrapSam}(1^n, 1^{m_2}, q)$. *Sample* $\mathbf{D}_1 \leftarrow D_{\mathbb{Z},\sigma}^{m_1 \times k}$. *Let* $\mathbf{U} \leftarrow U(\mathbb{Z}_q^{n \times k})$, *sample* $\mathbf{D}_2 \leftarrow \mathbf{A}_2^{-1}((\mathbf{U} + \mathbf{Z}), \sigma)$ *using* τ_2. *Let* $\mathbf{D} := \binom{\mathbf{D}_1}{\mathbf{D}_2}$. *Output* $\mathbf{D}$.

Then Distributions 1 and 1.1 are statistically close following Lemma 3.14. Distributions 2 and 1.2 are statistically close following Lemma 3.13.

It remains to prove that Distribution 1.1 $\approx_c$ Distribution 1.2 assuming $\mathsf{LWE}_{m_1,k,q,U(\mathbb{Z}_q),D_{\mathbb{Z},\sigma},D_{\mathbb{Z},\sigma}}$. This follows by taking $(\mathbf{D}_1, -\mathbf{A}_1 \cdot \mathbf{D}_1 + \mathbf{E})$ as the LWE sample, where $\mathbf{A}_1$ is the concatenation of n independent uniform secret vectors, $\mathbf{D}_1$ is the low-norm public matrix and $\mathbf{E}$ is the error matrix.

Formally, suppose there exists a p.p.t. distinguisher A for Distribution 1.1 and Distribution 1.2, we build a distinguisher A' for $\mathsf{LWE}_{m_1,k,q,U(\mathbb{Z}_q),D_{\mathbb{Z},\sigma},D_{\mathbb{Z},\sigma}}$. Given the challenge sample $(\mathbf{D}_1, \mathbf{Y}_1)$, A' runs $(\mathbf{A}_2, \tau_2) \leftarrow \mathsf{TrapSam}(1^n, 1^{m_2}, q)$, samples $\mathbf{D}_2 \leftarrow \mathbf{A}_2^{-1}((\mathbf{Y}_1 + \mathbf{Z}), \sigma)$ using τ_2, send $\mathbf{D} := \binom{\mathbf{D}_1}{\mathbf{D}_2}$ to the adversary A. If A says it is from Distribution 1.1, then A' chooses "LWE"; if A says Distribution 1.2, then A' chooses "random". The success probability of A' is same to the success probability of A.

5   Generalized GGH15 Encodings

We present the abstraction of *generalized GGH15 encodings*. The abstraction includes a construction framework and definitions of security notions.

5.1   The Construction Framework

We begin with a description of the construction:

Construction 5.1 (γ-GGH15 Encodings). *The randomized algorithm* ggh.encode *takes the following inputs*

- *Parameters[5] 1^λ, $h, n, m, q, t, w \in \mathbb{N}$, $\sigma \in \mathbb{R}^*$ and the description of a distribution χ over $\mathbb{Z}$.*
- *A function $\gamma : \mathbb{Z}^{w \times w} \times \mathbb{Z}^{n \times n} \to \mathbb{Z}^{t \times t}$.*
- *Matrices $\left\{ \mathbf{M}_{i,b} \in \mathbb{Z}_{i,b}^{w \times w} \right\}_{i \in [h], b \in \{0,1\}}$, $\left\{ \mathbf{S}_{i,b} \in \mathbb{Z}_{i,b}^{n \times n} \right\}_{i \in [h], b \in \{0,1\}}$.*
- *A matrix $\mathbf{A}_h \in \mathbb{Z}_q^{t \times m}$.*

It generates the output as follows

- *Samples $\{\mathbf{A}_i, \tau_i \leftarrow \mathsf{TrapSam}(1^t, 1^m, q)\}_{i \in \{0,1,\dots,h-1\}}$.*
- *Samples $\{\mathbf{E}_{i,b} \leftarrow \chi^{t \times m}\}_{i \in [h], b \in \{0,1\}}$.*
- *For $i \in [h], b \in \{0,1\}$, let $\hat{\mathbf{S}}_{i,b} := \gamma(\mathbf{M}_{i,b}, \mathbf{S}_{i,b})$, then samples*

$$\mathbf{D}_{i,b} \leftarrow \mathbf{A}_{i-1}^{-1}(\hat{\mathbf{S}}_{i,b} \cdot \mathbf{A}_i + \mathbf{E}_{i,b}, \sigma)$$

using τ_{i-1}.
- *Outputs $\mathbf{A}_0, \{\mathbf{D}_{i,b}\}_{i \in [h], b \in \{0,1\}}$.*

We require γ to be multiplicatively homomorphic:

$$\gamma(\mathbf{M}, \mathbf{S}) \cdot \gamma(\mathbf{M}', \mathbf{S}') = \gamma(\mathbf{M} \cdot \mathbf{M}', \mathbf{S} \cdot \mathbf{S}')$$

Remark 5.2 (Comparison with GGH15). The goal of the original GGH15 graded encodings in [23] was to emulate the functionality provided by multi-linear maps with respect to some underlying directed acyclic graph. The basic unit of the construction is an encoding of a low-norm matrix $\hat{\mathbf{S}}$ along $\mathbf{A}_0 \mapsto \mathbf{A}_1$ given by $\mathbf{A}_0^{-1}(\hat{\mathbf{S}}\mathbf{A}_1 + \mathbf{E})$, where $\hat{\mathbf{S}}$ must be drawn from some high-entropy distribution to achieve any meaningful notion of security.

Following [13, 26, 27, 38], we think of $\hat{\mathbf{S}}$ as being deterministically derived from an arbitrary low-norm matrix $\mathbf{M}$ and a random low-norm matrix $\mathbf{S}$ via some fixed function γ given by $\gamma : (\mathbf{M}, \mathbf{S}) \mapsto \mathbf{M} \otimes \mathbf{S}$ in the afore-mentioned constructions. Here, we make γ an explicit parameter to the construction, so that we obtain a family of constructions parameterized by γ, which we refer to as the "γ-GGH15 encodings".

---

[5] In the rest of the presentation, these parameters are omitted in the input of ggh.encode.

Looking ahead to Sect. 5.2, another advantage of decoupling $\hat{\mathbf{S}}$ into $\mathbf{M}$ and $\mathbf{S}$ is that we can now require semantic security for arbitrary inputs $\mathbf{M}$ and random choices of $\mathbf{S}$ (more precisely, arbitrary $\{\mathbf{M}_{i,b}\}_{i \in [h], b \in \{0,1\}}$ and random $\{\mathbf{S}_{i,b}\}_{i \in [h], b \in \{0,1\}}$), as considered in [38]. Moreover, this notion of semantic security can be achieved under the LWE assumption for some specific γ and classes of matrices $\mathbf{M}$. Here, we make explicit the idea that semantic security should be defined with respect to some fixed auxiliary function aux of the matrices $\{\mathbf{S}_{i,b}\}_{i \in [h], b \in \{0,1\}}, \mathbf{A}_0, \ldots, \mathbf{A}_h$.

Functionality. The next lemma captures the functionality provided by the construction, namely that for all $\mathbf{x} \in \{0,1\}^h$,

$$\mathbf{A}_0 \cdot \mathbf{D_x} \approx \gamma(\mathbf{M_x}, \mathbf{S_x}) \cdot \mathbf{A}_h$$

Lemma 5.3 (Functionality of γ-GGH15 encodings). *Suppose γ is multiplicatively homomorphic. For all inputs to the Construction 5.1 s.t. $\sigma > \Omega(\sqrt{t \log q})$, $m > \Omega(t \log q)$, $\|\chi\| \leq \sigma$; we have for all $\mathbf{x} \in \{0,1\}^h$, with all but negligible probability over the randomness in Construction 5.1,*

$$\|\mathbf{A}_0 \cdot \mathbf{D_x} - \gamma(\mathbf{M_x}, \mathbf{S_x}) \cdot \mathbf{A}_h\|_\infty \leq h \cdot \left(m\sigma \cdot \max_{i,b} \|\gamma(\mathbf{M}_{i,b}, \mathbf{S}_{i,b})\| \right)^h .$$

Proof. Recall $\hat{\mathbf{S}}_{i,b} = \gamma(\mathbf{M}_{i,b}, \mathbf{S}_{i,b})$. It is straight-forward to prove by induction that for all $h' = 0, 1, \ldots, h$:

$$\mathbf{A}_0 \cdot \prod_{k=1}^{h'} \mathbf{D}_{k,x_k} = \left(\prod_{i=1}^{h'} \hat{\mathbf{S}}_{i,x_i} \right) \mathbf{A}_{h'} + \sum_{j=1}^{h'} \left(\left(\prod_{i=1}^{j-1} \hat{\mathbf{S}}_{i,x_i} \right) \cdot \mathbf{E}_{j,x_j} \cdot \prod_{k=j+1}^{h} \mathbf{D}_{k,x_k} \right) \quad (10)$$

The base case $h' = 0$ holds trivially. The inductive step uses the fact that for all $h' = 1, \ldots, h$:

$$\mathbf{A}_{h'-1} \cdot \mathbf{D}_{h',x_{h'}} = \hat{\mathbf{S}}_{h',x_{h'}} \cdot \mathbf{A}_{h'} + \mathbf{E}_{h',x_{h'}}$$

From the homomorphic property of γ we can deduce that

$$\prod_{i=1}^{h} \hat{\mathbf{S}}_{i,x_i} = \prod_{i=1}^{h} \gamma(\mathbf{M}_{i,x_i}, \mathbf{S}_{i,x_i}) = \gamma(\mathbf{M_x}, \mathbf{S_x})$$

Finally, we bound the error term as follows:

$$\|\mathbf{A}_0 \cdot \mathbf{D_x} - \gamma(\mathbf{M_x}, \mathbf{S_x}) \cdot \mathbf{A}_h\|_\infty = \left\| \sum_{j=1}^{h} \left(\prod_{i=1}^{j-1} (\hat{\mathbf{S}}_{i,x_i}) \cdot \mathbf{E}_{j,x_j} \cdot \prod_{k=j+1}^{h} \mathbf{D}_{k,x_k} \right) \right\|_\infty$$

$$\leq h \cdot \sqrt{t} \cdot \sigma \cdot \left(\sqrt{t} \cdot \max_{i,b} \|\gamma(\mathbf{M}_{i,b}, \mathbf{S}_{i,b})\| \cdot \sigma \cdot \sqrt{m} \right)^{h-1}$$

$$\leq h \cdot \left(\max_{i,b} \|\gamma(\mathbf{M}_{i,b}, \mathbf{S}_{i,b})\| \cdot \sigma \cdot m \right)^h$$

Looking ahead, in the applications we will set the parameters to ensure that the threshold $B := h \cdot (m\sigma \cdot \max_{i,b} \|\gamma(\mathbf{M}_{i,b}, \mathbf{S}_{i,b})\|)^h$ is relatively small compared to the modulus q.

Remark 5.4 (Dimensions of $\mathbf{A}_h$). The construction and many analyses in this article can be obviously generalized to the cases where the dimensions of matrices are more flexible. As an example, the matrix $\mathbf{A}_h$ can be chosen from $\mathbb{Z}_q^t$ instead of $\mathbb{Z}_q^{t\times m}$ (as a result, $\mathbf{D}_{h,0}$, $\mathbf{D}_{h,1}$ are from $\mathbb{Z}^m$ instead of $\mathbb{Z}^{m\times m}$). This change maintains necessary functionalities, reduce the size of the construction, and is (more importantly) necessary for one of the proofs in the paper. For the ease of presentation we keep all the $\mathbf{A}$ matrices with the same dimension, all the $\mathbf{D}$ matrices with the same dimension, and mention the exceptions as they arise.

Interesting γ functions. We are interested in the following 3 γ functions:

- $\gamma_\otimes : \{0,1\}^{w\times w} \times \mathbb{Z}^{n\times n} \to \mathbb{Z}^{(wn)\times(wn)}$, $\mathbf{M}, \mathbf{S} \mapsto \mathbf{M} \otimes \mathbf{S}$.
  $\gamma_\otimes$ with permutation matrices $\mathbf{M}$ was introduced and studied in [13, 26, 27, 38].

- $\gamma_{\mathrm{diag}} : \mathbb{Z}^{w\times w} \times \mathbb{Z}^{n\times n} \to \mathbb{Z}^{(w+n)\times(w+n)}$, $\mathbf{M}, \mathbf{S} \mapsto \begin{pmatrix} \mathbf{M} & \\ & \mathbf{S} \end{pmatrix}$.

  γ_{diag} is implicit in the constructions in [21, 29] and is central to the security analysis in this work.

- $\gamma_{\otimes\mathrm{diag}} : \{0,1\}^{w\times w} \times \mathbb{Z}^{n\times n} \to \mathbb{Z}^{(wn+n)\times(wn+n)}$, $\mathbf{M}, \mathbf{S} \mapsto \begin{pmatrix} \mathbf{M} \otimes \mathbf{S} & \\ & \mathbf{S} \end{pmatrix}$.

  We introduce $\gamma_{\otimes\mathrm{diag}}$ in this work, which would be central to the applications in this paper.

Note that all of the three γ functions are multiplicatively homomorphic and norm-preserving.

5.2   Security Notions

Intuitively, semantic security says that for all $\mathbf{M}$, the output of the γ-GGH15 encodings

$$\mathbf{A}_0, \{\mathbf{D}_{i,b}\}_{i\in[h],b\in\{0,1\}}$$

hides $\{\mathbf{M}_{i,b}\}_{i\in[h],b\in\{0,1\}}$, for random choices of $\{\mathbf{S}_{i,b}\}_{i\in[h],b\in\{0,1\}}$ and $\mathbf{A}_0,\ldots,\mathbf{A}_h$. We consider a more general notion parameterized by some fixed function aux of $\{\mathbf{S}_{i,b}\}_{i\in[h],b\in\{0,1\}}$, $\mathbf{A}_0,\ldots,\mathbf{A}_h$, and we require that aux, $\{\mathbf{D}_{i,b}\}_{i\in[h],b\in\{0,1\}}$ hides $\{\mathbf{M}_{i,b}\}_{i\in[h],b\in\{0,1\}}$.

Definition 5.5 (Semantic security with auxiliary input). *We say that the γ-GGH15 encodings satisfies semantic security with auxiliary input aux for a family of matrices $\mathcal{M} \subseteq \mathbb{Z}^{w\times w}$ if for all $\{\mathbf{M}_{i,b} \in \mathcal{M}\}_{i\in[h],b\in\{0,1\}}$, we have*

$$\mathsf{aux}, \{\mathbf{D}_{i,b}\}_{i\in[h],b\in\{0,1\}} \approx_c \mathsf{aux}, \left\{(D_{\mathbb{Z},\sigma}^{m\times m})_{i,b}\right\}_{i\in[h],b\in\{0,1\}}$$

where

$$\mathbf{S}_{i,b} \leftarrow D_{\mathbb{Z},\sigma}^{n\times n}, \mathbf{A}_h \leftarrow U(\mathbb{Z}_q^{t\times m}), \{\mathbf{D}_{i,b}\} \leftarrow \mathsf{ggh.encode}(\gamma, \{\mathbf{M}_{i,b}\}_{i\in[h],b\in\{0,1\}}, \{\mathbf{S}_{i,b}\}_{i\in[h],b\in\{0,1\}}, \mathbf{A}_h)$$

and aux is a fixed function of $\{\mathbf{S}_{i,b}\}_{i\in[h],b\in\{0,1\}}$, $\mathbf{A}_0,\ldots,\mathbf{A}_h$.

Remark 5.6 ($\gamma_\otimes$-GGH encodings with permutation matrices). Canetti and Chen [13] (also, [26,38]) showed that the $\gamma_\otimes$-GGH15 encoding satisfies semantic security with auxiliary input $(\mathbf{A}_0, \mathbf{A}_1, \ldots, \mathbf{A}_h)$ for the family of permutation matrices in $\{0,1\}^{w \times w}$.

We can prove that the $\gamma_\otimes$-GGH15 encoding satisfies semantic security with auxiliary input $(\mathbf{A}_0, \{\mathbf{S}_{i,b}\}_{i \in [\ell], b \in \{0,1\}})$ for the family of permutation matrices in $\{0,1\}^{w \times w}$, by using the LWE assumption with the $\mathbf{S}_{i,b}$ as the public matrices. Such a proof requires a multiplicative blow-up (of roughly $O(\log q)$) in the dimensions of the $\mathbf{S}_{i,b}$ matrices. One of the advantages of using the $\mathbf{S}$ matrices as the public matrices is that we can use the same $\mathbf{S}_0, \mathbf{S}_1$ across all the h levels, similar to the PRF construction in [7].

5.3   Semantic Security for γ_{diag}-GGH15 and $\gamma_{\otimes\text{diag}}$-GGH15 Encodings

In this section, we prove semantic security of the γ_{diag}-GGH15 and $\gamma_{\otimes\text{diag}}$-GGH15 encodings in Construction 5.1 under the LWE assumption, where

$$\gamma_{\text{diag}}(\mathbf{M}, \mathbf{S}) = \begin{pmatrix} \mathbf{M} & \\ & \mathbf{S} \end{pmatrix}, \ \gamma_{\otimes\text{diag}}(\mathbf{M}, \mathbf{S}) = \begin{pmatrix} \mathbf{M} \otimes \mathbf{S} & \\ & \mathbf{S} \end{pmatrix}.$$

In fact, we show that this holds given auxiliary input about $\mathbf{A}_0$ and $\{\mathbf{S}_{i,b}\}_{i \in [h], b \in \{0,1\}}$.

$\mathbf{S}$-*dependent security.* Concretely, we will derive semantic security of $\gamma_{\otimes\text{diag}}$ from that of γ_{diag} by showing that the construction γ_{diag} satisfies a stronger notion of $\mathbf{S}$-dependent security where the matrices $\{\mathbf{M}_{i,b}\}_{i \in [h], b \in \{0,1\}}$ may depend on $\{\mathbf{S}_{i,b}\}_{i \in [h], b \in \{0,1\}}$:

Definition 5.7 (S-dependent semantic security with auxiliary input). *We say that the γ-GGH15 encodings satisfies $\mathbf{S}$-dependent semantic security with auxiliary input* aux *for a family of matrices $\mathcal{M} \subseteq \mathbb{Z}^{w \times w}$ if for every polynomial-size circuit $f : (\mathbb{Z}^{n \times n})^{2h} \to \mathcal{M}^{2h}$, we have*

$$\mathsf{aux}, \{\mathbf{D}_{i,b}\}_{i \in [h], b \in \{0,1\}} \approx_c \mathsf{aux}, \left\{ (D_{\mathbb{Z},\sigma}^{m \times m})_{i,b} \right\}_{i \in [h], b \in \{0,1\}}$$

where

$$\mathbf{S}_{i,b} \leftarrow D_{\mathbb{Z},\sigma}^{n \times n}, \mathbf{A}_h \leftarrow U(\mathbb{Z}_q^{t \times m}), \{\mathbf{M}_{i,b}\}_{i \in [h], b \in \{0,1\}} = f(\{\mathbf{S}_{i,b}\}_{i \in [h], b \in \{0,1\}}),$$

$$\{\mathbf{D}_{i,b}\} \leftarrow \mathsf{ggh.encode}(\gamma, \{\mathbf{S}_{i,b}\}_{i \in [h], b \in \{0,1\}}, \{\mathbf{M}_{i,b}\}_{i \in [h], b \in \{0,1\}}, \mathbf{A}_h)$$

and aux *is a fixed function of $\{\mathbf{S}_{i,b}\}_{i \in [h], b \in \{0,1\}}, \mathbf{A}_0, \ldots, \mathbf{A}_h$.*

Theorem 5.8 (S-dependent semantic security of γ_{diag}). *Assuming* $\mathsf{LWE}_{n,2m,q,U(\mathbb{Z}_q),D_{\mathbb{Z},\sigma},D_{\mathbb{Z},\sigma}}$, *the γ_{diag}-GGH15 encodings in Construction 5.1 satisfies $\mathbf{S}$-dependent semantic security for $\mathcal{M} = \mathbb{Z}^{w \times w}$ with auxiliary input*

$$\mathsf{aux} = \{\mathbf{S}_{i,b}\}_{i \in [h], b \in \{0,1\}}, \mathbf{J} \cdot \mathbf{A}_0, \overline{\mathbf{A}}_h$$

where $\overline{\mathbf{A}}_h \in \mathbb{Z}_q^{w \times m}$ *is the top w rows of $\mathbf{A}_h$ and $\mathbf{J} \in \{0,1\}^{n \times (t-n)} \mid \mathbf{I}^{n \times n}$.*

Remark 5.9 (Necessity of $\mathbf{J}\mathbf{A}_0$). Ideally, we would liked to have shown that semantic security holds with auxiliary input $\mathbf{A}_0$ (as opposed to $\mathbf{J}\mathbf{A}_0$). However, such a statement is false for general $\mathcal{M} \in \mathbb{Z}^{w \times w}$. Concretely, given $\mathbf{A}_0, \mathbf{D}_{1,0}$, we can compute $\mathbf{A}_0 \cdot \mathbf{D}_{1,0}$ which leaks information about the structure of $\mathbf{M}_{1,0}$. In particular, we can distinguish between $\begin{pmatrix} 1 & 0 \\ 0 & 1 \end{pmatrix}$ and $\begin{pmatrix} 0 & 1 \\ 0 & 1 \end{pmatrix}$.

As an immediate corollary, we then have:

Corollary 5.10 (semantic security of $\gamma_{\otimes\mathbf{diag}}$). *Assuming* $\mathsf{LWE}_{n,2m,q,U(\mathbb{Z}_q)}$, $D_{\mathbb{Z},\sigma}, D_{\mathbb{Z},\sigma}$, *the $\gamma_{\otimes diag}$-GGH15 encodings in Construction 5.1 satisfies semantic security for $\mathcal{M} = \mathbb{Z}^{w \times w}$ with auxiliary input*

$$\mathsf{aux} = \{\mathbf{S}_{i,b}\}_{i \in [h], b \in \{0,1\}}, \mathbf{J} \cdot \mathbf{A}_0, \overline{\mathbf{A}}_h$$

where $\overline{\mathbf{A}}_h \in \mathbb{Z}_q^{wn \times m}$ *is the top wn rows of $\mathbf{A}_h$ and $\mathbf{J} \in \{0,1\}^{n \times (t-n)} \mid \mathbf{I}^{n \times n}$.*

5.4 Proof of the Main Theorem

Proof (Proof of Theorem 5.8). For $t, n, w \in \mathbb{N}$ such that $t = w + n$. For any matrix $\mathbf{X} \in \mathbb{Z}^{t \times *}$, let $\mathbf{X} = \begin{pmatrix} \overline{\mathbf{X}} \\ \underline{\mathbf{X}} \end{pmatrix}$, where $\overline{\mathbf{X}} \in \mathbb{Z}^{w \times *}$, $\underline{\mathbf{X}} \in \mathbb{Z}^{n \times *}$. For the sake of completeness we spell out the details of the real and simulated distributions which will be proven indistinguishable.

The real and simulated distributions. In the real distribution the adversary is given

$$\mathbf{J} \cdot \mathbf{A}_0, \left\{ \boxed{\mathbf{D}_{i,b}}, \mathbf{S}_{i,b}, \mathbf{M}_{i,b} \right\}_{i \in [h], b \in \{0,1\}}, \overline{\mathbf{A}}_h$$

where

- $\{\mathbf{A}_i, \tau_i \leftarrow \mathsf{TrapSam}(1^t, 1^m, q)\}_{i \in \{0,1,...,h-1\}}, \mathbf{A}_h \leftarrow U(\mathbb{Z}_q^{t \times m})$
- $\mathbf{S}_{i,b} \leftarrow D_{\mathbb{Z},\sigma}^{n \times n}, \{\mathbf{M}_{i,b}\}_{i \in [h], b \in \{0,1\}} \leftarrow f(\{\mathbf{S}_{i,b}\}_{i \in [h], b \in \{0,1\}})$
- $\mathbf{D}_{i,b} \leftarrow \mathbf{A}_{i-1}^{-1} \begin{pmatrix} \mathbf{M}_{i,b}\overline{\mathbf{A}}_i + \overline{\mathbf{E}}_{i,b} \\ \mathbf{S}_{i,b}\underline{\mathbf{A}}_i + \underline{\mathbf{E}}_{i,b} \end{pmatrix}, \mathbf{E}_{i,b} \leftarrow \chi^{t \times m}$

The simulated distribution is generated in the same way except that the adversary is given

$$\mathbf{J} \cdot \mathbf{A}_0, \left\{ \boxed{\mathbf{V}_{i,b}}, \mathbf{S}_{i,b}, \mathbf{M}_{i,b} \right\}_{i \in [h], b \in \{0,1\}}, \overline{\mathbf{A}}_h$$

where $\mathbf{V}_{i,b} \leftarrow D_{\mathbb{Z},\sigma}^{m \times m}$.

To show that the real distribution is computationally indistinguishable from the simulated one, we introduce the following intermediate distributions.

Distributions 1.i, for $i \in \{h+1, h, ..., 1\}$. Let Distribution $1.(h+1)$ be identical to the real distribution. For $i = h$ down to 1, let Distributions $1.i$ be the same to Distributions $1.(i+1)$, except that $\mathbf{A}_{i-1}, \mathbf{D}_{i,0}, \mathbf{D}_{i,1}$ are sampled differently. Let $(\overline{\mathbf{A}}_{i-1}, \tau_{i-1}) \leftarrow \mathsf{TrapSam}(1^w, 1^m, q)$, $\underline{\mathbf{A}}_{i-1} \leftarrow U(\mathbb{Z}_q^{n \times m})$. Sample $\mathbf{D}_{i,b} \leftarrow \overline{\mathbf{A}}_{i-1}^{-1}((\mathbf{M}_{i,b}\overline{\mathbf{A}}_i + \overline{\mathbf{E}}_{i,b}), \sigma)$ using τ_{i-1}, $b \in \{0,1\}$.

Distributions 2.0. Distribution 2.0 is sampled identically to Distribution 1.1, except that $\mathbf{J} \cdot \mathbf{A}_0$ is replaced with a uniformly random matrix $\mathbf{U} \xleftarrow{\$} \mathbb{Z}^{n \times m}$. Since $\mathbf{J} \in \{0,1\}^{n \times (t-n)} \mid \mathbf{I}^{n \times n}$, $\mathbf{U} \approx_s \mathbf{J} \cdot \mathbf{A}_0$ for $\mathbf{A}_0, \tau_0 \leftarrow \mathsf{TrapSam}(1^t, 1^m, q)$ due to Lemma 3.11.

Distributions 2.j, for $j \in \{1, ..., h\}$. For $j = 1, 2, ..., h$, let Distributions $2.j$ be the same to Distributions $2.(j-1)$, except that $\mathbf{D}_{j,0}, \mathbf{D}_{j,1}$ are sampled simply from $D_{\mathbb{Z},\sigma}^{m \times m}$. Note that Distribution $2.h$ is identical to the simulated distribution, except that in Distribution $2.h$, $\mathbf{U} \xleftarrow{\$} \mathbb{Z}^{n \times m}$ is in the place where $\mathbf{J} \cdot \mathbf{A}_0$ is in the simulated distribution, so they are statistically close again due to Lemma 3.11.

The sequence. We will show that:

$$\mathrm{Real} = 1.(h+1) \approx_c 1.h \approx_c \cdots \approx_c 1.1 \approx_s 2.0 \approx_c 2.1 \approx_c \cdots \approx_c 2.h \approx_s \mathrm{Simulated}$$

In particular, the $\approx_c$'s will rely on the LWE assumption, using $\mathbf{A}_1, ..., \mathbf{A}_\ell$ as LWE secrets in the following order: $\mathbf{A}_\ell, ..., \underline{\mathbf{A}}_1, \overline{\mathbf{A}}_0, ..., \overline{\mathbf{A}}_{\ell-1}$.

Lemma 5.11. *For* $i \in [h]$, *Distribution* $1.(i+1) \approx_c$ *Distribution* $1.i$ *assuming* $\mathsf{LWE}_{n,2n,q,U(\mathbb{Z}_q),D_{\mathbb{Z},\sigma},D_{\mathbb{Z},\sigma}}$.

Roughly speaking, we will show that for all $i \in [h]$,

$$\left\{ \mathbf{A}_{i-1}^{-1} \begin{pmatrix} \mathbf{M}_{i,b}\overline{\mathbf{A}}_i + \overline{\mathbf{E}}_{i,b} \\ \mathbf{S}_{i,b}\underline{\mathbf{A}}_i + \underline{\mathbf{E}}_{i,b} \end{pmatrix} \right\}_{b \in \{0,1\}} \approx_c \left\{ \overline{\mathbf{A}}_{i-1}^{-1}(\mathbf{M}_{i,b}\overline{\mathbf{A}}_i + \overline{\mathbf{E}}_{i,b}) \right\}_{b \in \{0,1\}}$$

where the distinguisher is also given $\mathbf{A}_{i-1}, \tau_{i-1}, \mathbf{S}_{i,0}, \mathbf{S}_{i,1}, \mathbf{M}_{i,0}, \mathbf{M}_{i,1}, \overline{\mathbf{A}}_i$, but not $\underline{\mathbf{A}}_i$, so that we can treat $\underline{\mathbf{A}}_i$ as a LWE secret, cf. Lemma 4.4.

Proof. We introduce an intermediate distribution $1.i^*$, which is generated in the same way as Distributions $1.(i+1)$, except that $\mathbf{D}_{i,0}, \mathbf{D}_{i,1}$ are sampled as:

$$\mathbf{D}_{i,b} \leftarrow \mathbf{A}_{i-1}^{-1}\left(\begin{pmatrix} \mathbf{M}_{i,b}\overline{\mathbf{A}}_i + \overline{\mathbf{E}}_{i,b} \\ \mathbf{U}_{i,b} \end{pmatrix}, \sigma \right), b \in \{0,1\}.$$

where $(\mathbf{U}_{i,0}, \mathbf{U}_{i,1}) \leftarrow U(\mathbb{Z}_q^{n \times m} \times \mathbb{Z}_q^{n \times m})$.

The intermediate distribution $1.i^*$ is statistically close to Distribution $1.i$ due to Lemma 4.1. It remains to prove that $1.i^*$ is computationally indistinguishable from Distribution $1.(i+1)$. This follows Lemma 3.10, by treating $\underline{\mathbf{A}}_i$ as the LWE secret, and $\mathbf{S}_{i,0}, \mathbf{S}_{i,1}$ as the public matrices.

Formally, if there's an adversary A that distinguishes Distributions $1.(i + 1)$ and $1.i^*$, we build a distinguisher A' for $\mathsf{LWE}_{n,2n,q,U(\mathbb{Z}_q),D_{\mathbb{Z},\sigma},D_{\mathbb{Z},\sigma}}$ as follows. Once given the LWE challenge

$$\mathbf{S}_{i,0}, \mathbf{S}_{i,1}, \underline{\mathbf{Y}}_{i,0}, \underline{\mathbf{Y}}_{i,1}$$

where $\mathbf{S}_{i,0}, \mathbf{S}_{i,1}$ are the low-norm public matrices, $\underline{\mathbf{Y}}_{i,0}, \underline{\mathbf{Y}}_{i,1}$ are either the $\mathsf{LWE}_{n,2n,q,U(\mathbb{Z}_q),D_{\mathbb{Z},\sigma},D_{\mathbb{Z},\sigma}}$ samples with the common secret $\underline{\mathbf{A}}_i \leftarrow U(\mathbb{Z}_q^{n \times m})$, or independent uniform samples from $\mathbb{Z}_q^{n \times m} \times \mathbb{Z}_q^{n \times m}$. The LWE distinguisher A' proceeds as follows:

1. Sample $\left\{ \mathbf{S}_{k,b} \leftarrow D_{\mathbb{Z},\sigma}^{n \times n} \right\}_{k \in [h], k \neq i, b \in \{0,1\}}$.
2. For $k \in [h], b \in \{0,1\}$, compute $\mathbf{M}_{k,b} \in \mathbb{Z}^{w \times w}$ using $f(\{\mathbf{S}_{k,b}\}_{k \in [h], b \in \{0,1\}})$.
3. For $k \in \{0,1,...,i-1\}$, sample $\mathbf{A}_k, \tau_k \leftarrow \mathsf{TrapSam}(1^t, 1^m, q)$. For $k \in \{i, i+1, ..., h-1\}$, sample $\overline{\mathbf{A}}_k, \bar{\tau}_k \leftarrow \mathsf{TrapSam}(1^w, 1^m, q)$. Sample $\overline{\mathbf{A}}_h \leftarrow U(\mathbb{Z}_q^{t \times m})$.
4. For $k \in [h], b \in \{0,1\}$, samples

$$\mathbf{D}_{k,b} \leftarrow \begin{cases} \mathbf{A}_{k-1}^{-1} \left(\begin{smallmatrix} \mathbf{M}_{k,b}\overline{\mathbf{A}}_k + \overline{\mathbf{E}}_{k,b} \\ \mathbf{S}_{k,b}\underline{\mathbf{A}}_k + \underline{\mathbf{E}}_{k,b} \end{smallmatrix} \right) & \text{using } \tau_{k-1} \text{ if } k \leq i-1 \\ \mathbf{A}_{i-1}^{-1} \left(\begin{smallmatrix} \mathbf{M}_{i,b}\overline{\mathbf{A}}_i + \overline{\mathbf{E}}_{i,b} \\ \underline{\mathbf{Y}}_{i,b} \end{smallmatrix} \right) & \text{using } \tau_{i-1} \text{ if } k = i \\ \overline{\mathbf{A}}_{k-1}^{-1} (\mathbf{M}_{k,b}\overline{\mathbf{A}}_k + \overline{\mathbf{E}}_{k,b}) & \text{using } \bar{\tau}_{k-1} \text{ if } k \geq i+1 \end{cases}$$

with standard deviation σ.

The LWE distinguisher A' then sends

$$\mathbf{J} \cdot \mathbf{A}_0, \left\{ \boxed{\mathbf{D}_{k,b}}, \mathbf{S}_{k,b}, \mathbf{M}_{k,b} \right\}_{k \in [h], b \in \{0,1\}}, \overline{\mathbf{A}}_h.$$

to the adversary A. If A says it is Distribution $1.(i+1)$, it corresponds to the LWE samples with low-norm public matrices; if A says Distribution $1.i^*$, it corresponds to the uniform distribution.

Lemma 5.12. *For $j \in [h]$, Distribution $2.(j-1) \approx_c$ Distributions $2.j$ assuming* $\mathsf{LWE}_{m,2m,q,U(\mathbb{Z}_q),D_{\mathbb{Z},\sigma},D_{\mathbb{Z},\sigma}}$.

Roughly speaking, we will show that for all $j \in [h]$,

$$\left\{ \overline{\mathbf{A}}_{j-1}^{-1}(\mathbf{M}_{j,b}\overline{\mathbf{A}}_j + \overline{\mathbf{E}}_{j,b}) \right\}_{b \in \{0,1\}} \approx_c \left\{ D_{\mathbb{Z},\sigma}^{m \times m} \right\}_{b \in \{0,1\}}$$

where the distinguisher is also given $\mathbf{M}_{j,0}, \mathbf{M}_{j,1}, \overline{\mathbf{A}}_j$, but not $\overline{\mathbf{A}}_{j-1}$, so as to trigger Lemma 4.4.

Proof. For $j \in [h]$, suppose there exists an adversary A that distinguishes Distributions $2.(j-1)$ and $2.j$, we build a distinguisher A' for Distributions 1 and 2 in Lemma 4.4 as follows. Given challenging samples

$$\mathbf{D}_{j,0} \mid \mathbf{D}_{j,1} \in \mathbb{Z}^{m \times 2m}$$

either obtained from $\overline{\mathbf{A}}_{j-1}^{-1}([\mathbf{M}_{j,0}\overline{\mathbf{A}}_j + \overline{\mathbf{E}}_{j,0} \mid \mathbf{M}_{j,1}\overline{\mathbf{A}}_j + \overline{\mathbf{E}}_{j,1}])$ which corresponds to Distribution 1 in Lemma 4.4 (by treating $[\mathbf{M}_{j,0}\overline{\mathbf{A}}_j \mid \mathbf{M}_{j,1}\overline{\mathbf{A}}_j]$ as the arbitrary matrix $\mathbf{Z}$); or from $D_{\mathbb{Z},\sigma}^{m \times 2m}$ which corresponds to Distribution 2 in Lemma 4.4. The distinguisher A' proceeds as follows:

1. For $k \in [h], b \in \{0,1\}$, sample $\mathbf{S}_{k,b} \leftarrow D_{\mathbb{Z},\sigma}^{n \times n}$.
2. For $k \in [h], b \in \{0,1\}$, compute $\mathbf{M}_{k,b} \in \mathbb{Z}^{w \times w}$ using $f(\{\mathbf{S}_{k,b}\}_{k \in [h], b \in \{0,1\}})$.
3. For $k \in \{j, j+1, ..., h-1\}$, sample $\overline{\mathbf{A}}_k, \bar{\tau}_k \leftarrow \mathsf{TrapSam}(1^w, 1^m, q)$. Sample $\overline{\mathbf{A}}_h \leftarrow U(\mathbb{Z}_q^{t \times m})$.
4. For $k \in \{1, 2, ..., j-1, j+1, ..., h\}, b \in \{0,1\}$, samples

$$\mathbf{D}_{k,b} \leftarrow \begin{cases} D_{\mathbb{Z},\sigma}^{m \times m} & \text{if } k \leq j-1 \\ \overline{\mathbf{A}}_{k-1}^{-1}(\mathbf{M}_{k,b}\overline{\mathbf{A}}_k + \overline{\mathbf{E}}_{k,b}, \sigma) \text{ using } \bar{\tau}_{k-1} & \text{if } k \geq j+1 \end{cases}.$$

5. Sample $\mathbf{U} \leftarrow U(\mathbb{Z}_q^{n \times m})$.

A' then sends

$$\mathbf{U}, \left\{ \boxed{\mathbf{D}_{k,b}}, \mathbf{S}_{k,b}, \mathbf{M}_{k,b} \right\}_{k \in [h], b \in \{0,1\}}, \overline{\mathbf{A}}_h.$$

to the adversary A. Note that A' correctly produce the output without $\overline{\mathbf{A}}_{j-1}$. So if A determines that the samples are from Distribution 2.$(j-1)$, A' chooses Distribution 1 in Lemma 4.4; if A determines that the samples are from Distribution 2.j, A' chooses Distribution 2 in Lemma 4.4.

Theorem 5.8 follows from Lemmas 5.11 and 5.12.

Acknowledgments. Y.C. is supported by the NSF MACS project. Part of this work was done while visiting ENS. V.V. is supported in part by NSF Grants CNS-1350619 and CNS-1414119, Alfred P. Sloan Research Fellowship, Microsoft Faculty Fellowship, the NEC Corporation and a Steven and Renee Finn Career Development Chair from MIT. This work was also sponsored in part by the Defense Advanced Research Projects Agency (DARPA) and the U.S. Army Research Office under contracts W911NF-15-C-0226 and W911NF-15-C-0236. H.W. is supported by ERC Project aSCEND (H2020 639554). Part of this work was done while visiting CQT.

References

1. Ajtai, M.: Generating hard instances of the short basis problem. In: Wiedermann, J., van Emde Boas, P., Nielsen, M. (eds.) ICALP 1999. LNCS, vol. 1644, pp. 1–9. Springer, Heidelberg (1999). https://doi.org/10.1007/3-540-48523-6_1
2. Alamati, N., Peikert, C.: Three's compromised too: circular insecurity for any cycle length from (ring-)LWE. In: Robshaw, M., Katz, J. (eds.) CRYPTO 2016, Part II. LNCS, vol. 9815, pp. 659–680. Springer, Heidelberg (2016). https://doi.org/10.1007/978-3-662-53008-5_23
3. Alwen, J., Peikert, C.: Generating shorter bases for hard random lattices. Theory Comput. Syst. **48**(3), 535–553 (2011)
4. Apon, D., Döttling, N., Garg, S., Mukherjee, P.: Cryptanalysis of indistinguishability obfuscations of circuits over GGH13. In: ICALP, volume 80 of LIPIcs, pp. 38:1–38:16. Schloss Dagstuhl - Leibniz-Zentrum fuer Informatik (2017)

5. Mix Barrington, D.A.: Bounded-width polynomial-size branching programs recognize exactly those languages in nc^1. In: Hartmanis, J. (ed.) STOC, pp. 1–5. ACM (1986)
6. Boneh, D., Kim, S., Montgomery, H.W.: Private puncturable PRFs from standard lattice assumptions. In: Coron, J.-S., Nielsen, J.B. (eds.) EUROCRYPT 2017, Part I. LNCS, vol. 10210, pp. 415–445. Springer, Cham (2017). https://doi.org/10.1007/978-3-319-56620-7_15
7. Boneh, D., Lewi, K., Montgomery, H.W., Raghunathan, A.: Key homomorphic PRFs and their applications. In: Canetti, R., Garay, J.A. (eds.) CRYPTO 2013, Part I. LNCS, vol. 8042, pp. 410–428. Springer, Heidelberg (2013). https://doi.org/10.1007/978-3-642-40041-4_23
8. Boneh, D., Silverberg, A.: Applications of multilinear forms to cryptography. Contemp. Math. **324**(1), 71–90 (2003)
9. Brakerski, Z., Langlois, A., Peikert, C., Regev, O., Stehlé, D.: Classical hardness of learning with errors. In: Proceedings of the Forty-Fifth Annual ACM Symposium on Theory of Computing, pp. 575–584. ACM (2013)
10. Brakerski, Z., Rothblum, G.N.: Obfuscating conjunctions. In: Canetti, R., Garay, J.A. (eds.) CRYPTO 2013, Part II. LNCS, vol. 8043, pp. 416–434. Springer, Heidelberg (2013). https://doi.org/10.1007/978-3-642-40084-1_24
11. Brakerski, Z., Tsabary, R., Vaikuntanathan, V., Wee, H.: Private constrained PRFs (and more) from LWE. In: Kalai, Y., Reyzin, L. (eds.) TCC 2017, Part I. LNCS, vol. 10677, pp. 264–302. Springer, Cham (2017). https://doi.org/10.1007/978-3-319-70500-2_10
12. Brakerski, Z., Vaikuntanathan, V., Wee, H., Wichs, D.: Obfuscating conjunctions under entropic ring LWE. In: ITCS, pp. 147–156. ACM (2016)
13. Canetti, R., Chen, Y.: Constraint-hiding constrained PRFs for NC^1 from LWE. In: Coron, J.-S., Nielsen, J.B. (eds.) EUROCRYPT 2017, Part I. LNCS, vol. 10210, pp. 446–476. Springer, Cham (2017). https://doi.org/10.1007/978-3-319-56620-7_16
14. Cash, D., Hofheinz, D., Kiltz, E., Peikert, C.: Bonsai trees, or how to delegate a lattice basis. J. Cryptol. **25**(4), 601–639 (2012)
15. Chen, Y., Gentry, C., Halevi, S.: Cryptanalyses of candidate branching program obfuscators. In: Coron, J.-S., Nielsen, J.B. (eds.) EUROCRYPT 2017, Part III. LNCS, vol. 10212, pp. 278–307. Springer, Cham (2017). https://doi.org/10.1007/978-3-319-56617-7_10
16. Cheon, J.H., Han, K., Lee, C., Ryu, H., Stehlé, D.: Cryptanalysis of the multilinear map over the integers. In: Oswald, E., Fischlin, M. (eds.) EUROCRYPT 2015, Part I. LNCS, vol. 9056, pp. 3–12. Springer, Heidelberg (2015). https://doi.org/10.1007/978-3-662-46800-5_1
17. Coron, J.-S., Lee, M.S., Lepoint, T., Tibouchi, M.: Cryptanalysis of GGH15 multilinear maps. In: Robshaw, M., Katz, J. (eds.) CRYPTO 2016, Part II. LNCS, vol. 9815, pp. 607–628. Springer, Heidelberg (2016). https://doi.org/10.1007/978-3-662-53008-5_21
18. Coron, J.-S., Lee, M.S., Lepoint, T., Tibouchi, M.: Zeroizing attacks on indistinguishability obfuscation over CLT13. In: Fehr, S. (ed.) PKC 2017, Part I. LNCS, vol. 10174, pp. 41–58. Springer, Heidelberg (2017). https://doi.org/10.1007/978-3-662-54365-8_3
19. Coron, J.-S., Lepoint, T., Tibouchi, M.: Practical multilinear maps over the integers. In: Canetti, R., Garay, J.A. (eds.) CRYPTO 2013, Part I. LNCS, vol. 8042, pp. 476–493. Springer, Heidelberg (2013). https://doi.org/10.1007/978-3-642-40041-4_26

20. Garg, S., Gentry, C., Halevi, S.: Candidate multilinear maps from ideal lattices. In: Johansson, T., Nguyen, P.Q. (eds.) EUROCRYPT 2013. LNCS, vol. 7881, pp. 1–17. Springer, Heidelberg (2013). https://doi.org/10.1007/978-3-642-38348-9_1

21. Garg, S., Gentry, C., Halevi, S., Raykova, M., Sahai, A., Waters, B.: Candidate indistinguishability obfuscation and functional encryption for all circuits. In: FOCS, pp. 40–49 (2013)

22. Garg, S., Miles, E., Mukherjee, P., Sahai, A., Srinivasan, A., Zhandry, M.: Secure obfuscation in a weak multilinear map model. In: Hirt, M., Smith, A. (eds.) TCC 2016, Part B2. LNCS, vol. 9986, pp. 241–268. Springer, Heidelberg (2016). https://doi.org/10.1007/978-3-662-53644-5_10

23. Gentry, C., Gorbunov, S., Halevi, S.: Graph-induced multilinear maps from lattices. In: Dodis, Y., Nielsen, J.B. (eds.) TCC 2015, Part II. LNCS, vol. 9015, pp. 498–527. Springer, Heidelberg (2015). https://doi.org/10.1007/978-3-662-46497-7_20

24. Gentry, C., Lewko, A.B., Waters, B.: Witness encryption from instance independent assumptions. In: Garay, J.A., Gennaro, R. (eds.) CRYPTO 2014, Part I. LNCS, vol. 8616, pp. 426–443. Springer, Heidelberg (2014). https://doi.org/10.1007/978-3-662-44371-2_24

25. Gentry, C., Peikert, C., Vaikuntanathan V.: Trapdoors for hard lattices and new cryptographic constructions. In: STOC, pp. 197–206 (2008)

26. Goyal, R., Koppula, V., Waters, B.: Lockable obfuscation. In: FOCS, pp. 612–621 (2017)

27. Goyal, R., Koppula, V., Waters, B.: Separating semantic and circular security for symmetric-key bit encryption from the learning with errors assumption. In: Coron, J.-S., Nielsen, J.B. (eds.) EUROCRYPT 2017, Part II. LNCS, vol. 10211, pp. 528–557. Springer, Cham (2017). https://doi.org/10.1007/978-3-319-56614-6_18

28. Goyal, R., Koppula, V., Waters, B.: Collusion resistant traitor tracing from learning with errors. In: STOC (2018)

29. Halevi, S., Halevi, T., Shoup, V., Stephens-Davidowitz, N.: Implementing BP-obfuscation using graph-induced encoding. In: ACM CCS, pp. 783–798 (2017)

30. Koppula, V., Waters, B.: Circular security separations for arbitrary length cycles from LWE. In: Robshaw, M., Katz, J. (eds.) CRYPTO 2016, Part II. LNCS, vol. 9815, pp. 681–700. Springer, Heidelberg (2016). https://doi.org/10.1007/978-3-662-53008-5_24

31. Micciancio, D., Peikert, C.: Trapdoors for lattices: simpler, tighter, faster, smaller. In: Pointcheval, D., Johansson, T. (eds.) EUROCRYPT 2012. LNCS, vol. 7237, pp. 700–718. Springer, Heidelberg (2012). https://doi.org/10.1007/978-3-642-29011-4_41

32. Micciancio, D., Regev, O.: Worst-case to average-case reductions based on Gaussian measure. SIAM J. Comput. **37**(1), 267–302 (2007)

33. Peikert, C.: Public-key cryptosystems from the worst-case shortest vector problem: extended abstract. In: STOC, pp. 333–342 (2009)

34. Peikert, C., Regev, O., Stephens-Davidowitz, N.: Pseudorandomness of ring-LWE for any ring and modulus. In: STOC, pp. 461–473. ACM (2017)

35. Peikert, C., Rosen, A.: Efficient collision-resistant hashing from worst-case assumptions on cyclic lattices. In: Halevi, S., Rabin, T. (eds.) TCC 2006. LNCS, vol. 3876, pp. 145–166. Springer, Heidelberg (2006). https://doi.org/10.1007/11681878_8

36. Regev, O.: On lattices, learning with errors, random linear codes, and cryptography. In: Gabow, H.N., Fagin, R. (eds.) Proceedings of the 37th Annual ACM Symposium on Theory of Computing, Baltimore, MD, USA, 22–24 May 2005, pp. 84–93. ACM (2005)
37. Regev, O.: On lattices, learning with errors, random linear codes, and cryptography. J. ACM **56**(6), 34 (2009)
38. Wichs, D., Zirdelis, G.: Obfuscating compute-and-compare programs under LWE. In: FOCS, pp. 600–611 (2017)

Lower Bounds on Lattice Enumeration
with Extreme Pruning

Yoshinori Aono[1], Phong Q. Nguyen[2,3]([envelope]), Takenobu Seito[4], and Junji Shikata[5]

[1] National Institute of Information and Communications Technology,
Tokyo, Japan
[2] Inria Paris, Paris, France
Phong.Nguyen@inria.fr
[3] CNRS, JFLI, University of Tokyo, Tokyo, Japan
[4] Bank of Japan, Tokyo, Japan
[5] Yokohama National University, Yokohama, Japan

Abstract. At Eurocrypt '10, Gama, Nguyen and Regev introduced lattice enumeration with extreme pruning: this algorithm is implemented in state-of-the-art lattice reduction software and used in challenge records. They showed that extreme pruning provided an exponential speed-up over full enumeration. However, no limit on its efficiency was known, which was problematic for long-term security estimates of lattice-based cryptosystems. We prove the first lower bounds on lattice enumeration with extreme pruning: if the success probability is lower bounded, we can lower bound the global running time taken by extreme pruning. Our results are based on geometric properties of cylinder intersections and some form of isoperimetry. We discuss their impact on lattice security estimates.

1 Introduction

Among all the candidates submitted in 2017 to the NIST standardization of post-quantum cryptography, the majority are based on hard lattice problems, such as LWE and NTRU problems. Unfortunately, security estimates for lattice problems are known to be difficult: many different assessments exist in the research literature, which is reflected in the wide range of security estimates in NIST submissions (see [2]), depending on the model used. One reason is that the performance of lattice algorithms depends on many parameters: we do not know how to select these parameters optimally, and we do not know how far from optimal are current parameter selections. The most sensitive issue is the evaluation of the cost of a subroutine to find shortest or nearly shortest lattice vectors in certain dimensions (typically the blocksize of blockwise reduction algorithms). In state-of-the-art lattice reduction software [7,9,11], this subroutine is implemented by lattice enumeration with extreme pruning, introduced at

---

The views expressed in this paper are those of authors and do not necessarily reflect the official views of the Bank of Japan.

H. Shacham and A. Boldyreva (Eds.): CRYPTO 2018, LNCS 10992, pp. 608–637, 2018.
https://doi.org/10.1007/978-3-319-96881-0_21

Eurocrypt '10 by Gama, Nguyen and Regev [16] as a generalization of pruning methods introduced by Schnorr et al. [34,35] in the 90s. Yet, most lattice-based NIST submissions chose their parameters based on the assumption that sieving [1,8,20,22,28] (rather than enumeration) is the most efficient algorithm for this subroutine. This choice goes back to the analysis of NewHope [3, Sect. 6], which states that sieving is more efficient than enumeration in dimension ≥ 250 for both classical and quantum computers, based on a lower bound on the cost of sieving (ignoring subexponential terms) and an upper bound on the cost of enumeration (either [11, Table 4] or [10, Table 5.2]). In dimensions around $140 - 150$, this upper bound is very close to actual running times for solving the largest record SVP challenges [32], which does not leave much margin for future progress; and for dimensions ≥ 250, a numerical extrapolation has been used, which is also debatable.

It would be more consistent to compare the sieving lower bound by a lower bound on lattice enumeration with extreme pruning. Unfortunately, no such lower bound is known: the performances of extreme pruning strongly depends on the choice of bounding function, and it is unknown how good can be such a function. There is only a partial lower bound on the cost of extreme pruning in [11], assuming that the choice of step bounding function analyzed in [16] is optimal. And this partial lower bound is much lower than the upper bound given in [10,11].

Our results. We study the limitations of lattice enumeration with extreme pruning. We prove the first lower bound on the cost of extreme pruning, given a lower bound on the global success probability. This is done by studying the case of a single enumeration with cylinder pruning, and generalizing it to the extreme pruning case of multiple enumerations, possibly infinitely many. Our results are based on geometric properties of cylinder intersections and a probabilistic form of isoperimetry: usually, isoperimetry refers to a geometric inequality involving the surface area of a set and its volume.

Our lower bounds are easy to compute and appear to be reasonably tight in practice, at least in the single enumeration case: we introduce a cross-entropy-based method which experimentally finds upper bounds somewhat close to our lower bounds.

Impact. By combining our lower bounds with models of strongly-reduced lattice bases introduced in [7,11,26] and quantum speed-ups for enumeration [6], we obtain more sound comparisons with sieving: see Fig. 1 for an overview. It suggests that enumeration is faster than sieving up to higher dimensions than previously considered by lattice-based submissions to NIST post-quantum cryptography standardization: the cost lower bound used by many NIST submissions is not as conservative as previously believed, especially in the quantum setting. Concretely, in the quantum setting, the lower bounds of enumeration and sieving cross in dimensions roughly 300–400 in the HKZ-basis model or beyond 500 in the Rankin-basis model, depending on how many enumerations are allowed. We note that in high dimension, our lower bound for enumeration with 10^{10}

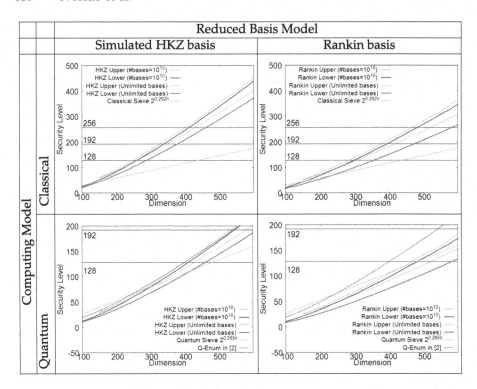

Fig. 1. Upper/lower bounds on the classical/quantum cost of enumeration with cylinder pruning, using strongly-reduced basis models. See Sect. 5 for the exact meaning of these curves: the lower bounds correspond to (16) and (17) and the upper bounds are found by the algorithm in Sect. 4. For comparison, we also displayed several curves from [2]: $2^{0.292n}$ and $2^{0.265n}$ as the simplified classical/quantum complexity of sieve algorithms, and the numerical extrapolation of enumeration cost of [17, (2)]. (Color figure online)

HKZ bases is somewhat close to the numerical extrapolation of [17, (2)], called Core-Enum+$O(1)$ in [2].

Technical overview. Enumeration is the simplest algorithm to solve hard lattice problems: it outputs $L \cap B$, given a lattice L and an n-dimensional ball $B \subseteq \mathbb{R}^n$. It dates back to the early 1980s [15,18,29] but has been significantly improved in practice in the past twenty years, thanks to pruning methods introduced by Schnorr et al. [33–35], and later revisited and generalized as respectively cylinder pruning by Gama, Nguyen and Regev [16] and discrete pruning by Aono and Nguyen [5]: pruning methods offer a trade-off by enumerating over a special subset $S \subseteq B$, at the expense of missing solutions. Gama et al. [16] introduced the idea of extreme pruning where one repeats pruned enumeration many times over different sets S: this can be globally faster than full enumeration, even if a single enumeration has a negligible probability of returning solutions. In the case of cylinder pruning, [16] showed that the speed-up can be asymptotically exponential for simple choices of the pruning subset S.

Cylinder pruning uses the intersection S of n cylinders defined by a lattice basis and a bounding function f: by using different lattice bases B, one obtains different sets S. The running time and the success probability of cylinder pruning depend on the quality of the basis, and the bounding function f. But when one uses different bases, these bases typically have approximately the same quality, which allows to focus on f, which determines the radii of S.

The probability of success of cylinder pruning is related to the volume of S, whereas its cost is related to the volumes of the 'canonical' projections of S. We show that if the success probability is lower bounded, that is, if S is sufficiently big (with respect to its volume, or its Gaussian measure for the case of solving LWE), then the function f defining S can be lower bounded: as a special case, if S occupies a large fraction of the ball, f is lower bounded by essentially the linear pruning function of [16]. This immediately gives lower bounds on the volumes of the projections of S, but we significantly improve these direct lower bounds using the following basic form of isoperimetry: for certain distributions such as the Gaussian distribution, among all Borel sets of a given volume, the ball centered at the origin has the largest probability. The extreme pruning case is obtained by a refinement of isoperimetry over finitely many sets: it is somewhat surprising that we obtain a lower bound even in the extreme case where we allow infinitely many sets S.

All our lower bounds are easy to compute. To evaluate their tightness, we introduce a method based on cross-entropy to compute good upper bounds in practice, i.e., good choices of f. This is based on earlier work by Chen [10].

Open problem. Our lower bounds are specific to cylinder pruning [16]. It would be interesting to obtain tight lower bounds for discrete pruning [5].

Roadmap. In Sect. 2, we introduce background and notation on lattices, enumeration and its cost estimations. Section 3 presents our lower bounds as geometric properties of cylinder intersections. Section 4 shows how to obtain good upper bounds in practice, by finding nice cylinder intersections using cross-entropy. Finally, in Sect. 5, we evaluate the tightness of our lower bounds and discuss security estimates for the hardness of finding nearly shortest lattice vectors. The appendix includes proofs of technical results. The full version of this paper on eprint also includes sage scripts to compute our lower bounds.

2   Background

2.1   Notation

Throughout the paper, we use row representations of matrices. The Euclidean norm of a vector $\mathbf{v} \in \mathbb{R}^n$ is denoted $\|\mathbf{v}\|$. The 'canonical' projection of $\mathbf{u} \in \mathbb{R}^n$ onto $\mathbb{R}^k$ for $1 \leq k \leq n$ is the truncation $\tau_k(\mathbf{u}) = (u_1, \ldots, u_k)$.

Measures. We denote by vol the standard Lebesgue measure over $\mathbb{R}^n$. We denote by $\rho_{n,\sigma}$ the centered Gaussian measure of variance σ^2, whose pdf over $\mathbb{R}^n$ is

$$(2\pi\sigma^2)^{-n/2}e^{-\|\mathbf{x}\|^2/(2\sigma^2)}.$$

The standard Gaussian measure is $\rho_n = \rho_{n,1}$.

Balls. We denote by $\mathrm{Ball}_n(R)$ the n-dimensional zero-centered ball of radius R. Let $V_n(R) = \mathrm{vol}(\mathrm{Ball}_n(R))$. Let $\mathbf{u} = (u_1, \ldots, u_n)$ be a point chosen uniformly at random from the unit sphere S^{n-1}, e.g. $u_i = x_i/\sqrt{\sum_{j=1}^n x_j^2}$, where $x_1, \ldots, x_n$ are independent, normally distributed random variables with mean 0 and variance 1. Then $\|\tau_k(\mathbf{u})\|^2 = \frac{\sum_{i=1}^k x_i^2}{\sum_{i=1}^k x_i^2 + \sum_{i=k+1}^n x_i^2} = \frac{X}{X+Y}$, where X and Y have distributions Gamma$(k/2, \theta = 2)$ and Gamma$((n-k)/2, \theta = 2)$ respectively. Here, we use the scale parametrization to represent Gamma distributions. Hence, $\|\tau_k(\mathbf{u})\|^2$ has distribution Beta$(k/2, (n-k)/2)$. In particular, $\|\tau_{n-2}(\mathbf{u})\|^2$ has distribution Beta$(n/2 - 1, 1)$, whose pdf is $x^{(n/2)-2}/B(n/2 - 1, 1) = (n/2 - 1)x^{(n/2)-2}$. It follows that the truncation $\tau_{n-2}(\mathbf{u})$ is uniformly distributed over $\mathrm{Ball}_{n-2}(1)$, which allows to transfer our results to random points in balls.

Recall that the cumulative distribution function of the Beta(a, b) distribution is the regularized incomplete beta function $I_x(a, b)$ defined as:

$$I_x(a, b) = \frac{1}{B(a, b)} \int_0^x u^{a-1}(1-u)^{b-1}du, \tag{1}$$

where $B(a, b) = \frac{\Gamma(a)\Gamma(b)}{\Gamma(a+b)}$ denotes the beta function. We have the following elementary bounds (by integrating by parts):

$$\frac{x^a(1-x)^{b-1}}{aB(a, b)} \leq I_x(a, b) \qquad \forall a > 0, b \geq 1, 0 \leq x \leq 1 \tag{2}$$

$$I_x(a, b) \leq \frac{x^a}{a \cdot B(a, b)} \qquad \forall a > 0, b \geq 1, 0 \leq x \leq 1 \tag{3}$$

For $z \in [0, 1]$ and $a, b > 0$, $I_z^{-1}(a, b) + I_{1-z}^{-1}(b, a) = 1$ which is immediate from the relation $I_x(a, b) + I_{1-x}(b, a) = 1$.

Finally, $P(s, x) = \int_0^x t^{s-1}e^{-t}dt/\Gamma(s)$ is the regularized incomplete gamma function.

Lattices. A *lattice* L is a discrete subgroup of $\mathbb{R}^m$, or equivalently the set $L(\mathbf{b}_1, \ldots, \mathbf{b}_n) = \{\sum_{i=1}^n x_i\mathbf{b}_i : x_i \in \mathbb{Z}\}$ of all integer combinations of n linearly independent vectors $\mathbf{b}_1, \ldots, \mathbf{b}_n \in \mathbb{R}^m$. Such $\mathbf{b}_i$'s form a *basis* of L. All the bases of L have the same number n of elements, called the dimension or rank of L, and the same n-dimensional volume of the parallelepiped $\{\sum_{i=1}^n a_i\mathbf{b}_i : a_i \in [0, 1)\}$ they generate. We call this volume the co-volume, or determinant, of L, and denote it by $\mathrm{covol}(L)$. The lattice L is said to be *full-rank* if $n = m$. The most famous lattice problem is the *shortest vector problem* (SVP), which asks to find a non-zero lattice vector of minimal Euclidean norm. The *closest vector problem* (CVP) asks to find a lattice vector closest to a target vector.

Orthogonalization. For a basis $B = (\mathbf{b}_1, \ldots, \mathbf{b}_n)$ of a lattice L and $i \in \{1, \ldots, n\}$, we denote by π_i the orthogonal projection on $\text{span}(\mathbf{b}_1, \ldots, \mathbf{b}_{i-1})^\perp$. The *Gram-Schmidt orthogonalization* of the basis B is defined as the sequence of orthogonal vectors $B^\star = (\mathbf{b}_1^\star, \ldots, \mathbf{b}_n^\star)$, where $\mathbf{b}_i^\star := \pi_i(\mathbf{b}_i)$. We can write each $\mathbf{b}_i$ as $\mathbf{b}_i^\star + \sum_{j=1}^{i-1} \mu_{i,j} \mathbf{b}_j^\star$ for some unique $\mu_{i,1}, \ldots, \mu_{i,i-1} \in \mathbb{R}$. Thus, we may represent the $\mu_{i,j}$'s by a lower-triangular matrix μ with unit diagonal. The projection of a lattice may not be a lattice, but $\pi_i(L)$ is an $n+1-i$ dimensional lattice generated by $\pi_i(\mathbf{b}_i), \ldots, \pi_i(\mathbf{b}_n)$, with $\text{covol}(\pi_i(L)) = \prod_{j=i}^{n} \|\mathbf{b}_j^\star\|$.

The Gaussian Heuristic. For a full-rank lattice L in $\mathbb{R}^n$ and a measurable set $C \subset \mathbb{R}^n$, the Gaussian heuristic estimates the number of lattice points inside of C to be approximately $\text{vol}(C)/\text{vol}(L)$. Accordingly, we would expect that $\lambda_1(L)$ might be close to $\text{GH}(L) = V_n(1)^{-1/n} \text{vol}(L)^{1/n}$, which holds for a random lattice L.

Cylinders. The performances of cylinder pruning are directly related to the following bodies. Define the (k-dimensional) cylinder-intersection of radii $R_1 \leq \cdots \leq R_k$ as the set

$$C_{R_1, \ldots, R_k} = \left\{ (x_1, \ldots, x_k) \in \mathbb{R}^k, \ \forall j \leq k, \ \sum_{\ell=1}^{j} x_\ell^2 \leq R_j^2 \right\} \subseteq \text{Ball}_k(R_k).$$

Gama *et al.* [16] showed how to efficiently compute tight lower and upper bounds for $\text{vol}(C_{R_1, \ldots, R_k})$, thanks to the Dirichlet distribution and special integrals.

2.2 Enumeration with Cylinder Pruning

To simplify notations, we assume that we focus on the SVP setting, *i.e.* to find short lattice vectors, rather than the more general CVP setting. Let L be a full-rank lattice in $\mathbb{R}^n$. Given a basis $B = (\mathbf{b}_1, \ldots, \mathbf{b}_n)$ of L and a radius $R > 0$, Enumeration [15,18,29] outputs $L \cap S$ where $S = \text{Ball}_n(R)$ by a depth-first tree search: by comparing all the norms of the vectors obtained, one extracts a shortest non-zero lattice vector.

We follow the general pruning framework of [5], which replaces S by a subset of S depending on B. Given a function $f : \{1, \ldots, n\} \to [0, 1]$, Gama *et al.* [16] introduced the following set to generalize the pruned enumeration of [34,35]:

$$P_f(B, R) = \{\mathbf{x} \in \mathbb{R}^n \text{ s.t. } \|\pi_{n+1-i}(\mathbf{x})\| \leq f(i)R \text{ for all } 1 \leq i \leq n\}, \quad (4)$$

where the π_i is the projection over $\text{span}(\mathbf{b}_1, \ldots, \mathbf{b}_{i-1})^\perp$. The set $P_f(B, R)$ should be viewed as a random variable. Note that $P_f(B, R) \subseteq \text{Ball}_n(R)$ and if g is the constant function equal to 1, then $P_g(B, R) = \text{Ball}_n(R)$.

Gama *et al.* [16] noticed that the basic enumeration algorithm can actually compute $L \cap P_f(B, R)$ instead of $L \cap \text{Ball}_n(R)$, just by changing its parameters. We call *cylinder pruning* this form of pruned enumeration, because $P_f(B, R)$ is an intersection of cylinders, since each equation $\|\pi_{n+1-i}(\mathbf{x})\| \leq f(i)R$ defines a cylinder. Cylinder pruning was historically introduced in the SVP setting, but its adaptation to CVP is straightforward, as was shown by Liu and Nguyen [21].

Complexity of Enumeration. The advantage is that for suitable choices of f, enumerating $L \cap P_f(B, R)$ is much cheaper than enumerating $L \cap \text{Ball}_n(R)$: indeed, [16] shows that cylinder pruning runs in $\sum_{k=1}^{n} N_k$ poly-time operations, where N_k is the number of points of $\pi_{n+1-k}(L \cap P_f(B, R))$: this is because N_k is exactly the number of nodes at depth $n - k + 1$ of the enumeration tree which is searched by cylinder pruning. By the Gaussian heuristic, we have heuristically $N_k \approx H_k$ where:

$$H_k = \frac{\text{vol}(\pi_{n+1-k}(P_f(B, R)))}{\text{covol}(\pi_{n+1-k}(L))} = \frac{\text{vol}(C_{Rf(1),...,Rf(k)})}{\text{covol}(\pi_{n+1-k}(L))}.$$

It follows that the complexity of cylinder pruning is heuristically:

$$N = \sum_{k=1}^{n} \frac{\text{vol}(C_{Rf(1),...,Rf(k)})}{\prod_{i=n-k+1}^{n} \|\mathbf{b}_i^\star\|} \tag{5}$$

This N is a heuristic estimate of the number of nodes in the tree searched by cylinder pruning. It depends on one hand on R and the bounding function f, but on the other hand on the quality of the basis B, because of the term $\prod_{i=n-k+1}^{n} \|\mathbf{b}_i^\star\|$. In the SVP setting, one can further divide (5) by two, because of symmetries in the enumeration tree.

Success Probability. We consider two settings:

Approximation Setting: The algorithm is successful if and only if we find at least one non-zero point of $L \cap P_f(B, R)$, that is $L \cap P_f(B, R) \not\subseteq \{0\}$. This is the situation studied in [5] and corresponds to the use of cylinder pruning in blockwise lattice reduction. By the Gaussian heuristic, the number of points of $L \cap P_f(B, R)$ is heuristically:

$$\frac{\text{vol}(P_f(B, R))}{\text{covol}(L)} = \frac{\text{vol}(C_{Rf(1),...,Rf(n)})}{\text{covol}(L)}.$$

So we estimate the probability of success as:

$$\Pr_{\text{succ}} = \min\left(1, \frac{\text{vol}(C_{Rf(1),...,Rf(n)})}{\text{covol}(L)}\right). \tag{6}$$

Since $\text{covol}(L) = V_n(\text{GH}(L))$, if $R = \beta \text{GH}(L)$, then (6) becomes

$$\Pr_{\text{succ}} = \min\left(1, \beta^n \frac{\text{vol}(C_{Rf(1),...,Rf(n)})}{V_n(R)}\right). \tag{7}$$

Unique Setting: This corresponds to the situation studied in [16] and to bounded distance decoding (BDD). There is a secret vector $\mathbf{v} \in L$, whose distribution is assumed to be the Gaussian distribution over $\mathbb{R}^n$ of parameter σ. The algorithm is successful if and only if $\mathbf{v}$ is returned by the algorithm, *i.e.* if and only if $\mathbf{v} \in P_f(B, R)$. So we estimate the probability of success as:

$$\Pr_{\text{succ}} = \rho_{n,\sigma}(P_f(B, R)) = \rho_{n,\sigma}(C_{f(1)R,...,f(n)R}). \tag{8}$$

3   Lower Bounds for Cylinder Pruning

In this section, we prove novel geometric properties of cylinder intersections: if a cylinder intersection is sufficiently big (with respect to its volume or its Gaussian measure), we can lower bound the radii defining the intersection, as well as the volume of all its canonical projections, which are also cylinder intersections.

A basic ingredient behind these properties is a special case of cylinder intersections, corresponding to the step-bounding functions used in [16]. More precisely, we consider the intersection of a ball with a cylinder, which we call a ball-cylinder:

$$D_{k,n}(R, R') = \left\{ (x_1, \ldots, x_n) \in \mathbb{R}^n, \ \sum_{l=1}^{k} x_l^2 \leq R^2 \ \text{and} \ \sum_{l=1}^{n} x_l^2 \leq R'^2 \right\}.$$

In other words, $D_{k,n}(R, R') = C_{R,\ldots,R,R',\ldots,R'}$ where R is repeated k times, and R' is repeated $n - k$ times. The following result is trivial:

Lemma 1. *Let $R_1 \leq R_2 \leq \cdots \leq R_n$ and $1 \leq k \leq n$. Then:*

$$C_{R_1,\ldots,R_n} \subseteq D_{k,n}(R_k, R_n).$$

Note that for fixed k, n and R', $\mathrm{vol}(D_{k,n}(R, R'))$ is an increasing function of R. The following lemma gives properties of the volume and Gaussian measures of ball-cylinders, based on the background:

Lemma 2. *Let $R \leq R'$ and $1 \leq k \leq n$. Then:*

$$\mathrm{vol}(D_{k,n}(R, R')) = V_n(R') \times I_{(R/R')^2}(k/2, 1 + (n-k)/2)$$
$$\rho_{k,\sigma}(\mathrm{Ball}_k(R)) \geq \rho_{n,\sigma}(D_{k,n}(R, R')) \geq \rho_{k,\sigma}(\mathrm{Ball}_k(R))\rho_{n,\sigma}(\mathrm{Ball}_n(R'))$$
$$\rho_{n,\sigma}(\mathrm{Ball}_n(R)) = P(n/2, R^2/(2\sigma^2)).$$

Proof. Because $D_{k,n}(R, R') \subseteq \mathrm{Ball}_n(R')$, $\mathrm{vol}(D_{k,n}(R, R'))/V_n(R')$ is the probability that a random vector $(x_1, \ldots, x_n)$ (chosen uniformly at random from the n-dimensional ball of radius R') satisfies $\sum_{l=1}^{k} x_l^2 \leq R^2$, that is, $\sum_{l=1}^{k}(x_l/R')^2 \leq (R/R')^2$. It follows that this probability is also the probability that a random vector $(y_1, \ldots, y_n)$ (chosen uniformly at random from the n-dimensional unit ball) satisfies: $\sum_{l=1}^{k} y_l^2 \leq (R/R')^2$. From the background, we know that $\sum_{l=1}^{k} y_l^2$ has distribution $\mathrm{Beta}(k/2, (n+2-k)/2)$, which proves the first equality.

Note that $D_{k,n}(R, R') \subseteq D_{k,n}(R, +\infty)$, which proves that $\rho_{n,\sigma}(D_{k,n}(R, R')) \leq \rho_{k,\sigma}(\mathrm{Ball}_k(R))$. Furthermore, by the Gaussian correlation inequality on convex symmetric sets, we have:

$$\rho_{n,\sigma}(D_{k,n}(R, R')) \geq \rho_{n,\sigma}(\mathrm{Ball}_n(R')) \times \rho_{n,\sigma}\left(\{(x_1, \ldots, x_n) \in \mathbb{R}^n : \sum_{i=1}^{k} x_i^2 \leq R^2\} \right)$$

$$= \rho_{k,\sigma}(\mathrm{Ball}_k(R))\rho_{n,\sigma}(\mathrm{Ball}_n(R'))$$

which proves that $\rho_{n,\sigma}(D_{k,n}(R, R')) \geq P(k/2, R^2/(2\sigma^2))P(n/2, R'^2/(2\sigma^2))$.

Finally, let $x_1, \ldots, x_n$ be independent, normally distributed random variables with mean 0 and variance 1. Then $X = \sum_{i=1}^{n} x_i^2$ has the distribution Gamma$(n/2, \theta = 2)$ whose CDF is $P(n/2, x/2)$. Therefore $\rho_n(\text{Ball}_n(R)) = P(n/2, R^2/2)$.   □

3.1   Lower Bounds on Cylinder Radii

The following theorem lower bounds the radii of any cylinder intersection covering a fraction of the ball:

Theorem 1. *Let $0 \le R_1 \le \cdots \le R_n$ be such that $\text{vol}(C_{R_1,\ldots,R_n}) \ge \alpha V_n(R_n)$, where $0 \le \alpha \le 1$. If for all $1 \le k \le n$, we define $\alpha_k > 0$ by $I_{\alpha_k}(k/2, 1 + (n - k)/2) = \alpha$, then $\text{vol}(D_{k,n}(\sqrt{\alpha_k}R_n, R_n)) \le \text{vol}(C_{R_1,\ldots,R_n})$ and:*

$$R_k \ge \sqrt{\alpha_k}R_n.$$

Proof. Lemma 1 shows that:

$$\text{vol}(C_{R_1,\ldots,R_n}) \le \text{vol}(D_{k,n}(R_k, R_n)).$$

On the other hand, Lemma 2 shows that by definition of α_k:

$$\text{vol}(D_{k,n}(\sqrt{\alpha_k}R_n, R_n))$$
$$= V_n(R_n) \times I_{\alpha_k}\left(\frac{k}{2}, 1 + \frac{n-k}{2}\right) = \alpha V_n(R_n) \le \text{vol}(C_{R_1,\ldots,R_n}),$$

which proves the first statement. Hence:
$\text{vol}(D_{k,n}(\sqrt{\alpha_k}R_n, R_n)) \le \text{vol}(D_{k,n}(R_k, R_n))$, which implies that $R_k \ge \sqrt{\alpha_k}R_n$.
                                                         □

The parameter α in Theorem 1 is directly related to our success probability (7) in the approximation setting: indeed, if $R_n = \beta GH(L)$ and $\text{Pr}_{\text{succ}} \ge \gamma$, then $\alpha = \gamma/\beta^n$ satisfies the condition of Theorem 1. We have the following Gaussian analogue of Theorem 1, where the lower bound on the volume is replaced by a lower bound on the Gaussian measure:

Theorem 2. *Let $0 \le R_1 \le \cdots \le R_n$ be such that $\rho_{n,\sigma}(C_{R_1,\ldots,R_n}) \ge \beta$, where $0 \le \beta \le 1$. If for all $1 \le k \le n$ we define $\beta_k > 0$ by $P(k/2, \beta_k/(2\sigma^2)) = \beta$, then $\rho_{n,\sigma}(D_{k,n}(\sqrt{\beta_k}, R_n)) \le \rho_{n,\sigma}(C_{R_1,\ldots,R_n})$ and $R_k \ge \sqrt{\beta_k}$.*

Proof. On the one hand, Lemma 1 shows that:

$$\rho_{n,\sigma}(C_{R_1,\ldots,R_n}) \le \rho_{n,\sigma}(D_{k,n}(R_k, R_n)).$$

On the other hand, Lemma 2 shows that by definition of β_k:

$$\rho_{n,\sigma}(D_{k,n}(\sqrt{\beta_k}, R_n)) \le P(k/2, \beta_k/2(\sigma^2)) = \beta \le \rho_{n,\sigma}(C_{R_1,\ldots,R_n}),$$

which proves the first statement. Hence:

$$\rho_{n,\sigma}(D_{k,n}(\sqrt{\beta_k}, R_n)) \le \rho_{n,\sigma}(D_{k,n}(R_k, R_n)),$$

which implies that $R_k \ge \sqrt{\beta_k}$.   □

In Theorem 2, β can be chosen as any lower bound on the success probability in the unique setting (8).

Theorem 1 allows to derive numerical lower bounds on the radii, from any lower bound on the success probability. However, there is a special case for which the lower bound has a simple algebraic form, thanks to the following technical lemma (proved in Appendix A):

Lemma 3. *If $1 \leq k \leq n$, then:*

$$1 - P(1/2, 1/2) \leq I_{k/n}(k/2, (n-k)/2) \leq P(1/2, 1/2) \tag{9}$$

By coupling Theorem 1 and Lemma 3, we obtain that the squared radii of any high-volume cylinder intersection are lower bounded by linear functions:

Theorem 3. *Let $0 \leq R_1 \leq \cdots \leq R_n$ such that $\mathrm{vol}(C_{R_1,\ldots,R_n}) \geq P(1/2, 1/2) \times V_n(R_n)$. Then for all $1 \leq k \leq n$:*

$$R_k \geq \sqrt{\frac{k}{n+2}} R_n.$$

Proof. The assumption and (9) imply that

$$\mathrm{vol}(C_{R_1,\ldots,R_n}) \geq I_{k/(n+2)}(k/2, 1 + (n-k)/2) V_n(R_n).$$

Hence, we can apply Theorem 1 with $\alpha_k = \sqrt{k/(n+2)}$. $\square$

Note that $P(1/2, 1/2) \approx 0.683\ldots$, so any bounding function with high success probability must have a cost lower bounded by that of some linear pruning, which means that its speed-up (compared to full enumeration) is at most single-exponential (see [16]).

3.2   Lower Bounds on Cylinder Volumes from Isoperimetry

The lower bounds on radii given by Theorems 1 and 2 provide lower bounds on $\mathrm{vol}(C_{R_1,\ldots,R_k})$ for all $1 \leq k \leq n-1$. Indeed, if $R_k \geq \sqrt{\alpha_k} R_n$, then:

$$\mathrm{vol}(C_{R_1,\ldots,R_k}) \geq \mathrm{vol}(C_{\sqrt{\alpha_1} R_n,\ldots,\sqrt{\alpha_k} R_n}).$$

Such lower bounds immediately provide a lower bound on the cost of enumeration with cylinder pruning, because of (5).

In this subsection, we show that this direct lower bound can be significantly improved, namely it can be replaced by $V_k(\sqrt{\alpha_k} R_n)$. Our key ingredient is the following isoperimetric result, which says that among all Borel sets of given volume, the ball centered at the origin has the largest measure, for any isotropic measure which decays monotonically radially away :

Theorem 4 (Isoperimetry). *Let A be a Borel set of $\mathbb{R}^k$. Let $\mathcal{D}$ be a distribution over $\mathbb{R}^k$ such that its probability density function f is radial and decays* *monotonically radially away:* $f(\mathbf{x}) \le f(\mathbf{y})$ *whenever* $\|\mathbf{x}\| \ge \|\mathbf{y}\|$. *If a random variable* X *has distribution* $\mathcal{D}$, *then:*

$$\Pr(X \in A) \le \Pr(X \in B),$$

where B *is the ball of* $\mathbb{R}^k$ *centered at the origin such that* $\mathrm{vol}(B) = \mathrm{vol}(A)$.

Proof. The statement is proved in [38, pp. 498–499] for the special case where $\mathcal{D}$ is the Gaussian distribution over $\mathbb{R}^k$. However, the proof actually works for any radial probability density function which decays monotonically radially away. □

It implies the following:

Lemma 4. *Let* $1 \le k \le n$. *Let* $\pi = \tau_k$ *be the canonical projection of* $\mathbb{R}^n$ *over* $\mathbb{R}^k$. *Let* C *be a subset of the* n-*dimensional ball of radius* R' *such that both* C *and* $\pi(C)$ *are measurable. If* R *is the radius of the* k-*dimensional ball of volume* $\mathrm{vol}(\pi(C))$, *then:*

$$\mathrm{vol}(C) \le \mathrm{vol}(D_{k,n}(R, R')) \text{ and } \rho_{n,\sigma}(C) \le \rho_{n,\sigma}(D_{k,n}(R, R')).$$

Proof. Let B' be the n-dimensional centered ball of radius R'. Let B be the k-dimensional centered ball of radius R. Let $\mathbf{x}$ be chosen uniformly at random from B'. Since $C \subseteq B'$, $\mathrm{vol}(C)/V_n(R')$ is exactly $\Pr(\mathbf{x} \in C)$, and we have:

$$\Pr(\mathbf{x} \in C) \le \Pr(\pi(\mathbf{x}) \in \pi(C)).$$

Let $\mathcal{D}$ be the distribution of $\mathbf{y} = \pi(\mathbf{x}) \in \mathbb{R}^k$. Then by Theorem 4,

$$\Pr(\mathbf{y} \in \pi(C)) \le \Pr(\mathbf{y} \in B).$$

Hence:

$$\Pr(\mathbf{x} \in C) \le \Pr(\mathbf{y} \in B) = \frac{\mathrm{vol}(D_{k,n}(R, R'))}{V_n(R')},$$

which proves the first statement. Similarly, if $\mathbf{x}$ is chosen from the Gaussian distribution corresponding to $\rho_{n,\sigma}$, then

$$\rho_{n,\sigma}(C)/\rho_{n,\sigma}(B') = \Pr(\mathbf{x} \in C) \le \Pr(\pi(\mathbf{x}) \in \pi(C)).$$

Let $\mathcal{D}'$ be the distribution of $\mathbf{y} = \pi(\mathbf{x}) \in \mathbb{R}^k$: this is a Gaussian distribution. Then by Theorem 4,

$$\Pr(\mathbf{y} \in \pi(C)) \le \Pr(\mathbf{y} \in B) = \frac{\rho_{n,\sigma}(D_{k,n}(R, R'))}{\rho_{n,\sigma}(B')}.$$

□

It has the following geometric consequence:

Corollary 1. *Let* $R_1 \le R_2 \le \cdots \le R_n$ *and* $1 \le k \le n$. *Let* $R > 0$ *such that* $\mathrm{vol}(C_{R_1,\ldots,R_n}) \ge \mathrm{vol}(D_{k,n}(R, R_n))$ *or* $\rho_{n,\sigma}(C_{R_1,\ldots,R_n}) \ge \rho_{n,\sigma}(D_{k,n}(R, R_n))$. *Then:*

$$\mathrm{vol}(C_{R_1,\ldots,R_k}) \ge V_k(R).$$

Proof. Let $C = C_{R_1,\dots,R_n}$ and $\pi = \tau_k$ be the canonical projection of $\mathbb{R}^n$ over $\mathbb{R}^k$. Then $\pi(C) = C_{R_1,\dots,R_k}$. If r is the radius the k-dimensional ball of volume $\mathrm{vol}(\pi(C))$, Lemma 4 implies that: $\mathrm{vol}(C) \leq \mathrm{vol}(D_{k,n}(r, R_n))$ and $\rho_{n,\sigma}(C) \leq \rho_{n,\sigma}(D_{k,n}(r, R_n))$. Thus, by definition of R, we have either $\mathrm{vol}(D_{k,n}(R, R_n)) \leq \mathrm{vol}(C) \leq \mathrm{vol}(D_{k,n}(r, R_n))$ or $\rho_{n,\sigma}(D_{k,n}(R, R_n)) \leq \rho_{n,\sigma}(C) \leq \rho_{n,\sigma}(D_{k,n}(r, R_n))$, which each imply that $r \geq R$. $\qquad\square$

Note that $C_{R_1,\dots,R_k}$ and $\mathrm{Ball}_k(R)$ are the projections of respectively $C_{R_1,\dots,R_n}$ and $D_{k,n}(R, R_n)$ over $\mathbb{R}^k$. So the corollary is a bit surprising: if one particular body is "bigger" than the other, then so are their projections. Obviously, this cannot hold for arbitrary bodies in the worst case.

This corollary implies the following lower bounds, which strengthens Theorem 1:

Corollary 2. *Under the same assumptions as Theorem 1, we have:*

$$\mathrm{vol}(C_{R_1,\dots,R_k}) \geq V_k(\sqrt{\alpha_k} R_n).$$

Proof. From Theorem 1, we have: $\mathrm{vol}(C_{R_1,\dots,R_n}) \geq \mathrm{vol}(D_{k,n}(\sqrt{\alpha_k} R_n, R_n))$. And we apply Corollary 1. $\qquad\square$

Similarly, we obtain:

Corollary 3. *Under the same assumptions as Theorem 2, we have:*

$$\mathrm{vol}(C_{R_1,\dots,R_k}) \geq V_k(\sqrt{\beta_k} R_n).$$

It would be interesting to study if the lower bounds of the last two corollaries can be further improved.

3.3 Generalisation to Finitely Many Cylinder Intersections

In this section, we give an analogue of the results of Sect. 3.2 to finitely many cylinder intersections, which corresponds to the extreme pruning setting. The key ingredient is the following refinement of isoperimetry:

Theorem 5 (Isoperimetry). *Let $A_1, \dots, A_m$ be Borel sets of $\mathbb{R}^k$. Let $\mathcal{D}$ be a distribution over $\mathbb{R}^k$ such that its probability density function f is radial and decays monotonically radially away: $f(\mathbf{x}) \leq f(\mathbf{y})$ whenever $\|\mathbf{x}\| \geq \|\mathbf{y}\|$. If a random variable X has distribution $\mathcal{D}$, then:*

$$\frac{1}{m} \sum_{i=1}^{m} \Pr(X \in A_i) \leq \Pr(X \in B),$$

where B is the ball of $\mathbb{R}^k$ centered at the origin such that $\mathrm{vol}(B) = \frac{1}{m} \sum_{i=1}^{m} \mathrm{vol}(A_i)$.

Proof. The statement is proved in [38, pp. 499–500] for the special case where $\mathcal{D}$ is the Gaussian distribution over $\mathbb{R}^k$. However, the proof actually works for any radial probability density function which decays monotonically radially away. $\square$

Lemma 5. *Let $1 \leq k \leq n$. Let $\pi = \tau_k$ be the canonical projection of $\mathbb{R}^n$ over $\mathbb{R}^k$. Let $C_1, \ldots, C_m \subseteq \text{Ball}_n(R')$ such that all the C_i's and $\pi(C_i)$'s are measurable. If R is the radius of the k-dimensional ball of volume $\frac{1}{m} \sum_{i=1}^{m} \text{vol}(\pi(C_i))$, then:*

$$\frac{1}{m} \sum_{i=1}^{m} \text{vol}(C_i) \leq \text{vol}(D_{k,n}(R, R')) \text{ and } \frac{1}{m} \sum_{i=1}^{m} \rho_{n,\sigma}(C_i) \leq \rho_{n,\sigma}(D_{k,n}(R, R')).$$

Proof. Let B' be the n-dimensional centered ball of radius R'. Let B be the k-dimensional centered ball of radius R such that $\text{vol}(B) = \frac{1}{m} \sum_{i=1}^{m} \text{vol}(\pi(C_i))$. Let $\mathbf{x}$ be chosen uniformly at random from B'. Since $C_i \subseteq B'$, $\text{vol}(C_i)/V_n(R')$ is exactly $\Pr(\mathbf{x} \in C_i)$, and we have:

$$\Pr(\mathbf{x} \in C_i) \leq \Pr(\pi(\mathbf{x}) \in \pi(C_i)).$$

Let $\mathcal{D}$ be the distribution of $\mathbf{y} = \pi(\mathbf{x}) \in \mathbb{R}^k$. Then by Theorem 5,

$$\frac{1}{m} \sum_{i=1}^{m} \Pr(\mathbf{y} \in \pi(C_i)) \leq \Pr(\mathbf{y} \in B).$$

Hence:

$$\frac{1}{m} \sum_{i=1}^{m} \Pr(\mathbf{x} \in C_i) \leq \Pr(\mathbf{y} \in B) = \frac{\text{vol}(D_{k,n}(R, R'))}{V_n(R')},$$

which proves the first statement.   □

It has the following geometric consequence:

Corollary 4. *Let $C_1, \ldots, C_m \subseteq \text{Ball}_n(R_n)$ be n-dimensional cylinder intersections. Let $1 \leq k \leq n$ and denote by $\pi = \tau_k$ the canonical projection of $\mathbb{R}^n$ over $\mathbb{R}^k$. Let $R > 0$ such that $\frac{1}{m} \sum_{i=1}^{m} \text{vol}(C_i) \geq \text{vol}(D_{k,n}(R, R_n))$ or $\frac{1}{m} \sum_{i=1}^{m} \rho_{n,\sigma}(C_i) \geq \rho_{n,\sigma}(D_{k,n}(R, R_n))$. Then:*

$$\frac{1}{m} \sum_{i=1}^{m} \text{vol}(\pi(C_i)) \geq V_k(R).$$

Proof. If r is the radius of the k-dimensional ball of volume $\frac{1}{m} \sum_{i=1}^{m} \text{vol}(\pi(C_i))$, the Lemma 5 implies that: $\frac{1}{m} \sum_{i=1}^{m} \text{vol}(C_i) \leq \text{vol}(D_{k,n}(r, R_n))$ and $\frac{1}{m} \sum_{i=1}^{m} \rho_{n,\sigma}(C_i) \leq \rho_{n,\sigma}(D_{k,n}(r, R_n))$. Thus, by definition of R, we have either $\text{vol}(D_{k,n}(R, R_n)) \leq \text{vol}(C) \leq \text{vol}(D_{k,n}(r, R_n))$ or $\rho_{n,\sigma}(D_{k,n}(R, R_n)) \leq \rho_n(C) \leq \rho_{n,\sigma}(D_{k,n}(r, R_n))$, which each imply that $r \geq R$.   □

Theorem 6. *Let $C_1, \ldots, C_m \subseteq \text{Ball}_n(R_n)$ be n-dimensional cylinder intersections such that $\sum_{i=1}^{m} \text{vol}(C_i) \geq m\alpha V_n(R_n)$, where $0 \leq \alpha \leq 1$. If for all $1 \leq k \leq n$, we define $\alpha_k > 0$ by $I_{\alpha_k}(k/2, 1 + (n-k)/2) = \alpha$, then $\text{vol}(D_{k,n}(\sqrt{\alpha_k}R_n, R_n)) \leq \frac{1}{m} \sum_{i=1}^{m} \text{vol}(C_i)$ and:*

$$\sum_{i=1}^{m} \text{vol}(\pi(C_i)) \geq mV_k(\sqrt{\alpha_k}R_n),$$

where $\pi = \tau_k$ denotes the canonical projection of $\mathbb{R}^n$ over $\mathbb{R}^k$.

Proof. Lemma 2 shows that by definition of α_k:

$$\text{vol}(D_{k,n}(\sqrt{\alpha_k}R_n, R_n)) = \alpha V_n(R_n) \leq \frac{1}{m} \sum_{i=1}^{m} \text{vol}(C_i),$$

which proves the first statement. And the rest follows by Lemma 4.   □

Again, the parameter α in Theorem 6 is directly related to our global success probability (7) in the approximation setting: the global success probability is $\leq \sum_{i=1}^{m} \text{vol}(C_i)/\text{covol}(L)$ so if $R_n = \beta GH(L)$ and the global success probability is $\geq \gamma$, then $\alpha = \gamma/(m\beta^n)$ satisfies the condition of Theorem 1.

We have the following Gaussian analogue of Theorem 6:

Theorem 7. *Let $C_1, \ldots, C_m \subseteq \text{Ball}_n(R_n)$ be n-dimensional cylinder intersections such that $\sum_{i=1}^{m} \rho_{n,\sigma}(C_i) \geq m\beta$, where $0 \leq \beta \leq 1/m$. If for all $1 \leq k \leq n$, we define $\beta_k > 0$ by $P(k/2, \beta_k/(2\sigma^2)) = \beta$, then $\rho_{n,\sigma}(D_{k,n}(\sqrt{\beta_k}R_n, R_n)) \leq \frac{1}{m} \sum_{i=1}^{m} \rho_{n,\sigma}(C_i)$ and:*

$$\sum_{i=1}^{m} \text{vol}(\pi(C_i)) \geq mV_k(\beta_k),$$

where $\pi = \tau_k$ denotes the canonical projection of $\mathbb{R}^n$ over $\mathbb{R}^k$.

In the unique setting, the global success probability is $\leq \sum_{i=1}^{m} \rho_{n,\sigma}(C_i)$, so if the global success probability is $\geq \gamma$, then $\beta = \gamma/m$ satisfies the condition of Theorem 7.

Surprisingly, we will show that Theorems 6 and 7 imply that we can lower bound the cost of extreme pruning, independently of the number m of cylinder intersections:

Lemma 6. *Let the global probability $0 \leq \alpha' \leq 1$ and $1 \leq k \leq n$. Let $\alpha = \alpha'/m$ and $\alpha_k > 0$ such that $I_{\alpha_k}(k/2, 1 + (n-k)/2) = \alpha$. Then, $mV_k(\sqrt{\alpha_k})$ is strictly decreasing w.r.t. m, yet lower bounded by some linear function of α':*

$$mV_k(\sqrt{\alpha_k}) > \alpha' \cdot \frac{kV_k(1)}{2} \cdot B\left(\frac{k}{2}, 1 + \frac{n-k}{2}\right).$$

Furthermore, for fixed α', k and n, the left-hand side converges to the right-hand side when m goes to infinity and α_k is defined as above.

Lemma 6 implies that the cost of enumeration decreases as the number of cylinder intersections increases, if the global probability α' is fixed. However, there is a limit given by some linear function of α' which depends only on n.

To prove the lemma, we use the following two lemmas:

Lemma 7. *For $a \geq 0, b \geq 1, 0 < z \leq 1$:*

$$\frac{\partial}{\partial z} I_z^{-1}(a, b) \geq \frac{1}{az} I_z^{-1}(a, b)$$

Proof. Substituting $x = I_z^{-1}(a, b)$ in (3) we obtain:

$$\frac{(1 - I_z^{-1}(a, b))^{b-1}(I_z^{-1}(a, b))^a}{aB(a, b)} \leq z.$$

This implies that

$$\frac{\partial}{\partial z}I_z^{-1}(a, b) = B(a, b)(1 - I_z^{-1}(a, b))^{1-b}(I_z^{-1}(a, b))^{1-a} \geq \frac{1}{az}I_z^{-1}(a, b).$$

$\square$

Lemma 8. *For $a \geq 0, b \geq 1$:*

$$\lim_{y \to 0+} \frac{y}{(I_y^{-1}(a, b))^a} = \frac{1}{a \cdot B(a, b)}$$

Proof. Bounding inequalities (2) and (3) from both sides implies that

$$\lim_{x \to 0+} \frac{I_x(a, b)}{x^a} = \frac{1}{a \cdot B(a, b)}.$$

Letting $x = I_y^{-1}(a, b)$, the claim holds. $\square$

Proof of Lemma 6
    We have $I_{\alpha_k}(k/2, 1 + (n - k)/2) = \alpha'/m$ and $\alpha_k = I_{\alpha'/m}^{-1}(k/2, 1 + (n - k)/2)$. This gives:

$$mV_k(\sqrt{\alpha_k}) = V_k(1)m \cdot \left(I_{\alpha'/m}^{-1}(k/2, 1 + (n - k)/2)\right)^{k/2}.$$

Thus, to show the first claim, it suffices to prove that

$$g(y) = \frac{1}{y}\left(I_{\alpha'y}^{-1}(k/2, 1 + (n - k)/2)\right)^{k/2}$$

is strictly increasing over $0 < y \leq 1$.
    For simplicity, we write $I := I_{\alpha'y}^{-1}(k/2, 1 + (n - k)/2)$ and we have:

$$g'(y) = \frac{\alpha'k}{2y}I^{k/2-1} \cdot \frac{\partial I}{\partial y} - \frac{I^{k/2}}{y^2}$$

By Lemma 7, we can see that $\frac{\partial I}{\partial y} \geq \frac{2}{\alpha'ky} > I$ and $g'(y) > 0$ which proves the first claim. The lower bound can be derived by the limit of the function. By the relationship

$$\lim_{m \to \infty} mV_k(\sqrt{\alpha_k}) = V_k(1) \cdot \lim_{y \to 0+} g(y),$$

and the straightforward consequence of Lemma 8,

$$\lim_{y \to 0+} g(y) = \alpha' \cdot \frac{k}{2} \cdot B\left(\frac{k}{2}, 1 + \frac{n - k}{2}\right),$$

we obtain the second claim. $\square$

    By a similar technique, we can show a similar result for the Gaussian case: the proof is postponed to Appendix A.3.

Lemma 9. *Let the global probability* $0 \leq \beta' \leq 1$ *and* $1 \leq k \leq n$. *Let* $\beta = \beta'/m$ *and* $\beta_k > 0$ *such that* $P(k/2, \beta_k/(2\sigma^2)) = \beta$. *Then,* $mV_k(\sqrt{\beta_k})$ *is strictly decreasing w.r.t.* m, *yet lower bounded by some linear function of* β':

$$mV_k(\sqrt{\beta_k}) > \beta'(2\pi\sigma^2)^{k/2}.$$

Moreover, for fixed β', k *and* σ, *the left-hand side converges to the right-hand side when* m *goes to infinity and* β_k *is defined as above.*

4   Efficient Upper Bounds Based on Cross-Entropy

In order to guess how tight are our lower bounds in practice, we need to be able to find efficiently very good bounding functions for cylinder pruning. Different methods have been used over the years (see [7,9,10,16]). In this section, we present the method that we used to generate bounding functions that try to minimize the enumeration cost, under the constraint that the success probability is greater than a given $p_0 > 0$. From our experience, different methods usually give rise to close bounding functions, but their running time can vary significantly.

4.1   Our Formulation and Previous Algorithms

Usually, the problem to find optimal cost has two formulations and our algorithm targets the first one:

1. [7,11] for a given basis B, radius R, and target probability p_0, minimize the cost (5) subject to the constraint that the probability (6) is greater than p_0. The variables are $R_1, \ldots, R_n$. This kind of constrained optimization is known as *monotonic optimization* because the objective function and constraint functions are both monotonic, i.e., $f(x_1, \ldots, x_n) \leq f(x'_1, \ldots, x'_n)$ if $x_i \leq x'_i$ for all i. It is known that the optimal value is on the border (see, for example [12]). A heuristic random perturbation is implemented in the progressive BKZ library [7], and an outline of the cross-entropy method is mentioned in Chen's thesis [10].
2. [9] for a given basis B and radius, minimize the expected cost of extreme pruning [16]: $m \cdot EnumCost + (m-1) \cdot PreprocessCost$ where m is a variable defining the number of bases, and therefore the success probability of the enumeration. The variables are $R_1, \ldots, R_n$ and m. This is an unconstrained optimization problem. A heuristic gradient descent and the Nelder-Mead method are implemented in the fpLLL library [9].

We explain why we introduce a new approach. All the known approaches try to minimize an approximate upper bound of the enumeration cost: this approximation is the sum of n terms, where each term can be derived from the computation of a simplex volume (following [16]) which costs $O(n^2)$, where the unit is number of floating-point operations and the required precision might be linear in n. Although there exists an $O(n^2)$ algorithm to compute the approximate upper bound [4, Sect. 3.3], a naive random perturbation strategy is too slow to converge.

Besides, we think that the Nelder-Mead and gradient descent are not suitable for our optimization problem. If we want to apply such methods to the constrained problem, a usual approach converts the problem into a corresponding global optimization problem by introducing penalty functions. Then, we find a near-optimal solution to the original problem by using the optimized variable of the converted problem. However, we know that the optimal point is on the border at which the penalty functions must change drastically. It could make the optimal point of the new problem far from the original one. Hence, we need an algorithm to solve our constrained problem directly.

For this purpose, we revisit Chen's partial description [10] of the cross-entropy method to solve the problem (i). In Sect. 4.2, we give a brief overview of the cross-entropy method, and in Sect. 4.3, we explain how we modify it for our purpose.

4.2 A Brief Introduction to the Cross Entropy Method

The original motivation of the cross entropy method is to speed up Monte-Carlo simulation for approximating a probability. If the target probability is extremely small, the number of sampling points must be huge. To solve this issue, Rubinstein [30] introduced the cross entropy method and showed that the algorithm could be used for combinatorial optimization problems. This subsection gives a general presentation of the cross-entropy method: we will apply it to the optimization of pruning functions. For more information, see for example [14,30].

Let χ be the whole space of combinations and consider a cost function $S : \chi \to \mathbb{R}_{\geq 0}$ that we want to minimize. Assume that we have a probability distribution $D_{\chi,\mathbf{u}}$ defined over χ and parametrized by a vector $\mathbf{u}$. We fix the corresponding probability density function $f_{\mathbf{u}}(x)$. A cross-entropy algorithm to find the optimal combination $X^* := \operatorname{argmin}_{X \in \chi} S(X)$ is outlined in Algorithm 1; here we use the description in the textbook [14, Algorithm 2.3].

The stochastic program in Step 4 is the problem of finding the parameter vector $\mathbf{v}$ which optimizes

$$\arg\max_{\mathbf{v}} \sum_{i=1}^{N} I_{S(X_i) \leq \gamma_t} \log f_{\mathbf{v}}(X_i) \tag{10}$$

where

$$I_{S(X_i) \leq \gamma_t} = \begin{cases} 1 & \text{if } S(X_i) \leq \gamma_t \\ 0 & \text{if } S(X_i) > \gamma_t \end{cases}$$

is the characteristic function. It is known that the new distribution $D_{\chi,\mathbf{v}_t}$ derived from the solution is closer to the ideal distribution $D_{\chi,\mathbf{opt}}$ that outputs the optimal $X^{\mathbf{opt}} = \arg\min_X S(X)$ with probability 1, than the previous distribution $D_{\chi,\mathbf{v}_{t-1}}$. In other words, the cost of sampled elements from $D_{\chi,\mathbf{v}_t}$ are likely to

---

Algorithm 1. A Generic Framework of the Cross-Entropy Method

Input: Searching space χ, cost function $S : \chi \to \mathbb{R}_{\geq 0}$, initial parameter vector $\mathbf{v}_0$, algorithm parameter ρ, N, d; for example, $N = 1000$, $\rho = 0.1$ and $d = 10$.
Output: An approximation $S(x^*)$ of the minimal and corresponding x^*.
1: $t \leftarrow 1$
2: According to $D_{\chi, \mathbf{v}_{t-1}}$, sample $X_1, \dots, X_N$ from χ
3: Let the threshold γ_t be the $\lceil \rho N \rceil$-th smallest value of $S(X_i)$
4: Solve the stochastic program (10) for the inputs $(X_1, \dots, X_N, \gamma_t, \mathbf{v}_{t-1})$ and find the new parameter $\mathbf{v}_t$
5: **if** the found minimum $S(X^*)$ during the execution of the algorithm is not updated in the last d loop **then**
6:     output the smallest $S(X^*)$ and X^*
7: **else**
8:     let $t \leftarrow t + 1$ and **goto Step 2**
9: **end if**

---

smaller than that of samples from $D_{\chi, \mathbf{v}_{t-1}}$. This is quantified by the function to measure the distance between two probability distributions:

$$D(g, f_{\mathbf{v}}) := \int g(x) \log \frac{g(x)}{f_{\mathbf{v}}(x)} dx$$

which is known as the *cross-entropy*, or Kullback-Leibler distance. The above algorithm wants to minimize the distance from the optimal state g by changing the parameter vector $\mathbf{v}$.

The stochastic program (10) can be easily solved analytically if the family of distribution function $\{f_{\mathbf{v}}(x)\}_{\mathbf{v} \in V}$ is a natural exponential family (NEF) [31]. In particular, if the function $f_{\mathbf{v}}(x)$ is convex and differentiable with respect to $\mathbf{v}$, the solution of (10) is obtained by solving the simultaneous equations

$$\sum_{i=1}^{N} I_{S(X_i) \leq \gamma_t} \nabla \log f_{\mathbf{v}}(X_i) = \mathbf{0}. \tag{11}$$

The Gaussian product (12) used in the next section is one of the simplest examples of such functions.

4.3   Our Algorithm

For the generic algorithm (Algorithm 1), we substitute our cost function and constraints. Then, we modify the sampler and introduce the FACE strategy as explained in this section. Recall that the input is a lattice basis and its Gram-Schmidt lengths, a radius R and a target probability p_0. We mention that our algorithm follows [19, Algorithm 2] for optimization over a subset of $\mathbb{R}^m$ by Kroese, Porotsky and Rubinstein.

Modified sampler: The sampling parameter is $\mathbf{u} = (c_1, \ldots, c_{n-1}, \sigma_1, \ldots, \sigma_{n-1}) \in \mathbb{R}_{\geq 0}^{2n-2}$ where c and σ correspond to the center and deviation respectively.

Since the bounding radii must increase and the last coordinate is $R_n = 1$, the searching space is

$$\chi = \{(x_1, \ldots, x_{n-1}) \in (0,1]^n : x_1 \leq x_2 \leq \cdots \leq x_{n-1}\} \subset \mathbb{R}^{n-1}.$$

To sample from the space following the parameter $\mathbf{u}$, define the corresponding probability distribution $D_{\chi,\mathbf{u}}$ as follows: sample each u_i from $N(c_i, \sigma_i^2)$ independently, if all $u_i \geq 0$, then let $(x_1, \ldots, x_n)$ be $(u_1, \ldots, u_n)$ sorted in increasing order and output it. We sort the output because because we do not know a suitable distribution from which the sampling from χ is easy. As we will see later, when the algorithm is about to converge, the Gaussian parameters σ_i become small, and the distributions of u_i's and x_i become close. Below we assume that the probability density function of $D_{\chi,\mathbf{u}}$ is sufficiently close to that of the Gaussian product

$$f_{\mathbf{u}}(X) = \frac{1}{(2\pi)^{n/2}} \prod_{i=1}^{n-1} \left(\frac{1}{\sigma_i} \exp(-(x_i - c_i)^2/(2\sigma_i^2)) \right). \tag{12}$$

The gradients of log of the function are

$$\frac{\partial}{\partial c_i} \log f_{\mathbf{u}}(X) = \frac{x_i - c_i}{\sigma_i^2},$$

and

$$\frac{\partial}{\partial \sigma_i} \log f_{\mathbf{u}}(X) = -\frac{1}{\sigma_i} + \frac{(x_i - c_i)^2}{\sigma_i^3}.$$

Substituting them into (11), we obtain the formulas to update c_i and σ_i as follows

$$c_i^{new} \leftarrow \frac{\sum_{j:S(X_j)\leq\gamma_t} x_{j,i}}{|\{j : S(X_j) \leq \gamma_t\}|}$$

$$\sigma_i^{new} \leftarrow \sqrt{\frac{\sum_{j:S(X_j)\leq\gamma_t} (x_{j,i} - c_i)^2}{|\{j : S(X_j) \leq \gamma_t\}|}} \tag{13}$$

where we denote $x_{j,i}$ for the i-th coordinate of X_j.

The FACE strategy: For practical speedup, we can employ the fully-automated cross-entropy (FACE) strategy described in [14, Sect. 4.2]. It simply replaces the full sampling in Step 2 in Fig. 1 by a recycling strategy. Consider a list $L = \{X_1, \ldots, X_N\}$. If the cost of a new sample is less than $\max_{i\in[N]} S(X_i)$, replace the new sample to the maximum element in the list, and update the parameter vector by (13) using all items in the list, i.e., with $\gamma_t = +\infty$.

We did preliminary experiments on this strategy and found that our problem has a typical trend, *i.e.* if the size N of list is small (≈ 10), the minimum cost $\min_{i\in[N]} S(X_i)$ decreases very fast but seems to stay near a local minimum. On the other hand, if we choose a large N (≈ 1000), the speed of convergence is slow, but the pruning function found is better than in the small case if we use many loop iterations. Hence, we start with a small N and increase it little by little.

Integrating the above, we give the pseudocode of our optimizing algorithm in Algorithm 2. We used a heuristic parameter set $N_{init} = 10$ and $N_{max} = 50$, and terminate the computation if $\mathbf{v}$ is not updated in the last 10 loop iterations.

Algorithm 2. Cross-Entropy Method for Optimizing Pruning Radii

---

Input: Gram-Schmidt lengths $(\|\mathbf{b}_1^\star\|, \ldots, \|\mathbf{b}_n^\star\|)$, Radius of the ball R, Target probability p_0, initial and maximum size of list N, N_{max}, initial parameter vector $\mathbf{u} = (\mathbf{c}, \sigma)$, parameter to increase list size d.

Output: A near optimal cost and corresponding radii $(R_1, \ldots, R_n)$

1: Sample new $X = (R_1, \ldots, R_m)$ from $D_{\chi,\mathbf{u}}$
2: **if** $Pr(X) < p_0$ **then**
3:     goto Step 1
4: **end if**
5: **if** $|L| < N$ **then**
6:     $L \leftarrow L \cup X$
7: **else**
8:     $X_i \leftarrow \text{argmax}_{X_i \in L} Cost(X_i)$
9: **end if**
10: **if** $Cost(X) < Cost(X_i)$ **then**
11:     Replace X_i by X
12:     Update $\mathbf{u}$ by using list L
13: **end if**
14: **if** $\mathbf{u}$ is not updated in the last d loops **then**
15:     $N \leftarrow N + 1$
16: **end if**
17: **if** $N > N_{max}$ **then**
18:     output minimum among $X_1, \ldots, X_{N-1}$ and **exit**
19: **end if**
20: goto Step 1

---

5   Tightness and Applications to Security Estimates

In this section, we study the heuristic cost N of (5) divided by two (SVP setting).

5.1   Modeling Strongly Reduced Bases

The cost (5) of cylinder pruning over $P_f(B, R)$ depends both on the quality of the basis B, the radius R and the pruning function f. The results of Sect. 3 allow to lower bound the numerator of each term of (5), but we also need to lower bound the part depending on the basis B. This was already discussed in [7,11,25] using two models of strongly reduced bases: the Rankin model used in [11,25] which provides conservative bounds by anticipating progress in lattice reduction, and the HKZ model used in [7,11] which is closer to the state-of-the-art. This part is more heuristic than Sect. 3.

The HKZ model. The BKZ algorithm tries to approximate HKZ-reduced bases, which are bases B such that $\|\mathbf{b}_i^\star\| = \lambda_1(\pi_i(L))$ for all $1 \le i \le n$. When running BKZ, an HKZ basis is the best output one can hope for. On the other hand, a BKZ-reduced basis with large blocksize will be close to an HKZ-basis, so this model is somewhat close to the state-of-the-art. It corresponds to an idealized Kannan's algorithm [18] where enumerations are only performed over HKZ-reduced bases (see [23] for more practical variants). Unfortunately, in theory, we do not know what the $\|\mathbf{b}_i^\star\|$'s of an HKZ basis will look like exactly, except for $i = 1$, but we can make a guess. Following [7,11], we assume that for $1 \le i \le n-50$, $\|\mathbf{b}_i^\star\| \approx \mathrm{GH}(\pi_i(L)) = V_{n-i+1}(1)^{-1/(n-i+1)} \left(\prod_{k=i}^n \|\mathbf{b}_k^\star\|\right)^{1/(n-i+1)}$, which means that we assume that $\pi_i(L)$ behaves like a random lattice. Then we can simulate $\|\mathbf{b}_i^\star\|$ for $1 \le i \le n-50$ by a simple recursive formula. We stop at $n-50$, because Chen and Nguyen [11] reported that the last projected lattices do not behave like random lattices. For the remaining indices, they proposed to use a numerical table from experimental results in low dimension: we use the same table. Note that for a large dimension such as 200, errors in the last coordinates are not an issue because the contribution of the terms $k \le 50$ in N is negligible.

The Rankin model. It is known that HKZ bases are not optimal for minimizing the running time of enumeration. For instance, Nguyen [27, Chap. 3] noticed a link between the cost of enumeration and the Rankin invariants of a lattice, which provides lower bounds on heuristic estimates of the number of nodes and identifies better bases than HKZ. However, finding these better bases is currently more expensive [13] than finding HKZ-reduced bases. Recall that the Rankin invariants $\gamma_{n,m}(L)$ of an n-rank lattice L satisfy:

$$\gamma_{n,m}(L) := \min_{\substack{S:\text{ sublattice of } L \\ \mathrm{rank}(S)=m}} \left(\frac{\mathrm{vol}(S)}{\mathrm{covol}(L)^{m/n}}\right)^2 \le \frac{\prod_{i=1}^m \|\mathbf{b}_i^\star\|^2}{\mathrm{covol}(L)^{2m/n}}, \qquad (14)$$

for any basis $(\mathbf{b}_1, \ldots, \mathbf{b}_n)$ of L. We have the following lower bound [37, Corollary 1] for Rankin's constant $\gamma_{n,m} := \max_L \gamma_{n,m}(L)$:

$$\gamma_{n,m} \ge \left(n \cdot \frac{\prod_{n-m+1}^n Z(j)}{\prod_{j=2}^m Z(j)}\right)^{2/n} \qquad \text{where} \quad Z(j) := \zeta(j)\Gamma(j/2)\pi^{-j/2}. \qquad (15)$$

According to [36], it seems plausible that most lattices come close to realizing Rankin constants: for any $\varepsilon > 0$ and sufficiently large n, most lattices L "should" verify $\gamma_{n,m}(L)^{1/(2m)} \ge \gamma_{n,m}^{1/(2m)} - \varepsilon$ for all m.

Ignoring ε, if we lower bound any term of the form $\frac{\prod_{i=1}^{m}\|\mathbf{b}_i^\star\|^2}{\text{covol}(L)^{2m/n}}$ in the simplified cost (5) by the right-hand side of (15), we obtain the following heuristic lower bound formula:

$$N = \frac{1}{2}\sum_{k=1}^{n}\frac{\text{vol}(C_{R_1,\ldots,R_k})\prod_{i=1}^{n-k}\|\mathbf{b}_i^\star\|}{\text{vol}(L)} > \frac{1}{2}\sum_{k=1}^{n}\frac{\text{vol}(C_{R_1,\ldots,R_k})}{\text{vol}(L)^{k/n}}\left((n-k)\frac{\prod_{j=k+1}^{n}Z(j)}{\prod_{j=2}^{n-k}Z(j)}\right)^{\frac{1}{n-k}}$$

In both cases, substituting the volume lower bounds in Sects. 3.2 and 3.3, we obtain closed formulas to find the lower bound complexity which are suitable for numerical analyses.

On the other hand, for any n-rank lattice L, and any fixed $m \in \{1,\ldots,n-1\}$, there is a basis $(\mathbf{b}_1,\ldots,\mathbf{b}_n)$ of L such that $\frac{\prod_{i=1}^{m}\|\mathbf{b}_i^\star\|^2}{\text{covol}(L)^{2m/n}} = \gamma_{n,m}(L)$. This existence would only be guaranteed for fixed m, such as for the m maximizing the corresponding number N_{n+1-m} of nodes in the enumeration tree at depth m. By idealization, we call Rankin basis a basis such that for all $m \in \{1,\ldots,n-1\}$, $\frac{\prod_{i=1}^{m}\|\mathbf{b}_i^\star\|^2}{\text{covol}(L)^{2m/n}}$ is approximately less than the right-hand side of (15): since such bases may not exist, this is an over-simplification to guess how much speed-up might be possible with the best bases. We use Rankin bases to compute speculative upper bounds, anticipating progress in lattice reduction.

5.2 Explicit Lower Bounds

We summarize the applications of the results of Sects. 3.2 and 3.3, to compute lower bounds on the number of nodes searched by cylinder pruning with lower bounded success probability.

Single Enumeration. By Corollary 2, if α is a lower bound on the success probability,

$$N \geq \frac{1}{2}\sum_{k=1}^{n}\frac{V_k(\sqrt{\alpha_k}R_n)}{\prod_{i=n-k+1}^{n}\|\mathbf{b}_i^\star\|} \tag{16}$$

where α_k is defined by $I_{\alpha_k}(k/2, 1+(n-k)/2) = \alpha$.

For the Gaussian case with success probability $\geq \beta$, from Corollary 3,

$$N \geq \frac{1}{2}\sum_{k=1}^{n}\frac{V_k(\sqrt{\beta_k})}{\prod_{i=n-k+1}^{n}\|\mathbf{b}_i^\star\|}$$

where β_k is defined by $P(k/2, \beta_k/(2\sigma^2)) = \beta$.

Multiple Enumerations. For the situation where one can use m bases, let α' be a lower bound on the global success probability. Then by Lemma 6,

$$N \geq \frac{\alpha'}{4} \sum_{k=1}^{n} \frac{k V_k(R_n) B(k/2, 1 + (n-k)/2)}{\prod_{i=n-k+1}^{n} \|\mathbf{b}_i^\star\|} \tag{17}$$

where α' satisfies $\mathrm{vol}(\cup_{i=1}^{m} C_i) \geq \alpha' \mathrm{vol}(R_n)$.

Lemma 9 also implies a lower bound for the Gaussian setting with global success probability $\rho_{n,\sigma}(\cup_{i=1}^{m} C_i) \geq \beta'$:

$$N \geq \frac{\beta'}{2} \sum_{k=1}^{n} \frac{(2\pi\sigma^2)^{k/2}}{\prod_{i=n-k+1}^{n} \|\mathbf{b}_i^\star\|}.$$

5.3   Radii Tightness

To check tightness, we give two figures (Fig. 2) that compare the lower bound of radii from Corollary 2, and the best radii generated by our cross entropy method. The comparison is for two regimes: high and low success probability. Note that the left probability 0.6827 is an approximation of $P(\frac{1}{2}, \frac{1}{2})$ for which the linear pruning is the best known proved lower bound.

We see that the radii bounds are reasonably tight in both cases. We deduce that in these examples, the enumeration cost bounds will also be tight, because the cost is dominated by what happens around $k \approx n/2$.

We note that it is to easier to compute lower bounds than upper bounds.

5.4   Security Estimates for Enumeration

Figure 1 (in the introduction) displays four bounds on the cost of enumeration in several situations, for varying dimension and simulated HKZ bases and Rankin bases:

- The thin red curve is an upper bound of the enumeration cost using $M = 10^{10}$ bases with single success probability $\alpha = 10^{-10}$ computed by the cross-entropy method.
- The bold red curve is a lower bound of the enumeration cost using $M = 10^{10}$ bases with single success probability $\alpha = 10^{-10}$ computed by M times (16).
- The thin green curve is an upper bound of the enumeration cost w.r.t. infinitely many bases with global success probability $\alpha' = 1$. This is computed by M times an upper bound of the enumeration cost with single success probability $1/M$ for a very large M where the single cost is greater than lattice dimension.
- The bold green curve is a lower bound of the enumeration cost w.r.t. infinitely many bases with a large global success probability. This is computed by (17) with $\alpha' = 1$.

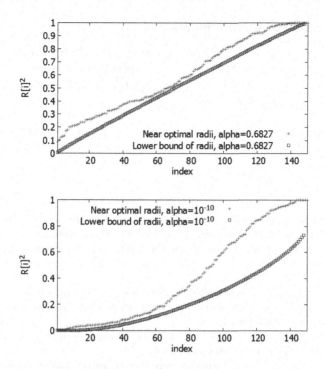

Fig. 2. Comparison of lower bound and near optimal radii; for the 150-dimensional simulated HKZ basis, compute near optimal radii and lower bound radii for $\alpha = 0.6827 \gtrsim P(\frac{1}{2}, \frac{1}{2})$ (Top) and $\alpha = 10^{-10}$ (Bottom).

In all experiments, we take the radius by $R_n = GH(L)$. The cost is the number of nodes of the enumeration tree in the classical computing model. The security level is the base-2 logarithm of the cost, which is divided by two in the quantum computing model [6,24].

We also draw the curve of $2^{0.292n}$ and $2^{0.265n}$ which are simplified lower bounds of the cost for solving SVP-n used in [2] for classical and quantum computers, respectively.

In all the situations where we use 10^{10} bases, the upper bounds (thin red curve) and the lower bounds (bold red curve) are close to each other, which demonstrates the tightness of our lower bound.

In the classical setting, our lower bounds for enumeration are higher than sieve lower bounds. On the other hand, in the quantum setting, there are cases where enumeration is faster than quantum sieving. For instance, if an attacker could find many quasi-Rankin bases by some new lattice reduction algorithm, the claimed 2^{128} quantum security might be dropped to about 2^{96} security. In such a situation, the required blocksize would increase from about 480 to 580.

5.5   Experimental Environments

All experiments were performed by a standard server with two Intel Xeon E5-2660 CPUs and 256-GB RAM. We used the boost library version 1.56.0, which has efficient subroutines to compute (incomplete) beta, (incomplete) gamma and zeta functions with high precision.

Acknowledgements. This work was supported by JSPS KAKENHI Grant Numbers 16H02780, 16H02830 and 18H03238, and JST CREST JPMJCR168A.

References

1. Ajtai, M., Kumar, R., Sivakumar, D.: A sieve algorithm for the shortest lattice vector problem. In: Proceedings of the 33rd STOC, pp. 601–610. ACM (2001)
2. Albrecht, M.R., et al.: Estimate all the LWE, NTRU schemes! Posted on the PQC-forum, 1 February 2018. https://estimate-all-the-lwe-ntru-schemes.github.io/paper.pdf
3. Alkim, E., Ducas, L., Pöppelmann, T., Schwabe, P.: Post-quantum key exchange - a new hope. In: Proceedings of the 25th USENIX Security Symposium, pp. 327–343. USENIX Association (2016)
4. Aono, Y.: A faster method for computing Gama-Nguyen-Regev's extreme pruning coefficients. CoRR, abs/1406.0342 (2014)
5. Aono, Y., Nguyen, P.Q.: Random sampling revisited: lattice enumeration with discrete pruning. In: Coron, J.-S., Nielsen, J.B. (eds.) EUROCRYPT 2017. LNCS, vol. 10211, pp. 65–102. Springer, Cham (2017). https://doi.org/10.1007/978-3-319-56614-6_3
6. Aono, Y., Nguyen, P.Q., Shen, Y.: Quantum lattice enumeration and tweaking discrete pruning (2018). https://eprint.iacr.org/2018/546
7. Aono, Y., Wang, Y., Hayashi, T., Takagi, T.: Improved progressive BKZ algorithms and their precise cost estimation by sharp simulator. In: Fischlin, M., Coron, J.-S. (eds.) EUROCRYPT 2016. LNCS, vol. 9665, pp. 789–819. Springer, Heidelberg (2016)
8. Becker, A., Ducas, L., Gama, N., Laarhoven, T.: New directions in nearest neighbor searching with applications to lattice sieving. In: Proceedings of the 27th ACM-SIAM Symposium on Discrete Algorithms (SODA), pp. 10–24 (2016)
9. The FPLLL Development Team.: FPLLL, a lattice reduction library (2016). https://github.com/fplll/fplll
10. Chen, Y.: Réduction de réseau et sécurité concrète du chiffrement complètement homomorphe. Ph.D. thesis, Univ. Paris 7 (2013)
11. Chen, Y., Nguyen, P.Q.: BKZ 2.0: better lattice security estimates. In: Lee, D.H., Wang, X. (eds.) ASIACRYPT 2011. LNCS, vol. 7073, pp. 1–20. Springer, Heidelberg (2011)
12. Cheon, M.-S.: Global optimization of monotonic programs: applications in polynomial and stochastic programming. Ph.D. thesis, Georgia Institute of Technology (2005)
13. Dadush, D., Micciancio, D.: Algorithms for the densest sub-lattice problem. In: Proceedings of the 24th ACM-SIAM Symposium on Discrete Algorithms, SODA 2013, pp. 1103–1122 (2013)

14. de Boer, P.-T., Kroese, D.P., Mannor, S., Rubinstein, R.Y.: A tutorial on the cross-entropy method. Ann. Oper. Res. **134**(1), 19–67 (2005)
15. Fincke, U., Pohst, M.: Improved methods for calculating vectors of short length in a lattice, including a complexity analysis. Math. Comput. **44**(170), 463–471 (1985)
16. Gama, N., Nguyen, P.Q., Regev, O.: Lattice enumeration using extreme pruning. In: Gilbert, H. (ed.) EUROCRYPT 2010. LNCS, vol. 6110, pp. 257–278. Springer, Heidelberg (2010). https://doi.org/10.1007/978-3-642-13190-5
17. Hülsing, A., Rijneveld, J., Schanck, J.M., Schwabe, P.: NTRU-HRSS-KEM: algorithm specifications and supporting documentation. NIST submission, 30 November 2017
18. Kannan, R.: Improved algorithms for integer programming and related lattice problems. In: Proceedings of the 15th ACM STOC, pp. 193–206 (1983)
19. Kroese, D.P., Porotsky, S., Rubinstein, R.Y.: The cross-entropy method for continuous multi-extremal optimization. Methodol. Comput. Appl. Probab. V **8**(3), 383–407 (2006)
20. Laarhoven, T.: Sieving for shortest vectors in lattices using angular locality-sensitive hashing. In: Gennaro, R., Robshaw, M. (eds.) CRYPTO 2015. LNCS, vol. 9215, pp. 3–22. Springer, Heidelberg (2015). https://doi.org/10.1007/978-3-662-47989-6_1
21. Liu, M., Nguyen, P.Q.: Solving BDD by enumeration: an update. In: Dawson, E. (ed.) CT-RSA 2013. LNCS, vol. 7779, pp. 293–309. Springer, Heidelberg (2013). https://doi.org/10.1007/978-3-642-36095-4_19
22. Micciancio, D., Voulgaris, P.: Faster exponential time algorithms for the shortest vector problem. In: Proceedings of the ACM-SIAM SODA, pp. 1468–1480 (2010)
23. Micciancio, D., Walter, M.: Fast lattice point enumeration with minimal overhead. In: Proceedings of the SODA 2015, pp. 276–294 (2015)
24. Montanaro, A.: Quantum walk speedup of backtracking algorithms. ArXiv e-prints (2015)
25. Nguyen, P.Q.: Public-key cryptanalysis. In: Luengo, I. (ed.) Recent Trends in Cryptography. Contemporary Mathematics, vol. 477. AMS-RSME (2009)
26. Nguyen, P.Q.: Hermite's constant and lattice algorithms. In: The LLL Algorithm: Survey and Applications. Springer, Heidelberg (2010). In [27]
27. Nguyen, P.Q., Vallée, B. (eds.): The LLL Algorithm: Survey and Applications. Information Security and Cryptography. Springer, Heidelberg (2009). https://doi.org/10.1007/978-3-642-02295-1
28. Nguyen, P.Q., Vidick, T.: Sieve algorithms for the shortest vector problem are practical. J. Math. Cryptol. **2**, 181–207 (2008)
29. Pohst, M.: On the computation of lattice vectors of minimal length, successive minima and reduced bases with applications. SIGSAM Bull. **15**(1), 37–44 (1981)
30. Rubinstein, R.Y.: Optimization of computer simulation models with rare events. Eur. J. Oper. Res. **99**, 89–112 (1996)
31. Rubinstein, R.Y., Kroese, D.P.: The Cross-Entropy Method, A Unified Approach to Combinatorial Optimization, Monte-Carlo Simulation and Machine Learning. Information Science and Statistics. Springer, New York (2004). https://doi.org/10.1007/978-1-4757-4321-0
32. Schneider, M., Gama, N.: SVP challenge. http://www.latticechallenge.org/svp-challenge/
33. Schnorr, C.P.: Lattice reduction by random sampling and birthday methods. In: Alt, H., Habib, M. (eds.) STACS 2003. LNCS, vol. 2607, pp. 145–156. Springer, Heidelberg (2003). https://doi.org/10.1007/3-540-36494-3_14

34. Schnorr, C.-P., Euchner, M.: Lattice basis reduction: improved practical algorithms and solving subset sum problems. Math. Program. **66**, 181–199 (1994)
35. Schnorr, C.P., Hörner, H.H.: Attacking the Chor-Rivest cryptosystem by improved lattice reduction. In: Guillou, L.C., Quisquater, J.-J. (eds.) EUROCRYPT 1995. LNCS, vol. 921, pp. 1–12. Springer, Heidelberg (1995). https://doi.org/10.1007/3-540-49264-X_1
36. Shapira, U., Weiss, B.: A volume estimate for the set of stable lattices. Comptes Rendus Mathématique **352**(11), 875–879 (2014)
37. Thunder, J.L.: Higher-dimensional analogs of Hermite's constant. Michigan Math. J. **45**(2), 301–314 (1998)
38. Venkatesh, S.A.: The Theory of Probability: Explorations and Applications. Cambridge University Press, Cambridge (2012)

A   Proof of Lemma 3

Let

$$p(k,n) := I_{k/n}\left(\frac{k}{2}, \frac{n-k}{2}\right) = \frac{\int_0^{k/n} z^{\frac{k}{2}-1}(1-z)^{\frac{n-k}{2}-1}dz}{B(\frac{k}{2}, \frac{n-k}{2})} \tag{18}$$

To prove Lemma 3, it suffices to show that: for any integers $1 \le k < n$,

$$p(n,k) \le P(\frac{1}{2}, \frac{1}{2}) = \frac{\int_0^{1/2} t^{-1/2}e^{-t}}{\Gamma(\frac{1}{2})} \approx 0.682689...$$

A.1   Formulas and Lemmas

We have

$$\Gamma(a+1) = a\Gamma(a) \quad \text{and} \quad B(a,b+1) = B(a,b)\frac{b}{a+b}. \tag{19}$$

The following recurrence formulas hold (see **8.17.18** and **8.17.21** of *NIST Digital Library of Mathematical Functions* http://dlmf.nist.gov/8.17 respectively):

$$I_x(a,b) = I_x(a+1, b-1) + \frac{x^a(1-x)^{b-1}}{aB(a,b)}. \tag{20}$$

$$I_x(a,b) = I_x(a, b+1) - \frac{x^a(1-x)^b}{bB(a,b)}. \tag{21}$$

We recall:

Theorem 8 *(Chebyshev integral inequality). For any nonnegative, monotonically increasing function $f(x)$ and monotonically decreasing function $g(x)$, we have*

$$\int_a^b f(x)g(x)dx \le \frac{1}{b-a}\left(\int_a^b f(x)dx\right) \cdot \left(\int_a^b g(x)dx\right).$$

Lemma 10. *For $a, b > 1$, the function $z^a(1-z)^b$ is maximized at $z_{max} = \frac{a}{a+b}$. Furthermore, it is strictly increasing over $z \in [0, z_{max}]$ and strictly decreasing over $z \in [z_{max}, 1]$.*

A.2 Proof Body

The proof of Lemma 3 can be derived from the following three lemmas.

Lemma 11. *If $n \geq 2$, then: $p(1, n) < p(1, n + 2)$.*

Proof. By (21), we have

$$
p(1, n) = I_{\frac{1}{n}}\left(\frac{1}{2}, \frac{n+1}{2}\right) - \frac{n^{-1/2}(1 - 1/n)^{\frac{n-1}{2}}}{\frac{n-1}{2} \cdot B\left(\frac{1}{2}, \frac{n-1}{2}\right)}
$$

$$
= I_{\frac{1}{n+2}}\left(\frac{1}{2}, \frac{n+1}{2}\right) + \frac{\int_{\frac{1}{n+2}}^{\frac{1}{n}} z^{-1/2}(1 - z)^{\frac{n-1}{2}}\, dz}{B\left(\frac{1}{2}, \frac{n+1}{2}\right)} - \frac{n^{-1/2}(1 - 1/n)^{\frac{n-1}{2}}}{\frac{n-1}{2} \cdot B\left(\frac{1}{2}, \frac{n-1}{2}\right)}.
$$

Then $J = p(1, n) - p(1, n + 2)$ is equal to the last two terms. We will show that $J < 0$. From (19), we have $B\left(\frac{1}{2}, \frac{n+1}{2}\right) = \frac{n-1}{n}B\left(\frac{1}{2}, \frac{n-1}{2}\right)$ and we get

$$
J' = J \cdot (n - 1)B\left(\frac{1}{2}, \frac{n-1}{2}\right) = n \int_{\frac{1}{n+2}}^{\frac{1}{n}} z^{-1/2}(1 - z)^{\frac{n-1}{2}}\, dz - 2n^{-1/2}(1 - 1/n)^{\frac{n-1}{2}}
$$

of which we want to show negativeness.

Since the integral function $z^{-1/2}(1 - z)^{\frac{n-1}{2}}$ is strictly decreasing, the trivial bound

$$
n \int_{\frac{1}{n+2}}^{\frac{1}{n}} z^{-1/2}(1 - z)^{\frac{n-1}{2}}\, dz
$$

$$
< n\left(\frac{1}{n} - \frac{1}{n+2}\right)\left(\frac{1}{n+2}\right)^{-1/2}\left(1 - \frac{1}{n+2}\right)^{\frac{n-1}{2}} = \frac{2}{\sqrt{n+2}}\left(1 - \frac{1}{n+2}\right)^{\frac{n-1}{2}}
$$

holds. Thus, letting $f(x) = \frac{1}{\sqrt{x}}(1 - 1/x)^{\frac{n-1}{2}}$, we have $J' < 2(f(n+2) - f(n))$ and it suffices to show that $f(x)$ is strictly decreasing over the range $x \in (n, n + 2)$. It is equivalent to check that the derivative of $g(x) = f(1/x) = \sqrt{x}(1 - x)^{\frac{n-1}{2}}$ is > 0 for $\frac{1}{n+2} < x < \frac{1}{n}$. We have:

$$
(\log g(x))' = \frac{g'(x)}{g(x)} = \frac{1}{2x} + \frac{n-1}{2}\frac{1}{x - 1} = \frac{nx - 1}{2x(x - 1)}
$$

which is > 0 if $0 < x < \frac{1}{n}$. Hence, $g(1/(n + 2)) < g(1/n)$, $f(n + 2) < f(n)$, and

$$
J' = J \cdot (n - 1)B\left(\frac{1}{2}, \frac{n-1}{2}\right) = 2(f(n + 2) - f(n)) < 0.
$$

Therefore, $p(1, n) = p(1, n + 2) + J < p(1, n + 2)$ for any $n \geq 2$. □

Corollary 5. *If $n \geq 2$, then $p(1, n) < P(\frac{1}{2}, \frac{1}{2})$.*

Proof. With $p(1, 2) = \frac{1}{2}$ and $p(1, 3) = \frac{1}{\sqrt{3}} \approx 0.5773$ and the known result $p(1, n) \to P(\frac{1}{2}, \frac{1}{2})$ $(n \to \infty)$, we obtain that $p(1, n) < P(\frac{1}{2}, \frac{1}{2})$ for $n \geq 2$. □

Lemma 12. $p(2, n) < P(\frac{1}{2}, \frac{1}{2})$ *for any* $n \geq 2$

Proof. By definition,

$$p(2, n) = \frac{\Gamma\left(\frac{n}{2}\right)}{\Gamma(1)\Gamma\left(\frac{n}{2} - 1\right)} \int_0^{\frac{2}{n}} (1 - z)^{\frac{n-4}{2}} dz = \frac{n - 2}{2} \int_0^{\frac{2}{n}} (1 - z)^{\frac{n-4}{2}} dz$$

$$= 1 - \left(1 - \frac{2}{n}\right)^{\frac{n}{2} - 1}.$$

For $2 \leq n \leq 8$, we can check it is smaller than 0.68 numerically, Also, for $n \geq 9$, since the function $(1 - 1/x)^x$ is monotonically increasing with x, we have

$$1 - \left(1 - \frac{2}{n}\right)^{\frac{n}{2} - 1} < 1 - \left(1 - \frac{2}{n}\right)^{\frac{n}{2}} \leq 1 - (1 - 2/9)^{9/2} < 0.68 < P\left(\frac{1}{2}, \frac{1}{2}\right).$$

$\square$

Lemma 13. $p(k + 2, n) < p(k, n)$ *for any* $1 \leq k < n$.

Proof. By definition and (20)

$$p(k + 2, n)$$

$$= I_{\frac{k+2}{n}}\left(\frac{k}{2} + 1, \frac{n - k}{2} - 1\right) = I_{\frac{k+2}{n}}\left(\frac{k}{2}, \frac{n - k}{2}\right) - \frac{2}{k} \frac{\left(\frac{k+2}{n}\right)^{\frac{k}{2}}\left(\frac{n-k-2}{n}\right)^{\frac{n-k-2}{2}}}{B\left(\frac{k}{2}, \frac{n-k}{2}\right)}$$

$$= p(k, n) + \frac{\int_{\frac{k}{n}}^{\frac{k+2}{n}} z^{\frac{k}{2} - 1}(1 - z)^{\frac{n-k}{2} - 1} dz}{B\left(\frac{k}{2}, \frac{n-k}{2}\right)} - \frac{2}{k} \frac{\left(\frac{k+2}{n}\right)^{\frac{k}{2}}\left(\frac{n-k-2}{n}\right)^{\frac{n-k-2}{2}}}{B\left(\frac{k}{2}, \frac{n-k}{2}\right)}.$$

Thus, it suffices to show

$$\int_{\frac{k}{n}}^{\frac{k+2}{n}} z^{\frac{k}{2} - 1}(1 - z)^{\frac{n-k}{2} - 1} dz - \frac{2}{k}\left(\frac{k + 2}{n}\right)^{\frac{k}{2}}\left(\frac{n - k - 2}{n}\right)^{\frac{n-k-2}{2}} := I - J < 0.$$

Let us define $g(z) = z^{\frac{k}{2} + 1}(1 - z)^{\frac{n-k}{2} - 1}$ which is strictly increasing over $[0, \frac{k+2}{n}]$. Since z^{-2} is strictly decreasing, Chebyshev's integral inequality implies that

$$I = \int_{\frac{k}{n}}^{\frac{k+2}{n}} z^{-2} g(z) dz < \frac{n}{2} \int_{\frac{k}{n}}^{\frac{k+2}{n}} z^{-2} dz \int_{\frac{k}{n}}^{\frac{k+2}{n}} g(z) dz = \frac{n^2}{k(k + 2)} \int_{\frac{k}{n}}^{\frac{k+2}{n}} g(z) dz$$

$$< \frac{n^2}{k(k + 2)} \cdot \frac{2}{n} g\left(\frac{k + 2}{n}\right) = J.$$

Therefore, we have $I < J$ and it derives $p(k + 2, n) < p(k, n)$.

$\square$

A.3   Proof of Lemma 9

Recall that $P(a, z) := \frac{\int_0^z x^{a-1} e^{-x} dx}{\Gamma(a)}$ which implies:

$$\frac{e^{-z} z^a}{\Gamma(a+1)} < P(a, z) < \frac{z^a}{\Gamma(a+1)} \quad \text{for } a > 0, z > 0. \tag{22}$$

Also, they imply the bound

$$P^{-1}(a, x) > (\Gamma(a+1)x)^{1/a} \quad \text{for } a > 0, 0 < x < 1 \tag{23}$$

and the limits

$$\lim_{z \to 0+} \frac{P(a, z)}{z^a} = \frac{1}{\Gamma(a+1)} \quad \text{and} \quad \lim_{x \to 0+} \frac{x}{(P^{-1}(a, x))^a} = \frac{1}{\Gamma(a+1)}. \tag{24}$$

Hence, we have

$$\lim_{m \to \infty} m V_k(\sqrt{\beta_k}) = V_k(1) \lim_{m \to \infty} m \cdot \left(2\sigma^2 P^{-1}(k/2, \beta)\right)^{k/2}$$
$$= V_k(1) \cdot \beta' \cdot \Gamma(k/2 + 1)(2\sigma^2)^{k/2} = \beta' \cdot (2\pi\sigma^2)^{k/2}.$$

To show the decreasing property, it suffices to show that $g(y) = \frac{1}{y} \cdot (P^{-1}(k/2, \beta'y))^{k/2}$ is strictly increasing over $0 < y \leq 1$.

We use the inequality

$$\frac{\partial}{\partial x} P^{-1}(a, x) = \Gamma(a) e^{P^{-1}(a,x)} P^{-1}(a, x)^{1-a} \geq \frac{P^{-1}(a, x)}{ax}$$

which is immediate from the left hand side of (22) with $z = P^{-1}(a, x)$.

Hence, denoting $P := P^{-1}(k/2, \beta'y)$ for simplicity,

$$g'(y) = \frac{\beta' k}{2y} P^{k/2-1} \cdot \frac{\partial P}{\partial y} - \frac{P^{k/2}}{y^2} > \frac{\beta' k}{2y} P^{k/2-1} \cdot \frac{P}{(k/2)\beta'y} P^{k/2-1} - \frac{P^{k/2}}{y^2} = 0$$

This completes the proof.   □

Dissection-BKW

Andre Esser[1(✉)], Felix Heuer[1], Robert Kübler[1], Alexander May[1], and Christian Sohler[2]

[1] Horst Görtz Institute for IT Security, Ruhr University Bochum, Bochum, Germany
{andre.esser,felix.heuer,robert.kuebler,alexander.may}@rub.de
[2] Department of Computer Science, TU Dortmund, Dortmund, Germany
christian.sohler@tu-dortmund.de

Abstract. The slightly subexponential algorithm of Blum, Kalai and Wasserman (BKW) provides a basis for assessing LPN/LWE security. However, its huge memory consumption strongly limits its practical applicability, thereby preventing precise security estimates for cryptographic LPN/LWE instantiations.

We provide the first time-memory trade-offs for the BKW algorithm. For instance, we show how to solve LPN in dimension k in time $2^{\frac{4}{3}\frac{k}{\log k}}$ and memory $2^{\frac{2}{3}\frac{k}{\log k}}$. Using the Dissection technique due to Dinur et al. (Crypto '12) and a novel, slight generalization thereof, we obtain fine-grained trade-offs for any available (subexponential) memory while the running time *remains subexponential.*

Reducing the memory consumption of BKW below its running time also allows us to propose a first quantum version QBKW for the BKW algorithm.

1 Introduction

The Learning Parity with Noise (LPN) problem [4] and its generalization to arbitrary moduli, the Learning with Errors (LWE) problem [29], lie at the heart of our most promising coding-based and lattice-based post-quantum cryptographic constructions [2,26,28]. With the NIST standardization [1], we have the urgent pressure to identify LPN/LWE instantiations that allow for efficient constructions, but yet give us the desired level of classic and quantum security.

Hence, we have to run cryptanalytic algorithms on medium-scale parameter sets in order to properly extrapolate towards cryptographic instantiations.

In LPN of dimension k and error-rate $0 \leq p < 1/2$, one has to recover a secret $\mathbf{s} \in \mathbb{F}_2^k$ from samples $(\mathbf{a}_i, \langle \mathbf{a}_i, \mathbf{s} \rangle + e_i)$ for uniformly random $\mathbf{a}_i \in \mathbb{F}_2^k$ and inner products with Bernoulli distributed error e_i, i.e., $\Pr[e_i = 1] = p$.

It is not hard to see that for constant error p, any candidate solution $\mathbf{s}'$ can be checked for correctness in time polynomial in p and k. This gives a simple brute-force LPN algorithm with time complexity 2^k and constant memory.

The algorithm of Blum, Kalai and Wassermann [5] solves the faulty system of linear equations from LPN/LWE by a block-wise Gaussian elimination. In a nutshell, BKW takes sums of two vectors whenever they cancel a block of

© International Association for Cryptologic Research 2018
H. Shacham and A. Boldyreva (Eds.): CRYPTO 2018, LNCS 10992, pp. 638–666, 2018.
https://doi.org/10.1007/978-3-319-96881-0_22

$\Theta(\frac{k}{\log k})$ bits to keep the accumulating error under control. In cryptographic constructions we usually have constant p, for which the BKW algorithm runs in time $2^{\frac{k}{\log k}(1+o(1))}$, albeit using the same amount of memory.

These two algorithms, brute-force and BKW, settle the initial endpoints for our time-memory trade-offs. Hence, for gaining a $\log(k)$-factor in the run time exponent one has to invest memory up to the point where memory equals run time. Interestingly, this behavior occurs in the second method of choice for measuring LWE security, lattice reduction, too.

Whereas on lattices of dimension n, lattice enumeration such as Kannan's algorithm [21] takes time $2^{\mathcal{O}(n \log n)}$ with polynomial memory only, lattice sieving methods [12, 22–24] require $2^{\mathcal{O}(n)}$ time and memory. Due to their large memory requirements, in practice lattice sieving is currently outperformed by enumeration, and there is an increasing interest in constructing time-memory trade-offs, e.g., by lattice tuple sieving [3, 18, 19].

For BKW, the research so far mainly concentrated on run time, where many optimizations have been proposed in the cryptographic literature, e.g. [7, 16, 17, 25, 32]. While these improvements may significantly reduce the running time for breaking concrete LPN instances such as $(k, p) = (512, 1/4)$ or $(512, 1/8)$, to the best of our knowledge for the running time exponent $\frac{k}{\log k}(1 + o(1))$ all improvements only affect the $o(1)$-term. Moreover, all proposals share the same huge memory requirements as original BKW, making it impossible to run them even in moderately large dimensions.

As a consequence state-of-the-art BKW implementations are currently only possible in dimension k up to around 100. For instance [14] reported a break of $(k, p) = (135, 1/4)$. However, of the total 6 days running time, the authors spent 2.5 days for an *exponential* preprocessing, followed by less than 2 h BKW in dimension 99, and another 3.5 days of *exponential* decoding. The reason for this run-time imbalance is that BKW in dimension 99 had already consumed all available memory, namely 2^{40} bits.

Hence, if we really want to break larger LPN instances in practice, we must study time-memory trade-offs that sacrifice a bit of running time, but stay in the *sub-exponential time* regime at the benefit of a manageable memory.

Our contribution. We provide the first time-memory trade-offs for the BKW algorithm. These trade-offs give us a smooth interpolation for the complexities of solving LPN between the known endpoints 2^k time for brute-force and $2^{\frac{k}{\log k}}$ for BKW.

Since our algorithms' running times remain subexponential even for given memory below the requirement $2^{\frac{k}{\log k}}$ of classic BKW, we (asymptotically) outperform all previous algorithms (e.g. [14]) that solved LPN in exponential time when classic BKW was not applicable due to memory restrictions.

As a starting point, we consider—instead of 2-sums as in the original BKW algorithm—c-sums for (constant) $c > 2$ that cancel some blocks of bits. The use of sums of more than 2 vectors has already been discussed in the literature for improving the running time of BKW, e.g. by Zhang et al. [32] as an extension

Table 1. c-sum-algorithms: Given a list L and some target t, the algorithms output $|L|$ sets each containing c entries from L adding to t. Memory consumption of the algorithms coincides with the size of list L. Let $N_c := (M_{\mathrm{BKW}})^{\frac{\log c}{c-1}} = 2^{\frac{\log c}{c-1}\frac{k}{\log k}}$.

	c-sum Algorithm	Memory	Time	for		
classic	sorting (BKW)	N_2	N_2	$c = 2$		[5]
	Naive	N_c	$N_c{}^{c-1}$	$c \geq 2$		Sect. 4.1
	Dissection	N_c	$N_c{}^{c-\sqrt{2c}}$	$c = 4, 7, 11, 16, \ldots$		Sect. 5.2
	Tailored Dissection	$N_c{}^{\alpha}$	$N_c{}^{c-\alpha\sqrt{2c}}$	$c = 4, 7, 11, 16, \ldots$	$\alpha \in [1, \frac{\sqrt{c}}{\sqrt{c-1}}]$	Sect. 5.3
quantum	Naive + Grover	N_c	$N_c{}^{c/2}$	$c \geq 2$		Sect. 4.2

$LF(k)$ of the BKW variants $LF1$ and $LF2$ by Levieil and Fouque [25], using Wagner's k-list algorithm [31].

Since the number of c-sums grows exponentially in c, so does the number of c-sums whose sum cancels some block of bits. In turn, we systematically use c-sums to significantly lower the number of samples N that need to be stored, at the slightly increased cost of finding such c-sums.

We show that the complexities of any c-sum BKW algorithm are dominated by the cost of computing c-sums. As a consequence we abstract the *c-sum-problem* from the BKW algorithm and study various memory-friendly algorithms to solve it. We ensure that our c-sum algorithms do not require more memory than already consumed by c-sum BKW for storing its samples. In fact, our BKW algorithms have sample and (thus) memory complexity as little as $N_c := M_{\mathrm{BKW}}^{\frac{\log c}{c-1}}$ for any constant $c \in \mathbb{N}$, where $M_{\mathrm{BKW}} := 2^{\frac{k}{\log k}}$ denotes the memory (and sample) requirement of classic BKW.

In Table 1, we give a brief overview of our c-sum algorithms complexities, and therefore also of our c-sum BKW complexities. We stress that all c-sum algorithms from Table 1, including those that use the Dissection technique [10,30], may be studied for arbitrary list sizes outside of the BKW context.

NAIVE. We first consider a naive approach that computes all $(c-1)$-sums of list entries and looks for some matching c^{th} vector. This naive approach already gives us a smooth first time-memory trade-off, informally captured in the following theorem.

Theorem 1.1 (Naive BKW Trade-Off, informal). *Let $c \in \mathbb{N}$. The LPN problem in dimension k can be solved in Time T and space M where*

$$\log T = \log c \cdot \frac{k}{\log k} \quad , \quad \log M = \frac{\log c}{c-1} \cdot \frac{k}{\log k} \quad .$$

Observe that the trade-off behaves quite nicely as a function of c. While we can reduce the memory consumption almost by a factor of $\frac{1}{c}$ this comes at the cost of only a $(\log c)$-factor in the run time exponent.

Note that for $c = 2$ Theorem 1.1 yields the well-known BKW complexities. While we consider constant c throughout this work, we point out that our results hold up to a choice of $c(k) = k^{1 - \frac{\log \log k}{\log k}}$ for which the formulas in Theorem 1.1 (as well as for the upcoming trade-offs) result in exponential running time in k with polynomial memory, matching the endpoint of the LPN brute-force algorithm. See Fig. 1 (stars) for an illustration of this time-memory trade-off.

QBKW. Using a standard Grover-search in our naive c-sum algorithm to identify $(c-1)$-sums for which there exists a matching c^{th} vector, we halve the running time complexity exponent from $\log c \cdot \frac{k}{\log k}$ down to $\frac{\log c}{2} \cdot \frac{k}{\log k}$. See Fig. 1 (triangles) for the resulting trade-off curve.

DISSECTION. We replace our naive c-sum algorithm by more advanced time-memory techniques like Schroeppel-Shamir [30] and its generalization, Dissection [10], to reduce the classic running time. We call the resulting algorithm DISSECTION-BKW. To give some illustrative results, with the Schroeppel-Shamir technique DISSECTION-BKW achieves exponents

$$\log T = \frac{4}{3}\frac{k}{\log k} \quad , \quad \log M = \frac{2}{3}\frac{k}{\log k}$$

(see the diamond at $\log M = \frac{2}{3}\frac{k}{\log k}$ in Fig. 1). Using 7-Dissection, DISSECTION-BKW achieves exponents

$$\log T = 1.87\frac{k}{\log k} \quad , \quad \log M = 0.47\frac{k}{\log k}$$

(see the diamond at $\log M \approx 0.47\frac{k}{\log k}$ in Fig. 1).

Theorem 1.2 (Dissection BKW Trade-Off, informal). *Let $c \in \mathbb{N}$ be sufficiently large. The LPN problem in dimension k can be solved in Time T and space M where*

$$\log T = \left(1 - \sqrt{\frac{2}{c}}\right) \cdot \log c \cdot \frac{k}{\log k} \quad , \quad \log M = \frac{\log c}{c-1} \cdot \frac{k}{\log k} \quad .$$

Hence, in comparison to Theorem 1.1 Dissection mitigates the price we pay for saving a factor of $\frac{\log c}{c-1}$ in memory from 1 down to $\left(1 - \sqrt{2/c}\right)$.

The trade-off is depicted by the diamonds in Fig. 1. Interestingly, when classically employing Schroeppel-Shamir we are on par (see point $(\frac{2}{3}, \frac{4}{3})$ in Fig. 1) with the complexities from the quantum trade-off as Schroeppel-Shamir allows for a square-root gain in the running time; the same as using a Grover-search in a quantum algorithm.

TAILORED DISSECTION. Eventually, we introduce a new slight generalization of the Dissection technique that we call *tailored Dissection*. It allows us to achieve a piece-wise continuous trade-off (line segments depicted in Fig. 1) covering the sub-exponential memory regime entirely.

The full version of this work [13] also contains a discussion how our results translate from the LPN setting to LWE.

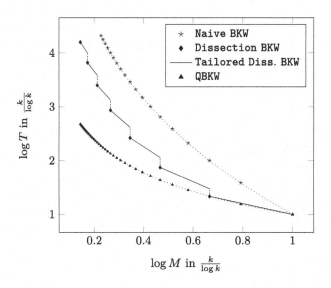

Fig. 1. Illustration of our BKW trade-offs. Instantiations exist exactly for marks as well as everywhere on solid lines. Naive BKW trade-off in stars (see Theorem 1.1), QBKW trade-off in triangles and Dissection-BKW trade-offs in diamonds and solid line segments (see Theorem 1.2).

2   Preliminaries

2.1   Notation

For $a \leq b \in \mathbb{N}$ let $[a,b] := \{a, a+1, \ldots, b\}$ and $[a] := [1,a]$. For a set S and $s \leq |S|$ let $\binom{S}{s}$ denote the set of all size-s subsets of S. A *list* $L = (l_1, \ldots, l_i)$ is an element $L \in S^i$ and is of length $|L| = i$. We let $\emptyset$ denote the empty list. For two lists L_1, L_2 we write $L_1 \subseteq L_2$ if all elements from L_1 are contained in L_2 at least as often as in L_1. We write shortly $l \in L_2$ for $(l) \subseteq L_2$. For lists $L_1 = (l_1, \ldots, l_i)$ and $L_2 = (l_{i+1}, \ldots, l_j)$ we let $L_1 \cup L_2 := (l_1, \ldots, l_i, l_{i+1}, \ldots, l_j)$. Logarithms are always base 2.

For $v \in \mathbb{F}_2^a$ and $b \leq a$ we denote the last b coordinates of v by $\text{low}_b(v)$. We let $\mathbf{u}_i$ denote the ith unit vector. 0^b denotes the zero vector of dimension b.

By $\mathcal{U}_M$ we denote the uniform distribution on a finite set M, by Ber_p we denote the Bernoulli distribution, i.e., $X \sim \text{Ber}_p$ means that $\Pr[X = 1] = 1 - \Pr[X = 0] = p$. For n independent random variables $X_1, \ldots, X_n \overset{iid}{\sim} \text{Ber}_p$ their sum X is binomial distributed with parameters n and p, denoted $X \sim \text{Bin}_{n,p}$. A probability $p(k)$ is called *overwhelming* in k, if $1 - p(k)$ is negligible in k. We denote deterministic assignments in algorithms by $\leftarrow$.

Theorem 2.1 (Chernoff Bound, [27]). *Let* $X \sim \text{Bin}_{n,p}$. *Then*

$$\Pr[X \leq (1-r)np] \leq \exp\left(-\frac{1}{2}r^2np\right) \quad \text{for any } r \in [0,1]. \tag{1}$$

2.2 The LPN Problem

Definition 2.1 ((Search) LPN Problem). *Let $k \in \mathbb{N}$, $s \in \mathbb{F}_2^k$ and $p \in [0, \frac{1}{2})$ be a constant. Let* Sample *denote an oracle that, when queried, samples $a \sim \mathcal{U}_{\mathbb{F}_2^k}$, $e \sim \mathrm{Ber}_p$ and outputs a sample of the form $(a, b) := (a, \langle a, s \rangle + e)$. The* LPN$_k$ *problem consists of recovering s given access to* Sample. *In the following we call k the* dimension, *s the* secret, *p the* error rate, *b the* label *of a and e the* noise.

Brute-Force Sampling Algorithm. A straight-forward way to recover the first bit s_1 of the secret s is to query Sample until we obtain a sample of the form (u_1, b). Then $b = \langle u_1, s \rangle + e = s_1 + e$. Hence, $\Pr[s_1 = b] = 1 - p > \frac{1}{2}$. However, as Sample draws a uniformly from $\mathbb{F}_2^k$, we expect to have to query the oracle 2^k times to have $a = u_1$.

Further, to boost the confidence in recovering s_1 correctly from merely $1 - p$ to being overwhelming (in k) one may collect many samples (u_1, b_i) and decide on s_1 by majority vote, whose error is bounded in the following lemma.

Lemma 2.1 (Majority Vote). *Let $q > \frac{1}{2}$ and $X_1, \ldots, X_n \sim \mathrm{Ber}_q$ independently. Then*

$$\Pr\left[\sum_{i=1}^n X_i > \frac{n}{2}\right] \geq 1 - \exp\left(-\frac{n}{2q}\left(q - \frac{1}{2}\right)^2\right) .$$

Proof. Since $X := \sum_{i=1}^n X_i \sim \mathrm{Bin}_{n,q}$, using Theorem 2.1 with $r = 1 - \frac{1}{2q}$ gives

$$\Pr\left[X > \frac{n}{2}\right] \geq 1 - \exp\left(-\frac{1}{2}\left(1 - \frac{1}{2q}\right)^2 nq\right) = 1 - \exp\left(-\frac{n}{2q}\left(q - \frac{1}{2}\right)^2\right) .$$

$\square$

Corollary 2.1. *For $n := \frac{2(1-p)k}{(\frac{1}{2}-p)^2}$ many samples, a majority vote recovers s_1 correctly with probability at least $1 - \exp(-k)$.*

Proof. Let us define $X_i = 1$ iff $b_i = s_1$, which implies $q = 1 - p$. Lemma 2.1 yields the desired result. $\square$

Therefore, for any constant error rate p, the majority vote requires only a linear number $n = \mathcal{O}(k)$ of labels of the form (u_1, b_i). Clearly, we can recover the remaining bits s_j, $j = 2, \ldots, k$ of the secret s by querying Sample until we obtained sufficiently many samples with $a = u_j$. Overall, the probability that we recover all bits of s correctly is at least $(1 - \exp(-k))^k \geq 1 - k \cdot \exp(-k) = 1 - \mathrm{negl}(k)$.

2.3 Combining Samples

In [5], Blum, Kalai and Wasserman introduced the idea to construct $a = u_1$ from a collection of N arbitrary samples rather than merely waiting for a sample where

$\mathbf{a} = \mathbf{u}_1$. Their core idea is based on synthesizing a new sample from two existing ones $(\mathbf{a}_1, b_1)$, $(\mathbf{a}_2, b_2)$ via addition

$$(\mathbf{a}_1 \oplus \mathbf{a}_2, b_1 \oplus b_2) = (\mathbf{a}_1 \oplus \mathbf{a}_2, \langle \mathbf{a}_1 \oplus \mathbf{a}_2, s \rangle \oplus e_1 \oplus e_2) \ .$$

For such a synthesized sample, which we call a *2-sum of samples*, we have $\mathbf{a}_1 \oplus \mathbf{a}_2 \sim \mathcal{U}_{\mathbb{F}_2^k}$ and $e_1 \oplus e_2 \sim \text{Ber}_{p'}$ where $p' = \frac{1}{2} - \frac{1}{2}(1 - 2p)^2 > p$ according to the following Piling-Up lemma.

Lemma 2.2 (Piling-Up Lemma [14]). *Let $p \in [0, 1]$ and $e_i \sim \text{Ber}_p$, $i \in [n]$ be identically, independently distributed. Then*

$$\bigoplus_{i=1}^{n} e_i \sim \text{Ber}_{\frac{1}{2} - \frac{1}{2}(1-2p)^n} \ .$$

Summing up two or more samples enables us to synthesize samples at the expense of an error rate approaching $\frac{1}{2}$ exponentially fast in the number of summands.

3   The c-Sum-Problem and its Application to BKW

3.1   A Generalized BKW Algorithm

While BKW repeatedly adds *pairs* of samples to zero out chunks of coordinates, we add $c > 2$ samples to accomplish the same. Beneficially, as the number of size-c subsets grows exponentially in c, this allows for a drastic reduction in the number of initially required samples (thus, memory as well) while still finding sufficiently many sums of c vectors adding up to zero on a block of coordinates.

We give our c-sum-BKW in Algorithm 1. For a *block-size* b and $j \in [a]$ we refer to the coordinates $[k - jb + 1, k - (j-1)b]$ as the jth *stripe*. Essentially, c-sum-BKW consists of a **for**-loop (line 4) that generates zeros (resp. the first unit vector) on the jth stripe for $j \in [a-1]$ (resp. the ath stripe). This step is repeated multiple times (see line 2) to obtain sufficiently many labels of $\mathbf{u}_1$ samples in order to let a majority vote determine the first bit s_1 of the secret $\mathbf{s}$ with overwhelming probability. This process is repeated k times to recover all bits of $\mathbf{s}$.

For a list L as constructed in line 3, $j \in [a]$ and $t \in \mathbb{F}_2^b$ we let c-sum(L, j, t) denote an algorithm that outputs a new list L where the coordinates of each entry match t on the jth stripe (see lines 5, 6). If L should shrink to size 0 throughout an execution, we abort and return a failure symbol (see lines 7, 8).

We point out that (essentially) the original BKW algorithm may be obtained by letting c-sum add pairs of vectors whose sum matches t on the jth stripe to L'.

Let us introduce the *c-sum-problem* lying at the heart of any algorithm that shall be used to instantiate c-sum. In short, given a list of vectors $L \in (\mathbb{F}_2^b)^*$, i.e., a stripe from the c-sum-BKW point of view, the c-sum-problem asks to collect sums of c vectors that add up to some target $t \in \mathbb{F}_2^b$.

Algorithm 1. c-sum-BKW(k, p, ε_a, N) $\triangleright$ c $\in \mathbb{N}$

Input: dimension k, error rate p, $\varepsilon_a > 0$, $N \geq 2^{\frac{b+c\log c+1}{c-1}}$, access to **Sample**
Output: s $\in \mathbb{F}_2^k$
 1: $a := \frac{\log k}{(1+\varepsilon_a)\log c}$, $b := \frac{k}{a}$, $n := \frac{8(1-p)k}{(1-2p)^{2c^a}}$
 2: **for** $i \leftarrow 1, \dots, n$ **do**
 3:     Query N samples from **Sample** and save them in L.
 4:     **for** $j \leftarrow 1, \dots, a-1$ **do**
 5:         $L \leftarrow$ c-sum$(L, j, 0^b)$
 6:     $L \leftarrow$ c-sum$(L, a, \mathbf{u}_1)$
 7:     **if** $L = \emptyset$ **then**
 8:         **return** $\perp$
 9:     Pick $(\mathbf{u}_1, b_i)$ uniformly from L.
10: $s_1 \leftarrow$ majorityvote$(b_1, \dots, b_n)$
11: Determine $s_2, \dots, s_k$ the same way.
12: **return** s $= s_1 \dots s_k$

Definition 3.1 (The c-Sum-Problem (c-SP)). *Let $b, c, N \in \mathbb{N}$ with $c \geq 2$. Let $L := (l_1, \dots, l_N)$ be a list where $l_i \sim \mathcal{U}_{\mathbb{F}_2^b}$ for all i and let $t \in \mathbb{F}_2^b$ be a target. A single-solution of the c-SP$_b$ is a size-c set $\mathcal{L} \in \binom{[N]}{c}$ such that*

$$\bigoplus_{j \in \mathcal{L}} l_j = t \ .$$

A solution is a set of at least N distinct single-solutions. The c-sum-problem c-SP$_b$ consists of finding a solution when given L, t while c is usually fixed in advance. We refer to (L, t, c) as an instance of the c-SP$_b$, concisely (L, t) if c is clear from the context.

Note that by definition a solution to the c-sum-problem c-SP$_b$ consists of at least N single-solutions. These may again be combined into a new list of size (at least) N. Thus, we may apply a c-SP$_b$ solving algorithm on different b-bit stripes of a list. Further, the list does not shrink if a solution exists in each iteration.

Obviously, a solution should exist whenever the list size N is large enough, since then sufficiently many c-sums add up to some given target t. In the following, we show that the lower bound for the list-size N from Algorithm 1 guarantees the existence of such a solution with overwhelming probability under the following heuristic assumption that is regularly used in the analysis of BKW-type algorithms [6,7,32].

Independence Heuristic. Obviously, c-sums $\bigoplus_{j \in \mathcal{L}} l_j$ are stochastically dependent for $\mathcal{L} \subseteq [N]$ with $|\mathcal{L}| = c$. However, their dependency should only mildly affect the runtime of an iterative collision search as in BKW-type algorithms. For instance, it has been shown in [9] that the dependence between 2-sums $\bigoplus_{j \in \mathcal{L}} l_j$ merely affects the overall runtime exponent by an $o(1)$-term. We heuristically assume that this also holds for $c > 2$, and therefore treat (iterative) c-sums as independent in our run time analyses.

We provide various experiments in Sect. 6.1 that support the Independence Heuristic.

For Algorithm 1, we need the following lemma only for the special case $\alpha = 1$. However, our Tailored Dissection approach in Sect. 5.3 also requires $\alpha > 1$.

Lemma 3.1. *Let* (L, t) *be a* c-SP$_b$ *instance with*

$$|L| = N^\alpha, \text{ where } N = 2^{\frac{b+c \log c+1}{c-1}} \text{ and } \alpha \geq 1 .$$

Then, under the Independence Heuristic, (L, t) *has at least* N^α *single-solutions with probability* $1 - \exp(-N/4)$.

Proof. For every $\mathcal{L} \subseteq [N]$ with $|\mathcal{L}| = c$ define an indicator variable that takes value $X_\mathcal{L} = 1$ iff $\bigoplus_{j \in \mathcal{L}} l_j = t$.

Let $X = \sum_\mathcal{L} X_\mathcal{L}$ be the number of single-solutions to the c-SP$_b$. Under the Independence Heuristic, the $X_\mathcal{L}$ can be analyzed as if independent, thus $X \sim \text{Bin}_{\binom{N^\alpha}{c}, 2^{-b}}$ is binomially distributed. Hence,

$$\mathbb{E}[X] = \binom{N^\alpha}{c} \cdot 2^{-b} \geq \left(\frac{N^\alpha}{c}\right)^c \cdot 2^{-b} . \tag{2}$$

Since $\log N = \frac{b+c \log c+1}{c-1}$, we obtain

$$\log \mathbb{E}[X] \geq c(\alpha \log N - \log c) - b \geq \alpha \left(c(\log N - \log c) - b\right)$$
$$= \alpha \cdot \left(c\left(\frac{b + c \log c + 1 - (c-1)\log c}{c-1}\right) - b\right)$$
$$= \alpha \cdot \frac{cb + c \log c + c - (c-1)b}{c-1} = \alpha \cdot \frac{b + c \log c + 1 + c - 1}{c-1}$$
$$= \alpha \cdot (\log N + 1) \geq \alpha \log N + 1 . \tag{3}$$

Thus, our choice of N guarantees $\mathbb{E}[X] \geq 2N^\alpha$. We can upper-bound the probability that the c-sum-problem has less than N^α single-solutions solution using our Chernoff bound from Theorem 2.1 as

$$\Pr\left[X < N^\alpha\right] \leq \Pr\left[X < \frac{1}{2}\mathbb{E}[X]\right] \leq \exp\left(-\frac{\mathbb{E}[X]}{8}\right) \leq \exp\left(-\frac{N}{4}\right) . \qquad \square$$

Observation 3.1. Clearly, any algorithm solving the c-sum-problem may be used to replace c-sum in lines 5 and 6 of c-sum-BKW (Algorithm 1). As a consequence we do not distinguish between c-sum and an algorithm solving the c-sum-problem.

We now give Theorem 3.2 stating that c-sum-BKW inherits its complexities from c-sum. As a result, we may focus on solving the c-sum-problem in the remainder of this work.

Theorem 3.2 (Correctness and Complexities of c-sum-BKW). *Let* c-sum *denote an algorithm solving the* c-SP$_b$ *in expected time* $T_{c,N}$ *and expected memory* $M_{c,N}$ *with overwhelming success probability, where* $N \geq 2^{\frac{b+c\log c+1}{c-1}}$. *Under the Independence Heuristic* c-sum-BKW *solves the* LPN$_k$ *problem with overwhelming probability in time* T, *memory* M, *where*

$$T = (T_{c,N})^{1+o(1)} \, , \quad M = (M_{c,N})^{1+o(1)} \, ,$$

using $N^{1+o(1)}$ *samples.*

Proof. Let $a = \frac{\log k}{(1+\varepsilon_a)\log c}$ and $b = \frac{k}{a}$ as in Algorithm 1. Consider one iteration of the **for**-loop in line 2. As stated in Lemma 3.1 there exists a solution to the c-SP$_b$ instance (implicitly defined via the jth stripe of L and target 0^b (resp. $\mathbf{u}_1$)) with probability at least $1 - \exp(-\frac{N}{4})$. Hence, the probability that there is a solution to the instance in each iteration is greater than

$$\left(1 - \exp\left(-\frac{N}{4}\right)\right)^{an} \geq 1 - an \cdot \exp\left(-\frac{N}{4}\right) \, .$$

We now analyze the probability that a single bit of the secret gets recovered correctly. Since we build c-sums iteratively a times in lines 4–6, eventually we obtain vectors being a sum of at most c^a samples, having an error of $\frac{1}{2} - \frac{1}{2}(1-2p)^{c^a}$ according to Lemma 2.2.

Note that the labels $b_1, \ldots, b_n$ collected in line 10 are stochastically independent as each b_i is obtained from freshly drawn samples. Now Corollary 2.1 yields that $n := \frac{8(1-p)k}{(1-2p)^{2c^a}}$ samples are sufficient for the majority vote to determine a bit of $\mathbf{s}$ correctly with error probability at most $\exp(-k)$. Using the Union Bound, one bit of the secret $\mathbf{s}$ gets successfully recovered with probability at least

$$1 - an \cdot \exp\left(-\frac{N}{4}\right) - \exp(-k) \, .$$

As we have to correctly recover all, i.e., k bits of $\mathbf{s}$, the overall success probability of c-sum-BKW is at least

$$\left(1 - 2an \cdot \exp\left(-\frac{N}{4}\right) - \exp(-k)\right)^k \geq 1 - 2ank \cdot \exp\left(-\frac{N}{4}\right) - k\exp(-k) \, .$$

Let us look at the term $2ank \cdot \exp\left(-\frac{N}{4}\right)$. Since $n = \tilde{\mathcal{O}}(2^{\kappa_p c^a})$ for some constant κ_p, we obtain for constant c

$$2ank = \tilde{\mathcal{O}}(n) = 2^{\mathcal{O}(k^{\epsilon'})} \text{ with } \epsilon' < 1, \text{whereas } N = 2^{\Theta(b)} = 2^{\Theta(\frac{k}{a})} = 2^{\Theta(\frac{k}{\log k})}. \quad (4)$$

Thus, the factor $\exp\left(-\frac{N}{4}\right)$ clearly dominates and makes the overall success probability overwhelming in k.

Let us now analyze the time and memory complexity of c-sum-BKW. Since c-sum has only *expected* time/memory complexity, this expectation will be inherited to c-sum-BKW. We later show how to remove the expectation from c-sum-BKW's complexities by a standard technique.

Let us start with the running time of c-sum-BKW, where we ignore the negligible overhead of iterations of line 2 caused by failures in the c-sum-algorithm. Clearly, $T_{c,N} \geq N$. Hence, one iteration of the **for**-loop can be carried out in time $\tilde{\mathcal{O}}(\max\{N, a \cdot T_{c,N}\}) = \tilde{\mathcal{O}}(T_{c,N})$. Thus, for recovering the whole secret we get a running time of $\tilde{\mathcal{O}}(n \cdot T_{c,N})$. From Equation (4) we already know that N dominates n, which implies that $T_{c,N}$ dominates n. More precisely, we have $n \cdot T_{c,N} = (T_{c,N})^{1+o(1)}$. Hence, we can also express the overall *expected* running time as $(T_{c,N})^{1+o(1)}$.

The memory consumption is dominated by c-sum, which gives us in total *expected* $\tilde{\mathcal{O}}(M_{c,N}) = (M_{c,N})^{1+o(1)}$. The sample complexity of c-sum-BKW is $\tilde{\mathcal{O}}(knN) = \tilde{\mathcal{O}}(nN) = N^{1+o(1)}$.

It remains to remove the expectations from the complexity statements for time and memory, while keeping the success probability overwhelming. We run c-sum-BKW k times aborting each run if it exceeds its expected running time or memory by a factor of 4. A standard Markov bound then shows that this modified algorithm fails to provide a solution with probability at most 2^{-k}. For details see the full version [13].   □

In the following section, we discuss an algorithm to naively solve the c-sum-problem leading to a first trade-off in the subexponential time/memory regime that also allows for a quantum speedup.

4   First Time-Memory Trade-Offs for BKW

4.1   A Classic Time-Memory Trade-Off

A straight-forward algorithm to solve an instance of the c-sum-problem is to compute all sums of c elements from L. For $N = |L|$ this approach takes time $\mathcal{O}(N^c)$ while it requires memory $\mathcal{O}(N)$.

With little effort, we can do slightly better: Let L be sorted. Now let us brute-force all $(c-1)$-sums from L, add t, and check whether the result appears in L. This gives us by construction a c-sum that matches t.

The details of this c-sum-naive approach are given in Algorithm 2. Notice that whenever we call c-sum-naive, we should first sort the input list L, which can be done in additional time $\tilde{\mathcal{O}}(N)$.

The following lemma shows correctness and the complexities of Algorithm 2.

Lemma 4.1. c-sum-naive *finds a solution of the* c-SP$_b$ *in time* $\tilde{\mathcal{O}}\left(N^{c-1}\right)$ *and memory* $\tilde{\mathcal{O}}(N)$.

Proof. See full version [13].

Let us now replace in the c-sum-BKW algorithm the c-sum subroutine with Algorithm 2 c-sum-naive, and call the resulting algorithm c-sum-naive-BKW.

Algorithm 2. c-sum-naive(L, t) ⊳ $c \in \mathbb{N}$

Input: Sorted list $L = (v_1, \ldots, v_N) \in (\mathbb{F}_2^b)^N$, target $t \in \mathbb{F}_2^b$
Output: $S \subseteq \binom{[N]}{c}$ or $\bot$
1: **for all** $\mathcal{V} = \{i_1, \ldots i_{c-1}\} \subseteq [N]$ **do**
3: **for all** $i_c \in [N] \setminus \mathcal{V}$ satisfying $v_{i_c} = t \oplus (\oplus_{i \in \mathcal{V}} v_i)$ **do**
4:   $S \leftarrow S \cup \{\{i_1, \ldots, i_c\}\}$
5:   **if** $|S| = N$ **then**
6:    **return** S
7: **return** $\bot$

Theorem 4.1 (Naive Trade-Off). *Let* $c \in \mathbb{N}$. *For all* $\varepsilon > 0$ *and sufficiently large* k, *under the Independence Heuristic* c-sum-naive-BKW *solves the* LPN_k *problem with overwhelming success probability in time* $T = 2^{\vartheta(1+\varepsilon)}$, *using* $M = 2^{\mu(1+\varepsilon)}$ *memory and samples, where*

$$\vartheta = \log c \cdot \frac{k}{\log k} , \quad \mu = \frac{\log c}{c-1} \cdot \frac{k}{\log k} .$$

Proof. Let $N := 2^{\frac{b+c \cdot \log c+1}{c-1}}$. According to Lemma 4.1 c-sum-naive is correct and we can apply Theorem 3.2 to conclude that c-sum-naive-BKW solves LPN with overwhelming success probability.

Further Lemma 4.1 shows that c-sum-naive runs in time

$$T_{c,N} = \tilde{\mathcal{O}}(N^{c-1}) = \tilde{\mathcal{O}}(2^{b+c \log c+1}) = \tilde{\mathcal{O}}(2^b) \text{ for constant } c.$$

Thus, by Theorem 3.2 c-sum-naive-BKW runs in time $T = 2^{b(1+o(1))}$. Since c-sum-BKW operates on stripes of width $b = \log c \cdot \frac{k(1+\varepsilon_a)}{\log k}$ (see the definition in Algorithm 1), we obtain the claimed complexity $T = 2^{\vartheta(1+\varepsilon_a+o(1))} = 2^{\vartheta(1+\varepsilon)}$ for every $\varepsilon > \varepsilon_a$ and sufficiently large k.

Since c-sum-naive requires memory $M_{c,N} = \tilde{\mathcal{O}}(N)$, by Theorem 3.2 the memory complexity of c-sum-BKW is (for constant c)

$$M = (M_{c,N})^{1+o(1)} = N^{1+o(1)} = (2^{\frac{b}{c-1}})^{1+o(1)} = (2^{\frac{\log c}{c-1} \cdot \frac{k}{\log k}})^{1+o(1)}.$$

The sample complexity of c-sum-BKW is $N^{1+o(1)}$ (see Theorem 3.2) and therefore identical to M. □

Figure 1 shows the time-memory trade-off from Theorem 4.1 depicted by stars.

4.2 A Quantum Time-Memory Trade-Off

Grover's algorithm [15] identifies a marked element in an *unsorted* database D in time $\mathcal{O}(\sqrt{|D|})$ with overwhelming probability. A matching lower bound $\Omega(\sqrt{|D|})$ by Donotaru and Høyer [11] shows that Grover's algorithm is optimal. We use a modification of Grover's algorithm due to [8], denoted Grover, that applies even in case the number of marked elements is unknown.

Theorem 4.2 (Grover Algorithm [8]). *Let $f\colon D \to \{0,1\}$ be a function with non-empty support. Then* **Grover** *outputs with overwhelming probability a uniformly random preimage of 1, making q queries to f, where*

$$q = \tilde{\mathcal{O}}\left(\sqrt{\frac{|D|}{|f^{-1}(1)|}}\right) .$$

We use Grover's algorithm to speed up our naive approach to solving the c-sum-problem. While we previously brute-forced all $(c-1)$-sums in list L and checked if there is a fitting c^{th} entry in L, we now employ a Grover-search to immediately obtain $(c-1)$-sums for which there exists a suitable c^{th} element in L. Let us define the Grover function f_t as

$$f_t\colon \binom{[|L|]}{c-1} \to \{0,1\}, \mathcal{V} \mapsto \begin{cases} 1 & \exists i_c \in [|L|] \setminus \mathcal{V}\colon \sum_{j=1}^{c-1} l_{ij} = l_{i_c} + t \\ 0 & \text{else} \end{cases} .$$

Given some $\mathcal{V} \in f_t^{-1}(1)$ we can recover all i_c such that $\mathcal{V} \cup \{i_c\}$ is a single-solution of instance (L,t) in time $\tilde{\mathcal{O}}(\log|L|)$ if L is sorted.

Algorithm 3. Q-c-sum(L,t) $\triangleright\, \mathsf{c} \in \mathbb{N}$

Input: Sorted list $L = (v_1, \ldots, v_N) \in (\mathbb{F}_2^b)^N$, target $t \in \mathbb{F}_2^b$
Output: $S \subseteq \binom{[N]}{c}$ or $\bot$
1: **repeat** $\tilde{\mathcal{O}}(N)$ times
2:     $\mathcal{V} = (i_1, \ldots, i_{c-1}) \leftarrow$ **Grover**^{f_t}
3:     **for all** $i_c \in [N] \setminus \mathcal{V}$ satisfying $v_{i_c} = t \oplus (\oplus_{i \in \mathcal{V}} v_i)$ **do**
4:         $S \leftarrow S \cup \{\{i_1, \ldots, i_c\}\}$
5:         **if** $|S| = N$ **then**
6:             **return** S
7: **return** $\bot$

Lines 3–7 of Q-c-sum and c-sum-naive are identical. We merely replaced the brute-force search (line 1 in Algorithm 2) by a Grover-search (lines 1, 2 in Algorithm 3).

Lemma 4.2. Q-c-sum *solves the* c-SP$_b$ *with overwhelming probability in time* $\tilde{\mathcal{O}}(N^{c/2})$ *and memory* $\tilde{\mathcal{O}}(N)$.

Proof. See full version [13]. ∎

Let QBKW denote algorithm c-sum-BKW where c-sum is instantiated using Q-c-sum.

Theorem 4.3. *Let $c \in \mathbb{N}$. For all $\varepsilon > 0$ and sufficiently large k, under the Independence Heuristic* QBKW *solves the* LPN$_k$ *problem with overwhelming success probability in time $T = 2^{\vartheta(1+\varepsilon)}$, using $M = 2^{\mu(1+\varepsilon)}$ memory and samples, where*

$$\vartheta = \frac{c}{2 \cdot (c-1)} \cdot \log c \cdot \frac{k}{\log k} , \quad \mu = \frac{\log c}{c-1} \cdot \frac{k}{\log k} .$$

Proof. The proof proceeds along the lines of the proof of Theorem 4.1.

The trade-off from Theorem 4.3 is depicted in Fig. 1 on Page 5 by triangles.

5   Time-Memory Trade-Offs for BKW via Dissection

While a naive approach already led to a first time-memory trade-off, a meet-in-the-middle approach for solving the c-sum-problem prohibits a trade-off, as we explain in Sect. 5.1. As a consequence, we resort to the more advanced Dissection technique [10,30] in Sect. 5.2. However, as Dissection merely leads to instantiations for a rather sparse choice of available memory, we give a slight generalization of Dissection *tailored* to any given amount of memory. This allows for a trade-off covering the whole range of possible memory (see Sect. 5.3).

Let us define the specific structure of single-solutions that are recovered by all c-sum-problem algorithms in this section.

Definition 5.1 (Equally-split (Single-)Solution). *Let (L, t) be an* c-SP$_b$ *instance. Partition L into lists $L_1, \ldots, L_c$ of size $\frac{L}{c}$ each. A single-solution is equally-split (wrt. $L_1, \ldots, L_c$) if it corresponds to list elements $l_1, \ldots, l_c$ whereby $l_i \in L_i$ for all $i \in [c]$. An equally-split solution is a collection of N equally-split single-solutions.*

Lemma 5.1. *Let (L, t) be a* c-SP$_b$ *instance with*

$$|L| = N^\alpha, \text{ where } N = 2^{\frac{b + c \log c + 1}{c - 1}} \text{ and } \alpha \geq 1 .$$

Then, under the Independence Heuristic, (L, t) has at least N^α equally-split single-solutions with probability $1 - \exp(-N/4)$.

Proof. Let X be a random variable for the number of *equally-split* single-solutions. Then $\mathbb{E}[X] = \left(\frac{N^\alpha}{c}\right)^c \cdot 2^{-b}$. Hence, Eq. (2) is satisfied, and the rest follows as in the proof of Lemma 3.1. $\qquad\square$

5.1   Meet-in-the-Middle and Beyond

Let (L, t) be an instance of the c-SP$_b$. In a meet-in-the-middle approach one splits a c-sum $t = v_{i_1} \oplus \ldots \oplus v_{i_c}$ into two parts $t = \left(v_{i_1} \oplus \ldots \oplus v_{i_{\frac{c}{2}}}\right) \oplus \left(v_{i_{\frac{c}{2}+1}} \oplus \ldots \oplus v_{i_c}\right)$. Let us define $L_1 := (v_1, \ldots, v_{\frac{|L|}{2}})$, $L_2 := (v_{\frac{|L|}{2}+1}, \ldots, v_{|L|})$ and consider a single-solution corresponding to $\frac{c}{2}$ elements from L_1 and L_2 each:

$$\left(v_{i_1}, \ldots, v_{i_{\frac{c}{2}}}\right) \subseteq L_1 \text{ and } \left(v_{i_{\frac{c}{2}+1}}, \ldots, v_{i_c}\right) \subseteq L_2 .$$

If we compute all $\frac{c}{2}$-sums of elements from L_1 and save them in a new list $L_1^{\frac{c}{2}}$, then for each $\frac{c}{2}$-sum v of L_2 we can check if $w := v \oplus t \in L_1^{\frac{c}{2}}$. If so, v and w form a single-solution since $v \oplus w = t$. Obviously, this approach has expected time and memory complexity $\tilde{\mathcal{O}}(\max(|L|, |L|^{\frac{c}{2}})) = \tilde{\mathcal{O}}(|L|^{\frac{c}{2}})$ for $c \geq 2$. Yet, choosing $c > 2$

only leads to worse complexities, time and memory-wise, while for $c = 2$ the complexities for the meet-in-the-middle approach are as bad as for c-sum-naive.

Schroeppel and Shamir's Meet-in-the-Middle. We present a heuristic simplification of the Schroeppel-Shamir algorithm [30] due to Howgrave-Graham and Joux [20].

In a nutshell, the idea of Schroeppel and Shamir is to run a meet-in-the-middle attack but impose an artificial constraint τ on the $\frac{c}{2}$-sums. This results in lists $L_1^{\frac{c}{2},\tau}$ that are significantly smaller than $L_1^{\frac{c}{2}}$ in the original meet-in-the-middle approach. In order to find all single-solutions, one iterates τ over its whole domain. $L_1^{\frac{c}{2},\tau}$ is in turn built from smaller lists as follows. Let $t = v_{i_1} \oplus \ldots \oplus v_{i_c}$ and write

$$t = \underbrace{v_{i_1} \oplus \ldots \oplus v_{i_{\frac{c}{4}}}}_{\ell_{11}} \oplus \underbrace{v_{i_{\frac{c}{4}+1}} \oplus \ldots \oplus v_{i_{\frac{c}{2}}}}_{\ell_{12}} \oplus \underbrace{v_{i_{\frac{c}{2}+1}} \oplus \ldots \oplus v_{i_{\frac{3c}{4}}}}_{\ell_{21}} \oplus \underbrace{v_{i_{\frac{3c}{4}+1}} \oplus \ldots \oplus v_{i_c}}_{\ell_{22}} .$$

Create four lists $L_{11}^{\frac{c}{4}}, L_{12}^{\frac{c}{4}}, L_{21}^{\frac{c}{4}}, L_{22}^{\frac{c}{4}}$ containing all $\frac{c}{4}$-sums of elements from the first, second, third, and fourth quarter of L. Let $\ell_{i,j}$ denote elements from $L_{ij}^{\frac{c}{4}}$ for $i, j = 1, 2$. As a constraint we choose $\text{low}_{\frac{c}{4}\log|L|}(\ell_{11} \oplus \ell_{12}) = \tau$ for some fixed τ. Now we construct $L_1^{\frac{c}{2},\tau}$ from $L_{11}^{\frac{c}{4}}$ and $L_{12}^{\frac{c}{4}}$ using a meet-in-the-middle approach requiring expected time $\tilde{\mathcal{O}}(|L|^{\frac{c}{4}})$. Similarly, we can compute all elements of list $L_2^{\frac{c}{2},t\oplus\tau}$ to obtain sums of $\frac{c}{2}$ vectors ($\frac{c}{4}$ from $L_{2,1}^{\frac{c}{4}}$ and $L_{2,2}^{\frac{c}{4}}$ each) matching $t \oplus \tau$ on the last $|\tau| = \frac{c}{4}\log|L|$ bits. Eventually, given the elements from $L_2^{\frac{c}{2},t\oplus\tau}$ and list $L_1^{\frac{c}{2},\tau}$ one can some recover single-solutions as before. Thereby list $L_1^{\frac{c}{2},\tau}$ is of expected size

$$\mathbb{E}\left[\left|L_1^{\frac{c}{2},\tau}\right|\right] = \left|L_{11}^{\frac{c}{4}}\right| \cdot \left|L_{12}^{\frac{c}{4}}\right| \cdot 2^{-|\tau|} = |L|^{2 \cdot \frac{c}{4} - \frac{c}{4}} = |L|^{\frac{c}{4}} .$$

We conclude that the expected memory consumption of the algorithm is given by $\tilde{\mathcal{O}}(\max\{|L|, |L|^{\frac{c}{4}}\})$.

As we iterate over $2^{|\tau|} = |L|^{\frac{c}{4}}$ choices of τ requiring expected time $\tilde{\mathcal{O}}(|L|^{\frac{c}{4}})$ per iteration, the overall expected running time is given by $\tilde{\mathcal{O}}(|L|^{\frac{c}{2}})$ for all $c \geq 4$. Hence, for $c = 4$ we obtain an algorithm as fast as the meet-in-the-middle approach, while consuming only expected memory $\tilde{\mathcal{O}}(|L|)$.

Note that it is sufficient to store list $L_1^{\frac{c}{2},\tau}$ while all elements from $L_2^{\frac{c}{2},t\oplus\tau}$ may be computed and checked on-the-fly, i.e., without storing its elements.

The Schroeppel-Shamir algorithm is a special case of Dissection run on 4 lists in the subsequent section, which further exploits the asymmetry between storing lists and computing (memory-free) lists on the fly.

5.2   Dissection

Dissection can be considered as a memory-friendly member of the class of k-list algorithms [31]. A Dissection algorithm is given c lists $L_c, \ldots, L_1$ and a target t.

For simplicity the algorithm merely sums list elements to obtain target t rather than outputting a single-solution explicitly. One could keep track of indices of those elements that sum to t, but for ease of notation we omit this. Instead, we employ some abstract "index recovering" procedure later.

HIGH-LEVEL STRUCTURE OF DISSECTION. A Dissection identifying sums of vectors adding up to some target t consists of the following steps

(1) A loop iterates over an artificially introduced constraint τ. For each τ:

    (1.1) A meet-in-the-middle approach is run to obtain a list L of sums from the first few lists that add up to τ on a some bits. List L is kept in memory.

    (1.2) Dissection is called recursively to find sums from the remaining lists that sum to $t \oplus \tau$ on a some bits. Found sums are passed to the parent call on-the-fly.

    (1.3) For all sums passed from the recursive call in step (1.2) list L is searched to construct sums adding up to τ on some more bits.

Before giving the fully-fledged Dissection algorithm, let us give an 11-Dissection example.

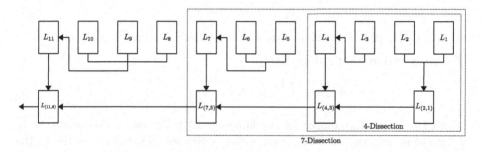

Fig. 2. High-level structure of an 11-Dissection on input lists $L_{11}, \ldots, L_1$. Recursively called 7- and 4-Dissection enclosed in dashed boxes. Arrows entering a list from the right side indicate a check on-the-fly. Arrows leaving a list on the left side indicate that a found match is returned on-the-fly. Arrows entering a list from the top indicate that the list below is populated with entries from above and stored entirely.

Example 5.1 (11-Dissection). An 11-Dissection is run on lists $L_{11}, \ldots, L_1$ and some target t. It loops through an artificial constraint τ_3. Within each iteration: A list $L_{(11,8)}$ containing sums $l_{11} \oplus \ldots \oplus l_8$ consistent with constraint τ_3 where $l_{11} \in L_{11}, \ldots, l_8 \in L_8$ is computed and stored. Then, still within the first iteration of the loop, a 7-Dissection is run (see Fig. 2) on lists $L_7, \ldots, L_1$ and a modified target $t \oplus \tau_3$. The 7-Dissection itself introduces a constraint τ_2 and stores a list $L_{(7,5)}$ containing sums of elements from L_7, L_6, L_5 fulfilling τ_2. It recursively calls a 4-Dissection, i.e. Schroeppel-Shamir (Sect. 5.1), on target $t \oplus \tau_3 \oplus \tau_2$. Internally, the 4-Dissection introduces another constraint τ_1.

    Whenever a partial sum is identified by the 4-Dissection, it is passed to the 7-Dissection on-the-fly while the 4-Dissection carries on. See the "chain" at the bottom in Fig. 2 traversing lists from right to left. Once, the 7-Dissection receives a sum, it immediately checks for a match in list $L_{(7,5)}$ and discards or returns it—in case of the latter—enriched by a matching element from $L_{(7,5)}$ to the 11-Dissection and continues.

Whenever the 11-Dissection receives a sum from the 7-Dissection, it instantly checks for a match in list $L_{(11,8)}$ to detect if a single-solution has been found.

Definition 5.2 (Join Operator). *Let $d \in \mathbb{N}$ and L_1, $L_2 \in (\mathbb{F}_2^d)^*$ be lists. The join of L_1 and L_2 is defined as*

$$L_1 \bowtie L_2 := (l_1 \oplus l_2 : l_1 \in L_1, l_2 \in L_2) \ .$$

For $t \in \mathbb{F}_2^{\leq d}$ the join of L_1 and L_2 on t is defined as

$$L_1 \bowtie_t L_2 := (l_1 \oplus l_2 : l_1 \in L_1, l_2 \in L_2 \wedge \text{low}_{|t|}(l_1 \oplus l_2) = t) \ .$$

If $L_2 = (l_2)$ we write $L_1 \bowtie_t l_2$ instead of $L_1 \bowtie_t (l_2)$.

Clearly, computing elements contained in a sequence of joins can be implemented memory-friendly without having to explicitly compute intermediate lists.

Definition 5.3 (The Magic Sequence [10]). *Let $c_{-1} := 1$ and*

$$c_i := c_{i-1} + i + 1 \tag{5}$$

for all $i \in \mathbb{N} \cup \{0\}$. The magic *sequence is defined as* $\text{magic} := (c_i)_{i \in \mathbb{N}^{\geq 1}}$.

One easily verifies that, alternatively,

$$\text{magic} = \left(\frac{1}{2} \cdot (i^2 + 3i + 4) \right)_{i \in \mathbb{N}^{\geq 1}} \ . \tag{6}$$

As Dissection formulated in the language of k-*list algorithms* might be of independent interest we deter from adding c-SP$_b$-solving related details to the Dissection algorithm presented next, but rather introduce a simple wrapper algorithm (see Algorithm 5) to solve the c-sum-problem afterwards.

We define the class of Dissection algorithms recursively. Let $L_2, L_1 \in (\mathbb{F}_2^d)^*$, $d \in \mathbb{N}$ and $t \in \mathbb{F}_2^{\leq d}$. Then

$$c_0\text{-Dissect}(L_2, L_1, t, \text{inner}) := L_2 \bowtie_t L_1 \ . \tag{7}$$

Here, "inner" indicates that c_0-Dissect was called recursively by another Dissection algorithm in contrast to an initial, explicit call to run Dissection that will be called with parameter "outer".

We proceed to define c_i-Dissect for $i \geq 1$. Lists are denoted by L and input-lists are numbered L_{c_i} down to L_1 for $c_i \in \text{magic}$. As a reading aid, list and element indices keep track of input-lists they originated from: A list $L_{(j,i)}$ is the output of a join of lists $L_j \bowtie \ldots \bowtie L_i$ for $j > i$. List elements are denoted l. We write $l_{(j,i)}$ to indicate that $l_{(j,i)}$ is a sum of elements $l_\kappa \in L_\kappa$ for $\kappa = j, \ldots, i$.

The optimality of this recursive structure is shown in [10]. We now establish the required properties of Algorithm 4 in a series of lemmata. We give detailed proofs in the full version [13].

Algorithm 4. c_i-Dissect$(L_{c_i}, \ldots, L_1, t, \text{pos})$ $\triangleright$ $c_i \in$ magic

---

Input: Lists $L_{c_i}, \ldots, L_1 \in (\mathbb{F}_2^b)^{2^\lambda}$ where $\lambda \leq \frac{b}{i}$, target $t \in \mathbb{F}_2^b$, pos $\in \{\text{outer}, \text{inner}\}$
Output: $S \subseteq \binom{[N]}{c_i}$ or $\perp$
1: **for all** $\tau_i \in \mathbb{F}_2^{i \cdot \lambda}$ **do**
2:      $L_{(c_i, c_{i-1}+1)} \leftarrow L_{c_i} \bowtie_{\tau_i} (L_{c_i-1} \bowtie \ldots \bowtie L_{c_{i-1}+1})$
3:      **for all** $l_{(c_{i-1},1)}$ **passed from** c_{i-1}-Dissect$(L_{c_{i-1}}, \ldots, L_1, \text{low}_{i \cdot \lambda}(t) \oplus \tau_i, \text{inner})$ **do**
4:          **for all** $l_{(c_i,1)} \in L_{(c_i, c_{i-1}+1)} \bowtie_t l_{(c_{i-1},1)}$ **do**
5:             **if** pos $=$ **inner then**
                pass $l_{(c_i,1)}$ to c_{i+1}-Dissect
6:             **else**
                $S \leftarrow S \cup \{\text{recover indices}(l_{(c_i,1)})\}$
7: **return** S

Algorithm 5. c_i-sum-Dissect(L, t) $\triangleright$ $c_i \in$ magic

---

Input: $L \in (\mathbb{F}_2^b)^N$, target $t \in \mathbb{F}_2^b$
Output: $S \subseteq \binom{[N]}{c_i}$ or $\perp$
1: Partition L into c_i lists $L_{c_i}, \ldots, L_1$ of size $\frac{N}{c_i}$ each
2: $S \leftarrow c_i$-Dissect$(L_{c_i}, \ldots, L_1, t, \text{outer})$
3: **if** $|S| < N$ **then**
4:      **return** $\perp$
5: **return** S

Lemma 5.2 (Correctness of c_i-Dissect). *For some fixed j_a let $l_a := L_a(j_a)$ denote the j_a^{th} element of list L_a. When c_i-Dissect$(L_{c_i}, \ldots, L_1, t, \text{outer})$ halts, set S contains $(j_{c_i}, \ldots, j_1) \in [2^\lambda]^{c_i}$ if and only if $\bigoplus_{a=1}^{c_i} l_a = t$.*

Proof. See full version [13].

Lemma 5.3 (Memory Consumption of c_i-Dissect). *For all $i \geq 1$ algorithm c_i-Dissect requires expected memory $\tilde{\mathcal{O}}(\max\{2^\lambda, \mathbb{E}[|S|]\})$.*

Proof. See full version [13].

Lemma 5.4. *Let $i \geq 1$ and consider one iteration of the **for**-loop in line 1 within a call of c_i-Dissect$(\cdots, \text{inner})$. Then, in total, expected $\tilde{\mathcal{O}}(2^{c_{i-2} \cdot \lambda})$ elements are returned in line 5.*

Proof. See full version [13].

Lemma 5.5. *Let $i \geq 1$. Algorithm c_i-Dissect$(\cdots, \text{inner})$ runs in expected time $\tilde{\mathcal{O}}(2^{c_{i-1} \cdot \lambda})$.*

Proof. See full version [13].

Lemma 5.6 (Running Time of c_i-Dissect). *Let $i \geq 1$. A call of algorithm c_i-Dissect($\cdots$, outer) runs in expected time $\tilde{\mathcal{O}}(\max\{2^{c_{i-1} \cdot \lambda}, \mathbb{E}[\|S\|]\})$.*

Proof. See full version [13].

Lemma 5.7. *Let $b \in \mathbb{N}$ and $c_i \in$ magic. For $t \in \mathbb{F}_2^b$ let (L, t) be an instance of the c_i-SP_b where $|L| = N := 2^{\frac{b+c_i \cdot \log c_i+1}{c_i-1}}$. Under the Independence Heuristic c_i-sum-Dissect solves the c_i-SP_b with overwhelming probability in expected time $T = \tilde{\mathcal{O}}(N^{c_{i-1}})$ and expected memory $M = \tilde{\mathcal{O}}(N)$.*

Proof. From Lemma 5.1 we know that at least N equally-split single-solutions exist with overwhelming probability. Lemma 5.2 ensures that c_i-Dissect recovers all of them. Note that the lists defined in line 1 are of length

$$2^\lambda = \frac{N}{c_i} = 2^{\frac{b+c_i \cdot \log c_i+1}{c_i-1} - \log c_i} = 2^{\frac{b+\log c_i+1}{c_i-1}} \ .$$

One easily verifies that $\lambda = \frac{b+\log c_i+1}{c_i-1} \leq \frac{b}{i}$ as syntactically required by c_i-Dissect. Hence, Algorithm 5 solves the c-SP_b with overwhelming probability. From Lemma 5.3 we have

$$M = \tilde{\mathcal{O}}(\max\{2^\lambda, \mathbb{E}[\|S\|]\}) = \tilde{\mathcal{O}}(\max\{N, \mathbb{E}[\|S\|]\}) \ .$$

Under the Independence Heuristic we obtain $\mathbb{E}[\|S\|] = \left(\frac{N}{c_i}\right)^{c_i} \cdot 2^{-b} = 2N$, where the last equality follows from Eq. (3). Therefore, $M = \tilde{\mathcal{O}}(N)$. From Lemma 5.6 we conclude

$$T = \tilde{\mathcal{O}}(\max\{2^{c_{i-1} \cdot \lambda}, \mathbb{E}[\|S\|]\}) = \tilde{\mathcal{O}}(N^{c_{i-1}}) \ . \qquad \square$$

Since $c_{i-1} = c_i - i - 1$ by Eq. (5) and $i \approx \sqrt{2c_i}$ by Eq. (6), we see that c_i-sum-Dissect reduces the time complexity of solving the c-sum-problem from N^{c-1} (c-sum-naive) down to roughly $N^{c-\sqrt{2c}}$ (see also Table 1). Let c_i-Dissect-BKW denote the variant of c-sum-BKW, where c-sum is instantiated using c_i-sum-Dissect.

Theorem 5.1 (Dissection Trade-Off). *Let $c_i \in$ magic, $\varepsilon > 0$ and $k \in \mathbb{N}$ sufficiently large. Under the Independence Heuristic c_i-Dissect-BKW solves the LPN_k problem with overwhelming success probability in time $T = 2^{\vartheta(1+\varepsilon)}$, using $M = 2^{\mu(1+\varepsilon)}$ memory and samples, where*

$$\vartheta = \left(1 - \frac{i}{c_i - 1}\right) \cdot \log c_i \cdot \frac{k}{\log k} \ , \qquad \mu = \frac{\log c_i}{c_i - 1} \cdot \frac{k}{\log k} \ .$$

Proof. Let $N := 2^{\frac{b+c_i \cdot \log c_i+1}{c_i-1}}$. It follows from Lemma 5.7 and Theorem 3.2 that c_i-Dissect-BKW solves LPN with overwhelming probability. We now combine Lemma 5.7 and Theorem 3.2 to compute the running time T and memory complexity M of c_i-Dissect-BKW. We have

$$\log T = c_{i-1} \cdot \frac{b + c_i \cdot \log c_i + 1}{c_i - 1} \cdot (1 + o(1)) \ ,$$

whereby c-sum-BKW operates on stripes of size $b = \log c_i \cdot \frac{k \cdot (1+\varepsilon_a)}{\log k}$. Hence

$$\log T = \left(\frac{c_{i-1} \log c_i}{c_i - 1} \cdot \frac{k \cdot (1 + \varepsilon_a)}{\log k} + \frac{c_{i-1} \cdot (c_i \log c_i + 1)}{c_i - 1} \right) \cdot (1 + o(1))$$

$$= \frac{c_{i-1} \log c_i}{c_i - 1} \cdot \frac{k}{\log k} \cdot (1 + \varepsilon_a + o(1))$$

$$= \frac{c_{i-1}}{c_i - 1} \cdot \log c_i \cdot \frac{k}{\log k} \cdot (1 + \varepsilon)$$

for every $\varepsilon > \varepsilon_a$ and sufficiently large k. Finally

$$\log T \overset{(5)}{=} \left(1 - \frac{i}{c_i - 1} \right) \cdot \log c_i \cdot \frac{k}{\log k} \cdot (1 + \varepsilon) .$$

Analogously we have for M:

$$\log M = \frac{\log c_i}{c_i - 1} \cdot \frac{k}{\log k} \cdot (1 + \varepsilon) ,$$

for every $\varepsilon > \varepsilon_a$ and sufficiently large k. The sample complexity of c-sum-BKW is $N^{1+o(1)} = M$. □

The trade-off of Theorem 5.1 clearly improves over the naive trade-off initially obtained in Theorem 4.1. While the memory consumption of the Dissection approach remains the same as for the naive trade-off, we can reduce the price we have to pay in time from $\log c_i$ down to $(1 - \frac{i}{c_i-1}) \cdot \log c_i$.

The trade-off from Theorem 5.1 is given in Fig. 1 on Page 5 as diamonds. Although it improves over the naive tradeoff from Sect. 4.1, this improvement comes at the price of covering only c_i-sums with $c_i \in$ magic. Given some available memory M, one would choose the minimal $c_i \in$ magic such that c_i-Dissect-BKW consumes at most memory M. However, such a choice of c_i is unlikely to fully use M. In the following section, we show how to further speed up the algorithm by using M entirely.

5.3   Tailored Dissection

Assume, we run c_i-sum-Dissect and our available memory is not fully used. Recall that c_i-sum-Dissect collects single-solutions while iterating an outmost loop over some constraint. In a nutshell, access to additional memory allows us to increase the size of lists $L_{c_i}, \dots, L_1$, where $N = |L_{c_i}| + \dots + |L_1|$. Thereby, the number of equally-split single-solutions of a c-sum-problem instance increases significantly beyond N. As it suffices to identify (roughly) N single-solutions, we may prune the outmost loop of c_i-Dissect to recover N (rather than all) equally-split single-solutions.

Yet, examining a fraction of the solution space only leads to recovering a respective fraction of single-solutions if the latter are distributed sufficiently uniformly.[1]

---

[1] Imagine many single-solutions concentrated on few constraints τ_i as a counterexample.

Let us briefly recall that the total number of existing single-solutions taken over the initial choice of input lists is close to a binomial distribution under the Independence Heuristic. This allowed us to show that c_i-sum-Dissect succeeds with high probability as sufficiently many single-solutions exist with high probability.

Now, let us denote the random variable of the number of single-solutions gained in the jth iteration of the outmost loop of c_i-Dissect by Z_j. In order to prove that a certain number of iterations is already sufficient to collect enough single-solutions with high probability we require information on the distribution of sums of Z_j. However, as we show shortly, already Z_j is distributed rather awkwardly and it seems to be a challenging task to obtain Chernoff-style results ensuring that the sum of Z_j does not fall too short from its expectation with high probability. In turn, we resort to the following heuristic.

Tailoring Heuristic. Let $c_i \in$ magic. Let random variable Z_j denote the number of single-solutions gained in the jth iteration of the outmost **for**-loop of c_i-Dissect taken over the initial choice of input lists. We heuristically assume that there exists a polynomial function $\text{poly}(\lambda)$, such that for all $\mathcal{J} \subseteq \{1, \dots, 2^{i\lambda}\}$ we have

$$\Pr\left[\sum_{j \in \mathcal{J}} Z_j < \frac{1}{\text{poly}(\lambda)} \cdot \mathbb{E}\left[\sum_{j \in \mathcal{J}} Z_j\right]\right] \leq \text{negl}(\lambda) \ . \tag{8}$$

In particular, it follows from Equation (8) that for all $\iota \leq 2^{i\lambda}$ we have

$$\Pr\left[\sum_{j=1}^{\iota \cdot \text{poly}(\lambda)} Z_j \geq \mathbb{E}\left[\sum_{j=1}^{\iota} Z_j\right]\right] \geq 1 - \text{negl}(\lambda) \ .$$

That is, we can compensate the deviation of the sums of Z_j below its expectation by iterating $\text{poly}(\lambda)$ more often.[2]

As for the Independence Heuristic we ran experiments to verify the Tailoring Heuristic (Sect. 6.2).

Algorithm 6. tailored–c_i–sum–Dissect(L, t) ▷ $c_i \in$ magic

---

Input: $L \in (\mathbb{F}_2^b)^{N^\alpha}$ where $N := 2^{\frac{b + c_i \cdot \log c_i + 1}{c_i - 1}}$ and $\alpha \geq 1$, target $t \in \mathbb{F}_2^b$
Output: $S \subseteq \binom{[N^\alpha]}{c_i}$ or $\bot$
1: Partition L into c_i lists $L_{c_i}, \dots, L_1$ of size $2^\lambda := \frac{N^\alpha}{c_i}$ each
2: $S \leftarrow c_i$-Dissect$(L_{c_i}, \dots, L_1, t, \text{outer})$ ▷ halt c_i-Dissect once $|S| = N^\alpha$
3: **if** $|S| < N^\alpha$ **then**
4:      **return** $\bot$
5: **return** S

---

[2] Clearly, it does not make sense to iterate $\iota \cdot \text{poly}(\lambda) > 2^{i \cdot \lambda}$ times. However, once we would have $\iota \cdot \text{poly}(\lambda) > 2^{i \cdot \lambda}$ iterating $2^{i\lambda}$ times is sufficient to collect enough single-solutions as shown in Lemma 3.1.

We stress that the only syntactical difference of `tailored-c_i-sum-Dissect` compared to `c_i-sum-Dissect` (Algorithm 5) is the increase of the size of list L from N to N^α for $\alpha \geq 1$ and the halt condition added as a comment in line 2.

Lemma 5.8 (Tailored Dissection). *Let $b \in \mathbb{N}, c_i \in$ magic and $\alpha \in [1, \frac{c_i-1}{c_{i-1}}]$. For $t \in \mathbb{F}_2^b$ let (L,t) be an instance of the c_i-SP_b for $|L| = N^\alpha$ whereby $N := 2^{\frac{b+c_i \cdot \log c_i + 1}{c_i - 1}}$. Under the Independence and Tailoring Heuristic `tailored-c_i-sum-Dissect` solves the c_i-SP_b with overwhelming probability in expected time $T = \tilde{\mathcal{O}}\left(N^{c_{i-1}-i\cdot(\alpha-1)}\right)$ and expected memory $M = \tilde{\mathcal{O}}(N^\alpha)$.*

Proof. See full version [13].

The complexities of `tailored-c_i-sum-Dissect` are given in Table 1 where we simplified α's upper bound using $c_{i-1} \approx c_i - \sqrt{2c_i}$. Let `tailored-c_i-BKW` denote c-sum-BKW, where the c-sum-problem is solved via `tailored-c_i-sum-Dissect`.

Theorem 5.2 (Tailored-Dissection Trade-Off). *Let $c_i \in$ magic and further $\alpha \in [1, \frac{c_i-1}{c_{i-1}}]$, $\varepsilon > 0$ and $k \in \mathbb{N}$ sufficiently large. Under the Independence and Tailoring Heuristic `tailored-c_i-BKW` solves the LPN_k problem with overwhelming success probability in time $T = 2^{\vartheta(1+\varepsilon)}$, using $M = 2^{\mu(1+\varepsilon)}$ memory and samples, where*

$$\vartheta = \left(1 - \frac{\alpha \cdot i}{c_i - 1}\right) \cdot \log c_i \cdot \frac{k}{\log k} \quad , \quad \mu = \frac{\alpha \cdot \log c_i}{c_i - 1} \cdot \frac{k}{\log k} \quad .$$

Proof. See full version [13].

Intuitively, it is clear how to choose optimal parameters for `tailored-c_i-BKW` for any given amount of memory M: Find the minimal $c_i \in$ magic such that `c_i-Dissect-BKW` uses at most memory M. Then, resort to `tailored-c_i-BKW` using memory M entirely by choosing the right α. The trade-off achieved via this approach is given in Fig. 1 on page 5 (line segments). A formal justification of the approach is contained in the full version [13].

6   Experimental Verification of Heuristics

We present experimental results to verify our Independence Heuristic as well as our Tailoring Heuristic.

6.1   Experiments for the Independence Heuristic

We tested the Independence Heuristic for $c_i \in \{4, 7\}$. We iteratively monitored the number of single-solutions found after a run of `c_i-sum-Dissect` on successive stripes starting with a list of size N. For each c_i we repeatedly called `c_i-sum-Dissect` on three stripes. After each call we stored the number of single-solutions found. To analyze the impact of dependencies amongst the

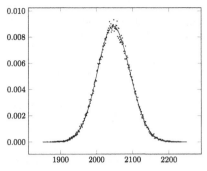

(a) Distribution of the number of single-solutions after run 1 of 4-sum-Dissect. Sample size in thousands: 108.

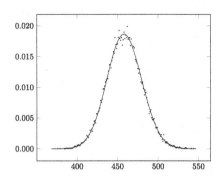

(d) Distribution of the number of single-solutions after run 1 of 7-sum-Dissect. Sample size in thousands: 29.

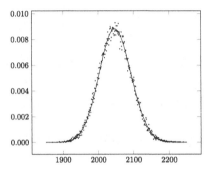

(b) Distribution of the number of single-solutions after run 2 of 4-sum-Dissect. Sample size in thousands: 100.

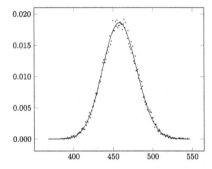

(e) Distribution of the number of single-solutions after run 2 of 7-sum-Dissect. Sample size in thousands: 23.

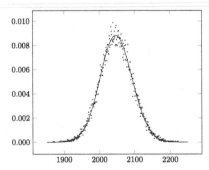

(c) Distribution of the number of single-solutions after run 3 of 4-sum-Dissect. Sample size in thousands: 58.

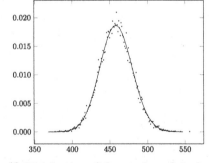

(f) Distribution of the number of single-solutions after run 3 of 7-sum-Dissect. Sample size in thousands: 18.

Fig. 3. Distribution of the number of single-solutions over successive runs of c_i-sum-Dissect. Under the Independence Heuristic this distribution is close to $\mathrm{Bin}_{(N/c_i)^{c_i},2^{-b}}$. All parameters are given in Table 2.

list elements—rather than influences due to variations in the number of single-solutions found—we pruned lists of more than N single-solutions down to N before starting the next run, and discarded lists where less than N single-solutions were found.

Note that during the first run all list elements are independent and uniformly distributed, even if their c-sums are not. While the list elements remain uniform on a "fresh" stripe in subsequent runs of c_i-sum-Dissect they are not independent anymore what could affect (besides c-sums being dependent) the distribution of existing single-solutions even further. Under the Independence Heuristic the number of single-solutions found is close to being $\text{Bin}_{(N/c_i)^{c_i}, 2^{-b}}$ distributed after any run of c_i-sum-Dissect.

Our experiments with parameters as given in Table 2 lead to the plots given in Fig. 3. The measured relative frequencies are given by points, while the continuous plots are the benchmark distributions $\text{Bin}_{(N/c_i)^{c_i}, 2^{-b}}$ for our Independence Heuristic.

Table 2. Parameters for testing the Independence Heuristic. Parameter a denotes the number of stripes of width b.

c_i	a	b	N	run	sample size in thous.	given in
				1	108	Fig. 3a
$c_1 = 4$	3	25	2048	2	100	Fig. 3b
				3	58	Fig. 3c
				1	29	Fig. 3d
$c_2 = 7$	3	33	441	2	23	Fig. 3e
				3	18	Fig. 3f

We see from Fig. 3 that the distribution of the output list-size is close to their benchmark, even after three iterations of the c-sum subroutine, where already $4^3 = 64$-sums (resp. $7^3 = 343$-sums) haven been built.

We also used the Independence Heuristic in Lemma 5.8 to show that the random variables Z_j of the number of single-solutions gained in the jth iteration over a constraint is close to being binomially $\text{Bin}_{x \cdot y, 2^{-(b-i\lambda)}}$ distributed, where $x \sim \text{Bin}_{2^{(i+1)\cdot\lambda}, 2^{-i\lambda}}$ and $y \sim \text{Bin}_{2^{\lambda c_i - 1}, 2^{-i\lambda}}$. In order to verify this experimentally, we computed several instances with parameter set

$$i = 1 \ (c_1 = 4), \ b = 25, \ a = 3, \ N = 8192 \ .$$

Each time we performed three consecutive runs of 4-sum-Dissect on successive stripes and stored the number of single-solutions obtained per constraint after each iteration. The results are given in Fig. 4. Again, the obtained relative frequencies accurately match the benchmark curve $\text{Bin}_{x \cdot y, 2^{-(b-i\lambda)}}$.

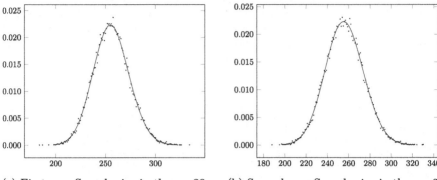

(a) First run. Sample size in thous.: 20.   (b) Second run. Sample size in thous.: 22.

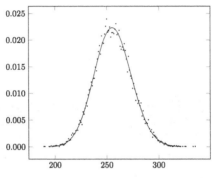

(c) Third run. Sample size in thous.: 14.

Fig. 4. Distribution of the number of single-solutions per constraint in the first (Fig. 4a), second (Fig. 4b) and third run (Fig. 4c) of 4-sum-Dissect.

6.2   Experiments on the Tailoring Heuristic

As in the previous subsection, let Z_j be the number of single-solutions obtained per constraint iteration in c_i-sum-Dissect. In Tailored Dissection it is required that the sum of these random variables is close to its expectation. The Tailoring Heuristic states that this is true with overwhelming probability, if we slightly increase the expected number of required iterations by a polynomial factor.

To test the Tailoring Heuristic we ran 4-sum-Dissect (without tailoring) on three stripes ($a = 3$) with $N = 8192$ and varying choice of b. We summed the numbers Z_j of single-solutions found per randomized constraint τ_j during the last run in a list, until their sum exceeded N. The results can be found in Table 3 and Fig. 5.

Table 3. Parameters and results for testing the Tailoring Heuristic for 4-sum-Dissect, $N = 8192$.

	E[iterations to reach N]				
b	theory	experiments	99% confidence interval	sample size in thous.	given in
25	32	32.50	$32.50 \cdot (1 \pm 0.031)$	50	
28	256	255.40	$255.40 \cdot (1 \pm 0.031)$	100	Fig. 5a
29	512	511.78	$511.78 \cdot (1 \pm 0.026)$	150	Fig. 5b
30	1024	1024.20	$1024.20 \cdot (1 \pm 0.021)$	250	Fig. 5c

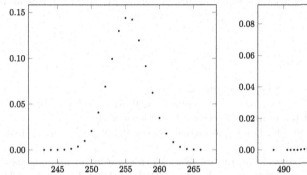 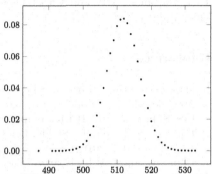

(a) $b = 28$. Parameters of sample set X_1: $\mathbb{E}[X_1] = 255.40$, $\mathrm{Var}[X_1] = 7.55$, $\sigma_{X_1} = 2.75$, 99% confidence interval $\mathbb{E}[X_1] \pm 8$.

(b) $b = 29$. Parameter of sample set X_2: $\mathbb{E}[X_2] = 511.78$, $\mathrm{Var}[X_2] = 22.81$, $\sigma_{X_2} = 4.78$, 99% confidence interval $\mathbb{E}[X_2] \pm 13$.

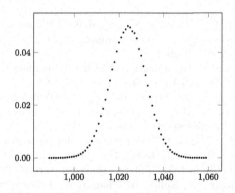

(c) $b = 30$. Parameter of sample set X_3: $\mathbb{E}[X_3] = 1024.20$, $\mathrm{Var}[X_3] = 63.99$, $\sigma_{X_3} = 7.99$, 99% confidence interval $\mathbb{E}[X_3] \pm 21$.

Fig. 5. Required number of iterations to collect at least N single-solutions. $N = 8192$.

We see in Table 3 that the experimentally required numbers of iteration very accurately match their theoretical predictions (that were computed under the

Independence Heuristic). Moreover, we experimentally need only a small factor to achieve a 99% confidence interval, even for low expectations. This means that the distribution has small variance and sharply concentrates around its mean, as can also been seen in Fig. 5. This all supports the validity of our Tailoring Heuristic for the analysis of Tailored Dissection BKW.

Acknowledgements. We would like to thank Eamonn Postlethwaite for his detailed feedback and helpful suggestions on an earlier version of this paper. We are grateful to the anonymous CRYPTO reviewers for their valuable comments.

Andre Esser was supported by DFG Research Training Group GRK 1817. Felix Heuer, Alexander May and Christian Sohler were supported by Mercator Research Center Ruhr, project "LPN-Krypt".

References

1. http://csrc.nist.gov/groups/ST/post-quantum-crypto/
2. Alekhnovich, M.: More on average case vs approximation complexity. In: 44th FOCS, pp. 298–307. IEEE Computer Society Press, October 2003
3. Bai, S., Laarhoven, T., Stehlé, D.: Tuple lattice sieving. LMS J. Comput. Math. **19**(A), 146–162 (2016)
4. Blum, A., Furst, M.L., Kearns, M.J., Lipton, R.J.: Cryptographic primitives based on hard learning problems. In: Stinson, D.R. (ed.) CRYPTO 1993. LNCS, vol. 773, pp. 278–291. Springer, Heidelberg (1994). https://doi.org/10.1007/3-540-48329-2_24
5. Blum, A., Kalai, A., Wasserman, H.: Noise-tolerant learning, the parity problem, and the statistical query model. In: 32nd ACM STOC, pp. 435–440. ACM Press, May 2000
6. Bogos, S., Tramèr, F., Vaudenay, S.: On solving LPN using BKW and variants - implementation and analysis. Crypt. Commun. **8**(3), 331–369 (2016). https://doi.org/10.1007/s12095-015-0149-1
7. Bogos, S., Vaudenay, S.: Optimization of LPN solving algorithms. In: Cheon, J.H., Takagi, T. (eds.) ASIACRYPT 2016, Part I. LNCS, vol. 10031, pp. 703–728. Springer, Heidelberg (2016). https://doi.org/10.1007/978-3-662-53887-6_26
8. Boyer, M., Brassard, G., Høyer, P., Tapp, A.: Tight bounds on quantum searching. arXiv preprint quant-ph/9605034 (1996)
9. Devadas, S., Ren, L., Xiao, H.: On iterative collision search for LPN and subset sum. In: Kalai, Y., Reyzin, L. (eds.) TCC 2017, Part II. LNCS, vol. 10678, pp. 729–746. Springer, Cham (2017). https://doi.org/10.1007/978-3-319-70503-3_24
10. Dinur, I., Dunkelman, O., Keller, N., Shamir, A.: Efficient dissection of composite problems, with applications to cryptanalysis, knapsacks, and combinatorial search problems. In: Safavi-Naini, R., Canetti, R. (eds.) CRYPTO 2012. LNCS, vol. 7417, pp. 719–740. Springer, Heidelberg (2012). https://doi.org/10.1007/978-3-642-32009-5_42
11. Dohotaru, C., Hoyer, P.: Exact quantum lower bound for grover's problem. arXiv preprint arXiv:0810.3647 (2008)
12. Ducas, L.: Shortest vector from lattice sieving: a few dimensions for free. In: Nielsen, J.B., Rijmen, V. (eds.) EUROCRYPT 2018, Part I. LNCS, vol. 10820, pp. 125–145. Springer, Cham (2018). https://doi.org/10.1007/978-3-319-78381-9_5

13. Esser, A., Heuer, F., Kübler, R., May, A., Sohler, C.: Dissection-BKW. Cryptology ePrint Archive, Report 2018/569 (2018). https://eprint.iacr.org/2018/569

14. Esser, A., Kübler, R., May, A.: LPN decoded. In: Katz, J., Shacham, H. (eds.) CRYPTO 2017, Part II. LNCS, vol. 10402, pp. 486–514. Springer, Cham (2017). https://doi.org/10.1007/978-3-319-63715-0_17

15. Grover, L.K.: A fast quantum mechanical algorithm for database search. In: 28th ACM STOC, pp. 212–219. ACM Press, May 1996

16. Guo, Q., Johansson, T., Löndahl, C.: Solving LPN using covering codes. In: Sarkar, P., Iwata, T. (eds.) ASIACRYPT 2014, Part I. LNCS, vol. 8873, pp. 1–20. Springer, Heidelberg (2014). https://doi.org/10.1007/978-3-662-45611-8_1

17. Guo, Q., Johansson, T., Stankovski, P.: Coded-BKW: solving LWE using lattice codes. In: Gennaro, R., Robshaw, M.J.B. (eds.) CRYPTO 2015, Part I. LNCS, vol. 9215, pp. 23–42. Springer, Heidelberg (2015). https://doi.org/10.1007/978-3-662-47989-6_2

18. Herold, G., Kirshanova, E.: Improved algorithms for the approximate k-list problem in euclidean norm. In: Fehr, S. (ed.) PKC 2017, Part I. LNCS, vol. 10174, pp. 16–40. Springer, Heidelberg (2017). https://doi.org/10.1007/978-3-662-54365-8_2

19. Herold, G., Kirshanova, E., Laarhoven, T.: Speed-Ups and time–memory trade-offs for tuple lattice sieving. In: Abdalla, M., Dahab, R. (eds.) PKC 2018, Part I. LNCS, vol. 10769, pp. 407–436. Springer, Cham (2018). https://doi.org/10.1007/978-3-319-76578-5_14

20. Howgrave-Graham, N., Joux, A.: New generic algorithms for hard knapsacks. In: Gilbert, H. (ed.) EUROCRYPT 2010. LNCS, vol. 6110, pp. 235–256. Springer, Heidelberg (2010). https://doi.org/10.1007/978-3-642-13190-5_12

21. Kannan, R.: Improved algorithms for integer programming and related lattice problems. In: 15th ACM STOC, pp. 193–206. ACM Press, April 1983

22. Laarhoven, T.: Sieving for shortest vectors in lattices using angular locality-sensitive hashing. In: Gennaro, R., Robshaw, M.J.B. (eds.) CRYPTO 2015, Part I. LNCS, vol. 9215, pp. 3–22. Springer, Heidelberg (2015). https://doi.org/10.1007/978-3-662-47989-6_1

23. Laarhoven, T., Mariano, A.: Progressive lattice sieving. In: Lange, T., Steinwandt, R. (eds.) PQCrypto 2018. LNCS, vol. 10786, pp. 292–311. Springer, Cham (2018). https://doi.org/10.1007/978-3-319-79063-3_14

24. Laarhoven, T., de Weger, B.: Faster sieving for shortest lattice vectors using spherical locality-sensitive hashing. In: Lauter, K.E., Rodríguez-Henríquez, F. (eds.) LATINCRYPT 2015. LNCS, vol. 9230, pp. 101–118. Springer, Cham (2015). https://doi.org/10.1007/978-3-319-22174-8_6

25. Levieil, É., Fouque, P.-A.: An improved LPN algorithm. In: De Prisco, R., Yung, M. (eds.) SCN 2006. LNCS, vol. 4116, pp. 348–359. Springer, Heidelberg (2006). https://doi.org/10.1007/11832072_24

26. Lyubashevsky, V., Peikert, C., Regev, O.: A toolkit for ring-LWE cryptography. In: Johansson, T., Nguyen, P.Q. (eds.) EUROCRYPT 2013. LNCS, vol. 7881, pp. 35–54. Springer, Heidelberg (2013). https://doi.org/10.1007/978-3-642-38348-9_3

27. Mitzenmacher, M., Upfal, E.: Probability and Computing: Randomized Algorithms and Probabilistic Analysis. Cambridge University Press, New York (2005)

28. Regev, O.: New lattice based cryptographic constructions. In: 35th ACM STOC, pp. 407–416. ACM Press, June 2003

29. Regev, O.: On lattices, learning with errors, random linear codes, and cryptography. J. ACM 56(6), 34:1–34:40 (2009). https://doi.org/10.1145/1568318.1568324

30. Schroeppel, R., Shamir, A.: A T=O($2^{n/2}$), S=O($2^{n/4}$) algorithm for certain np-complete problems. SIAM J. Comput. **10**(3), 456–464 (1981). https://doi.org/10.1137/0210033

31. Wagner, D.: A Generalized birthday problem. In: Yung, M. (ed.) CRYPTO 2002. LNCS, vol. 2442, pp. 288–304. Springer, Heidelberg (2002). https://doi.org/10.1007/3-540-45708-9_19

32. Zhang, B., Jiao, L., Wang, M.: Faster algorithms for solving LPN. In: Fischlin, M., Coron, J.-S. (eds.) EUROCRYPT 2016, Part I. LNCS, vol. 9665, pp. 168–195. Springer, Heidelberg (2016). https://doi.org/10.1007/978-3-662-49890-3_7

Lattice-Based ZK

Sub-linear Lattice-Based Zero-Knowledge Arguments for Arithmetic Circuits

Carsten Baum[1], Jonathan Bootle[2], Andrea Cerulli[2], Rafael del Pino[3],
Jens Groth[2], and Vadim Lyubashevsky[3(✉)]

[1] Bar-Ilan University, Ramat Gan, Israel
carsten.baum@biu.ac.il
[2] University College London, London, UK
{jonathan.bootle.14,andrea.cerulli.13,j.groth}@ucl.ac.uk
[3] IBM Research - Zurich, Rüschlikon, Switzerland
vadim.lyubash@gmail.com

Abstract. We propose the first zero-knowledge argument with sublinear communication complexity for arithmetic circuit satisfiability over a prime p whose security is based on the hardness of the short integer solution (SIS) problem. For a circuit with N gates, the communication complexity of our protocol is $O\left(\sqrt{N\lambda\log^3 N}\right)$, where λ is the security parameter. A key component of our construction is a surprisingly simple zero-knowledge proof for pre-images of linear relations whose amortized communication complexity depends only logarithmically on the number of relations being proved. This latter protocol is a substantial improvement, both theoretically and in practice, over the previous results in this line of research of Damgård et al. (CRYPTO 2012), Baum et al. (CRYPTO 2016), Cramer et al. (EUROCRYPT 2017) and del Pino and Lyubashevsky (CRYPTO 2017), and we believe it to be of independent interest.

Keywords: Sigma-protocol · Zero-knowledge argument
Arithmetic circuit · SIS assumption

1 Introduction

Zero-knowledge proofs and arguments are used throughout cryptography as a key ingredient to ensure security in complex protocols. They form an important part of applications such as authentication protocols, electronic voting systems,

Jonathan Bootle, Andrea Cerulli and Jens Groth were supported by funding from the European Research Council under the European Union's Seventh Framework Programme (FP/2007-2013)/ERC Grant Agreement n. 307937. Rafael del Pino and Vadim Lyubashevsky were supported in part by the SNSF ERC Transfer Starting Grant CRETP2-166734-FELICITY. Carsten Baum acknowledges support by the BIU Center for Research in Applied Cryptography and Cyber Security in conjunction with the Israel National Cyber Bureau in the Prime Ministers Office.

© International Association for Cryptologic Research 2018
H. Shacham and A. Boldyreva (Eds.): CRYPTO 2018, LNCS 10992, pp. 669–699, 2018.
https://doi.org/10.1007/978-3-319-96881-0_23

encryption primitives, multi-party computation schemes, and verifiable computation protocols. Therefore, designing zero-knowledge protocols with strong security and high efficiency is of the utmost importance.

A zero-knowledge argument allows a prover to convince a verifier that a particular statement is true, without the prover revealing any other information that she knows about the statement. Statements are of the form $u \in \mathcal{L}$, where $\mathcal{L}$ is a language in NP. We call w a witness for statement u if $(u, w) \in R$, where R is a polynomial time decidable binary relation associated with $\mathcal{L}$. Zero-knowledge arguments must be complete, sound and zero-knowledge.

Completeness: A prover with witness w for $u \in \mathcal{L}$ can convince the verifier.
Soundness: A prover cannot convince the verifier when $u \notin \mathcal{L}$.
Zero-knowledge: The interaction should not reveal anything to the verifier except that $u \in \mathcal{L}$. In particular, it should not reveal the prover's witness w.

We wish to design a zero-knowledge argument based on the short integer solution (SIS) assumption. Lattice problems appear to resist quantum attacks, and possess attractive worst-case to average-case reductions, in stark contrast with number theoretic assumptions such as the hardness of factoring or computing discrete logarithms. Moreover, using SIS (and the even more efficient Ring-SIS) yields better computational efficiency, which is a significant bottleneck in many zero-knowledge arguments.

1.1   Our Contributions

We provide an honest verifier zero-knowledge argument for arithmetic circuit satisfiability over $\mathbb{Z}_p$, for an arbitrary prime p. Our argument is based on the SIS assumption [Ajt96, MR04], which is conjectured to be secure even against a quantum adversary. Our argument has an expected constant number of moves and sub-linear communication complexity, as shown in Table 1. Moreover, it achieves small soundness error in a single protocol execution. Moreover, both the prover and verifier have quasi-linear computational complexity in the amount of computation it would require to evaluate the arithmetic circuit directly. The argument therefore improves on the state-of-the-art in communication complexity for lattice proof systems and is efficient on all performance parameters.

Table 1. Performance of our zero-knowledge argument for arithmetic circuit satisfiability. Here N is the number of gates in the arithmetic circuit, and λ is the security parameter.

Expected # Moves	Communication (bits)	Prover Complexity (bit ops)	Verifier Complexity (bit ops)
$O(1)$	$O(\sqrt{N\lambda}\log^3 N)$	$O(N \log N (\log \lambda)^2)$	$O(N(\log \lambda)^3)$

Techniques. We draw inspiration from the discrete logarithm based arithmetic circuit satisfiability argument of Bootle et al. [BCC+16], which requires 5 moves and has square root communication complexity in the number of multiplication gates. In their argument the prover commits to all the wires using homomorphic commitments, and embeds the wire values into a polynomial that verifies products and linear relations simultaneously, avoiding the cost for addition gates.

Almost all parts of the original arguments adapt seamlessly to the SIS setting, except for two important issues:

- To achieve sub-linear communication, we need a technique for proving knowledge of commitment openings in sub-linear space.
- Due to the new algebraic setting, we require new techniques for achieving negligible soundness in a single run of the protocol.

The first of these issues has been an open problem in a fairly active area of research, and we sketch our solution below.

Proof of Knowledge. Suppose that we have a linear relation

$$\boldsymbol{As} = \boldsymbol{t} \bmod q, \tag{1}$$

where $\boldsymbol{A} \in \mathbb{Z}_q^{r \times v}, \boldsymbol{t} \in \mathbb{Z}_q^r$ are public and $\boldsymbol{s} \in \mathbb{Z}_q^v$ is a vector with small coefficients, and we want to give a zero-knowledge proof of knowledge of an $\bar{\boldsymbol{s}}$ with small coefficients (the coefficients of $\bar{\boldsymbol{s}}$ may be larger than those of $\boldsymbol{s}$) that satisfies

$$\boldsymbol{A}\bar{\boldsymbol{s}} = \boldsymbol{t} \bmod q. \tag{2}$$

We do not currently know of any an efficient linear-communication protocol for proving knowledge of a single relation of the above form in a direct way. There are protocols, however, that allow for proofs of many such relations for the same $\boldsymbol{A}$ but different $\boldsymbol{s}_i$ (and thus different $\boldsymbol{t}_i$) in linear amortized complexity. We will mention these previous works in more detail in Sect. 1.2.

In this work, we give a protocol for proving (1) where the proof length is a factor $\frac{\lambda}{\ell} \cdot O(\log v\ell\lambda)$ larger than the total bit-length of ℓ pre-images $\boldsymbol{s}_1, \ldots, \boldsymbol{s}_\ell$ of the relations, where λ is the security parameter. More specifically, to prove knowledge of ℓ pre-images $\boldsymbol{s}_1, \ldots, \boldsymbol{s}_\ell$ whose coefficients have $\log s$ bits each, the prover needs to send λ vectors in $\mathbb{Z}_q^v$ whose coefficients require $O(\log v\ell\lambda s)$ bits to represent. Ignoring logarithmic terms, our proof essentially requires a fixed-size proof regardless of the number of relations being proved. The previously best results had proofs that were at least linear in the total size of the pre-images.

Surprisingly, the proof of knowledge protocol turns out to just be a parallel repetition of λ copies of the ZKPoK implicit in the signing protocol from [Lyu12]. In particular, if we write the ℓ relations as $\boldsymbol{AS} = \boldsymbol{T} \bmod q$, where $\boldsymbol{S} \in \mathbb{Z}_q^{v \times \ell}$, then the protocol begins with the prover selecting a "masking" value $\boldsymbol{Y}$ with small coefficients and sending $\boldsymbol{W} = \boldsymbol{A}\boldsymbol{Y} \bmod q$. The verifier then picks a random challenge matrix $\boldsymbol{C} \in \{0,1\}^{\ell \times (\lambda+2)}$, and sends it to the prover. The prover computes $\boldsymbol{Z} = \boldsymbol{SC} + \boldsymbol{Y}$ and performs a rejection sampling step in order to make the distribution of Z independent from S, and if it passes, sends Z to the verifier. The verifier checks that all columns comprising Z have small norms and that $AZ = TC + W \bmod q$. This protocol can be shown to be zero-knowledge using exactly the same techniques as in [Lyu09, Lyu12].

To show that the protocol is a proof of knowledge, we make the following observation: if the prover succeeds with probability $\epsilon > 2^{-\lambda}$, and she succeeded for a random C, then there is a probability of $\epsilon - 2^{-\lambda-2}$ that she would successfully answer another challenge $C' \neq C$ that is constructed such that all rows except the ith are the same as that of C, and the ith row is picked uniformly at random. This property follows from an averaging (or "heavy row") type argument. The implication is that if the prover succeeds in time t with probability ϵ, then the extractor can extract responses to two such commitments C, C' in expected time $O(t/\epsilon)$. Obtaining two responses Z, Z' for two such challenges allows the extractor to compute $A(Z - Z') = T(C - C')$ where $C - C'$ is 0 everywhere except in row i. Since $C \neq C'$, this implies that some position in row i is ± 1. If t_i is the ith column of T and z_i is the ith column of $Z - Z'$, then we have a solution $Az_i = \pm t_i$. Repeating this extraction ℓ times, each time rewinding by fixing all rows in the challenge except for the ith, results in an algorithm that runs in expected time $O(\ell \cdot t/\epsilon)$, which is only a factor of ℓ larger than the expected running time of a successful prover.

In the case that we are proving (1) over the polynomial ring $\mathbb{Z}[X]/(X^d + 1)$, the proof can be even shorter, as we can reduce the number of columns in C to $\approx \lambda/\log 2d$ because we can use challenges of the form $\pm X^i$ and prove the knowledge of $\bar{s}$ such that $A\bar{s} = 2t$ using the observation from [BCK+14].

Commitment Scheme. Central to the main proof of proving circuit satisfiability is being able to commit to N values in $\mathbb{Z}_p$ and giving a ZKPoK for the values such that the total size of the commitments and the proofs is sub-linear in N. For this, it is necessary to use a compressing commitment scheme – i.e. one in which we can commit to n elements of $\mathbb{Z}_p$ in space less than n elements. The scheme that we will use is the "classic" statistically-hiding commitment scheme based on the hardness of SIS that was already implicit in the original work of Ajtai [Ajt96]. The public randomness consists of two matrices $A \in \mathbb{Z}_q^{r \times 2r \log_p q}$, $B \in \mathbb{Z}_q^{r \times n}$, and committing to a message string $s \in \mathbb{Z}_p^n$ where $p < q$ involves picking a random vector $r \in \mathbb{Z}_p^{2r \log_p q}$ and outputting the commitment $t = Ar + Bs \bmod q$. Thus the commitment of n elements of $\mathbb{Z}_p$ requires $r \log q$ bits. One can set the parameters such that $n = \text{poly}(r)$ and the commitment scheme will still be computationally binding based on the worst-case hardness of approximating SIVP for all lattices of dimension r.

We now explain the intuition for putting together this commitment scheme with the zero-knowledge proof system we described above to produce a commitment to N values in $\mathbb{Z}_p$ such that the total size of the commitments and the ZKPoK of the committed values is $O(\sqrt{N\lambda \log N})$. The idea is to create N/n commitments (for some choice of n which will be optimized later), with each one committing to n values. Our motivation is that an arithmetic circuit over

$\mathbb{Z}_p$ with N gates has $3N$ wire values in $\mathbb{Z}_p$. Now, we can arrange all of the wire values in the circuit into, for example, a $3N/n \times n$ matrix over $\mathbb{Z}_p$, and make one homomorphic commitment to all of the elements in each row of the matrix. Then, we can employ techniques from [Gro09a, BCC+16], where checking arithmetic circuit satisfiability is reduced to checking linear-algebraic statements over committed matrices, using a homomorphic commitment scheme.

The total space requirement for these commitments is therefore $\frac{N}{n} \cdot r \log_p q$.

We now have a linear equation of the form $\begin{bmatrix} A & B \end{bmatrix} \begin{bmatrix} R \\ S \end{bmatrix} = T \bmod q$. Using our new zero-knowledge proof, the communication complexity of proving the knowledge of a short $\begin{bmatrix} \bar{R} \\ \bar{S} \end{bmatrix} \in \mathbb{Z}_q^{(r \log_p q + n) \times N/n}$ such that $\begin{bmatrix} A & B \end{bmatrix} \begin{bmatrix} \bar{R} \\ \bar{S} \end{bmatrix} = T \bmod$ q requires sending λ vectors of length $r \log_p q + n$ with coefficients requiring $O(\log N \lambda p)$ bits, for a total bit-length of $n \cdot \lambda \cdot O(\log N \lambda p)$. Combining the proof size with the commitment size results in a total bit-size of

$$\frac{N}{n} \cdot r \log q + n \cdot \lambda \cdot O(\log N \lambda p).$$

We minimize the above by setting $n = \sqrt{\frac{N r \log_p q}{\lambda \log N \lambda p}}$, which makes the size

$$O\left(\sqrt{N r \lambda (\log_p q)(\log N \lambda p)}\right).$$

Based on the complexity of the best known algorithm against the SIS problem, one can set $\log q, r = O(\log N)$, thus making the proof size of order $O(\sqrt{N \lambda \log^3 N})$.

1.2   Related Work

Zero-knowledge proofs were invented by Goldwasser et al. [GMR85]. It is useful to distinguish between zero-knowledge *proofs*, with statistical soundness, and zero-knowledge *arguments* with computational soundness. The most efficient proofs have communication proportional to the size of the witness [IKOS07, KR08, GGI+15] and proofs cannot in general have communication that is smaller than the witness size unless surprising results about the complexity of solving SAT instances hold [GH98, GVW02]. Kilian [Kil92] showed that in contrast to proofs, zero-knowledge arguments can have very low communication complexity. His construction relied on the PCP theorem, and thus incurred a large computational cost.

Group theoretic zero-knowledge arguments. Schnorr [Sch91] and Guillou and Quisquater [GQ88] gave early examples of practical zero-knowledge arguments for concrete number theoretic problems. Extending Schnorr's protocols, there have been many constructions of zero-knowledge arguments based on the discrete logarithm assumption, for instance [CD97, Gro09a]. The most efficient discrete logarithm based zero-knowledge arguments for arithmetic circuits are by

Bootle et al. [BCC+16] and later optimised in [BBB+17], which have logarithmic communication complexity and require a linear number of exponentiations.

An exciting line of research [Gro10a, Lip12, BCCT12, GGPR13, BCCT13, PHGR13, Gro16] on succinct non-interactive arguments (SNARGs) has yielded pairing-based constructions where the arguments consist of a constant number of group elements. However, it can be shown that all SNARKs must rely on non-falsifiable knowledge extractor assumptions [GW11]. In contrast, since our argument is interactive, we do not need to rely on these strong assumptions.

Lattice-based zero-knowledge arguments. The first zero-knowledge proofs from lattice-based assumptions were aimed at lattice problems themselves. Goldreich and Goldwasser [GG98] presented constant round interactive zero knowledge proofs for the complements of the approximate Shortest Vector Problem (SVP) and the approximate Closest Vector Problem (CVP). Micciancio and Vadhan [MV03] later constructed statistical zero knowledge proofs for these problems which had efficient provers.

Stern's protocol [Ste94] was one of the first zero-knowledge identification protocols to be based on a post-quantum assumption, namely, on the hardness of syndrome decoding for a random linear code, which is essentially proving (1) where $q = 2$ and $\|s\| \ll \sqrt{v}$. The protocol achieves constant soundness error, and thus requires many parallel repetitions. Stern's work prompted many variants and similar protocols. For example, [LNSW13] adapts the protocol for larger q, which implies proving knowledge of SIS solutions.

Another technique for creating zero-knowledge proofs is the "Fiat-Shamir with Aborts" approach [Lyu09, Gro10b, Lyu12]. When working over polynomial rings R, it gives a proof of knowledge of a vector $\bar{s}$ with small coefficients (though larger than those in s) and a ring element $\bar{c}$ with very small coefficients satisfying $A\bar{s} = \bar{c}t$. As long as the ring R has many elements with small coefficients, such proofs are very efficient, producing soundness of $1 - 2^{-128}$ with just one iteration. While these proofs are good enough for constructing practical digital signatures (e.g. [GLP12, DDLL13, BG14]), commitment schemes with proofs of knowledge [BKLP15, BDOP16], and certain variants of verifiable encryption schemes [LN17], they prove less than what the honest prover knows. In many applications where zero-knowledge proofs are used, in particular those that need to take advantage of additive homomorphisms, the presence of the element $\bar{c}$ makes these kinds of "approximate" proofs too weak to be useful. As of today, we do not have any truly practical zero-knowledge proof systems that give a proof of (1).

The situation is more promising when one considers *amortized* proofs. The work of [BD10] uses MPC-in-the-head to prove knowledge of plaintexts for multiple Regev [Reg05] ciphertexts. Damgård and López-Alt [DL12] extend the [BD10] results to prove knowledge of plaintext in $\mathbb{Z}_p$, rather than bits, and provide a proof for the correctness of multiplications. Combining these together gives a zero-knowledge proof for the satisfiability of arithmetic circuits with linear communication in the circuit size.

Another idea for proving the relation in (1) is to use the above-mentioned "Fiat-Shamir with Aborts" protocol, but with challenges that come from the set $\{0, 1\}$. The works of [BDLN16, CDXY17, dPL17] gave a series of improved protocols that were able to employ this technique in the amortized setting. Their proofs had a small polynomial "slack" (i.e. the ratio between the original committed s and the extracted $\bar{s}$) and were of approximate linear size when the number of commitments was a couple of thousand. The schemes are considerably less efficient when one is proving fewer relations.

The amortized zero-knowledge proof in the current work improves on the above series of papers in two important ways. First, the number of relations necessary before the size of our proof is linear only in λ. But more importantly, if we have more than λ relations, the communication complexity does not increase except for small logarithmic factors (i.e. the proof size becomes sub-linear).

Hash-based zero-knowledge arguments. Recently Bootle et al. [BCG+17] used error-correcting codes and linear-time collision-resistant hash functions to give proof systems for the satisfiability of an arithmetic circuit where the prover uses a linear number of field multiplications. Verification is even more efficient, requiring only a linear number of additions. While their proofs and arguments are asymptotically very efficient, they are not quite practical as their choices of error-correcting codes and hash functions involves very large constants.

An another effective way to construct efficient zero-knowledge proofs is to follow the so-called MPC-in-the-head paradigm of [IKOS07]. This approach proved itself to give very efficient constructions both theoretically and practically. Most notably, ZKBOO [GMO16] and subsequent optimisation ZKB++ [CDG+17] use hash functions to construct zero-knowledge arguments for the satisfiability of boolean circuits. Their communication complexity is linear in the circuit size, but the use of symmetric primitives gives good performances in practice. Ligero [AHIV17] provides another implementation of the MPC-in-the-head paradigm and used techniques similar to [BCG+17] to construct sublinear arguments for arithmetic circuits.

2 Preliminaries

Algorithms in our schemes receive a security parameter λ as input (sometimes implicitly) written in unary. The intuition is that the higher the security parameter, the lower the risk of the scheme being broken. Given two functions $f, g : \mathbb{N} \to [0, 1]$ we write $f(\lambda) \approx g(\lambda)$ when $|f(\lambda) - g(\lambda)| = \lambda^{-\omega(1)}$. We say that f is *negligible* when $f(\lambda) \approx 0$ and that f is *overwhelming* when $f(\lambda) \approx 1$. For any integer N, $[N]$ denotes the set $\{0, 1, \ldots, N - 1\}$ of integers.

2.1 Notation

Throughout this paper we will consider a ring $\mathcal{R}$, which will be either $\mathbb{Z}$ or the polynomial ring $\mathbb{Z}[X]/(X^d + 1)$ for d some power of 2. We will denote elements of $\mathcal{R}$ by lowercase letters, (column) vectors over $\mathcal{R}$ in bold lowercase and matrices over $\mathcal{R}$ in bold uppercase. e.g. $\boldsymbol{A} = [\boldsymbol{a}_1, \ldots, \boldsymbol{a}_k] \in \mathcal{R}^{l \times k}$ with $\boldsymbol{a}_i = (a_{i1}, \ldots, a_{im})^T \in \mathcal{R}^l$. We will consider the norm of elements in $\mathcal{R}$ to be $\|a\|_2 = |a|$ if $a \in \mathbb{Z}$, and $\|a\|_2 = \sqrt{\sum a_i^2}$ if $a = \sum a_i X^i \in \mathbb{Z}[X]/(X^d + 1)$. We extend the notation to vectors and matrices $\|\boldsymbol{a}\|_2 = \sqrt{\sum \|a_i\|_2^2}$, $\|\boldsymbol{A}\|_2 = \sqrt{\sum \|\boldsymbol{a}_i\|_2^2}$. We will also consider the quotient ring $\mathcal{R}_q = \mathcal{R}/q\mathcal{R}$ for odd q. In the quotient ring, the norm of an element $\mathcal{R}_q$ will be the norm of its unique representative $\mathcal{R}$ with coefficients in $\left[-\frac{q-1}{2}, \frac{q-1}{2}\right]$.

We will also consider the operator norm of matrices over $\mathcal{R}$ defined as $s_1(\boldsymbol{A}) = \max_{\|x\|_2 \neq 0} \left(\frac{\|\boldsymbol{A}x\|_2}{\|x\|_2} \right)$.

Probability Distributions. Let $\mathcal{D}$ denote a distribution over some set. Then, $d \leftarrow \mathcal{D}$ means that d was sampled from the distribution $\mathcal{D}$. If we write $d \xleftarrow{\$} S$ for some finite set S without a specified distribution this means that d was sampled uniformly random from S. We let $\Delta(X, Y)$ indicate the statistical distance between two distributions X, Y. Define the function $\rho_\sigma(x) = \exp\left(\frac{-x^2}{2\sigma^2}\right)$ and the discrete Gaussian distribution over the integers, D_σ, as

$$D_\sigma(x) = \frac{\rho(x)}{\rho(\mathbb{Z})} \text{ where } \rho(\mathbb{Z}) = \sum_{v \in \mathbb{Z}} \rho(v).$$

We will write $\boldsymbol{X} \leftarrow D_\sigma^{r \times m}$ to mean that every coefficient of the matrix $\boldsymbol{X}$ is distributed according to D_σ.

Using the tail bounds for the 0-centered discrete Gaussian distribution (cf. [Ban93]), we can show that for any $\sigma > 0$ the norm of $x \leftarrow D_\sigma$ can be upper-bounded using σ. Namely, for any $k > 0$ it holds that

$$\Pr_{x \leftarrow D_\sigma} [|x| > k\sigma] \leq 2e^{-k^2/2}, \tag{3}$$

and when $\boldsymbol{x}$ is drawn from D_σ^r, we have

$$\Pr_{x \leftarrow D_\sigma^r} [\|\boldsymbol{x}\|_2 > \sqrt{2r} \cdot \sigma] < 2^{-r/4}. \tag{4}$$

We will abuse the notation $x \leftarrow D_\sigma$ when $x \in \mathbb{Z}[X]/(X^d + 1)$ to denote the distribution in which each coefficient of x is taken from D_σ. It is clear that in this case $\|x\|_2$ can be bounded using Eq. 4 with d instead of r.

2.2   Lattice-Based Commitment Schemes

A commitment scheme allows a sender to create commitments to secret values, which she might then decide to reveal later. The main properties of commitment schemes are hiding and binding. Hiding guarantees that commitments do not leak information about the committed values, while binding guarantees that the sender cannot change her mind and open commitments to different values.

Formally, a non-interactive commitment scheme is a pair of probabilistic polynomial-time algorithms $(\mathrm{Gen}, \mathrm{Com})$. The setup algorithm $ck \leftarrow \mathrm{Gen}(1^\lambda)$ generates a commitment key ck, which specifies message, randomness and commitment spaces $\mathsf{M}_{ck}, \mathsf{R}_{ck}, \mathsf{C}_{ck}$. It also specifies an efficiently sampleable probability distribution $D_{\mathsf{R}_{ck}}$ over R_{ck} and a binding set $\mathsf{B}_{ck} \subset \mathsf{M}_{ck} \times \mathsf{R}_{ck}$. The commitment key also specifies a deterministic polynomial-time commitment function $\mathrm{Com}_{ck} : \mathsf{M}_{ck} \times \mathsf{R}_{ck} \rightarrow \mathsf{C}_{ck}$. We define $\mathrm{Com}_{ck}(\boldsymbol{m})$ to be the probabilistic algorithm that given $\boldsymbol{m} \in \mathsf{M}_{ck}$ samples $\boldsymbol{r} \leftarrow D_{\mathsf{R}_{ck}}$ and returns $\boldsymbol{c} = \mathrm{Com}_{ck}(\boldsymbol{m}; \boldsymbol{r})$.

The commitment scheme is homomorphic, if the message, randomness and commitment spaces are abelian groups (written additively) and we have for all $\lambda \in \mathbb{N}$, and for all $ck \leftarrow \mathrm{Gen}(1^\lambda)$, for all $\boldsymbol{m}_0, \boldsymbol{m}_1 \in \mathsf{M}_{ck}$ and for all $\boldsymbol{r}_0, \boldsymbol{r}_1 \in \mathsf{R}_{ck}$

$$\mathrm{Com}_{ck}(\boldsymbol{m}_0; \boldsymbol{r}_0) + \mathrm{Com}_{ck}(\boldsymbol{m}_1; \boldsymbol{r}_1) = \mathrm{Com}_{ck}(\boldsymbol{m}_0 + \boldsymbol{m}_1; \boldsymbol{r}_0 + \boldsymbol{r}_1).$$

Definition 1 (Hiding). *The commitment scheme is computationally hiding if a commitment does not reveal the committed value. Formally, we say the commitment scheme is hiding if for all probabilistic polynomial time stateful interactive adversaries $\mathcal{A}$*

$$\Pr\left[\begin{matrix} ck \leftarrow \mathrm{Gen}(1^\lambda); (\boldsymbol{m}_0, \boldsymbol{m}_1) \leftarrow \mathcal{A}(ck); b \leftarrow \{0,1\}; \\ \boldsymbol{r} \leftarrow D_{\mathsf{R}_{ck}}; \boldsymbol{c} \leftarrow \mathrm{Com}_{ck}(\boldsymbol{m}_b; \boldsymbol{r}) : \mathcal{A}(\boldsymbol{c}) = b \end{matrix}\right] \approx \frac{1}{2},$$

where $\mathcal{A}$ outputs $\boldsymbol{m}_0, \boldsymbol{m}_1 \in \mathsf{M}_{ck}$.

Definition 2 (Binding). *The commitment scheme is computationally binding if a commitment can only be opened to one value within the binding set B_{ck}. For all probabilistic polynomial time adversaries $\mathcal{A}$*

$$\Pr\left[\begin{matrix} ck \leftarrow \mathrm{Gen}(1^\lambda); (\boldsymbol{m}_0, \boldsymbol{r}_0, \boldsymbol{m}_1, \boldsymbol{r}_1) \leftarrow \mathcal{A}(ck) : \\ \boldsymbol{m}_0 \neq \boldsymbol{m}_1 \text{ and } \mathrm{Com}_{ck}(\boldsymbol{m}_0; \boldsymbol{r}_0) = \mathrm{Com}_{ck}(\boldsymbol{m}_1; \boldsymbol{r}_1) \end{matrix}\right] \approx 0,$$

where $\mathcal{A}$ outputs $(\boldsymbol{m}_0, \boldsymbol{r}_0), (\boldsymbol{m}_1, \boldsymbol{r}_1) \in \mathsf{B}_{ck}$.

The commitment scheme is compressing if the sizes of commitments are smaller than the sizes of the committed values.

Ajtai's One-Way Function. The standard one-way function used in lattice cryptography maps a vector $\mathcal{R}^n$ to $\mathcal{R}^r$ via the function

$$f_{\boldsymbol{A}}(\boldsymbol{s}) = \boldsymbol{A}\boldsymbol{s},$$

where $\boldsymbol{A}$ is a fixed, randomly-chosen matrix in $\mathcal{R}^{r \times n}$. Ajtai's seminal result [Ajt96] stated that when $\mathcal{R} = \mathbb{Z}_q$, it is as hard to find elements $\boldsymbol{s}$ with some bounded norm $\|\boldsymbol{s}\| \leq B$ such that $f_{\boldsymbol{A}}(\boldsymbol{s}) = 0$ for random $\boldsymbol{A}$, as it is to find short vectors in any lattice of dimension r. This is called the short integer solution (SIS) problem and its hardness increases as r, q increase and B decreases; but somewhat surprisingly, the hardness of SIS is essentially unaffected by n as soon as n is large enough. The independence of the hardness from n holds both theoretically and in practice.

When solving SIS, one can ignore, if one wishes, any columns of $\boldsymbol{A}$ by setting the corresponding coefficient of $\boldsymbol{s}$ to 0, and solving SIS over the remaining columns. It was computed in [MR08] that if n is very large, then one should solve SIS for a submatrix where the number of columns is $n' = \sqrt{r \log q / \log \delta}$ for some constant δ.[1] With such a setting of n', one expects to find a vector of length approximately

$$\min\{q, 2^{\sqrt{r \log q \log \delta}}\}. \tag{5}$$

Compressing Commitments Based on SIS. The fact that a larger n (after a certain point) does not decrease the security of the scheme allows one to construct simple compressing commitment schemes where the messages are elements in $\mathbb{Z}_p$ for $p < q$. The commitment scheme, which was already implicit in the aforementioned work of Ajtai [Ajt96], uses uniformly-random matrices $\boldsymbol{A}_1 \in \mathbb{Z}_q^{r \times 2r \log_p q}$ and $\boldsymbol{A}_2 \in \mathbb{Z}_q^{r \times n}$ as a commitment key, where n is the number of elements that one wishes to commit to. A commitment to a vector $\boldsymbol{m} \in \mathbb{Z}_p^n$ involves choosing a random vector $\boldsymbol{r} \in \mathbb{Z}_p^{2r \log_p q}$ and outputting the commitment vector $\boldsymbol{v} = \boldsymbol{A}_1 \boldsymbol{r} + \boldsymbol{A}_2 \boldsymbol{m} \bmod q$. By the leftover hash lemma, $(\boldsymbol{A}_1, \boldsymbol{A}_1 \boldsymbol{r} \bmod q)$ is statistically close to uniform, and so the commitment scheme is statistically hiding.[2]

To prove binding, note that if there are two different $(\boldsymbol{r}, \boldsymbol{m}) \neq (\boldsymbol{r}', \boldsymbol{m}')$ such that $\boldsymbol{v} = \boldsymbol{A}_1 \boldsymbol{r} + \boldsymbol{A}_2 \boldsymbol{m} = \boldsymbol{A}_1 \boldsymbol{r}' + \boldsymbol{A}_2 \boldsymbol{m}' \bmod q$, then $\boldsymbol{A}_1(\boldsymbol{r} - \boldsymbol{r}') + \boldsymbol{A}_2(\boldsymbol{m} - \boldsymbol{m}') = \boldsymbol{0} \bmod q$, and the non-zero vector $\boldsymbol{s} = \begin{bmatrix} \boldsymbol{r} - \boldsymbol{r}' \\ \boldsymbol{m} - \boldsymbol{m}' \end{bmatrix}$ is a solution to the SIS problem for the matrix $\boldsymbol{A} = [\boldsymbol{A}_1 \ \boldsymbol{A}_2]$. As long as the parameters are set such that $\|\boldsymbol{s}\|$ is smaller than the value in (5), the binding property of the commitment is based on an intractable version of the SIS problem.

The commitment scheme we will be working with in this paper works as follows:

$\mathrm{Gen}(1^\lambda) \rightarrow ck$: Select a ring $\mathcal{R}$ (either $\mathbb{Z}$ or $\mathbb{Z}[X]/(X^d + 1)$), and parameter p, q, r, v, N, B, σ according to Table 2, and let $\mathcal{R}_q = \mathcal{R}/q\mathcal{R}$.

Pick uniformly at random matrices $\boldsymbol{A}_1 \leftarrow \mathcal{R}_q^{r \times r \log_p q}$ and $\boldsymbol{A}_2 \leftarrow \mathcal{R}_q^{r \times n}$.

Return $ck = (p, q, r, v, \ell, N, B, \mathcal{R}_q, A_1, A_2)$.

The commitment key defines message, randomness, commitment and binding spaces and distribution $\mathsf{M}_{ck} = \mathcal{R}_q^n$, $\mathsf{R}_{ck} = \mathcal{R}_q^{2r \log_p q}$, $\mathsf{C}_{ck} = \mathcal{R}_q^r$, $\mathsf{B}_{ck} = \left\{ \boldsymbol{s} = \begin{bmatrix} \boldsymbol{m} \\ \boldsymbol{r} \end{bmatrix} \in \mathcal{R}_q^{n+2r \log_p q} \ \middle| \ \|\boldsymbol{s}\| < B \right\}$, $\mathsf{D}_{\mathsf{R}_{ck}} = D_\sigma^r$.

---

[1] This constant δ is related to the optimal block-size in BKZ reduction [GN08], which is the currently best way of solving the SIS problem. Presently, the optimal lattice reductions set $\delta \approx 1.005$.

[2] For improved efficiency, one could reduce the number of columns in $\boldsymbol{A}_1$ and make the commitment scheme computationally-hiding based on the hardness of the LWE problem.

$\text{Com}_{ck}(m; r)$: Given $m \in \mathcal{R}_q^n$ and $r \in \mathcal{R}_q^{2r \log_p q}$ return $c = A_1 r + A_2 s$.

In the following, when we make multiple commitments to vectors $m_1, \ldots,$ $m_\ell \in \mathsf{M}_{ck}$ we write $C = \text{Com}_{ck}(M; R)$ when concatenating the commitment vectors as $C = [c_1, \cdots, c_\ell]$. It corresponds to computing $C = A_1 R + A_2 M$ with $M = [m_1, \cdots, m_\ell]$ and randomness $R = [r_1, \cdots, r_\ell]$.

2.3   Arguments of Knowledge

We aim to give efficient lattice-based proofs for arithmetic circuit satisfiability over $\mathbb{Z}_p$. The strategy we will employ is to commit to the values of a satisfying assignment to the wires, execute a range proof to demonstrate the committed values are within a suitable range, and to prove the committed values satisfy the constraints imposed by the arithmetic circuit. We will now formally define arguments of knowledge.

Let R be a polynomial time decidable ternary relation. The first input will contain some public parameters (aka common reference string) pp. We define the corresponding language L_{pp} indexed by the public parameters that consists of elements u with a witness w such that $(pp, u, w) \in R$. This is a natural generalisation of standard NP languages, which can be cast as the special case of relations that ignore the first input.

A proof system consists of a PPT parameter generator PGen, and interactive and stateful PPT algorithms $\mathcal{P}$ and $\mathcal{V}$ used by the prover and verifier. We write $(tr, b) \leftarrow \langle \mathcal{P}(pp), \mathcal{V}(pp, t) \rangle$ for running $\mathcal{P}$ and $\mathcal{V}$ on inputs pp, s, and t and getting communication transcript tr and the verifier's decision bit b. Our convention is $b = 0$ means reject and $b = 1$ means accept.

Definition 3 (Argument of knowledge). *The proof system* (PGen, $\mathcal{P}, \mathcal{V}$) *is called an* argument of knowledge *for the relation R if it is complete and knowledge sound as defined below.*

Definition 4 (Statistical completeness). (PGen, $\mathcal{P}, \mathcal{V}$) *has statistical completeness with completeness error* $\rho : \mathbb{N} \to [0; 1]$ *if for all adversaries* $\mathcal{A}$

$$\Pr \left[\begin{array}{c} pp \leftarrow \text{PGen}(1^\lambda); (u, w) \leftarrow \mathcal{A}(pp); (tr, b) \leftarrow \langle \mathcal{P}(pp, u, w), \mathcal{V}(pp, u) \rangle : \\ (pp, u, w) \in R \text{ and } b = 0 \end{array} \right] \leq \rho(\lambda).$$

Definition 5 (Computational knowledge soundness). $(\mathcal{K}, \mathcal{P}, \mathcal{V})$ *is knowledge sound with knowledge soundness error* $\epsilon : \mathbb{N} \to [0; 1]$ *if for all deterministic polynomial time* $\mathcal{P}^*$ *there exists an expected polynomial time extractor* $\mathcal{E}$ *such that for all PPT adversaries* $\mathcal{A}$

$$\Pr \left[\begin{array}{c} pp \leftarrow \text{PGen}(1^\lambda); (u, s) \leftarrow \mathcal{A}(pp); (tr, b) \leftarrow \langle \mathcal{P}^*(pp, u, s), \mathcal{V}(pp, u) \rangle; \\ w \leftarrow \mathcal{E}^{\mathcal{P}^*(pp, u, s)}(pp, u, tr, b) : (pp, u, w) \notin R \text{ and } b = 1 \end{array} \right] \leq \epsilon(\lambda).$$

It is sometimes useful to relax the definition of knowledge soundness to hold only for a larger relation $\bar{R}$ such that $R \subset \bar{R}$. In this work, our zero-knowledge proofs of pre-images will for instance have "slack". Thus, even though v is constructed using r, m with coefficients in $\mathbb{Z}_p$, we will only be able to prove knowledge of vectors $\bar{r}, \bar{m}$ with larger norms. This extracted commitment is still binding as long as the parameters are set such that the vector $\bar{s} = \begin{bmatrix} \bar{r} - \bar{r}' \\ \bar{m} - \bar{m}' \end{bmatrix}$ has norm smaller than the bound in (5).[3]

Concretely, if we would like to make a commitment to N values in $\mathbb{Z}_p$, then to satisfy (5) we need to make sure that $q > \|\bar{s}\|$ and $\sqrt{r \log q \log \delta} > \log \|\bar{s}\|$. In the protocols in our paper, we will have $\|\bar{s}\| < N^2 p^2$ and $p < N$, which implies that $r = O(\log N)$.

We say the proof system is *public coin* if the verifier's challenges are chosen uniformly at random independently of the prover's messages. A proof system is special honest verifier zero-knowledge if it is possible to simulate the proof without knowing the witness whenever the verifier's challenges are known in advance.

Definition 6 (Special honest-verifier zero-knowledge). *A public-coin argument of knowledge* $(\mathrm{PGen}, \mathcal{P}, \mathcal{V})$ *is said to be* statistical special honest-verifier zero-knowledge (SHVZK) *if there exists a PPT simulator $\mathcal{S}$ such that for all interactive and stateful adversaries $\mathcal{A}$*

$$\Pr \left[\begin{array}{c} pp \leftarrow \mathrm{PGen}(1^\lambda); (u, w, \varrho) \leftarrow \mathcal{A}(pp); (tr, b) \leftarrow \langle \mathcal{P}(pp, u, w), \mathcal{V}(\sigma, u; \varrho) \rangle : \\ (pp, u, w) \in R \text{ and } \mathcal{A}(tr) = 1 \end{array} \right]$$

$$\approx \Pr \left[\begin{array}{c} pp \leftarrow \mathrm{PGen}(1^\lambda); (u, w, \varrho) \leftarrow \mathcal{A}(pp); (tr, b) \leftarrow \mathcal{S}(pp, u, \varrho) : \\ (pp, u, w) \in R \text{ and } \mathcal{A}(tr) = 1 \end{array} \right],$$

where ϱ is the randomness used by the verifier.

Full Zero-Knowledge. In real life applications special honest verifier zero-knowledge may not suffice since a malicious verifier may give non-random challenges. However, it is easy to convert an SHVZK argument into a full zero-knowledge argument secure against *arbitrary* verifiers in the common reference string model using standard techniques, and when using the Fiat-Shamir heuristic to make the argument non-interactive SHVZK suffices to get zero-knowledge in the random oracle model.

3   Amortized Proofs of Knowledge

We will consider amortized proofs of knowledge for preimages of the Ajtai one-way function. Formally, given a matrix $A \in \mathcal{R}_q^{r \times v}$ the relation we want to give

---

[3] Commitments over other rings, such as $\mathbb{Z}_q[X]/(X^d + 1)$ can be done in the same manner as above based on the hardness of the Ring-SIS problem [PR06, LM06] for which the bound in (5) still appears to hold in practice.

a zero-knowledge proof of knowledge for is

$$
R = \left\{ \begin{array}{c} (pp, u, w) = ((q, \ell, \beta, \mathcal{R}, \boldsymbol{A}, c), \boldsymbol{T}, \boldsymbol{S}) \\ (\boldsymbol{A}, \boldsymbol{S}, \boldsymbol{T}) \in \mathcal{R}_q^{r \times v} \times \mathcal{R}^{v \times \ell} \times \mathcal{R}_q^{r \times \ell} \wedge \ \boldsymbol{A}\boldsymbol{S} = c \cdot \boldsymbol{T} \wedge \left[\|\boldsymbol{s}_i\|_2 \le \beta \right]_{i \in [\ell]} \end{array} \right\}
$$

with $\boldsymbol{S} = [\boldsymbol{s}_1, \cdots, \boldsymbol{s}_\ell]$ where $\mathcal{R}$ is implicitly fixed in advance. The multiplier c depends on the instantiation of the proof: for $\mathcal{R} = \mathbb{Z}$ our proof achieves $c = 1$ and is exact, while for $\mathcal{R} = \mathbb{Z}[X]/(X^d + 1)$ it only guarantees that $c = 2$.

<table>
<tr><td>$\mathcal{P}$</td><td></td><td>$\mathcal{V}$</td></tr>
<tr><td>$\boldsymbol{A} \in \mathcal{R}_q^{r \times v}, \boldsymbol{S} \in \mathcal{R}^{v \times \ell}, \boldsymbol{T} \in \mathcal{R}_q^{r \times \ell}$
s.t $\boldsymbol{A}\boldsymbol{S} = \boldsymbol{T}$</td><td></td><td>$\boldsymbol{A}, \boldsymbol{T}$</td></tr>
<tr><td>$\boldsymbol{Y} \leftarrow D_\sigma^{v \times n}$
$\boldsymbol{W} = \boldsymbol{A}\boldsymbol{Y}$</td><td>$\xrightarrow{\ \boldsymbol{W}\ }$

$\xleftarrow{\ \boldsymbol{C}\ }$</td><td>$\boldsymbol{C} \xleftarrow{\$} C^{\ell \times n}$</td></tr>
<tr><td>$\boldsymbol{Z} := \boldsymbol{S}\boldsymbol{C} + \boldsymbol{Y}$
Abort if $\mathrm{Rej}(\boldsymbol{Z}, \boldsymbol{B}, \sigma, \rho) = 1$</td><td>$\xrightarrow{\ \boldsymbol{Z}\ }$</td><td>$[\boldsymbol{z}_1, \ldots, \boldsymbol{z}_n] := \boldsymbol{Z}$
Check: $\begin{cases} \forall i \in [n], \|\boldsymbol{z}_i\|_2 \le B \\ \boldsymbol{A}\boldsymbol{Z} = \boldsymbol{T}\boldsymbol{C} + \boldsymbol{W} \end{cases}$</td></tr>
</table>

Fig. 1. Amortized proof for ℓ equations. The ring $\mathcal{R}$ can be either $\mathbb{Z}$ or $\mathbb{Z}[X]/(X^d + 1)$, the challenge set C will be respectively $\{0, 1\}$ or $\{0\} \bigcup \{\pm X^j\}_{j < d}$

We consider a generalization of Σ-Protocols in which honest instances only complete with some constant probability $1/\rho$, this is to accommodate the fact that the rejection sampling step described in Lemma 1 only outputs 1 with probability $1/\rho$. In practice such a restriction is not too inconvenient: though the interactive protocol has to be repeated an average of ρ times to terminate, what we are interested in is usually the non-interactive protocol obtained by using the Fiat-Shamir transform, in which case the prover only has to output a proof when she obtains a challenge which passes the rejection step.

In our zero-knowledge proof, the prover will want to output a matrix $\boldsymbol{Z}$ whose distribution should be independent of the secret matrix $\boldsymbol{S}$. During the protocol, the prover obtains $\boldsymbol{Z}' = \boldsymbol{B} + \boldsymbol{Y}$ where $\boldsymbol{B}$ depends on the secret $\boldsymbol{S}$ and $\boldsymbol{Y}$ is a "masking" matrix each of whose coefficients is a discrete Gaussian with standard deviation σ. To remove the dependency of $\boldsymbol{Z}'$ on $\boldsymbol{B}$, we use the rejection sampling procedure from [Lyu12] in Algorithm 1, which has the properties described in Lemma 1.

Algorithm 1. $\text{Rej}(\boldsymbol{Z}, \boldsymbol{B}, \sigma, \rho)$

$u \leftarrow [0, 1)$
if $u > \frac{1}{\rho} \cdot \exp\left(\frac{-2\langle \boldsymbol{Z}, \boldsymbol{B} \rangle + \|\boldsymbol{B}\|^2}{2\sigma^2}\right)$ **then**
    return 0
else
    return 1
end if

Lemma 1 ([Lyu12]). *Let* $\boldsymbol{B} \in \mathcal{R}^{r \times n}$ *be any matrix. Consider a procedure that samples a* $\boldsymbol{Y} \leftarrow D_\sigma^{r \times n}$ *and then returns the output of* $\text{Rej}(\boldsymbol{Z} := \boldsymbol{Y} + \boldsymbol{B}, \boldsymbol{B}, \sigma, \rho)$ *where* $\sigma \geq \frac{12}{\ln \rho} \cdot \|\boldsymbol{B}\|$*. The probability that this procedure outputs* 1 *is within* 2^{-100} *of* $1/\rho$*. The distribution of* $\boldsymbol{Z}$*, conditioned on the output being* 1*, is within statistical distance of* 2^{-100} *of* $D_\sigma^{r \times n}$*.*

We give a useful lemma for knowledge extraction. In essence this lemma will be used to show that a prover who can output a verifying output for a challenge $\boldsymbol{c}_1, \ldots, \boldsymbol{c}_\ell$ has a high probability of also being able to answer a challenge $\boldsymbol{c}_1', \boldsymbol{c}_2, \ldots, \boldsymbol{c}_\ell$ in which only $\boldsymbol{c}_1' \neq \boldsymbol{c}_1$.

Lemma 2 ([Dam10]). *Let* $\boldsymbol{H} \in \{0, 1\}^{\ell \times n}$ *for some* $n, \ell > 1$*, such that a fraction* ε *of the inputs of* $\boldsymbol{H}$ *are* 1*. We say that a row of* $\boldsymbol{H}$ *is "heavy" if it contains a fraction at least* $\varepsilon/2$ *of ones. Then more than half of the ones in* $\boldsymbol{H}$ *are located in heavy rows.*

We describe our proof system in Fig. 1. Our first instantiation is with $\mathcal{R} = \mathbb{Z}$ in which case the one-way function will rely on the SIS problem and the challenge set will be $\mathcal{C}^{\ell \times n}$ for $\mathcal{C} = \{0, 1\}$, this solution allows the extractor of the protocol to obtain exact preimages of the $\boldsymbol{t}_i$ and requires $n \geq \lambda + 2$. This ensures that communication only grows linearly in λ regardless of the size of ℓ (since $\boldsymbol{Z} \in \mathbb{Z}_q^{v \times n}$).

Theorem 1. *Let* $\mathcal{R} = \mathbb{Z}$*,* $\mathcal{C} = \{0, 1\}$*,* $v, r = poly(\lambda)$*, and* $n \geq \lambda + 2$*. Let* $s > 0$ *be an upper bound on* $s_1(\boldsymbol{S})$*,* $\rho > 1$ *be a constant,* $\sigma \in \mathbb{R}$ *be such that* $\sigma \geq \frac{12}{\ln \rho} s \sqrt{\ell n}$*, and* $B = \sqrt{2v}\sigma$*. Then the protocol described in Fig. 1 is a zero-knowledge proof of knowledge for* R*.*

Proof. We will prove correctness and zero-knowledge here as the proofs are straightforward and very similar to prior works. We will however defer the proof of soundness to Lemma 3.

Correctness: If $\mathcal{P}$ and $\mathcal{V}$ are honest then the probability of abort is exponentially close to $1 - 1/\rho$ since $\|\boldsymbol{S}\boldsymbol{C}\|_2 \leq s_1(\boldsymbol{S})\|\boldsymbol{C}\|_2 \leq s\sqrt{\ell n}$. The equation verified by $\mathcal{V}$ is true by construction of $\boldsymbol{Z}$. Since each coefficient of $\boldsymbol{Z}$ is statistically close to D_σ, then according to (4) we have $\|\boldsymbol{z}_i\|_2 \leq \sqrt{2v}\sigma$ with overwhelming probability.

Honest-Verifier Zero-Knowledge: We will now prove that our protocol is honest-verifier zero-knowledge. More concretely, we show that the protocol is zero-knowledge when the prover does not abort prior to sending Z. The reason that this is enough for practical purposes is that HVZK Σ-protocols can be turned into non-interactive proofs via the Fiat-Shamir transform. The non-interactive protocol generates the challenge C as the hash of W and T, and otherwise repeats the prover's part of the protocol until a non-abort occurs, whereupon the prover outputs the transcript (W, C, Z). Only the non-aborting transcripts will be seen by $\mathcal{V}$, and thus only they need to be simulated. Further below we will also sketch how to modify our protocol to obtain an interactive zero-knowledge proof.

Let $\mathcal{S}(A, T)$ be the following PPT algorithm:

1. Sample $C \leftarrow \{0,1\}^{\ell \times n}$
2. Sample $Z \leftarrow D_\sigma^{v \times n}$
3. Set $W = AZ - TC$
4. Output (W, C, Z)

It is clear that Z verifies with overwhelming probability. We already showed in the section on correctness that in the real protocol when no abort occurs the distribution of Z is within statistical distance 2^{-100} of $D_\sigma^{v \times n}$. Since W is completely determined by A, T, Z and C, the distribution of (W, C, Z) output by $\mathcal{S}$ is within 2^{-100} of the distribution of these variables in the actual non-aborting run of the protocol.

To turn our proof into a full interactive HVZK proof, one can use the above simulator together with a standard transformation: in the first message of the protocol, $\mathcal{P}$ will send a statistically hiding commitment of W to the verifier. Later in the third round, she will then send both the opening and the message Z, given that the protocol would not abort. The above simulator $\mathcal{S}(A, T)$ can then, in the beginning of the protocol, flip a coin to determine if the simulation is aborting. If so, then it can just commit to a uniformly random value, and otherwise to the correct value W. In order to make the protocol secure against arbitrary verifiers one can run an interactive coin-flipping protocol to generate C.

Lemma 3 (Knowledge Soundness). *For any prover $\mathcal{P}^*$ who succeeds with probability $\varepsilon > 2^{-\lambda}$ (i.e. $\geq 2^{-n+2}$) over her random tape $\chi \in \{0,1\}^x$ and the challenge choice $C \xleftarrow{\$} \mathcal{C}^{\ell \times n}$, there exists a knowledge extractor $\mathcal{E}$ running in expected time $\mathsf{poly}(\lambda)/\varepsilon$ who can extract a witness $S' := (s_1', \ldots, s_\ell') \in \mathcal{R}^{v \times \ell}$, such that $AS' = T$, and $\forall i \in [\ell] \; \|s_i'\|_2 \leq 2B$.*

Proof. For $i \in [\ell]$, let $t_i \in \mathcal{R}^n$ be the ith column of T, and $c_i^T \in \mathcal{R}^{1 \times n}$ be the ith row of C (note that c_i^T are not the transpose of the columns of C but really its rows). Note that $t_i c_i^T \in \mathcal{R}^{r \times n}$ and $TC = \sum_{i=1}^{\ell} t_i c_i^T$. For any fixed i, we describe an extractor $\mathcal{E}_i$ who can extract a preimage of t_i of norm less than $2B$ in expected $O(1/\varepsilon)$ executions, and the full result follows by running each extractor (of which there are $\ell = \mathsf{poly}(\lambda)$).

Consider a matrix $\boldsymbol{H}_i \in \{0,1\}^{2^{n(\ell-1)+x} \times 2^n}$ whose rows are indexed by the value of $(\chi, \boldsymbol{c}_1^T, \ldots, \boldsymbol{c}_{i-1}^T, \boldsymbol{c}_{i+1}^T, \ldots, \boldsymbol{c}_\ell^T)$ and whose columns are indexed by the value of $\boldsymbol{c}_i^T$. An entry of $\boldsymbol{H}_i$ will be 1 if $\mathcal{P}^*$ succeeds for the corresponding challenge (i.e. produces an accepting $\boldsymbol{Z}$). We will say that a row of $\boldsymbol{H}_i$ is "heavy" if it contains a fraction of at least $\varepsilon/2$ ones, i.e. if it contains more than $2^k * \varepsilon/2 > 2$ ones. The extractor $\mathcal{E}_i$ will proceed as follow:

1. Run $\mathcal{P}^*$ on random challenges $\boldsymbol{C}'$ until it succeeds, and obtains $\boldsymbol{Z}'$ that verifies. This takes expected time $1/\varepsilon$.
2. Run $\mathcal{P}^*$ on random challenges $\boldsymbol{C}''$ where $\forall j \neq i, \boldsymbol{c}_j''^T = \boldsymbol{c}_j'^T$ and $\boldsymbol{c}_i''^T$ is freshly sampled. If after λ/ε attempts $\mathcal{P}^*$ has not output a valid response $\boldsymbol{Z}''$, abort.

The extractor $\mathcal{E}_i$ runs in expected time $poly(\lambda)/\varepsilon$, and aborts with probability less than $1/2 + 2^{-\lambda}$. The running time is clear from the definition of $\mathcal{E}_i$. To compute the abort probability note that in step 2 all the challenges $\boldsymbol{C}''$ considered are in the same row of $\boldsymbol{H}_i$ as $\boldsymbol{C}'$, if we call Abort the event where $\mathcal{E}_i$ aborts and Heavy the event that $\boldsymbol{C}'$ is in a row of $\boldsymbol{H}_i$, we have:

$$\Pr[\text{Abort}] = \Pr[\text{Abort}|\text{Heavy}] \Pr[\text{Heavy}] + \Pr[\text{Abort}|\neg\text{Heavy}] \Pr[\neg\text{Heavy}]$$

According to Lemma 2, $\Pr[\neg\text{Heavy}] < 1/2$. On the other hand if the row is heavy then for a random sample in this row $\mathcal{P}^*$ has probability at least $\varepsilon/2 - 2^{-n} > \varepsilon/4$ of outputting a valid answer (the probability is $\varepsilon/2 - 2^{-n}$ and not $\varepsilon/2$ because we want a reply for a challenge different from $\boldsymbol{C}'$). Thus the probability that $\mathcal{P}^*$ does not succeed on any of the λ/ε challenges $\boldsymbol{C}''$ is $\Pr[\text{Abort}|\text{Heavy}] < (1 - \varepsilon/4)^{\lambda\varepsilon} < e^{-4\lambda} < 2^{-\lambda}$, and therefore $\Pr[\text{Abort}] < 1/2 + 2^{-\lambda}$. By running $\mathcal{E}_i$ $O(\lambda)$ times we obtain an extractor that runs in expected time $poly(\lambda)/\varepsilon$ and outputs two valid pairs $\boldsymbol{C}', \boldsymbol{Z}'$ and $\boldsymbol{C}'', \boldsymbol{Z}''$ such that $\forall j \neq i, \boldsymbol{c}_j'^T = \boldsymbol{c}_j''^T$, and $\boldsymbol{c}_i'^T \neq \boldsymbol{c}_i''^T$.

Since both transcripts verify we know that $\boldsymbol{A}\boldsymbol{Z}' = \boldsymbol{T}\boldsymbol{C}' + \boldsymbol{W} = \sum_{j=1}^r t_j \boldsymbol{c}_j'^T + \boldsymbol{W}$ and that $\boldsymbol{A}\boldsymbol{Z}'' = \boldsymbol{T}\boldsymbol{C}'' + \boldsymbol{W} = \sum_{j=1}^r t_j \boldsymbol{c}_j''^T + \boldsymbol{W}$, which implies that $\boldsymbol{A}(\boldsymbol{Z}' - \boldsymbol{Z}'') = \sum_{j=1}^r t_j(\boldsymbol{c}_j'^T - \boldsymbol{c}_j''^T) = t_i(\boldsymbol{c}_i'^T - \boldsymbol{c}_i''^T)$ If we consider an index $l \in [\ell]$ such that $\boldsymbol{c}_i'^T[l] \neq \boldsymbol{c}_i''^T[l]$, and assume w.l.o.g that $\boldsymbol{c}_i'^T[l] - \boldsymbol{c}_i''^T[l] = 1$, then by only considering the lth column of the previous equation we obtain $\boldsymbol{A}(\boldsymbol{z}_l' - \boldsymbol{z}_l'') = t_i$ where $\|\boldsymbol{z}_l' - \boldsymbol{z}_l''\|_2 \leq 2B$.

Our second instantiation uses $\mathcal{R} = \mathbb{Z}[X]/(X^d + 1)$ and $\mathcal{C} = \{0\} \bigcup \{\pm X^j\}_{j<d}$. This protocol only proves R with $c = 2$, i.e. the extractor will only obtain preimages of $2t_i$ but the number of columns in the response matrix $\boldsymbol{Z}$ can be reduced by a factor of $\log(2d + 1)$ as the soundness now only requires that $n\log(2d+1) \geq \lambda+2$. It is worth noting that in this protocol the values of r and v would typically be chosen to be around d times smaller than in the instantiation with $\mathcal{R} = \mathbb{Z}$, because $\boldsymbol{A}$ will be a matrix of polynomials of degree d. We first give a lemma about the difference on monomials in $\mathbb{Z}[X]/(X^d + 1)$ which will be useful in the extraction.

Lemma 4 ([BCK+14] Lemma 3.2). *Let d be a power of 2, let $a, b \in \{\pm X^i : i \geq 0\} \cup \{0\}$. Then $2(a - b)^{-1} \mod X^d + 1$ only has coefficients in $\{-1, 0, 1\}$. In particular $\|2(a - b)^{-1}\|_2 \leq \sqrt{d}$.*

Theorem 2. *Let $\mathcal{R} = \mathbb{Z}[X]/X^d + 1$, $\mathcal{C} = \{0\} \cup \{\pm X^j\}$, $v, r = poly(\lambda)$, and $n \geq (\lambda + 2)/\log(2d + 1)$. Let $s \in \mathbb{R}$ be an upper bound on $s_1(\boldsymbol{S})$, $\rho > 1$ be a constant, $\sigma \in \mathbb{R}$ be such that $\sigma \geq \frac{12}{\ln \rho} s \sqrt{\ell n}$, and $B = \sqrt{2md}\sigma$. Then the protocol described in Fig. 1 is a SHVZK proof of knowledge.*

Proof. The proofs for correctness and zero-knowledge are nearly identical to the ones of Theorem 1. We will prove soundness in Lemma 5. $\quad\square$

Lemma 5 (Knowledge Soundness). *For any prover $\mathcal{P}^*$ who succeeds with probability $\varepsilon > 2^{-\lambda}(\geq 2^{-n \log(2d+1)+2})$ over his random tape $\chi \in \{0, 1\}^x$ and the challenge choice $\boldsymbol{C} \leftarrow \mathcal{C}^{\ell \times n}$ there exists a knowledge extractor $\mathcal{E}$ who can extract a witness $\boldsymbol{S}' := (\boldsymbol{s}'_1, \ldots, \boldsymbol{s}'_\ell) \in \mathcal{R}^{v \times \ell}$, such that $\boldsymbol{A}\boldsymbol{S}' = 2\boldsymbol{T}$, and $\forall i \in [\ell]$ $\|\boldsymbol{s}'_i\|_2 \leq 2\sqrt{d}B$, in expected time $poly(\lambda)/\varepsilon$.*

Proof. The first part of the proof (obtaining $\boldsymbol{C}', \boldsymbol{Z}'$ and $\boldsymbol{C}'', \boldsymbol{Z}''$) is identical to the one of Lemma 3 except for the fact that the matrix $\boldsymbol{H}_i$ has different dimensions. Let $\delta = \log(2d + 1)$. Since for each $j \in [\ell]$, $\boldsymbol{c}_j^T$ is sampled from a set of size $2^{n\delta}$, we have $\boldsymbol{H}_i \in \{0, 1\}^{2^{n\delta(\ell-1)+x} \times 2^{n\delta}}$. The heavy rows of $\boldsymbol{H}_i$ will contain $2^{n\delta}\varepsilon/2 > 2$ ones, and the extractor can proceed as in the proof of Lemma 3. Assume that $\mathcal{E}_i$ has extracted $\boldsymbol{C}', \boldsymbol{Z}''$ and $\boldsymbol{C}'', \boldsymbol{Z}''$ such that $\forall j \neq i, \boldsymbol{c}_j^T = \boldsymbol{c}_j''^T$, and $\boldsymbol{c}_i'^T \neq \boldsymbol{c}_i''^T$. As previously we have $\boldsymbol{A}(\boldsymbol{Z}' - \boldsymbol{Z}'') = \sum_{j=1}^{\ell} \boldsymbol{t}_j(\boldsymbol{c}_j'^T - \boldsymbol{c}_j''^T) = \boldsymbol{t}_i(\boldsymbol{c}_i'^T - \boldsymbol{c}_i''^T)$ If we consider an index $l \in [\ell]$ such that $\boldsymbol{c}_i'^T[l] \neq \boldsymbol{c}_i''^T[l]$, since $\mathcal{C} = \{0\} \cup \{\pm X^j\}_{0 \leq j \leq d-1}$, we have according to Lemma 4 that there exists a $\boldsymbol{g} \in \mathcal{R}$ such that $2^{-1}(\boldsymbol{c}_i'^T[l] - \boldsymbol{c}_i''^T[l])\boldsymbol{g} = 1$ and $\|\boldsymbol{g}\|_2 \leq \sqrt{d}$. Hence $\boldsymbol{A}(\boldsymbol{z}'_l - \boldsymbol{z}''_l)\boldsymbol{g} = 2\boldsymbol{t}_i \cdot 2^{-1}(\boldsymbol{c}_i'^T[l] - \boldsymbol{c}_i''^T[l])\boldsymbol{g} = 2\boldsymbol{t}_i$, with $\|(\boldsymbol{z}'_l - \boldsymbol{z}''_l)\boldsymbol{g}\|_2 \leq 2\sqrt{d}B$. $\quad\square$

4   Argument for the Satisfiability of an Arithmetic Circuit

In this section, we show how to construct arguments for the satisfiability of an arithmetic circuit based on the SIS assumption. We take inspiration from the arguments of [Gro09a, BCC+16] which rely on homomorphic commitments based on the hardness of discrete logarithm and translate them into the lattice settings. We obtain sublinear communication arguments with improved computational efficiency with respect to [Gro09a, BCC+16].

At a high level, [BCC+16] reduces the satisfiability of an arithmetic circuit to the verification of two sets of constraints: multiplication constraints, arising from multiplication gates; linear constraints, arising from additions and multiplication by constant gates. Then, it shows how to embed each of these sets of constraints into a polynomial equation over $\mathbb{Z}_p$. An argument for the satisfiability of an arithmetic circuit can then be constructed by giving arguments for the satisfiability of such polynomial equations, evaluating at random challenge points and using the Schwarz-Zippel lemma to argue soundness.

We give arithmetic circuit arguments over $\mathbb{Z}_p$ for much smaller p (e.g. $p = poly(\lambda)$). Therefore, a straightforward translation of the above approach yield arguments which only have inverse polynomial soundness error, as $O(1/p)$ is inverse-polynomial in the security parameter in this setting. The soundness error could be reduced by repeated the protocol multiple times in parallel, resulting into a significant computational and communication overhead.

Therefore, we devise a more complex embedding technique in order to apply the Schwarz-Zippel lemma over larger fields. Cramer, Damgård and Keller give in [CDK14] an amortised proof of knowledge of k commitments over $\mathbb{Z}_p$ are embedded into $GF(p^k)$, with soundness error $O(1/p^k)$. We follow a similar approach and embed the constraints for the satisfiability of the circuit into polynomial equations over an extension field. While [CDK14] only give a proof of knowledge, we also construct a product argument for the openings of k commitments over $\mathbb{Z}_p$ embedded into an extension field of degree $2k$ with soundness $O(1/p^{2k})$.

We start by recalling how [BCC+16] embedded the satisfiability of an arithmetic circuit into a polynomial equations over $\mathbb{Z}_p$ and then extend it to $GF(p^{2k})$.

Reduction of Circuit Satisfiability to a Hadamard Matrix Product and Linear Constraints over $\mathbb{Z}_p$. We consider arithmetic circuits with fan-in 2 addition and multiplication gates. Multiplication gates are directly represented as equations of the form $a \cdot b = c$, and we refer to a, b, c as the left, right and output wires, respectively.

The satisfiability of an arithmetic circuit can be described as a system of equations in the entries of three matrices A, B, C. The multiplication gates define a set of N equations $A \circ B = C$, where $\circ$ is the Hadamard (entry-wise) product.

The circuit description also contains constraints on the wires between multiplication gates. Denoting the rows of the matrices A, B, C as

$$\boldsymbol{a}_i = (a_{i,1}, \ldots, a_{i,n}) \quad \boldsymbol{b}_i = (b_{i,1}, \ldots, b_{i,n}) \quad \boldsymbol{c}_i = (c_{i,1}, \ldots, c_{i,n}) \quad \text{for } i \in \{1, \ldots, m\}$$

these constraints can be expressed as $U < 2N$ linear equations of inputs and outputs of multiplication gates of the form

$$\sum_{i=1}^{m} \boldsymbol{a}_i \cdot \boldsymbol{w}_{u,a,i} + \sum_{i=1}^{m} \boldsymbol{b}_i \cdot \boldsymbol{w}_{u,b,i} + \sum_{i=1}^{m} \boldsymbol{c}_i \cdot \boldsymbol{w}_{u,c,i} = K_u \quad \text{for } u \in \{1, \ldots, U\} \quad (6)$$

for constant vectors $\boldsymbol{w}_{u,a,i}, \boldsymbol{w}_{u,b,i}, \boldsymbol{w}_{u,c,i}$ and scalars K_u. We refer to [BCC+16] for a more detailed explanation of this process.

In total, to capture all multiplications and linear constraints, we have $N + U$ equations that the wires must satisfy in order for the circuit to be satisfiable.

Reduction to Two Polynomial Equations. Let Y be a formal indeterminate. We will reduce the $N+U$ equations above to a two polynomial equations in Y by embedding distinct equations into distinct powers of Y. In our argument we will then require the prover to prove that these two equations hold when replacing Y by a random challenge received from the verifier. More explanation behind this process can be found in the full version of this paper.

Let us define $\boldsymbol{w}_{a,i}(Y) = \sum_{u=1}^{U} \boldsymbol{w}_{u,a,i} Y^{N+1+u}$, $\boldsymbol{w}_{b,i}(Y) = \sum_{u=1}^{U} \boldsymbol{w}_{u,b,i} Y^{N+1+u}$
$\boldsymbol{w}_{c,i}(Y) = \sum_{u=1}^{U} \boldsymbol{w}_{u,c,i} Y^{N+1+u}$, $K(Y) = \sum_{u=1}^{U} K_u Y^{N+1+u}$
Then the circuit is satisfied if and only if

$$\sum_{i=1}^{m} \boldsymbol{a}_i \cdot \boldsymbol{w}_{a,i}(Y) + \sum_{i=1}^{m} \boldsymbol{b}_i \cdot \boldsymbol{w}_{b,i}(Y) + \sum_{i=1}^{m} \boldsymbol{c}_i \cdot \boldsymbol{w}_{c,i}(Y) - K(Y) = 0 \qquad (7)$$

$$\sum_{i=1}^{m} \boldsymbol{a}_i \circ \boldsymbol{b}_i Y^i = \sum_{i=1}^{m} \boldsymbol{c}_i Y^i \qquad (8)$$

Sublinear Communication Product Argument. To give an argument for the satisfiability of an arithmetic circuit it is sufficient to give arguments showing that (7) and (8) are satisfied. For the purpose of constructing sublinear communication arguments, we craft polynomials which will have particular terms equal to zero if and only if (7) and (8) are satisfied. This can then be proved by having the prover reveal evaluations of the polynomials at random points to the verifier, who can check that the evaluations are correct using the homomorphic property of the commitment scheme. We define $\boldsymbol{a}(X) := \boldsymbol{a}_0 + \sum_{i=1}^{m} \boldsymbol{a}_i y^i X^i$, $\boldsymbol{b}(X) := \boldsymbol{b}_{m+1} + \sum_{i=1}^{m} \boldsymbol{b}_i X^{m+1-i}$ and $\boldsymbol{c} := \sum_{i=1}^{m} \boldsymbol{c}_i y^i$.

We have designed these polynomials such that the X^{m+1} term of $\boldsymbol{a}(X) \circ \boldsymbol{b}(X)$ is equal to $\sum_{i=1}^{m} \boldsymbol{c}_i y^i$. We conclude that the X^{m+1} term of $\boldsymbol{a}(X) \circ \boldsymbol{b}(X)$ is exactly $\boldsymbol{c}$ if and only if (8) is satisfied. A similar approach can followed to embed the satisfiability of (7) into the constant term of polynomial which is tested at random challenge evaluation points.

4.1 Amortisation Over Field Extensions

We now show how to extend the previous approach to work over field extensions. This will allow us to give an efficient amortised argument for the product of openings of commitments. This will be used to give efficient arguments for the satisfiability of an arithmetic circuit achieving sublinear communication and $O(1/p^{2k})$ soundness error.

Let $GF(p^{2k}) \simeq \mathbb{Z}_p[\phi]/\langle f(\phi) \rangle$, where f is a polynomial of degree $2k$ that is irreducible over $\mathbb{Z}_p$. Our goal is to embed k elements of $\mathbb{Z}_p$ into the extension field in a way so that we can multiply two $GF(p^{2k})$ elements in a way that does not interfere with the products of the original $\mathbb{Z}_p$ elements. Let $e_1, \ldots, e_k$ be distinct interpolation points in $\mathbb{Z}_p$ (note that in particular, this forces $p > k$). Let $l_1(X), \ldots, l_k(X)$ be the Lagrange polynomials associated with the points e_i, which have degree $k - 1$. Let $l_0(X) = \prod_{j=1}^{k}(X - e_i)$, which has degree k.

Now, suppose that we have $a_1, \ldots, a_k, b_1, \ldots, b_k$ and $c_1, \ldots, c_k$ in $\mathbb{Z}_p$ such that $a_j \cdot b_j = c_j \bmod p$ for each j. By evaluating the expression at each interpolation point, we see that the following statement about polynomials holds over $\mathbb{Z}_p$:
$$\left(\textstyle\sum_{j=1}^{k} a_j l_j(X)\right) \cdot \left(\textstyle\sum_{j=1}^{k} b_j l_j(X)\right) \equiv \left(\textstyle\sum_{j=1}^{k} c_j l_j(X)\right) \bmod l_0(X).$$

Therefore, there are $c_0', \ldots, c_{k-2}' \in \mathbb{Z}_p$ such that $\left(\sum_{j=1}^{k} a_j l_j(X)\right) \cdot \left(\sum_{j=1}^{k} b_j l_j(X)\right) = \left(\sum_{j=1}^{k} c_j l_j(X)\right) + l_0(X) \sum_{j=0}^{k-2} c_j' X^j$.

The degree of f is $2k$, so if we choose the basis $\mathcal{B} = \{l_1(\phi), \ldots, l_k(\phi), l_0(\phi), \phi l_0(\phi), \ldots, \phi^{k-1} l_0(\phi)$ for $GF(p^{2k})\}$, we can perform multiplications of extension field elements without any overflow modulo f interfering with the individual product relations $a_i b_i = c_i$ in $\mathbb{Z}_p$. We can therefore port he above equality into $GF(p^{2k})$ as the equality $\left(\sum_{j=1}^{k} a_j l_j(\phi)\right) \cdot \left(\sum_{j=1}^{k} b_j l_j(\phi)\right) = \left(\sum_{j=1}^{k} c_j l_j(\phi)\right) + l_0(\phi) \sum_{j=0}^{k-2} c_j' \phi^j$.

This allows one multiplication of committed values to be performed without any overflow modulo f. As we shall see in the next subsection, this is sufficient for verifying multiplication triples for arithmetic circuit satisfiability.

We also need to be able to view single commitments to elements of $\mathbb{Z}_p$ as elements of the extension field in a way that helps to verify linear consistency relations between the elements.

Now, suppose that we have $a_1, \ldots, a_k, b_1, \ldots, b_k$ and $c_1, \ldots, c_k$ in $\mathbb{Z}_p$, and coefficients $w_{a,1}, \ldots, w_{a,k}, w_{b,1}, \ldots, w_{b,k}$ and $w_{c,1}, \ldots, w_{c,k}$ in $\mathbb{Z}_p$ such that $\sum_{j=1}^{k} a_j w_{a,j} + \sum_{j=1}^{k} b_j w_{b,j} + \sum_{j=1}^{k} c_j w_{c,j} = K \bmod p$. By comparing coefficients, we see that the following statement about polynomials holds over $\mathbb{Z}_p$: $\left(\sum_{j=1}^{k} a_j X^{j-1}\right) \cdot \left(\sum_{j=1}^{k} w_{a,j} X^{k-j}\right) + \left(\sum_{j=1}^{k} b_j X^{j-1}\right) \cdot \left(\sum_{j=1}^{k} w_{b,j} X^{k-j}\right) + \left(\sum_{j=1}^{k} c_j X^{j-1}\right) \cdot \left(\sum_{j=1}^{k} w_{c,j} X^{k-j}\right) = K X^{k-1} + \sum_{j=0, j \neq k-1}^{2k-2} K_j X^j$, where the K_j are extra terms determined from the a, b, c and w values.

If we choose the basis $\mathcal{B}' = 1, \phi, \phi^2, \ldots, \phi^{2k-1}$ for $GF(p^{2k})$, we can perform multiplications of extension field elements in a way that always yields a useful linear relation in the ϕ^{k-1} term without any overflow modulo f.

By viewing multiplication in $GF(p^{2k})$ as a linear map over $\mathbb{Z}_p^{2k}$, we can simulate arithmetic in the extension field using arithmetic in $\mathbb{Z}_p^{2k}$.

Let $A_1, \ldots, A_{2k} \in \mathcal{C}^{2k}$ be homomorphic commitments to single elements, $a_1, \ldots, a_k \in \mathbb{Z}_p$. We can consider the tuple $\boldsymbol{A} = (A_1, \ldots, A_k)$ to be a commitment to an element $\boldsymbol{a} = (a_1, \ldots, a_{2k})$ of $GF(p^{2k})$. Now, if we consider $\boldsymbol{x} \in \mathbb{Z}_p^{2k}$ as an element of $GF(p^{2k})$, then there is a matrix $M_{\boldsymbol{x}}$ which simulates multiplication by $\boldsymbol{x}$ in $\mathbb{Z}_p^{2k}$ when we multiply on the left by $M_{\boldsymbol{x}}$. Since the A_i are homomorphic commitments, we can obtain a commitment to $\boldsymbol{x} * \boldsymbol{a}$ by computing $M_{\boldsymbol{x}} \boldsymbol{A}$, where $*$ represents multiplication in $GF(p^{2k})$.

Reduction of Circuit Satisfiability to a Hadamard Matrix Product and Linear Constraints over $GF(p^{2}k)$. Let $N = mnk$ be the number of multiplication gates in the arithmetic circuit. To reduce circuit satisfiability to constraints over $GF(p^{2k})$, we can consider the same polynomial equations as before, written over $GF(p^{2k})$ rather than $\mathbb{Z}_p$. We consider the rows of matrices A, B, and C as before, but this time, we label the row vectors of the matrices $\boldsymbol{a}_{i,j}, \boldsymbol{b}_{i,j}$ and $\boldsymbol{c}_{i,j} \in \mathbb{Z}_p^n$, for $1 \leq i \leq m$ and $1 \leq j \leq k$. Now, we consider the row vectors $\boldsymbol{a}_{i,1}, \ldots, \boldsymbol{a}_{i,k}$, which are elements of $\mathbb{Z}_p^n$, as an element in $GF(p^{2k})^n$.

Let $a_i = (\boldsymbol{a}_{i,1}, \boldsymbol{a}_{i,2}, \ldots, \boldsymbol{a}_{i,k}, \boldsymbol{0}, \ldots, \boldsymbol{0})^T$ represent this element in $GF(p^{2k})^n$. Each column of the matrix represents a separate element of $GF(p^{2k})$.

Satisfiability conditions over $\mathbb{Z}_p$ were embedded using scalar products, denoted by $\cdot$, and element-wise products, denoted by $\circ$. If a and b in $\mathbb{Z}_p^{2k \times n}$ represent elements of $GF(p^{2k})^n$, then each column represents an element of $GF(p^{2k})$, and the scalar products and element-wise products of a and b are computed using the columns. We denote the element-wise product by $a \bigcirc b$ and the scalar product by $a \bigodot b$ to avoid confusion with any other matrix products on a and b.

$$a = \left(\begin{array}{c} \boldsymbol{v}_1 \ \boldsymbol{v}_2 \ \ldots \ \boldsymbol{v}_n \end{array} \right), b = \left(\begin{array}{c} \boldsymbol{w}_1 \ \boldsymbol{w}_2 \ \ldots \ \boldsymbol{w}_n \end{array} \right)$$

$$a \bigcirc b = \left(\begin{array}{c} M_{\boldsymbol{v}_1} \boldsymbol{w}_1 \ M_{\boldsymbol{v}_2} \boldsymbol{w}_2 \ \ldots \ M_{\boldsymbol{v}_n} \boldsymbol{w}_n \end{array} \right)$$

$$a \bigodot b = M_{\boldsymbol{v}_1} \boldsymbol{w}_1 + M_{\boldsymbol{v}_2} \boldsymbol{w}_2 + \ldots + M_{\boldsymbol{v}_n} \boldsymbol{w}_n$$

Note that in the verification equations, although the verifier computes high powers of random challenges $\boldsymbol{x}$ and $\boldsymbol{y}$, the verifier only computes quadratic polynomials of values such as a and b which have been sent by the prover. This is important, because when we expand a and b in terms of their coefficients a_i and b_i, we see that the verifier only computes expressions which have degree 2 in the prover's secret committed wire values, embedded as elements of $GF(p^{2k})$. Therefore, considering a field extension of degree $2k$ with the basis $\mathcal{B}$ is sufficient for our purposes: we only need to ensure that a single multiplication in $GF(p^{2k})$ preserves the individual product relations embedded in the $GF(p)$ elements.

When embedding satisfiability conditions into a polynomial over $\mathbb{Z}_p$, using random challenges $x, y \in \mathbb{Z}_p$, the prover could send linear combinations of vectors $\boldsymbol{a}_i \in \mathbb{Z}_p^n$ such as $\boldsymbol{a}(x) = \boldsymbol{a}_0 + \sum_{i=1}^{m} \boldsymbol{a}_i y^i x^i$ to the verifier.

However, when embedding satisfiability conditions into a polynomial over $GF(p^{2k})$, using random challenges $\boldsymbol{x}, \boldsymbol{y} \in GF(p^{2k})$, the prover sends linear combinations of vectors $a_i \in GF(p^{2k})^n$ such as $a(x) = a_0 + \sum_{i=1}^{m} (M_y)^i (M_x)^i a_i$.

Committing and Performing Calculations in a Lattice Setting. Commitment schemes based on lattice assumptions often require messages to be 'small' elements of the base ring in which the commitment is computed. Therefore, we consider the wire values in the arithmetic circuit to be integers in $[p]$ inside a larger ambient ring $\mathbb{Z}_q$ where the commitments are computed.

We can still simulate the action of $GF(p^{2k})$ over the integers by applying the same multiplication matrices over the integers rather than working modulo p. Whenever the prover and verifier multiply by powers of random challenges $\boldsymbol{x} \in [p]^{2k}$, they reduce powers of matrices such as M_x and M_y modulo p before applying these matrices to commitments or openings. For example, the prover will send openings a and b to the verifier: $a = \sum_{i=0}^{m}(M_x^i M_y^i \mod p)a_i$ and $b = \sum_{i=0}^{m}(M_x^{(m+1-i)} \mod p)b_i$.

For this reason, the verification equations will compare quantities that are congruent modulo p, but not equal over the integers, or in $\mathbb{Z}_q$, as the prover and verifier will have computed and reduced various terms modulo p, but performed this reduction at different times during the computation. Therefore, the prover will send an additional commitment D containing a message which is a multiple of p and corrects the discrepancy.

5   Parameter Selection

In this section we introduce notation for the parameters in our arithmetic circuit argument, and specify the choice of values in our arguments to ensure asymptotic security. Due to the large number of different variables used in the arithmetic circuit argument, and the fact that the arithmetic circuit argument and earlier proof of knowledge are quite independent of one another, we redefine certain variable names which were used earlier on for use in the arithmetic circuit argument. Parameter λ is dictated by the desired security level, and p and N come from the arithmetic circuit whose satisfiability is to be proven. All other parameters are derived from the table below, can be written in terms of λ, p and N, and are chosen in order to ensure that the commitment scheme is binding on a large enough message space for security.

Parameters and Asymptotic Sizes. In order to satisfy the constraints above, we choose the parameters in Table 2. Let λ be the security parameter, and suppose that we wish to verify an arithmetic circuit with N gates, over $\mathbb{Z}_p$.

Table 2. Parameter choices for our arithmetic circuit argument.

Parameter	Size	Description
λ		Security parameter for our arguments
p	$poly(\lambda)$	Underlying field for the arithmetic circuit
N	$kmn = poly(\lambda)$	Number of multiplication gates in the arithmetic circuit
P	$O(nk^2m^2p^2)$	Maximum size of elements committed by honest prover
B	$O(PN)$	Soundness slack from proof of knowledge
P'	$P' = BP$	Commitment scheme must be binding up to elements in $[P']$.
n	$n \approx \sqrt{\frac{Nr \log q}{\lambda \log N\lambda p}}$	Controls length of vectors in the SAT argument
k	$k \approx \lambda / \log_2 p$	Controls soundness error of the SAT argument
m	$m = N/kn$	Number of commitments in SAT argument is $O(mk)$
q	$q \approx P'\sqrt{r}$	Modulus for SIS instances.
r	$r = O(\log n)$	Commitments lie in $\mathbb{Z}_q^d$.

6   Product Argument

The following protocol allows the prover to prove that they know $N = nmk$ triples satisfying multiplicative relations.

We give parameters for our protocol in Sect. 5.

Consider the commitment scheme $\mathrm{Com}_{ck} : \mathbb{Z}_q^n \times \mathbb{Z}_q^{n'} \mapsto \mathcal{C}$ introduced earlier in Sect. 2.2, where ck consists of the public matrices used to generate a SIS instance. Let $A \in \mathbb{Z}_q^{2k \times n}$ and $R \in \mathbb{Z}_q^{2k \times n'}$. Define the extended commitment scheme $\mathrm{Com}_{ck}{}^*$ as

$$
\mathrm{Com}_{ck}{}^*(A; R) := \begin{pmatrix} \mathrm{Com}_{ck}(\boldsymbol{a}_1; \boldsymbol{r}_1) \\ \mathrm{Com}_{ck}(\boldsymbol{a}_2, \boldsymbol{r}_2) \\ \vdots \\ \mathrm{Com}_{ck}(\boldsymbol{a}_{2k}; \boldsymbol{r}_{2k}) \end{pmatrix}
$$

where $\boldsymbol{a}_i \in \mathbb{Z}_p^n$, $\boldsymbol{r}_i \in \mathbb{Z}_p^{n'}$ are the row vectors of A and R.

Common Reference String: Commitment key ck. The basis $\mathcal{B}$ for the extension field $GF(p^{2k})$, which specifies how elements should be multiplied.

Statement: Description of a set of $N = kmn$ multiplication relations over $\mathbb{Z}_p$.

Prover's Witness: Values $A_i, B_i, C_i \in \mathbb{Z}_p^{k \times n}$, $1 \leq i \leq m$, such that $\forall i$, $A_i \circ B_i \equiv C_i \mod p$.

Argument:

$\mathcal{P}$ Since $\forall i$, $A_i \circ B_i \equiv C_i \mod p$, then for $1 \leq i \leq m$, we can write

$$
\begin{bmatrix} A_i \\ \mathbf{0}^{k \times n} \end{bmatrix} \bigcirc \begin{bmatrix} B_i \\ \mathbf{0}^{k \times n} \end{bmatrix} = \begin{bmatrix} C_i \\ C_i' \end{bmatrix} \quad \mod p
$$

for some $C_i' \in [p]^{k \times n}$, $1 \leq i \leq m$, by our choice of basis $\mathcal{B}$.

The prover randomly selects $A_0, B_{m+1} \leftarrow D_{\sigma_1}^{2k \times n}$.

The prover selects α_i and β_i uniformly at random from $[p]^{k \times n'}$ and γ_i uniformly at random from $[p]^{2k \times n'}$ for $1 \leq i \leq m$, and selects $\alpha_0, \beta_{m+1} \leftarrow D_{\sigma_1}^{2k \times n'}$.

For $1 \leq i \leq m$, the prover computes

$$
\boldsymbol{A}_i = \mathrm{Com}_{ck}{}^* \left(\begin{bmatrix} A_i \\ \mathbf{0}^{k \times n} \end{bmatrix} ; \begin{bmatrix} \alpha_i \\ \mathbf{0}^{k \times n'} \end{bmatrix} \right) \qquad \boldsymbol{C}_i = \mathrm{Com}_{ck}{}^* \left(\begin{bmatrix} C_i \\ C_i' \end{bmatrix} ; \gamma_i \right)
$$

$$
\boldsymbol{B}_i = \mathrm{Com}_{ck}{}^* \left(\begin{bmatrix} B_i \\ \mathbf{0}^{k \times n} \end{bmatrix} ; \begin{bmatrix} \beta_i \\ \mathbf{0}^{k \times n'} \end{bmatrix} \right)
$$

Note that by definition, $\boldsymbol{A}_i$ and $\boldsymbol{B}_i \in \mathcal{C}^{2k}$ consist of k commitments and k trivial commitments in the k final components. The prover also computes

$$
\boldsymbol{A}_0 = \mathrm{Com}_{ck}{}^*(A_0; \alpha_0), \qquad \boldsymbol{B}_{m+1} = \mathrm{Com}_{ck}{}^*(B_{m+1}; \beta_{m+1})
$$

The prover sends $\{\boldsymbol{A}_i\}_{i=0}^m, \{\boldsymbol{B}_i\}_{i=1}^{m+1}, \{\boldsymbol{C}_i\}_{i=1}^m$ to the verifier.

$\mathcal{V}$ The verifier picks $\boldsymbol{y} \leftarrow [p]^{2k}$, and sends $\boldsymbol{y}$ to the prover.

$\mathcal{P}$ The prover computes polynomials $A(\boldsymbol{X}), B(\boldsymbol{X})$, which have matrix coefficients, in the indeterminate $\boldsymbol{X} \in \mathbb{Z}_q^{2k}$, and also computes C.

$$A(\boldsymbol{X}) = A_0 + \sum_{i=1}^{m} M_{\boldsymbol{X}}^i (M_{\boldsymbol{y}}^i \mod p) \begin{bmatrix} A_i \\ \mathbf{0}^{k \times n} \end{bmatrix}$$

$$B(\boldsymbol{X}) = B_{m+1} + \sum_{i=1}^{m} M_{\boldsymbol{X}}^{m+1-i} \begin{bmatrix} B_i \\ \mathbf{0}^{k \times n} \end{bmatrix}$$

$$C = \sum_{i=1}^{m} M_{\boldsymbol{y}}^i \begin{bmatrix} C_i \\ C_i' \end{bmatrix} \mod p$$

The prover computes $A(\boldsymbol{X}) \bigcirc B(\boldsymbol{X}) \mod p$.

$$A(\boldsymbol{X}) \bigcirc B(\boldsymbol{X}) \mod p = M_{\boldsymbol{X}}^{m+1} C + \sum_{l=0, l \neq m+1}^{2m} M_{\boldsymbol{X}}^l H_l \mod p$$

where $H_l \in [p]^{2k \times n}$.

For $0 \leq l \leq 2m, l \neq 0$, the prover selects η_l uniformly at random from $[p]^{2k \times n'}$, and computes $\boldsymbol{H}_l = \mathrm{Com}_{ck}{}^*(H_l; \eta_l)$.

The prover sends $\{\boldsymbol{H}_l\}_{l=0, l \neq m}^{2m}$ to the verifier.

$\mathcal{V}$ The verifier picks $\boldsymbol{x} \leftarrow [p]^{2k}$, and sends $\boldsymbol{x}$ to the prover.

$\mathcal{P}$ The prover computes the following values modulo p.

$$A = A_0 + \sum_{i=1}^{m} (M_{\boldsymbol{x}}^i M_{\boldsymbol{y}}^i \mod p) \begin{bmatrix} A_i \\ \mathbf{0}^{k \times n} \end{bmatrix}$$

$$\alpha = \alpha_0 + \sum_{i=1}^{m} (M_{\boldsymbol{x}}^i M_{\boldsymbol{y}}^i \mod p) \begin{bmatrix} \alpha_i \\ \mathbf{0}^{k \times n'} \end{bmatrix}$$

$$B = B_{m+1} + \sum_{i=1}^{m} (M_{\boldsymbol{x}}^{m+1-i} \mod p) \begin{bmatrix} B_i \\ \mathbf{0}^{k \times n} \end{bmatrix}$$

$$\beta = \beta_{m+1} + \sum_{i=1}^{m} (M_{\boldsymbol{x}}^{m+1-i} \mod p) \begin{bmatrix} \beta_i \\ \mathbf{0}^{k \times n'} \end{bmatrix}$$

Note that $A \equiv A(\boldsymbol{x}) \mod p$ and $B \equiv B(\boldsymbol{x}) \mod p$.

The prover computes

$$D = (A \bigcirc B \mod p) - \sum_{i=1}^{m} (M_{\boldsymbol{y}}^i \mod p) \begin{bmatrix} C_i \\ C_i' \end{bmatrix} - \sum_{l=0, l \neq m+1}^{2m} (M_{\boldsymbol{x}}^l \mod p) H_l$$

The prover randomly selects $\delta \leftarrow D_{\sigma_2}^{2k \times n'}$ and computes $\boldsymbol{D} = \mathrm{Com}_{ck}{}^*(D; \delta)$.

The prover randomly selects $E \leftarrow p \cdot D_{\sigma_3}^{2k \times n}$, $\epsilon \leftarrow D_{\sigma_4}^{2k \times n'}$ and computes $\boldsymbol{E} = \mathrm{Com}_{ck}{}^*(E; \epsilon)$. Note that E is 0 modulo p.

The prover sends $\boldsymbol{D}$ and $\boldsymbol{E}$ to the verifier.

$\mathcal{V}$ The verifier picks $z \leftarrow [p]^{2k}$, and sends z to the prover.

$\mathcal{P}$ The prover runs $\mathsf{Rej}((A||\alpha||B||\beta), (A||\alpha||B||\beta) - (A_0||\alpha_0||B_{m+1}||\beta_{m+1}), \sigma_1, e)$, and aborts according to the result.

The prover computes the following

$$\rho = \sum_{i=1}^{m} (M_x^{m+1} M_y^i \mod p)\gamma_i + \sum_{l=0, l\neq m+1}^{2m} (M_x^l \mod p)\eta_l + \delta$$

The prover runs $\mathsf{Rej}(\rho, \rho - \delta, \sigma_2, e)$.

The prover computes $\bar{D} = (M_z \mod p)D + E$ and $\bar{\delta} = (M_z \mod p)\delta + \epsilon$.

The prover runs $\mathsf{Rej}(\bar{D}/p, D/p, \sigma_3, e)$.

The prover runs $\mathsf{Rej}(\bar{\delta}, \delta, \sigma_4, e)$.

The prover sends $A, \alpha, B, \beta, \rho, \bar{D}, \bar{\delta}$ to the verifier.

$\mathcal{V}$ The prover and the verifier engage in a proof-of-knowledge, as shown in Fig. 1, including every commitment sent from the prover to the verifier.

The verifier accepts if and only if

$$\mathsf{Com}_{ck}{}^*(A; \alpha) = \sum_{i=0}^{m} (M_x^i M_y^i \mod p)\boldsymbol{A}_i$$

$$\mathsf{Com}_{ck}{}^*(B; \beta) = \sum_{i=1}^{m+1} (M_x^{m+1-i} \mod p)\boldsymbol{B}_i$$

$$\mathsf{Com}_{ck}{}^*(A \bigcirc B \mod p; \rho) = \sum_{i=1}^{m} (M_x^{m+1} M_y^i \mod p)\boldsymbol{C}_i$$

$$+ \sum_{l=0, l\neq m+1}^{2m} (M_x^l \mod p)\boldsymbol{H}_l + \boldsymbol{D}$$

$$\mathsf{Com}_{ck}{}^*(\bar{D}; \bar{\delta}) = (M_z \mod p)\boldsymbol{D} + \boldsymbol{E}$$

$$\bar{D} = 0 \mod p \qquad \|\bar{D}\|_2 \leq 2\sqrt{kn}\sigma_3 p$$

$$\|(A||\alpha||B||\beta)\|_2 \leq 4\sqrt{kn}\sigma_1 \qquad \|\rho\|_2 \leq 2\sqrt{kn}\sigma_2 \qquad \|\bar{\delta}\|_2 \leq 2\sqrt{kn}\sigma_4$$

and the proof-of-knowledge is accepting.

Sizes of Standard Deviations

$$\sigma_1 = 48\sqrt{kn}kmp^2, \qquad\qquad \sigma_2 = 72\sqrt{2kn}kmp,$$
$$\sigma_3 = 24\sqrt{2kn}kp(1 + 6kmp), \qquad\qquad \sigma_4 = 24\sqrt{2}k^2pn\sigma_2$$

Security Analysis

Theorem 3. *Given the statistically hiding, computationally binding commitment scheme based on SIS, the argument for multiplication triples has statistical completeness, statistical special honest verifier zero-knowledge and computational knowledge-soundness.*

The proof of Theorem 3 can be found in the full version of this paper.

Efficiency. The above argument uses 7 moves of interaction and results in an overall 9 move argument when combined with the proof-of-knowledge sub-protocols. For the product argument, the prover must send $8mk + 6k$ commitments to the verifier, and $14nk$ integers as commitments openings, plus the communication for the proof-of-knowledge. Sub-linear communication is achieved by setting parameters as in Table 2. This gives communication of approximately $O(\sqrt{N \log N})$ elements of $\mathbb{Z}_q$.

For $q = \text{poly}(\lambda)$, the prover's computational costs are given by $O(N \log N (\log \lambda)^2)$ bit operations for the prover. The verifier's computational costs are dominated by computing the same types of linear combinations as the prover, giving computational costs of $O(N(\log \lambda)^3)$ bit operations.

7   Linear Constraint Argument Description

Using similar ideas to those in the multiplication protocol, in the full version of this paper, we give a protocol which allows the prover to prove that $N = nmk$ committed values satisfy the linear consistency relations

$$\sum_{i=1,j=1}^{m,k} a_{i,j} \cdot w_{u,a,i,j} + \sum_{i=1,j=1}^{m,k} b_{i,j} \cdot w_{u,b,i,j} + \sum_{i=1,j=1}^{m,k} c_{i,j} \cdot w_{u,c,i,j} = K_u \quad \text{for } u \in \{1, \ldots, U\} \tag{9}$$

Without loss of generality, we pad the linear consistency relations so that U is divisible by k.

The protocol, security proof, and complexity analysis are very similar to that of the argument for proving multiplication triples in the previous section.

We select parameters for our protocol in Sect. 5.

Security Analysis

Theorem 4. *Given the statistically hiding, computationally binding commitment scheme based in SIS, the argument for linear consistency constraints has statistical completeness, statistical special honest verifier zero-knowledge and computational knowledge-soundness.*

The proof of Theorem 4 can be found in the full version of this paper.

Efficiency. The above argument uses 7 moves of interaction and results in an overall 9 move argument when combined with the proof-of-knowledge sub-protocols. For the product argument, the prover must send $7km + 9k - 1$ commitments to the verifier, and $10nk + 2k$ integers as commitment openings, plus the communication for the proof-of-knowledge. The asymptotic costs of the protocol are the same as for the argument for multiplication triples in the previous section. Combined with the proof of knowledge, this gives an arithmetic circuit argument with the stated efficiency.

8   Arithmetic Circuit Argument

The product protocol given in Sect. 6 and the linear consistency protocol given in Sect. 7 imply an arithmetic circuit protocol with the same asymptotic efficiency as the two subprotocols, in which the prover forms $O(mk)$ commitments, each to n wire values in p, and runs both subprotocols in order to prove that they satisfy the arithmetic circuit, reusing the same commitments $\boldsymbol{A}_i, \boldsymbol{B}_i, \boldsymbol{C}_i$ to the wires in both subprotocols.

This yields a zero-knowledge argument for arithmetic circuit satisfiability with communication costs $O(\sqrt{N \log N})$ elements of $\mathbb{Z}_q$, computational costs of $O(N \log N)$ for the prover, and approximately $O(N)$ for the verifier.

References

[AHIV17]   Ames, S., Hazay, C., Ishai, Y., Venkitasubramaniam, M.: Ligero: lightweight sublinear arguments without a trusted setup. In: Thuraisingham et al. [TEMX17], pp. 2087–2104

[Ajt96]   Ajtai, M.: Generating hard instances of lattice problems (extended abstract). In: 28th ACM STOC, pp. 99–108. ACM Press, May 1996

[Ban93]   Banaszczyk, W.: New bounds in some transference theorems in the geometry of numbers. Mathematische Annalen **296**, 625–635 (1993)

[BBB+17]   Bunz, B., Bootle, J., Boneh, D., Poelstra, A., Maxwell, G.: Bulletproofs: short proofs for confidential transactions and more. Cryptology ePrint Archive, Report 2017/1066 (2017). https://eprint.iacr.org/2017/1066

[BCC+16]   Bootle, J., Cerulli, A., Chaidos, P., Groth, J., Petit, C.: Efficient zero-knowledge arguments for arithmetic circuits in the discrete log setting. In: Fischlin and Coron [FC16], pp. 327–357

[BCCT12]   Bitansky, N., Canetti, R., Chiesa, A., Tromer, E.: From extractable collision resistance to succinct non-interactive arguments of knowledge, and back again. In: Goldwasser, S. (ed.) ITCS 2012, pp. 326–349. ACM, January 2012

[BCCT13]   Bitansky, N., Canetti, R., Chiesa, A., Tromer, E.: Recursive composition and bootstrapping for SNARKS and proof-carrying data. In: Boneh, D., Roughgarden, T., Feigenbaum, J. (eds.) 45th ACM STOC, pp. 111–120. ACM Press, June 2013

[BCG+17]   Bootle, J., Cerulli, A., Ghadafi, E., Groth, J., Hajiabadi, M., Jakobsen, S.K.: Linear-time zero-knowledge proofs for arithmetic circuit satisfiability. In: Takagi, T., Peyrin, T. (eds.) ASIACRYPT 2017, Part III. LNCS, vol. 10626, pp. 336–365. Springer, Cham (2017). https://doi.org/10.1007/978-3-319-70700-6_12

[BCK+14]   Benhamouda, F., Camenisch, J., Krenn, S., Lyubashevsky, V., Neven, G.: Better zero-knowledge proofs for lattice encryption and their application to group signatures. In: Sarkar, P., Iwata, T. (eds.) ASIACRYPT 2014, Part I. LNCS, vol. 8873, pp. 551–572. Springer, Heidelberg (2014). https://doi.org/10.1007/978-3-662-45611-8_29

[BD10]   Bendlin, R., Damgård, I.: Threshold decryption and zero-knowledge proofs for lattice-based cryptosystems. In: Micciancio, D. (ed.) TCC 2010. LNCS, vol. 5978, pp. 201–218. Springer, Heidelberg (2010). https://doi.org/10.1007/978-3-642-11799-2_13

[BDLN16] Baum, C., Damgård, I., Larsen, K.G., Nielsen, M.: How to prove knowledge of small secrets. In: Robshaw, M., Katz, J. (eds.) CRYPTO 2016, Part III. LNCS, vol. 9816, pp. 478–498. Springer, Heidelberg (2016). https://doi.org/10.1007/978-3-662-53015-3_17

[BDOP16] Baum, C., Damgård, I., Oechsner, S., Peikert, C.: Efficient commitments and zero-knowledge protocols from ring-SIS with applications to lattice-based threshold cryptosystems. Cryptology ePrint Archive, Report 2016/997 (2016). http://eprint.iacr.org/2016/997

[BG14]   Bai, S., Galbraith, S.D.: An improved compression technique for signatures based on learning with errors. In: Benaloh, J. (ed.) CT-RSA 2014. LNCS, vol. 8366, pp. 28–47. Springer, Cham (2014). https://doi.org/10.1007/978-3-319-04852-9_2

[BKLP15] Benhamouda, F., Krenn, S., Lyubashevsky, V., Pietrzak, K.: Efficient zero-knowledge proofs for commitments from learning with errors over rings. In: Pernul, G., Ryan, P.Y.A., Weippl, E. (eds.) ESORICS 2015, Part I. LNCS, vol. 9326, pp. 305–325. Springer, Cham (2015). https://doi.org/10.1007/978-3-319-24174-6_16

[CD97]   Cramer, R., Damgård, I.: Linear zero-knowledge - a note on efficient zero-knowledge proofs and arguments. In: 29th ACM STOC, pp. 436–445. ACM Press, May 1997

[CDG+17] Chase, M., Derler, D., Goldfeder, S., Orlandi, C., Ramacher, S., Rechberger, C., Slamanig, D., Zaverucha, G.: Post-quantum zero-knowledge and signatures from symmetric-key primitives. In: Thuraisingham et al. [TEMX17], pp. 1825–1842

[CDK14]   Cramer, R., Damgård, I., Keller, M.: On the amortized complexity of zero-knowledge protocols. J. Cryptol. **27**(2), 284–316 (2014)

[CDXY17] Cramer, R., Damgård, I., Xing, C., Yuan, C.: Amortized complexity of zero-knowledge proofs revisited: achieving linear soundness slack. In: Coron and Nielsen [CN17], pp. 479–500

[CN17]   Coron, J.-S., Nielsen, J.B. (eds.): EUROCRYPT 2017, Part I. LNCS, vol. 10210. Springer, Cham (2017). https://doi.org/10.1007/978-3-319-56620-7

[Dam10]   Damgård, I.: On Σ-protocols (2010). http://www.cs.au.dk/~ivan/Sigma.pdf

[DDLL13] Ducas, L., Durmus, A., Lepoint, T., Lyubashevsky, V.: Lattice signatures and bimodal gaussians. In: Canetti, R., Garay, J.A. (eds.) CRYPTO 2013, Part I. LNCS, vol. 8042, pp. 40–56. Springer, Heidelberg (2013). https://doi.org/10.1007/978-3-642-40041-4_3

[DL12]   Damgård, I., López-Alt, A.: Zero-knowledge proofs with low amortized communication from lattice assumptions. In: Visconti, I., De Prisco, R. (eds.) SCN 2012. LNCS, vol. 7485, pp. 38–56. Springer, Heidelberg (2012). https://doi.org/10.1007/978-3-642-32928-9_3

[dPL17]   del Pino, R., Lyubashevsky, V.: Amortization with fewer equations for proving knowledge of small secrets. In: Katz, J., Shacham, H. (eds.) CRYPTO 2017, Part III. LNCS, vol. 10403, pp. 365–394. Springer, Cham (2017). https://doi.org/10.1007/978-3-319-63697-9_13

[FC16] Fischlin, M., Coron, J.-S. (eds.): EUROCRYPT 2016, Part II. LNCS, vol. 9666. Springer, Heidelberg (2016). https://doi.org/10.1007/978-3-662-49896-5

[GG98] Goldreich, O., Goldwasser, S.: On the limits of non-approximability of lattice problems. In: 30th ACM STOC, pp. 1–9. ACM Press, May 1998

[GGI+15] Gentry, C., Groth, J., Ishai, Y., Peikert, C., Sahai, A., Smith, A.D.: Using fully homomorphic hybrid encryption to minimize non-interative zero-knowledge proofs. J. Cryptol. **28**(4), 820–843 (2015)

[GGPR13] Gennaro, R., Gentry, C., Parno, B., Raykova, M.: Quadratic span programs and succinct NIZKs without PCPs. In: Johansson, T., Nguyen, P.Q. (eds.) EUROCRYPT 2013. LNCS, vol. 7881, pp. 626–645. Springer, Heidelberg (2013). https://doi.org/10.1007/978-3-642-38348-9_37

[GH98] Goldreich, O., Håstad, J.: On the complexity of interactive proofs with bounded communication. Inf. Process. Lett. **67**, 205–214 (1998)

[GLP12] Güneysu, T., Lyubashevsky, V., Pöppelmann, T.: Practical lattice-based cryptography: a signature scheme for embedded systems. In: Prouff, E., Schaumont, P. (eds.) CHES 2012. LNCS, vol. 7428, pp. 530–547. Springer, Heidelberg (2012). https://doi.org/10.1007/978-3-642-33027-8_31

[GMO16] Giacomelli, I., Madsen, J., Orlandi, C.: Zkboo: faster zero-knowledge for boolean circuits. In: 25th USENIX Security Symposium, pp. 1069–1083 (2016)

[GMR85] Goldwasser, S., Micali, S., Rackoff, C.: The knowledge complexity of interactive proof-systems (extended abstract). In: 17th ACM STOC, pp. 291–304. ACM Press, May 1985

[GN08] Gama, N., Nguyen, P.Q.: Predicting lattice reduction. In: Smart, N. (ed.) EUROCRYPT 2008. LNCS, vol. 4965, pp. 31–51. Springer, Heidelberg (2008). https://doi.org/10.1007/978-3-540-78967-3_3

[GQ88] Guillou, L.C., Quisquater, J.-J.: A practical zero-knowledge protocol fitted to security microprocessor minimizing both transmission and memory. In: Barstow, D., et al. (eds.) EUROCRYPT 1988. LNCS, vol. 330, pp. 123–128. Springer, Heidelberg (1988). https://doi.org/10.1007/3-540-45961-8_11

[Gro09a] Groth, J.: Linear algebra with sub-linear zero-knowledge arguments. In: Halevi, S. (ed.) CRYPTO 2009. LNCS, vol. 5677, pp. 192–208. Springer, Heidelberg (2009). https://doi.org/10.1007/978-3-642-03356-8_12

[Gro10a] Groth, J.: Short pairing-based non-interactive zero-knowledge arguments. In: Abe, M. (ed.) ASIACRYPT 2010. LNCS, vol. 6477, pp. 321–340. Springer, Heidelberg (2010). https://doi.org/10.1007/978-3-642-17373-8_19

[Gro10b] Groth, J.: A verifiable secret shuffle of homomorphic encryptions. J. Cryptol. **23**(4), 546–579 (2010)

[Gro16] Groth, J.: On the size of pairing-based non-interactive arguments. In: Fischlin and Coron [FC16], pp. 305–326

[GVW02] Goldreich, O., Vadhan, S.P., Wigderson, A.: On interactive proofs with a laconic prover. Comput. Complex. **11**(1–2), 1–53 (2002)

[GW11] Gentry, C., Wichs, D.: Separating succinct non-interactive arguments from all falsifiable assumptions. In: Fortnow, L., Vadhan, S.P. (eds.) 43rd ACM STOC, pp. 99–108. ACM Press, June 2011

[IKOS07] Ishai, Y., Kushilevitz, E., Ostrovsky, R., Sahai, A.: Zero-knowledge from secure multiparty computation. In: Johnson, D.S., Feige, U. (eds.) 39th ACM STOC, pp. 21–30. ACM Press, June 2007

[Kil92] Kilian, J.: A note on efficient zero-knowledge proofs and arguments (extended abstract). In: 24th ACM STOC, pp. 723–732. ACM Press, May 1992

[KR08] Kalai, Y.T., Raz, R.: Interactive PCP. In: Aceto, L., Damgård, I., Goldberg, L.A., Halldórsson, M.M., Ingólfsdóttir, A., Walukiewicz, I. (eds.) ICALP 2008, Part II. LNCS, vol. 5126, pp. 536–547. Springer, Heidelberg (2008). https://doi.org/10.1007/978-3-540-70583-3_44

[Lip12] Lipmaa, H.: Progression-free sets and sublinear pairing-based non-interactive zero-knowledge arguments. In: Cramer, R. (ed.) TCC 2012. LNCS, vol. 7194, pp. 169–189. Springer, Heidelberg (2012). https://doi.org/10.1007/978-3-642-28914-9_10

[LM06] Lyubashevsky, V., Micciancio, D.: Generalized compact knapsacks are collision resistant. In: Bugliesi, M., Preneel, B., Sassone, V., Wegener, I. (eds.) ICALP 2006, Part II. LNCS, vol. 4052, pp. 144–155. Springer, Heidelberg (2006). https://doi.org/10.1007/11787006_13

[LN17] Lyubashevsky, V., Neven, G.: One-shot verifiable encryption from lattices. In: Coron and Nielsen [CN17], pp. 293–323

[LNSW13] Ling, S., Nguyen, K., Stehlé, D., Wang, H.: Improved zero-knowledge proofs of knowledge for the ISIS problem, and applications. In: Kurosawa, K., Hanaoka, G. (eds.) PKC 2013. LNCS, vol. 7778, pp. 107–124. Springer, Heidelberg (2013). https://doi.org/10.1007/978-3-642-36362-7_8

[Lyu09] Lyubashevsky, V.: Fiat-Shamir with aborts: applications to lattice and factoring-based signatures. In: Matsui, M. (ed.) ASIACRYPT 2009. LNCS, vol. 5912, pp. 598–616. Springer, Heidelberg (2009). https://doi.org/10.1007/978-3-642-10366-7_35

[Lyu12] Lyubashevsky, V.: Lattice signatures without trapdoors. In: Pointcheval, D., Johansson, T. (eds.) EUROCRYPT 2012. LNCS, vol. 7237, pp. 738–755. Springer, Heidelberg (2012). https://doi.org/10.1007/978-3-642-29011-4_43

[MR04] Micciancio, D., Regev, O.: Worst-case to average-case reductions based on Gaussian measures. In: 45th FOCS, pp. 372–381. IEEE Computer Society Press, October 2004

[MR08] Micciancio D., Regev O.: Lattice-based Cryptography. In: Bernstein, D.J., Buchmann, J., Dahmen, E. (eds.) Post-Quantum Cryptography. Springer, Heidelberg (2009). https://doi.org/10.1007/978-3-540-88702-7_5

[MV03] Micciancio, D., Vadhan, S.P.: Statistical zero-knowledge proofs with efficient provers: lattice problems and more. In: Boneh, D. (ed.) CRYPTO 2003. LNCS, vol. 2729, pp. 282–298. Springer, Heidelberg (2003). https://doi.org/10.1007/978-3-540-45146-4_17

[PHGR13] Parno, B., Howell, J., Gentry, C., Raykova, M.: Pinocchio: nearly practical verifiable computation. In: 2013 IEEE Symposium on Security and Privacy, pp. 238–252. IEEE Computer Society Press, May 2013

[PR06] Peikert, C., Rosen, A.: Efficient collision-resistant hashing from worst-case assumptions on cyclic lattices. In: Halevi, S., Rabin, T. (eds.) TCC 2006. LNCS, vol. 3876, pp. 145–166. Springer, Heidelberg (2006). https://doi.org/10.1007/11681878_8

[Reg05] Regev, O.: On lattices, learning with errors, random linear codes, and cryptography. In: Gabow, H.N., Fagin, R. (eds.) 37th ACM STOC, pp. 84–93. ACM Press, May 2005

[Sch91] Schnorr, C.-P.: Efficient signature generation by smart cards. J. Cryptol. 4(3), 161–174 (1991)

[Ste94] Stern, J.: A new identification scheme based on syndrome decoding. In: Stinson, D.R. (ed.) CRYPTO 1993. LNCS, vol. 773, pp. 13–21. Springer, Heidelberg (1994). https://doi.org/10.1007/3-540-48329-2_2

[TEMX17] Thuraisingham, B.M., Evans, D., Malkin, T., Xu, D. (eds.): ACM CCS 17. ACM Press, October/November (2017)

Lattice-Based Zero-Knowledge Arguments for Integer Relations

Benoît Libert[1,2](✉), San Ling[3], Khoa Nguyen[3], and Huaxiong Wang[3]

[1] CNRS, Laboratoire LIP, Lyon, France
benoit.libert@ens-lyon.fr
[2] ENS de Lyon, Laboratoire LIP (U. Lyon, CNRS, ENSL, Inria, UCBL),
Lyon, France
[3] School of Physical and Mathematical Sciences,
Nanyang Technological University, Singapore, Singapore

Abstract. We provide lattice-based protocols allowing to prove relations among committed integers. While the most general zero-knowledge proof techniques can handle arithmetic circuits in the lattice setting, adapting them to prove statements over the integers is non-trivial, at least if we want to handle exponentially large integers while working with a polynomial-size modulus q. For a polynomial L, we provide zero-knowledge arguments allowing a prover to convince a verifier that committed L-bit bitstrings x, y and z are the binary representations of integers X, Y and Z satisfying $Z = X + Y$ over $\mathbb{Z}$. The complexity of our arguments is only linear in L. Using them, we construct arguments allowing to prove inequalities $X < Z$ among committed integers, as well as arguments showing that a committed X belongs to a public interval $[\alpha, \beta]$, where α and β can be arbitrarily large. Our range arguments have logarithmic cost (i.e., linear in L) in the maximal range magnitude. Using these tools, we obtain zero-knowledge arguments showing that a committed element X does *not* belong to a public set S using $\widetilde{\mathcal{O}}(n \cdot \log |S|)$ bits of communication, where n is the security parameter. We finally give a protocol allowing to argue that committed L-bit integers X, Y and Z satisfy multiplicative relations $Z = XY$ over the integers, with communication cost subquadratic in L. To this end, we use our protocol for integer addition to prove the correct recursive execution of Karatsuba's multiplication algorithm. The security of our protocols relies on standard lattice assumptions with polynomial modulus and polynomial approximation factor.

1 Introduction

Lattice-based cryptography has been an extremely active area since the celebrated results of Ajtai [3] and Regev [58]. In comparison with discrete-logarithm and factoring-based techniques, it indeed offers numerous advantages like simpler arithmetic operations, a better asymptotic efficiency, advanced functionalities or a conjectured resistance to quantum computing. Its development was further

H. Shacham and A. Boldyreva (Eds.): CRYPTO 2018, LNCS 10992, pp. 700–732, 2018.
https://doi.org/10.1007/978-3-319-96881-0_24

boosted by breakthrough results of [26,53] showing how to safely use lattice trapdoors, which have been the cornerstone of many advanced primitives.

While lattices enable powerful functionalities that have no counterpart using traditional number theoretic tools, they do not easily lend themselves to the realization of certain fundamental tasks, like efficient zero-knowledge proofs. Zero-knowledge protocols [30] make it possible to prove properties about certain secret witnesses in order to have users demonstrate their correct behavior while protecting their privacy. For simple statements such as proving knowledge of a secret key, efficient solutions have been reported in [39,47,50,55]. In order to prove relations among committed values, the best known methods rely on the extra algebraic structure [5,8,60] offered by the ring-LWE or ring-SIS problems [51] and no truly efficient solution is known for standard (i.e., non-ideal) lattices.

In this paper, we investigate the problem of proving, under standard lattice assumptions, that large committed *integers* satisfy certain algebraic relations. Namely, if c_x, c_y and c_z are commitments to integers X, Y, Z of arbitrary polynomial bit-size $L = \mathsf{poly}(n)$, where n is the security parameter, we consider the problem of proving statements of the form $Z = X + Y$ and $Z = X \cdot Y$ over $\mathbb{Z}$. Note that this problem is different from the case of arithmetic circuits addressed in [8]: here, we are interested in proving relations over the integers. Furthermore, we would like to design zero-knowledge arguments for various other relations among large committed integers. As specific applications, we consider the problems of: (i) Proving that a committed integer X belongs to a publicly known range $[\alpha, \beta]$; (ii) Proving order relations $Y < X < Z$ between committed integers Y, X, Z; (iii) Proving that a committed element X does not belong to a public set (which allows users to prove their non-blacklisting).

While these problems received much attention in the literature, the most efficient solutions [21,34,48] handling large integers appeal to integer commitments [22,25] based on hidden-order groups (e.g., RSA groups), which are vulnerable to quantum computing. In particular, designing a solution based on mild assumptions in standard lattices is a completely open problem to our knowledge. Even in ideal lattices, handling integers of polynomial length L requires to work with exponentially large moduli, which affects both the efficiency and the approximation factor of the lattice assumption. Here, our goal is to realize the aforementioned protocols using polynomial moduli and approximation factors.

If we were to use known zero-knowledge proof systems [5,8,60] in ideal lattices to handle additive relations over $\mathbb{Z}$, we would need (super-)exponentially large moduli. In particular, in order to prove that committed integers X, Y, Z of bit-size $L = \mathsf{poly}(n)$ satisfy $Z = X + Y$, these protocols would require to prove that $Z = X + Y \mod q$ for a large modulus $q = 2^{\mathsf{poly}(n)}$. With current techniques, this would imply to work with a commitment scheme over rings R_q, for the same modulus q. In terms of efficiency, a single ring element would cost thousand times L bits to represent since the modulus should contain more than L bits. When it comes to proving smallness of committed values (in order to prove $Z = X + Y$ over $\mathbb{Z}$ via $Z = X + Y \mod q$, the prover should guarantee that X and Y are small w.r.t. q) together with relations among them, the prover may need to send hundreds of ring elements. As a consequence, the communication cost could be as large as $k \cdot L$, where k is up to hundreds of thousands. In terms of security, we note that such approaches may require at least sub-exponential approximation factors for the underlying ideal-lattice problems. Moreover, ensuring soundness may be non-trivial as the protocols of [5,8] only guarantee relaxed soundness.

OUR CONTRIBUTIONS. We provide statistical zero-knowledge arguments allowing to prove additive and multiplicative relations among committed integers of bit-size $L = \mathrm{poly}(n)$ under mild assumptions in standard (i.e., non-ideal) lattices. Our protocols can work with two flavors of the commitment scheme by Kawachi, Tanaka and Xagawa (KTX) [39]. If we commit to integers in a bit-by-bit fashion, the modulus q can be as small as $\widetilde{\mathcal{O}}(n)$ and the security of our protocols can rely on the worst-case hardness of SIVP_γ with $\gamma = \widetilde{\mathcal{O}}(n)$, which turns out to be one the weakest assumptions in the entire literature on lattice-based cryptography. On the other hand, if we rely on a stronger assumption with $\gamma = \widetilde{\mathcal{O}}(\sqrt{L} \cdot n)$ for a modulus $q = \widetilde{\mathcal{O}}(\sqrt{L} \cdot n)$, then we can commit to L bits at once and reduce the communication cost. For this all-at-once commitment variant, the complexities of our protocols are summarized as follows.

The protocol for integer additions has communication cost $(\zeta + 20L) \cdot \kappa$ bits, where $\zeta = \widetilde{\mathcal{O}}(n) + 6L \log q$ is the cost of proving knowledge of valid openings for the commitments to X, Y, Z and $\kappa = \omega(\log n)$ is the number of protocol repetitions to make the soundness error negligibly small. Thus, the actual cost for proving the additive relation is $20L \cdot \kappa$ bits. In terms of computation complexity, both the prover and the verifier only perform $\mathcal{O}(L)$ simple operations.

We offer two options for proving integer multiplications. For practically interesting values of L, e.g., $L \leq 8000$, we can emulate the schoolbook multiplication algorithm by proving L additive relations, and obtain communication cost $\widetilde{\mathcal{O}}(n + L^2) \cdot \kappa$ as well as computation costs $\mathcal{O}(L^2)$ for both parties. To our knowledge, all known methods for proving integer multiplications (sometimes implicitly) involve $\mathcal{O}(L^2)$ computation and/or communication complexities. Can we break this quadratic barrier?

As a theoretical contribution, we put forward the first protocol for multiplicative relations that does not incur any quadratic costs. Specifically, by proving in zero-knowledge the correct execution of a Karatsuba multiplication algorithm [38], we obtain both computation and communication complexities of order $\mathcal{O}(L^{\log_2 3})$.

Applications. While our protocol for additive relations only handles non-negative integers, it suffices for many applications, such as arguments of inequalities among committed integers, range membership for public/hidden ranges, and set non-membership. Moreover, it can also be used in higher-level protocols like zero-knowledge lists [27].[1] In particular, for a set of N elements with bit-size $\widetilde{\mathcal{O}}(n)$, our protocol for proving non-membership of a committed value only cost $\widetilde{\mathcal{O}}(n \cdot \log N)$ bits. In the lattice setting, this is the first non-membership proof

---

[1] These involve a prover wishing to convince a verifier that a committed list contains elements $\{a_i\}_i$ in a specific order without revealing anything else.

that achieves communication cost logarithmic in the cardinality of the set. Meanwhile, in our protocol for proving that a committed L-bit integer belongs to a given range $[\alpha, \beta]$, where $\beta - \alpha \approx 2^L$, besides the cost of proving knowledge of a valid opening for the commitment, the prover only has to send $23L \cdot \kappa$ bits to the verifier. In Table 1, we provide the concrete cost of the protocol variant achieving soundness error 2^{-80}, for commonly used lattice parameters.

Table 1. Concrete communication cost of our lattice-based zero-knowledge argument (Sect. 5.1) for proving knowledge of committed integer X belonging to a given range, w.r.t. various range sizes. We work with lattice parameters $n = 256$, $q \approx 2^{15}$, $m = 4608$. To achieve soundness error 2^{-80}, we set $\kappa = 137$.

Range size	2^{1000}	2^{2000}	2^{4000}	2^{8000}
Proving knowledge of committed X	3.16	3.65	4.63	6.59
Proving range membership of X	0.38	0.75	1.5	3
Total communication cost	3.54 MB	4.4 MB	6.13 MB	9.59 MB

We remark that, if we only had to prove the correct evaluation of binary addition circuits, MPC-based techniques [20,28,36] could perform slightly better than our protocols. However, they become much less efficient for the algebraic parts of the statements we have to prove (in particular, we also need to prove knowledge of openings of SIS-based commitments). Indeed, the MPC-in-the head paradigm [36] and its follow-ups [20,28] have linear complexities in the size of the circuit, which is much larger than the witness size as the commitment relation entails $\Theta(n(L + m))$ additions and multiplications over $\mathbb{Z}_q$. In our protocols, proving knowledge of an opening takes $\Theta((L + m) \log q)$ bits of communication.

Our Techniques. We proceed by emulating integer commitments by means of bit commitments. To commit to an L-bit integer X in an all-in-one fashion, we generate a KTX commitment $\mathbf{c}_x = \sum_{i=0}^{L-1} \mathbf{a}_i \cdot x_i + \mathbf{B} \cdot \mathbf{r} \in \mathbb{Z}_q^n$ to its binary representation $(x_{L-1}, \ldots, x_0)_2$ using public matrices $\mathbf{A} = [\mathbf{a}_0 \mid \ldots \mid \mathbf{a}_{L-1}] \in \mathbb{Z}_q^{n \times L}$ and $\mathbf{B} \in \mathbb{Z}_q^{n \times m}$ and random coins $\mathbf{r} \hookleftarrow U(\{0, 1\}^m)$.

Integer Additions. To prove additive relations among committed integers, we come up with an idea that may sound natural for computer processors, but, to the best of our knowledge, has not been considered in the context of zero-knowledge proofs. The idea is to view integer additions as binary additions *with carries*. Suppose that we add two bits x and y with carry-in c_{in} to obtain a bit z and carry-out c_{out}. Then, the relations among these bits are captured by equations

$$z = x + y + c_{in} \bmod 2, \qquad c_{out} = x \cdot y + z \cdot c_{in} + c_{in} \bmod 2,$$

which is equivalent to a homogeneous system of two equations over $\mathbb{Z}_2$. Using the above adder, we consider the addition of L-bit integers $X = (x_{L-1}, ..., x_0)_2$

and $Y = (y_{L-1}, ..., y_0)_2$ assuming that the committed sum is of length $L + 1$ and written as $Z = (z_L, z_{L-1}, ..., z_0)_2$. For each $i \in \{0, ..., L - 1\}$, we denote by c_{i+1} the carry-out of the i-th addition and define $c_L = z_L$. The equations become

$$z_0 + x_0 + y_0 = 0 \bmod 2$$
$$c_1 + x_0 \cdot y_0 = 0 \bmod 2$$
$$z_1 + x_1 + y_1 + c_1 = 0 \bmod 2$$
$$c_2 + x_1 \cdot y_1 + z_1 \cdot c_1 + c_1 = 0 \bmod 2$$
$$\vdots$$
$$z_{L-1} + x_{L-1} + y_{L-1} + c_{L-1} = 0 \bmod 2$$
$$z_L + x_{L-1} \cdot y_{L-1} + z_{L-1} \cdot c_{L-1} + c_{L-1} = 0 \bmod 2.$$

We observe that all the terms in the above equations are either bits or products of two bits. By adapting the Stern-like [59] techniques for hiding secret bits [44] and handling quadratic relations [42], we manage to prove that the bits of X, Y, Z satisfy the above equations modulo 2, which is equivalent to $X + Y = Z$ over $\mathbb{Z}$. Meanwhile, to prove that those bits coincide with the values committed under the KTX commitment requires to additionally prove a linear equation modulo q.

Interestingly, we show that, not only the problem of proving additive relations among committed integers can be reduced to proving secret bits satisfying linear and quadratic equations modulo 2 and one linear equation modulo q, such type of reduction is doable for all subsequently considered relations (multiplications, range membership, set non-membership). To handle the reduced statements in a modular manner, we thus design (in Sect. 3) a general zero-knowledge protocol that subsumes all argument systems of this work. In comparison with previous protocols [39,43,45,47] built on Stern's framework [59], this general protocol introduces a technical novelty which allows to reduce the communication cost.

Range Membership and Set Non-Membership. Our techniques for additions of non-negative integers directly yield a method for proving inequalities of the form $X \leq Z$, where it suffices to show the existence of non-negative integer Y such that $X + Y = Z$. This method can be further adapted to handle strict inequalities. To prove that $X < Z$, we demonstrate the existence of non-negative Y such that $X + Y + 1 = Z$, for which only a small additional treatment for the least significant bits of X, Y, Z is needed. Then, by combining two sub-protocols for inequalities, we can obtain range arguments for the statements "$X \in [\alpha, \beta]$", "$X \in [\alpha, \beta)$", "$X \in (\alpha, \beta]$" and "$X \in (\alpha, \beta)$", where X is committed under the KTX commitment, and α, β can be hidden/committed or public.

Given the techniques for proving inequalities, we can further obtain arguments of non-membership. In order to prove that a committed string $X \in \{0, 1\}^k$ does *not* belong to a public set $S = \{s_1, \ldots, s_N\}$, the prover generates a (publicly computable) Merkle tree [52] whose leaves are the elements of S arranged in lexicographical order. Then, the prover can use the technique of Libert *et al.* [44] – which allows arguing possession of a path in a lattice-based Merkle tree – to prove knowledge of two paths leading to adjacent leaves for which the corresponding set elements $Y, Z \in \{0,1\}^k$ satisfy $Y < X < Z$ in lexicographical order. Here, the adjacency of the leaves Y and Z is argued using our techniques for integers additions, which allows proving that their labels (i.e., the binary encoding of the path that connects them to the root) encode integers V, W such that $W = V + 1$.

Subquadratic Integer Multiplications. Proving multiplicative relations among L-bit committed integers with subquadratic complexity requires some additional tricks. Karatsuba's technique [38] divides integers X, Y into equal halves $X = X_1|X_0$ and $Y = Y_1|Y_0$, each of which has length $L/2$. If the length is odd, the factors must be padded with zeroes in the left halves, which raises technical difficulties as will be explained below. We have $X = 2^{L/2} \cdot X_1 + X_0$ and $Y = 2^{L/2} \cdot Y_1 + Y_0$, so that $X \cdot Y$ can be written

$$X \cdot Y = (2^L - 2^{L/2})(X_1 Y_1) + (1 - 2^{L/2})(X_0 Y_0) + 2^{L/2}(X_1 + X_0)(Y_1 + Y_0). \quad (1)$$

To prove this equation, we first prove knowledge of 3 partial products and then prove their correct shifting w.r.t. multiplication by powers of 2 before proving the correctness of additions. Each of the factors $X_1, Y_1, X_0, Y_0, X_1 + X_0, Y_1 + Y_0$ of (1) is recursively broken into 3 smaller products until reaching an easy-to-prove "base multiplication". One difficulty is that the length of $X_1 + X_0$ and $Y_1 + Y_0$ are one bit longer than the length $L/2$ of X_0, X_1, Y_0, Y_1. Since $L/2 + 1$ is odd, we need to pad with a zero before dividing any further and the same issue arises when dividing X_1, Y_1, X_0, Y_0. In the context of zero-knowledge proofs, it makes it very complicated to keep track of the lengths of witnesses in the underlying equations and determine where the original bits of X and Y should be.

To address the problems caused by carry-on bits in additions, Knuth [40] suggested to use subtractions and re-write the product $X \cdot Y$ as

$$(2^L + 2^{L/2}) \cdot (X_1 \cdot Y_1) + (1 + 2^{L/2}) \cdot (X_0 \cdot Y_0) - 2^{L/2} \cdot (X_1 - X_0) \cdot (Y_1 - Y_0). \quad (2)$$

The difference $X_1 - X_0$ is now guaranteed to have length $L/2$, which allows using $L = 2^k$ and recursively come down to base multiplications of two-bit integers. However, this modification introduces another problem as $X_1 - X_0$ and $Y_1 - Y_0$ can now be negative integers, which are more difficult to handle in our setting. For this reason, we need to make sure that we always subtract a smaller integer from a larger one, while preserving the ability to prove correct computations.

To this end, our idea is to compare X_1 and X_0 and let the smaller one be subtracted from the larger one. To do this, we define auxiliary variables X_1', X_0' such that $X_1' > X_0'$ and $\{X_1', X_0'\} = \{X_1, X_0\}$. Letting b be the bit such that $b = 1$ if $X_1' \geq X_0'$ and $b = 0$ otherwise, this can be expressed by the equation:

$$(X_1' - X_0') = b \cdot (X_1 - X_0) + (1 - b) \cdot (X_0 - X_1),$$

which is provable in zero-knowledge using our techniques for integer additions. If we repeat the above process and define variables Y_1', Y_0' such that $\{Y_1', Y_0'\} = \{Y_1, Y_0\}$ and an order control bit $c \in \{0,1\}$, if we define $d = b + c \bmod 2$, we have

$$(X_1 - X_0) \cdot (Y_1 - Y_0) = (X_1' - X_0') \cdot (Y_1' - Y_0') \qquad \text{if} \quad d = 0$$
$$(X_1 - X_0) \cdot (Y_1 - Y_0) = -(X_1' - X_0') \cdot (Y_1' - Y_0') \quad \text{if} \quad d = 1.$$

The term $(X_1 - X_0) \cdot (Y_1 - Y_0)$ appearing in Eq. (2) can thus be written as

$$(X_1 - X_0) \cdot (Y_1 - Y_0) = (1 - d) \cdot (X_1' - X_0') \cdot (Y_1' - Y_0') - d \cdot (X_1' - X_0') \cdot (Y_1' - Y_0'),$$

which yields an equation compatible our techniques while avoiding to handle negative integers. At each recursive step, we further divide the differences $X_1' - X_0'$ and $Y_1' - Y_0'$ and keep track of the control bits b, c, d which are part of the witnesses.

RELATED WORK. The first integer commitment scheme was proposed by Fujisaki and Okamoto [25] who suggested to use it to prove relation over the integers. They underlined the importance of zero-knowledge arguments over the integers in order to be able to prove modular relations when the modulus is not known in advance, when the commitment key is generated. Damgård and Fujisaki [22] corrected a flaw in the Fujisaki-Okamoto commitment and generalized it to abelian groups satisfying specific properties.

Lipmaa [48] highlighted the cryptographic importance of the class **D** of Diophantine sets[2] [1] and gave improved constructions of zero-knowledge proofs for Diophantine equations. As special cases, he obtained efficient zero-knowledge arguments for intervals, unions of intervals, exponential relations and gcd relations. In [33], Groth suggested another integer commitment scheme based on the Strong RSA assumption [4] which, like [22, 25], relies on groups of hidden order. Couteau, Peters and Pointcheval [21] recently suggested to combine integer commitments with a commitment scheme to field elements in order to improve the efficiency of zero-knowledge proofs over the integers. They also revisited the Damgård-Fujisaki commitment [22] and proved it the security of its companion argument system under the standard RSA assumption. While our results are not as general as those of [21, 48] as we do not handle negative integers, they suffice for many applications of integer commitments, as we previously mentioned.

Range proofs were introduced by Brickell *et al.* [10] and received a permanent attention [9, 12, 18, 19, 21, 31, 35, 48] since then. They served as a building block of countless cryptographic applications, which include anonymous credentials [14], anonymous e-cash [13], auction protocols [49], e-voting [34] and many more.

Currently known range proofs proceed via two distinct approaches. The first one proceeds by breaking integers into bits or small digits [7, 10, 12, 23, 31, 35], which allows communicating a sub-logarithmic (in the range size) number of group elements in the best known constructions [12, 31, 35]. The second approach [9, 21, 34, 48] appeals to integer commitments and groups of hidden order. This approach is usually preferred for very large ranges (which often arise in applications like anonymous credentials [14], where range elements are comprised of

---

[2] For $k, \ell \in \mathbb{N}$, a Diophantine set is a set of the form $S = \{ \boldsymbol{x} \in \mathbb{Z}^k \mid \exists \boldsymbol{w} \in \mathbb{Z}^\ell : P_S(\boldsymbol{x}, \boldsymbol{w}) = 0 \}$, for some representing polynomial $P_S(\boldsymbol{X}, \boldsymbol{W})$ defined over integer vectors $\boldsymbol{X} \in \mathbb{Z}^k$, $\boldsymbol{W} \in \mathbb{Z}^\ell$. Any recursively enumerable set is [24] Diophantine.

thousands of bits) where it tends to be more efficient and it does not require the maximal range length to be known when the commitment key is chosen.

Despite three decades of research, all known efficient range proofs (by "efficient", we mean that the communication complexity should be only logarithmic in the range size) build on quantum-vulnerable assumptions and the only candidates supporting very large integers rely on groups of hidden order. By proving knowledge of small secret vectors, lattice-based protocols [39,47] can be seen as providing a limited form of range proofs: if we can prove that a committed $\mathbf{x} \in \mathbb{Z}^m$ has infinity norm $\|\mathbf{x}\|_\infty < B$ for some basis $B < q$ of a B-ary representation, we can prove that $\mathbf{x}$ encodes an integer X in the range $[0, B^m - 1]$. However, it is not clear how to deal with arbitrary ranges. Using homomorphic integer commitments, any range $[\alpha, \beta]$ can be handled (see [17] and references therein) by exploiting the homomorphic properties of the commitment scheme and proving that $X - \alpha \in [0, \beta - \alpha]$. With homomorphic commitments used in the context of lattice-based cryptography, there is no obvious way to shift the committed value by an integer α when $\alpha > q$. Even with a sub-exponential modulus q, the size L of integers can be at most sub-linear in n. To our knowledge, no flexible solution has been proposed in the lattice setting, let alone under standard lattice assumptions with polynomial approximation factors and polynomial-size moduli. Our schemes thus provide a first answer to this question.

In the context of set non-membership, our construction bears resemblance with a technique used by Nakanishi *et al.* [56] to handle revocation in privacy-preserving protocols by proving inequalities over the integers. For a public set $S = \{s_1, \ldots, s_N\}$ arranged in lexicographical order, they rely on a trusted authority to create Camenisch-Lysyanskaya signatures [16] on all ordered pairs $\{\mathsf{Msg}_i = (s_i, s_{i+1})\}_{i=1}^{N-1}$ of adjacent set elements. To prove that a committed s is not in S, the prover proceeds with a proof of knowledge of two message-signature pairs (Msg_j, sig_j), $(\mathsf{Msg}_{j+1}, sig_{j+1})$ for which $\mathsf{Msg}_j = (s_j, s_{j+1})$ and $\mathsf{Msg}_{j+1} = (s_{j+1}, s_{j+2})$ contain elements s_j, s_{j+1} such that $s_j < s < s_{j+1}$. While this approach could be instantiated with our technique for proving integer inequalities, it would require proofs of knowledge of signatures and thus lattice trapdoors (indeed, all known lattice-based signatures compatible with proofs of knowledge rely on lattice trapdoors [26,53]). By using proofs of knowledge of a Merkle tree path [44] instead of signatures, our solution eliminates the need for lattice trapdoors, which allows for a better efficiency (note that proving inequalities $s_j < s < s_{j+1}$ incurs a complexity $\Omega(\log N)$ in both cases, so that using Merkle trees does not affect the asymptotic complexity). Moreover, the technique of Nakanishi *et al.* [56] involves a trusted entity to sign all pairs $(s_i, s_{i+1})\}_{i=1}^{N-1}$ in a setup phase whereas no trusted setup is required in our construction.

Other approaches to prove (non-)membership of a public set were suggested in [12,15,41,46]. However, they rely on a trusted entity to approve the sets of which (non-)membership must be proven during a setup phase. Setup-free accumulator-based set membership proofs were described in [11,44], but they are not known to support non-membership proofs.

In [6], Bayer and Groth cleverly used Σ protocols to handle proofs of non-membership without assuming a trusted setup. Their construction achieves logarithmic complexity in the cardinality of the set, but it crucially relies on commitment schemes, like Pedersen's discrete-log-based commitment [57], with homomorphic properties over the message space and the randomness space. For lack of a lattice-based commitment scheme with similar properties, their approach does not seem readily instantiable under lattice assumptions.

2   Preliminaries

NOTATIONS. When working with an integer $X \in [0, 2^L - 1]$, we use the notation $X = (x_{L-1}, \ldots, x_0)_2$ to describe its bits, and use bold lower-case letter $\mathbf{x}$ to denote the representation of X as binary column vector $(x_{L-1}, \ldots, x_0) \in \{0,1\}^L$. The column concatenation of matrices $\mathbf{A} \in \mathbb{Z}^{n \times k}$ and $\mathbf{B} \in \mathbb{Z}^{n \times m}$ is denoted by $[\mathbf{A}|\mathbf{B}] \in \mathbb{Z}^{n \times (k+m)}$. When concatenating column vectors $\mathbf{x} \in \mathbb{Z}^k$ and $\mathbf{y} \in \mathbb{Z}^m$, for simplicity, we often use the notation $(\mathbf{x}\|\mathbf{y}) \in \mathbb{Z}^{k+m}$ (instead of $(\mathbf{x}^\top\|\mathbf{y}^\top)^\top$).

2.1   Lattice-Based Cryptographic Building Blocks

We first recall the average-case problem SIS and its hardness.

Definition 1 ($\mathsf{SIS}^\infty_{n,m,q,\beta}$ [2,26]). *Given uniformly random matrix $\mathbf{A} \in \mathbb{Z}_q^{n \times m}$, find a non-zero vector $\mathbf{x} \in \mathbb{Z}^m$ such that $\|\mathbf{x}\|_\infty \leq \beta$ and $\mathbf{A} \cdot \mathbf{x} = \mathbf{0}$ mod q.*

If $m, \beta = \mathsf{poly}(n)$, and $q > \beta \cdot \widetilde{\mathcal{O}}(\sqrt{n})$, the $\mathsf{SIS}^\infty_{n,m,q,\beta}$ problem is at least as hard as worst-case lattice problem SIVP_γ for some $\gamma = \beta \cdot \widetilde{\mathcal{O}}(\sqrt{nm})$ (see, e.g., [26,54]).

We will use two SIS-based cryptographic ingredients: the commitment scheme of Kawachi, Tanaka and Xagawa [39] (KTX) and the Merkle hash tree from [44].

The KTX commitment scheme. The scheme works with security parameter n, prime modulus $q = \mathcal{O}(\sqrt{L} \cdot n)$, and dimension $m = n(\lceil \log_2 q \rceil + 3)$. We will consider several flavours of the scheme.

In the variant that allows committing to $L \leq \mathsf{poly}(n)$ bits, the commitment key is $(\mathbf{a}_0, \ldots, \mathbf{a}_{L-1}, \mathbf{B}) \hookleftarrow U(\mathbb{Z}_q^{n \times (m+L)})$. To commit to a bitstring $x_0, \ldots, x_{L-1}$, one samples $\mathbf{r} \hookleftarrow U(\{0,1\}^m)$, and outputs $\mathbf{c} = \sum_{i=0}^{L-1} \mathbf{a}_i \cdot x_i + \mathbf{B} \cdot \mathbf{r}$ mod q. Then, to open the commitment, one simply reveals $x_0, \ldots, x_{L-1} \in \{0,1\}$ and $\mathbf{r} \in \{0,1\}^m$.

If one can compute two valid openings $(x'_0, \ldots, x'_{L-1}, \mathbf{r}')$ and $(x''_0, \ldots, x''_{L-1}, \mathbf{r}'')$ for the same commitment $\mathbf{c}$, where $(x'_0, \ldots, x'_{L-1}) \neq (x''_0, \ldots, x''_{L-1})$, then one can compute a solution to the $\mathsf{SIS}^\infty_{n,m+L,q,1}$ problem associated with the uniformly random matrix $[\mathbf{a}_0 \mid \ldots \mid \mathbf{B}] \in \mathbb{Z}_q^{n \times (m+L)}$. Thus, the scheme is computationally binding, assuming the worst-case hardness of $\mathsf{SIVP}_{\widetilde{\mathcal{O}}(\sqrt{L} \cdot n)}$. On the other hand, by the Leftover Hash Lemma [29], the distribution of a commitment $\mathbf{c}$ is statistically close to uniform over $\mathbb{Z}_q^n$. This implies that the scheme is statistically hiding.

In the special case when $L = 1$, the scheme becomes a bit commitment scheme, in which case it can use a small modulus $q = \widetilde{\mathcal{O}}(n)$ and rely on a weak SIVP assumption with $\gamma = \widetilde{\mathcal{O}}(n)$.

Kawachi *et al.* [39] extended the above fixed-length commitment scheme to a string commitment scheme $\mathsf{COM} : \{0,1\}^* \times \{0,1\}^m \to \mathbb{Z}_q^n$. The obtained scheme is also statistically hiding for the given setting of parameters, and computationally binding assuming that $\mathsf{SIVP}_{\widetilde{\mathcal{O}}(n)}$ is hard.

Here, we will use the first commitment variant to commit to secret bits and the string commitment scheme COM as a building block for Stern-like protocols.

Lattice-based Merkle hash tree. The construction relies on the following collision-resistant hash function. Let n be the security parameter, $q = \widetilde{\mathcal{O}}(n)$, $k = n\lceil\log_2 q\rceil$ and $m = 2k$. Define the "powers-of-2" matrix

$$\mathbf{G} = \mathbf{I}_n \otimes [1\ 2\ 4\ \cdots\ 2^{\lceil\log_2 q\rceil-1}] \in \mathbb{Z}_q^{n\times k}.$$

Note that for every $\mathbf{v} \in \mathbb{Z}_q^n$, we have $\mathbf{v} = \mathbf{G} \cdot \mathrm{bin}(\mathbf{v})$, where $\mathrm{bin}(\mathbf{v}) \in \{0,1\}^k$ denotes the binary representation of $\mathbf{v}$.

For matrix $\mathbf{B} = [\mathbf{B}_0 \mid \mathbf{B}_1] \hookleftarrow U(\mathbb{Z}_q^{n\times m})$, where $\mathbf{B}_0, \mathbf{B}_1 \in \mathbb{Z}_q^{n\times k}$, define the function $h_{\mathbf{B}} : \{0,1\}^k \times \{0,1\}^k \to \{0,1\}^k$ as follows:

$$(\mathbf{u}_0, \mathbf{u}_1) \mapsto h_{\mathbf{B}}(\mathbf{u}_0, \mathbf{u}_1) = \mathrm{bin}\big(\mathbf{B}_0 \cdot \mathbf{u}_0 + \mathbf{B}_1 \cdot \mathbf{u}_1 \bmod q\big).$$

Note that $h_{\mathbf{B}}(\mathbf{u}_0, \mathbf{u}_1) = \mathbf{u} \Leftrightarrow \mathbf{B}_0 \cdot \mathbf{u}_0 + \mathbf{B}_1 \cdot \mathbf{u}_1 = \mathbf{G} \cdot \mathbf{u} \bmod q$. This hash function was shown collision-resistant if $\mathsf{SIVP}_{\widetilde{\mathcal{O}}(n)}$ is hard [2,44]. It allows building Merkle trees to securely accumulate data. In particular, for an ordered set $S = \{\mathbf{d}_0, \ldots, \mathbf{d}_{2^\ell-1}\}$ consisting of $2^\ell \in \mathsf{poly}(n)$ elements of bit-size k, one builds the binary tree of depth ℓ on top of elements of the set, as follows. First, associate the 2^ℓ leaf nodes with elements of the set, with respect to the order of these elements. Then, every non-leaf node of the tree is associated with the hash value of its two children. Finally, output the root of the tree $\mathbf{u} \in \{0,1\}^k$. Note that, the collision resistance of the hash function $h_{\mathbf{B}}$ guarantees that it is infeasible to find a tree path starting from the root $\mathbf{u}$ and ending with $\mathbf{d}' \notin S$.

2.2 Zero-Knowledge Argument Systems and Stern-Like Protocols

We will work with statistical zero-knowledge argument systems, where remain zero-knowledge for *any* cheating verifier while the soundness property only holds against *computationally bounded* cheating provers. More formally, let the set of statements-witnesses $\mathrm{R} = \{(y, w)\} \in \{0,1\}^* \times \{0,1\}^*$ be an NP relation. A two-party game $\langle \mathcal{P}, \mathcal{V} \rangle$ is called an interactive argument system for the relation R with soundness error e if the following conditions hold:

- Completeness. If $(y, w) \in \mathrm{R}$ then $\Pr\big[\langle \mathcal{P}(y, w), \mathcal{V}(y) \rangle = 1\big] = 1$.
- Soundness. If $(y, w) \notin \mathrm{R}$, then $\forall$ PPT $\widehat{\mathcal{P}}$: $\Pr[\langle \widehat{\mathcal{P}}(y, w), \mathcal{V}(y) \rangle = 1] \le e$.

B. Libert et al.

An argument system is called statistical zero-knowledge if there exists a PPT simulator $\mathcal{S}(y)$ having oracle access to any $\widehat{\mathcal{V}}(y)$ and producing a simulated transcript that is statistically close to the one of the real interaction between $\mathcal{P}(y, w)$ and $\widehat{\mathcal{V}}(y)$. A related notion is argument of knowledge, which requires the witness-extended emulation property. For protocols consisting of 3 moves (*i.e.*, commitment-challenge-response), witness-extended emulation is implied by *special soundness* [32], where the latter assumes that there exists a PPT extractor which takes as input a set of valid transcripts with respect to all possible values of the "challenge" to the same "commitment", and outputs w' such that $(y, w') \in R$.

The statistical zero-knowledge arguments of knowledge presented in this work are Stern-like [59] protocols. In particular, they are Σ-protocols in the generalized sense defined in [37] (where 3 valid transcripts are needed for extraction, instead of just 2). The basic protocol consists of 3 moves: commitment, challenge, response. If a statistically hiding and computationally binding string commitment scheme, such as the KTX scheme [39], is employed in the first move, then one obtains a statistical zero-knowledge argument of knowledge (ZKAoK) with perfect completeness, constant soundness error $2/3$. In many applications, the protocol is repeated $\kappa = \omega(\log n)$ times to make the soundness error negligibly small in n.

3 A General Zero-Knowledge Argument of Knowledge

This section presents a general Stern-like zero-knowledge argument system that subsumes all the subsequent constructions in Sects. 4, 5 and 6. Before describing the protocol, we first recall two previous Stern-like techniques that it will use.

3.1 Some Previous Extending-then-Permuting Techniques

Let us recall the techniques for proving knowledge of a single secret bit x, and for proving knowledge of bit product $x_1 \cdot x_2$, from [42,44], respectively. These techniques will be employed in the protocol presented in Sect. 3.2.

For any bit $b \in \{0, 1\}$, denote by $\bar{b}$ the bit $\bar{b} = b + 1 \bmod 2$, and by $\mathsf{ext}_2(b)$ the 2-dimensional vector $(\bar{b}, b) \in \{0, 1\}^2$.

For any bit $c \in \{0, 1\}$, define P_c^2 as the permutation that transforms the integer vector $\mathbf{v} = (v_0, v_1) \in \mathbb{Z}^2$ into $P_c^2(\mathbf{v}) = (v_c, v_{\bar{c}})$. Namely, if $c = 0$ then P_c^2 keeps the arrangement the coordinates of $\mathbf{v}$; or swaps them if $c = 1$. Note that:

$$\mathbf{v} = \mathsf{ext}_2(b) \quad \Longleftrightarrow \quad P_c^2(\mathbf{v}) = \mathsf{ext}_2(b + c \bmod 2). \tag{3}$$

As shown in [44], the equivalence (3) helps proving knowledge of a secret bit x that may appear in several correlated linear equations. To this end, one extends x to $\mathsf{ext}_2(x) \in \{0, 1\}^2$, and permutes the latter using P_c^2, where c is a uniformly random bit. Seeing the permuted vector $\mathsf{ext}_2(x + c \bmod 2)$ convinces the verifier that the original vector $\mathsf{ext}_2(x)$ is well-formed – which in turn implies knowledge of some bit x – while c acts as a "one-time pad" that completely hides x.

To prove that a bit is the product $x_1 \cdot x_2$ of two secret bits, Libert $et\ al.$ [42] introduced the following t echnique. For any two bits b_1, b_2, define

$$\mathsf{ext}_4(b_1, b_2) = (\bar{b}_1 \cdot \bar{b}_2, \bar{b}_1 \cdot b_2, b_1 \cdot \bar{b}_2, b_1 \cdot b_2) \in \{0,1\}^4,$$

which is an extension of the bit product $b_1 \cdot b_2$. Next, define a specific type of permutation associated with two bits, as follows.

For any two bits $c_1, c_2 \in \{0,1\}$, define P_{c_1,c_2}^4 as the permutation that transforms the integer vector $\mathbf{v} = (v_{0,0}, v_{0,1}, v_{1,0}, v_{1,1}) \in \mathbb{Z}^4$ into

$$P_{c_1,c_2}^4(\mathbf{v}) = (v_{c_1,c_2}, v_{c_1,\bar{c}_2}, v_{\bar{c}_1,c_2}, v_{\bar{c}_1,\bar{c}_2}) \in \mathbb{Z}^4.$$

For any bits b_1, b_2, c_1, c_2 and any vector $\mathbf{v} = (v_{0,0}, v_{0,1}, v_{1,0}, v_{1,1}) \in \mathbb{Z}^4$, we have

$$\mathbf{v} = \mathsf{ext}_4(b_1, b_2) \quad \Longleftrightarrow \quad P_{c_1,c_2}^4(\mathbf{v}) = \mathsf{ext}_4(b_1 + c_1 \bmod 2, b_2 + c_2 \bmod 2). \quad (4)$$

As a result, to prove the well-formedness of $x_1 \cdot x_2$, one can extend it to the vector $\mathsf{ext}_4(x_1, x_2)$, permute the latter using P_{c_1,c_2}^4, where c_1, c_2 are uniformly random bits, and send the permuted vector to the verifier who should be convinced that the original vector, i.e., $\mathsf{ext}_4(x_1, x_2)$, is well-formed, while learning nothing else about x_1 and x_2, thanks to the randomness of c_1 and c_2. Furthermore, this sub-protocol can be combined with other Stern-like protocols, where one has to additionally prove that x_1, x_2 satisfy other conditions. This is done by using the same "one-time pads" c_1, c_2 at all occurrences of x_1 and x_2, respectively.

3.2   Our General Protocol

Let $N, \mathsf{m}_1, \mathsf{m}_2$ be positive integers, where $\mathsf{m}_1 \leq N$. Let $T = \{(i_1, j_1), \ldots, (i_{|T|}, j_{|T|})\}$ be a non-empty subset of $[N] \times [N]$. Define $d_1 = 2(\mathsf{m}_1 + \mathsf{m}_2)$, $d_2 = 2N + 4|T|$ and $d = d_1 + d_2$. Let $n_1 \leq d_1, n_2 \leq d_2$ and $q > 2$ be positive integers. The argument system we aim to construct can be summarized as follows.

Public input consists of $\mathbf{g}_1, \ldots, \mathbf{g}_{\mathsf{m}_1}, \mathbf{b}_1, \ldots, \mathbf{b}_{\mathsf{m}_2}, \mathbf{u}_1 \in \mathbb{Z}_q^{n_1}$ and

$$\{h_{\ell,k}\}_{(\ell,k)\in[n_2]\times[N]}; \ \{f_{\ell,t}\}_{(\ell,t)\in[n_2]\times[|T|]}; \ v_1, \ldots, v_{n_2} \in \mathbb{Z}_2.$$

Prover's witness is $(N + \mathsf{m}_2)$-bit vector $\mathbf{s} = (s_1, \ldots, s_{\mathsf{m}_1}, \ldots, s_N, \ldots, s_{N+\mathsf{m}_2})$.

Prover's goal is to prove in zero-knowledge that:

1. The first m_1 bits $s_1, \ldots, s_{\mathsf{m}_1}$ and the last m_2 bits $s_{N+1}, \ldots, s_{N+\mathsf{m}_2}$ satisfy the following linear equation modulo q.

$$\sum_{i\in[\mathsf{m}_1]} \mathbf{g}_i \cdot s_i + \sum_{j\in[\mathsf{m}_2]} \mathbf{b}_j \cdot s_{N+j} = \mathbf{u}_1 \bmod q. \quad (5)$$

2. The first N bits $s_1, \ldots, s_{\mathfrak{m}_1}, \ldots, s_N$ satisfy the following n_2 equations modulo 2 that contain N linear terms and a total of $|T|$ quadratic terms $\{s_{i_t} \cdot s_{j_t}\}_{t=1}^{|T|}$.

$$\forall \ell \in [n_2] : \sum_{k=1}^{N} h_{\ell,k} \cdot s_k + \sum_{t=1}^{|T|} f_{\ell,t} \cdot (s_{i_t} \cdot s_{j_t}) = v_\ell \bmod 2. \tag{6}$$

Looking ahead, all the statements that we will consider in Sects. 4, 5 and 6 can be handled as special cases of the above general protocol, which will serve as an "umbrella" for all of our subsequent constructions.

As a preparation for the protocol construction, let us first introduce a few notations and techniques.

Encoding vector $\mathsf{ENC}(\cdot)$. In the protocol, we will work with a binary vector of length $\mathbf{d}$ that has a very specific constraint determined by $N + \mathfrak{m}_2$ bits. For any $\mathbf{b} = (b_1, \ldots, b_{\mathfrak{m}_1}, \ldots, b_N, \ldots, b_{N+\mathfrak{m}_2}) \in \{0,1\}^{N+\mathfrak{m}_2}$, we denote by $\mathsf{ENC}(\mathbf{b}) \in \{0,1\}^{\mathbf{d}}$ the vector encoding $\mathbf{b}$ as follows:

$$\mathsf{ENC}(\mathbf{b}) = \big(\ \mathsf{ext}_2(b_1)\ \|\ \ldots\ \|\ \mathsf{ext}_2(b_{\mathfrak{m}_1})\ \|\ \mathsf{ext}_2(b_{N+1})\ \|\ \ldots\ \|\ \mathsf{ext}_2(b_{N+\mathfrak{m}_2})$$
$$\|\ \mathsf{ext}_2(b_1)\ \|\ \ldots\ \|\ \mathsf{ext}_2(b_N)\ \|\ \mathsf{ext}_4(b_{i_1}, b_{j_1})\ \|\ \ldots\ \|\ \mathsf{ext}_4(b_{i_{|T|}}, b_{j_{|T|}})\ \big),$$

where $\mathsf{ext}_2(\cdot)$ and $\mathsf{ext}_4(\cdot, \cdot)$ are as in Sect. 3.1.

Permutation Γ. To prove in zero-knowledge of a vector that has the form $\mathsf{ENC}(\cdot)$, we will need to a specific type of permutation. To this end, we associate each $\mathbf{c} = (c_1, \ldots, c_N, \ldots, c_{N+\mathfrak{m}_2}) \in \{0,1\}^{N+\mathfrak{m}_2}$ with a permutation $\Gamma_{\mathbf{c}}$ that acts as follows. When being applied to vector

$$\mathbf{v} = \big(\mathbf{v}_1 \| \ldots \| \mathbf{v}_{\mathfrak{m}_1} \| \mathbf{v}_{\mathfrak{m}_1+1} \| \ldots \| \mathbf{v}_{\mathfrak{m}_1+\mathfrak{m}_2} \| \mathbf{v}_{\mathfrak{m}_1+\mathfrak{m}_2+1} \| \ldots \| \mathbf{v}_{\mathfrak{m}_1+\mathfrak{m}_2+N} \|$$
$$\| \mathbf{v}_{\mathfrak{m}_1+\mathfrak{m}_2+N+1} \| \ldots \| \mathbf{v}_{\mathfrak{m}_1+\mathfrak{m}_2+N+|T|}\big) \in \mathbb{Z}^{\mathbf{d}},$$

whose first $\mathfrak{m}_1 + \mathfrak{m}_2 + N$ blocks are of length 2 and last $|T|$ blocks are of length 4, it transforms these blocks as described below.

$$\mathbf{v}_i \mapsto P_{c_i}^2(\mathbf{v}_i), \forall i \in [\mathfrak{m}_1]; \qquad \mathbf{v}_{\mathfrak{m}_1+j} \mapsto P_{c_{N+j}}^2(\mathbf{v}_{\mathfrak{m}_1+j}), \forall j \in [\mathfrak{m}_2];$$
$$\mathbf{v}_{\mathfrak{m}_1+\mathfrak{m}_2+k} \mapsto P_{c_k}^2(\mathbf{v}_{\mathfrak{m}_1+\mathfrak{m}_2+k}), \forall k \in [N];$$
$$\mathbf{v}_{\mathfrak{m}_1+\mathfrak{m}_2+N+t} \mapsto P_{c_{i_t}, c_{j_t}}^4(\mathbf{v}_{\mathfrak{m}_1+\mathfrak{m}_2+N+t}), \forall t \in [|T|].$$

Based on the equivalences observed in (3)–(4), it can be checked that the following holds. For all $\mathbf{b}, \mathbf{c} \in \{0,1\}^{N+\mathfrak{m}_2}$, all $\mathbf{v} \in \mathbb{Z}^{\mathbf{d}}$,

$$\mathbf{v} = \mathsf{ENC}(\mathbf{b}) \quad \Longleftrightarrow \quad \Gamma_{\mathbf{c}}(\mathbf{v}) = \mathsf{ENC}(\mathbf{b} + \mathbf{c} \bmod 2). \tag{7}$$

Let us now present the protocol, based on the above notations and techniques. First, we perform the following extensions for the secret objects:

$$\begin{cases} \forall k \in [N + \mathfrak{m}_2] : \mathbf{s}_k = \mathsf{ext}_2(s_k) \in \{0,1\}^2 \\ \forall (i_t, j_t) \in T : \mathbf{y}_{i_t, j_t} = \mathsf{ext}_4(s_{i_t}, s_{j_t}) \in \{0,1\}^4. \end{cases} \tag{8}$$

Now, we will perform some transformations regarding Eq. (5). Observe that, for each $i \in [\mathsf{m}_1]$, if we form matrix $\mathbf{G}_i = [\mathbf{0}^{n_1} \mid \mathbf{g}_i] \in \mathbb{Z}_q^{n_1 \times 2}$, then we will have $\mathbf{G}_i \cdot \mathbf{s}_i = \mathbf{g}_i \cdot s_i \bmod q$. Similarly, for each $j \in [\mathsf{m}_2]$, if we form $\mathbf{B}_j = [\mathbf{0}^{n_1} \mid \mathbf{b}_j] \in \mathbb{Z}_q^{n_1 \times 2}$, then we will have $\mathbf{B}_j \cdot \mathbf{s}_{N+j} = \mathbf{b}_j \cdot s_{N+j} \bmod q$.

Therefore, if we build matrix $\mathbf{M}_1 = [\mathbf{G}_1 \mid \ldots \mid \mathbf{G}_{\mathsf{m}_1} \mid \mathbf{B}_1 \mid \ldots \mid \mathbf{B}_{\mathsf{m}_2}] \in \mathbb{Z}_q^{n_1 \times d_1}$, Eq. (5) can be expressed as $\mathbf{M}_1 \cdot \mathbf{w}_1 = \mathbf{u}_1 \bmod q$, where $\mathbf{w}_1 = (\mathbf{s}_1 \| \ldots \| \mathbf{s}_{\mathsf{m}_1} \| \mathbf{s}_{N+1} \| \ldots \| \mathbf{s}_{N+\mathsf{m}_2}) \in \{0,1\}^{d_1}$.

Next, we will unify all the n_2 equations in (6) into just one equation modulo 2, in the following manner. We form matrices

$$\begin{cases} \mathbf{H}_{\ell,k} = [0 \mid h_{\ell,k}] \in \mathbb{Z}_2^{1 \times 2}, \forall (\ell, k) \in [n_2] \times [N]; \\ \mathbf{F}_{\ell,t} = [0 \mid 0 \mid 0 \mid f_{\ell,t}] \in \mathbb{Z}_2^{1 \times 4}, \forall (\ell, t) \in [n_2] \times [|T|], \end{cases}$$

and note that $\mathbf{H}_{\ell,k} \cdot \mathbf{s}_k = h_{\ell,k} \cdot s_k \bmod 2$ and $\mathbf{F}_{\ell,t} \cdot \mathbf{y}_{i_t, j_t} = f_{\ell,t} \cdot (s_{i_j} \cdot s_{i_t}) \bmod 2$. Thus, (6) can be rewritten as:

$$\mathbf{H}_{1,1} \cdot \mathbf{s}_1 + \ldots + \mathbf{H}_{1,N} \cdot \mathbf{s}_N + \mathbf{F}_{1,1} \cdot \mathbf{y}_{i_1, j_1} + \cdots + \mathbf{F}_{1,|T|} \cdot \mathbf{y}_{i_{|T|}, j_{|T|}} = v_1 \bmod 2$$
$$\mathbf{H}_{2,1} \cdot \mathbf{s}_1 + \ldots + \mathbf{H}_{2,N} \cdot \mathbf{s}_N + \mathbf{F}_{2,1} \cdot \mathbf{y}_{i_1, j_1} + \cdots + \mathbf{F}_{2,|T|} \cdot \mathbf{y}_{i_{|T|}, j_{|T|}} = v_2 \bmod 2$$
$$\vdots \qquad\qquad \vdots \qquad\qquad \vdots$$
$$\mathbf{H}_{n_2,1} \cdot \mathbf{s}_1 + \cdots + \mathbf{H}_{n_2,N} \cdot \mathbf{s}_N + \mathbf{F}_{n_2,1} \cdot \mathbf{y}_{i_1, j_1} + \cdots + \mathbf{F}_{n_2,|T|} \cdot \mathbf{y}_{i_{|T|}, j_{|T|}} = v_{n_2} \bmod 2.$$

Letting $\mathbf{u}_2 = (v_1, \ldots, v_{n_2})^\top \in \mathbb{Z}_2^{n_2}$, the above equations can be unified into

$$\mathbf{M}_2 \cdot \mathbf{w}_2 = \mathbf{u}_2 \bmod 2, \tag{9}$$

where matrix $\mathbf{M}_2 \in \mathbb{Z}_2^{n_2 \times d_2}$ is built from $\mathbf{H}_{\ell,k}, \mathbf{F}_{\ell,t}$, and

$$\mathbf{w}_2 = (\mathbf{s}_1 \| \ldots \| \mathbf{s}_N \| \mathbf{y}_{i_1, j_1} \| \ldots \| \mathbf{y}_{i_{|T|}, j_{|T|}}) \in \{0,1\}^{2N+4|T|}.$$

Now, let us construct the vector $\mathbf{w} = (\mathbf{w}_1 \| \mathbf{w}_2) \in \{0,1\}^d$, which has the form

$$(\mathbf{s}_1 \| \ldots \| \mathbf{s}_{\mathsf{m}_1} \| \mathbf{s}_{N+1} \| \ldots \| \mathbf{s}_{N+\mathsf{m}_2} \| \mathbf{s}_1 \| \ldots \| \mathbf{s}_N \| \mathbf{y}_{i_1, j_1} \| \ldots \| \mathbf{y}_{i_{|T|}, j_{|T|}}),$$

where its components blocks are as described in (8). Then, by our above definition of encoding vectors, we have $\mathbf{w} = \mathsf{ENC}(\mathbf{s})$.

The transformations we have done so far allow us to reduce the original statement to proving knowledge of vector $\mathbf{s} \in \{0,1\}^{N+\mathsf{m}_2}$, such that the component vectors $\mathbf{w}_1 \in \{0,1\}^{d_1}$, $\mathbf{w}_2 \in \{0,1\}^{d_2}$ of $\mathbf{w} = \mathsf{ENC}(\mathbf{s})$ satisfy the equations $\mathbf{M}_1 \cdot \mathbf{w}_1 = \mathbf{u}_1 \bmod q$ and $\mathbf{M}_2 \cdot \mathbf{w}_2 = \mathbf{u}_2 \bmod 2$. The derived statement can be handled in Stern's framework, based on the following main ideas.

- To prove that $\mathbf{w} = \mathsf{ENC}(\mathbf{s})$, we will use the equivalence (7). To this end, we sample a uniformly random $\mathbf{c} \in \{0,1\}^{N+\mathsf{m}_2}$ and prove instead that $\Gamma_{\mathbf{c}}(\mathbf{w}) = \mathsf{ENC}(\mathbf{s} + \mathbf{c} \bmod 2)$. Seeing this, the verifier is convinced in ZK that $\mathbf{w}$ indeed satisfies the required constraint, thanks to the randomness of $\mathbf{c}$.

- To prove that equations $\mathbf{M}_1 \cdot \mathbf{w}_1 = \mathbf{u}_1 \bmod q$ and $\mathbf{M}_2 \cdot \mathbf{w}_2 = \mathbf{u}_2 \bmod 2$ hold, we sample uniformly random $\mathbf{r}_1 \in \mathbb{Z}_q^{d_1}$, $\mathbf{r}_2 \in \mathbb{Z}_2^{d_2}$, and demonstrate that

$$\mathbf{M}_1 \cdot (\mathbf{w}_1 + \mathbf{r}_1) = \mathbf{u}_1 + \mathbf{M}_1 \cdot \mathbf{r}_1 \bmod q; \mathbf{M}_2 \cdot (\mathbf{w}_2 + \mathbf{r}_2) = \mathbf{u}_2 + \mathbf{M}_2 \cdot \mathbf{r}_2 \bmod 2.$$

The interactive protocol. Our interactive protocol goes as follows.

- The public input consists of matrices $\mathbf{M}_1, \mathbf{M}_2$ and vectors $\mathbf{u}_1, \mathbf{u}_2$, which are constructed from the original public input, as discussed above.
- The prover's witness consists of the original secret vector $\mathbf{s} \in \{0,1\}^{N+\mathfrak{m}_2}$ and vector $\mathbf{w} = (\mathbf{w}_1 \| \mathbf{w}_2) = \mathsf{ENC}(\mathbf{s})$ derived from $\mathbf{s}$, as described above.

The prover $\mathcal{P}$ and the verifier $\mathcal{V}$ interact as described in Fig. 1. The protocol uses the KTX string commitment scheme COM, which is statistically hiding and computationally binding. For simplicity of presentation, for vectors $\mathbf{w} = (\mathbf{w}_1 \| \mathbf{w}_2) \in \mathbb{Z}^d$ and $\mathbf{r} = (\mathbf{r}_1 \| \mathbf{r}_2) \in \mathbb{Z}^d$, we denote by $\mathbf{w} \boxplus \mathbf{r}$ the operation that computes $\mathbf{z}_1 = \mathbf{w}_1 + \mathbf{r}_1 \bmod q$, $\mathbf{z}_2 = \mathbf{w}_2 + \mathbf{r}_2 \bmod 2$, and outputs d-dimensional integer vector $\mathbf{z} = (\mathbf{z}_1 \| \mathbf{z}_2)$. We note that, for all $\mathbf{c} \in \{0,1\}^{N+\mathfrak{m}_2}$, if $\mathbf{t} = \Gamma_{\mathbf{c}}(\mathbf{w})$ and $\mathbf{s} = \Gamma_{\mathbf{c}}(\mathbf{r})$, then we have $\Gamma_{\mathbf{c}}(\mathbf{w} \boxplus \mathbf{r}) = \mathbf{t} \boxplus \mathbf{s}$.

The described protocol can be seen as an improved version of a Stern-like protocol presented in [45], in the following aspect. In the case $Ch = 1$, instead of sending $\Gamma_{\mathbf{c}}(\mathbf{w}) = \mathsf{ENC}(\mathbf{c}^\star)$ - which costs $d = 2(\mathfrak{m}_1 + \mathfrak{m}_2) + 2N + 4|T|$ bits, we let the prover send $\mathbf{c}^\star$ which enables the verifier to compute the value $\mathsf{ENC}(\mathbf{c}^\star)$ and which costs only $N + \mathfrak{m}_2$ bits. Due to this modification, the results from [45] are not directly applicable to our protocol, and thus, in the proof of Theorem 1, we will analyze the protocol from scratch.

Theorem 1. *Suppose that* COM *is a statistically hiding and computationally binding string commitment. Then, the protocol described above is a statistical* ZKAoK *for the considered relation, with perfect completeness, soundness error* $2/3$ *and communication cost* $\zeta + 2 + N + \mathfrak{m}_2 + 2(\mathfrak{m}_1 + \mathfrak{m}_2)\lceil \log_2 q \rceil + 2N + 4|T|$, *where* $\zeta = \mathcal{O}(n \log n)$ *is the total bit-size of* CMT *and two commitment randomness.*

Proof. We first analyze the completeness and efficiency of the protocol. Then we prove that it is a zero-knowledge argument of knowledge.

Completeness. Suppose that the prover is honest and follows the protocol. Then, observe that the verifier outputs 1 under the following conditions.

1. $\mathbf{t} \boxplus \mathbf{v} = \Gamma_{\mathbf{c}}(\mathbf{z})$. This conditions holds, since $\mathbf{w} = \mathsf{ENC}(\mathbf{s})$, and by equivalence (7), we have $\mathbf{t} = \mathsf{ENC}(\mathbf{c}^\star) = \mathsf{ENC}(\mathbf{s} + \mathbf{c} \bmod 2) = \Gamma_{\mathbf{c}}(\mathsf{ENC}(\mathbf{s})) = \Gamma_{\mathbf{c}}(\mathbf{w})$. Hence, $\mathbf{t} \boxplus \mathbf{v} = \Gamma_{\mathbf{c}}(\mathbf{w}) \boxplus \Gamma_{\mathbf{c}}(\mathbf{r}) = \Gamma_{\mathbf{c}}(\mathbf{w} \boxplus \mathbf{r}) = \Gamma_{\mathbf{c}}(\mathbf{z})$.
2. $\mathbf{M}_1 \cdot \mathbf{x}_1 - \mathbf{u}_1 = \mathbf{M}_1 \cdot \mathbf{r}_1 \bmod q$ and $\mathbf{M}_2 \cdot \mathbf{x}_2 - \mathbf{u}_2 = \mathbf{M}_2 \cdot \mathbf{r}_2 \bmod 2$. These two equations hold, because $\mathbf{x}_1 = \mathbf{w}_1 + \mathbf{r}_1 \bmod q$, $\mathbf{x}_2 = \mathbf{w}_2 + \mathbf{r}_2 \bmod 2$ and $\mathbf{M}_1 \cdot \mathbf{w}_1 = \mathbf{u}_1 \bmod q$, $\mathbf{M}_2 \cdot \mathbf{w}_2 = \mathbf{u}_2 \bmod 2$.

Therefore, the protocol has perfect completeness.

---

1. **Commitment:** $\mathcal{P}$ samples $\mathbf{c} \leftarrow U(\{0,1\}^{N+\mathsf{m}_2})$, $\mathbf{r}_1 \leftarrow U(\mathbb{Z}_q^{d_1})$, $\mathbf{r}_2 \leftarrow U(\mathbb{Z}_2^{d_2})$, and computes $\mathbf{r} = (\mathbf{r}_1 \| \mathbf{r}_2)$, $\mathbf{z} = \mathbf{w} \boxplus \mathbf{r}$.
   Then $\mathcal{P}$ samples randomness ρ_1, ρ_2, ρ_3 for COM, and sends $\mathrm{CMT} = (C_1, C_2, C_3)$ to $\mathcal{V}$, where $C_1 = \mathsf{COM}(\mathbf{c}, \mathbf{M}_1 \cdot \mathbf{r}_1 \bmod q, \mathbf{M}_2 \cdot \mathbf{r}_2 \bmod 2; \rho_1)$, and

$$C_2 = \mathsf{COM}(\Gamma_{\mathbf{c}}(\mathbf{r}); \rho_2), \quad C_3 = \mathsf{COM}(\Gamma_{\mathbf{c}}(\mathbf{z}); \rho_3).$$

2. **Challenge:** $\mathcal{V}$ sends a challenge $Ch \leftarrow U(\{1,2,3\})$ to $\mathcal{P}$.
3. **Response:** $\mathcal{P}$ sends RSP computed according to Ch, as follows:
   - $Ch = 1$: $\mathrm{RSP} = (\mathbf{c}^\star, \mathbf{v}, \rho_2, \rho_3)$, where $\mathbf{c}^\star = \mathbf{s} + \mathbf{c} \bmod 2$ and $\mathbf{v} = \Gamma_{\mathbf{c}}(\mathbf{r})$.
   - $Ch = 2$: $\mathrm{RSP} = (\mathbf{b}, \mathbf{x}, \rho_1, \rho_3)$, where $\mathbf{b} = \mathbf{c}$ and $\mathbf{x} = \mathbf{z}$.
   - $Ch = 3$: $\mathrm{RSP} = (\mathbf{e}, \mathbf{y}, \rho_1, \rho_2)$, where $\mathbf{e} = \mathbf{c}$ and $\mathbf{y} = \mathbf{r}$.

Verification: Receiving RSP, $\mathcal{V}$ proceeds as follows:

- $Ch = 1$: Let $\mathbf{t} = \mathsf{ENC}(\mathbf{c}^\star)$. Check that $C_2 = \mathsf{COM}(\mathbf{v}; \rho_2)$, $C_3 = \mathsf{COM}(\mathbf{t} \boxplus \mathbf{v}; \rho_3)$.
- $Ch = 2$: Parse $\mathbf{x} = (\mathbf{x}_1 \| \mathbf{x}_2)$, where $\mathbf{x}_1 \in \mathbb{Z}_q^{d_1}$ and $\mathbf{x}_2 \in \mathbb{Z}_2^{d_2}$, and check that

$$C_1 = \mathsf{COM}(\mathbf{b}, \mathbf{M}_1 \cdot \mathbf{x}_1 - \mathbf{u}_1 \bmod q, \mathbf{M}_2 \cdot \mathbf{x}_2 - \mathbf{u}_2 \bmod 2; \rho_1), \quad C_3 = \mathsf{COM}(\Gamma_{\mathbf{b}}(\mathbf{x}); \rho_3).$$

- $Ch = 3$: Parse $\mathbf{y} = (\mathbf{y}_1 \| \mathbf{y}_2)$, where $\mathbf{y}_1 \in \mathbb{Z}_q^{d_1}$ and $\mathbf{y}_2 \in \mathbb{Z}_2^{d_2}$, and check that

$$C_1 = \mathsf{COM}(\mathbf{e}, \mathbf{M}_1 \cdot \mathbf{y}_1 \bmod q, \mathbf{M}_2 \cdot \mathbf{y}_2 \bmod 2; \rho_1), \quad C_2 = \mathsf{COM}(\Gamma_{\mathbf{e}}(\mathbf{y}); \rho_2).$$

In each case, $\mathcal{V}$ outputs 1 if and only if all the conditions hold.

Fig. 1. The interactive protocol.

Efficiency. Both prover and verifier only have to carry out $\mathcal{O}(d)$ simple operations modulo q and modulo 2. In terms of communication cost, apart from ζ bits needed for transferring CMT and two commitment randomness, the prover has to send a vector in $\{0,1\}^{N+\mathsf{m}_2}$, a vector in $\mathbb{Z}_q^{d_1}$ and a vector in $\mathbb{Z}_2^{d_2}$, while the verifier only has to send 2 bits. Thus, the total cost is $\zeta + 2 + N + \mathsf{m}_2 + 2(\mathsf{m}_1 + \mathsf{m}_2)\lceil \log_2 q \rceil + 2N + 4|T|$ bits. (When COM is the KTX string commitment scheme, we have $\zeta = 3n\lceil \log_2 q \rceil + 2m$.)

Zero-Knowledge Property. We construct a PPT simulator SIM interacting with a (possibly dishonest) verifier $\widehat{\mathcal{V}}$, such that, given only the public input, it outputs with probability negligibly close to $2/3$ a simulated transcript that is statistically close to the one produced by the honest prover in the real interaction.

The simulator first chooses a random $\overline{Ch} \in \{1,2,3\}$ as a prediction of the challenge value that $\widehat{\mathcal{V}}$ will *not* choose.

Case $\overline{Ch} = 1$: SIM uses linear algebra over $\mathbb{Z}_q$ and $\mathbb{Z}_2$ to find $\mathbf{w}_1' \in \mathbb{Z}_q^{d_1}$ and $\mathbf{w}_2' \in \mathbb{Z}_2^{d_2}$ s.t. $\mathbf{M}_1 \cdot \mathbf{w}_1' = \mathbf{u}_1 \bmod q$ and $\mathbf{M}_2 \cdot \mathbf{w}_2' = \mathbf{u}_2 \bmod 2$. Let $\mathbf{w}' = (\mathbf{w}_1' \| \mathbf{w}_2')$.

Next, it samples $\mathbf{c} \leftarrow U(\{0,1\}^{N+\mathsf{m}_2})$, $\mathbf{r}_1 \leftarrow U(\mathbb{Z}_q^{d_1})$, $\mathbf{r}_2 \leftarrow U(\mathbb{Z}_2^{d_2})$, and computes $\mathbf{r} = (\mathbf{r}_1 \| \mathbf{r}_2)$, $\mathbf{z}' = \mathbf{w}' \boxplus \mathbf{r}$. Then, it samples randomness ρ_1, ρ_2, ρ_3 for COM and sends the commitment $\mathrm{CMT} = (C'_1, C'_2, C'_3)$ to $\widehat{\mathcal{V}}$, where

$$C'_1 = \mathsf{COM}(\mathbf{c}, \mathbf{M}_1 \cdot \mathbf{r}_1 \bmod q, \mathbf{M}_2 \cdot \mathbf{r}_2 \bmod 2; \rho_1),$$
$$C'_2 = \mathsf{COM}(\varGamma_{\mathbf{c}}(\mathbf{r}); \rho_2), \quad C'_3 = \mathsf{COM}(\varGamma_{\mathbf{c}}(\mathbf{z}'); \rho_3).$$

Receiving a challenge Ch from $\widehat{\mathcal{V}}$, the simulator responds as follows:

- If $Ch = 1$: Output $\bot$ and abort.
- If $Ch = 2$: Send $\mathrm{RSP} = (\mathbf{c}, \mathbf{z}', \rho_1, \rho_3)$.
- If $Ch = 3$: Send $\mathrm{RSP} = (\mathbf{c}, \mathbf{r}, \rho_1, \rho_2)$.

Case $\overline{Ch} = 2$: SIM samples $\mathbf{s}' \leftarrow U(\{0,1\}^{N+\mathsf{m}_2})$ and computes $\mathbf{w}' = \mathsf{ENC}(\mathbf{s}')$. Next, it picks $\mathbf{c} \leftarrow U(\{0,1\}^{N+\mathsf{m}_2})$, and $\mathbf{r}_1 \leftarrow U(\mathbb{Z}_q^{d_1}), \mathbf{r}_2 \leftarrow U(\mathbb{Z}_2^{d_2})$, and computes $\mathbf{r} = (\mathbf{r}_1 \| \mathbf{r}_2)$, $\mathbf{z}' = \mathbf{w}' \boxplus \mathbf{r}$. Then, it samples randomness ρ_1, ρ_2, ρ_3 for COM and sends the commitment $\mathrm{CMT} = (C'_1, C'_2, C'_3)$ to $\widehat{\mathcal{V}}$, where

$$C'_1 = \mathsf{COM}(\mathbf{c}, \mathbf{M}_1 \cdot \mathbf{r}_1 \bmod q, \mathbf{M}_2 \cdot \mathbf{r}_2 \bmod 2; \ \rho_1),$$
$$C'_2 = \mathsf{COM}(\varGamma_{\mathbf{c}}(\mathbf{r}); \rho_2), \quad C'_3 = \mathsf{COM}(\varGamma_{\mathbf{c}}(\mathbf{z}'); \rho_3).$$

Receiving a challenge Ch from $\widehat{\mathcal{V}}$, the simulator responds as follows:

- If $Ch = 1$: Send $\mathrm{RSP} = (\mathbf{s}' + \mathbf{c} \bmod 2, \varGamma_{\mathbf{c}}(\mathbf{r}), \rho_2, \rho_3)$.
- If $Ch = 2$: Output $\bot$ and abort.
- If $Ch = 3$: Send $\mathrm{RSP} = (\mathbf{c}, \mathbf{r}, \rho_1, \rho_2)$.

Case $\overline{Ch} = 3$: SIM prepares $\mathrm{CMT} = (C'_1, C'_2, C'_3)$ as in the case $\overline{Ch} = 2$ above, except that C'_1 is computed as

$$C'_1 = \mathsf{COM}(\mathbf{c}, \mathbf{M}_1 \cdot (\mathbf{w}'_1 + \mathbf{r}_1) - \mathbf{u}_1 \bmod q, \mathbf{M}_2 \cdot (\mathbf{w}'_2 + \mathbf{r}_2) - \mathbf{u}_2 \bmod 2; \ \rho_1).$$

Receiving a challenge Ch from $\widehat{\mathcal{V}}$, it responds as follows:

- If $Ch = 1$: Send RSP computed as in the case $(\overline{Ch} = 2, Ch = 1)$.
- If $Ch = 2$: Send RSP computed as in the case $(\overline{Ch} = 1, Ch = 2)$.
- If $Ch = 3$: Output $\bot$ and abort.

In all the above cases, since COM is statistically hiding, the distribution of the commitment CMT and that of the challenge Ch from $\mathcal{V}$ are statistically close to those of the real interaction. Hence, the probability that the simulator outputs $\bot$ is negligibly far from $1/3$. Moreover, whenever the simulator does not halt, it provides an accepting transcript, of which the distribution is statistically close to that of the prover in a real interaction. We thus described a simulator that can successfully emulate the honest prover with probability negligibly close to $2/3$.

Argument of Knowledge. Suppose that we have $\mathrm{RSP}_1 = (\mathbf{c}^\star, \mathbf{v}, \rho_2^{(1)}, \rho_3^{(1)})$, $\mathrm{RSP}_2 = (\mathbf{b}, \mathbf{x}, \rho_1^{(2)}, \rho_3^{(2)})$, and $\mathrm{RSP}_3 = (\mathbf{e}, \mathbf{y}, \rho_1^{(3)}, \rho_2^{(3)})$, which are accepting transcripts for the three possible values of the challenge and the same commitment

$\mathsf{CMT} = (C_1, C_2, C_3)$. Let us parse $\mathbf{x}$ and $\mathbf{y}$ as $\mathbf{x} = (\mathbf{x}_1 \| \mathbf{x}_2)$, $\mathbf{y} = (\mathbf{y}_1 \| \mathbf{y}_2)$, where $\mathbf{x}_1, \mathbf{y}_1 \in \mathbb{Z}_q^{d_1}$ and $\mathbf{x}_2, \mathbf{y}_2 \in \mathbb{Z}_2^{d_2}$. The validity of the given responses implies that:

$$\begin{cases} C_1 = \mathsf{COM}(\mathbf{b}, \mathbf{M}_1 \cdot \mathbf{x}_1 - \mathbf{u}_1 \bmod q, \mathbf{M}_2 \cdot \mathbf{x}_2 - \mathbf{u}_2 \bmod 2; \rho_1^{(2)}); \\ C_1 = \mathsf{COM}(\mathbf{e}, \mathbf{M}_1 \cdot \mathbf{y}_1 \bmod q, \mathbf{M}_2 \cdot \mathbf{y}_2 \bmod 2; \rho_1^{(3)}); \\ C_2 = \mathsf{COM}(\mathbf{v}; \rho_2^{(1)}) = \mathsf{COM}(\Gamma_{\mathbf{e}}(\mathbf{y}); \rho_2^{3}); \\ C_3 = \mathsf{COM}(\mathbf{t} \boxplus \mathbf{v}; \rho_3^{(1)}) = \mathsf{COM}(\Gamma_{\mathbf{b}}(\mathbf{x}); \rho_3^{(2)}), \end{cases}$$

where $\mathbf{t} = \mathsf{ENC}(\mathbf{c}^\star)$. Since COM is computationally binding, we can deduce that:

$$\mathbf{b} = \mathbf{e}; \quad \mathbf{v} = \Gamma_{\mathbf{e}}(\mathbf{y}); \quad \mathbf{t} \boxplus \mathbf{v} = \Gamma_{\mathbf{b}}(\mathbf{x});$$
$$\mathbf{M}_1 \cdot \mathbf{x}_1 - \mathbf{u}_1 = \mathbf{M}_1 \cdot \mathbf{y}_1 \bmod q; \quad \mathbf{M}_2 \cdot \mathbf{x}_2 - \mathbf{u}_2 = \mathbf{M}_2 \cdot \mathbf{y}_2 \bmod 2.$$

Let $\mathbf{s}' = \mathbf{c}^\star + \mathbf{e} \bmod 2$ and $\mathbf{w}' = [\Gamma_{\mathbf{e}}]^{-1}(\mathbf{t})$. Since $\mathbf{t} = \mathsf{ENC}(\mathbf{c}^\star)$, by equivalence (7), we have that $\mathbf{w}' = \mathsf{ENC}(\mathbf{s}')$. Furthermore, note that $\Gamma_{\mathbf{e}}(\mathbf{w}') \boxplus \Gamma_{\mathbf{e}}(\mathbf{y}) = \Gamma_{\mathbf{e}}(\mathbf{x})$, which implies that $\mathbf{w}' \boxplus \mathbf{y} = \mathbf{x}$.

Now, parse $\mathbf{w}'$ as $\mathbf{w}' = (\mathbf{w}_1' \| \mathbf{w}_2')$, where $\mathbf{w}_1' \in \{0,1\}^{d_1}$ and $\mathbf{w}_2' \in \{0,1\}^{d_2}$. Then, we have $\mathbf{w}_1' + \mathbf{y}_1 = \mathbf{x}_1 \bmod q$, $\mathbf{w}_2' + \mathbf{y}_2 = \mathbf{x}_2 \bmod 2$, and

$$\mathbf{M}_1 \cdot \mathbf{w}_1' = \mathbf{M}_1 \cdot \mathbf{x}_1 - \mathbf{M}_1 \cdot \mathbf{y}_1 = \mathbf{u}_1 \bmod q;$$
$$\mathbf{M}_2 \cdot \mathbf{w}_2' = \mathbf{M}_2 \cdot \mathbf{x}_2 - \mathbf{M}_2 \cdot \mathbf{y}_2 = \mathbf{u}_2 \bmod 2.$$

This implies $\mathbf{w}' = (\mathbf{w}_1' \| \mathbf{w}_2') = \mathsf{ENC}(\mathbf{s}')$, as well as $\mathbf{M}_1 \cdot \mathbf{w}_1' = \mathbf{u}_1 \bmod q$ and $\mathbf{M}_2 \cdot \mathbf{w}_2' = \mathbf{u}_2 \bmod 2$. Let $\mathbf{s}' = (s_1', \ldots, s_{m_1}', \ldots, s_N', \ldots, s_{N+m_2}') \in \{0,1\}^{N+m_2}$. By reversing the transformations, it can be seen that the bits of $\mathbf{s}'$ satisfy

$$\sum_{i \in [m_1]} \mathbf{g}_i \cdot s_i' + \sum_{j \in [m_2]} \mathbf{b}_j \cdot s_{N+j}' = \mathbf{u}_1 \bmod q;$$

$$\forall \ell \in [n_2]: \quad \sum_{k=1}^{N} h_{\ell,k} \cdot s_k' + \sum_{t=1}^{|T|} f_{\ell,t} \cdot (s_{i_t}' \cdot s_{j_t}') = v_\ell \bmod 2.$$

Hence, we have extracted $\mathbf{s}' = (s_1', \ldots, s_{m_1}', \ldots, s_N', \ldots, s_{N+m_2}')$, which is a valid witness for the considered relation. $\square$

As we mentioned earlier, all the statements we will consider in the next sections will be reduced into instances of the presented general protocol. For each of them, we will employ the same strategy. First, we demonstrate that the considered statement can be expressed as an equation modulo q of the form (5) and equations modulo 2 of the form (6). This implies that we can run the general protocol to handle the statement, and obtain a statistical ZKAoK via Theorem 1. Next, as the complexity of the protocol depends on $m_1 + m_2, N, |T|$, we count these respective numbers in order to evaluate its communication cost.

4 Zero-Knowledge Arguments for Integer Additions

This section presents our lattice-based ZK argument system for additive relation among committed integers. Let n be the security parameter, and let

$L = \mathsf{poly}(n)$. Given KTX commitments to L-bit integers $X = (x_{L-1}, \ldots, x_0)_2$, $Y = (y_{L-1}, \ldots, y_0)_2$ and $(L+1)$-bit integer $Z = (z_L, z_{L-1}, \ldots, z_0)_2$, the protocol allows the prover to convince the verifier in ZK that $X + Y = Z$ over $\mathbb{Z}$.

As discussed in Sects. 1 and 2.1, using different flavors of the KTX commitment scheme, we can commit to all the bits of X, Y, Z at once or a bit-by-bit fashion. Both approaches are both compatible with (and independent of) our ZK techniques. Depending on which commitments we use, we obtain different give trade-offs in terms of parameters, key sizes, security assumptions and communication costs. In the following, we will use the former variant, which yields communication complexity $\widetilde{\mathcal{O}}(L + n)$. Our protocol can be easily adjusted to handle the bit-wise commitment variant, which yields complexity $\widetilde{\mathcal{O}}(L \cdot n)$, but allows smaller parameters, smaller keys and weaker lattice assumption.

Commitments. Let a prime $q = \widetilde{\mathcal{O}}(\sqrt{L} \cdot n)$ and $m = n(\lceil \log_2 q \rceil + 3)$. Choose a commitment key $(\mathbf{a}_0, \ldots, \mathbf{a}_{L-1}, \mathbf{a}_L, \mathbf{b}_1, \ldots, \mathbf{b}_m) \hookleftarrow U(\mathbb{Z}_q^{n \times (L+m+1)})$. To commit to X, Y, Z, sample $r_{i,1}, \ldots, r_{i,m} \hookleftarrow U(\{0,1\})$, for $i \in \{1, 2, 3\}$, and compute

$$\begin{cases} \sum_{i=0}^{L-1} \mathbf{a}_i \cdot x_i + \sum_{j=1}^{m} \mathbf{b}_j \cdot r_{1,j} = \mathbf{c}_x \bmod q; \\ \sum_{i=0}^{L-1} \mathbf{a}_i \cdot y_i + \sum_{j=1}^{m} \mathbf{b}_j \cdot r_{2,j} = \mathbf{c}_y \bmod q; \\ \sum_{i=0}^{L} \mathbf{a}_i \cdot z_i + \sum_{j=1}^{m} \mathbf{b}_j \cdot r_{3,j} = \mathbf{c}_z \bmod q, \end{cases} \tag{10}$$

and output commitments $\mathbf{c}_x, \mathbf{c}_y, \mathbf{c}_z \in \mathbb{Z}_q^n$. The scheme relies on the worst-case hardness of SIVP_γ, for $\gamma = \widetilde{\mathcal{O}}(\sqrt{L} \cdot n)$.

Before presenting our protocol, we note that the three equations (10) can be unified into one equation of the form

$$\sum_{i=0}^{L-1} \mathbf{a}_i^{(1)} \cdot x_i + \sum_{i=0}^{L-1} \mathbf{a}_i^{(2)} \cdot y_i + \sum_{i=0}^{L} \mathbf{a}_i^{(3)} \cdot z_i + \sum_{(i,j) \in [3] \times [m]} \mathbf{b}_j^{(i)} \cdot r_{i,j} = \mathbf{c} \bmod q, \tag{11}$$

where $\mathbf{a}_i^{(1)}, \mathbf{a}_i^{(2)}, \mathbf{a}_i^{(3)} \in \mathbb{Z}_q^{3n}$ are extensions of $\mathbf{a}_i$; $\mathbf{b}_j^{(1)}, \mathbf{b}_j^{(2)}, \mathbf{b}_j^{(3)} \in \mathbb{Z}_q^{3n}$ are extensions of $\mathbf{b}_j$; and $\mathbf{c} = (\mathbf{c}_x \| \mathbf{c}_y \| \mathbf{c}_z) \in \mathbb{Z}_q^{3n}$. Having done this simple transformation, we observe that Eq. (11) does have the form captured by Eq. (5) in the protocol we put forward in Sect. 3. Here, the secret bits contained in the equations are the bits of X, Y, Z and those of the commitment randomness.

Proving Integer Additions. At a high level, our main idea consists in translating the addition operation $X + Y$ over the integers into the binary addition operation *with carries* of $(x_{L-1}, \ldots, x_0)_2$ and $(y_{L-1}, \ldots, y_0)_2$ and proving that this process indeed yields result $(z_L, z_{L-1}, \ldots, z_0)_2$. For the latter statement, we capture the whole process as equations modulo 2 that contain linear and quadratic terms, and show how this statement, when combined with the commitment equations (11), reduces to an instance of the protocol of Sect. 3.

Let us first consider the addition of two bits x, y with carry-in bit c_{in}. Let the output be bit z and the carry-out bit be c_{out}. Then, observe that the relation among $x, y, z, c_{\mathsf{in}}, c_{\mathsf{out}} \in \{0, 1\}$ is captured by equations

$$\begin{cases} z = x + y + c_{\mathsf{in}} \bmod 2 \\ c_{\mathsf{out}} = x \cdot y + z \cdot c_{\mathsf{in}} + c_{\mathsf{in}} \bmod 2 \end{cases} \Longleftrightarrow \begin{cases} z + x + y + c_{\mathsf{in}} = 0 \bmod 2 \\ c_{\mathsf{out}} + x \cdot y + z \cdot c_{\mathsf{in}} + c_{\mathsf{in}} = 0 \bmod 2. \end{cases}$$

Therefore, the addition with carries of $(x_{L-1}, \ldots, x_0)_2$ and $(y_{L-1}, \ldots, y_0)_2$ results in $(z_L, z_{L-1}, \ldots, z_0)_2$ if and only if the following equations hold:

$$\begin{cases} z_0 + x_0 + y_0 = 0 \bmod 2; \\ c_1 + x_0 \cdot y_0 = 0 \bmod 2; \\ z_1 + x_1 + y_1 + c_1 = 0 \bmod 2; \\ c_2 + x_1 \cdot y_1 + z_1 \cdot c_1 + c_1 = 0 \bmod 2; \\ \quad \vdots \\ z_{L-1} + x_{L-1} + y_{L-1} + c_{L-1} = 0 \bmod 2; \\ z_L + x_{L-1} \cdot y_{L-1} + z_{L-1} \cdot c_{L-1} + c_{L-1} = 0 \bmod 2. \end{cases} \qquad (12)$$

Here, for each $i \in \{1, \ldots, L-1\}$, c_i denotes the carry-out bit at the i-th step which is also the carry-in bit at the $(i+1)$-th step. (The last carry-out bit is z_L.)

Now, observe that, together with Eq. (11), the $2L$ equations in (12) lead us to an instance of the protocol of Sect. 3. It indeed fits the pattern if we let $N := 4L$, $\mathfrak{m}_1 := 3L + 1$, $\mathfrak{m}_2 := 3m$ and denote the ordered tuple of $N + \mathfrak{m}_2$ secret bits $(x_0, \ldots, x_{L-1}, y_0, \ldots, y_{L-1}, z_0, \ldots, z_L, c_1, \ldots, c_{L-1}, r_{1,1}, \ldots, r_{3,m})$ by $(s_1, \ldots, s_{N+\mathfrak{m}_2})$. Then, note that the first $\mathfrak{m}_1$ bits $s_1, \ldots, s_{\mathfrak{m}_1}$ and the last $\mathfrak{m}_2$ bits $s_{N+1}, \ldots, s_{N+\mathfrak{m}_2}$ satisfy the linear equation modulo q from (11), while the first N bits $s_1, \ldots, s_N$ satisfy the equations modulo 2 in (12), which contain N linear terms and a total of $|T| := 2L - 1$ quadratic terms, i.e.:

$$x_0 \cdot y_0, \ x_1 \cdot y_1, \ z_1 \cdot c_1, \ \ldots, \ x_{L-1} \cdot y_{L-1}, \ z_{L-1} \cdot c_{L-1}.$$

As a result, our ZK argument system can be obtained from the protocol constructed in Sect. 3. The protocol is a statistical ZKAoK assuming the security of two variants of the KTX commitment scheme: the variant used to commit to X, Y, Z - which relies on the hardness of $\mathsf{SIVP}_{\widetilde{\mathcal{O}}(\sqrt{L} \cdot n)}$, and the commitment COM used in the interaction between two parties - which relies on the hardness of $\mathsf{SIVP}_{\widetilde{\mathcal{O}}(n)}$. By Theorem 1, each execution of the protocol has perfect completeness, soundness error $2/3$ and communication cost

$$\mathcal{O}(n \log n) + 3m + 2(3L + 1 + 3m)\lceil \log_2 q \rceil + 20L$$

bits, where $\mathcal{O}(n \log n)$ is the total bit-size of 3 KTX commitments (sent by the prover in the first move) and 2 commitment randomness. Here, it is important to note that the cost of proving knowledge of valid openings for $\mathbf{c}_x, \mathbf{c}_y, \mathbf{c}_z$ is $\mathcal{O}(n \log n) + 3m + 2(3L + 1 + 3m)\lceil \log_2 q \rceil$ bits. Thus, the actual cost for proving the addition relation is $20L$ bits.

We further remark that the protocol can easily be adapted to less challenging situations such as: (i) The bit-size of the sum Z is public known to be exactly L (instead of $L+1$); (ii) Not all elements X, Y, Z need to be hidden and committed.

Indeed, in those scenarios, our strategy of expressing the considered relations as equations modulo q and modulo 2 easily goes through. Moreover, it even simplifies the resulting protocols and reduces their complexity because the number of secret bits to deal with is smaller than in the above protocol.

5 Logarithmic-Size Arguments for Range Membership and Set Non-Membership

We present two applications of our zero-knowledge protocol for integer additions from Sect. 4: range membership and set non-membership arguments.

5.1 Range Membership Arguments

Our range arguments build on the integer addition protocol of Sect. 4. We consider the problem of proving in ZK that a committed integer X satisfies $X \in [\alpha, \beta]$, i.e., $\alpha \leq X \leq \beta$, for publicly known integers α, β.

Let $L = \mathsf{poly}(n)$, $q = \widetilde{\mathcal{O}}(\sqrt{L} \cdot n)$ and $m = n(\lceil \log_2 q \rceil + 3)$. Suppose that L-bit integer $X = (x_{L-1}, \ldots, x_0)_2$ is committed via the KTX commitment scheme, using a public commitment key $\mathbf{a}_0, \ldots, \mathbf{a}_{L-1}, \mathbf{b}_1, \ldots, \mathbf{b}_m \in \mathbb{Z}_q^n$ and randomness $r_1, \ldots, r_m \in \{0, 1\}$. Namely, the commitment $\mathbf{c} \in \mathbb{Z}_q^n$ is computed as

$$\sum_{i=0}^{L-1} \mathbf{a}_i \cdot x_i + \sum_{j=1}^{m} \mathbf{b}_j \cdot r_j = \mathbf{c} \bmod q. \tag{13}$$

Our goal is to prove in ZK that $X \in [\alpha, \beta]$, for publicly given L-bit integers $\alpha = (\alpha_{L-1}, \ldots, \alpha_0)_2$ and $\beta = (\beta_{L-1}, \ldots, \beta_0)_2$.

The main idea. We observe that X satisfies $\alpha \leq X \leq \beta$ if and only if there exist non-negative L-bit integers Y, Z such that

$$\alpha + Y = X \quad \text{and} \quad X + Z = \beta. \tag{14}$$

We thus reduce the task of proving $X \in [\alpha, \beta[$ to proving two addition relations among integers, which can be achieved using the techniques of Sect. 4. To this end, it suffices to demonstrate that the relations among the secret bits of X, Y, Z and public bits of α, β can be expressed as equations modulo 2 of the form (6).

The underlying equations modulo 2. Let the bits of integers Y, Z be $(y_{L-1}, \ldots, y_0)_2$ and $(z_{L-1}, \ldots, z_0)_2$, respectively. The addition $\alpha + Y = X$ over $\mathbb{Z}$, when viewed as a binary addition with carries, can be expressed as the following $2L$ equations modulo 2 which contain $L - 1$ quadratic terms $x_1 \cdot c_1, \ldots, x_{L-1} \cdot c_{L-1}$.

$$\begin{cases} x_0 + y_0 = \alpha_0 \bmod 2; \\ c_1 + \alpha_0 \cdot y_0 = 0 \bmod 2; & /\!/ \text{ First carry-bit} \\ x_1 + y_1 + c_1 = \alpha_1 \bmod 2; \\ c_2 + \alpha_1 \cdot y_1 + x_1 \cdot c_1 + c_1 = 0 \bmod 2; & /\!/ \text{ Second carry-bit} \\ \quad \vdots \\ c_{L-1} + \alpha_{L-2} \cdot y_{L-2} + x_{L-2} \cdot c_{L-2} + c_{L-2} = 0 \bmod 2; \\ x_{L-1} + y_{L-1} + c_{L-1} = \alpha_{L-1} \bmod 2; \\ \alpha_{L-1} \cdot y_{L-1} + x_{L-1} \cdot c_{L-1} + c_{L-1} = 0 \bmod 2. & /\!/ \text{ Last carry-bit is } 0. \end{cases} \quad (15)$$

The relation $X + Z = \beta$ is handled similarly. We obtain the following $2L$ equations modulo 2, which contain L quadratic terms $x_0 \cdot z_0, x_1 \cdot z_1, \ldots,$ $x_{L-1} \cdot z_{L-1}$.

$$\begin{cases} x_0 + z_0 = \beta_0 \bmod 2; \\ e_1 + x_0 \cdot z_0 = 0 \bmod 2; & /\!/ \text{ First carry-bit} \\ x_1 + z_1 + e_1 = \beta_1 \bmod 2; \\ e_2 + x_1 \cdot z_1 + \beta_1 \cdot e_1 + e_1 = 0 \bmod 2; & /\!/ \text{ Second carry-bit} \\ \quad \vdots \\ e_{L-1} + x_{L-2} \cdot z_{L-2} + \beta_{L-2} \cdot e_{L-2} + e_{L-2} = 0 \bmod 2; \\ x_{L-1} + z_{L-1} + e_{L-1} = \beta_{L-1} \bmod 2; \\ x_{L-1} \cdot z_{L-1} + \beta_{L-1} \cdot e_{L-1} + e_{L-1} = 0 \bmod 2. & /\!/ \text{ Last carry-bit is } 0. \end{cases} \quad (16)$$

Combining (15) and (16), we obtain a system of $4L$ equations modulo 2, which contain $N := 5L - 2$ linear terms

$$x_0, \ldots, x_{L-1}, y_0, \ldots, y_{L-1}, z_0, \ldots, z_{L-1}, c_1, \ldots, c_{L-1}, e_1, \ldots, e_{L-1},$$

and a total of $|T| = 2L - 1$ quadratic terms

$$x_1 \cdot c_1, \ldots, x_{L-1} \cdot c_{L-1}, x_0 \cdot z_0, x_1 \cdot z_1, \ldots, x_{L-1} \cdot z_{L-1}.$$

Putting it altogether. Based on the above transformations, we have translated the task of proving that committed integer X satisfies $X \in [\alpha, \beta]$ to proving knowledge of $N + \mathsf{m}_2 = 5L - 2 + m$ secret bits

$$x_0, \ldots, x_{L-1}, y_0, \ldots, y_{L-1}, z_0, \ldots, z_{L-1}, c_1, \ldots, c_{L-1}, e_1, \ldots, e_{L-1}, r_1, \ldots, r_m, \quad (17)$$

where the first $\mathsf{m}_1 = L$ bits and the last $\mathsf{m}_2 = m$ bits satisfy Eq. (13) modulo q, while the first $N = 5L - 2$ bits satisfy a system of equations modulo 2 containing N linear terms and $|T| = 2L - 1$ quadratic terms. In other words, we have reduced the considered statement to an instance of the general protocol of Sect. 3.2. By running the latter with the witness described in (17), we obtain a statistical ZKAoK hardness of based on the hardness of SIVP_γ with factor $\gamma \leq \widetilde{\mathcal{O}}(\sqrt{L} \cdot n)$.

Each execution of the protocol has perfect completeness, soundness error $2/3$ and communication cost

$$\mathcal{O}(n \log n) + m + 2(L + m)\lceil \log_2 q \rceil + 23L$$

bits, where $\mathcal{O}(n \log n)$ is the total bit-size of 3 KTX commitments (sent by the prover in the first move) and 2 commitment randomness. Here, the cost of proving knowledge of a valid opening for $\mathbf{c}$ is $\mathcal{O}(n \log n) + m + 2(L + m)\lceil \log_2 q \rceil$ bits. The actual cost for proving the range membership thus amounts to $23L$ bits.

Variants. Our techniques can be easily adapted to handle other variants of range membership arguments. To prove a strict inequality, e.g., $X < \beta$ for a given β, we can simply prove that $X \leq \beta - 1$ using the above approach. In the case of hidden ranges, e.g., when we need prove that $Y < X < Z$ where X, Y, Z are all committed, then we proceed by proving the existence of non-negative L-bit integers Y_1, Z_1 such that $Y + Y_1 + 1 = X$ and $X + Z_1 + 1 = Z$. This can be done by executing two instances of the protocol for addition relation among committed integers from Sect. 4.

5.2 Set Non-Membership Arguments

In this section, we construct a protocol allowing to prove that a committed element is not in a public set Set. The goal is to do this without relying on a trusted third party to approve the description of Set by signing its elements or any other means. To this end, we combine our protocols for integer addition and inequalities with arguments of knowledge of a path in a Merkle tree [44]. While Merkle trees were introduced for proving set membership, we (somewhat counter-intuitively) use them for dual purposes.

For security parameter n, choose $q = \widetilde{\mathcal{O}}(n)$, $k = n\lceil \log_2 q \rceil$ and $m = 2k$. Sample uniformly random matrices $\mathbf{A}, \mathbf{B}_0, \mathbf{B}_1 \in \mathbb{Z}_q^{n \times k}$, and denote their columns as $\mathbf{a}_0, \ldots, \mathbf{a}_{k-1}, \mathbf{b}_{0,0}, \ldots, \mathbf{b}_{0,k-1}, \mathbf{b}_{1,0}, \ldots, \mathbf{b}_{1,k-1} \in \mathbb{Z}_q^n$. These vectors will serve as public key for the KTX commitment scheme with k-bit committed values, while matrix $\mathbf{B} = [\mathbf{B}_0 \mid \mathbf{B}_1] \in \mathbb{Z}_q^{n \times 2k}$ will also serve as the public key for the Merkle tree from [43]. Let $\mathbf{G} \in \mathbb{Z}_q^{n \times k}$ be the "powers-of-2" matrix of Sect. 2.1.

Let $X = (x_{k-1}, \ldots, x_0)_2$ be a k-bit integer, and let $\mathbf{c} \in \mathbb{Z}_q^n$ be a KTX commitment to X, i.e., we have the following equation modulo q:

$$\sum_{i=0}^{k-1} \mathbf{a}_i \cdot x_i + \sum_{(i,j) \in \{0,1\} \times k} \mathbf{b}_{i,j} \cdot r_{i,j} = \mathbf{c} \bmod q, \tag{18}$$

where bits $r_{0,1}, \ldots, r_{1,k} \in \{0,1\}$ are the commitment randomness.

Let Set $= \{S_1, \ldots, S_M\}$ be a public set containing $M = \mathsf{poly}(n)$ integers of bit-size k, where $S_1 < S_2 < \ldots < S_M$. We wish to prove in ZK that an integer X, which has been committed to via $\mathbf{c} \in \mathbb{Z}_q^n$, does not belong to Set. We aim at communication complexity $\mathcal{O}(\log M)$, so that the protocol scales well for large sets. To this end, we will use the lattice-based Merkle hash tree from [44].

Without loss of generality, assuming that $M = 2^\ell - 2$ for some positive integer ℓ.[3] For each $i = 0, \ldots, M$, let $\mathbf{s}_i \in \{0,1\}^k$ be the binary-vector representation of S_i. Let $\mathbf{s}_0 = (0, \ldots, 0)$ and $\mathbf{s}_{M+1} = (1, \ldots, 1)$ be the all-zero and all-one vectors of length k, which represent 0 and $2^k - 1$, the smallest and the largest non-negative integers of bit-size k, respectively. Using the SIS-based hash function $h_{\mathbf{B}}$ (see Sect. 2.1), we build a Merkle tree of depth ℓ on top of 2^ℓ vectors $\mathbf{s}_0, \mathbf{s}_1, \ldots, \mathbf{s}_M, \mathbf{s}_{M+1}$ and obtain the root $\mathbf{u} \in \{0,1\}^k$. For each $i \in [0, M+1]$, the tree path from leaf $\mathbf{s}_i$ to root $\mathbf{u}$ is determined by the ℓ bits representing integer i.

We prove knowledge of two *consecutive* paths from leaves $\mathbf{y} \in \{0,1\}^k$ and $\mathbf{z} \in \{0,1\}^k$ to the public root $\mathbf{u}$ such that the k-bit integers Y and Z corresponding to $\mathbf{y}$ and $\mathbf{z}$ satisfy $Y < X < Z$, where X is the integer committed in $\mathbf{c}$.

Let $v_{\ell-1}, \ldots, v_0$ and $w_{\ell-1}, \ldots, w_0$ be the bits determining the paths from the leaves $\mathbf{y}$ and $\mathbf{z}$, respectively, to root $\mathbf{u}$. Then, by "consecutive", we mean that the ℓ-bit integers $V = (v_{\ell-1}, \ldots, v_0)_2$ and $W = (w_{\ell-1}, \ldots, w_0)_2$ satisfy $V + 1 = W$.

We remark that the truth of the statement – which is ensured by the soundness of the argument – implies that the integer committed in $\mathbf{c}$ does not belong to Set, assuming the collision-resistance of the Merkle hash tree and the security of the commitment scheme. This is because: (i) The existence of the two tree paths guarantees that $\mathbf{y}, \mathbf{z} \in$ Set; (ii) The fact that they are consecutive further ensures that $(\mathbf{y}, \mathbf{z}) = (\mathbf{s}_i, \mathbf{s}_{i+1})$, for some $i \in [0, M]$; (iii) The inequalities $Y < X < Z$ then implies that either $X < S_1$ or $S_M < X$ or $S_j < X < S_{j+1}$, for some $j \in [1, M-1]$. In either case, it must be true that $X \notin$ Set.

The considered statement can be divided into 4 steps: (1) Proving knowledge of X committed in $\mathbf{c}$; (2) Proving knowledge of the tree paths from $\mathbf{y}$ and $\mathbf{z}$; (3) Proving the range membership $Y < Z < X$; (4) Proving the addition relation $V + 1 = W$. We show that the entire statement can be expressed as one linear equation modulo q together with linear and quadratic equations modulo 2, which allows reducing it to an instance of the general protocol from Sect. 3.2. Regarding (1), we have obtained Eq. (18). As for (2), we use the techniques from [44] to translate Merkle tree inclusions into a set of provable equations modulo q and modulo 2. The sub-statement (3) can be handled as in Sect. 5.1. Finally, (4) can easily be expressed as $2\ell - 1$ simple equations modulo 2.

The details of these steps are provided in the full version of the paper. We finally remark that set elements can have a longer representation than $k = n\lceil \log q \rceil$ bits if we hash them into k-bit string before building the Merkle tree. For this purpose, a SIS-based hash function $H_{\mathsf{SIS}} : \{0,1\}^m \to \mathbb{Z}_q^n$ like [2] should be used to preserve the compatibility with zero-knowledge proofs.

---

[3] If M does not have this form, one can duplicate S_1 sufficiently many times until the cardinality of the set has this property. Our protocol remains the same in this case.

6   Subquadratic Arguments for Integer Multiplications

For $L = \mathsf{poly}(n)$, we consider the problem of proving that committed integers $X = (x_{L-1}, \ldots, x_0)_2$, $Y = (y_{L-1}, \ldots, y_0)_2$, $Z = (z_{2L-1}, \ldots, z_0)_2$ satisfy the multiplicative relation $Z = XY$. This task can be realized by running L instances of the protocol for integer additions from Sect. 4, but this naive method would yield complexity at least $\mathcal{O}(L^2)$. Our target here is to design an asymptotically more efficient protocol with computation/communication cost subquadratic in L. From a theoretical point of view, such a protocol is particularly interesting, because its execution must somehow employ a subquadratic multiplication algorithm. This inspires us to consider for the first time in the context of ZK proofs the Karatsuba multiplication algorithm [38] that achieves subquadratic complexity $\mathcal{O}(L^{\log_2 3})$. Specifically, we will prove that the result of applying the Karatsuba algorithm to committed integers X, Y is exactly the committed integer Z.

Commitments. Choose a prime $q = \widetilde{\mathcal{O}}(\sqrt{L} \cdot n)$ and let $m = n(\lceil \log_2 q \rceil + 3)$. We use the KTX commitment scheme with public key $(\mathbf{a}_0, \ldots, \mathbf{a}_{2L-1}, \mathbf{b}_1, \ldots, \mathbf{b}_m) \hookleftarrow U(\mathbb{Z}_q^{n \times (2L+m)})$. Let $\mathbf{c}_x, \mathbf{c}_y, \mathbf{c}_z \in \mathbb{Z}_q^n$ be commitments to X, Y, Z, where

$$
\begin{cases}
\sum_{i=0}^{L-1} \mathbf{a}_i \cdot x_i + \sum_{j=1}^{m} \mathbf{b}_j \cdot r_{1,j} = \mathbf{c}_x \bmod q; \\
\sum_{i=0}^{L-1} \mathbf{a}_i \cdot y_i + \sum_{j=1}^{m} \mathbf{b}_j \cdot r_{2,j} = \mathbf{c}_y \bmod q; \\
\sum_{i=0}^{2L-1} \mathbf{a}_i \cdot z_i + \sum_{j=1}^{m} \mathbf{b}_j \cdot r_{3,j} = \mathbf{c}_z \bmod q,
\end{cases}
$$

where bits $\{r_{i,j}\}_{(i,j)\in[3]\times[m]}$ are the commitment randomness. Then, as in Sect. 4, we can unify the 3 equations into one linear equation modulo q:

$$
\sum_{i=0}^{L-1} \mathbf{a}_i^{(1)} \cdot x_i + \sum_{i=0}^{L-1} \mathbf{a}_i^{(2)} \cdot y_i + \sum_{i=0}^{2L-1} \mathbf{a}_i^{(3)} \cdot z_i + \sum_{(i,j)\in[3]\times[m]} \mathbf{b}_j^{(i)} \cdot r_{i,j} = \mathbf{c} \bmod q. \quad (19)
$$

6.1   An Interpretation of the Karatsuba Algorithm

Let $L = 2^k$ for some positive integer k. We will employ a variant of the Karatsuba algorithm, suggested by Knuth [40, Sect. 4.3.3]. First, we need to interpret the execution of the algorithm in a fashion compatible with our ZK technique.

The First Iteration. For the first application of Karatsuba algorithm, we break X and Y into their "most significant" and "least significant" halves:

$$
X = [X^{(1)}, X^{(0)}] \text{ and } Y = [Y^{(1)}, Y^{(0)}], \quad (20)
$$

where $X^{(1)}, X^{(0)}, Y^{(1)}, Y^{(0)}$ are $L/2$-bit integers. Then, as suggested by Knuth, the product Z can be written as:

$$
\begin{aligned}
Z = XY = (2^L + 2^{L/2}) \cdot X^{(1)}Y^{(1)} + (2^{L/2} + 1) \cdot X^{(0)}Y^{(0)} \\
- 2^{L/2} \cdot (X^{(1)} - X^{(0)})(Y^{(1)} - Y^{(0)}). \quad (21)
\end{aligned}
$$

The advantage of Knuth's approach over Karatsuba's is that it allows working with the differences $(X^{(1)} - X^{(0)})$, $(Y^{(1)} - Y^{(0)})$ that guarantee to have bit-size $L/2$, rather than working with the sums $(X^{(1)} + X^{(0)})$, $(Y^{(1)} + Y^{(0)})$ that cause a burden of carry-on bits. However, this modification introduces a new issue as these differences may be negative, which are more difficult to handle in our setting. For this reason, we need to make sure that we always subtract a smaller integer from a larger one, while preserving the ability to prove correct computations.

Let $\widehat{X}^{(1)}, \widehat{X}^{(0)}$ such that $\widehat{X}^{(1)} \geq \widehat{X}^{(0)}$ and $\{\widehat{X}^{(1)}, \widehat{X}^{(0)}\} = \{X^{(1)}, X^{(0)}\}$. If we use an order control bit b that is assigned value 1 if $X^{(1)} \geq X^{(0)}$, or value 0 otherwise, and let $X^{(2)} = \widehat{X}^{(1)} - \widehat{X}^{(0)} \geq 0$, then we have the relations

$$\widehat{X}^{(1)} = b \cdot X^{(1)} + \overline{b} \cdot X^{(0)}; \quad \widehat{X}^{(0)} = \overline{b} \cdot X^{(1)} + b \cdot X^{(0)}; \quad X^{(2)} + \widehat{X}^{(0)} = \widehat{X}^{(1)}. \quad (22)$$

Conversely, if non-negative integers $X^{(1)}, X^{(0)}, \widehat{X}^{(1)}, \widehat{X}^{(0)}, X^{(2)}$ and bit b satisfy (22), then it holds that $\{\widehat{X}^{(1)}, \widehat{X}^{(0)}\} = \{X^{(1)}, X^{(0)}\}$ and $\widehat{X}^{(1)} \geq \widehat{X}^{(0)}$ and $X^{(2)} = \widehat{X}^{(1)} - \widehat{X}^{(0)}$.

Similarly, we can obtain $\widehat{Y}^{(1)}, \widehat{Y}^{(0)}$ such that $\widehat{Y}^{(1)} \geq \widehat{Y}^{(0)}$, non-negative $Y^{(2)}$ such that $Y^{(2)} = \widehat{Y}^{(1)} - \widehat{Y}^{(0)}$, as well as a control bit d satisfying

$$\widehat{Y}^{(1)} = d \cdot Y^{(1)} + \overline{d} \cdot Y^{(0)}; \quad \widehat{Y}^{(0)} = \overline{d} \cdot Y^{(1)} + d \cdot Y^{(0)}; \quad Y^{(2)} + \widehat{Y}^{(0)} = \widehat{Y}^{(1)}. \quad (23)$$

Relations (22)–(23) essentially establish a "bridge" that allows us to work (in the subtractions $X^{(1)} - X^{(0)}$ and $Y^{(1)} - Y^{(0)}$ incurring in (21)) with non-negative integers $X^{(2)}$ and $Y^{(2)}$ instead of possibly negative integers. Indeed, letting $s = b + d \bmod 2$, we have

$$(X^{(1)} - X^{(0)})(Y^{(1)} - Y^{(0)}) = \overline{s} \cdot X^{(2)}Y^{(2)} - s \cdot X^{(2)}Y^{(2)}.$$

Then, Eq. (21) can be expressed as

$$Z = XY = (2^L + 2^{L/2})Z^{(1)} + (2^{L/2} + 1)Z^{(0)} + 2^{L/2}(s \cdot Z^{(2)}) - 2^{L/2}(\overline{s} \cdot Z^{(2)}), \quad (24)$$

where $Z^{(1)} = X^{(1)}Y^{(1)}$, $Z^{(0)} = X^{(0)}Y^{(0)}$ and $Z^{(2)} = X^{(2)}Y^{(2)}$ are L-bit integers. These values are computed based on recursive applications of the Karatsuba algorithm until we reach integers of bit-size $L/2^{k-1} = 2$, as described below.

The Recursion. For $t = 1$ to $k - 2$, and for string $\alpha \in \{0,1,2\}^t$, on input of $L/2^t$-bit integers $X^{(\alpha)}$ and $Y^{(\alpha)}$, we recursively obtain $L/2^{t+1}$-bit integers

$$X^{(\alpha 1)}; \ X^{(\alpha 0)}; \ \widehat{X}^{(\alpha 1)}; \ \widehat{X}^{(\alpha 0)}; \ X^{(\alpha 2)}; \ Y^{(\alpha 1)}; \ Y^{(\alpha 0)}; \ \widehat{Y}^{(\alpha 1)}; \ \widehat{Y}^{(\alpha 0)}; \ Y^{(\alpha 2)},$$

and bits $b^{(\alpha)}, d^{(\alpha)}, s^{(\alpha)}$ satisfying the following relations.

$$
\begin{cases}
X^{(\alpha)} = [X^{(\alpha 1)}, X^{(\alpha 0)}]; \\
\widehat{X}^{(\alpha 1)} = b^{(\alpha)} \cdot X^{(\alpha 1)} + \overline{b}^{(\alpha)} \cdot X^{(\alpha 0)}; \quad \widehat{X}^{(\alpha 0)} = \overline{b}^{(\alpha)} \cdot X^{(\alpha 1)} + b^{(\alpha)} \cdot X^{(\alpha 0)}; \\
X^{(\alpha 2)} + \widehat{X}^{(\alpha 0)} = \widehat{X}^{(\alpha 1)}; \\
Y^{(\alpha)} = [Y^{(\alpha 1)}, Y^{(\alpha 0)}]; \\
\widehat{Y}^{(\alpha 1)} = d^{(\alpha)} \cdot Y^{(\alpha 1)} + \overline{d}^{(\alpha)} \cdot Y^{(\alpha 0)}; \quad \widehat{Y}^{(\alpha 0)} = \overline{d}^{(\alpha)} \cdot Y^{(\alpha 1)} + d^{(\alpha)} \cdot Y^{(\alpha 0)}; \\
Y^{(\alpha 2)} + \widehat{Y}^{(\alpha 0)} = \widehat{Y}^{(\alpha 1)}; \\
s^{(\alpha)} = b^{(\alpha)} + d^{(\alpha)} \bmod 2.
\end{cases}
\tag{25}
$$

Let $Z^{(\alpha 1)} = X^{(\alpha 1)} Y^{(\alpha 1)}$, $Z^{(\alpha 0)} = X^{(\alpha 0)} Y^{(\alpha 0)}$, $Z^{(\alpha 2)} = X^{(\alpha 2)} Y^{(\alpha 2)}$. Note that these $L/2^t$-bit integers satisfy the equation:

$$
Z^{(\alpha)} := X^{(\alpha)} Y^{(\alpha)} = \left(2^{L/2^t} + 2^{L/2^{t+1}} \right) \cdot Z^{(\alpha 1)} + \left(2^{L/2^{t+1}} + 1 \right) \cdot Z^{(\alpha 0)}
$$
$$
+ 2^{L/2^{t+1}} \cdot \left(s^{(\alpha)} \cdot Z^{(\alpha 2)} \right) - 2^{L/2^{t+1}} \cdot \left(\overline{s}^{(\alpha)} \cdot Z^{(\alpha 2)} \right). \tag{26}
$$

We remark that the number of secret bits contained in the integers

$$
\{ X^{(\alpha 1)}; \; X^{(\alpha 0)}; \; \widehat{X}^{(\alpha 1)}; \; \widehat{X}^{(\alpha 0)}; \; X^{(\alpha 2)} \}, \quad \text{where } \alpha \in \{0, 1, 2\}^t, \forall t = 0, \ldots, k-2,
$$

derived from X in the above process is

$$
5 \cdot \sum_{t=0}^{k-2} \left(3^t \cdot \frac{L}{2^{t+1}} \right) = \frac{5L}{3} \cdot \sum_{t=0}^{k-2} \left(\frac{3}{2} \right)^{t+1} = \frac{10L}{3} \cdot \left(\frac{3}{2} \right)^k - 5L = \frac{10}{3} \cdot 3^{\log_2 L} - 5L.
$$

That is also the number of secret bits in the integers derived from Y. Meanwhile, the number of control bits $b^{(\alpha)}, d^{(\alpha)}, s^{(\alpha)}$ is $3 \cdot \sum_{t=0}^{k-2} 3^t = (3^{\log_2 L} - 3)/2$. In total, the process gives us $\mathcal{O}(3^{\log_2 L}) = \mathcal{O}(L^{\log_2 3})$ secret bits.

6.2   Representing All Relations as Equations Modulo 2

As shown in Sects. 4 and 5, to prove that committed integers satisfy some statement, it suffices to demonstrate that the statement can be expressed as one linear equation modulo q together with linear and quadratic equations modulo 2, which effectively reduces it to an instance of the general protocol of Sect. 3.2. We have already obtained the linear equation modulo q from (19). Our main task is now to show that all the relations among $\mathcal{O}(L^{\log_2 3})$ secret bits obtained in Sect. 6.1 can be expressed in terms of linear and quadratic equations modulo 2.

We observe that, apart from the linear equations $s^{(\alpha)} = b^{(\alpha)} + d^{(\alpha)} \bmod 2$, there are several common types of relations among the secret objects derived in Sect. 6.1, for which we handle as follows.

The first type is relation of the form $X^{(\alpha)} = [X^{(\alpha 1)}, X^{(\alpha 0)}]$, between an $L/2^t$-bit integer $X^{(\alpha)}$ and its halves $X^{(\alpha 1)}$ and $X^{(\alpha 0)}$. Let $X^{(\alpha)} = (x_{\frac{L}{2^t}-1}^{(\alpha)}, \ldots, x_0^{(\alpha)})_2$

and $X^{(\alpha 1)} = (x^{(\alpha 1)}_{\frac{L}{2^{t+1}}-1}, \ldots, x^{(\alpha 1)}_0)_2$, $X^{(\alpha 0)} = (x^{(\alpha 0)}_{\frac{L}{2^{t+1}}-1}, \ldots, x^{(\alpha 0)}_0)_2$. This type of relation can be expressed as the following linear equations modulo 2:

$$\forall i = 0, \ldots, \frac{L}{2^{t+1}} - 1 : x^{(\alpha 0)}_i + x^{(\alpha)}_i = 0 \bmod 2; \quad x^{(\alpha 1)}_i + x^{(\alpha)}_{i+\frac{L}{2^{t+1}}} = 0 \bmod 2.$$

The second type is relation of the form

$$\widehat{X}^{(\alpha 1)} = b^{(\alpha)} \cdot X^{(\alpha 1)} + \overline{b}^{(\alpha)} \cdot X^{(\alpha 0)}; \quad \widehat{X}^{(\alpha 0)} = \overline{b}^{(\alpha)} \cdot X^{(\alpha 1)} + b^{(\alpha)} \cdot X^{(\alpha 0)},$$

reflecting how $L/2^{t+1}$-bit integers $\widehat{X}^{(\alpha 1)}, \widehat{X}^{(\alpha 0)}$ are computed from $X^{(\alpha 1)}, X^{(\alpha 0)}$ based on a control bit $b^{(\alpha)}$. This type of relation can be translated into the following equations modulo 2, with respect to the bits of those integers

$$\forall i = 0, \ldots, L/2^{t+1} - 1 : \widehat{x}^{(\alpha 1)}_i + b^{(\alpha)} \cdot x^{(\alpha 1)}_i + \overline{b}^{(\alpha)} \cdot x^{(\alpha 0)}_i = 0 \bmod 2;$$

$$\forall i = 0, \ldots, L/2^{t+1} - 1 : \widehat{x}^{(\alpha 0)}_i + \overline{b}^{(\alpha)} \cdot x^{(\alpha 1)}_i + b^{(\alpha)} \cdot x^{(\alpha 0)}_i = 0 \bmod 2,$$

that contains $4 \cdot \frac{L}{2^{t+1}}$ quadratic terms.

The third type is the addition relation $X^{(\alpha 2)} + \widehat{X}^{(\alpha 0)} = \widehat{X}^{(\alpha 1)}$ among $L/2^{t+1}$-bit integers. This can be handled using our techniques from Sect. 4, resulting in equations modulo 2 with less than $2 \cdot \frac{L}{2^{t+1}}$ quadratic terms in total.

The fourth type of relations appears when we reach the base multiplication of 2-bit integers: e.g., $Z^{(\alpha 1)} = X^{(\alpha 1)} Y^{(\alpha 1)}$, where $\alpha \in \{0, 1, 2\}^{k-2}$. Let $X^{(\alpha 1)} = (x^{(\alpha 1)}_1, x^{(\alpha 1)}_0)_2$, $Y^{(\alpha 1)} = (y^{(\alpha 1)}_1, y^{(\alpha 1)}_0)_2$ and $Z^{(\alpha 1)} = (z^{(\alpha 1)}_3, z^{(\alpha 1)}_2, z^{(\alpha 1)}_1, z^{(\alpha 1)}_0)_2$. This relation can then be expressed by the following equations modulo 2, which contain 6 quadratic terms.

$$
\begin{cases}
z^{(\alpha 1)}_0 + x^{(\alpha 1)}_0 \cdot y^{(\alpha 1)}_0 = 0 \bmod 2; \\
t^{(\alpha 1)}_{1,0} + x^{(\alpha 1)}_1 \cdot y^{(\alpha 1)}_0 = 0 \bmod 2; \quad // \text{ assign value } x^{(\alpha 1)}_1 \cdot y^{(\alpha 1)}_0 \text{ to } t^{(\alpha 1)}_{1,0} \\
t^{(\alpha 1)}_{0,1} + x^{(\alpha 1)}_0 \cdot y^{(\alpha 1)}_1 = 0 \bmod 2; \quad // \text{ assign value } x^{(\alpha 1)}_0 \cdot y^{(\alpha 1)}_1 \text{ to } t^{(\alpha 1)}_{0,1} \\
z^{(\alpha 1)}_1 + t^{(\alpha 1)}_{1,0} + t^{(\alpha 1)}_{0,1} = 0 \bmod 2; \\
c^{(\alpha 1)}_1 + t^{(\alpha 1)}_{1,0} \cdot t^{(\alpha 1)}_{0,1} = 0 \bmod 2; \quad // \text{ carry bit} \\
t^{(\alpha 1)}_{1,1} + x^{(\alpha 1)}_1 \cdot y^{(\alpha 1)}_1 = 0 \bmod 2; \quad // \text{ assign value } x^{(\alpha 1)}_1 \cdot y^{(\alpha 1)}_1 \text{ to } t^{(\alpha 1)}_{1,1} \\
z^{(\alpha 1)}_2 + t^{(\alpha 1)}_{1,1} + c^{(\alpha 1)}_1 = 0 \bmod 2; \\
z^{(\alpha 1)}_3 + t^{(\alpha 1)}_{1,1} \cdot c^{(\alpha 1)}_1 = 0 \bmod 2,
\end{cases}
$$

The other types of relations come into the scene when we add up partial products and their shifts to compute the $Z^{(\alpha)}$'s and finally reach Z, which are reflected by equations (26) and (24). To handle the shifts, e.g., left-shifting integer $Z^{(\alpha 1)}$ by $L/2^{t+1}$ positions, we assign an auxiliary variable $\widetilde{Z}^{(\alpha 1)} := 2^{L/2^{t+1}} \cdot Z^{(\alpha 1)}$ and express the relations between bits of $\widetilde{Z}^{(\alpha 1)}$ and $Z^{(\alpha 1)}$ as linear equations modulo 2, as is done for the first type of relation considered above. After performing all the shifts, we will need to handle a few additions of integers to compute a partial product such as $Z^{(\alpha)}$ in (26). There, the subtraction by $2^{L/2^{t+1}} \cdot (\overline{s}^{(\alpha)} \cdot Z^{(\alpha 2)})$

can be transformed into an equivalent addition relation. Then, we can represent each of the addition operations in (26) as linear and quadratic equations modulo 2.

Based on the above discussion, it can be seen that the whole execution of the Karatsuba algorithm can be expressed as linear and quadratic equations modulo 2. Combining with the linear equation modulo q from (19), we thus obtain an instance of the general protocol from Sect. 3.2. As a result, we achieve a statistical ZKAoK of committed integers X, Y, Z satisfying $XY = Z$. The security of the argument system relies on the binding of the COM used in the interaction and the binding of the commitment variant used for committing to X, Y, Z. Overall, the protocol is secure assuming the hardness of $\mathsf{SIVP}_{\tilde{\mathcal{O}}(\sqrt{L} \cdot n)}$.

We remark that, in our process of translating the relations in Sect. 6.1 into equations modulo 2, for each type of relations, the number of secret bits and the number of quadratic terms we need to handle are only a constant times larger than those before translating. Thus, the final numbers N and $|T|$ are of order $\mathcal{O}(L^{\log_2 3})$. Meanwhile, from Eq. (19), we obtain that $\mathfrak{m}_1 + \mathfrak{m}_2 = 4L + 3m$. Therefore, when repeating the protocol $\kappa = \omega(\log n)$ times to achieve negligible soundness error, the total communication cost is of order $\big(\mathcal{O}(L + m)\log q\big) + \mathcal{O}(L^{\log_2 3})\big) \cdot \kappa$. In terms of computation cost, the total number of bit operations performed by the prover and the verifier is of order $\mathcal{O}(L^{\log_2 3})$, i.e., subquadratic in L.

Acknowledgements. Part of this research was funded by Singapore Ministry of Education under Research Grant MOE2016-T2-2-014(S) and by the French ANR ALAMBIC project (ANR-16-CE39-0006). Another part was funded by BPI-France in the context of the national project RISQ (P141580). This work was also supported in part by the European Union PROMETHEUS project (Horizon 2020 Research and Innovation Program, grant 780701).

References

1. Adleman, L., Mander, K.: Diophantine complexity. In: SFCS, pp. 81–88. IEEE Computer Society (1976)
2. Ajtai, M.: Generating hard instances of lattice problems (extended abstract). In: STOC 1996 (1996)
3. Ajtai, M.: Generating hard instances of the short basis problem. In: Wiedermann, J., van Emde Boas, P., Nielsen, M. (eds.) ICALP 1999. LNCS, vol. 1644, pp. 1–9. Springer, Heidelberg (1999). https://doi.org/10.1007/3-540-48523-6_1
4. Barić, N., Pfitzmann, B.: Collision-free accumulators and fail-stop signature schemes without trees. In: Fumy, W. (ed.) EUROCRYPT 1997. LNCS, vol. 1233, pp. 480–494. Springer, Heidelberg (1997). https://doi.org/10.1007/3-540-69053-0_33
5. Baum, C., Damgård, I., Oechsner, S., Peikert, C.: Efficient commitments and zero-knowledge protocols from ring-sis with applications to lattice-based threshold cryptosystems. IACR Cryptology ePrint Archive, 2016:997 (2016)

6. Bayer, S., Groth, J.: Zero-knowledge argument for polynomial evaluation with application to blacklists. In: Johansson, T., Nguyen, P.Q. (eds.) EUROCRYPT 2013. LNCS, vol. 7881, pp. 646–663. Springer, Heidelberg (2013). https://doi.org/10.1007/978-3-642-38348-9_38
7. Bellare, M., Goldwasser, S.: Verifiable partial key escrow. In: ACM-CCS (1997)
8. Benhamouda, F., Krenn, S., Lyubashevsky, V., Pietrzak, K.: Efficient zero-knowledge proofs for commitments from learning with errors over rings. In: Pernul, G., Ryan, P.Y.A., Weippl, E. (eds.) ESORICS 2015. LNCS, vol. 9326, pp. 305–325. Springer, Cham (2015). https://doi.org/10.1007/978-3-319-24174-6_16
9. Boudot, F.: Efficient proofs that a committed number lies in an interval. In: Preneel, B. (ed.) EUROCRYPT 2000. LNCS, vol. 1807, pp. 431–444. Springer, Heidelberg (2000). https://doi.org/10.1007/3-540-45539-6_31
10. Brickell, E.F., Chaum, D., Damgård, I.B., van de Graaf, J.: Gradual and verifiable release of a secret (Extended Abstract). In: Pomerance, C. (ed.) CRYPTO 1987. LNCS, vol. 293, pp. 156–166. Springer, Heidelberg (1988). https://doi.org/10.1007/3-540-48184-2_11
11. Camacho, P., Hevia, A., Kiwi, M.A., Opazo, R.: Strong accumulators from collision-resistant hashing. Int. J. Inf. Sec. 11(5), 349–363 (2012)
12. Camenisch, J., Chaabouni, R., Shelat, A.: Efficient protocols for set membership and range proofs. In: Pieprzyk, J. (ed.) ASIACRYPT 2008. LNCS, vol. 5350, pp. 234–252. Springer, Heidelberg (2008). https://doi.org/10.1007/978-3-540-89255-7_15
13. Camenisch, J., Hohenberger, S., Lysyanskaya, A.: Compact e-cash. In: Cramer, R. (ed.) EUROCRYPT 2005. LNCS, vol. 3494, pp. 302–321. Springer, Heidelberg (2005). https://doi.org/10.1007/11426639_18
14. Camenisch, J., Lysyanskaya, A.: An efficient system for non-transferable anonymous credentials with optional anonymity revocation. In: Pfitzmann, B. (ed.) EUROCRYPT 2001. LNCS, vol. 2045, pp. 93–118. Springer, Heidelberg (2001). https://doi.org/10.1007/3-540-44987-6_7
15. Camenisch, J., Lysyanskaya, A.: Dynamic accumulators and application to efficient revocation of anonymous credentials. In: Yung, M. (ed.) CRYPTO 2002. LNCS, vol. 2442, pp. 61–76. Springer, Heidelberg (2002). https://doi.org/10.1007/3-540-45708-9_5
16. Camenisch, J., Lysyanskaya, A.: Signature schemes and anonymous credentials from bilinear maps. In: Franklin, M. (ed.) CRYPTO 2004. LNCS, vol. 3152, pp. 56–72. Springer, Heidelberg (2004). https://doi.org/10.1007/978-3-540-28628-8_4
17. Chaabouni, R.: Enhancing privacy protection: set membership, range proofs, and the extended access control. Ph.D. thesis, EPFL, Lausanne (2017)
18. Chaabouni, R., Lipmaa, H., Zhang, B.: A non-interactive range proof with constant communication. In: Keromytis, A.D. (ed.) FC 2012. LNCS, vol. 7397, pp. 179–199. Springer, Heidelberg (2012). https://doi.org/10.1007/978-3-642-32946-3_14
19. Chan, A., Frankel, Y., Tsiounis, Y.: Easy come — easy go divisible cash. In: Nyberg, K. (ed.) EUROCRYPT 1998. LNCS, vol. 1403, pp. 561–575. Springer, Heidelberg (1998). https://doi.org/10.1007/BFb0054154
20. Chase, M., Derler, D., Goldfeder, S., Orlandi, C., Ramacher, S., Rechberger, C., Slamanig, D., Zaverucha, G.: Post-quantum zero-knowledge and signatures from symmetric-key primitives. In: ACM-CCS (2017)
21. Couteau, G., Peters, T., Pointcheval, D.: Removing the strong RSA assumption from arguments over the integers. In: Coron, J.-S., Nielsen, J.B. (eds.) EUROCRYPT 2017. LNCS, vol. 10211, pp. 321–350. Springer, Cham (2017). https://doi.org/10.1007/978-3-319-56614-6_11

22. Damgård, I., Fujisaki, E.: A statistically-hiding integer commitment scheme based on groups with hidden order. In: Zheng, Y. (ed.) ASIACRYPT 2002. LNCS, vol. 2501, pp. 125–142. Springer, Heidelberg (2002). https://doi.org/10.1007/3-540-36178-2_8

23. Damgård, I., Jurik, M.: A generalisation, a simplification and some applications of Paillier's probabilistic public-key system. In: Kim, K. (ed.) PKC 2001. LNCS, vol. 1992, pp. 119–136. Springer, Heidelberg (2001). https://doi.org/10.1007/3-540-44586-2_9

24. Davis, M., Putnam, H., Robinson, J.: The decision problem for exponential diophantine equations. Ann. Math. **74**, 425–436 (1961)

25. Fujisaki, E., Okamoto, T.: Statistical zero knowledge protocols to prove modular polynomial relations. In: Kaliski, B.S. (ed.) CRYPTO 1997. LNCS, vol. 1294, pp. 16–30. Springer, Heidelberg (1997). https://doi.org/10.1007/BFb0052225

26. Gentry, C., Peikert, C., Vaikuntanathan, V.: Trapdoors for hard lattices and new cryptographic constructions. In: STOC (2008)

27. Ghosh, E., Ohrimenko, O., Tamassia, R.: Zero-knowledge authenticated order queries and order statistics on a list. In: Malkin, T., Kolesnikov, V., Lewko, A.B., Polychronakis, M. (eds.) ACNS 2015. LNCS, vol. 9092, pp. 149–171. Springer, Cham (2015). https://doi.org/10.1007/978-3-319-28166-7_8

28. Giacomelli, I., Madsen, J., Orlandi, C.: ZKBoo: faster zero-knowledge for Boolean circuits. In: USENIX Security Symposium (2016)

29. Goldwasser, S., Kalai, Y.T., Peikert, C., Vaikuntanathan, V.: Robustness of the learning with errors assumption. In: ICS 2010, pp. 230–240 (2010)

30. Goldwasser, S., Micali, S., Rackoff, C.: The knowledge complexity of interactive proof-systems. In: STOC (1985)

31. González, A., Ráfols, C.: New techniques for non-interactive shuffle and range arguments. In: Manulis, M., Sadeghi, A.-R., Schneider, S. (eds.) ACNS 2016. LNCS, vol. 9696, pp. 427–444. Springer, Cham (2016). https://doi.org/10.1007/978-3-319-39555-5_23

32. Groth, J.: Evaluating security of voting schemes in the universal composability framework. In: Jakobsson, M., Yung, M., Zhou, J. (eds.) ACNS 2004. LNCS, vol. 3089, pp. 46–60. Springer, Heidelberg (2004). https://doi.org/10.1007/978-3-540-24852-1_4

33. Groth, J.: Cryptography in subgroups of $\mathbb{Z}_n^*$. In: Kilian, J. (ed.) TCC 2005. LNCS, vol. 3378, pp. 50–65. Springer, Heidelberg (2005). https://doi.org/10.1007/978-3-540-30576-7_4

34. Groth, J.: Non-interactive zero-knowledge arguments for voting. In: Ioannidis, J., Keromytis, A., Yung, M. (eds.) ACNS 2005. LNCS, vol. 3531, pp. 467–482. Springer, Heidelberg (2005). https://doi.org/10.1007/11496137_32

35. Groth, J.: Efficient zero-knowledge arguments from two-tiered homomorphic commitments. In: Lee, D.H., Wang, X. (eds.) ASIACRYPT 2011. LNCS, vol. 7073, pp. 431–448. Springer, Heidelberg (2011). https://doi.org/10.1007/978-3-642-25385-0_23

36. Ishai, Y., Kushilevitz, E., Ostrovksy, R., Sahai, A.: Zero-knowledge from secure multiparty computation. In: STOC (2007)

37. Jain, A., Krenn, S., Pietrzak, K., Tentes, A.: Commitments and efficient zero-knowledge proofs from learning parity with noise. In: Wang, X., Sako, K. (eds.) ASIACRYPT 2012. LNCS, vol. 7658, pp. 663–680. Springer, Heidelberg (2012). https://doi.org/10.1007/978-3-642-34961-4_40

38. Karatsuba, A., Ofman, Y.: Multiplication of many-digital numbers by automatic computers. Phys. Dokl. **7**, 595–596 (1963)

39. Kawachi, A., Tanaka, K., Xagawa, K.: Concurrently secure identification schemes based on the worst-case hardness of lattice problems. In: Pieprzyk, J. (ed.) ASI-ACRYPT 2008. LNCS, vol. 5350, pp. 372–389. Springer, Heidelberg (2008). https://doi.org/10.1007/978-3-540-89255-7_23

40. Knuth, D.E.: The Art of Computer Programming. Seminumerical Algorithms, vol. 2, 3rd edn. Addison-Wesley, Reading (1998)

41. Li, J., Li, N., Xue, R.: Universal accumulators with efficient nonmembership proofs. In: Katz, J., Yung, M. (eds.) ACNS 2007. LNCS, vol. 4521, pp. 253–269. Springer, Heidelberg (2007). https://doi.org/10.1007/978-3-540-72738-5_17

42. Libert, B., Ling, S., Mouhartem, F., Nguyen, K., Wang, H.: Zero-knowledge arguments for matrix-vector relations and lattice-based group encryption. In: Cheon, J.H., Takagi, T. (eds.) ASIACRYPT 2016. LNCS, vol. 10032, pp. 101–131. Springer, Heidelberg (2016). https://doi.org/10.1007/978-3-662-53890-6_4

43. Libert, B., Ling, S., Mouhartem, F., Nguyen, K., Wang, H.: Signature schemes with efficient protocols and dynamic group signatures from lattice assumptions. In: Cheon, J.H., Takagi, T. (eds.) ASIACRYPT 2016. LNCS, vol. 10032, pp. 373–403. Springer, Heidelberg (2016). https://doi.org/10.1007/978-3-662-53890-6_13

44. Libert, B., Ling, S., Nguyen, K., Wang, H.: Zero-knowledge arguments for lattice-based accumulators: logarithmic-size ring signatures and group signatures without trapdoors. In: Fischlin, M., Coron, J.-S. (eds.) EUROCRYPT 2016. LNCS, vol. 9666, pp. 1–31. Springer, Heidelberg (2016). https://doi.org/10.1007/978-3-662-49896-5_1

45. Libert, B., Ling, S., Nguyen, K., Wang, H.: Zero-knowledge arguments for lattice-based PRFs and applications to e-cash. In: Takagi, T., Peyrin, T. (eds.) ASI-ACRYPT 2017. LNCS, vol. 10626, pp. 304–335. Springer, Cham (2017). https://doi.org/10.1007/978-3-319-70700-6_11

46. Libert, B., Peters, T., Yung, M.: Scalable group signatures with revocation. In: Pointcheval, D., Johansson, T. (eds.) EUROCRYPT 2012. LNCS, vol. 7237, pp. 609–627. Springer, Heidelberg (2012). https://doi.org/10.1007/978-3-642-29011-4_36

47. Ling, S., Nguyen, K., Stehlé, D., Wang, H.: Improved zero-knowledge proofs of knowledge for the ISIS problem, and applications. In: Kurosawa, K., Hanaoka, G. (eds.) PKC 2013. LNCS, vol. 7778, pp. 107–124. Springer, Heidelberg (2013). https://doi.org/10.1007/978-3-642-36362-7_8

48. Lipmaa, H.: On Diophantine complexity and statistical zero-knowledge arguments. In: Laih, C.-S. (ed.) ASIACRYPT 2003. LNCS, vol. 2894, pp. 398–415. Springer, Heidelberg (2003). https://doi.org/10.1007/978-3-540-40061-5_26

49. Lipmaa, H., Asokan, N., Niemi, V.: Secure vickrey auctions without threshold trust. In: Blaze, M. (ed.) FC 2002. LNCS, vol. 2357, pp. 87–101. Springer, Heidelberg (2003). https://doi.org/10.1007/3-540-36504-4_7

50. Lyubashevsky, V.: Lattice-based identification schemes secure under active attacks. In: Cramer, R. (ed.) PKC 2008. LNCS, vol. 4939, pp. 162–179. Springer, Heidelberg (2008). https://doi.org/10.1007/978-3-540-78440-1_10

51. Lyubashevsky, V., Peikert, C., Regev, O.: On ideal lattices and learning with errors over rings. In: Gilbert, H. (ed.) EUROCRYPT 2010. LNCS, vol. 6110, pp. 1–23. Springer, Heidelberg (2010). https://doi.org/10.1007/978-3-642-13190-5_1

52. Merkle, R.C.: A certified digital signature. In: Brassard, G. (ed.) CRYPTO 1989. LNCS, vol. 435, pp. 218–238. Springer, New York (1990). https://doi.org/10.1007/0-387-34805-0_21

53. Micciancio, D., Peikert, C.: Trapdoors for lattices: simpler, tighter, faster, smaller. In: Pointcheval, D., Johansson, T. (eds.) EUROCRYPT 2012. LNCS, vol. 7237, pp. 700–718. Springer, Heidelberg (2012). https://doi.org/10.1007/978-3-642-29011-4_41

54. Micciancio, D., Peikert, C.: Hardness of SIS and LWE with small parameters. In: Canetti, R., Garay, J.A. (eds.) CRYPTO 2013. LNCS, vol. 8042, pp. 21–39. Springer, Heidelberg (2013). https://doi.org/10.1007/978-3-642-40041-4_2

55. Micciancio, D., Vadhan, S.P.: Statistical zero-knowledge proofs with efficient provers: lattice problems and more. In: Boneh, D. (ed.) CRYPTO 2003. LNCS, vol. 2729, pp. 282–298. Springer, Heidelberg (2003). https://doi.org/10.1007/978-3-540-45146-4_17

56. Nakanishi, T., Fujii, H., Hira, Y., Funabiki, N.: Revocable group signature schemes with constant costs for signing and verifying. In: Jarecki, S., Tsudik, G. (eds.) PKC 2009. LNCS, vol. 5443, pp. 463–480. Springer, Heidelberg (2009). https://doi.org/10.1007/978-3-642-00468-1_26

57. Pedersen, T.: Non-interactive and information-theoretic secure verifiable secret sharing. In: Feigenbaum, J. (ed.) CRYPTO 1991. LNCS, vol. 576, pp. 129–140. Springer, Heidelberg (1992). https://doi.org/10.1007/3-540-46766-1_9

58. Regev, O.: On lattices, learning with errors, random linear codes, and cryptography. In: STOC (2005)

59. Stern, J.: A new paradigm for public key identification. IEEE Trans. Inf. Theory **42**(6), 2757–2768 (1996)

60. Xie, X., Xue, R., Wang, M.: Zero knowledge proofs from Ring-LWE. In: Abdalla, M., Nita-Rotaru, C., Dahab, R. (eds.) CANS 2013. LNCS, vol. 8257, pp. 57–73. Springer, Cham (2013). https://doi.org/10.1007/978-3-319-02937-5_4

Multi-Theorem Preprocessing NIZKs
from Lattices

Sam Kim[(✉)] and David J. Wu[(✉)]

Stanford University, Stanford, USA
{skim13,dwu4}@cs.stanford.edu

Abstract. Non-interactive zero-knowledge (NIZK) proofs are fundamental to modern cryptography. Numerous NIZK constructions are
known in both the random oracle and the common reference string (CRS)
models. In the CRS model, there exist constructions from several classes
of cryptographic assumptions such as trapdoor permutations, pairings,
and indistinguishability obfuscation. Notably absent from this list, however, are constructions from standard *lattice* assumptions. While there
has been partial progress in realizing NIZKs from lattices for specific
languages, constructing NIZK proofs (and arguments) for all of NP from
standard lattice assumptions remains open.

In this work, we make progress on this problem by giving the first
construction of a *multi-theorem* NIZK argument for NP from standard
lattice assumptions in the *preprocessing* model. In the preprocessing
model, a (trusted) setup algorithm generates proving and verification
keys. The proving key is needed to construct proofs and the verification
key is needed to check proofs. In the multi-theorem setting, the proving
and verification keys should be reusable for an unbounded number of
theorems without compromising soundness or zero-knowledge. Existing constructions of NIZKs in the preprocessing model (or even the
designated-verifier model) that rely on weaker assumptions like one-
way functions or oblivious transfer are only secure in a single-theorem
setting. Thus, constructing multi-theorem NIZKs in the preprocessing
model does not seem to be inherently easier than constructing them in
the CRS model.

We begin by constructing a multi-theorem preprocessing NIZK
directly from context-hiding homomorphic signatures. Then, we show
how to efficiently implement the preprocessing step using a new cryptographic primitive called *blind homomorphic signatures*. This primitive
may be of independent interest. Finally, we show how to leverage our
new lattice-based preprocessing NIZKs to obtain new malicious-secure
MPC protocols purely from standard lattice assumptions.

1 Introduction

The concept of zero-knowledge is fundamental to theoretical computer science. Introduced in the seminal work of Goldwasser, Micali, and Rackoff [62],

The full version of this paper is available at https://eprint.iacr.org/2018/272.pdf.

H. Shacham and A. Boldyreva (Eds.): CRYPTO 2018, LNCS 10992, pp. 733–765, 2018.
https://doi.org/10.1007/978-3-319-96881-0_25

a zero-knowledge proof system enables a prover to convince a verifier that some statement is true without revealing *anything more* than the truth of the statement. Traditionally, zero-knowledge proof systems for NP are interactive, and in fact, interaction is essential for realizing zero-knowledge (for NP) in the standard model [61].

Non-interactive zero-knowledge. Nonetheless, Blum, Feldman, and Micali [16] showed that meaningful notions of zero-knowledge are still realizable in the non-interactive setting, where the proof consists of just a *single* message from the prover to the verifier. In the last three decades, a beautiful line of works has established the existence of NIZK proof (and argument) systems for all of NP in the random oracle model [45,81] or the common reference string (CRS) model [40,44,65,66,86], where the prover and the verifier are assumed to have access to a common string chosen by a trusted third party. Today, we have NIZK candidates in the CRS model from several classes of cryptographic assumptions:[1] (doubly-enhanced) trapdoor permutations [40,44,65], pairings [66], and indistinguishability obfuscation [86]. Notably absent from this list are constructions from lattice assumptions [6,83]. While some partial progress has been made in the case of specific languages [7,79], the general case of constructing NIZK proofs (or even arguments) for all of NP from standard lattice assumptions remains a longstanding open problem.

NIZKs in a preprocessing model. In this work, we make progress on this problem by giving the first *multi-theorem* NIZK argument for NP from standard lattice assumptions in the *preprocessing* model. In the NIZK with preprocessing model [42], there is an initial (trusted) setup phase that generates a proving key k_P and a verification key k_V. The proving key is needed to construct proofs while the verification key is needed to check proofs. In addition, the setup phase is run *before* any statements are proven (and thus, must be statement-independent). In the multi-theorem setting, we require that soundness holds against a prover who has oracle access to the verifier (but does not see k_V), and that zero-knowledge holds against a verifier who has oracle access to the prover (but does not see k_P). The NIZK with preprocessing model generalizes the more traditional settings under which NIZKs have been studied. For instance, the case where k_P is public (but k_V is secret) corresponds to designated-verifier NIZKs [34,36,39], while the case where both k_P and k_V are public corresponds to the traditional CRS setting, where the CRS is taken to be the pair (k_P, k_V).

Why study the preprocessing model? While the preprocessing model is weaker than the more traditional CRS model, constructing multi-theorem NIZK

---

[1] There are also NIZK candidates based on number-theoretic assumptions [15,16,41] which satisfy weaker properties. We discuss these in greater detail in Sect. 1.2 and Remark 4.7.

arguments (and proofs) in this model does not appear to be any easier than constructing them in the CRS model. Existing constructions of NIZKs in the preprocessing model from weaker assumptions such as one-way functions [38,42,69,75] or oblivious transfer [73] are only secure in the *single-theorem* setting. As we discuss in greater detail in Remark 4.7, the constructions from [38,42,75] only provide single-theorem zero-knowledge, while the constructions in [69,73] only provide single-theorem soundness. Even in the designated-verifier setting [34,36,39] (where only the holder of a verification key can verify the proofs), the existing constructions of NIZKs for NP based on linearly-homomorphic encryption suffer from the so-called "verifier-rejection" problem where soundness holds only against a *logarithmically-bounded* number of statements. Thus, the only candidates of multi-theorem NIZKs where soundness and zero-knowledge hold for an *unbounded* number of theorems are the constructions in the CRS model, which all rely on trapdoor permutations, pairings, or obfuscation. Thus, it remains an interesting problem to realize multi-theorem NIZKs from lattice assumptions even in the preprocessing model.

Moreover, as we show in Sect. 6.1, multi-theorem NIZKs in the preprocessing model suffice to instantiate many of the classic applications of NIZKs for boosting the security of multiparty computation (MPC) protocols. Thus, our new constructions of reusable NIZK arguments from standard lattice assumptions imply new constructions of round-optimal, near-optimal-communication MPC protocols purely from lattice assumptions. Our work also implies a *succinct* version of the classic Goldreich-Micali-Wigderson compiler [59,60] for boosting semi-honest security to malicious security, again purely from standard lattice assumptions. Furthermore, studying NIZKs in the preprocessing model may also serve as a stepping stone towards realizing NIZKs in the CRS model from standard lattice assumptions. For example, the starting point of the first multi-theorem NIZK construction by Feige, Lapidot, and Shamir [44] was a NIZK proof for graph Hamiltonicity in the preprocessing model.

1.1 Multi-Theorem Preprocessing NIZKs from Lattices

The focus of this work is on constructing NIZKs in the preprocessing model (which we will often refer to as a "preprocessing NIZK") from standard lattice assumptions. As we discuss in Sect. 1.2 and in Remark 4.7, this is the first candidate of reusable (i.e., multi-theorem) NIZK arguments from a standard lattice assumption. Below, we provide a high-level overview of our main construction.

Homomorphic signatures. A *homomorphic signature* scheme [5,18,19,63] enables computations on *signed* data. Specifically, a user can sign a message x using her private signing key to obtain a signature σ. Later on, she can delegate the pair (x, σ) to an untrusted data processor. The data processor can then compute an arbitrary function g on the signed data to obtain a value $y = g(x)$ along with a signature $\sigma_{g,y}$. The computed signature $\sigma_{g,y}$ should certify that the value y corresponds to a *correct* evaluation of the function g on the original input x. In a *context-hiding* homomorphic signature scheme [18,22], the computed signature $\sigma_{g,y}$ also *hides* the input message x. Namely, the pair $(y, \sigma_{g,y})$ reveals no information about x other than what could be inferred from the output $y = g(x)$. Gorbunov et al. [63] gave the first construction of a context-hiding homomorphic signature scheme for general Boolean circuits (with bounded depth) from standard lattice assumptions.

From homomorphic signatures to zero-knowledge. The notion of context-hiding in a homomorphic signature scheme already bears a strong resemblance to zero-knowledge. Namely, a context-hiding homomorphic signature scheme allows a user (e.g., a prover) to certify the result of a computation (e.g., the output of an NP relation) without revealing any additional information about the input (e.g., the NP witness) to the computation. Consider the following scenario. Suppose the prover has a statement-witness pair (x, w) for some NP relation $\mathcal{R}$ and wants to convince the verifier that $\mathcal{R}(x, w) = 1$ without revealing w. For sake of argument, suppose the prover has obtained a signature σ_w on the witness w (but does not have the signing key for the signature scheme), and the verifier holds the verification key for the signature scheme. In this case, the prover can construct a zero-knowledge proof for x by evaluating the relation $\mathcal{R}_x(w) := \mathcal{R}(x, w)$ on (w, σ_w). If $\mathcal{R}(x, w) = 1$, then this yields a new signature $\sigma_{\mathcal{R},x}$ on the bit 1. The proof for x is just the signature $\sigma_{\mathcal{R},x}$. Context-hiding of the homomorphic signature scheme says that the signature $\sigma_{\mathcal{R},x}$ reveals no information about the input to the computation (the witness w) other than what is revealed by the output of the computation (namely, that $\mathcal{R}(x, w) = 1$). This is precisely the zero-knowledge property. Soundness of the proof system follows by unforgeability of the homomorphic signature scheme (if there is no w such that $\mathcal{R}_x(w) = 1$, the prover would not be able to produce a signature on the value 1 that verifies according to the function $\mathcal{R}_x$).

While this basic observation suggests a connection between homomorphic signatures and zero-knowledge, it does not directly give a NIZK argument. A key problem is that to construct the proof, the prover must already possess a signature on its witness w. But since the prover does not have the signing key (if it did, then the proof system is no longer sound), it is unclear how the prover obtains this signature on w without interacting with the verifier (who could hold the signing key). This is the case even in the preprocessing model, because we require that the preprocessing be statement-independent (and in fact, reusable for arbitrarily many adaptively-chosen statements).

Preprocessing NIZKs from homomorphic signatures. Nonetheless, the basic observation shows that if we knew ahead of time which witness w the prover would use to construct its proofs, then the setup algorithm can simply give the prover a homomorphic signature σ_w on w. To support this, we add a layer of indirection. Instead of proving that it knows a witness w where $\mathcal{R}(x, w) = 1$, the prover instead demonstrates that it has an encryption ct_w of w (under some key sk), and that it knows some secret key sk such that ct decrypts to a valid witness

w where $\mathcal{R}(x, w) = 1$.[2] A proof of the statement x then consists of the encrypted witness ct_w and a proof $\pi_{\mathcal{R},x,\mathsf{ct}_w}$ that ct_w is an encryption of a satisfying witness (under *some* key). First, if the encryption scheme is semantically-secure and the proof is zero-knowledge, then the resulting construction satisfies (computational) zero-knowledge. Moreover, the witness the prover uses to construct $\pi_{\mathcal{R},x,\mathsf{ct}_w}$ is always the same: the secret key sk. Notably, the witness is statement-independent and can be reused to prove arbitrarily many statements (provided the encryption scheme is CPA-secure).

This means we can combine context-hiding homomorphic signatures (for general circuits) with any CPA-secure symmetric encryption scheme to obtain NIZKs in the preprocessing model as follows:

- **Setup:** The setup algorithm generates a secret key sk for the encryption scheme as well as parameters for a homomorphic signature scheme. Both the proving and verification keys include the public parameters for the signature scheme. The proving key k_P additionally contains the secret key sk and a signature σ_{sk} on sk.
- **Prove:** To generate a proof that an NP statement x is true, the prover takes a witness w where $\mathcal{R}(x, w) = 1$ and encrypts w under sk to obtain a ciphertext ct_w. Next, we define the witness-checking function $\mathsf{CheckWitness}[\mathcal{R}, x, \mathsf{ct}_w]$ (parameterized by $\mathcal{R}$, x, and ct_w) that takes as input a secret key sk and outputs 1 if $\mathcal{R}(x, \mathsf{Decrypt}(\mathsf{sk}, \mathsf{ct}_w)) = 1$, and 0 otherwise. The prover homomorphically evaluates $\mathsf{CheckWitness}[\mathcal{R}, x, \mathsf{ct}_w]$ on $(\mathsf{sk}, \sigma_{\mathsf{sk}})$ to obtain a new signature σ^* on the value 1. The proof consists of the ciphertext ct_w and the signature σ^*.
- **Verify:** Given a statement x for an NP relation $\mathcal{R}$ and a proof $\pi = (\mathsf{ct}, \sigma^*)$, the verifier checks that σ^* is a valid signature on the bit 1 according to the function $\mathsf{CheckWitness}[\mathcal{R}, x, \mathsf{ct}]$. Notice that the description on the function only depends on the relation $\mathcal{R}$, the statement x, and the ciphertext ct, all of which are known to the verifier.

Since the homomorphic signature scheme is context-hiding, the signature σ^* hides the input to $\mathsf{CheckWitness}[\mathcal{R}, x, \mathsf{ct}_w]$, which in this case, is the secret key sk. By CPA-security of the encryption scheme, the ciphertext hides the witness w, so the scheme provides zero-knowledge. Soundness again follows from unforgeability of the signature scheme. Thus, by combining a lattice-based homomorphic signature scheme for general circuits [63] with any lattice-based CPA-secure symmetric encryption scheme, we obtain a (multi-theorem) preprocessing NIZK from lattices. In fact, the verification key in our construction only consists of the public parameters for the homomorphic signature scheme, and thus, can be made public. This means that in our construction, only the proving key needs to be kept secret, so we can equivalently view our construction as a multi-theorem "designated-prover" NIZK. We discuss this in greater detail in Remark 4.6.

---

[2] This is a classic technique in the construction of non-interactive proof systems and has featured in many contexts (e.g., [56,87]).

An appealing property of our preprocessing NIZKs is that the proofs are short: the length of a NIZK argument for an NP relation $\mathcal{R}$ is $|w| + \mathsf{poly}(\lambda, d)$ bits, where $|w|$ is the length of a witness for $\mathcal{R}$ and d is the depth of the circuit computing $\mathcal{R}$. The proof size in NIZK constructions from trapdoor permutations or pairings [40,44,65,66] typically scale with the *size* of the circuit computing $\mathcal{R}$ and *multiplicatively* with the security parameter. Previously, Gentry et al. [56] gave a generic approach using fully homomorphic encryption (FHE) to reduce the proof size in any NIZK construction. The advantage of our approach is that we naturally satisfy this succinctness property, and the entire construction can be based only on lattice assumptions (without needing to mix assumptions). We discuss this in greater detail in the full version of this paper [74]. We also give the complete description of our preprocessing NIZK and security analysis in Sect. 4.

Blind homomorphic signatures for efficient preprocessing. A limitation of preprocessing NIZKs is we require a trusted setup to generate the proving and verification keys. One solution is to have the prover and verifier run a (malicious-secure) two-party computation protocol (e.g., [76]) to generate the proving and verification keys. However, generic MPC protocols are often costly and require making *non-black-box* use of the underlying homomorphic signature scheme.

In this work, we describe a conceptually simpler and more efficient way of implementing the preprocessing without relying on general MPC. We do so by introducing a new cryptographic notion called *blind homomorphic signatures*. First, we observe that we can view the two-party computation of the setup phase as essentially implementing a "blind signing" protocol where the verifier holds the signing key for the homomorphic signature scheme and the prover holds the secret key sk. At the end of the blind signing protocol, the prover should learn σ_{sk} while the verifier should not learn anything about sk. This is precisely the properties guaranteed by a blind signature protocol [35,47]. In this work, we introduce the notion of a blind homomorphic signature scheme which combines the blind signing protocol of traditional blind signature schemes while retaining the ability to homomorphically operate on ciphertexts. Since the notion of a blind homomorphic signatures is inherently a two-party functionality, we formalize it in the model of universal composability [24]. We provide the formal definition of the ideal blind homomorphic signature functionality in Sect. 5.

In Sect. 5.1, we show how to securely realize our ideal blind homomorphic signature functionality in the presence of *malicious* adversaries by combining homomorphic signatures with any UC-secure oblivious transfer (OT) protocol [27]. Note that security against malicious adversaries is critical for our primary application of leveraging blind homomorphic signatures to implement the setup algorithm of our preprocessing NIZK candidate. At a high-level, we show how to construct a blind homomorphic signature scheme from any "bitwise" homo-morphic signature scheme—namely, a homomorphic signature scheme where the signature on an ℓ-bit message consists of ℓ signatures, one for each bit of the message. Moreover, we assume that the signature on each bit position only depends on the value of that particular bit (and not the value of any of the other bits of the message); of course, the ℓ signatures can still be generated using common or correlated randomness. Given a bitwise homomorphic signature scheme, we can implement the blind signing protocol (on ℓ-bit messages) using ℓ independent 1-out-of-2 OTs. Specifically, the signer plays the role of the sender in the OT protocol and for each index $i \in [\ell]$, the signer signs both the bit 0 as well as the bit 1. Then, to obtain a signature on an ℓ-bit message, the receiver requests the signatures corresponding to the bits of its message.

While the high-level schema is simple, there are a few additional details that we have to handle to achieve robustness against a malicious signer. For instance, a malicious signer can craft the parameters of the homomorphic signature scheme so that when an evaluator computes on a signature, the resulting signatures no longer provide context-hiding. Alternatively, a malicious signer might mount a "selective-failure" attack during the blind-signing protocol to learn information about the receiver's message. We discuss how to address these problems by giving strong definitions of malicious context-hiding for homomorphic signatures in Sect. 3, and give the full construction of blind homomorphic signatures from oblivious transfer in Sect. 5.1. In particular, we show that the Gorbunov et al. [63] homomorphic signature construction satisfies our stronger security notions, and so coupled with the UC-secure lattice-based OT protocol of Peikert et al. [80], we obtain a UC-secure blind homomorphic signature scheme from standard lattice assumptions. Moreover, the blind signing protocol is a two-round protocol, and only makes black-box use of the underlying homomorphic signature scheme.

UC-secure preprocessing NIZKs. Finally, we show that using our UC-secure blind homomorphic signature candidate, we can in fact realize the stronger notion of UC-secure NIZK arguments in a preprocessing model from standard lattice assumptions. This means that our NIZKs can be arbitrarily composed with other cryptographic protocols. Our new candidates are thus suitable to instantiate many of the classic applications of NIZKs for boosting the security of general MPC protocols. As we show in Sect. 6, combining our preprocessing UC-NIZKs with existing lattice-based semi-malicious MPC protocols such as [78] yields malicious-secure protocols purely from standard lattice assumptions (in a reusable preprocessing model). We also show that our constructions imply a *succinct* version of the classic GMW [59,60] protocol compiler (where the total communication overhead of the compiled protocol depends only on the *depth*, rather than the *size* of the computation).

Towards NIZKs in the CRS model. In this paper, we construct the first multi-theorem preprocessing NIZK arguments from standard lattice assumptions. However, our techniques do not directly generalize to the CRS setting. While it is possible to obtain a *publicly-verifiable* preprocessing NIZK (i.e., make the verification key k_V public), our construction critically relies on the prover state being hidden. This is because the prover state contains the *secret key* the prover uses to encrypt its witness in the proofs, so publishing this compromises zero-knowledge. Nonetheless, we believe that having a better understanding of

NIZKs in the preprocessing model provides a useful stepping stone towards the goal of building NIZKs from lattices in the CRS model, and we leave this as an exciting open problem.

Preprocessing NIZKs from other assumptions? Our work gives the first construction of a multi-theorem preprocessing NIZK from standard lattice assumptions. It is an interesting challenge to obtain multi-theorem preprocessing NIZKs from other assumptions that are currently not known to imply NIZKs in the CRS model. For instance, a natural target would be to construct multi-theorem NIZKs in the preprocessing model from the decisional Diffie-Hellman (DDH) assumption.

1.2   Additional Related Work

In this section, we survey some additional related work on NIZK constructions, blind signatures, and homomorphic signatures.

Other NIZK proof systems. In the CRS model, there are several NIZK constructions based on specific number-theoretic assumptions such as quadratic residuosity [15,16,41]. These candidates are also secure in the *bounded-theorem* setting where the CRS can only be used for an *a priori* bounded number of proofs. Exceeding this bound compromises soundness or zero-knowledge. In the preprocessing model, Kalai and Raz [70] gave a single-theorem *succinct* NIZK proof system for the class LOGSNP from polylogarithmic private information retrieval (PIR) and *exponentially-hard* OT. In this work, we focus on constructing multi-theorem NIZKs, where an *arbitrary* number of proofs can be constructed after an initial setup phase.

NIZKs have also been constructed for specific algebraic languages in both the publicly-verifiable setting [64,67] as well as the designated-verifier setting [33]. In the specific case of lattice-based constructions, there are several works on building hash-proof systems, (also known as smooth projective hash functions [37]) [14,71,91], which are designated-verifier NIZK proofs for a *specific* language (typically, this is the language of ciphertexts associated with a particular message). In the random oracle model, there are also constructions of lattice-based NIZK arguments from Σ-protocols [77,90]. Recently, there has also been work on instantiating the random oracle in Σ-protocols with lattice-based correlation-intractable hash functions [26]. However, realizing the necessary correlation-intractable hash functions from lattices requires making the non-standard assumption that Regev's encryption scheme [83] is *exponentially KDM-secure* against all polynomial-time adversaries. In our work, we focus on NIZK constructions for general NP languages in the plain model (without random oracles) from the *standard* LWE assumption (i.e., polynomial hardness of LWE with a subexponential approximation factor).

Very recently, Rothblum et al. [84] showed that a NIZK proof system for a decisional variant of the bounded distance decoding (BDD) problem suffices for building NIZK proof system for NP.

Blind signatures. The notion of blind signatures was first introduced by Chaum [35]. There are many constructions of blind signatures from a wide range of assumptions in the random oracle model [1,12,13,17,21,82,85,88], the CRS model [2–4,23,47,49,57,72], as well as the standard model [50–52,68].

Homomorphic signatures. There are many constructions of linearly homomorphic signatures [5,8–10,18–20,31,43,48,53,89]. Beyond linear homomorphisms, a number of works [11,19,32] have constructed homomorphic signatures for polynomial functions from lattices or multilinear maps. For general circuits, Gorbunov et al. [63] gave the first homomorphic signature scheme from lattices, and Fiore et al. [46] gave the first "multi-key" homomorphic signature scheme from lattices (where homomorphic operations can be performed on signatures signed under *different* keys).

2   Preliminaries

We begin by introducing some basic notation. For an integer $n \geq 1$, we write $[n]$ to denote the set of integers $\{1, \ldots, n\}$. For a positive integer $q > 1$, we write $\mathbb{Z}_q$ to denote the ring of integers modulo q. For a finite set S, we write $x \xleftarrow{R} S$ to denote that x is sampled uniformly at random from S. For a distribution $\mathcal{D}$, we write $x \leftarrow \mathcal{D}$ to denote that x is sampled from $\mathcal{D}$. Throughout this work, we use λ to denote a security parameter. We typically use bold uppercase letters (e.g., $\mathbf{A}$, $\mathbf{B}$) to denote matrices and bold lowercase letters (e.g., $\mathbf{u}$, $\mathbf{v}$) to denote vectors.

We say that a function f is negligible in λ, denoted $\mathsf{negl}(\lambda)$, if $f(\lambda) = o(1/\lambda^c)$ for all constants $c \in \mathbb{N}$. We say that an event happens with negligible probability if the probability of the event occurring is bounded by a negligible function, and we say that an event happens with overwhelming probability if its complement occurs with negligible probability. We say an algorithm is efficient if it runs in probabilistic polynomial time in the length of its input. We write $\mathsf{poly}(\lambda)$ to denote a quantity whose value is upper-bounded by a fixed polynomial in λ. We say that two families of distributions $\mathcal{D}_1 = \{\mathcal{D}_{1,\lambda}\}_{\lambda \in \mathbb{N}}$ and $\mathcal{D}_2 = \{\mathcal{D}_{2,\lambda}\}_{\lambda \in \mathbb{N}}$ are computationally indistinguishable if no efficient algorithm can distinguish samples from either $\mathcal{D}_1$ or $\mathcal{D}_2$, except with negligible probability. We denote this by writing $\mathcal{D}_1 \overset{c}{\approx} \mathcal{D}_2$. We write $\mathcal{D}_1 \overset{s}{\approx} \mathcal{D}_2$ to denote that $\mathcal{D}_1$ and $\mathcal{D}_2$ are statistically indistinguishable (i.e., the statistical distance between $\mathcal{D}_1$ and $\mathcal{D}_2$ is bounded by a negligible function). In the full version of this paper [74], we provide additional preliminaries in on CPA-secure encryption as well as lattice-based cryptography.

3   Homomorphic Signatures

A homomorphic signature scheme enables computations on signed data. Given a function C (modeled as a Boolean circuit) and a signature σ_x that certifies a message x, one can homomorphic derive a signature $\sigma_{C(x)}$ that certifies the value

$C(x)$ with respect to the function C. The two main security notions that we are interested in are unforgeability and context-hiding. We first provide a high-level description of the properties:

- **Unforgeability:** We say a signature scheme is unforgeable if an adversary who has a signature σ_x on a message x cannot produce a valid signature on any message $y \neq C(x)$ that verifies with respect to the function C.
- **Context-hiding:** Context-hiding says that when one evaluates a function C on a message-signature pair (x, σ_x), the resulting signature $\sigma_{C(x)}$ on $C(x)$ should not reveal any information about the original message x other than the circuit C and the value $C(x)$. In our definition, the homomorphic signature scheme contains an explicit "hide" function that implements this transformation.

Syntax and notation. Our construction of blind homomorphic signatures from standard homomorphic signatures (Sect. 5.1) will impose some additional structural requirements on the underlying scheme. Suppose the message space for the homomorphic signature scheme consists of ℓ-tuples of elements over a set $\mathcal{X}$ (e.g., the case where $\mathcal{X} = \{0,1\}$ corresponds to the setting where the message space consists of ℓ-bit strings). Then, we require that the public parameters $\overrightarrow{\mathsf{pk}}$ of the scheme can be split into a vector of public keys $\overrightarrow{\mathsf{pk}} = (\mathsf{pk}_1, \ldots, \mathsf{pk}_\ell)$. In addition, a (fresh) signature on a vector $\boldsymbol{x} \in \mathcal{X}^\ell$ can also be written as a tuple of ℓ signatures $\boldsymbol{\sigma} = (\sigma_1, \ldots, \sigma_\ell)$ where σ_i can be verified with respect to the verification key vk and the ith public key pk_i for all $i \in [\ell]$. In our description below, we often use vector notation to simplify the presentation.

Definition 3.1 (Homomorphic Signatures [19,63]). *A homomorphic signature scheme with message space $\mathcal{X}$, message length $\ell \in \mathbb{N}$, and function class $\mathcal{C} = \{\mathcal{C}_\lambda\}_{\lambda \in \mathbb{N}}$, where each $\mathcal{C}_\lambda$ is a collection of functions from $\mathcal{X}^\ell$ to $\mathcal{X}$, is defined by a tuple of algorithms $\Pi_{\mathsf{HS}} = $ (PrmsGen, KeyGen, Sign, PrmsEval, SigEval, Hide, Verify, VerifyFresh, VerifyHide) with the following properties:*

- PrmsGen$(1^\lambda, 1^\ell) \to \overrightarrow{\mathsf{pk}}$*: On input the security parameter λ and message length ℓ, the parameter-generation algorithm returns a set of ℓ public keys $\overrightarrow{\mathsf{pk}} = (\mathsf{pk}_1, \ldots, \mathsf{pk}_\ell)$.*
- KeyGen$(1^\lambda) \to (\mathsf{vk}, \mathsf{sk})$*: On input the security parameter λ, the key-generation algorithm returns a verification key vk, and a signing key sk.*
- Sign$(\mathsf{pk}_i, \mathsf{sk}, x_i) \to \sigma_i$*: On input a public key pk_i, a signing key sk, and a message $x_i \in \mathcal{X}$, the signing algorithm returns a signature σ_i.*
  Vector variant: For $\overrightarrow{\mathsf{pk}} = (\mathsf{pk}_1, \ldots, \mathsf{pk}_\ell)$, and $\boldsymbol{x} = (x_1, \ldots, x_\ell) \in \mathcal{X}^\ell$, we write Sign$(\overrightarrow{\mathsf{pk}}, \mathsf{sk}, \boldsymbol{x})$ *to denote component-wise signing of each message. Namely,* Sign$(\overrightarrow{\mathsf{pk}}, \mathsf{sk}, \boldsymbol{x})$ *outputs signatures $\boldsymbol{\sigma} = (\sigma_1, \ldots, \sigma_\ell)$ where $\sigma_i \leftarrow$* Sign$(\mathsf{pk}_i, \mathsf{sk}, x_i)$ *for all $i \in [\ell]$.*
- PrmsEval$(C, \overrightarrow{\mathsf{pk}'}) \to \mathsf{pk}_C$*: On input a function $C : \mathcal{X}^\ell \to \mathcal{X}$ and a collection of public keys $\overrightarrow{\mathsf{pk}'} = (\mathsf{pk}'_1, \ldots, \mathsf{pk}'_\ell)$, the parameter-evaluation algorithm returns an evaluated public key pk_C.*

Vector variant: For a circuit $C \colon \mathcal{X}^\ell \to \mathcal{X}^k$, we write $\mathsf{PrmsEval}(C, \overrightarrow{\mathsf{pk}'})$ to denote component-wise parameter evaluation. Namely, let $C_1, \ldots, C_k$ be functions such that $C(x_1, \ldots, x_\ell) = \big(C_1(x_1, \ldots, x_\ell), \ldots, C_k(x_1, \ldots, x_\ell)\big)$. Then, $\mathsf{PrmsEval}(C, \overrightarrow{\mathsf{pk}'})$ evaluates $\mathsf{pk}_{C_i} \leftarrow \mathsf{PrmsEval}(C_i, \overrightarrow{\mathsf{pk}'})$ for $i \in [k]$, and outputs $\mathsf{pk}_C = (\mathsf{pk}_{C_1}, \ldots, \mathsf{pk}_{C_k})$.

- $\mathsf{SigEval}(C, \overrightarrow{\mathsf{pk}'}, \boldsymbol{x}, \boldsymbol{\sigma}) \to \sigma$: On input a function $C \colon \mathcal{X}^\ell \to \mathcal{X}$, public keys $\overrightarrow{\mathsf{pk}'} = (\mathsf{pk}'_1, \ldots, \mathsf{pk}'_\ell)$, messages $\boldsymbol{x} \in \mathcal{X}^\ell$, and signatures $\boldsymbol{\sigma} = (\sigma_1, \ldots, \sigma_\ell)$, the signature-evaluation algorithm returns an evaluated signature σ.
  Vector variant: We can define a vector variant of $\mathsf{SigEval}$ analogously to that of $\mathsf{PrmsEval}$.

- $\mathsf{Hide}(\mathsf{vk}, x, \sigma) \to \sigma^*$: On input a verification key vk, a message $x \in \mathcal{X}$, and a signature σ, the hide algorithm returns a signature σ^*.
  Vector variant: For $\boldsymbol{x} = (x_1, \ldots, x_k)$ and $\boldsymbol{\sigma} = (\sigma_1, \ldots, \sigma_k)$, we write $\mathsf{Hide}(\mathsf{vk}, \boldsymbol{x}, \boldsymbol{\sigma})$ to denote component-wise evaluation of the hide algorithm. Namely, $\mathsf{Hide}(\mathsf{vk}, \boldsymbol{x}, \boldsymbol{\sigma})$ returns $(\sigma_1^*, \ldots, \sigma_k^*)$ where $\sigma_i^* \leftarrow \mathsf{Hide}(\mathsf{vk}, x_i, \sigma_i)$ for all $i \in [k]$.

- $\mathsf{Verify}(\mathsf{pk}, \mathsf{vk}, x, \sigma) \to \{0, 1\}$: On input a public key pk, a verification key vk, a message $x \in \mathcal{X}$, and a signature σ, the verification algorithm either accepts (returns 1) or rejects (returns 0).
  Vector variant: For a collection of public keys $\overrightarrow{\mathsf{pk}'} = (\mathsf{pk}'_1, \ldots, \mathsf{pk}'_k)$, messages $\boldsymbol{x} = (x_1, \ldots, x_k)$, and signatures $\boldsymbol{\sigma} = (\sigma_1, \ldots, \sigma_k)$, we write $\mathsf{Verify}(\overrightarrow{\mathsf{pk}'}, \mathsf{vk}, \boldsymbol{x}, \boldsymbol{\sigma})$ to denote applying the verification algorithm to each signature component-wise. In other words, $\mathsf{Verify}(\overrightarrow{\mathsf{pk}'}, \mathsf{vk}, \boldsymbol{x}, \boldsymbol{\sigma})$ accepts if and only if $\mathsf{Verify}(\mathsf{pk}'_i, \mathsf{vk}, x_i, \sigma_i)$ accepts for all $i \in [k]$.

- $\mathsf{VerifyFresh}(\mathsf{pk}, \mathsf{vk}, x, \sigma) \to \{0, 1\}$: On input a public key pk, a verification key vk, a message $x \in \mathcal{X}$, and a signature σ, the fresh verification algorithm either accepts (returns 1) or rejects (returns 0).
  Vector variant: We can define a vector variant of $\mathsf{VerifyFresh}$ analogously to that of Verify.

- $\mathsf{VerifyHide}(\mathsf{pk}, \mathsf{vk}, x, \sigma^*) \to \{0, 1\}$: On input a public key pk, a verification key vk, a message $x \in \mathcal{X}$, and a signature σ^*, the hide verification algorithm either accepts (returns 1) or rejects (returns 0).
  Vector variant: We can define a vector variant of $\mathsf{VerifyHide}$ analogously to that of Verify.

Correctness. We now state the correctness requirements for a homomorphic signature scheme. Our definitions are adapted from the corresponding ones in [63]. Our homomorphic signature syntax has three different verification algorithms. The standard verification algorithm Verify can be used to verify fresh signatures (output by Sign) as well as homomorphically-evaluated signatures (output by $\mathsf{SigEval}$). The hide verification algorithm $\mathsf{VerifyHide}$ is used for verifying signatures output by the context-hiding transformation Hide, which may be structurally different from the signatures output by Sign or $\mathsf{SigEval}$. Finally, we have a special verification algorithm $\mathsf{VerifyFresh}$ that can be used to verify signatures output by Sign (before any homomorphic evaluation has taken place).

While Verify subsumes VerifyFresh, having a separate VerifyFresh algorithm is useful for formulating a strong version of evaluation correctness. Due to space limitations, we defer the formal correctness definitions to the full version of this paper [74].

Unforgeability. Intuitively, a homomorphic signature scheme is unforgeable if no efficient adversary who only possesses signatures $\sigma_1, \ldots, \sigma_\ell$ on messages $x_1, \ldots, x_\ell$ can produce a signature σ_y that is valid with respect to a function C where $y \neq C(x_1, \ldots, x_\ell)$. We give the formal definition in the full version.

Context-hiding. The second security requirement on a homomorphic signature scheme is *context-hiding*, which roughly says that if a user evaluates a function C on a message-signature pair (x, σ) to obtain a signature $\sigma_{C(x)}$, and then runs the hide algorithm on $\sigma_{C(x)}$, the resulting signature $\sigma^*_{C(x)}$ does not contain any information about x other than what is revealed by C and $C(x)$. We define this formally in the full version.

Compactness. The final property that we require from a homomorphic signature scheme is compactness. Roughly speaking, compactness requires that given a message-signature pair (x, σ), the size of the signature obtained from homomorphically evaluating a function C on σ depends only on the size of the output message $|C(x)|$ (and the security parameter) and is *independent* of the size of the original message $|x|$.

Structural properties of homomorphic signatures. Definition 3.1 specifies a *bitwise* homomorphic signature scheme where the signature on an ℓ-bit message $x = x_1 \cdots x_\ell$ consists of ℓ separate signatures $\sigma = (\sigma_1, \ldots, \sigma_\ell)$ with respect to ℓ public keys $\overrightarrow{\mathsf{pk}} = (\mathsf{pk}_1, \ldots, \mathsf{pk}_\ell)$, one for each bit of the message. As discussed in Sect. 1.1, this property is essentially to our construction of blind homomorphic signatures from homomorphic signatures and oblivious transfer. In addition to a bitwise homomorphic signature scheme, we also require a *decomposable homomorphic signature scheme* for our full construction. In a decomposable homomorphic signature scheme, a signature σ of a message x can be decomposed into a message-independent σ^{pk} that contains no information about x, and a message-dependent component σ^{m}. In the full version of this paper [74], we use this decomposability property to show that the homomorphic signature construction of Gorbunov et al. [63] simultaneously satisfies full unforgeability and context-hiding (against malicious signers).

4 Preprocessing NIZKs from Homomorphic Signatures

In this section, we begin by formally defining the notion of a non-interactive zero-knowledge argument in the preprocessing model (i.e., "preprocessing NIZKs").

This notion was first introduced by De Santis et al. [42], who also gave the first candidate construction of a preprocessing NIZK from one-way functions. Multiple works have since proposed additional candidates of preprocessing NIZKs from one-way functions [38,69,75] or oblivious transfer [73]. However, all of these constructions are *single-theorem*: the proving or verification key cannot be reused for multiple theorems without compromising either soundness or zero-knowledge. We provide a more detailed discussion of existing preprocessing NIZK constructions in Remark 4.7.

Definition 4.1 (NIZK Arguments in the Preprocessing Model). *Let $\mathcal{R}$ be an NP relation, and let $\mathcal{L}$ be its corresponding language. A non-interactive zero-knowledge (NIZK) argument for $\mathcal{L}$ in the preprocessing model consists of a tuple of three algorithms $\Pi_{\text{PPNIZK}} = (\text{Setup}, \text{Prove}, \text{Verify})$ with the following properties:*

- Setup(1^λ) $\rightarrow$ (k_P, k_V): *On input the security parameter λ, the setup algorithm (implemented in a "preprocessing" step) outputs a proving key k_P and a verification key k_V.*
- Prove(k_P, x, w) $\rightarrow$ π: *On input the proving key k_P, a statement x, and a witness w, the prover's algorithm outputs a proof π.*
- Verify(k_V, x, π) $\rightarrow$ $\{0,1\}$: *On input the verification key k_V, a statement x, and a proof π, the verifier either accepts (with output 1) or rejects (with output 0).*

Moreover, Π_{PPNIZK} should satisfy the following properties:

- **Completeness:** *For all x, w where $\mathcal{R}(x,w) = 1$, if we take $(k_P, k_V) \leftarrow$ Setup(1^λ);*

$$\Pr[\pi \leftarrow \text{Prove}(k_P, x, w) : \text{Verify}(k_V, x, \pi) = 1] = 1.$$

- **Soundness:** *For all efficient adversaries $\mathcal{A}$, if we take $(k_P, k_V) \leftarrow$ Setup(1^λ), then*

$$\Pr[(x, \pi) \leftarrow \mathcal{A}^{\text{Verify}(k_V, \cdot, \cdot)}(k_P) : x \notin \mathcal{L} \wedge \text{Verify}(k_V, x, \pi) = 1] = \text{negl}(\lambda).$$

- **Zero-Knowledge:** *For all efficient adversaries $\mathcal{A}$, there exists an efficient simulator $\mathcal{S} = (\mathcal{S}_1, \mathcal{S}_2)$ such that if we take $(k_P, k_V) \leftarrow$ Setup(1^λ) and $\tau_V \leftarrow \mathcal{S}_1(1^\lambda, k_V)$, we have that*

$$\left| \Pr[\mathcal{A}^{\mathcal{O}_0(k_P, \cdot, \cdot)}(k_V) = 1] - \Pr[\mathcal{A}^{\mathcal{O}_1(k_V, \tau_V, \cdot, \cdot)}(k_V) = 1] \right| = \text{negl}(\lambda),$$

where the oracle $\mathcal{O}_0(k_P, x, w)$ outputs Prove(k_P, x, w) if $\mathcal{R}(x, w) = 1$ and $\perp$ otherwise, and the oracle $\mathcal{O}_1(k_V, \tau_V, x, w)$ outputs $\mathcal{S}_2(k_V, \tau_V, x)$ if $\mathcal{R}(x, w) = 1$ and $\perp$ otherwise.

Remark 4.2 (Comparison to NIZKs in the CRS Model). Our zero-knowledge definition in Definition 4.1 does *not* allow the simulator to choose the verification state k_V. We can also consider a slightly weaker notion of zero-knowledge where the simulator also chooses the verification state:

- **Zero-Knowledge:** For all efficient adversaries $\mathcal{A}$, there exists an efficient simulator $\mathcal{S} = (\mathcal{S}_1, \mathcal{S}_2)$ such that if we take $(k_P, k_V) \leftarrow \mathsf{Setup}(1^\lambda)$ and $(\tilde{k}_V, \tilde{\tau}_V) \leftarrow \mathcal{S}_1(1^\lambda)$, we have that

$$\left| \Pr[\mathcal{A}^{\mathsf{Prove}(k_P, \cdot, \cdot)}(k_V) = 1] - \Pr[\mathcal{A}^{\mathcal{O}(\tilde{k}_V, \tilde{\tau}_V, \cdot, \cdot)}(\tilde{k}_V) = 1] \right| = \mathsf{negl}(\lambda),$$

where the oracle $\mathcal{O}(\tilde{k}_V, \tilde{\tau}_V, x, w)$ outputs $\mathcal{S}_2(\tilde{k}_V, \tilde{\tau}_V, x)$ if $\mathcal{R}(x, w) = 1$ and $\perp$ otherwise.

We note that this definition of zero-knowledge captures the standard notion of NIZK arguments in the common reference string (CRS) model. Specifically, in the CRS model, the Setup algorithm outputs a single CRS σ. The proving and verification keys are both defined to be σ.

Preprocessing NIZKs from homomorphic signatures. As described in Sect. 1.1, we can combine a homomorphic signature scheme (for general circuits) with any CPA-secure symmetric encryption scheme to obtain a preprocessing NIZK for general NP languages. We give our construction and security analysis below. Combining the lattice-based construction of homomorphic signatures of [63] with any lattice-based CPA-secure encryption [6,58], we obtain the first multi-theorem preprocessing NIZK from standard lattice assumptions (Corollary 4.5). In Remark 4.6, we note that a variant of Construction 4.3 also gives a *publicly-verifiable* preprocessing NIZK.

Construction 4.3 (Preprocessing NIZKs from Homomorphic Signatures). Fix a security parameter λ, and define the following quantities:

- Let $\mathcal{R}: \{0,1\}^n \times \{0,1\}^m \to \{0,1\}$ be an NP relation and $\mathcal{L}$ be its corresponding language.
- Let $\Pi_{\mathsf{SE}} = (\mathsf{SE.KeyGen}, \mathsf{SE.Encrypt}, \mathsf{SE.Decrypt})$ be a symmetric encryption scheme with message space $\{0,1\}^m$ and secret-key space $\{0,1\}^\rho$.
- For a message $x \in \{0,1\}^n$ and ciphertext ct from the ciphertext space of Π_{SE}, define the function $f_{x,\mathsf{ct}}(k_{\mathsf{SE}}) := \mathcal{R}(x, \mathsf{SE.Decrypt}(k_{\mathsf{SE}}, \mathsf{ct}))$.
- Let $\Pi_{\mathsf{HS}} = (\mathsf{PrmsGen}, \mathsf{KeyGen}, \mathsf{Sign}, \mathsf{PrmsEval}, \mathsf{SigEval}, \mathsf{Hide}, \mathsf{Verify}, \mathsf{VerifyFresh}, \mathsf{VerifyHide})$ be a homomorphic signature scheme with message space $\{0,1\}$, message length ρ, and function class $\mathcal{C}$ that includes all functions of the form $f_{x,\mathsf{ct}}$.[3]

We construct a preprocessing NIZK argument $\Pi_{\mathsf{NIZK}} = (\mathsf{Setup}, \mathsf{Prove}, \mathsf{Verify})$ as follows:

- $\mathsf{Setup}(1^\lambda) \to (k_P, k_V)$: First, generate a secret key $k_{\mathsf{SE}} \leftarrow \mathsf{SE.KeyGen}(1^\lambda)$. Next, generate $\overrightarrow{\mathsf{pk}}_{\mathsf{HS}} \leftarrow \mathsf{PrmsGen}(1^\lambda, 1^\rho)$ and a signing-verification key-pair $(\mathsf{vk}_{\mathsf{HS}}, \mathsf{sk}_{\mathsf{HS}}) \leftarrow \mathsf{KeyGen}(1^\lambda)$. Next, sign the symmetric key $\boldsymbol{\sigma}_k \leftarrow \mathsf{Sign}(\overrightarrow{\mathsf{pk}}_{\mathsf{HS}}, \mathsf{sk}_{\mathsf{HS}}, k_{\mathsf{SE}})$ and output

$$k_P = (k_{\mathsf{SE}}, \overrightarrow{\mathsf{pk}}_{\mathsf{HS}}, \mathsf{vk}_{\mathsf{HS}}, \boldsymbol{\sigma}_k) \quad \text{and} \quad k_V = (\overrightarrow{\mathsf{pk}}_{\mathsf{HS}}, \mathsf{vk}_{\mathsf{HS}}, \mathsf{sk}_{\mathsf{HS}}).$$

---

[3] Since it is more natural to view $x \in \{0,1\}^n$ as a string rather than a vector, we drop the vector notation $\boldsymbol{x}$ and simply write x in this section.

- Prove(k_P, x, w) → π: If $\mathcal{R}(x, w) = 0$, output $\bot$. Otherwise, parse $k_P = (k_{\mathsf{SE}}, \vec{\mathsf{pk}}_{\mathsf{HS}}, \mathsf{vk}_{\mathsf{HS}}, \boldsymbol{\sigma}_k)$. Let $\mathsf{ct} \leftarrow \mathsf{SE.Encrypt}(k_{\mathsf{SE}}, w)$, and $C_{x,\mathsf{ct}}$ be the circuit that computes the function $f_{x,\mathsf{ct}}$ defined above. Compute the signature $\sigma'_{x,\mathsf{ct}} \leftarrow \mathsf{SigEval}(C_{x,\mathsf{ct}}, \vec{\mathsf{pk}}_{\mathsf{HS}}, k_{\mathsf{SE}}, \boldsymbol{\sigma}_k)$ and then $\sigma^*_{x,\mathsf{ct}} \leftarrow \mathsf{Hide}(\mathsf{vk}_{\mathsf{HS}}, 1, \sigma'_{x,\mathsf{ct}})$. It outputs the proof $\pi = (\mathsf{ct}, \sigma^*_{x,\mathsf{ct}})$.

- Verify(k_V, x, π) → $\{0, 1\}$: Parse $k_V = (\vec{\mathsf{pk}}_{\mathsf{HS}}, \mathsf{vk}_{\mathsf{HS}}, \mathsf{sk}_{\mathsf{HS}})$ and $\pi = (\mathsf{ct}, \sigma^*_{x,\mathsf{ct}})$. Let $C_{x,\mathsf{ct}}$ be the circuit that computes $f_{x,\mathsf{ct}}$ defined above. Then, compute $\mathsf{pk}_{x,\mathsf{ct}} \leftarrow \mathsf{PrmsEval}(C_{x,\mathsf{ct}}, \vec{\mathsf{pk}}_{\mathsf{HS}})$, and output $\mathsf{VerifyHide}(\mathsf{pk}_{x,\mathsf{ct}}, \mathsf{vk}_{\mathsf{HS}}, 1, \sigma^*_{x,\mathsf{ct}})$.

Theorem 4.4 (Preprocessing NIZKs from Homomorphic Signatures).
Let λ be a security parameter and $\mathcal{R}$ be an NP relation (and let $\mathcal{L}$ be its corresponding language). Let Π_{NIZK} be the NIZK argument in the preprocessing model from Construction 4.3 (instantiated with a symmetric encryption scheme Π_{SE} and a homomorphic signature scheme Π_{HS}). If Π_{SE} is CPA-secure and Π_{HS} satisfies evaluation correctness, hiding correctness, selective unforgeability, and context-hiding, then Π_{NIZK} is a NIZK argument for $\mathcal{R}$ in the preprocessing model.

We give the proof of Theorem 4.4 in the full version [74]. Combining Construction 4.3 with a lattice-based homomorphic signature scheme [63] and any LWE-based CPA-secure encryption scheme [6,58], we have the following corollary.

Corollary 4.5 (Preprocessing NIZKs from Lattices). *Under the LWE assumption, there exists a multi-theorem preprocessing NIZK for NP.*

Remark 4.6 (Publicly-Verifiable Preprocessing NIZK). Observe that the verification algorithm in Construction 4.3 does not depend on the signing key $\mathsf{sk}_{\mathsf{HS}}$ of the signature scheme. Thus, we can consider a variant of Construction 4.3 where the verification key does *not* contain $\mathsf{sk}_{\mathsf{HS}}$, and thus, the verification state can be made *public*. This does not compromise soundness because the prover's state already includes the other components of the verification key. However, this publicly-verifiable version of the scheme does not satisfy zero-knowledge according to the strong notion of zero-knowledge in Definition 4.1. This is because without the signing key, the simulator is no longer able to simulate the signatures in the simulated proofs. However, if we consider the weaker notion of zero-knowledge from Remark 4.2 where the simulator chooses the verification key for the preprocessing NIZK, then the publicly-verifiable version of the scheme is provably secure. Notably, when the simulator constructs the verification key, it also chooses (and stores) the signing key for the homomorphic signature scheme. This enables the simulator to simulate signatures when generating the proofs. The resulting construction is a publicly-verifiable preprocessing NIZK (i.e., a "designated-prover" NIZK).

Remark 4.7 (Preprocessing NIZKs from Weaker Assumptions). By definition, any NIZK argument (or proof) system in the CRS model is also a preprocessing NIZK (according to the notion of zero-knowledge from Remark 4.2). In the CRS model (and without random oracles), there are several main families of assumptions known to imply NIZKs: number-theoretic conjectures such as quadratic residuosity [15,16,41],[4] trapdoor permutations [40,44,65], pairings [66], or indistinguishability obfuscation [86]. In the designated-verifier setting, constructions are also known from additively homomorphic encryption [34,36,39]. A number of works have also studied NIZKs in the preprocessing model, and several constructions have been proposed from one-way functions [38,42,69,75] and oblivious transfer [73]. Since lattice-based assumptions imply one-way functions [6,83], oblivious transfer [80], and homomorphic encryption [55,83], one might think that we can already construct NIZKs in the preprocessing model from standard lattice assumptions. To our knowledge, this is not the case:

– The NIZK constructions of [38,42,75] are *single-theorem* NIZKs, and in particular, zero-knowledge does not hold if the prover uses the same proving key to prove multiple statements. In these constructions, the proving key contains secret values, and each proof reveals a subset of the prover's secret values. As a result, the verifier can combine multiple proofs together to learn additional information about each statement than it could have learned had it only seen a single proof. Thus, the constructions in [38,42,75] do not directly give a multi-theorem NIZK.

  A natural question to ask is whether we can use the transformation by Feige et al. [44] who showed how to generically boost a NIZK (in the CRS model) with single-theorem zero-knowledge to obtain a NIZK with multi-theorem zero-knowledge. The answer turns out to be negative: the [44] transformation critically relies on the fact that the prover algorithm is publicly computable, or equivalently, that the prover algorithm does not depend on any secrets.[5] This is the case in the CRS model, since the prover algorithm depends only on the CRS, but in the preprocessing model, the prover's algorithm can depend on a (secret) proving key k_P. In the case of [38,42,75], the proving key must be kept private for zero-knowledge. Consequently, the preprocessing NIZKs of [38,42,75] do not give a general multi-theorem NIZK in the preprocessing model.

– The (preprocessing) NIZK constructions based on oblivious transfer [73], the "MPC-in-the-head" paradigm [69], and the ones based on homomorphic encryption [34,36,39] are designated-verifier, and in particular, are vulnerable to the "verifier rejection" problem. Specifically, soundness is compromised if the prover can learn the verifier's response to multiple adaptively-chosen

---

[4] Some of these schemes [16,41] are "bounded" in the sense that the prover can only prove a small number of theorems whose total size is bounded by the length of the CRS.

[5] At a high-level, the proof in [44] proceeds in two steps: first show that single-theorem zero knowledge implies single-theorem witness indistinguishability, and then that single-theorem witness indistinguishability implies multi-theorem witness indistinguishability. The second step relies on a hybrid argument, which requires that it be possible to *publicly* run the prover algorithm. This step does not go through if the prover algorithm takes in a secret state unknown to the verifier.

statements and proofs. For instance, in the case of [73], an oblivious transfer protocol is used to hide the verifier's challenge bits; namely, the verifier's challenge message is fixed during the preprocessing, which means the verifier uses the *same* challenge to verify every proof. A prover that has access to a proof-verification oracle is able to reconstruct the verifier's challenge bit-by-bit and compromise soundness of the resulting NIZK construction. A similar approach is taken in the preprocessing NIZK construction of [69].

From the above discussion, the only candidates of general multi-theorem NIZKs in the preprocessing model are the same as those in the CRS model. Thus, this work provides the first candidate construction of a multi-theorem NIZK in the preprocessing model from standard lattice assumptions. It remains an open problem to construct multi-theorem NIZKs from standard lattice assumptions in the standard CRS model.

In the full version of this paper [74], we highlight several additional properties of our multi-theorem preprocessing NIZK. We also describe another approach for instantiating our construction using context-hiding homomorphic MACs [28–30,54]. While existing homomorphic MAC constructions from one-way functions do not suffice for our constructions (they are not context-hiding), they do provide another potential avenue towards realizing multi-theorem preprocessing NIZKs from weaker assumptions.

5 Blind Homomorphic Signatures

One limitation of preprocessing NIZKs is that we require a trusted setup to generate the proving and verification keys. One solution is to have the prover and the verifier run a (malicious-secure) two-party computation protocol (e.g., [76]) to generate the proving and verification keys. However, generic MPC protocols are often costly and require making *non-black-box* use of the underlying homomorphic signature scheme. In this section, we describe how this step can be efficiently implemented using a new primitive called *blind homomorphic signatures*. We formalize our notion in the model of universal composability [24]. This has the additional advantage of allowing us to realize the stronger notion of a preprocessing universally-composable NIZK (UC-NIZK) from standard lattice assumptions. We give our UC-NIZK construction and then describe several applications to boosting the security of MPC in Sect. 6. We refer to the full version for a review of the UC model.

We now define the ideal blind homomorphic signature functionality $\mathcal{F}_{\mathrm{BHS}}$. Our definition builds upon existing definitions of the ideal signature functionality $\mathcal{F}_{\mathrm{SIG}}$ by Canetti [25] and the ideal blind signature functionality $\mathcal{F}_{\mathrm{BLSIG}}$ by Fischlin [47]. To simplify the presentation, we define the functionality in the two-party setting, where there is a special signing party (denoted **S**) and a single receiver who obtains the signature (denoted **R**). While this is a simpler model than the multi-party setting considered in [25,47], it suffices for the applications we describe in this work.

Ideal signature functionalities. The $\mathcal{F}_{\text{SIG}}$ functionality from [25] essentially provides a "registry service" where a distinguished party (the signer) is able to register message-signature pairs. Moreover, any party that possesses the verification key can check whether a particular message-signature pair is registered (and thus, constitutes a valid signature). The ideal functionality does not impose any restriction on the structure of the verification key or the legitimate signatures, and allows the adversary to choose those values. In a blind signature scheme, the signing process is replaced by an interactive protocol between the signer and the receiver, and the security requirement is that the signer does not learn the message being signed. To model this, the $\mathcal{F}_{\text{BLSIG}}$ functionality from [47] asks the adversary to provide the description of a *stateless* algorithm IdealSign in addition to the verification key to the ideal functionality $\mathcal{F}_{\text{BLSIG}}$. For blind signing requests involving an *honest* receiver, the ideal functionality uses IdealSign to generate the signatures. The message that is signed (i.e., the input to IdealSign) is not disclosed to either the signer or the adversary. This captures the intuitive requirement that the signer does not learn the message that is signed in a blind signature scheme. Conversely, if a corrupt user makes a blind signing request, then the ideal functionality asks the adversary to supply the signature that could result from such a request.

Capturing homomorphic operations. In a homomorphic signature scheme, a user possessing a signature σ on a message x should be able to compute a function g on σ to obtain a new signature σ^* on the message $g(x)$. In turn, the verification algorithm checks that σ^* is a valid signature on the value $g(x)$ *and* importantly, that it is a valid signature with respect to the function g. Namely, the signature is bound not only to the computed value $g(x)$ but also to the function g.[6] To extend the ideal signature functionality to support homomorphic operations on signatures, we begin by modifying the ideal functionality to maintain a mapping between *function-message pairs* and signatures (rather than a mapping between messages and signatures). In this case, a fresh signature σ (say, output by the blind signing protocol) on a message x would be viewed as a signature on the function-message pair (f_{id}, x), where f_{id} here denotes the identity function. Then, if a user subsequently computes a function g on σ, the resulting signature σ^* should be viewed as a signature on the new pair $(g \circ f_{\text{id}}, g(x)) = (g, g(x))$. In other words, in a homomorphic signature scheme, signatures are bound to a function-message pair, rather than a single message.

Next, we introduce an additional *signature-evaluation* operation to the ideal functionality. There are several properties we desire from our ideal functionality:

– The ideal signature functionality allows the adversary to decide the structure of the signatures, so it is only natural that the adversary also decides the structure of the signatures output by the signature evaluation procedure.

---

[6] If there is no binding between σ^* and the function g, then we cannot define a meaningful notion of unforgeability.

- Signature evaluation should be compatible with the blind signing process. Specifically, the receiver should be able to compute on a signature it obtained from the blind signing functionality, and moreover, the computation (if requested by an honest receiver) should not reveal to the adversary on which signature or message the computation was performed.
- The computed signature should also hide the input message. In particular, if the receiver obtains a blind signature on a message x and later computes a signature σ^* on $g(x)$, the signature σ^* should not reveal the original (blind) message x.

To satisfy these properties, the ideal functionality asks the adversary to additionally provide the description of a *stateless* signature evaluation algorithm IdealEval (in addition to IdealSign). The ideal functionality uses IdealEval to generate the signatures when responding to evaluation queries. We capture the third property (that the computed signatures hide the input message to the computation) by setting the inputs to IdealEval to only include the function g that is computed and the output value of the computation $g(x)$. The input message x is not provided to IdealEval.

   Under our definition, the signature evaluation functionality takes as input a function-message pair (f_{id}, x), a signature σ on (f_{id}, x) (under the verification key vk of the signature scheme), and a description of a function g (to compute on x). The output is a new signature σ^* on the pair $(g, g(x))$. That is, σ^* is a signature on the value $g(x)$ with respect to the function g. When the evaluator is honest, the signature on $(g, g(x))$ is determined by IdealEval$(g, g(x))$ (without going through the adversary). As discussed above, IdealEval only takes as input the function g and the value $g(x)$, and not the input; this means that the computed signature σ^* hides all information about x other than what is revealed by $g(x)$. When the evaluator is corrupt, the adversary chooses the signature on $(g, g(x))$, subject to basic consistency requirements.[7] Once an evaluated signature is generated, the functionality registers the new signature σ^* on the pair $(g, g(x))$. Our definition implicitly requires that homomorphic evaluation be non-interactive. Neither the adversary nor the signer is notified or participates in the protocol.

Preventing selective failures. In our definition, the functionalities IdealSign and IdealEval must either output $\bot$ on *all* inputs, or output $\bot$ on *none* of the inputs. This captures the property that a malicious signer cannot mount a *selective failure* attack against an honest receiver, where the function of whether the receiver obtains a signature or not in the blind signing protocol varies depending on its input message. In the case of the blind signing protocol, we do allow a malicious signer to cause the protocol to fail, but this failure event must be *independent* of the receiver's message. We capture this in the ideal functionality by allowing a corrupt signer to dictate whether a blind signing execution completes

---

[7] The adversary is not allowed to re-register a signature that was previously declared invalid (according to the verification functionality) as a valid signature.

successfully or not. However, the corrupt signer must decide whether a given protocol invocation succeeds or fails *independently* of the receiver's message.

Simplifications and generalizations. In defining our ideal blind homomorphic signature functionality, we impose several restrictions to simplify the description and analysis. We describe these briefly here, and note how we could extend the functionality to provide additional generality. Note that all of the applications we consider (Sect. 6) only require the basic version of the functionality (Fig. 1), and not its generalized variants.

- **One-time signatures.** The ideal blind homomorphic signature functionality supports blind signing of a *single* message. Namely, the ideal blind signing functionality only responds to the first signing request from the receiver and ignores all subsequent requests. Moreover, the ideal functionality only supports signature evaluation requests after a signature has been successfully issued by the ideal signing functionality. We capture this via a ready flag that is only set at the conclusion of a successful signing operation. We can relax this single-signature restriction, but at the cost of complicating the analysis.
- **Single-hop evaluation.** Our second restriction on the ideal blind homomorphic signature functionality is we only consider "single-hop" homomorphic operations: that is, we only allow homomorphic operations on fresh signatures. In the ideal functionality, we capture this by having the signature evaluation functionality ignore all requests to compute on function-message pairs (f, x) where $f \neq f_{\mathsf{id}}$ is not the identity function. A more general definition would also consider "multi-hop" evaluation where a party can perform arbitrarily many sequential operations on a signature. The reason we present our definition in the simpler single-hop setting is because existing constructions of homomorphic signatures [63] (which we leverage in our construction) do not support the multi-hop analog of our definition. This is because under our definition, the ideal evaluation functionality essentially combines the homomorphic evaluation with the context-hiding transformation in standard homomorphic signature schemes. The current homomorphic signature candidate [63] does not support homomorphic computation after performing context-hiding, and so, cannot be used to realize the more general "multi-hop" version of our functionality. For this reason, we give our definition in the single-hop setting.

We give the formal specification of the ideal blind homomorphic signature functionality $\mathcal{F}_{\mathrm{BHS}}$ in Fig. 1.

5.1 Constructing Blind Homomorphic Signatures

In Fig. 2, we give the formal description of our blind homomorphic signature protocol Π_{BHS} in the $\mathcal{F}_{\mathrm{OT}}^{\ell, s}$-hybrid model.[8] Here, we provide a brief overview of

---

[8] For the protocol description and its security proof, we use the vector notation $\boldsymbol{x}$ to represent the messages (in order to be consistent with the homomorphic signature notation).

Functionality $\mathcal{F}_{\text{BHS}}$

The ideal blind homomorphic signature functionality $\mathcal{F}_{\text{BHS}}$ runs with a signer **S**, a receiver **R**, and an ideal adversary $\mathcal{S}$. The functionality is parameterized by a message length ℓ and a function class $\mathcal{H}$. We write f_{id} to denote the identity function.

Key Generation: Upon receiving a value (sid, keygen) from the signer **S**, send (sid, keygen) to the adversary $\mathcal{S}$. After receiving (sid, vkey, vk) from $\mathcal{S}$, give (sid, vkey, vk) to **S** and record vk. Then, initialize an empty list $\mathcal{L}$, and a ready flag (initially unset).

Signature Generation: If a signature-generation request has already been processed, ignore the request. Otherwise, upon receiving a value (sid, sign, vk, x) from the receiver **R** (for some message $x \in \{0,1\}^\ell$), send (sid, signature) to $\mathcal{S}$, and let (sid, IdealSign, IdealEval) be the response from $\mathcal{S}$, where IdealSign and IdealEval are functions that either output $\perp$ on *all* inputs or on *no* inputs. Record the tuple (IdealSign, IdealEval). If **S** is honest, send (sid, signature) to **S** to notify it that a signature request has taken place. If **S** is corrupt, then send (sid, sig-success) to $\mathcal{S}$ and let (sid, b) be the response from $\mathcal{S}$. If $b \neq 1$, send (sid, signature, $(f_{\text{id}}, x), \perp$) to **R**. Otherwise, proceed as follows:

- If **R** is honest, generate $\sigma \leftarrow \text{IdealSign}(x)$, and send (sid, signature, $(f_{\text{id}}, x), \sigma$) to **R**.
- If **R** is corrupt, send (sid, sign, x) to $\mathcal{S}$ to obtain (sid, signature, $(f_{\text{id}}, x), \sigma$).

If (vk, $(f_{\text{id}}, x), \sigma, 0) \in \mathcal{L}$, abort. Otherwise, add (vk, $(f_{\text{id}}, x), \sigma, 1$) to $\mathcal{L}$, and if $\sigma \neq \perp$, set the flag ready.

Signature Verification: Upon receiving an input (sid, verify, vk$'$, $(f, x), \sigma$) from a party $\mathbf{P} \in \{\mathbf{S}, \mathbf{R}\}$, proceed as follows:

- *Correctness:* If $f \notin \mathcal{H}$, then set $t = 0$. If vk = vk$'$ and (vk, $(f, x), \sigma, 1) \in \mathcal{L}$, then set $t = 1$.
- *Unforgeability:* Otherwise, if vk = vk$'$, the signer **S** has not been corrupted, and there does not exist (vk, $(f_{\text{id}}, x'), \sigma', 1) \in \mathcal{L}$ for some x', σ' where $x = f(x')$, then set $t = 0$, and add (vk, $(f, x), \sigma, 0$) to $\mathcal{L}$.
- *Consistency:* Otherwise, if there is already an entry (vk$'$, $(f, x), \sigma, t') \in \mathcal{L}$ for some t', set $t = t'$.
- Otherwise, send (sid, verify, vk$'$, $(f, x), \sigma$) to the adversary $\mathcal{S}$. After receiving (sid, verified, $(f, x), \sigma, \tau$) from $\mathcal{S}$, set $t = \tau$ and add (vk$'$, $(f, x), \sigma, \tau$) to $\mathcal{L}$.

Send (sid, verified, $(f, x), \sigma, t$) to **P**. If $t = 1$, we say the signature successfully verified.

Fig. 1. The $\mathcal{F}_{\text{BHS}}$ functionality. The description continues on the next page.

Functionality $\mathcal{F}_{\text{BHS}}$ (Continued)

Signature Evaluation: If the ready flag has not been set, then ignore the request. Otherwise, upon receiving an input $(\text{sid}, \text{eval}, \text{vk}, g, (f, x), \sigma)$ from a party $\mathbf{P} \in \{\mathbf{S}, \mathbf{R}\}$, ignore the request if $f \neq f_{\text{id}}$. If $f = f_{\text{id}}$, then apply the signature verification procedure to $(\text{sid}, \text{verify}, \text{vk}, (f, x), \sigma)$, but do *not* forward the output to $\mathbf{P}$. If the signature does not verify, then ignore the request. Otherwise, proceed as follows:

- If $g \notin \mathcal{H}$, then set $\sigma^* = \perp$.
- Otherwise, if $\mathbf{P}$ is honest, compute $\sigma^* \leftarrow \text{IdealEval}(g, g(x))$.
- Otherwise, if $\mathbf{P}$ is corrupt, send $(\text{sid}, \text{eval}, g, (f, x), \sigma)$ to $\mathcal{S}$ to obtain $(\text{sid}, \text{signature}, (g, g(x)), \sigma^*)$.

Finally, send $(\text{sid}, \text{signature}, (g, g(x)), \sigma^*)$ to $\mathbf{P}$. If $\sigma^* \neq \perp$ and $(\text{vk}, (g, g(x)), \sigma^*, 0) \in \mathcal{L}$, abort. If $\sigma^* \neq \perp$ and $(\text{vk}, (g, g(x)), \sigma^*, 0) \notin \mathcal{L}$, add $(\text{vk}, (g, g(x)), \sigma^*, 1)$ to $\mathcal{L}$.

Fig. 1. (*continued*)

the construction. As discussed in Sect. 1.1, our construction combines homomorphic signatures with any UC-secure oblivious transfer protocol [27]. The key-generation, signature-verification, and signature-evaluation operations in Π_{BHS} just correspond to running the underlying Π_{HS} algorithms.

The blind signing protocol is interactive and relies on OT. Since we use a bitwise homomorphic signature scheme, a signature on an ℓ-bit message consists of ℓ signatures, one for each bit of the message. In the first step of the blind signing protocol, the signer constructs two signatures (one for the bit 0 and one for the bit 1) for each bit position of the message. The receiver then requests the signatures corresponding to the bits of its message using the OT protocol. Intuitively, the OT protocol ensures that the signer does not learn which set of signatures the receiver requested and the receiver only learns a single signature for each bit position. However, this basic scheme is vulnerable to a "selective-failure" attack where the signer strategically generates *invalid* signatures for certain bit positions of the message x. As a result, whether the receiver obtains a valid signature on its entire message becomes *correlated* with its message itself. To prevent this selective-failure attack, we use the standard technique of having the receiver first split its message x into a number of random shares $w_1, \ldots, w_t$ where $x = \bigoplus_{i \in [t]} w_i$. Instead of asking for a signature on x directly, it instead asks for a signature on the shares $w_1, \ldots, w_t$. Since the signatures on the shares $w_1, \ldots, w_t$ are homomorphic, the receiver can still compute a signature on the original message x and hence, correctness of signing is preserved. Moreover, as we show in the proof of Theorem 5.1, unless the malicious signer correctly guesses *all* of the shares of $w_1, \ldots, w_t$ the receiver chose, the probability that the receiver aborts (due to receiving an invalid signature) is *independent* of x no matter how the malicious signer generates the signatures. We formally summarize the security properties of Π_{BHS} in the following theorem, but defer its proof to the full version [74].

Theorem 5.1 (Blind Homomorphic Signatures). *Fix a security parameter* λ. *Define parameters* ℓ, t, *and* s *as in* Π_{BHS} *(Fig. 2) where* $t = \omega(\log \lambda)$. *Let* $\mathcal{H}$ *be a function class over* $\{0,1\}^{\ell}$ *and let* Π_{HS} *be a homomorphic signature scheme for the message space* $\{0,1\}$ *and function class* $\mathcal{H}'$ *such that for any function* $f \in \mathcal{H}$, *we have* $f \circ f_{\text{recon}} \in \mathcal{H}'$, *where* f_{recon} *is the share-reconstruction function from Fig. 2. Suppose that* Π_{HS} *satisfies correctness, unforgeability, and context-hiding. Then, the protocol* Π_{BHS} *(when instantiated with* Π_{HS}*) securely realizes the ideal functionality* $\mathcal{F}_{\text{BHS}}$ *(Fig. 1) with respect to function class* $\mathcal{H}$ *in the presence of (static) malicious adversaries in the* $\mathcal{F}_{\text{OT}}^{\ell,s}$*-hybrid model.*

Blind homomorphic signatures from LWE. Combining the fully-secure homomorphic signature scheme described in the full version [74] (based on [63]) with the lattice-based UC-secure oblivious transfer protocol from [80], we obtain a blind homomorphic signature scheme from standard lattice assumptions. We describe our instantiation below.

Fact 5.2 (Oblivious Transfer from LWE [80]). *Let* λ *be a security parameter and define parameters* $\ell, s = \text{poly}(\lambda)$. *Then, under the LWE assumption, there exists a protocol* Π_{OT} *that security realizes the ideal OT functionality* $\mathcal{F}_{\text{OT}}^{\ell,s}$ *in the presence of malicious adversaries in the CRS model (and assuming static corruptions). Moreover, the protocol* Π_{OT} *is round-optimal: it consists of one message from the receiver to the signer and one from the receiver to the signer.*

Corollary 5.3 (Blind Homomorphic Signatures from LWE). *Let* λ *be a security parameter. Then, under the LWE assumption, for all* $d = \text{poly}(\lambda)$, *there exists a protocol* Π'_{BHS} *that securely realizes* $\mathcal{F}_{\text{BHS}}$ *for the class of depth-d Boolean circuits in the presence of malicious adversaries in the CRS model (and assuming static corruptions). Moreover, the protocol* Π'_{BHS} *satisfies the following properties:*

- *The key-generation, signature-verification, and signature-evaluation protocols are non-interactive.*
- *The signature-generation protocol (i.e., blind signing) is a two-round interactive protocol between the signer and the receiver (one message each way).*
- *The length of a signature is* $\text{poly}(\lambda, d)$.

Proof. Let Π_{BHS} be the protocol from Fig. 2 instantiated with a lattice-based homomorphic signature scheme (see the full version [74]). By Theorem 5.1, protocol Π_{BHS} securely realizes $\mathcal{F}_{\text{BHS}}$ in the $\mathcal{F}_{\text{OT}}^{\ell,s}$-hybrid model, for some $\ell, s = \text{poly}(\lambda)$. We let Π'_{BHS} be the protocol obtained by instantiating the functionality $\mathcal{F}_{\text{OT}}^{\ell,s}$ in Π_{BHS} with the protocol from Fact 5.2. Security of Π'_{BHS} then follows from the universal composition theorem. Key generation, signature verification, and signature evaluation in Π'_{BHS} simply corresponds to invoking the associated functionalities of the underlying homomorphic signature scheme, and thus, are non-interactive. The signature length is also inherited from Π_{HS}. The blind signing protocol reduces to a single invocation of $\mathcal{F}_{\text{OT}}^{\ell,s}$, which by Fact 5.2, can be implemented by just two rounds of interaction.

Protocol Π_{BHS} in the $\mathcal{F}_{\text{OT}}^{\ell,s}$-Hybrid Model

Let λ be a security parameter and $\mathcal{H}$ be a class of functions from $\{0,1\}^\ell$ to $\{0,1\}$. For a parameter $t \in \mathbb{N}$, we define $f_{\text{recon}} \colon \{0,1\}^{t\ell} \to \{0,1\}^\ell$ to be a share-reconstruction function $(\boldsymbol{w}_1, \ldots, \boldsymbol{w}_t) \mapsto \bigoplus_{i \in [t]} \boldsymbol{w}_i$. Let $\Pi_{\text{HS}} = (\text{PrmsGen}, \text{KeyGen}, \text{Sign}, \text{PrmsEval}, \text{SigEval}, \text{Hide}, \text{Verify}, \text{VerifyFresh}, \text{VerifyHide})$ be a decomposable homomorphic signature scheme with message space $\{0,1\}$, message length ℓ, and function class $\mathcal{H}'$ where $\mathcal{H}'$ contains all functions of the form $f \circ f_{\text{recon}}$ where $f \in \mathcal{H}$. We assume that the signer $\mathbf{S}$ and receiver $\mathbf{R}$ has access to the ideal functionality $\mathcal{F}_{\text{OT}}^{\ell,s}$ where s is the length of the signatures in Π_{HS}.

Key Generation: Upon receiving an input $(\text{sid}, \text{keygen})$, the signer $\mathbf{S}$ computes a set of public parameters $\overrightarrow{\text{pk}} = \{\text{pk}_{i,j}\}_{i \in [t], j \in [\ell]} \leftarrow \text{PrmsGen}(1^\lambda, 1^{t\ell})$, and a pair of keys $(\text{vk}', \text{sk}) \leftarrow \text{KeyGen}(1^\lambda)$. It stores (sid, sk), sets $\text{vk} = (\overrightarrow{\text{pk}}, \text{vk}')$, and outputs $(\text{sid}, \text{vkey}, \text{vk})$. Finally, the signer initializes the **ready** flag (initially unset).

Signature Generation: If the signer or receiver has already processed a signature-generation request, then they ignore the request. Otherwise, they proceed as follows:

– **Receiver:** On input $(\text{sid}, \text{sign}, \text{vk}, \boldsymbol{x})$, where $\text{vk} = (\overrightarrow{\text{pk}}, \text{vk}')$ and $\boldsymbol{x} \in \{0,1\}^\ell$, the receiver chooses t shares $\boldsymbol{w}_1, \ldots, \boldsymbol{w}_t \xleftarrow{\text{R}} \{0,1\}^\ell$ where $\bigoplus_{i \in [t]} \boldsymbol{w}_i = \boldsymbol{x}$. Then, for each $i \in [t]$, it sends $((\text{sid}, i), \text{receiver}, \boldsymbol{w}_i)$ to $\mathcal{F}_{\text{OT}}^{\ell,s}$. It also initializes the **ready** flag (initially unset). Note that if vk is not of the form $(\overrightarrow{\text{pk}}, \text{vk}')$ where $\text{pk}' = \{\text{pk}_{i,j}\}_{i \in [t], j \in [\ell]}$, the receiver outputs $(\text{sid}, \text{signature}, (f_{\text{id}}, \boldsymbol{x}), \bot)$.

– **Signer:** On input $(\text{sid}, \text{signature})$, the signer generates signatures $\sigma_{i,j}^{\text{pk}} \leftarrow \text{SignPK}(\text{pk}_{i,j}, \text{sk})$ and $\sigma_{i,j,b}^{\text{m}} \leftarrow \text{SignM}(\text{pk}_{i,j}, \text{sk}, b, \sigma_{i,j}^{\text{pk}})$, and sets $\sigma_{i,j,b} = (\sigma_{i,j}^{\text{pk}}, \sigma_{i,j,b}^{\text{m}})$ for all $i \in [t]$, $j \in [\ell]$ and $b \in \{0,1\}$. The signer then sends $((\text{sid}, i), \text{sender}, \{(\sigma_{i,j,0}, \sigma_{i,j,1})\}_{j \in [\ell]})$ to $\mathcal{F}_{\text{OT}}^{\ell,s}$. In addition, $\mathbf{S}$ sends the message-independent components $\{\sigma_{i,j}^{\text{pk}}\}_{i \in [t], j \in [\ell]}$ to $\mathbf{R}$, and sets the **ready** flag.

Let $\{\tilde{\sigma}_{i,j}^{\text{pk}}\}_{i \in [t], j \in [\ell]}$ be the message-independent signatures that $\mathbf{R}$ receives from $\mathbf{S}$, and $\{\tilde{\sigma}_{i,j}\}_{i \in [t], j \in [\ell]}$ be the signatures $\mathbf{R}$ receives from the different $\mathcal{F}_{\text{OT}}^{\ell,s}$ invocations. For all $i \in [t]$ and $j \in [\ell]$, the receiver checks that $\text{VerifyFresh}(\text{pk}_{i,j}, \text{vk}', w_{i,j}, \tilde{\sigma}_{i,j}) = 1$, and moreover, that the message-independent component of $\tilde{\sigma}_{i,j}$ matches $\tilde{\sigma}_{i,j}^{\text{pk}}$ it received from the signer. If any check fails, then $\mathbf{R}$ outputs $(\text{sid}, \text{signature}, (f_{\text{id}}, \boldsymbol{x}), \bot)$. Otherwise, it evaluates $\sigma \leftarrow \text{SigEval}(f_{\text{recon}}, \overrightarrow{\text{pk}}, (\boldsymbol{w}_1, \ldots, \boldsymbol{w}_t), (\sigma_1, \ldots, \sigma_t))$, where $\sigma_i = (\tilde{\sigma}_{i,1}, \ldots, \tilde{\sigma}_{i,\ell})$ for all $i \in [t]$. The receiver also sets the **ready** flag and outputs $(\text{sid}, \text{signature}, (f_{\text{id}}, \boldsymbol{x}), \sigma)$.

Fig. 2. The Π_{BHS} protocol. The protocol description continues on the next page.

Protocol Π_{BHS} in the $\mathcal{F}_{\text{OT}}^{\ell,s}$-Hybrid Model (Continued)

Signature Verification: Upon receiving an input $(\text{sid}, \text{verify}, \text{vk}, (f, \boldsymbol{x}), \boldsymbol{\sigma})$ where $\text{vk} = (\overrightarrow{\text{pk}}, \text{vk}')$, party $\mathbf{P} \in \{\mathbf{S}, \mathbf{R}\}$ first checks if $f \notin \mathcal{H}$ and sets $t = 0$ if this is the case. Otherwise, it computes $\text{pk}_f \leftarrow \text{PrmsEval}(f \circ f_{\text{recon}}, \overrightarrow{\text{pk}})$. If $f = f_{\text{id}}$, then it sets $t \leftarrow \text{Verify}(\text{pk}_f, \text{vk}', \boldsymbol{x}, \boldsymbol{\sigma})$, and if $f \neq f_{\text{id}}$, it sets $t \leftarrow \text{VerifyHide}(\text{pk}_f, \text{vk}', \boldsymbol{x}, \boldsymbol{\sigma})$. It outputs $(\text{sid}, \text{verified}, \boldsymbol{x}, \boldsymbol{\sigma}, t)$.

Signature Evaluation: If the ready flag has not been set, then ignore the request. Otherwise, upon receiving an input $(\text{sid}, \text{eval}, \text{vk}, g, (f, \boldsymbol{x}), \boldsymbol{\sigma})$, party $\mathbf{P} \in \{\mathbf{S}, \mathbf{R}\}$ ignores the request if $f \neq f_{\text{id}}$. If $f = f_{\text{id}}$, $\mathbf{P}$ runs the signature-verification procedure on input $(\text{sid}, \text{verify}, \text{vk}, (f, \boldsymbol{x}), \boldsymbol{\sigma})$ (but does not produce an output). If the signature does not verify, then ignore the request. Otherwise, it parses $\text{vk} = (\overrightarrow{\text{pk}}, \text{vk}')$, computes $\text{pk}_{\text{recon}} \leftarrow \text{PrmsEval}(f_{\text{recon}}, \overrightarrow{\text{pk}})$ and computes $\sigma' \leftarrow \text{SigEval}(g, \text{pk}_{\text{recon}}, \boldsymbol{x}, \boldsymbol{\sigma})$, and $\sigma^* \leftarrow \text{Hide}(\text{vk}', g(\boldsymbol{x}), \sigma')$. It outputs $(\text{sid}, \text{signature}, (g, g(\boldsymbol{x})), \sigma^*)$.

Fig. 2. (*continued*)

6 Universally-Composable Preprocessing NIZKs

In this section, we show how to combine blind homomorphic signatures with CPA-secure encryption to obtain UC-NIZKs in the preprocessing model from standard lattice assumptions. We give our protocol Π_{ZK} in the $\mathcal{F}_{\text{BHS}}$-hybrid model in Fig. 3. Next, we state the formal security theorem and describe how to instantiate it from standard lattice assumptions. We give the proof of Theorem 6.1 in the full version of this paper [74].

Theorem 6.1 (Preprocessing Zero-Knowledge Arguments). *Let $\Pi_{\text{SE}} = (\text{KeyGen}, \text{Encrypt}, \text{Decrypt})$ be a CPA-secure encryption scheme. Then, the protocol Π_{ZK} in Fig. 3 (instantiated with Π_{SE}) securely realizes $\mathcal{F}_{\text{ZK}}$ in the presence of (static) malicious adversaries in the $\mathcal{F}_{\text{BHS}}$-hybrid model.*

Corollary 6.2 (Preprocessing UC-NIZKs from LWE). *Let λ be a security parameter. Then, under the LWE assumption, for all $d = \text{poly}(\lambda)$, there exists a protocol Π'_{NIZK} that securely realizes $\mathcal{F}_{\text{ZK}}$ in the presence of (static) malicious adversaries in the CRS model for all NP relations $\mathcal{R}$ that can be computed by a circuit of depth at most d. The protocol Π'_{NIZK} satisfies the following properties:*

- *The (one-time) preprocessing phase is a two-round protocol between the prover and the verifier.*
- *The prover's and verifier's algorithms are both non-interactive.*
- *If $\mathcal{R}$ is an NP relation, then the length of a proof of membership for the language associated with $\mathcal{R}$ is $m + \text{poly}(\lambda, d)$, where m is the size of the witness associated with $\mathcal{R}$.*

Protocol Π_{ZK} in the $\mathcal{F}_{BHS}$-Hybrid Model

Let λ be a security parameter and $\Pi_{SE} = (\mathsf{KeyGen}, \mathsf{Encrypt}, \mathsf{Decrypt})$ be a CPA-secure encryption scheme. We assume that the prover $\mathcal{P}$ and the verifier $\mathcal{V}$ have access to the ideal functionality $\mathcal{F}_{BHS}$, where $\mathcal{P}$ is the receiver $\mathbf{R}$ and $\mathcal{V}$ is the signer $\mathbf{S}$. For any NP relation $\mathcal{R}$, define the Boolean-valued function $\mathsf{CheckWitness}_{\mathcal{R},ct,x}$, parameterized by $\mathcal{R}$, a statement x, and a ciphertext ct as follows: on input a secret key sk, $\mathsf{CheckWitness}_{\mathcal{R},ct,x}(sk)$ outputs 1 if and only if $\mathcal{R}(x, \mathsf{Decrypt}(sk, ct)) = 1$, and 0 otherwise. We implicitly assume that $\mathsf{CheckWitness}_{\mathcal{R},ct,x} \in \mathcal{H}$, where $\mathcal{H}$ is the function class associated with $\mathcal{F}_{BHS}$.

Preprocessing phase: In the preprocessing phase, the prover and verifier do the following:

1. The verifier sends (sid, keygen) to $\mathcal{F}_{BHS}$ and receives in response a verification key vk. The verifier sends vk to the prover. Subsequently, when the verifier receives $(sid, \mathsf{signature})$ from $\mathcal{F}_{BHS}$, it sets the ready flag.
2. The prover begins by sampling a secret key $sk \leftarrow \mathsf{KeyGen}(1^\lambda)$. Then, it requests a signature on sk under vk by sending $(sid, \mathsf{sign}, vk, sk)$ to $\mathcal{F}_{BHS}$. The prover receives a signature σ_{sk} from $\mathcal{F}_{BHS}$. If $\sigma_{sk} = \bot$, then the prover aborts.

Prover: On input a tuple $(sid, ssid, \mathsf{prove}, \mathcal{R}, x, w)$ where $\mathcal{R}(x, w) = 1$, the prover proceeds as follows:

1. Encrypt the witness w to obtain a ciphertext $ct \leftarrow \mathsf{Encrypt}(sk, w)$.
2. Submit $(sid, \mathsf{eval}, vk, \mathsf{CheckWitness}_{\mathcal{R},ct,x}, (f_{id}, sk), \sigma_{sk})$ to $\mathcal{F}_{BHS}$ to obtain a signature σ^*.
3. Set $\pi = (ct, \sigma^*)$ and send $(sid, ssid, \mathsf{proof}, \mathcal{R}, x, \pi)$ to the verifier.

Verifier: When the verifier receives a tuple $(sid, ssid, \mathsf{proof}, \mathcal{R}, x, \pi)$, it ignores the request if the ready flag has not been set. Otherwise, it parses $\pi = (ct, \sigma)$, and ignores the message if π does not have this form. Otherwise, it submits $(sid, \mathsf{verify}, vk, (\mathsf{CheckWitness}_{\mathcal{R},ct,x}, 1), \sigma)$ to $\mathcal{F}_{BHS}$. If the signature is valid (i.e., $\mathcal{F}_{BHS}$ replies with 1), then the verifier accepts and outputs $(sid, ssid, \mathsf{proof}, \mathcal{R}, x)$. Otherwise the verifier ignores the message.

Fig. 3. Preprocessing ZK argument in the $\mathcal{F}_{BHS}$-hybrid model.

Proof. Fix a depth bound $d = \mathsf{poly}(\lambda)$. First, we can instantiate the CPA-secure encryption scheme $\Pi_{SE} = (\mathsf{KeyGen}, \mathsf{Encrypt}, \mathsf{Decrypt})$ in Fig. 3 from lattices using any lattice-based CPA-secure symmetric encryption scheme [6,58]. Let d' be a bound on the depth of the circuit that computes the $\mathsf{CheckWitness}_{\mathcal{R},ct,x}$ function in Fig. 3. Note that $d' = \mathsf{poly}(\lambda, d)$, since the depth of the relation $\mathcal{R}$ is bounded by d and the depth of the $\mathsf{Decrypt}$ function is $\mathsf{poly}(\lambda)$. By Corollary 5.3, under the LWE assumption, there exists a protocol Π'_{BHS} that securely realizes $\mathcal{F}_{BHS}$ for the class of all depth-d' Boolean circuits in the presence of (static) malicious adversaries. The claim then follows by combining Theorem 6.1 with Corollary 5.3 and the universal composition theorem. We now check the additional properties:

- The preprocessing phase corresponds to the blind signing protocol of Π'_{BHS}, which is a two-round protocol between the signer and the verifier.
- The prover's algorithm corresponds to signature evaluation while the verifier's algorithm corresponds to signature verification. Both of these are non-interactive in Π'_{BHS}.
- The length of a proof for an NP relation $\mathcal{R}$ consists of an encryption of the witness under Π_{SE} (of size $m + \mathsf{poly}(\lambda)$) and a signature under Π'_{BHS} (of size $\mathsf{poly}(\lambda, d)$). The total size is bounded by $m + \mathsf{poly}(\lambda, d)$.   □

6.1 Applications to MPC

In the full version of this paper, we describe several applications of our preprocessing UC-NIZKs to boosting the security of MPC protocols. Specifically, we show that combining our construction with the round-optimal, semi-malicious MPC protocol of Mukherjee-Wichs [78] yields a round-optimal, malicious-secure MPC protocol from lattices in a *reusable preprocessing* model where the communication complexity only depends on the size of the inputs/outputs. Then, we show how to obtain a *succinct* version of the GMW [59,60] compiler from lattice assumptions.

Acknowledgments. We thank Dan Boneh and Akshayaram Srinivasan for many insightful comments and discussions on this work. We thank the anonymous reviewers for helpful comments on the presentation. This work was funded by NSF, DARPA, a grant from ONR, and the Simons Foundation. Opinions, findings and conclusions or recommendations expressed in this material are those of the authors and do not necessarily reflect the views of DARPA.

References

1. Abe, M.: A secure three-move blind signature scheme for polynomially many signatures. In: Pfitzmann, B. (ed.) EUROCRYPT 2001. LNCS, vol. 2045, pp. 136–151. Springer, Heidelberg (2001). https://doi.org/10.1007/3-540-44987-6_9
2. Abe, M., Fuchsbauer, G., Groth, J., Haralambiev, K., Ohkubo, M.: Structure-preserving signatures and commitments to group elements. In: Rabin, T. (ed.) CRYPTO 2010. LNCS, vol. 6223, pp. 209–236. Springer, Heidelberg (2010). https://doi.org/10.1007/978-3-642-14623-7_12
3. Abe, M., Haralambiev, K., Ohkubo, M.: Signing on elements in bilinear groups for modular protocol design. IACR Cryptology ePrint Archive (2010)
4. Abe, M., Ohkubo, M.: A framework for universally composable non-committing blind signatures. In: Matsui, M. (ed.) ASIACRYPT 2009. LNCS, vol. 5912, pp. 435–450. Springer, Heidelberg (2009). https://doi.org/10.1007/978-3-642-10366-7_26

5. Ahn, J.H., Boneh, D., Camenisch, J., Hohenberger, S., Shelat, A., Waters, B.: Computing on authenticated data. J. Cryptol. **28**(2), 351–395 (2015)
6. Ajtai, M.: Generating hard instances of lattice problems. In: STOC (1996)
7. Alamati, N., Peikert, C., Stephens-Davidowitz, N.: New (and old) proof systems for lattice problems. In: Abdalla, M., Dahab, R. (eds.) PKC 2018. LNCS, vol. 10770, pp. 619–643. Springer, Cham (2018). https://doi.org/10.1007/978-3-319-76581-5_21
8. Ateniese, G., et al.: Provable data possession at untrusted stores. In: ACM CCS (2007)
9. Ateniese, G., Kamara, S., Katz, J.: Proofs of storage from homomorphic identification protocols. In: Matsui, M. (ed.) ASIACRYPT 2009. LNCS, vol. 5912, pp. 319–333. Springer, Heidelberg (2009). https://doi.org/10.1007/978-3-642-10366-7_19
10. Attrapadung, N., Libert, B.: Homomorphic network coding signatures in the standard model. In: Catalano, D., Fazio, N., Gennaro, R., Nicolosi, A. (eds.) PKC 2011. LNCS, vol. 6571, pp. 17–34. Springer, Heidelberg (2011). https://doi.org/10.1007/978-3-642-19379-8_2
11. Backes, M., Fiore, D., Reischuk, R.M.: Verifiable delegation of computation on outsourced data. In: ACM CCS (2013)
12. Baldimtsi, F., Lysyanskaya, A.: Anonymous credentials light. In: ACM CCS (2013)
13. Bellare, M., Namprempre, C., Pointcheval, D., Semanko, M.: The one-more-RSA-inversion problems and the security of Chaum's blind signature scheme. J. Cryptol. **16**(3), 185–215 (2003)
14. Benhamouda, F., Blazy, O., Ducas, L., Quach, W.: Hash proof systems over lattices revisited. In: Abdalla, M., Dahab, R. (eds.) PKC 2018. LNCS, vol. 10770, pp. 644–674. Springer, Cham (2018). https://doi.org/10.1007/978-3-319-76581-5_22
15. Blum, M., De Santis, A., Micali, S., Persiano, G.: Noninteractive zero-knowledge. SIAM J. Comput. **20**(6), 1084–1118 (1991)
16. Blum, M., Feldman, P., Micali, S.: Non-interactive zero-knowledge and its applications. In: STOC (1988)
17. Boldyreva, A.: Threshold signatures, multisignatures and blind signatures based on the Gap-Diffie-Hellman-Group signature scheme. In: Desmedt, Y.G. (ed.) PKC 2003. LNCS, vol. 2567, pp. 31–46. Springer, Heidelberg (2003). https://doi.org/10.1007/3-540-36288-6_3
18. Boneh, D., Freeman, D.M.: Homomorphic signatures for polynomial functions. In: Paterson, K.G. (ed.) EUROCRYPT 2011. LNCS, vol. 6632, pp. 149–168. Springer, Heidelberg (2011). https://doi.org/10.1007/978-3-642-20465-4_10
19. Boneh, D., Freeman, D.M.: Linearly homomorphic signatures over binary fields and new tools for lattice-based signatures. In: Catalano, D., Fazio, N., Gennaro, R., Nicolosi, A. (eds.) PKC 2011. LNCS, vol. 6571, pp. 1–16. Springer, Heidelberg (2011). https://doi.org/10.1007/978-3-642-19379-8_1
20. Boneh, D., Freeman, D.M., Katz, J., Waters, B.: Signing a linear subspace: signature schemes for network coding. In: Jarecki, S., Tsudik, G. (eds.) PKC 2009. LNCS, vol. 5443, pp. 68–87. Springer, Heidelberg (2009). https://doi.org/10.1007/978-3-642-00468-1_5
21. Brands, S.A.: Rethinking Public Key Infrastructures and Digital Certificates: Building in Privacy. MIT Press, Cambridge (2000)
22. Brzuska, C., et al.: Security of sanitizable signatures revisited. In: Jarecki, S., Tsudik, G. (eds.) PKC 2009. LNCS, vol. 5443, pp. 317–336. Springer, Heidelberg (2009). https://doi.org/10.1007/978-3-642-00468-1_18

23. Camenisch, J., Koprowski, M., Warinschi, B.: Efficient blind signatures without random oracles. In: Blundo, C., Cimato, S. (eds.) SCN 2004. LNCS, vol. 3352, pp. 134–148. Springer, Heidelberg (2005). https://doi.org/10.1007/978-3-540-30598-9_10

24. Canetti, R.: Universally composable security: a new paradigm for cryptographic protocols. In: FOCS (2001)

25. Canetti, R.: Universally composable signature, certification, and authentication. In: CSFW (2004)

26. Canetti, R., Chen, Y., Reyzin, L., Rothblum, R.D.: Fiat-Shamir and correlation intractability from strong KDM-Secure encryption. In: Nielsen, J.B., Rijmen, V. (eds.) EUROCRYPT 2018. LNCS, vol. 10820, pp. 91–122. Springer, Cham (2018). https://doi.org/10.1007/978-3-319-78381-9_4

27. Canetti, R., Lindell, Y., Ostrovsky, R., Sahai, A.: Universally composable two-party and multi-party secure computation. In: STOC (2002)

28. Catalano, D.: Homomorphic signatures and message authentication codes. In: Abdalla, M., De Prisco, R. (eds.) SCN 2014. LNCS, vol. 8642, pp. 514–519. Springer, Cham (2014). https://doi.org/10.1007/978-3-319-10879-7_29

29. Catalano, D., Fiore, D.: Practical homomorphic MACs for arithmetic circuits. In: Johansson, T., Nguyen, P.Q. (eds.) EUROCRYPT 2013. LNCS, vol. 7881, pp. 336–352. Springer, Heidelberg (2013). https://doi.org/10.1007/978-3-642-38348-9_21

30. Catalano, D., Fiore, D., Gennaro, R., Nizzardo, L.: Generalizing homomorphic MACs for arithmetic circuits. In: Krawczyk, H. (ed.) PKC 2014. LNCS, vol. 8383, pp. 538–555. Springer, Heidelberg (2014). https://doi.org/10.1007/978-3-642-54631-0_31

31. Catalano, D., Fiore, D., Warinschi, B.: Efficient network coding signatures in the standard model. In: Fischlin, M., Buchmann, J., Manulis, M. (eds.) PKC 2012. LNCS, vol. 7293, pp. 680–696. Springer, Heidelberg (2012). https://doi.org/10.1007/978-3-642-30057-8_40

32. Catalano, D., Fiore, D., Warinschi, B.: Homomorphic signatures with efficient verification for polynomial functions. In: Garay, J.A., Gennaro, R. (eds.) CRYPTO 2014. LNCS, vol. 8616, pp. 371–389. Springer, Heidelberg (2014). https://doi.org/10.1007/978-3-662-44371-2_21

33. Chaidos, P., Couteau, G.: Efficient designated-verifier non-interactive zero-knowledge proofs of knowledge. IACR Cryptology ePrint Archive (2017)

34. Chaidos, P., Groth, J.: Making sigma-protocols non-interactive without random oracles. In: Katz, J. (ed.) PKC 2015. LNCS, vol. 9020, pp. 650–670. Springer, Heidelberg (2015). https://doi.org/10.1007/978-3-662-46447-2_29

35. Chaum, D.: Blind signatures for untraceable payments. In: Chaum, D., Rivest, R.L., Sherman, A.T. (eds.) Advances in Cryptology, pp. 199–203. Springer, Boston (1983). https://doi.org/10.1007/978-1-4757-0602-4_18

36. Cramer, R., Damgård, I.: Secret-key zero-knowlegde and non-interactive verifiable exponentiation. In: Naor, M. (ed.) TCC 2004. LNCS, vol. 2951, pp. 223–237. Springer, Heidelberg (2004). https://doi.org/10.1007/978-3-540-24638-1_13

37. Cramer, R., Shoup, V.: Universal hash proofs and a paradigm for adaptive chosen ciphertext secure public-key encryption. In: Knudsen, L.R. (ed.) EUROCRYPT 2002. LNCS, vol. 2332, pp. 45–64. Springer, Heidelberg (2002). https://doi.org/10.1007/3-540-46035-7_4

38. Damgård, I.: Non-interactive circuit based proofs and non-interactive perfect zero-knowledge with preprocessing. In: Rueppel, R.A. (ed.) EUROCRYPT 1992. LNCS, vol. 658, pp. 341–355. Springer, Heidelberg (1993). https://doi.org/10.1007/3-540-47555-9_28

39. Damgård, I., Fazio, N., Nicolosi, A.: Non-interactive zero-knowledge from homomorphic encryption. In: Halevi, S., Rabin, T. (eds.) TCC 2006. LNCS, vol. 3876, pp. 41–59. Springer, Heidelberg (2006). https://doi.org/10.1007/11681878_3

40. De Santis, A., Di Crescenzo, G., Ostrovsky, R., Persiano, G., Sahai, A.: Robust non-interactive zero knowledge. In: Kilian, J. (ed.) CRYPTO 2001. LNCS, vol. 2139, pp. 566–598. Springer, Heidelberg (2001). https://doi.org/10.1007/3-540-44647-8_33

41. De Santis, A., Micali, S., Persiano, G.: Non-interactive zero-knowledge proof systems. In: Pomerance, C. (ed.) CRYPTO 1987. LNCS, vol. 293, pp. 52–72. Springer, Heidelberg (1988). https://doi.org/10.1007/3-540-48184-2_5

42. De Santis, A., Micali, S., Persiano, G.: Non-interactive zero-knowledge with preprocessing. In: Goldwasser, S. (ed.) CRYPTO 1988. LNCS, vol. 403, pp. 269–282. Springer, New York (1990). https://doi.org/10.1007/0-387-34799-2_21

43. Dodis, Y., Vadhan, S.P., Wichs, D.: Proofs of retrievability via hardness amplification. In: Reingold, O. (ed.) TCC 2009. LNCS, vol. 5444, pp. 109–127. Springer, Heidelberg (2009). https://doi.org/10.1007/978-3-642-00457-5_8

44. Feige, U., Lapidot, D., Shamir, A.: Multiple non-interactive zero knowledge proofs based on a single random string. In: FOCS (1990)

45. Fiat, A., Shamir, A.: How to prove yourself: practical solutions to identification and signature problems. In: Odlyzko, A.M. (ed.) CRYPTO 1986. LNCS, vol. 263, pp. 186–194. Springer, Heidelberg (1987). https://doi.org/10.1007/3-540-47721-7_12

46. Fiore, D., Mitrokotsa, A., Nizzardo, L., Pagnin, E.: Multi-key homomorphic authenticators. In: Cheon, J.H., Takagi, T. (eds.) ASIACRYPT 2016. LNCS, vol. 10032, pp. 499–530. Springer, Heidelberg (2016). https://doi.org/10.1007/978-3-662-53890-6_17

47. Fischlin, M.: Round-optimal composable blind signatures in the common reference string model. In: Dwork, C. (ed.) CRYPTO 2006. LNCS, vol. 4117, pp. 60–77. Springer, Heidelberg (2006). https://doi.org/10.1007/11818175_4

48. Freeman, D.M.: Improved security for linearly homomorphic signatures: a generic framework. In: Fischlin, M., Buchmann, J., Manulis, M. (eds.) PKC 2012. LNCS, vol. 7293, pp. 697–714. Springer, Heidelberg (2012). https://doi.org/10.1007/978-3-642-30057-8_41

49. Fuchsbauer, G.: Automorphic signatures in bilinear groups and an application to round-optimal blind signatures. IACR Cryptology ePrint Archive (2009)

50. Fuchsbauer, G., Hanser, C., Kamath, C., Slamanig, D.: Practical round-optimal blind signatures in the standard model from weaker assumptions. In: Zikas, V., De Prisco, R. (eds.) SCN 2016. LNCS, vol. 9841, pp. 391–408. Springer, Cham (2016). https://doi.org/10.1007/978-3-319-44618-9_21

51. Fuchsbauer, G., Hanser, C., Slamanig, D.: Practical round-optimal blind signatures in the standard model. In: Gennaro, R., Robshaw, M. (eds.) CRYPTO 2015. LNCS, vol. 9216, pp. 233–253. Springer, Heidelberg (2015). https://doi.org/10.1007/978-3-662-48000-7_12

52. Garg, S., Rao, V., Sahai, A., Schröder, D., Unruh, D.: Round optimal blind signatures. In: Rogaway, P. (ed.) CRYPTO 2011. LNCS, vol. 6841, pp. 630–648. Springer, Heidelberg (2011). https://doi.org/10.1007/978-3-642-22792-9_36

53. Gennaro, R., Katz, J., Krawczyk, H., Rabin, T.: Secure network coding over the integers. In: Nguyen, P.Q., Pointcheval, D. (eds.) PKC 2010. LNCS, vol. 6056, pp. 142–160. Springer, Heidelberg (2010). https://doi.org/10.1007/978-3-642-13013-7_9

54. Gennaro, R., Wichs, D.: Fully homomorphic message authenticators. In: Sako, K., Sarkar, P. (eds.) ASIACRYPT 2013. LNCS, vol. 8270, pp. 301–320. Springer, Heidelberg (2013). https://doi.org/10.1007/978-3-642-42045-0_16

55. Gentry, C.: Fully homomorphic encryption using ideal lattices. In: STOC (2009)
56. Gentry, C., Groth, J., Ishai, Y., Peikert, C., Sahai, A., Smith, A.D.: Using fully homomorphic hybrid encryption to minimize non-interative zero-knowledge proofs. J. Cryptol. **28**(4), 820–843 (2015)
57. Ghadafi, E., Smart, N.P.: Efficient two-move blind signatures in the common reference string model. In: Gollmann, D., Freiling, F.C. (eds.) ISC 2012. LNCS, vol. 7483, pp. 274–289. Springer, Heidelberg (2012). https://doi.org/10.1007/978-3-642-33383-5_17
58. Goldreich, O., Goldwasser, S., Micali, S.: How to construct random functions. In: FOCS (1984)
59. Goldreich, O., Micali, S., Wigderson, A.: How to prove all NP statements in zero-knowledge and a methodology of cryptographic protocol design (extended abstract). In: Odlyzko, A.M. (ed.) CRYPTO 1986. LNCS, vol. 263, pp. 171–185. Springer, Heidelberg (1987). https://doi.org/10.1007/3-540-47721-7_11
60. Goldreich, O., Micali, S., Wigderson, A.: How to play any mental game or a completeness theorem for protocols with honest majority. In: STOC (1987)
61. Goldreich, O., Oren, Y.: Definitions and properties of zero-knowledge proof systems. J. Cryptol. **7**(1), 1–32 (1994)
62. Goldwasser, S., Micali, S., Rackoff, C.: The knowledge complexity of interactive proof-systems (extended abstract). In: STOC (1985)
63. Gorbunov, S., Vaikuntanathan, V., Wichs, D.: Leveled fully homomorphic signatures from standard lattices. In: STOC (2015)
64. Groth, J.: Simulation-sound NIZK proofs for a practical language and constant size group signatures. In: Lai, X., Chen, K. (eds.) ASIACRYPT 2006. LNCS, vol. 4284, pp. 444–459. Springer, Heidelberg (2006). https://doi.org/10.1007/11935230_29
65. Groth, J.: Short non-interactive zero-knowledge proofs. In: Abe, M. (ed.) ASIACRYPT 2010. LNCS, vol. 6477, pp. 341–358. Springer, Heidelberg (2010). https://doi.org/10.1007/978-3-642-17373-8_20
66. Groth, J., Ostrovsky, R., Sahai, A.: Perfect non-interactive zero knowledge for NP. In: Vaudenay, S. (ed.) EUROCRYPT 2006. LNCS, vol. 4004, pp. 339–358. Springer, Heidelberg (2006). https://doi.org/10.1007/11761679_21
67. Groth, J., Sahai, A.: Efficient non-interactive proof systems for bilinear groups. In: Smart, N. (ed.) EUROCRYPT 2008. LNCS, vol. 4965, pp. 415–432. Springer, Heidelberg (2008). https://doi.org/10.1007/978-3-540-78967-3_24
68. Hanzlik, L., Kluczniak, K.: A short paper on blind signatures from knowledge assumptions. In: Grossklags, J., Preneel, B. (eds.) FC 2016. LNCS, vol. 9603, pp. 535–543. Springer, Heidelberg (2017). https://doi.org/10.1007/978-3-662-54970-4_31
69. Ishai, Y., Kushilevitz, E., Ostrovsky, R., Sahai, A.: Zero-knowledge proofs from secure multiparty computation. SIAM J. Comput. **39**(3), 1121–1152 (2009)
70. Kalai, Y.T., Raz, R.: Succinct non-interactive zero-knowledge proofs with preprocessing for LOGSNP. In: FOCS (2006)
71. Katz, J., Vaikuntanathan, V.: Smooth projective hashing and password-based authenticated key exchange from lattices. In: Matsui, M. (ed.) ASIACRYPT 2009. LNCS, vol. 5912, pp. 636–652. Springer, Heidelberg (2009). https://doi.org/10.1007/978-3-642-10366-7_37
72. Kiayias, A., Zhou, H.-S.: Concurrent blind signatures without random oracles. In: De Prisco, R., Yung, M. (eds.) SCN 2006. LNCS, vol. 4116, pp. 49–62. Springer, Heidelberg (2006). https://doi.org/10.1007/11832072_4

73. Kilian, J., Micali, S., Ostrovsky, R.: Minimum resource zero-knowledge proofs. In: Brassard, G. (ed.) CRYPTO 1989. LNCS, vol. 435, pp. 545–546. Springer, New York (1990). https://doi.org/10.1007/0-387-34805-0_47

74. Kim, S., Wu, D.J.: Multi-theorem preprocessing NIZKs from lattices. IACR Cryptology ePrint Archive 2018:272 (2018)

75. Lapidot, D., Shamir, A.: Publicly verifiable non-interactive zero-knowledge proofs. In: Menezes, A.J., Vanstone, S.A. (eds.) CRYPTO 1990. LNCS, vol. 537, pp. 353–365. Springer, Heidelberg (1991). https://doi.org/10.1007/3-540-38424-3_26

76. Lindell, Y., Pinkas, B.: An efficient protocol for secure two-party computation in the presence of malicious adversaries. In: Naor, M. (ed.) EUROCRYPT 2007. LNCS, vol. 4515, pp. 52–78. Springer, Heidelberg (2007). https://doi.org/10.1007/978-3-540-72540-4_4

77. Ling, S., Nguyen, K., Stehlé, D., Wang, H.: Improved zero-knowledge proofs of knowledge for the ISIS problem, and applications. In: Kurosawa, K., Hanaoka, G. (eds.) PKC 2013. LNCS, vol. 7778, pp. 107–124. Springer, Heidelberg (2013). https://doi.org/10.1007/978-3-642-36362-7_8

78. Mukherjee, P., Wichs, D.: Two round multiparty computation via multi-key FHE. In: Fischlin, M., Coron, J.-S. (eds.) EUROCRYPT 2016. LNCS, vol. 9666, pp. 735–763. Springer, Heidelberg (2016). https://doi.org/10.1007/978-3-662-49896-5_26

79. Peikert, C., Vaikuntanathan, V.: Noninteractive statistical zero-knowledge proofs for lattice problems. In: Wagner, D. (ed.) CRYPTO 2008. LNCS, vol. 5157, pp. 536–553. Springer, Heidelberg (2008). https://doi.org/10.1007/978-3-540-85174-5_30

80. Peikert, C., Vaikuntanathan, V., Waters, B.: A framework for efficient and composable oblivious transfer. In: Wagner, D. (ed.) CRYPTO 2008. LNCS, vol. 5157, pp. 554–571. Springer, Heidelberg (2008). https://doi.org/10.1007/978-3-540-85174-5_31

81. Pointcheval, D., Stern, J.: Security proofs for signature schemes. In: Maurer, U. (ed.) EUROCRYPT 1996. LNCS, vol. 1070, pp. 387–398. Springer, Heidelberg (1996). https://doi.org/10.1007/3-540-68339-9_33

82. Pointcheval, D., Stern, J.: Security arguments for digital signatures and blind signatures. J. Cryptol. **13**(3), 361–396 (2000)

83. Regev, O.: On lattices, learning with errors, random linear codes, and cryptography. In: STOC (2005)

84. Rothblum, R.D., Sealfon, A., Sotiraki, K.: Towards non-interactive zero-knowledge for NP from LWE. IACR Cryptology ePrint Archive (2018)

85. Rückert, M.: Lattice-based blind signatures. In: Abe, M. (ed.) ASIACRYPT 2010. LNCS, vol. 6477, pp. 413–430. Springer, Heidelberg (2010). https://doi.org/10.1007/978-3-642-17373-8_24

86. Sahai, A., Waters, B.: How to use indistinguishability obfuscation: deniable encryption, and more. In: STOC (2014)

87. Santis, A.D., Persiano, G.: Zero-knowledge proofs of knowledge without interaction. In: FOCS (1992)

88. Schnorr, C.P.: Efficient identification and signatures for smart cards. In: Brassard, G. (ed.) CRYPTO 1989. LNCS, vol. 435, pp. 239–252. Springer, New York (1990). https://doi.org/10.1007/0-387-34805-0_22

89. Shacham, H., Waters, B.: Compact proofs of retrievability. In: Pieprzyk, J. (ed.) ASIACRYPT 2008. LNCS, vol. 5350, pp. 90–107. Springer, Heidelberg (2008). https://doi.org/10.1007/978-3-540-89255-7_7

90. Xie, X., Xue, R., Wang, M.: Zero knowledge proofs from Ring-LWE. In: Abdalla, M., Nita-Rotaru, C., Dahab, R. (eds.) CANS 2013. LNCS, vol. 8257, pp. 57–73. Springer, Cham (2013). https://doi.org/10.1007/978-3-319-02937-5_4
91. Zhang, J., Yu, Y.: Two-round PAKE from approximate SPH and instantiations from lattices. In: Takagi, T., Peyrin, T. (eds.) ASIACRYPT 2017. LNCS, vol. 10626, pp. 37–67. Springer, Cham (2017). https://doi.org/10.1007/978-3-319-70700-6_2

Efficient MPC

SPDZ$_{2^k}$: Efficient MPC mod 2^k for Dishonest Majority

Ronald Cramer[1,2], Ivan Damgård[3]($\boxtimes$), Daniel Escudero[3],
Peter Scholl[3], and Chaoping Xing[4]

[1] CWI, Amsterdam, The Netherlands
[2] Leiden University, Leiden, The Netherlands
[3] Aarhus University, Aarhus, Denmark
ivan@cs.au.dk
[4] Nanyang Technological University, Singapore, Singapore

Abstract. Most multi-party computation protocols allow secure computation of arithmetic circuits over a finite field, such as the integers modulo a prime. In the more natural setting of integer computations modulo 2^k, which are useful for simplifying implementations and applications, no solutions with active security are known unless the majority of the participants are honest.

We present a new scheme for information-theoretic MACs that are homomorphic modulo 2^k, and are as efficient as the well-known standard solutions that are homomorphic over fields. We apply this to construct an MPC protocol for dishonest majority in the preprocessing model that has efficiency comparable to the well-known SPDZ protocol (Damgård et al., CRYPTO 2012), with operations modulo 2^k instead of over a field. We also construct a matching preprocessing protocol based on oblivious transfer, which is in the style of the MASCOT protocol (Keller et al., CCS 2016) and almost as efficient.

1   Introduction

In the context of secure multi-party computation (MPC) there are n parties $P_1, \ldots, P_n$ who want to compute a function $f : \mathcal{R}^n \to \mathcal{R}^n$ securely on an input $(x_1, \ldots, x_n)$, where each party P_i holds x_i, without revealing the inputs to each other and only by exchanging messages between them. The main security guarantee we would like to achieve is that at the end of the interaction each party P_i only learns x_i and the i-th component of $f(x_1, \ldots, x_n)$, and nothing else. This should hold even if an adversary corrupts some of the parties and, in case of active or malicious corruption, takes control of the corrupted parties and have them do what the adversary wants. These ideas are formalized by requiring that using the protocol should be essentially equivalent to having a trusted third party compute the function. For such a formalization see, for example, the Universal Composability Framework (UC) [4].

It is well known that the hardest case to handle efficiently is the dishonest majority case, where $t \geq n/2$ parties are actively corrupted. Here we cannot

© International Association for Cryptologic Research 2018
H. Shacham and A. Boldyreva (Eds.): CRYPTO 2018, LNCS 10992, pp. 769–798, 2018.
https://doi.org/10.1007/978-3-319-96881-0_26

guarantee that the protocol terminates correctly, and we have to use computationally heavy public-key technology — unconditional security is not possible in this scenario. However, in a recent line of work [2,9], it was observed that we can push the use of public-key tools into a preprocessing phase, where one does not need to know the inputs or even the function to be computed. This phase produces "raw material" (correlated randomness) that can be used later in an online phase to compute the function much more efficiently and with unconditional security (given the correlated randomness).

In all existing protocols that handle a dishonest majority and active corruptions, the function being computed must be expressed in terms of arithmetic operations (i.e. additions and multiplications) over a finite field, such as the integers modulo a prime. However, in many applications one would like to use numbers modulo some M that is chosen by the application and is not necessarily a prime. In particular, $M = 2^k$ is interesting because computation modulo 2^k matches closely what happens on standard CPUs and hence protocol designers can take advantage of the tricks found in this domain. For instance, functions containing comparisons and bitwise operations are typically easier to implement using arithmetic modulo 2^k; these kinds of operations are expensive to emulate with finite field arithmetic, and also very common in applications of MPC such as secure benchmarking based on linear programming [6]. This has been done successfully by the team behind the Sharemind suite of protocols [3], which allows bitwise operations and integer arithmetic mod 2^{32}. However, in their basic setting, they could only get a passively secure solution: here, even corrupt players are assumed to follow the protocol. Also, the security of Sharemind completely breaks down if half (or more) of the players are corrupted, and the efficiency does not scale well beyond three parties.

To obtain active security over fields, the main idea of modern protocols is to use unconditionally secure message authentication codes (MACs) to prevent players from lying about the data they are given in the preprocessing phase. A typical example is the SPDZ protocol [7,9], where security reduces to the following game: we have a data value x, a random MAC key α and a MAC $m = \alpha x$, all in some finite field $\mathbb{F}$. The adversary is given x but not α or αx. He may now specify errors to be added to x, α and m, and we let x', α', m' be the resulting values. The adversary wins if $x \neq x'$ and $m' = \alpha' x'$. It is easy to see that the adversary must guess α to win, and so the probability of winning is $1/|\mathbb{F}|$. This authentication scheme is additively homomorphic, which is exploited heavily in the SPDZ protocol and is crucial for its efficiency.

However, the security proof depends on the fact that any non-zero value in $\mathbb{F}$ is invertible, and it is easy to see that if we replace the field by a ring, say $\mathbb{Z}_{2^k}$, then the adversary can cheat with large probability. For instance, in the ring $\mathbb{Z}_{2^k}$ he can choose $x' = x + 2^{k-1}$ and cheat with probability $1/2$. Up to now, it has been an open problem to design a homomorphic authentication scheme that would work over $\mathbb{Z}_{2^k}$ or more generally $\mathbb{Z}_M$ for any M, and is as efficient as the SPDZ scheme.

1.1 Our Contributions

In this paper we solve the above question: we design a new additively homomorphic authentication scheme that works in $\mathbb{Z}_{2^k}$[1], and is as efficient as the standard solution over a field. The main idea is to choose the MAC key α randomly in $\mathbb{Z}_{2^s}$, where s is the security parameter, and compute the MAC αx in $\mathbb{Z}_{2^{k+s}}$. We explain below why this helps. We also design a method for checking large batches of MACs with a communication complexity that does not depend on the size of the batch. We believe that these techniques will be of independent interest.

We then use the MAC scheme to design a SPDZ-style online protocol that securely computes an arithmetic circuit over $\mathbb{Z}_{2^k}$ with statistical security, assuming access to a preprocessing functionality that outputs multiplication triples in a suitable format. The total computational work done is dominated by $O(|C|n)$ elementary operations in the ring $\mathbb{Z}_{2^{k+s}}$, where C is the circuit to be computed. So if $k \geq s$, the work needed per player is equal to the work needed to compute C in the clear, up to a constant factor — as is the case for the SPDZ protocol. As in other protocols from this line of work, the overhead becomes more significant when k is small. Each player stores data from the preprocessing of size $O(|C|(k+s))$ bits. However, the communication complexity is $O(|C|k)$ bits plus an overhead that does not depend on C. This is due to the batch-checking of MACs mentioned above.

Our final result is an implementation of the preprocessing functionality to generate multiplication triples. It has communication complexity $O((k+s)^2)$ bits per multiplication gate, and is roughly as efficient as the MASCOT protocol [14], which is the state of the art for preprocessing over a field using oblivious transfer. Concretely, our triple generation protocol has around twice the communication cost of MASCOT, due to the overhead incurred when we have to work over larger rings in certain scenarios. However, this additional cost seems like a small price to pay for the potential benefits to applications from working modulo 2^k instead of in a field.

1.2 Overview of Our Techniques

For the authentication scheme, as mentioned, we have a data item $x \in \mathbb{Z}_{2^{k+s}}$, a key $\alpha \in \mathbb{Z}_{2^{k+s}}$ and we define the MAC as $m = \alpha x \mod 2^{k+s}$. Note that we want to authenticate k-bit values, so although $x \in \mathbb{Z}_{2^{k+s}}$, only the least significant k bits matter. The adversary is given x, and specifies errors e_x, e_α, e_m, which define modified values $x' = x + e_x, \alpha' = \alpha + e_\alpha, m' = m + e_m$. He wins if $m' = \alpha'x' \mod 2^{k+s}$, but note that since we store data in the least significant k bits only, this is only a forgery if $e_x \mod 2^k \neq 0$. As we show in detail in Sect. 3, if the adversary wins, he is able to compute $e_x\alpha \mod 2^{k+s}$. From this, and $e_x \mod 2^k \neq 0$, it follows that the adversary can effectively guess $\alpha \mod 2^s$, which is only possible with probability 2^{-s}.

We also want to batch-check many MACs using only a small amount of communication. The SPDZ protocol [9] uses a method that basically takes a random

---

[1] We use modulus 2^k throughout, but the scheme easily extends to any modulus.

linear combination of all messages and MACs and checks only the resulting message and MAC. Unfortunately, applying the analysis we just sketched to this scenario does not give a negligible probability of cheating, unless we 'lift' again and compute MACs modulo 2^{k+2s}, but then our storage and preprocessing costs would become significantly bigger. We provide a more complicated but tighter analysis showing that we can still compute MACs mod 2^{k+s} and the batch checking works with $2^{-s+\log s}$ error probability, so we only need increase s by a few bits.

Using these MACs, we can create an information-theoretically secure MPC protocol over $\mathbb{Z}_{2^k}$ in the preprocessing model, similar to the online phase of SPDZ from [7]. To implement the preprocessing phase, we follow the style of MASCOT [14], which uses oblivious transfer to produce shares of authenticated multiplication triples. We first design a protocol for authenticating values using correlated oblivious transfer, which allows creating the secret-shared MACs that will be added to the preprocessing data. This stage is similar to MASCOT, whereby first a passively secure protocol is used to compute shares of the MACs αx_i, for each value x_i that is to be authenticated, and then a random linear combination of these values is opened, and the resulting MAC checked for correctness. The main change we need to make here is that, depending on the size of the x_i's being authenticated, we may need to first compute the MACs over a larger ring in order to apply our analysis of taking random linear combinations.

Once the authentication scheme has been implemented, the main task is to create the multiplication triples needed in the online phase of our protocol. For this we also follow a similar approach to MASCOT, where the overall idea is that each party P_i chooses its shares (a^i, b^i) and then is engaged in an oblivious transfer subprotocol with P_j for each $j \neq i$, where shares of the cross products $a^i b^j$ and $a^j b^i$ are obtained. This yields shares of the product $(\sum_{i=1}^n a^i)(\sum_{j=1}^n b^j) = \sum_{i=1}^n a^i b^i + \sum_{i \neq j}(a^i b^j + a^j b^i)$, as required. Behind this simplification lies the problem that some information about the honest parties' shares can be leaked to a cheating adversary. In MASCOT this potential leakage is mitigated by "spreading out" the randomness by taking random linear combinations on correlated triples (with the same b value). When working over fields, the inner product yields a 2-universal hash function so the new distribution can be argued to be close to uniform using the Leftover Hash Lemma. However, this is not true anymore over rings like $\mathbb{Z}_{2^k}$. We overcome this issue by starting with triples where the shares of a are *bits* instead of ring elements, and then taking linear combinations over the bits. These combinations correspond to a subset sum over $\mathbb{Z}_{2^k}$, which *is* a 2-universal hash function, so allows for removing the leakage.

Additionally, random combinations are used in MASCOT to check the correctness of a triple by "sacrificing" another one. The security argument is that if the adversary manages to authenticate an incorrect triple, then it will have to guess the randomness used in the sacrifice step, which is unlikely. This is argued by deriving an equation from which we can solve for the random value. In order to extend this argument to the ring case, we use the technique sketched at the beginning of this section, working over $\mathbb{Z}_{2^{k+s}}$ to check correctness modulo 2^k.

Organization of this document. Section 2 introduces the notation we will use throughout this document. It also introduces the oblivious transfer and coin tossing functionalities, $\mathcal{F}_{\mathsf{ROT}}$ and $\mathcal{F}_{\mathsf{Rand}}$, which constitute our most basic building blocks and will be used to implement the offline phase of our protocol. We then describe our information-theoretic MAC scheme in Sect. 3, and we show how to check correctness of several authenticated values assuming a functionality $\mathcal{F}_{\mathsf{MAC}}$ that generates keys and MACs. Next, in Sect. 4 we show how to use our scheme to realise the functionality $\mathcal{F}_{\mathsf{Online}}$, i.e. to evaluate securely any arithmetic circuit modulo 2^k, in the preprocessing model.

The next two sections are concerned with the implementation of the preprocessing functionality $\mathcal{F}_{\mathsf{Prep}}$. Section 5 deals with the implementation of the functionality $\mathcal{F}_{\mathsf{MAC}}$, i.e. the distribution of the MAC key and the generation of MACs. Our construction is based on a primitive called vector Oblivious Linear Function Evaluation ($\mathcal{F}_{\mathsf{vOLE}}$). This can be implemented using Correlated Oblivious Transfer ($\mathcal{F}_{\Delta\text{-}\mathsf{OT}}$), which as we mention in that section can be implemented using our basic primitive $\mathcal{F}_{\mathsf{ROT}}$. On the other hand, Sect. 6 builds on top of our MAC scheme and generates multiplication triples that will be used during the online phase of our protocol to evaluate multiplication gates. Finally, in Sect. 7 we provide an efficiency analysis of our protocol.

Related work. There are only a few previous works that study MPC over rings, and none of these offer security against an active adversary who corrupts a dishonest majority of the parties. Cramer et al. showed how to contruct actively secure MPC over black-box rings [5] using secret-sharing techniques for honest majority, but this is only a feasibility result and the concrete efficiency is not clear. As already mentioned, Sharemind [3] allows mixing of secure computation over the integers modulo 2^k with boolean computations, but is restricted to the three-party setting when at most one party is corrupted. In some settings Sharemind can also provide active security [18].

More recently, Damgård, Orlandi and Simkin [8] present a compiler that transforms a semi-honest secure protocol for t corruptions into a maliciously secure protocol that is secure against a smaller number of corruptions (approximately $\sqrt{t}$). This also works for protocols in the preprocessing model, but will always result in a protocol for honest majority, so they can tolerate a smaller number of corruptions. On the other hand, their compiler is perfectly secure, so it introduces no overhead that depends on the security parameter. Thus, their results are incomparable to ours.

2 Preliminaries

Notation. We denote by $\mathbb{Z}_M$ the set of integers x such that $0 \leq x \leq M - 1$. The congruence $x \equiv y \mod 2^k$ will be abbreviated as $x \equiv_k y$. We let $x \mod M$ denote the remainder of x when divided by M, and we take this representative as an element of the set $\mathbb{Z}_M$. Given two vectors $\boldsymbol{x}$ and $\boldsymbol{y}$ of the same dimensions, $\boldsymbol{x} * \boldsymbol{y}$ denotes their component-wise product, $\langle \boldsymbol{x}, \boldsymbol{y} \rangle$ denotes their dot product and $\boldsymbol{x}[i]$ denotes the i-th entry of $\boldsymbol{x}$.

2.1 Oblivious Transfer and Coin Tossing Functionalities

We use a standard functionality for oblivious transfer on random ℓ-bit strings, shown in Fig. 1. This can be efficiently realised using OT extension techniques with an amortized cost of κ bits per random OT, where κ is a computational security parameter [13]. We use the notation $\mathcal{F}_{\mathsf{ROT}}^{\tau}$ to denote τ parallel copies of $\mathcal{F}_{\mathsf{ROT}}$ functionalities.

Functionality $\mathcal{F}_{\mathsf{ROT}}$

On input $(\mathsf{Sender}, P_j, \ell)$ from P_j and $(\mathsf{Receiver}, b, P_i)$ from P_i, the functionality samples random values $r_0, r_1 \leftarrow_R \mathbb{Z}_{2^\ell}$, then sends (r_0, r_1) to P_j and r_b to P_i.
If P_j is corrupted then the functionality instead allows the adversary to choose (r_0, r_1) before sending r_b to P_i.

Fig. 1. Random Oblivious Transfer functionality between a sender and receiver

We also use a coin tossing functionality, which on input (Rand) from all parties, sample $r \leftarrow_R \mathcal{R}$ and output r to all parties. This can be implemented in the random oracle model by having each party P_i first commit to a random seed s_i with $H(i \| s_i)$, then opening all commitments and using $\bigoplus_i s_i$ as a seed to sample from $\mathcal{R}$.

3 Information-Theoretic MAC Scheme

In this section we introduce our secret-shared, information-theoretic message authentication scheme. This forms the backbone of our MPC protocol over $\mathbb{Z}_{2^k}$. The scheme has two parameters, k, where 2^k is the size of the ring in which computations are performed, and a security parameter s. In the MAC scheme itself and the online phase of our MPC protocol there is no restriction on k, whilst in the preprocessing phase k also affects security.

There is a single, global key $\alpha = \sum_i \alpha^i \bmod 2^{k+s}$, where each party holds a random additive share $\alpha^i \in \mathbb{Z}_{2^s}$. For every authenticated, secret value $x \in \mathbb{Z}_{2^k}$, the parties will have additive shares on this value over the *larger ring* modulo 2^{k+s}, namely shares $x_i \in \mathbb{Z}_{2^{k+s}}$ such that $x' = \sum_i x^i \bmod 2^{k+s}$ and $x \equiv_k x'$. The parties will also have additive shares modulo 2^{k+s} of the MAC $m = \alpha \cdot x' \bmod 2^{k+s}$. We will denote this representation by $[x]$, so we have:

$$[x] = \left(x^i, m^i, \alpha^i \right)_{i=1}^n \in (\mathbb{Z}_{2^{k+s}} \times \mathbb{Z}_{2^{k+s}} \times \mathbb{Z}_{2^s})^n, \quad \sum_i m^i \equiv_{k+s} \left(\sum_i x^i \right) \cdot \left(\sum_i \alpha^i \right)$$

Notice that if the parties have $[x]$ and $[y]$, then it is straightforward to obtain by means of local operations $[x + y]$, $[c \cdot x]$ and $[x + c]$, where the arithmetic is modulo 2^{k+s} and c is a constant. We state the procedures that allow the parties to do this in Fig. 2.

Procedure AffineComb

This procedure allows the parties to compute authenticated shares of $y = c + c_1 \cdot x_1 + \cdots + c_t \cdot x_t \mod 2^{k+s}$ given $c, c_1, \ldots, c_t, [x_1], \ldots, [x_t]$. The input to this procedure are the constants $c, c_1, \ldots, c_t \in \mathbb{Z}_{2^{k+s}}$, the shares of the values $\{x_i^j\}_{i=1}^t$, the shares of the MACs $\{m_i^j\}_{i=1}^t$, owned by each party P_j, and the shares of the MAC key $\{\alpha^j\}_j$.

1. Party P_1 sets $y^1 = c + c_1 \cdot x_1^1 + \cdots + c_t \cdot x_t^1 \mod 2^{k+s}$;
2. Each party P_j, $j \neq 1$, sets $y^j = c_1 \cdot x_1^j + \cdots + c_t \cdot x_t^j \mod 2^{k+s}$;
3. Each party P_j sets $m^j = \alpha_j \cdot c + c_1 \cdot m_1^j + \cdots + c_t \cdot m_t^j \mod 2^{k+s}$.

At the end of the procedure $\{y^j\}_j$ are additive shares of y modulo 2^{k+s} and $\{m^j\}_j$ are shares of $\alpha \cdot y \mod 2^{k+s}$, the MAC of y. To simplify the exposition, we write

$$[c + c_1 \cdot x_1 + \cdots + c_t \cdot x_t] = c + c_1 \cdot [x_1] + \cdots + c_t \cdot [x_t]$$

whenever this procedure is called.

Fig. 2. Procedure for obtaining authenticated shares of affine combinations of shared values

In Fig. 3 we define the functionality $\mathcal{F}_{\mathsf{MAC}}$, which acts as a trusted dealer who samples and distributes shares of the MAC key, and creates secret-shared MACs of additively shared values input by the parties. As with previous works, it allows corrupt parties to choose their own shares instead of sampling them at random, since our protocols allow the adversary to influence the distribution of these. We will show how to implement this functionality in Sect. 5.

3.1   Opening Values and Checking MACs

Given an authenticated sharing $[x]$, a natural (but insufficient) approach to opening and reconstructing x is for each party to first broadcast the share x^i and then compute $x' = \sum_i x^i \mod 2^{k+s}$. The parties can then check the MAC relation $x' \cdot \alpha$ without revealing the key α using the method from [7]. Although this method guarantees *integrity* of the opened result modulo 2^k (by the same argument sketched in the introduction), it does not suffice for *privacy* when accounting for the fact that x may be a result of applying linear combinations on other private inputs. For example, suppose $x = y + z$ for some previous

---

Functionality $\mathcal{F}_{\text{MAC}}$

The functionality generates shares of a global MAC key and, on input shares of a value, distributes shares of a tag of this value. Let A be the set of corrupted parties and s be a security parameter.

Initialize: On receiving (Init) from all parties, sample random values $\alpha^j \leftarrow_R \mathbb{Z}_{2^s}$ for $j \notin A$ and receive shares $\alpha^j \in \mathbb{Z}_{2^s}$, for $j \in A$, from the adversary. Store the MAC key $\alpha = \sum_{j=1}^{n} \alpha^j$ (over $\mathbb{Z}$) and output α^j to party P_j.

Macro $\text{Auth}(\ell, x^1, \ldots, x^n)$ (this is an internal subroutine only)
 1. Let $x = \sum_{j=1}^{n} x^j \mod 2^{\ell}$ and $m = \alpha \cdot x \mod 2^{\ell}$
 2. Wait for input $\{m^j\}_{j \in A}$ from the adversary and sample $\{m^j\}_{j \notin A}$ at random conditioned on $m \equiv_{\ell} \sum_{j=1}^{n} m^j$. Output $(m^1, \ldots, m^n)$.

Authentication: On input $(\text{MAC}, \ell, r, \{x_i^j\}_{i=1}^t)$ from each party P_j, where $x_i^j \in \mathbb{Z}_{2^r}$ and $\ell \geq r$:
 1. Wait for the adversary to send messages (guess, j, S_j), for every $j \notin A$, where S_j efficiently describes a subset of $\{0, 1\}^s$. If $\alpha^j \in S_j$ for all j then send (success) to $\mathcal{A}$. Otherwise, send $\perp$ to all parties and abort.
 2. Execute $\text{Auth}(\ell, x_i^1, \ldots, x_i^n)$ for $i = 1, \ldots, t$, and then wait for the adversary to send either OK or Abort. If the adversary sends OK then send the MAC shares $m_i^j \in \mathbb{Z}_{2^{\ell}}$ to party P_j, otherwise abort.

Fig. 3. Functionality for generating shares of global MAC key, distributing shares of inputs and tags

inputs y, z. When opening x modulo 2^{k+s}, although for correctness we only care about the lower k bits of x, to verify the MAC relation we have to reveal the *entire* shares modulo 2^{k+s}. This leaks whether or not the sum $y + z$ overflowed modulo 2^k.

To prevent this leakage we use an authenticated, random s-bit mask to hide the upper s bits of x when opening. The complete protocol for doing this is shown below.

Procedure SingleCheck($[x]$):

1. Generate a random, shared value $[r]$ using $\mathcal{F}_{\text{MAC}}$, where $r \in \mathbb{Z}_{2^s}$
2. Compute $[y] = [x + 2^k r]$
3. Each party broadcasts their shares y^i and reconstructs $y = \sum_i y^i \mod 2^{k+s}$
4. P_i commits to $z^i = m^i - y \cdot \alpha^i \mod 2^{k+s}$, where m^i is the MAC share on y
5. All parties open their commitments and check that $\sum_i z^i \equiv_{k+s} 0$
6. If the check passes then output $y \mod 2^k$

Claim 1. *If the MAC check passes then* $y \equiv_k x$, *except with probability at most* 2^{-s}.

Proof. Suppose a corrupted party opens $[y]$ to some $y' = y + \delta$, where $\delta \in \mathbb{Z}_{2^{k+s}}$ can be chosen by $\mathcal{A}$, and $\delta \not\equiv_k 0$. To pass the MAC check, they must also come up with an additive error Δ in the committed values z^i such that $\sum_i z^i + \Delta$ is zero modulo 2^{k+s}. This simplifies to finding $\Delta \in \mathbb{Z}_{2^{k+s}}$ such that

$$\sum_i (m^i - (x + \delta) \cdot \alpha^i) + \Delta \equiv_{k+s} 0$$

$$\Leftrightarrow \delta \cdot \alpha \equiv_{k+s} -\Delta$$

Let v be the largest integer such that 2^v divides δ, and note that because $\delta \not\equiv_k 0$ we have $v < k$. This means that we can divide the above by 2^v, reducing the modulus from 2^{k+s} to 2^{k+s-v} accordingly:

$$\frac{\delta}{2^v} \cdot \alpha \equiv_{k+s-v} -\frac{\Delta}{2^v}$$

By definition of v, $\frac{\delta}{2^v}$ must be an odd integer, hence invertible modulo 2^{k+s-v}. Multiply by its inverse gives

$$\alpha \equiv_{k+s-v} -\frac{\Delta}{2^v} \cdot \left(\frac{\delta}{2^v}\right)^{-1}$$

Note that $k + s - v > s$, since $v < k$, which implies that $\mathcal{A}$ must have guessed $\alpha \bmod 2^s$ to come up with δ and Δ which pass the check. This requires guessing the s least significant bits of α, which are uniformly random, so the probability of success is at most 2^{-s}.   □

3.2 Batch MAC Checking with Random Linear Combinations

The method described in the previous section allows the parties to open and then check one shared value $[x]$. However, in our MPC protocol many such values will be opened, and using the previous method to check each one of these would have the drawback that we need shared, authenticated random masks for each value to be opened, consuming a lot of additional preprocessing data.[2] In order to avoid this, we present a batch MAC checking procedure for opening and checking t shared values $[x_1], \ldots, [x_t]$, which uses just *one random mask* to check the whole batch.

Technically speaking, our main contribution here is a new analysis of the distribution of random linear combinations of adversarially chosen errors modulo 2^k, when lifting these combinations to the larger ring $\mathbb{Z}_{2^{k+s}}$. If we naively apply the analysis from Claim 1 to this case, then we would have to lift to an even bigger ring $\mathbb{Z}_{2^{k+2s}}$ to prove security, adding extra overhead when creating and

---

[2] Note that in previous SPDZ-like protocols these extra masks are not needed.

Procedure BatchCheck

Procedure for opening and checking the MACs on t shared values $[x_1], \ldots, [x_t]$. Let x_i^j, m_i^j, α^j be P_j's share, MAC share and MAC key share for $[x_i]$.

Open phase:

1. Each party P_j broadcasts for each i the value $\tilde{x}_i^j = x_i^j \bmod 2^k$.
2. The parties compute $\tilde{x}_i = \sum_{j=1}^n \tilde{x}_i^j \bmod 2^{k+s}$.

MAC check phase:

3. The parties call $\mathcal{F}_{\mathsf{Rand}}(\mathbb{Z}_{2^s}^t)$ to sample public random values $\chi_1, \ldots, \chi_t \in \mathbb{Z}_{2^s}$ and then compute $\tilde{y} = \sum_{i=1}^t \chi_i \cdot \tilde{x}_i \bmod 2^{k+s}$.
4. Each party P_j samples $r^j \leftarrow_R \mathbb{Z}_{2^s}$, and then calls $\mathcal{F}_{\mathsf{MAC}}$ on input $(s, s, r^j, \mathsf{MAC})$ to obtain $[r]$. Denote P_j's MAC share on r by ℓ^j.
5. Each party P_j computes $p^j = \sum_{i=1}^t \chi_i \cdot p_i^j \bmod 2^s$ where $p_i^j = \frac{x_i^j - \tilde{x}_i^j}{2^k}$ and broadcasts $\tilde{p}^j = p^j + r^j \bmod 2^s$.
6. Parties compute $\tilde{p} = \sum_{j=1}^n \tilde{p}^j \bmod 2^s$.
7. Each party P_j computes $m^j = \sum_{i=1}^t \chi_i \cdot m_i^j \bmod 2^{k+s}$ and $z^j = m^j - \alpha^j \cdot \tilde{y} - 2^k \cdot \tilde{p} \cdot \alpha^j + 2^k \cdot \ell^j \bmod 2^{k+s}$. Then it commits to z^j, and then all parties open their commitments.
8. Finally, the parties verify that $\sum_{j=1}^n z^j \equiv_{k+s} 0$. If the check passes then the parties accept the values $\tilde{x}_i \bmod 2^k$, otherwise they abort.

Fig. 4. Procedure for checking a batch of MACs

storing the MACs. With our more careful analysis in Lemma 1 below, we can still work over $\mathbb{Z}_{2^{k+s}}$ and obtain failure probability around $2^{-s+\log s}$, which gives a significant saving.

Suppose the parties wish to open $[x_1], \ldots, [x_t]$, hence learn the values $x_1, \ldots, x_t$ modulo 2^k. Denote the shares, MAC shares and MAC key share held by P_j as x_i^j, m_i^j, α^j respectively. To initially open the values, the parties simply broadcast their shares $\tilde{x}_i^j = x_i^j \bmod 2^k$ and reconstruct $\tilde{x}_i = \sum_j \tilde{x}_i^j$ (as before, we cannot send the upper s bits of x_i^j for privacy reasons). As the parties do not have MACs on the values modulo 2^k, these s dropped bits will have to be used at some point during the MAC check, by adding them back in to the linear combination of MACs being checked. Crucially, by postponing the use of these s bits until the MAC check phase, our protocol only needs one authenticated random value to mask them, instead of t. The procedure that achieves this is described in Fig. 4, and its guarantees are stated in the following theorem.

Theorem 1. *Suppose that the inputs $[x_1], \ldots, [x_t]$ to the BatchCheck procedure are consistent sharings of $x_1, \ldots, x_t$ under the MAC key $\alpha = \sum_i \alpha^i \bmod 2^s$, and the honest parties' shares $\alpha^j \in \mathbb{Z}_{2^s}$ are uniformly random in the view of* *an adversary corrupting at most $n - 1$ parties. Then, if the procedure does not abort, the values $\tilde{x}_i$ accepted by the parties satisfy $x_i \equiv_k \tilde{x}_i$ with probability at least $1 - 2^{-s+\log(s+1)}$.*

The following lemma will be used in the proof of this theorem. The lemma is very general, which will allow us to use it also when we prove the security of the preprocessing phase of our protocol. However, in the current context, this lemma will be used with $\ell = k + s$, $r = k$ and $m = s$, and the δ's can be thought of as the errors introduced by the adversary during the opening phases.

Lemma 1. *Let ℓ, r and m be positive integers such that $\ell - r \le m$. Let $\delta_0, \delta_1, \ldots, \delta_t \in \mathbb{Z}$, and suppose that not all the δ_i's are zero modulo 2^r, for $i > 0$. Let Y be a probability distribution on $\mathbb{Z}$. Then, if the distribution Y is independent from the uniform distribution sampling α below, we have*

$$\Pr_{\substack{\alpha, \chi_1, \ldots, \chi_t \leftarrow_R \mathbb{Z}_{2^m}, \\ y \leftarrow_R Y}} \left[\alpha \cdot \left(\delta_0 + \sum_{i=1}^{t} \chi_i \cdot \delta_i \right) \equiv_\ell y \right] \le 2^{-\ell+r+\log(\ell-r+1)},$$

Proof. Define $S := \delta_0 + \sum_{i=1}^{t} \chi_i \cdot \delta_i$, and define E to be the event that $\alpha \cdot S \equiv_\ell y$. Let W be the random variable defined as $\min(\ell, e)$, where 2^e is the largest power of two dividing S. We will use the following claims.

Proposition 1.

   i. $\Pr[E \mid W = r + c] \le 2^{-(\ell-r-c)}$ for any $c \in \{1, \ldots, \ell - r\}$
   ii. $\Pr[E \mid 0 \le W \le r] \le 2^{-(\ell-r)}$
   iii. $\Pr[W = r + c] \le 2^{-c}$ for any $c \in \{1, \ldots, \ell - r\}$

Proof. For the first part, suppose that $0 < c < \ell - r$ (the case $c = \ell - r$ is trivial), in particular, $w = r + c$ is the largest exponent such that 2^w divides S and therefore $S/2^w$ is an odd integer. From the definitions of E and w we have that E holds if and only if $\alpha \cdot S \equiv_\ell y$, which in turn is equivalent to $\alpha \cdot \frac{S}{2^w} \equiv_{\ell-w} \frac{y}{2^w}$ and therefore to $\alpha \equiv_{\ell-w} \frac{y}{2^w} \cdot \left(\frac{S}{2^w}\right)^{-1}$. Since α is uniformly random in $\mathbb{Z}_{2^m}$ and independent of the right-hand side, and also $\ell - w < m$ (as $r < w$ and $\ell - r \le m$), we conclude that the event holds with probability $2^{-(\ell-w)} = 2^{-(\ell-r-c)}$, conditioned on $W = r + c$.

Similarly, if $0 \le w \le r$ then $\ell - w \ge \ell - r$ and so $\alpha \equiv_{\ell-r} \frac{y}{2^w} \cdot \left(\frac{S}{2^w}\right)^{-1}$. As $\ell - r \le m$, the event holds with probability at most $2^{-(\ell-r)}$ if conditioned on $0 \le W \le r$. This proves the second part.

For the third part, we must also look at the randomness from the χ_i coefficients. Suppose without loss of generality that δ_t is non-zero modulo 2^r, and suppose that $W = r + c$ some $1 \le c \le \ell - r$. Since $2^W | S$, we have $S \equiv_{r+c} 0$, and so

$$\chi_t \cdot \delta_t \equiv_{r+c} \underbrace{-\delta_0 - \sum_{i \ne t} \chi_i \cdot \delta_i}_{= S'}$$

Let 2^v be the largest power of two dividing δ_t, and note that by assumption we have $v < r$ so $r + c - v > c$. Therefore,

$$\chi_t \cdot \frac{\delta_t}{2^v} \equiv_{r+c-v} \frac{S'}{2^v}$$

$$\chi_t \equiv_{r+c-v} \frac{S'}{2^v}\left(\frac{\delta_t}{2^v}\right)^{-1}$$

$$\chi_t \equiv_c \frac{S'}{2^v}\left(\frac{\delta_t}{2^v}\right)^{-1}$$

By the same argument as previously, and from the fact that $c \leq \ell - r \leq m$, this holds with probability 2^{-c}, over the randomness of $\chi_t \leftarrow_R \mathbb{Z}_{2^m}$, as required.

Putting things together, we apply the law of total probability over all possible values of w, obtaining:

$$\Pr[E] = \Pr[E \mid 0 \leq W \leq r] \cdot \Pr[0 \leq W \leq r] + \sum_{c=1}^{\ell-r} \Pr[E \mid W = r + c] \cdot \Pr[W = r + c]$$

$$\leq 2^{-\ell+r} \cdot 1 + \sum_{c=1}^{\ell-r} 2^{-\ell+r+c} \cdot 2^{-c} = 2^{-\ell+r} + \sum_{c=1}^{\ell-r} 2^{-\ell+r}$$

$$= (\ell - r + 1) \cdot 2^{-\ell+r} \leq 2^{-\ell+r+\log(\ell-r+1)}$$

where the first inequality comes from applying item ii of Proposition 1 on the left, and items i and iii on the right. $\qquad\square$

Now we proceed with the proof of Theorem 1.

Proof (of Theorem 1). We first assume that $\mathcal{A}$ sends no **Key Query** messages to $\mathcal{F}_{\mathsf{MAC}}$, and later discuss how the claim still holds when this is not the case.

First of all notice that if no error is introduced by the adversary, then the check passes. Now, let $y = \sum_{i=1}^{t} \chi_i \cdot x_i \mod 2^{s+k}$, $p_i = \sum_{j=1}^{n} p_i^j \mod 2^s$ and $p = \sum_{j=1}^{n} p^j \mod 2^s$. If all parties followed the protocol then the following chain of congruences holds

$$\sum_{j=1}^{n} z^j \equiv_{k+s} \sum_{j=1}^{n} m^j - \tilde{y} \cdot \sum_{j=1}^{n} \alpha^j - 2^k \cdot \tilde{p} \cdot \sum_{j=1}^{n} \alpha^j + 2^k \cdot \sum_{j=1}^{n} \ell^j$$

$$\equiv_{k+s} \alpha \cdot y - \alpha \cdot \tilde{y} - \alpha \cdot 2^k \cdot \tilde{p} + 2^k \cdot \alpha \cdot r$$

$$\equiv_{k+s} \alpha \cdot (y - \tilde{y} - 2^k \cdot (\tilde{p} - r))$$

$$\equiv_{k+s} \alpha \cdot (y - \tilde{y} - 2^k \cdot p)$$

$$\equiv_{k+s} \alpha \cdot \sum_{i=1}^{t} \chi_i \cdot (x_i - \tilde{x}_i - 2^k p_i) \equiv_{k+s} 0$$

where the last equality holds due to the fact that for all $i = 1, \ldots, t$ we have $x_i = \tilde{x}_i + 2^k \cdot p_i$.

Now, consider the case in which the adversary does not open correctly to $\tilde{x}_i$ and $\tilde{p}$ in the execution of the procedure. Let $\tilde{x}_i + \delta_i \mod 2^{k+s}$ and $\tilde{p}+\epsilon \mod 2^s$ be the values opened in steps 1 and 5 respectively, so the value computed in step 3 is equal to $\tilde{y}' = \tilde{y} + \delta \mod 2^{k+s}$, where $\delta = \sum_{i=1}^{t} \chi_i \cdot \delta_i \mod 2^{k+s}$. As a consequence, the share that an honest P_j should open in step 7 is $z^j - \alpha^j \cdot (\delta + 2^k \epsilon) \mod 2^{k+s}$. However, the adversary can open this value plus some errors that sum up to a value $\Delta \in \mathbb{Z}_{2^{k+s}}$. If the check passes, this means that

$$0 \equiv_{k+s} \sum_{j=1}^{n} \left(z^j - \alpha^j \cdot (\delta + 2^k \epsilon)\right) + \Delta \quad \Leftrightarrow \quad \alpha \cdot (\delta + 2^k \epsilon) \equiv_{k+s} \Delta.$$

Suppose that for some index it holds that $\delta_i \not\equiv_k 0$. By setting $\delta_0 = 2^k \epsilon$, $\ell = k + s$, $r = k$, $m = s$ and Y to be the distribution of Δ produced by the adversary, we observe we are in the same setting as the hypothesis of Lemma 1. This allows us to conclude that the probability that the check passes is bounded by $2^{-\ell+r+\log(\ell-r+1)} = 2^{-s+\log(s+1)}$.

Handling key queries. We now show that this probability is the same for an adversary who makes some successful queries to an honest party's α^j using the (guess) command of $\mathcal{F}_{\mathsf{MAC}}$. Let S be the set of possible keys guessed by $\mathcal{A}$ (if there is more than one query then we take S to be the intersection of all sets). The probability that all these queries are successful is no more than $|S|/2^s$, and conditioned on this event, the min-entropy of the honest party's key share is reduced to $\log|S| \le s$. Therefore, instead of success probability $2^{-s+\log(s+1)}$ as above, the overall probability of $\mathcal{A}$ performing successful key queries *and* passing the check is bounded by

$$|S|/2^s \cdot 2^{-\log|S|+\log(\log|S|+1)} = 2^{-s+\log(\log|S|+1)} \le 2^{-s+\log(s+1)}$$

as required. $\qquad\qquad\qquad\qquad\qquad\qquad\qquad\qquad\qquad\qquad\qquad\qquad\qquad\square$

4   Online Phase

Our protocol is divided in two phases, a preprocessing phase and an online phase. The preprocessing, which is independent of each party's input, implements a functionality $\mathcal{F}_{\mathsf{Prep}}$ which generates the necessary shared, authenticated values needed to compute the given function securely. This functionality is stated in Fig. 5.

The main difference, with respect to SPDZ, is that instead of generating the random input masks and multiplication triples over the same space as the inputs, we sample them over $\mathbb{Z}_{2^{k+s}}$, even though we are doing computations in $\mathbb{Z}_{2^k}$. In the input phase, this is necessary to mask the parties' input whilst also obtaining a correct MAC over $\mathbb{Z}_{2^{k+s}}$. For the triples, we sample the shares and compute the MACs in $\mathbb{Z}_{2^{k+s}}$, but only care about *correctness* of the multiplication modulo 2^k, so the upper s bits of a triple are just random.[3]

---

[3] These s bits are not actually required to be random, since whenever we open a value using BatchCheck the upper s bits of all shares are masked anyway. However, it simplifies the description of the functionality to use random shares.

Modulo these differences, the online phase of our protocol, shown in Fig. 7, is similar to that in other secret sharing-based protocols like GMW, BeDOZa, SPDZ and MASCOT [2,9,11,14].

Shares of the inputs are distributed by means of the random shares provided by $\mathcal{F}_{\mathsf{Prep}}$. When an addition gate is found, the parties obtain the output by

---

Functionality $\mathcal{F}_{\mathsf{Prep}}$

The preprocessing functionality has all the same features as $\mathcal{F}_{\mathsf{MAC}}$, with the additional commands:

Input: On input (Input, P_i) from all parties, do the following:
1. Sample a random value $r \in \mathbb{Z}_{2^{k+s}}$ and generate random shares $r = \sum_{j=1}^{n} r^j$ mod 2^{k+s}. If P_i is corrupted, instead let the adversary choose all shares r^j and compute r accordingly.
2. Run the Auth macro to generate shares and MAC shares of $[r]$.
3. Send r to P_i, and the relevant shares of $[r]$ to each party.

Triple: On input (Triple) from all parties, the functionality performs the following steps
1. Sample random shares $\{(a^j, b^j)\}_{j \notin A} \subseteq (\mathbb{Z}_{2^{k+s}})^2$
2. Wait for input $\{(a^j, b^j, c^j)\}_{j \in A} \subseteq (\mathbb{Z}_{2^{k+s}})^3$ from the adversary and set $c = a \cdot b$ mod 2^k, where $a = \sum_{j=1}^{n} a^j$ mod 2^k and $b = \sum_{j=1}^{n} b^j$ mod 2^k.
3. Sample $\{c^j\}_{j \notin A} \subseteq \mathbb{Z}_{2^{k+s}}$ and $r \in \mathbb{Z}_{2^s}$ subject to $c + 2^k r \equiv_{k+s} \sum_{j=1}^{n} c^j$.
4. Finally, the functionality runs the Auth macro to generate sharings $[a], [b], [c]$ and sends the j-th output of each result to party P_j.

Fig. 5. Functionality for the preprocessing phase

Functionality $\mathcal{F}_{\mathsf{Online}}$

Initialization: The functionality receives input (Init, k) from all parties.
Input: On input (Input, P_i, vid, x) from party P_i and input (Input, P_i) from the other parties, where vid is a fresh, valid identifier, the functionality stores $(vid, x$ mod $2^k)$.
Add: On input (add, vid_1, vid_2, vid_3) from all parties, the functionality retrieves (if present in memory) the values (vid_1, x_1), (vid_2, x_2) and stores $(vid_3, x_1 + x_2$ mod $2^k)$.
Multiply: On input (multiply, vid_1, vid_2, vid_3) from all parties, the functionality retrieves (if present in memory) the values (vid_1, x_1), (vid_2, x_2) and stores $(vid_3, x_1 \cdot x_2$ mod $2^k)$.
Output: On input (output, vid) from all honest parties, the functionality looks for (vid, y) in memory and if present, sends y to the adversary. The functionality then waits for a message Abort or Proceed from the adversary: if it sends Abort then the functionality aborts, otherwise the value y is delivered to all parties.

Fig. 6. Ideal functionality for the online phase

Protocol Π_{Online}

The protocol is parameterized by k, which specifies the word size on which the operations are to be performed, and a security parameter s.

Initialize: The parties call the functionality $\mathcal{F}_{\mathsf{Prep}}$ as follows:
1. On input (Init) to get MAC key shares $\alpha^j \in \mathbb{Z}_{2^s}$.
2. On input (Input, P_i) for all parties to obtain random sharings $[r]$ where P_i learns r, for every input that P_i will provide.
3. On input (Triple) to get enough triples $([a], [b], [c])$.

Input: To share an input x^i held by P_i:
1. P_i broadcasts $\epsilon = x^i - r \mod 2^{k+s}$, where $[r]$ is the next unused input mask.
2. The parties compute $[x^i] = [r] + \epsilon$.

Add: To add two values $[x]$ and $[y]$ the parties compute locally $[z] = [x] + [y]$.

Multiply: To multiply two values $[x]$ and $[y]$:
1. Open $[x] - [a]$ as ϵ and $[y] - [b]$ as δ using the **Open** phase of BatchCheck, where $([a], [b], [c])$ is the next unused triple.
2. Locally compute $[x \cdot y] = [c] + \epsilon \cdot [b] + \delta \cdot [a] + \epsilon \cdot \delta$.

Output: To output a value $[y]$:
1. Call the procedure BatchCheck to check the MACs on the values that have been opened so far in multiplications.
2. If this does not abort, the parties open and check the MAC on $[y]$ using the procedure SingleCheck from Section 3.1.

Fig. 7. Protocol for reactive secure multi-party computation over $\mathbb{Z}_{2^k}$

adding their shares locally. On the other hand, multiplication triples are used for the multiplication gates, where the fact that $x \cdot y = c + \epsilon \cdot b + \delta \cdot a + \epsilon \cdot \delta$ for $c = a \cdot b$, $\epsilon = x - a$ and $\delta = y - b$ allows us to evaluate multiplications as affine operations on x and y, once the values of ϵ and δ are known. Finally, after checking correctness of all the values opened in multiplications using the batch MAC checking procedure from Sect. 3, the values for the output wires are revealed (Fig. 6).

The proof of the following theorem is quite straightforward, given the analysis of the MACs in Sect. 3.

Theorem 2. *The protocol Π_{Online} implements $\mathcal{F}_{\mathsf{Online}}$ in the $\mathcal{F}_{\mathsf{Prep}}$-hybrid model, with statistical security parameter s.*

5 Preprocessing: Creating the MACs

We now show how to authenticate additively shared values with the linear MAC scheme, realising the functionality $\mathcal{F}_{\mathsf{MAC}}$ from Sect. 3 (Fig. 3). Recall that after sampling shares of the MAC key $\alpha \in \mathbb{Z}_{2^s}$, the functionality takes as input secret-shared values $x \in \mathbb{Z}_{2^r}$, and produces shares of the MAC $x \cdot \alpha \mod 2^\ell$. The input and output widths r and ℓ are parameters with $\ell \geq r$. In our protocol we actually require $\ell \geq 2s$ and $\ell \geq r + s$, where s is the security parameter, but if these do not hold then we work with $\ell' = \max(r + s, 2s)$ and reduce the outputs modulo 2^{ℓ}.

Building block: vector oblivious linear function evaluation. To create the MACs, we will use a functionality for random vector oblivious linear function evaluation (vector-OLE) over the integers modulo 2^{ℓ}. This is a protocol between two parties, P_A and P_B, that takes as input a fixed element $\alpha \in \mathbb{Z}_{2^s}$ from party P_A, a vector $\boldsymbol{x}$ from party P_B, then samples a random vector $\boldsymbol{b} \in \mathbb{Z}_{2^{\ell}}$ as output to P_B, and sends $\boldsymbol{a} = \boldsymbol{b} + \alpha \cdot \boldsymbol{x} \mod 2^{\ell}$ to P_A. In the specification of our ideal functionality in Fig. 8, $\boldsymbol{x}$ is a vector of length $t + 1$, with the first t components from $\mathbb{Z}_{2^r}$ and the final component from $\mathbb{Z}_{2^{\ell}}$. This is because our MAC generation protocol will create a batch of t MACs at once on r-bit elements, but to do this securely we also need to authenticate an additional random mask of ℓ bits.

Notice that the functionality also allows a corrupted P_B to try to guess a subset of $\mathbb{Z}_{2^s}$ in which α lies, but if the guess is incorrect the protocol aborts. This is needed in order to efficiently implement $\mathcal{F}_{\mathsf{vOLE}}$ using oblivious transfer on correlated messages, based on existing oblivious transfer extension techniques.

Functionality $\mathcal{F}_{\mathsf{vOLE}}^s$

Initialize: On receiving $(sid, \mathsf{Init}, \alpha)$ from P_A, where $\alpha \in \mathbb{Z}_{2^s}$, and (sid, Init) from P_B, store α and ignore any subsequent (sid, Init) messages.

Vector-OLE: On input $(sid, \ell, r, t, \boldsymbol{x})$ from P_B, where $\boldsymbol{x} \in \mathbb{Z}_{2^r}^t \times \mathbb{Z}_{2^{\ell}}$:
1. Sample $\boldsymbol{b} \leftarrow_R \mathbb{Z}_{2^{\ell}}^{t+1}$. If P_B is corrupted, instead receive $\boldsymbol{b}$ from $\mathcal{A}$.
2. Compute $\boldsymbol{a} = \boldsymbol{b} + \alpha \cdot \boldsymbol{x} \mod 2^{\ell}$
3. If P_A is corrupted, receive $\boldsymbol{a} \in \mathbb{Z}_{2^{\ell}}^t$ from $\mathcal{A}$ and recompute $\boldsymbol{b} = \boldsymbol{a} - \alpha \cdot \boldsymbol{x}$.
4. If P_B is corrupted, wait for $\mathcal{A}$ to input a message (guess, S), where S efficiently describes a subset of $\{0,1\}^s$. If $\alpha \in S$ then send $(\mathsf{success})$ to $\mathcal{A}$. Otherwise, send $\perp$ to both parties and terminate.
5. Output $\boldsymbol{a}$ to P_A and $\boldsymbol{b}$ to P_B.

Fig. 8. Random vector oblivious linear function evaluation functionality over $\mathbb{Z}_{2^{k+s}}$

MAC generation protocol. Each party samples a random MAC key share α^i, and uses this to initialize an instance of $\mathcal{F}_{\mathsf{vOLE}}$ with every other party. On input a vector of additive secret shares $\boldsymbol{x}^i = (x_1^i, \ldots, x_t^i)$ from every P_i, each party samples a random ℓ'-bit mask x_{t+1}^i, and then uses $\mathcal{F}_{\mathsf{vOLE}}$ to compute two-party secret-sharings of the products $\alpha^i \cdot (\boldsymbol{x}^j \| x_{t+1}^j)$ for all $j \neq i$. Each party can then obtain a share of the MACs $\alpha \cdot \boldsymbol{x}$ (where $\alpha = \sum \alpha^i$ and $\boldsymbol{x} = \sum \boldsymbol{x}^i$), by adding up all the two-party sharings together with the product $\alpha^i \cdot \boldsymbol{x}^i$.

So far, the protocol is only passively secure, since there is nothing to prevent a corrupt P_j from using inconsistent values of α^j or $\boldsymbol{x}^j$ with two different honest parties, so the corrupt parties' inputs may not be well-defined. To prevent this issue, and ensure that in the security proof the simulator can correctly extract the adversary's inputs, we add a consistency check in steps 6–11: this challenges the parties to open a random linear combination of all authenticated values. This is where we need the additional random mask x_{t+1}, to prevent any leakage on the parties inputs from opening this linear combination. The check does not rule out *all* possible deviations in the protocol, however, in what follows we show that it ensures that the *sum* of all the errors directed towards any given honest party is zero, so these errors all cancel out. Intuitively, this suffices to realise $\mathcal{F}_{\mathsf{MAC}}$ because the functionality only adds a MAC to the sum of all parties' inputs, and not the individual shares themselves (Fig. 9).

Protocol Π_{Auth}

Initialize: Each party P_i samples a MAC key share $\alpha^i \leftarrow_R \mathbb{Z}_{2^s}$. Every pair of parties (P_i, P_j) initializes an instance of $\mathcal{F}_{\mathsf{vOLE}}$, where P_i inputs α_i.

Authentication: To authenticate the values $\boldsymbol{x} = (x_1, \ldots, x_t)$ over $\mathbb{Z}_{2^\ell}$, where each party P_j inputs an additive share $\boldsymbol{x}^j \in \mathbb{Z}_{2^r}^t$:

    1. Let $\ell' = \max(\ell, r + s, 2s)$.

    2. Each party P_j samples a random mask $x_{t+1}^j \leftarrow_R \mathbb{Z}_{2^{\ell'}}$ and defines $\tilde{\boldsymbol{x}}^j :=$ $(\boldsymbol{x}^j, x_{t+1}^j) \in \mathbb{Z}_{2^r}^t \times \mathbb{Z}_{2^{\ell'}}$.

    3. Every pair (P_i, P_j) (for $i \neq j$) calls their $\mathcal{F}_{\mathsf{vOLE}}$ instance with input $(\ell', r, t, \tilde{\boldsymbol{x}}^j)$ from P_j.

    4. P_j receives $\boldsymbol{b}^{j,i}$ and P_i receives $\boldsymbol{a}^{i,j}$, such that $\boldsymbol{a}^{i,j} = \boldsymbol{b}^{j,i} + \alpha^i \cdot \tilde{\boldsymbol{x}}^j \mod 2^{\ell'}$.

    5. For $h = 1, \ldots, t+1$, each party P_j defines the MAC share

$$m_h^j = \alpha^j \cdot x_h^j + \sum_{i \neq j}(\boldsymbol{a}^{j,i} - \boldsymbol{b}^{j,i})[h] \mod 2^{\ell'}$$

Consistency check:

    6. Sample $\chi_1, \ldots, \chi_t \leftarrow_R \mathbb{Z}_{2^s}^t$ using $\mathcal{F}_{\mathsf{Rand}}$.

    7. Each party P_j computes and broadcasts $\hat{x}^j = \sum_{i=1}^t x_i^j \cdot \chi_i + x_{t+1}^j \mod 2^{\ell'}$.

    8. Each party P_j defines $\hat{m}^j = \sum_{h=1}^t m_h^j \cdot \chi_h + m_{t+1}^j \mod 2^{\ell'}$ and $\hat{x} = \sum_i \hat{x}^i$.

    9. Each party P_j commits to and then opens $z^j = \hat{m}^j - \hat{x} \cdot \alpha^j \mod 2^{\ell'}$.

    10. All parties check that $\sum_i z^i = 0 \mod 2^{\ell'}$ and abort if the check fails.

    11. Each party P_j outputs the MAC shares $m_1^j, \ldots, m_t^j \mod 2^\ell$.

Fig. 9. Protocol for authenticating secret-shared values

5.1   Security

We now analyse the consistency check of the MAC creation protocol. There are two main types of deviations that a corrupt P_j can perform, namely (1) Input inconsistent values of α^j to the initialization phase of $\mathcal{F}_{\mathsf{vOLE}}$ with different honest parties, and (2) Input inconsistent shares $\boldsymbol{x}^j$ in the authentication stage.

For both types of errors, we define the *correct* values α^j, $\boldsymbol{x}^j$ to be those used in the $\mathcal{F}_{\mathsf{vOLE}}$ instance with an arbitrary, fixed honest party, say P_{i_0}. We then define the errors

$$\gamma^{j,i} = \alpha^{j,i} - \alpha^j \quad \text{and} \quad \boldsymbol{\delta}^{j,i} = \boldsymbol{x}^{j,i} - \boldsymbol{x}^j,$$

for each $j \in A$ and $i \notin A$. For an honest party P_i, we also define $\alpha^{i,j}$, $\boldsymbol{x}^{i,j}$ to be equal to α^i, $\boldsymbol{x}^i$ for all $j \neq i$.

In Claims 2 and 3 below we will show that, if the consistency check passes, then with overwhelming probability the *sum* of all corrupted parties' values is well-defined. That is, the values $\sum_{j \in A} \alpha^j$ and $\sum_{j \in A} \boldsymbol{x}^j$ would be exactly same even if they were defined using the inputs from P_j with a *different* honest party $P_{i_1} \neq P_{i_0}$. Since the MACs are computed based only on the sum of the MAC key shares and input shares, this suffices to prove security of the protocol.

Suppose that the corrupted parties compute the MAC shares $\boldsymbol{m}^j$ as an honest P_j would, using the values α^j, $\boldsymbol{x}^j$ we defined above, as well as the values $\boldsymbol{a}^{j,i}$, $\boldsymbol{b}^{j,i}$ sent to $\mathcal{F}_{\mathsf{vOLE}}$. Note that even though a corrupt P_j need not do this, any deviation here can be modelled by an additive error in the commitment to z^j in step 9, so we do not lose any generality.

The sum of the vector of MAC shares on $\boldsymbol{x}$ is then given by

$$\sum_i \boldsymbol{m}^i = \sum_i \alpha^i \cdot \boldsymbol{x}^i + \sum_i \sum_{j \neq i} (\boldsymbol{a}^{i,j} - \boldsymbol{b}^{j,i})$$

$$= \sum_i \alpha^i \cdot \boldsymbol{x}^i + \sum_i \sum_{j \neq i} \alpha^{i,j} \cdot \boldsymbol{x}^{j,i})$$

$$= \alpha \cdot \boldsymbol{x} + \sum_{i \notin A} \boldsymbol{x}^i \cdot \underbrace{\sum_{j \in A} \gamma^{j,i}}_{=\gamma^i} + \sum_{i \notin A} \alpha_i \cdot \underbrace{\sum_{j \in A} \boldsymbol{\delta}^{j,i}}_{=\boldsymbol{\delta}^i}$$

After taking random linear combinations with the vector $\boldsymbol{\chi} = (\chi_1, \ldots, \chi_t)$ to compute the MAC on $\hat{x}$, these MAC shares satisfy

$$\sum_i \hat{m}^i = \alpha \cdot \hat{x} + \sum_{i \notin A} (\langle \boldsymbol{x}^i, \boldsymbol{\chi} \rangle + x_{t+1}^i) \cdot \gamma^i + \sum_{i \notin A} \alpha^i \cdot \langle \boldsymbol{\delta}^j, \boldsymbol{\chi} \rangle \qquad (1)$$

To pass the consistency check, the adversary must first open the random linear combination $\hat{x}$ to some (possibly incorrect) value, say $\hat{x} + \varepsilon$, in step 7. Then they must come up with an error $\Delta \in \mathbb{Z}_{2^{\ell'}}$ such that

$$0 \equiv_{\ell'} \sum_i z^i + \Delta$$

$$\equiv_{\ell'} \sum_i (m^i - (\hat{x} + \varepsilon) \cdot \alpha^i) + \Delta$$

$$\Leftrightarrow -\Delta \equiv_{\ell'} \sum_i m^i - (\hat{x} + \varepsilon) \cdot \alpha$$

$$\equiv_{\ell'} \alpha \cdot \varepsilon + \sum_{i \notin A} \underbrace{(\langle x^i, \chi \rangle + x^i_{t+1})}_{=u^i} \cdot \gamma^i + \sum_{i \notin A} \alpha^i \cdot \langle \delta^j, \chi \rangle$$

$$-\Delta - \sum_{j \in A} \alpha^j \cdot \varepsilon \equiv_{\ell'} \sum_{i \notin A} u^i \cdot \gamma^i + \sum_{i \notin A} \alpha^i \cdot (\langle \delta^j, \chi \rangle + \delta^j_{t+1} + \varepsilon)$$

where the last two congruences come from substituting (1) and moving information known by the adversary to the left-hand side.

When proving the two claims below we assume that the adversary does not send any (guess) messages to $\mathcal{F}_{\mathsf{vOLE}}$. Similarly to the proof of Theorem 1, these can easily be extended to handle this case.

Claim 2. *If at least one $\gamma^i \neq 0$ then the probability of passing the check is no more than $2^{-s+\log n}$.*

Proof. Let i be an index for where $\gamma^i \neq 0$. Recall that $\gamma^i = \sum_{j \notin A} \gamma^{j,i}$, where each $\gamma^{j,i} < 2^s$, therefore $\gamma^i < 2^{s+\log n}$. Note that the distribution of u^i is uniform in $\mathbb{Z}_{2^{\ell'}}$ and independent of all other terms, due to the extra mask x^i_{t+1}, so we can write $u^i \cdot \gamma^i \equiv_{\ell'} \Delta'$, for some Δ' that is independent of u^i. Dividing by 2^v, the largest power of two dividing γ^i, we get

$$u^i \cdot \frac{\gamma^i}{2^v} \equiv_{\ell'-v} \frac{\Delta'}{2^v}$$

$$u^i \equiv_{\ell'-v} \frac{\Delta'}{2^v} \cdot \left(\frac{\gamma^i}{2^v}\right)^{-1}$$

Since $v < s + \log n$, this holds with probability at most $2^{-\ell'+s+\log n} \leq 2^{-s+\log n}$ since $\ell' \geq 2s$.

Claim 3. *Suppose $\gamma^i = 0$ for all $i \notin A$, and δ^j is non-zero modulo 2^k in at least one component for some j. Then, the probability of passing the check is no more than $2^{-s+\log(\ell'-r+1)}$.*

Proof. Pick an honest party, say P_{i_0}, and similarly to the previous claim, we can write the equivalence as

$$\alpha_{i_0} \cdot (\langle \delta^i, \chi \rangle + \delta^i_{t+1} + \varepsilon) \equiv_{\ell'} \Delta'$$

for some Δ' that is independent of the honest party's MAC key share α_{i_0}. We can then apply Lemma 1 with $r = r, m = s, \ell = \ell'$ and $\delta_0 = \delta^i_{t+1} + \varepsilon$ to obtain the bound $2^{-\ell'+r+\log(\ell'-r+1)}$, which proves the claim since $\ell' \geq r + s$.

The above two claims show that, except with negligible probability in s and r, the sum of all errors directed towards any given honest party is zero, so all errors introduced by corrupt parties cancel out and the outputs form a correct MAC on the underlying shared value. In particular, for the security proof, this implies that in the ideal world the MAC shares seen by the environment (including those of honest parties') are identically distributed to the MAC shares output in the real world.

We have the following theorem.

Theorem 3. *The protocol Π_{Auth} securely realises $\mathcal{F}_{\mathsf{MAC}}$ in the $(\mathcal{F}_{\mathsf{vOLE}}, \mathcal{F}_{\mathsf{Rand}})$-hybrid model.*

6   Preprocessing: Creating Multiplication Triples

In this section we focus on developing a protocol that implements the Triple command in the preprocessing functionality. More precisely, let $\mathcal{F}_{\mathsf{Triple}}$ be the functionality that has the same features as $\mathcal{F}_{\mathsf{Prep}}$ (Fig. 5), but without the **Input** command. Our protocol, described in Fig. 10, implements the functionality $\mathcal{F}_{\mathsf{Triple}}$ in the $(\mathcal{F}_{\mathsf{ROT}}, \mathcal{F}_{\mathsf{MAC}}, \mathcal{F}_{\mathsf{Rand}})$-hybrid model (Fig. 11).

The protocol itself is very similar to the one used in MASCOT [14], with several changes introduced in order to cope with the fact that our ring $\mathbb{Z}_{2^k}$ has non-invertible elements. Most of these changes involve taking the coefficients of random linear combinations in a different ring $\mathbb{Z}_{2^s}$, which is useful to argue that certain equations of the form $r \cdot a \equiv_{k+s} b$ are satisfied with low probability. This can be seen for example in the sacrifice step, where the random value t is chosen to have at least s random bits, instead of k. Additionally, in our protocol (like in MASCOT) random linear combinations must be used to extract randomness from partially leaked values $a_1, \ldots, a_t$, which still have reasonably high entropy. In order to use the Leftover Hash Lemma in this context one needs to make sure that taking random linear combinations yields a universal hash function. However, in contrast to the field case it is not true in general that the function $r_1 \cdot a_1 + \cdots + r_t \cdot a_t \bmod 2^k$ is universal, unless we make some assumptions about the set the values a_i are picked from. In the case of our protocol, we force the a_i to be $-1, 0$ or 1. With this additional condition it can be shown that the function above is universal.

The **Multiply** phase generates shares $\{(\boldsymbol{a}^i, b^i, \boldsymbol{c}^i)\}_{i=1}^n$ such that P_i has $(\boldsymbol{a}^i, b^i, \boldsymbol{c}^i)$, where $\boldsymbol{a}^i$ is a vector of bits, b^i is a random element of $\mathbb{Z}_{2^{k+s}}$ and $\boldsymbol{c}^i$ is a vector of random elements of $\mathbb{Z}_{2^{k+s}}$. These values satisfy $\boldsymbol{c} = \boldsymbol{a} \cdot b$, where $\boldsymbol{c} = \sum_{i=1}^n \boldsymbol{c}^i \bmod 2^{k+s}$, $\boldsymbol{a} = \sum_{i=1}^n \boldsymbol{a}^i \bmod 2^{k+s}$ and $b = \sum_{i=1}^n b^i \bmod 2^{k+s}$. This is achieved by letting the parties choose their shares on $\boldsymbol{a}$ and b, and using oblivious transfer to compute the cross products $\boldsymbol{a}^i \cdot b^j$. However, this is not a fully functional multiplication triple yet as it might not satisfy the right multiplicative relation (besides other technical issues like $\boldsymbol{a}$ being a short vector, and not a value in $\mathbb{Z}_{2^{k+s}}$). To check that the triple is correct, the **Sacrifice** phase uses another triple to check correctness. As the name suggests, one triple is "sacrificed" (i.e. opened) so that we can check correctness of the other while keeping it secret.

On the other hand, we must also ensure that the triple looks random to all parties. As we will see shortly in the proof of Theorem 4, if the triple is correct

---

Protocol Π_{Triple}

The integer parameter $\tau = 4s + 2k$ specifies the size of the input triple used to generate each output triple.

Multiply:
1. Each party P_i samples $\boldsymbol{a}^i = (a_1^i, \ldots, a_\tau^i) \leftarrow_R (\mathbb{Z}_2)^\tau$, $b^i \leftarrow_R \mathbb{Z}_{2^{k+s}}$
2. Every ordered pair of parties (P_i, P_j) does the following:
   (a) Both parties call $\mathcal{F}_{\text{ROT}}^\tau$ with P_i as the receiver and P_j as the sender. P_i inputs the bits $(a_1^i, \ldots, a_\tau^i) \in (\mathbb{Z}_2)^\tau$.
   (b) P_j receives $q_{0,h}^{j,i}, q_{1,h}^{j,i} \in \mathbb{Z}_{2^{k+s}}$ and P_i receives $s_h^{i,j} = q_{a_h^i,h}^{j,i}$ for $h = 1, \ldots, \tau$.
   (c) P_j sends $d_h^{j,i} = q_{0,h}^{j,i} - q_{1,h}^{j,i} + b^j \mod 2^{k+s}$, for $h = 1, \ldots, \tau$.
   (d) P_i sets $t_h^{i,j} = s_h^{i,j} + a_h^i \cdot d_j^{j,i} \mod 2^{k+s}$ for $h = 1, \ldots, \tau$. In particular

$$t_h^{i,j} \equiv_{k+s} s_h^{i,j} + a_h^i \cdot d_j^{j,i}$$

$$\equiv_{k+s} q_{a_h^i,h}^{j,i} + a_h^i \cdot \left(q_{0,h}^{j,i} - q_{1,h}^{j,i} + b^j \right)$$

$$\equiv_{k+s} q_{0,h}^{j,i} + a_h^i b^j.$$

Therefore, the following equation holds modulo 2^{k+s} on each entry

$$\begin{pmatrix} t_1^{i,j} \\ t_2^{i,j} \\ \vdots \\ t_\tau^{i,j} \end{pmatrix} = \begin{pmatrix} q_{0,1}^{j,i} \\ q_{0,2}^{j,i} \\ \vdots \\ q_{0,\tau}^{j,i} \end{pmatrix} + b^j \begin{pmatrix} a_1^i \\ a_2^i \\ \vdots \\ a_\tau^i \end{pmatrix}$$

   (e) P_i sets $\boldsymbol{c}_{i,j}^i = \left(t_1^{i,j}, t_2^{i,j}, \ldots, t_\tau^{i,j} \right) \in (\mathbb{Z}_{2^{k+s}})^\tau$.
   (f) P_j sets $\boldsymbol{c}_{i,j}^j = - \left(q_{0,1}^{j,i}, q_{0,2}^{j,i}, \ldots, q_{0,\tau}^{j,i} \right) \in (\mathbb{Z}_{2^{k+s}})^\tau$.
   (g) The following congruence holds

$$\boldsymbol{c}_{i,j}^i + \boldsymbol{c}_{i,j}^j \equiv_{k+s} \boldsymbol{a}^i \cdot b^j,$$

   where the modulo congruence is component-wise.
3. Each party P_i computes:

$$\boldsymbol{c}^i = \boldsymbol{a}^i \cdot b^i + \sum_{j \neq i} (\boldsymbol{c}_{i,j}^i + \boldsymbol{c}_{j,i}^i) \mod 2^{k+s}$$

Fig. 10. Triple generation protocol

---

this will reveal some partial information about the honest parties' shares to the adversary. This means that the adversary can guess a particular bit of these shares, which would allow him to distinguish in the simulation. This issue is addressed by the step **Combine**, which takes place before the Sacrifice step. Here the parties take a random linear combination of $\boldsymbol{a}$. Now, in order to pass

---

Protocol Π_{Triple} (continuation)

Combine:
    1. Sample $r, \hat{r} \leftarrow_R \mathcal{F}_{\text{Rand}}((\mathbb{Z}_{2^{k+s}})^\tau)$.
    2. Each party P_i sets

$$a^i = \sum_{h=1}^{\tau} r_h a^i[h] \mod 2^{k+s}, \qquad c^i = \sum_{h=1}^{\tau} r_h c^i[h] \mod 2^{k+s} \qquad \text{and}$$

$$\hat{a}^i = \sum_{h=1}^{\tau} \hat{r}_h a^i[h] \mod 2^{k+s}, \qquad \hat{c}^i = \sum_{h=1}^{\tau} \hat{r}_h c^i[h] \mod 2^{k+s}$$

Authenticate: Each party P_i runs $\mathcal{F}_{\text{MAC}}$ on their shares to obtain authenticated shares $[a], [b], [c], [\hat{a}], [\hat{c}]$.

Sacrifice: Check correctness of the triple $([a], [b], [c])$ by sacrificing $[\hat{a}], [\hat{c}]$.
    1. Sample $t := \mathcal{F}_{\text{Rand}}(\mathbb{Z}_{2^s})$.
    2. Execute the procedure AffineComb to compute $[\rho] = t \cdot [a] - [\hat{a}]$
    3. Execute the procedure BatchCheck on $[\rho]$ to obtain ρ.
    4. Execute the procedure AffineComb to compute $[\sigma] = t \cdot [c] - [\hat{c}] - [b] \cdot \rho$.
    5. Run BatchCheck on $[\sigma]$ to obtain σ, and abort if this value is not zero modulo 2^{k+s}.

Output: Generate using $\mathcal{F}_{\text{MAC}}$ a random value $[r]$ with $r \in \mathbb{Z}_{2^s}$. Output $([a], [b], [c + 2^k r])$ as a valid triple.

Fig. 11. Triple generation protocol (continuation)

the check, the adversary has to guess a random combination of the bits of a, which is much harder.

At this point a triple $([a], [b], [c])$ has been created, with $c \equiv_k a \cdot b$. However, the s most significant bits of c have some information that could allow the adversary to guess the shares of a of the honest parties. Moreover, correctness of the triple is only required modulo 2^k, as this is the modulus in the circuit the parties want to compute. Therefore, in order to mitigate this issue the parties use a random authenticated mask to hide the s most significant bits of c. This mask is very similar to the one used in the procedure SingleCheck from Sect. 3.1. In fact, in an actual implementation we could ignore the mask on the triples, as these will be masked before opening in the MAC checking procedures. However, if we wish to apply the Composition Theorem to our final protocol, each subprotocol must be UC secure by itself, regardless of any further composition.

Now we proceed with the main theorem of the section, which states the security of the protocol in Fig. 10.

Theorem 4. *If $\tau \geq 4k + 2s$, then the protocol Π_{Triple} (Fig. 10) securely implements $\mathcal{F}_{\text{Triple}}$ in the $(\mathcal{F}_{\text{ROT}}, \mathcal{F}_{\text{MAC}}, \mathcal{F}_{\text{Rand}})$-hybrid model, with statistical security parameter k.*

Proof. Let $\mathcal{Z}$ be an environment, which we also refer to as adversary, corrupting a set A of at most $n - 1$ parties. We construct a simulator $\mathcal{S}$ that has access to the ideal functionality $\mathcal{F}_{\mathsf{Triple}}$ and interacts with $\mathcal{Z}$ in such a way that the real interaction and the simulated interaction are indistinguishable to $\mathcal{Z}$. Our simulator $\mathcal{S}$ proceeds as follows:

Simulating the Multiply phase. The simulator emulates the functionality $\mathcal{F}_{\mathsf{ROT}}^\tau$ and sends $q_{0,h}^{j,i}, q_{1,h}^{j,i} \in \mathbb{Z}_{2^k}$ for $h \in \{1, \ldots, \tau\}$ to every $j \in A$ (on behalf of each honest party P_i). When a corrupted party P_j sends $d_h^{j,i}$ to an honest party P_i, $h \in \{1, \ldots, \tau\}$, the simulator uses its knowledge on the q's to extract the values of b used by the adversary as $b_h^j = d_h^{j,i} - q_{0,h}^{j,i} + q_{1,h}^{j,i} \mod 2^k$ (notice that if all the parties were honest we would have that all b_h^j for $h \in \{1, \ldots, \tau\}$ are equal, however, the adversary can take any strategy and this may not be the case here). The simulator then emulates the multiplication procedure according to the protocol using a fixed consistent value b^j for each $j \in A$ (say the value of b_1^j used with a fixed honest party P_{i_0}). We let $\boldsymbol{b}^{j,i} \in (\mathbb{Z}_{2^{k+s}})^\tau$ denote the vector of values of b that P_j tried to use in interaction with the emulated honest party P_i in step (c) and we define $\boldsymbol{\delta}_b = \boldsymbol{b}^{j,i} - \boldsymbol{b}^j$ (modulo 2^{k+s} on each entry) where $\boldsymbol{b}^j$ is the vector $(b^j, \ldots, b^j)$.

In a similar way, we define $\boldsymbol{\delta}_a^{j,i} = \boldsymbol{a}^{j,i} - \boldsymbol{a}^j$ where $\boldsymbol{a}^j = \boldsymbol{a}^{j,i_0}$ (these are the errors introduced by P_j when interacting with P_i with respect to the values used in the interaction with P_{i_0}) and $\boldsymbol{a}^{j,i}$ is the vector that the corrupt party P_j used in the random OT when interacting with honest party P_i. Notice that $\boldsymbol{\delta}_a^{j,i} \in \{-1, 0, 1\}^\tau$.

Simulating the Combining phase. All the computations are local, so $\mathcal{S}$ just emulates $\mathcal{F}_{\mathsf{Rand}}$ and proceeds according to the protocol.

Simulating the Authentication phase. Now $\mathcal{S}$ emulates $\mathcal{F}_{\mathsf{MAC}}$ with inputs from the corrupt parties provided by $\mathcal{Z}$. Notice that $\mathcal{S}$ can compute the actual values that each corrupt party should authenticate. The simulator authenticates these and defines e_{Auth} and $\hat{e}_{Auth}$ to be the total error introduced by the adversary in this step. Note that here $e_{Auth}, \hat{e}_{Auth} \neq 0$ essentially means that the adversary authenticates values different from those computed in the previous phases. If $\mathcal{Z}$ sends Abort to $\mathcal{F}_{\mathsf{MAC}}$ then $\mathcal{S}$ sends Abort to $\mathcal{F}_{\mathsf{Triple}}$.

Simulating the Sacrifice step. The simulator opens a uniform value in $\mathbb{Z}_{2^{k+s}}$ as the value of ρ, and aborts if the triple that it has internally stored is incorrect modulo 2^k. Otherwise it stores this triple as a valid triple.

Now we argue that the environment $\mathcal{Z}$ cannot distinguish between the hybrid execution and the simulated one. We begin by noticing that in the **Multiply** phase the adversary only learns the mask $d_h^{i,j}$ for each $i \in A$, but they look perfectly random as the values $q_{1-a_h^j,h}^{i,j}$ are uniformly random and never revealed to $\mathcal{Z}$. On the other hand, we still need to argue that the value ρ during the **Sacrifice** step has indistinguishable distributions in both executions, and that the triple $([a], [b], [c])$ obtained in the real execution is indistinguishable from the triple generated in the ideal execution (where a and b are uniformly random).

In order to analyze these distributions, we study what is the effect of the adversarial behavior in the final shared value $\boldsymbol{c}$, and we do this by considering what happens in the real execution at the end of step 2 when executed by a pair of parties (P_i, P_j). If both j and i are honest, then the vectors $\boldsymbol{c}_{i,j}^i$ and $\boldsymbol{c}_{i,j}^j$ computed at the end of the execution satisfy $\boldsymbol{c}_{i,j}^i + \boldsymbol{c}_{i,j}^j \equiv_{k+s} \boldsymbol{a}^i \cdot b^j$. Also, if j and i are both corrupt then we can safely assume that $\boldsymbol{c}_{i,j}^i + \boldsymbol{c}_{i,j}^j \equiv_{k+s} \boldsymbol{a}^i \cdot b^j$ also holds, since any variation on this will result in an additive error term which depends only in adversarial values and therefore it will get absorbed by the authentication phase. Now suppose that j is corrupt and i is honest, then P_i uses $\boldsymbol{a}^i$ and P_j uses $\boldsymbol{b}^{j,i}$, so the vectors $\boldsymbol{c}_{i,j}^i$ and $\boldsymbol{c}_{i,j}^j$ computed at the end of the execution satisfy

$$\boldsymbol{c}_{i,j}^i + \boldsymbol{c}_{i,j}^j \equiv_{k+s} \boldsymbol{a}^i \cdot \boldsymbol{b}^{j,i} \equiv_{k+s} \boldsymbol{a}^i \cdot \boldsymbol{\delta}_b^{j,i} + \boldsymbol{a}^i \cdot b^j.$$

Similarly, if i is corrupt and j is honest, then P_i uses $\boldsymbol{a}^{i,j}$ and P_j uses b^j, so the vectors $\boldsymbol{c}_{i,j}^i$ and $\boldsymbol{c}_{i,j}^j$ computed at the end of the execution satisfy

$$\boldsymbol{c}_{i,j}^i + \boldsymbol{c}_{i,j}^j \equiv_{k+s} \boldsymbol{a}^{i,j} \cdot b^j \equiv_{k+s} \boldsymbol{\delta}_a^{i,j} \cdot b^j + \boldsymbol{a}^i \cdot b^j.$$

Now, if $\boldsymbol{c}^i$ is the vector obtained by party P_i at the end of the multiplication, then we have that

$$\boldsymbol{c} \equiv_{k+s} \boldsymbol{a} \cdot b + \underbrace{\sum_{i \notin A} \boldsymbol{a}^i * \boldsymbol{\delta}_b^i}_{e_a} + \underbrace{\sum_{j \notin A} \boldsymbol{\delta}_a^j \cdot b^j}_{e_b}$$

where $\boldsymbol{a} = \sum_{i=1}^n \boldsymbol{a}^i$, $b = \sum_{i=1}^n b^i$, $\boldsymbol{\delta}_b^i = \sum_{j \in A} \boldsymbol{\delta}_b^{j,i}$ and $\boldsymbol{\delta}_a^j = \sum_{i \in A} \boldsymbol{\delta}_a^{i,j}$, and all congruences are considered component-wise. Notice that each entry in $\boldsymbol{\delta}_a^j$ is the sum of at most n bits and therefore it is upper bounded strictly by n, since we assume that $n \ll 2^{k+s}$ we can consider the sum $\boldsymbol{a} = \sum_{i=1}^n \boldsymbol{a}^i$ (without the modulus).

Assume all parties (including corrupt ones) take the right linear combination in the combine phase (every adversarial misbehavior will result in an additive error term that only depends on values that the adversary has, and this term will be absorbed by the error term in the authentication phase). Therefore, after the combination and authentication phases the parties obtain values $[b], [a], [c], [\hat{a}], [\hat{c}]$ where $b, a, c, \hat{a}, \hat{c} \in \mathbb{Z}_{2^{k+s}}$ satisfy

$$c \equiv_{k+s} a \cdot b + e_a + e_b + e_{Auth}$$
$$\hat{c} \equiv_{k+s} \hat{a} \cdot b + \hat{e}_a + \hat{e}_b + \hat{e}_{Auth}$$

and

$$c \equiv_{k+s} \sum_{h=1}^{\tau} r_h \cdot \boldsymbol{c}[h], \qquad \hat{c} = \sum_{h=1}^{\tau} \hat{r}_h \cdot \boldsymbol{c}[h]$$

$$a \equiv_{k+s} \sum_{h=1}^{\tau} r_h \cdot \boldsymbol{a}[h], \qquad \hat{a} \equiv_{k+s} \sum_{h=1}^{\tau} \hat{r}_h \cdot \boldsymbol{a}[h]$$

$$e_a \equiv_{k+s} \sum_{h=1}^{\tau} r_h \cdot e_a[h], \qquad \hat{e}_a \equiv_{k+s} \sum_{h=1}^{\tau} \hat{r}_h \cdot e_a[h]$$

$$e_b \equiv_{k+s} \sum_{h=1}^{\tau} r_h \cdot e_b[h], \qquad \hat{e}_b \equiv_{k+s} \sum_{h=1}^{\tau} \hat{r}_h \cdot e_b[h].$$

We prove the following two claims can be proven using the same techniques as in the single and batch MAC checking protocols from Sect. 3, and Lemma 1.

Claim 4. *If the sacrifice step passes, then it holds that $e := e_a + e_b + e_{Auth} \equiv_k 0$ and $\hat{e} := \hat{e}_a + \hat{e}_b + \hat{e}_{Auth} \equiv_k 0$ with probability at least $1 - 2^{-s}$.*

Claim 5. *Suppose that the sacrificing step passes, then all the errors $\{\delta_a^i[h]\}_{h, i \notin A}$ are zero except with probability at most $2^{-k+\log(n \cdot (k+1-\log n))}$.*

The previous claim allows us to conclude that $e_b = \hat{e}_b \equiv_{k+s} 0$, except with negligible probability. Now we would like to claim that the value $\rho \in \mathbb{Z}_{2^{k+s}}$ opened in the sacrifice step is indistinguishable from the one opened in the real execution. Since in the ideal execution the simulator opens a uniform value, what we actually need to show is that in a real execution ρ looks (close to) uniform. Given that $\rho = t \cdot a - \hat{a} \mod 2^k$, this can be accomplished by showing that $\hat{a}$ looks uniform to the environment. In order to see that $\hat{a} \equiv_{k+s} \sum_{h=1}^{\tau} \hat{r}_h \cdot a[h] \equiv_{k+s} \sum_{i=1}^{n} \left(\sum_{h=1}^{\tau} \hat{r}_h \cdot a^i[h] \right)$ is uniformly distributed it suffices to show that at least for one $i_0 \notin A$ it holds that $\hat{a}^{i_0}$ looks uniform to the environment, where $\hat{a}^i = \sum_{h=1}^{\tau} \hat{r}_h \cdot a^i[h] \mod 2^{k+s}$, and that all these values are actually independent. This can be shown using the Leftover Hash Lemma by giving a good lower bound on the min-entropy of a^{i_0}. We proceed with the details below.

Using Claims 4 and 5, we have that whenever the sacrifice step passes it holds that

$$-e_{Auth} \equiv_k e_a \equiv_k \sum_{h=1}^{\tau} r_h \cdot e_a[h] \equiv_k \sum_{h=1}^{\tau} r_h \sum_{i \notin A} a^i[h] \cdot \delta_b^i[h].$$

and

$$-\hat{e}_{Auth} \equiv_k \hat{e}_a \equiv_k \sum_{h=1}^{\tau} \hat{r}_h \cdot e_a[h] \equiv_k \sum_{h=1}^{\tau} \hat{r}_h \sum_{i \notin A} a^i[h] \cdot \delta_b^i[h].$$

Intuitively, the only information that the adversary has about the honest party's shares is that the sacrifice step passed, which in turn implies that the above equation holds. Ideally, the fact that this relation holds should not reveal so much information about $\{a^i\}_{i \notin A}$ to the adversary. Indeed, this will be the case, which will be seen when we bound by below the entropy of this random variable. To this end, let $m = n - |A|$ be the number of honest parties and let $S \subseteq \mathbb{Z}_2^{m \cdot \tau}$ be the set of all possible honest shares $(a^i)_{i \notin A}$ for which the sacrifice step would pass. Notice that in particular, these shares satisfy the equations above and therefore they are completely determined by the errors that are introduced by the adversary. Moreover, since the shares $(\boldsymbol{a}^i)_{i \notin A}$ are uniformly distributed in S, the min-entropy of these shares is $\log|S|$. Additionally, the vectors in $(\boldsymbol{a}^i)_{i \notin A}$ are independent one from each other, hence there is at least one honest party P_{i_0} such that the min entropy of $\boldsymbol{a}^{i_0}$ is at least $\frac{\log|S|}{m}$. In the following we show that $a^{i_0} = \sum_{h=1}^{\tau} r_h \cdot \boldsymbol{a}^{i_0}[h] \mod 2^{k+s}$ and $\hat{a}^{i_0} = \sum_{h=1}^{\tau} \hat{r}_h \cdot \boldsymbol{a}^{i_0}[h] \mod 2^{k+s}$ look random to the environment.

Let β be the probability of passing the sacrifice step, i.e. $\beta = \frac{|S|}{2^{m\tau}} = 2^{-c}$ where $c = m\tau - \log|S|$. We get that

$$H_\infty\left(\boldsymbol{a}^{i_0}\right) \geq \frac{\log|S|}{m} = \tau - \frac{c}{m} \geq \tau - c.$$

Now consider the function $h_{r,\hat{r}} : (\mathbb{Z}_2)^\tau \to (\mathbb{Z}_{2^{k+s}})^2$ given by

$$h_{r,\hat{r}}(\boldsymbol{a}) = \left(\sum_{h=1}^{\tau} \boldsymbol{r}[h] \cdot \boldsymbol{a}[h] \mod 2^{k+s}, \quad \sum_{h=1}^{\tau} \hat{\boldsymbol{r}}[h] \cdot \boldsymbol{a}[h] \mod 2^{k+s} \right),$$

We claim that this family of functions is $2-$universal. Let $\boldsymbol{a}, \boldsymbol{a}' \in (\mathbb{Z}_2)^\tau$ such that $\boldsymbol{a} \neq \boldsymbol{a}'$, say $\boldsymbol{a}[h_0] \not\equiv_{k+s} \boldsymbol{a}'[h_0]$. If $h_{r,\hat{r}}(\boldsymbol{a}) = h_{r,\hat{r}}(\boldsymbol{a}')$ then $\sum_{h=1}^{\tau} \boldsymbol{r}[h] \cdot (\boldsymbol{a}[h] - \boldsymbol{a}'[h]) \equiv_{k+s} 0$ and $\sum_{h=1}^{\tau} \hat{\boldsymbol{r}}[h] \cdot (\boldsymbol{a}[h] - \boldsymbol{a}'[h]) \equiv_{k+s} 0$. Given that $\boldsymbol{a}$ and $\boldsymbol{a}'$ are vectors of bits, we have that $\boldsymbol{a}[h_0] - \boldsymbol{a}'[h_0] = \pm 1$, so we can solve for $\boldsymbol{r}[h_0]$ and $\hat{r}[h_0]$ in the equations above. Therefore, these equations hold with probability at most $\frac{1}{2^{k+s}} \cdot \frac{1}{2^{k+s}} = \frac{1}{2^{2(k+s)}}$ over the choice of $(\boldsymbol{r}, \hat{\boldsymbol{r}})$, and hence the family is 2-universal.

According to the Leftover Hash Lemma, even if the adversary knows $\boldsymbol{r}$ and $\hat{\boldsymbol{r}}$, the statistical distance between $h_{r,\hat{r}}(X)$ and the uniform distribution in $(\mathbb{Z}_{2^{k+s}})^2$ is at most $2^{-\kappa}$, provided that $H_\infty(X) \geq 2\kappa + 2(k+s)$. This is satisfied if we take $\kappa = \frac{1}{2} \cdot (\tau - c - 2 \cdot (k+s))$.

Finally, ignoring the event in which the check passes with some non-zero errors, which happens with negligible probability, the distinguishing advantage of $\mathcal{Z}$ is the multiplication between the probability of passing the sacrifice step and the probability of distinguishing the output distribution from random, given that the check passed. This is equal to

$$\beta \cdot 2^{-\kappa} = 2^{-c} \cdot 2^{-\frac{1}{2} \cdot (\tau - c - 2 \cdot (k+s))} = 2^{-\frac{\tau - 2 \cdot (k+s)}{2} - \frac{c}{2}}.$$

Since we want this probability to be bounded by 2^{-s} for any c, we take τ so that $s \leq \frac{\tau - 2 \cdot (k+s)}{2}$, which is equivalent to $\tau \geq 4s + 2k$.   □

7   Efficiency Analysis

We now turn to estimating the efficiency of our preprocessing protocol, focusing on the triple generation phase since this is likely to be the bottleneck in most applications. We emphasise that the costs presented here, compared with those of previous protocols, do not take into account the benefits to applications from working over $\mathbb{Z}_{2^k}$ instead of a finite field with arithmetic modulo a prime. Supporting natural arithmetic modulo 2^k offers advantages on several levels: it simplifies implementations by avoiding the need for modular arithmetic, it reduces the complexity of compiling existing programs into arithmetic circuits, and we believe that it will also be beneficial in performing operations such as secure comparison and bit decomposition of shared values more efficiently than standard techniques using arithmetic modulo p.

Cost of the preprocessing. When authenticating a secret-shared value $x \in \mathbb{Z}_{2^k}$, the main cost is running the vector OLEs, which have inputs over $\mathbb{Z}_{2^k}$ and outputs over $\mathbb{Z}_{2^{k+s}}$, when the MAC key $\alpha \in \mathbb{Z}_{2^s}$. Each vector OLE requires s correlated OTs on messages over $\mathbb{Z}_{2^\ell}$, where $\ell = \max(k+s, 2s)$, which gives an amortized cost of $s \cdot \ell$ bits for each component of the vector OLE. We ignore the cost of the consistency check, since this is independent of the number of values being authenticated.

To generate a triple, we need τ random OTs on strings of length $k + s$ bits, which cost $k + s$ bits of communication each using [13], followed by $\tau \cdot (k + s)$ bits to send the $d^{j,i}$ values. The parties then authenticate 5 values in $\mathbb{Z}_{2^{k+s}}$, which requires generating MACs modulo $\mathbb{Z}_{2^{k+2s}}$ for security. Generating these MACs costs $5 \cdot s \cdot (k + 2s) \cdot n(n - 1)$ bits of communication using Π_{Auth} based on correlated OT, since the vector OLEs are performed with $\ell = k + 2s$. The costs of $\mathcal{F}_{\mathsf{Rand}}$ and the sacrifice check are negligible compared to this, since the MAC check can be performed in a batch when producing many triples at once. This gives a total cost estimate of $5s(k + 2s) + 2\tau(k + s)$ bits per triple. Setting $\tau = 4s + 2k$ (to give failure probability 2^{-s}) this becomes $2(k + 2s)(9s + 4k)$.

Comparison with MASCOT. Table 1 shows the estimated communication complexity of our protocol for two parties creating a triple in different rings. Note that like MASCOT [14] — the most practical OT-based protocol for actively secure, dishonest majority MPC over finite fields — we expect that communication will be the bottleneck, since the protocol has very simple computational costs. In the table we fix the computational security parameter to 128, and set the statistical security parameter to $s = 64$ in a 64 or 128-bit ring, or $s = 32$ in the 32-bit ring, giving the claimed security bounds (cf. Theorem 1 and Claim 5). Compared with MASCOT, our protocol needs around twice as much communication for 64 or 128-bit triples, with roughly the same level of statistical security. Over the integers modulo 2^{32}, the overhead reduces to around 50% more than MASCOT, although here the statistical security parameters of 26 and 32 bits may be too low for some applications. Note that many applications will not be possible with MASCOT or SPDZ over a 32-bit field, since here integer overflow (modulo p) occurs more easily, and emulating operations such as secure comparison and bit decomposition over a field requires working with a much larger modulus to avoid overflow. When working over $\mathbb{Z}_{2^{32}}$ instead, this should not be necessary.

These overheads for triple generation, compared with MASCOT, come from the fact that our protocol sometimes needs to work in larger rings to ensure security. For example, for the triple check to be secure, our protocol authenticates shares of triples modulo 2^{k+s}, even though the triples are only ever used modulo 2^k in the online phase. This means that when creating these MACs with the protocol from Sect. 5, we need to work over $\mathbb{Z}_{2^{k+2s}}$ to ensure security. We leave it to future work to try to avoid these costs and improve efficiency.

Table 1. Communication cost of our protocol and previous protocols for various rings and fields, and statistical security parameters

Protocol	Message space	Stat. security	Input cost (kbit)	Triple cost (kbit)
Ours	$\mathbb{Z}_{2^{32}}$	26	3.17	79.87
	$\mathbb{Z}_{2^{64}}$	57	12.48	319.49
	$\mathbb{Z}_{2^{128}}$	57	16.64	557.06
MASCOT	32-bit field	32	1.06	51.20
	64-bit field	64	4.16	139.26
	128-bit field	64	16.51	360.44

Comparison with SPDZ using homomorphic encryption. In very recent work [15], Keller, Pastro and Rotaru presented a new variant of the SPDZ protocol that improves upon the performance of MASCOT. In the two-party setting, they show that an optimized implementation of the original SPDZ [9] runs around twice as fast as MASCOT, and give a new variant that performs 6 times as fast in 64-bit fields; this would probably be around 12 times as fast as our protocol for 64-bit rings. The original SPDZ uses somewhat homomorphic encryption based on the ring-LWE assumption, while their newer variant uses additively homomorphic encryption, and the conjecture that ring-LWE based additively homomorphic encryption has "linear-only" homomorphism. It seems likely that both of these protocols could be adapted to generate triples over $\mathbb{Z}_{2^k}$ using our techniques. One challenge, however, is to adapt the ciphertext packing techniques used in SPDZ for messages over $\mathbb{F}_p$ to the case of $\mathbb{Z}_{2^k}$, to allow parallel homomorphic operations on ciphertexts; it was shown how this can be done in [10], but it's not clear how efficient this method is in practice.

Acknowledgements. This work has been supported by the European Research Council (ERC) under the European Unions's Horizon 2020 research and innovation programme under grant agreement No 669255 (MPCPRO); the European Union's Horizon 2020 research and innovation programme under grant agreement No 731583 (SODA); the European Union's Horizon 2020 research and innovation programme under grant agreement No 74079 (ALGSTRONGCRYPTO); and the Danish Independent Research Council under Grant-ID DFF-6108-00169 (FoCC).

References

1. Asharov, G., Lindell, Y., Schneider, T., Zohner, M.: More efficient oblivious transfer extensions with security for malicious adversaries. In: Oswald, E., Fischlin, M. (eds.) EUROCRYPT 2015, Part I. LNCS, vol. 9056, pp. 673–701. Springer, Heidelberg (2015). https://doi.org/10.1007/978-3-662-46800-5_26
2. Bendlin, R., Damgård, I., Orlandi, C., Zakarias, S.: Semi-homomorphic encryption and multiparty computation. In: Paterson, K.G. (ed.) EUROCRYPT 2011. LNCS, vol. 6632, pp. 169–188. Springer, Heidelberg (2011). https://doi.org/10.1007/978-3-642-20465-4_11
3. Bogdanov, D., Laur, S., Willemson, J.: Sharemind: a framework for fast privacy-preserving computations. In: Jajodia, S., Lopez, J. (eds.) ESORICS 2008. LNCS, vol. 5283, pp. 192–206. Springer, Heidelberg (2008). https://doi.org/10.1007/978-3-540-88313-5_13
4. Canetti, R.: Universally composable security: a new paradigm for cryptographic protocols. In: 42nd FOCS, pp. 136–145. IEEE Computer Society Press, October 2001
5. Cramer, R., Fehr, S., Ishai, Y., Kushilevitz, E.: Efficient multi-party computation over rings. In: Biham, E. (ed.) EUROCRYPT 2003. LNCS, vol. 2656, pp. 596–613. Springer, Heidelberg (2003). https://doi.org/10.1007/3-540-39200-9_37
6. Damgård, I., Damgård, K., Nielsen, K., Nordholt, P.S., Toft, T.: Confidential benchmarking based on multiparty computation. In: Grossklags, J., Preneel, B. (eds.) FC 2016. LNCS, vol. 9603, pp. 169–187. Springer, Heidelberg (2017). https://doi.org/10.1007/978-3-662-54970-4_10
7. Damgård, I., Keller, M., Larraia, E., Pastro, V., Scholl, P., Smart, N.P.: Practical covertly secure MPC for dishonest majority – or: breaking the SPDZ limits. In: Crampton, J., Jajodia, S., Mayes, K. (eds.) ESORICS 2013. LNCS, vol. 8134, pp. 1–18. Springer, Heidelberg (2013). https://doi.org/10.1007/978-3-642-40203-6_1
8. Damgård, I., Orlandi, C., Simkin, M.: Yet another compiler for active security or: efficient MPC over arbitrary rings. In: Shacham, H., Boldyreva, A. (eds.) CRYPTO 2018. LNCS, vol. 10992, pp. 799–829. Springer, Cham (2018)
9. Damgård, I., Pastro, V., Smart, N.P., Zakarias, S.: Multiparty computation from somewhat homomorphic encryption. In: Safavi-Naini, R., Canetti, R. (eds.) CRYPTO 2012. LNCS, vol. 7417, pp. 643–662. Springer, Heidelberg (2012). https://doi.org/10.1007/978-3-642-32009-5_38
10. Gentry, C., Halevi, S., Smart, N.P.: Better bootstrapping in fully homomorphic encryption. In: Fischlin, M., Buchmann, J., Manulis, M. (eds.) PKC 2012. LNCS, vol. 7293, pp. 1–16. Springer, Heidelberg (2012). https://doi.org/10.1007/978-3-642-30057-8_1
11. Goldreich, O., Micali, S., Wigderson, A.: How to play any mental game or a completeness theorem for protocols with honest majority. In: Aho, A. (ed.) 19th ACM STOC, pp. 218–229. ACM Press, May 1987
12. Impagliazzo, R., Levin, L.A., Luby, M.: Pseudo-random generation from one-way functions (extended abstracts). In: 21st ACM STOC, pp. 12–24. ACM Press, May 1989
13. Keller, M., Orsini, E., Scholl, P.: Actively secure OT extension with optimal overhead. In: Gennaro, R., Robshaw, M. (eds.) CRYPTO 2015, Part I. LNCS, vol. 9215, pp. 724–741. Springer, Heidelberg (2015). https://doi.org/10.1007/978-3-662-47989-6_35

14. Keller, M., Orsini, E., Scholl, P.: MASCOT: faster malicious arithmetic secure computation with oblivious transfer. In: Weippl, E.R., Katzenbeisser, S., Kruegel, C., Myers, A.C., Halevi, S. (eds.) ACM CCS 2016, pp. 830–842, ACM Press, October 2016

15. Keller, M., Pastro, V., Rotaru, D.: Overdrive: making SPDZ great again. In: Nielsen, J.B., Rijmen, V. (eds.) EUROCRYPT 2018. LNCS, vol. 10822, pp. 158–189. Springer, Cham (2018). https://doi.org/10.1007/978-3-319-78372-7_6

16. Nielsen, J.B., Nordholt, P.S., Orlandi, C., Burra, S.S.: A new approach to practical active-secure two-party computation. In: Safavi-Naini, R., Canetti, R. (eds.) CRYPTO 2012. LNCS, vol. 7417, pp. 681–700. Springer, Heidelberg (2012). https://doi.org/10.1007/978-3-642-32009-5_40

17. Nielsen, J.B., Schneider, T., Trifiletti, R.: Constant round maliciously secure 2PC with function-independent preprocessing using LEGO. In: 24th NDSS Symposium. The Internet Society (2017). http://eprint.iacr.org/2016/1069

18. Pettai, M., Laud, P.: Automatic proofs of privacy of secure multi-party computation protocols against active adversaries. In: IEEE 28th Computer Security Foundations Symposium, CSF 2015, Verona, Italy, 13–17 July 2015, pp. 75–89. IEEE (2015)

19. Scholl, P.: Extending oblivious transfer with low communication via key-homomorphic PRFs. In: Abdalla, M., Dahab, R. (eds.) PKC 2018. LNCS, vol. 10769, pp. 554–583. Springer, Cham (2018). https://doi.org/10.1007/978-3-319-76578-5_19

Yet Another Compiler for Active Security or: Efficient MPC Over Arbitrary Rings

Ivan Damgård, Claudio Orlandi, and Mark Simkin$^{(\boxtimes)}$

Aarhus University, Aarhus, Denmark
{ivan,orlandi,simkin}@cs.au.dk

Abstract. We present a very simple yet very powerful idea for turning any passively secure MPC protocol into an actively secure one, at the price of reducing the threshold of tolerated corruptions.

Our compiler leads to a very efficient MPC protocols for the important case of secure evaluation of arithmetic circuits over arbitrary rings (e.g., the natural case of $\mathbb{Z}_{2^\ell}$) for a small number of parties. We show this by giving a concrete protocol in the preprocessing model for the popular setting with three parties and one corruption. This is the first protocol for secure computation over rings that achieves active security with constant overhead.

1 Introduction

Secure Computation. Secure Multiparty Computation (MPC) allows a set of participants $P_1, \ldots, P_n$ with private inputs respectively $x_1, \ldots, x_n$ to learn the output of some public function f evaluated on their private inputs i.e., $z = f(x_1, \ldots, x_n)$ without having to reveal *any other information* about their inputs. Seminal MPC results from the 80s [3,6,18,26] have shown that with MPC it is possible to securely evaluate any boolean or arithmetic circuit with information theoretic security (under the assumption that a strict minority of the participants are corrupt) or with computational security (when no such honest majority can be assumed).

As is well known, the most efficient MPC protocols are only passively secure. What is perhaps less well known is that by settling for passive security, we also get a wider range of domains over which we can do MPC. In addition to the standard approach of evaluating boolean or arithmetic circuits over fields, we can also efficiently perform computations over other rings. This has been demonstrated by the Sharemind suite of protocols [5], which works over the ring $\mathbb{Z}_{2^\ell}$. Sharemind's success in practice is probably, to a large extent, due to the choice of the underlying ring, which closely matches the kind of ring CPUs naturally use. Closely matching an actual CPU architecture allows easier programming of algorithms for MPC, since programmers can reuse some of the tricks that CPUs use to do their work efficiently.

While passive security is a meaningful security notion that is sometimes sufficient, one would of course like to have security against active attacks. However,

H. Shacham and A. Boldyreva (Eds.): CRYPTO 2018, LNCS 10992, pp. 799–829, 2018.
https://doi.org/10.1007/978-3-319-96881-0_27

the known techniques, such as the GMW compiler, for achieving active security incur a significant overhead, and while more efficient approaches exist, they usually need to assume that the computation is done over a field, and they always have an overhead that depends on the security parameter. Typically, such protocols, like the BeDOZa or SPDZ protocols [4,11,13], start with a *preprocessing phase* which generates the necessary correlated randomness [19] in the form of so called *multiplication triples.* This is followed by an information theoretic and therefore very fast *online phase* where the triples are consumed to evaluate the arithmetic circuit. To get active security in the on-line phase, protocols employ information-theoretic MACs that allow to detect whether incorrect information is sent. Using such MACs forces the domain of computation to be a field which excludes, of course, the ring $\mathbb{Z}_{2^\ell}$. The only exception is recent work subsequent to ours [10]. This is not a compiler but a specific protocol for the preprocessing model which allows MACs for the domain $\mathbb{Z}_{2^\ell}$. This is incomparable to our result for this setting: compared to our result, the protocol from [10] tolerates larger number of corruptions, but it introduces an overhead in storage and computational work proportional to the product of the security parameter and the circuit size.

Another alternative is to use garbled circuits. However, they incur a rather large overhead when active security is desired, and cannot be used at all if we want to do arithmetic computation directly over a large ring. Thus, a very natural question is:

Can we go from passive to active security at a small cost and can we do so in a general way which allows us to do computations over general rings?

Our results. In this paper we address the above question by making three main contributions:

1. A generic transformation that compiles a protocol with passive security against at least 2 corruptions into one that is actively secure (but against a smaller number of corruptions). This works both for the preprocessing and the standard model. The transformation preserves perfect and statistical security and its overhead depends only on the number of players, and not on the security parameter. Thus, for a constant number of parties it loses only a constant factor in efficiency.

2. We present a preprocessing protocol for 3 parties. It generates multiplication triples to be used by a particular protocol produced by our compiler. This preprocessing can generate triples over any ring $\mathbb{Z}_m$ and has constant computational overhead for large enough m; more precisely, if m is exponential in the statistical security parameter. We build this preprocessing from scratch, not by using our compiler. This, together with our compiler, gives a plug-in replacement for the Sharemind protocol as explained below.

3. A generic transformation that works for a large class of protocols including those output by our passive-to-active compiler. It takes as input a protocol that is secure with abort and satisfies certain extra conditions, and produces a new protocol with complete fairness [8]. In security with abort, the adversary gets the output and can then decide if the protocol should abort.

In complete fairness the adversary must decide whether to abort without seeing the output. This is relevant in applications where the adversary might "dislike" the result and would prefer that it is not delivered. The transformation has an additive overhead that only depends on the size of the output and not the size of the computation. It works in the honest majority model without broadcast. In this model we cannot guarantee termination in general so security with complete fairness is essentially the best we can hope for.

Discussion of results. Our passive-to-active compiler can, for instance, be applied to the straightforward 3-party protocol that represents secret values using additive secret sharing over $\mathbb{Z}_{2^\ell}$ and does secure multiplication using multiplication triples created in a preprocessing phase. This protocol is secure against 2 passive corruptions. Applying our compiler results in a 3-party protocol Π in the preprocessing model that is information theoretically secure against 1 corruption and obtains active security with abort. Π can be used as plug-in replacement for the Sharemind protocol. It has better (active) instead of passive security and is essentially as efficient. This, of course, is only interesting if we can implement the required preprocessing efficiently, which is exactly what we do as our second result, discussed in more detail below.

The compiler is based on the idea of turning each party in the passively secure protocol into a "virtual" party, and then each virtual party is independently emulated by 2 or more of the real parties (i.e., each real party will locally run the code of the virtual party). Intuitively, if the number of virtual parties for which a corrupt party is an emulator is not larger than the privacy threshold of the original protocol, then our transform preserves the *privacy* guarantees of the original protocol. Further, if we can guarantee that each virtual party is emulated by at least one honest party, then this party can detect faulty behaviour by the other emulators and abort if needed, thus guaranteeing *correctness*. Moreover, if we set the parameters in a way that we are guaranteed an honest majority among the emulators, then we can even decide on the correct behaviour by majority vote and get full active security. While this in hindsight might seem like a simple idea, proving that it actually works in general requires us to take care of some technical issues relating, for instance, to handling the randomness and inputs of the virtual parties.

The approach is closely related to replicated secret sharing which has been used for MPC before [17,22] (see the related work section for further discussion), but to the best of our knowledge, this is the first general construction that transforms an entire passively secure protocol to active security. From this point of view, it can be seen as a construction that unifies and "explains" several earlier constructions.

While our construction works for any number of parties it unfortunately does not scale well, and the resulting protocol will only tolerate corruptions of roughly $\sqrt{n}$ of the n parties and has a multiplicative overhead of order n compared to the passively secure protocol. This is far from the constant fraction of corruptions we know can be tolerated with other techniques. We show two ways to improve this. First, while our main compiler preserves adaptive security, we also present an alternative construction that only works for static security but tolerates $n/\log n$ active corruptions, and has overhead $\log^2 n$. Second, we show that using results from [7], we get a protocol for any number n of parties tolerating roughly $n/4$ malicious corruptions. We do this by starting from a protocol for 5 parties tolerating 2 passive corruptions, use our result to constructs a 5 party protocol tolerating 1 active corruption, and then use a generic construction from [7] based on monotone formulae. Note that a main motivation for the results from [7] was to introduce a new approach to the design of multiparty protocols. Namely, first design a protocol for a constant number of parties tolerating 1 active corruption, and then apply player emulation and monotone formulae to get actively secure multiparty protocols. From this point of view, adding our result extends their idea in an interesting way: using a generic transformation one can now get active and information theoretic security for a constant fraction of corruptions from a seemingly even simpler object: a protocol for a constant number of parties that is *passively* secure against 2 corruptions.

Our second result, the preprocessing protocol, is based on the idea that we can quite easily create multiplication triples involving secret shared values $a, b, c \in \mathbb{Z}_m$ and where $ab = c \bmod m$ if parties behave honestly. The problem now is that the standard efficient approach to checking whether $ab = c \bmod m$ only works if m is prime, or at least has only large prime factors. We solve this by finding a way to embed the problem into a slightly larger field $\mathbb{Z}_p$ for a prime p. We can then check efficiently if $ab = c \bmod p$. In addition we make sure that a, b are small enough so that this implies $ab = c$ over the integers and hence also that $ab = c \bmod m$.

Our final result, the compiler for complete fairness, works for protocols where the output is only revealed in the last round, as is typically the case for protocols based on secret sharing. Roughly speaking, the idea is to execute the protocol up to its last round just before the outputs are delivered. We then compute verifiable secret sharings of the data that parties would send in the last round – as well as one bit that says whether sending these messages would cause an abort in the original protocol. Of course, this extra computation may abort, but if it does not and we are told that the verifiably shared messages are correct, then it is too late for the adversary to abort; as we assume an honest majority the shared messages can always be reconstructed. While this basic idea might seem simple, the proof is trickier than one might expect – as we need to be careful with the assumptions on the original protocol to avoid selective failure attacks.

1.1 Related Work

Besides what is already mentioned above, there are several other relevant works. Previous compilers, notably the GMW [18] and the IPS compiler [20,21], allow to transform passively secure protocols into maliciously secure ones. The GMW compiler uses zero-knowledge proofs and, hence, is not blackbox in the underlying construction. It produces protocols which are far from practically efficient. The IPS compiler works, very roughly speaking, by using an inner protocol to simulate the protocol execution of an outer protocol. The outer protocol computes the desired functionality. The inner protocol protocols computes the individual computation steps of the outer protocol. The compiler is blackbox with respect to the inner, but not the outer protocol and it requires the existence of oblivious transfer. It is unclear whether the IPS compiler can be used to produce practically efficient protocols.

In contrast, our compiler does not require any computational assumption and thus preserves any information theoretic guarantees the underlying protocol has. Our transform does not have any large hidden constants and can produce actively secure protocols with efficiency that may be of practical interest.

In a recent work by Furukawa et al. [17], a practically very efficient three-party protocol with one active corruption was proposed. Their protocol uses replicated secret sharing and only works for bits. As the authors state themselves, it is not straightforward to generalize their protocol to more than three parties, while maintaining efficiency. In contrast, our protocol works over any arbitrary ring and can easily be generalized to any number of players. Furthermore our transform produces protocols with constant overhead, whereas their protocol does not have constant overhead.

The idea of using replication to detect active corruptions has been used before. For instance, Mohassel et al. [23] propose a three-party version of Yao's protocol. In a nutshell, their approach is to let two parties garble a circuit separately and to let the third party check that the circuits are the same. Our results in this work are more general in the sense that we propose a general transform to obtain actively secure protocols from passively secure ones. In [14], Desmedt and Kurosawa use replication to design a mix-net with t^2 servers secure against (roughly) t actively corrupted servers. A simple approach to MPC based on replicated secret sharing was proposed by Maurer in [22]. It has been the basis for practical implementations like [5].

2   Preliminaries

Notation. If $\mathcal{X}$ is a set, then $v \leftarrow \mathcal{X}$ means that v is a uniformly random value chosen from $\mathcal{X}$. When A is an algorithm, we write $v \leftarrow A(x)$ to denote a run of A on input x that produces output v. For $n \in \mathbb{N}$, we write $[n]$ to denote the set $\{1, 2, \ldots, n\}$. For n party protocols, we will write P_{i+1} and implicitly assume a wrap-around of the party's index, i.e. $\mathrm{P}_{n+1} = \mathrm{P}_1$ and $\mathrm{P}_{1-1} = \mathrm{P}_n$. All logarithms are assumed to be base 2.

Security Definitions. We will use the UC model throughout the paper, more precisely the variant described in [9]. We assume the reader has basic knowledge about the UC model and refer to [9] for details. Here we only give a very brief introduction: We consider the following entities: a *protocol* $\Pi_{\mathcal{F}}$ for n players that is meant to implement an *ideal functionality* $\mathcal{F}$. An *environment* Z that models everything external to the protocol which means that Z chooses inputs for the players and is also the adversarial entity that attacks the protocol. Thus Z may corrupt players passively or actively as specified in more detail below. We have an *auxiliary functionality* $\mathcal{G}$ that the protocol may use to accomplish its goal. Finally we have a *simulator* S that is used to demonstrate that $\Pi_{\mathcal{F}}$ indeed implements $\mathcal{F}$ securely.

In the definition of security we compare two processes: First, the *real process* executes Z, $\Pi_{\mathcal{F}}$ and $\mathcal{G}$ together, this is denoted $Z \diamond \Pi_{\mathcal{F}} \diamond \mathcal{G}$. Second, we consider the *ideal process* where we execute Z, S and $\mathcal{F}$ together, denoted $Z \diamond S \diamond \mathcal{F}$. The role of the simulator S is to emulate Z's view of the attack on the protocol, this includes the views of the corrupted parties as well as their communication with $\mathcal{G}$. To be able to do this, S must send inputs for corrupted players to $\mathcal{F}$ and will get back outputs for the corrupted players. A simulator in the UC model is not allowed to rewind the environment.

Both processes are given a security parameter k as input, and the only output is one bit produced by Z. We think of this bit as Z's guess at whether it has been part of the real or the ideal process. We define p_{real} respectively p_{ideal} to be the probabilities that the real, respectively the ideal process outputs 1, and we say that $Z \diamond \Pi_{\mathcal{F}} \diamond \mathcal{G} \equiv Z \diamond S \diamond \mathcal{F}$ if $|p_{real} - p_{ideal}|$ is negligible in k.

Definition 1. *We say that protocol $\Pi_{\mathcal{F}}$ securely implements functionality $\mathcal{F}$ with respect to a class of environments Env in the $\mathcal{G}$-hybrid model if there exists a simulator S such that for all $Z \in Env$ we have $Z \diamond \Pi_{\mathcal{F}} \diamond \mathcal{G} \equiv Z \diamond S \diamond \mathcal{F}$.*

Different types of security can now be captured by considering different classes of environments: For *passive t-security*, we consider any Z that corrupts at most t players. Initially, it chooses inputs for the players. Corrupt players follow the protocol so Z only gets read access to their views. For *biased passive t-security*, we consider any Z that corrupts at most t players. Initially, it chooses inputs for the players, as well as random coins for the corrupt players. Then corrupt players follow the protocol so Z only gets read access to their views. This type of security has been considered in [1,24] and intuitively captures passively secure protocols where privacy only depends on the honest players choosing their randomness properly. This is actually true for almost all known passively secure protocols. Finally, for *active t-security*, we consider any Z that corrupts at most t players, and Z takes complete control over corrupt players.

One may also distinguish between unconditional or computational security depending on whether the environment class contains all environments of a certain type or only polynomial time ones. We will not be concerned much with this distinction, as our main compiler is the same regardless, and preserves both unconditional and computational security. For simplicity, we will consider unconditional security by default. We also consider by default adaptive security, meaning that Z is allowed to adaptive choose players to corrupt during the protocol.

We will consider synchronous protocols throughout, so protocols proceed in rounds in the standard way, with a rushing adversary. We will always assume that point-to-point secure channels are available. In addition, we will also sometimes make use of other auxiliary functionalities, as specified in the next subsection.

Ideal Functionalities. The broadcast functionality $\mathcal{F}_{\mathsf{bcast}}$ (Fig. 1) allows a party to send a value to a set of other parties, such that either all receiving parties receive the same value or all parties jointly abort by outputting $\bot$. This functionality is known as detectable broadcast [15] and while unconditionally secure broadcast with termination among n parties requires that strictly less than $n/3$ parties are corrupted [25], this bound does not apply to detectable broadcast, which can be instantiated with information-theoretic security tolerating any number of corruptions [16].

Functionality $\mathcal{F}_{\mathsf{bcast}}$

The ideal functionality runs with parties $P_1, \ldots, P_n$ and environment Z.

- P_i sends $(v, \mathbb{P})$ to $\mathcal{F}_{\mathsf{bcast}}$, where $v \in \{0,1\}^*$ and $\mathbb{P} \subset \{P_1 \ldots P_n\}$.
- If $\mathbb{P}$ contains a corrupted party, then Z receives v. Otherwise it only receives notification that a broadcast has been started. Z then decides whether to continue or to abort by sending a bit to the ideal functionality.
  - If Z continues, then $\mathcal{F}_{\mathsf{bcast}}$ sends v to all $P_j \in \mathbb{P}$.
  - If Z aborts, then $\mathcal{F}_{\mathsf{bcast}}$ sends $\perp$ to all $P_j \in \mathbb{P}$.

Fig. 1. The broadcast functionality

Functionality $\mathcal{F}_{\mathsf{cflip}}$

The ideal functionality runs with parties $P_1, \ldots, P_n$ and environment Z.

- The functionality waits for messages of the form $(\mathsf{cflip}, \mathbb{P})$ from all parties.
- After receiving all such messages, and a deliver message from the environment Z, the functionality $\mathcal{F}_{\mathsf{cflip}}$ picks a random string $r \leftarrow \{0,1\}^\lambda$ and outputs r to all parties in $\mathbb{P}$.

Fig. 2. The coin flip functionality

Using the coin flip functionality $\mathcal{F}_{\mathsf{cflip}}$ (Fig. 2), a set of parties can jointly generate and agree on a uniformly random λ-bit string. In the case of an honest majority, this functionality can be implemented with information-theoretic security via verifiable secret sharing (VSS) [9] as follows: Let $\mathbb{P}$ be the set of players that want to perform a coin flip. To realize the functionality, every participating party $P_i \in \mathbb{P}$ secret shares a random bit string r_i among *all* the other players. Once every player in $\mathbb{P}$ shared its bit string r_i, we let all players in $\mathbb{P}$ reconstruct all bit strings and output $\bigoplus_i r_i$. This is done by having all players send all their shares to players in $\mathbb{P}$. Here we assume that reconstruction is non-interactive, i.e., players send shares to each other and each player locally computes the secret. Such VSS schemes exist, as is well known. It is important to note that a VSS needs broadcast in the sharing phase, and since we only assume detectable broadcast, the adversary may force the VSS to abort. However, since the decision to abort or not must be made without knowing the shared secret (by privacy of the VSS) the adversary cannot use this to bias the output of the coinflip.

The standard functionality $\mathcal{F}_{\text{triple}}$ (Fig. 3) allows three parties P_1, P_2, and P_3 to generate a replicated secret sharing of multiplication triples. In this functionality, the adversary can corrupt one party and pick its shares. The remaining shares of the honest parties are chosen uniformly at random. The intuition behind this ideal functionality is that, even though the adversary can pick its own shares, it does not learn anything about the remaining shares, and hence it does not learn anything about the actual value of the multiplication triple that is secret shared. We will present a communication efficient implementation of this functionality in Sect. 5.

Functionality $\mathcal{F}_{\text{triple}}$

The ideal functionality is parameterized by an integer m, runs with parties P_1, P_2, P_3 and environment Z.

- If party P_i is corrupted, then the environment Z can input (corrupt, v) where $v = (a_{i+1}, a_{i+2}, b_{i+1}, b_{i+2}, c_{i+1}, c_{i+2})$ all in $\mathbb{Z}_m$.
- Upon receiving init from all honest parties the functionality $\mathcal{F}_{\text{triple}}$ picks the undefined (a_i, b_i, c_i) uniformly at random, such that $(a_1 + a_2 + a_3) \cdot (b_1 + b_2 + b_3) = (c_1 + c_2 + c_3) \in \mathbb{Z}_m$ and outputs:
  - (a_1, b_1, c_1) to P_2 and P_3,
  - (a_2, b_2, c_2) to P_3 and P_1,
  - (a_3, b_3, c_3) to P_1 and P_2.

Fig. 3. Triple generation functionality

Finally, for any function f with n inputs and one output, we will let $\mathcal{F}_f$ denote a UC functionality for computing f securely with (individual) abort. That is, once it receives inputs from all n parties it computes f and then sends the output to the environment Z. Z returns for each player a bit indicating if this player gets the output or will abort. F_f sends the output to the selected players and sends $\perp$ to the rest. We consider three (stronger) variants of this: $\mathcal{F}_f^{\text{unanimous}}$ where Z must give the output to all players or have them all abort; $\mathcal{F}_f^{\text{fair}}$ where Z is not given the output when it decides whether to abort; and $\mathcal{F}_f^{\text{fullactive}}$ where the adversary cannot abort at all.

3   Our Passive to Active Security Transform

The goal of our transform is to take a passively secure protocol and convert it into a protocol that is secure against a small number of active corruptions.

For simplicity, let us start with a passively secure n-party protocol $(n \geq 3)$ that we will convert into an n-party protocol in the $\mathcal{F}_{\mathsf{cflip}}$-hybrid model that is secure against *one* active corruption.

The main challenge in achieving security against an actively corrupted party, is to prevent it from deviating from the protocol description and sending malformed messages. Our protocol transform is based upon the observation that, assuming one active corruption, every pair of parties contains at least one honest party. Now instead of letting the real parties directly run the passively secure protocol, we will let pairs of real parties simulate virtual parties that will compute, using the passively secure protocol, the desired functionality on behalf of the real parties. More precisely, for $1 \leq i \leq n$, the real parties P_i and P_{i+1} will simulate virtual party $\mathbb{P}_i$. In the first phase of our protocol, P_i and P_{i+1} will agree on some common input and randomness that we will specify in a moment. In the second phase, the virtual parties will run a passively secure protocol on the previously agreed inputs and randomness. Whenever virtual party $\mathbb{P}_i$ sends a message to $\mathbb{P}_j$, we will realize this by letting P_i and P_{i+1} both send the same message to P_j and P_{j+1}. Note that when both P_i and P_{i+1} are honest, these two messages will be identical since they are constructed according to the same (passively secure) protocol, using the same shared randomness and the previously received messages. The "action" of receiving a message at the virtual party $\mathbb{P}_j$ is emulated by having the real parties P_j and P_{j+1} both receive two messages each. Both parties now check locally whether the received messages are identical and, if not, broadcast an "abort" message. Otherwise they continue to execute the passively secure protocol. The high-level idea behind this approach is that the adversary controlling one real party cannot send a malformed message and at the same time be consistent with the other honest real party simulating the same virtual party. Hence, either the adversary behaves honestly or the protocol will be aborted.

Remember that we need all real parties emulating the same virtual party to agree on a random tape and a common input. Agreeing on a random tape is trivial in the $\mathcal{F}_{\mathsf{cflip}}$-hybrid model, we can just invoke $\mathcal{F}_{\mathsf{cflip}}$ for each virtual $\mathbb{P}_i$ and have it send the random string to the corresponding real parties P_i and P_{i+1}. Moreover, in the process of agreeing on inputs for the virtual parties we need to be careful in not leaking any information about the real parties' original inputs. Towards this goal, we will let every real party secret share, e.g. XOR, its input among all virtual parties. Now, instead of letting the underlying passively secure protocol compute $f(x_1, \ldots, x_n)$, where real P_i holds input x_i, we will use it to compute $f'((x_1^1, \ldots, x_n^1), \ldots, (x_1^n, \ldots, x_n^n)) := f(\bigoplus_i x_1^i, \ldots, \bigoplus_i x_n^i)$, where virtual party $\mathbb{P}_i$ has input $(x_1^i, \ldots, x_n^i)$, i.e. one share of every original input.

As a small example, for the case of three parties, we would get $\mathbb{P}_1 = \{P_1, P_2\}$ holding input (x_1^1, x_2^1, x_3^1), $\mathbb{P}_2 = \{P_2, P_3\}$ with input (x_1^2, x_2^2, x_3^2), and $\mathbb{P}_3 = \{P_3, P_1\}$ with (x_1^3, x_2^3, x_3^3). Since every real party only participates in the simulation of two virtual parties, no real party learns enough shares to reconstruct the other parties' inputs. More precisely, for arbitrary $n \geq 3$ and one corruption, each real party will participate in the simulation of two virtual parties, thus the underlying passively secure protocol needs to be at least passively 2-secure. Actually, each real party will learn not only two full views, but also one of the inputs of each other virtual party, since it knows the shares it distributed itself. As we will see in the security proof this is not a problem and passive 2-security is, for one active corruption, a sufficient condition on the underlying passively secure protocol.

The approach described above can be generalized to a larger number of corrupted parties. The main insight for one active corruption was that each set of two parties contains one honest party. For more than one corruption, we need to ensure that each set of parties of some arbitrary size contains at least one honest party that will send the correct message. Given n parties and t corruptions, each virtual party needs to be simulated by at least $t + 1$ real parties. We let real parties $P_i, \ldots, P_{i+t}$ simulate virtual party $\mathbb{P}_i$[1]. This means that every real party will participate in the simulation of $t + 1$ virtual parties. Since we have t corruptions, the adversary can learn at most $t(t + 1)$ views of virtual parties, which means that our underlying passively secure protocol needs to have at least passive $(t^2 + t)$-security.

In the following formal description, let $\mathbb{P}_i$ be the virtual party that is simulated by $P_i, \ldots, P_{i+t}$. By slight abuse of notation, we use the same notation for the virtual party $\mathbb{P}_j$ and the set of real parties that emulate it. When we say $\mathbb{P}_i$ sends a message to $\mathbb{P}_j$, we mean that each real party in $\mathbb{P}_i$ will send one message to every real party in $\mathbb{P}_j$. Let $\mathbb{V}_i$ be the set of virtual parties in whose simulation P_i participates.

Let f be the n-party functionality we want to compute, and $\Pi_{f'}$ be a passive $(t^2 + t)$-secure protocol that computes f', i.e., it computes f on secret shares as described above. We construct $\tilde{\Pi}_f$ that computes f and is secure against t active corruption as follows:

The protocol $\tilde{\Pi}_f$:

1. P_i splits its input x_i into n random shares, s.t. $x_i = \bigoplus_{1 \leq j \leq n} x_i^j$, and for all $j \in [n]$ send $(x_i^j, \mathbb{P}_j)$ to $\mathcal{F}_{\text{bcast}}$ (which then sends x_i^j to all parties in $\mathbb{P}_j$).
2. For $i \in [n]$ invoke $\mathcal{F}_{\text{cflip}}$ on input $\mathbb{P}_i$. Each P_i receives $\{r_j | \mathbb{P}_j \in \mathbb{V}_i\}$ from the functionality.
3. P_i receives $\left(x_1^j, \ldots, x_n^j\right)$ for every $\mathbb{P}_j \in \mathbb{V}_i$ from $\mathcal{F}_{\text{bcast}}$. If any $x_i^j = \bot$, abort the protocol.
4. All virtual parties, simulated by the real parties, jointly execute $\Pi_{f'}$, where each real party in $\mathbb{P}_i$ uses the same randomness r_i that it obtained through $\mathcal{F}_{\text{cflip}}$. Whenever $\mathbb{P}_i$ receives a message from $\mathbb{P}_j$, each member of $\mathbb{P}_i$ checks that it received the same message from all parties in $\mathbb{P}_j$. If not, it aborts (this includes the case where a message is missing). Once a player makes it to the end of $\Pi_{f'}$ without aborting, it outputs whatever is output in $\Pi_{f'}$.

---

[1] Any other distribution of real party among virtual parties that ensures that each real party simulates equally many virtual parties would work as well.

Theorem 1. *Let $n \geq 3$. Suppose $\Pi_{f'}$ implements $\mathcal{F}_{f'}$ with passive $(t^2 + t)$-security. Then $\tilde{\Pi}_f$ as described above implements $\mathcal{F}_f$ in the $(\mathcal{F}_{\text{bcast}}, \mathcal{F}_{\text{cflip}})$-hybrid model with active t-security.*

Remark 1. We construct a protocol where the adversary can force some honest players to abort while others terminate normally. We can trivially extend this to a protocol implementing $\mathcal{F}_f^{\text{unanimous}}$ where all players do the same: we just do a round of detectable broadcast in the end where players say whether they would abort in the original protocol. If a player hears "abort" from anyone, he aborts.

Remark 2. In Step 1 of the protocol the parties perform a XOR based n-out-of-n secret sharing. We remark that any n-out-of-n secret sharing scheme could be used here instead. In particular, when combining the transform with the preprocessing protocol of Sect. 5, it will be more efficient to do the sharing in the ring $(\mathbb{Z}_m, +)$.

Remark 3. Our compiler is information-theoretically secure. This means that our compiler outputs a protocol that is computationally, statistically, or perfectly secure if the underlying protocol was respectively computationally, statistically, or perfectly secure. This is particularly interesting, since, to the best of our knowledge, our compiler is the first one to preserve statistical and perfect security of the underlying protocol.

Remark 4. The theorem trivially extends to compilation of protocols that use an auxiliary functionality $\mathcal{G}$, such as a preprocessing functionality. We would then obtain a protocol in the $(\mathcal{F}_{\text{bcast}}, \mathcal{F}_{\text{cflip}}, \mathcal{G})$-hybrid model. We leave the details to the reader.

Proof. Before getting into the details of the proof, let us first roughly outline the possibilities of an actively malicious adversary and our approach to simulating his view in the ideal world. The protocol can be split into two separate phases. First all real parties secret share their inputs among the virtual parties through the broadcast functionality. A malicious party P_i^* can pick an arbitrary input x_i, but the broadcast functionality ensures that all parties simulating some virtual party $\mathbb{P}_j$ will receive the same consistent share x_i^j from the adversary. Since every virtual party is simulated by at least one honest real party, the simulator will obtain all secret shares of all inputs belonging to $\mathcal{A}$. This allows the simulator to reconstruct these inputs and query the ideal functionality to retrieve $f(x'_1, \ldots, x'_n)$ where if P_j is honest then $x'_j = x_j$ is the input chosen by the environment and if P_j is corrupt $x'_j = \bigoplus_i x_j^i$ is the input extracted by the simulator. Having the inputs of all corrupted parties and the output from the ideal functionality, we can use the simulator of $\Pi_{f'}$ to simulate the interaction with the adversary. At this point, there are two things to note.

First, we have n real parties that simulate n virtual parties. Since the adversary can corrupt at most t real parties, we simulate each virtual party by $t + 1$ real parties. As each real party participates in the same amount of simulations of virtual parties, we get that each real party simulates $t + 1$ virtual parties.

This means that the adversary can learn at most $t^2 + t$ views of the virtual parties and, hence, since $\Pi_{f'}$ is passively $(t^2 + t)$-secure, the adversary cannot distinguish the simulated transcript from a real execution.

Second, the random tapes are honestly generated by $\mathcal{F}_{\text{cflip}}$. The simulator knows the exact messages that the corrupted parties should be sending and how to respond to them. Upon receiving an honest message from a corrupted party, the simulator responds according to underlying simulator. If the adversary tries to cheat, the simulator aborts. Aborting is fine, since, in a real world execution, the adversary would be sending a message, which is inconsistent with at least one honest real party that simulates the same virtual party, and this would make some receiving honest party abort.

Given this intuition, let us now proceed with the formal simulation. Let Z be the environment (that corrupts at most t parties). Let $\mathbb{P}^*$ be the set of real parties that are corrupted before the protocol execution starts. Let $\mathbb{V}^*$ be the set of virtual parties that are simulated by at least one corrupt real party from $\mathbb{P}^*$. We will construct a simulator $S_{\tilde{\Pi}_f}$ using the simulator $S_{\Pi_{f'}}$ for f'. In the specification of the simulator we will often say that it sends some message to a corrupt player. This will actually mean that Z gets the message as Z plays for all the corrupted parties.

$S_{\tilde{\Pi}_f}$:

1. For each $P_i \in \mathbb{P}^*$ and $j \in [n]$, Z sends $(x_i^j, \mathbb{P}_j)$ to $\mathcal{F}_{\text{bcast}}$ (which is emulated by $S_{\tilde{\Pi}_f}$). For each $\mathbb{P}_j \in \mathbb{V}^*$ and each corrupt emulator in $\mathbb{P}_j$, send to Z the shares this emulator would receive from $\mathcal{F}_{\text{bcast}}$, that is, $\{x_i^j\}_{i=1..n}$ where for a corrupt P_i we use the share specified by Z before and for honest P_i we use a random value.

2. For each $P_i \in \mathbb{P}^*$, compute $x_i = \bigoplus_j x_i^j$ and send it to the ideal functionality $\mathcal{F}_f$ to retrieve $z = f(x_1, \ldots, x_n)$, where all x_i with $P_i \notin \mathbb{P}^*$ are the honest parties' inputs in the ideal execution.

3. To simulate the calls to $\mathcal{F}_{\text{cflip}}$, for each corrupt $\mathbb{P}_j$, choose r_j at random and send it to each corrupt emulator of $\mathbb{P}_j$.

   Note that, at this point, we know the inputs and random tapes of all currently corrupted parties. With this, we can check in the following whether corrupt players follow the protocol.

4. Start the simulator $S_{\Pi_{f'}}$ and tell it that the initial set of corrupted players is $\mathbb{V}^*$. We will emulate both its interface towards $\mathcal{F}_{f'}$ and towards its environment, as described below.

5. When $S_{\Pi_{f'}}$ queries $\mathcal{F}_{f'}$ for inputs of corrupted players, we return, for each $\mathbb{P}_j \in \mathbb{V}^*$, $x_1^j, \ldots, x_n^j$. When it queries for the output we return z.

6. For each round in $\Pi_{f'}$ the following is done until the protocol ends or aborts:
   (a) Query $S_{\Pi_{f'}}$ for the messages sent from honest to corrupt virtual parties in the current round. For each such message to be received by a corrupted $\mathbb{P}_j$, send this message to all corrupt real parties in $\mathbb{P}_j$.

(b) Get from Z the messages from corrupt to honest real players in the current round. Compute the set A of honest real players that, given these message, will abort. For all corrupt $\mathbb{P}_j$ and honest $\mathbb{P}_i$, compute the correct message $m_{j,i}$ to be sent in this round from $\mathbb{P}_j$ to $\mathbb{P}_i$. Tell $S_{\Pi_{f'}}$ that $\mathbb{P}_j$ sent $m_{j,i}$ to $\mathbb{P}_i$ in this round.

(c) If we completed the final round, stop the simulation. Else, if A contains all real honest parties, send "abort" to $\mathcal{F}_f$ and stop the simulation. Else, If $A = \emptyset$ go to step 6a. Else, do as follows in the next round (in which the protocol will abort because $A \neq \emptyset$): Query $S_{\Pi_{f'}}$ for the set of messages M sent from honest to corrupt virtual parties in the current round. For all real parties in A tell Z that they send nothing in this round. For all other real honest players compute, as in step 6a, what messages they would send to corrupt real players given M and send these to Z. Send "abort" to F_f and stop the simulation.

It remains to specify how adaptive corruptions are handled: Whenever the adversary adaptively corrupts a new party P_i, we go through all virtual parties $\mathbb{P}_j$ in $\mathbb{V}_i$ (the virtual parties simulated by P_i) and consider the following two cases. First, if $\mathbb{P}_j$ already contained a corrupted party, then we already know how to simulate the view for this virtual player. Second, if P_i is the first corrupted party in $\mathbb{P}_j$, then we add $\mathbb{P}_i$ to $\mathbb{V}^*$ and tell $S_{\Pi_{f'}}$ that $\mathbb{P}_j$ is now corrupt and we forward the response of $S_{\Pi_{f'}}$ to Z, namely the (simulated) current view of $\mathbb{P}_j$. Since the view of $\mathbb{P}_j$ contains this virtual party's random tape, we can continue our overall simulation as above.

We now need to show that $S_{\tilde{\Pi}_f}$ works as required. For contradiction assume that we have an environment Z for which $Z \diamond S_{\tilde{\Pi}_f} \diamond F_f \not\equiv Z \diamond \Pi_f \diamond \mathcal{F}_{\mathsf{cflip}} \diamond \mathcal{F}_{\mathsf{bcast}}$. We will use Z to construct an environment Z' that breaks the assumed security of $\Pi_{f'}$ and so reach a contradiction.

Z':

1. Run internally a copy of Z, and get the initial set of corrupted real players from Z, this determines the set $\mathbb{V}^*$ of corrupt virtual players as above, so Z' will corrupt this set (recall that Z' acts as environment for $\Pi_{f'}$).
2. For each real honest party P_i, get its input x_i from Z. Choose random shares x_i^j subject to $x_i = \bigoplus_j x_i^j$.
3. Execute with Z Step 1 of $S_{\tilde{\Pi}_f}$'s algorithm, but instead of choosing random shares on behalf of honest players, use the shares chosen in the previous step. This will fix the inputs $\{x_i^j\}_{i=1..n}$ of every virtual player $\mathbb{P}_j$. Z' specifies these inputs for the parties in $\Pi_{f'}$.
4. Recall that Z' (being a passive environment) has access to the views of the players in $\mathbb{V}^*$. This initially contains the randomness r_j of corrupt $\mathbb{P}_j$. Z' uses this r_j to execute Step 3 of $S_{\tilde{\Pi}_f}$.

5. Now Z' can expect to see the views of the corrupt $\mathbb{P}_j$'s as they execute the protocol Therefore Z' can perform Step 6 of $S_{\tilde{\Pi}_f}$ with one change only: it will get the messages from honest to corrupt players by looking at the views of the corrupt $\mathbb{P}_j$'s, but will forward these messages to Z exactly as $S_{\tilde{\Pi}_f}$ would have done. In the end Z' outputs the guess produced by Z.

Now, all we need to observe is that if Z' runs in the ideal process, the view seen by its copy of Z is generated using effectively the same algorithm as in $S_{\tilde{\Pi}_f}$, since the views of corrupt virtual parties come from $S_{\Pi_{f'}}$. On the other hand, if Z' runs in the real process, its copy of Z will see a view distributed exactly as what it would see in a normal real process. This is because the first 4 steps of Z' is a perfect simulation of the real Π_f, and the last step aborts exactly when the real protocol would have aborted and otherwise provides real protocol messages to Z. Therefore Z' can distinguish real from ideal process with exactly the same advantage as Z.   □

Efficiency of our transform. In our transform every real party emulates $t + 1$ virtual parties which constitutes the only computational overhead of our transform (if we ignore the computational effort in checking that the $t + 1$ received messages are equal).

Since our transform mainly works by sending messages in a redundant fashion, it incurs a multiplicative bandwidth overhead that depends on the number of active corruptions we want to tolerate. Assume the underlying protocol $\Pi_{f'}$ sends a total of m messages and further assume that we want to tolerate t corruptions. This means that every virtual party $\mathbb{P}_i$ will be simulated by $t + 1$ real parties. Whenever a virtual party $\mathbb{P}_i$ sends a message to $\mathbb{P}_j$, we send $(t + 1) \cdot (t + 1) = t^2 + 2t + 1$ real messages. Ignoring messages sent for the coin-flips and share distribution, our transform produces a protocol that sends at most $m \cdot (t^2 + 2t + 1)$ messages.

For the special case, where $n = 3$, $t = 1$, and $\mathbb{P}_1 = \{\mathrm{P}_1, \mathrm{P}_2\}$, $\mathbb{P}_2 = \{\mathrm{P}_2, \mathrm{P}_3\}$, and $\mathbb{P}_3 = \{\mathrm{P}_3, \mathrm{P}_1\}$, it holds that for all $i \neq j$, $|\mathbb{P}_i \cap \mathbb{P}_j| = 1$. Hence, every message from $\mathbb{P}_i$ to $\mathbb{P}_j$ is realized by sending 3 real messages, which results in $3m$ total messages sent during the second phase of our transform.

Active security without $\mathcal{F}_{\mathsf{cflip}}$ and $\mathcal{F}_{\mathsf{bcast}}$: By the UC composition theorem, we can replace the functionalities $\mathcal{F}_{\mathsf{cflip}}$ and $\mathcal{F}_{\mathsf{bcast}}$ in our compiled protocol by secure implementations and still have a secure protocol. It should be noted that for t corruptions we have $n \geq (t^2 + t) + 1$ and thus we are always in an honest majority setting. This means that both functionalities can be implemented with information theoretic security in the basic point-to-point secure channels model as described in Sect. 2.

The implementation of $\mathcal{F}_{\mathsf{cflip}}$ uses verifiable secret sharing (VSS). Note that even though VSS in itself is powerful enough to realize secure multiparty computation, we only use it for the coin flip functionality. Thus, the number of VSSs we need depends only on the amount of randomness used in the passively secure protocol, and this can be reduced using a pseudorandom generator. Besides (and perhaps more importantly) for the large class of protocols with biased passive security we do not need $\mathcal{F}_{\mathsf{cflip}}$ at all to compile them. Recall that, in the biased passive security model, we still assume that all parties follow the protocol execution honestly, but corrupted parties have the additional power of choosing their random tapes in a non-adaptive, but arbitrary manner. Adversaries who behave honestly, but tamper with their random tapes have been previously considered in [1,24].

If our compiler starts with a protocol $\Pi_{f'}$ that is secure against biased passive adversaries, then we can avoid the use of a coin-flipping functionality, since any random tape is secure to use. We can modify our compiler in a straightforward fashion. Rather than executing one coin-flip for every $\mathbb{P}_i$ to agree on a random tape, we simply let one party from each $\mathbb{P}_i$ broadcast an arbitrarily chosen random tape to the other members of $\mathbb{P}_i$. Now, since we do not need $\mathcal{F}_{\mathsf{cflip}}$, and we do not need to implement VSS for this purpose.

Guaranteed Output Delivery. At the cost of reducing the threshold t of active corruptions that our transform can tolerate, we can obtain guaranteed output delivery. For this we need to ensure that an adversary cannot abort in neither the first phase, nor the second phase of our protocol. In the first phase, when each real party broadcasts its input shares to the virtual parties, we can ensure termination by simply letting every $\mathbb{P}_i$ to be simulated by $3t + 1$ real parties. In this case each $\mathbb{P}_i$ contains less than $1/3$ corruptions and unconditionally secure broadcast (with termination) exists among the members of $\mathbb{P}_i$. Using this approach, the adversary can learn $t(3t + 1)$ views and thus the underlying protocol needs to have passive $(3t^2 + t)$-security.

Another approach that gives slightly better parameters is to only assume an honest majority in each $\mathbb{P}_i$ and use detectable broadcast. In this case the underlying protocol needs to be passively $(2t^2 + t)$-secure and thus, since $n \geq (2t^2 + t) + 1$, unconditionally secure broadcast with termination exists among *all* parties. If a real party simulating a virtual party aborts during a detectable broadcast (to members of $\mathbb{P}_i$), it will broadcast (with guaranteed termination) this abort to all parties. At this point an honest sender, who initiated the broadcast, can broadcast its share for that virtual party among all parties in the protocol. Intuitively, since the broadcast failed, there is at least one corrupted party in the virtual party and thus the adversary already learned the sender's input share, so we do not need to keep it secret any more. If the sender is corrupt and does not broadcast its share after an abort, then all parties replace the sender's input by some default value.

In the second phase of our protocol, real parties simulating virtual parties are currently aborting as soon as they receive inconsistent messages, as they cannot distinguish a correct message from a malformed one. If we ensure that every virtual party is simulated by an honest majority, then, whenever a real party receives a set of messages representing a message from a virtual party, it makes a majority decision. That is, it considers the most frequent message as the correct one and continues the protocol based on this message. Let $\tilde{\Pi}_f$ denote the modified protocol as described above. We then have the following corollary whose proof is a trivial modification of the proof of Theorem 1.

Corollary 1. *Let $n \geq 3$. Suppose $\Pi_{f'}$ implements $\mathcal{F}_{f'}$ with passive $(2t^2 + t)$-security. Then $\tilde{\Pi}_f$ as described above implements $\mathcal{F}_f^{fullactive}$ with active t-security in the $(\mathcal{F}_{bcast}, \mathcal{F}_{cflip})$-hybrid model.*

3.1 Tolerating More Corruptions Assuming Static Adversaries

In this section we sketch a technique that allows to improve the number of corruptions tolerated by our compiler if we restrict the adversary to only perform static corruptions, i.e., if the adversary must choose the corrupted parties before the protocol starts, and we assume a sufficiently large number of parties.

In contrast to our compiler from Theorem 1, instead of choosing which real parties will emulate which virtual party in a deterministic way, we will now map real parties to virtual parties in a probabilistic fashion. Intuitively, since the adversary has to choose who to corrupt before the assignment and since the assignment is done in a random way, this can lead to better bounds when transforming protocols with a large number of parties.

Our new transform works as follows: At the start of the protocol, the parties invoke $\mathcal{F}_{cflip}$ and use the obtained randomness to select uniformly at random a set of real parties to emulate each virtual party. Then we execute the transformed protocol Π_f exactly as we specified above.

Let us define a virtual party in our transform to be *controlled by the adversary* if it is only emulated by corrupt real parties, and let us define a virtual party to be *observed by the adversary* if it is emulated by at least one corrupt real party. In the proof of Theorem 1, we need to ensure two conditions for our transform to be secure. (1) No virtual party can be *controlled by the adversary* and, (2) the number of virtual parties *observed by the adversary* must be smaller than the privacy threshold of the passively secure protocol $\Pi_{f'}$.

We now show that we can set the parameters of the protocol in a way that these two properties are satisfied (except with negligible probability) and in a way that produces better corruption bounds than our original transform.

In the analysis we assume that $n = \Theta(\lambda)$, where n is, as before, the number of virtual and real parties, while λ is the statistical security parameter. We also assume that the security threshold of the underlying passively secure protocol $\Pi_{f'}$ is cn for some constant c. Finally, let e be the number of real parties that emulate each virtual party, and let $e = u \log n$ for a constant u. The number of corrupt real parties that can be tolerated by our transform is then at most $d \cdot n / \log n$ for some constant d. We choose the constants d and u such that $c < 1 - du$.

To show (1), it is easy to see that (by a union bound) the probability that at least one virtual party is fully controlled by the adversary (i.e., it is emulated only by corrupt real parties) is at most:

$$n \left(\frac{dn}{n \log n} \right)^e = n \left(\frac{d}{\log n} \right)^e$$

Since we set $e = u \log n$, this probability is negligible.

As for (2), the probability that a virtual party is *not* observed by the adversary (i.e., it is emulated only by honest parties) is $(1 - d/\log n)^e$, so that the expected number of such parties is $n(1 - d/\log n)^e$ which for large n (and hence small values of $d/\log n$) converges to

$$n(1 - de/\log n) = n(1 - du).$$

As we choose d and u such that $c < 1 - du$, it then follows immediately from a Chernoff bound that the number of virtual parties with only honest emulators is at least cn with overwhelming probability. Let $\bar{\Pi}_f$ denote the protocol using this probabilistic emulation strategy. We then have:

Corollary 2. *Let* $n = \Theta(\lambda)$. *Suppose* $\Pi_{f'}$ *realizes the n-party functionality* $\mathcal{F}_{f'}$ *with passive and static cn-security for a constant c. Then* $\bar{\Pi}_f$ *realizes* F_f *with active and static* $d \cdot n/\log n$-*security in the* $(\mathcal{F}_{bcast}, \mathcal{F}_{cflip})$-*hybrid model, for a constant d.*

Moreover, compared to the protocol obtained using our adaptively secure transform, $\bar{\Pi}_f$ has asymptotically better multiplicative overhead of only $O((\log n)^2)$.

3.2   Achieving Constant Fraction Corruption Threshold

A different approach for improving the bound of corruptions that we can tolerate is to combine our compiler with the results of Cohen et al. [7].

In [7], the authors show how to construct a multiparty protocol for any number of parties from a protocol for a constant number k of parties and a log-depth threshold formula of a certain form. The formula must contain no constants and consist only of threshold gates with k inputs that output 1 if at least j input bits are 1. The given k-party protocol should be secure against $j-1$ (active) corruptions. In [7], constructions are given for such formulae, and this results in multiparty protocols tolerating essentially a fraction $(j-1)/(k-1)$ corruptions.

For instance, from a protocol for 5 parties tolerating 2 passive corruptions (in the model without preprocessing), our result constructs a 5 party protocol tolerating 1 active corruption. Applying the results from [7], we get a protocol for any number n of parties tolerating $n/4 - o(n)$ malicious corruptions. This protocol is maliciously secure with abort, but we can instead start from a protocol for 7 parties tolerating 3 passive corruptions and use Corollary 1 to get a protocol for 7 parties, 1 active corruption and guaranteed output delivery. Applying again the results from [7], we get a protocol for any number n of parties tolerating $n/6 - o(n)$ malicious corruptions with guaranteed output delivery. These results also imply that if we accept that the protocol construction is not explicit, or we make a computational assumption, then we get threshold exactly $n/4$, respectively $n/6$.

4   Achieving Security with Complete Fairness

The security notion achieved by our previous results is active security with abort, namely the adversary gets to see the output and then decides whether the protocol should abort – assuming we want to tolerate the maximal number of corruptions the construction can handle. However, security with abort is often not very satisfactory: it is easy to imagine cases where the adversary may for some reason "dislike" the result and hence prefers that it is not delivered.

However, there is a second version that is stronger than active security with abort, yet weaker than full active security, which is called *active security with complete fairness* [8]. Here the adversary may tell the functionality to abort or ask for the output, but once the output is given, it will also be delivered to the honest parties.

In this section we show how to get general MPC with complete fairness from MPC with abort, with essentially the same efficiency. This will work if we have honest majority and if the given MPC protocol has a *compute-then-open* structure, a condition that is satisfied by a large class of protocols. The skeptical reader may ask why such a result is interesting, since with honest majority we can get full active security without abort anyway. Note, however, that this is only possible if we assume that unconditionally secure broadcast with termination is given as an ideal functionality. In contrast, we do not need this assumption as our results above can produce compute-then-open protocols that only need detectable broadcast (which can be implemented from scratch) and our construction below that achieves complete fairness does not need broadcast with termination either.

We define the following:

Definition 2. Π_f *is a compute-then-open protocol for computing function f if it satisfies the following:*

- *It implements $\mathcal{F}_f$ with active t-security, where $t < n/2$.*[2]
- *One can identify a particular round in the protocol, called the* output round, *that has properties as defined below. The rounds up to but not including the output round are called the* computation phase.
- *The adversary's view of the computation phase is independent of the honest party's input. More formally, we assume that the simulator always simulates the protocol up to the output round without asking for the output.*
- *The total length of the messages sent in the output round depends only on the number of players, the size of the output and (perhaps) on the security parameter*[3]. *We use $d_{i,j}$ to denote the message sent from party i to party j in the output round.*

---

[2] We believe that our results also extend to the computational case, but since we are in an honest majority setting, we only focus on statistical and perfect security.

[3] In particular, it does not depend on the size of the evaluated function.

- At the end of the computation phase, the adversary knows whether a given set of messages sent by corrupt parties in the output round will cause an abort. More formally, there is an efficiently computable Boolean function f_{abort} which takes as input the adversary's view v of the computation phase and messages $\boldsymbol{d} = \{d_{i,j}| \ 1 \leq i \leq t, 1 \leq j \leq n\}$, where we assume without loss of generality that the first t parties are corrupted. Now, when corrupt parties have state v and send $\boldsymbol{d}$ in the output round, then if $f_{abort}(v, \boldsymbol{d}) = 0$ then all honest players terminate the protocol normally, otherwise at least one aborts, where both properties hold except with negligible probability.
- One can decide whether the protocol aborts based only on all messages sent in the output round[4]. More formally, we assume the function f_{abort} can also take as input messages $\boldsymbol{d}_{all} = \{d_{i,j}| \ 1 \leq i \leq t, 1 \leq j \leq n\}$. Then, if parties $P_1, ..., P_n$ send messages $\boldsymbol{d}_{all}$ in the output round and $f_{abort}(\boldsymbol{d}_{all}) = 0$, then all honest players terminate the protocol, otherwise some player aborts (except with negligible probability).

Note that the function f_{abort} is assumed to be computable in two different ways: from the set of all messages sent in the output round, or from adversary's view. The former is used by our compiled protocol, while the latter is only used by the simulator of that protocol.

A typical example of a compute-then-open protocol can be obtained by applying our compiler from Sect. 3 to a secret-sharing based and passively secure protocol, such as BGW: In the compiled protocol, the adversary can only make it to the output round by following the protocol. Therefore he knows what he should send in the output round and that the honest players will abort if they don't see what they expect. From the set of all messages sent in the output round, one can determine if an abort will occur by simple equality checks. More generally, it is straightforward to see that if one applies the compiler to a compute-then-open passively secure protocol, then the resulting protocol also has the same structure.

We can now show the following:

Theorem 2. *Assume we are given a compiler that constructs from the circuit for a function f a compute-then-open protocol Π_f that realizes $\mathcal{F}_f$, with active t-security. Then we can construct a new compiler that constructs a compute-then-open protocol Π'_f that realizes $\mathcal{F}_f^{fair}$ with active t-security. The complexity of Π'_f is larger than that of Π_f by an additive term that only depends on the number of players, the size of the outputs and the security parameter.*

Proof. Let *Deal* be a probabilistic algorithm that on input a string s produces shares of s in a verifiable secret sharing scheme with perfect t-privacy and non-interactive reconstruction, we write $Deal(s) = (Deal_1(s), \ldots, Deal_n(s))$ where $Deal_i(s)$ is the $i'th$ share produced. For $t < n/2$ this is easily constructed,

---

[4] This restriction is only for simplicity, our results extend to the more general case where termination also depends on some state information that parties keep private, as long as the size of this state only depends on the size of the output.

e.g., by first doing Shamir sharing with threshold t and then appending to each share unconditionally secure MACs that can be checked by the other parties. Such a scheme will reconstruct the correct secret except with negligible probability (statistical correctness) and has the extra property that given a secret s and an unqualified set of shares, we can efficiently compute a complete set $Deal(s)$ that is consistent with s and the shares we started from.

Now given function f, we construct the protocol Π'_f from Π_f as follows:

1. Run the computation phase of Π_f (where we abort if Π_f aborts) and let $\boldsymbol{d}_{all} = \{d_{i,j}|\ 1 \leq i \leq t, 1 \leq j \leq n\}$ denote the messages that parties would send in the output round of Π_f. Note that each party P_i can compute what he would send at this point.
2. Let f' be the following function: it takes as input a set of strings $\boldsymbol{d}_{all} = \{d_{i,j}|\ 1 \leq i \leq t, 1 \leq j \leq n\}$. It computes $Deal(d_{i,j})$ for $1 \leq i,j \leq n$ and outputs to party $P_l\ Deal(d_{i,j})_l$. Finally, it outputs $f_{abort}(\boldsymbol{d}_{all})$ to all parties. Now we run $\Pi_{f'}$, where parties input the $d_{i,j}$'s they have just computed.
3. Each player uses detectable broadcast to send a bit indicating if he terminated $\Pi_{f'}$ or aborted.
4. If any player sent abort, or if $\Pi_{f'}$ outputs 1, all honest players abort. Otherwise parties reconstruct each $d_{i,j}$ from $Deal(d_{i,j})$ (which we have from the previous step): each party P_l sends $Deal(d_{i,j})_l$ to P_j, for $1 \leq i \leq n$ (recall that P_j is the receiver of $d_{i,j}$), and parties apply the reconstruction algorithm of the VSS.
5. Finally parties complete protocol Π_f, assuming $\boldsymbol{d}_{all} = \{d_{i,j}|\ 1 \leq i \leq t, 1 \leq j \leq n\}$ were sent in the output round.

The claim on the complexity of Π'_f is clear, since Π_f is a compute-then-open protocol and steps 2–4 only depend on the size of the messages in the output round and not on the size of the total computation.

As for security, the idea is that just before the output phase of the original protocol, instead of sending the d_i's we use a secure computation $\Pi_{f'}$ to VSS them instead and also to check if they would cause an abort or not. This new computation may abort or tell everyone that the d_i's are bad, but the adversary already knew this by assumption since Π_f is a compute-then-open protocol. So by privacy of the VSS, nothing is revealed by doing this. On the other hand, if there is no abort and we are told the d_i's are good, the adversary can no longer abort, as he cannot stop the reconstruction of the VSSs.

More formally, we construct a simulator T as follows:

1. First run the simulator S for Π_f up to the output round. Then run the simulator S' for $\Pi_{f'}$ where T also emulates the functionality $\mathcal{F}_{f'}$. In particular, T can observe the inputs S' produced for f' on behalf of the corrupt parties, that is, messages $\boldsymbol{d} = \{d_{i,j}|\ 1 \leq i \leq t, 1 \leq j \leq n\}$ where we assume without loss of generality that the first t parties are corrupt.

2. Note that T now has the adversary's view v of the computation phase of Π_f (from S) and messages $\boldsymbol{d}$, so T computes $f_{abort}(v, \boldsymbol{d})$. Since Π_f is a compute-then-open protocol, this bit equals the output from f', so we give this bit to S', who will now, for each honest player, say whether that player aborts or gets the output.

3. T can now trivially simulate the round of detectable broadcasts, as it knows what each honest player will send. If anyone broadcasts "abort", or the output from f' was 1, T sends "abort" to $\mathcal{F}_f$ and stops. Otherwise, T asks for the output y from f which we pass to S, who will now produce a set of messages $\boldsymbol{d}_{honest}$ to be sent by honest players in the output round. In response, we tell S the corrupt parties sent $\boldsymbol{d}$. By assumption we know that this will not cause S to abort. So we now have a complete set of messages $\boldsymbol{d}_{all}$ (including messages from the honest parties) that is consistent with y.

4. Now T exploits t-privacy of the VSS: during the run of $\Pi_{f'}$ t shares of each $Deal(d_{i,j})$ have been given to the adversary. T now completes each set of shares to be consistent with $d_{i,j}$, and sends the resulting shares on behalf of the honest parties in Π'_f.

5. Finally, we let S complete its simulation of the execution of Π_f after the output round (if anything is left).

It is clear that T does not abort after it asks for the output. Further the output of T working with f is statistically close to that of the real protocol. This follows easily from the corresponding properties of S and S' and statistical correctness of the VSS.   □

The construction in Theorem 2 is quite natural, and works for a more general class of protocols than those produced by our main result, but we were unable to find it in the literature.

It should also be noted that when applying the construction to protocols produced by our main result, we can get a protocol that is much more efficient than in the general case. This is because the computation done by the function f' becomes quite simple: we just need a few VSSs and some secure equality checks.

5   Efficient Three-Party Computation Over Rings

To illustrate the potential of our compiler from Sect. 3, we provide a protocol for secure three-party computation over arbitrary rings $\mathbb{Z}_m$ that is secure against one active corruption, and has *constant* online communication overhead for any value of m. That is, during the online phase, the communication overhead does not depend on the security parameter.

The protocol uses the preprocessing/online circuit evaluation approach firstly introduced by Beaver [2]. During the preprocessing phase, independently of the inputs and the function to be computed, the parties jointly generate a sufficient amount of additively secret shared multiplication triples of the form $c = a \cdot b \in \mathbb{Z}_m$. During the online phase, the parties then consume these triples to evaluate an arithmetic circuit over their secret inputs.

The online phase of Beaver's protocol tolerates 2 passive corruptions and thus we can directly apply Theorem 1 to obtain a protocol for the online phase that is secure against one active corruption. What is left is the preprocessing phase, i.e., how to generate the multiplicative triples. Our technical contribution here is a novel protocol for this task. Note that this protocol *does not* use our compiler. Instead it produces the triples to be used by the compiled online protocol. Furthermore, since Beaver's online phase is deterministic, our protocol, as opposed to the general compiler, does not require to use any coin flip protocol.

For the sake of concreteness, in this section we give an explicit description of the entire protocol. In the preprocessing protocol we create replicated secret shares of multiplication triples[5]. Afterwards we briefly describe the online phase we obtain from applying our compiler to Beaver's online phase. The communication of our preprocessing protocol is only $O(\log m + \lambda)$ many bits per generated triple, meaning that the overhead for active security is a constant when m is exponential in the (statistical) security parameter.

5.1   The Preprocessing Protocol

The goal of our preprocessing protocol is to generate secret shared multiplication triples of the form $c = a \cdot b \in \mathbb{Z}_m$, where m is an arbitrary ring modulus. Our approach can be split into roughly three steps. First, we optimistically generate a possibly incorrect multiplication triple over the integers. In the second step, we optimistically generate another possibly incorrect multiplication triple in $\mathbb{Z}_p$, where p is some sufficiently large prime. We interpret our integer multiplication triple from step one as a triple in $\mathbb{Z}_p$ and "sacrifice" our second triple from $\mathbb{Z}_p$ to check its validity. In the third step we exploit the fact that the modulo operation and the product operation are interchangeable. That is, each party reduces its integer share modulo m to obtain a share of a multiplication triple in $\mathbb{Z}_m$.

The main idea in step one is, that we can securely secret share a value $a \in \mathbb{Z}_m$ over the integers by using shares that are $\log m + \lambda$ bits large. The extra λ bits in the share size ensure that for any two values in $\mathbb{Z}_m$ the resulting distributions of shares are statistically close.

We now proceed with a more formal description of the different parts of the protocol. We start by introducing some useful notation for replicated secret sharing:

Replicated Secret Sharing – Notation and Invariant: We write $[a]_{\mathbb{Z}} = (a_1, a_2, a_3)$ for a replicated integer secret sharing of a and $[a]_p = (a_1, a_2, a_3)$ for a replicated secret sharing modulo p. In both cases it holds that $a = a_1 + a_2 + a_3$ (where the additions are over the integer in the first case and modulo p in the latter). As an invariant for both kinds of secret sharing, each party P_i will know the shares a_{i+1} and a_{i-1}.

---

[5] Note that for the three-party case an additively secret shared value among virtual parties, corresponds to a replicated additively secret shared value among the real parties.

Replicated Secret Sharing – Input: When a party P_i wants to share a value $a \in \mathbb{Z}_p$, P_i picks uniformly random $a_1, a_2 \leftarrow \mathbb{Z}_p$ and defines $a_3 = a - a_1 - a_2$ mod p. Then P_i sends shares a_{j-1} and a_{j+1} to P_j. Finally P_{i+1} and P_{i-1} echo a_i to each other and abort if the value they received in this echo phase differs from what they received from P_i. When using integer secret sharing instead, the shares need to be large enough to statistically hide the secret. That is, when a party P_i wants to share a value $a \in \{0, \ldots, m-1\}$, P_i picks uniformly random $a_1, a_2 \leftarrow \{0, \ldots, 2^{\lceil \log m \rceil + \lambda} - 1\}$ and defines $a_3 = a - a_1 - a_2$. Then P_i sends shares a_{j-1} and a_{j+1} to P_j. Now, P_j checks if $|a_{j\pm1}| \leq 2^{\lceil \log m \rceil + \lambda + 1}$ and aborts otherwise.[6] Finally P_{i+1} and P_{i-1} echo a_i to each other and abort if the value they received in this echo phase differs from what they received from P_i.

Replicated Secret Sharing – Reveal: When parties want to open a share $[a]$, P_i sends its shares a_{i+1} and a_{i-1} to P_{i+1} and P_{i-1} respectively. When P_i receives share a_i from P_{i+1} and share a_i' from P_{i-1}, P_i aborts if $a_i \neq a_i'$ or outputs $a = a_1 + a_2 + a_3$ otherwise.[7]

Replicated Secret Sharing – Linear Combination: Since the secret sharing we use here is linear, we can compute linear functions without interaction i.e., when executing $[c] = [a] + [b]$ each party will locally add its shares[8]. We consider three kind of additions:

- $[c]_p = [a]_p + [b]_p$, where all the shares are added modulo p;
- $[c]_\mathbb{Z} = [a]_\mathbb{Z} + [b]_\mathbb{Z}$, where the shares are added over the integers (note that the magnitude of the shares will increase when using integer secret sharing);
- $[c]_p = [a]_p + [b]_\mathbb{Z}$, where the shares are added modulo p. Note that in the this case, if a is uniform modulo p then c is uniform modulo p.[9]

Replicated Secret Sharing – Multiplication: Given two sharings $[a]_p, [b]_p$, we can compute a secret sharing of the product $[c = a \cdot b]$ in the following way:

1. P_i samples a random $s_i \leftarrow \mathbb{Z}_p$ and computes $u_i = a_{i+1}b_{i+1} + a_{i+1}b_{i-1} + a_{i-1}b_{i+1} + s_i$;
2. P_i sends u_i to P_{i+1} and s_i to party P_{i-1};
3. Finally, party P_i defines its own two shares of c as $c_{i+1} = u_{i-1} - s_i$ and $c_{i-1} = u_i - s_{i+1}$;

When performing multiplications with integer secret sharings, we need to ensure that the chosen randomness is large enough to hide the underlying secrets.

---

[6] To keep the protocol symmetric, we use the bound for a_3 for all three shares.

[7] There is no need to explicitly check for the size of a share in the reconstruction phase since, by the assumption that at least one among P_{i+1} and P_{i-1} is honest, one of the received shares will be the correct one.

[8] The implementation of $[c] = [a] + k$ and $[c] = k \cdot [a]$ i.e., addition and multiplication by constant, follows trivially.

[9] We will use this property twice in the protocol: once, when mixing integer triples and p-modular triples in the multiplication checking phase, and finally, to argue that the resulting triples will be uniform modulo m.

In particular, given two sharings $[a]_{\mathbb{Z}}$, $[b]_{\mathbb{Z}}$, such that all shares are bounded by B, we can compute a secret sharing of the product $[c = a \cdot b]_{\mathbb{Z}}$ in the following way:

1. P_i samples a random $s_i \leftarrow \{0, \ldots, 2^{2\lceil \log B \rceil + \lambda + 2} - 1\}$ and computes $u_i = a_{i+1}b_{i+1} + a_{i+1}b_{i-1} + a_{i-1}b_{i+1} + s_i$;
2. P_i sends u_i to P_{i+1} and s_i to party P_{i-1};
3. P_i checks that the received shares are of the correct size i.e., $|u_{i-1}| \leq 2^{2\lceil \log B \rceil + \lambda + 3}$ and $|s_{i+1}| \leq 2^{2\lceil \log B \rceil + \lambda + 2}$
4. Finally, party P_i defines its own two shares of c as $c_{i+1} = u_{i-1} - s_i$ and $c_{i-1} = u_i - s_{i+1}$;

Armed with these tools we are now ready to describe our preprocessing protocol. The protocol is similar in spirit to previous protocols (e.g., [12,13]) for generating multiplication triples, and like in previous work we start by generating two possibly incorrect triples, and then "sacrificing" one to check the correctness of the other. The main novelty of this protocol is that the two triples actually live in different domains. One is a an integer secret sharing, while the others is a modular secret sharing. For the sake of exposition we describe the protocol to generate a single multiplicative triple but, as with previous work, it will be more efficient to generate many triples in parallel.

The Preprocessing Protocol – Generate Random Triples:

1. Every P_i picks random $a_i, b_i \leftarrow \mathbb{Z}_m$ and generates sharings of $[a_i]_{\mathbb{Z}}, [b_i]_{\mathbb{Z}}$;
2. All parties jointly compute $[a]_{\mathbb{Z}} = [a_1]_{\mathbb{Z}} + [a_2]_{\mathbb{Z}} + [a_3]_{\mathbb{Z}}$ and $[b]_{\mathbb{Z}} = [b_1]_{\mathbb{Z}} + [b_2]_{\mathbb{Z}} + [b_3]_{\mathbb{Z}}$;[10]
3. All parties jointly compute $[c]_{\mathbb{Z}} = [a]_{\mathbb{Z}} \cdot [b]_{\mathbb{Z}}$ (optimistically using the multiplication protocol described above);
4. Every P_i picks random $x_i, y_i, r_i \leftarrow \mathbb{Z}_p$ and generates sharings of $[x_i]_p, [y_i]_p, [r_i]_p$;
5. All parties jointly compute $[x]_p = [x_1]_p + [x_2]_p + [x_3]_p$ and $[y]_p = [y_1]_p + [y_2]_p + [y_3]_p$ and $[r]_p = [r_1]_p + [r_2]_p + [r_3]_p$;
6. All parties jointly compute $[z]_p = [x]_p \cdot [y]_p$ (optimistically using the multiplication protocol described above);
7. All parties open r;
8. All parties jointly compute $[e]_p = r[x]_p + [a]_{\mathbb{Z}}$;
9. All parties jointly compute $[d]_p = [y]_p + [b]_{\mathbb{Z}}$;
10. All parties jointly open e, d, then compute and open

$$[t]_p = de - rd[x]_p - e[y]_p + r[z]_p - [c]_{\mathbb{Z}}$$

and abort if the result is not 0;

---

[10] Note that if now we convert the sharing of $[a]_{\mathbb{Z}}$ to $[a]_m$ by having each party take their shares and locally reduce modulo m, we get that, from the adversary's point of view, a is uniformly random in $\mathbb{Z}_m$, since at least one honest party choose a_i as a uniform value modulo m; the same argument applies symmetrically to $[b]_{\mathbb{Z}}$.

11. If the protocol did not abort, all parties output (modular) sharings $[a]_m, [b]_m, [c]_m$ by reducing their integer shares modulo m;

We now argue that:

Theorem 3. *The above protocol securely realizes $\mathcal{F}_{\mathsf{triple}}$ with statistical security parameter λ in the presence of one active corruption when $|p| = O(\log m + \lambda)$.*

Proof. We only give an informal argument for the security of the protocol, since its proof is quite similar to the proof of many previous protocols in the literature (such as [4,12,13], etc.).

We first argue for correctness of the protocol, focusing on steps 1,2 and 9: Note that, if there is an output, the output is correct and uniform modulo m. It is correct since, if $c = ab$ over the integer then $c = ab \mod m$ as well. And the values a, b, c are distributed uniformly since there is at least one honest party (in fact, two), who will pick a_i uniformly at random in $\mathbb{Z}_m$, therefore $a = a_1 + a_2 + a_3 \mod m$ will be uniform over $\mathbb{Z}_m$ as well (the same applies of course also to b and c).

We now describe the simulator strategy for the individual subroutines, and then we build the overall simulator for the protocol in a bottom-up fashion. To keep the notation simpler we assume that P_1 is corrupt. This is w.l.o.g. due to the symmetry of the protocol. To account for rushing adversaries, we always let the adversary send their message after seeing the message output by the simulator on behalf of the honest parties. As usual, the simulator keeps track of the shares that all parties (honest and corrupt) are supposed to hold at all times.

Simulator – Honest Parties Inputs: To simulate an honest party inputting a value a the simulator follows the share procedure but replacing a with 0. The simulator then sends a_2, a_3 to the adversary P_1 and stores a_1, a_2, a_3. Now the simulator receives a_2' (or a_3' depending on whether we are simulating a P_2 input or a P_3 input) back from the adversary and aborts if $a_2' \neq a_2$ (as an honest party would do).

When performing sharings modulo p, the distribution of the simulated a_2, a_3 are identical as in the real protocol (trivially for a_2, and since a_1 is random and unknown to the adversary, a_3 will be uniformly distributed in both cases). When performing integer sharings, the distribution of the simulated a_2 is trivially identical in the real and simulated execution while a_3 is statistically close. This can be easily seen considering the distribution of $a_3 + a_2$ which is $a - a_1$ in the real protocol and $-a_1$ in the simulated execution. Since $a < m$ and a_1 is uniform between 0 and $m \cdot 2^\lambda$ the distributions are statistically close with parameter λ.

Simulator – Corrupt Party Input: When simulating the input of the corrupt party P_1 the simulator receives (a_1, a_3) (on behalf of P_2) and (a_1', a_2) on behalf of P_3. The simulator aborts if $a_1 \neq a_1'$ (like the two honest party would do). When simulating an input in $\mathbb{Z}_p$ the simulator reconstructs $a = \sum_i a_i \mod p$. When simulating an integer input the simulator checks in addition that the shares received are of the right size and then reconstructs $a = \sum_i a_i$. Note that now $|a| < 3 \cdot 2^{\lceil \log m \rceil + \lambda + 1}$ which could be larger than m, but not larger than p given our parameters.

Simulator – Multiplication: When simulating multiplications the simulator picks random (u_3, s_2) (see below for the distribution) and sends them to P_1. Then the simulator receives (u_1, s_1) from P_1. This uniquely defines the corrupt party shares of c, namely $c_2 = u_3 - s_1$ and $c_3 = u_1 - s_2$. Note that the simulator can already now compute the error $\delta_c = c - ab$ from the stored shares of a, b and the received values u_1, s_1 i.e., $\delta_c = u_1 - (a_2 b_2 + a_2 b_3 + a_3 b_2 + s_1)$. The simulator sets the final share of c to be $c_1 = ab + \delta_c - c_2 - c_3$ and remembers (c_1, c_2, c_3) and δ_c.

When simulating multiplications in $\mathbb{Z}_p$ the simulator picks (u_3, s_2) uniformly at random, thus the view of the adversary is perfectly indistinguishable in the real and simulated execution: this is trivial for s_2, and for u_3 we can see that it will also be uniformly random as well since in the real protocol s_3 is chosen uniformly at random.

When simulating integer multiplications the simulator picks (u_3, s_2) uniformly at random in $\{0, \ldots, 2^{2\lceil \log B \rceil + \lambda + 2} - 1\}$, thus the view of the adversary is statistically close in the real and simulated execution (trivially for s_2, and since in the protocol s_3 is used to mask a value of magnitude at most $3B^3$, the distributions are statistically close with parameter λ. Note that when simulating integer multiplications the simulator will also abort if the received shares (u_1, s_1) exceed their bounds. This means that at this point the value of $|c| = |\sum_i c_i|$ is bounded by $24B^2 2^\lambda$. As we know from the input phase that all shares are bound by $B = 2^{\lceil \log m \rceil + \lambda + 1}$ we get that by setting p to be e.g., larger than $100m^2 2^{2\lambda}$ we can ensure that even in the presence of a corrupt party the value of c will not exceed p.

Simulator – Fake Reveal: At any point the simulator can open a sharing (a_1, a_2, a_3) to any value $a + \delta_1$ of its choice. To do so, the simulator sends two identical shares $(a_1 + \delta_1)$ to P_1 (simulating that both the honest P_2 and P_3 send the same share to P_1). Then, P_1 sends its (possibly malicious) shares $a_2 + \delta_2$ and $a_3 + \delta_3$ to the simulator. Now the simulator aborts if $\delta_2 \neq 0$ or if $\delta_3 \neq 0$. Note the aborting condition is exactly the same as in the real protocol, where e.g., the honest P_2 receives a_2 from P_1 and a_2' from P_3 and aborts if the two values are different. Finally note that the view of the adversary is exactly the same in the real and simulated execution.

Putting Things Together – Overall Simulator Strategy: We are now ready to describe the overall simulation strategy. Note that all the settings in which the simulator aborts in the previous subroutines are identical to the abort conditions of the honest parties in the protocol and moreover are "predictable" by the adversary (i.e., the adversary knows that sending a certain message will make the protocol abort). The labels of the steps of the simulator refer to the respective steps in the protocol.

  0. As already described, the simulator keeps track of the shares that all parties (honest and corrupt) are supposed to hold at all times.

1a. (Send on behalf of P_2 and P_3) The simulator simulates P_2 and P_3 sharing values a_2, a_3, b_2, b_3 as described above (e.g., the input are set to be 0);

1b. (Receive from P_1) The simulator receives the (maliciously chosen) shares of a_1 using the procedure described above. In particular, now a_1 is well defined and bounded.

2. The simulator keeps track of the shares of a and b that all parties are supposed to store after the addition; (note that since the shares of the honest parties are simulated to 0 we have $a = a_1$ and $b = b_1$ at this point);

3. The simulator uses the simulation strategy for the multiplication protocol as explained above. If the simulation does not abort the value of c and δ_c are now well defined and bounded.

4. The simulator runs the sharing subroutine for $x_2, y_2, r_2, x_3, y_3, r_3$ (e.g., all values are set to 0).

5. The simulator keeps track of the shares of x, y and r that all parties are supposed to store after the addition; (at this point x, y and r are well defined);

6. The simulator uses the simulation strategy for the multiplication protocol as explained above. If the simulation does not abort the value of z and δ_z are now well defined.

7. The simulator now runs the fake reveal subroutine and opens r to a uniformly random value;

8–9. The simulator keeps track of the shares of e, d that all parties are supposed to store after the executions of the linear combination;

10a. The simulator runs the fake reveal subroutine and opens e, d to two uniformly random values;

10b. If the simulation did not abort so far the simulator runs the fake reveal subroutine and opens t to $r\delta_z - \delta_c \mod p$. The simulator aborts if $t \neq 0$ as an honest party do, but also aborts if $\delta_c \neq 0$ or $\delta_z \neq 0$.

11. If the simulator did not abort yet, then the simulator inputs the shares of the multiplicative triple owned by the adversary $(a_2, a_3, b_2, b_3, c_2, c_3)$ to the ideal functionality $\mathcal{F}_{\text{triple}}$.

We have already argued for indistinguishability for the various subroutines (thanks to the large masks used in the integer secret sharings). Note that when we combine them in the overall simulator we add an extra aborting condition between a real world execution of the protocol and a simulated execution, namely that the simulation always aborts when the triple is incorrect (during the triple check phase). We conclude that the view of the adversary in these two cases are statistically close in λ thanks to the correctness check at steps 4–10: assume that the multiplication triples are correct i.e., that $z = xy \mod p$ and $c = ab$ over the integers. Now, if we make sure that p is large enough such that the shares of a, b, and c are the same over the integers and modulo p, then the resulting t will always be 0. Note that this is guaranteed by the check, during the sharing phase, of the magnitude of the shares chosen by the other parties. Finally, assume that $c \neq ab$ e.g., $c = ab + \delta_c$ (with $\delta_c \neq 0$) and $z = xy + \delta_z$.

Now the result of the check will be $t = r\delta_z - \delta_c \mod p$: Since the value r is picked by the simulator *after* the values δ_c, δ_z have already been defined, we finally have that t is equal to 0 with probability p^{-1} which is negligible as desired.

5.2   Online Phase

Here we briefly sketch the online phase of our protocol i.e., the protocol resulting by applying our compiler to Beaver's passively protocol, which is secure against 1 active corruption. In what follows we describe the protocol explicitly i.e., we describe directly the steps to be performed by the real parties and with no access to helping ideal functionalities: since the online phase of Beaver's protocol is completely deterministic, we do not need the coin flip functionality and, since we only have 3 parties, the broadcast functionality is easily implemented: when P_i broadcasts to a set $\{P_i, P_j\}$, this is implemented by sending a message to P_j and, when P_i broadcasts to a set $\{P_j, P_k\}$, this is implemented by sending the same message to both parties, who then echo it to each other and abort if the two received messages are different. Finally, note that an additive secret sharing $a = a_1 + a_2 + a_3 \mod m$ among the virtual parties $\mathbb{P}_1, \mathbb{P}_2, \mathbb{P}_3$ (i.e., where $\mathbb{P}_i$ knows a_i) is exactly the same as a replicated secret sharing $[a]_m$ (as described above) between the real parties P_1, P_2, P_3, and therefore we can continue using the notation introduced for the preprocessing phase.

Online Phase – Setup and Invariant: Let C be the arithmetic circuit that the real parties wish to evaluate, where every input wire is associated to some party P_i. As before, for a value $x \in \mathbb{Z}_m$ we write $[x]_m$ to denote the situation where P_i knows two shares x_{i+1}, x_{i-1} such that $\sum_i x_i = x$.

Online Phase – Input Gates: Remember that in our general compiler the secret sharing happened "outside" of the passive MPC protocol and then we modified the circuit to be evaluated by adding a layer of linear operations to reconstruct the secret sharings of the inputs. This is not necessary in the special case of Beaver's protocol, since after a single sharing we already have the inputs in the desired, replicated secret shared format. Therefore, for every input wire in C associated to P_i with input $x \in \mathbb{Z}_m$, we let P_i pick random shares $(x_1, x_2, x_3) \in \mathbb{Z}_m^3$ s.t., $\sum_i x_i = x$, and sends x_i to P_{i-1} and P_{i+1}. Finally P_{i-1} and P_{i+1} echo x_i to each other and abort if the value they received in this echo phase differs from what they received from P_i.

Online Phase – Output Gates/Open Subroutine: Whenever the parties need to be able to reveal the content of a shared value $[z]_m$, we let P_i sends its shares z_{i+1} and z_{i-1} to P_{i+1} and P_{i-1} respectively. When P_i receives share z_i from P_{i+1} and share z_i' from P_{i-1}, P_i aborts if $z_i \neq z_i'$ or outputs $z = z_1 + z_2 + z_3$ otherwise. During the circuit evaluation we open wires to output the result of the computation and as a subroutine during the evaluation of multiplication gates.

Online Phase – Linear Gates: Linear gates (binary additions, unary additions by constant and multiplication by constant) can be locally implemented by share manipulations in the same way as for the preprocessing phase.

Online Phase – Multiplication Gates: Binary multiplication of two shared values $[x]_m, [y]_m$ is performed by finding an unused preprocessed multiplication triple $[a]_m, [b]_m, [c]_m$ and then running Beaver's protocol, i.e.:

1. Open $e = [a]_m + [x]_m$
2. Open $d = [b]_m + [y]_m$
3. Locally compute $[z]_m = [c]_m + e \cdot [y]_m + d \cdot [x]_m - ed$

Acknowledgements. We thank the anonymous reviewers for their useful feedback. This project has received funding from: the European Research Council (ERC) under the European Unions's Horizon 2020 research and innovation programme (grant agreement No 669255); the Danish Independent Research Council under Grant-ID DFF-6108-00169 (FoCC); the European Union's Horizon 2020 research and innovation programme under grant agreement No 731583 (SODA).

References

1. Asharov, G., Jain, A., López-Alt, A., Tromer, E., Vaikuntanathan, V., Wichs, D.: Multiparty computation with low communication, computation and interaction via threshold FHE. In: Pointcheval, D., Johansson, T. (eds.) EUROCRYPT 2012. LNCS, vol. 7237, pp. 483–501. Springer, Heidelberg (2012). https://doi.org/10.1007/978-3-642-29011-4_29
2. Beaver, D.: Efficient multiparty protocols using circuit randomization. In: Feigenbaum, J. (ed.) CRYPTO 1991. LNCS, vol. 576, pp. 420–432. Springer, Heidelberg (1992). https://doi.org/10.1007/3-540-46766-1_34
3. Ben-Or, M., Goldwasser, S., Wigderson, A.: Completeness theorems for non-cryptographic fault-tolerant distributed computation (extended abstract). In: Proceedings of the 20th Annual ACM Symposium on Theory of Computing, 2–4 May 1988, Chicago, Illinois, USA, pp. 1–10 (1988)
4. Bendlin, R., Damgård, I., Orlandi, C., Zakarias, S.: Semi-homomorphic encryption and multiparty computation. In: Paterson, K.G. (ed.) EUROCRYPT 2011. LNCS, vol. 6632, pp. 169–188. Springer, Heidelberg (2011). https://doi.org/10.1007/978-3-642-20465-4_11
5. Bogdanov, D., Laur, S., Willemson, J.: Sharemind: a framework for fast privacy-preserving computations. In: Jajodia, S., Lopez, J. (eds.) ESORICS 2008. LNCS, vol. 5283, pp. 192–206. Springer, Heidelberg (2008). https://doi.org/10.1007/978-3-540-88313-5_13
6. Chaum, D., Crépeau, C., Damgård, I.: Multiparty unconditionally secure protocols (extended abstract). In: 20th ACM STOC, pp. 11–19. ACM Press, May 1988
7. Cohen, G., et al.: Efficient multiparty protocols via log-depth threshold formulae. Electronic Colloquium on Computational Complexity (ECCC), 20:107 (2013)
8. Cohen, R., Lindell, Y.: Fairness versus guaranteed output delivery in secure multiparty computation. In: Sarkar, P., Iwata, T. (eds.) ASIACRYPT 2014, Part II. LNCS, vol. 8874, pp. 466–485. Springer, Heidelberg (2014). https://doi.org/10.1007/978-3-662-45608-8_25

9. Cramer, R., Damgård, I., Nielsen, J.B.: Secure Multiparty Computation and Secret Sharing. Cambridge University Press, New York (2015)
10. Cramer, R., Damgrd, I., Escudero, D., Scholl, P., Xing, C.: SPDZ2k: efficient MPC mod 2^k for dishonest majority. CRYPTO (2018). https://eprint.iacr.org/2018/482
11. Damgård, I., Keller, M., Larraia, E., Pastro, V., Scholl, P., Smart, N.P.: Practical covertly secure MPC for dishonest majority – or: breaking the SPDZ limits. In: Crampton, J., Jajodia, S., Mayes, K. (eds.) ESORICS 2013. LNCS, vol. 8134, pp. 1–18. Springer, Heidelberg (2013). https://doi.org/10.1007/978-3-642-40203-6_1
12. Damgård, I., Orlandi, C.: Multiparty computation for dishonest majority: from passive to active security at low cost. In: Rabin, T. (ed.) CRYPTO 2010. LNCS, vol. 6223, pp. 558–576. Springer, Heidelberg (2010). https://doi.org/10.1007/978-3-642-14623-7_30
13. Damgård, I., Pastro, V., Smart, N.P., Zakarias, S.: Multiparty computation from somewhat homomorphic encryption. In: Safavi-Naini, R., Canetti, R. (eds.) CRYPTO 2012. LNCS, vol. 7417, pp. 643–662. Springer, Heidelberg (2012). https://doi.org/10.1007/978-3-642-32009-5_38
14. Desmedt, Y., Kurosawa, K.: How to break a practical MIX and design a new one. In: Preneel, B. (ed.) EUROCRYPT 2000. LNCS, vol. 1807, pp. 557–572. Springer, Heidelberg (2000). https://doi.org/10.1007/3-540-45539-6_39
15. Fitzi, M., Gisin, N., Maurer, U.M., von Rotz, O.: Unconditional Byzantine agreement and multi-party computation secure against dishonest minorities from scratch. In: Knudsen, L.R. (ed.) EUROCRYPT 2002. LNCS, vol. 2332, pp. 482–501. Springer, Heidelberg (2002). https://doi.org/10.1007/3-540-46035-7_32
16. Fitzi, M., Gottesman, D., Hirt, M., Holenstein, T., Smith, A.: Detectable Byzantine agreement secure against faulty majorities. In: Ricciardi, A. (ed.) 21st ACM PODC, pp. 118–126. ACM, July 2002
17. Furukawa, J., Lindell, Y., Nof, A., Weinstein, O.: High-throughput secure three-party computation for malicious adversaries and an honest majority. In: Coron, J.-S., Nielsen, J.B. (eds.) EUROCRYPT 2017, Part II. LNCS, vol. 10211, pp. 225–255. Springer, Cham (2017). https://doi.org/10.1007/978-3-319-56614-6_8
18. Goldreich, O., Micali, S., Wigderson, A.: How to play any mental game or a completeness theorem for protocols with honest majority. In: Aho, A. (ed.) 19th ACM STOC, pp. 218–229. ACM Press, May 1987
19. Ishai, Y., Kushilevitz, E., Meldgaard, S., Orlandi, C., Paskin-Cherniavsky, A.: On the power of correlated randomness in secure computation. In: Sahai, A. (ed.) TCC 2013. LNCS, vol. 7785, pp. 600–620. Springer, Heidelberg (2013). https://doi.org/10.1007/978-3-642-36594-2_34
20. Ishai, Y., Prabhakaran, M., Sahai, A.: Founding cryptography on oblivious transfer – efficiently. In: Wagner, D. (ed.) CRYPTO 2008. LNCS, vol. 5157, pp. 572–591. Springer, Heidelberg (2008). https://doi.org/10.1007/978-3-540-85174-5_32
21. Lindell, Y., Oxman, E., Pinkas, B.: The IPS compiler: optimizations, variants and concrete efficiency. In: Rogaway, P. (ed.) CRYPTO 2011. LNCS, vol. 6841, pp. 259–276. Springer, Heidelberg (2011). https://doi.org/10.1007/978-3-642-22792-9_15
22. Maurer, U.M.: Secure multi-party computation made simple. In: Cimato, S., Persiano, G., Galdi, C. (eds.) SCN 2002. LNCS, vol. 2576, pp. 14–28. Springer, Heidelberg (2003). https://doi.org/10.1007/3-540-36413-7_2
23. Mohassel, P., Rosulek, M., Zhang, Y.: Fast and secure three-party computation: the garbled circuit approach. In: Proceedings of the 22nd ACM SIGSAC Conference on Computer and Communications Security, Denver, CO, USA, 12–16 October 2015, pp. 591–602 (2015)

24. Mukherjee, P., Wichs, D.: Two round multiparty computation via multi-key FHE. In: Fischlin, M., Coron, J.-S. (eds.) EUROCRYPT 2016, Part II. LNCS, vol. 9666, pp. 735–763. Springer, Heidelberg (2016). https://doi.org/10.1007/978-3-662-49896-5_26

25. Pease, M., Shostak, R., Lamport, L.: Reaching agreement in the presence of faults. J. ACM (JACM) **27**(2), 228–234 (1980)

26. Yao, A.C.-C.: How to generate and exchange secrets (extended abstract). In: 27th FOCS, pp. 162–167. IEEE Computer Society Press, October 1986

Author Index

Printed in the United States
By Bookmasters